WORK LAW: CASES AND MATERIALS

Third Edition

WORK LAW: CASES AND MATERIALS

Third Edition

Marion G. Crain
Vice Provost, Washington University in St. Louis
Wiley B. Rutledge Professor of Law
Washington University School of Law

Pauline T. Kim
Charles Nagel Chair of Constitutional Law and Political Science
Washington University School of Law

Michael Selmi
Samuel Tyler Research Professor of Law
George Washington University Law School

CAROLINA ACADEMIC PRESS
Durham, North Carolina

Print: 978-1-6328-1538-5
ebook: 978-1-6328-1539-2
Looseleaf: 978-1-6328-1598-9

Library of Congress Cataloging-in-Publication Data

Crain, Marion G., author.
Work law : cases and materials / Marion G. Crain, Vice Provost, Washington University, Wiley B. Rutledge Professor of Law, Washington University School of Law ; Pauline T. Kim, Charles Nagel Professor of Law, Washington University School of Law; Michael Selmi, Samuel Tyler Research Professor of
Law, George Washington University Law School.—Third Edition.
pages cm
Includes index.
ISBN 978-1-63281-538-5 (hardbound)
1. Labor laws and legislation—United States—Cases. I. Kim, Pauline T., author. II. Selmi, Michael,
author. III. Title.
IV. Title: Worklaw.
KF3455.C73 2015
344.7301—dc23

2015002898

Carolina Academic Press, LLC
700 Kent Street
Durham, North Carolina 27701
Telephone (919) 489-7486
Fax (919) 493-5668
www.caplaw.com

Printed in the United States of America
2016 Printing

Acknowledgments

The authors would like to thank the authors and publishers for permission to reprint portions of the following copyrighted material:

Abrams, Roger L. & Nolan, Dennis R., *Toward a Theory of "Just Cause" in Employee Discipline Cases* , 1985 DUKE L.J. 594. Copyright © 1985 Duke Law Journal. All rights reserved. Reprinted with permission.

Anderson, Deborah J., Binder, Melissa & Krause, Kate, *The Motherhood Wage Penalty Revisited: Experience, Heterogeneity, Work Effort and Work-Schedule Flexibility*, 56 INDUS. & LAB. REL. REV. 273 (2003). Copyright © 2003. All rights reserved. Reprinted with permission.

Ansley, Frances Lee, *Rethinking Law in Globalization Labor Markets*, 1 U. PA. J. LAB. & EMP. L. 369 (1998). Copyright © 1998 University of Pennsylvania Journal of Labor and Employment Law. All rights reserved. Reprinted with permission.

Arnow-Richman, Rachel, *Accommodation Subverted: The Future of Work/Family Initiatives in a "Me, Inc." World*, 12 TEX. J. WOMEN & L. 345 (2003). Copyright © 2003 Rachel Arnow-Richman. All rights reserved. Reprinted with permission.

Arnow-Richman, Rachel, *Just Notice: Re-reforming Employment at Will*, 58 UCLA L. REV. 1 (2010). Copyright © 2010. All rights reserved. Reprinted with permission.

Avery, Dianne & Crain, Marion, *Branded: Corporate Image, Sexual Stereotyping, and the New Face of Capitalism*, 14 DUKE J. OF GENDER L. & POLICY 13 (2007). Copyright © 2007 Duke University. All rights reserved. Reprinted with permission.

Bales, Richard A., COMPULSORY ARBITRATION: THE GRAND EXPERIMENT IN EMPLOYMENT 3–10 (1997). Copyright © 1997 by Cornell University. All rights reserved. Used by permission of the publisher, Cornell University Press.

Bales, Richard A., *The Discord Between Collective Bargaining and Individual Employment Rights: The Theoretical Origins and a Proposed Reconciliation*, 77 B.U. L. REV. 687 (1997). Reprinted with permission of the author.

Barstow, David, *A Trench Caves in: A Young Worker Is Dead, Is It a Crime?*, N.Y. TIMES, Dec. 21, 2003 at 1. Copyright © 2003 by The New York Times Co. Reprinted with permission.

Befort, Stephen F., *Labor and Employment Law at the Millenium: A Historical Review and Critical Assessment*, 43 B.C. L. REV. 351 (2002). Copyright © 2002 Boston College Law Review. All rights reserved. Reprinted with permission.

Befort, Stephen F., *Revisiting the Black Hole of Worplace Regulation: A Historical and Comparative Perspective on Contingent Work*, 24 BERKELEY J. EMP. & LAB. L. 153 (2003). Copyright © 2003 Berkeley Journal of Employment and Labor Law. All rights reserved. Reprinted with permission.

Bidwell, Matthew, Briscoe, Forrest, Fernandez-Mateo, Isabel & Sterling, Adina, *The Employment Relationship and Inequality: How and Why Changes in Employment Practices are Reshaping Rewards in Organizations*, THE ACADEMY OF MANAGEMENT ANNALS 4 (2013). Copyright © 2013. All rights reserved. Reprinted with permission.

Blades, Lawrence E., *Employment at Will vs. Individual Freedom: On Limiting the*

Acknowledgments

Abusive Exercise of Employer Power, 67 COLUM. L. REV. 1404, 1404 (1967). Copyright © 1967 Directors of the Columbia Law Review Association, Inc. All rights reserved. Reprinted with permission.

Casebeer, Kenneth M., *Unemployment Insurance: American Social Wage, Labor Organization, and Legal Ideology*, 35 B.C. L. REV. 259 (1994). Copyright © 1994. All rights reserved. Reprinted with permission.

Carbado, Devon W. & Gulati, Mitu, *The Law and Economics of Critical Race Theory*, 112 YALE L.J. 1757 (2003). Reprinted with permission of The Yale Law Journal Company and William S. Hein Company from The Yale Law Journal, Vol. 112, pages 1757–1828.

Colvin, Alexander J.S. & Pike, Kelly, *Saturns and Rickshaws Revisited: What Kind of Arbitration System has Developed?*, 29 OH. ST. J. ON DISP. RES. 59 (2014). Copyright © 2014. All rights reserved. Reprinted with permission.

Crain, Marion, *Managing Identity: Buying into the Brand at Work*, 95 IOWA L. REV. 1179 (2010). Copyright © 2010 Iowa Law Review. All rights reserved. Reprinted with permission.

Crain, Marion, *The Transformation of the Professional Workplace*, 79 CHI.-KENT L. REV. 543 (2004). Copyright © 2004 Chicago-Kent Law Review. All rights reserved. Reprinted with permission.

Crain, Marion, *"Where Have All the Cowboys Gone?" Marriage and Breadwinning in Postindustrial Society*, 6 OH. ST. L.J. 1877 (1999). Copyright © 1999 Ohio State Law Journal. Originally published in 6 OH. ST. L.J. 1877 (1999). All rights reserved. Reprinted with permission.

Crain, Marion & Matheny, Ken, *"Labor's Divided Ranks": Privilege and the United Front Ideology*, 84 CORNELL L. REV. 1542 (1999). Copyright © 1999 Cornell University. All rights reserved. Reprinted with permission.

Craver, Charles B., *The American Worker: Junior Partner in Success and Senior Partner in Failure*, 37 U.S.F. L. REV. 587 (2003). Copyright © 2003 University of San Francisco Law Review. All rights reserved. Reprinted with permission.

Dau-Schmidt, Kenneth G., *Employment in the New Age of Trade and Technology: Implications for Labor and Employment Law*, 76 IND. L.J. 1 (2001). Copyright © 2001 Indiana Law Journal. All rights reserved. Reprinted with permission.

Epstein, Richard A., *A Common Law for Labor Relations: A Critique of the New Deal Labor Legislation*, 92 YALE L.J. 1357 (1983). Reprinted with permission of The Yale Law Journal Company and William S. Hein Company from The Yale Law Journal, Vol. 92, pages 1357–1408.

Epstein, Richard A., *In Defense of the Contract at Will*, 51 U. CHI. L. REV. 947 (1984). Copyright © 1984 University of Chicago Law Review. All rights reserved. Reprinted with permission.

Estlund, Cynthia L., *Free Speech and Due Process in the Workplace*, 71 IND. L.J. 101 (1995). Copyright © 1995 Indiana Law Journal. All rights reserved. Reprinted with permission.

Estlund, Cynthia L., *How Wrong Are Employees About Their Rights, and Why Does It*

Acknowledgments

Matter?, 77 N.Y.U. L. REV. 6 (2002). Copyright © 2002 N.Y.U. Law Review. All rights reserved. Reprinted with permission.

Estlund, Cynthia L., *Labor, Property, and Sovereignty After* Lechmere, 46 STAN. L. REV. 305 (1994). Copyright © 1994 The Board of Trustees of the Leland Stanford Junior University. All rights reserved. Reprinted with permission.

Estlund, Cynthia L., *The Ossification of American Labor Law*, 102 COLUM. L. REV. 1527 (2002). Copyright © 2002 Directors of the Columbia Law Review Association, Inc. All rights reserved. Reprinted with permission.

Estlund, Cynthia L., *Working Together: The Workplace, Civil Society, and the Law*, 89 GEO. L.J. 1 (2000). Reprinted with permission of the publisher, Georgetown Law Journal © 2000.

Estlund, Cynthia L., *Rebuilding the Law of the Workplace in an Era of Self-Regulation*, 105 COLUM. L. REV. 319 (20005). Copyright © 2002 Directors of the Columbia Law Review Association, Inc. All rights reserved. Reprinted with permission.

Estreicher, Samuel, *Saturns for Rickshaws: The Stakes in the Dispute over Predispute Employment Arbitration Agreements*, 16 OH. ST. J. DISP. RES. 559 (2001). Copyright © 2001 Ohio State Journal of Dispute Resolution. All rights reserved. Reprinted with permission.

Estreicher, Samuel & Gold, Laurence, *The Shift from Defined Benefit Plans to Defined Contribution Plans*, 11 LEWIS & CLARK L. REV. 331 (2007). Copyright © 2007 Lewis & Clark Law Review. All rights reserved. Reprinted with permission.

Feinman, Jay M., *The Development of the Employment at Will Rule*, 20 AM. J. LEGAL HIST. 118 (1976). Copyright © 1976 Temple University School of Law. All rights reserved. Reprinted with permission.

Finkin, Matthew W., *Employee Privacy, American Values, and the Law*, 72 CHI.-KENT L. REV. 221 (1996). Copyright © 1996 Chicago-Kent Law Review. All rights reserved. Reprinted with permission.

Flanagan, Julie A., Note, *Restricting Electronic Monitoring in the Private Workplace*, 43 DUKE L.J. 1256. Copyright © Duke Law Journal. All rights reserved. Reprinted with permission.

Freed, Mayer G. & Polsby, Daniel D., *The Doubtful Provenance of "Wood's Rule" Revisted*, 22 ARIZ. ST. L.J. 551 (1990). Reprinted with permission.

Freeman, Richard B., *What Will a 10% . . . 50% . . . 100% Increase in the Minimum Wage Do?*, 48 IND. & LAB. REL. REV. 830 (1995). Copyright © 1995 Industrial & Labor Relations Review. All rights reserved. Reprinted with permission.

Freeman, Richard & Medoff, James L., WHAT DO UNIONS DO? 7–9 (1984). Copyright © 1984 by Basic Books, Inc. Reprinted with permission of Basic Books, Inc., a member of Perseus Books, L.L.C.

Greenfield, Kent, *The Unjustified Absence of Federal Fraud Protection in the Labor Market*, 107 YALE L.J. 715 (1997). Reprinted with permission of The Yale Law Journal Company and William S. Hein Company from The Yale Law Journal, Vol. 107, pages 715–789.

Grossman, Joanna L., *Job Security Without Equality: The Family and Medical Leave*

Acknowledgments

Act of 1993, 15 WASH. U. J.L. & POL'Y 17 (2004). Copyright © 2004. All rights reserved. Reprinted with permission.

Hyde, Alan, *Who Speaks for the Working Poor?: A Preliminary Look at the Emerging Tetralogy of Representation of Law-Wage Service Workers*, 12 CORNELL J. L. & POL'Y 599 (2004). Copyright © 2004 by the Cornell Journal of Law and Policy. All rights reserved. Reprinted with permission.

Hyde, Alan, WORKING IN SILICON VALLEY: ECONOMIC AND LEGAL ANALYSIS OF A HIGH-VELOCITY LABOR MARKET 31 (Armonk, NY: M.E. Sharpe 2003). Copyright © 2003 M.E. Sharpe. All rights reserved. Reprinted with permission.

Issacharoff, Samuel, *Contracting for Employment: The Limited Return of the Common Law*, 74 TEX. L. REV. 1783 (1996). Copyright © 1996 Texas Law Review Association. All rights reserved. Reprinted with permission.

Karst, Kenneth L., *The Coming Crisis of Work in Constitutional Perspective*, 82 CORNELL L. REV. 523 (1997). Copyright © 1997 Cornell University. All rights reserved. Reprinted with permission.

Kim, Pauline T., *Bargaining with Imperfect Information: A Study of Worker Perceptions of Legal Protection in an At-Will World*, 83 CORNELL L. REV. 105 (1997). Copyright © 1997 Cornell University. All rights reserved. Reprinted with permission.

Kim, Pauline T., *Genetic Discrimination, Genetic Privacy: Rethinking Employee Protections for a Brave New Workplace*, 96 NW. U.L. REV. 1497 (2002). Copyright © 2002 Northwestern University Law Review. All rights reserved. Reprinted with special permission of Northwestern University, *Northwestern University Law Review*.

Kim, Pauline T., *Privacy Rights, Public Policy, and the Employment Relationship*, 57 OH. ST. L.J. 671, 728 (1996) Copyright © 1996 Ohio State Law Journal. Originally published in 57 Oh. St. L.J. 671 (1996). All rights reserved. Reprinted with permission.

Kim, Pauline T., *Collective and Individual Approaches to Protecting Employee Privacy: The Experience with Workplace Drug Testing*, 66 LA. L. REV. 1009 (2006). Copyright © 2006. All rights reserved. Reprinted with permission.

Kohler, Thomas C., *The Employment Relation and Its Ordering at Century's End: Reflections on Emerging Trends in the United States*, 41 B.C. L. REV. 103 (1999). Copyright © 1999 Boston College Law Review. All rights reserved. Reprinted with permission.

Korobkin, Russell, *The Failed Jurisprudence of Managed Care, and How to Fix It: Reinterpreting ERISA Preemption*, 51 UCLA L. REV. 457 (2003). Originally published in 51 UCLA L. REV. 457 (2003). Copyright © 2003 UCLA Law Review. All rights reserved. Reprinted with permission.

Larson, Arthur, *The Nature and Origins of Workmen's Compensation*, 37 CORNELL L.Q. 206 (1952). Copyright © 1952 Cornell University. All rights reserved. Reprinted with permission.

Larson, Arthur & Larson, Lex K., LARSON'S WORKERS' COMPENSATION LAW (2004). Copyright © 2004 by Matthew Bender & Co., Inc., a member of the LexisNexis Group. All rights reserved. Reprinted with permission.

Linder, Marc, *Farm Workers and the Fair Labor Standards Act: Racial Discrimination in the New Deal*, 65 TEX. L. REV. 1335 (1987). Copyright © 1987 Texas Law Review

Acknowledgments

Association. All rights reserved. Reprinted with permission.

Lobel, Jules, *Losers, Fools & Prophets: Justice as Struggle*, 80 CORNELL L. REV. 1331 (1995). Copyright © 1995 Cornell University. All rights reserved. Reprinted with permission.

Lynd, Staughton, *Communal Rights*, 62 TEX. L. REV. 1417 (1984). Copyright © 1984 Texas Law Review Association. All rights reserved. Reprinted with permission.

Malamud, Deborah C., *Engineering the Middle Classes: Class Line-Drawing in New Deal Hours Legislation*, 96 MICH. L. REV. 2212 (1998). Copyright © 1998 the Michigan Law Review Association. All rights reserved. Reprinted with permission.

Matheny, Ken & Crain, Marion, *Disloyal Workers and the "Un-American" Labor Law*, 82 N.C. L. REV. 1705 (2004). Copyright © 2004 North Carolina Law Review. All rights reserved. Reprinted with permission.

Matsuda, Mari J., *Voices of America: Accent, Antidiscrimination Law, and a Jurisprudence for the Last Reconstruction*, 100 YALE L.J. 1329 (1991). Reprinted with permission of The Yale Law Journal Company and William S. Hein Company from The Yale Law Journal, Vol. 100, pages 1329–1407.

Miller, Scott D., *Revitalizing the FLSA*, 19 HOFSTRA LAB. & EMP. L.J. 1 (2001). Copyright © 2001 Hofstra Labor & Employment Law Journal. All rights reserved. Reprinted with permission.

Morris, Charles J., *NLRB Protection in the Nonunion Workplace: A Glimpse at a General Theory of Section 7 Conduct*, 137 U. PA. L. REV. 1673 (1989). Copyright © 1989 University of Pennsylvania Law Review. All rights reserved. Reprinted with permission of The University of Pennsylvania Law Review and William S. Hein Company.

Newman, Nathan, *Trade Secrets and Collective Bargaining: A Solution to Resolving Tensions in the Economics of Innovation*, 6 EMPLOYEE RTS. & EMP. POL'Y J. 1 (2002). Copyright © 2002 Workplace Fairness. All rights reserved. Reprinted with permission.

Quigley, William, *Full-Time Workers Should Not Be Poor: The Living Wage Movement*, 70 MISS. L.J. 889 (2001). Copyright © 2001 Mississippi Law Journal. All rights reserved. Reprinted with permission.

RESTATEMENT OF AGENCY. Copyright © 1957 by the American Law Institute. All rights reserved. Reprinted with permission.

RESTATEMENT (SECOND) OF CONTRACTS. Copyright © 1981 by the American Law Institute. All rights reserved. Reprinted with permission.

RESTATEMENT (SECOND) OF TORTS. Copyright © 1977 by the American Law Institute. All rights reserved. Reprinted with permission.

Ramirez, Steven A., *Diversity and the Boardroom*, 6 STAN. J.L. BUS. & FIN. 85 (2000). Copyright © 2000. All rights reserved. Reprinted with permission.

Riskin, Victoria & Farrell, Mike, *Profiting of the Backs of Child Laborers*, LOS ANGELES TIMES, Oct. 12, 2000, at B-11. Copyright © 2000 Victoria Riskin and Mike Farrell. All rights reserved. Reprinted with permission.

Rogers, Brishen, *Justice at Work: Minimum Wage Laws and Social Equality*, 92 TEX. L. REV. 1543 (2014). Copyright © 2014. All rights reserved. Reprinted with permission.

Acknowledgments

Rose-Ackerman, Susan, *Progressive Law and Economics—And the New Administrative Law*, 98 YALE L.J. 341 (1988). Reprinted with permission of The Yale Law Journal Company and William S. Hein Company from The Yale Law Journal, Vol. 98, pages 341–368.

Schultz, Vicki, *Life's Work*, 100 COLUM. L. REV. 1881, 1882, 1890–93, 1939–40 (2000). Copyright © 2000 Directors of the Columbia Law Review Association, Inc. All rights reserved. Reprinted with permission.

Schultz, Vicki, *The Sanitized Workplace*, 112 YALE L.J. 2061 (2003). Reprinted with permission of The Yale Law Journal Company and William S. Hein Company from The Yale Law Journal, Vol. 112, pages 2061–2193.

Schwab, Stewart J., *Wrongful Discharge Law and the Search for Third-Party Effects*, 74 TEX. L. REV. 1943 (1996). Copyright © 1996 Texas Law Review. All rights reserved. Reprinted with permission.

Schwartz, David S., *Mandatory Arbitration and Fairness*, 84 NOTRE DAME L. REV. 1247 (2009). Copyright © 2009. All rights reserved. Reprinted with permission.

Selmi, Michael, *The Price of Discrimination: The Nature of Class Action Employment Discrimination Litigation and Its Effects*, 81 TEX. L. REV. 1249 (2003). Copyright © 2003 Texas Law Review Association. All rights reserved. Reprinted with permission.

Selmi, Michael & Cahn, Naomi, *Caretaking and the Contradictions of Contemporary Policy*, 55 ME. L. REV. 289 (2003). Copyright © 2003 University of Maine Law School. All rights reserved. Reprinted with permission.

Shaviro, Daniel, *The Minimum Wage, the Earned Income Tax Credit, and Optimal Subsidy Policy*, 64 U. CHI. L. REV. 407 (1997). Copyright © 1997 University of Chicago Law Review. All rights reserved. Reprinted with permission.

Singer, Joseph William, *The Reliance Interest in Property*, 40 STAN. L. REV. 611 (1988). Copyright © 1988 The Board of Trustees of the Leland Stanford Junior University. All rights reserved. Reprinted with permission.

Slawson, W. David, *Unilateral Contracts of Employment: Does Contract Law Conflict With Public Policy?*, 10 TEX. WESLEYAN L. REV. 9, 30–31 (2003). Copyright © Texas Wesleyan Law Review and W. David Slawson. All rights reserved. Reprinted with permission.

Sturm, Susan, *Second Generation Employment Discrimination: A Structural Approach*, 101 COLUM. L. REV. 458 (2001). Copyright © 2001 Directors of the Columbia Law Review Association, Inc. All rights reserved. Reprinted with permission.

Summers, Clyde W., *Contingent Employment in the United States*, 19 COMP. LAB. L.J. 503 (1997). Copyright © 1997 Clyde W. Summers. All rights reserved. Reprinted with permission.

Summers, Clyde W., *Employment at Will in the United States: The Divine Right of Employers*, 3 U. PA. J. LAB. & EMP. L. 65 (2000). Copyright © 2000 University of Pennsylvania Journal of Labor and Employment Law. All rights reserved. Reprinted with permission.

Summers, Clyde W., *Individualism, Collectivism and Autonomy in American Labor Law*, 5 EMPLOYEE RTS. & EMP. POL'Y J. 453 (2001). Copyright © 2001 Workplace Fairness. All rights reserved. Reprinted with permission.

Acknowledgments

Preface

The law of work has evolved as a patchwork of legal interventions in the labor market, sometimes by statute, and sometimes through the common law of judicial decisions. Most law school curricula divide the law of work into three topical areas—Labor Law, Employment Law, and Employment Discrimination—and offer separate courses in each area. Labor law in the United States is understood to encompass the study of the National Labor Relations Act, the law governing union organizing and collective bargaining. It is the law of collective rights at work. Employment law refers to the statutes and common law governing individual rights at work. It ranges from minimum standards legislation to judicially created doctrines based in tort and contract law. Employment discrimination law deals with the statutes and interpretative case law advancing the antidiscrimination norm in the workplace. These statutes address the problem of status discrimination at work (e.g., discrimination on the basis of race, sex, national origin, ethnicity, religion, disability, or sexual orientation).

Regulation of the employment relation defies such categorical thinking, however. The law has struggled with the tension between the desire to leave things to private contract and market forces, and the impulse to intervene to redress inequitable results occasioned by the imbalance of power between employees and employers. In some areas freedom of contract principles have prevailed. In other areas the law has considered it essential to extend protection to employees to act collectively in dealing with the employer, as in the labor laws. An increasingly prevalent response is government legislation to afford minimum standards of protection to all workers, and particularly to those historically disadvantaged in the American labor market, such as people of color, women, and persons with disabilities. These legal regimes overlap and relate to one another in complex ways that are obscured by categorical study.

We believe that acquaintance with historical context and the multiple legal structures governing the workplace is vital for today's lawyers. Historical legal context affords important insights about how the law may evolve in the future. Understanding the story behind the decline of labor unions and labor law provides critical assistance in evaluating new employee representation systems and conceptualizing rights. Minimum standards legislation was established partly because gaps in union representation left many workers unprotected at the workplace. Antidiscrimination law responded to union failures to represent the rights of subordinated groups. Is there any logical stopping point to this progression? As each new right is conceptualized and political momentum builds for legal protection, will laws continue to proliferate? Similarly, as groups of employees previously excluded from protection against discrimination press for legal agency, will new employment discrimination statutes be enacted? Where is the sunset? Yet at the same time, the politics of the global economy militate in favor of more flexibility for U.S. employers attempting to compete in an international market. Will employers block such legislation? Will legislative impasse ensue, as it ultimately did in the area of labor law? What, then, might evolve to replace individual statutory rights?

A comprehensive study of the law of work also provides an opportunity to assess critically what form enforcement of rights should take. Should conflicts between employers and employees be channeled into private resolution systems such as collective bargaining or contractual arbitration, or is the public interest sufficient to justify committing administrative, judicial and legislative resources to it? What is the significance of casting employee rights as collective—and therefore entrusting their enforcement to an employee representative such as a union—versus conceptualizing them as individual? Must such a collective representative be independent of the employer, or do employer-initiated employee committees further worker voice just as effectively? Doesn't history also warn of the risks of subordinating individual interests to those of the collective, particularly in the context of a diverse workforce with minority groups characterized by race, ethnicity or gender?

Accordingly, we have denominated this text "Work Law" and endeavor here to present basic materials on each system of labor market regulation. We identify core themes of conflict and concern in the workplace, canvass the governing law, and offer a vantage point for assessment. Several themes furnish the organizing structure for the book. We ask how law should mediate the perennial conflict between employer and employee rights; what difference it makes whether employee rights are conceptualized individually or collectively; what significance the increasing racial, ethnic, and gender diversity of the workforce should have for legal policy; whether dispute resolution systems should be privatized (via collective bargaining or individual contract) or remain in the public fora (courts and legislatures); and whether law is the most effective way to address interests of employers and employees (as contrasted, for example, with human resource practices, employer initiatives, or employee self-help measures).

The book will be most useful in Employment Law courses that address the significance of conceptualizing rights at work individually as opposed to collectively. Its strength, we believe, is its refusal to categorize the law of the workplace in doctrinal boxes that may be out-of-date by the time the book reaches maturity. We advert to Labor Law principles at a number of points throughout the book, but at a policy level rather than a doctrinal level, as a way of introducing and evaluating an alternative model of employee representation; we assume no knowledge of Labor Law on the part of teacher or student and make no effort here to provide a satisfactory substitute for a Labor Law text. We offer some detail in the law of Employment Discrimination but do so primarily with an eye toward surveying the field and assessing antidiscrimination regulation as a response to an increasingly diverse workforce, rather than providing an in-depth study of Employment Discrimination principles.

This text surveys the existing legal landscape, but it does not stop there. Work Law is an exciting and intellectually stimulating practice area because it is of necessity in a constant state of flux, responding to labor market innovations. Flexibility in thinking is vital to this area of practice. We urge students to reject traditional rigid categories and to ask: what new paths might emerge from a holistic conception of Work Law, and the demolition of categorical divides between Labor Law, Employment Law, and Employment Discrimination Law? Toward that end, we offer the following specific questions as a guide for study. We suggest that professors and students consider them in each area covered throughout the course:

1. Which worker desires predominate in this area? Which employer desires predominate? What public interests, if any, are at stake? In short, what is the justification for law to enter the market in this area?

2. What form has the law assumed in this area: e.g., statutory, common law, agency regulation/decisionmaking?

Preface

    A.   What is the substance of the law?

    B.   Who is covered by it (how are covered employees defined, which employers are covered)?

    C.   What are the catalysts for change and is the law in this area receptive to change?

3. What remedies does the law offer for the harms/problems it conceptualizes? Are they adequate?

    A.   How is the law enforced and what are the enforcement mechanisms? Who enforces it (e.g., watchdog system or individuals, agency or union, etc.)? Is the law enforced by federal or state authorities?

    B.   What is the interaction between systems of law addressing a given area (e.g. collective bargaining and individual statutory rights; federal vs. state regulation)?

    C.   Is adjudication private or public? What is the significance of this choice?

4. What extralegal alternatives are available? What human resource strategies have employers developed to manage their workforces? What self-help strategies do employees utilize, both individually and collectively? Are they adequate?

Several colleagues were instrumental in getting this project off the ground. We owe a huge debt to Professor Charles Craver, whose encouragement and vision made this book possible. Without his careful planning, insight, and enthusiasm we might not have attempted this task. Professor Cynthia Estlund collaborated on the outline and philosophy of the text, and was a guiding force in the project's early days. Much of her work appears throughout these pages, as well. Professor Clyde Summers' thoughtful scholarly assessment of the law of work was a powerful influence on our conceptualization of the materials presented here and his voice is audible through many excerpts from his work. We are grateful to him, and to the many other authors whose work graces these pages, for permission to use their words to tell the story of Work Law.

We owe thanks to all who have assisted us in our day-to-day work on this project. We offer special thanks to Washington University School of Law and George Washington University Law Center who provided research support; to our hardworking and enthusiastic student research assistants Kelly Behr, Erika Hanson, Lisa Mays, Michelle Seares, Robert Sonnenfelt, Sylvia Tsakos, and Alex Zuckerman and our clerical support, Nancy Cummings.

We have included relevant statutory provisions at appropriate points in the text for convenience; accordingly, use of a Statutory Supplement is not necessary. We chose to edit the cases according to the following conventions: parallel citations and other distracting material have been removed to make the cases as readable as possible. Extraneous detail was omitted to conserve space and focus attention on the issues in the principal cases we included, using ellipses to indicate all deletions of text other than footnotes or citations to authority. Original footnote numbers for included footnotes are shown in brackets at the outset of the footnote. We conformed to bluebook citation format wherever possible to ensure consistency, but ignored the rules when they were silly or unhelpful.

We hope you enjoy this journey through the law of work!

Marion Crain
Pauline Kim
Mike Selmi

TABLE OF CONTENTS

Table of Contents

Table of Contents

Table of Contents

Table of Contents

Table of Contents

Table of Contents

Table of Contents

Table of Contents

Table of Contents

Table of Contents

Table of Contents

Table of Contents

Part One

INTRODUCTION: REGULATING WORK

We begin the journey through Work Law with an overview of the evolving nature of the employment relation and a survey of the predominant systems of legal regulation: private individual contract, unionization and collective bargaining, and government intervention to establish minimum protections for workers. Chapter 1 begins by exploring the public's interest in regulating the employment relation. The law of work is one of the most politically divisive issues in the public arena. What is it about work that makes this terrain so hotly contested?

Chapter 1 next traces the historical regulation of the employment relation, beginning with the primacy of freedom of contract as applied to individual contracts between presumed equals and the theoretical foundations of the American rule of employment at-will. We will see the rise of collective action and unionization and the contemporaneous effort by states to enact worker protective legislation. Although such efforts were initially turned back by the courts, national labor policy eventually shifted, and courts embraced a vision of workers as dependent and in need of protection from exploitation by more powerful employers. New Deal legislation—including laws protecting the right of workers to organize unions and to bargain collectively with their employers over wages, hours, and working conditions, and the early worker-protection statutes—was sustained against constitutional challenge on this theory. A new era was born, characterized by private ordering of the employment relationship through unionism and collective bargaining augmented by a social safety net of legislation enacted to protect workers and to spur the economy by encouraging consumption.

Ultimately, however, unionism and collective bargaining declined and government intervention in the public interest became the dominant model of workplace regulation. A new wave of statutory and judicially-created employee rights supplanted unionism and labor law as the primary source of workers' rights. Significantly, these new rights were conceptualized as individual rights, not collective rights. Individual contract again took on more importance as the vast bulk of workers were forced to negotiate individually, without union representation.

In Chapter 2, we consider more recent shifts in workforce demographics and the structure of work. The pressures of workforce diversification by gender, race, and ethnicity and the aging of the workforce create new challenges for employers and for Work Law. Further, the structure of employment has morphed significantly in response to a globalized labor market undergoing rapid transformation. The advent of new technologies, global competition, and shifting social norms pose both new threats and new opportunities. We ask how the employment relationship is being reformulated in the modern labor market, and what the implications for Work Law are. We also provide an introduction to the important questions of which relationships count as employment and who qualifies as an employee for purposes of protection under the various sources of Work Law, as well as which entities count as employers for purposes of imposing liability.

Chapter 1

ORIGINS

In this opening chapter, we will briefly consider how the employment relation has been characterized and regulated at law. At common law, employment was originally viewed as a master-servant relation in which the master's authority to exercise control over the work done and the persons who would perform it was absolute. Employer sovereignty emanated from property rights to control the business and to direct the workers who labored in it. American law soon developed a presumption that employment was at will and could be terminated by either party without notice or cause. The parties were free to contract to any terms they wished. The inherent inequality of bargaining power between employers and individual employees, however, made such freedom illusory. Workers responded by organizing labor unions and demanding collective bargaining rights. Widespread strikes and disruption of the economy soon led the government to enter the fray, first with laws promoting unionization and collective bargaining designed to channel workplace disputes into the private law mechanisms of bargaining and arbitration, and later with laws mandating minimum employment terms. Statutes prohibiting discrimination in employment followed.

The powerful ethos of individualism and freedom of contract were not easily subdued, however. Unionism and collective bargaining soon suffered a dramatic decline in popularity. As union density declined, the government found it necessary to intervene to regulate the employment relation more and more frequently to restrain employer power and protect individual employee rights. A new individual rights model of employment law began to emerge, enforced primarily by administrative agencies and individual workers. Courts once again became the ultimate arbiters of the employment relation, interpreting and applying statutory language and eventually authoring new common law doctrines that limited the force of the employment at will doctrine.

The struggle to define the nature of the employment relation and to control how work is done, who does it, and under what conditions has occupied a central role in American law. Before turning to the historical details of this struggle, we pause briefly to consider what is at stake. What is the social and economic significance of work in our culture?

A. THE MEANING OF WORK

Kenneth L. Karst, *The Coming Crisis of Work in Constitutional Perspective*
82 Cornell L. Rev. 523, 530–34 (1997)

. . . For countless millions, work is a chore, a burden to be borne, a source of anxiety and conflict. In Studs Terkel's memorable words, for a large proportion of Americans work is "a Monday through Friday sort of dying," a kind of "violence—to the spirit as well as to the body." So, these people might ask, what is so liberating about work?

Probably the most vivid answers to that question would come from people who are unemployed. They seek work not for its own sake, but for the rewards it brings, both tangible and intangible. As far back as the colonial era, New Englanders invested work with an almost religious character, and white Americans generally spoke of the dignity of work, recognizing that work had much to do with defining the person. Yet, it was not work in general that they dignified, but the autonomy that was both expressed and reinforced by the free choice to work. The delegates to the Constitutional Convention reflected this attitude in the wicked bargain that recognized a sharp distinction between free persons and slaves. The legal conditions of free men (such was the usual locution) came to be defined in contrast to slavery. If a slave was dependent, bound by law to work for another's profit and under that person's control, a free citizen was independent, mobile, with the liberty to work in one pursuit or another, and for his or her own family's benefit. To be a citizen is to be a respected and responsible participant in the public life of the community. Even in those early times, work was a medium through which a free man might demonstrate that he was a citizen.

Today, I concede, other social meanings of work usually are more conspicuous. . . . Most obviously, jobs are "the entry tickets to provisions." Whatever other meanings work may bear, for most of us it is a crucial means of sustaining ourselves and our families. Work can be a teacher, offering the chance to learn tasks at increasing levels of authority and increasing levels of pay. Central to "the American dream" is the notion that a free and independent individual can rise to a better condition through hard work, and that his or her family can join in the rise. Especially vital to family security today are the health care and pension benefits that attach to many jobs. Where there are young children, decent child care becomes an additional family concern.

To speak of family status and family security is to recognize that work means much more than a paycheck; it is the exercise of responsibility. The responsibilities involved in work extend not just to our loved ones but to our coworkers, and even to the larger community. Work is still seen as connected to the citizenship values of respect, independence, and participation. In our society, as much as anywhere else in the world, work is a means of proving yourself worthy in your own eyes and in the eyes of others. Even a person who hates his or her job can understand the idea of "[t]he dignity of work and of personal achievement." . . .

Many years ago I was at a big party, among strangers. Some small talk had suggested that the woman next to me was a teacher in a local school. Lacking anything better to say, I opened with, "So, you're a school teacher?" Her reply was chilly: "It's what I do; it's not who I am." I was duly chastened; of course there is more to a person than the way she earns her living. But there is also truth in the comment, "You become your job." Work shapes individual identities in ways both general and particular. Consider such terms as initiative, dependability, industry, attention to detail, and cooperativeness—or still more general terms such as work habits or the work ethic. Terms like these—or their opposites accenting irresponsibility and sloth—are internalized, made a part of the individual worker's sense of self. Furthermore, particular jobs have their own socializing effects, from the do-it-by-the-book mindset of the clerks in a welfare office to the hypermasculinity of the "splicers" who maintain heavy cables that are strung on towers and under the ground.

The idea that we become our jobs has another dimension: the work we do affects other people's evaluations of us. Prominent among the social meanings of work is a rough popular status-ordering of types of work. These status evaluations are strongly influenced by differences in pay, but they are also affected by other kinds of perceptions that are widely shared: the power associated with the job (police officer), the importance of the work to society at large (school teacher), the difficulty of entry into the job (opera conductor), the individual's independence in performing the task (architect), the complexity of the work (scientific researcher), the level of creativity demanded by the work (sculptor), or the level of training required (veterinarian). These public perceptions of what we do—or, more precisely, our assumptions about other people's perceptions—become part of our own sense of what our work is worth, and, more generally, what we are worth as individuals.

What happens to individuals and families when the formal freedom to work becomes hollow because stable work with a decent wage, decent health and retirement benefits, and access to decent child care just isn't available? Most obviously, family income is sharply reduced. But other harms of unemployment and underemployment are less tangible, growing out of the positive social meanings that Americans have invested in work:

—If stable, adequately paid work is a source of independence, its absence means dependence on others.

—If stable, adequately paid work is an avenue to personal achievement, its absence signifies failure.

—If stable, adequately paid work offers advancement up the socioeconomic ladder, its absence means that one's social station is either fixed or in decline.

—If stable, adequately paid work provides family security, its absence means insecurity.

—If stable, adequately paid work elicits the esteem of others, its absence means shame. . . .

NOTES

1.   Work as Burden, or Benefit? Karst begins with the stark statement that for many, work is drudgery. He then describes a perspective at the opposite end of the continuum in which work brings meaning and identity to those fortunate enough to be employed. Can both be true at the same time? What factors might influence a worker's outlook on work?

2.   Work as Virtue. The significance of work in the lives of most Americans resonates with themes of Protestantism, particularly self-sufficiency and industriousness. While some past civilizations viewed work as a "degrading pursuit to be carried out by those at the bottom of their cultural hierarchy," modern Western culture sees hard work and diligence as positive virtues, marks of good character. If industriousness is a virtue, wealth becomes a sign of God's blessing. In this vision of the world, it is axiomatic that unemployment and poverty are evidence of wickedness and sin. *See* SHARON BEDER, SELLING THE WORK ETHIC 10–14, 16–19 (2000); MICHELLE LAMONT, THE DIGNITY OF WORKING MEN 26 (2000); Edward J. McCaffery, *The Burden of Benefits*, 44 VILL. L. REV. 445, 473–78 (1999) (describing how early federal welfare programs conditioned receipt of benefits on an assessment of a family's perceived "worthiness").

3.   The Relationship Between Identity and Work. Reflect upon your own experience of work. In what ways is your identity linked to the work you do? How has the work you have done so far changed you as a person? How does your occupation impact others' perception of you? Vicki Schultz observes:

> The process of adapting ourselves to our work roles does not stop at the office door or factory gate. As human beings, we are not purely instrumental, and we cannot easily compartmentalize the selves we learn to become during working hours. In fact, most of us spend more time working than doing anything else. So, it should not be surprising that the strategies we use to succeed as workers become infused into our behavior, thoughts, feelings, and senses of ourselves—our very beings—with real spillover effects in our so-called "private" lives.

Vicki Schultz, *Life's Work*, 100 COLUM. L. REV. 1881, 1890–91 (2000).

4.   Work and Gender. Is the significance of work the same regardless of gender? Beginning with the industrial revolution, government policy was premised on a male-headed nuclear family with a gendered division of labor in which the husband served as breadwinner and the wife performed unpaid homemaking and childcare. While this vision of appropriate gender roles no longer describes the vast majority of households, it continues to influence employment policy—as well as family policy—at many levels. *See* Marion Crain, *"Where Have All the Cowboys Gone?" Marriage and Breadwinning in Postindustrial Society*, 60 OHIO ST. L.J. 1877, 1917–20 (1999).

What is the relationship between work and sex equality? What should it be? Vicki Schultz suggests that the structure of employment shapes workers' attitudes about gender roles and their identities themselves; workers' views about work and gender roles are not fixed at the point in time that they first enter the workforce, but are shaped by their experience of work. Therefore, she argues, Work Law reform should play a central role in furthering sex equality. *See* Vicki Schultz, *Telling Stories About Women and Work: Judicial Interpretations of Sex Segregation on the Job in Title VII Cases Raising the Lack of Interest Argument*, 103 HARV. L. REV. 1749 (1990). Consider Schultz's vision of the norms that Work Law could impart:

> The idea that work shapes identity may not be controversial when applied to men who work in high-status occupations. We understand that "the job makes the man." However, we almost never assume that the same is true of women. Despite women's presence in the paid labor force in overwhelming numbers, we still tend to see women as inauthentic workers. . . .

> In the conventional conception of femininity, women are first and foremost committed to domesticity—as wives, mothers, daughters, sisters, general nurturers, and providers of care and cleanup. Sometimes, this connection is portrayed as natural and essential, either biologically endowed or so deeply ingrained in our psyches that it would be almost impossible to change. In other theories, it is learned through early childhood socialization or constructed through mass culture (such as the media). But even in the versions in which women's attachment to home and hearth is seen as acquired rather than given, that attachment is seen as fixed firmly in place long before women ever begin working (or searching for work). If women's domestic orientation is fixed by the time we enter the labor force, then women's actions, aspirations, and self-understandings cannot and will not change much in response to our experiences in the world of paid work. Thus, in the conventional view, paid work neither creates nor offers any hope of relief from the material and other disadvantages that mark women's lives. . . .

> In my vision, paid work should serve as a foundation that secures to women and men from all walks of life a source of equal citizenship, economic wherewithal, social ties, and personal identity. Everyone would have a right to train for and pursue work of their own choosing, and each of us would earn a living wage by doing that work (our wages supplemented by the state, if necessary). Individual adults, rather than families (however defined), would be the unit of analysis for purposes of wages and other state subsidies, guaranteeing that no adult would have to depend on another for basic economic support. No one would have to work the death-and-disability-dealing hours that many of us do now. Everyone would work saner, and more similar hours, so that all of us would have an opportunity to participate fully in family, friendship, politics, and civic life. Following current trends, a great deal of housework and caregiving would be converted into bundles of services that some people would do for a living—and a living wage. Most of us would continue to do a fair amount of housework and caregiving on our own, both in households that are not necessarily heterosexual or even nuclear in form, as well as in collective, community-based arrangements with friends, neighbors, and newcomers. To supplement such private initiatives, we would create and publicly finance a variety of different child care arrangements—including well-respected, state-financed child care programs that are so good for children that

everyone, including the middle-classes—would use them. In addition to child care, all adults would have access to the basic services they need to engage in suitable work, including health care, transportation, and continuing training. We would also have periodic sabbaticals, in which some portion of our wages is paid by the state, to allow us to fulfill our caregiving commitments and to perform public service work needed by the community or nation. Because everyone—men and women alike—would have access to work that provides economic security, social ties, and a strong source of selfhood, no one would be forced to stay in an intimate relationship that is not supportive or satisfying. Over time, the family would be reconstituted as a primarily affective realm in which adults come (and stay) together mainly for love rather than economic need.

This, to me, is a forward-thinking vision that builds on current trends and age-old aspirations to enable women and men of all walks of life to become full citizens—and fuller human beings—in the twenty-first century. This is what it means to secure the right to pursue a life's work.

Vicki Schultz, *Life's Work*, 100 Colum. L. Rev. 1881, 1882–93, 1939–40 (2000).

Should employers bear all the burdens and responsibility for fostering work-and-family balance? What role do gendered social norms about the distribution of family care work and household duties play in reinforcing the structure of paid work? Studies consistently find that despite some progress in the division of labor on household chores, women still do significantly more child care and housework than men. *See* Suzanne M. Bianchi, John P. Robinson, & Melissa A. Milkie, Changing Rhythms of Family Life 64, tbl. 4.1; 93, tbl. 5.1 (2006); Alexandra Sifferlin, *Women Are Still Doing Most of the Housework*, Time Mag., June 18, 2014 (summarizing data from the Bureau of Labor Statistics). Why should employers change their practices to facilitate egalitarian distribution of family work if men have not changed their behavior? *See* Michael Selmi, *The Work-Family Conflict: An Essay on Employers, Men and Responsibility*, 4 U. St. Thomas L.J. 573 (2007) (evaluating arguments).

5. **Work and Race.** Is the significance of work the same across racial lines? Many scholars argue that it is not. For example, members of outsider groups may be required to perform identity work to counter negative stereotypes associated with their race or ethnicity in order to satisfy seemingly objective work standards. *See* Mitu Gulati & Devon W. Carbado, *Working Identity*, 85 Cornell L. Rev. 1259 (2000). Several studies also suggest that African-American workers place a higher priority on solidarity with other workers than do whites, in part because of their experience of resisting racial segregation and discrimination. *See, e.g.*, Michele Lamont, The Dignity of Working Men 20–21 (2000). This propensity for collective action has translated into higher union organizing win rates for African-Americans than for whites, particularly in racially homogenous work units. *See* Kate Bronfenbrenner & Tom Juravich, *It Takes More than House Calls: Organizing to Win with a Comprehensive Union-Building Strategy, in* Organizing to Win: New Research on Union Strategies 19, 32 (Kate Bronfenbrenner *et al.*, eds., 1998).

6. **Work as a Constitutional Right?** If work is so important, why doesn't it rise to the level of a constitutional right? Karst provides a partial answer:

[I]t may seem incongruous that the Supreme Court in the modern era has not given constitutional recognition to a free-standing right to work. Even in the days when the Court was invalidating wage-and-hour laws and other governmental restrictions on the liberty of the employment contract, the Justices gave no hint of any individual right to be afforded work. The liberty in question was a formal freedom from governmental regulation of private bargains, grounded on a formal equality of right—and never mind the huge differences in the bargaining power of employers and workers. But even this formal legal equality could be submerged. For one example among many, a potential worker who claimed a freedom to be idle might be imprisoned because his idleness was made into the crime of vagrancy, but the idea of imposing on potential employers a correlative legal duty to provide work was unthinkable. Any assertion of an employer's constitutional duty would encounter the "state action" limitation that had been read into the Fourteenth Amendment, and a statute imposing a similar duty would be an unconstitutional invasion of the employer's sphere of private liberty. Nor could any comparable duties be imposed on the states or Congress. Government's constitutional duty was noninterference, and no one in authority thought that judges could compel legislators or executive officials either to employ the unemployed or to take other positive action on their behalf.

Kenneth L. Karst, *The Coming Crisis of Work in Constitutional Perspective*, 82 Cornell L. Rev. 523, 535–36 (1997).

William Forbath has argued for recognition of a constitutional right to work that would place responsibility on Congress and on state legislatures to ensure decent work and an acceptable income for all. Re-envisioning the right to work as grounded in the constitution, Forbath suggests, would afford a constitutional dimension to governmental decisions about the structure of labor markets, the financial order, and other economic realms. *See* William E. Forbath, *Why Is This Rights Talk Different from All Other Rights Talk? Demoting the Court and Reimagining the Constitution*, 46 Stan. L. Rev. 1771, 1790–92 (1994); *see also* William P. Quigley, *The Right to Work and Earn a Living Wage: A Proposed Constitutional Amendment*, 2 CUNY L. Rev. 139 (1998) (proposing an amendment to the federal Constitution that would guarantee a right to work and a right to receive a living wage). If there were a constitutional dimension to the right to work, would it be acceptable for governments to target an unemployment rate higher than zero?

B.   THE RISE AND FALL OF FREEDOM OF CONTRACT

The employment relation in the United States originated as an amalgam of free contract and master-servant status. As we will see in Chapter 3, the default rule was that employment contracts were mutually terminable at will. At the same time, however, the law was laced with assumptions concerning the presumed authority of the master (employer) to exercise authority and control over the servant (employee), as well as duties of loyalty and obedience owed by the servant to his master. The law's deference to the employer's prerogative to manage its business was shored up by a belief that employers would act as guardians of the social welfare in ways that individual employees would not. Employers whose capital-intensive operations were located in a particular city could be expected to further the interests of the community, while a transient workforce that lacked a permanent stake in the area could not be trusted to do the same. The laws permitting incorporation and the "locking in" of financial capital dovetailed with this under-standing of employer interests as coextensive with those of the community. *See* Margaret M. Blair, *Locking in Capital: What Corporate Law Achieved for Business Organizers in the Nineteenth Century*, 51 UCLA L. REV. 387, 454 (2003). By contrast, workers' efforts to collectively organize and alter the paradigm of managerial control were viewed as disloyal, selfish, and even greedy. Unsurpris-ingly, judicial reaction to early efforts at labor organizing was hostile. State court judges conceptualized labor organizing as a criminal conspiracy designed to injure the public welfare because demands for wage increases inevitably resulted in higher prices for consumer goods. Employers, on the other hand, were viewed as lacking in "vindictive passions" and stood as "guardians of the community from imposition and rapacity." *Philadelphia Cordwainers' Case [Commonwealth v. Pullis]*, Phila-delphia Mayor's Court (1806), 3 DOC. HIST. OF AM. IND. SOC. 59, 137–38 (2d ed. Commons 1910).

These assumptions were ultimately cloaked in constitutional garb when the Court elevated the employer's right to discharge to a due process right of constitutional stature. The two earliest cases embodying this idea involved workers who were discharged because of their membership in labor unions. In *Adair v. United States*, 208 U.S. 161 (1908), the Court struck down a federal statute prohibiting discrimination against union members in employment. The Court reiterated the general rule that "the right of the employee to quit the service of the employer, for whatever reason, is the same as the right of the employer, for whatever reason, to dispense with the services of such employee." *Id.* at 174–75. The Court then declared that federal legislation that infringes on this two-sided bargain by compelling an employer to retain a worker is "an invasion of the personal liberty as well as of the right of property, guaranteed by [the 5th] Amendment." *Id.* at 172. The Court explained:

> . . . [I]t is not within the functions of government—at least in the absence of contract between the parties—to compel any person in the course of his business and against his will to accept or retain the personal services of another, or to compel any person, against his will, to perform personal services for another. . . .

> It was the legal right of the defendant Adair—however unwise such a course might have been—to discharge Coppage because of his being a member of a labor organization, as it was the legal right of Coppage, if he saw fit to do so—however unwise such a course on his part might have been—to quit the service in which he was engaged, because the defendant employed some persons who were not members of a labor organization. In all such particulars the employer and the employee have equality of right, and any legislation that disturbs that equality is an arbitrary interference with the liberty of contract which no government can legally justify in a free land.

Id. at 174–75. Subsequently, similar state legislation was invalidated under the due process clause of the Fourteenth Amendment. *See Coppage v. Kansas*, 236 U.S. 1 (1915).

Once employers' power to dictate conditions of employment through private contract on pain of discharge was recognized as a constitutional right, it followed that employers also possessed the right to establish standards of employment (rates and hours of pay, for example) through private contract. Courts soon applied the freedom of contract rationale more broadly to strike down minimum standards legislation enacted by the states.

LOCHNER v. NEW YORK
United States Supreme Court
198 U.S. 45 (1905)

[The Court was called upon to pass on the constitutionality of the New York state labor law limiting the number of hours that workers could work per week in bakeries. The statute provided:

> § 110, *Hours of labor in bakeries and confectionery establishments.*—No employee shall be required or permitted to work in a biscuit, bread, or cake bakery or confectionery establishment more than sixty hours in any one week, or more than ten hours in any one day, unless for the purpose of making a shorter work day on the last day of the week; nor more hours in any one week than will make an average of ten hours per day for the number of days during such week in which such employee shall work. . . .]

statute @ issue

Mr. Justice Peckham, after making the foregoing statement of the facts, delivered the opinion of the Court.

The indictment . . . charges that the plaintiff . . . wrongfully and unlawfully required and permitted an employee working for him to work more than sixty hours in one week. . . . The mandate of the statute, that "no employee shall be required or permitted to work," is the substantial equivalent of an enactment that "no employee shall contract or agree to work," more than ten hours per day; and, as there is no provision for special emergencies, the statute is mandatory in all cases. It is not an act merely fixing the number of hours which shall constitute a legal day's work, but an absolute prohibition upon the employer permitting, under any circumstances, more than ten hours work to be done in his establishment. The employee may desire to earn the extra money which would arise from his working more than the prescribed time, but this statute forbids the employer from permitting the employee to earn it.

The statute necessarily interferes with the right of contract between the employer and employees, concerning the number of hours in which the latter may labor in the bakery of the employer. The general right to make a contract in relation to his business is part of the liberty of the individual protected by the 14th Amendment of the Federal Constitution. Under that provision no state can deprive any person of life, liberty, or property without due process of law. The right to purchase or to sell labor is part of the liberty protected by this amendment, unless there are circumstances which exclude the right. There are, however, certain powers, existing in the sovereignty of each state in the Union, somewhat vaguely termed police powers, the exact description and limitation of which have not been attempted by the courts. Those powers, broadly stated, and without, at present, any attempt at a more specific limitation, relate to the safety, health, morals, and general welfare of the public. Both property and liberty are held on such reasonable conditions as may be imposed by the governing power of the state in the exercise of those powers, and with such conditions the 14th Amendment was not designed to interfere.

The state, therefore, has power to prevent the individual from making certain kinds of contracts, and in regard to them the Federal Constitution offers no protection. If the contract be one which the state, in the legitimate exercise of its police power, has the right to prohibit, it is not prevented from prohibiting it by the 14th Amendment. Contracts in violation of a statute, either of the Federal or state government, or a contract to let one's property for immoral purposes, or to do any other unlawful act, could obtain no protection from the Federal Constitution, as coming under the liberty of person or of free contract. Therefore, when the state, by its legislature, in the assumed exercise of its police powers, has passed an act which seriously limits the right to labor or the right of contract in regard to their means of livelihood between persons who are *sui juris* (both employer and employee), it becomes of great importance to determine which shall prevail—the right of the individual to labor for such time as he may choose, or the right of the state to prevent the individual from laboring, or from entering into any contract to labor, beyond a certain time prescribed by the state.

This court has recognized the existence and upheld the exercise of the police powers of the states in many cases which might fairly be considered as border ones, and it has, in the course of its determination of questions regarding the asserted invalidity of such statutes, on the ground of their violation of the rights secured by the Federal Constitution, been guided by rules of a very liberal nature, the application of which has resulted, in numerous instances, in upholding the validity of state statutes thus assailed. Among the later cases where the state law has been upheld by this court is that of *Holden v. Hardy, 169 U. S. 366* [1898]. A provision in the act of the legislature of Utah was there under consideration, the act limiting the employment of workmen in all underground mines or workings, to eight hours per day, "except in cases of emergency, where life or property is in imminent danger." It also limited the hours of labor in smelting and other institutions for the reduction or refining of ores or metals to eight hours per day, except in like cases of emergency. The act was held to be a valid exercise of the police powers of the state. A review of many of the cases on the subject, decided by this and other courts, is given in the opinion. It was held that the kind of employment, mining, smelting, etc., and the character of the employees in such kinds of labor, were such as to make it reasonable and proper for the state to interfere to prevent the employees from being constrained by the rules laid down by the proprietors in regard to labor. . . .

The question whether this act is valid as a labor law, pure and simple, may be dismissed in a few words. There is no reasonable ground for interfering with the liberty of person or the right of free contract, by determining the hours of labor, in the occupation of a baker. There is no contention that bakers as a class are not equal in intelligence and capacity to men in other trades or manual occupations, or that they are not able to assert their rights and care for themselves without the protecting arm of the state, interfering with their independence of judgment and of action. They are in no sense wards of the state. Viewed in the light of a purely labor law, with no reference whatever to the question of health, we think that a law like the one before us involves neither the safety, the morals, nor the welfare, of the public, and that the interest of the public is not in the slightest degree affected by such an act. The law must be upheld, if at all, as a law pertaining to the health of the individual engaged in the occupation of a baker. It does not affect any other portion of the public than those who are engaged in that occupation. Clean and wholesome bread does not depend upon whether the baker works but ten hours per day or only sixty hours a week. The limitation of the hours of labor does not come within the police power on that ground.

It is a question of which of two powers or rights shall prevail—the power of the state to legislate or the right of the individual to liberty of person and freedom of contract. The mere assertion that the subject relates, though but in a remote degree, to the public health, does not necessarily render the enactment valid. The act must have a more direct relation, as a means to an end, and the end itself must be appropriate and legitimate, before an act can be held to be valid which interferes with the general right of an individual to be free in his person and in his power to contract in relation to his own labor. . . .

We think the limit of the police power has been reached and passed in this case. There is, in our judgment, no reasonable foundation for holding this to be necessary or appropriate as a health law to safeguard the public health, or the health of the individuals who are following the trade of a baker. If this statute be valid, and if, therefore, a proper case is made out in which to deny the right of an individual, *sui juris*, as employer or employee, to make contracts for the labor of the latter under the protection of the provisions of the Federal Constitution, there would seem to be no length to which legislation of this nature might not go. . . .

We think that there can be no fair doubt that the trade of a baker, in and of itself, is not an unhealthy one to that degree which would authorize the legislature to interfere with the right to labor, and with the right of free contract on the part of the individual, either as employer or employee. In looking through statistics regarding all trades and occupations, it may be true that the trade of a baker does not appear to be as healthy as some other trades, and is also vastly more healthy than still others. . . . It might be safely affirmed that almost all occupations more or less affect the health. There must be more than the mere fact of the possible existence of some small amount of unhealthiness to warrant legislative interference with liberty. It is unfortunately true that labor, even in any department, may possibly carry with it the seeds of unhealthiness. But are we all, on that account, at the mercy of legislative majorities? A printer, a tinsmith, a locksmith, a carpenter, a cabinetmaker, a dry goods clerk, a bank's, a lawyer's, or a physician's clerk, or a clerk in almost any kind of business, would all come under the power of the legislature, on this assumption. No trade, no occupation, no mode of earning one's living, could escape this all-pervading power, and the acts of the legislature in limiting the hours of labor in all employments would be valid, although such limitation might seriously cripple the ability of the laborer to support himself and his family. In our large cities there are many buildings into which the sun penetrates for but a short time in each day, and these buildings are occupied by people carrying on the business of bankers, brokers, lawyers, real estate, and many other kinds of business, aided by many clerks, messengers, and other employees. . . . It might be said that it is unhealthy to work more than that number of hours in an apartment lighted by artificial light during the working hours of the day; that the occupation of the bank clerk, the lawyer's clerk, the real estate clerk, or the broker's clerk, in such offices is therefore unhealthy, and the legislature, in its paternal wisdom, must, therefore, have the right to legislate on the subject of, and to limit, the hours for such labor; and, if it exercises that power, and its validity be questioned, it is sufficient to say, it has reference to the public health; it has reference to the health of the employees condemned to labor day after day in buildings where the sun never shines; it is a health law, and therefore it is valid, and cannot be questioned by the courts.

It is also urged, pursuing the same line of argument, that it is to the interest of the state that its population should be strong and robust, and therefore any legislation which may be said to tend to make people healthy must be valid as health laws, enacted under the police power. . . . The act is not, within any fair meaning of the term, a health law, but is an illegal interference with the rights of individuals, both employers and employees, to make contracts regarding labor upon such terms as they may think best, or which they may agree upon with the other parties to such contracts. Statutes of the nature of that under review, limiting the hours in which grown and intelligent men may labor to earn their living, are mere meddlesome interferences with the rights of the individual, and they are not saved from condemnation by the claim that they are passed in the exercise of the police power and upon the subject of the health of the individual whose rights are interfered with, unless there be some fair ground, reasonable in and of itself, to say that there is material danger to the public health, or to the health of the employees, if the hours of labor are not curtailed. . . .

It is manifest to us that the limitation of the hours of labor as provided for in this section of the statute under which the indictment was found, and the plaintiff in error convicted, has no such direct relation to, and no such substantial effect upon, the health of the employee, as to justify us in regarding the section as really a health law. It seems to us that the real object and purpose were simply to regulate the hours of labor between the master and his employees (all being men, *sui juris*), in a private business, not dangerous in any degree to morals, or in any real and substantial degree to the health of the employees. Under such circumstances the freedom of master and employee to contract with each other in relation to their employment, and in defining the same, cannot be prohibited or interfered with, without violating the Federal Constitution.

The judgment of the Court of Appeals of New York, as well as that of the Supreme Court and of the County Court of Oneida County, must be reversed and the case remanded to the County Court for further proceedings not inconsistent with this opinion.

Reversed.

MR. JUSTICE HARLAN, with whom MR. JUSTICE WHITE and MR. JUSTICE DAY concurred, dissenting.

DISSENT

It is plain that this statute was enacted in order to protect the physical wellbeing of those who work in bakery and confectionery establishments. It may be that the statute had its origin, in part, in the belief that employers and employees in such establishments were not upon an equal footing, and that the necessities of the latter often compelled them to submit to such exactions as unduly taxed their strength. Be this as it may, the statute must be taken as expressing the belief of the people of New York that, as a general rule, and in the case of the average man, labor in excess of sixty hours during a week in such establishments may endanger the health of those who thus labor. Whether or not this be wise legislation it is not the province of the court to inquire. Under our systems of government the courts are not concerned with the wisdom or policy of legislation. So that, in determining the question of power to interfere with liberty of contract, the court may inquire whether the means devised by the state are germane to an end which may be lawfully accomplished and have a real or substantial relation to the protection of health, as involved in the daily work of the persons, male and female, engaged in bakery and confectionery establishments. But when this inquiry is entered upon I find it impossible, in view of common experience, to say that there is here no real or substantial relation between the means employed by the state and the end sought to be accomplished by its legislation. Nor can I say that the statute has no appropriate or direct connection with that protection to health which each state owes to her citizens; or that it is not promotive of the health of the employees in question, or that the regulation prescribed by the state is utterly unreasonable and extravagant or wholly arbitrary. Still less can I say that the statute is, beyond question, a plain, palpable invasion of rights secured by the fundamental law. Therefore I submit that this court will transcend its functions if it assumes to annul the statute of New York. It must be remembered that this statute does not apply to all kinds of business. It applies only to work in bakery and confectionery establishments, in which, as all know, the air constantly breathed by workmen is not as pure and healthful as that to be found in some other establishments or out of doors.

ct is stepping on legislature toes

— & the dissenter think yes

Professor Hirt in his treatise on the "Diseases of the Workers" has said: "The labor of the bakers is among the hardest and most laborious imaginable, because it has to be performed under conditions injurious to the health of those engaged in it. It is hard, very hard, work, not only because it requires a great deal of physical exertion in an overheated workshop and during unreasonably long hours, but more so because of the erratic demands of the public, compelling the baker to perform the greater part of his work at night, thus depriving him of an opportunity to enjoy the necessary rest and sleep,—a fact which is highly injurious to his health." Another writer says: "The constant inhaling of flour dust causes inflammation of the lungs and of the bronchial tubes. The eyes also suffer through this dust, which is responsible for the many cases of running eyes among the bakers. The long hours of toil to which all bakers are subjected produce rheumatism, cramps, and swollen legs. The intense heat in the workshops induces the workers to resort to cooling drinks, which, together with their habit of exposing the greater part of their bodies to the change in the atmosphere, is another source of a number of diseases of

condition of baking

(rem: this case = 1905)

various organs. Nearly all bakers are palefaced and of more delicate health than the workers of other crafts, which is chiefly due to their hard work and their irregular and unnatural mode of living, whereby the power of resistance against disease is greatly diminished. The average age of a baker is below that of other workmen; they seldom live over their fiftieth year, most of them dying between the ages of forty and fifty. During periods of epidemic diseases the bakers are generally the first to succumb to the disease, and the number swept away during such periods far exceeds the number of other crafts in comparison to the men employed in the respective industries. . . . "

We judicially know that the question of the number of hours during which a workman should continuously labor has been, for a long period, and is yet, a subject of serious consideration among civilized peoples, and by those having special knowledge of the laws of health. Suppose the statute prohibited labor in bakery and confectionery establishments in excess of eighteen hours each day. No one, I take it, could dispute the power of the state to enact such a statute. But the statute before us does not embrace extreme or exceptional cases. It may be said to occupy a middle ground in respect of the hours of labor. What is the true ground for the state to take between legitimate protection, by legislation, of the public health and liberty of contract is not a question easily solved, nor one in respect of which there is or can be absolute certainty. There are very few, if any, questions in political economy about which entire certainty may be predicated. . . .

. . . [T]he state is not amenable to the judiciary, in respect of its legislative enactments, unless such enactments are plainly, palpably, beyond all question, inconsistent with the Constitution of the United States. We are not to presume that the state of New York has acted in bad faith. Nor can we assume that its legislature acted without due deliberation, or that it did not determine this question upon the fullest attainable information and for the common good. We cannot say that the state has acted without reason, nor ought we to proceed upon the theory that its action is a mere sham. Our duty, I submit, is to sustain the statute as not being in conflict with the Federal Constitution, for the reason—and such is an all-sufficient reason—it is not shown to be plainly and palpably inconsistent with that instrument. Let the state alone in the management of its purely domestic affairs, so long as it does not appear beyond all question that it has violated the Federal Constitution. This view necessarily results from the principle that the health and safety of the people of a state are primarily for the state to guard and protect. . . .

The judgment, in my opinion, should be affirmed.

MR. JUSTICE HOLMES dissenting. . . .

This case is decided upon an economic theory which a large part of the country does not entertain. If it were a question whether I agreed with that theory, I should desire to study it further and long before making up my mind. But I do not conceive that to be my duty, because I strongly believe that my agreement or disagreement has nothing to do with the right of a majority to embody their opinions in law. It is settled by various decisions of this court that state constitutions and state laws may regulate life in many ways which we as legislators might think as injudicious, or if you like as tyrannical, as this, and which, equally with this, interfere with the liberty to contract. Sunday laws and usury laws are ancient examples. A more modern one is the prohibition of lotteries. The liberty of the citizen to do as he likes so long as he does not interfere with the liberty of others to do the same, which has been a shibboleth for some well-known writers, is interfered with by school laws, by the Postoffice, by every state or municipal institution which takes his money for purposes thought desirable, whether he likes it or not. . . . Some of these laws embody convictions or prejudices which judges are likely to share. Some may not. But a Constitution is not intended to embody a particular economic theory, whether of paternalism and the organic relation of the citizen to the state or of *laissez faire*. It is made for people of fundamentally differing views, and the accident of our finding certain opinions natural and familiar, or novel, and even shocking, ought not to conclude our judgment upon the question whether statutes embodying them conflict with the Constitution of the United States. . . .

NOTES

1. **The Slippery Slope of Government Intervention in the Market.** The *Lochner* majority worried that if it were to sustain the maximum hours statute as an exercise of the state's police power to protect the public health or the bakers' health, there would be "no length to which legislation of this nature might not go." Did the Court overstate this concern?

Just a few years earlier, the Court had upheld similar legislation setting maximum hours for underground miners. *See Holden v. Hardy,* 169 U.S. 366 (1898). How did the Court distinguish *Holden*? Are you persuaded that the distinction between bakers and underground miners is viable? According to the Court, in what contexts would legislative intervention be sustainable? Would legislative findings that this particular occupation was unhealthful and dangerous be sufficient?

[handwritten margin note: safety of occup.]

2. **The Role of Labor Unions in Supporting Maximum Hours Legislation.** The Bakery and Confectionery Workers' International Union was instrumental in bringing about the maximum hours legislation challenged in *Lochner*. By the 1890s, many of the larger commercial bakeries in New York were unionized. Most of the unionized bakers in large bakeries did not actually work more than 10 hours per day and 60 hours per week. The unionized bakers were worried, however, that union jobs would be threatened by the smaller non-unionized bakeries' propensity to require their employees to work much longer hours. The initial publicity that exposed the unsanitary conditions in the smaller bakeries was spurred by a member of the Bakery and Confectionery Workers' International Union, who persuaded news reporters to investigate the working conditions in these bakeries. The maximum hours law was passed with the support of the union and the larger commercial bakeries, who believed the law would help limit competition from the smaller bakeries. The unions' support for maximum hours legislation was thus motivated not only by the health concerns discussed in *Lochner*, but by the unions' interest in protecting members' jobs at the larger bakeries by squeezing out of the market the smaller bakeries with which they competed. An organization of smaller bakeries, the New York Association of Master Bakers, eventually brought the legal challenge to the maximum hours statute. *See* David Bernstein, Rehabilitating Lochner (2010).

3.   Protective Legislation for Women Workers. *Lochner* was something of an aberration in its historical context. It was one of very few cases decided before the 1920s invalidating protective labor legislation. In addition to *Holden v. Hardy*, the Court upheld several general protective workplace laws in the same time frame. *See, e.g., Atkin v. Kansas*, 191 U.S. 207 (1903) (upholding legislation regulating employment on public works projects); *Dayton Coal & Iron Co. v. Barton*, 183 U.S. 23 (1901) (upholding legislation requiring mining company to pay workers in cash rather than in "scrip").

Just a few years after rendering its opinion in *Lochner*, the Court upheld an Oregon statute limiting the employment of women in mechanical establishments, factories, or laundries to no more than ten hours per day. *See Muller v. Oregon*, 208 U.S. 412 (1908). The Court distinguished *Lochner* on the grounds that the regulation of the working hours of women rested upon powerful justifications that did not apply to the regulation of hours of male workers. Specifically, "the physical organization of women," "her maternal functions," "the rearing and education of the children," and "the maintenance of the home" justified state intervention to protect women, whose "physical structure and . . . performance of maternal functions place her at a disadvantage in the struggle for subsistence," especially "when the burdens of motherhood are upon her." *Id.* at 419, 421. Noting the "injurious effects" of prolonged working hours on women's bodies and the public interest in fostering women's health "in order to preserve the strength . . . of the race," *id.* at 421, the Court concluded that the maximum hours legislation did not offend the liberty of contract. Subsequently, the Court issued several other rulings upholding maximum hours legislation for women. *See, e.g., Bosley v. McLaughlin*, 236 U.S. 385 (1915); *Miller v. Wilson*, 236 U.S. 373 (1915). Cases involving protective legislation for women became established as "a separate category within due process" principles. *See* JULIE NOKOV, CONSTITUTING WORKERS, PROTECTING WOMEN: GENDER, LAW, AND LABOR IN THE PROGRESSIVE NEW ERA AND NEW DEAL YEARS 138 (2001).

4.   *Lochner's* Revival: A Gender-Neutral Freedom of Contract? Soon thereafter, *Lochner's* freedom of contract rationale was revived and expanded to invalidate protective legislation for women workers, as well. In *Adkins v. Children's Hospital*, 261 U.S. 525 (1923), the Court struck down a minimum wage law applicable to women and children employed in the District of Columbia, reasoning that the statute interfered with the freedom of contract guaranteed by the Fifth Amendment's due process clause. The *Adkins* Court limited *Muller v. Oregon* to its historical context, noting that revolutionary changes in the intervening years had reduced the inequality of the sexes in contractual, political, and civil status "almost, if not quite, to the vanishing point." *Adkins*, 261 U.S. at 553. Further, the D.C. statute did not single out particular occupations where work of long hours would pose a detriment to health, so it could not be sustained on that basis. Instead, it sought to regulate the "heart of the [employment] contract, that is, the amount of wages to be paid and received." *Id.* at 554. Despite a detailed legislative history justifying the minimum wage, including studies showing that the wage was the smallest amount with which a woman could purchase the bare necessities for survival, the Court found that the regulation was not defensible as an exercise of the state's police power:

. . . [The statute in question] does not prescribe hours of labor or conditions under which labor is to be done. It is not for the protection of persons under legal disability or for the prevention of fraud. It is simply and exclusively a price-fixing law, confined to adult women . . . who are legally as capable of contracting for themselves as men. It forbids two parties having lawful capacity—under penalties as to the employer—to freely contract with one another in respect of the price for which one shall render service to the other in a purely private employment where both are willing, perhaps anxious, to agree, even though the consequence may be to oblige one to surrender a desirable engagement and the other to dispense with the services of a desirable employee. The price fixed by the board [a three-person board authorized to hold public hearings and to determine the minimum wages payable] need have no relation to the capacity or earning power of the employee, the number of hours which may happen to constitute the day's work, the character of the place where the work is to be done, or the circumstances or surroundings of the employment. . . . It is based wholly on the opinions of the members of the board and their advisers . . . as to what will be necessary to provide a living for a woman, keep her in health and preserve her morals. It applies to any and every occupation in the District, without regard to its nature or the character of the work.

. . . .

[A] statute which prescribes payment . . . solely with relation to circumstances apart from the contract of employment, the business affected by it and the work done under it, is so clearly the product of a naked, arbitrary exercise of power that it cannot be allowed to stand under the Constitution of the United States.

Adkins, 261 U.S. at 554–55, 558. The gender-neutral heyday of freedom of contract continued into the 1930s, resulting in the invalidation of almost 200 state statutes.

5. **A Turning Point.** In *West Coast Hotel v. Parrish*, 300 U.S. 379 (1937), the Court abruptly shifted course and upheld a minimum wage law for women. Acknowledging the economic hardship of the Great Depression and the public interest in guaranteeing a minimum wage, the Court signaled its acceptance of protective legislation for men and women. The Court rejected arguments that the minimum wage law hurt workers who could not command the minimum, *id.* at 398–400, and noted that the continuation of inequalities in bargaining power ultimately burdened the state and more specifically the taxpayers, who were "bound to provide what is in effect a subsidy for unconscionable employers." *Id.* Citing *Muller*, the Court explained:

The exploitation of a class of workers who are in an unequal position with respect to bargaining power and are thus relatively defenceless [sic] against the denial of a living wage is not only detrimental to their health and well-being but casts a direct burden for their support upon the community. What these workers lose in wages the taxpayers are called upon to pay.

Id. One commentator assessed the dramatic turnaround from the *Lochner* principles to those adopted in *West Coast Hotel* in this way:

> *West Coast Hotel* signaled a significant theoretical shift during the New Deal Era, recognizing that government, through inaction (relying on "traditional market mechanisms within the common law framework") or action (enforcing labor standards), is making a choice to either subsidize "unconscionable employers," or a living wage for workers, respectively. . . .
>
> For the *Lochner* Era judiciary, "it was neutrality that the due process clause commanded, and neutrality was served only by the general or 'public' purposes comprehended by the police power." Common law categories were natural (pre-political) constructs forming the baseline "from which to measure deviations from neutrality, or self-interested deals." Under this logic, maximum hours legislation was unprincipled and partisan, rather than neutral, and therefore invalid. Popular opinion viewed such reasoning to reflect the courts' "laissez faire philosophy" and "general lack of interest and insufficiency of knowledge upon the subject of the effect of long hours of employment." As a lesson of the Civil War (e.g., the evils of slavery), such logic exposed market defects (unfettered buying and selling of labor producing coercion and dominance rather than protecting self-ownership and self-direction, e.g., freedom) requiring government protection of workers (minimum wage and maximum hours regulations). . . .
>
> Under the *West Coast Hotel* . . . labor standards baseline, the common law appeared less natural and inviolate. As President Franklin Roosevelt opined, "we must lay hold of the fact that economic laws are not made by nature. They are made by human beings." The baseline thus shifted from the common (contract) law to a system of labor standards (statutes and regulations) addressing wages, hours, and other conditions of employment.

Scott D. Miller, *Revitalizing the FLSA*, 19 HOFSTRA LAB. & EMP. L.J. 21–23 (2001). *West Coast Hotel* paved the way for enactment of the next wave of protective statutes that became the foundation for much of modern employment law: The New Deal.

    6.   The Legacy of *Muller* and *West Coast Hotel*. The Court's descriptions of women in *Muller, supra* at n. 3, and *West Coast Hotel, supra* at n.5, have a foreign ring to the modern ear. What is the significance of the fact that the justification for the state's intervention in the labor market to protect workers was a conception of women as victims in need of protection lest they (and their offspring) become public charges? The issues raised in *Muller* and *West Coast Hotel* with regard to the intersection between women's reproductive capacities and their role as employees were not easily put to rest. For example, in *UAW v. Johnson Controls, Inc.*, 499 U.S. 187 (1991) the Court struck down an employer's policy prohibiting fertile women from participating in relatively high-paying positions involving lead exposure that could be detrimental to their reproductive capacities. The Court reasoned that despite evidence of risks to the reproductive capacities of male employees, the employer's policy addressed only potential harm to women. Citing *Muller*, the Court observed:

> Concern for a woman's existing or potential offspring historically has been the excuse for denying women equal employment opportunities. . . . It is no more appropriate for the courts than it is for individual employers to decide whether a woman's reproductive role is more important to herself and her family than her economic role. Congress has left this choice to the woman as hers to make.

Id. at 211. Similarly, in 2014 the EEOC issued new enforcement guidance on pregnancy discrimination, requiring employers to make reasonable accommodation for pregnant workers and advising employers to develop specific job-related qualification standards that minimize the potential for gender stereotyping and discrimination on the basis of pregnancy, child birth, or related medical conditions. *See* U.S. EQUAL EMPLOYMENT OPPORTUNITY COMMISSION, ENFORCEMENT GUIDANCE: PREGNANCY DISCRIMINATION AND RELATED ISSUES, July 14, 2014, *available at* http://www.eeoc.gov/laws/guidance/pregnancy_guidance.cfm. We will consider these issues further in connection with discussions of stereotypes about working mothers in Chapter 10.

C.　THE NEW DEAL LABOR LEGISLATION

In 1933, President Roosevelt's administration put forth the "New Deal," a program of regulation designed to spur the economic recovery following the Great Depression. The New Deal policy was to reduce wage competition so that American workers would enjoy higher wages and more secure employment and therefore would spend more money, stimulating business growth which in turn would create more jobs. The New Deal labor and employment policies were committed to the regulation of employment at the local level, by agreement between the employer and the workers, who knew best the particular issues and needs of their industry. Thus, the core of the New Deal was the commitment to labor unionism as a vehicle for worker representation and collective bargaining between employer and union as a means to establish the terms and conditions of employment. Federal labor law protected the right to organize and imposed an obligation on employers to bargain collectively with the representative of their employees, first through the Railway Labor Act of 1926, 45 U.S.C. §§ 151–63, then through the short-lived National Industrial Recovery Act of 1933 (struck down by the Court in *A.L.A. Schechter Poultry Corp. v. United States*, 295 U.S. 495 (1935), as an unconstitutional delegation of government power to private interests), and finally through the National Labor Relations Act (Wagner Act) of 1935, 29 U.S.C. §§ 151–68. Federal wage and hour law, first through the Davis-Bacon Act of 1931, 40 U.S.C. § 276a (establishing minimum wage standards on public projects) and the Walsh-Healey Public Contracts Act of 1936, 41 U.S.C. §§ 35–45 (requiring government contractors to adopt an 8-hour day and a 40-hour workweek, to pay a prevailing minimum wage determined by the Secretary of Labor, and restricting the hiring of children), and later through the Fair Labor Standards Act of 1938, 29 U.S.C. §§ 201–19 (establishing a threshold minimum wage and providing incentives for employers to spread work and create new jobs by requiring the payment of overtime wages for hours worked in excess of 40 per week). We will study the Fair Labor Standards Act in Chapter 11 (Wages and Hours).

1. The Labor Laws

The Wagner Act was the first in a trilogy of Congressional enactments that have come collectively to be called the National Labor Relations Act (NLRA), or more popularly, the labor laws. (The Labor Management Relations Act of 1947 (Taft-Hartley amendments) and the Labor Management Reporting and Disclosure Act of 1959 (Landrum-Griffin amendments) complete the trilogy.) The Wagner Act declared it to be the "policy of the United States" to encourage worker self-organization and collective bargaining as a means to facilitate labor peace and the uninterrupted flow of interstate commerce. The theory of the Act was that requiring the exchange of information and establishing a therapeutic outlet for discussion would encourage employers and unions to resolve their differences through bargaining rather than through the exercise of economic weapons (the strike and the lockout). As the Court explained in an early case: "The basic theme of the Act was that through collective bargaining the passions, arguments, and struggles of prior years would be channeled into constructive, open discussions leading, hopefully, to mutual agreement." *H.K. Porter Co. v. NLRB*, 397 U.S. 99, 103 (1970). Nevertheless, effective bargaining required leverage, and the right to strike was accordingly protected as an incidental necessity. The Wagner Act conferred rights to organize and to bargain collectively on employees, and proscribed employer "unfair labor practices" that interfered with those rights. The Act created the National Labor Relations Board, charged with authority to settle representation questions arising under the Act and to prosecute violations of its unfair labor practice provisions.

The selection of collective bargaining as the preferred means of resolving workplace disputes was no accident in a democratic society. By establishing the vehicles for asserting collective voice—unionization and collective bargaining—Congress hoped to enhance and support the larger political democracy. Senator Wagner, the principal proponent of the new labor law in Congress, wrote this justification for the legislation:

> Under modern conditions government by the people is not so simple. Politics in the narrower sense is becoming impersonalized. People cannot join in as they joined in the old New England town meeting. The country is too large, its problems too complex, the pace of life too rapid. For the masses of men and women the expression of the democratic impulse must be within the industries they serve—it must fall within the ambit of their daily work.

> That is why the struggle for a voice in industry, through the processes of collective bargaining is at the heart of the struggle for the preservation of political as well as economic democracy in America. Let men become the servile pawns of their masters in the factories of the land and there will be destroyed the bone and sinew of resistance to political dictatorship.

Robert F. Wagner, *The Ideal Industrial State—As Wagner Sees It*, N.Y. TIMES, May 9, 1937, at 23. The Act's supporters touted an additional benefit of worker representation and participation in workplace management through collective bargaining: They argued that it would promote efficiency and productivity by combating feelings of powerlessness and worker alienation.

Shortly after its enactment, the Supreme Court upheld the Wagner Act against a constitutional challenge in the following case.

NLRB v. Jones & Laughlin Steel Corp., 301 U.S. 1 (1937). The NLRB found that a large company that manufactured steel and iron had committed unfair labor practices by coercing and intimidating employees who were seeking to organize a union, and discharging employees in retaliation for union organizing. The Board ordered the company to reinstate the workers with backpay, to cease and desist from further discriminatory acts, and to post notices stating that it would no longer engage in such discriminatory actions. The company refused to comply, and the NLRB petitioned the Court of Appeals for enforcement of its order. The court denied the petition, finding that the order exceeded the Board's power. The Board petitioned the Supreme Court for review.

The employer argued that the NLRA represented an unconstitutional incursion by the federal government on powers reserved to the states over local concerns, placing all industrial relations under federal supervision. The Supreme Court rejected the argument, finding that the Act's sweep was much more limited: it applied only to activities that burden or obstruct interstate commerce. Further, the Act's goal—to facilitate industrial peace—was closely linked to the Act's protection of collective bargaining, which had been shown to reduce labor strife. The Court explained:

> . . . [I]n its present application, the statute goes no further than to safeguard the right of employees to self-organization and to select representatives of their own choosing for collective bargaining or other mutual protection without restraint or coercion by their employer.
>
> That is a fundamental right. Employees have as clear a right to organize and select their representatives for lawful purposes as the respondent has to organize its business and select its own officers and agents. Discrimination and coercion to prevent the free exercise of the right of employees to self-organization and representation is a proper subject for condemnation by competent legislative authority. Long ago we stated the reason for labor organizations. We said that they were organized out of the necessities of the situation; that a single employee was helpless in dealing with an employer; that he was dependent ordinarily on his daily wage for the maintenance of himself and family; that, if the employer refused to pay him the wages that he thought fair, he was nevertheless unable to leave the employ and resist arbitrary and unfair treatment; that union was essential to give laborers opportunity to deal on an equality with their employer. . . . Fully recognizing the legality of collective action on the part of employees in order to safeguard their proper interests, we said [in a case construing the Railway Labor Act] that Congress was not required to ignore this right but could safeguard it. Congress could seek to make appropriate collective action of employees an instrument of peace rather than of strife. We said that such collective action would be a mockery if representation were made futile by interference with freedom of choice. . . .

The stoppage of [respondent's] operations by industrial strife would have a most serious effect upon interstate commerce. In view of respondent's far-flung activities [the company boasted 19 subsidiaries and a completely integrated operation that included transportation facilities], it is idle to say that the effect would be indirect or remote. It is obvious that it would be immediate and might be catastrophic. We are asked to shut our eyes to the plainest facts of our national life and to deal with the question of direct and indirect effects in an intellectual vacuum. Because there may be but indirect and remote effects upon interstate commerce in connection with a host of local enterprises throughout the country, it does not follow that other industrial activities do not have such a close and intimate relation to interstate commerce as to make the presence of industrial strife a matter of the most urgent national concern. When industries organize themselves on a national scale, making their relation to interstate commerce the dominant factor in their activities, how can it be maintained that their industrial labor relations constitute a forbidden field into which Congress may not enter when it is necessary to protect interstate commerce from the paralyzing consequences of industrial war? We have often said that interstate commerce itself is a practical conception. It is equally true that interferences with that commerce must be appraised by a judgment that does not ignore actual experience.

Experience has abundantly demonstrated that the recognition of the right of employees to self-organization and to have representatives of their own choosing for the purpose of collective bargaining is often an essential condition of industrial peace. Refusal to confer and negotiate has been one of the most prolific causes of strife. This is such an outstanding fact in the history of labor disturbances that it is a proper subject of judicial notice and requires no citation of instances. . . .

Id. at 33–42. To the employer's objection that the NLRA represented an excessive intrusion on its right to manage and control its business, the Court responded:

The Act does not compel agreements between employers and employees. It does not compel any agreement whatever. It does not prevent the employer 'from refusing to make a collective contract and hiring individuals on whatever terms' the employer 'may by unilateral action determine.' The Act expressly provides in section 9(a) that any individual employee or a group of employees shall have the right at any time to present grievances to their employer. The theory of the Act is that free opportunity for negotiation with accredited representatives of employees is likely to promote industrial peace and may bring about the adjustments and agreements which the Act in itself does not attempt to compel. . . . The Act does not interfere with the normal exercise of the right of the employer to select its employees or to discharge them. The employer may not, under cover of that right, intimidate or coerce its employees with respect to their self-organization and representation, and, on the other hand, the Board is not entitled to make its authority a pretext for interference with the right of discharge when that right is exercised for other reasons than such intimidation and coercion. The true purpose [of the employer's discharge decision] is the subject of investigation with full opportunity to show the facts. It would seem that when employers freely recognize the right of their employees to their own organizations and their unrestricted right of representation there will be much less occasion for controversy in respect to the free and appropriate exercise of the right of selection and discharge.

. . .

Id. at 45–46.

NOTES

1. **The Impact of Strikes on the American Economy.** One of the central justifications for enactment of the Wagner Act was the need for federal control over labor policy towards the goal of achieving industrial peace. In the era of *Jones & Laughlin*, work stoppages were widespread and had an extraordinarily disruptive impact on the economy. The disruptive impact of strikes was a particular concern in periods surrounding wartime. First, labor organizing and labor unionism were seen as fundamental acts of disloyalty, not only to the employer, but to the state. American legislatures and courts considered unions to be dangerously subversive societies creating their own constitutions, rules, and social aims in an attempt to legislate without constitutional authority—a direct threat to judicial and legislative authority. To these lawmakers, worker organizing and pressure strategies evidenced contempt for the state and the law itself—a form of dissent that the state could ill afford to tolerate within its boundaries when at war. *See* Ken Matheny & Marion Crain, *Disloyal Workers and the "Un-American" Labor Law*, 82 N.C. L. Rev. 1705 (2004). Second, strikes interfered directly with military readiness. Thus, wartime pressures were important forces shaping the development of federal labor law. Ross E. Davies, *Strike Season: Protecting Labor-Management Warfare in the Age of Terror*, 93 Geo. L.J. 1783, 1795 (2005). After World War II ended, every major industry in America—including steel, coal, automobile manufacturing, electric products, meatpacking, and railroads—endured strikes. In this historical context, Congress's concern with achieving labor peace is understandable. *See* Philip Yale Nicholson, Labor's Story in the United States 243–44 (2004).

Would *Jones & Laughlin* be decided the same way today? In the modern era work stoppages have declined dramatically and are currently near their lowest level since the government began collecting statistics in 1947. *See* Bureau of Labor Statistics, Major Work Stoppages Involving 1000 or More Workers, 1947–2013, Table 1 (Feb. 12, 2014), *available at* http://www.bls.gov/news.release/wkstp.t01.htm. What weight, if any, should this fact receive?

2. **The Wagner Act as Amended.** The Wagner Act was subsequently amended by the Taft-Hartley Amendments in 1947 and the Landrum-Griffin Amendments in 1959. The Taft-Hartley Amendments were aimed at curbing organized labor, which had grown dramatically in numbers (from two million to 15 million in the 10 years following the Wagner Act) and in power in the years following the Wagner Act. The Taft-Hartley Amendments added a right of employees to refrain from organizing or becoming union members, eliminated the closed shop (a union clause requiring that employees become union members as a condition of obtaining employment), added union unfair labor practice provisions, conferred power on the Board to prevent

unfair labor practices by unions, and imposed limits on "blackmail" picketing by unions (picketing directed at forcing employees to join the union or to change their union affiliation, regardless of the results of elections or where the representation issue was unsettled). The Landrum-Griffin Amendments were aimed at curbing union power further and banned the use of the secondary boycott: direct union pressure on employers doing business with the primary "struck" employer in order to bring economic pressure indirectly to bear on the primary employer. Landrum-Griffin also targeted internal union corruption and the lack of democratic process within unions, establishing a bill of rights for union members.

The National Labor Relations Act (NLRA), as the sum of these amendments is known, created the National Labor Relations Board, an administrative body consisting of five members appointed by the President and charged with interpreting and enforcing the provisions of the Act. The heart of the Act, contained in § 7, provides:

> Employees shall have the right to self-organization, to form, join, or assist labor organizations, to bargain collectively through representatives of their own choosing, and to engage in concerted activities, for the purpose of collective bargaining or other mutual aid or protection, and shall also have the right to refrain from any or all of such activities. . . .

Section 7 rights are enforceable by filing unfair labor practice charges under § 8(a) (workers) or § 8(b) (employers). Note that section 7 rights are conferred on employees, not unions, and they encompass group activities other than union organizing or collective bargaining. Thus, even employees in nonunion workplaces who act together but are not seeking to organize a union have such rights. If employees do elect a union by majority vote, the employer is obligated to bargain with it. The collective bargaining obligation is defined in § 8(d), which provides:

> [T]o bargain collectively is the performance of the mutual obligation of the employer and the representative of the employees to meet at reasonable times and confer in good faith with respect to wages, hours, and other terms and conditions of employment, or the negotiation of an agreement, or any question arising thereunder . . . but such obligation does not compel either party to agree to a proposal or require the making of a concession.
>
> . . .

Collective bargaining is required over "mandatory" subjects: wages, hours, and terms and conditions of employment, but not on "permissive" subjects, such as plant closings and product marketing, which go to the core of an employer's entrepreneurial control. The parties are obligated to negotiate in good faith to impasse, but as the Court noted *in Jones & Laughlin*, the Act does not compel agreement.

3. **Enforcement of the NLRA.** The NLRA is enforced by the NLRB, which through its General Counsel is responsible for investigating and prosecuting unfair labor practices under the Act. The NLRB's quasi-judicial arm resolves the cases, first through administrative law judges who conduct hearings and take testimony, and subsequently through a five-member Board that reviews the decisions of the ALJs. The Board's decisions can be appealed directly to the U.S. Courts of Appeals, and from there to the U.S. Supreme Court.

The Act's remedial shortcomings have been widely criticized. First, the Act provides for only "make-whole" equitable relief: back pay, reinstatement, orders to post notices detailing the violation and the remedy ordered, and injunctive relief. Fines, punitive damages, and other penalties are generally not available (except against unions who violate the Act's secondary boycott prohibitions). Second, the Board's processes are characterized by lengthy procedural delays; it is not unusual for cases to require three years for resolution by the Board, and appeals through the judicial system easily extend that time frame. Stephen Befort explains in the following excerpt how the cumulative effects of the limited remedies and delay before the NLRB undermine the Act's ability to accomplish its goals:

> . . . [A] common employer tactic in opposing union organizational campaigns is to discharge the leading employee organizers. While the NLRA makes this conduct unlawful, it does little to deter its occurrence. The usual remedy under the NLRA for the illegal discharge of an employee organizer is a cease and desist order coupled with reinstatement and back pay. The NLRA does not provide for fines, punitive damages, or any other "penalty," and the discharged employee is subject to a duty to mitigate losses by finding alternative work. This "make whole" approach provides little deterrence against employers who realize that they can chill union organization efforts by immediately firing the employee organizers. The lack of remedial clout is compounded by the fact that lengthy procedural delays in resolving the resulting unfair labor practice charges operate to dissipate union support.
>
> The NLRA's relatively weak remedial scheme also diminishes the effectiveness of the Act's bargaining mandate. The only remedy recognized under the NLRA for a party's refusal to engage in good faith bargaining is an order requiring that party to return to the bargaining table. The Supreme Court of the United States has ruled that the NLRB is without power to impose substantive contract terms in the event of a violation even where the NLRB has concluded that an employer has acted in a manner designed to frustrate the bargaining process. Thus, an employer may engage in protracted "surface" bargaining with little fear of meaningful administrative intervention. The problem of "surface" bargaining is particularly acute when used by an employer as a tactic to avoid the consummation of an initial collective bargaining agreement. Approximately one-third of all newly certified union representatives fail to conclude a first contract. At this early stage, a union's inability to obtain a collective bargaining agreement virtually dooms it to an eventual decertification.
>
> Finally, an additional shortcoming of the NLRA scheme flows from an employer's ability to hire permanent replacements to fill the positions of striking employees. An employer lawfully may decline to reinstate a striker at the conclusion of a strike so long as the position continues to be occupied by a replacement employee. This practice significantly undercuts the power of unions in two respects. First, the threat of being permanently replaced serves to deter strikes and decreases the union's ability to use the threat of a strike as leverage in collective bargaining. Secondly, the permanent replacements have the right to vote in representation elections, while the

voting rights of displaced strikers typically cease twelve months after the beginning of the strike. These electoral rules, accordingly, permit an employer to rid itself of a union by pushing the employees into a strike and then hiring permanent replacements who vote to decertify the union in an election held a little more than twelve months after being hired.

Stephen F. Befort, *Labor and Employment Law at the Millennium: A Historical Review and Critical Assessment*, 43 B.C. L. Rev. 351, 373–75 (2002).

2.   The Philosophy of Unionism, Industrial Pluralism, and the Practice of Collective Bargaining

Richard B. Freeman & James L. Medoff, What Do Unions Do? 7–9 (1984)

As Hirschman pointed out in his important book [Albert O. Hirschman, Exit, Voice, and Loyalty (1970)], societies have two basic mechanisms for dealing with social or economic problems. The first is the classic market mechanism of exit-and-entry, in which individuals first respond to a divergence between desired and actual social conditions by exercising freedom of choice or mobility: the dissatisfied consumer switches products; the diner whose soup is too salty seeks another restaurant; the unhappy couple divorces. In the labor market, exit is synonymous with quitting, while entry consists of new hires by the firm. By leaving less desirable for more desirable jobs, or by refusing bad jobs, individuals penalize the bad employer and reward the good, leading to an overall improvement in the efficiency of the economic system. . . .

As long as the exit-entry market mechanism is viewed as the *only* adjustment mechanism, institutions like unions are invariably seen as impediments to the optimal operation of the economy.

 The second mode of adjustment is the political mechanism that Hirschman termed "voice." "Voice" refers to the use of direct communication to bring actual and desired conditions closer together. It means talking about problems: complaining to the store about a poor product rather than taking business elsewhere; telling the chef that the soup had too much salt; discussing marital problems rather than going directly to the divorce court. In a political context, "voice" refers to participation in the democratic process, through voting, discussion, bargaining, and the like. . . .

In the job market, voice means discussing with an employer conditions that ought to be changed, rather than quitting the job. In modern industrial economies, and particularly in large enterprises, a trade union is the vehicle for collective voice—that is, for providing workers as a group with a means of communicating with management.

Collective rather than individual bargaining with an employer is necessary for effective voice at the workplace for two reasons. First, many important aspects of an industrial setting are "public goods," that is, goods which will affect the well-being (negatively or positively) of every employee in such a way that one

benefits every 1 (handwritten margin note)

individual's partaking of the good does not preclude someone else from doing so. Safety conditions, lighting, heating, the speed of the production line, the firm's formal grievance procedure, pension plan, and policies on matters such as layoffs, work-sharing, cyclical wage adjustment, and promotion all obviously affect the entire workforce in the same way that defense, sanitation, and fire protection affect the community at large. . . .

Without a collective organization, the incentive for the individual to take into account the effects of his or her actions on others, or to express his or her preferences, or to invest time and money in changing conditions, is likely to be too small to spur action. . . .

collective voice is protected (handwritten margin note)

A second reason why collective action is necessary is that workers who are tied to a firm are unlikely to reveal their true preferences to an employer, for fear the employer may fire them. In a world in which workers could find employment at the same wages immediately, the market would offer adequate protection for the individual, but that is not the world we live in. The danger of job loss makes expression of voice by an individual risky. Collective voice, by contrast, is protected both by the support of all workers and by the country's labor law. . . .

NOTES

1.   **The Effects of Unionism.** By the late 1940s and early 1950s, American trade unionism had reached its zenith. The largest industries of mass production were heavily organized, including the crucial transport and infrastructure occupations—railroads, trucking, shipping, municipal transit, commercial construction, and electric power generation. Steel, auto, coal mining, meatpacking, and rubber industries were over 80% organized by the decade after World War II. Labor's claims commanded respect by the media, and labor's support was vital in political elections. Unions obtained wage increases with almost every contract negotiated. The most powerful unions secured cost-of-living adjustments protecting wages from inflationary erosion, and real wages doubled between 1940 and 1967. Wage differentials between racial groups were reduced as unions sought a uniform wage to avoid the potential for employers to undercut unionized workers' wages by shifting work to those who could be induced to perform it for less. Nelson Lichtenstein, State of the Unions 54–59 (2002). At the same time, unions negotiated for and obtained significant fringe benefits for their members, including health insurance, pension benefits, paid medical leave, vacation time, and enhanced overtime pay. These fringe benefits became standardized in the unionized sector and later spread to much of the nonunionized sector as well.

Nevertheless, a significant gap remains between the wages and benefits of unionized and nonunionized workers, and the gap has widened in recent years. In 2011, the union wage premium was 13.6% overall, and was highest for men, immigrants, and racial and ethnic minorities. Union workers were 28.2% more likely to have employer-provided health insurance, and 53.9% more likely to have employer-provided pensions. Lawrence Mishel, *Unions, Inequality, and the Faltering Middle Class*, Economic Policy Institute, Aug. 29, 2012, *available at* http://www.epi.org/publication/ib342-unions-inequality-faltering-middle-class/; George I. Long, *Differences Between Union and Nonunion Compensation,*

MONTHLY LAB. REV., April 2013, *available at* http://www.bls.gov/opub/mlr/2013/04/art2full.pdf.

Unions were also very successful in obtaining due process protections for workers that reduced the tyranny of the shop foreman over the workers by protecting workers against arbitrary discharge. Most labor contracts contained just-cause-for-discharge clauses that established a system of progressive discipline, ensuring that the workplace version of capital punishment—discharge—could not be imposed without warning and an opportunity to reform conduct. In addition, nearly every collective bargaining agreement established and administered a seniority system. Seniority systems served three functions, all beneficial in a unionized environment: they protected against favoritism by supervisors, furnishing an objective method for distributing benefits and opportunities; they provided union leaders with an objective means to settle disputes between union members over job entitlement; and they offered a basis upon which workers could predict their future employment position. At bottom, however, seniority principles were grounded in notions of equity:

> A company should not take from a man the best working years of his life and then, if times turn bad or he slows down, throw him out like so much spent machinery. A worker who has provided his employer with many years of faithful service is entitled to some protection when, no longer young, he can no longer protect himself.

Caroline Poplin, *Fair Employment in a Depressed Economy: The Layoff Problem*, 23 UCLA L. REV. 177, 196–97 (1975); *see also* Benjamin Aaron, *Reflections on the Legal Nature and Enforceability of Seniority Rights*, 75 HARV. L. REV. 1532, 1534 (1962).

2. Unions as a Lobbying Force for Workers' Rights. A less well-known but vitally important contribution made by unions during the 1960s and beyond is their role in lobbying for legislation protecting the rights of all workers, not just those in the unionized sector. Unions were an important political force in the enactment of Title VII, the Occupational Safety and Health Act, the Employee Retirement Income Security Act, the Worker Adjustment Retraining and Notification Act, the Family and Medical Leave Act, and other legislation conferring individual rights on workers. Unions also finance and pursue important impact litigation, including sex and race discrimination cases under Title VII, cases involving the constitutional rights of public sector employees, and cases involving the scope of minimum standards legislation such as the Fair Labor Standards Act and the Occupational Safety and Health Act. *See* Charlotte Garden, *Union Made: Labor's Litigation for Social Change*, 88 TUL. L. REV. 193 (2013).

Does it undermine the union marketing pitch for unions to lobby for such legislation and advance causes that benefit the nonunion sector? If workers possess individual rights by virtue of statutory enactment or judicial decisionmaking, why do they need unions to whom they must pay dues? Why, then, do unions spend such a significant portion of their budgets on lobbying and litigation?

3. The Theory of Industrial Pluralism. The system of collective bargaining implemented by the NLRA is premised on the model of industrial pluralism.

Richard Bales describes the model in the following excerpt:

Industrial pluralism is a model of social interaction between employers and employees that eschews outside interference, envisioning workers as sufficiently empowered to fend for themselves. According to this model, the NLRA establishes a framework through which employees can organize, thus acquiring the bargaining power necessary to demand better wages and working conditions. Industrial pluralism analogizes workplace relations to miniature political democracies. Employers and employees, roughly coequal, jointly negotiate and enforce an agreement that establishes the terms and conditions of employment. It is this agreement, rather than external sources of law, that creates the rights and duties of employers and employees. This process of collective bargaining, and its expressly contractarian ideology, thus gives employees a voice in decisions that significantly influence their lives. The NLRA, according to the industrial pluralist model, confers no substantive employment rights, but rather establishes the framework through which employees may jointly negotiate rights on their own behalf. Indeed, industrial pluralism seeks to put an end to individual bargaining and non-contractual employment rights. The collective bargaining process is thought to be adequate to protect whatever rights workers feel are worth negotiating for, and the essentially democratic nature of union representation ensures that workers' voices are adequately represented at the bargaining table.

The NLRA shifted workplace sovereignty from employers and courts to employers and employees, creating a framework for the joint determination of workplace rights through the collective bargaining process. Finding an internal mechanism for resolving disputes between employers and employees was critical to maintaining this shift in sovereignty. Arbitration became the mechanism. In the metaphor of industrial democracy, the workplace "legislature," composed of management and union representatives, negotiated and ultimately promulgated the law, or the "constitution" of the shop—the collective bargaining agreement. Arbitration, as an analog to courts of law, provided the mechanism by which that law was interpreted and applied. Not only did arbitration serve the instrumental function of interpreting and applying the law, it also fit the theoretical model of an autonomous system. The arbitrator was chosen by, and served at the whim of, the parties. The arbitrator's authority was derived exclusively from the terms of the collective bargaining agreement and from the "common law" of shop custom. Arbitration thus completed the metaphor of industrial organization as a self-contained mini-democracy—"an island of self-rule whose self-regulating mechanisms must not be disrupted by judicial intervention or other scrutiny by outsiders."

Richard A. Bales, *The Discord Between Collective Bargaining and Individual Employment Rights: Theoretical Origins and a Proposed Reconciliation*, 77 B.U. L. Rev. 687, 745–48 (1997).

4. **The Practice of Collective Bargaining.** The typical collective bargaining agreement contains clauses pertaining to four basic topics: union security and

management rights; the wage and effort bargain; individual job security; and contract administration:

(1) *Union Security and Management Rights*: includes a recognition clause describing the bargaining unit (employee positions covered), a clause specifying that the employer recognizes the union as the representative of the employees; union security provisions giving the union power over employment (requiring employees to either join the union or pay an equivalent fee to dues for the services the union provides); a clause requiring that the employer withhold union dues or their equivalent from employee paychecks, and remit them to the union (a dues checkoff clause); a clause reserving certain power to management (such as freedom to direct the business objectives of the company, to determine the scope and direction of the business, and to discipline or discharge workers for cause); and a duration and renewal clause specifying the duration of the collective agreement.

(2) *The Wage and Effort Bargain*: includes provisions specifying pay, hours, job classifications and rate ranges, premium pay for overtime or shift differential work; paid holidays and vacations; contingent benefits such as pensions, insurance plans, and other supplemental benefits.

(3) *Individual Job Security*: includes seniority provisions, provisions conferring superseniority (for example, on union shop stewards); just cause for discharge provision; progressive disciplinary procedures; and due process protections (known as the grievance procedure).

(4) *Administration*: clauses covering machinery designed to enforce the agreement, including scope of authority delegated to arbitrators under the grievance procedure clause.

See EDWIN BEAL & EDWARD WICKERSHAM, THE PRACTICE OF COLLECTIVE BARGAINING 259–64 (1972).

Additional clauses negotiated by modern unions and employers include "protected plant status" clauses (clauses that restrict management's right to close or downsize plants, source products, lay off employees or contract out work, invest capital, sell plants, etc.), successorship clauses (clauses that prohibit the employer from selling the plant except to a buyer who recognizes the union and negotiates a contract with it), protection against "runaway executive salaries" (clauses that place limits on executives' salaries), productivity and efficiency agreements (which establish a system for improving worker productivity), and organizing neutrality pledges and/or card check agreements by employers (promises by employers to remain neutral in organizing campaigns conducted in other units and/or to recognize new unions based upon a majority authorization card count rather than requiring an NLRB election).

3. The Decline of Unionism, Collective Bargaining, and Labor Law

The enactment of the Wagner Act gave union organizing a significant boost. Organizers told prospective members that the President wanted them to join a union, and workers responded. In the post-World War II industrial era, union membership reached its all-time high: by 1954, 35% of the American workforce covered by the NLRA was unionized. Between 1954 and 1980, union membership continued to grow but at a much slower rate than it had in the period immediately following the enactment of the Wagner Act. By 1970 union membership exceeded nineteen million, and by 1980 it was approximately 22 million, with much of the growth in those years coming from the public sector. However, the workforce expanded faster than unionization, and the relative position of unions declined steadily to 27% of the covered workforce by 1980. During the 1980s and 1990s, organized labor's share of the workforce dropped in both absolute and relative numbers.

By the end of 2014, the overall union membership rate had sagged to 11.1% of the nonagricultural workforce. The decline in private sector union membership has been even more dramatic than this figure suggests—just 6.6% of the nonagricultural workforce is unionized. *See* Bureau of Labor Statistics, Union Members in 2014, Table 1 (Jan. 23, 2015), *available at* http://www.bls.gov/news. release/pdf/union2.pdf. The growth of public sector union membership has compensated somewhat for the private sector decline (private sector employees account for about 60% of total union membership), although government cutbacks during the recent recession and political attacks on public sector unionism have resulted in public sector union membership declines, as well. *See* Joseph E. Slater, *The Assault on Public Sector Collective Bargaining: Real Harms and Imaginary Benefits, "The American Rule" That Swallows the Exception*, Issue Brief, The American Constitution Society for Law and Policy (June 2011), *available at* http://www.acslaw.org/sites/default/files/Slater_Collective_Bargaining.pdf

The decline in union membership has been attributed to a constellation of factors: (1) the shift in employment from industrial production, historically the core of union strength, to white-collar and service work; (2) the substitution of new technology for manufacturing workers and corresponding loss of union membership; (3) the shifting demographics of the labor force by age, sex, race, ethnicity, and education and labor's failure to adapt its organizing and representation to the new workforce; (4) the growth of the contingent workforce with its weaker labor market affiliation and reduced expectation of job tenure, which make it more difficult to unionize; (5) the globalization of labor and outsourcing of manufacturing and other low-skilled jobs to the south or to western states where union density is low and more recently to low-waged foreign countries; (6) the hardening of employer resistance to unionization, the remedial shortcomings of the NLRA, and the law's hostility toward organized labor; and (7) a tendency toward bureaucracy and complacency in union leadership, loss of militancy, and a concomitant drop in class consciousness of workers. *See generally* Charles C. Craver, Can Unions Survive? (1993); Michael Goldfield, The Decline of Organized Labor in the United States (1987).

Other western industrialized countries have experienced stagnation or declines in union density but at far slower rates. What might account for the relative steepness of the American decline? Some studies suggest that structural factors—in particular, the drop in the historically unionized goods-producing sector accompanied by a simultaneous rise in the nonunionized service sector, the decline in public sector employment, and the increase in part-time employment—are primarily responsible for the steep decline in the United States. *See* David Fairris & Edward Levine, *Declining Union Density in Mexico*, MONTHLY LAB. REV., Sept. 2004, at 14. These factors are not as significant in Canada, for example, where union density has hovered around 30% since 1998. *See id*; *Union Coverage in Canada*, 2013, *available at* http://www.labour.gc.ca/eng/resources/info/publications/union_coverage/union_cov2013_en.pdf.

Several studies emphasize the relationship between the uniquely unfavorable legal climate in the United States and union decline. Canadian law permits recognition and certification of unions in more expeditious fashion than in the United States. In most Canadian provinces, the union is automatically certified and a bargaining duty is imposed on the employer when the union presents evidence— usually in the form of signed authorization cards—that a majority of workers or other fixed percentage in the bargaining unit desires union representation for purposes of collective bargaining. (Some provinces have recently shifted from a card-check procedure to a mandatory election vote system for union certification similar to that which exists in the United States.) Mexican workers enjoy constitutional protection for organizing, and employers are obligated to bargain with any group of twenty workers who agree to become union members, regardless of whether they comprise a majority of the bargaining unit. *See* Stephen J. Befort & Virginia E. Cornett, *Beyond the Rhetoric of the NAFTA Treaty Debate: A Comparative Analysis of Labor and Employment Law in Mexico and the United States*, 17 COMP. LAB. L. 269 (1996); David L. Gregory, *The Right to Unionize in the United States, Canada, and Mexico: A Comparative Assessment*, 10 HOFSTRA LAB. L.J. 537 (1993). By contrast, American workers desiring unionization must produce signed authorization cards from a significant segment of the bargaining unit (30% or more) in order to petition the NLRB for an election. Following a period during which both parties vigorously campaign, the union must obtain greater than 50% of the vote in a secret ballot election in order to obtain bargaining rights. Once it does so, it becomes the exclusive representative for all the employees in the unit.

Employer resistance to unionism in the United States has also become increasingly aggressive relative to that in other western industrialized countries. In a landmark article published in 1983, Paul Weiler demonstrated empirically that employers resisting initial union organizing drives terminate approximately one in twenty and perhaps as many as one in five workers on the basis of their union organizing activity, an action specifically proscribed by the NLRA. This use of illegal and coercive tactics, he argued, was a major factor in the decline of union density. *See* Paul Weiler, *Promises to Keep: Securing Workers' Rights to Self-Organization Under the NLRA*, 96 HARV. L. REV. 1769, 1778–81 (1983); *see also* PAUL WEILER, GOVERNING THE WORKPLACE (1991); Richard W. Hurd & Joseph B. Uehlein, *Patterned Responses to Organizing: Case Studies of the Union-Busting Convention, in* SHELDON FRIEDMAN ET AL., RESTORING THE PROMISE OF AMERICAN LABOR LAW

61 (1994). More recent studies show more widespread violations: over half of all employers in a study of elections held between 1998 and 1999 made illegal threats to close all or part of their plants in retaliation for union organizing activities, with the threat rate considerably higher—approaching 70%—in mobile industries where the threat was especially credible, such as manufacturing and communications. The union win rate associated with campaigns in which employers made such threats was significantly lower than it was in those in which threats were not made. The overwhelming majority of the employers in the same sample also opposed the union campaign through a combination of threats, discharges, promises of improvements, unscheduled unilateral changes in wages or benefits, bribes, and surveillance—all illegal under the NLRA. *See* Kate Bronfenbrenner, *Uneasy Terrain: The Impact of Capital Mobility on Workers, Wages, and Union Organizing*, submitted to the U.S. Trade Deficit Review Commission, Sept. 6, 2000. A 2009 report of the Economic Policy Institute revealed that employers threatened plant closures in 57% of all union elections, discharged workers in 34% of elections, and threatened wage and benefit cuts in 47% of elections. Kate Bronfenbrenner, *No Holds Barred: The Intensification of Employer Opposition to Organizing* 1–2 (Econ. Pol'y Inst., Briefing Paper No. 235, 2009).

Over three-quarters of all employers now utilize anti-union consultants during the campaign and, if the union wins the election, during bargaining. Consultant use is highly correlated with union election losses and failure to obtain a first contract. Consultants advise employers on how to exploit the weaknesses in the NLRA's remedial scheme, how to produce and distribute effective anti-union propaganda, and in many cases, how to use illegal tactics—particularly those involving discharge of union activists, surveillance, interrogation, and threats. *See* John Logan, *Consultants, Lawyers, and the "Union Free" Movement in the USA Since the 1970s*, 33 INDUS. REL. L.J. 197, 198, 207–08 (2002); *see generally* MARTY LEVITT, CONFESSIONS OF A UNION BUSTER (1993). Many consultants are lawyers; some law firms routinely sponsor lucrative seminars on how to remain "union-free." Do such activities raise any ethical concerns?

State government officials, particularly in southern states, have sometimes been hostile to union organizing, as well. In 2011, Boeing announced plans to open a new production line for its 787 Dreamliner passenger plane. Concerned about a pattern of strikes by its unionized workers at its factory in Washington state in support of demands at the collective bargaining table, Boeing sought to locate the new production line in South Carolina, which is well-known for its low unionization rate. When unions in South Carolina sought to organize the new plant, Governor Nikki Haley made a series of public speeches and statements designed to discourage unionization, particularly at Boeing. South Carolina labor unions attempting to organize Boeing brought suit, arguing that Haley and appointed administrators were using the machinery of state government to prevent workers from joining or organizing unions, in violation of workers' First Amendment rights to free association and their rights to organize under the NLRA. Organizers complained that employees were unwilling to talk with them about unionization as a result. Steven Greenhouse, *Boeing Labor Dispute Is Making New Factory a Political Football*, N.Y. TIMES, June 30, 2011. A South Carolina district court ruled that these comments were mere political rhetoric rather than a threat of particular action that would violate the NLRA. *Int'l Ass'n of Machinists & Aerospace Workers v. Haley*, 832 F. Supp. 2d 612 (D.S.C. 2011). The court found that Haley's general public statements to the effect that she would do everything possible to maintain the state's right-to-work position were nothing more than comments consistent with her political identity, which the people of the state had endorsed by electing her. As to the comments specific to Boeing made by one of Haley's political appointees, the court explained:

> Although the defendants were more specific in alluding to potential labor issues at the Boeing plant in North Charleston, their comments still cannot be characterized as threats. Templeton [Haley's Director of Labor, Licensing, and Regulation] whose comments about Boeing were arguably the most specific, said, "[W]e will do everything we can to work with Boeing and make sure that their workforce is taken care of, that they run efficiently, and that we don't add anything unnecessarily." Following her confirmation, Templeton said, "Let me be very clear . . . this is an anti-union administration. We don't want Boeing or anybody else to introduce extra bureaucracy into the administration." These statements indicate that Templeton does not want workers at the Boeing plant to unionize. They do not, however, convey any threat of prosecution or regulatory punishment to unions, union organizers, or workers.

Id. at 629–30. The court reasoned that absent proof of an act of adverse regulation or a specific threat, such statements were nothing more than predictable political rhetoric. The Fourth Circuit affirmed in an unpublished opinion. 2012 U.S. App. LEXIS 9175 (4th Cir. May 3, 2012).

Union organizing efforts at Volkswagen encountered similar resistance from elected officials in Tennessee when Volkswagen opened a new plant in Chattanooga. Accustomed to dealing with unions in Germany, VW expressed support for unionization during the UAW representation election held in early 2014, raising hopes that unions would gain a foothold in the state. Republican lawmakers reacted by predicting that auto parts suppliers would not locate businesses in the area if the plant unionized, stating that the Republican-controlled legislature was "unlikely" to approve additional tax subsidies if workers' unionization drive prevailed ($300 million in incentives promised if the company would bring a new SUV production line to the state), and by arguing that the union had contributed to the downfall of Detroit automakers and would have the same effect at VW. They also stated (erroneously) that VW executives had said that VW would bring a second production line to the plant only if workers voted against the union. The union lost the election by a narrow margin, which most attributed to the combination of political resistance and southern workers' unfamiliarity and traditional hostility toward unions. Steven Greenhouse, *Defeat of Auto Union in Tennessee Casts Its Strategy into Doubt*, N.Y. Times, Feb. 15, 2014. The union filed a charge with the NLRB alleging that threats by Tennessee lawmakers had destroyed the conditions necessary for a fair election and seeking a new election; the union later dropped the charge because the NLRB's lengthy administrative process for election challenges would delay filing for a new election, which the union may do one year after the election loss. Steven Greenhouse, *UAW Drops Appeal of VW Vote in Tennessee*, N.Y. Times, Apr. 21, 2014.

Finally, other commentators suggest that American workers and unions themselves may bear some responsibility for the decline in unionism. Consider Stephen Befort's comments below on the historical origins of American unionism and the continuing legacy of workers' lack of enthusiasm for collective responses to workplace problems. Is hostility toward unions the inevitable byproduct of American culture and the Horatio Alger dream?

Although some early organizations such as the Knights of Labor in the 1870s and the International Workers of the World some forty years later urged a broad platform of political and social reform, the mainstream of the American labor movement chartered a very different course. The American Federation of Labor (AFL), founded in 1886, advocated a strategy of economic empowerment as opposed to political upheaval. Composed mostly of craft workers, the AFL concentrated on a policy of "business unionism" that sought not to replace capitalism but to share in its gains. Even during the heady years of the New Deal era, organized labor focused on bettering the lot of its members through collective bargaining rather than attempting to craft a new social and economic landscape through political activism.

Business unionism fit America's lack of class-consciousness, but it came with a price. American unions today are relatively unpopular and isolated. Many Americans view unions as just another self-serving, special interest group. And having gone it alone when times were good, American unions lack the strong support of allied social partners that many of their European counterparts receive. . . .

One additional factor warrants a brief mention—unionism always has been an awkward fit with the rugged individualism of the American psyche. This may explain why the United States has never fully embraced the union movement, as illustrated by the fact that even at its zenith, union density in the United States fell far short of that in most industrialized countries.

Unionization, of course, is a matter of collective action. The dominant American self-image, in contrast, is squarely grounded in the cult of the individual. Fueled by generations of Horatio Alger stories, working-class Americans dream of a middle-class future. Indeed, Americans popularly view unions as reserved for the "lower class." Since most Americans, whether by hard work or good luck, plan not to be part of that lower class some day, union membership is symbolic of opting out of the American dream.

Stephen F. Befort, *Labor and Employment Law at the Millennium: A Historical Review and Critical Assessment*, 43 B.C. L. REV. 351, 375–77 (2002).

Data gathered by Joel Rogers and Richard Freeman, however, establishes the existence of a "representation gap." Rogers and Freeman found that a large majority of workers still desire some form of representation and voice at work, albeit not necessarily a traditional labor union. Most workers want a jointly run enterprise in which workers elect their own representatives and disputes are resolved through arbitration. Approximately 44% would like to be represented by a union. Overwhelming support, however, exists for a system of representation supported by management and empowered to engage in cooperative labor-management relations rather than the traditional adversarial system of unionization and collective bargaining. *See* RICHARD B. FREEMAN & JOEL ROGERS, WHAT DO WORKERS WANT? 6–7, 41–43, 89 (1999).

Nonetheless, a growing number of workers disapprove of unions, citing union corruption, union political influence and spending dues to support political candidates, and mandatory dues payment requirements for those who don't wish to be union members but work in a union-represented bargaining unit that has obtained a union security clause. *See Public, Union Members View Unions Positively, but with Reservations, Poll Finds,* DAILY LAB. REP. (BNA) No. 43, Mar. 5, 2004 (reporting results of survey). The economic recession that gripped the country in 2008–09 further eroded union support among the general public: a 2009 Gallup Poll found that just under half of all Americans—48%—support labor unions, down from 59% the previous year. In addition, 51% of those surveyed said they believed unions mostly hurt rather than helped the U.S. economy. *See Majority Believes Unions Harm U.S. Economy but Benefit Individual Members, Gallup Finds,* DAILY LAB. REP. (BNA) No. 172, Sept. 9, 2009; James Surowiecki, *State of the Unions,* THE NEW YORKER, Jan. 17, 2011. Why might the public support for unions erode during a recession?

A final explanation advanced for the decline of unionism and the increasing marginalization of collective bargaining as a system of workplace participative management is that labor law itself has "ossified" at the legislative, judicial and administrative levels. Cynthia Estlund argues that legislative gridlock and judicial application of a strong federal preemption doctrine have operated to prevent labor law from adapting to suit modern work practices, and to isolate it from the creative innovations that have characterized the common law of employment and the evolution of constitutional theory and doctrine. *See* Cynthia L. Estlund, *The Ossification of American Labor Law,* 102 COLUM. L. Rev. 1527 (2002).

D.   THE INDIVIDUAL RIGHTS MODEL

In the decades after the New Deal enactments, state and federal legislatures enacted a host of statutes that conferred individual rights on workers. A common law of workers' rights also began to evolve, primarily through contract and tort law doctrinal development. The remainder of this book is devoted to a study of these developments. Modern Work Law appears caught between two systems, a system of private autonomy (collective bargaining or laissez-faire market ordering) and the system of public (legislative and judicial) intervention. What are the advantages and disadvantages of each system of workplace governance? Is legislative regulation an acceptable substitute for collective bargaining from the perspective of workers? Which system would employers prefer? Why? We encourage you to ask these questions as we study each topical area that follows.

As an introduction to some of the concerns that have been raised about the adequacy of the individual rights model, consider the following critiques.

Katherine Van Wezel Stone, *The Legacy of Industrial Pluralism: The Tension Between Individual Employment Rights and the New Deal Collective Bargaining System*
59 U. Chi. L. Rev. 575, 593, 624, 637–38 (1992)

First, providing individual employment rights without a union does not allow employees to participate in corporate decisionmaking. To the extent that we value not only minimal employment standards, but also the opportunity for employees to have a say about workplace issues that concern them, the nonunion rights model is not an adequate substitute.

Second, there is some evidence that productivity improves when employees have an avenue for expressing discontent with voice rather than exit. Some nonunion firms have established internal grievance mechanisms to gain the benefits of a voice mechanism without incurring the costs and disadvantages of having a union. However, some have argued that such mechanisms, when not truly independent, ultimately breed distrust, cynicism, and low morale.

Third, minimal terms are too uniform and rigid to address the preferences of employees at all workplaces; they cannot accommodate local differences. Therefore they are not a particularly efficient way to improve wages and working conditions. They can provide basic minima, but above a very low level they cannot provide meaningful improvements.

Fourth, minimal terms often are not effective. For example, the Occupational Safety and Health Act of 1970 directed the Labor Department and the National Institute of Safety and Health to set standards for all potentially hazardous industrial substances in use, to apply to all workplaces. Such a project is so vast, and the interests affected so varied, that today, twenty years after the enactment of the legislation, standards have only been set for a small number of the tens of thousands of industrial chemicals in common use. As a result, the effort to establish minimum terms at the national level has left most workplaces without any terms at all.

The fifth and final flaw in the individual rights/minimal terms model is that it is inherently unstable. Any improvements in protections for individual employees that occur without the presence of a strong union movement are vulnerable and transitory. This is because employees who are not in unions are not organized into a political constituency that can protect the minimal terms in the future. Without an organized constituency, any minimal terms enacted can always be repealed or negated through judicial interpretation.

Within a democratic polity, if there is no organized constituency that can articulate and advocate the interests of a segment of the population, those interests almost certainly will be ignored. . . .

. . . As the labor movement continues to decline, there may soon be no organized pressure group that is capable of defending or improving individual employment rights in the future. Thus the individual rights/minimal terms model of labor relations contains a built-in self-destruct dynamic. It functions to disorganize labor, to prevent the very group formation that is necessary to retain or improve the minimal terms.

Cynthia Estlund, *Rebuilding the Law of the Workplace in an Era of Self-Regulation*
105 Colum. L. Rev. 319, 333 (2005)

[T]he law of the workplace, once dominated by New Deal labor law and the collective bargaining model it established, is now dominated by regulatory statutes administered by government agencies and by individual rights enforceable through private litigation. This shift has fundamentally altered the law's conception of employees: the rights-litigation model of wrongful discharge law casts employees as rights bearers, but also, and perhaps more visibly, as victims seeking redress for past wrongs. The regulatory model renders employees the passive beneficiaries of the government's protection. Neither conceives of employees, as the NLRA does, as citizens who actively participate in the governance of the workplace. Especially in the wake of union decline, modern employment law suffers from a serious democratic deficit. That democratic deficit has become particularly disquieting as the enforcement of rights and regulations has been pulled increasingly into the firm itself, through parallel trends toward self-regulation and internalization in the enforcement of both labor standards and employee rights.

NOTES

1. **"Employment Law as Labor Law"?** What role, if any, will remain for unions under the new individual rights model of employment regulation? Robert Rabin suggests that unions might utilize the rights guaranteed to workers by individual employment law statutes to pressure employers for expanded gains during collective bargaining. For example, unions could use potential wage and hour claims under the FLSA as leverage to pressure an employer for improved wages. Alternatively, unions might treat the protections afforded workers by individual rights statutes as a floor from which to begin in collective bargaining. For example, they might seek to expand the right to unpaid leave guaranteed to workers under the FMLA to paid leave. *See* Robert J. Rabin, *The Role of Unions in the Rights-Based Workplace*, 25 U.S.F. L. Rev. 169, 174–87, 192 (1991).

Benjamin Sachs has expanded on this idea, rejecting altogether the traditional view that employment law's individual rights model is inimical to collective organizing and collective action. Sachs argues that workers might harness the legal architecture of the FLSA and Title VII to galvanize group action by framing wage and hour and discrimination complaints in ways that facilitate a common understanding of workplace issues and thus further the group consciousness necessary for collective action, by using the anti-retaliation protections in those statutes to insulate workers' collective efforts from employer interference, and by achieving significant early successes that in turn generate successive forms of collective activity that move beyond assertion of statutory rights. *See* Benjamin I. Sachs, *Employment Law as Labor Law*, 29 Cardozo L. Rev. 2685 (2008).

2. **Differential Enforcement of Individual Employment Statutes.** Employment-related topics appear regularly on legislative agendas at the state and

federal level, occupy a significant percentage of courts' time, and offer an expanding practice area for lawyers. As you work through the following materials, consider whether legislation and litigation are effective and efficient means of balancing the conflict of interests between employers and workers. Do legislation and litigation function equitably, distributing benefits and burdens fairly across workers as a class? Consider the following:

> The profile of those most likely to pursue claims under this growing body of law [employment law and employment discrimination] . . . strongly tends to follow the patterns of income distribution. Thus, litigants pursuing employment discrimination claims today tend to be relatively better educated and compensated employees who are challenging their discharges from employment rather than an initial failure to be hired. Similarly, some observers estimate that 60 to 80% of successful plaintiffs in wrongful discharge cases are middle or upper managerial or professional employees, and that lower-level workers "only infrequently" prevail in such cases, which they are in any event less likely to bring.

Thomas C. Kohler, *The Employment Relation and Its Ordering at Century's End: Reflections on Emerging Trends in the United States*, 41 B.C. L. REV. 103, 122–23 (1999).

Chapter 2

THE CONTEMPORARY ERA—SHIFTS IN THE DEMOGRAPHICS AND STRUCTURE OF WORK

Five assumptions guided the model of Work Law that held sway during the historical period surveyed in Chapter 1. First, the U.S. economy was assumed to be relatively self-contained; because foreign competition was not a factor, standardization of wages and working conditions could be implemented without fear of undermining the national economy. Second, the public economy was supported by the private, nonwaged work of women who were primarily committed to homemaking for a (presumed male) breadwinner upon whose wages and benefits the family relied. Third, the employment norm was full-time, long-term, and stable. Fourth, the corporation itself was a large, often industrial firm with well-defined boundaries between itself and the external business environment; clear distinctions were also drawn internally between the supervising and managing class and the rank-and-file workers. Finally, labor unions had a powerful influence on wages, benefits and working conditions within the firm both directly (through their representation of rank-and-file workers) and indirectly (as benefits gained for rank-and-file workers trickled up to those who occupied positions above them in the workplace hierarchy). The social contract came to embody the expectation that wages would rise with seniority and job tenure and that the fortunes of employers and workers would be linked so that earnings would rise with prosperity. *See* Paul Osterman et. al., Working in America: A Blueprint for the New Labor Market 8 (2001).

The contemporary era has been characterized by the steady undermining of all of these assumptions. This chapter surveys the changes that have occurred during this transition. We begin in Part A by examining the shift in the demographic composition of the workforce. Workforce diversification (along racial, ethnic, and gender lines) and the aging of the workforce have the potential to alter the work relation significantly. Part B assesses changes in the structure of work itself linked to the transition from an industrial economy to a service sector and information-based economy, and from a domestic economy to a global labor market. Part C explores the difficulties courts have faced in defining the boundaries of the employment relationship: which relationships count as employment, which workers count as "employees" for purposes of coverage under employment legislation, and which entities count as employers for liability purposes.

A. THE WORKFORCE OF THE FUTURE

Mitra Toossi, *Labor Force Projections to 2022: The Labor Force Participation Rate Continues to Fall*

MONTHLY LABOR REVIEW (December 2013), *available at* http://www.bls.gov/
opub/mlr/2013/article/labor-force-projections-to-2022-the-labor-force-
participation-rate-continues-to-fall-16.htm

The U.S. civilian labor force—the number of people working or looking for work—has gone through substantial changes in its size and demographic composition over the last half of the 20th century. During the 1970s and 1980s, the labor force grew vigorously as women's labor force participation rates surged and the baby-boom generation entered the labor market. However, the dynamic demographic, economic, and social forces that once spurred the level, growth, and composition of the labor force have changed and are now damping labor force growth. The labor force participation rate of women, which peaked in 1999, has been on a declining trend. In addition, instead of entering the labor force, baby boomers are retiring in large numbers and exiting the workforce. Once again, the baby-boom generation has become a generator of change, this time in its retirement. Moreover, the jobless recovery of the 2001 recession, coupled with the severe economic impact of the 2007–2009 recession, caused disruptions in the labor market. In the first 12 years of the 21st century, the growth of the population has slowed and labor force participation rates generally have declined. As a result, labor force growth also has slowed. The Bureau of Labor Statistics (BLS) projects that the next 10 years will bring about an aging labor force that is growing slowly, a declining overall labor force participation rate, and more diversity in the racial and ethnic composition of the labor force.

NOTES

1. **Labor Force Growth Slows and Participation Rates Decline.** The Bureau of Labor Statistics projects that the civilian workforce (the number of people working or looking for work) will grow by 8.5 million between 2012 and 2022, an annual growth rate of 0.5. Toossi, *supra.* This continues a decline in labor force growth that began in the 1980s and 1990s and is largely traceable to decreased birth rates in the years following the baby boom generation. For perspective, labor force growth hovered at 1.6% per year during the 1980s, dropped to 1.1% per year during the 1990s, and to 0.7% in the 2002–2012 period. *See id.*; Marlene A. Lee & Mark Mather, *U.S. Labor Force Trends*, 63 POPULATION BULLETIN 3 (June 2008) (a publication of the Population Reference Bureau). Nevertheless, the U.S. is better positioned than most countries in Europe and East Asia, where workforces are also shrinking. For example, Japan is projected to experience a 12% drop in its labor force between 2000 and 2020. Lee & Mather, *supra.* Why are policymakers concerned with a slow labor force growth rate?

Labor force participation rates represent the proportion of the civilian non-institutional population that is currently in the labor force. U.S. labor force participation rates peaked at 67.1% from 1997 to 2000 and have been on a downward spiral since then, accelerating during the 2007–2009 recession. In 2008, the aggregate participation rate was 66%; by 2012, it had decreased to 63.7%, and it is projected to decline further to 61.6% by 2022. Toossi, *supra*. These rates of change are relatively rapid by historical measures, and are attributed primarily to the aging of the baby boom generation (since participation rates decline with age). In addition, the Congressional Budget Office predicts that the passage of the Affordable Care Act will lead to a decrease in full-time workers (particularly lower-wage workers), as employees choose to forego work because of the availability of government-sponsored health insurance exchanges. Ben Penn, *ACA to Reduce Workforce by 2 Million, Mostly by Voluntary Choices, CBO Projects*, DAILY LAB. REP. (BNA) No. 23, Feb. 4, 2014.

Labor force participation rates vary by demographic group. The participation rate of workers 55 years and older is rising. Toossi, *supra*. On the other hand, the participation rate of workers ages 16–54 has declined since 2000 and is projected to continue to do so. *Id.* A particularly sharp decline has occurred among youths aged 16-to-24 years, whose participation rate has dropped from 63.3% in 2002 to 54.9% in 2012; it is projected to drop to 49.6% by 2022. This decrease is largely attributable to increased school attendance at all levels, including summer school, secondary school, and college. *Id.* Should policymakers be concerned about these trends?

2.   **The Graying Workforce.** In 1992, the median age for workers in the U.S. labor force was 37.1 years, compared with a median age in 2012 of 41.9 years. The Bureau of Labor Statistics projects that the median age of the labor force will increase to 42.6 years in 2022. Toossi, *supra*. In 2002, 14.3% of the labor force was 55 or older. By 2012, the workforce share of the total labor force had increased to 20.9%. By 2022, that percentage is projected to rise to 25.6%—one in four workers. Toossi, *supra*. Nevertheless, the U.S. workforce is youthful in relative terms: by 2050, a third or more of the populations of developed countries in Europe or East Asia will be over age 65, compared with 20% of the U.S. population. Joel Kotkin, *The Kids Will Be Alright*, WALL ST. J., Jan. 23–24, 2010.

How should law respond to this shift? The Comptroller General discussed the reasons for this trend, which has been evident for some time, and the challenges that it presents for policymakers:

The aging of the baby boom generation, increased life expectancy, and declining birth rates have created a demographic tsunami that poses serious future challenges for individuals, employers, and the economy. In the 21st century, older Americans are expected to make up a larger share of the U.S. population, live longer, and spend more years in retirement than previous generations. At the same time, by 2025 labor force growth is expected to be less than a fifth of what it is today. Without a major increase in productivity or higher than projected immigration, low labor force growth will ultimately lead to slower growth in the economy and slower growth of federal revenues. These circumstances in turn will accentuate the overall pressure on the federal budget, which will be encumbered with increased claims for Medicare and Social Security benefits while relatively fewer workers are paying into the benefits systems.

An additional concern is the possible loss of many experienced workers as the baby boomers retire. Employers face challenges in engaging and retaining older workers, that is, recruiting seasoned workers, adapting job designs and making workplace accommodations, and keeping workers past the traditional retirement age. Some research has indicated that the impending retirements of the baby boom generation and the decline in the growth of the labor supply could affect certain industries and occupations more than others. These trends could create gaps in skilled workers and managerial occupations in particular, leading to further adverse effects on productivity and economic growth. . . .

While many, including the GAO, have reported on these trends and their likely consequences, not enough has been done to address them. Many employers are still unaware of these trends, and few have implemented programs to engage or retain older workers. Similarly, despite their increased risk, many workers are not adequately preparing for retirement. . . . [T]he time to prepare for these challenges is running out, and employers and employees, as well as government, have a role to play.

Comptroller General, INTRODUCTION TO ENGAGING AND RETAINING OLDER WORKERS, GAO-07-438SP, 1–2 (Feb. 2007), *available at* http://www.gao.gov/new.items/ d07438sp.pdf. *See also* KEN DYCHTWALD ET AL., WORKFORCE CRISIS: HOW TO BEAT THE COMING SHORTAGE OF SKILLS AND TALENT (2006) (discussing changing demographics and what they portend for the workforce and the economy in the future).

Nevertheless, some other factors point toward longer labor force participation by older workers and thus less rapid shrinkage of the workforce. Many jobs have become less physically demanding and improved health care has increased life expectancy, making it possible and even advisable for workers to stay in the workforce longer. Moreover, changes to the Social Security program have pushed back the retirement age for full benefits eligibility (from 65 to 67, with additional incentives to work to age 70), encouraging longer labor force participation. Almost 75% of workers ages 25 to 75 say they intend to work beyond the age of 65; the sentiment is particularly common among those in higher-paying occupations. Chris Opfer, *Record Total of Americans Work Past Age 65, but Many Seeking Jobs Cannot Get Them*, DAILY LAB. REP. (BNA) No. 99, May 22, 2012. Financial necessity has also been a powerful motivator, however: about half of employees in their 50s currently lack the resources to retire at traditional ages, and the 2007–2009 recession negatively impacted retirement savings, investment accounts and housing equity for many workers, who responded by delaying retirement or returning to the workforce. Larry Swisher, *Youth Faring Poorly in Job Market, as Older Workers Delay Retirement*, DAILY LAB. REP. (BNA) No. 146, July 29, 2011; Jennifer Levitz, *Americans Delay Retirement as Housing, Stocks Swoon*, WALL ST. J., Apr. 2, 2008. Working longer may not be realistic, however, for workers whose jobs involve significant physical labor. *See* Opfer, *supra.*

As the Comptroller's Report above suggests, even as workers' interest in continuing their labor force participation into their golden years rises, most employers are lukewarm about the prospect and have done little to create new opportunities for them to do so. Why do you suppose this is? There are exceptions, however: some employers have redesigned work spaces to minimize strain on muscles and joints, or are exploring new methodologies (for example, new surgical techniques that put less strain on doctors' bodies) to retain older workers who can serve as role models and mentors for younger workers. *See* James R. Hagerty, *Keeping Boomers Fit for Work*, WALL ST. J., Dec. 28, 2011.

Must work be all (full-time) or nothing? Phased retirement (in which older full-time workers gradually reduce work hours with a concomitant reduction in pay) has been suggested as a transition strategy to ease the path from full-time work to retirement for workers and to preserve access to experienced workers with specialized knowledge of the job and the firm. Phased retirements also relieve pressure on employer-sponsored pensions and on the Social Security system. Nevertheless, most employers eschew formal phased-retirement programs, and those who do implement them prefer informal case-by-case arrangements. *See* Robert Hutchens, *Phased Retirement: Problems and Prospects*, Center for Retirement Research, Feb. 2007, at 4–6. Several structural issues relating to employee benefits also tend to dissuade employers from implementing phased retirement programs. Pension systems may disincentivize phased retirements by basing benefits calculations on the last several years of a worker's salary. If part-time employees are not covered under the employer's health insurance, phased retirement plans may result in loss of coverage. Finally, some jobs are simply not compatible with part-time work. *See id.*

3. Women's Workforce Participation Stabilizes While Men's Declines. Women's labor force participation more than doubled between 1950 and 2000, reaching its highest level of 60% in 1999. It has declined slowly since then and is projected to be around 56% by 2022 (compared with 67.6% for men). Toossi, *supra*; U.S. DEPARTMENT OF LABOR, *Latest Annual Data: Women of Working Age, available at* http://www.dol.gov/wb/stats/recentfacts.htm#mothers. Meanwhile, the recession of 2007–2009 had particularly dramatic effects on men's labor force participation, prompting some commentators to refer to the recession as the "man-cession." *See* Joan C. Williams & Allison Tait, *"Mancession" or "Momcession"?: Good Providers, a Bad Economy, and Gender Discrimination*, 86 CHI.-KENT L. REV. 857, 860–62 (2011). Some argued that the "mancession" was simply a myth: while men lost jobs with higher wages and better benefits, women held onto or moved into lower paying jobs with no benefits. *See id.* at 876–77. Much of the drop for men was attributable to their heavy concentration in the construction and building trades, which were hardest hit by the recession. By contrast, women were concentrated in education, the public sector, and health care, which were at least initially less volatile. *Id.* Men have benefitted most from the economic recovery that has occurred since then, however, landing 88% of the non-farm jobs created since the recession officially ended in June 2009. Lorraine Woellert, *American Men Dominate Job Gains, Taking 88% of Spots: Economy*, BLOOMBERG, Apr. 3, 2012, *available at* http://www.bloomberg.com/news/2012-04-03/american-men-dominate-jobs-recovery-taking-88-of-spots-economy.html.

The gender demographics of the new workforce present serious challenges to an employment regime designed around the life patterns of male breadwinners with a female caregiver at home. Mothers are the primary breadwinners or sole breadwinners in 40% of U.S. households. Catherine Rampell, *U.S. Women on the Rise as*

Family Breadwinner, N.Y. TIMES, May 29, 2013. The labor force participation rate of mothers with children under 18 years of age was nearly 70% in 2013. U.S. DEPARTMENT OF LABOR, *Latest Annual Data: Women of Working Age, available at* http://www.dol.gov/wb/stats/recentfacts.htm#mothers. Further, evolving gender norms mean that many workers—men as well as women—now juggle caregiving obligations. Baby boomers frequently find themselves caring for aging parents as well as children, a financial burden and time bind that has earned them the moniker "the sandwich generation." Kim Parker & Eileen Patten, *The Sandwich Generation*, Jan. 30, 2013, *available at* http://www.pewsocialtrends.org/2013/01/30/the-sandwich-generation/.

Flexible schedules (compressed work weeks, flex-time), flex-place (telecommuting or working from sites closer to home), job sharing, and other alternative work arrangements may be needed to attract and retain skilled workers and to maximize their productivity. Some have suggested that employee benefits should include not only child care alternatives, but access to paid household help, arguing that firms should think of housework as part of the structural cost of doing business. *See Study Says Paid Household Help Could Boost Productivity of Women Research Scientists*, DAILY LAB. REP. (BNA) No. 16, Jan. 27, 2010 (finding that female scientists perform nearly twice as much housework as their male counterparts, and proposing that "institutions provide a package of flexible benefits that employees can customize to support aspects of their private lives in ways that save time and enhance professional productivity"). Does this seem feasible? Would workers be more likely to take advantage of these sorts of benefits than to utilize benefits that afford them flex-time to perform the tasks themselves? *Cf.* ARLIE RUSSELL HOCHSCHILD, THE TIME BIND: WHEN WORK BECOMES HOME AND HOME BECOMES WORK (1997) (reporting that many workers choose not to take advantage of family-friendly policies that would reduce work time in favor of family time, preferring to spend more time at work where their efforts are socially valued and supported). We discuss the legal issues raised by the work-family time conflict further in Chapter 10.

4.   Increased Racial and Ethnic Diversity. Hispanics remain the most rapidly growing segment of the labor force, due to high birth rates, strong immigration patterns, and high labor force participation rates (since most immigrants are drawn to the U.S. by the prospect of better job opportunities, this is not surprising). The Bureau of Labor Statistics projects that Hispanics will make up 19.1% of the labor force by 2022, up from 12.4% in 2002. Toossi, *supra*. By contrast, white non-Hispanics accounted for 71.3% of the labor force in 2002, and are projected to account for just 60.3% in 2022. *Id.* African Americans are projected to increase from their 11.4% share in 2002 to 12.4% by 2022. Asians will account for 6.2% of the workforce by 2022, up from 4.6% in 2002. *Id.* What challenges do these demographic shifts present for employers? For the law?

5.   Immigration. In recent years, the largest portion of immigrants to the United States has been of Hispanic origin. A large number are permanent lawful immigrants. Many others have come as guest workers. Douglas S. Massey, *Immigration and the Great Recession*, Oct. 2012, THE RUSSELL SAGE FOUNDATION AND THE STANFORD CENTER ON POVERTY AND INEQUALITY, *available at* http://web.stanford.edu/group/recessiontrends/cgi-bin/web/sites/all/themes/barron/pdf/Immigration_ fact_sheet.pdf. Immigrants tend to be concentrated in low-wage, low-skilled sectors such as hotel and restaurant work, landscaping, janitorial work, meat packing, construction, agriculture, and garment manufacturing.

The majority of unauthorized immigrants in the U.S.—52% in 2012—are from Mexico. Jeffrey Passel, D'Vera Cohn, & Ana Gonzalez Barrera, *Population Decline of Unauthorized Immigrants Stalls, May Have Reversed* (Pew Hispanic Trends Project, Sept. 23, 2013), *available at* http://www.pewhispanic.org/2013/09/23/population-decline-of-unauthorized-immigrants-stalls-may-have-reversed/.   The combination of the recession, America's slow economic recovery, and tighter border controls has slowed the rate of immigration from Latin America and Mexico, particularly of unauthorized workers. Rakesh Kochhar, *Latino Jobs Growth Driven by U.S. Born*, Pew Research Hispanic Trends Project, June 19, 2014, *available at* http://www.pewhispanic.org/2014/06/19/latino-jobs-growth-driven-by-u-s-born/. Although it is difficult to say with accuracy how many unauthorized workers currently reside in the U.S., a report by the Pew Hispanic Center estimated that there were likely over 11.7 million undocumented workers in the United States in 2012, down from the high point of 12.2 million in 2007, before the recession. The majority of unauthorized immigrants reside in California, Florida, Illinois, New Jersey, New York, and Texas.

B. CHANGES IN THE STRUCTURE OF WORK

The structure of work and the employment practices that shape it have shifted dramatically over the last century. Many of the statutes that we will study were designed to apply to the workplace regimes in place at the time of their enactment. It is helpful, therefore, to have some appreciation for how work has changed over that period. Shifts in how work is organized have significant legal implications, particularly when a mismatch develops between the evolving structure of work and the applicable legislation.

As the following excerpts explain, the traditional understanding of employment was a lifetime relationship of dependency in which the employer insulated employees from external markets, guaranteeing benefits in exchange for loyalty; job turnover was relatively low, and workers advanced during their careers through internal job ladders. Modern employment relationships, on the other hand, tend to be characterized by a shorter-term, entrepreneurial relationship in which each employee is self-sufficient, accepting responsibility for his or her own training and career development. In this regime, employees adopt a nomadic life pattern in which loyalty to an employer is replaced by contingent commitment until a better deal surfaces elsewhere. Some workers have flourished in this new regime, while others have been casualties of economic downsizings, layoffs and productivity-based standards.

[handwritten margin note: old employ view vs. now]

How should law respond to the demise of the old social contract and the creation of new social norms concerning job tenure and loyalty to the firm? How can statutes predicated on the old model of long-term employment and dependence be retrofitted to apply to the arrangements that characterize the modern era? What new challenges are presented for employers by the shift to increased worker turnover?

Matthew Bidwell, Forrest Briscoe, Isabel Fernandez-Mateo, & Adina Sterling, *The Employment Relationship and Inequality: How and Why Changes in Employment Practice Are Reshaping Rewards in Organizations*
The Academy of Management Annals 4–19 (2013)

The Changing Nature of the Employment Relationship

Where We Have Come From

A defining feature of postwar employment systems was the dominant role played by administrative hierarchies. The middle of the twentieth century saw the emergence of an employment model, the "internal labor market" (ILM), under which internal administrative procedures played a central role in determining the allocation of jobs and rewards. . . . [T]hese ILMs insulated employment from external labor markets in a number of ways. First, in allocating jobs, ILMs strongly favored internal promotions over external hiring. Indeed . . . hiring was sometimes restricted to only a few ports of entry at lower levels of the organization. Second, seniority played a role in determining which workers were eligible to be promoted or transferred to other kinds of jobs. Seniority also had a substantial impact on pay and yielded increasing wages as a worker's tenure increased.

The[re] . . . was little movement of workers between organizations, as employees sought instead to gain and then secure the advantages of tenure. This detachment of workers from the external labor market meant that compensation systems became internally focused; in other words, their aim was to maintain appropriate pay differentials within the organization and not to balance supply and demand with respect to the external labor market. Many nonwage benefits provided by employers—most notably, health insurance, and old age pensions—were also structured to reward employees for loyalty and long tenure. . . .

However, the protections stemming from ILMs were never universally available. Research on dual labor markets argues that workers populated two distinct segments. The primary (core) sector provided long-term, stable relationships with employers; the secondary (peripheral) sector, comprising mostly low-wage workers, did not afford such benefits and held little opportunity for advancement. Women, racial minorities, and low-skilled workers were more apt to be located in the periphery.

. . . .

What Has Changed

The postwar period witnessed the dominance of internal hierarchy in the governance of employment relationships, but the years since the 1970s have seen a resurgence of extra-organizational forces. . . . Much of this change can be characterized as an increase in the influence of external market forces on the organizational distribution of work and rewards. Stable long-term exchanges between employers and employees have been replaced by more flexible arrangements that allow organizations to adapt to changing demands for their goods and services by restructuring, downsizing, and outsourcing.

Market-based practices. One manifestation of these market-based forces is a decline in employee tenure. Although there was initial debate as to whether the average duration of employment relationships was actually declining, recent studies demonstrate substantial changes in worker tenure. These changes have been especially large among those groups that were previously most isolated from market conditions—namely, men and employees of large organizations. . . .

Another route by which markets have penetrated the employment relationship is through firms' use of downsizing to restructure their workforces. Rather than seeking to retrain or redeploy workers, firms have been abandoning them to the external labor market during reorganization. That being said, it is not clear that the rate of layoffs has increased much in recent decades: studies drawing on different data have come to different conclusions. . . .

. . . Analyses of layoff announcements indicate that layoffs have become less likely to occur in response to declining demand or poor profitability and more likely to reflect reorganizations and attempts to control costs. Such evidence suggests that employers have come to see the reallocation of workers into the external labor market as a normal business practice rather than a last resort.

There have also been increasing market influences on how employees are paid. Organizations have implemented contingent-based pay practices that reward workers for their productivity. Pay-for-performance practices embody arguments from neoclassical economics that firms should pay employees at their marginal product and that incentives are needed to induce worker efforts. Performance—contingent pay systems initially gained popularity after World War II, when organizations began to implement formal evaluation systems; however, they did not become widespread until after the 1982 recession, when firms faced enormous pressure to improve workforce efficiency. By the mid-1980s, more than 80% of US organizations had implemented performance—contingent pay plans, and this high rate continued into the twenty-first century.

. . . [Additionally,] employees' exposure to the market has been increased in a more subtle way: by changes in firms' benefits practices. First, many organizations no longer offer any benefits to their employees. Benefit availability has declined fastest for health insurance . . . and has also declined for pensions . . . . An even more dramatic change occurred in retiree health benefits, which are exempt from legislative protection. . . . Hence, more employees are purchasing benefits for themselves in the open market, increasing their exposure to market forces.

Second, even for those employees who retain access to benefits through their employer, changes in benefit format have transferred market risk from employers to employees. A key change has been the shift from a "defined benefit" to "defined contribution" format. The pure form of a defined benefit plan prescribes a specific benefit (e.g. fully paid health insurance, a guaranteed retirement income) to workers with sufficient tenure. In contrast, the pure form of a defined contribution plan provides a set amount of pretax money in each year of employment, money that the employee can use toward the purchase of benefits (e.g. a health insurance product, a 401 k investment). . . . [T]he shift in the format of benefit plans has been relatively swift: of the workers covered by retirement plans, from 1981 to 2001, the portion with defined benefit plans fell from 60% to 23%. Although the shift in health benefits is more complex to trace, one indicator is the amount employees must contribute toward the purchase of their own health insurance . . . . [For employees at large firms who continue to be covered under employer-provided plans, costs borne by the employee to purchase health insurance more than doubled between 1999 and 2011.]

Just as regular employment relationships have become more exposed to market forces, so the use of contingent work and outsourcing has also grown. Under these alternative arrangements, firms no longer enter into a traditional employment relationship with their workforce. Instead, companies are able to employ workers using arm's-length agreements and thereby bring the flexibility of the market into their dealings with workers.

One focus of the research on such market-like relationships is the use of contingent workers, who lack any implicit or explicit expectation of long-term employment. There is a general consensus among management scholars that the use of contingent workers—including independent contractors and both on-call and direct-hire temporary workers—has grown in the recent decades, although the lack of historical data on the contingent workforce makes it hard to substantiate that claim. . . . Recent data from employer surveys indicate that about 8% of workers across establishments are in some sort of contingent employment relationship, and there has been a moderate (but uneven) increase in that figure over time. However, there is considerable variance across establishments.

Studies of the temporary help services industry provide more conclusive evidence of change, with temporary help employment increasing from less than a quarter of a million in the early 1970s to some 2.3 million at the end of the 2000s and accounting for nearly 10% of US employment growth for the period 1990–2000. . . . The contingent employment of workers through labor market intermediaries such as temporary help agencies has received particular attention in the literature. Introducing a labor market intermediary into the mix changes the nature of the employment relationship by turning it into a triadic exchange. Workers employed through an intermediary are employees of the intermediary and not of the firm where they work, so in principle, the intermediary is in charge of managing and supervising them. Such arrangements thus turn a hierarchical, firm—employee relation into a market-based, firm-to-firm relation.

Another way in which firms have been able to make increasing use of markets to shape employment is by the outsourcing of entire functions that were previously carried out internally. Whereas contingent employment typically involves hiring small groups of short-term workers alongside regular employees, outsourcing involves the firm severing its employment relationships with an entire group of workers and then contracting with another firm to replace their output. Although there is a general belief that outsourcing has increased over the last few decades, the evidence is again somewhat fragmentary. . . .

. . . .

THE REASONS FOR CHANGE

. . . As we have moved from nationally based manufacturing economies to a technology-enabled and services-heavy global market, the nature of work is much different from what it used to be. . . .

The Turbulent Environment: Technology and Globalization

The era of increased market penetration into employment relationships was also an era of rapid technological change, as digital technology spread into practically every area of economic activity. By altering the ways in which activities are coordinated, both in organizations and in markets, these changes had substantial effect on employment relations. For example, some scholars have suggested that technological changes made it easier to coordinate across market interfaces, leading to a decline in the use of organizations to govern such activities as employment. Other work suggests that new technologies have required firms to organize work in fundamentally different ways, drawing on new skills and new production methods. Such wholesale changes in the organization of work—and the skills required—may have put substantial pressure on the less responsive, organizationally based employment relationships that characterized the postwar period.

. . . .

Global competition is another frequently cited source of pressure on the employment system. Early commentary on changes to employment emphasized the challenges that foreign competition posed to previously stable markets, especially in manufacturing. Such accounts suggest that rapidly declining market shares triggered a perceived need for aggressive cost cutting, prompting employers to negotiate greater flexibility from their employees. There is no doubt that foreign competition has had a devastating impact on several US industries, including some (e.g. automotive) that were once the most likely to close off their employment systems to external labor markets. There is also evidence that these forces have affected employment relationships. . . . Yet, just as in the case of technological change, we lack systematic evidence on the extent to which globalization has been responsible for widespread changes in employment.

Changing Nature of the Workforce

At the same time that firms' environments were experiencing substantial changes, the nature of the workforce was also evolving. In particular, some of the changes in employment relationships already described could be partly driven by shifts in the composition of the labor force as well as by workers' preferences for different types of employment arrangements. . . .

. . . [O]ne of the most significant trends in the last few decades has been the increase in women's participation in the labor market—not only in the USA, but also in other industrialized countries. The growth of women's labor force participation is associated with an increase in the number of dual-career families. This phenomenon may also be associated with some of the changes observed in employment patterns, including the spread of work—family benefits, increased worker mobility, and the growth of nonstandard work. There is clear evidence, for example, that the increasing number of women and dual-career workers of both sexes helps to explain firms' offering work—family benefits. . . .

Some authors argue that women may prefer such flexible employment arrangements as part-time work and other forms of nonstandard employment, perhaps because many women still do most of the household work. Temporary and other nontraditional employment relationship may also be favored by older workers, who remain in the workforce for longer than they used to—either by choice or necessity—and may often prefer to work fewer or more flexible hours. Such older workers may thus welcome transitioning to nonstandard work arrangements.

These discussions of demographic shifts suggest that workers' preferences for less traditional employment arrangements may underlie part of the growth in new forms of working. Such preferences may not be limited to women and older workers; some authors claim that younger generations may be more open to the idea of moving frequently across firms and managing their careers in a flexible way. . . . The assumption underpinning much of this literature is that individuals' decisions are the main driver of changes in career trajectories. However . . . there is no strong empirical evidence that macro changes in employment relationships are driven by the predilection of individuals for an independent career. So even though demographic shifts and preferences have probably contributed to some of the observed changes in employment patterns, especially in the area of benefits, they seem not to be the main driver of these transformations.

Stakeholder Power Struggles

Our review of the available literature leads us to argue that technological change, global competition, and demographic shifts provided a favorable context for renegotiating the terms of the employment relationship but did not shape them in a deterministic manner. Technology and globalization did offer a ready justification for the need to change that was often used by managers during the 1990s and 2000s. Yet, there is no convincing evidence that this trend fully dictated the direction, pace, or nature of changes to be made. Instead, the changes that developed can be seen as the outcomes of struggles among stakeholders seizing opportunities to advance their own agendas and interests.

Decline in Workers' Class-Based Collective Action

. . . [T]he long sweep of employment history in the USA can be described as a struggle between the advocates of laissez-faire markets and those of employment protection and social security. One side gaining the upper hand triggers a backlash, which leads to pendulum-like swings between free markets and increased protections for workers.

Arguing along these lines explains many of the changes of the last three decades. Following increased regulation during the 1960s and 1970s and the subsequent crisis in corporate profitability, employers have been more assertive in attempting to reshape the institutional landscape in ways that increase their flexibility and limit worker protections. [Some researchers have documented] the tremendous increase in resources that corporations have committed to influencing government from the late 1970s onward. . . .

Most important for our purposes, powerful corporations were able to defeat attempts to adapt industrial relations law to the changing economy and were also able to blunt the political influence of unions. . . . As workers lost power relative to other groups, their ability to demand protections from their employers also declined. Most observers conclude that political organizations allied with labor presented little in the way of countervailing force to corporate influences on federal employment policy-making during the 1980s and 1990s.

Probably the starkest indicator of the shift in power from workers to employers is the decline in union membership, which has been the focus of much research in the last few decades. By providing workers with collective organization and voice, unions substantially increase worker bargaining power. Although that power is most salient in workplaces that have been unionized, there is considerable evidence that a strong union movement affects all workers because even the threat of unionization serves to discipline employers. Although . . . union power is most obviously used to raise wages, that power has also been exercised to insulate workers from the external labor market. . . . Although there is some dispute over exactly when union organizing began to decline, the timing roughly coincides with employers' increased push into the political arena . . . . [To some degree] union organizing always relied on the tacit support of the state. As the state withdrew its support and as employers prevented the updating of industrial relations policy to reflect the modern work-place, unions were effectively removed from the employment stage.

. . . [In addition, researchers have found] a strong association between local industry unionization levels and wage inequality, [demonstrating] that unions impose norms of equity on the labor market. . . . [T]he decline of unionization could thereby explain from a fifth to a third of the growth in inequality. There is also evidence that unions inhibit the spread of contingent work. . . . Unionized workplaces are also more likely to stave off reductions in health insurance and pensions.

Identity-Based Social Movements

Although there is evidence that the US labor movement has been in decline, research also suggests that the last few decades have seen an increase among workers in new forms of collective action based on social identity rather than social class. These new forms of action are intriguing because, at first blush, they represent a kaleidoscope of potentially conflicting identities. Despite this challenge, participation has cut across class and occupational lines, drawing in frontline workers as well as managers, consultants, and others working in and around corporations who have served as effective advocates for new employment practices. Recent research has demonstrated the influence of these identity-based movements in shaping specific practices related to employee benefits, work—family policies, and workforce diversity.

. . . [A]n identity-based social movement [is] a group of individuals who share a social identity (e.g. race, ethnicity, gender, age, disability, immigrant status, sexual orientation) and who are trying to change society through collective action aimed at influencing the policies of institutional actors such as governments and corporations. The initial waves of civil rights activism were aimed mainly at the state during the 1960 and 1970s. Since then, however, identity-based social movements have become more active in influencing corporate employment practices by applying direct pressure to firms and their leaders. . . .

Marion Crain, *Managing Identity: Buying into the Brand at Work*
95 Iowa L. Rev. 1179, 1187–92 (2010)

In an influential book [The New Deal at Work: Managing the Market-Driven Workforce (1999)], Peter Cappelli described a fundamental shift in the nature of the employment relation that took hold in the 1990s. Once a relatively secure and stable relationship in which shareholders bore the risks associated with the market and firms buffered the risks vis-à-vis their workers, employment morphed into a fluid, dynamic relationship more directly linked to volatile external product markets. As global competition forced firms to cut costs, reduce time to market and strive to differentiate themselves from competitors, long-term investments in people and products no longer made good business sense. These changes brought market norms inside the firm and displaced internal labor market structures. Flexibility and efficiency replaced more traditional norms of long-term commitment and equity. New management practices took hold, as well: benchmarking, outsourcing and pay-for-performance replaced job security, employee development practices, internal job ladders and seniority systems. Employers calibrated compensation to the external labor market rather than to the firm's internal market structure.

As a part of this shift, workers were encouraged to assume responsibility for their own training and to substitute loyalty to themselves and their careers for loyalty to the firm. Significantly, in the late 1990s almost half of U.S. employers added new material to their employee handbooks outlining the "new deal" for employees. The language was designed to reorient and limit employee expectations and clarify employees' personal responsibility for job security. . . . Cappelli summarized the transformation in employment norms in these compelling terms: "If the traditional lifetime employment relationship was like a marriage, then the new employment relationship is like a lifetime of divorces and remarriages, a series of close relationships governed by the expectation going in that they . . . will inevitably not last."

Expanding upon Cappelli's description of the new deal, Katherine Van Wezel Stone described the evolution of the "new psychological contract" associated with the new deal at work, in which employees gave up job security in exchange for promises of training to enhance employability, access to networks to enhance employees' social capital, and compensation geared to market rates, reflecting differential talent rather than seniority. [*See* Katherine Van Wezel Stone, From Widgets to Digits: Employment Regulation for the Changing Workplace (2004)]. Stone argued that the shift from the old deal to the new deal was widespread, and enumerated the elements of the new psychological contract offered by employers in lieu of the old model: a promise of training to enhance employability; a promise of access to networks to enhance employees' social capital; and compensation geared to market rates, reflecting differential talent rather than seniority.

Although not all commentators accept Stone's claim of the demise of the old deal, it seems clear that a significant shift has occurred in social norms concerning job tenure and employee attachment to the firm. Moreover, attitudes towards the acceptability of shifting market risks onto employees have changed in dramatic ways, paving the way for the development of new workplace practices. Not only did the calibration of compensation change to a more market-oriented approach, but traditional health and pension benefits that had been designed to bind the employee to the firm also shifted to accommodate a mobile workforce and to afford the new entrepreneurial worker more control and choice over the health insurance and retirement vehicles that were still linked to employment. These shifts in turn created new challenges: decreased employee loyalty and difficulties in supervising and controlling a workforce that was critical to retaining customers and expanding into new markets.

NOTES

1. Internal Labor Markets and Seniority Principles. As Bidwell *et al.* explain, the internal labor markets that characterized the old social contract of employment structured jobs into hierarchical ladders within firms; each job provided the skills and training for the job on the next rung. Employers hired at the entry level, and employees scaled the ladder throughout their careers. Wages rose as length of service increased and benefits were linked to tenure with the firm. Katherine V. W. Stone, *Employee Representation in the Boundaryless Workplace*, 77 CHI.-KENT L. REV. 773, 779–80 (2002); *see generally* PETER DOERINGER & MICHAEL PIORE, INTERNAL LABOR MARKETS AND MANPOWER ANALYSIS (1971).

Seniority principles are an important feature of internal labor markets. Developed by unions in conjunction with collective bargaining, seniority systems function as a form of shared governance, wresting from management some control over who is promoted and who is not. In addition, seniority systems protect workers with the most significant investment in the firm (and therefore, the lowest mobility) against arbitrary treatment, ensuring that workers with the longest service are the last to be laid off or terminated and first in line for promotions. Worker seniority is also the determining factor in entitlement to levels of fringe benefits, such as vacation time and pension benefits. Seniority systems were especially important in the industrial context, where they offered artificial protection for those whose lack of skill rendered them easily replaceable and hence vulnerable to discharge or layoff.

What benefits do internal labor markets and seniority systems offer employers? What risks do they pose? What benefits do they afford to workers? What are the downsides to them from the perspective of workers? *See* RICHARD B. FREEMAN & JAMES L. MEDOFF, WHAT DO UNIONS DO? 122 (1984); Caroline Poplin, *Fair Employment in a Depressed Economy: The Layoff Problem*, 23 UCLA L. REV. 177, 196–97 (1975). How important are they in the largely nonunion postindustrial era? Why do so many nonunionized employers continue to give some weight to seniority in promotion and hiring decisions, as well as fringe benefit levels? What values might guide termination decisions when workforce cutbacks are necessary if a firm does not adhere to seniority principles?

2. **Shifting Risks to Workers**. Bidwell *et al.* and Crain explain that in the old model of employment, firms assumed the responsibility for insuring workers against events that would interrupt or end employment, such as illness, disability, or retirement. In the modern employment relation, employers have shifted many of those risks to workers. These shifts track the transition away from long-term employment and toward labor market flexibility. *See* Katherine V. W. Stone, *A Fatal Mismatch: Employer-Centric Benefits in a Boundaryless World*, 11 LEWIS & CLARK L. REV. 451 (2007); *see generally* JACOB S. HACKER, THE GREAT RISK SHIFT (2006) (describing trends in public policy that combine to shift risk and responsibility away from governments and employers and onto workers, and noting that this risk-shift is the "defining feature of the contemporary economy"). How should work law respond to this risk-shift?

3. **Rising Income Inequality**. Income inequality has been growing since the late 1970s. In 1980, the richest 10% of Americans collected about one-third of the nation's income; by 2012, they were receiving one-half. The top 1% of income earners saw their share more than double between 1973 and 2011. Annie Lowrey, *The Wealth Gap in America Is Growing, Too*, N.Y. TIMES, April 2, 2014; Marion Crain & Ken Matheny, *Unionism, Law, and the Collective Struggle for Economic Justice*, *in* WORKING AND LIVING IN THE SHADOW OF ECONOMIC FRAGILITY 101 (Marion Crain & Michael Sherraden eds., 2014). Researchers have documented a correlation between rising income inequality and declining union density. *See* Bruce Western & Jake Rosenfeld, *Unions, Norms, and the Rise in U.S. Wage Inequality*, 76 AM. SOC. REV. 513 (2011). Moreover, a higher percentage of workers are employed in what the Center for Economic and Policy Research defines as "bad jobs"—those that pay less than $37,000 per year, lack employer-provided health insurance and have no retirement plan. In 2010, nearly 24% of workers occupied such jobs, up from 18% in 1979. John Schmitt & Janelle Jones, *Bad Jobs on the Rise*, CENTER FOR ECONOMIC AND POLICY RESEARCH, Sept. 2012, *available at* http://www.cepr.net/documents/publications/bad-jobs-2012-09.pdf.

Should policy makers be concerned with these trends? If so, why?

4. **Rising Contingent Employment**. As Bidwell *et al.* explain, contingent employment is on the rise. The temporary staffing industry reached an all-time high in 2014. Gayle Cinquegrani, *Report Says Hike in Use of Staffing Agencies Means More Worker Protections Are Needed*, DAILY LAB. REP. (BNA) No. 170, Sept. 3, 2014. Temporary workers hired through staffing agencies generally have lower pay rates than regular employees hired directly by employers, are less likely to have health and retirement benefits, and are rarely represented by unions. In addition, their injury rates are higher because they are less likely to receive safety training, even though many work in hazardous industries. Racial minorities and former recipients of public assistance are overrepresented among temporary workers. *Id.* Though temporary hiring often increases following an economic downturn, many believe that this shift has morphed into a structural change as employers realized the cost savings possible. Damian Paletta, *Temp Jobs Surge as Firms Contain Expenses*, WALL ST. J., Apr. 7, 2014.

The number of part-time workers is also increasing. Part-time and temporary workers generally earn less per hour than full-time workers and customarily are afforded no benefits. Advancement opportunities are limited, and job security is negligible. Why do you think this might be? *See id.*; Barry T. Hirsch, *The Relative Compensation of Part-Time and Full-Time Workers*, EMPLOYMENT POLICIES INSTITUTE, July 2000 (discussing role of lower skill levels and work preferences in the wage differential between part-time and full-time employees). Seventy percent of the part-time workforce is female; disabled persons, teenagers, and persons over 65 are also disproportionately represented in the part-time workforce. Part-time work is voluntary for about 72% of those who work part-time, often because they seek to balance family or school obligations or to accommodate limitations on working hours necessitated by health problems or disabilities. Heidi Shierholz, *A Primer: What's Going on with Part-Time Work*, ECONOMIC POLICY INSTITUTE, Aug. 4, 2014, *available at* http://www.epi.org/blog/primer-whats-part-time-work/. For others, however, part-time work is "involuntary"; these part-timers frequently patch together two or more jobs to make ends meet.

Is the real problem under-employment? Can you think of policy responses that would be more effective if the phenomenon of contingent work was redefined in this way? *See* Gillian Lester, *Careers and Contingency*, 51 STAN. L. REV. 73 (1998) (suggesting that the growth of the contingent workforce is evidence of market failure to match workers with jobs that fully exploit their human capital and preferences).

The dramatic growth of the contingent workforce has raised vexing legal questions in a system modeled upon an assumption of full-time, continuous employment. In general, contingent workers fall outside the safety net of statutory protection in employment. Some statutes contain gatekeeping eligibility requirements that exclude part-time and temporary workers from coverage on the basis that they have formed an impermanent attachment to the employer. For example, the Affordable Care Act applies only to employees defined as those who work at least 30 hours per week. Most statutes also specifically exclude independent contractors from coverage. Thus, legal incentives exist for employers to manipulate the status of full-time employees in order to avoid application of employment laws, increase flexibility and reduce labor costs. Should these statutes be amended or re-interpreted to cover the contingent workforce? On the other hand, not all contingent workers are vulnerable, insecure, and low-waged. In fact, many independent contractors are older, highly educated persons who work in high-paying management, business and financial fields, typically as consultants or free-lance workers. *Id. See also* Sarah E. Needleman, *Negotiating the Freelance Economy*, WALL ST. J., May 6, 2009 (describing growth of contract workers—many of whom are professionals—who are employed on a project basis). Should employment laws apply to them? If so, on what rationale(s)?

5. The "New Psychological Contract." Crain discusses Katherine Stone's theory of the new psychological contract. Stone explained and defended her theory of the rise of a new psychological contract in a series of articles and a book. *See* Katherine V. W. Stone, *The New Psychological Contract: Implications of the Changing Workplace for Labor and Employment Law*, 48 UCLA L. REV. 519 (2001); Katherine Van Wezel Stone, FROM WIDGETS TO DIGITS: EMPLOYMENT REGULA-

TION FOR THE CHANGING WORKPLACE (2004). Management theorists and CEOs have embraced the idea, although commitment to all the elements that Stone lists as part of the new "deal," particularly training, appears uneven. Former General Electric CEO Jack Welch reportedly told his workforce, "At the end of the week, we cut you a paycheck; you don't owe me anything and I don't owe you anything. We start fresh on Monday." Daniel J. B. Mitchell & Christopher L. Erickson, *The Individual Employee in the Context of Employer Ascendancy: New-Old Economic Analysis*, 10 J. INDIVID. EMP. RTS. 197, 200–01, 203–04 (2002–03). Still other executives have denounced the value of company loyalty, another feature of the old social contract, telling managers, "if you want loyalty, get a dog." PETER CAPPELLI, THE NEW DEAL AT WORK: MANAGING THE MARKET-DRIVEN WORKFORCE 216 (1999).

On the other hand, a number of commentators have pointed out that the majority of workers still hold jobs in the primary labor market that feature training, prospects of continuity, and advancement. Sanford Jacoby evaluated the data on the asserted demise of long-term employment relationships and found only a modest decline in aggregate job stability in the 1990s, along with a slight drop in the overall prevalence of long-term jobs over the past 20 years. He argues that internal job markets remain the norm in the U.S. and that reports of their extinction are an exaggeration. *See* Sanford M. Jacoby, *Melting into Air? Downsizing, Job Stability, and the Future of Work*, 76 CHI.-KENT L. REV. 1195 (2000); *see also* Stephen F. Befort, *Labor and Employment Law at the Millennium: A Historical Review and Critical Assessment*, 43 B.C. L. REV. 351, 390–91 (2002) (expressing doubt that the new psychological contract is as prevalent as some have portrayed it to be).

6.   Changes in Job Tenure over Time. Others have challenged the assumption that job tenure has declined, at least for workers as a class. *See, e.g.*, RICHARD FREEMAN & JOEL ROGERS, WHAT WORKERS WANT 10–11 (1999) (contesting the claim of lowered job tenure and noting intragroup differences according to age and job category that affect tenure data). An analysis of employee job tenure based on Census Data from 2012 concludes that there is little basis for the perception that past generations of workers held career jobs. Median employee tenure for adults aged 25 or older actually increased slightly over the last 30 years, rising from 5.0 years in 1983 to 5.4 years in 2012. A small but significant decrease in men's median job tenure is apparent (down from 5.9 years in 1983 to 5.5 years in 2012); however, women's tenure increased from 4.2 in 1983 to 5.4 years in 2012, more than offsetting the drop in male tenure. Craig Copeland, *Employee Tenure Trends, 1983–2102* (Employee Benefit Research Institute), *available at* http://www.ebri.org/pdf/notespdf/EBRI. Median tenure for all workers was 4.6 years in January 2012. Bureau of Labor Statistics, Employee Tenure in 2012, Sept. 18, 2012, *available at* http://www.bls.gov/news.release/tenure.nr0.htm.

Part of the difficulty in interpreting the data is that job tenure data do not necessarily correlate with job security. An increase in job tenure could be associated with a slack labor market and an increased termination rate for lower-tenured workers, leaving longer-tenured workers employed but less secure. Alternatively, a decrease in median tenure could occur in a tight labor market when more jobs are open to new labor market entrants, job opportunities are plentiful and experienced workers feel comfortable shifting to other employment. Demographic shifts in the labor market—such as more older workers staying in the market longer—also affect job tenure rates, as younger workers tend to have shorter job tenure than older workers. *See id.* (reporting that median job tenure for workers aged 65 and over was 10.3 years in 2012, compared with 3.2 years for workers aged 25–34). More than half of workers aged 55 years and over had been employed with their current employer for at least 10 years, compared with just 13% of workers aged 30 to 34. What reasons might explain why younger workers are more likely to have shorter job tenure than older workers?

7. **Training for Workers.** Stone theorized that the new psychological contract included an implied promise of training to enhance re-employability as part of the quid pro quo for the shift away from long-term employment. Does this make sense from an employer perspective? Isn't it just as likely that short-term employers will *decrease* their investment in training, preferring to hire employees with the skills they need rather than investing in creating them? Rachel Arnow-Richman has made this argument:

> In the current economy, employers are less willing than in the past to make costly initial investments in workers, due to the likelihood that their need for the skills in question will change or that, in better economic times, trained workers will be inclined to take their careers and skills elsewhere. Instead, employers are outsourcing the skills-acquisition process or are looking for employees who come to the job with the requisite training or experience. . . . The prevailing expectation is that employers will extract as much work product as possible from the employee at the outset of the relationship, while her function and skills are relevant, giving only limited attention to long-term productivity. This makes sense from the perspective of the employer who may find it difficult to assess its long-term needs or the transferability of an employee's skill set to the employer's future undetermined endeavors. . . .

Accommodation Subverted: The Future of Work/Family Initiatives in a "Me, Inc." World, 12 TEX. J. WOMEN & L. 345, 384 (2003). Whose job should it be to train workers?

8. **A Loyal, Hard-Working Labor Force.** Crain points out that employers relied upon internal labor markets, seniority principles and benefits structured to reward longevity at the firm to build employee loyalty and make it easier to control and discipline the workforce. In a labor market where longevity is not the norm, how will managers adjust their incentive structures to motivate employees? Might profit-sharing or stock option purchase plans help to align the interests of workers and employers, providing an incentive for workers to invest discretionary effort in their jobs? As Bidwell *et al.* explain, motivating workers by having them share in the company's economic performance is not a new idea; indeed, it was associated with the welfare capitalism of the 1920s. Myron J. Roomkin, *Preface* to PROFIT SHARING AND GAIN SHARING at ix (Myron J. Roomkin ed., 1990). Could employee stock ownership furnish an alternative vehicle to enhance worker voice? Some commentators believe so. *See* Dana Muir, *Employee Profit Sharing, Voice, and Peace,* 35 VAND. J. TRANSNAT'L L. 485 (2003).

Crain observes that service sector employers are more dependent upon front-line employees' loyalty and willingness to go the extra mile to further the firm's mission than manufacturing employers because service businesses offer no tangible product; the firms' service *is* the product, and it cannot be separated from the workers who provide it. Some "encounter-styled" service businesses (such as fast food businesses) simply accept high turnover and lack of attachment to the firm as industrial realities and develop rigid control practices designed to accommodate turnover, such as scripting interactions and requiring all employees to present a uniform image to consumers. Others whose service entails more "relationship-styled" sustained contact with customers (such as airlines) have developed internal marketing programs aimed at inducing buy-in from workers to the firm's brand in order to incentivize the extra-role behavior and "organizational citizenship" that is linked to profitability:

> [R]elationship-styled businesses have been at the forefront of developing new strategies aimed at replacing the old norm of "blind loyalty" to the firm as a whole with a more targeted commitment to the firm's vision and values. These new strategies, collectively referred to as "identity-based brand management" or simply "internal branding programs," are more sophisticated than simple scripting and routinization (though they may contain elements of both). Directed by or in collaboration with the corporate marketing department, identity-based brand management programs go beyond traditional loyalty-enhancing programs such as family-friendly workplace policies, retirement vehicles based on longevity or stock options linked to performance, typically administered by human resources departments. Instead of acting on employee behavior, internal branding programs function to transform employee identity. Employees are persuaded to internalize brand values through a systematic recruiting, training, development, and compensation program that fosters a psychological commitment to the firm and a "consciousness of kind" that translates into deeper attachment to the firm. The goal is to produce a workforce that reacts and behaves instinctively "on-brand," effectively managing itself.

Crain, *supra*, at 1199–1200. Crain discusses internal branding programs at Southwest Airlines and Disney. Can you think of others? Are there any downsides to such programs for workers?

9.   Forced Distribution Performance Evaluation Systems. Preferring the stick to the carrot, some companies have experimented with performance evaluation plans referred to as "grading on a curve," in which employees are grouped together into bands by performance. Such forced distribution plans began as a means to combat evaluation inflation or "easy grading" that had tended to undermine previous evaluation systems. Forced distribution curves are characterized by a system in which a specific percentage of workers must fall into each category, with employment consequences then attaching to their placement. Forced distribution curves facilitate the eradication of low-performing workers and downsizing, and are sometimes referred to as the "rank and yank" model of evaluation. Those at the top of the bell curve are promoted, and those at the bottom of the curve are discharged. A typical distribution plan ranks employees into three categories: the top 5%, the middle 90%, and the bottom 5%. There are many variations, however, and the middle 90% is often further broken down into categories of very good, good, and room for improvement, with corresponding formal feedback, including pay raises based upon the percentile in which the employee is classified. Estimates are that 60% of Fortune 500 employers utilize some form of this ranking system, with 14% adopting the most rigid form. Leslie Kwoh, *'Rank and Yank' Retains Vocal Fans*, WALL ST. J., Jan. 31, 2012.

Forced distribution systems that visit disproportionate effects on older employees or on workers of color have been challenged under the antidiscrimination laws. Plaintiffs complained that forced distribution systems were subjectively applied and masked discriminatory animus. Most actions were settled, with some employers abandoning the systems; others continue to use them. *See* Norihiko Shirouzo, *Ford Stops Using Letter Ranking to Rate Workers*, WALL ST. J., July 11, 2001; Reed Abelson, *Employees Sue over Ranking Systems; Gradings Favor Certain Workers, Lawsuits Allege*, CHI. TRIB., Mar. 19, 2001.

What are the advantages and disadvantages of forced distribution systems? If safeguards against discriminatory implementation are in place, do they raise any other concerns about legal liability? What impact are they likely to have on morale? Why do you think they are so widely used?

10. Restructuring Work. Some employers have restructured work itself in ways that reframe core employees to look more like peripheral employees, at least in terms of work time. Among low-wage service sector employers, Wal-Mart set the tone with adoption of a "preferred scheduling" policy. This system uses computerized scheduling to match employee work schedules with fluctuating data on peak customer activity and traffic, concentrating the greatest number of workers on the busiest nights and weekends in order to streamline personnel costs. Some observers bemoaned the policy, saying that it would effectively push out full-time and long-term workers who earn more money and receive benefits because they must conform to unpredictable shiftwork and weekly hours allocations, straining their financial, personal, and family lives. Wal-Mart defended the policy as an efficient deployment of company resources designed to maximize customer service. Steven Greenhouse & Michael Barbaro, *Wal-Mart to Add Wage Caps and Part-Timers*, N.Y. TIMES, Oct. 2, 2006. Large retail employers soon adopted the same strategies, drawn by the prospect of reduced labor costs and increased productivity. *See* Rhonda Smith, *Use of Employee Scheduling Software Raises Union Concerns About Seniority, Work Hours*, DAILY LAB. REP. (BNA) No. 97, May 20, 2014 (noting use of scheduling software at the Gap, Banana Republic, and other large retailers).

Some employers have moved away from these strategies in response to union pressure, complaints by workers, or adverse publicity. Employers that have done so include UPS, Costco, Macy's, and Starbucks. *See id*; Jodi Kantor, *Working Anything but 9 to 5*, N.Y. TIMES, Aug. 13, 2014; Leslie Patton, *Starbucks Changes Scheduling Rules to Make Its Employees' Lives Easier*, DAILY LAB. REP. (BNA) No. 157, Aug.14, 2014. Scholars and advocacy groups have called for legislation to address the hardships imposed by unpredictable work schedules, particularly for parents trying to arrange child care. *See* Michael Rose, *Need for Scheduling Legislation Is Backed up by Research, Advocates Say*, DAILY LAB. REP. (BNA) No. 175, Sept. 10, 2104 (describing Schedules That Work Act, introduced by Sen. Elizabeth Warren in July 2014).

In addition, home-based work and telework that accommodate work/life balance have become increasingly common, although there are wide variations by occupation and industry. Advances in technology and communications have driven these trends, allowing workers to perform their jobs from remote locations and facilitating workforce monitoring and risk management by employers. *See 13.4 Million Workers Home-Based in 2010, Up 18 Percent over Five Years, Agency Says*, DAILY LAB. REP. (BNA) No. 195, Oct. 9, 2012; Leslie Clark, *Cornell Survey Finds Remote Work Has Pluses for Employees and Businesses*, DAILY LAB. REP. (BNA) No. 220, Nov. 15, 2011. Best Buy experimented with a scheduling policy for its corporate employees called ROWE ("results-only work environment"). Begun as a covert "bottom up" experiment in which employees set their own schedules and performed their work from the locations they chose (such as at home), ROWE quickly caught on as a way to avoid long commutes and increase worker satisfaction and therefore, productivity. The official policy was that employees were "free to work wherever they want, whenever they want, as long as they get their work done." Best Buy claimed that the program reduced employee turnover, enhanced productivity, and improved job satisfaction. *See* Michelle Conlin, *Smashing the Clock*, BUS. WEEK, Dec. 11, 2006, at 60. With the arrival of a new CEO, however, the experiment ended and ROWE was eliminated. Convinced that ROWE was "fundamentally flawed from a leadership standpoint," the CEO reversed corporate philosophy and instituted "top down accountability" throughout the company. *See* Gary Peterson, *Cutting ROWE Won't Cure Best Buy*, FORBES, Mar. 12, 2013, *available at* http://www.forbes.com/sites/garypeterson/2013/03/12/cutting-rowe-wont-cure-best-buy/.

Note the dramatic difference in the types of policies aimed at low-waged, low-skilled workers who are relatively fungible, and high-waged, high-skilled workers who are likely to have more bargaining leverage: these policies restrict the autonomy of low-waged workers, while enhancing the autonomy of high-waged workers. Are such trends novel? What do the modern versions of these policies add to historical patterns of oversight of low-skilled workers with time clocks and hourly wages versus salaries and flexible hours for high-skilled workers?

C. DEFINING THE BOUNDARIES OF THE EMPLOYMENT RELATIONSHIP

It may seem obvious that labor and employment laws apply to employment relationships, but the question of what counts as an employment relationship for legal purposes has proved to be far from simple. Labor and employment statutes typically contain only the most superficial definitions, leaving courts to flesh out their meaning. The majority of the cases on this question have centered around the meaning to be accorded to the term "employee" in various statutory contexts. In those cases, the question has typically been whether the individual is an employee or an independent contractor. We explore that issue in more depth in subsection 2, below. Closely related is the question of which entity should be held liable for labor and employment law violations—who is the employer? This question has taken on added complexity in a market characterized by franchising and outsourcing. We cover these issues in subsection 3.

More recent challenges have made it clear, however, that our conception of the employment relationship itself is in considerable flux. What counts as work? Who works? We explore these questions first.

1.   What Is the Nature of Employment?

Historically courts have assumed that employment is characterized by compensation flowing from employer to worker, and employer control over the worker's duties. But how should we think about less traditional arrangements in which labor occurs and value is received? For example, do unpaid student internships create employment relationships governed by work law? Are scholar-athletes who receive athletic scholarships employed by the university? What about cheerleaders for professional sports teams who receive minimal compensation but gain publicity necessary to launch a modeling career? Are prisoners who receive no compensation or minimal compensation for the work they perform employees? These new questions challenge historical assumptions and raise fundamental issues about the nature of employment. The first case below illustrates the use of the compensation requirement as a threshold issue: without a "hiring," there can be no employment. The vignettes that follow highlight some additional contexts that challenge traditional assumptions about the essential characteristics of an employment relationship.

O'CONNOR v. DAVIS
United States Court of Appeals for the Second Circuit
126 F.3d 112 (1997)

WALKER, CIRCUIT JUDGE.

. . . .

While enrolled as a student at Marymount College ("Marymount"), a private Catholic college located in Tarrytown, New York, Bridget O'Connor majored in social work. As a component of her major, O'Connor was required during her senior year to perform 200 hours of field work at one of several Marymount-approved organizations which, in the past, had included schools, day-care centers, community organizations, correctional facilities, and social service agencies. Marymount arranged for O'Connor to be placed for her senior-year internship with Rockland, a hospital for the mentally disabled operated by New York State. Because this internship was considered to be "work study" for financial aid purposes, O'Connor received, through Marymount, federal work study funds for the time she spent performing her volunteer work with Rockland.

O'Connor's internship with Rockland began on September 20, 1994. The hours O'Connor worked were flexible, although she generally chose to work on Mondays and Wednesdays from approximately 8:00 a.m. to 4:30 p.m. because that schedule did not conflict with her regular Marymount classes. O'Connor regularly attended morning staff meetings with Rockland employees and other volunteers, met with the patients assigned to her both one-on-one and in groups. She then documented the results of these patient sessions in "process recordings" which were given first to her Rockland supervisor, Lisa Punzone ("Punzone"), and then to faculty at Marymount.

Dr. James Davis ("Davis") worked as a licensed psychiatrist at Rockland. Approximately two days after O'Connor began her internship, Davis referred to O'Connor, in her presence, as "Miss Sexual Harassment"—a term Davis later explained was intended, as a compliment, to convey the idea that O'Connor was physically attractive and, as such, was likely to be the object of sexual harassment. O'Connor promptly complained about Davis's comment to Punzone, who explained that Davis made similar comments to her, and that O'Connor should try her best to ignore him.

Not only did Davis continue to address O'Connor as "Miss Sexual Harassment," he added to his repertoire of inappropriate sexual remarks. For instance, on one Monday morning, Davis told O'Connor that she looked tired, and that she and her boyfriend must have had "a good time" the night before. On another occasion, Davis pointed to a picture in a newspaper of a woman dressed only in underwear and announced that O'Connor was the woman photographed. He also suggested to O'Connor (and other women present) that they should participate in an "orgy." Finally, on yet another occasion, Davis told O'Connor to remove her clothing in preparation for a meeting with him; he explained, "Don't you always take your clothes off before you go in the doctor's office?"

O'Connor was apparently not Davis's only target; he also commented regularly on the physical appearance of a number of women employed at Rockland, and directed sexual jokes and sexually suggestive noises at them—particularly, as Davis put it, on occasions when he thought the women "looked very well that day." Davis also made "jokes" about female patients—suggesting in one instance that a woman patient would benefit from sterilization and, on another occasion, when considering a woman patient who was an incest victim, stating: "the family that plays together stays together."

Although O'Connor reported a good deal of this conduct to Punzone, Punzone did not report any of O'Connor's complaints to James Wagner, her own supervisor, until January of 1995. And when Wagner learned of O'Connor's encounters with Davis, he, like Punzone, did nothing to remedy the situation.

Also in January of 1995, O'Connor complained to Virginia Kaiser, Marymount's social work field instructor, who in turn brought Davis's conduct to the attention of Madeline Connolly, Rockland's director of social work. Connolly then notified Wilbur T. Aldridge, Rockland's affirmative action administrator, who thereafter investigated O'Connor's complaint.

Finally, at some point in January of 1995, O'Connor left Rockland; however, Marymount arranged for her to complete her internship at another facility.

In March of 1995, O'Connor filed the instant action against Marymount, Rockland, the State of New York, and various Marymount and Rockland employees, alleging, *inter alia*, sexual harassment in violation of Title VII, 42 U.S.C. § 2000e, et seq., and Title IX, 20 U.S.C. §§ 1681, *et seq.* The action was eventually discontinued against Marymount, Punzone, Wagner, Connolly, and Davis himself. The remaining defendants (Rockland and New York State) moved for summary judgment on several grounds. First, they argued that the plaintiff's Title VII claim should be dismissed because O'Connor was not an "employee" of Rockland within the meaning of Title VII. Second, the defendants argued that the Title IX claim should be dismissed because Rockland was not an "educational institution" as set forth in Title IX. Finally, the defendants argued that O'Connor failed to establish a prima facie case of sexual harassment.

In an opinion and order dated May 20, 1996, the district court granted the defendants' summary judgment motion, agreeing that O'Connor was not an "employee" under Title VII and that Rockland was not an "educational institution" under Title IX. Because of this disposition, the district court did not reach the defendants' assertion that O'Connor failed to establish a prima facie case of sexual harassment.

DISCUSSION

. . . .

O'Connor's first argument on appeal is that the district court improperly concluded that she was not a Rockland employee within the meaning of Title VII. She argues that although she worked at Rockland as an unpaid intern, she nevertheless satisfies the common-law agency definition of "employee." We disagree. The definition of the term "employee" provided in Title VII is circular: the Act states only that an "employee" is an "individual employed by an employer." 42 U.S.C. § 2000e(f); *see also EEOC v. Johnson & Higgins*, 91 F.3d 1529, 1538 (2d Cir. 1996). However, it is well established that when Congress uses the term "employee" without defining it with precision, courts should presume that Congress had in mind "the conventional master-servant relationship as understood by the common-law agency doctrine." *Nationwide Mut. Ins. Co. v. Darden*, 503 U.S. 318, 322–23 (1992) (quoting *Community for Creative Non-Violence v. Reid*, 490 U.S. 730, 739–40 (1989)) . . . .

In most cases where an attempt has been made to discern the contours of the "conventional master-servant relationship," it has been because a court has been asked to consider whether, under a particular statute, a party is an employee or an independent contractor. *See, e.g., Reid*, 490 U.S. at 739–40 (considering the Copyright Act of 1976, 17 U.S.C. § 101); *Darden*, 503 U.S. 318, 322–23 (1992) (considering ERISA, 29 U.S.C. § 1132(a)); *Alford v. United States*, 116 F.3d 334, 337–38 (8th Cir. 1997) (considering 26 U.S.C. § 62(a)(1) of the Internal Revenue Code); *Cilecek v. Inova Health Sys.* Servs., 115 F.3d 256, 260 (4th Cir. 1997) (considering Title VII); *Sharkey v. Ultramar Energy Ltd.*, 70 F.3d 226, 232 (2d Cir. 1995) (considering ERISA). In this context, the Supreme Court has outlined the following factors, culled from the Restatement of Agency, *see Reid*, 490 U.S. at 752 n.31, and from caselaw, as relevant to the inquiry:

> In determining whether a hired party is an employee under the general common law of agency, we consider the hiring party's right to control the manner and means by which the product is accomplished. Among the other factors relevant to this inquiry are the skill required; the source of the instrumentalities and tools; the location of the work; the duration of the

relationship between the parties; whether the hiring party has the right to assign additional projects to the hired party; the extent of the hired party's discretion over when and how long to work; the method of payment; the hired party's role in hiring and paying assistants; whether the work is part of the regular business of the hiring party; whether the hiring party is in business; the provision of employee benefits; and the tax treatment of the hired party. *Reid*, 490 U.S. at 751–752 (footnotes omitted).

Both parties on appeal (and the district court below) addressed themselves to the question of whether or not O'Connor was an employee within this framework. However, we think that this analysis is flawed because it ignores the antecedent question of whether O'Connor was hired by Rockland for any purpose. As the Supreme Court suggests, the common feature shared by both the employee and the independent contractor is that they are "hired parties," *id.*, and thus, a prerequisite to considering whether an individual is one or the other under common-law agency principles is that the individual have been hired in the first instance. That is, only where a "hire" has occurred should the common-law agency analysis be undertaken.

Other courts have agreed with this view. As the Eighth Circuit has explained, courts turn to common-law principles to analyze the character of an economic relationship "only in situations that plausibly approximate an employment relationship." *Graves v. Women's Prof'l Rodeo Assoc.*, 907 F.2d 71, 74 (8th Cir. 1990). Where no financial benefit is obtained by the purported employee from the employer, no "plausible" employment relationship of any sort can be said to exist because although "compensation by the putative employer to the putative employee in exchange for his services is not a sufficient condition, . . . it is an essential condition to the existence of an employer-employee relationship." *Graves*, 907 F.2d at 73. *See also Neff v. Civil Air Patrol*, 916 F. Supp. 710, 712–13 (S.D. Ohio, 1996); *Smith v. Berks Community Television*, 657 F. Supp. 794, 796 (E.D. Pa. 1987); *cf. Haavistola v. Community Fire Co.*, 6 F.3d 211, 219 (4th Cir. 1993).

This "essential condition" of remuneration has been recognized in this Circuit as well. In *Tadros v. Coleman*, 898 F.2d 10, 11 (2d Cir. 1990), we explicitly upheld the dismissal of the Title VII claims of a plaintiff who worked as a volunteer on the faculty of Cornell Medical College on the ground that the plaintiff was not an employee under Title VII. As a volunteer, the plaintiff received no salary, health benefits, retirement benefits, and also had no regular hours assigned to him by the hospital. In concluding that the plaintiff was not an employee, the district court in *Tadros* held that "[a] Title VII plaintiff is only an 'employee' if the defendant both pays him and controls his work." 717 F. Supp. 996, 1004 (S.D.N.Y. 1989).

We believe that the preliminary question of remuneration is dispositive in this case. It is uncontested that O'Connor received from Rockland no salary or other wages, and no employee benefits such as health insurance, vacation, or sick pay, nor was she promised any such compensation. This case thus differs from *Haavistola v. Community Fire Co.*, in which the Fourth Circuit considered whether a volunteer member of a fire company was an employee for Title VII purposes where "on the one hand, [plaintiff] did not receive direct compensation as a member of the Fire Company, but, on the other hand, she did not affiliate with the company without reward entirely." 6 F.3d 211, 221 (4th Cir. 1993). The court then noted that the plaintiff received, through her volunteer position, a state-funded disability pension, survivors' benefits for dependents, scholarships for dependents upon death or disability, group life insurance, and several other benefits. *See id.* The court concluded that the district court granted summary judgment improvidently, given that a factfinder should determine whether "the benefits represent indirect but significant remuneration . . . or inconsequential incidents of an otherwise gratuitous relationship." *Id.* at 222.

Because the absence of either direct or indirect economic remuneration or the promise thereof is undisputed in this case, we agree with the district court that O'Connor was not a Rockland employee within the meaning of Title VII and thus that her discrimination claim under that statute must fail.

We reject O'Connor's claim that she was compensated to the extent that she received, through Marymount, federal work study funding for the hours of volunteer work performed at Rockland. Plainly, it was Marymount—not Rockland—that made these payments to O'Connor.

[The court went on to find that Rockland was not functioning as an educational institution covered by Title IX, which prohibits sex discrimination against students and employees in educational institutions that receive federal funding].

Conclusion

By allowing an intern to perform the fieldwork required of her by the wholly unaffiliated college she attends, Rockland is not transformed into an employer under Title VII or into an administrator of an education program or activity under Title IX. We conclude by saying only that we are not unsympathetic to O'Connor's situation. We recognize, for example, that from her perspective, her success at Marymount was dependent to some degree on successfully completing her internship with Rockland, and that her dependency on Rockland made her vulnerable to continued harassment much as an employee dependent on a regular wage can be vulnerable to ongoing misconduct. In a similar vein, we recognize that O'Connor was not in quite the same position to simply walk away from the alleged harassment as are many other volunteers. However, it is for Congress, if it should choose to do so, and not this court, to provide a remedy under either Title VII or Title IX for plaintiffs in O'Connor's position. We therefore affirm the judgment of the district court.

NOTES

1. **Uncompensated Interns and Volunteers.** *O'Connor v. Davis* remains the dominant rule applicable to claims by unpaid interns under antidiscrimination statutes. *See Wang v. Phoenix Satellite Television US*, 976 F. Supp. 2d 527 (S.D.N.Y. 2013) (unpaid intern was not an employee for purposes of her sexual harassment and discriminatory retaliation claim under New York's human rights laws, but instead a volunteer). According to the EEOC, interns are not employees covered by Title VII unless they receive "significant remuneration" in some form; unpaid interns are conceptualized as volunteers. *See Federal EEO Laws: When Interns May Be Employees*, INFORMAL DISCUSSION LETTER, December 8, 2011, *available at*

http://www.eeoc.gov/eeoc/foia/letters/2011/eeo_laws_when_interns_may_be_ employees.html; EEOC Compliance Manual, Section 2: *Threshold Issues*, at part 2-III.A.1.c. (discussing coverage for volunteers), *available at* http://www.eeoc.gov/ policy/docs/threshold.html (hereinafter *Threshold Issues Guidance*). Some jurisdictions, disturbed by this result, have legislated coverage for unpaid interns. In response to *Wang*, for example, the New York City Council amended its Human Rights law to provide interns (paid and unpaid) protection against workplace discrimination and harassment, joining Washington, D.C., California, and Oregon. *Intern Rights May Be Next Trend in Employment Law*, LAW 360, Apr. 28, 2014; Laura Mahoney, *California Governor Signs Sick Leave, Anti-Bullying and Interns' Rights Bills*, DAILY LAB. REP. (BNA) No. 175, Sept. 10, 2014. As we shall see, interns may be viewed as employees for purposes of application of some other employment legislation, such as wage and hour laws.

The *Davis* analysis treating the existence of compensation as an independent antecedent inquiry established by proof of a "hiring" also reflects the majority approach to discrimination cases involving volunteers. *See also United States v. City of New York*, 359 F.3d 83 (2d Cir. 2004) (adopting a two-step test for determining whether an individual is an employee under Title VII, which requires a plaintiff to establish first that she is a "hired party" by showing that she received "substantial benefits not merely incidental to the activity performed," and second that she qualifies as an employee under the common law agency test); *Seattle Opera v. NLRB*, 292 F.3d 757 (D.C. Cir. 2002) (applying the two-step test in determining whether auxiliary choristers were employees of the opera under the National Labor Relations Act). However, in *Bryson v. Middlefield Volunteer Fire Dep't, Inc.*, 656 F.3d 348 (6th Cir. 2011), a divided Sixth Circuit ruled that volunteer firefighters count for purposes of establishing the minimum number of employees for coverage under Title VII, allowing a paid administrative aide's sexual harassment claim against the fire chief to proceed. The court considered the question of remuneration as one factor among several, applying a common law agency test drawn from *Nationwide Mutual Insurance Co. v. Darden*, 503 U.S. 318 (1992) that requires analysis of the method of payment, the hiring party's right to control the manner and means by which work is accomplished, the skills required, the location of the work, ownership of the job's instrumentalities and tools, and other similar factors. And some courts have considered benefits other than wages as sufficient to satisfy the compensation hurdle, including small payments, insurance coverage, gift cards, personal use and access rights to facilities, and training. *See, e.g., Bryson, supra*, at 355–56.

In any event, it is clear that the label "volunteer" is not sufficient to exempt the relationship from analysis as a possible employment relation. *See Mendel v. City of Gibraltar*, 727 F.3d 565 (6th Cir. 2013) (noting that volunteer firefighters who receive a $15 per hour wage for responding to calls when they choose to do so are "employees" for Family and Medical Leave Act purposes because they work in contemplation of compensation, despite the common use of the term "volunteer" to describe their obligations). Should volunteers be treated as employees for purposes of protection under at least some employment statutes? Whose interests are harmed if volunteers are not counted as employees? *See* Mitchell H. Rubenstein, *Our Nation's Forgotten Workers: The Unprotected Volunteers*, 9 U. PA. J. LAB. &

EMP. L. 147 (2006) (proposing legislation to address gaps in coverage).

2. The Nature of Employment. Larger questions about what counts as employment continue to perplex the courts. Should compensation be the only criterion? Consider this summary of the primary characteristics of work—does it help?

> Setting aside the technicalities of legal tests, four features seem significant: (1) the employee gets paid and thereby 'makes a living' (livelihood); (2) the employer makes money selling the products of the employee's labor, which are valued by those who pay for them (production); (3) the employee's time and conduct are subject to the employer's control—at work she is on 'the company's time' (discipline); (4) as someone who 'works for a living' and 'plays by the rules' the employee is accorded social respect and granted access to social citizenship (status).

Noah D. Zatz & Eileen Boris, *Seeing Work, Envisioning Citizenship*, 18 EM. RTS. & EMP. POL'Y J. 95, 96 (2014).

The following vignettes challenge the traditional criteria for finding an employment relationship governed by labor and employment laws. In each case, consider whether the situation should be viewed as employment, and if so, for what purposes. What policy goals or larger economic trends suggest treating these relationships as employment? What considerations counsel against treating them as employment? The factors listed by Zatz & Boris, *supra*, may also be helpful in guiding your analysis.

Unpaid Student Interns

The *O'Connor* court focused on the existence of compensation flowing from the putative employer to the alleged employee as the key attribute of the employment relation for purposes of applying anti-discrimination protections. Compensation is not a threshold requirement in cases litigated under the wage and hour laws, however. In these cases, interns argue that the violation was the lack of pay itself; the policy underlying the law is to ensure a minimum level of pay for all workers and to spread work (create jobs) by requiring payment of a premium for overtime hours. We will explore the rapidly evolving law applying to unpaid internships under the FLSA in more depth in Chapter 11. For now, consider the following scenario:

> A solo practitioner hires law students to work as interns for the summer months. The interns perform the following tasks: translating for clients who are not proficient in English, stuffing envelopes, cleaning offices, making coffee, and hand-delivering legal documents around the city. The interns receive no pay; the firm explains that the internship affords students the opportunity to supplement academic training with practical experience, exposing them to the inner workings of a litigation practice in New York City. Should the interns be permitted to bring claims under the wage and hour laws for minimum wage? For overtime pay if their hours exceed 40 per week? [*See Poff v. The Portela Law Firm*, settled 2013]

Scholar-Athletes

In some cases the compensation element is clearly satisfied and the would-be employer appears to exercise significant control over the work performed, but the relationship has traditionally been seen as falling into another category—an academic relationship, for example. Much of the law in this area has developed under the National Labor Relations Act when students have sought organizing and collective bargaining rights vis-à-vis the university. The NLRB has ruled that medical interns, residents and fellows who are paid to spend 80% of their time providing direct patient care with limited supervision are primarily functioning as employees, not as students, and thus are protected under the NLRA. *Boston Med. Ctr. Corp.*, 330 N.L.R.B. 152 (1999). On the other hand, a closely divided NLRB found that graduate teaching assistants and undergraduate research assistants who assist with teaching were primarily students: their teaching duties were a core element of the educational process for which they received academic credit and financial aid, they were closely supervised by academic faculty, and the amount of time spent teaching was small compared to the amount of time spent on their own studies. Because their relationship with the university was primarily academic rather than economic, they were not employees for NLRA purposes. *Brown Univ.*, 342 N.L.R.B. 483 (2004). Can these two rulings be harmonized? Now consider this scenario:

> A private university competing in Division I athletics provides scholarships to its football players that cover tuition, room and board, health insurance, fees and books for up to five years; benefits may total as much as $76,000 per calendar year. The scholarships are tied to performing on the playing field and can be withdrawn if the player withdraws from the team or abuses team rules. The football team is profitable for the university, generating as much as $235 million in revenue with only $159 million in expenses. The players are engaged in athletic pursuits 50–60 hours per week and their daily itineraries are strictly controlled from 5:45 a.m. until 10:30 p.m. They are required to follow strict rules and policies that other students are not, including restrictions on where they live, on outside employment, on the vehicles they drive, on their interactions with the press and social media, on swearing in public, on selling merchandise or autographs that allow them to profit from their athletic abilities (mirroring an NCAA rule), and on gambling, drug and alcohol use. Their class schedules are organized around their athletic activities. The players seek to organize a union in order to advocate for the right to control the use of their own images and to obtain post-graduation health care coverage for injuries sustained while on the team. Is their relationship with the university primarily academic, like the graduate students in *Brown*, or primarily economic, like the medical interns and residents in *Boston University*? [*See Northwestern University*, 2014 NLRB LEXIS 221, review granted by full Board, 2014 NLRB LEXIS 298 (Apr. 24, 2014), pending]

Cheerleaders for Professional Sports Teams

In many situations, individuals are compensated but their pay averages out to less than minimum wage after taking into account work that they must do "off-the-clock" to retain their positions. In some contexts, the prestige and public platform offered by the position induces individuals to accept this substandard pay because the position advances their future aspirations (in the case of cheerleaders for professional sports teams, a modeling, acting, or dancing career), or more abstract reputational gains (a prestigious or sexy image). Consider the following scenario based upon recently filed complaints:

> Cheerleaders for the New York Jets, the Oakland Raiders, the Cincinnati Bengals, the Tampa Buccaneers and the Buffalo Bills allege that they are paid subminimum wage for their work as cheerleaders. This came about because although they are paid minimum wage for the time they spent providing entertainment at the games, they were also required to make appearances at many events as ambassadors for the team, to attend unpaid rehearsals three times per week, and to perform work at home, all without compensation. In addition, they are subject to strict rules regarding attire, demeanor, weight and fitness (one team reportedly requires cheerleaders to pass a "jiggle test"), are required to agree to a "morals" clause, and must comply with restrictions on social media communications. Violations of these rules are sometimes punished with fines, further reducing their compensation. Should they be paid at least minimum wage and overtime pay for all the hours they spend preparing and making appearances as directed? How far should this extend? Should it include time spent straightening curly hair to conform to appearance requirements? If the cheerleaders are not employees, what are they—volunteers? Independent contractors? [*See* Eric Morath, *Ex-NFL Cheerleaders Tackle Wages*, WALL ST. J., Sept. 6–7, 2014]

Prisoners

Another context where work performed challenges the boundaries of traditional employment is the correctional system. Prison laborers who work inside the prison may provide services that would otherwise have to be done by paid employees; they may also generate revenue for the prison by producing products that are sold outside the prison. In addition, they increasingly work outside prisons for private companies as part of work-release programs. Is prison labor different from other sorts of labor, justifying its exemption from employment and labor laws? If so, why? Consider the following:

> Arizona state law requires all able-bodied prison inmates to work at least 40 hours per week in a "hard labor" job as part of their sentences. Prisoners fulfill this requirement either by working in the corrections department's work incentive pay program, which allows them to earn 10 to 50 cents per hour in jobs performed onsite at the prisons where they are incarcerated, or in off-site programs operated by statutorily-created business entities that contract out inmate labor to private companies. The latter program is designed to help offenders obtain marketable skills. Workers in the off-site programs are paid more than those in the on-site programs, but less than minimum wage. Under this program, a prison inmate worked 40 hours per week in a private greenhouse picking tomatoes for $2.25 an hour. The job involved pushing a 600-pound tomato cart and being on one's feet

for the entire shift. When the inmate began experiencing pain and swelling in one of his ankles, he sought permission from the prison and the private company to take short breaks during his shift; this request was declined, and he was told that he would be fired if he insisted on taking them. On a doctor's advice, he sought a job change or an accommodation to allow him to continue to work, both of which were denied. Should the inmate have a claim under the Americans with Disabilities Act, which prohibits discrimination on the basis of disability and requires employers to make reasonable accommodations to facilitate work? [*See Castle v. Eurofresh*, 731 F.3d 901 (9th Cir. 2013)].

2. Who Is an "Employee"?

The question whether a worker is an independent contractor or an employee cannot be answered in the abstract and there is no uniform doctrinal test for status. Instead, the issue must be examined in the context of the legislative purpose of the particular statutory rights at issue. Moreover, the decisions are fact-intensive and seemingly small differences in the way in which work is structured may have significant ramifications. Compare the following cases.

FEDEX HOME DELIVERY v. NATIONAL LABOR RELATIONS BOARD
United States Court of Appeals for the D.C. Circuit
563 F.3d. 492 (2009)

BROWN, CIRCUIT JUDGE:

[In 2006, the International Brotherhood of Teamsters, Local Union 25 organized and was certified as the collective bargaining representative for FedEx single route drivers in two locations in Wilmington, Delaware. FedEx refused to bargain with the Teamsters, claiming that the organized drivers were not employees within the meaning of the National Labor Relations Act. The National Labor Relations Board ruled that FedEx had violated §§ 8(a)1 and 8(a)5 of the National Labor Relations Act. FedEx appealed the decision to the Court of Appeals for the DC Circuit and the National Labor Relations Board filed a cross-application for enforcement. The Union intervened in support of the Board's position.]

II.

To determine whether a worker should be classified as an employee or an independent contractor, the Board and this court apply the common-law agency test, a requirement that reflects clear congressional will. *See NLRB v. United Ins. Co.*, 390 U.S. 254, 256 (1968). While this seems simple enough, the Restatement's non-exhaustive ten-factor test is not especially amenable to any sort of bright-line rule,[1] a long-recognized rub. Thus, "there is no shorthand formula or magic phrase

---

[1] [n. 1] The common law factors include, *inter alia*, "the extent of control which, by the agreement, the master may exercise over the details of the work"; "the kind of occupation"; whether the worker

that can be applied to find the answer, but all of the incidents of the relationship must be assessed and weighed with no one factor being decisive," *United Ins. Co.*, 390 U.S. at 258, always bearing in mind the "legal distinction between 'employees' . . . and 'independent contractors' . . . is permeated at the fringes by conclusions drawn from the factual setting of the particular industrial dispute." *North Am. Van Lines, Inc. v. NLRB*, 869 F.2d 596, 599 (D.C. Cir. 1989) ("*NAVL*").

This potential uncertainty is particularly problematic because the line between worker and independent contractor is jurisdictional—the Board has no authority whatsoever over independent contractors. *See id.* at 598. Consequently, it is "one of this court's principal functions" to "ensur[e] that the Board exercises power only within the channels intended by Congress," especially as determining status from undisputed facts "involves no special administrative expertise that a court does not possess." *Id.* We thus do not grant great or even "normal[ ]" deference to the Board's status determinations; instead, we will only uphold the Board if at least "it can be said to have 'made a choice between two fairly conflicting views.' " *C.C. Eastern, Inc. v. NLRB*, 60 F.3d 855, 858 (D.C.Cir.1995) (quoting *NAVL*, 869 F.2d at 599).

For a time, when applying this common law test, we spoke in terms of an employer's right to exercise control, making the extent of actual supervision of the means and manner of the worker's performance a key consideration in the totality of the circumstances assessment. Though all the common law factors were considered, the meta-question, as it were, focused on the sorts of controls employers could use without transforming a contractor into an employee. . . .

Gradually, however, a verbal formulation emerged that sought to identify the essential quantum of independence that separates a contractor from an employee . . . a process where we used words like control but struggled to articulate exactly what we meant by them. "Control," for instance, did not mean *all* kinds of controls, but only *certain* kinds. . . .

. . . [I]n *Corporate Express Delivery Systems v. NLRB*, 292 F.3d 777 (D.C.Cir.2002) . . . both this court and the Board, while retaining all of the common law factors, "shift[ed the] emphasis" away from the unwieldy control inquiry in favor of a more accurate proxy: whether the "putative independent contractors have 'significant entrepreneurial opportunity for gain or loss.' " *Id.* at 780 (quoting *Corp. Express Delivery Sys.*, 332 N.L.R.B. No. 144, at 6 (Dec. 19, 2000)). This subtle refinement was done at the Board's urging in light of a comment to the Restatement that explains a " 'full-time cook is regarded as a servant,' "—and not "an independent contractor"—" 'although it is understood that the employer will exercise no control over the cooking.' " *Id.* (quoting RESTATEMENT (SECOND) OF AGENCY § 220(1) cmt. d). Thus, while all the considerations at common law remain in play, an important animating principle by which to evaluate those factors in cases where some factors cut one way and some the other is whether the position presents the

---

"supplies the instrumentalities, tools, and the place of work"; "the method of payment, whether by the time or by the job"; "the length of time for which the person is employed"; whether "the work is a part of the regular business of the employer"; and the intent of the parties. RESTATEMENT (SECOND) OF AGENCY § 220(2).

opportunities and risks inherent in entrepreneurialism. *Id.*[2]

Although using this "emphasis" does not make applying the test purely mechanical, the line drawing is easier, or at least this court and the Board in *Corporate Express* seem to have so hoped. *See id.* ("We agree with the Board's suggestion that [entrepreneurial opportunity] better captures the distinction between an employee and an independent contractor."). In *C.C. Eastern*, for instance, we decided drivers for a cartage company who owned their own tractors, signed an independent contractor agreement, "retain[ed] the rights, as independent entrepreneurs, to hire their own employees" and could "use their tractors during non-business hours," and who were "paid by the job" and received no employee benefits, should be characterized as independent contractors. 60 F.3d at 858–59. We also noted the company did not require "specific work hours" or dress codes, nor did it subject workers to conventional employee discipline. *Id.* at 858. Conversely, in *Corporate Express*, emphasizing entrepreneurialism, we straightforwardly concluded that where the owner-operators "were not permitted to employ others to do the Company's work or to use their own vehicles for other jobs," they "lacked all entrepreneurial opportunity and consequently functioned as employees rather than as independent contractors." 292 F.3d at 780–81.

This struggle to capture and articulate what is meant by abstractions like "independence" and "control" also seems to play a part in the Board's own cases, though we readily concede the Board's language has not been as unambiguous as this court's binding statement in *Corporate Express*. For instance, in the latest but far from only statement of the principle . . . , *Arizona Republic*, 349 N.L.R.B. 1040, 1040 (2007), the Board held that where carriers sign an independent contractor agreement; own, maintain, and control their own vehicles; hire full-time substitutes and control the substitutes' terms and conditions of employment; are permitted to hold contracts on multiple routes; select the delivery sequence; and are not subject to the employer's progressive discipline system, the evidence establishes that the carriers are independent contractors, *id.* at 1040–41, 1046. Importantly, the Board, noting many drivers had "multiple routes" and could deliver newspapers for another publisher, also concluded significant entrepreneurial opportunity existed, even if most failed to make the extra effort. "[T]he fact that many carriers choose not to take advantage of this opportunity to increase their income does not mean that they do not have the entrepreneurial *potential* to do so." *Id.* at 1045.

The record here shares many of the same characteristics of entrepreneurial potential. In the underlying representation decision, the Regional Director found the contractors sign a Standard Contractor Operating Agreement that specifies the contractor is not an employee of FedEx "for any purpose" and confirms the "manner and means of reaching mutual business objectives" is within the contractor's discretion, and FedEx "may not prescribe hours of work, whether or when the

---

[2] [n. 3] The common law test, after all, is not merely quantitative. We do not just count the factors that favor one camp, and those the other, and declare that whichever side scores the most points wins. Instead, there also is a qualitative assessment to evaluate which factors are determinative in a particular case, and why. In *Corporate Express*, we said this qualitative evaluation "focus[es] not upon the employer's control of the means and manner of the work but instead upon whether the putative independent contractors have a 'significant entrepreneurial opportunity for gain or loss.'" 292 F.3d at 780 (quoting *Corp. Express*, 332 N.L.R.B. at 6).

contractors take breaks, what routes they follow, or other details of performance"; "contractors are not subject to reprimands or other discipline"; contractors must provide their own vehicles, although the vehicles must be compliant with government regulations and other safety requirements; and "contractors are responsible for all the costs associated with operating and maintaining their vehicles." *FedEx Home Delivery and Local 25*, N.L.R.B. Case Nos. 1-RC-22034, 22035, slip op. at 10–14 (First Region, Sept. 20, 2006) ("*Representation Decision*"). They may use the vehicles "for other commercial or personal purposes . . . so long as they remove or mask all FedEx Home logos and markings," and, even on this limited record, some do use them for personal uses like moving family members, and in the past "Alan Douglas[ ] used his FedEx truck for his 'Douglas Delivery' delivery service, in which he delivered items such as lawn mowers for a repair company." *Id.* at 14, 15. Contractors can independently incorporate, and at least two in Wilmington have done so. At least one contractor has negotiated with FedEx for higher fees. *Id.* at 20.

Tellingly, contractors may contract to serve multiple routes or hire their own employees for their single routes; more than twenty-five percent of contractors have hired their own employees at some point. "The multiple route contractors have sole authority to hire and dismiss their drivers"; they are responsible for the "drivers' wages" and "all expenses associated with hiring drivers, such as the cost of training, physical exams, drug screening, employment taxes, and work accident insurance." Representation Decision, slip op. at 27. The drivers' pay and benefits, as well as responsibility for fuel costs and the like, are negotiated "between the contractors and their drivers." *Id.* In addition, "both multiple and single route contractors may hire drivers" as "temporary" replacements on their own routes; though they can use FedEx's "Time Off Program" to find replacement drivers when they are ill or away, they need not use this program, and not all do. *Id.* at 28–29. Thus, contrary to the dissent's depiction, contractors do not need to show up at work every day (or ever, for that matter); instead, at their discretion, they can take a day, a week, a month, or more off, so long as they hire another to be there. "FedEx [also] is not involved in a contractor's decision to hire or terminate a substitute driver, and contractors do not even have to tell FedEx [ ] they have hired a replacement driver, as long as the driver is 'qualified.' " *Representation Decision*, slip op. at 29. "Contractors may also choose to hire helpers" without notifying FedEx at all; at least six contractors in Wilmington have done so. *Id.* at 29–30. This ability to hire "others to do the Company's work" is no small thing in evaluating "entrepreneurial opportunity." *Corp. Express*, 292 F.3d at 780–81.

Another aspect of the Operating Agreement is significant, and is novel under our precedent. Contractors can assign at law their contractual rights to their routes, without FedEx's permission. The logical result is they can sell, trade, give, or even bequeath their routes, an unusual feature for an employer-employee relationship. In fact, the amount of consideration for the sale of a route is negotiated "strictly between the seller and the buyer," with no FedEx involvement at all other than the new route owner must also be "qualified" under the Operating Agreement, *Representation Decision*, slip op. at 30, with "qualified" merely meaning the new owner of the route also satisfies Department of Transportation ("DOT") regulations, *see id.* at 8–10. Although FedEx assigns routes without nominal charge, the record contains evidence, as the Regional Director expressly found, that at least two contractors were able to sell routes for a profit ranging from $3,000 to nearly $16,000. *See id.* at 30–32, 38–39.

In its argument to this court, the Board . . . discounts this evidence of entrepreneurial opportunity by saying any so-called profit merely represents the value of the vehicles, which were sold along with the routes. But if a vehicle depreciates in value, it is not worth as much as it was before; that is tautological. Here, buyers paid more for a vehicle and route than just the depreciated value of the vehicle—in one instance more than $10,000 more. Therefore, as the Regional Director did, we find this value *is* profit. The *amount* of profit may be "murky," as it may be as high as $6,000 and $16,000 or as low as $3,000 or $11,000, respectively, but the profit is real. *Representation Decision*, slip op. at 38. That this potential for profit exists is unsurprising: routes are geographically defined, and they likely have value dependent on those geographic specifics which some contractors can better exploit than others. For example, as people move into an area, the ability to profit from that migration varies; some contractors using more efficient methods can continue to serve the entire route, while others cannot.

It is similarly confused to conclude FedEx gives away routes for free. A contractor agrees to provide a service in return for compensation, i.e., both sides give consideration. If a contractor does not do what she says, FedEx suffers damages, just as she does if FedEx does not pay what is owed. Servicing a route is not cheap; one needs a truck (which the contractor pays for) and a driver (which the contractor also pays for, either directly or in kind). To say this is giving away a route is to say when one hires a contractor to build a house, one is just giving away a construction opportunity. All of this evidence thus supports finding these contractors to be independent.

The Regional Director, however, thought FedEx's business model distinguishable from those where the Board had concluded the drivers were independent contractors. For example, FedEx requires: contractors to wear a recognizable uniform and conform to grooming standards; vehicles of particular color (white) and within a specific size range; and vehicles to display FedEx's logo in a way larger than that required by DOT regulations. The company insists drivers complete a driving course (or have a year of commercial driving experience, which need not be with FedEx) and be insured, and it "conducts two customer service rides per year" to audit performance. FedEx provides incentive pay (as well as fuel reimbursements in limited instances) and vehicle availability allotments, and requires contractors have a vehicle and driver available for deliveries Tuesday through Saturday. *Id.* at 508–14. Moreover, FedEx can reconfigure routes if a contractor cannot provide adequate service, though the contractor has five days to prove otherwise, and is entitled to monetary compensation for the diminished value of the route. *Id.* at 512. These aspects of FedEx's operation are distinguishable from the business models in *Dial-A-Mattress*, 326 N.L.R.B. 884 (contractors arranged their own training, could decline work, did not wear uniforms, could use any vehicle, and were provided no subsidies or minimum compensation) and *Argix Direct, Inc.*, 343 N.L.R.B. 1017 (2004) (contractors could decline work, delivered to major retailers using any vehicle, and had no guaranteed income).

But those distinctions, though not irrelevant, reflect differences in the type of service the contractors are providing rather than differences in the employment relationship. In other words, the distinctions are significant but not sufficient. FedEx Home's business model is somewhat unique. The service is delivering small packages, mostly to residential customers. Unlike some trucking companies, its drivers are not delivering goods that FedEx sells or manufacturers, nor does FedEx move freight for a limited number of large clients. Instead, it is an intermediary between a diffuse group of senders and a broadly diverse group of recipients. With this model comes certain customer demands, including safety. . . . And once a driver wears FedEx's logo, FedEx has an interest in making sure her conduct reflects favorably on that logo, for instance by her being a safe and insured driver-which is required by DOT regulations in any event. *See Representation Decision*, slip op. at 8–9, 14, 24.

. . . .

The Regional Director also emphasized that these "contractors perform a function that is a regular and essential part of FedEx Home's normal operations, the delivery of packages," and that few have seized any of the alleged entrepreneurial opportunities. *Representation Decision*, slip op. at 34, 38. While the essential nature of a worker's role is a legitimate consideration, it is not determinative in the face of more compelling countervailing factors, otherwise companies like FedEx could never hire delivery drivers who *are* independent contractors. . . . And both the Board and this court have found the failure to take advantage of an opportunity is beside the point. *See C.C. Eastern*, 60 F.3d at 860 (opportunities cannot be ignored unless they are the sort workers "cannot realistically take," and even "one instance" of a driver using such an opportunity can be sufficient to "show [ ] there is no unwritten rule or invisible barrier preventing other drivers from likewise exercising their contractual right"); *Arizona Republic*, 349 N.L.R.B. at 1045. Instead, "it is the worker's retention of the right to engage in entrepreneurial activity rather than his regular exercise of that right that is most relevant for the purpose of determining whether he is an independent contractor." *C.C. Eastern*, 60 F.3d at 860.[3]

. . . .

IV.

We have considered all the common law factors, and, on balance, are compelled to conclude they favor independent contractor status. The ability to operate multiple routes, hire additional drivers (including drivers who substitute for the contractor) and helpers, and to sell routes without permission, as well as the parties' intent expressed in the contract, augurs strongly in favor of independent contractor status. Because the indicia favoring a finding the contractors are employees are clearly outweighed by evidence of entrepreneurial opportunity, the Board cannot be

---

[3] [n. 8] The Regional Director noted too that "FedEx Home offers what is essentially a take-it-or-leave-it agreement." But we will "draw no inference of employment status from merely the economic controls which many corporations are able to exercise over independent contractors with whom they contract." *NAVL*, 869 F.2d at 599.

said to have made a choice between two fairly conflicting views. Though evidence can be marshaled and debater's points scored on both sides, the evidence supporting independent contractor status is more compelling under our precedent. . . . But even as the record stands, the Board's determination was legally erroneous.

Accordingly, we grant the petition, vacate the Board's order, and deny the cross-application for enforcement.

So ordered.

[The dissenting opinion of JUDGE GARLAND is omitted.]

ALEXANDER v. FEDEX GROUND PACKAGE SYSTEM
United States Court of Appeals for the Ninth Circuit
765 F.3d 981 (9th Cir. 2014)

W. FLETCHER, CIRCUIT JUDGE:

As a central part of its business, FedEx Ground Package System, Inc. ("FedEx"), contracts with drivers to deliver packages to its customers. The drivers must wear FedEx uniforms, drive FedEx-approved vehicles, and groom themselves according to FedEx's appearance standards. FedEx tells its drivers what packages to deliver, on what days, and at what times. Although drivers may operate multiple delivery routes and hire third parties to help perform their work, they may do so only with FedEx's consent.

FedEx contends its drivers are independent contractors under California law. Plaintiffs, a class of FedEx drivers in California, contend they are employees. We agree with plaintiffs.

I. Background

. . . .

[Plaintiffs, a class comprising 2300 full-time delivery drivers who worked for FedEx in California between 2000 and 2007, asserted claims in state court for employment expenses and unpaid wages under California Labor Code provisions applicable to "employees." FedEx removed the case to federal court on the basis of diversity jurisdiction, and the case was ultimately consolidated with others filed across the country, all of which turned on the common question whether the drivers were "employees" for purposes of state employment laws. The court granted summary judgment in favor of FedEx, finding as a matter of law that plaintiffs were independent contractors. Plaintiffs appealed.]

 FedEx characterizes its drivers as independent contractors. FedEx's Operating Agreement ("OA") governs its relationship with the drivers. The OA's "Background Statement" provides:

[T]his Agreement will set forth the mutual business objectives of the two parties . . . but the manner and means of reaching these results are within the discretion of the [driver], and no officer or employee of FedEx . . . shall have the authority to impose any term or condition on [the driver] . . . which is contrary to this understanding. A provision of the OA titled "Discretion of Contractor to Determine Method and Means of Meeting Business Objectives," states:

OA

stating ICs

[N]o officer, agent or employee of FedEx . . . shall have the authority to direct [the driver] as to the manner or means employed . . . . For example, no officer, agent or employee of FedEx . . . shall have the authority to prescribe hours of work, whether or when the [driver] is to take breaks, what route the [driver] is to follow, or other details of performance.

FedEx's relationship with its drivers also is governed by various policies and procedures prescribed by FedEx.

. . . .

III. Discussion

. . . .

Right-to-Control Test

California's right-to-control test requires courts to weigh a number of factors: "The principal test of an employment relationship is whether the person to whom service is rendered has the right to control the manner and means of accomplishing the result desired." *S.G. Borello & Sons, Inc. v. Department of Industrial Relations*, 769 P.2d 399, 404 (Cal. 1989). California courts also consider "several 'secondary' indicia of the nature of a service relationship." *Id.* The right to terminate at will, without cause, is "[s]trong evidence in support of an employment relationship." *Id.* Additional factors include:

*

(a) whether the one performing services is engaged in a distinct occupation or business; (b) the kind of occupation, with reference to whether, in the locality, the work is usually done under the direction of the principal or by a specialist without supervision; (c) the skill required in the particular occupation; (d) whether the principal or the worker supplies the instrumentalities, tools, and the place of work for the person doing the work; (e) the length of time for which the services are to be performed; (f) the method of payment, whether by the time or by the job; (g) whether or not the work is a part of the regular business of the principal; and (h) whether or not the parties believe they are creating the relationship of employer-employee.

Id. These factors "[g]enerally . . . cannot be applied mechanically as separate tests; they are intertwined and their weight depends often on particular combinations."

1. "Manner and Means"

FedEx argues that the OA creates an independent-contractor relationship. California law is clear that "[t]he label placed by the parties on their relationship is not dispositive, and subterfuges are not countenanced." *Id.* at 403. What matters is what the contract, in actual effect, allows or requires. The OA and FedEx's policies and procedures unambiguously allow FedEx to exercise a great deal of control over the manner in which its drivers do their jobs. Therefore, this factor strongly favors plaintiffs.

First, FedEx can and does control the appearance of its drivers and their vehicles. FedEx controls its drivers' clothing from their hats down to their shoes and socks. It requires drivers to be "clean shaven, hair neat and trimmed, [and] free of body odor." FedEx's detailed appearance requirements clearly constitute control over its drivers. *See Ruiz v. Affinity Logistics Corp.*, 754 F.3d 1093 (9th Cir. June 16, 2014) (finding right to control under California law where a delivery company controlled " 'every exquisite detail' of the drivers' appearance, including the 'color of their socks' and 'the style of their hair' ").

FedEx requires drivers to paint their vehicles a specific shade of white, mark them with the distinctive FedEx logo, and to keep their vehicles "clean and presentable [and] free of body damage and extraneous markings." These requirements go well beyond those imposed by federal regulations. *See* 49 C.F.R. § 390.21. FedEx dictates the vehicles' dimensions, including the dimensions of their "package shelves" and the materials from which the shelves are made. Managers may prevent drivers from working if they are improperly dressed or groomed, or if their vehicles do not meet specifications.

Second, FedEx can and does control the times its drivers can work. Although the OA does not allow FedEx to set specific working hours down to the last minute, it is clear from the OA that FedEx has a great deal of control over drivers' hours. FedEx structures drivers' workloads so that they have to work 9.5 to 11 hours every working day. FedEx argues that, because drivers can hire helpers to do their work for them, they are free to complete a full day's work in less than 9.5 hours. But managers may adjust drivers' workloads to ensure that they never have more or less work than can be done in 9.5 to 11 hours. Drivers are not supposed to leave their terminals in the morning until all of their packages are available, and they must return to the terminals no later than a specified time. If drivers want their vehicles loaded, they must leave them at the terminal overnight. The combined effect of these requirements is substantially to define and constrain the hours that FedEx's drivers can work.

Third, FedEx can and does control aspects of how and when drivers deliver their packages. It assigns each driver a specific service area, which it "may, in its sole discretion, reconfigure." It tells drivers what packages they must deliver and when. It negotiates the delivery window for packages directly with its customers. The OA requires drivers to comply with "standards of service," including requirements to "[f]oster the professional image and good reputation of FedEx" and to "conduct all business activities with . . . proper decorum at all times."

FedEx notes that there are details of its drivers' work that it does not control.

[handwritten: FedEx arg where details it does not control]

For instance, it does not require drivers to follow specific routes or to deliver packages in a specific order. Taking the evidence in the light most favorable to FedEx, it does not require drivers to follow managers' recommendations after ride-along evaluations. But the right-to-control test does not require absolute control. Employee status may still be found where "[a] certain amount of . . . freedom is inherent in the work." *Air Couriers Int'l v. Emp't Dev. Dep't*, 59 Cal. Rptr. 3d 37, 44 (Ct. App. 2007); *see also id.* at 47 (upholding trial court's finding that there was "no inconsistency between employee status and the driver's discretion on when to take breaks or vacation"). FedEx's lack of control over some parts of its drivers' jobs does not counteract the extensive control it does exercise.

FedEx argues that it controls its drivers only with respect to the results it seeks, not the manner and means in which drivers achieve those results. *See Millsap v. Fed. Express Corp.*, 277 Cal. Rptr. 807, 811 (Ct. App. 1991) ("If control may be exercised only as to the result of the work and not the means by which it is accomplished, an independent contractor relationship is established."). We agree with FedEx that "results," reasonably understood, refers in this context to timely and professional delivery of packages. Some but not all of FedEx's requirements go to the "results" of its drivers' work so understood. Most obviously, no reasonable jury could find that the "results" sought by FedEx includes detailed specifications as to the delivery driver's fashion choices and grooming. *See Ruiz*, 2014 WL 2695534, at *7 & n.5. And no reasonable jury could find that the "results" FedEx seeks include having all of its vehicles containing shelves built to exactly the same specifications. Other aspects of FedEx's control—such as limiting drivers to a specific service area with specific delivery locations—also are not merely control of results under California law.

[handwritten margin: FedEx arg does not control manner means]

[handwritten margin: Ct resp]

Notably, in *Estrada v. FedEx Ground Package System, Inc.*, 64 Cal. Rptr. 3d 327 (Ct. App. 2007), the California Court of Appeal affirmed a trial court's determination, following a bench trial, that a class of FedEx drivers, working under the same OA as plaintiffs in this case during an overlapping time period, were employees based on "FedEx's control over every exquisite detail of the drivers' performance." *Id.* at 336. FedEx attempts to distinguish *Estrada* on two grounds. First, the trial court in *Estrada* specifically excluded multiple-route drivers from the class, deciding the question of employment status only with respect to single-route drivers, whereas here, while limited to drivers who personally drive full time for FedEx, the class includes a number of drivers who operate more than one route. Second, FedEx contends that "*Estrada* involved a fundamentally different evidentiary record." However, the OA grants FedEx identical rights to control both single-route and multiple-route drivers. And while *Estrada*'s reliance on specific factual findings by the trial court means that *Estrada* is not dispositive here, the *Estrada* court's reasoning is nonetheless apposite.

[handwritten margin: FedEx distinguishing Estrada]

FedEx argues that the OA gives drivers "flexibility and entrepreneurial opportunities that no 'employee' has." However, in *Borello*, the California Supreme Court reasoned that "[a] business entity may not avoid its statutory obligations by carving up its production process into minute steps, then asserting that it lacks 'control' over the exact means by which one such step is performed by the responsible workers." 769 P.2d at 408. There, S.G. Borello & Sons, a commercial produce grower, hired agricultural laborers under written "sharefarmer" agreements. The agreements

[handwritten margin: FedEx arg that drivers have entrepeneur opp.]

recited that the parties deemed themselves "principal and independent contractor rather than employer and employee." *Id.* at 401.

The sharefarmers agreed to harvest the crop, assisted by members of their families. They could "contract for the amount of land they wish[ed] to harvest on a first-come, first-served basis." *Id.* at 402. The sharefarmers were "totally responsible for the care of the plants in their assigned plots during the harvest period." *Id.* (internal quotation marks omitted). They were required to furnish their own tools and their own transportation to and from the field. "The method and manner of accomplishing" the harvest was left solely to the sharefarmers, though they agreed to "utilize accepted agricultural practices in order to provide for the maximum harvest." *Id.*

The sharefarmers set their own hours. They were free to decide when to pick the crop in order to maximize the profit. "Profit incentive [was] the only guaranty of performance and quality control." *Id.* Borello had "no right to discharge a sharefarmer or his workers during the harvest, and no recourse if the harvesters abandon[ed] the field." *Id.* Although the sharefarmers had significant autonomy over the harvest itself, the California Supreme Court reasoned that Borello retained "all *necessary* control over the harvest portion of its operations," and held that the sharefarmers were employees as a matter of law. *Id.* at 408, 410.

California courts have since applied *Borello's* "all *necessary* control" test and found employee status in several cases involving delivery drivers. . . . [The court discussed these cases and noted that FedEx exercised even greater control over its drivers than the employers in those cases had, since FedEx assigns each driver a specified service area and tells them where in their service area to deliver packages, affords drivers no control over which packages they deliver, sets the rates charged, bills the customers, and collects payment, and pays the drivers on a regular schedule.]

. . . .

According to FedEx, its drivers' "entrepreneurial opportunities"—the ability to take on multiple routes and vehicles and to hire third-party helpers—are inconsistent with employee status. FedEx relies not on California law for this argument, but on the D.C. Circuit's decision in *FedEx Home Delivery v. National Labor Relations Board*, 563 F.3d 492 (D.C. Cir. 2009). In *FedEx Home Delivery*, a divided panel of the D.C. Circuit reversed an agency decision that FedEx drivers were employees. *Id.* at 495. The majority "shift[ed the] emphasis away from the unwieldy control inquiry," asking instead "whether the putative independent contractors have significant entrepreneurial opportunity for gain or loss." *Id.* at 497 (alteration in original) (internal quotation marks omitted). It held that the evidence "favoring a finding the [drivers] are employees [was] clearly outweighed by evidence of entrepreneurial opportunity." *Id.* at 504.

The D.C. Circuit's decision in *FedEx Home Delivery*, even if correct, has no bearing on this case. There is no indication that California has replaced its longstanding right-to-control test with the new entrepreneurial-opportunities test developed by the D.C. Circuit. Instead, California cases indicate that entrepreneurial opportunities do not undermine a finding of employee status. In *Arzate v. Bridge*

Terminal Transport, Inc., 121 Cal. Rptr. 3d 400 (Cal. App. 2011), the California Court of Appeal reversed a trial court's grant of summary judgment to the defendant where, as here, the "plaintiffs drove their own trucks and paid the related expenses, [and] could have leased more than one truck to defendant and hired other drivers." *Id.* at 405–06. The court found that these opportunities did not override other factors in California's multi-factor analysis such that the drivers were independent contractors as a matter of law. *Id.* In *Narayan [v. EGL, Inc.*, 616 F.3d 895, 900 (9th Cir. 2010)] we concluded that, where drivers "retained the right to employ others to assist in performing their contractual obligations," but the company had to approve all helpers, this was indicative of control of the details of the drivers' performance under California law. 616 F.3d at 902. And in *Ruiz*, we found that drivers were employees where the company "retained ultimate discretion to approve or disapprove of those helpers and additional drivers." 754 F.3d 1093, 1102. "[A]pproval was largely based upon neutral factors, such as background checks required under federal regulations," but the drivers nonetheless "did not have an unrestricted right to choose these persons, which is an "important right[] [that] would normally inure to a self-employed contractor." *Id.* (alterations in original) (quoting *Borello*, 769 P.2d at 408 n.9). Further, "any additional drivers were subject to the same degree of control exerted by Affinity over the drivers generally." *Id.*

The entrepreneurial opportunities available to FedEx's drivers are equivalent to those in *Narayan* and *Ruiz.* The OA allows drivers to operate more than one vehicle or route only if FedEx consents, and only if doing so is "consistent with the capacity of the [driver's] terminal." Drivers must be "in good standing" in order to assign their contractual rights, and any replacement driver must be "acceptable to FedEx." Nothing in the OA limits FedEx's discretion to withhold consent to additional vehicles or routes, or to decide whether a replacement driver is "acceptable." Daniel Sullivan, FedEx's founder and CEO until January 2007, testified in his deposition that FedEx may refuse to let a driver take on additional routes or sell his route to a third party. He further testified that FedEx's senior managers have the authority to reject proposed replacement drivers based on failure to meet FedEx standards such as grooming requirements. "The existence of the right of control and supervision establishes the existence of an agency relationship." *Ayala*, 327 P.3d at 173. Whether FedEx ever exercises its right of refusal is irrelevant; what matters is that the right exists. *See id.*

2. Secondary Factors

In light of the powerful evidence of FedEx's right to control the manner in which drivers perform their work, none of the remaining right-to-control factors sufficiently favors FedEx to allow a holding that plaintiffs are independent contractors. *See Borello*, 769 P.2d at 404 (identifying evidence of the right to control as the "principal" factor); *JKH Enter[prises, Inc. v. Department of Industrial Relations*, 48 Cal. Rptr. 3d 563 (Ct. App. 2006)], at 579–80 (holding, where JKH's retention of "all *necessary* control over the operation as a whole" was, under *Borello*, "enough to find an employment relationship," that no "single factor, either alone or in combination, mandate[d] a different result").

The first factor, the right to terminate at will, slightly favors FedEx. The OA contains an arbitration clause and does not give FedEx an unqualified right to terminate. Under California law, the right to discharge at will is "[s]trong evidence in support of an employment relationship," *Tieberg*, 471 P.2d at 979, even though termination for cause is consistent with both employee and independent contractor status, *see Ruiz*, 2014 WL 2695534, at *11 ("[T]he parties' mutual termination provision is consistent with either an employer-employee or independent contractor relationship."); *cf. Foley v. Interactive Data Corp.*, 765 P.2d 373, 376 (Cal. 1988) (noting that, while California Labor Code § 2922 provides a presumption of at-will employment when employment is for no specified term, "[t]his presumption may be superseded by a contract, express or implied, limiting the employer's right to discharge the employee").

FedEx's right under the OA to terminate its drivers, while broad, is somewhat constrained. FedEx may fire a driver for any "breach [ ] or fail[ure] to perform . . . contractual obligations," which would cover, for example, any failure to act "with proper decorum at all times," or to "foster the professional image and good reputation of FedEx." We conclude that this factor does not favor FedEx enough to allow a finding that its drivers are independent contractors. *See Toyota Motor Sales*, 269 Cal. Rptr. at 653 ("The real test [for ascertaining whether the right to control exists] has been said to be whether the employee was subject to the employer's orders and control and was liable to be discharged for disobedience or misconduct." (internal quotation marks omitted)).

The second factor, distinct occupation or business, favors plaintiffs. As the California Court of Appeal reasoned in *Estrada*, "the work performed by the drivers is wholly integrated into FedEx's operation. The drivers look like FedEx employees, act like FedEx employees, [and] are paid like FedEx employees." 64 Cal. Rptr. 3d at 334. "The customers are FedEx's customers, not the drivers' customers." *Id.* at 336–37. . . .

The third factor, whether the work is performed under the principal's direction, slightly favors plaintiffs. As explained above, although drivers retain freedom to determine several aspects of their day-to-day work, FedEx also closely supervises their work through various methods.

The fourth factor, the skill required in the occupation, also favors plaintiffs. FedEx drivers "need no experience to get the job in the first place and [the] only required skill is the ability to drive." *Id.* at 337; *see JKH Enters.*, 48 Cal. Rptr. 3d at 579 ("[T]he functions performed by the drivers, pick-up and delivery of papers or packages and driving in between, did not require a high degree of skill.").

The fifth factor, the provision of tools and equipment, slightly favors FedEx. The drivers provide their own vehicles and are not required to get other equipment from FedEx. On the other hand, "FedEx is involved in the purchasing process, providing funds and recommending vendors." *Estrada*, 64 Cal. Rptr. 3d at 334. Indeed, the drivers' scanners are not readily available anywhere else. . . .

The sixth factor, length of time for performance of services, favors plaintiffs. Drivers enter into the OA for a term of one to three years. At the end of the initial term, the OA provides for automatic renewal for successive one-year terms if there is no notice of non-renewal by either party.

> [T]he length and indefinite nature of the plaintiff [d]rivers' tenure with [FedEx] . . . point toward an employment relationship. . . . This was not a circumstance where a contractor was hired to perform a specific task for a defined period of time. There was no contemplated end to the service relationship at the time that the plaintiff [d]rivers began working for [FedEx].

Narayan, 616 F.3d at 903 . . . .

The seventh factor, method of payment, is neutral. FedEx pays its drivers according to a complicated scheme that includes fixed and variable components and ties payment to, among other things, packages, stops, and the ratio of driving time to deliveries. This payment method cannot easily be compared to either hourly payment (which favors employee status) or per-job payment (which favors independent contractor status). . . .

The eighth factor, whether the work is part of the principal's regular business, favors plaintiffs. The work that the drivers perform, the pickup and delivery of packages, is "essential to FedEx's core business." *Estrada*, 64 Cal. Rptr. 3d at 334 . . . .

The final factor, the parties' beliefs, slightly favors FedEx. The OA expressly identifies the relationship as one of an independent contractor, and disclaims any authority on FedEx's part to direct drivers as to the manner or means of their work. . . . Ultimately, though, "neither [FedEx]'s nor the drivers' own perception of their relationship as one of independent contracting" is dispositive. *See JKH Enters.*, 48 Cal. Rptr. 3d at 580.

3. Summary

Viewing the evidence in the light most favorable to FedEx, the OA grants FedEx a broad right to control the manner in which its drivers' perform their work. The most important factor of the right-to-control test thus strongly favors employee status. The other factors do not strongly favor either employee status or independent contractor status. Accordingly, we hold that plaintiffs are employees as a matter of law under California's right-to-control test. . . .

REVERSED and REMANDED.

TROTT, CIRCUIT JUDGE, with whom GOODWIN, CIRCUIT JUDGE, joins, concurring:

The resolution of this case as a matter of granting summary judgment to the drivers is far from simple, as the length and complexity of Judge Fletcher's meticulous opinion demonstrates. It has not been made easier by FedEx's brief, which, by quoting part of a sentence from an admission—but not all of it—creates a rosier picture of the drivers' state of mind than the record supports.

FedEx represents in its brief, and I quote, that each of the drivers personally "intended to enter an independent contractor relationship with [FedEx]." What the brief omits are the important words that precede this language and the final sentence in the drivers' response. This is what the drivers admitted:

> Named plaintiffs admit that on the day they signed their original Operating Agreement, *in reliance on Defendants' statements that they would be an independent contractor*, they intended to enter into an independent contractor relationship with Defendants. Named Plaintiffs deny, however, that an independent contractor relationship ever, in fact, existed between them and Defendants.

Response to Request for Admission No. 1 (emphasis supplied). The meaning of this response read as a whole is that the drivers believed they were becoming true independent contractors, but the reality they encountered was different.

We also find the actual meaning of the drivers' "admission" in this case in a companion case, *Slayman v. FedEx Ground Package System, Inc.*, Nos. 12-35525 and 12-35559. In that case, drivers pursued a personal claim in Oregon district court for rescission, claiming fraud. In denying summary judgment to both parties on the sole ground that the claim was not timely, the district court noted that "[d]eposition testimony indicate[d] that soon after becoming a driver, each plaintiff believed that the [Operating Agreement], despite its express terms, did not give the driver the control he expected as an independent contractor." *Slayman v. FedEx Ground Package Sys., Inc.*, 3:05-cv-1127-HZ, 2012 U.S. Dist. LEXIS 73450, at *20 (D. Or. May 25, 2012). All that glittered turned out not to be gold.

. . . .

Abraham Lincoln reportedly asked, "If you call a dog's tail a leg, how many legs does a dog have?" His answer was, "Four. Calling a dog's tail a leg does not make it a leg." Justice Cardozo made the same point in *W.B. Worthen Co. v. Kavanaugh*, 295 U.S. 56, 62 (1935), counseling us, when called upon to characterize a written enactment, to look to the "underlying reality rather than the form or label." The California Supreme Court echoed this wisdom in *Borello*, saying that the "label placed by the parties on their relationship is not dispositive, and subterfuges are not countenanced." 769 P.2d at 403. As noted by Judge Fletcher, "[N]either [FedEx's] nor the drivers' own perception of their relationship as one of independent contracting" is dispositive. *JKH Enters., Inc.*, 48 Cal. Rptr. at 580.

Bottom line? Labeling the drivers "independent contractors" in FedEx's Operating Agreement does not conclusively make them so when viewed in the light of (1) the entire agreement, (2) the rest of the relevant "common policies and procedures" evidence, and (3) California law. As Judge Fletcher points out, the [lower court's] decision to the contrary relied on an inappropriate consideration: the entrepreneurial opportunities factor.

Although our decision substantially unravels FedEx's business model, FedEx was not entitled to "write around" the principles and mandates of California Labor Law by constructing a contract which, after a contested trial, the California trial court in *Estrada* called:

> [A] brilliantly drafted contract creating the constraints of an employment arrangement with [the drivers] in the guise of an independent contractor

model—because FedEx not only has the right to control, but has close to absolute control over [the drivers] based upon interpretation and obfuscation.

Estrada, 64 Cal. Rptr. 3d at 334. The Court of Appeal in that case appropriately called the trial court's observation an application of the looks like, walks like, swims like, and quacks like a duck test. *See id.* at 335.

Accordingly, I concur in JUDGE FLETCHER'S persuasive opinion.

NOTES

1. Comparing *FedEx Home Delivery* and *Alexander*. The D.C. Circuit determined that the drivers were independent contractors (despite the NLRB's initial determination that they were employees), while the Ninth Circuit concluded that the FedEx drivers were employees, reversing the lower court's determination in the multidistrict litigation. What accounts for the difference in the outcomes of the two cases?

Which facts seemed most important to the D.C. Circuit in *FedEx Home Delivery*? Which facts seemed most important to the Ninth Circuit in *Alexander*? Would either court have reached a different result if some of the circumstances of the drivers' employment were altered? For example, would it make a difference if the FedEx drivers were paid by the job? If they were not required to wear uniforms or conform to an appearance code? If they could choose to utilize any kind of truck, and didn't have to comply with the FedEx truck logo requirement? Suppose they were permitted to do work for other delivery services as well as FedEx?

Note that the D.C. Circuit discussed and considered the "entrepreneurial potential" for drivers to work multiple routes, even though the action before it involved only the single work area drivers (the multiple route drivers had been found to be supervisors and therefore were excluded from the bargaining unit). Did this change the way in which the court framed the relevant facts? How did the Ninth Circuit deal with the fact that the multiple route drivers in the *Alexander* plaintiff class had at least some potential to function as entrepreneurs by hiring others to work for them?

What difference, if any, do the different legal contexts in which the cases arose make in the doctrinal test used or the way in which it was applied? *FedEx Home Delivery* involved classification for purposes of bargaining rights under the NLRA. In a more recent decision considering application of the D.C. Circuit's standard to another group of FedEx drivers who had unionized and were seeking to compel bargaining, the Board reaffirmed its commitment to using common law agency principles to evaluate independent contractor status, with no single factor being dispositive. *FedEx Home Delivery*, 361 N.L.R.B. No. 55 (2014). *Alexander* involved the workers' classification for purposes of reimbursement of employee expenses under the CALIFORNIA LABOR CODE. The Ninth Circuit confirmed its analysis recently in *Ruiz v. Affinity Logistics Corp.*, 754 F.3d 1093 (9th Cir. 2014) (discussed in *Alexander*), ruling that California truck drivers were employees under the right to control test for purposes of sick leave, vacation pay, holiday and severance benefits governed by state law.

2.   **Other Cases Involving FedEx Drivers.** FedEx has been a defendant in a number of other cases that challenge its classification of drivers under various statutes, including a multi-district class action claim under ERISA, administrative claims before the IRS, and numerous state law claims including fraud, workers' compensation claims and wage and hour litigation. *Alexander* itself was part of a larger multi-district litigation that involved claims against FedEx in 40 states under various state laws. Why has FedEx been such a popular target? First, many of these cases have been litigated by the same network of plaintiffs' lawyers, who have developed a significant knowledge base about FedEx's business practices. Second, the FedEx operating model contrasts with those of its competitors, including UPS, the industry leader. UPS's delivery drivers are heavily unionized and have successfully resisted UPS's efforts to classify them as independent contractors. *See UPS Settles Wage and Hour Lawsuit over Driver Classification for $12.8 Million,* DAILY LAB. REP. (BNA) No. 235, Dec. 10, 2009. The Teamsters union had organized the drivers at FedEx in Wilmington and was an intervenor in the *FedEx Home Delivery* litigation.

3.   **Challenges to FedEx's Business Model.** The concurring judges in *Alexander* acknowledged that the Ninth Circuit's decisions in *Alexander* and in a companion case from Oregon, *Slayman v. FedEx Ground Package System, Inc.*, 765 F.3d 1033 (9th Cir. 2014) "substantially unravel[ ] FedEx's business model." Fed Ex's independent contractor model features significant labor cost savings—perhaps as much as 30%—over a more traditional employer-employee relationship, avoiding obligations imposed on employers by wage and hour laws, the Social Security Act, the Affordable Care Act, and workers' compensation laws. *See AFL-CIO Official Discusses Dangers of Misclassifying Workers as Contractors,* DAILY LAB. REP. (BNA) No. 85, May 5, 2010. Loss of the independent contractor model would place FedEx on more even footing with its largest competitor, UPS. *See* Martha Neil, *'Seismic' 9th Cir. Rulings Nix FedEx Claim Its Drivers Aren't Employees, Could Cost Company Millions,* ABA JOURNAL, Aug. 27, 2014, *available at* www.abajournal. com.

How effective is the common law at curtailing an employer's ability to manipulate the status of its workers for purposes of protection under employment legislation? FedEx responded to the *Estrada* ruling that its single work area drivers were employees (discussed in *Alexander*) by eliminating them: it refused to renew the operating agreements for single work area drivers and offered them the choice of quitting, signing a release and accepting severance benefits, or applying for a multiple work area contract under new terms. Multiple route arrangements were left intact because, as the D.C. Circuit explained in *FedEx Home Delivery*, the drivers' ability to subcontract work to others created the kind of entrepreneurial potential that rendered them independent contractors rather than employees. *See Delivery Services: FedEx Will Pay $27 Million to Settle Lawsuit over Classification of Drivers,* DAILY LAB. REP. (BNA) No. 236, Dec. 9, 2008; Nora L. Macey, *Contractor Status of FedEx Ground Drivers Challenged,* 36 A.B.A. J. LAB. & EMP. L., Fall 2007, at 1, 12. How do you think FedEx will respond to *Alexander*? Suppose that FedEx requires the employees to form their own businesses as a condition of employment, and contracts with those businesses instead of with the drivers personally. Would this convert the drivers to independent contractors? *See Ruiz v. Affinity Logistics*

Corp., supra, at 1104 (finding that such a requirement was irrelevant because "in the real world, such businesses were in name only" where the company did not permit drivers to use their trucks for any purpose other than their work for Affinity, and holding that drivers were employees).

4.   **Exotic Dancers and Piece/Project Workers.** Some workers' employment circumstances defy easy categorization. For example, exotic dancers who perform in strip clubs pay for the opportunity to dance for tips. Are they "employees" entitled to receive minimum wages and overtime pay, or independent contractors? In *Chaves v. King Arthur's Lounge, Inc.*, 2009 Mass. Super. LEXIS 298 (July 30, 2009), exotic dancers who paid the club $35 per night to dance for tips complained that they did not earn minimum wage and that they were entitled to overtime compensation. The strip club argued that its principal business was selling food and liquor, and characterized the dancers as "a form of entertainment . . . provide[d] for its patrons, akin to the television and pool tables in a sports bar." *Id.* at *9. The court rejected the club's argument, stating: "[a] court would need to be blind to human instinct to decide that live nude entertainment was equivalent to the wallpaper of routinely-televised matches, games, tournaments and sports talk," and found that the dancers were an integral part of the company's business, and thus employees. *Id.* at *11. The test, said the court, was whether the worker wears "the hat of an employee" or "the hat of his own independent enterprise." The court took judicial notice of the fact that inexpensive and ready access to adult media on the internet made it unlikely that exotic dancing would amount to a "commercial opportunity—over the long term—that would rise to an independently established trade or occupation." The fact that the plaintiffs had to pay in order to ply their trade confirmed the fact that exotic dancing was not "an independently established occupation" in a "free market." *Id.* at *15. A number of federal district courts have reached a similar conclusion, applying the "economic realities" test under the FLSA which requires consideration of multiple factors including the degree of control exercised by the club over the dancers, the dancers' opportunity for profit and loss, the dancers' relative investment, the lack of specialized skill required to be a dancer, and the integral nature of nude entertainment to the club's business. *See, e.g., Thompson v. Linda and A, Inc.,* 779 F. Supp. 2d 139 (D.D.C. 2011); *Clincy v. Galardi South Enters., Inc.,* 808 F. Supp. 2d 1326 (N.D. Ga. 2011).

Do you agree with these rulings? Which test is more useful, the "hat of an employee" versus "hat of [his/her] own independent enterprise" test, or the economic realities test?

Many workers are paid on a piece-work or project basis, and work at home. Are they employees or independent contractors? Courts in these cases typically focus on whether the work is vital to the putative employer's business. For example, knitters and sewers have been held to be employees rather than independent contractors even where they work at home at their own pace on their own machines and are paid by the piece (or job). Courts reason that they are performing a core function vital to the production of the particular product sold by the employer and made to its specifications. *See, e.g., Fleece on Earth v. Dep't of Employment and Training,* 923 A.2d 594 (Vt. 2007) (finding knitters employees for purposes of unemployment insurance). By contrast, a computer programmer who worked for a company for ten years was an independent contractor rather than an employee, even though he performed information technology services using computer equipment supplied by the employer and according to a work schedule established by the employer, because using the company's equipment was the inevitable and logical result of hiring a consultant to work on the system. *See Estate of Suskovich v. Anthem Health Plans of Va., Inc.*, 553 F.3d 559 (7th Cir. 2009) (finding computer programmer an independent contractor for purposes of overtime pay under the FLSA). How can these cases be squared with one another?

5. Governmental Efforts to Control Misclassification. The misclassification of employees as independent contractors has consequences not only for workers themselves, but for the public fisc. Because the workers are not treated as employees for minimum wage, Social Security, unemployment compensation or workers' compensation purposes, the state may end up picking up the tab in the case of poverty, disability, termination, or injury). Federal and state budget concerns have prompted the IRS and state tax authorities to mount particularly aggressive enforcement efforts in recent years. In addition, employers face penalties under the Affordable Care Act if they have misclassified workers as independent contractors rather than employees and do not provide the minimum requisite health care coverage. Penalties may include health plan premiums and potential medical claims associated with misclassified workers. Sean Forbes, *Worker Misclassification May Result in Higher ACA Penalties, Consultant Says*, DAILY LAB. REP. (BNA) No. 242, Dec. 16, 2013.

The Department of Labor's Wage and Hour Division focuses on business models that raise red flags that misclassification may be occurring, such as the creation of business entities that have no independence beyond being described as a franchisee or limited liability corporation. *See* Rhonda Smith, *Government Agencies Expanding Efforts to Target Problems Contingent Workers Face*, DAILY LAB. REP. (BNA) No. 92, May 13, 2014. In addition, the Department of Labor has established information-sharing programs with other federal and state agencies (including the IRS), designed to coordinate and enhance enforcement efforts. *See Employee Misclassification as Independent Contractors*, U.S. DEPARTMENT OF LABOR, WAGE AND HOUR DIVISION, *available at* http://www.dol.gov/whd/workers/misclassification/.

Legislation has been considered at the federal level in an effort to curtail misclassification. The Employee Misclassification Prevention Act, S. 3648/H.R. 6111 was introduced in Congress in 2008 and again in 2010. It was designed to amend the Fair Labor Standards Act to impose special penalties on employers who misclassify employees as independent contractors. The Payroll Fraud Prevention Act of 2014, H.R. 4611/S. 1687, introduced previously in 2011 and 2013, would have expanded the Fair Labor Standards Act to cover "non-employees," require employers to provide every employee with a notice of his or her classification and rights under law, and would create a new offense of misclassification of employees with penalties of up to $5,000 for each violation. To date, none of these proposed bills have gained traction.

Employee misclassification statutes have been enacted in a number of states. *See Employee Misclassification*, NATIONAL CONFERENCE OF STATE LEGISLATURES, Aug. 26, 2013, *available at* http://www.ncsl.org/research/labor-and-employment/employee-misclassification-resources.aspx. Some state laws attempt to standardize the definition of an employee across statutes and then penalize employers for misclassification, regardless of intent. Other statutes simply provide for enhanced penalties ranging from stiff fines to criminal penalties, particularly for intentional misclassification. *Id.* California, for example, provides for penalties of $15,000 to $25,000 per violation for willful misclassification, with penalties highest for repeat offenders. *See* CAL. LAB. CODE §§ 226.8, 2753. New York prescribes criminal penalties for intentional misclassification. *See* N.Y. LAB. LAW § 862(d).

3.   Who Is the Employer?

A vexing question that arises under every employment statute and under the NLRA is the difficulty of defining which entities should be held accountable for violations of law: who is the "employer"? In a subcontracting scenario, for example, is the employer the contracting entity or the subcontractor? Or should both be subject to liability? Courts confronting such situations look behind labels and ostensible relationships to determine whether an employment relationship exists.

Under the "joint employer" doctrine, both entities—the contracting employer and the subcontractor—may be held liable for statutory violations if the contracting entity maintains significant control over the work and the workers are economically dependent upon the contracting entity. Courts have developed various tests to determine whether such a relationship is present. *Compare Zheng v. Liberty Apparel Co.*, 2010 U.S. App. LEXIS 16637 (2d Cir. Aug. 10, 2010) (applying six-factor test to hold garment manufacturer and "jobber" liable for wage and hour violations against workers employed to stitch and sew garments in Chinatown factory) with *Martinez-Mendoza v. Champion International Corp.*, 340 F.3d 1200 (11th Cir. 2003) (applying seven-factor "economic realities" test and finding no liability under Fair Labor Standards Act or Migrant and Seasonal Agricultural Worker Protection Act for large paper company that utilized farm labor contractors to re-plant trees on its forest land, because the seasonal relationship lacked permanency and duration and the hand-planting of seeds was not an integral part of the paper company's business). Because it arises most frequently in the area of low-wage work, this doctrine will be examined further *infra* in Chapter 11 (Wages and Hours).

One development with far-ranging impact across work law, however, is the application of the joint employer doctrine to the franchising context. Franchise relationships usually involve a contract that allows the franchisee to use the trademarks and trade secrets of the franchisor at a single business outlet, such as a restaurant or motel. Trade secrets may include the labor cost structures, supervisory model, and other labor-related aspects of the business as well as the brand name, recipes, and marketing formula. The franchisee pays royalties to the franchisor and covers the operational costs of operating the outlet, and retains the remainder of the profits for itself. There exists a built-in incentive for the franchisee to cut operating costs in order to increase profits, thus potentially deviating from the franchisor's standards of quality and uniformity to the ultimate disadvantage of the franchisor's brand. Accordingly, franchisors typically wield some significant degree of control over franchisees, accomplished either through contract provisions or the use of market sanctions (such as permitting another franchisee to open a store nearby). *See* Adam B. Badawi, *Relational Governance and Contract Damages: Evidence from Franchising*, 7 J. EMPIRICAL LEGAL STUD. 743, 746–47 (2010). Extensions of liability to franchisors are most likely to affect those that maintain strict control over franchisees, such as McDonald's, which imposes standards on its franchisees addressing appearance, food quality and business management, among other subjects, and provides labor efficiency software to its franchisees that instructs managers when to take employees on and off the clock.

Although most circuit courts have concluded that franchisors are not liable as joint employers for wage and hour violations of their franchisees, *see, e.g., Orozco v. Plackis*, 757 F.3d 445 (5th Cir. 2014), some courts have noted that the fact-bound specificity of the joint employer doctrine makes this a possibility, and have denied motions to dismiss wage and hour claims against franchisors, allowing cases to move forward. *See, e.g., Cordova v. SCCF, Inc.*, 2014 U.S. Dist. LEXIS 97388 (S.D.N.Y. July 16, 2014). Further, the NLRB's General Counsel has indicated that his office will treat McDonald's Corporation as a joint employer alongside its franchisees in unfair labor practices cases arising out of nationwide strikes by nonunion fast food workers seeking higher wages. *See NLRB Office of the General Counsel Authorizes Complaints Against McDonald's Franchisees, and Determines McDonald's, USA, LLC, Is a Joint Employer*, July 29, 2014, *available at* http://www.nlrb.gov/news-outreach/news-story/nlrb-office-general-counsel-authorizes-complaints-against-mcdonalds. Some suggest that the Department of Labor might follow suit in cases arising under the Occupational Safety and Health Act, extending liability to franchisors like McDonald's. *See NLRB Joint Employer Stance Could Affect OSHA Position on Franchisors, Franchisees*, DAILY LAB. REP. (BNA) No. 151, Aug. 6, 2014.

On the other hand, the California Supreme Court refused to hold Domino's Pizza liable for alleged sexual harassment at one of its franchise locations, reasoning that although Domino's "vigorously enforced" control over pizza making, delivery, store operation, and branding, it was not sufficiently involved in day-to-day hiring, firing and supervision to be held liable as a joint employer. The court viewed the "contract-based operational division" between the franchisor and its franchisees as critical, noting the longstanding existence and "profound" economic effects of the franchising model on American business. *Patterson v. Domino's Pizza, LLC*, 2014 Cal. LEXIS 6251, at *5, *28–*30, *55–*57 (Cal. 2014). The court did leave open, however, the possibility that a franchisor might be held responsible for sexual harassment at a franchisee's store if it retains control over relevant day-to-day operations. *See id.* at *61–*62. Should the fact that a business model is well-established and dominant have any relevance to a court's analysis of employer liability for violations of employment discrimination law?

Does the fact that courts may reach different conclusions about the applicability of joint employer doctrine depending upon the legal context raise any concerns?

Another challenging question involves employer liability for outsourced work that occurs beyond U.S. borders. In *Doe I v. Wal-Mart Stores, Inc.*, 572 F.3d 677 (9th Cir. 2009) foreign workers employed by companies that supply goods to Wal-Mart sought to hold Wal-Mart liable for the suppliers' noncompliance with local labor laws. The workers argued that they were third-party beneficiaries of the supply contracts, that Wal-Mart was their joint employer, that Wal-Mart had negligently failed to monitor its suppliers, and that Wal-Mart was unjustly enriched by the suppliers' mistreatment of their workers. The court rejected the claims, reasoning that although Wal-Mart did set standards for its suppliers with regard to quality of products and deadlines for delivery, it had not promised to monitor its suppliers' labor conditions, did not exercise sufficient day-to-day control over the suppliers' employees to justify liability as an employer, and its relationship to the plaintiffs was too attenuated to ground a claim of unjust enrichment. *Id.* at 681–83, 685.

A number of commentators have argued that the problem of determining employer liability under work law stems from a mismatch between laws developed in a stable domestic economy and the way business is done in a volatile global economy. Brishen Rogers contends that the shift from an economy characterized by vertically integrated production to a global economy in which firms have extended their production supply chains to encompass networks of independent firms demands more than simply liberalizing tests for joint employer liability. He advocates "holding firms to a duty of reasonable care to prevent wage and hour violations within their domestic supply chains, regardless of whether they enjoy a contractual relationship with the primary wrongdoer." Brishen Rogers, *Toward Third-Party Liability for Wage Theft*, 31 BERKELEY J. EMP. & LAB. L. 1, 2 (2010). Timothy Glynn has suggested holding corporate decisionmakers personally liable for violations of work law under a negligence standard. *See* Timothy P. Glynn, *Taking Self-Regulation Seriously: High-Ranking Officer Sanctions for Work-Law Violations*, 32 BERKELEY J. EMP. & LAB. L. 279 (2011). Would these standards alter the outcome in *Doe I*? Would they change corporate behavior? Do they seem feasible to you?

Even where legal liability for outsourced work does not exist, pressure from consumer and labor groups may convince U.S. companies to engage in more oversight of the labor conditions in factories located outside U.S. borders, particularly where attention is drawn to the outsourcing by media coverage of tragic events. When a garment factory that produced apparel for Wal-Mart collapsed and killed more than 1100 workers, for example, public pressure induced Wal-Mart to put in place new safety measures at factories it uses in Bangladesh. Among other things, Wal-Mart assigned factory monitors to conduct in-depth safety inspections, announced that it would post the results on its website, promised to stop production if urgent safety problems were revealed, and vowed to notify factory owners and government authorities of the problems. It did not agree to underwrite the improvements, however, as some European retailers had done. Steven Greenhouse, *As Firms Line up on Factories, Wal-Mart Plans Solo Effort*, N.Y. TIMES, May 14, 2013. Nor was Wal-Mart alone; the Gap and several other American retailers also refused to sign onto a plan to commit retailers to help finance safety upgrades in Bangladesh factories. The companies raised concerns about incurring legal liability for problems beyond their control in the global supply chain. Steven Greenhouse, *U.S. Retailers See Big Risk in Safety Plan for Factories in Bangladesh*, N.Y. TIMES, May 22, 2013.

The question "who is the employer?" has other legal implications. Traditionally, unions organized workers within a single store or plant, and utilized pressure tactics against that single employer. But suppose that the joint employer concept were applied to franchisees, might unions seek to organize workers nationally, across multiple franchisees? Could this re-invigorate unionism? *See* Steven Greenhouse, *McDonald's Ruling Could Open Door for Unions*, N.Y. TIMES, July 29, 2014; Scott Flaherty, *McDonald's 'Joint Employer' Directive Goes Beyond Fast Food*, LAW 360, July 30, 2014; Ben Penn, *To Unions, McDonald's Joint Employer Status No Slam Dunk, as Fast Food Push Intensifies*, DAILY LAB. REP. (BNA) No. 177, Sept. 12, 2014.

Part Two

BALANCING EMPLOYER AND EMPLOYEE INTERESTS: INDIVIDUAL VERSUS COLLECTIVE RESPONSES

In this Part, we examine the common law and statutory frameworks that have developed to resolve the basic tensions arising in the employment relationship. We have grouped the issues loosely around the most powerful conflicts that characterize the work relation. What most employees want today is some measure of security in maintaining the wages and benefits that work provides and on which they depend for their most basic needs. In addition, employees want to work under conditions that respect their interests in dignity, privacy and autonomy, to have a greater voice in the workplace, and to participate in a cooperative mechanism for workplace governance. And workers desire to be treated fairly on the job, particularly in the sense of not being discriminated against on the basis of arbitrary personal characteristics.

But what about employers? Aren't their desires entitled to significant weight? Are they not the owners of the enterprise that produces the wages and benefits to which employees claim an entitlement? Employers need flexibility in structuring their production processes in order to respond to rapidly changing economic conditions and global competition. In order to maximize the profitability of the firm, they desire unfettered authority to make decisions regarding the hiring, firing and deployment of the workforce. In addition, employers typically claim that their property rights in their business give their interests in control over the workplace priority over the desires of workers to shape their own working lives.

Given these conflicting interests, why not allow the parties to reach their own agreement about the terms of the employment relationship? In American jurisprudence, the notion of freedom of contract has deep resonance, although as we saw in Part I, the meaning and strength of that concept has varied over time. In the context of the employment relationship, the impulse to leave things to private contracting and market forces exists in deep tension with a recognition of the imbalance of bargaining power between employees and employers.

Congress explicitly recognized this imbalance of bargaining power in the preamble to the Wagner Act, which articulated part of the justification for conferring on employees the right to organize and bargain collectively with employers:

> The inequality of bargaining power between employees who do not possess full freedom of association or actual liberty of contract, and employers who are organized in the corporate or other forms of ownership association substantially burdens and affects the flow of commerce, and tends to aggravate recurrent business depressions, by depressing wage rates and the purchasing power of wage earners in industry. . . .

National Labor Relations Act, 29 U.S.C. § 151.

Although the Wagner Act intended to address this inequality of bargaining power by encouraging collective bargaining, the decline of labor unionism left a vacuum in which an imbalance of power persisted between individual employees and employers organized in the corporate form. In an influential article published in 1967, Lawrence Blades emphasized the consequences of such an imbalance of power:

> It is a widely accepted proposition that large corporations now pose a threat to individual freedom comparable to that which would be posed if governmental power were unchecked. The proposition need not, however, be limited to the mammoth business corporation, for the freedom of the individual is threatened whenever he becomes dependent upon a private entity possessing greater power than himself. Foremost among the relationships of which this generality is true is that of employer and employee.
>
> The threat to individual freedom posed by employer power has special significance because "We have become a nation of employees. We are dependent upon others for our means of livelihood, and most of our people have become completely dependent upon wages. If they lose their jobs they lose every resource, except for the relief supplied by the various forms of social security. Such dependence of the mass of the people upon others for *all* of their income is something new in the world. *For our generation, the substance of life is in another man's hands.*"

Lawrence E. Blades, *Employment at Will vs. Individual Freedom: On Limiting the Abusive Exercise of Employer Power*, 67 COLUM. L. REV. 1404, 1404 (1967) (quoting F. TANNENBAUM, A PHILOSOPHY OF LABOR 9 (1951) (emphasis in original)).

Throughout Part II, we consider the various ways in which courts and legislatures have intervened—or refused to do so—to address the imbalance of bargaining power between employee and employer. In considering the response of the law, we contrast individual and collective intervention strategies, posing questions about whether regulation is warranted, and if so, which approach is most effective or desirable in each context.

In the first three chapters of this Part, we consider the conflict between employees' interest in job security and the employer's need for flexibility.

Chapter 3 begins with the basic presumption of at-will employment and explores the various ways in which that presumption may be overcome by the words or actions of the parties, while Chapter 4 examines the situations in which considerations of public policy protect the job security of individual employees in particular circumstances. The materials in Chapter 5 consider the collective job security concerns of workers—those threatened not by an individual firing, but by capital investment decisions that threaten the jobs of entire categories of employees.

The remaining chapters address other conflicts between employee and employer interests. Chapter 6 considers how employees' interests in moving freely to new job opportunities may conflict with employers' desires to control the competitive activities of their former employees after the employment relationship has ended. The materials in Chapter 7 juxtapose employees' interests in human dignity, personal privacy, and autonomy against the profit-driven efficiency pressures employers feel to maximize output and to commodify labor. Chapter 8 presents materials highlighting the tension between employees' desire for voice and participation in workplace decisionmaking and the employer's desire to control its property and production processes.

Chapter 3

CONTRACTING FOR INDIVIDUAL JOB SECURITY

As we saw in Part I, American law understands the employment relationship as fundamentally contractual in nature. Over time, conceptions about the appropriate role of the law have changed, and both courts and legislatures have become more willing to intervene in the relation between employer and employee. However, even though numerous laws now regulate the employment relationship, the underlying assumption remains that the terms and conditions of employment are primarily determined by private agreement between the parties.

We begin this Part with an exploration of how this fundamental understanding shapes the basic nature of the employment relationship, with a particular focus on the employee's interest in job security. Obviously, job security is a concern for employees who are dependent upon their wages to provide for the basic needs of themselves and their families. Employees also have an interest in job security because they invest in their jobs over time. This investment may be financial, as when an employee incurs moving or other expenses to take or keep a job. Employees also invest in their jobs by learning skills, expending effort and committing psychologically to the goals of the employer. The employee's interests in ensuring her job security, however, run up against the employer's need or desire for discretion and flexibility to manage its workforce.

Regarding job security, the presumption that employment is at will is the dominant rule, having been adopted in every American jurisdiction by the early twentieth century. Today, it is still the rule in every state except Montana, which in 1987 passed the Wrongful Discharge from Employment Act requiring employers to have good cause to fire an employee. *See* Mont. Stat. Ann. § 39-2-901 *et seq*. Despite its predominance, the at-will rule merely states a presumption; in theory, employee and employer remain free to contract around it by reaching an alternative agreement.

This chapter explores the efforts of individual employees to assert that they have legal rights, growing out of specific agreements they had with their employers, to something other than at-will employment. Part A briefly discusses the historical development of the at-will rule in America in the late nineteenth and early twentieth centuries, as well as some alternative approaches to dealing with employee job security that have developed in the contexts of union and government employment. In the remaining parts of this chapter, we consider modern applications of contract law to the employment relationship. Part B considers express and implied agreements restricting employers' rights to discharge, and Part C explores the meaning of a requirement that the employer have "cause" for termination. Part D addresses some additional contract-based theories limiting at-will employment.

A. THE PRESUMPTION OF EMPLOYMENT AT-WILL

1. Historical Background

Up until the late nineteenth century, American law offered few clear rules governing the duration of a service contract. Prior to that time, the question had been thought part of the law of masters and servants, and English precedent was influential. Increasingly, however, the circumstances of the typical service relationship were shifting—from that of the domestic servant with a personal relationship with the employer to the mass of workers employed by a large corporation—and it was unclear what rules should apply to the emerging modern employment relationship. By the early twentieth century, a contract-based approach to understanding the employment relationship was firmly entrenched in American jurisprudence. The following excerpt traces these developments:

Jay M. Feinman, *The Development of the Employment at Will Rule*
20 Am. J. Legal Hist. 118, 119–124, 126, 129–131 (1976)

I. The English Law

. . . The duration of service relationships was a concern in early stages of English law, but the law was best formulated and made prominent only with the statement of a rule and policy by Blackstone:

> If the hiring be general, without any particular time limited, the law construes it to be a hiring for a year; upon a principle of natural equity, that the servant shall serve, and the master maintain him, throughout all the revolutions of the respective seasons, as well when there is work to be done as when there is not.

The rule thus stated expressed a sound principle: injustice would result if, for example, masters could have the benefit of servants' labor during planting and harvest seasons but discharge them to avoid supporting them during the unproductive winter, or if servants who were supported during the hard season could leave their masters' service when their labor was most needed. . . . [D]espite a concern with the "revolution of the seasons," the rule articulated by Blackstone was not restricted to agricultural and domestic workers. The presumption that an indefinite hiring was a hiring for a year extended to all classes of servants. . . .

presumption

The presumption of a yearly hiring could be rebutted in specific cases by other means, especially . . . when the parties were alleged to have contracted with reference to a custom of the trade for a shorter period of employment. The frequency of periodic payments was a material factor in determining whether the parties intended the contract to be for a shorter period, but periodic payment of wages alone would not ordinarily rebut the presumption. Because the central question in each case was the factual one of the intention of the parties, the court decisions are sometimes apparently in conflict.

rebutting presumption

As the law was faced with an increasing variety of employment situations, mostly far removed from the domestic relations which had shaped the earlier law, the importance of the duration of contract question diminished and the second issue, the notice required to terminate the contract, moved to the fore. Even when they recognized hirings as yearly ones, the courts refused to consider the contracts as entire and instead developed the rule that, unless specified otherwise, service contracts could be terminated on reasonable notice. . . . What constituted reasonable notice was a question of fact to be decided anew in each case, but certain conventions grew up. . . . Although notice was a separate question in each case, the custom of the trade was often determinative. In the twentieth century the required notice decreased considerably and is now regulated for many employees by the Contracts of Employment Act of 1963, which prescribes periods of required notice from one to eight weeks. . . .

II. The American Development

[handwritten: U. S.]

While English law followed a relatively clear path, American law at the same time exhibited a confusion of principles and rules. Through the middle of the nineteenth century, American courts and lawyers relied heavily on English precedents but often came to different results. . . . Not until Horace Gray Wood's crucial 1877 master and servant treatise . . . was a clean break made. Wood argued effectively that master and servant could no longer be considered one of the domestic relations, and that "all who are in the employ of another" belonged to a single category. . . .

Wood sliced through the confusion and stated the employment at will doctrine in absolutely certain terms:

> With us the rule is inflexible, that a general or indefinite hiring is *prima facie* a hiring at will, and if the servant seeks to make it out a yearly hiring, the burden is upon him to establish it by proof. . . . [I]t is an indefinite hiring and is determinable at the will of either party, and in this respect there is no distinction between domestic and other servants.

The puzzling question is what impelled Wood to state the rule that has since become identified with his name. Wood's master and servant treatise, like his other works, won him acclaim for his painstaking scholarship, but that comprehensiveness and concern for detail were absent in his treatment of the duration of service contracts. First, the four American cases he cited in direct support of the rule were in fact far off the mark. Second, his scholarly disingenuity was extraordinary; he stated incorrectly that no American courts in recent years had approved the English rule, that the employment at will rule was inflexibly applied in the United States, and that the English rule was only for a yearly hiring, making no mention of notice. Third, in the absence of valid legal support, Wood offered no policy grounds for the rule he proclaimed.

Whatever its origin and the inadequacies of its explanation, Wood's rule spread across the nation until it was generally adopted. . . . The courts substituted a new presumption of termination at will for their earlier differences as to presumption of long-term hiring or reasonable notice, and the new presumption was not easily rebutted. . . .

Perhaps the most common hypothesis [to explain the change to the at-will rule]

[handwritten margin note: maybe why they changed to at will]

[handwritten margin note: or →]

considers Wood's rule to be an outgrowth of the concurrently-developing theory of contract. . . . [C]ontrasting [contract doctrine] with the rule and the reality of the cases shows that the contract hypothesis is improbable. Pure contract law was designed to give effect to the manifest joint intention of the parties regardless of the nature of the transaction. Under Wood's rule, however, the nature of the transaction is crucial. Because employment contracts were at issue, an artificial presumption of terminability was introduced; the parties' intentions were secondary, to be considered only rarely to rebut the presumption. . . . If master and servant law had similarly followed true contract theory, the rule would be that the duration of employment and any notice required would be subject to factual determination in each case.

A second possible explanation of the employment at will rule is that it was a response to changing social conditions and its presumption accurately reflected the usual duration of employment contracts. Little collected evidence on the duration of hirings and people's perceptions of them exists, but several factors suggest that this is not a likely explanation, that contracts were not generally terminable at will, especially for those middle-level workers with whom the cases dealt. First, the contracts in several of the New York cases, like those in other states, were clearly for definite periods, often a year. Some of these were brought within the rule anyway; the cases in which Wood's rule was applied are not easily distinguishable factually from others in which yearly contracts were allowed to stand. Second, the great propensity of trial juries to find contracts of long duration suggests a common perception of permanence in at least certain types of employment. Third, even though short-term or at-will contracts were used for some workers, the employees for whom the rule was initially fashioned were not in that category. These were not day laborers or factory operatives whose talents were fungible. Rather, they were responsible agents and managers who were well-paid for their efforts on behalf of enterprises of significant size. Such employees would most likely have expectations of some permanence in their jobs. . . . It is unlikely, therefore, that, before the advent of Wood's rule, either employees or employers usually regarded this type of relationship as severable on a moment's notice.

NOTES

1. **The Revolution of the Seasons.** What was the rationale behind Blackstone's rule that the law construes a hiring to be for a year? What understanding of the nature of the service relationship underlies the rule? Do the concerns that animated Blackstone's rule have any relevance to the contemporary employment relationship? *[handwritten note: they both can't leave during down or busy season]*

2. **Notice.** Feinman's account indicates that the focus of English law shifted to the question of how much notice is required to terminate an employment contract. What interests do employees and employers have in defining a period of notice before the employment relationship ends? Is there any reason to regulate the amount of notice required, as opposed to leaving the question to the private agreement of the parties? *[handwritten note: perhaps regulation = consistency]* *[handwritten note: Er won't be left high & dry]*

3. **Wood's Rule.** Feinman and others criticize Wood's 1877 treatise, arguing that the four American cases he cited did not in fact support the at-will rule he

articulated. *See, e.g.*, J. Peter Shapiro & James F. Tune, Note, *Implied Contract Rights to Job Security*, 26 STAN. L. REV. 335, 341 (1974). In two of the cases, appellate courts affirmed jury verdicts for employees who alleged that they had employment contracts for a definite duration. Another case concerned a contract between the army and a private company for transportation of goods, not an employment contract. And the other involved an action by a bartender who was discharged by a tavern and given notice to leave the room he occupied at the end of the month. When he failed to leave, he was forcibly ejected and he sued for damages for unlawful ejection, apparently without challenging his dismissal. None of these cases entailed judgments against an employee challenging a dismissal without cause, leaving Wood vulnerable to the charge that the at-will rule sprang "full-blown in 1877 from [his] busy and perhaps careless pen." Theodore J. St. Antoine, *You're Fired!*, HUMAN RIGHTS at 32, 33 (Winter 1982).

[handwritten margin note: cases wood cited to]

On the other hand, Mayer G. Freed and Daniel D. Polsby have argued that the cases *do* support Wood's rule, at least in the sense that each of the cases is consistent with Wood's formulation—that indefinite hirings are terminable at will unless the employee can establish that the parties intended otherwise. *See* Mayer G. Freed & Daniel D. Polsby, *The Doubtful Provenance of "Wood's Rule" Revisited*, 22 ARIZ. ST. L.J. 551 (1990).

[handwritten margin note: arguing for cases wood cited & defending wood]

Freed and Polsby also defend Wood's rule against the charge that it is unduly rigid or inflexible:

> Wood does not suggest that it should be impermissible or even difficult for a plaintiff to prove that the parties intended that the employment relationship would last for a certain length of time. All it says is that plaintiff has the burden of proving that a contract of employment with no express duration was nevertheless intended by the parties to continue for a fixed duration. Nothing in the rule forecloses a jury from considering all the facts and circumstances from which inferences might be drawn concerning what the contract had been.
>
> Of course, that is the role of a presumption: to decide issues where facts are skimpy or absent; presumptions are not supposed to keep facts from being introduced into evidence, nor are they supposed to decide what "surrounding circumstances" may count as a fact.

Freed & Polsby, *supra*, at 553.

Wood's own explanation was that "[i]t is competent for either party to show what the mutual understanding of the parties was in reference to the matter; but unless their understanding was mutual that the service was to extend for a certain fixed and definite period, it is an indefinite hiring and is determinable at the will of either party . . . ." H. WOOD, THE LAW OF MASTER AND SERVANT § 134 (1877).

Aside from the issue of its accuracy, scholars also dispute whether or not Wood's rule was influential in establishing the dominance of the at-will rule in American jurisdictions. Feinman points out that treatises summarizing the law were an important resource for both the bench and bar in the late nineteenth century. Although he argues that social and economic factors were primarily responsible for the spread of the at-will rule, he argues that the rule would not have been established as quickly and uniformly in the absence of Wood's treatise. *See* Jay M. Feinman, *The Development of the Employment at Will Rule*, 20 AM. J. LEGAL HIST. 118, 127 (1976). Andrew Morriss disagrees, asserting that the at-will rule had already been adopted in several states prior to the publication of Wood's treatise, and was subsequently adopted in numerous other states without citing Wood as authority. Thus, he concludes that Wood's role was one of "relative insignificance." *See* Andrew P. Morriss, *Exploding Myths: An Empirical and Economic Reassessment of the Rise of Employment At-Will*, 59 Mo. L. REV. 679, 697–98 (1994).

4.   **A Classic Statement.** *Payne v. Western & Atlantic Railroad Co.*, 81 Tenn. 507 (1884) is frequently quoted for its classic statement of the at-will rule: employers "may dismiss their employees at will . . . for good cause, for no cause, or even for cause morally wrong, without being thereby guilty of legal wrong." *Payne*, however, was not an employment case, but a suit brought by a merchant against a railroad that employed a large number of workers nearby. The plaintiff, Payne, operated a store in Chattanooga, Tennessee, selling goods to the employees of the railroad. Plaintiff brought suit for interference with business relations after the defendant prohibited its employees from trading with Payne on penalty of discharge. The sufficiency of the allegations turned in part on whether the defendant employer had the right to discharge employees for trading with the plaintiff or "for any other cause." Judge Ingersoll, writing for the majority in *Payne* reasoned:

> Is it unlawful for one person, or a number of persons in conspiracy, to threaten to discharge employees if they trade with a certain merchant? . . .
>
> For any one to do this without cause is censurable and unjust. But is it legally wrong? Is it unlawful? May I not refuse to trade with any one? May I not forbid my family to trade with any one? May I not dismiss my domestic servant for dealing, or even visiting, where I forbid? And if my domestic, why not my farm-hand, or my mechanic, or teamster? And, if one of them, then why not all four? And, if all four, why not a hundred or a thousand of them? . . . [M]en must be left, without interference to buy and sell where they please, and to discharge or retain employees at will for good cause or for no cause, or even for bad cause without thereby being guilty of an unlawful act per se. It is a right which an employee may exercise in the same way, to the same extent, for the same cause or want of cause as the employer. He may refuse to work for a man or company, that trades with any obnoxious person, or does other things which he dislikes. He may persuade his fellows, and the employer may lose all his hands and be compelled to close his doors; or he may yield to the demand and withdraw his custom or cease his dealings, and the obnoxious person be thus injured or wrecked in business. Can it be pretended that for this either of the injured parties has a right of action against the employees? Great loss may result, indeed has often resulted from such conduct; but loss alone gives no right of action. Great corporations, strong associations, and wealthy individuals may thus do great mischief and wrong; may make and break merchants at will; may crush out competition, and foster monopolies, and thus greatly injure individuals and the public; but power is inherent in size and strength and wealth; and the law cannot set bound to it, unless it is

exercised illegally. Then it is restrained because of its illegality, not because of its quantity or quality. The great and rich and powerful are guaranteed the same liberty and privilege as the poor and weak. All may buy and sell when they choose; they may refuse to employ or dismiss whom they choose, without being thereby guilty of a legal wrong, though it may seriously injure and even ruin others.

All [employers] may dismiss their employees at will, be they many or few, for good cause, for no cause or even for cause morally wrong, without being thereby guilty of legal wrong. *A fortiori* they may "threaten" to discharge them without thereby doing an illegal act, per se. . . . The law cannot compel them to employ workmen, nor to keep them employed. . . . Trade is free; so is employment. The law leaves employer and employee to make their own contracts; and these, when made, it will enforce; beyond this it does not go. Either the employer or employee may terminate the relation at will, and the law will not interfere. . . .

Id. at 517–20. Judge Freeman, with Judge Turney, concurring, dissented:

It is argued that a man ought to have the right to say where his employees shall trade. I do not recognize any such right. . . . This is not in any way to interfere with the legal right to discharge an employee for good cause, or without any reason assigned if the contract justifies it, but only that he shall not do this solely for the purpose of injury to another, or hold the threat over the employee *in terrorem* to fetter the freedom of the employee, and for the purpose of injuring an obnoxious party. . . .

In view of the immense development and large aggregations of capital in this favored country—a capital to be developed and aggregated within the life of the present generation more than a hundred fold—giving the command of immense numbers of employees, by such means as we have before us in this case, it is the demand of a sound public policy, for the future more especially, as well as now, that the use of this power should be restrained within legitimate boundaries. Take for instance the larger manufacturing establishments of the country—of which we will in time have our full share, when thousands upon thousands of hard-working operatives will be employed. It will be to their interest to have free competition in the purchase of supplies for their wants, and its beneficial influences in keeping prices at the normal standard. The merchant and groceryman, and other traders should be untrammeled to furnish these, and the employees untrammeled in the exercise of his right to purchase where his interest will best be subserved. If, however, these masters of aggregated capital can use their power over their employees as in this case, all other traders except such as they choose to permit will be driven away or crushed out, and their capital probably alone have a monopoly to furnish his employees at his own rates freed from competition. The result is that capital may crush legitimate trade, and thus cripple the general property of the country and the employee be subject to its grinding exactions at will.

The principle of the majority opinion will justify employers, at any rate allow them to require employees to trade where they may demand, to vote as they may require, or do anything not strictly criminal that employer may dictate, or feel the wrath of employer by dismissal from service. Employment is the means of sustaining life to himself and family to the employee, and so he is morally though not legally compelled to submit. Capital may thus not only find its own legitimate employment, but may control the employment of others to an extent that in time may sap the foundations of our free institutions. Perfect freedom in all legitimate uses is due to capital, and should be zealously enforced, but public policy and all the best interests of society demands it shall be restrained within legitimate boundaries, and any channel by which it may escape or overleap these boundaries, should be carefully but judiciously guarded. For its legitimate uses I have perfect respect, against its illegitimate use I feel bound, for the best interests both of capital and labor, to protest. . . .

Id. at 542–44. What justifications does the majority offer for permitting employers to an unfettered right to terminate employees at will? What is the point of disagreement between the majority and dissenting judges?

Despite incursions on the employment-at-will rule through legislative enactment and common law development, employment at will remains the default rule. Clyde Summers explains that the doctrine is rooted in assumptions about the primacy of property rights over the value of labor. The employer, as owner of the business, has the legal right to control the operation of its enterprise. Workers have only the right to be paid for labor performed. Accordingly, they serve at the will of the master:

> [T]he premises of the doctrine [of employment at will] are quite clear; the employer has sovereignty except to the extent it has expressly granted its employees rights. The doctrine thus expresses and implements the subordination of workers to those who control the enterprise. In the absence of a protective provision in the contract of employment—and only upper level managers have such contracts—workers are totally subordinate. Their terms and conditions of employment can be changed in any way at any time and they can be dismissed without reason and without notice.

Clyde W. Summers, *Employment at Will in the United States: The Divine Right of Employers*, 3 U. Pa. J. Lab. & Emp. L. 65, 68 (2000).

5. At-Will Employment as a Default Rule. If the at-will rule merely establishes a presumption when an employment contract is silent as to its duration, then the parties remain free to contract around it. In economic parlance, such a presumption is a "default" rule, one that operates merely as a gap-filler, supplying necessary terms when the parties to a contract have failed to specify every aspect of their relationship. Because the parties can avoid an undesirable default rule simply by agreeing to different terms, not much is at stake, in theory, in selecting what the default rule will be. Bargaining can be costly, however, and so standard economic theory suggests that a default rule should be set at the terms that the parties would most likely choose themselves in the absence of transactions costs. *See, e.g.*, Charles J. Goetz & Robert E. Scott, *The Mitigation Principle: Toward a General Theory of Contractual Obligation*, 69 Va. L. Rev. 967, 971 (1983).

Feinman argues that the presumption of at-will employment did not in fact reflect the expectations of the typical employer and employee at the time the rule became dominant. What about today? If default rules should be set at the terms most parties would want if they actually bargained over the issue, should the default rule today be employment at will? Does the fact that very few individuals have negotiated contracts that limit the employer's right to discharge at will mean that the current at-will default accurately captures the preferences of the parties in most cases? Is the fact that virtually all collective bargaining agreements require just cause for dismissal at all relevant to determining the appropriate default rule?

SAVAGE v. SPUR DISTRIBUTING CO.
Court of Appeals of Tennessee
228 S.W.2d 122 (1949)

FELTS, JUDGE.

This is an action for damages for breach of an alleged employment contract. At the close of plaintiff's evidence the trial judge directed a verdict for defendant and dismissed the action. Plaintiff appealed. . . .

Plaintiff lived in Pittsburgh, Pennsylvania, and was employed as an accountant by Price-Waterhouse, a firm of accountants in that city. They had been doing work for defendant, and through them he learned that there was soon to be a vacancy in the accounting department of defendant's Nashville office. On or about April 25, 1946, he came to Nashville and applied for the position.

He discussed the matter with defendant's vice president, Mr. Hines, and its secretary, Mr. Peterson. He asked whether the position would be temporary or permanent. They told him that it would be permanent and he would have it as long as he performed the work satisfactorily and that he would be paid a salary of $300 a month and a bonus to be determined by the company's earnings. . . .

As a result of this discussion the secretary, Mr. Peterson, employed plaintiff to be his assistant to take charge of defendant's accounting department. There was no written contract but only the oral understanding reached in their discussion. Plaintiff began work June 9, 1946, and later moved his family to Nashville. He was paid his moving expenses and was paid his salary each month and a bonus of $150 at the end of 1946. . . .

He continued to receive his salary each month until October 20, 1947, when he was discharged by Mr. Knestric, who had succeeded Peterson as secretary. He was given a month's salary in advance in lieu of notice, and his discharge slip gave this explanation: "Reorganization of Secretary's Office which decentralized the duties performed by this employee." But it appears there had been some disagreement between him and the new secretary, which might have been the cause of his discharge. . . .

We think there was no evidence of any breach of contract. There was no contract for employment for any definite time. It was an indefinite hiring, merely a promise by defendant to employ plaintiff permanently as long as he did the work satisfactorily. But there was no counterpromise by him to work for it for any length of time. He was free to quit any time—to accept other employment whenever he chose. It is a general principle that unless both parties are bound neither is bound.

The general rule in the United States is that such an indefinite hiring is a hiring at the will of both parties and may be terminated by either at any time.

Such a contract for permanent employment means nothing more than that the employment is to continue indefinitely subject to the continuing satisfaction of both parties and may be terminated at the will of either party. " 'A contract of employment for an indefinite term may, in the United States, be terminated at the will of either party. A contract for permanent employment where the consideration is paid wholly or partly in advance, as by the relinquishment of a claim for personal injuries, or which is supported by a consideration other than the promise to render services, is not such an indefinite contract as to come within the rule. But a contract for permanent employment, so long as it is satisfactorily performed, which is not supported by any consideration other than the obligation of service to be performed on the one hand and wages to be paid on the other, is terminable at the pleasure of either party.' " *Combs v. Standard Oil Co.*, 59 S.W. (2d) [525,] 526.

There is a line of cases where the employee paid his employer in advance a valuable consideration in addition to his promise to render the services for the wages paid, such as a release of a claim for damages for personal injuries (*East Tennessee, V. & G. R. Co. v. Staub*, 75 Tenn. 397), or giving up of a competitive business. *Carnig v. Carr*, 46 N.E. 117. In such cases it is said that the employee purchased an option for permanent employment terminable only at his will.

parg

Plaintiff likens this case to the Staub, Carr, and like cases. He insists that he gave up his former employment and had the expenses of moving his family here, of finding living quarters, and of buying a home here at an inflated price; and that these things constituted an additional advance consideration sufficient to support a contract for permanent employment—sufficient to purchase an option binding defendant to employ him so long as he remained able and chose to continue the employment.

ct
resp:

These things, however, do not appear to have been mutually understood by the parties as any part of the agreed exchange or consideration. Defendant's offer was only for plaintiff's services as its assistant secretary. This was the only consideration moving to it. These other things were of no benefit to it. At most they were merely a detriment to him incident to preparing himself to accept its offer—only the same sort of detriment that ordinarily results to any employee who leaves one employment and goes elsewhere to accept another.

Some cases do hold that such a detriment in itself is a sufficient consideration to bring the case within the rule of the Staub, Carr, and like cases. In the latter class of cases, however, the employee not only sustained a detriment to himself but also passed a benefit to his employer. We think the better view, and the one supported by the weight of authority, is that a mere detriment sustained by the employee in preparing himself to accept the employer's offer, such as here shown, is not a sufficient consideration to make an indefinite hiring terminable only at the will of

H/R
again

the employee. . . .

NOTES

1.   The Weight of a Presumption. What kind of contract did Savage allege that he had? Did the parties express their intent as to the expected duration of the contract or the conditions under which it could be terminated? How does the court apply the at-will presumption in resolving Savage's breach of contract claim?

2.   Additional Consideration. *Savage* is fairly typical of how courts dealt with employee suits challenging dismissals in the first half of the 20th century. Courts required employees alleging that they had been promised "permanent" employment to prove that they had provided some additional consideration, beyond the services performed, in order to support such a promise. And as the *Savage* opinion suggests, their view of what constituted such consideration was quite narrow. Generally, courts found sufficient additional consideration only in the two situations mentioned in the opinion—when an employee agreed to release a claim for damages or agreed to give up a competing business.

ex of where ct finds considerati

What consideration did Savage allege that he provided in exchange for the promise of permanent employment? Why did the court find it inadequate? Suppose Savage had agreed to accept a lower salary in exchange for the employer's promise of permanent employment. Should that be considered sufficient additional consideration?

3.   Mutuality. The *Savage* court's conclusion that no contract existed also rested on the absence of any "counter-promise" by the plaintiff to continue working for any length of time. Stating that "[i]t is a general principle that unless both parties are bound neither is bound," the court reasoned that because Savage was free to quit at any time, the employer could not be bound to any promise to continue to employ plaintiff. *Id.* at 124. This requirement of mutuality of promises was justified in greater detail by the Supreme Court of Louisiana in *Pitcher v. United Oil & Gas Syndicate, Inc.*, 139 So. 760 (1932):

> An employee is never presumed to engage his services permanently, thereby cutting himself off from all chances of improving his condition; indeed, in this land of opportunity it would be against public policy and the spirit of our institutions that any man should thus handicap himself; and the law will presume almost juris et de jure that he did not so intend. And if the contract of employment be not binding on the employee for the whole term of such employment, then it cannot be binding upon the employer; there would be lack of 'mutuality.' . . . An employment which is to continue as long as the employer shall do business is such an employment as might effectively deprive the employee, for the rest of his natural life, of all opportunity to improve his condition. Such a contract, as we have said, would be against public policy and the spirit of our institutions.

Id. at 761, 762. Do concerns about the ability of employees to pursue better opportunities justify a rule that courts will not enforce a contract for "permanent" employment?

4.   Default vs. Substantive Rules. Default rules are typically contrasted with substantive or immutable rules—regulations that economic actors cannot avoid through private agreements. Thus, for example, the federal minimum wage law is a substantive rule in that an employer cannot pay a covered employee less than the mandated minimum wage, even if she is willing to accept less. The distance between a default and a substantive rule, however, depends upon the strength of the presumption and what evidence is required to overcome it. The higher the barriers are to avoiding a default rule, the more closely it may come in practice to a substantive rule. An important question for the law, then, is how difficult it should be for parties to contract around a default term. In the early 20th century, the courts applied doctrines such as mutuality of obligation and additional consideration in such a way as to raise the barriers for employees seeking to overcome the at-will presumption and establish contractual rights to job security.

Clyde Summers criticizes these doctrines relied on in the early cases as "spurious contract law," writing that:

> Contracts require only exchanged consideration, not mutual obligations. The employee, by coming to work, provides sufficient consideration to make the employer's promise of continued or permanent employment binding. . . . Mutuality of obligation, particularly in the form of mirrored obligations as required by the courts in these cases, has never been considered essential to make promises binding.

> Another spurious contractual doctrine . . . was that to overcome the presumption that employment for an indefinite term was employment at will the employee must give some additional consideration. Coming to work, even working for a number of years, was not consideration for a promise of future employment. An employee must give something more. Why something more than faithful service was required was never clearly explained. There seemed to be an assumption that because wages for work performed had been paid, the work could not be consideration for a promise of continued employment. As any first semester law student knows, however, one performance can be consideration to support two or even twenty promises. The work performed could be consideration for both the wages paid and the promise of future employment. The requirement of additional consideration was but a device for converting Wood's presumption into a substantive rule so that even an express promise of permanent employment would not bind the employer.

Clyde W. Summers, *The Contract of Employment and the Rights of Individual Employees: Fair Representation and Employment at Will*, 52 FORDHAM L. REV. 1082, 1098–99 (1984).

Is Summers right that the early cases converted the at-will presumption into a substantive rule? How could an employee and employer create a contract that provided greater job security? What advantages and disadvantages might such a contract have for each?

What sort of showing should be required to overcome the at-will presumption? Are there any reasons to make it difficult to overcome the at-will presumption?

2. Alternative Models

At the same time that the common law courts were strictly applying the at-will rule, two alternative models for addressing concerns about job security were evolving for employees covered by collective bargaining agreements or employed by the government. Before exploring in detail the operation of the at-will rule in the contemporary context, we first briefly consider these alternative models.

a. The Union Sector

As discussed above, the courts applied the at-will rule with particular vigor up through the mid-20th century. Discharged employees rarely challenged their terminations in court, and on the few occasions they did so, their claims were likely to be rejected out of hand by courts invoking the at-will rule. Only the rare employee who could prove an express contract for a definite term, or who could demonstrate that he had in essence "purchased" the job, was likely to prevail. The typical individual employee thus lacked any enforceable guarantees of job security.

This same period saw the passage of the National Labor Relations Act, and the growth of unions until they reached the peak of their strength in the mid-1950s. Because most collective bargaining agreements place "just cause" restrictions on the employer's right to discharge workers, individual employees in unionized workplaces receive legal protection against arbitrary discharge. Although most collective bargaining agreements do not define the term "just cause," an extensive body of arbitral decisions exists interpreting the term in individual employee discipline and discharge cases. In addition, collective bargaining agreements typically establish a grievance procedure beginning with informal attempts at resolution and culminating in a hearing before a neutral arbitrator in those cases the union elects to pursue. The following excerpts describe the industrial due process model characteristic of unionized workplaces.

Roger I. Abrams & Dennis R. Nolan, *Toward a Theory of "Just Cause" in Employee Discipline Cases*
1985 DUKE L.J. 594, 611–12

A. Just cause for discipline exists only when an employee has failed to meet his obligations under the fundamental understanding of the employment relationship. The employee's general obligation is to provide satisfactory work. Satisfactory work has four components:

1. Regular attendance.

2. Obedience to reasonable work rules.

3. A reasonable quality and quantity of work.

4. Avoidance of conduct, either at or away from work, which would interfere with the employer's ability to carry on the business effectively.

B. For there to be just cause, the discipline must further one or more of management's three legitimate interests:

1. Rehabilitation of a potentially satisfactory employee.

2. Deterrence of similar conduct, either by the disciplined employee or by other employees.

3. Protection of the employer's ability to operate the business successfully.

C. The concept of just cause includes certain employee protections that reflect the union's interest in guaranteeing "fairness" in disciplinary situations.

1. The employee is entitled to *industrial due process*. This includes:

a. actual or constructive notice of expected standards of conduct and penalties for wrongful conduct;

b. a decision based on facts, determined after an investigation that provides the employee an opportunity to state his case, with union assistance if he desires it;

c. the imposition of discipline in gradually increasing degrees, except in cases involving the most extreme breaches of the fundamental understanding. In particular, discharge may be imposed only when less severe penalties will not protect legitimate management interests, for one of the following reasons: (1) the employee's past record shows that the unsatisfactory conduct will continue, (2) the most stringent form of discipline is needed to protect the system of work rules, or (3) continued employment would inevitably interfere with the successful operation of the business; and

d. proof by management that just cause exists.

2. The employee is entitled to *industrial equal protection*, which requires like treatment of like cases.

3. The employee is entitled to *individualized treatment*. Distinctive facts in the employee's record or regarding the reason for discipline must be given appropriate weight.

Cynthia L. Estlund, *Free Speech and Due Process in the Workplace*
71 IND. L.J. 101, 136–38 (1995)

Virtually all employees represented by a union are protected by a just cause requirement for discipline and discharge, together with a grievance-arbitration system for enforcing it. The just cause clause has generated a body of arbitral law known as "industrial due process." . . .

Under a just cause provision, the employer must have a valid basis for discipline or discharge. If an employee "grieves" the decision, the union may take the grievance through several steps of discussion with successively higher management officials, and eventually to arbitration. The arbitrator is an impartial third party with experience in labor relations, and often in the particular collective bargaining relationship, who is chosen jointly by the employer and the union, and whose future employment as an arbitrator depends on a reputation for impartiality and even-handedness. The hearing, at which the employer bears the burden of proof, resembles a trial, but is less formal. An attorney or other representative for each side presents arguments, documents, and witnesses, but briefing is limited or nonexistent. The arbitrator is typically required to render a decision and some short explanation within a few weeks. The standard remedy for a discharge without "just cause" is reinstatement and backpay. The entire process, from the employer's discharge decision to the arbitrator's ruling, may take as little as two to four months. . . .

In addition, on the purely procedural front the employee may challenge the adequacy of the employer's pre-termination process, including the adequacy of notice, compliance with "progressive discipline" in the form of warnings and suspensions prior to discharge, and equitable treatment vis-à-vis other offenders. These procedural requirements are supplemented by the grievance process itself, the first steps of which give the union employee an opportunity to probe the employer's case and often to settle the dispute prior to arbitration. All of this process enforces norms of fair and equal treatment that make it hard for the employer to seize upon minor infractions or lags in performance to discharge employee dissenters.

The employee may also challenge the substantive justification for discipline: she may contest the reasonableness of the employer's rules, the job-relatedness of alleged misconduct, and the severity of the penalty. . . .

The employee protected by a just cause clause, like the tenured civil servant, has a kind of property right in continued employment, the termination of which must be justified by good reasons and preceded by fair procedures. . . . [T]he employee may challenge her discharge and demand a prompt hearing before an impartial arbitrator, at which <u>the employer must show just cause.</u> The delay and the cost of the proceeding is minimal, and the burdens of proof and uncertainty fall on the employer. . . .

[I]ndustrial due process is a collective right. Under a collective bargaining agreement, the union decides whether to carry a grievance through arbitration. . . . The union is subject to a duty to fairly represent employees, but that does not guarantee every employee a hearing. Moreover, the duty of fair representation is enforceable only through litigation. . . .

On the other hand, the presence of an active, effective collective bargaining representative bolsters the employee's position in a number of ways. The union is a repeat player standing in a position of rough equality with the employer in selecting an arbitrator; the arbitrator's future livelihood depends on dealing fairly with both sides. The union also provides representation, either by a union official experienced in handling arbitrations or by an attorney. Moreover, if the arbitrator reinstates the individual, the union remains on the scene to help protect the employee's position.

NOTES

1. **Substance and Procedure.** The meaning of "just cause" as applied in the union setting has both a substantive and procedural dimension. What are the elements of each? Are these two aspects of "just cause" entirely independent, or are

they linked in some way?

2. **Application of Theory.** In addition to their theoretical account of "just cause," Abrams and Nolan's article discusses how the principles they articulate apply in concrete factual situations. For example, continual tardiness or absenteeism constitutes just cause, particularly when the absences adversely affect the employer's operations. Such a rule is not absolute, however. The notion of "industrial due process" may require that the employer put the worker on notice of its behavioral expectations before taking disciplinary action. Except in cases of serious violations, progressive discipline might also be required—by first giving the worker a warning, then a brief suspension if the absences continue, followed by discharge if her attendance record does not improve. Abrams & Nolan, *supra*, at 613–14.

Under a just cause standard, the employer's right to enforce reasonable work rules will also permit discharge of an employee for reasons like fighting, sleeping on the job, engaging in horseplay that threatens the company's property or operations, failing to meet reasonably established production standards, violating required safety procedures, or becoming physically or psychologically incapable of performing assigned work.

b. Public Employment

Government employment also entails protections for employee job security not generally available in the non-unionized private sector workplace. Civil service statutes at both the state and federal levels typically restrict the ability of public employers to discharge covered employees without cause. And because constitutional restraints extend to the actions of government when acting in its capacity as an employer, public employees may enjoy additional rights under the Constitution.

The Fourteenth Amendment provides that no state shall "deprive any person of life, liberty or property without due process of law." The following materials explore what this clause means in the context of public employment.

BOARD OF REGENTS OF STATE COLLEGES v. ROTH
United States Supreme Court
408 U.S. 564 (1972)

Mr. Justice Stewart delivered the opinion of the Court.

In 1968 the respondent, David Roth, was hired for his first teaching job as assistant professor of political science at Wisconsin State University-Oshkosh. He was hired for a fixed term of one academic year. The notice of his faculty appointment specified that his employment would begin on September 1, 1968, and would end on June 30, 1969. The respondent completed that term. But he was informed that he would not be rehired for the next academic year.

 The respondent had no tenure rights to continued employment. Under Wisconsin statutory law a state university teacher can acquire tenure as a "permanent" employee only after four years of year-to-year employment. Having acquired tenure, a teacher is entitled to continued employment "during efficiency and good behavior." A relatively new teacher without tenure, however, is under Wisconsin law entitled to nothing beyond his one-year appointment. There are no statutory or administrative standards defining eligibility for re-employment. State law thus clearly leaves the decision whether to rehire a nontenured teacher for another year to the unfettered discretion of university officials. . . .

The respondent then brought this action in Federal District Court alleging that the decision not to rehire him for the next year infringed his Fourteenth Amendment rights. . . . [He] alleged that the failure of University officials to give him notice of any reason for nonretention and an opportunity for a hearing violated his right to procedural due process of law. . . .

The requirements of procedural due process apply only to the deprivation of interests encompassed by the Fourteenth Amendment's protection of liberty and property. When protected interests are implicated, the right to some kind of prior hearing is paramount. But the range of interests protected by procedural due process is not infinite. . . .

There might be cases in which a State refused to re-employ a person under such circumstances that interests in liberty would be implicated. But this is not such a case.

The State, in declining to rehire the respondent, did not make any charge against him that might seriously damage his standing and associations in his community. It did not base the nonrenewal of his contract on a charge, for example, that he had been guilty of dishonesty, or immorality. Had it done so, this would be a different case. For "[w]here a person's good name, reputation, honor, or integrity is at stake because of what the government is doing to him, notice and an opportunity to be heard are essential." *Wisconsin v. Constantineau*, 400 U.S. 433 (1971). In such a case, due process would accord an opportunity to refute the charge before University officials.[1] In the present case, however, there is no suggestion whatever that the respondent's "good name, reputation, honor, or integrity" is at stake.

Similarly, there is no suggestion that the State, in declining to re-employ the respondent, imposed on him a stigma or other disability that foreclosed his freedom to take advantage of other employment opportunities. The State, for example, did not invoke any regulations to bar the respondent from all other public employment in state universities. Had it done so, this, again, would be a different case. . . .

Hence, on the record before us, all that clearly appears is that the respondent was not rehired for one year at one university. It stretches the concept too far to suggest that a person is deprived of "liberty" when he simply is not rehired in one job but remains as free as before to seek another.

The Fourteenth Amendment's procedural protection of property is a safeguard of the security of interests that a person has already acquired in specific benefits. . . . To have a property interest in a benefit, a person clearly must have more than

---

[1] [n. 12] The purpose of such notice and hearing is to provide the person an opportunity to clear his name. Once a person has cleared his name at a hearing, his employer, of course, may remain free to deny him future employment for other reasons.

an abstract need or desire for it. He must have more than a unilateral expectation of it. He must, instead, have a legitimate claim of entitlement to it. It is a purpose of the ancient institution of property to protect those claims upon which people rely in their daily lives, reliance that must not be arbitrarily undermined. It is a purpose of the constitutional right to a hearing to provide an opportunity for a person to vindicate those claims.

Property interests, of course, are not created by the Constitution. Rather they are created and their dimensions are defined by existing rules or understandings that stem from an independent source such as state law—rules or understandings that secure certain benefits and that support claims of entitlement to those benefits. . . . [T]he respondent's "property" interest in employment at Wisconsin State University-Oshkosh was created and defined by the terms of his appointment. Those terms secured his interest in employment up to June 30, 1969. But the important fact in this case is that they specifically provided that the respondent's employment was to terminate on June 30. They did not provide for contract renewal absent "sufficient cause." Indeed, they made no provision for renewal whatsoever.

Thus, the terms of the respondent's appointment secured absolutely no interest in re-employment for the next year. They supported absolutely no possible claim of entitlement to re-employment. Nor, significantly, was there any state statute or University rule or policy that secured his interest in re-employment or that created any legitimate claim to it. In these circumstances, the respondent surely had an abstract concern in being rehired, but he did not have a property interest sufficient to require the University authorities to give him a hearing when they declined to renew his contract of employment. . . .

[JUSTICE POWELL took no part in the decision of this case.]

[JUSTICE DOUGLAS's dissenting opinion is omitted.]

MR. JUSTICE MARSHALL, dissenting.

. . . In my view, every citizen who applies for a government job is entitled to it unless the government can establish some reason for denying the employment. This is the "property" right that I believe is protected by the Fourteenth Amendment and that cannot be denied "without due process of law." And it is also liberty— liberty to work—which is the "very essence of the personal freedom and opportunity" secured by the Fourteenth Amendment.

This Court has often had occasion to note that the denial of public employment is a serious blow to any citizen. Thus, when an application for public employment is denied or the contract of a government employee is not renewed, the government must say why, for it is only when the reasons underlying government action are known that citizens feel secure and protected against arbitrary government action.

Employment is one of the greatest, if not the greatest, benefits that governments offer in modern-day life. When something as valuable as the opportunity to work is at stake, the government may not reward some citizens and not others without demonstrating that its actions are fair and equitable. And it is procedural due process that is our fundamental guarantee of fairness, our protection against arbitrary, capricious, and unreasonable government action. . . .

[A] requirement of procedural regularity at least renders arbitrary action more difficult. Moreover, proper procedures will surely eliminate some of the arbitrariness that results, not from malice, but from innocent error. "Experience teaches . . . that the affording of procedural safeguards, which by their nature serve to illuminate the underlying facts, in itself often operates to prevent erroneous decisions on the merits from occurring." *Silver v. New York Stock Exchange*, 373 U.S. 341 (1963). When the government knows it may have to justify its decisions with sound reasons, its conduct is likely to be more cautious, careful, and correct. . . .

NOTES

1. **A Companion Case.** On the same day that *Roth* was decided, the United States Supreme Court also issued a decision in *Perry v. Sindermann,* 408 U.S. 593 (1972). Like Roth, Robert Sindermann was a teacher whose contract was not renewed at the end of the 1968–69 academic year. Sindermann, however, had taught in the Texas state college system for 10 years, the last four at Odessa Junior College, under a series of one-year contracts. Although he was not formally tenured, he alleged that the college had a *de facto* tenure system, citing the Faculty Guide which stated, "Odessa College has no tenure system. The Administration of the College wishes the faculty member to feel that he has permanent tenure as long as his teaching services are satisfactory and as long as he displays a cooperative attitude toward his co-workers and his superiors, and as long as he is happy in his work." In addition, he relied on guidelines promulgated by the Texas College and University System that provided that teachers employed for seven years or more have some form of job tenure.

Based on these factual allegations, the Court concluded that Sindermann had raised a genuine issue regarding whether he had a legitimate interest in continued employment sufficient to trigger due process protection. The Court wrote:

We have made clear in *Roth*, that "property" interests subject to procedural due process protection are not limited by a few rigid, technical forms. Rather, "property" denotes a broad range of interests that are secured by "existing rules or understandings." A person's interest in a benefit is a "property" interest for due process purposes if there are such rules or mutually explicit understandings that support his claim of entitlement to the benefit and that he may invoke at a hearing.

A written contract with an explicit tenure provision clearly is evidence of a formal understanding that supports a teacher's claim of entitlement to continued employment unless sufficient "cause" is shown. Yet absence of such an explicit contractual provision may not always foreclose the possibility that a teacher has a "property" interest in re-employment. For example, the law of contracts in most, if not all, jurisdictions long has employed a process by which agreements, though not formalized in writing, may be "implied." 3 A. Corbin on Contracts §§ 561–572A (1960). Explicit contractual provisions may be supplemented by other agreements implied from "the promisor's words and conduct in the light of the surrounding circumstances." *Id.* at § 562. And, "the meaning of [the promisor's] words and acts is found by relating them to the usage of the past." *Ibid.*

A teacher, like the respondent, who has held his position for a number of years, might be able to show from the circumstances of this service—and from other relevant facts—that he has a legitimate claim of entitlement to job tenure. Just as this Court has found there to be a "common law of a particular industry or of a particular plant" that may supplement a collective-bargaining agreement, *Steelworkers v. Warrior & Gulf Co.*, 363 U.S. 574, 579, so there may be an unwritten "common law" in a particular university that certain employees shall have the equivalent of tenure. This is particularly likely in a college or university, like Odessa Junior College, that has no explicit tenure system even for senior members of its faculty, but that nonetheless may have created such a system in practice.[2] . . .

Id. at 601–02.

2. Procedural Protections for Substantive Rights. To what extent does the due process clause of the Constitution provide protection for public employees' job security under the Supreme Court's decisions in *Roth* and *Sindermann*? When are such protections triggered?

Roth and Sindermann each had one-year teaching contracts. From a doctrinal perspective, explain why the Court treated the two cases quite differently. Does this difference in treatment make sense from a practical point of view? Does it make any sense to provide procedural protections before discharge if an employee has no substantive right to continued employment?

In addition to his due process claim, Sindermann alleged that his discharge violated the First Amendment. During the 1968–69 academic year, he had been involved in public disagreements with the Board of Regents concerning efforts to change the status of the institution to a four-year college. He believed that his advocacy on the issue motivated the Board's decision not to offer him a teaching contract for the following year. Although the issue was not presented before the Supreme Court, Roth made a similar claim in the trial court, alleging that the University had decided not to renew his teaching contract in retaliation for his criticism of the administration. As we shall see in Chapter 8, *infra*, the First Amendment affords some protection to public employees by limiting government employers' ability to fire them because of their speech. Should the fact that both Roth and Sindermann alleged that their employers' actions violated their First Amendment rights be relevant to their claims that they were entitled to certain

---

[2] [n. 7] We do not now hold that the respondent has any such legitimate claim of entitlement to job tenure. For "property interests . . . are not created by the Constitution. Rather, they are created and their dimensions are defined by existing rules or understandings that stem from an independent source such as state law . . . ." *Board of Regents v. Roth, supra*, at 577. If it is the law of Texas that a teacher in the respondent's position has no contractual or other claim to job tenure, the respondent's claim would be defeated.

procedural rights? *See Board of Regents v. Roth*, 408 U.S. 564, 585 (1972) (Douglas, J., dissenting) ("Without a statement of the reasons for the discharge and an opportunity to rebut those reasons . . . there is no means short of a lawsuit to safeguard the right not to be discharged for the exercise of First Amendment guarantees."). *See also* Cynthia L. Estlund, *Free Speech and Due Process in the Workplace*, 71 IND. L.J. 101, 124–29 (1995) (arguing that due process rights are critical to protecting the freedom of speech of public employees).

3. **The Value of Process.** Justice Marshall's dissent in *Roth* suggests some of the reasons due process rights are important in our constitutional scheme: they protect against arbitrary government action, insure fairness in government decision-making, and avoid mistaken decisions. These concerns are obviously pressing when the government acts as sovereign—for example, to deprive an individual of liberty based on asserted criminal conduct. But are these concerns also relevant when the government acts *as an employer*? Are there any countervailing concerns about imposing due process requirements in the context of the public workplace? What about the private sector workplace—do notions of due process have any relevance in that setting? Or is the notion of due process meaningless in the context of at-will employment?

4. **What Process Is Due?** In a subsequent case, the United States Supreme Court considered the question of what procedures are required prior to terminating a public employee with job tenure rights. *Cleveland Board of Education v. Loudermill*, 470 U.S. 532 (1985). The plaintiff, James Loudermill, was employed by the Board of Education as a security guard, a civil service position. Under Ohio law, such an employee could be terminated only for cause, and could challenge a discharge by filing an administrative appeal after the fact. When Loudermill was fired for alleged dishonesty on his employment application, he filed suit alleging that the Ohio statute was unconstitutional in that it failed to provide any kind of a hearing prior to dismissal, thereby depriving him of property without due process. The Court first rejected the government's argument that public employees are limited to whatever procedures are provided by the state statute creating the substantive right to remain in their jobs absent good cause. The Court described as "the root requirement" of the Due Process Clause the necessity "that an individual be given an opportunity for a hearing *before* he is deprived of any significant property interest." *Id.* at 542, (quoting *Boddie v. Connecticut*, 401 U.S. 371, 379 (1971)) (emphasis in original). The Court then considered the competing interests at stake when a public employee faced the loss of a job:

> First, the significance of the private interest in retaining employment cannot be gainsaid. We have frequently recognized the severity of depriving a person of the means of livelihood. While a fired worker may find employment elsewhere, doing so will take some time and is likely to be burdened by the questionable circumstances under which he left his previous job.
>
> Second, some opportunity for the employee to present his side of the case is recurringly of obvious value in reaching an accurate decision. Dismissals for cause will often involve factual disputes. Even where the facts are clear, the appropriateness or necessity of the discharge may not

be; in such cases, the only meaningful opportunity to invoke the discretion of the decisionmaker is likely to be before the termination takes effect. . . .

The governmental interest in immediate termination does not outweigh these interests. [A]ffording the employee an opportunity to respond prior to termination would impose neither a significant administrative burden nor intolerable delays. Furthermore, the employer shares the employee's interest in avoiding disruption and erroneous decisions; and until the matter is settled, the employer would continue to receive the benefit of the employee's labors. . . . [I]n those situations where the employer perceives a significant hazard in keeping the employee on the job, it can avoid the problem by suspending with pay.

The foregoing considerations indicate that the pretermination "hearing," though necessary, need not be elaborate. We have pointed out that "[t]he formality and procedural requisites for the hearing can vary, depending upon the importance of the interests involved and the nature of the subsequent proceedings." . . . The only question is what steps were required before the termination took effect. . . . Here, the pretermination hearing need not definitively resolve the propriety of the discharge. It should be an initial check against mistaken decisions—essentially a determination of whether there are reasonable grounds to believe that the charges against the employee are true and support the proposed action.

The essential requirements of due process . . . are notice and an opportunity to respond. The opportunity to present reasons, either in person or in writing, why proposed action should not be taken is a fundamental due process requirement. The tenured public employee is entitled to oral or written notice of the charges against him, an explanation of the employer's evidence, and an opportunity to present his side of the story. To require more than this prior to termination would intrude to an unwarranted extent on the government's interest in quickly removing an unsatisfactory employee. . . .

Id. at 543–46.

3. The Contemporary Era

By the 1970s, workers in the private non-union workplace on the one hand, and those in the government and union sectors on the other, faced quite different situations in terms of their enforceable rights to job security. While the latter had various due process protections under the Constitution and civil service statutes or through the grievance arbitration machinery established through collective bargaining, the unorganized private sector employee had little legal protection against arbitrary discharge. In some ways, however, the actual employment patterns in the different sectors were not so distinct. Unionized workplaces were characterized by long-term career employment, promotion from within the firm, and a strong reliance on seniority to distribute benefits. These practices tended to spill over into the nonunion setting, such that the careers of unorganized employees often followed a similar pattern involving long-term investments in

unionized workplaces benefited unorganized EEs [handwritten]

training and expectations of loyalty on both sides of the employment relationship.

Employers who were already dealing with a portion of their workforce through collective bargaining, or alternatively, those who wished to discourage unionization, had strong incentives to adopt some of the same practices found in the organized workplace. In particular, many large firms adopted a form of "internal due process," putting into place procedures by which employees could challenge adverse employment actions, perhaps by going up the chain of command, or seeking resolution with the assistance of a separate human resources department. Ideas about rational personnel management spread with the growth in the number of human resources professionals, leading many employers to adopt specific policies directing line supervisors on matters such as performance evaluation, record-keeping, and how progressive discipline should be implemented.

why nonunion workpla internal procedur [handwritten margin note]

Eventually, the expectations generated by these practices, as well as the contrasting models provided by the unionized and public sector models, put pressure on the strict at-will regime of the common law. Beginning in the 1970s and 1980s, courts became increasingly willing to find that the presumption of at-will employment had been overcome in individual cases. Doing so, however, required courts to rethink what kind of a showing was necessary to rebut the at-will presumption, and, in particular, the traditional doctrines of mutuality and additional consideration.

As we saw in *Savage v. Spur Distributing Co.*, 228 S.W.2d 122 (Tenn. Ct. App. 1949), *supra*, the older cases held that a promise not to discharge without cause was not binding unless the employee was similarly bound. They also typically required that an employee prove that he had provided "additional consideration" beyond the services to be performed to support a promise by the employer not to discharge without cause. In the 1980s, however, many courts rejected these doctrines, opening the way for discharged employees to assert that an employer's express or implied promises not to discharge without cause were enforceable even if the employee remained free to quit and had not provided any consideration apart from his labor. For example, in upholding a discharged employee's breach of contract claim, the court in *Pine River State Bank v. Mettille*, 333 N.W.2d 622 (Minn. 1983), expressly rejected the employer's reliance on the doctrines of mutuality and additional consideration to avoid enforcement of its earlier assurances of job security. It reasoned:

> The requirement of additional consideration, like the at-will rule itself, is more a rule of construction than of substance, and it does not preclude the parties, if they make clear their intent to do so, from agreeing that the employment will not be terminable by the employer except pursuant to their agreement, even though no consideration other than services to be performed is expected by the employer or promised by the employee. . . .
> [N]one of our cases purport to hold that additional, independent consideration is the exclusive means for creating an enforceable job security provision in a contract of indefinite duration. . . . The consideration here for the job security provision is Mettille's continued performance despite his freedom to leave. As such, the job security provisions are enforceable.
> . . .

don't need add'l consideratio [handwritten margin note]

add'l independent consideration is not the exclusive means for enforceable job security [handwritten note]

[handwritten: mutuality is also unnecessary]

[Regarding defendant's argument that] job security provisions lack enforceability because mutuality of obligation is lacking. . . . The demand for mutuality of obligation, although appealing in its symmetry, is simply a species of the forbidden inquiry into the adequacy of consideration, an inquiry in which this court has, by and large, refused to engage. "If the requirement of consideration is met, there is no additional requirement of . . . equivalence in the values exchanged; or . . . 'mutuality of obligation.'" Restatement (Second) of Contracts § 79 (1981). We see no merit in the lack of mutuality argument. . . .

Id. at 629.

Even with the hurdles of mutuality and additional consideration removed, individual employees who wish to challenge their dismissals as a violation of their contractual rights must still come forward with some evidence to overcome the presumption that employment is at-will. In the remainder of this chapter, we consider the various ways in which unorganized private sector workers have established contractually enforceable rights to job security under contemporary doctrines.

B. OVERCOMING THE PRESUMPTION BY AGREEMENT

1. Written Contracts *[handwritten: — can set forth grounds for termination such as for cause]*

Even when the at-will rule was at its zenith, the presumption could be overcome by evidence that the parties had contracted for the employment to continue for a definite period of time, and a written contract for a fixed term remains the most straightforward way to overcome the at-will presumption. Once a written contract exists, the terms of employment are governed by the parties' intentions regarding job security, determined through the application of ordinary contract principles. When a fixed-term contract fails to address the grounds for termination, courts generally presume that the employee cannot be discharged during the term of the contract without cause. *See, e.g., Nelson Trabue, Inc. v. Professional Management-Automotive, Inc.*, 589 S.W.2d 661, 663 (Tenn. 1979) (contracts for a definite term may not be terminated before the end of the term, except for cause or by mutual agreement).

In other cases, the contract will set out the permissible grounds for termination, and in that situation, the terms of the agreement will govern. Disputes may nevertheless arise over whether the employee was dismissed "for cause" or not, either because the contract terms are themselves ambiguous or because the parties disagree about the facts—for example, whether the discharged employee actually engaged in wrongdoing which would justify discharge. The meaning of "cause" is discussed in greater detail in section C, below, but it is important to keep in mind that where a written contract exists, the definitions in the agreement will determine what constitutes "cause."

[handwritten: what defines cause in K]

Remedies for breach of a contract also follow basic contract principles. If an employee shows her termination breached the agreement, she is entitled to expectation damages—the amount of compensation she would have received if the contract had been fulfilled. The discharged employee is also required to mitigate damages, and therefore, she must search for another job and any subsequent earnings will reduce the amount of her damages.

Because the parties may believe that the usual measure of expectation damages over- or under-compensates the discharged employee, employment contracts sometimes provide for liquidated damages in case of early termination without cause. Alternatively, an employment contract may permit termination at any time, but require the employer to pay a fixed amount to the discharged employee in the form of a severance payment if the termination is without cause. In addition, written employment contracts sometimes specify a required notice period or procedure for terminating the contract—for example, requiring 90 days written notice by either side to end the employment.

[handwritten: expectation damages + security]

Very few published opinions deal with definite-term, written employment agreements, perhaps because relatively few employees, aside from high-level executives, have such contracts, and when disputes arise, they are likely to be resolved by settlement or arbitration. Aside from the unique, highly skilled employee, or those working for employers that operate on a fixed cycle, like schools, individual employees today are unlikely to have written contracts for a fixed period of time. When an employee does have such a contract, it is likely to deal with a wide variety of issues beyond job security, such as benefits, job responsibilities, post-employment competition, and arbitration of disputes.

Written contracts for a fixed term are clearly enforceable, but what about written contracts for an indefinite term that promise not to discharge without just cause? Although the traditional view was that any employment contract that was not for a definite term must be construed as at-will, most modern courts are willing to enforce indefinite-term contracts restricting the employer's power to terminate where the parties' intentions are clear. Thus, the Supreme Court of Nevada in *Shoen v. Amerco, Inc.*, 896 P.2d 469 (Nev. 1995), held a contract for permanent employment was enforceable based on a written contract that specifically stated that the parties intended to provide the plaintiff with lifetime employment.

[handwritten: written Ks for indefinite term] [handwritten: some say ok]

However, some courts persist in the traditional view that indefinite-term contracts are per se unenforceable, even when a promise of job security is included in a written contract. In *Main v. Skaggs Community Hospital*, 812 S.W.2d 185 (Mo. Ct. App. 1991), the plaintiff was hired pursuant to a written contract that provided that "either party may terminate this agreement, with just cause, by giving sixty days' written notice." The Missouri Court of Appeals found that because the contract "purports to grant plaintiff the right to perpetual employment by Hospital unless plaintiff's performance becomes deficient enough to constitute 'just cause' for firing him," it was "a contract imposing an obligation in perpetuity" which is disfavored by the law. *Id.* at 189. Because the plaintiff could not show that he had a contract for a definite term, the court upheld summary judgment for the employer.

[handwritten: some say not OK]

As discussed in section A.2., collective bargaining agreements typically contain provisions requiring an employer to have "just cause" to terminate an employee, thereby overcoming the at-will presumption for the workers covered by it. Although both collective bargaining agreements and individual employment contracts may restrict an employer's ability to discharge without cause, they tend to differ significantly in other ways. Individual contracts are most often written for executives, managers, professionals, and other highly skilled employees, while collective bargaining agreements typically cover rank-and-file production and service workers. In addition, Kenneth G. Dau-Schmidt and Timothy A. Haley report that individual employment contracts show far more variability than collective bargaining agreements, which tend to have standardized terms across employers. Kenneth G. Dau-Schmidt & Timothy A. Haley, *Governance of the Workplace: The Contemporary Regime of Individual Contract*, 28 COMP. LAB. L. & POL'Y J. 313, 321 (2007). While both types of contracts deal with salary and benefits, individual contracts tend to emphasize employers' concerns with flexibility (including employer rights of termination), protection of intellectual property and trade secrets, and preventing post-employment competition, while collectively bargained agreements are more focused on job security, seniority, and occupational health and safety issues. *Id.*

NOTES

1. **Remedies.** Consider a situation in which an executive is hired under an agreement that states,

> You will serve the Company on a full-time basis as a senior executive employee, and the company will employ you as such, for a period of three years commencing November 1, 2012 and ending October 31, 2015 unless you are terminated at an earlier date for good cause as defined by this Agreement. Your annual salary will be $150,000.

Suppose the employee is terminated on April 30, 2014 and the court determines that there was not good cause for the discharge. How much is the employee entitled to in damages?

Now suppose that the former employee found a new job and began working on November 1, 2014, earning an annual salary of $70,000 in his new job. Then how much would his damages be?

What if the employee was hired under an indefinite-term good cause contract? In those states which have held such a contract can be enforceable, what would be the measure of damages if an employee were discharged without cause? Because the contract was indefinite in length, does that mean that the employee fired without cause is entitled to receive lost wages for the duration of her working life? What contract principle would limit plaintiff's recovery? If you represented one of the parties to such a dispute, what evidence would you offer to establish or limit the amount of the plaintiff's damages?

2. **Employee Breach.** What if an employee working under a fixed-term contract leaves the job before the end of the term? Should the employer be able to sue the employee for damages? If the contract is silent on the issue, should the courts imply terms permitting the employee to quit under certain circumstances? What should those circumstances be? Although this type of case does not often arise, employers do occasionally sue employees who quit before the end of a fixed-term contract. *See, e.g., Equity Insurance Managers of Illinois v. McNichols,*

755 N.E.2d 75 (Ill. App. Ct. 2001) (affirming arbitration award of $91,000 against former employee who left for a better paying job prior to the end of a three-year contract); *Handicapped Children's Education Board of Sheboygan County v. Lukaszewski*, 332 N.W.2d 774 (Wis. 1983) (upholding award of damages against speech and language therapist who repudiated contract to provide services for upcoming school year).

2. Oral Contracts

The at-will presumption may be overcome by oral agreements regarding the terms of the employment relationship, as well as by written agreements. However, because the agreement between the parties is not memorialized, difficulties may arise in determining whether an oral agreement was reached and on what terms. Consider the following pair of cases decided by the Michigan Supreme Court about a decade apart:

Toussaint v. Blue Cross & Blue Shield of Mich., 292 N.W.2d 880 (Mich. 1980). Charles Toussaint was employed in a "middle management" position with Blue Cross for five years. He testified that he had inquired about job security when he was hired, and that he was told that he would be with the company "as long as I did my job." Walter Ebling, the plaintiff in a companion case, *Ebling v. Masco Corp.*, was told that "if he was 'doing the job' he would not be discharged." When they were fired, each sued his employer, alleging breach of contract. The court held that the oral statements were sufficient for a jury to find the existence of contracts for employment terminable only for cause:

> When a prospective employee inquires about job security and the employer agrees that the employee shall be employed as long as he does the job, a fair construction is that the employer has agreed to give up his right to discharge at will without assigning cause and may discharge only for cause. . . .

> Where the employment is for a definite term—a year, 5 years, 10 years—it is implied, if not expressed, that the employee can be discharged only for good cause and collective bargaining agreements often provide that discharge shall only be for good or just cause. There is, thus, no public policy against providing job security or prohibiting an employer from agreeing not to discharge except for good or just cause. That being the case, we can see no reason why such a provision in a contract having no definite term of employment with a single employee should necessarily be unenforceable and regarded, in effect, as against public policy and beyond the power of the employer to contract.

> Toussaint and Ebling were hired for responsible positions. They negotiated specifically regarding job security with the persons who interviewed and hired them. If Blue Cross or Masco had desired, they could have established a company policy of requiring prospective employees to acknowledge that they served at the will or the pleasure of the company and, thus, have avoided the misunderstandings that generated this litigation.

Id. at 890–91.

Rowe v. Montgomery Ward & Co., 473 N.W.2d 268 (Mich. 1991). When Mary Rowe was hired for a sales position at Montgomery Ward, she was told that she would have a job as long as she achieved her sales quota. Eight years later, she was fired after she left the store for a personal emergency without permission from her supervisor. The court looked to the facts in *Toussaint* to guide its evaluation of the oral statement made to Rowe:

> Prior to being hired, Toussaint had several interviews with the cotreasurer of the company, and the position he sought was assistant to the treasurer. Toussaint claimed he was promised he would not be terminated " 'as long as I did my job.' " Further, upon inquiring about job security, he was handed a manual which expressly confirmed that he could be released " 'for just cause only.' "

> Ebling also had several interviews prior to being hired. He was interviewed by the executive vice president and the general manager about a marketing director position. He expressed concerns specifically about job security to the vice president. In particular, he voiced concerns about a personality conflict with his supervisor. Subsequent to negotiations, the vice president agreed not to terminate Ebling as long as he was doing his job.

> In the instant case, plaintiff was interviewed for the job by Vern Harryman, sales manager of the appliance department. Although defendant had been advertising to attract salespersons, plaintiff told Harryman " 'Well, I hadn't seen the ad, I just kind of stumbled in there. . . . ' " With regard to representations pertinent to job security, plaintiff testified that "[h]e said that he needed somebody to sell sewing machines and vacuum cleaners and that this job would involve selling, *and as long as I sold, I would have a job at Montgomery Ward.*" (Emphasis added.)

> Contrasting the surrounding circumstances of this case with *Toussaint* and *Ebling* to determine if there was mutual assent on a provision for permanent employment, or if the statements were noncontractual expressions of "optimistic hope of a long relationship," we find the oral statements insufficient to rise to the level of an agreement providing termination only for just cause. Although the "as long as" statement bears resemblance to remarks made in *Toussaint*, we find objective evidence lacking to permit a reasonable juror to find that a reasonable promisee would interpret Harryman's statements and actions as a promise of termination only for cause implied in fact.

> Unlike *Toussaint*, plaintiff did not engage in preemployment negotiations regarding security. She simply "stumbled" into the store one day and had one interview before being hired. Nor is there any testimony suggesting that plaintiff inquired about job security. Therefore, Harryman's statements could not have been addressed to any inquiry regarding job security. In short, no objective evidence exists that their minds met on the

subject of continued employment. In addition, we note that in *Toussaint*, the plaintiffs were applying for singular, executive job positions. That the positions were unique supports the finding that the terms were specifically negotiated. Here, plaintiff was one of many departmental salespersons. The fact that plaintiff applied for one of several identical positions militates against the likelihood that the contract terms were negotiable and suggests that company policy was more likely to govern. . . .

Thus, we conclude that the oral statements of job security must be clear and unequivocal to overcome the presumption of employment at will. . . .

Harryman's words were couched in general terms, more akin to stating a policy as opposed to offering an express contract. His words were vague when discussing termination (e.g., "*generally*, as long as *they* generated sales and were honest . . . *they* had a job at Wards;" "*about* the only way that you could be terminated would be if you failed to make your draw. . . . "). (Emphasis added.) We find that these words do not clearly indicate an intent to form a contract for permanent employment. Rather, the context of Harryman's comments suggests that they were merely intended to emphasize the number one priority of plaintiff's job—sales. . . .

Id. at 273–75.

NOTES

1.   Establishing Oral Contracts for Job Security. In theory, contracts requiring just cause or good cause for termination can be created by oral agreement as well as written agreement. In practice, however, claims based on purely oral promises face substantial hurdles. Although the Michigan Supreme Court's opinion in *Toussaint* suggested that such oral contracts would be enforced like any other contract, it retreated significantly from that expansive holding in *Rowe*.

One of the difficulties with enforcing oral contracts lies in distinguishing between "puffery and promise," especially in the context of the hiring process in which mutual wooing between the parties occurs. As the court in *Broussard v. CACI, Inc.—Federal*, 780 F.2d 162 (1st Cir. 1986), describes:

> Employment negotiations resulting in employment are by definition conducted in an atmosphere of optimism and mutual hope. The air is redolent with expectation of duration on the part of the employee and of satisfactory performance by the employer. But to equate general expressions of hope for a long relationship with an express promise to discharge only for good cause would effectively eliminate [the at-will rule].

Id. at 163.

Another problem with oral contracts is the difficulty of determining exactly what was said long after the fact. For this reason, courts often look to the circumstances surrounding the hiring for evidence that the parties intended job security to be part of the bargain. For example, in *Ohanian v. Avis Rent-a-Car System, Inc.*, 779 F.2d 101 (2d Cir. 1985), the court considered a claim of breach of an oral promise of lifetime employment. The plaintiff in that case, Robert Ohanian, was recruited from the company's Western Region to become Vice President of Sales for the Northeast Region. The Western Region, headed by Ohanian, "stood out as the one region that was growing and profitable." *Id.* at 103. By contrast, the Northeast Region was "dying," and the company sought new leadership for that division. Ohanian was very reluctant to move to the Northeast for both personal and professional reasons, but finally agreed after a series of phone calls from upper management, which included assurances that "his future was secure" with the company. *Id.* at 104. About a year and a half later, he was fired.

Ohanian sued Avis, alleging breach of an oral contract for lifetime employment. After trial, a jury awarded him more than $300,000 for lost wages and pension benefits. On appeal, the defendant argued that the jury verdict for the plaintiff should be reversed, citing *Brown v. Safeway Stores, Inc.*, 190 F. Supp. 295 (E.D.N.Y. 1960), a case in which the court found evidence of an oral promise of lifetime employment insufficient as a matter of law. The court in *Ohanian* distinguished the two cases:

> In [*Brown*], the claimed assurances were made in several ways including meetings of a group of employees—the purpose of which was not to discuss length of employment—or during casual conversation. The conversations were not conducted in an atmosphere, as here, of critical one-on-one negotiations regarding the terms of future employment. . . . [I]n the instant case the evidence was ample to permit the jury to decide whether statements made to Ohanian by defendant were more than casual comments or mere pep talks delivered by management to a group of employees. All of the surrounding circumstances . . . were sufficient for the jury in fact to find that there was a promise of lifetime employment to a "star" employee who, it was hoped, would revive a "dying" division of defendant corporation.

Ohanian, 779 F.2d at 109.

Given the approach taken by the courts in *Rowe* and *Ohanian*, what factors would you look for in order to determine whether an employee has an enforceable contract for job security? What types of employees are most likely to succeed in proving the existence of such claims? What can less skilled employees, who are unlikely to engage in extensive pre-hire negotiations, do to try to protect their job security?

2. Implied-in-Fact Contracts. Because of the difficulty in establishing the precise terms of an oral agreement, some courts have viewed oral promises not as creating contracts by themselves, but as one aspect of a long-term relationship that, together with other factors, may implicitly give rise to enforceable expectations of job security. In *Pugh v. See's Candies, Inc.*, 116 Cal. App. 3d 311 (1981) the California Court of Appeals held that the entire course of dealing between the employer and employee, including oral assurances of job security, could give rise to an implied-in-fact promise that the plaintiff would not be discharged without cause. The plaintiff, Wayne Pugh, had worked his way up over a 32-year career at See's Candies from dishwasher to a position as vice-president and member of the board of directors. Pugh had received repeated assurances that his job was secure as long as he did a good job. He received regular raises and bonuses and his work performance had never been criticized, nor had he ever received disciplinary warnings. The court found that a jury could find the existence of an implied promise not to discharge without cause based on evidence of "the duration of appellant's employment, the commendations and promotions he received, the apparent lack of any direct criticism of his work, the assurances he was given, and the employer's acknowledged policies." *Id.* at 927.

The California Supreme Court endorsed the holding of *Pugh*, explaining that "[i]n the employment context, factors apart from consideration and express terms may be used to ascertain the existence and content of an employment agreement." *Foley v. Interactive Data Corp.*, 765 P.2d 373, 387 (Cal. 1988). It identified a number of factors relevant to finding an implied-in-fact contract, including "the personnel policies or practices of the employer, the employee's longevity of service, actions or communications by the employer reflecting assurances of continued employment, and the practices of the industry in which the employee is engaged." *Id.*

In a subsequent case, *Guz v. Bechtel National, Inc.*, 8 P.3d 1089 (Cal. 2000), the California Supreme Court emphasized that the purpose of the implied-in-fact contract theory was to enforce the *actual* understanding of the parties. The court reaffirmed that "the totality of the circumstances" should be examined "to determine whether the parties' conduct . . . gave rise to an implied-in-fact contract limiting the employer's termination rights." *Id.* at 1101. However, it also noted that its decision in *Foley* "did not suggest . . . that every vague combination of *Foley* factors, shaken together in a bag, necessarily allows a finding that the employee had a right to be discharged only for good cause, as determined in court." *Id.* Rather the focus of the inquiry should be on the *particular* terms and conditions of employment impliedly agreed to by the parties. And if there was evidence the parties had expressly agreed to at-will employment, that agreement would negate any argument that an implied agreement to the contrary existed.

Although a few states have followed *Pugh* or adopted similar analyses, *see, e.g., Kestenbaum v. Pennzoil Co.*, 766 P.2d 280, 286 (N.M. 1988); *Berube v. Fashion Centre, Ltd.*, 771 P.2d 1033, 1044–45 (Utah 1989), the case has also been criticized as overly vague and essentially undermining employment-at-will. *See, e.g., Calleon v. Miyagi*, 876 P.2d 1278 (Haw. 1994).

3. Longevity of Service. According to the *Pugh* court, one of the factors relevant to determining whether an implied contract exists is the longevity of the plaintiff's employment. Why should longevity matter? Does the 32-year employee have a stronger claim to his job than the two-year employee? If so, why? Should longevity of employment alone be enough to support an implied contract claim?

The California Supreme Court considered this question in *Guz*:

> [A]n employee's *mere* passage of time in the employer's service, even where marked with tangible indicia that the employer approves the employee's work, cannot *alone* form an implied-in-fact contract that the employee is no longer at will. Absent other evidence of the employer's intent, longevity, raises and promotions are their own rewards for the employee's continuing valued service; they do not, *in and of themselves*, additionally constitute a contractual guarantee of future employment

> security. A rule granting such contract rights on the basis of successful longevity alone would discourage the retention and promotion of employees.
>
> On the other hand, long and successful service is not necessarily irrelevant to the existence of such a contract. Over the period of an employee's tenure, the employer can certainly communicate, by its written and unwritten policies and practices, or by informal assurances, that seniority and longevity *do* create rights against termination at will. The issue is whether the employer's words or conduct, on which an employee reasonably relied, gave rise to that *specific* understanding.

Guz, 8 P.3d at 1104–05. The court's approach in *Guz* is based on its understanding of the employment relationship as "fundamentally contractual." *Id.* at 1105. On this view, the length of employment is relevant because it shows whether there has been "sufficient time for *conduct to occur* on which a trier of fact could find the existence of an implied contract," *id.* at 1105 (citing *Foley*, 47 Cal. 3d 654, 681), not because an employee's long years of service themselves give rise to any right to job security.

Is there any other reason to take longevity into account in determining whether an employee has rights to individual job security?

Paul Weiler argues that for the career employee, involuntary termination is particularly significant. He points out that many firms have wage structures that pay employees more money the longer they have worked there, such that compensation rewards loyalty, rather than reflecting a market valuation of the worker's productivity. In addition, a variety of fringe benefits such as vacation pay and pension benefits, are linked to the number of years a worker has been employed by the firm. Seniority also may provide opportunities for advancement, as well as protection against economic layoff. Together, these policies create "an elaborate set of financial incentives for employees to stay and penalties if they quit." PAUL C. WEILER, GOVERNING THE WORKPLACE 66 (1990). Because career employment is often structured to reward longevity, Weiler argues that for the long-term employee,

> [A] new job is not fungible with an old job even if the jobs are virtually the same in type, pay, and conditions. An employee who has worked his way up the seniority ladder with one firm and now enjoys all the perquisites that long service provides loses this major advantage when he leaves his current job. The loss cannot be repaired even if he were to find an otherwise identical job the very next day, because in the new position he would have to begin at or near the bottom of the seniority ladder, with all the disadvantages that entails. . . .
>
> New employees come to work under a regime in which they initially earn less in pay and benefits than they produce, and they enjoy less favorable jobs, shifts, and security than their senior fellow workers. This system has been designed by the firm to induce workers to remain in its employ, because the employees realize that eventually they will reap the benefits of the system when they have put in sufficient time under it. . . . If an employer suddenly exercises its unilateral prerogative to terminate that contract when the employee has obtained more senior status (and, by the

way, has thereby become more expensive), the employee is deprived of what he expected would be the return on his bargain with the firm: he suffers the irreversible loss of his investment of a significant part of his working life making his way up the ladder in this job rather than somewhere else. . . .

Id. at 66–67.

4. Statute of Frauds. Another hurdle confronting discharged employees who wish to rely on oral promises of job security is the statute of frauds. Generally, the statute of frauds bars enforcement of oral contracts that are not capable of performance within a year. However, many states interpret the statute of frauds narrowly, such that it bars only those contracts that could not possibly have been completed within a year, even when performance in fact continues well beyond a year. In the context of employment contracts, many courts take the position that indefinite-term just-cause contracts are not barred by the statute of frauds because performance *could* be completed within a year, if, for example, the employment ended due to the death, retirement or voluntary departure of the employee, or because of a layoff or discharge for cause. *See, e.g., Nutt v. Knutson*, 795 P.2d 30 (Kan. 1989); *Foley v. Interactive Data Corp.*, 765 P.2d 373 (Cal. 1988); *Kestenbaum v. Pennzoil C/o.*, 766 P.2d 280 (N.M. 1988). In other states, the rule is strictly enforced, such that oral contracts of employment for longer than one year, including indefinite-term contracts, are unenforceable. *See, e.g., McInerney v. Charter Golf, Inc.*, 680 N.E.2d 1347 (Ill. 1997); *Graham v. Central Fidelity Bank*, 428 S.E.2d 916 (Va. 1993).

3.　Implied Agreements

In addition to relying on express promises, whether written or oral, employees have argued that employers' written policies may also create contractual rights to job security. In these cases, individually negotiated agreements are absent; nevertheless, courts have sometimes been willing to recognize enforceable contract rights for a group of employees based on language in a personnel manual or employee handbook. This section explores the conditions under which courts have found that employer policies create enforceable promises not to discharge at will.

WOOLLEY v. HOFFMANN-LA ROCHE, INC.
Supreme Court of New Jersey
491 A.2d 1257 (1985)

Wilentz, C.J.

. . . Plaintiff, Richard Woolley, was hired by defendant, Hoffmann-La Roche, Inc., in October 1969, as an Engineering Section Head in defendant's Central Engineering Department at Nutley. There was no written employment contract between plaintiff and defendant. Plaintiff began work in mid-November 1969. Some time in December, plaintiff received and read the personnel manual on which his claims are based.

In 1976, plaintiff was promoted, and in January 1977 he was promoted again, this latter time to Group Leader for the Civil Engineering, the Piping Design, the Plant

Layout, and the Standards and Systems Sections. In March 1978, plaintiff was directed to write a report to his supervisors about piping problems in one of defendant's buildings in Nutley. This report was written and submitted to plaintiff's immediate supervisor on April 5, 1978. On May 3, 1978, stating that the General Manager of defendant's Corporate Engineering Department had lost confidence in him, plaintiff's supervisors requested his resignation. Following this, by letter dated May 22, 1978, plaintiff was formally asked for his resignation, to be effective July 15, 1978.

Plaintiff refused to resign. Two weeks later defendant again requested plaintiff's resignation, and told him he would be fired if he did not resign. Plaintiff again declined, and he was fired in July.

Plaintiff filed a complaint alleging breach of contract. . . . The gist of plaintiff's breach of contract claim is that the express and implied promises in defendant's employment manual created a contract under which he could not be fired at will, but rather only for cause, and then only after the procedures outlined in the manual were followed. Plaintiff contends that he was not dismissed for good cause, and that his firing was a breach of contract.

Defendant's motion for summary judgment was granted by the trial court, which held that the employment manual was not contractually binding on defendant, thus allowing defendant to terminate plaintiff's employment at will.[3] The Appellate Division affirmed. . . .

What is before us in this case is not a special contract with a particular employee, but a general agreement covering all employees. There is no reason to treat such a document with hostility.

The trial court viewed the manual as an attempt by Hoffmann-La Roche to avoid a collective bargaining agreement.[4] Implicit is the thought that while the employer viewed a collective bargaining agreement as an intrusion on management preroga-

---

[3] [n. 2] . . . It may be of some help to point out some of the manual's general provisions here. It is entitled "Hoffmann-La Roche, Inc. Personnel Policy Manual" and at the bottom of the face page is the notation "issued to: [and then in handwriting] Richard Woolley 12/1/69." The portions of the manual submitted to us consist of eight pages. It describes the employees "covered" by the manual ("all employees of Hoffmann-La Roche"), the manual's purpose ("a practical operating tool in the equitable and efficient administration of our employee relations program"); five of the eight pages are devoted to "termination." In addition to setting forth the purpose and policy of the termination section, it defines "the types of termination" as "layoff," "discharge due to performance," "discharge, disciplinary," "retirement" and "resignation." As one might expect, layoff is a termination caused by lack of work, retirement a termination caused by age, resignation a termination on the initiative of the employee, and discharge due to performance and discharge, disciplinary, are both terminations for cause. There is no category set forth for discharge without cause. The termination section includes "Guidelines for discharge due to performance," consisting of a fairly detailed procedure to be used before an employee may be fired for cause. Preceding these definitions of the five categories of termination is a section on "Policy," the first sentence of which provides: "It is the policy of Hoffmann-La Roche to retain to the extent consistent with company requirements, the services of all employees who perform their duties efficiently and effectively."

[4] [n. 6] The trial court, after noting that if Hoffmann-La Roche had been unionized, Woolley would not be litigating the question of whether the employer had to have good cause to fire him, said "[T]here is no question in my mind that Hoffmann-La Roche offered these good benefits to their employees to steer them away from this kind of specific collective bargaining contract. . . . "

tives, it recognized, in addition to the advantages of an employment manual to both sides, that unless this kind of company manual were given to the workforce, collective bargaining, and the agreements that result from collective bargaining, would more likely take place.

A policy manual that provides for job security grants an important, fundamental protection for workers. If such a commitment is indeed made, obviously an employer should be required to honor it. When such a document, purporting to give job security, is distributed by the employer to a workforce, substantial injustice may result if that promise is broken. . . .

Given the facts before us and the common law of contracts interpreted in the light of sound policy applicable to this modern setting, we conclude that the termination clauses of this company's Personnel Policy Manual, including the procedure required before termination occurs, could be found to be contractually enforceable. Furthermore, we conclude that when an employer of a substantial number of employees circulates a manual that, when fairly read, provides that certain benefits are an incident of the employment (including, especially, job security provisions), the judiciary, instead of "grudgingly" conceding the enforceability of those provisions, should construe them in accordance with the reasonable expectations of the employees.

The employer's contention here is that the distribution of the manual was simply an expression of the company's "philosophy" and therefore free of any possible contractual consequences. The former employee claims it could reasonably be read as an explicit statement of company policies intended to be followed by the company in the same manner as if they were expressed in an agreement signed by both employer and employees. From the analysis that follows we conclude that a jury, properly instructed, could find, in strict contract terms, that the manual constituted an offer; put differently, it could find that this portion of the manual (concerning job security) set forth terms and conditions of employment.

In determining the manual's meaning and effect, we must consider the probable context in which it was disseminated and the environment surrounding its continued existence. The manual, though apparently not distributed to all employees ("in general, distribution will be provided to supervisory personnel . . . "), covers all of them. Its terms are of such importance to all employees that in the absence of contradicting evidence, it would seem clear that it was intended by Hoffmann-La Roche that all employees be advised of the benefits it confers.

We take judicial notice of the fact that Hoffmann-La Roche is a substantial company with many employees in New Jersey. The record permits the conclusion that the policy manual represents the most reliable statement of the terms of their employment. At oral argument counsel conceded that it is rare for any employee, except one on the medical staff, to have a special contract. Without minimizing the importance of its specific provisions, the context of the manual's preparation and distribution is, to us, the most persuasive proof that it would be almost inevitable for an employee to regard it as a binding commitment, legally enforceable, concerning the terms and conditions of his employment. Having been employed, like hundreds of his co-employees, without any individual employment contract, by an employer whose good reputation made it so attractive, the employee is given this one document that purports to set forth the terms and conditions of his employment, a document obviously carefully prepared by the company with all of the appearances of corporate legitimacy that one could imagine. If there were any doubt about it (and there would be none in the mind of most employees), the name of the manual dispels it, for it is nothing short of the official *policy* of the company, it is the Personnel *Policy* Manual. As every employee knows, when superiors tell you "it's company policy," they mean business.

The mere fact of the manual's distribution suggests its importance. Its changeability—the uncontroverted ability of management to change its terms—is argued as supporting its non-binding quality, but one might as easily conclude that, given its importance, the employer wanted to keep it up to date, especially to make certain, given this employer's good reputation in labor relations, that the benefits conferred were sufficiently competitive with those available from other employers, including benefits found in collective bargaining agreements. The record suggests that the changes actually made almost always favored the employees.

Given that background, then, unless the language contained in the manual were such that no one could reasonably have thought it was intended to create legally binding obligations, the termination provisions of the policy manual would have to be regarded as an obligation undertaken by the employer. It will not do now for the company to say it did not mean the things it said in its manual to be binding. Our courts will not allow an employer to offer attractive inducements and benefits to the workforce and then withdraw them when it chooses, no matter how sincere its belief that they are not enforceable.

Whatever else the manual may deal with (as noted above, we do not have the entire manual before us), one of its major provisions deals with the single most important objective of the workforce: job security. The reasons for giving such provisions binding force are particularly persuasive. Wages, promotions, conditions of work, hours of work, all of those take second place to job security, for without that all other benefits are vulnerable. . . . Job security is the assurance that one's livelihood, one's family's future, will not be destroyed arbitrarily; it can be cut off only "for good cause," fairly determined. Hoffmann-La Roche's commitment here was to what working men and women regard as their most basic advance. It was a commitment that gave workers protection against arbitrary termination.

Many of these workers undoubtedly know little about contracts, and many probably would be unable to analyze the language and terms of the manual. Whatever Hoffmann-La Roche may have intended, that which was read by its employees was a promise not to fire them except for cause.

Under all of these circumstances, therefore, it would be most unrealistic to construe this manual and determine its enforceability as if it were the same as a lifetime contract with but one employee. . . .[5]

---

[5] [n. 8] The contract arising from the manual is of indefinite duration. It is *not* the extraordinary "lifetime" contract. . . . For example, a contract arising from a manual ordinarily may be terminated when the employee's performance is inadequate; when business circumstances require a general reduction in the employment force, the positions eliminated including that of plaintiff; when those same circumstances require the elimination of employees performing a certain function, for instance, for

[Having concluded that a jury could find the Personnel Policy Manual to constitute an offer, we deal with what most cases deem the major obstacle to construction of the terms as constituting a binding agreement, namely, the requirement under contract law that consideration must be given in exchange for the employer's offer in order to convert that offer into a binding agreement./The cases on this subject deal with such issues as whether there was a promise in return for the employer's promise (the offer contained in the manual constituting, in effect, a promise), or whether there was some benefit or detriment bargained for and in fact conferred or suffered, sufficient to create a unilateral contract; whether the action or inaction, the benefit or the detriment, was done or not done in reliance on the employer's offer or promise; whether the alleged agreement was so lacking in "mutuality" as to be insufficient for contractual purposes—in other words, whether the fundamental requirements of a contract have been met.

considera [margin]

mutualit [margin]

We conclude that these job security provisions contained in a personnel policy manual widely distributed among a large workforce are supported by consideration and may therefore be enforced as a binding commitment of the employer.

yes consideration [margin]

In order for an offer in the form of a promise to become enforceable, it must be accepted. Acceptance will depend on what the promisor bargained for: he may have bargained for a return promise that, if given, would result in a bilateral contract, both promises becoming enforceable. Or he may have bargained for some action or nonaction that, if given or withheld, would render his promise enforceable as a unilateral contract. In most of the cases involving an employer's personnel policy manual, the document is prepared without any negotiations and is voluntarily distributed to the workforce by the employer. It seeks no return promise from the employees. It is reasonable to interpret it as seeking continued work from the employees, who, in most cases, are free to quit since they are almost always employees at will, not simply in the sense that the employer can fire them without cause, but in the sense that they can quit without breaching any obligation. Thus analyzed, the manual is an offer that seeks the formation of a unilateral contract—the employees' bargained-for action needed to make the offer binding being their continued work when they have no obligation to continue.

acceptan [margin]

The unilateral contract analysis is perfectly adequate for that employee who was aware of the manual and who continued to work intending that continuation to be the action in exchange for the employer's promise; it is even more helpful in support of that conclusion if, but for the employer's policy manual, the employee would have quit.

unilatera k [margin]

[Rather than requiring proof of reliance, the court held that reliance was to be

---

technological reasons, and plaintiff performed such functions; when business conditions require a general reduction in salary, a reduction that brings plaintiff's pay below that which he is willing to accept; or when any change, including the cessation of business, requires the elimination of plaintiff's position, an elimination made in good faith in pursuit of legitimate business objectives: all of these terminations, long before the expiration of "lifetime" employment, are ordinarily contemplated in a contract arising from a manual, although the list does not purport to be exhaustive. The essential difference is that the "lifetime" contract purports to protect the employment against any termination; the contract arising from the manual protects the employment only from arbitrary termination.

presumed under the circumstances.][6]

The lack of definiteness concerning the other terms of employment—its duration, wages, precise service to be rendered, hours of work, etc., does not prevent enforcement of a job security provision. The lack of terms (if the complete manual is similarly lacking) can cause problems of interpretation about these other aspects of employment, but not to the point of making the job security term unenforceable. Realistically, the objection has force only when the agreement is regarded as a special one between the employer and an individual employee. There it might be difficult to determine whether there was good cause for termination if one could not determine what it was that the employee was expected to do. That difficulty is one factor that suggests the employer did not intend a lifetime contract with one employee. Here the question of good cause is made considerably easier to deal with in view of the fact that the agreement applies to the entire workforce, and the workforce itself is rather large. Even-handedness and equality of treatment will make the issue in most cases far from complex; the fact that in some cases the "for cause" provision may be difficult to interpret and enforce should not deprive employees in other cases from taking advantage of it. If there is a problem arising from indefiniteness, in any event, it is one caused by the employer. . . .

Defendant expresses some concern that our interpretation will encourage lawsuits by disgruntled employees. As we view it, however, if the employer has in fact agreed to provide job security, plaintiffs in lawsuits to enforce that agreement should not be regarded as disgruntled employees, but rather as employees pursuing what is rightfully theirs. The solution is not deprivation of the employees' claim, but enforcement of the employer's agreement. The defendant further contends that its future plans and proposed projects are premised on continuance of the at-will employment status of its workforce. We find this argument unpersuasive. There are many companies whose employees have job security who are quite able to plan their future and implement those plans. If, however, the at-will employment status of the workforce was so important, the employer should not have circulated a document so likely to lead employees into believing they had job security. . . .

Our opinion need not make employers reluctant to prepare and distribute company policy manuals. Such manuals can be very helpful tools in labor relations,

---

[6] [n. 10] If reliance is not presumed, a strict contractual analysis might protect the rights of some employees and not others. For example, where an employee is not even aware of the existence of the manual, his or her continued work would not ordinarily be thought of as the bargained-for detriment. *See* S. Williston, *Contracts* §§ 101, 102A (1957). *But see* A. Corbin, *Contracts* § 59 (1963) (suggesting that knowledge of an offer is not a prerequisite to acceptance). Similarly, if it is quite clear that those employees who knew of the offer knew that it sought their continued work, but nevertheless continued without the slightest intention of putting forth that action as consideration for the employer's promise, it might not be sufficient to form a contract. *See* S. Williston, *Contracts* § 67 (1957). *But see Pine River, supra*, 333 N.W.2d at 627, 630. In this case there is no proof that plaintiff, Woolley, relied on the policy manual in continuing his work. Furthermore, as the Appellate Division correctly noted, Woolley did "not bargain for" the employer's promise. The implication of the presumption of reliance is that the manual's job security provisions became binding the moment the manual was distributed. Anyone employed before or after became one of the beneficiaries of those provisions of the manual. . . . [E]mployees neither had to read it, know of its existence, or rely on it to benefit from its provisions any more than employees in a plant that is unionized have to read or rely on a collective-bargaining agreement in order to obtain its benefits.

helpful both to employer and employees, and we would regret it if the consequence of this decision were that the constructive aspects of these manuals were in any way diminished. We do not believe that they will, or at least we certainly do not believe that that constructive aspect *should* be diminished as a result of this opinion.

All that this opinion requires of an employer is that it be fair. It would be unfair to allow an employer to distribute a policy manual that makes the workforce believe that certain promises have been made and then to allow the employer to renege on those promises. What is sought here is basic honesty: if the employer, for whatever reason, does not want the manual to be capable of being construed by the court as a binding contract, there are simple ways to attain that goal. All that need be done is the inclusion in a very prominent position of an appropriate statement that there is no promise of any kind by the employer contained in the manual; that regardless of what the manual says or provides, the employer promises nothing and remains free to change wages and all other working conditions without having to consult anyone and without anyone's agreement; and that the employer continues to have the absolute power to fire anyone with or without good cause.

Reversed and remanded for trial.

NOTES

1.　**Doctrine and Policy.** *Woolley* is one of the leading cases holding that an employer's policy manual could give rise to binding contractual obligations.

The decision of the New Jersey Supreme Court in *Woolley* operates on two levels: formal contract doctrine and policy. How does the court argue that the promises contained in Hoffman-La Roche's employment manual should be enforceable as a matter of contract law? How well does the unilateral contract analysis fit the facts of Woolley's situation? Are there any problems with this approach? Does the fact that the manual covered many employees rather than just Woolley help the court's contract analysis?

What are the policy concerns that motivate the *Woolley* decision? Why do employers issue employment handbooks? If the employer did not intend such policies to be enforceable, why should the courts enforce them?

The court suggests that a desire to avoid unionization motivated the employer in *Woolley*. Why would the existence of a handbook affect the likelihood of unionization? Should the outcome of the case be different if there were no prospect of unionization at all among Hoffman-La Roche's employees? What should the position of unions be regarding the enforceability of handbook promises?

2.　**Alternative Theories.** A majority of states have held that personnel manuals can give rise to binding obligations, although they vary as to the specific factors necessary to make handbook promises enforceable. In addition, courts rely on different theories to explain why employee handbooks may create binding contracts. Perhaps most common is the approach taken by the New Jersey Supreme Court in *Woolley*—that employee handbooks give rise to unilateral contracts, thus making negotiation over terms and an exchange of promises unnecessary. A few states have also relied on a promissory estoppel theory. For example, in *Continen-*

tal Airlines, Inc. v. Keenan, 731 P.2d 708 (Colo. 1987), the Colorado Supreme Court held that the termination procedures contained in a personnel manual are enforceable if the employee can demonstrate that the employer should reasonably have expected the employee to consider the manual a commitment by the employer to follow the procedure, that the employee reasonably relied on that commitment, and that injustice can only be avoided by enforcing those procedures.

Other courts, however, rely on basic fairness arguments rather than formal contract theory to justify holding employers to the promises contained in employee handbooks. The classic expression of this argument is found in the Michigan Supreme Court's opinion in *Toussaint v. Blue Cross & Blue Shield of Mich.*, 292 N.W.2d 880 (Mich. 1980):

> While an employer need not establish personnel policies or practices, where an employer chooses to establish such policies and practices and makes them known to its employees, the employment relationship is presumably enhanced. The employer secures an orderly, cooperative and loyal work force, and the employee the peace of mind associated with job security and the conviction that he will be treated fairly. No pre-employment negotiations need take place and the parties' minds need not meet on the subject; nor does it matter that the employee knows nothing of the particulars of the employer's policies and practices or that the employer may change them unilaterally. It is enough that the employer chooses, presumably in its own interest, to create an environment in which the employee believes that, whatever the personnel policies and practices, they are established and official at any given time, purport to be fair, and are applied consistently and uniformly to each employee. The employer has then created a situation "instinct with an obligation."

Id. at 892.

Such an approach emphasizes the benefit to employers and the reasonable expectations of employees, rather than trying to conform the cases to technical contract doctrine. On the other hand, a handful of states refuse to consider promises contained in employee handbooks binding at all, insisting upon the traditional contract elements of offer, acceptance, and bargained-for consideration. *See, e.g., Johnson v. McDonnell Douglas Corp.*, 745 S.W.2d 661 (Mo. 1988) (holding that handbook was "merely an informational statement of McDonnell's self-imposed policies").

3. Reliance. The court in *Woolley* held that it was unnecessary for the plaintiff to prove that he had knowledge of the particular promises that allegedly gave rise to the employer's contractual obligations. What justifications exist for presuming reliance on employer statements in a handbook, whether or not the employee was even aware of them?

Other courts insist that the employee actually rely on the provisions in an employment manual before they will find them to be contractually binding. *See, e.g., DePetris v. Union Settlement Ass'n*, 657 N.E.2d 269 (N.Y. 1995) (holding that employee must show that he was aware of the written policy limiting employer's right of discharge and that he detrimentally relied on that policy in accepting the employment); *Bulman v. Safeway, Inc.*, 27 P.3d 1172 (Wash. 2001) (in order to enforce handbook promises, employee must show justifiable reliance on these promises).

4.   **Terms of Agreement.** Although courts in many states are willing to enforce promises contained in employee handbooks, whether they will do so in a particular case depends upon the actual language of the handbook or policy. For example, the Supreme Court of Idaho wrote:

> Statements made and policies promulgated by the employer, whether in an employment manual or otherwise, may give rise to such an implied-in-fact agreement. However, such statements must be more than vague statements of opinion or prediction, and policies must manifest an intent that they become part of the employment agreement.

Bollinger v. Fall River Rural Elec. Coop., 272 P.3d 1263, 1269 (Idaho 2012). The Supreme Court of Iowa similarly determines the existence of an offer by looking for "terms with precise meaning that provide certainty of performance." *Anderson v. Douglas & Lomason Co.*, 540 N.W.2d 277, 286 (Iowa 1995). If the language is indefinite, the court will not find an intent to be bound. As it explained:

> . . . When considering whether a handbook is objectively definite to create a contract we consider its language and context. Our analysis of case law reveals three factors to guide this highly fact-intensive inquiry: (1) Is the handbook in general and the progressive disciplinary procedures in particular mere guidelines or a statement of policy, or are they directives? (2) Is the language of the disciplinary procedures detailed and definite or general and vague? and (3) Does the employer have the power to alter the procedures at will or are they invariable? We ask these questions to determine whether an employee is reasonably justified in understanding a commitment has been made.

Id. at 286–87. Thus, courts will not find contractual rights to exist if the language in a particular handbook is not sufficiently clear to create a promise. *See, e.g., Hoendermis v. Advanced Physical Therapy*, 251 P.3d 346, 355 (Alaska 2011); *Fogel v. Trustees of Iowa College*, 446 N.W.2d 451, 456 (Iowa 1989).

In addition, the language of the handbook must be examined to determine *what* the employer has promised. In the early cases, terminated employees sought to overcome the at-will presumption by showing that the language in a personnel manual or handbook constitutes a promise not to discharge without cause. Even aside from language limiting the *reasons* an employer may discharge an employee, an employer's policies may commit it to following certain *procedures* before an employee may be terminated. Many personnel manuals contain "progressive discipline" policies, which assure employees that, except in cases of gross misconduct, they will be given warnings and an opportunity to improve before being terminated for performance problems. These sorts of policies may give employees enforceable contract rights if such procedures are not followed, independent of any substantive limitation on an employer's right to discharge. *See, e.g., Strass v. Kaiser Foundation Health Plan of Mid-Atlantic*, 744 A.2d 1000 (D.C. 2000) (holding that progressive discipline policies contained in employee handbook established preconditions to termination); *Feges v. Perkins Restaurants, Inc.*, 483 N.W.2d 701 (Minn. 1992) (finding progressive discipline procedures set forth in policy manual to be contractually binding).

Is a right to progressive discipline prior to discharge meaningful if the employer's policy does not also place some substantive limits on its right to terminate? What reasons do employers have for establishing progressive discipline policies even while retaining the right to discharge without cause?

Although the focus of this chapter is on job security, employment manuals may give employees other types of contractual rights, such as a right to severance pay or other benefits, to the extent that they contain clear language to that effect. *See, e.g., Dow v. Columbus-Cabrini Medical Center*, 655 N.E.2d 1, 3 (Ill. App. Ct. 1995) (promise to pay accumulated sick time in employee handbook is enforceable); *Maloney v. Connecticut Orthopedics*, P.C., 47 F. Supp. 2d 244, 249 (D. Conn. 1999) (promises of vacation and severance pay in personnel manual enforceable); *Langdon v. Saga Corp.*, 569 P.2d 524, 524–28 (Okla. Civ. App. 1976) (same). Conversely, personnel manuals may contain terms that bind employees, for example, agreements to arbitrate any disputes that arise, *see, e.g., Davis v. Nordstrom, Inc.*, 755 F.3d 1089, 1093 (9th Cir. 2014), an issue discussed in detail in Chapter 14.

Because contract theories underlie courts' willingness to find promises of job security in employee handbooks, an examination of the actual language used by the employer is key to determining whether and what rights were in fact created.

5. Disclaimers. The court in *Woolley* suggests that an employer may avoid having a court construe its policy manual as a binding contract simply by including an "appropriate statement" to that effect. As other courts began to follow *Woolley*'s lead in finding enforceable promises in policy manuals and employee handbooks, employers responded by disclaiming any contractual intent. Courts were then faced with the task of interpreting the effect of these disclaimers. The court in *Anderson* described the issues:

> Although in theory disclaimers protect employers, many courts have imposed requirements that make it more difficult to give effect to them. For example, many jurisdictions require the disclaimer be "clear and conspicuous" to be enforceable and negate any contractual relationship between an employer and employee. . . . The requirement that a disclaimer be conspicuous has given rise to much litigation. [The opinion lists numerous cases reaching differing conclusions on the effect of a disclaimer after examining such factors as the size, typeface and color of the disclaimer, and the location and surrounding text with which it appears.]

> We think such uncertainty is unnecessary. A disclaimer should be considered in the same manner as any other language in the handbook to ascertain its impact on our search for the employer's intent. Therefore, we reject any special requirements for disclaimers; we simply examine the language and context of the disclaimer to decide whether a reasonable employee, reading the disclaimer, would understand it to mean that the employer has not assented to be bound by the handbook's provisions.

. . . Here the disclaimer appears on page fifty-three, the last page of the handbook, two inches below the preceding paragraph:

> This Employee Handbook is not intended to create any contractual rights in favor of you or the Company. The Company reserves the right to change the terms of this handbook at any time.

. . . We believe DLC's disclaimer is clear in its disavowal of any intent to create a contract. . . . The disclaimer is found in the handbook itself and unequivocally applies to the entire employee handbook.

We think a reasonable person reading the handbook could not believe that DLC has assented to be bound to the provisions contained in the manual. Thus, we hold DLC's handbook is not sufficiently definite to constitute a valid offer. . . .

Anderson v. Douglas & Lomason Co., 540 N.W.2d 277, 287–89 (Iowa 1995).

Consider a contrasting approach taken by the Vermont Supreme Court in *Dillon v. Champion Jogbra, Inc.*, 819 A.2d 703 (Vt. 2002). The employer in that case distributed a manual to all employees at the time of hire that stated in capital letters on the first page:

> The policies and procedures contained in this manual constitute guidelines only. They do not constitute part of an employment contract, nor are they intended to make any commitment to any employee concerning how individual employment action can, should, or will be handled. Champion Jogbra offers no employment contracts nor does it guarantee any minimum length of employment. Champion Jogbra reserves the right to terminate any employee at any time "at will," with or without cause.

The manual detailed a "Corrective Action Procedure" that established a progressive discipline system for employees and different categories of disciplinary infractions. The plaintiff, who was reassigned and then terminated without any prior warning that her performance was inadequate, sued, alleging breach of contract based on the company's employment manual and practices.

The Supreme Court of Vermont reversed the trial court's grant of summary judgment for the employer, holding that "[w]hen the terms of a manual are ambiguous . . . or send mixed messages regarding an employee's status, the question of whether the presumptive at-will status has been modified *is* properly left to the jury." *Id.* at 708. Examining Champion Jogbra's manual, the court found that:

> Notwithstanding the disclaimer contained on the first page of the manual quoted above, the manual goes on to establish . . . an elaborate system governing employee discipline and discharge. It states as its purpose: "To establish Champion Jogbra policy for all employees." It states that actions will be carried out "in a fair and *consistent* manner." (Emphasis added.) It provides that "[t]he Corrective Action Policy *requires* management to use training and employee counseling to achieve the desired actions of employees." (Emphasis added.) It establishes three categories of violations of company policy and corresponding actions to be generally taken in

each case. It delineates progressive steps to be taken for certain types of cases, including "[u]nsatisfactory quality of work," and time periods governing things such as how long a reprimand is considered "active." All of these terms are inconsistent with the disclaimer at the beginning of the manual, in effect sending mixed messages to employees. Furthermore, these terms appear to be inconsistent with an at-will employment relationship, its classic formulation being that an employer can fire an employee "for good cause or for no cause, or even for bad cause."

The court also reviewed evidence that the company had followed the procedures in the manual when terminating employees in the past. Finding that "the manual itself is at the very least ambiguous regarding employees' status, and Jogbra's employment practices appear from the record to be both consistent with the manual *and* inconsistent with an at-will employment arrangement," it concluded that the plaintiff should be permitted to proceed with a breach of implied contract claim. *Id.* at 708–09.

Should courts impose special requirements on disclaimers in order for them to be effective? Given the policy reasons that courts enforced handbook terms in the first place, how should courts deal with personnel manuals that send mixed messages? Should the legal effect of a disclaimer depend upon employees' perceptions or only on the words themselves? How can an employer ensure that its employees understand a disclaimer?

Additional questions arise if the disclaimer was not part of the original handbook, but the employer attempts to modify its promises at a later date. The next case explores the issues raised by modifications to an employee handbook or policy.

ASMUS v. PACIFIC BELL
Supreme Court of California
999 P.2d 71 (2000)

CHIN, J.

. . . In 1986, Pacific Bell issued the following "Management Employment Security Policy" (MESP): "It will be Pacific Bell's policy to offer all management employees who continue to meet our changing business expectations employment security through reassignment to and retraining for other management positions, even if their present jobs are eliminated. This policy will be maintained so long as there is no change that will materially affect Pacific Bell's business plan achievement."

In January 1990, Pacific Bell notified its managers that industry conditions could force it to discontinue its MESP. In a letter to managers, the company's chief executive officer wrote: "[W]e intend to do everything possible to preserve our Management Employment Security policy. However, given the reality of the marketplace, changing demographics of the workforce and the continued need for cost reduction, the prospects for continuing this policy are diminishing—perhaps, even unlikely. We will monitor the situation continuously; if we determine that business conditions no longer allow us to keep this commitment, we will inform you immediately."

Nearly two years later, in October 1991, Pacific Bell announced it would terminate its MESP on April 1, 1992, so that it could achieve more flexibility in conducting its business and compete more successfully in the marketplace. That same day, Pacific Bell announced it was adopting a new layoff policy (the Management Force Adjustment Program) that replaced the MESP but provided a generous severance program designed to decrease management through job reassignments and voluntary and involuntary terminations. Employees who chose to continue working for Pacific Bell would receive enhanced pension benefits. Those employees who opted to retire in December 1991 would receive additional enhanced pension benefits, including increases in monthly pension and annuity options. Employees who chose to resign in November 1991 would receive these additional enhanced pension benefits as well as outplacement services, medical and life insurance for one year, and severance pay equaling the employee's salary and bonus multiplied by a percentage of the employee's years of service.

Plaintiffs . . . chose to remain with the company for several years after the policy termination and received increased pension benefits for their continued employment while working under the new Management Force Adjustment Program. . . . [After a couple of years under the new policy, plaintiffs were laid off, and they sued, alleging breach of contract.]

The district court granted summary judgment on the breach of contract claim . . . conclud[ing] that Pacific Bell could not terminate its MESP unless it first demonstrated (paraphrasing the words of the MESP) "a change that will materially alter Pacific Bell's business plan achievement."

The parties agree that California law permits employers to implement policies that may become unilateral implied-in-fact contracts when employees accept them by continuing their employment. . . . The parties here disagree on how employers may terminate or modify a unilateral contract that has been accepted by the employees' performance. . . .

Pacific Bell points to the rule in the majority of jurisdictions that have addressed the question whether and how an employer may terminate or modify an employment security policy that has become an implied-in-fact unilateral contract. Regardless of the legal theory employed, the majority of other jurisdictions that have addressed the question conclude that an employer may terminate or modify a contract with no fixed duration period after a reasonable time period, if it provides employees with reasonable notice, and the modification does not interfere with vested employee benefits. *[handwritten: Rule]*

Most of these courts refer to general contract law in deciding whether an employer may terminate or modify an employment contract. They reason that because the employer created the policy's terms unilaterally, the employer may terminate or modify them unilaterally with reasonable notice. . . .

As plaintiffs observe, a minority of jurisdictions today hold that an employer cannot terminate or modify a unilateral employment contract without the employees' express knowledge and consent. Like the dissent, they reason that *any* termination or modification of a unilateral employment contract requires additional consideration and acceptance by the affected employees, because their only choices in light of a pending termination would be to resign or to continue working.

[We agree with Vice Chief Justice Jones's dissent in *Demasse v. ITT Corp.*, 984 P.2d 1138 (Ariz. 1999), which] rejected the notion that in order to free itself of future obligations, the company would be required to provide employees with a wage increase or other bonus amounting to new consideration. . . . As the dissent observed, "employers may be unilaterally forced by economic circumstance to curtail or shut down an operation, something employers have the absolute right to do. When the employer chooses in good faith, in pursuit of legitimate business objectives, to eliminate an employee policy as an alternative to curtailment or total shutdown, there has been forbearance by the employer. Such forbearance constitutes a benefit to the employee in the form of an offer of continuing employment. The employer who provides continuing employment, albeit under newly modified contract terms, also provides consideration to support the amended policy manual." (*Demasse, supra*, 984 P.2d at p. 1155 (dis. opn. of Jones, V.C.J.).) . . .

Application of Legal Principles

1. *Consideration*

Plaintiffs contend that Pacific Bell gave no valid consideration to bind the proposed MESP termination and subsequent modification. According to plaintiffs, when Pacific Bell unilaterally terminated the contract to create a new contract with different terms, it left its employees with no opportunity to bargain for additional benefits or other consideration. The parties' obligations were unequal, and hence, there was no mutuality of obligation for the change.

We disagree. The general rule governing the proper termination of unilateral contracts is that once the promisor determines after a reasonable time that it will terminate or modify the contract, and provides employees with reasonable notice of the change, additional consideration is not required. The mutuality of obligation principle requiring new consideration for contract termination applies to bilateral contracts only. In the unilateral contract context, there is no mutuality of obligation. For an effective modification, there is consideration in the form of continued employee services. . . . Here, Pacific Bell replaced its MESP with a subsequent layoff policy. Plaintiffs' continued employment constituted acceptance of the offer of the modified unilateral contract. As we have observed, a rule requiring separate consideration in addition to continued employment as a limitation on the ability to terminate or modify an employee security agreement would contradict the general principle that the law will not concern itself with the adequacy of consideration.

The corollary is also true. Just as employers must accept the employees' continued employment as consideration for the original contract terms, employees must be bound by amendments to those terms, with the availability of continuing employment serving as adequate consideration from the employer. When Pacific Bell terminated its original MESP and then offered continuing employment to employees who received notice and signed an acknowledgment to that effect, the employees accepted the new terms, and the subsequent modified contract, by continuing to work. . . .

2. *Illusoriness*

Plaintiffs alternatively claim that Pacific Bell's MESP would be an illusory contract if Pacific Bell could unilaterally modify it. Plaintiffs rely on the rule that when a party to a contract retains the unfettered right to terminate or modify the agreement, the contract is deemed to be illusory. . . . [A]n unqualified right to modify or terminate the contract is not enforceable. But the fact that one party reserves the implied power to terminate or modify a unilateral contract is not fatal to its enforcement, if the exercise of the power is subject to limitations, such as fairness and reasonable notice.

As Pacific Bell observes, the MESP was not illusory because plaintiffs obtained the benefits of the policy while it was operable. In other words, Pacific Bell was obligated to follow it as long as the MESP remained in effect. Although a permanent no-layoff policy would be highly prized in the modern workforce, it does not follow that anything less is without significant value to the employee or is an illusory promise. As long as the MESP remained in force, Pacific Bell could not treat the contract as illusory by refusing to adhere to its terms; the promise was not optional with the employer and was fully enforceable until terminated or modified.

3. *Vested Benefits*

Plaintiffs next allege that the MESP conferred a vested benefit on employees, like an accrued bonus or a pension. But as Pacific Bell observes, no court has treated an employment security policy as a vested interest for private sector employees. In addition, plaintiffs do not allege that Pacific Bell terminated its MESP in bad faith. Although we agree with plaintiffs that an employer may not generally interfere with an employee's vested benefits, we do not find that the MESP gave rise to, or created, any vested benefits in plaintiffs' favor.

4. *Condition as Definite Duration Clause*

. . . Because Pacific Bell declared that it would maintain its MESP "so long as" its business conditions did not substantially change, plaintiffs, like the dissent, assert that the specified condition is automatically one for a definite duration that Pacific Bell is obliged to honor until the condition occurs. . . . As Pacific Bell observes . . . the condition did not state an ascertainable event that could be measured in any reasonable manner. . . . Therefore, the condition in the MESP did not restrict Pacific Bell's ability to terminate or modify it, as long as the company made the change after a reasonable time, on reasonable notice, and in a manner that did not interfere with employees' vested benefits.

The facts show that those conditions were met here. Pacific Bell implemented the MESP in 1986, and it remained in effect until 1992, when the company determined that maintaining the policy was incompatible with its need for flexibility in the marketplace. The company then implemented a new Management Force Adjustment Program in which employees whose positions were eliminated would be given 60 days to either find another job within the company, leave the company with severance benefits after signing a release of any claims, or leave the company without severance benefits. The employees were provided with a booklet entitled Voluntary Force Management Programs detailing the new benefits the company provided following the MESP cancellation.

Thus, the MESP was in place for a reasonable time and was effectively terminated after Pacific Bell determined that it was no longer a sound policy for the company. Contrary to the dissent, Pacific Bell did not engage in behavior that one could characterize as "manipulative" or "oppressive." Employees were provided ample advance notice of the termination, and the present plaintiffs even enjoyed at least two more years of employment and corresponding benefits under a modified policy before they were eventually laid off. In sum, Pacific Bell maintained the MESP for a reasonable time, it provided more than reasonable notice to the affected employees that it was terminating the policy, and it did not interfere with employees' vested benefits. The law requires nothing more. . . .

Dissenting Opinion by George, C.J.

. . . Under the majority's contract analysis, an employer unilaterally may terminate an express promise of job security to a current employee—offered specifically to induce employees not to resign in good economic times, when there is a shortage of labor and a high demand for qualified employees—simply because the promise later becomes inconvenient or financially disadvantageous to the employer during an economic downturn, a time when the employee would most expect to be able to rely upon and benefit from the employer's promise. Not only is such a result entirely inconsistent with fundamental tenets of contract law, but it also condones and encourages manipulative, oppressive, and unfair treatment of employees. An employer's implied-in-fact contractual promise would not be binding upon the employer but would be only as good as the employer's desire to keep the promise at some unspecified point in the future. . . . If an employer wishes to escape its own voluntarily incurred contractual obligations, it may do so prospectively with regard to new employees, and it may negotiate with those employees covered under existing agreements by offering additional consideration and obtaining the individual assent of the employees to the termination of the employer's obligations. . . .

[T]he fallacy underlying decisions upholding unilateral modification in this context is that the modification of a contract is completely analogous to its formation. The general rule that the act of continuing employment with knowledge of new or changed conditions may create binding obligations was framed initially in decisions in which the courts considered the *formation* of a unilateral contract. Continuing to perform and insisting upon one's rights under an existing contract, however, are not proper grounds from which to imply a party's assent to a subsequent *modification* of that contract. In addition, as with all contracts, in order to modify an employment security agreement, the employer must provide some new term or benefit that inures to the advantage of all affected employees.

Under contract law, we cannot simply ignore the original agreement and find that the employer has offered a new agreement that is accepted by continued performance, as was the original agreement. When the employment relationship begins, or when the employer confers additional benefits upon the employee such as a job security policy, it is reasonable to conclude that the employee accepts the unilateral offer by continuing employment. The employee provides services and forgoes the right to obtain employment elsewhere as consideration for the employer's promises, while the employer enjoys the extra productivity and loyalty conferred by the job security term. When the employee already is employed under an enforceable agreement, however, the *employer* is the party that must provide new consideration in exchange for the employee's agreement to forgo the valuable right to job security. This right is vested in the sense that, once the contract giving rise to the right has been created, Pacific Bell must honor its contractual commitment. (*See Hunter v. Sparling* (1948) 87 Cal.App.2d 711, 722–725, 197 P.2d 807.). . . .

Because the majority concludes that *plaintiffs* provided the necessary consideration for cancellation of the MESP by continuing their employment, it does not reach Pacific Bell's contention that it provided its own consideration by conferring increased pension benefits upon plaintiffs. As explained above, I disagree that plaintiffs' continued employment provided consideration supporting the modification. The additional pension benefits provided by Pacific Bell to plaintiffs conceivably could constitute consideration given by Pacific Bell. A question of fact also remains whether plaintiffs, by continuing to work, accepted the offer of modification accompanied by these increased pension benefits.

NOTES

1.   **The Middle Ground?** In *Demasse v. ITT Corp.*, 984 P.2d 1138 (Ariz. 1999), a case cited in *Asmus*, the Supreme Court of Arizona held that once an implied contract was formed by issuance of an employee handbook, its terms could not be modified unilaterally. *Id.* at 1144. In order to effectively modify such a contract, "there must be: (1) an offer to modify the contract, (2) assent to or acceptance of that offer, and (3) consideration." The court was concerned that if the employer could unilaterally alter the policy terms and immediately fire an employee, then the original contract was illusory. *Id.* at 1147. It held that the employee's continued work alone could not constitute consideration for the modification; separate consideration was required. *Id.* at 1144–45. Similarly, it rejected the argument that the continued employment after issuance of the new handbook could constitute acceptance of the new terms, "otherwise the 'illusion (and the irony) is apparent: to preserve their right under the [existing contract] . . . plaintiffs would be forced to quit.'" *Id.* at 1145 (quoting *Doyle v. Holy Cross Hosp.*, 682 N.E.2d 68 (Ill. App. Ct. 1997)).

Govier v. North Sound Bank, 957 P.2d 811 (Wash. Ct. App. 1998) represents the opposite approach. When the plaintiff, Deborah Govier, was initially hired, she was given a personnel handbook that assured employees that once they passed a 90-day probationary period, they were permanent employees so long as they "continued satisfactory performance." *Id.* at 813. It also mandated certain procedures, including warnings and an opportunity to improve prior to discharge, and stated that dismissals were "for cause." The Bank's officers believed that they could not terminate non-probationary employees except for cause. *Id.* at 814. Several years after the plaintiff was hired, the Bank presented her with a new employment agreement and told her that she must sign the contract within a few days or be terminated. *Id.* The new agreement was for a one-year period, renegotiable at the end of that time, and permitted either party to terminate the contract upon 20 days' written notice. When Govier refused to sign the new agreement, she was fired. *Id.* Although the court found that the provisions in the earlier personnel manual were legally binding, it held that "its obligations existed only while its policies were in effect." *Id.* at 816. The Bank was permitted to unilaterally amend the earlier policies, and the new policy was effective upon giving actual notice to the affected employees. *Id.* at 817.

Given these two contrasting approaches, one might regard *Asmus* as taking a middle ground position on employer modifications of contractual rights based on handbook provisions. *See also Bollinger v. Fall River Rural Elec. Coop.*, 272 P.3d 1263, 1269 (Idaho 2012) (holding that an employer may unilaterally amend its policies by providing "reasonable notice" of the change to its employees).

How does the holding in *Asmus* differ from the two approaches exemplified by *Govier* and *Demasse*? Are the limits the *Asmus* court places on an employer's ability to unilaterally modify promises contained in an employee handbook dictated by contract doctrine? Are they supportable for policy reasons? Do they adequately protect employees' reasonable expectations? What specific facts in *Asmus* might argue for permitting Pacific Bell to change its "Management Employment Security Policy"? What facts argue against such a result?

   2. Employer Interests? In *Toussaint v. Blue Cross & Blue Shield of Michigan*, 292 N.W.2d 880 (Mich. 1980), the Michigan Supreme Court suggested that employee handbook provisions guaranteeing job security should be enforced because the employer derives the benefit of "an orderly, cooperative and loyal work force" as a result of its promises. *Id.* at 892. In a later case, the same court found that an employer could unilaterally modify those written policy statements, even if it had not expressly reserved the right to make changes. *In re Certified Question: Bankey v. Storer Broadcasting Co.*, 443 N.W.2d 112 (Mich. 1989). It reasoned that once the employer changed its for cause discharge policy to employment-at-will, "the employer's benefit is correspondingly extinguished, as is the rationale for the court's enforcement of the discharge-for-cause policy." *Id.* at 119. The court further cited the need for flexibility, finding that "[i]n the modern economic climate, the operating policies of a business enterprise must be adaptable and responsive to change." *Id.* at 120.

Does a rule that permits employers to make unilateral changes to their policy statements always benefit employers? Consider the following argument:

   [The rule] deprives employers of any means of making enforceable promises of employment security. No matter how absolutely and unquali- fiedly an employer promises its employees that it will not discharge them except for cause or promises them other employment rights, it can thereafter unilaterally change the rights with impunity. Even if the employees would be willing to trust their employer's existing management to keep its unenforceable promises, they would have no way of protecting themselves against changes in ownership or, if the employer was a corporation, changes the shareholders or board of directors demanded. The [ ] law thus deprives employers of a valuable bargaining chip with their employees, and of a valuable means of attracting and keeping desirable employees, and of increasing its employees' job satisfaction and loyalty. . . .

The employer's inability to make enforceable promises of employment security will also put both employees who do not want to join unions and their employers who do not want them to join at an unfair disadvantage. . . . Union organizers in the states where the courts [permit unilateral modification] can now tell employees that no matter what their employers may promise them, the only way they can obtain rights—rather than just unenforceable promises—of employment security is to join a union. . . .

W. David Slawson, *Unilateral Contracts of Employment: Does Contract Law Conflict with Public Policy?*, 10 Tex. Wesleyan L. Rev. 9, 30–31 (2003).

Is it true under *Asmus* that employers have no way of making enforceable promises of job security to their workforce? Why don't employers take steps to insure that their promises are binding, for example, by entering into bilateral agreements with consideration, if that is what they intend?

3. Modifications That Bind Employees. In addition to avoiding promises previously made, employers may also seek modification of handbook policies in order to bind their employees. In *Davis v. Nordstrom, Inc.*, 755 F.3d 1089 (9th Cir. 2014), an employer argued that she was not bound by an amendment to the employee handbook that required employees to arbitrate individual employment claims and precluded them from filing class action lawsuits. Citing *Asmus*, the Ninth Circuit held that the revised handbook was binding because the employer had provided reasonable notice of the modification by sending a letter to all employees informing them of the modification and not enforcing the new provision for 30 days. *Id.* at 1094.

C. WHAT IS "CAUSE"?

Once the existence of a contract promising job security has been established, a court must determine whether a discharged employee was terminated "for cause" or whether the firing breached the agreement. Courts have used the terms "cause," "good cause," and "just cause" without a great deal of consistency or clarity. Sometimes these terms are used more or less interchangeably; at other times, "just cause" suggests a more demanding standard—something akin to objective reasonableness—while good cause connotes the exercise of good faith. The terms have proven extremely difficult to define. As one court explained, "The concept of 'just cause' does not lend itself to a mathematically precise definition. Indeed, '[t]here is no single definition of what constitutes good cause for discharge.' " *Shapiro v. Massengill*, 661 A.2d 202, 211 (Md. Ct. Spec. App. 1995). *Cause* has been defined as "reasons that relate to performance of [an employee's] job and the impact of that performance on an employer's ability to attain its reasonable goals" as opposed to "reasons which are arbitrary, unfair or generated out of some petty vendetta." *Kern v. Palmer College of Chiropractic*, 757 N.W.2d 651, 658 (Iowa 2008). Another court stated that good cause is "that which a reasonable employer, acting in good faith, would regard as good and sufficient reason for terminating the services of an employee, as distinguished from an arbitrary whim or caprice." *Koster v. P & P Enterprises, Inc.*, 539 N.W.2d 274, 278 (Neb. 1995). Are these definitions helpful in determining whether a particular discharge constitutes a breach? Do you see any common elements in these definitions?

Despite the vagueness of these judicial definitions, some clear understandings have emerged as the concept of "cause" has been applied in different factual circumstances. As discussed in section A, above, "just cause" has come to have a fairly well defined meaning in the collective bargaining context. And when an individual contract expressly defines acceptable reasons for termination, those terms will clearly govern the parties' relationship. Thus, examining the actual language of a contract is crucial. Consider the following definitions of "cause" taken from actual executive contracts:

Example 1: "Cause" shall mean dishonesty, gross negligence, or willful misconduct in the performance of your duties or a willful or material breach of this Agreement.

Example 2: For purposes of this Agreement, "Cause" shall consist of a termination due to the following, as specified in the written notice of termination (and in each case following written notice a failure by Executive to cure within thirty (30) days of such notice except as to clauses (E) or (F) which shall not be subject to cure): (A) Executive's failure to substantially perform the fundamental duties and responsibilities associated with Executive's position, including Executive's failure or refusal to carry out reasonable instructions; (B) Executive's material breach of any material written Company policy; (C) Executive's gross misconduct in the performance of Executive's duties for the Company; (D) Executive's material breach of the terms of this Agreement; (E) Executive's conviction of any fraudulent or felony criminal offense or any other criminal offense which reflects adversely on the Company or reflects conduct or character that the Board reasonably concludes is inconsistent with continued employment; or (F) Executive's conviction of any criminal conduct that is a "statutory disqualifying event" (as defined under federal securities laws, rules and regulations). Prior to any termination for Cause, and following the thirty (30) day cure period, Executive will be given five (5) business days written notice specifying the alleged Cause event and will be entitled to appear (with counsel) before the full Board to present information regarding his views on the Cause event. A termination for cause will occur if after such hearing, there is at least a majority vote of the full Board (other than Executive) to terminate for Cause.

Example 3: For purposes of this Agreement, "Cause" will mean any of the following, whether occurring before or after the Effective Date: (i) the commission of a felony or other crime involving moral turpitude or the commission of any other act or omission involving misappropriation, dishonesty, unethical business conduct, including bribery or similar conduct, disloyalty, fraud or breach of fiduciary duty, (ii) reporting to work under the influence of alcohol, (iii) the use of illegal drugs (whether or not at the workplace) or other conduct, even if not in conjunction with his duties hereunder, which could reasonably be expected to, or which does, cause the Company or any of its Subsidiaries public disgrace or disrepute or economic harm, (iv) repeated failure to perform duties as reasonably directed by the Board, (v) gross negligence or willful misconduct with respect to the Company or any of its Subsidiaries or in the performance of the Executive's duties hereunder, (vi) obtaining any personal profit not thoroughly disclosed to and approved by the Board in connection with any transaction entered into by, or on behalf of, the Company or any of its Subsidiaries, (vii) violating the expense reimbursement policies of the Company or any of its Subsidiaries, (viii) violating any of the terms of the Company's or any of its Subsidiaries' rules or policies which, if curable, is not cured to the Board's reasonable satisfaction within fifteen (15) days after written notice thereof to the Executive, or (ix) any other material breach of this Agreement or any other agreement between the Executive and the Company or any of its Subsidiaries which, if curable, is not cured to the Board's reasonable satisfaction within fifteen (15) days after written notice thereof to the Executive.

How do these contractual provisions differ from the court definitions quoted above and from one another? What factors might lead the parties to adopt one of these approaches over the others?

An analysis of hundreds of contracts between CEOs and publicly-held companies found that these agreements most commonly define "cause" to include wilful misconduct, moral turpitude, and failure to perform duties. *See* Stewart J. Schwab & Randall S. Thomas, *An Empirical Analysis of CEO Employment Contracts: What Do Top Executives Bargain for?*, 63 WASH. & LEE L. REV. 231, 248 (2006). The next most common terms defining "cause" were breach of fiduciary duties and gross misconduct. *Id.* Perhaps surprisingly, poor performance on the job is not listed as a basis for "cause" permitting termination in most CEO contracts. *Id.* at 249. Why do you think this is the case?

Some employment contracts, particularly those that are not intensively negotiated, may be silent about the acceptable reasons for termination and courts must supply default terms. What if the parties have agreed to a contract for employment for a two-year period, but the contract says nothing about termination. Should a court imply a term allowing the employer to terminate the employee for dishonesty or gross misconduct? Or should it simply enforce the contract for the period of time agreed to? What if the employer discharges the employee because of its need to save money in the face of changed business circumstances? Should it be permitted to do so?

Most courts to consider these questions have implied a term permitting termination of a definite-term contract for misconduct or inability to perform job duties. *See, e.g., Rosecrans v. Intermountain Soap & Chemical Co.*, 605 P.2d 963 (Idaho 1980); *Nelson Trabue, Inc. v. Professional Management-Automotive, Inc.*, 589 S.W.2d 661, 663 (Tenn. 1979). However, they have generally assumed that the contract could not be terminated for financial reasons. For example, in *Drake v. Geochemistry and Environmental Chemistry Research, Inc.*, 336 N.W.2d 666 (S.D. 1983), the court refused to release the employer from its obligations under a fixed-term employment contract even though the government contract that the plaintiff was hired to fulfill was seriously delayed. The court held that the possibility that the defendant might not receive the contract or that it would be delayed was "a risk [the defendant] undertook to accept." Finding that "the one-year contract was not conditioned upon the performance of work on any specific project," the court was "not inclined to read such a limitation into it," and upheld judgment against the employer on plaintiff's breach of contract claim. *Id.* at 668; *see also Ryan v. Brown Motors*, 39 A.2d 70 (N.J. 1944); RESTATEMENT (THIRD) OF EMPLOYMENT LAW § 2.04(a) cmt. b (Proposed Final Draft, April 18, 2014).

On the other hand, when interpreting indefinite term contracts, most courts interpret "cause" to include both employee malfeasance *and* economic circumstances. *See, e.g., Braun v. Alaska Commercial Fishing and Agriculture Bank*, 816 P.2d 140 (Alaska 1991); *Wilde v. Houlton Regional Hospital*, 537 A.2d 1137 (Me. 1988); RESTATEMENT (THIRD) OF EMPLOYMENT LAW § 2.04(b) (Proposed Final Draft, April 18, 2014). Can you think of reasons why the default rules should differ between fixed-term and indefinite-term contracts in this way? What about the meaning of "just cause" that has evolved in the collective bargaining context? Should courts look to that existing body of arbitral law when interpreting the meaning of "cause" in fixed-term contracts? When interpreting indefinite term contracts? Why or why not? Once again, it is important to remember that these debates are over the appropriate default terms. If the parties clearly agree to different terms, those terms will govern, rather than any judicially implied default term.

Even if the meaning of "cause" is clear, what standard should be applied to determine whether "cause" actually existed? The following case considers how courts should go about answering that question.

COTRAN v. ROLLINS HUDIG HALL INTERNATIONAL, INC.
Supreme Court of California
948 P.2d 412 (1998)

BROWN, J.

When an employee hired under an *implied* agreement not to be dismissed except for "good cause" is fired for misconduct and challenges the termination in court, what is the role of the jury in deciding whether misconduct occurred? Does it decide whether the acts that led to the decision to terminate happened? Or is its role to decide whether the employer had reasonable grounds for *believing* they happened and otherwise acted fairly? . . .[7]

---

[7] [n. 1] In this case, the contractual limitation on the employer's at-will power of termination is implied, arising, as the trial judge apparently determined, from preliminary negotiations and the text of a letter defendants sent plaintiff in response to a request for additional assurances of "permanent employment" before accepting their employment offer. The letter stated that if plaintiff's efforts to

In 1987, Rollins Hudig Hall International, Inc. (Rollins), an insurance brokerage firm, approached plaintiff, then a vice-president of a competitor, with a proposal to head its new West Coast international office. Following a series of telephone conferences, meetings and exchanges of letters, plaintiff joined Rollins in January 1988 as senior vice-president and western regional international manager. He held that position until 1993 when he was fired.

The events leading to plaintiff's termination began in March 1993, when an employee in Rollins's international department reported to Deborah Redmond, the firm's director of human resources, that plaintiff was sexually harassing two other employees, Carrie Dolce and Shari Pickett. On March 24, Redmond called both women to her office. In separate interviews, she asked each if they had been harassed. Both said yes; each accused plaintiff as the harasser. Two days later, both women furnished statements to Redmond stating that plaintiff had exposed himself and masturbated in their presence more than once; both also accused plaintiff of making repeated obscene telephone calls to them at home. Redmond sent copies of these statements to Rollins's equal employment opportunity (EEO) office in Chicago. Rollins's president, Fred Feldman, also was given copies. He arranged for a meeting with plaintiff at Rollins's Chicago office, attended by Robert Hurvitz, the firm's head of EEO, and Susan Held, Rollins's manager for EEO compliance. At the meeting, Feldman reviewed the accusations made by Dolce and Pickett against plaintiff. He explained that an investigation would ensue and that its outcome would turn on credibility. After reading the Dolce and Pickett statements to plaintiff, Held explained how the investigation would proceed. Plaintiff said nothing during the meeting about having had consensual relations with either of his two accusers, and offered no explanation for the complaints.

Pending completion of the EEO investigation, Rollins suspended plaintiff. Over the next two weeks, Held interviewed 21 people who had worked with plaintiff, including 5 he had asked her to interview. Held concluded that both Dolce and Pickett, who reiterated the incidents described in their statements, appeared credible. Her investigation failed to turn up anyone else who accused plaintiff of harassing them while at Rollins. One Rollins account executive, Gail Morris, told Held that plaintiff had made obscene telephone calls to her when they both worked for another company, soon after a sexual relationship between the two had ended. . . . Held's investigation also confirmed that plaintiff had telephoned Dolce and Pickett at home. In April, both women signed sworn affidavits reciting in detail the charges made against plaintiff in their original statements.

On the basis of her investigation, her assessment of Dolce's and Pickett's credibility, and the fact that no one she interviewed had said it was "impossible" to believe plaintiff had committed the alleged sexual harassment, Held concluded it was more likely than not the harassment had occurred. She met with Feldman and Hurvitz to present her conclusions and gave Feldman copies of the affidavits of Dolce, Pickett, and Gail Morris. After reviewing Held's investigative report and the

---

develop an international brokerage department failed to succeed, "other opportunities" within the organization would be "made available" to him. . . . Wrongful termination claims founded on an *explicit* promise that termination will not occur except for just or good cause may call for a different standard, depending on the precise terms of the contract provision.

affidavits, Feldman fired plaintiff on April 23, 1993. This suit followed.

[At trial, the plaintiff testified that he had been involved in sexual relationships with both Dolce, from early 1991 through February 1993, and with Pickett from January to April 1992.] He had not disclosed these liaisons during the Chicago interview with Feldman because he was upset, "frightened," and felt "ambushed." Plaintiff presented additional evidence through several witnesses suggesting Dolce had been "flirtatious" in front of others, that both she and Pickett were angry because he had been "two-timing" them, and that Dolce's real motive was to force plaintiff to grant her a substantial raise in pay. . . .

[Dolce and Pickett both testified at trial in detail about the incidents reported in their affidavits. Both denied ever having sex with plaintiff.] . . .

Rollins defended its decision to fire plaintiff on the ground that it had been reached honestly and in good faith, not that Rollins was required to prove the acts of sexual harassment occurred. . . . [T]he trial judge remarked, the case was nothing more than "a contract dispute" and it was Rollins's burden to *prove* plaintiff committed the acts that led to his dismissal. . . .

The jury returned a special verdict. Asked whether plaintiff "engaged in any of the behavior on which [Rollins] based its decision to terminate plaintiff's employment," it answered "no." It set the present cash value of plaintiff's lost compensation at $1.78 million. Rollins appealed. . . .

In *Wilkerson* [*v. Wells Fargo Bank*, 212 Cal. App. 3d 1217 (*Wilkerson*), the California Court of Appeal] held that in a wrongful termination suit by an employee terminable only for good cause, the employer must prove, as part of its defense burden, that the misconduct leading to dismissal actually occurred. That is, *Wilkerson* directs the jury to reexamine the facts on which the employer relied in terminating the employee and, if it finds them erroneous, to award damages.

"[I]n contract law," the court in *Wilkerson* reasoned, "the belief of the breaching party does not determine whether a breach of the contract . . . occurred. Obviously, a defaulting borrower's good faith belief he or she has repaid a loan is not a defense to a lender's claim for payment. Similarly, an employer's subjective belief it possessed good cause does not dispose of a wrongfully discharged employee's claim for breach of contract. . . . [A]n employer's belief is not a substitute for good cause. For that reason, the employer's broad latitude does not extend to being *factually* incorrect . . . ."

Instead of adopting the de novo rule [of *Wilkerson*] . . . we adopt a different standard under which the jury assesses the factual basis for the decision to terminate employment. . . . A middle ground—combining a balanced regard for the employee's interest in continuing employment with the employer's interest in efficient personnel decisions—exists. As we explain, . . . the jury's role is to assess the *objective reasonableness* of the employer's factual determination of misconduct. . . .

Southwest Gas v. Vargas 901 P.2d 693 (1995) discusses some of the concerns raised by an instruction directing the jury to reexamine the factual accuracy supporting the employer's decision to terminate employment. "[A]llowing a jury to trump the factual findings of an employer that an employee has engaged in misconduct rising to the level of 'good cause' for discharge, made in good faith and in pursuit of legitimate business objectives, is a highly undesirable prospect," the Nevada high court said. (Vargas, supra, 901 P.2d at p. 699.) "In effect, such a system would create the equivalent of a preeminent fact-finding board unconnected to the challenged employer, that would have the ultimate right to determine anew whether the employer's decision to terminate an employee was based upon an accurate finding of misconduct. . . . This ex officio 'fact-finding board,' unattuned to the practical aspects of employee suitability over which it would exercise consummate power, and unexposed to the entrepreneurial risks that form a significant basis of every state's economy, would be empowered to impose substantial monetary consequences on employers whose employee termination decisions are found wanting." (*Ibid.*). . . .

As several courts have pointed out, a standard permitting juries to reexamine the factual basis for the decision to terminate for misconduct—typically gathered under the exigencies of the workaday world and without benefit of the slow-moving machinery of a contested trial—dampens an employer's willingness to act, intruding on the "wide latitude" . . . recognized as a reasonable condition for the efficient conduct of business. . . .

Equally significant is the jury's relative remoteness from the everyday reality of the workplace. The decision to terminate an employee for misconduct is one that not uncommonly implicates organizational judgment and may turn on intractable factual uncertainties, even where the grounds for dismissal are fact specific. If an employer is required to have in hand a signed confession or an eyewitness account of the alleged misconduct before it can act, the workplace will be transformed into an adjudicatory arena and effective decisionmaking will be thwarted. Although these features do not justify a rule permitting employees to be dismissed arbitrarily, they do mean that asking a civil jury to reexamine in all its factual detail the triggering cause of the decision to dismiss—including the retrospective accuracy of the employer's comprehension of that event—months or even years later, in a context distant from the imperatives of the workplace, is at odds with . . . the need for a sensible latitude for managerial decisionmaking and its corollary, an optimum balance point between the employer's interest in organizational efficiency and the employee's interest in continuing employment.

Plaintiff argues that withdrawing from the jury the factual issue underlying the decision to terminate employment will destroy the protections afforded by the implied good cause contract term. It will permit the discharge decision to be based on subjective reasons, the argument runs, reasons that may be pretextual, and mask arbitrary and unlawful motives made practically unreviewable by a standard-less "good faith" rule. But as we have tried to show, this argument is founded on a misunderstanding of the nature and effect of an *objective* good faith standard. The rule we endorse today, carefully framed as a jury instruction and honestly administered, will not only *not* have the effects plaintiff claims, but by balancing the interests of *both* parties, will ensure that "good cause" dismissals continue to be scrutinized by courts and juries under an objective standard, without infringing more than necessary on the freedom to make efficient business decisions. At least one state high court has reasoned that striking a fair balance between the interests of the parties to the employment contract through an objective just-cause standard will *promote* the continued use of such limitations on the at-will doctrine; imbalances, on the other hand, encourage employers to adopt defensive measures by "remov[ing] such [just-cause] provisions from their [employment] handbooks." (Baldwin, supra, 769 P.2d at p. 304.)

The proper inquiry for the jury, in other words, is not, "Did the employee *in fact* commit the act leading to dismissal?" It is, "Was the factual basis on which the employer concluded a dischargeable act had been committed reached honestly, after an appropriate investigation and for reasons that are not arbitrary or pretextual?" The jury conducts a factual inquiry in both cases, but the questions are not the same. In the first, the jury decides the ultimate truth of the employee's alleged misconduct. In the second, it focuses on the *employer's response* to allegations of misconduct. . . . We give operative meaning to the term "good cause" in the context of implied employment contracts by defining it . . . as fair and honest reasons, regulated by good faith on the part of the employer, that are not trivial, arbitrary or capricious, unrelated to business needs or goals, or pretextual. A reasoned conclusion, in short, supported by substantial evidence gathered through an adequate investigation that includes notice of the claimed misconduct and a chance for the employee to respond. . . .

Because it was error to instruct that Rollins could prevail only if the jury was satisfied sexual harassment actually occurred, the case must be retried. . . .

Mosk, J., concurring.

. . . I write separately to make three points. First, "substantial evidence" that the employee committed misconduct is not synonymous with "any" evidence. The ultimate determination is whether a *reasonable* employer could have found that an employee committed the charged misconduct based on all the evidence before it. Similarly, the requirement that an employee receive notice and an opportunity to be heard is not fulfilled by a charade of due process by an employer that has already made up its mind, but rather signifies "*adequate* notice of the 'charges' . . . and a *reasonable* opportunity to respond." *Pinsker v. Pacific Coast Society of Orthodontists* (1974) 526 P.2d 253, (italics added). Although we do not dictate the precise form that the employer must adopt, fair procedure requires that the employee have a truly meaningful opportunity to tell his or her side of the story and to influence the employer's decision.

Second, there is nothing, of course, in the majority's standard that precludes an employer and an employee from negotiating or impliedly forming a contract with a "good cause" clause that defines that term more explicitly, in which case the jury's good cause determination would be shaped by this contractual definition. For example, the employment contract may spell out in greater detail the due process protections enjoyed by the employee. A court may also reasonably interpret an implied or express employment agreement that contains particularly strong promises of employment security to embody a more protective good cause standard. In short, the majority's definition of "good cause" is a "default" definition that applies only in the absence of more specific contractual provisions.

Third, I note that nothing in the majority opinion is intended to alter the different manner in which the term "good cause" is construed by arbitrators pursuant to a collective bargaining agreement between unions and employers. In such agreements the contract is express, the remedies more limited, the role of the arbitrator in policing collective bargaining agreements well established both contractually and customarily, and the contractual language supplemented by a well developed body of arbitration law concerning the meaning of "good cause" that the parties can be presumed to be aware of at the time they entered the agreement. The majority's good cause standard does not extend beyond the context in which it is articulated, i.e., implied contracts between employers and individual employees.

[OPINION OF KENNARD, J., concurring and dissenting, is omitted.]

NOTES

1.   **Burdens of Proof.** When an employee alleges that his termination breached an agreement limiting the employer's power to discharge at will, who should bear the burden of proving whether "good cause" for the discharge existed, and what should that burden be? The court in *Cotran* suggests that its approach represents the "middle ground." What alternative standards could the court have adopted, and do you see any problems with these alternatives? Do you think the holding in *Cotran* adequately balances the interests of terminated employees and their employers? Are there any other interests that should be taken into account in striking the proper balance?

Ordinarily, a party alleging failure to perform bears the burden of proving the existence of a breach. And in the collective bargaining setting, most arbitrators interpret "just cause" provisions to require the employer to prove that the conduct justifying the dismissal actually occurred. In *Cotran*, the plaintiff's claim was based on an implied contract that arose out of the pre-hiring negotiations between the parties, including a letter sent to the plaintiff in response to a request for additional assurances of "permanent employment" before accepting the offer. Does the nature of the contract in *Cotran* warrant a different rule?

Other courts have taken a different approach. For example, the Supreme Court of Michigan, in interpreting an implied contract based on an employee handbook held that "the jury as trier of facts decides whether the employee was, in fact, discharged for unsatisfactory work." In its view, "[a] promise to terminate employment for cause only would be illusory if the employer were permitted to be the sole judge and final arbiter of the propriety of the discharge." *Toussaint v. Blue Cross & Blue* Shield, 292 N.W.2d 880, 895 (Mich. 1980). Similarly, in *Kern v. Palmer College of Chiropractic*, 757 N.W.2d 651 (Iowa 2008), the Supreme Court of Iowa refused to defer to the employer's judgment that "cause" for termination existed and held instead that the question was one for the fact-finder. In *Kern*, the for-cause limitation on termination was based on a handbook that specifically listed the reasons a faculty member could be dismissed. Can these two cases be reconciled with *Cotran*? If not, which is the better approach?

In the union context, employers bear the burden of proving that just cause exists for disciplining or discharging an employee. ELKOURI & ELKOURI, HOW ARBITRATION WORKS 15.23 (7th ed. 2012). The *quantum* of proof required to justify a discharge under a collective bargaining agreement is less clear. Most arbitrators use the "preponderance of the evidence" standard; however, in some cases, arbitrators have imposed a "clear and convincing evidence" standard or even a "beyond a reasonable doubt" standard. These higher standards of proof are most likely to be required in situations in which the employee's alleged conduct constituted criminal behavior or involved moral turpitude or social stigma, or where the sanction was discharge rather than some lesser discipline. *Id.* at 15.25–.27.

2.   **Managerial Discretion.** In *Cotran*, the plaintiff did not dispute that the employer's reason for dismissing him was the charge of sexual harassment, nor did he contend that such conduct, if it actually occurred, constituted good cause. But what if the discharge was allegedly for poor job performance? How much deference should the trier of fact give to the employer's assessment that a particular employee's performance was inadequate for the job? This question becomes particularly difficult with high-level employees whose performance cannot be measured objectively. Consider one court's answer:

> In any free enterprise system, an employer must have wide latitude in making independent, good faith judgments about high-ranking employees without the threat of a jury second-guessing its business judgment. Measuring the effective performance of such an employee involves the consideration of many intangible attributes such as personality, initiative, ability to function as part of the management team and to motivate subordinates, and the ability to conceptualize and effectuate management style and goals. . . . Although the jury must assess the legitimacy of the employer's decision to discharge, it should not be thrust into a managerial role.

Pugh v. See's Candies, Inc., 203 Cal. App. 3d 743, 767–71 (1988) (*Pugh II*). Is such deference to managerial discretion consistent with a finding of a contractual guarantee of job security? Should the class status of the employee influence how much deference is given the employer's judgment?

3.   **Pretext.** In some cases, the dispute may not turn on what the employee actually did, but rather on a disagreement over the employer's real motivation for the termination. This type of issue arises when a defendant alleges that it terminated an employee for a legitimate reason, but the employee contends it was a pretext for another reason not constituting good cause. If the plaintiff produces evidence casting doubt on the motives of the employer, the jury may have to decide which was the true motive. For example, in *Coelho v. Posi-Seal International*, 544 A.2d 170 (Conn. 1988), the plaintiff, who was ostensibly discharged in a reduction in force, produced evidence that the employer was in fact motivated by conflicts that the plaintiff, as quality control manager, had with the director of manufacturing. Although it acknowledged that a reduction in force would constitute good cause, the court held that a question of fact remained as to whether the plaintiff was *actually* terminated for legitimate economic reasons or for other reasons that violated the employer's contractual obligations. *Id.* at 178.

D.   OTHER CONTRACT-BASED LIMITS ON EMPLOYMENT-AT-WILL

1. Promissory Estoppel

GOFF-HAMEL v. OBSTETRICIANS
& GYNECOLOGISTS, P.C.
Supreme Court of Nebraska
588 N.W.2d 798 (1999)

WRIGHT, J.

. . . Goff-Hamel worked for Hastings Family Planning for 11 years. Prior to leaving Hastings Family Planning, Goff-Hamel was earning $24,000 plus the following benefits: 6 weeks' paid maternity leave, 6 weeks' vacation, 12 paid holidays, 12 sick days, an educational reimbursement, and medical and dental insurance coverage.

In July 1993, Goff-Hamel met with representatives of Obstetricians regarding the possibility of employment. Present at the meeting were Janet Quackenbush, the office manager; Dr. George Adam, a part owner of Obstetricians; and Larry Draper, a consultant of Obstetricians involved in personnel decisions. Adam had approached Goff-Hamel in June 1993 about working for him as a patient relations and outreach coordinator at Obstetricians. Goff-Hamel initially declined the offer, explaining that she had made commitments to do some training in the fall and to hire and help train a new bookkeeper. Adam spoke to Goff-Hamel approximately 1 month later, asking her to reconsider and whether she was ready to "jump ship and come work for him." Goff-Hamel told Adam she would be interested in hearing some details, and an interview was set for July 27 at Adam's office.

At the meeting, Adam represented to Goff-Hamel that the position would be full time and would start at a salary of $10 per hour and that she would be provided 2 weeks' paid vacation, three or four paid holidays, uniforms, and an educational stipend. A retirement plan would start after the end of the second year, retroactive to the end of the first year. The job would not provide health insurance.

Goff-Hamel was offered a job with Obstetricians during the July 27, 1993, meeting, and she accepted the job offer at that time. She expressed concern that she be given time to finish some projects at Hastings Family Planning, and it was agreed that she would start her employment on October 4. Goff-Hamel gave notice to Hastings Family Planning in August, informing them that she would be resigning to take a job with Obstetricians.

Subsequently, Goff-Hamel went to Obstetricians' office and was provided with uniforms for her job. She was given a copy of her schedule for the first week of work, but did not receive a copy of the employee handbook.

On October 3, 1993, Goff-Hamel was told by Draper that she should not report to work the next morning as had been planned. Draper told her that Janel Foote, the wife of a part owner of Obstetricians, Dr. Terry Foote, opposed the hiring of

Goff-Hamel. . . . Goff-Hamel sought replacement employment, but was unable to obtain employment until April 1995, when she was employed part time at the rate of $11 per hour. . . .

It is undisputed that on July 27, 1993, Obstetricians offered Goff-Hamel employment and that she accepted. The oral agreement did not specify that the employment was for a definite period. We have consistently held that when employment is not for a definite term and there are no contractual, statutory, or constitutional restrictions upon the right of discharge, an employer may lawfully discharge an employee whenever and for whatever cause it chooses. Therefore, the trial court correctly determined as a matter of law that Goff-Hamel could not bring a claim for breach of an employment contract.

Goff-Hamel's second cause of action was based upon promissory estoppel. " '[T]he development of the law of promissory estoppel "is an attempt by the courts to keep remedies abreast of increased moral consciousness of honesty and fair representations in all business dealings." ' " *Rosnick v. Dinsmore*, 457 N.W.2d 793, 801 (1990).

Promissory estoppel provides for damages as justice requires and does not attempt to provide the plaintiff damages based upon the benefit of the bargain. *Id.* It requires only that reliance be reasonable and foreseeable. It does not impose the requirement that the promise giving rise to the cause of action must be so comprehensive in scope as to meet the requirements of an offer that would ripen into a contract if accepted by the promisee.

We have not specifically addressed whether promissory estoppel may be asserted as the basis for a cause of action for detrimental reliance upon a promise of at-will employment. In *Merrick v. Thomas*, 522 N.W.2d 402 (1994), the employee was terminated from her job approximately 4 months after she had been hired. We determined that because the employee had worked for a time, the employer had kept his promise to employ the plaintiff and that promissory estoppel was not available. We did not consider whether a cause of action based upon promissory estoppel could be stated by a prospective at-will employee who had been induced to leave previous gainful employment based upon the promise of other employment, but who did not commence employment at the new job.

Other jurisdictions which have addressed the question of whether a cause of action for promissory estoppel can be stated in the context of a prospective at-will employee are split on the issue. Some have held that an employee can recover damages incurred as a result of resigning from the former at-will employment in reliance on a promise of other at-will employment. They have determined that when a prospective employer knows or should know that a promise of employment will induce an employee to leave his or her current job, such employer shall be liable for the reliant's damages. Recognizing that both the prospective new employer and the prior employer could have fired the employee without cause at any time, they have concluded that the employee would have continued to work in his or her prior employment if it were not for the offer by the prospective employer. Although damages have not been allowed for wages lost from the prospective at-will employment, damages have been allowed based upon wages from the prior employment and other damages incurred in reliance on the job offer.

In contrast, other jurisdictions have held as a matter of law that a prospective employee cannot recover damages incurred in reliance on an unfulfilled promise of at-will employment, concluding that reliance on a promise consisting solely of at-will employment is unreasonable as a matter of law because the employee should know that the promised employment could be terminated by the employer at any time for any reason without liability. These courts have stated that an anomalous result occurs when recovery is allowed for an employee who has not begun work, when the same employee's job could be terminated without liability 1 day after beginning work. . . .

[W]e conclude under the facts of this case that promissory estoppel can be asserted in connection with the offer of at-will employment and that the trial court erred in granting Obstetricians summary judgment. A cause of action for promissory estoppel is based upon a promise which the promisor should reasonably expect to induce action or forbearance on the part of the promisee which does in fact induce such action or forbearance. Here, promissory estoppel is appropriate where Goff-Hamel acted to her detriment in order to avail herself of the promised employment.

We next consider whether the trial court should have granted summary judgment in favor of Goff-Hamel. . . .

In the present context, the questions are (1) whether Obstetricians made a definite promise of employment to Goff-Hamel which Obstetricians reasonably expected or should have expected would induce Goff-Hamel to terminate her present employment; (2) whether Goff-Hamel was, in fact, induced to act by such offer; (3) whether the action taken by Goff-Hamel was detrimental to her; and (4) whether justice requires that Obstetricians reimburse Goff-Hamel for damages incurred as a result of the promise of employment.

The facts are not disputed that Obstetricians offered Goff-Hamel employment. Apparently, at the direction of the spouse of one of the owners, Obstetricians refused to honor its promise of employment. It is also undisputed that Goff-Hamel relied upon Obstetricians' promise of employment to her detriment in that she terminated her employment of 11 years. Therefore, under the facts of this case, the trial court should have granted summary judgment in favor of Goff-Hamel on the issue of liability.

However, there remains a material issue of fact regarding the amount of damages sustained by Goff-Hamel. . . . Promissory estoppel provides for damages as justice requires and does not attempt to provide the plaintiff damages based upon the benefit of the bargain. For example, the damages sustained by an employee who quits current employment to accept another job are different than the damages sustained by an employee who had no prior employment but may have moved to a new location in reliance upon a job offer. In the latter case, wages from prior employment are not considered in the determination of damages because the party did not give up prior employment in reliance upon the new offer. In neither case are damages to be based upon the wages the employee would have earned in the prospective employment because the employment was terminable at will. . . .

STEPHAN, J., dissenting.

. . . I cannot reconcile the result reached by the majority or its rationale with our firmly established legal principles governing at-will employment. As succinctly and, in my view, correctly stated by the district court: "Since plaintiff could have been terminated after one day's employment without the defendant incurring liability, logic dictates she could also be terminated before the employment started." . . .

I would follow what I consider to be the better reasoned view that promissory estoppel may not be utilized to remedy an unfulfilled promise of at-will employment. I acknowledge that this reasoning would produce a seemingly harsh result from the perspective of Goff-Hamel under the facts of this case, but to some degree, this is inherent in the concept of at-will employment. . . . Similarly, an employer which has made a significant expenditure in training an at-will employee may feel harshly treated if, upon completing the training, the employee immediately utilizes his or her newly acquired skills to secure more remunerative employment with a competitor. If the law of at-will employment were regularly bent to circumvent what some may consider a harsh result in a particular case, its path would soon become hopelessly circuitous and impossible to follow.

Employment for a specific duration imposes certain benefits and burdens upon each party to the relationship. Under our established law, parties wishing to create such a relationship must do so by contract. Where, as in this case, the parties have not chosen to impose contractual obligations upon themselves, it is my view that a court should not utilize the principle of promissory estoppel to impose the subjective expectations of either party upon the other.

NOTES

1. **Restatement Elements.** Promissory estoppel is an implied contract doctrine intended to enforce promises that induce reasonable detrimental reliance when the factual circumstances fall short of establishing a formally bargained-for exchange. *The Restatement of Contracts* set out the elements:

> A promise which the promisor should reasonably expect to induce action or forbearance . . . on the part of the promisee and which does induce such action or forbearance is binding if injustice can be avoided only by enforcement of the promise.

RESTATEMENT (SECOND) OF CONTRACTS § 90 (1981). Were each of these elements met in Goff-Hamel's case? Which element presents the greatest difficulty given the nature of the employment offer she received?

Promissory estoppel also differs from ordinary breach of contract claims in the type of damages that are available. According to the court, how should Goff-Hamel's damages be measured? Are there any difficulties in determining the amount of damages given that her employment would have been at-will?

2. **Reasonable Reliance on At-Will Employment?** Is it reasonable for a worker to rely on a promise of at-will employment? In a case involving an offer of prospective employment like in *Goff-Hamel*, the court thought it could be reason-

able, because even though an employer has the legal right to fire, an employee might reasonably believe that right would not be exercised before the employee begins work. *Cocchiara v. Lithia Motors, Inc.*, 297 P.3d 1277, 1284 (Or. 2013). Moreover, the court expressed concern that barring a promissory estoppel claim might "allow an employer to abuse its ability to induce the reliance of prospective employees." For example, the employer "could promise an at-will job to multiple people to keep them available while the employer continued to vet them or to prevent them from accepting a position with a competitor." *Id.* at 1285–86. Does such a concern justify permitting promissory estoppel claims based on at-will promises? Or is that possibility simply an inevitable consequence of at-will employment?

One argument made against permitting a promissory estoppel claim is that it creates an anomaly, because it protects the at-will employee who could be fired on the first day of work. The court in *Grouse v. Group Health Plan, Inc.*, 306 N.W.2d 114 (Minn. 1981), a case cited by the majority in *Goff-Hamel*, considered this argument in a similar case. The defendant, Group Health Plan, had offered the plaintiff, John Grouse, a position as pharmacist at one of its clinics. Grouse accepted the offer, but informed defendant that he needed to give his current employer two weeks notice. He gave notice, and also turned down another offer of employment. Ten days later, when Grouse called Group Health ready to report to work, he was told that someone else had been hired. Grouse had difficulty finding another fulltime job.

Because the employment would have been at-will, the court found that "neither party is committed to performance and the promises are, therefore, illusory." *Id.* at 116. However, in the absence of an actual contract, the court held that a promissory estoppel claim was appropriate:

> Group Health contends that recognition of a cause of action on these facts would result in the anomalous rule that an employee who is told not to report to work the day before he is scheduled to begin has a remedy while an employee who is discharged after the first day does not. We cannot agree since under appropriate circumstances we believe section 90 would apply even after employment has begun. . . . The conclusion we reach does not imply that an employer will be liable whenever he discharges an employee whose term of employment is at will. What we do hold is that under the facts of this case the appellant had a right to assume he would be given a good faith opportunity to perform his duties to the satisfaction of respondent once he was on the job. He was not only denied that opportunity but resigned the position he already held in reliance on the firm offer which respondent tendered him. . . .

Id. The dissent in *Goff-Hamel* criticized the *Grouse* case, arguing that the notion that an at-will employee has "a right to assume he would be given a good faith opportunity to perform his duties to the satisfaction" of the employer is entirely inconsistent with "the established principle . . . that in the absence of contractual, statutory, or constitutional restrictions, an employer may discharge an at-will employee 'whenever and for whatever cause it chooses.' "

Some courts, like the dissent in *Goff-Hamel*, view the promissory estoppel claim as inconsistent with at-will employment and simply refuse to recognize such a claim by an at-will employee. *See Knowlton v. Shaw*, 791 F. Supp. 2d 220, 258 (D. Me. 2011); *Rosatone v. GTE Sprint Communications*, 761 S.W.2d 670, 673 (Mo. Ct. App. 1988) (rejecting employee's promissory estoppel claim as "an attempt to 'outflank' the employment-at-will doctrine").

3.   **Estoppel After Commencing Work.** The court in *Goff-Hamel* mentions its earlier decision in *Merrick v. Thomas*, 522 N.W.2d 402 (Neb. 1994), in which it held that an employee terminated four months after she was hired could not bring a promissory estoppel claim. Can its decision in *Goff-Hamel* be reconciled with the earlier case?

The court in *Grouse* stated that "under appropriate circumstances" a promissory estoppel claim would apply even after an at-will employment relationship had begun. What circumstances would make recognition of a promissory estoppel claim "appropriate" after an employee has started working? By making such a claim available, is the court converting at-will employment into an indefinite-term just cause contract? Or are there some inherent limits to the doctrine? In what ways would a promissory estoppel claim differ in the protection it provided compared with an indefinite-term just cause contract?

Promissory estoppel claims may also be based on a promise of something other than at-will employment. In *Blinn v. Beatrice Community Hosp.*, 708 N.W.2d 235 (Neb. 2006), the plaintiff, an at-will employee, alleged that he gave up an offer of a better job elsewhere when his current employer assured him that he would be employed for at least five more years, but then terminated him several months later. Even though the employer's promise was not definite enough to create an oral contract of job security, the court held that a genuine issue of material fact existed as to whether the promise could reasonably be expected to induce Blinn to forego the other job offer, and thus permitted the plaintiff to proceed on his promissory estoppel claim.

4.   **Low Success Rates.** One might expect promissory estoppel to have particular force in the employment setting, where employers, seeking to build loyalty and morale among their workers, use promissory language or assurances of fair treatment, and employees, in the absence of formal negotiations over the terms of employment, are likely to rely on those statements in committing themselves psychologically to a particular job. In fact, however, promissory estoppel claims appear to have only limited success in the employment context.

Robert Hillman concludes that employment-based promissory estoppel claims have been "monumentally unsuccessful," based on an empirical study of all reported decisions involving promissory estoppel claims in the United States over a two-year period in the mid-1990s. *See* Robert A. Hillman, *The Unfulfilled Promise of Promissory Estoppel in the Employment Setting*, 31 RUTGERS L.J. 1, 21 (1999). Among the cases he examined, only 4.23% of claims brought by employees succeeded on the merits. Although this low success rate is part of a larger judicial trend disfavoring the promissory estoppel theory, employment-based claims still fared significantly worse than such claims brought in other contexts, 14.65% of which succeeded on the merits. Hillman suggests that although some of the claims were clearly weak claims, it appears that "judicial veneration of the employment-at-will rule" contributes to a situation in which courts rarely permit promissory estoppel claims to proceed, and then "only on the strongest showing of each element." *Id.* at 25–26. As a result, he argues, meritorious claims are often precluded.

5. The Relevance of Relocation. In addition to resigning from their current jobs, employees sometimes relocate their homes and families a great distance in order to take a new job. Should the financial and psychic costs of doing so be relevant to the legal analysis?

As we saw in *Savage v. Spur Distributing Co.*, 228 S.W.2d 122 (Tenn. Ct. App. 1949), *supra*, discharged employees sometimes argued that the costs of moving to accept new employment constituted additional consideration sufficient to support an employer's promise not to discharge without cause. Like the court in *Savage*, however, most courts in the first half of the 20th century rejected such arguments.

Today, an employee's relocation could be relevant to the legal analysis in several different ways. Under a promissory estoppel theory, moving might establish that the plaintiff acted in reliance on an employer's promises. *See, e.g., Peck v. Imedia, Inc.*, 679 A.2d 745 (N.J. Super. Ct. App. Div. 1996) (holding that worker's moving from Boston to New Jersey and giving up her desktop publishing business for promise of employment stated claim for promissory estoppel because of detrimental reliance). In order to prevail, however, the plaintiff would also have to prove the other elements of promissory estoppel, including the reasonableness of the plaintiff's reliance.

Alternatively, evidence that an employee incurred the costs of moving might strengthen the plaintiff's claim that an express contract existed between the parties. For some courts, the employee's relocation and other visible forms of reliance serve an evidentiary function, providing extrinsic evidence that the parties had in fact agreed to some limitation on the employer's power to discharge. For example, in *Coelho v. Posi-Seal International, Inc.*, 544 A.2d 170 (Conn. 1988), the court wrote:

> The evidence that the plaintiff had foregone other job opportunities, had relocated from Massachusetts to the New London area, and had purchased a home and become obligated on a mortgage was material as proof of his reasonable expectations in light of the promises made to him, as it confirmed his testimony that special assurance concerning job security was given to him. This evidence, upon which the jury may reasonably have relied in finding the employment agreement could be terminated only for just cause, fulfilled its function in supporting the plaintiff's version of the terms of the agreement, whether or not it would satisfy the criteria for a separate consideration.

Id. at 177.

In contrast, in *Kurtzman v. Applied Analytical Industries, Inc.*, 493 S.E.2d 420 (N.C. 1997), the Supreme Court of North Carolina found no reason to give any weight to the fact that the plaintiff had recently moved from another state in reliance on the employment offer. The employer in that case had contacted

Kurtzman while he was working for another company in the northeast, and recruited him for a position in Wilmington, North Carolina. After some negotiation, including assurances about job security in response to his inquiries, Kurtzman accepted the offer, sold his home in Massachusetts and moved his family to Wilmington. After seven months on the job, he was terminated. The court dismissed the fact that Kurtzman had incurred the costs of relocation:

> The society to which the employment-at-will doctrine currently applies is a highly mobile one in which relocation to accept new employment is common. To remove an employment relationship from the at-will presumption upon an employee's change of residence, coupled with vague assurances of continued employment, would substantially erode the rule and bring considerable instability to an otherwise largely clear area of the law. *See House v. Cannon Mills Co.*, 713 F. Supp. 159, 164 (M.D.N.C. 1988) ("Recognition of a general exception whenever relocation or a job change is involved would emasculate the terminable-at-will rule, because many if not most hirings involve either a job change or a change of residence or both."). We thus hold that plaintiff-employee's change of residence in the wake of defendant-employer's statements here does not constitute additional consideration making what is otherwise an at-will employment relationship one that can be terminated by the employer only for cause.

Id. at 423. As we saw in Chapter 2, *supra*, labor markets have been characterized by greater mobility in recent years, with the breakdown of the traditional pattern of career employment with a single firm. Does the fact that it is increasingly common for employees to move between jobs and firms mean that relocating should be viewed as a less significant detriment to the employee today? Or does some other rationale underlie the *Kurtzman* court's refusal to attribute any legal significance to the plaintiff's relocation?

6. Other Promises. Promissory estoppel may also protect reasonable reliance on employer promises about issues other than job security. For example, in *Peters v. Gilead Sciences, Inc.*, 533 F.3d 594 (7th Cir. 2008), the court permitted an employee who was terminated while on medical leave to pursue a promissory estoppel claim based on provisions in the employer's handbook guaranteeing its employees twelve weeks of medical leave. Even though the employee had no statutory right to leave under the Family and Medical Leave Act, or any other federal or state statute, the court found that he had reasonably relied on the employer's promises that he was entitled to leave at the time of his termination.

2. The Implied Covenant of Good Faith and Fair Dealing

According to the Restatement, "Every contract imposes upon each party a duty of good faith and fair dealing in its performance and its enforcement." RESTATEMENT (SECOND) OF CONTRACTS § 205 (1981). The Uniform Commercial Code and the overwhelming majority of American jurisdictions have also endorsed the rule. U.C.C. § 1-304 (Supp. 2002). This duty—implied as a matter of law—allows courts "to effectuate the intentions of parties, or to protect their reasonable expectations." Steven J. Burton, *Breach of Contract and the Common Law Duty to Perform in Good Faith*, 94 HARV. L. REV. 369, 371 (1980). The following materials explore whether or how one can reconcile a covenant of good faith and fair dealing implied in all contracts with at-will employment.

FORTUNE v. NATIONAL CASH REGISTER CO.
Supreme Judicial Court of Massachusetts
364 N.E.2d 1251 (1977)

ABRAMS, JUSTICE.

Orville E. Fortune (Fortune), a former salesman of The National Cash Register Company (NCR), brought a suit to recover certain commissions allegedly due as a result of a sale of cash registers to First National Stores Inc. (First National) in 1968. . . .

Fortune was employed by NCR under a written "salesman's contract" which was terminable at will, without cause, by either party on written notice. The contract provided that Fortune would receive a weekly salary in a fixed amount plus a bonus for sales made within the "territory" (i.e., customer accounts or stores) assigned to him for "coverage or supervision," whether the sale was made by him or someone else. The amount of the bonus was determined on the basis of "bonus credits," which were computed as a percentage of the price of products sold. Fortune would be paid a percentage of the applicable bonus credit as follows: (1) 75% if the territory was assigned to him at the date of the order, (2) 25% if the territory was assigned to him at the date of delivery and installation, or (3) 100% if the territory was assigned to him at both times. The contract further provided that the "bonus interest" would terminate if shipment of the order was not made within eighteen months from the date of the order unless (1) the territory was assigned to him for coverage at the date of delivery and installation, or (2) special engineering was required to fulfil the contract. In addition, NCR reserved the right to sell products in the salesman's territory without paying a bonus. However, this right could be exercised only on written notice.

In 1968, Fortune's territory included First National. This account had been part of his territory for the preceding six years; he had been successful in obtaining several orders from First National, including a million dollar order in 1963. Sometime in late 1967, or early 1968, NCR introduced a new model cash register, Class 5. Fortune corresponded with First National in an effort to sell the machine. He also helped to arrange for a demonstration of the Class 5 to executives of First National on October 4, 1968. NCR had a team of men also working on this sale.

On November 27, 1968, NCR's manager of chain and department stores, and the Boston branch manager, both part of NCR's team, wrote to First National regarding the Class 5. The letter covered a number of subjects, including price protection, trade-ins, and trade-in protection against obsolescence. While NCR normally offered price protection for only an eighteen-month term, apparently the size of the proposed order from First National caused NCR to extend its price protection terms for either a two-year or four-year period. On November 29, 1968, First National signed an order for 2,008 Class 5 machines to be delivered over a four-year period at a purchase price of approximately $5,000,000. Although Fortune did not participate in the negotiation of the terms of the order, his name appeared on the order form in the space entitled "salesman credited." The amount of the bonus credit as shown on the order was $92,079.99.

On January 6, 1969, the first working day of the new year, Fortune found an envelope on his desk at work. It contained a termination notice addressed to his home dated December 2, 1968. Shortly after receiving the notice, Fortune spoke to the Boston branch manager with whom he was friendly. The manager told him, "You are through," but, after considering some of the details necessary for the smooth operation of the First National order, told him to "stay on," and to "[k]eep on doing what you are doing right now." Fortune remained with the company in a position entitled "sales support." In this capacity, he coordinated and expedited delivery of the machines to First National under the November 29 order as well as servicing other accounts.

Commencing in May or June, Fortune began to receive some bonus commissions on the First National order. Having received only 75% of the applicable bonus due on the machines which had been delivered and installed, Fortune spoke with his manager about receiving the full amount of the commission. Fortune was told "to forget about it." Sixty-one years old at that time, and with a son in college, Fortune concluded that it "was a good idea to forget it for the time being."

NCR did pay a systems and installations person the remaining 25% of the bonus commissions due from the First National order although contrary to its usual policy of paying only salesmen a bonus. NCR, by its letter of November 27, 1968, had promised the services of a systems and installations person; the letter had claimed that the services of this person, Bernie Martin (Martin), would have a forecasted cost to NCR of over $45,000. As promised, NCR did transfer Martin to the First National account shortly after the order was placed.

Approximately eighteen months after receiving the termination notice, Fortune, who had worked for NCR for almost twenty-five years, was asked to retire. When he refused, he was fired in June of 1970. Fortune did not receive any bonus payments on machines which were delivered to First National after this date. . . .

[The jury found that the defendant had acted in bad faith when it decided to terminate the Plaintiff's contract as a salesman by letter dated December 2, 1968, delivered on January 6, 1969 and when it let the Plaintiff go on June 5, 1970. It awarded plaintiff $45,649.62 in damages.[8]]

The central issue on appeal is whether this "bad faith" termination constituted a breach of the employment at will contract. Traditionally, an employment contract which is "at will" may be terminated by either side without reason. . . .

The contract at issue is a classic terminable at will employment contract. It is clear that the contract itself reserved to the parties an explicit power to terminate the contract without cause on written notice. It is also clear that under the express terms of the contract Fortune has received all the bonus commissions to which he

---

[8] [n. 6] The amount apparently represented 25% of the commission due during the eighteen months the machines were delivered to First National, and which was paid to Martin, and 100% of the commissions on the machines delivered after Fortune was fired.

is entitled. Thus, NCR claims that it did not breach the contract, and that it has no further liability to Fortune.[9] According to a literal reading of the contract, NCR is correct.

However, Fortune argues that, in spite of the literal wording of the contract, he is entitled to a jury determination on NCR's motives in terminating his services under the contract and in finally discharging him. We agree. We hold that NCR's written contract contains an implied covenant of good faith and fair dealing, and a termination not made in good faith constitutes a breach of the contract.

We do not question the general principles that an employer is entitled to be motivated by and to serve its own legitimate business interests; that an employer must have wide latitude in deciding whom it will employ in the face of the uncertainties of the business world; and that an employer needs flexibility in the face of changing circumstances. We recognize the employer's need for a large amount of control over its work force. However, we believe that where, as here, commissions are to be paid for work performed by the employee, the employer's decision to terminate its at will employee should be made in good faith. NCR's right to make decisions in its own interest is not, in our view, unduly hampered by a requirement of adherence to this standard. . . . In so holding we are merely recognizing the general requirement in this Commonwealth that parties to contracts and commercial transactions must act in good faith toward one another. Good faith and fair dealing between parties are pervasive requirements in our law; it can be said fairly, that parties to contracts or commercial transactions are bound by this standard. . . .

[Citing a New Hampshire case finding bad faith termination of an at-will employee, the court explained that the earlier case] merely extends to employment contracts the rule that " 'in *every* contract there is an implied covenant that neither party shall do anything which will have the effect of destroying or injuring the right of the other party to receive the fruits of the contract, which means that in *every* contract there exists an implied covenant of good faith and fair dealing' " (emphasis supplied).

In the instant case, we need not pronounce our adherence to so broad a policy nor need we speculate as to whether the good faith requirement is implicit in every contract for employment at will. It is clear, however, that, on the facts before us, a finding is warranted that a breach of the contract occurred. Where the principal seeks to deprive the agent of all compensation by terminating the contractual relationship when the agent is on the brink of successfully completing the sale, the principal has acted in bad faith and the ensuing transaction between the principal and the buyer is to be regarded as having been accomplished by the agent. Restatement (Second) of Agency § 454, and Comment a (1958). The same result obtains where the principal attempts to deprive the agent of any portion of a commission due the agent. Courts have often applied this rule to prevent overreaching by employers and the forfeiture by employees of benefits almost earned by the

---

[9] [n. 7] Damages were, by stipulation of the parties, set equal to the unpaid bonus amounts. Thus we need not consider whether other measures of damages might be justified in cases of bad faith termination. Nor do we now decide whether a tort action, with possible punitive damages, might lie in such circumstances. . . .

rendering of substantial services. In our view, the Appeals Court erroneously focused only on literal compliance with payment provisions of the contract and failed to consider the issue of bad faith termination.

NCR argues that there was no evidence of bad faith in this case; therefore, the trial judge was required to direct a verdict in any event. We think that the evidence and the reasonable inferences to be drawn therefrom support a jury verdict that the termination of Fortune's twenty-five years of employment as a salesman with NCR the next business day after NCR obtained a $5,000,000 order from First National was motivated by a desire to pay Fortune as little of the bonus credit as it could. The fact that Fortune was willing to work under these circumstances does not constitute a waiver or estoppel; it only shows that NCR had him "at their mercy."

NCR also contends that Fortune cannot complain of his firing in June, 1970, as his employment contract clearly indicated that bonus credits would be paid only for an eighteen-month period following the date of the order. As we have said, the jury could have found that Fortune was stripped of his "salesman" designation in order to disqualify him for the remaining 25% of the commissions due on cash registers delivered prior to the date of his first termination. Similarly, the jury could have found that Fortune was fired so that NCR would avoid paying him any commissions on cash registers delivered after June, 1970.

Conversely, the jury could have found that Fortune was assigned by NCR to the First National account; that all he did in this case was arrange for a demonstration of the product; that he neither participated in obtaining the order nor did he assist NCR in closing the order; and that nevertheless NCR credited him with the sale. This, however, did not obligate the trial judge to direct a verdict. Where evidence is conflicting, the rule is clear: "If upon any reasonable view of the evidence there is found any combination of circumstances from which a rational inference may be drawn in favor of the plaintiff, then there was no error in the denial of the motion, even if there may be other and different circumstances disclosed in the evidence which, if accepted as true by the jury, would support a conclusion adverse to the plaintiff." *Howes v. Kelman*, 96 N.E.2d 394, 395 (1951).

We think that NCR's conduct in June, 1970 permitted the jury to find bad faith. . . .

Judgment of the Superior Court affirmed.

MURPHY v. AMERICAN HOME PRODUCTS CORP.
Court of Appeals of New York
448 N.E.2d 86 (1983)

Jones, Judge.

. . . Plaintiff, Joseph Murphy, was first employed by defendant, American Home Products Corp., in 1957. He thereafter served in various accounting positions, eventually attaining the office of assistant treasurer, but he never had a formal contract of employment. On April 18, 1980, when he was 59 years old, he was discharged.

Plaintiff claims that he was fired . . . because of his disclosure to top management of alleged accounting improprieties on the part of corporate personnel. . . . [P]laintiff asserts that his firing was in retaliation for his revelation to officers and directors of defendant corporation that he had uncovered at least $50 million in illegal account manipulations of secret pension reserves which improperly inflated the company's growth in income and allowed high-ranking officers to reap unwarranted bonuses from a management incentive plan, as well as in retaliation for his own refusal to engage in the alleged accounting improprieties. He contends that the company's internal regulations required him to make the disclosure that he did. He also alleges that his termination was carried out in a humiliating manner. . . .

[In addition to several other claims,] plaintiff asserted that, although his employment contract was of indefinite duration, the law imposes in every employment contract "the requirement that an employer shall deal with each employee fairly and in good faith." On that predicate he alleged that defendant's conduct in stalling his advancement and ultimately firing him for his disclosures "breached the terms of its contract requiring good faith and fair dealing toward plaintiff and damaged plaintiff thereby." . . .

Although he concedes in his complaint that his employment contract was of indefinite duration (inferentially recognizing that, were there no more, under traditional principles his employer might have discharged him at any time), he asserts that in all employment contracts the law implies an obligation on the part of the employer to deal with his employees fairly and in good faith and that a discharge in violation of that implied obligation exposes the employer to liability for breach of contract. Seeking then to apply this proposition to the present case, plaintiff argues in substance that he was required by the terms of his employment to disclose accounting improprieties and that defendant's discharge of him for having done so constituted a failure by the employer to act in good faith and thus a breach of the contract of employment.

No New York case upholding any such broad proposition is cited to us by plaintiff (or identified by our dissenting colleague), and we know of none. New York does recognize that in appropriate circumstances an obligation of good faith and fair dealing on the part of a party to a contract may be implied and, if implied will be enforced (e.g., *Wood v. Duff-Gordon*, 222 N.Y. 88; *Pernet v. Peabody Eng. Corp.*, 20 A.D.2d 781). In such instances the implied obligation is in aid and furtherance of other terms of the agreement of the parties. No obligation can be implied, however, which would be inconsistent with other terms of the contractual relationship. Thus, in the case now before us, plaintiff's employment was at will, a relationship in which the law accords the employer an unfettered right to terminate the employment at any time. In the context of such an employment it would be incongruous to say that an inference may be drawn that the employer impliedly agreed to a provision which would be destructive of his right of termination. The parties may by express agreement limit or restrict the employer's right of discharge, but to imply such a limitation from the existence of an unrestricted right would be internally inconsistent. In sum, under New York law as it now stands, absent a constitutionally impermissible purpose, a statutory proscription, or an express limitation in the individual contract of employment, an employer's right at any time to terminate an employment at will remains unimpaired. . . .

Accordingly [plaintiff's breach of contract claim] should have been dismissed for failure to state a cause of action.

MEYER, J., dissenting in part.

. . . I cannot [ ] accept the majority's refusal to follow precedent decisional law recognizing an implied-in-law obligation on the part of the employer not to discharge an employee for doing that which the employment contract obligated him to do. . . . Plaintiff's complaint alleges that "defendant's internal regulations . . . required that plaintiff report any deviation from proper accounting practice to defendant's top management" and that he was dismissed as a result of his doing just that. . . .

[The implied-in-law obligation referred to is] the covenant implied by the law that the parties will not "frustrate the contracts into which they have entered" and that one party will "not intentionally and purposely do anything to prevent the other party from carrying out the agreement on his part" (*Grad v. Roberts*, 14 NY2d 70, 75) or that may hinder or obstruct his doing that which the contract stipulates he should do (*Patterson v. Meyerhofer*, 204 NY 96, 101). . . . To be borne in mind is the fact that we deal not with a contract which by its expressed term authorizes the employer to terminate without cause, but with one in which, because no durational term has been expressed, the law implies a right of termination. In the latter situation only the strongest of policy reasons can sustain reading the *implied* right of termination as a limitation upon the *express* obligation imposed upon the employee. . . .

NOTES

1. **Good Faith Contracting.** Good faith and fair dealing speaks in contractual terms, but the obligation is not based on any express promises made by the parties to deal in good faith. What is the appropriate relationship between the actual terms agreed to and the covenant of good faith and fair dealing?

In *Fortune*, the plaintiff had a written contract regarding his compensation structure. Why couldn't he recover based on the express terms of the contract rather than relying on an implied covenant of good faith?

Unlike Fortune, Murphy did not have any sort of express contract governing his employment relationship, although he alleged that his employer's internal regulations required him to disclose any accounting improprieties to top management. In a subsequent case, *Sabetay v. Sterling Drug, Inc.*, 506 N.E.2d 919 (N.Y. 1987), the obligation of the employee to report wrongdoing was even clearer. In that case, an accountant alleged that he was fired for doing precisely what he was required to do under his employer's written "Accounting Code." The code stated:

> [i]t is corporate policy to prohibit illegal or improper payments from company funds or assets . . . It is the responsibility of every employee promptly to report to General Counsel any knowledge of infractions of this policy. Any employee who fails to follow these policies will incur a penalty.

Such penalty will range from lack of promotion (censure), to demotion or dismissal.

Id. at 923 (Hancock, J., concurring). Citing *Murphy*, the New York Court of Appeals rejected the plaintiff's claim that his discharge violated the covenant of good faith and fair dealing. The concurring judge complained that

> Under the [majority's ruling, the plaintiff] is precluded from claiming that the law, under the circumstances he alleges, imposes an obligation on the employer not to fire him for doing what he may be fired for failing to do. [Recognizing] an implied duty under these circumstances would not require an abandonment of the *Murphy* rule that a good-faith obligation will not be read into all employment at-will contracts. Such limited exception—"that in every contract there is an implied undertaking on the part of each party that he will not intentionally and purposely do anything to prevent the other party from carrying out the agreement on his part" (*Grad v. Roberts*, 198 N.E.2d 26)—is consistent with basic rules of contract law and has ample support in precedent and other recognized authority.

Id. at 923–24.

Do you agree that even an at-will employee should be protected against discharge for fulfilling his job obligations as spelled out by the employer?

2.   Good Faith vs. At-Will. The *Fortune* court holds that there was no error in submitting the bad faith claim to the jury even though the plaintiff was clearly an at-will employee. Is the court's holding in fact consistent with Fortune's at-will status? Or is the court essentially saying that the employer had to have good cause to terminate Fortune's employment? Why did the New York Court of Appeals in *Murphy* reject application of the implied covenant of good faith and fair dealing in the employment context? Can a duty of good faith and fair dealing be implied by law into an employment at-will contract, or is such a theory incoherent?

Although many courts refuse to recognize a duty of good faith in employment at all, other courts have held that the duty exists, but does not limit the employer's ability to discharge an at-will employee without cause. For example, the Arizona Supreme Court explained the implied covenant this way:

> [W]e do not feel that we should treat employment contracts as a special type of agreement in which the law refuses to imply the covenant of good faith and fair dealing that it implies in all other contracts. . . . [T]he implied-in-law covenant of good faith and fair dealing protects the right of the parties to an agreement to receive the benefits of the agreement that they have entered into. . . . Thus, the relevant inquiry always will focus on the contract itself, to determine what the parties did agree to. In the case of an employment-at-will contract, it may be said that the parties have agreed, for example, that the employee will do the work required by the employer and that the employer will provide the necessary working conditions and pay the employee for work done. What cannot be said is that one of the agreed benefits to the at-will employee is a guarantee of continued employment or tenure. . . .

The covenant does not protect the employee from a "no cause" termination because tenure was never a benefit inherent in the at-will agreement. The covenant does protect an employee from a discharge based on an employer's desire to avoid the payment of benefits already earned by the employee, such as the sales commissions in *Fortune*, but not the tenure required to earn the pension and retirement benefits in *Cleary* [*v. American Airlines, Inc.*, 111 Cal. App. 3d 443 (1980)].

Wagenseller v. Scottsdale Memorial Hospital, 710 P.2d 1025, 1040 (Ariz. 1985). *See also Gram v. Liberty Mutual Insurance Co.*, 429 N.E.2d 21 (Mass. 1981) (holding that implied good faith covenant is not violated when employee is discharged without cause; however, employer may be liable for loss of compensation related to employee's past service).

Other than situations like *Fortune*, where an employee is owed commissions for work already performed, can you think of other "benefits of the agreement" that an at-will employee might assert are protected by the implied covenant? In *Metcalf v. Intermountain Gas Co.*, 778 P.2d 744 (Idaho 1989), the plaintiff, a full-time employee, had health problems which required her to miss work for eight weeks. Although the amount of sick leave she took exceeded the company average, it was still less than the amount she had accrued under her employer's sick leave policy. She alleged that because of her sick leave history, her employer reduced her work schedule to two hours per day, eventually leading her to resign. The Idaho Supreme Court permitted her to proceed on a claim of breach of the implied covenant, reasoning that "[a]ny action by either party which violates, nullifies or significantly impairs any benefit of the employment contract is a violation of the implied-in-law covenant." *Id.* at 749. Concerned about the imprecision and unpredictability of a standard that focuses on the subjective intentions of the employer, however, the court stated that: "we reject the 'amorphous concept of bad faith' as the standard for determining whether the covenant has been breached." *Id.* at 749–50. *See also Cook v. Zions First National Bank*, 919 P.2d 56 (Utah 1996) (permitting plaintiff to proceed on a good faith claim based on employer's alleged refusal to permit her to use sick leave accrued pursuant to an express contract).

A few other courts have taken different approaches. For example, the Delaware Supreme Court looks for employer conduct with an aspect of fraud or deceit. In *Merrill v. Crothall-American, Inc.*, 606 A.2d 96, 101 (Del. 1992), it held that an employer violated the implied covenant "when it induces another to enter into an employment contract through actions, words, or the withholding of information, which is intentionally deceptive in some way material to the contract." Alaska takes the broadest view, holding that the covenant "requires that the employer act in a manner that a reasonable person would regard as fair." *Charles v. Interior Regional Housing Authority*, 55 P.3d 57, 62 (Alaska 2002). *See also Hoendermis v. Advanced Physical Therapy*, 251 P.3d 346, 356 (Alaska 2011).

Many states, however, simply refused to recognize employee claims based on the covenant of good faith and fair dealing at all, viewing them as encroaching too far on management prerogatives. For example, the Wisconsin Supreme Court stated:

We refuse to impose a duty to terminate in good faith into employment contracts. To do so would "subject each discharge to judicial incursions into the amorphous concept of bad faith." *Parnar v. Americana Hotels, Inc.*, 652 P.2d 625 (Haw. 1982). Moreover, we feel it unnecessary and unwarranted for the courts to become arbiters of any termination that may have a tinge of bad faith attached. Imposing a good faith duty to terminate would unduly restrict an employer's discretion in managing the workforce.

Brockmeyer v. Dun & Bradstreet, 335 N.W.2d 834 (Wis. 1983). *See also Bollinger v. Fall River Rural Elec. Coop.*, 272 P.3d 1263, 1271 (Idaho 2012) (stating that the covenant of good faith and fair dealing "does not create new duties that are not inherent in the agreement itself and, thus, cannot create a for-cause termination limitation in an at-will employment agreement").

Chapter 4

PUBLIC POLICY PROTECTIONS FOR INDIVIDUAL JOB SECURITY

We saw in the previous chapter that the common law views employment primarily as a matter of private agreement between employer and employee. Sometimes, however, that relationship may have effects that reach beyond the parties to the contract. When the at-will rule was at its zenith, courts were not concerned with how the employer exercised its authority to discharge or what impact that power might have on its workers or others.

Recall that in *Payne v. The Western & Atlantic Railroad Co.*, 81 Tenn. 507 (1884), discussed *supra*, a merchant complained that a railroad corporation had harmed his business by forbidding its employees on pain of discharge from patronizing his store. In rejecting the merchant's claim, the court in *Payne* wrote:

> Great corporations, strong associations, and wealthy individuals may thus do great mischief and wrong; may make and break merchants at will; may crush out competition, and foster monopolies, and thus greatly injure individuals and the public; but power is inherent in size and strength and wealth; and the law cannot set bound to it, unless it is exercised illegally. Then it is restrained because of its illegality, not because of its quantity or quality. The great and rich and powerful are guaranteed the same liberty and privilege as the poor and weak. All may buy and sell when they choose; they may refuse to employ or dismiss whom they choose, without being thereby guilty of a legal wrong, though it may seriously injure and even ruin others. . . . The law leaves employer and employee to make their own contracts; and these, when made, it will enforce; beyond this it does not go.

Id. at 519–20.

The dissent complained that:

> The principle of the majority opinion will justify employers, at any rate allow them to require employees to trade where they may demand, to vote as they may require, or do anything not strictly criminal that employer may dictate, or feel the wrath of employer by dismissal from service. . . . Capital may thus not only find its own legitimate employment, but may control the employment of others to an extent that in time may sap the foundations of our free institutions. Perfect freedom in all legitimate uses is due to capital, and should be zealously enforced, but public policy and all the best interests of society demands it shall be restrained within legitimate boundaries. . . .

Id. at 543–44. (Freeman, J., dissenting)

For many decades after *Payne*, the position articulated by the majority was the dominant one, such that even when the employer's exercise of its power to discharge had effects beyond the operation of its business, the courts refused to intervene on the grounds that no contractual provision limited the employer's actions. As seen in Part I, *supra*, the first inroads on the employer's unfettered right to terminate were statutory. The National Labor Relations Act, passed in 1935, forbade discharging employees for their union activities, and Title VII of the Civil Rights Act of 1964 prohibited terminating employees because of their race, color, sex, national origin, or religion, thus making unlawful a few narrowly defined bad motives for discharge.

Then, in 1967, Lawrence Blades published an influential article calling for recognition of a right of employees to sue for abusive discharge, arguing that the fear of discharge rendered "the great majority of employees vulnerable to employer coercion." Lawrence E. Blades, *Employment at Will vs. Individual Freedom: On Limiting the Abusive Exercise of Employer Power*, 67 COLUM. L. REV. 1404, 1406 (1967). Blades argued that unchecked employer power threatened the freedom of the individual, particularly in areas of his life with no relevance to the employment relationship, and risked pressing the employee into engaging in immoral or unlawful activities.

In the following decades, the common law courts developed a number of doctrines that mitigated the harshness of the at-will rule. As we saw in Chapter 3, *supra*, some of these were based on contract law, and focused on the nature of the employment agreement. Others were grounded in tort law and sought to vindicate important interests irrespective of the nature of the contract. In this chapter, we focus on one particular claim that offers individual employees some protection for job security: wrongful discharge in violation of public policy.

A.   THE PUBLIC POLICY EXCEPTION

SHEETS v. TEDDY'S FROSTED FOODS, INC.
Supreme Court of Connecticut
427 A.2d 385 (1980)

PETERS, ASSOCIATE JUSTICE.

The issue in this case is whether an employer has a completely unlimited right to terminate the services of an employee whom it has hired for an indefinite term.
. . .

The complaint alleges that for a four-year period, from November, 1973, to November, 1977, the plaintiff was employed by the defendant, a producer of frozen food products, as its quality control director and subsequently also as operations manager. In the course of his employment, the plaintiff received periodic raises and bonuses. In his capacity as quality control director and operations manager, the plaintiff began to notice deviations from the specifications contained in the defendant's standards and labels, in that some vegetables were substandard and some meat components underweight. These deviations meant that the defendant's products violated the express representations contained in the defendant's labeling; false or misleading labels in turn violate the provisions of General Statutes § 19-222, the Connecticut Uniform Food, Drug and Cosmetic Act. In May of 1977, the plaintiff communicated in writing to the defendant concerning the use of substandard raw materials and underweight components in the defendant's finished products. His recommendations for more selective purchasing and conforming components were ignored. On November 3, 1977, his employment with the defendant was terminated. Although the stated reason for his discharge was unsatisfactory performance of his duties, he was actually dismissed in retaliation for his efforts to ensure that the defendant's products would comply with the applicable law relating to labeling and licensing. . . .

The issue before us is whether to recognize an exception to the traditional rules governing employment at will so as to permit a cause of action for wrongful discharge where the discharge contravenes a clear mandate of public policy. In addressing that claim, we must clarify what is not at stake in this litigation. The plaintiff does not challenge the general proposition that contracts of permanent employment, or for an indefinite term, are terminable at will. Nor does he argue that contracts terminable at will permit termination only upon a showing of just cause for dismissal. . . . There is a significant distinction between a criterion of just cause and what the plaintiff is seeking. "Just cause" substantially limits employer discretion to terminate, by requiring the employer, in all instances, to proffer a proper reason for dismissal, by forbidding the employer to act arbitrarily or capriciously. By contrast, the plaintiff asks only that the employer be responsible in damages if the former employee can prove a demonstrably *improper* reason for dismissal, a reason whose impropriety is derived from some important violation of public policy. . . .

It would be difficult to maintain that the right to discharge an employee hired at will is so fundamentally different from other contract rights that its exercise is never subject to judicial scrutiny regardless of how outrageous, how violative of public policy, the employer's conduct may be. The defendant does not seriously contest the propriety of cases in other jurisdictions that have found wrongful and actionable a discharge in retaliation for the exercise of an employee's right to: (1) refuse to commit perjury; *Petermann v. International Brotherhood of Teamsters*, 344 P.2d 25 (1959); (2) file a workmen's compensation claim; *Frampton v. Central Indiana Gas Co.*, 297 N.E.2d 425 (1973); *Sventko v. Kroger Co.*, 245 N.W.2d 151 (1976); *Brown v. Transcon Lines*, 588 P.2d 1087 (1978); (3) engage in union activity; *Glenn v. Clearman's Golden Cock Inn*, Inc., 13 Cal. Rptr. 769 (1961); (4) perform jury duty; *Nees v. Hocks*, 536 P.2d 512 (1975); *Reuther v. Fowler & Williams, Inc.*, 386 A.2d 119 (1978). While it may be true that these cases are supported by mandates of public policy derived directly from the applicable state statutes and constitutions, it is equally true that they serve at a minimum to establish the principle that public policy imposes some limits on unbridled discretion to terminate the employment of someone hired at will. . . .

The issue then becomes the familiar common-law problem of deciding where and how to draw the line between claims that genuinely involve the mandates of public policy and are actionable, and ordinary disputes between employee and employer that are not. We are mindful that courts should not lightly intervene to impair the exercise of managerial discretion or to foment unwarranted litigation. We are, however, equally mindful that the myriad of employees without the bargaining power to command employment contracts for a definite term are entitled to a modicum of judicial protection when their conduct as good citizens is punished by their employers.

The central allegation of the plaintiff's complaint is that he was discharged because of his conduct in calling to his employer's attention repeated violations of the Connecticut Uniform Food, Drug and Cosmetic Act. This act prohibits the sale of mislabeled food. General Statutes §§ 19-213,[1] 19-222.[2] The act, in § 19-215,[3] imposes criminal penalties upon anyone who violates § 19-213; subsection (b) of § 19-215 makes it clear that criminal sanctions do not depend upon proof of intent to defraud or mislead, since special sanctions are imposed for intentional misconduct. The plaintiff's position as quality control director and operations manager might have exposed him to the possibility of criminal prosecution under this act. The act was intended to "safeguard the public health and promote the public welfare by protecting the consuming public from injury by product use and the purchasing public from injury by merchandising deceit . . . ." General Statutes § 19-211.

It is useful to compare the factual allegations of this complaint with those of other recent cases in which recovery was sought for retaliatory discharge. In *Geary v. United States Steel Corporation*, [319 A.2d 174 (1974)], in which the plaintiff had disputed the safety of tubular steel casings, he was denied recovery because, as a company salesman, he had neither the expertise nor the corporate responsibility to "exercise independent, expert judgment in matters of product safety." By contrast, this plaintiff, unless his title is meaningless, did have responsibility for product quality control. Three other recent cases in which the plaintiff's claim survived demurrer closely approximate the claim before us. In *Trombetta v. Detroit, Toledo & Ironton R. Co.*, 265 N.W.2d 385 (1978), a cause of action was stated when an employee alleged that he had been discharged in retaliation for his refusal to manipulate and alter sampling results for pollution control reports required by Michigan law. There, as here, falsified reports would have violated state law. In *Harless v. First National Bank in Fairmont*, 246 S.E.2d 270, 276 (W. Va. 1978), an employee stated a cause of action when he alleged that he had been discharged in retaliation for his efforts to ensure his employer's compliance with state and federal consumer credit protection laws. There, as here, the legislature had established a public policy of consumer protection. In *Pierce v. Ortho Pharmaceutical Corpora-*

---

[1] [n. 4] "[General Statutes] Sec. 19-213. PROHIBITED ACTS. The following acts and the causing thereof shall be prohibited: (a) The sale in intrastate commerce of any food, drug, device or cosmetic that is adulterated or misbranded; (b) the adulteration or misbranding of any food, drug, device or cosmetic in intrastate commerce . . . ."

[2] [n. 5] Section 19-222 provides in relevant part: "MISBRANDED FOOD. A food shall be deemed to be misbranded: (a) If its labeling is false or misleading in any particular."

[3] [n. 6] Section 19-215 provides in relevant part: "PENALTIES. (a) Any person who violates any provision of section 19-213 shall, on conviction thereof, be imprisoned not more than six months or fined not more than five hundred dollars or both. . . . (b) Notwithstanding the provisions of subsection (a) of this section, any person who violates any provision of section 19-213, with intent to defraud or mislead, shall be imprisoned not more than one year or fined not more than one thousand dollars or both."

tion, 399 A.2d 1023 (1979), the plaintiff was entitled to a trial to determine whether she had been wrongfully discharged for refusing to pursue clinical testing of a new drug containing a high level of saccharin; the court noted that the plaintiff's status as a physician entitled her to invoke the Hippocratic Oath as well as state statutory provisions governing the licensing and the conduct of physicians. There, as here, the case might have been dismissed as a conflict in judgment.

In the light of these recent cases, which evidence a growing judicial receptivity to the recognition of a tort claim for wrongful discharge, the trial court was in error in granting the defendant's motion to strike. The plaintiff alleged that he had been dismissed in retaliation for his insistence that the defendant comply with the requirements of a state statute, the Food, Drug and Cosmetic Act. We need not decide whether violation of a state statute is invariably a prerequisite to the conclusion that a challenged discharge violates public policy. Certainly when there is a relevant state statute we should not ignore the statement of public policy that it represents. For today, it is enough to decide that an employee should not be put to an election whether to risk criminal sanction or to jeopardize his continued employment. . . .

COTTER, CHIEF JUSTICE, dissenting.

I cannot agree that, on the factual situation presented to us, we should abandon the well-established principle that an indefinite general hiring may be terminated at the will of either party without liability to the other. The majority by seeking to extend a "modicum" of judicial protection to shield employees from retaliatory discharges instead offers them a sword with which to coerce employers to retain them in their employ. In recognizing an exception to the traditional rules governing employment at will and basing a new cause of action for retaliatory discharge on the facts of this case, the majority is necessarily led to the creation of an overly broad new cause of action whose nuisance value alone may impair employers' ability to hire and retain employees who are best suited to their requirements. Other jurisdictions which have recognized a cause of action for retaliatory discharge have done so on the basis of a much clearer and more direct contravention of a mandate of public policy. . . .

[T]he purposes of the statute the majority would rely on, the Connecticut Uniform Food, Drug and Cosmetic Act, General Statutes §§ 19-211 through 19-239, can only be considered as, at most, marginally affected by an allegedly retaliatory discharge of an employee who observed the supposed sale of shortweight frozen entrees and the use of U.S. Government Certified "Grade B" rather than "Grade A" vegetables. A retaliatory discharge in the present case would not necessarily thwart or inhibit the Connecticut Uniform Food, Drug and Cosmetic Act's purpose of protecting the consumer. The plaintiff, if he desired to protect the consumer, could have communicated, even anonymously, to the commissioner of consumer affairs his concerns that his employer was violating the Food, Drug and Cosmetic Act so as to invoke the statute's enforcement mechanisms. To further and comply with the public policy expressed in Connecticut's Uniform Food, Drug and Cosmetic Act and to avoid the exceedingly remote possibility of criminal sanctions,[4] the plaintiff need not have jeopardized his continued employment. There is no indication that the plaintiff has either, before or after his discharge, informed or even attempted to inform the commissioner of consumer protection of violations the plaintiff claims to have first noted in his fourth year as the defendant's quality control director and fourth month as its operations manager. Unlike those cases where an employer allegedly discharged employees for engaging in union activities or filing workmen's compensation claims and the discharge itself contravened a statutory mandate, in the present case the discharge itself at most only indirectly impinged on the statutory mandate.

Consequently, the majority seemingly invites the unrestricted use of an allegation of almost any statutory or even regulatory violation by an employer as the basis for a cause of action by a discharged employee hired for an indefinite term. By establishing a cause of action, grounded upon "intentionally tortious conduct," for retaliatory discharges which do not necessarily in and of themselves directly contravene statutory mandates, the majority is creating an open-ended arena for judicial policy making and the usurpation of legislative functions. To base this new cause of action on a decision as to whether an alleged reason for discharge "is derived from some important violation of public policy" is not to create adequate and carefully circumscribed standards for this new cause of action but is to invite the opening of a Pandora's box of unwarranted litigation arising from the hope that the judicial estimate of derivation, importance, and public policy matches that of the plaintiff.

Moreover, this is policy making that the Connecticut legislature recently declined to undertake. In 1974, the Connecticut General Assembly considered and rejected a bill which would have provided that "[a]ny employee [including private sector employees] hired for an indefinite term, may be dismissed only for just cause or because of the employer's reduction in work force for business reasons." H.B. No. 5179, 1974 Sess. Representative Francis J. Mahoney, the bill's sponsor, gave examples of the kind of discharges he intended the bill to cover: discharges for overlooking violations of building codes or for campaigning for the wrong political party. 17 H.R. Proc., Pt. 5, 1974 Sess., pp. 2689, 2694–95. Thus, "just cause" in the overwhelmingly rejected 1974 bill was meant to encompass the kinds of retaliatory discharge that the majority approves as a new cause of action. Furthermore, the most recent legislature enacted a statute protecting "whistle blowing" state employees; Public Acts 1979, No. 79-599; and in Public Acts 1979, No. 153, addressed the problem of retaliatory dismissals of building officials. The legislature is thus adopting appropriate remedies for certain types of retaliatory discharges at its own considered pace and there appears to be no urgency for this court to violate that measured momentum by creating a broadly based new cause of action. In these circumstances, this court should consider itself precluded from substituting its own

---

[4] [n. 1] There is no allegation in the plaintiff's amended complaint that he was exposed to criminal liability by the defendant's alleged violations and it should be noted that those presumed violations could well fall within the Uniform Food, Drug and Cosmetic Act's provision for minor violations which the commissioner of consumer protection is not required to report to the state's attorney for possible institution of criminal proceedings. General Statutes § 19-218.

ideas of what might be wise policy in place of a clear expression of legislative will.
. . .

NOTES

1.   An Exception to At-Will Employment. According to the majority opinion, Sheets was not challenging his at-will status, only claiming that the reason that he was discharged was improper. What is the practical difference between the two arguments? What considerations argue for permitting Sheets to proceed with his wrongful discharge claim, even when he conceded that he was employed at will? Are there public policy concerns that argue against allowing his claim?

Consider one court's description of the interests at stake in creating a public policy exception:

> [A]n at will employee's interest in job security, particularly when continued employment is threatened not by genuine dissatisfaction with job performance but because the employee has refused to act in an unlawful manner or attempted to perform a statutorily prescribed duty, is deserving of recognition. Equally to be considered is that the employer has an important interest in being able to discharge an at will employee whenever it would be beneficial to his business. Finally, society as a whole has an interest in ensuring that its laws and important public policies are not contravened. Any modification of the at will rule must take into account all of these interests.

Adler v. American Standard Corp., 432 A.2d 464, 470 (Md. 1981). What kind of legal rule best accommodates all of these interests?

2.   Courts vs. Legislatures. The dissent in *Sheets* complains that the majority "is creating an open-ended arena for judicial policymaking and the usurpation of legislative functions." The Court of Appeals of New York, that state's highest court, relied on a similar argument in refusing to recognize a public policy exception to the at-will rule:

> [The] perception and declaration of relevant public policy . . . are best and more appropriately explored and resolved by the legislative branch of our government. The Legislature has infinitely greater resources and procedural means to discern the public will, to examine the variety of pertinent considerations, to elicit the views of the various segments of the community that would be directly affected and in any event critically interested, and to investigate and anticipate the impact of imposition of such liability. Standards should doubtless be established applicable to the multifarious types of employment and the various circumstances of discharge. If the rule of nonliability for termination of at-will employment is to be tempered, it should be accomplished through a principled statutory scheme, adopted after opportunity for public ventilation, rather than in consequence of judicial resolution of the partisan arguments of individual adversarial litigants.

Murphy v. American Home Products, 448 N.E.2d 86, 89–90 (N.Y. 1983). The New York legislature responded to the decision in *Murphy* by passing a statute prohibiting retaliation against an employee who objects to or discloses information about an employer activity "that is in violation of law, rule or regulation which violation creates and presents a substantial and specific danger to the public health or safety," and creating a private cause of action for employees subject to such retaliation. N.Y. LAB. LAW § 740.

Is the creation of exceptions to the employment-at-will doctrine exclusively within the province of the legislature, or do common law courts have a role to play in shaping the law in this area? Do you think that the political process can accurately and fairly weigh the competing interests of employees, employers, and the public? Are courts likely to do better or worse than the legislature in developing workable rules through individually litigated cases?

3.   **The Majority Rule.** In arguing that recognition of a public policy exception is best left to the legislature, the New York Court of Appeals articulates a distinctly minority view. An overwhelming majority of American jurisdictions have recognized a public policy exception to the at-will rule, although the scope of the exception varies significantly from state to state.

4.   **Mistaken Belief.** Sheets believed that his employer's labeling practices violated the law, but what if he was mistaken? How should courts treat the employee who *believes* that what her employer has asked her to do is illegal, but in fact, it is not? Most courts that recognize the public policy tort will protect the employee so long as she has a good faith, or at least objectively reasonable, belief that the act was illegal, even if she turns out to be wrong. *See, e.g., Phipps v. Clark Oil & Refining Corp.*, 408 N.W.2d 569 (Minn. 1987) (holding the employee may bring action if discharged for refusing to participate in an activity that the employee, in good faith, believes is illegal); *Ellis v. City of Seattle*, 13 P.3d 1065 (Wash. 2001) (recognizing cause of action where employee has an objectively reasonable belief an employer has violated the law). A few, however, require that the employee prove that the activity was *in fact* illegal. *See, e.g., Clark v. Modern Group*, 9 F.3d 321 (3d Cir. 1993) (holding that plaintiff bears the burden of proving that alleged actions by employer were in fact illegal).

5.   **Contract vs. Tort.** Given that the employment relationship is essentially a contractual one, should tort remedies be available in cases of wrongful discharge in violation of public policy? One of the early cases laid out the rationale for permitting such claims to proceed as torts:

> [W]e conclude that an employee's action for wrongful discharge is ex delicto and subjects an employer to tort liability. . . . [A]n employer's obligation to refrain from discharging an employee who refuses to commit a criminal act does not depend upon any express or implied "promises set forth in the [employment] contract," but rather reflects a duty imposed by law upon all employers in order to implement the fundamental public policies embodied in the state's penal statutes. As such, a wrongful discharge suit exhibits the classic elements of a tort cause of action. As Professor Prosser has explained: "[Whereas] contract actions are created to protect the interest in having promises performed," "tort actions are created to protect the

interest in freedom from various kinds of harm. The duties of conduct which give rise to them are imposed by law, and are based primarily upon social policy, and not necessarily upon the will or intention of the parties . . . " Prosser, Law of Torts (4th ed. 1971) p. 613.

Tameny v. Atlantic Richfield Co., 610 P.2d 1339 (Cal. 1980).

The Wisconsin Supreme Court has taken a different position, holding that only contract remedies are available for terminations that violate public policy. In its view, the claim is "predicated on the breach of an implied provision" that the employer will not discharge an employee for reasons that violate public policy. *Brockmeyer v. Dun & Bradstreet*, 335 N.W.2d 834 (Wis. 1983). Although a couple of other states limit remedies in public policy cases to contract damages, the overwhelming majority of states that recognize a public policy exception in employment agree with the California court that the claim sounds in tort, not contract.

What practical difference does it make whether the cause of action is denominated a contract claim or a tort claim?

6. Types of Public Policy Cases. The *Sheets* opinion lists several cases from other jurisdictions in which courts had found a discharge to be actionable. The seminal cases, each widely cited in other jurisdictions adopting a public policy exception, are *Petermann v. International Brotherhood of Teamsters, Frampton v. Central Indiana Gas Co.*, and *Nees v. Hock*. Each of these cases is excerpted below. Consider the rationale of the courts for finding a public policy exception in these cases.

Petermann v. International Brotherhood of Teamsters, **344 P.2d 25 (Cal. Ct. App. 1959).** Plaintiff, employed by the defendant union as a business agent, was subpoenaed to testify before a state legislative committee. He alleged that a union official instructed him to testify falsely, and when he failed to do so, he was discharged the next day. The California Court of Appeal reversed a judgment on the pleadings for defendant, permitting plaintiff to proceed on his claim. The court held that although plaintiff's employment was terminable at will, "the right to discharge an employee under such a contract may be limited by statute or by considerations of public policy." It explained:

> The commission of perjury is unlawful (Pen.Code, § 118). It is also a crime to solicit the commission of perjury. Pen.Code, § 653f. The presence of false testimony in any proceeding tends to interfere with the proper administration of public affairs and the administration of justice. It would be obnoxious to the interests of the state and contrary to public policy and sound morality to allow an employer to discharge any employee, whether the employment be for a designated or unspecified duration, on the ground that the employee declined to commit perjury, an act specifically enjoined by statute. The threat of criminal prosecution would, in many cases, be a sufficient deterrent upon both the employer and employee, the former from soliciting and the latter from committing perjury. However, in order to more fully effectuate the state's declared policy against perjury, the civil

law, too, must deny the employer his generally unlimited right to discharge an employee whose employment is for an unspecified duration, when the reason for the dismissal is the employee's refusal to commit perjury. To hold otherwise would be without reason and contrary to the spirit of the law. The public policy of this state as reflected in the penal code sections referred to above would be seriously impaired if it were to be held that one could be discharged by reason of his refusal to commit perjury. To hold that one's continued employment could be made contingent upon his commission of a felonious act at the instance of his employer would be to encourage criminal conduct upon the part of both the employee and employer and would serve to contaminate the honest administration of public affairs. This is patently contrary to the public welfare. The law must encourage and not discourage truthful testimony. . . .

Id. at 27.

Frampton v. Central Indiana Gas Co., 297 N.E.2d 425 (Ind. 1973). The plaintiff injured her arm while working for defendant and filed a claim for workers' compensation benefits. She received a settlement for her injury and was discharged one month later without being given any reason. She sued, alleging that her employer terminated her in retaliation for her claim for workers' compensation benefits. The Supreme Court of Indiana reversed the trial court's order dismissing her complaint:

Workmen's compensation acts are designed to afford injured workers "an expeditious remedy both adequate and certain, and independent of any negligence on their part or on the part of the employer." . . . The basic policy behind such legislation is to shift the economic burden for employment connected injuries from the employee to the employer. . . . But in order for the goals of the Act to be realized and for public policy to be effectuated, the employee must be able to exercise his right in an unfettered fashion without being subject to reprisal. If employers are permitted to penalize employees for filing workmen's compensation claims, a most important public policy will be undermined. The fear of being discharged would have a deleterious effect on the exercise of a statutory right. Employees will not file claims for justly deserved compensation— opting, instead, to continue their employment without incident. The end result, of course, is that the employer is effectively relieved of his obligation.

Since the Act embraces such a fundamental, well-defined and well-established policy, strict employer adherence is required. . . . Once an employee knows he is remediless if retaliatorily discharged, he is unlikely to file a claim. What then is to prevent an employer from coercing an employee? Upholding retaliatory discharge opens the door to coercion and other duress-provoking acts. Retaliatory discharge for filing a workmen's compensation claim is a wrongful, unconscionable act and should be actionable in a court of law. . . .

Id. at 427–28.

Nees v. Hock, 536 P.2d 512 (Or. 1975). The plaintiff was a clerical employee of defendant. She was called for jury duty and, after being granted one postponement, was again subpoenaed to serve on the jury. She told her employer, who did not want her to be gone for a month and gave her a letter asking that she be excused. She gave the letter to the court clerk, but said that should like to serve and the clerk declined to excuse her. She then informed her employer that she would have to serve a minimum of two weeks of jury duty. Several days after she started her jury duty, she was terminated. She found a new job about one week after she completed jury duty, but alleged that she suffered emotional distress because of her discharge. A jury awarded her compensatory and punitive damages. In reviewing the trial verdict, the Oregon Supreme Court wrote:

> We conclude that there can be circumstances in which an employer discharges an employee for such a socially undesirable motive that the employer must respond in damages for any injury done. The next question is, does the evidence in this case permit a finding that such circumstances are present? There is evidence from which the jury could have found that the defendants discharged the plaintiff because, after being subpoenaed, and contrary to the defendants' wishes, plaintiff told the clerk she would like to serve and she did serve on jury duty. Therefore, the immediate question can be stated specifically,—is the community's interest in having its citizens serve on jury duty so important that an employer, who interferes with that interest by discharging an employee who served on a jury, should be required to compensate his employee for any damages she suffered?

> Art. VII, § 3, of the Oregon Constitution provides that jury trial shall be preserved in civil cases. Art. I, § 11, provides a defendant in a criminal case has a right of trial by jury. Art VII, § 5, provides: 'The Legislative Assembly shall so provide that the most competent of the permanent citizens of the county shall be chosen for jurors.'

> ORS 10.040 provides for certain exemptions from jury duty. ORS 10.050 provides for certain excuses from jury duty including health, age and '(c) When serving as a juror would result in extreme hardship to the person including but not limited to unusual and extraordinary financial hardship.' ORS 10.055 provides for deferment of jury duty 'for good cause shown' for not more than one year. ORS 10.990 provides that if a juror 'without reasonable cause,' neglects to attend for jury service the sheriff may impose a fine, not exceeding $20 for each day the juror does not attend.

> *People v. Vitucci*, 199 N.E.2d 78 (1964), stated that an employer who discharged an employee who was absent because of jury duty was guilty of contempt of court. Massachusetts has a statute making such conduct contemptuous. 44 Mass. G.L.A., ch. 268, § 14A.

> These actions by the people, the legislature and the courts clearly indicate that the jury system and jury duty are regarded as high on the scale of American institutions and citizen obligations. If an employer were permitted with impunity to discharge an employee for fulfilling her obligation of jury duty, the jury system would be adversely affected. The

will of the community would be thwarted. For these reasons we hold that the defendants are liable for discharging plaintiff because she served on the jury. . . .

Id. at 515–16.

The Oregon Supreme Court then reversed the award of punitive damages on the grounds that prior to this case, no cases existed putting the employer on notice that it would be liable if it discharged an employee for serving on jury duty.

How would you describe the interests protected in *Petermann, Frampton,* and *Nees*? Are those interests sufficiently important to warrant an exception to the at-will rule? Do any of these three cases provide direct precedent for the holding in *Sheets*? If not, was judicial recognition of a public policy exception nevertheless warranted in that case?

B.   WHAT CONSTITUTES PUBLIC POLICY?

Once the courts recognize a claim for wrongful discharge in violation of public policy, they then face the task of defining what public policy is or at least providing guidance as to how relevant public policies can be identified. In considering what constitutes "clearly mandated public policy," the court in *Palmateer v. International Harvester Co.*, 421 N.E.2d 876 (Ill. 1981), stated:

> In general, it can be said that public policy concerns what is right and just and what affects the citizens of the State collectively. . . . Although there is no precise line of demarcation dividing matters that are the subject of public policies from matters purely personal, . . . a matter must strike at the heart of a citizen's social rights, duties, and responsibilities before the tort will be allowed.

Id. at 878–79. How helpful is such a definition in identifying when an employer should be liable for discharging an employee?

In order to delineate the boundaries of the public policy claim, some courts simply list the types of situations in which an exception will be recognized. The Supreme Court of Texas takes the narrowest approach, carving out a public policy exception only in the case of an employee discharged "for the sole reason that the employee refused to perform an illegal act that carried criminal penalties." *City of Midland v. O'Bryant*, 18 S.W.3d 209, 215 (Tex. 2000). More commonly, courts identify categories of public policy wrongful discharge cases, often corresponding to the fact patters in *Petermann, Frampton,* and *Nees*. Many also recognize whistle-blowing as a type of activity covered by the public policy exception in order to protect employees fired for reporting or complaining about their employer's unlawful acts. *See* RESTATEMENT (THIRD) OF EMPLOYMENT LAW § 5.02 (Proposed Final Draft, April 18, 2014) (listing types of employee activities protected by wrongful discharge in violation of public policy tort).

Can you identify any common theory that would justify recognizing all four of these exceptions? Do these categories of cases exhaust the situations in which it is appropriate to recognize a public policy exception, or are there other situations in which an employer should be held liable for discharging an employee? Alternative approaches to identifying public policy focus not on the specific fact pattern presented, but on identifying legitimate sources of public policy. The following cases illustrate how courts have attempted to define the contours of the public policy exception.

HAYES v. EATERIES, INC.
Supreme Court of Oklahoma
905 P.2d 778 (1995)

LAVENDER, JUSTICE.

. . . [In his trial court petition,] Hayes alleged essentially the following: In May 1990 he had been employed at the Stillwater Garfield's for about two years and had recently been promoted to assistant manager. He was led to believe he would be employed as long as he did an adequate job and performed his duties. On May 29, 1990, Hayes was terminated despite the fact he had at all times performed his job satisfactorily and there were no grounds for his discharge. . . . He [alleged that he] was discharged because he reported and was attempting to investigate theft of property and embezzlement from Garfield's. Accordingly, his discharge violated the public policy of Oklahoma and constituted the tort of wrongful discharge.

As can be seen, the allegations in Hayes' petition are extremely general. He does not indicate the person who terminated him, who he believed was embezzling from Garfield's, or who he reported any theft or embezzlement to. From what we can glean from Hayes' brief in the trial court and his submissions on appeal it appears he asserts it was his supervisor, i.e. the manager at the Stillwater Garfield's, that was embezzling money from the restaurant, that Hayes either directly or indirectly confronted this manager with his concern about missing money, that the manager had Hayes sign a statement that he, Hayes, had left the restaurant and/or restaurant safe unlocked on one occasion and that it was this manager who terminated him. We also glean from Hayes' submissions that he was going to continue to investigate the embezzlement he had uncovered and he was going to report it and this is the reason the manager fired Hayes. Hayes also informs us in his appellate submissions that after his discharge the manager was actually charged and convicted of six counts of embezzlement from Garfield's.

In essence then, Hayes asserted two claims. The first [is] a breach of contract claim. . . . Second, a tort claim, alleging violation of the public policy exception to the employment-at-will doctrine under *Burk v. K-Mart Corp.*, 770 P.2d 24 (Okla.1989). Garfield's moved to dismiss Hayes' petition for failure to state a claim upon which relief could be granted. The trial court granted the motion, Hayes appealed and the Court of Appeals affirmed. . . .

[The court first discusses, and rejects, the breach of contract claim.] . . .

THE PUBLIC POLICY TORT EXCEPTION.

In *Burk v. K-Mart*, supra, we adopted a public policy tort exception to the employment-at-will doctrine in "cases in which the discharge is contrary to a clear mandate of public policy as articulated by constitutional, statutory or decisional law." 770 P.2d at 28. We noted that the exception was to be tightly circumscribed in light of the vague meaning of the term public policy. *Id.* at 28–29. A public policy tort claim, as fashioned by *Burk*, was said to arise "where an employee is discharged for [1] refusing to act in violation of an established and well-defined public policy or [2] for performing an act consistent with a clear and compelling public policy." 770 P.2d at 29. Hayes claims his discharge falls within both of these branches of the public policy tort exception to the employment-at-will doctrine. In that we have held that the initial determination of public policy is a question of law to be resolved by the court [*Pearson v. Hope Lumber & Supply Co., Inc.*, 820 P.2d 443, 444 (Okla. 1991)] it falls initially to the trial court and ultimately to this Court to decide whether a sufficient discernable public policy is implicated by the discharge of an otherwise at-will employee to allow the employee to go forward within the *Burk* tort framework or whether, instead, the case may be resolved as a matter of law against the discharged employee. . . .

In essence, Hayes contends his reporting and investigating of criminal activity by his supervisor against the employer, i.e. embezzlement from Garfield's, which Hayes correctly points out is a violation of our criminal law, should be protected because in doing so he is performing an act consistent with a clear and compelling public policy, to wit: acting as a good citizen and loyal employee in reporting said crime committed by his co-employee, and an employer should not be allowed with impunity to terminate an employee for such "whistleblowing" activity. We believe Hayes is mistaken.

In the first instance, in that Hayes' petition does not indicate whether he reported the embezzlement to outside law enforcement officials or internally to company officials, we deal with both situations. In our view, neither external reporting, i.e. to outside law enforcement officials, or internal reporting, i.e. to company officials, of the crime of embezzlement from the employer, is imbued with the necessary clear and compelling public policy sufficient to protect the employee from discharge under the tort established in *Burk*.

Although we believe most people, including the members of this Court, would agree that, generally speaking, the reporting of crimes to appropriate law enforcement officials should be lauded and encouraged, and that an employee's reporting to appropriate company officials of crimes committed by co-employees against the interests of the employer is a likewise commendable endeavor, we must decide in this case whether the reporting of this particular crime against this particular victim, i.e. Garfield's, is so imbued with a clear and compelling public policy such that a tort claim is stated if the employer discharges the employee for so reporting. In our view, such reporting is not so protected.

Initially we note that an employee, in reporting a crime by a co-employee against the interest of his employer (such as the crime of embezzlement involved here) to outside law enforcement officials is not exercising any legal right or interest of his own. Thus, we start with the proposition the present situation must be distinguished from cases where the employee is terminated for seeking to vindicate his own legal rights or interests, such as where the employee is terminated for refusing to abandon (i.e. for continuing to pursue) a lawsuit against a third party to redress an on-the-job injury, *Groce v. Foster*, 880 P.2d 902 (Okla.1994), or where an employee has in good faith filed a workers' compensation claim against his employer to recover for an on-the-job injury, a situation specifically protected by legislative enactment. 85 O.S.Supp.1992, § 5. In the present case Hayes' reporting of a crime against the interest of his employer cannot be said to have been seeking to vindicate his own legal rights, but only those of the employer he says wrongfully terminated him.

Further, an employee, in reporting such a crime committed by a co-employee against the interest of his employer to outside law enforcement officials is not seeking to vindicate a public wrong where the victim of the crime could in any real or direct sense be said to be the general public, as where crimes or violations of health or safety laws are involved. Thus, the situation here must also be distinguished from those where sister jurisdictions have protected "whistleblowing" activity geared toward the good faith reporting of infractions by the employer or co-employees of rules, regulations or the law pertaining to the public health, safety or general welfare. These latter situations must be distinguished from those which involve merely private or proprietary interests because to support a viable tort claim the public policy must truly be public, rather than merely private or proprietary. We believe here the situation involves only the private or proprietary interests of the employer-employee relationship, not the direct interests of the general public as where the reporting involves the criminal wrongdoing of the employer or a co-employee perpetrated against the interests of the general public.[5]

Further, in regard to external reporting (assuming that is what Hayes did) it is not up to an individual employee to report to outside law enforcement agencies embezzlement from his employer by a co-employee, but it is up to the employer, who is the direct victim of the crime. Although the public in a very general way might be said to be the indirect victim of all crimes we are not aware of a general consensus sufficient to base a *Burk* tort claim upon that there is a public policy so thoroughly established in the public consciousness that would forbid an employer from making an informed business decision that its employees are prohibited from reporting crimes against the interest of the employer (here embezzlement from Garfield's) to law enforcement officials and if they do so termination is the result. After all it is the employer, Garfield's, whose money or property was stolen, not Hayes' money or the money of a relative or friend. Hayes makes no allegations otherwise.

This situation is also distinguishable from that dealt with in *Vannerson v. Board of Regents of University of Oklahoma*, 784 P.2d 1053 (Okla.1989), where we held a public employee working for the University of Oklahoma, a State institution, had a

---

[5] [n. 7] This case must also be distinguished from situations where the employee is discharged for performing an important public obligation which is also statutorily protected from employer retaliatory discharge, such as where the employee is terminated for performing jury duty. *See Brown v. MFC Finance Co. of Oklahoma*, 838 P.2d 524 (Okla. Ct. App. Div. 3, 1992) (employee's jury service statutorily protected against employer's retaliatory discharge by 38 O.S.1991, § 35). In such a situation the public policy is clear and compelling and the public nature of jury service is unmistakable. . . .

viable claim under *Burk* if he could show he was terminated for going over his supervisor's head in complaint of an illegal disposition of state property. Vannerson, 784 P.2d at 1055. In *Vannerson* the activity subject to the discharged employee's reporting involved the illegal transfer, by sale or gift, of public property, a situation which we believe concerns a clear and compelling public policy, protecting the public's interest in seeing to it that the peoples' tax dollars are not fraudulently stolen by State employees or officials, or other individuals, by either giving away or selling public property for their own private reasons or profit. In essence, the situation in *Vannerson* was one where public property was being pilfered or stolen. Here we can see no such overriding public interest, but merely the private and/or proprietary interests of the employer in its relationship with the employee as to whether the employer wishes to pursue in the first instance a criminal complaint against the accused co-employee. Again, this is, in our view, primarily a private business decision.

As to internal reporting to company officials (assuming that is what Hayes' claim is based upon) the same rationale applies, to wit: no clear and compelling public policy is involved, rather only a private internal business matter is implicated. Although we might think it would actually be contrary to good business decision-making for an employer to terminate an employee for uncovering co-employee embezzlement and reporting it to the company hierarchy, and we might even think it is morally wrong, the *Burk* tort does not protect an employee from his employer's poor business judgment, corporate foolishness or moral transgressions, but only protects the employee from termination by the employer when such discharge has violated a clear mandate of public policy. An employer's internal policies on how to deal with the actual affirmative reporting of crimes where the employer is the victim of the crime, as with the embezzlement involved here, simply does not implicate to a sufficient degree the second branch of the *Burk* formulation, i.e. performing an act consistent with a clear and compelling public policy. . . .

Hayes also asserts his refusal to forego reporting of the criminal activity of his manager at the Stillwater Garfield's falls under the *Burk* umbrella of refusing to act in violation of an established and well-defined public policy. Hayes put his argument as to this part of the *Burk* tort as follows in his trial court brief in response to Garfield's motion to dismiss:

> Under Oklahoma law, it is a serious criminal offense for an employee to embezzle funds from his employer. When, as is alleged by Plaintiff in this case, an employee becomes aware of such a crime, it is a critically important part of his duty of loyalty to his employer that it be investigated and reported to the responsible officers of the corporation. In substance, then, Plaintiff was discharged by his supervisor because he refused to ignore this duty of loyalty, continued to investigate, and must have appeared to threaten his supervisor with exposure. . . .

As with the second branch of the *Burk* tort, Hayes is mistaken as to his reliance in regard to the first branch. Aspects of loyalty to the employer involve merely private and proprietary interests insufficient to support a *Burk* claim. They simply do not sufficiently impact any public policy subject to protection under the *Burk* tort that we can discern. Further, we must note that generally mere presence at the scene of a crime or acquiescence therein, without participation, does not constitute a crime. Accordingly, it cannot be said as a general proposition that an employee's mere failure to report a crime of which he has knowledge is guilty of any violation of the criminal law. Hayes never alleges that his discharge was for a refusal to commit a crime.

This situation, accordingly, must be distinguished from those where a *Burk* tort has been sanctioned because the discharge was claimed to have been motivated by the employee's refusal to commit a crime. . . .

Hayes' petition was, thus, legally insufficient to state any viable tort claim which would take the matter out of the employment-at-will situation and the trial court properly dismissed Hayes' asserted tort claim.

NOTES

1. **Distinguishing Public Policy.** How does Hayes argue that his situation fits within the scope of the public policy exception as earlier defined by the Oklahoma Supreme Court? Why does his claim fail? How does the court distinguish Hayes' situation from other cases in which public policy exceptions have been found?

2. **Whistleblowers.** The facts of *Hayes* present a whistleblower situation— where the employee asserts that he was terminated because he reported wrong-doing or illegality on the part of the employer or other employees. Although such claims are closely related to the classic *Petermann* fact pattern—refusing to perform an illegal act—whistleblowing claims raise some particular difficulties. For example, Hayes lost his claim, even though the activity he objected to was clearly illegal. If he himself had been asked to participate in some illegality, and had refused, he would have had a stronger case. Is such a difference in treatment justified? Consider the reasoning of one court:

> The employee who chooses to report illegal or unsafe conduct by his employer differs significantly from the employee forced to choose between his job and actual participation in illegal behavior . . . [T]he whistleblower faces the arguably less onerous choice of either ignoring the known or suspected illegality or becoming an instrument of law enforcement.

Wagner v. City of Globe, 722 P.2d 250, 256 (Ariz. 1986).

If firing whistleblowers implicates public policy concerns, should every employee discharged in retaliation for reporting wrongdoing have a claim? As with claims that an employee was fired for refusing to perform an illegal act, courts must decide what standard to apply regarding the actual illegality of the employer's activity. Is the employee's subjective good faith or objectively reasonable belief enough, or should she have to prove the illegality of the activity she reports?

Whistleblowing cases also raise the question whether an employee should be required to report the alleged wrongdoing to government or other authorities outside the company in order to receive protection under the public policy exception, or whether reporting violations internally to management is sufficient. What arguments support limiting public policy protections to external whistleblow-ers only? What kinds of incentives are created by such a rule? Which rule best protects public policy—protecting internal whistleblowers, external whistleblowers or both?

And should it matter what *kind* of violation is alleged? Activities that threaten public health or safety, such as manufacturing defective automobile brakes, *White v. General Motors Corp.*, 908 F.2d 669 (10th Cir. 1990), or distributing spoiled milk to the public, *Garibaldi v. Lucky Food Stores, Inc.*, 726 F.2d 1367 (9th Cir. 1984), clearly raise public policy concerns, but what about financial wrongdoing? At least one court has imposed a higher standard of proof on financial whistleblowers, stating that "actual violations of law, policy or regulation [are] required in situations involving financial misconduct," while in the context of threats to public safety, an employee only has to show an objectively reasonable belief the law may be violated in the absence of his or her action. *Ellis v. City of Seattle*, 13 P.3d 1065, 1071 (Wash. 2001). Should protections for whistleblowers differ depending upon whether they are reporting threats to public health and safety or financial wrongdoing?

All of these issues must also be addressed if a legislature chooses to protect whistleblowers by statute. As discussed in Chapter 8 *infra*, both state legislatures and Congress have become more active in recent years in enacting whistleblower protections, although the types of employees covered and the scope of the protections vary widely. *See* DANIEL P. WESTMAN & NANCY M. MODESITT, WHISTLE-BLOWING: THE LAW OF RETALIATORY DISCHARGE app. A–C (2d ed. 2004 & Supp. 2013) (listing whistleblower statutes). As we shall see in Chapter 8, federal law is particularly focused on protecting the reporting of financial misconduct by publicly-held companies. State statutes vary considerably, with some narrowly defining the types of protected whistleblowing, *see, e.g.*, N.Y. LAB. LAW § 740 (prohibiting retaliation against employees only for reporting an actual violation that presents "a substantial and specific danger to the public health or safety"), while others extend protection more broadly. *See, e.g.*, CONN. GEN. STAT. ANN. § 31-51 m (protecting reports of a violation or suspected violation of any state or federal law, regulation, any municipal ordinance or regulation, unethical practices, mismanagement, or abuse of authority).

Where a state legislature has created statutory whistleblower protections, courts sometimes conclude that the statutory remedy is exclusive, and will not permit wrongful discharge in violation of public policy claims that allege retaliation for complaining about unlawful or unethical activities. *See, e.g., Dudewicz v. Norris-Schmid, Inc.*, 503 N.W.2d 645 (Mich. 1993) (holding that the remedies provided by Michigan's Whistleblowers' Protection Act are exclusive, barring wrongful discharge claims). However, as of 2014, less than half of the states had passed whistleblower statutes protecting employees in the private sector, and therefore, in those states, the common law wrongful discharge tort often remains an important potential source of protection for whistleblowers. *See, e.g., Combs v. City Electric Supply Co.*, 690 S.E.2d 719 (N.C. Ct. App. 2010) (permitting wrongful discharge claim by employee allegedly discharged for reporting illegal and fraudulent activity to management); *DeCarlo v. Bonus Stores*, 989 So. 2d 351 (Miss. 2008) (holding that discharge in retaliation for reporting illegal actions constitutes tort claim).

3. **Public Policy vs. Private Interests.** In recognizing a public policy claim, many courts have emphasized that it protects only *public* and not purely private

interests. Attempting to cabin the public policy exception in this way, however, raises the further question of how to distinguish between truly public and merely private interests.

One possible test was suggested by the California Supreme Court in *Foley v. Interactive Data Corp.*, 765 P.2d 373 (Cal. 1988), a case factually similar to *Hayes*. The plaintiff in *Foley* alleged that he was discharged because he reported to management that his supervisor, who had recently been hired by the company, was under investigation by the Federal Bureau of Investigation for embezzlement from his former employer, the Bank of America. He asserted that he disclosed this information "in the interest and for the benefit of his employer," because he believed the company had an interest in knowing about alleged criminal conduct, given that it did "business with the financial community on a confidential basis." *Id.* at 375. To support his claim of wrongful discharge, Foley argued that public policy imposed a duty on him as an employee and agent of the company to report relevant business information to his employer. He pointed to provisions of the state Labor Code imposing a duty of care on employees as evidence of this public policy.

The California Supreme Court held that identifying a "statutory touchstone" was insufficient: "we must still inquire whether the discharge is against public policy and affects a duty which inures to the benefit of the public at large rather than to a particular employer or employee." *Id.* at 379. In this case, the court found no "substantial public policy" barring the plaintiff's discharge, because the disclosure about his supervisor's background "serves only the private interest of the employer." *Id.* at 380. In a footnote, the court explained:

> The absence of a distinctly "public" interest in this case is apparent when we consider that if an employer and employee were *expressly* to agree that the employee has no obligation to, and should not, inform the employer of any adverse information the employee learns about a fellow employee's background, nothing in the state's public policy would render such an agreement void. By contrast, in the previous cases asserting a discharge in violation of public policy, the public interest at stake was invariably one which could not properly be circumvented by agreement of the parties. For example, in Tameny, supra, 27 Cal.3d 167, a contract provision purporting to obligate the employee to comply with an order of the employer directing the employee to violate the antitrust laws would clearly have been void as against public policy, and in Petermann, supra, [344 P.2d 25], a contract provision which purported to obligate the employee to commit perjury at the employer's behest would just as obviously have been invalid. Because here the employer and employee could have agreed that the employee had no duty to disclose such information, it cannot be said that an employer, in discharging an employee on this basis, violates a fundamental duty imposed on all employers for the protection of the public interest.

Id. at 380 n.12.

Does the "void if contracted for" test suggested by the California Supreme Court help to distinguish fundamental public policies from purely private interests? Are there any difficulties in applying it?

4. Third-Party Effects. Stewart Schwab has suggested another approach to identifying situations in which a public policy claim is warranted:

> The key articulated element [in the public policy cases] was that the firing implicate a public concern, rather than merely be a private overreaching by the employer. This appropriately reflects the predominant efficiency rationale for tort law—the control of externalities. In other words, tort law should intervene in contractual relationships to ensure that the parties consider the costs they impose on outsiders. . . .
>
> Imagine in these cases that the employer explained at the initial job interview, "This job pays extra-high wages because it is potentially dangerous. It may require you to be convicted of perjury, or to be held in contempt of court for refusing jury service, or simply to violate your moral beliefs against enabling drunk drivers. But the value to this company of perjury, or constant attendance, or serving customers, outweighs these high wages; that is why we offer the job." The employee then asks: "What happens if I don't agree to this perjury term, or refusing-jury-service term, or must-serve-drunks term?" "If you refuse the term now," the employer replies, "you won't be hired. If you refuse to perform later, you will be fired." If the employee accepts the job with this understanding, presumably it is because the high wages and other aspects of the job are worth the expected criminal/moral penalties from perjury, or refusing jury service, or serving drunks. Thus, the employer and employee are jointly better off with these conditions than without. But even [a] valiant [ ] freedom-of-contract buff . . . would refuse to enforce such contracts. The rationale is simple. The parties, while furthering their own self-interests, are ignoring the effects of their deal on others. Because the private contract has substantial adverse third-party effects, we refuse to enforce it.
>
> In theory, under this imaginary bargaining story, an employee taking the job agrees to commit perjury, or to refuse jury duty, or to serve drunks. If the employee maintains his end of the bargain, the investigating agency hears perjured testimony, the jury pool lacks a member, and a drunk-driving accident occurs. The employee keeps his job, and no wrongful discharge suit is filed. What the tort of wrongful discharge allows, however, is for the employee to change his mind. He can renege on the Faustian deal without fear of losing the job.
>
> In practice, employers and employees rarely expressly negotiate over job duties that violate the public interest. Even if they did, their agreement rarely would call for civic-minded action by the employee. A public-goods problem exists here. An employee acting in the public interest gets only a small share of the social benefit created. The public-good activity, therefore, will be underproduced unless tort law intervenes. The wrongful discharge tort gives the employee some backbone to look at the overall social interest. The employee deciding whether to testify against his employer or to take time off to perform jury duty knows that, if he is fired, he will be compensated with tort damages. Of course, compensatory damages at best put him in the same position had he not testified or been a juror (and

thereby not been fired). If the employee recognizes that he may not win his lawsuit because of the vagaries of trial, or recognizes that he must generally pay attorney fees out of his damage award, he may rationally decide to commit perjury or to reject jury duty. Perhaps an employee's sense of morality is enough to let him take the plunge. Tort law attempts to tip the balance by adding the possibility of punitive damages.

Stewart J. Schwab, *Wrongful Discharge Law and the Search for Third-Party Effects*, 74 Tex. L. Rev. 1943, 1950–53 (1996).

Does the search for third-party effects offer a more coherent way of identifying the boundaries of the public policy exception? Consider the four classic types of cases in which public policy exceptions have been found. Does a concern for third-party effects explain each of them? For which types of cases does it offer the strongest justification? The weakest? Are third-party effects *always* present when fundamental public policies are implicated?

GANTT v. SENTRY INSURANCE
Supreme Court of California
824 P.2d 680 (1992)

Arabian, Justice.

[Gantt was hired as a sales manager in Sentry's Sacramento office. Another employee, Joyce Bruno, who reported to Gantt, complained that she was being sexually harassed by another manager. Gantt recommended that Bruno report the harassment to a supervisor at regional headquarters and Gantt himself conveyed the complaints to two other managers, including the person responsible for receiving complaints of sex discrimination. Nevertheless, the harassment continued and Bruno was ultimately transferred and then fired.

Bruno filed a complaint with the Department of Fair Employment and Housing, the California state agency responsible for investigating claims of employment discrimination, alleging sexual harassment by her supervisor and Sentry's failure to act on her complaints.] Caroline Fribance, Sentry's house counsel in charge of labor-related matters, undertook to investigate the matter. Gantt informed Fribance that he had reported Bruno's complaints to personnel in [the regional headquarters in] Scottsdale. However, Gantt gained the impression that he was being pressured by Fribance to retract his claim that he had informed Scottsdale of the complaints. Later, following the interview with Fribance, Tailby [Gantt's supervisor] cautioned Gantt that [some managers] did not care for Gantt. In a follow-up memorandum, Tailby cautioned Gantt that "it sometimes appears that you are involved in some kind of 'intrigue' and 'undercover' operation." In December 1982, Tailby rated Gantt's overall work performance for the year as "acceptable." [The prior year Gantt had been ranked among Sentry's top district managers in premium growth.] Without directly informing Gantt, Singer changed the rating to "borderline acceptable/unacceptable."

Shortly thereafter, John Thompson, a DFEH investigator, contacted Fribance to arrange interviews with certain employees, including Gantt. . . . Gantt met with

Fribance the day before his formal DFEH interview. She repeatedly reminded him that he was the only management employee supporting Ms. Bruno's claim that she had notified management about the harassment. Plaintiff felt that Fribance was unhappy with his testimony and that her unstated intent was to induce him to change his story. She also told him about another employee who had been found guilty of sexual harassment but retained by the company because he was a loyal employee. It was also during this meeting that Gantt discovered the change in his December 1982 evaluation. These events confirmed his fears that the company was pressuring him to withhold testimony or face retaliation.

The official DFEH interviews took place the next day. Fribance was present during Thompson's interview with Gantt. Following the interview, Fribance asked Thompson why he was not investigating sexual harassment charges against Gantt; she indicated that Gantt had harassed Bruno and was trying to deflect attention from himself. Thompson was surprised by Fribance's statements since he had never experienced a company attorney suggesting that charges be brought against one of the company's own employees.

Less than two months later, on March 3, 1983, Gantt attended an awards ceremony in Scottsdale to accept a life insurance sales award on behalf of his office. The following morning, [he was demoted to sales representative, and] also informed that he would not be given a "book" of existing accounts to start his new job; according to Gantt, such a book was necessary to survive. [Several weeks later, Gantt resigned, and later sued Sentry alleging that he was forced to resign.]

[The jury returned a verdict in favor of Gantt, finding, that he had been constructively discharged in retaliation for his refusal to testify untruthfully or to withhold testimony in support of Joyce Bruno's sexual harassment allegations, and awarded Gantt $1.34 million in damages. Sentry appealed.]

III. Discussion

A. *Sources of the Public Policy Exception*

This court first recognized a public policy exception to the at-will employment doctrine in *Tameny*, [*v. Atlantic Richfield Co.*], 610 P.2d 1330 [(1980)], and has since reaffirmed its commitment to that principle on several occasions. . . . Indeed, the vast majority of states have recognized that an at-will employee possesses a tort action when he or she is discharged for performing an act that public policy would encourage, or for refusing to do something that public policy would condemn.

Yet despite its broad acceptance, the principle underlying the public policy exception is more easily stated than applied. The difficulty, of course, lies in determining where and how to draw the line between claims that genuinely involve matters of public policy, and those that concern merely ordinary disputes between employer and employee. This determination depends in large part on whether the public policy alleged is sufficiently clear to provide the basis for such a potent remedy. . . .

[T]hose courts which have addressed the issue appear to be divided over the question whether nonlegislative sources may ever provide the basis of a public policy claim. *Pierce v. Ortho Pharmaceutical Corp.* (1980) 417 A.2d 505 is the leading case for a broad interpretation. As the New Jersey Supreme Court explained: "The sources of public policy [which may limit the employer's right of discharge] include legislation; administrative rules, regulations or decisions; and judicial decisions. In certain instances, a professional code of ethics may contain an expression of public policy." (*Id.*, 417 A.2d at p. 512.) Several other states have adopted similarly broad views of the public policy exception. (See *Parnar v. Americana Hotels, Inc.* (1982) 652 P.2d 625, 631 ["In determining whether a clear mandate of public policy is violated, courts should inquire whether the employer's conduct contravenes the letter or purpose of a constitutional, statutory, or regulatory provision or scheme. Prior judicial decisions may also establish the relevant public policy."]; *Boyle v. Vista Eyewear, Inc.* (Mo.Ct.App.1985) 700 S.W.2d 859, 871 [" 'Public policy' is that principle of law which holds that no one can lawfully do that which tends to be injurious to the public or against the public good. . . . It finds its sources in the state constitution, . . . in the letter and purpose of a constitutional, statutory or regulatory provision or scheme, . . . in the judicial decisions of the state and national courts, . . . in 'the constant practice of the government officials,'. . . and, in certain instances, in professional codes of ethics."]

Other courts have applied a stricter definition to public policy claims. The leading case is *Brockmeyer v. Dun & Bradstreet* (1983) 335 N.W.2d 834. There, the Wisconsin Supreme Court, while recognizing a public policy exception to the employment-at-will doctrine, nevertheless limited plaintiffs to contract damages and confined such claims to statutory or constitutional violations. "Given the vagueness of the concept of public policy," the court explained, "it is necessary that we be more precise about the contours of the public policy exception. A wrongful discharge is actionable when the termination clearly contravenes the public welfare and gravely violates paramount requirements of public interest. The public policy must be evidenced by a constitutional or statutory provision." (*Id.*, 335 N.W.2d at p. 840.). . . .

Surveying the extensive and conflicting decisional law summarized above, several general observations are possible. First, notwithstanding the lively theoretical debate over the sources of public policy which may support a wrongful discharge claim, with few exceptions courts have, in practice, relied to some extent on statutory or constitutional expressions of public policy as a basis of the employee's claim.

Second, it is generally agreed that "public policy" as a concept is notoriously resistant to precise definition, and that courts should venture into this area, if at all, with great care and due deference to the judgment of the legislative branch, "lest they mistake their own predilections for public policy which deserves recognition at law." (*Hentzel v. Singer Co.*, supra, 138 Cal.App.3d 290, 297.). . . .

These wise caveats against judicial policymaking are unnecessary if one recognizes that courts in *wrongful discharge actions* may not declare public policy without a basis in either the constitution or statutory provisions. A public policy exception carefully tethered to fundamental policies that are delineated in constitutional or statutory provisions strikes the proper balance among the interests of employers, employees and the public. The employer is bound, at a minimum, to know the fundamental public policies of the state and nation as expressed in their constitutions and statutes; so limited, the public policy exception presents no impediment to employers that operate within the bounds of law. Employees are protected against employer actions that contravene fundamental state policy. And society's interests are served through a more stable job market, in which its most important policies are safeguarded.

B. *Application of the Public Policy Exception*

Here, we are *not* being asked to declare public policy. The issue as framed by the pleadings and the parties is whether there exists a clear constitutional or legislative declaration of fundamental public policy forbidding plaintiff's discharge under the facts and circumstances presented. . . .

Although Sentry did not discriminate against Gantt on account of his sex within the meaning of the constitutional provision [prohibiting sex discrimination], there is nevertheless direct statutory support for the jury's express finding that Sentry violated a fundamental public policy when it constructively discharged plaintiff "in retaliation for his refusal to testify untruthfully or to withhold testimony" in the course of the DFEH investigation. . . .

The FEHA specifically enjoins any obstruction of a DFEH investigation. Government Code section 12975 provides: "Any person who shall willfully resist, prevent, impede or interfere with any member of the department or the commission or any of its agents or employees in the performance of duties pursuant to the provisions of this part relating to employment discrimination, . . . is guilty of a misdemeanor" punishable by fine or imprisonment. Nowhere in our society is the need greater than in protecting well motivated employees who come forward to testify truthfully in an administrative investigation of charges of discrimination based on sexual harassment. It is self-evident that few employees would cooperate with such investigations if the price were retaliatory discharge from employment.

Thus, any attempt to induce or coerce an employee to lie to a DFEH investigator plainly contravenes the public policy of this State. Accordingly, we hold that plaintiff established a valid *Tameny* claim based on the theory of retaliation for refusal to withhold information or to provide false information to the DFEH. . . .

KENNARD, JUSTICE, concurring and dissenting.

. . . [T]he majority concludes, with only perfunctory analysis, that its rule that a wrongful discharge cause of action may be based only on public policies expressed in constitutional or statutory provisions "strikes the proper balance" because "[t]he employer is bound, at a minimum, to know the fundamental public policies of the state and nation as expressed in their constitutions and statutes . . . ." This creates the impression that only statutes or constitutional provisions provide employers with adequate notice of what is forbidden by public policy, and that it is somehow unfair for employers to be bound by other legitimate sources of public policy. This is wrong. Other legitimate sources of public policy, such as judicial decisions or codes of professional ethics, for instance, are readily available to employers or their counsel and thus provide no less "notice" than do statutes or constitutional provisions.

Implicit in the majority's objection to requiring employers to adhere to fundamental public policy set forth in published sources other than statutes or constitutional provisions is the notion that other sources express policies that are not "fundamental" or "substantial" enough. It may be somewhat easier to characterize as "fundamental" a public policy that is plainly based on the terms of a statute or constitutional provision than to so characterize one that is not so based. But it is a mistake to assume that only those policies based on statutes or constitutional provisions are firmly established and important.

An example is helpful. In *Verduzco v. General Dynamics, Convair Div.* (S.D. Cal.1990) 742 F. Supp. 559, the plaintiff, a production supervisor for a national defense project, alleged that he was terminated because he complained that workers without required security clearances had access to restricted documents, and that "security was so lax that workers at the plant could walk off with blueprints and other material," compromising the national security of the United States. (*Id.* at p. 560.)

The federal court found no statute that addressed this issue; it stated that "Verduzco is asking this court to recognize a public policy that is not based on or derived from a statute." (*Id.* at p. 560.) Nevertheless, applying California law on wrongful termination, the court held that Verduzco had stated a cause of action for retaliatory dismissal in violation of "a fundamental public interest in preventing unauthorized persons from obtaining access to important technical data relating to military projects." *(Id.* at p. 562.)

Under the majority's approach, a plaintiff in Verduzco's position could be discharged without fear of consequences, because he could point to no statute or constitutional provision that was violated by his discharge. But the absence of a statute or constitutional provision should not prevent the recognition of a fundamental public policy in preserving national security. . . .

Other examples are no doubt available. But the point is plain. Courts should not be foreclosed from adjudicating wrongful discharge cases based on violations of public policy springing from nonstatutory and nonconstitutional sources. The majority's attempt to constrain the development of the law in a one-size-fits-all judicial straitjacket ignores the essential wisdom of the common law: law is best developed case by case, with attention to the facts of particular cases and the patterns of cases as they develop over time.

NOTES

1. **Sources of Public Policy.** *Gantt* holds that an employee bringing a wrongful discharge claim must identify a public policy delineated in a constitutional or statutory provision. What rationale does it offer for limiting public policy to these sources? As the court acknowledges, a number of other states recognize non-legislative sources of public policy, such as administrative rules or regulations and judicial decisions. The California Supreme Court itself went beyond *Gantt* in a subsequent case, holding that administrative regulations are also a source of

fundamental public policy limiting the employer's right to discharge at will. *Green v. Ralee Engineering Co.*, 960 P.2d 1046 (Cal. 1998). The plaintiff in that case alleged that he was terminated after he objected to his employer's practice of shipping parts to airplane manufacturers even though they had failed in-house inspections. He cited certain administrative regulations implementing the Federal Aviation Act as the source of the public policy allegedly violated by his discharge. The California Supreme Court reasoned:

> if a statute that seeks to further a public policy objective delegates the authority to adopt administrative regulations to an administrative agency in order to fulfill that objective, and that agency adopts regulations that are within the scope of its statutory authority and effectuate the statutory policy, then those regulations may be manifestations of important public policy.

Id. at 1056.

The dissent complained that:

> [T]he majority have opened the door to virtually limitless litigation in California over what was once a narrowly contoured exception to the legislatively declared general rule of at-will employment. One cannot deny that there are thousands and thousands of administrative regulations that have been promulgated pursuant to state and federal statutes. That reality, coupled with the majority's utter failure to provide any meaningful standards for determining when a regulatory provision sufficiently expresses a fundamental public policy with respect to a particular employer, makes it inevitable that the once-limited exception will become the general rule and effectively nullify the concept of at-will employment.

Id. at 1066 (Baxter, J., dissenting).

Should administrative regulations or judicial decisions also be recognized as sources of fundamental public policy? By limiting acceptable sources of public policy can courts effectively cabin the exception to at-will employment? Does an employee's inability to point to a specific statutory or constitutional provision *always* mean that there is no public policy at stake?

As we will discuss in section D, *infra*, in some situations the existence of a statutory remedy may complicate efforts to base a common law claim on the public policy articulated in that statute.

2.   Codes of Professional Ethics. What about professional ethics codes? These codes impose particular duties on members of certain professions. Should an employee's termination for abiding by those codes of ethics give rise to a wrongful discharge claim? As we shall see in subsection E below, this question is particularly difficult when dealing with attorneys, because of the unique nature of the attorney-client relationship.

When dealing with other professionals, however, several courts have held that their ethical codes may provide a source of public policy. For example, in *Rocky Mountain Hospital and Medical Service v. Mariani*, 916 P.2d 519 (Colo. 1996), the plaintiff, a licensed certified public accountant, alleged that she was terminated after she discovered and complained to her supervisors about the company's questionable accounting practices. She claimed that her discharge violated public policy as articulated in the Colorado State Board of Accountancy Rules and Regulations. Noting that "[a] professional employee forced to choose between violating his or her ethical obligations or being terminated is placed in an intolerable position," *id.* at 525, the Colorado Supreme Court found that professional ethics codes may constitute public policy for purposes of establishing a wrongful discharge claim. The court cautioned, however, that "in order to qualify as public policy, the ethical provision must be designed to serve the interests of the public rather than the interests of the profession. The provision may not concern merely technical matters or administrative regulations. . . . [It] must serve the public interest and be sufficiently concrete to notify employers and employees of the behavior it requires." *Id.* at 525. Finding that the rules of professional conduct for accountants have an important public purpose in ensuring the accurate reporting of financial information to the public, the court held that they provided an adequate basis for a wrongful discharge claim. *See also Pierce v. Ortho Pharmaceutical Corp.*, 417 A.2d 505 (N.J. 1980) (holding that a professional code of ethics may contain an expression of public policy; however, plaintiff had no right to continued employment when she refused to conduct research based on her personal morals). For a contrary view, see *Suchodolski v. Mich. Consolidated Gas Co.*, 316 N.W.2d 710 (Mich. 1982) (holding that code of ethics of a private association does not establish public policy). The RESTATEMENT takes the position that "well-established principles of professional or occupational conduct protective of the public interest" are a source of public policy for purposes of the wrongful discharge tort. *See* RESTATEMENT (THIRD) OF EMPLOYMENT LAW § 5.03(d) (Proposed Final Draft, April 18, 2014).

3. Federal Law and State Public Policy. Can federal law provide a public policy basis for a state common law wrongful discharge claim? The courts are divided on this issue. The Supreme Court of Pennsylvania rejected the claim of an employee who alleged that she was discharged for complaining about the use of a toxic chemical without proper ventilation. *McLaughlin v. Gastrointestinal Specialists, Inc.*, 750 A.2d 283 (Pa. 2000). Although the federal Occupational Safety and Health Act (OSHA) prohibits retaliation against employees who complain about health and safety violations, the court held that the plaintiff must "do more than show a possible violation of a federal statute that implicates only her own personal interest. The Plaintiff in some way must allege that some *public* policy of *this* Commonwealth is implicated, undermined, or violated because of the employer's termination of the employee." *Id.* at 289. The court concluded that "it is a mistake to baldly point to a federal statute or administrative regulation and, without more, proclaim this as the public policy of the Commonwealth, such that every violation of any federal code, or statute becomes the basis for seeking a common law remedy against the employer." *Id.* at 290. *See also Darrow v. Integris Health, Inc.*, 176 P.3d 1204 (Okla. 2008) (holding that "a federal statute, standing alone, does not articulate Oklahoma's public policy").

Other courts disagree with this position, finding that "substantial public policy interests can reside in certain federal statutory provisions." *Strozinsky v. School District of Brown Deer*, 614 N.W.2d 443 (Wis. 2000). Thus, courts have permitted wrongful discharge claims to proceed based on public policies found in OSHA,

Cloutier v. Great Atlantic & Pacific Tea Co., 436 A.2d 1140 (N.H. 1981); the Internal Revenue Code, *Strozinsky*, 614 N.W.2d 443; *Peterson v. Browning*, 832 P.2d 1280 (Utah 1992); the Federal Aviation Act regulations, *Green v. Ralee Engineering Co.*, 960 P.2d 1046 (Cal. 1998); the Clean Air Act regulations, *Phipps v. Clark Oil & Refining Corp.*, 408 N.W.2d 569 (Minn. 1987); and regulations of the Food and Drug Administration, *Boyle v. Vista Eyewear, Inc.*, 700 S.W.2d 859 (Mo. Ct. App. 1985), among other federal sources of law.

Many of the early cases simply assumed that federal law could serve as a source of public policy. In later cases, courts have begun to analyze whether or under what circumstances that should be the case. *See* Nancy Modesitt, *Wrongful Discharge: The Use of Federal Law as a Source of Public Policy*, 8 U. Pa. J. Lab. & Emp. L. 623 (2006) (analyzing different approaches courts have taken regarding when public policy tort claim can be based on federal law).

After Congress passed the Sarbanes-Oxley Act (discussed in Chapter 8, *infra*), which protects certain types of corporate whistleblowers from retaliation, courts have again disagreed, reaching different conclusions as to whether Sarbanes-Oxley could be a source of public policy supporting the wrongful discharge tort. *Compare Walker v. West Publishing Corp.*, 2011 U.S. Dist. LEXIS 90262 (S.D. W. Va. Aug. 11, 2011) (permitting claim for wrongful discharge based on public policy found in Sarbanes-Oxley Act), *and Romaneck v. Deutsche Asset Mgmt.*, 25 I.E.R. Cas. (BNA) 71 (N.D. Cal. 2006) (same), *with Day v. Staples*, 555 F.3d 42 (1st Cir. 2009) (refusing to recognize claim for wrongful discharge in violation of public policy based on Sarbanes-Oxley), *and Repetti v. Sysco Corp.*, 730 N.W.2d 189 (Wis. Ct. App. 2007) (same).

4. Multi-Part Tests. In later cases, the California courts have read into *Gantt* a four-part test for determining whether a public policy exception applies. As the court in *Stevenson v. Huntington Memorial Hospital*, 941 P.2d 1157 (Cal. 1997), wrote, "to support a wrongful discharge claim, [the alleged policy] must be: (1) delineated in either constitutional or statutory provisions; (2) 'public' in the sense that it 'inures to the benefit of the public' rather than serving merely the interests of the individual; (3) well established at the time of the discharge; and (4) substantial and fundamental." *Id.* at 1161.

The Washington Supreme Court has also articulated a four-part test for analyzing claims of wrongful discharge in violation of public policy, the first two parts of which address the question of how to recognize public policy: "(1) The plaintiffs must prove the existence of a clear public policy (the *clarity* element). (2) The plaintiffs must prove that discouraging the conduct in which they engaged would jeopardize the public policy (the *jeopardy* element). (3) The plaintiffs must prove that the public-policy-linked conduct caused the dismissal (the *causation* element). (4) The defendant must not be able to offer an overriding justification for the dismissal (the *absence of justification* element)." *Ellis v. City of Seattle*, 13 P.3d 1065, 1070 (Wash. 2001). According to the Washington Supreme Court, the clarity element asks whether the employer's conduct violates the letter or purpose of a constitutional, statutory or regulatory provision or scheme, while the jeopardy element is intended to insure that a public policy is "genuinely threatened." *Id.*

Do these multi-part tests help answer the question: when should a public policy exception be recognized?

KIRK v. MERCY HOSPITAL TRI-COUNTY
Missouri Court of Appeals
851 S.W.2d 617 (1993)

MONTGOMERY, PRESIDING JUDGE.

. . . Plaintiff, a registered nurse, started working on a part-time basis for the Hospital on December 24, 1982. On July 12, 1983, Plaintiff was employed full time as a charge nurse with the duty to supervise other nurses and assistants on the ward during her shift. In this capacity, she reported directly to Norma Sellers, the Hospital's Director of Nursing.

Shortly before Plaintiff's termination, Debbie Crain was admitted to the Hospital as one of Plaintiff's patients. Soon after Debbie Crain's admission Plaintiff, as required, made a nursing assessment and nursing diagnosis of that patient's condition. Her nursing diagnosis was toxic shock syndrome, a condition that results in death, if untreated. Plaintiff anticipated immediate doctor's orders for antibiotics to combat the life-threatening infection. Time passed with no such orders, and Plaintiff repeatedly discussed the situation with Norma Sellers. After showing extreme concern, Plaintiff was instructed by Sellers to "document, report the facts and stay out of it." The treating doctor never gave the orders Plaintiff expected for the proper care of Debbie Crain. When protocol allowed, Plaintiff discussed Debbie Crain's condition with Dr. Jumper, the Chief of Medical Staff. Appropriate steps were then taken, but to no avail. Debbie Crain later died from the effects of massive internal infection.

Within a day or two prior to Plaintiff's termination on March 22, 1984, Norma Sellers was visited by a member of Debbie Crain's family who informed her that Plaintiff had offered to obtain Debbie Crain's medical records for the family. On the day of Plaintiff's termination, a Hospital employee reported to Sellers that Plaintiff had stated Debbie Crain's physician was "paving her way to heaven." Sellers advised Mr. Lorimer, the Hospital Administrator, of Plaintiff's statement. He directed Sellers to terminate Plaintiff that day, which she did.

Plaintiff received a letter from the Hospital's attorney soon after her discharge which admonished her to "immediately cease making any further false statement regarding [the Hospital]." Plaintiff then requested a service letter, and the Hospital made the following response:

> The reason and cause for your dismissal is that it came to the attention of the hospital administration that on several occasions you made certain statements concerning the hospital, its staff or employees which were untrue and detrimental to the hospital. These statements exhibited a lack of support for the hospital administration and medical staff.

Based on these facts, the trial court entered summary judgment in favor of the Hospital. . . . [W]e believe the trial court committed error by finding there is no clear mandate in "law or regulation" to prohibit the Hospital from discharging Plaintiff. . . .

Here, the trial court apparently concluded Plaintiff, as an at-will employee, could be lawfully discharged unless a specific "law or regulation" prohibited the Hospital from doing so. . . . A finding that no such law or regulation existed does not preclude Plaintiff from asserting her claim for wrongful discharge based on the public policy exception to the employment-at-will doctrine.

The gist of Plaintiff's claim here is that her discharge violated a clear mandate of public policy as reflected in The Nursing Practice Act (NPA), [R.S.Mo.] §§ 335.011 to 335.096. She makes no claim of any specific statute, regulation or constitutional provision that prohibited the actions taken by the Hospital. She is entitled to pursue her claim without reliance on any direct violation of "law or regulation" by the Hospital. In this regard, the trial court's determination was erroneous as a matter of law.

The Hospital argues the NPA on which Plaintiff relies "does not constitute a clear mandate of law on which a cause of action for wrongful discharge in violation of public policy may be based." In essence, the Hospital believes the trial court reached the right result for the wrong reason. . . . [W]e must decide if there is a clear mandate of public policy reflected by the NPA with application to the facts in this case.

"Public policy" as described in *Boyle* [*v. Vista Eyewear, Inc.*, 700 S.W.2d 859 (Mo. App. 1985),] is "that principle of law which holds that no one can lawfully do that which tends to be injurious to the public or against the public good. It finds its sources in the state constitution, in the letter and purpose of a constitutional, statutory or regulatory provision or scheme, in the judicial decisions of the state and national courts, in 'the constant practice of the government officials,' and, in certain instances, in professional codes of ethics." 700 S.W.2d at 871 (citations omitted).

Plaintiff, as a registered nurse, was licensed under the provisions of the NPA. Section 335.016(8) of the Act defines the profession in this manner:

> "Professional nursing" is the performance for compensation of any act which requires substantial specialized education, judgment and skill based on knowledge and application of principles derived from the biological, physical, social and nursing sciences, including, but not limited to:
>
> (a) Responsibility for the teaching of health care and the prevention of illness to the patient and his family; or
>
> (b) Assessment, nursing diagnosis, nursing care, and counsel of persons who are ill, injured or experiencing alterations in normal health processes; or
>
> (c) The administration of medications and treatments as prescribed by a person licensed in this state to prescribe such medications and treatments; or
>
> (d) The coordination and assistance in the delivery of a plan of health care with all members of the health team; or

(e) The teaching and supervision of other persons in the performance of any of the foregoing.

Section 335.021 creates "The Missouri State Board of Nursing," and § 335.036 gives the Board authority to adopt rules and regulations to carry into effect the provisions of the NPA. That statute also requires the Board to set minimum standards for educational programs preparing persons for licensure under the Act and to license qualified applicants. Further, the Board shall "[c]ause the prosecution of all persons violating provisions of [the NPA] . . . ." § 335.036.1(8). After a hearing, the Board is empowered to revoke or suspend the license of a registered nurse for causes listed under § 335.066.2. Among those grounds are:

. . . .

(5) Incompetency, misconduct, gross negligence, fraud, misrepresentation or dishonesty in the performance of the functions or duties of any profession licensed or regulated by this chapter;

(6) Violation of, or assisting or enabling any person to violate, any provision of this chapter, or of any lawful rule or regulation adopted pursuant to this chapter;

. . . .

(12) Violation of any professional trust or confidence.

Regulation of the registered nurse profession is extensive as shown by the regulations adopted by the State Board of Nursing in 4 CSR 200-2. That chapter sets minimum standards for accredited programs of professional nursing and registration of professional nurses. Noteworthy is 4 CSR 200-2.010(1)(A).1 which indicates the purpose of accreditation is to "[t]o promote the safe practice of professional nursing . . . ." Other regulations promulgated by the Board include a procedure for handling public complaints concerning violations of Chapter 335, RSMo by a registered nurse. 4 CSR 200-4.030. Subsection (8) of that regulation indicates the Board interprets this rule "to exist for the benefit of those members of the public who submit complaints to the board . . . ."

Public policy finds its sources "in the letter and purpose of a constitutional, statutory or regulatory provision or scheme . . . ." *Boyle*, 700 S.W.2d at 871. In this case, the public policy alleged to have been violated is set forth in the above NPA and regulations thereunder. That Act and the regulations reveal a clear mandate of public policy. The purpose is to train and license a person to engage in the safe and competent practice of nursing. By definition, a professional registered nurse applies her specialized skills to (1) the prevention of illness to her patient, (2) care and counsel of ill persons, (3) administration of prescribed treatment and medication, and (4) assisting in the delivery of a health care plan. § 335.016(8). Such duties reflect the public policy of this state that registered nurses licensed in this state have an obligation to faithfully serve the best interests of their patients.

Plaintiff could clearly risk discipline and prosecution by the State Board of Nursing if she ignored improper treatment of a patient under her care. Inaction in that situation could be viewed as incompetence, gross negligence or misconduct on the part of Plaintiff. It could be viewed as assisting or enabling another person to commit those acts, or a violation of Plaintiff's professional trust. § 335.066.2(5), (6) and (12). Registered nurses who do not engage in the safe and competent practice of nursing are disciplined under a regulation that exists for the benefit of the public who might suffer from the consequences of unsafe or incompetent nursing care. 4 CSR 200-4.030(8).

Here, Plaintiff perceived Debbie Crain was dying from improper medical treatment. After reporting her views to her direct superior, she was told to "stay out of it." We are convinced the NPA and regulations thereunder sets forth a clear mandate of public policy that Plaintiff not "stay out" of a dying patient's improper treatment. Plaintiff's constant and immediate involvement in seeking proper treatment for Debbie Crain was her absolute duty. Common sense dictates this is the highest duty in the nursing profession.

The Hospital argues the public policy we have discussed is vague and ambiguous. Plaintiff cites numerous cases, including *Boyle*, which contain specific provisions of statutes, regulations or constitutional provisions upon which the plaintiff relied. For example, Plaintiff points to the specific regulation in *Boyle* that requires a process of manufacturing eyeglasses designed to give eyeglass wearers maximum protection against eye injuries and blindness. Contrasting that regulation against the NPA and regulations thereunder, the Hospital believes the vagueness is obvious. We disagree. The definition of "public policy" as defined in *Boyle, supra,* is in itself vague until applied to the facts of each case. Here, that principle would hold that the Hospital cannot lawfully require that Plaintiff "stay out" of Debbie Crain's case because of the obvious injurious consequences. Therefore, on the facts of this case we hold that the NPA and regulations thereunder constitutes a clear mandate of law on which a cause of action for wrongful discharge in violation of public policy can be based.

We have not decided that Plaintiff's discharge resulted from her refusal to "stay out of it." On the contrary, our view of the record indicates a material issue of fact exists on the cause of Plaintiff's discharge. The Hospital's service letter indicates a basis for discharge other than the reason Plaintiff argues here. We reverse the grant of the summary judgment and remand for a trial at which the Plaintiff may be afforded an opportunity to establish her allegations that her discharge resulted from her performance of a mandated lawful act contrary to the directions of her employer.

Reversed and remanded.

NOTES

1. **"Carefully Tethered to Fundamental Policies."** The *Gantt* court said that the public policy exception should be "carefully tethered to fundamental policies that are delineated in constitutional or statutory provisions." What does it mean to be "carefully tethered"? How specifically must the statutory or constitutional provision speak to the particular circumstances of the plaintiff's discharge? In *Kirk*, the statute relied on as a source of public policy was quite general, speaking in broad aspirational terms. Was the court justified in relying on the Nursing Practices Act? Why or why not?

Alternatively, some courts have looked for quite specific statutory prohibitions, but this approach, too, can prove awkward. For example, in *Wagenseller v. Scottsdale Memorial Hospital*, 710 P.2d 1025 (Ariz. 1985), the plaintiff alleged that her relationship with her supervisor deteriorated and that she was eventually fired because, while on a group camping and rafting trip, she had refused to join in a parody of the song "Moon River" which concluded with members of the group "mooning" the audience. She challenged her discharge on public policy grounds, relying on Arizona's indecent exposure statute, which prohibits exposure of a person's genitals or anus when another would be offended or alarmed by the act. The Arizona Supreme Court permitted her claim to proceed, stating that

> [w]hile this statute may not embody a policy which "strikes at the heart of a citizen's social right, duties and responsibilities" as clearly and forcefully as a statute prohibiting perjury, we believe that it was enacted to preserve and protect the commonly recognized sense of public privacy and decency. The statute does, therefore, recognize bodily privacy as a "citizen's social right." . . . We thus uphold this state's public policy by holding that termination for refusal to commit an act which might violate [the indecent exposure statute] may provide the basis of a claim for wrongful discharge. . . . The relevant inquiry here is not whether the alleged "mooning" incidents were either felonies or misdemeanors or constituted purely technical violations of the statute, but whether they contravened the important public policy interests embodied in the law. The law enacted by the legislature establishes a clear policy that public exposure of one's anus or genitals is contrary to public standards of morality. We are compelled to conclude that termination of employment for refusal to participate in public exposure of one's buttocks is a termination contrary to the policy of this state, even if, for instance, the employer might have grounds to believe that all of the onlookers were voyeurs and would not be offended. In this situation, there might be no crime, but there would be a violation of public policy to compel the employee to do an act ordinarily proscribed by the law.

Id. at 1035. In the *Wagenseller* case, should it matter whether or not an actual violation would have occurred under the precise terms of the statute?

Some courts do not restrict public policy to violations of the "literal language" of a statutory or constitutional provision, but assert that they should consider whether a discharge contravenes the "spirit as well as the letter" of such a provision. *Strozinsky v. School District of Brown Deer*, 614 N.W.2d 443, 455 (Wis. 2000). Others have been far more reluctant to find public policy violations without a specific showing of an actual violation. *See, e.g., Babick v. Oregon Arena Corp.*, 40 P.3d 1059, 1063 (Or. 2002) (rejecting plaintiffs' public policy claims on the grounds that the statutes relied on are "far too general" and suffer from a "lack of focus"); *Adler v. American Standard Corp.*, 432 A.2d 464 (Md. 1981) (holding that plaintiff's complaint failed to state a cause of action for wrongful discharge where the allegations were too vague and lacking in specifics to show that the claimed misconduct actually violated the statute relied upon as a source of public policy).

2. Statutory Remedies. Suppose that Missouri's Nursing Practices Act had a provision that specifically prohibited an employer from firing a nurse in retaliation for advocating on behalf of a patient. Would Kirk's public policy claim rest on firmer ground? What if the statute not only specifically prohibited such retaliation, but also provided a remedy to the nurse subject to the retaliation? We will discuss how the common law public policy tort interacts with statutory remedies in section D *infra*.

C.   WHAT IS A "DISCHARGE"?

In the cases considered thus far in this chapter, the employees were clearly fired by their employers. Sometimes, however, employees bring claims after quitting their jobs, alleging that they were forced to resign—a "constructive discharge" in legal terms. What circumstances are necessary to show that a quit was in fact a constructive discharge?

Strozinsky v. School District of Brown Deer, 614 N.W.2d 443 (Wis. 2000). The plaintiff in *Strozinsky* was the payroll clerk for a school district. According to her complaint, she disagreed with her supervisors about how to handle tax withholding on a bonus check for the district superintendent. Strozinsky alleged that the superintendent insisted that she issue the check without any withholding, which she believed would violate the tax laws, and that during this conversation, the superintendent was assertive and threatening, yelling at her like she was a child. In a subsequent confrontation over the issue, the superintendent "screamed as his veins bulged and spittle came out of his mouth. . . . [he] leaned over the desk red-faced, pointed to the door, and warned that if Strozinsky engaged in similar behavior in the future, she would be 'out of here.' " This incident left Strozinsky shaken: "She cried, hyperventilated, and vomited." Shortly afterwards, Strozinsky left on a previously planned family vacation. When she returned, she alleged that her supervisors diminished her work responsibilities, stopped communicating with her, reprimanded her without cause and put undue pressure on her to meet deadlines. She felt threatened and believed she was being given "an ultimatum." A few weeks later, Strozinsky resigned. She then sued for wrongful discharge in violation of public policy.

The court first considered whether Strozinsky had identified a fundamental public policy sufficient to state a claim for wrongful discharge and concluded that she had. It next considered whether she had resigned or been constructively discharged:

> The doctrine of constructive discharge recognizes that some resignations are coerced, tantamount to a termination. Usually, employers do not "discharge" employees who resign: An employee can leave an at-will position at any time—for any reason or no reason at all—just as an employer can terminate an at-will employee at its discretion. An employee who departs from the workplace generally cannot pursue a claim against the employer for wrongful discharge. Nonetheless, many courts reason that employers should not escape liability simply because the employer forced a resignation:

>> Actual discharge carries significant legal consequences for employers, including possible liability for wrongful discharge. In an attempt to

avoid liability, an employer may refrain from actually firing an employee, preferring instead to engage in conduct causing him or her to quit. The doctrine of constructive discharge addresses such employer-attempted "end runs" around wrongful discharge and other claims requiring employer-initiated terminations of employment.

Balmer v. Hawkeye Steel, 604 N.W.2d 639, 641 (Iowa 2000) (quoting *Turner v. Anheuser-Busch, Inc.*, 876 P.2d 1022, 1025 (Cal. 1994)). Constructive discharge exposes "what is ostensibly a resignation [as] a discharge." *Turner*, 876 P.2d at 1030. The doctrine operates "to discard form for substance, to reject sham for reality" and recognizes that certain resignations are, in fact, actual firings.

. . . [C]onstructive discharge is not a generic, free-flowing cause of action. Other jurisdictions recognize that constructive discharge is not actionable by itself. Rather, the doctrine is ancillary to an underlying claim in which an express discharge otherwise would be actionable. Constructive discharge joins the actionable claim and operates as a defense against an employer's contention that the employee quit voluntarily. An employee who relies on a constructive discharge defense in a public policy exception case still must identify a fundamental and well defined public policy and then prove that the discharge, whether constructive or express, violated that policy. We therefore must determine whether the doctrine of constructive discharge can attach to a common-law claim based on the narrow public policy exception to the general rule of employment-at-will.

[handwritten margin notes: WD not an action by itself; if a PP exception case →; overall issue]

The concept of constructive discharge first arose in federal statutory claims brought under the National Labor Relations Act. In *Sure-Tan, Inc. v. NLRB*, 467 U.S. 883 (1984), the United States Supreme Court addressed the discrimination some employers exerted against workers engaged in labor organizations. The Court observed that an employer discriminates "not only when . . . it directly dismisses an employee, but also when it purposefully creates working conditions so intolerable that the employee has no option but to resign—a so-called 'constructive discharge.'" *Id.* at 894. Federal courts allowed the constructive discharge defense in discrimination actions launched under Title VII of the Civil Rights Act of 1964, the Age Discrimination in Employment Act of 1967, and the Americans with Disabilities Act of 1990. . . .

We . . . decide that to raise the constructive discharge defense, the employee must establish conditions so intolerable that he or she felt compelled to resign. If the plaintiff cannot show conditions so intolerable, the claim does not proceed.

[handwritten margin note: EE must establish]

We therefore must discern what conditions rise to this level of intolerability. A constructive discharge analysis implicates an objective inquiry, recognizing that employees cannot be overly sensitive to a working environment. The question hinges on whether a reasonable person in the position of the plaintiff would feel forced to quit. Stressful "disappointments, and possibly some injustices" are not actionable. Similarly, employees will not prevail in claims charging only that managers were heavy-handed, critical, or unpleasant. Inferior work assignments, transfers to less favorable job duties, and substandard performance reviews alone generally do not create intolerable conditions. Rather, the situation must be unusually aggravating and surpass "[s]ingle, trivial, or isolated" incidents of misconduct. *Turner*, 876 P.2d at 1027. . . .

PP

[E]mployers cannot escape liability by coercing a resignation instead of formally uttering the words "you're fired." Were we to prohibit this cause of action because the employer forced a resignation instead of expressly discharging the employee, we would elevate form over substance and eviscerate the essence of [the public policy exception to at-will employment]. Nonetheless, we emphasize that a plaintiff's burden to prove constructive discharge is stringent. The plaintiff must prevail under an objective standard, establishing that conditions were so intolerable that a reasonable person confronted with same circumstances would have been compelled to resign. The level of intolerability must be unusually aggravating and surpass isolated incidents of misconduct, injustice, or disappointment.

The court then concluded that the facts supported Strozinsky's claim that she was forced to resign because of intolerable conditions, and held that a jury should decide whether her resignation was voluntary or a constructive discharge.

NOTES

1. **Constructive Discharge.** What does the *Strozinsky* court mean when it says that "constructive discharge is not a generic, free-floating cause of action"? In what way is this statement consistent with the policy that lies behind recognition of constructive discharge theories?

As discussed by the court in *Strozinsky*, constructive discharge doctrines were first developed in the case law interpreting the National Labor Relations Act, and later, various anti-discrimination statutes, such as Title VII. Like the Wisconsin Supreme Court, most courts that have considered the issue have adopted the constructive discharge theory in the context of wrongful discharge in violation of public policy claims. This evolution in constructive discharge law is one example of how doctrines developed in one area of work law influence the evolution of the law in other areas as well.

What exactly must the plaintiff show in order to establish that she was constructively discharged? There are at least three issues that must be addressed in establishing the standards for determining when an employee has been constructively discharged: 1) what type of working conditions must the employee show? 2) by what standards should the alleged conditions be judged? and 3) what level of employer intent is required? How does the *Strozinsky* court answer the first two of these questions? *See also Mills v. Hankla*, 297 P.3d 158, 166 (Alaska 2013) (holding that constructive discharge may result from a " 'sustained campaign' of harassment" such that the employee was "forced into an involuntary resignation").

Courts have taken different approaches to the third question. Many adapt a "known or should have known" standard. The California Supreme Court takes a slightly different approach. In *Turner v. Anheuser-Busch, Inc.*, 876 P.2d 1022 (Cal. 1994), it held that a plaintiff must show that the employer had actual knowledge, not merely constructive knowledge, of the allegedly intolerable conditions giving rise to the constructive discharge claim. It reasoned that requiring employees to notify employers of intolerable working conditions permits employers unaware of wrongdoing to correct the situation. Because the conditions causing the employee's resignation "must be employer-caused and against the employee's will," it held that "the employer must either deliberately create the intolerable working conditions . . . or, at a minimum, must know about them and fail to remedy the situation." *Id.* at 249–50.

[handwritten: Cal]

Like *Strozinsky* and numerous other courts, however, the court in *Turner* agreed that the constructive discharge theory does not require proof that the employer expressly intended to make the employee quit. *See, e.g., Beye v. Bureau of National Affairs*, 477 A.2d 1197, 1202 (Md. Ct. Spec. App. 1984) (employer's express intent to cause employee to resign not necessary); *Slack v. Kanawha County Housing and Redevelopment Authority*, 423 S.E.2d 547 (W. Va. 1992) (plaintiff need not prove employer's actions were taken with a specific intent to cause plaintiff to quit).

[handwritten: do not need express intent to make EE quit]

2.   **Wrongful Retaliation.** What about employees who suffer retaliatory actions by their employers that fall short of discharge, and are not egregious enough to constitute conditions so intolerable that a reasonable employee would resign? Should the courts recognize claims for wrongful demotion or discipline in violation of public policy? Courts are divided on this issue. The Washington Supreme Court in *White v. State*, 929 P.2d 396 (Wash. 1997), rejected the claim of a nursing home employee that she was transferred to another position in retaliation for reporting an incident of alleged patient abuse. In declining to recognize a claim for "wrongful transfer in violation of public policy," the court expressed concern that extending the public policy exception to personnel actions short of discharge "would be opening a floodgate to frivolous litigation and substantially interfering with an employer's discretion to make personnel decisions." *Id.* at 408. Noting that the courts are "ill-equipped to act as super personnel agencies," the court held that "[s]ubjecting each disciplinary decision of an employer to the scrutiny of the judiciary would not strike the proper balance between the employer's right to run his business as he sees fit and the employee's right to job security." *Id.*

[handwritten: WA divided cts on wrongful demotion or discip in V of PP]

Taking the opposite view, the Supreme Court of Kansas in *Brigham v. Dillon Cos.*, 935 P.2d 1054 (Kan. 1997), permitted the plaintiff to proceed on a claim that he had been wrongfully demoted in retaliation for claiming workers' compensation benefits. Reasoning that "the loss or damage to the demoted employee differs in degree only" from the discharged employee, it held that "recognition of a cause of action for retaliatory demotion is a necessary and logical extension of the cause of action for retaliatory discharge." *Id.* at 1059–60. To hold otherwise, it suggested, would send "[t]he obvious message . . . [to] employers to demote rather than discharge employees in retaliation for filing a workers compensation claim or whistleblowing." *Id.* at 1060. The court dismissed concerns about a "torrent of litigation," arguing that "[t]he linchpin of the tort for retaliatory demotion is a violation of public policy. As such, the cause of action is strictly limited and would likewise prevent 'excessive judicial entanglement.' " *Id.* at 1059.

[handwritten: KS]

[handwritten: why KS took position of yes]

D.   THE RELATIONSHIP BETWEEN STATUTORY AND COMMON LAW REMEDIES

Because of the number and variety of statutes regulating the employment relationship, courts often confront situations in which a claim of wrongful discharge in violation of public policy potentially overlaps with a statutory remedy. Consider, for example, a situation in which an employer discharges an employee for complaining about unsafe working conditions. A state statute prohibits retaliation against employees who raise safety concerns, and the terminated employee brings a claim for wrongful discharge in violation of public policy relying on the statute as a source of public policy. The employee might bring the common law claim instead of or in addition to the statutory claim if more generous damages are available under the common law, or because the statute's protections do not encompass her precise factual situation. Alternatively, a statute may articulate an important public policy, such as the prohibition of sex discrimination, but have limited application, for example, by exempting small employers from its coverage. An employee whose employer is too small to be covered by the statute may bring a claim for wrongful discharge in violation of a public policy against sex discrimination. In these types of situations, should the existence of a statutory remedy bar a common law claim for wrongful discharge?

Some courts have held that claims of wrongful discharge in violation of public policy are premised on the absence of any other remedy for the alleged wrong. Thus, the court in *Wehr v. Burroughs Corp.*, 438 F. Supp. 1052, 1055 (E.D. Pa. 1977) wrote:

> It is clear then that the whole rationale undergirding the public policy exception is the vindication or the protection of certain strong policies of the community. If these policies or goals are preserved by other remedies, then the public policy is sufficiently served. Therefore, application of the public policy exception requires two factors: (1) that the discharge violate some well-established public policy; and (2) that there be no remedy to protect the interests of the aggrieved employee or society.

Id. at 565–66. *Wehr* and those courts that follow its reasoning conclude that if a statutory remedy exists for a given discharge, no common law wrongful discharge claim is necessary or warranted. *See, e.g., Kimmelman v. Heather Downs Management Ltd.*, 753 N.W.2d 265 (Mich. 2008).

Other courts have found that the existence of an alternative statutory remedy does not *automatically* preclude a common law wrongful discharge claim. *See, e.g., Amos v. Oakdale Knitting Co.*, 416 S.E.2d 166 (N.C. 1992); *Wilmot v. Kaiser Aluminum and Chemical Corp.*, 821 P.2d 18 (Wash. 1991). As the court in *Amos v. Oakdale Knitting Co.* explained:

> If the sole rationale for the adoption of the public policy exception . . . was to provide a remedy where no other remedy existed, then the reasoning of the Court of Appeals [following *Wehr*] would be persuasive. [Recognition of the public policy tort,] however, was not predicated on the "no alternative remedy" theory. . . . The underlying rationale was the recognition that the judicially created employment-at-will doctrine had its

limits and it was the role of this Court to define those limits. . . . The public policy exception adopted by this Court . . . is not just a remedial gap-filler. It is a judicially recognized outer limit to a judicially created doctrine, designed to vindicate the rights of employees fired for reasons offensive to the public policy of this State. The existence of other remedies, therefore, does not render the public policy exception moot.

Id. at 171.

Even if a court, like the *Amos* court, does not automatically bar a wrongful discharge claim because of the existence of a statutory remedy, the claim will nevertheless be barred if the legislative remedy was intended to be exclusive. Certainly in cases where the legislature's intent to provide an exclusive remedy is clear, a wrongful discharge claim will be barred. Thus, an examination of the statutory language and purpose is often decisive.

Comprehensive federal statutes sometimes preempt state laws relating to the same subjects. Congress may explicitly express its intent to preempt related state laws, or preemption may be implied when the legislation's scope indicates Congress' attempt to occupy the field. For example, in *Ingersoll-Rand v. McClendon*, 498 U.S. 133 (1990), the United States Supreme Court held that federal law preempted a common law claim that plaintiff was wrongfully discharged in order to prevent his pension from vesting. The Employee Retirement Income Security Act (ERISA), passed in 1974, imposes reporting, disclosure and vesting requirements on employee pension plans, and includes a broadly worded preemption clause: "the provisions of this subchapter . . . shall supercede any and all state laws insofar as they may now or hereafter relate to any employee benefit plan . . .." 29 U.S.C. § 1144. The Court found that the breadth of the preemption clause was "designed to 'establish pension plan regulation as exclusively a federal concern.' " *Id.* at 138. Similarly, the court in *Botz v. Omni Air International*, 286 F.3d 488 (8th Cir. 2002), held that a flight attendant's whistleblower claim based on a state statute was preempted by the federal Airline Deregulation Act, 49 U.S.C. § 41713. It pointed out that protecting her right to refuse an assignment based on her belief that it violated FAA regulations on flight times could ground scheduled flights and disrupt airline service, an area of closely regulated federal concern.

A strong legislative policy favoring a uniform approach to an issue gives a statute such as the ERISA or NLRA strong preemptive effects as a matter of federal law. In other areas, the federal statutory schemes contemplate overlapping state authority over the subject. For example, the federal Fair Labor Standards Act, which establishes a minimum wage and the requirement of overtime pay for work in excess of 40 hours in a week, does not preclude the states from establishing a higher minimum wage or a more protective overtime standard. Similarly, the federal Occupational Safety and Health Act encourages states to develop and administer their own workplace safety and health programs. In areas like these, the argument for federal preemption of state law remedies is weaker.

When common law wrongful discharge claims overlap *state* statutory schemes, the federalism concerns are absent. Nevertheless, common law courts must examine the legislative intent behind the state statutes to determine whether the common law claims should be precluded. The easiest cases are those in which the legislature explicitly addresses the question. For example, Montana's Wrongful Discharge from Employment Act expressly precludes common law claims of wrongful discharge, replacing them with a statutory cause of action if the employer discharges an employee for refusing to violate public policy or reporting a violation of public policy. MONT. CODE ANN. § 39-2-901 *et seq.* Similarly, New York's "whistle-blower" statute makes plain how its remedies interact with other claims:

when statutes plainly preclude cl claims

> Nothing in this section shall be deemed to diminish the rights, privileges, or remedies of any employee under any other law or regulation or under any collective bargaining agreement or employment contract; except that the institution of an action in accordance with this section shall be deemed a waiver of [any other available] rights and remedies.

N.Y. LABOR LAW § 740(7).

silent statutes

Quite often, however, statutes are silent as to the effect they should have on other overlapping remedies such as common law claims. In the case of legislative silence, the courts are left to discern whether recognition of the wrongful discharge claim is appropriate. Some courts look for the implied intent of the legislature, *see, e.g., Lederer v. Hargraves Tech. Corp.,* 256 F. Supp. 2d 467 (W.D.N.C. 2003), but where the legislature has not specifically addressed the issue, discerning "implied intent" is difficult, and courts have divided on the question whether the existence of a statutory remedy should bar a wrongful discharge claim. *Compare Dukowitz v. Hannon Sec. Serv.,* 841 N.W.2d 147 (Minn. 2014) (refusing to recognize public policy tort claim where legislature has already provided a remedy), *and Wiles v. Medina Auto Parts,* 773 N.E.2d 526 (Ohio 2002) (same), *with Fleshner v. Pepose Vision Institute,* 304 S.W.3d 81 (Mo. 2010) (holding that statutory remedy is not exclusive remedy and does not displace wrongful discharge claim), *and George v. D.W. Zinser Co.,* 762 N.W.2d 865 (Iowa 2009) (same).

rstmt

Because determining intent in the face of legislative silence is difficult, the Restatement of Employment Law takes the position that "it is more realistic to acknowledge that the inquiry does not turn so much on an elusive search for implied legislative intent, but on whether it is appropriate to recognize an additional judicial remedy given the presence of a relevant statute addressing the same subject matter." RESTATEMENT (THIRD) OF EMPLOYMENT LAW § 5.01, cmt. e (Proposed Final Draft, April 18, 2014). It identifies two concerns that underlie that inquiry. The first concern is that the "statutory remedy may reflect compromises between competing interests that are better handled in a legislative, as opposed to a judicial, forum." *Id.* The second concern is whether the public policy tort is not needed because the employee has an adequate alternative remedy under the statute.

concerns ① ②

discrimination

The first concern has led courts in many states to find that wrongful discharge claims premised on a violation of public policy against discrimination are precluded by the administrative procedures and remedies provided by federal or state anti-discrimination laws. Some state anti-discrimination statutes provide for only reinstatement and backpay in cases of employment discrimination, and Title VII imposes caps on the amount of compensatory and punitive damages that can be awarded. In addition, these statutes often require plaintiffs to follow certain administrative procedures prior to, or in lieu of, filing suit in court, or impose more stringent standards for establishing liability. Because they view these statutory schemes as comprehensive and reflecting a legislative judgment of the appropriate remedies, many courts have declined to permit wrongful discharge claims based on violation of anti-discrimination policies. *See, e.g., Makovi v. Sherwin-Williams Co.,* 561 A.2d 179, 190 (Md. 1989) (rejecting plaintiff's common law claim alleging sex discrimination on the grounds that allowing "full tort damages to be claimed in the name of vindicating the statutory public policy goals upsets the balance between right and remedy struck by the Legislature in establishing the very policy relied upon"); *Thibodeau v. Design Group One Architects,* 802 A.2d 731 (Conn. 2002) (barring wrongful discharge claim based on pregnancy discrimination where the state statute articulating the public policy exempted small employers such as defendant). *But see City of Moorpark v. Super. Ct.,* 959 P.2d 752 (Cal. 1998) (permitting disability discrimination claim even though state's anti-discrimination statute provided a remedy for disability discrimination); *Gandy v. Wal-Mart Stores,* 872 P.2d 859 (N.M. 1994) (holding that remedies in state Human Rights Act are not exclusive).

On the other hand, the judgment that a statutory remedy is inadequate may lead courts to conclude that the common law claim should not be precluded. For example, in *Flenkner v. Willamette Industries, Inc.,* 967 P.2d 295 (Kan. 1998), the court permitted a wrongful discharge claim after determining that the available statutory remedy was inadequate. The plaintiff in that case alleged that he was fired for reporting unsafe working conditions to the Occupational Safety and Health Administration (OSHA). Although OSHA permits an employee retaliated against for making a complaint to file a claim with the Secretary of Labor, the decision whether to bring an action on the employee's behalf rests within the sole discretion of the Secretary of Labor. The court found that the Secretary's discretion "is a significant limitation on the employee's right of redress. What would, in a common-law tort action, be the decision of the plaintiff and plaintiff's counsel is, under [OSHA], the decision of a government employee. The concerns of the government employee could range from budget constraints to political pressure." *Id.* at 302. Concluding that the remedy provided by the statute is inadequate, the Kansas Supreme Court held that the plaintiff's state tort claim for retaliatory discharge was not barred.

E.   THE SPECIAL CASE OF ATTORNEYS

As discussed in section B, professional codes of ethics may sometimes provide the basis for a wrongful discharge in violation of public policy claim. In the case of attorneys, those same codes also impose numerous duties owed to clients, particularly a duty of confidentiality. When an attorney's client is also his or her sole employer—as is the case for in-house counsel—those duties may be in tension with the rights normally available to employees, such as the right to sue for wrongful termination. Should attorneys who are employed as in-house counsel be permitted to sue on this basis?

In one of the earliest cases to consider the issue, *Balla v. Gambro, Inc.,* 584 N.E.2d 104 (Ill. 1991), the Supreme Court of Illinois said no. The plaintiff in that case, Roger Balla, was employed as general counsel for a company that distributed kidney dialysis equipment manufactured in Germany. He learned that the company planned to sell a shipment of dialyzers that did not meet established standards and presented a risk of serious bodily harm or death to patients dependent upon dialysis to treat kidney failure. After his recommendation that the company not distribute the equipment was ignored, he raised further objections, telling the company's president that he would "do whatever necessary to stop the sale of the dialyzers." The dialyzers were eventually seized by the Food and Drug Administration and found to be "adulterated." Balla was fired shortly after his complaints, and he sued for "retaliatory discharge," alleging that his discharge violated public policy.

The court acknowledged that Balla appeared to have stated a claim for retaliatory discharge in contravention of public policy under Illinois law. However, it concluded that in-house counsel cannot bring a claim for retaliatory discharge. It reached its conclusion based on the purpose of the retaliatory discharge tort and on the nature of the attorney-client relationship. The Illinois Rules of Professional Conduct at the time stated that "A lawyer shall reveal information about a client to the extent it appears necessary to prevent the client from committing an act that would result in death or serious bodily injury." The court reasoned that the public policy of protecting health and safety was "adequately safeguarded" because lawyers like Balla were under a mandatory duty to report information that threatens death or serious bodily injury, as the adulterated dialyzers did. Because Balla had no choice but to report under his ethical obligations, the retaliatory tort was unnecessary to protect public policy.

The court further reasoned that permitting in-house counsel to sue for retaliatory discharge "would have an undesirable effect on the attorney-client relationship." It explained:

> . . . Generally, a client may discharge his attorney at any time, with or without cause. (*Rhoades v. Norfolk & Western Ry. Co.* (1979) 399 N.E.2d 969.) This rule applies equally to in-house counsel as it does to outside counsel. Further, this rule "recognizes that the relationship between an attorney and client is based on trust and that the client must have confidence in his attorney in order to ensure that the relationship will function properly." (Rhoades, [399 N.E.2d 969]) As stated in *Herbster*, "the attorney is placed in the unique position of maintaining a close relationship with a client where the attorney receives secrets, disclosures, and information that otherwise would not be divulged to intimate friends." (Herbster, [501 N.E.2d 343].) We believe that if in-house counsel are granted the right to sue their employers for retaliatory discharge, employers might be less willing to be forthright and candid with their in-house counsel. Employers might be hesitant to turn to their in-house counsel for advice regarding potentially questionable corporate conduct knowing that their in-house counsel could use this information in a retaliatory discharge suit. . . .

> Our decision not to extend the tort of retaliatory discharge to in-house counsel also is based on other ethical considerations. Under the Rules of Professional Conduct, appellee was required to withdraw from representing Gambro if continued representation would result in the violation of the Rules of Professional Conduct by which appellee was bound, or if Gambro discharged the appellee. (See 134 Ill. 2d Rules 1.16(a)(2), (a)(4).) In this

case, Gambro did discharge appellee, and according to appellee's claims herein, his continued representation of Gambro would have resulted in a violation of the Rules of Professional Conduct.

We also believe that it would be inappropriate for the employer/client to bear the economic costs and burdens of their in-house counsel's adhering to their ethical obligations under the Rules of Professional Conduct. Presumably, in situations where an in-house counsel obeys his or her ethical obligations and reveals certain information regarding the employer/client, the attorney-client relationship will be irreversibly strained and the client will more than likely discharge its in-house counsel. In this scenario, if we were to grant the in-house counsel the right to sue the client for retaliatory discharge, we would be shifting the burden and costs of obeying the Rules of Professional Conduct from the attorney to the employer/client. The employer/client would be forced to pay damages to its former in-house counsel to essentially mitigate the financial harm the attorney suffered for having to abide by Rules of Professional Conduct. This, we believe, is impermissible for all attorneys know or should know that at certain times in their professional career, they will have to forgo economic gains in order to protect the integrity of the legal profession. . . .

Id. at 109–10.

The reasoning of the court in *Balla* has come under significant criticism. Consider the contrary arguments made in the following case:

CREWS v. BUCKMAN LABORATORIES INTERNATIONAL, INC.
Supreme Court of Tennessee
78 S.W.3d 852 (2002)

WILLIAM M. BARKER, JUSTICE.

. . . [P]laintiff was hired by Buckman in 1995 as associate general counsel in its legal department, and while working in this capacity, she reported to Buckman's General Counsel, Ms. Katherine Buckman Davis. Sometime in 1996, the plaintiff discovered that Ms. Davis, who "held herself out as a licensed attorney," did not possess a license to practice law in the State of Tennessee. The plaintiff became concerned that Ms. Davis was engaged in the unauthorized practice of law, and she discussed her suspicions with a member of Buckman's Board of Directors.[6]

Ms. Davis eventually took and passed the bar exam, but the plaintiff learned some time later that Ms. Davis had yet to complete the requirements for licensure by taking the Multi-State Professional Responsibility Examination. The plaintiff informed Buckman officials of the continuing problem, and she advised them on how

---

[6] [n. 1] This Director then requested an opinion from the Board of Professional Responsibility based on a hypothetical scenario mirroring the situation at Buckman. The Board replied that a person without a Tennessee law license may not be employed as general counsel in this state and that the failure to have such a license constitutes the unauthorized practice of law.

best to proceed. On June 17, 1999, Ms. Davis allegedly entered the plaintiff's office, yelling that she was frustrated with the plaintiff's actions. The plaintiff responded that she also was frustrated with the situation, to which Ms. Davis remarked that "maybe [the plaintiff] should just leave." The plaintiff declined to leave, and she later received a below-average raise for the first time during her tenure at Buckman, despite having been told earlier by Ms. Davis that she was "doing a good job in position of Associate Counsel."

In August, the plaintiff sought legal advice concerning her ethical obligations, and based on this advice, she informed the Board of Law Examiners of Ms. Davis's situation. The Board later issued a show-cause order asking Ms. Davis to clarify certain facts in her bar application. Upon receipt of the order, Ms. Davis demanded to know from the plaintiff what information the Board possessed in its application file. The plaintiff stated that she knew nothing of the file, and she told Ms. Davis that her actions were threatening and inappropriate. Ms. Davis then apologized, but she immediately proceeded to schedule the plaintiff's performance review.

The plaintiff then informed Mr. Buckman and the Vice-President of Human Resources that "the situation [had become] untenable and that she could not function under those circumstances." They agreed that the plaintiff should be immediately transferred to a position away from Ms. Davis's supervision and that she should eventually leave the company altogether within six to nine months. However, while the plaintiff was "in the midst of working out the new arrangement," Ms. Davis informed her that her services would no longer be needed. . . .

On April 10, 2000, the plaintiff filed suit against Buckman in the Shelby County Circuit Court, alleging a common-law action for retaliatory discharge in violation of public policy. . . .

Buckman then moved to dismiss the complaint under Rule of Civil Procedure 12.02(6) for failure to state a claim upon which relief may be granted. On June 11, 2000, the trial court granted Buckman's motion, [and the Court of Appeals affirmed]. . . .

Tennessee has long adhered to the employment-at-will doctrine in employment relationships not established or formalized by a contract for a definite term. . . . However, an employer's ability to discharge at-will employees was significantly tempered by our recognition in *Clanton v. Cain-Sloan Co.*, 677 S.W.2d 441 (Tenn. 1984), of a cause of action for retaliatory discharge. Since that time, we have further recognized that an at-will employee "generally may not be discharged for attempting to exercise a statutory or constitutional right, or for any other reason which violates a clear public policy which is evidenced by an unambiguous constitutional, statutory, or regulatory provision." *See Stein v. Davidson Hotel Co.*, 945 S.W.2d 714, 716–17 (Tenn. 1997). Therefore, in contrast to the purposes typically justifying the employment-at-will doctrine, an action for retaliatory discharge recognizes "that, in limited circumstances, certain well-defined, unambiguous principles of public policy confer upon employees implicit rights which must not be circumscribed or chilled by the potential of termination." *Id.*

This Court has not previously addressed the issue of whether a lawyer may pursue a claim of retaliatory discharge against a former employer. At least initially,

first impression issue

we must recognize that this case differs significantly from the usual retaliatory discharge case involving non-lawyer employees. When the discharged employee served as in-house counsel, the issue demands an inquiry into the corporation's expectations as the lawyer's sole employer and client, the lawyer's ethical obligations to the corporation, and the interest of the lawyer—in her character as an employee—in having protections available to other employees seeking redress of legal harm. . . .

[I]n *Balla v. Gambro, Inc.*, 584 N.E.2d 104 (Ill. 1991), . . . the Illinois Supreme Court . . . set forth several rationales why in-house counsel should not be permitted to assert an action for retaliatory discharge. These rationales included (1) that because "in-house counsel do not have a choice of whether to follow their ethical obligations as attorneys licensed to practice law," *id.* at 109, lawyers do not need an action for retaliatory discharge to encourage them to abide by their ethical duties; and (2) that recognizing such an action would affect the foundation of trust in attorney-client relationships, which would then make employers "naturally hesitant to rely upon in-house counsel for advice regarding [the employer's] potentially questionable conduct." *Id.* at 110.

case we just read

In more recent years, however, other states have permitted a lawyer, under limited circumstances, to pursue a claim of retaliatory discharge based upon termination in violation of public policy. The principal case permitting such an action is *General Dynamics Corp. v. Rose*, 876 P.2d 487 (Cal. 1994), in which the California Supreme Court rejected the views held by *Balla* and others and established an analytical framework permitting a lawyer to sue for retaliatory discharge. . . . However, the *General Dynamics* Court cautioned that the lawyer bringing the action could not rely upon confidential information to establish the claim and that any unsuccessful lawyer breaching his or her duty of confidentiality was subject to disciplinary sanctions. *Id.* at 503.

other states permit it

CAL

Following California's lead, the Supreme Judicial Court of Massachusetts has also permitted in-house counsel to assert a limited retaliatory discharge action. [*GTE Products Corp. v. Stewart*, 653 N.E.2d 161 (Mass. 1995).] . . . Finally, and most recently, the Montana Supreme Court also held that in-house counsel should be permitted to bring retaliatory discharge actions when necessary to protect public policy. In *Burkhart v. Semitool, Inc.*, 5 P.3d 1031 (Mont. 2000) . . . the court reasoned that "by making his or her attorney an employee, [the employer] has avoided the traditional attorney-client relationship and granted the attorney protections that do not apply to independent contractors, but do apply to employees . . . ." *Id.* at 1039. . . .

MA

MT

Considering these two general approaches to retaliatory discharge actions based upon termination in violation of public policy, we generally agree with the approaches taken by the courts in *General Dynamics, Stewart,* and *Burkhart.* The very purpose of recognizing an employee's action for retaliatory discharge in violation of public policy is to encourage the employee to protect the public interest, and it seems anomalous to protect only non-lawyer employees under these circumstances. Indeed, as cases in similar contexts show, in-house counsel do not generally forfeit employment protections provided to other employees merely because of their status or duties as a lawyer.[7] . . .

Balla's principal rationale was that recognition of a retaliatory discharge action was not necessary to protect the public interest so long as lawyers were required to follow a code of ethics. . . . We respectfully disagree that the public interest is adequately served in this context without permitting in-house counsel to sue for retaliatory discharge. It is true that counsel in this case was under a mandatory duty to not aid a non-lawyer in the unauthorized practice of law, see Tenn. Sup. Ct. R. 8, DR 3-101(A),[8] and the [court below] was also correct that lawyers do not have the option of disregarding the commandments of the Disciplinary Rules. This is not to say, however, that lawyers can never *choose* to violate mandatory ethical duties, as evidenced by the number of sanctions, some more severe than others, imposed upon lawyers by this Court and the Board of Professional Responsibility for such violations.

Ultimately, sole reliance on the mere presence of the ethical rules to protect important public policies gives too little weight to the actual presence of economic pressures designed to tempt in-house counsel into subordinating ethical standards to corporate misconduct. Unlike lawyers possessing a multiple client base, in-house counsel are dependent upon only *one* client for their livelihood. As the *General Dynamics* Court acknowledged,

> the economic fate of in-house attorneys is tied directly to a single employer, at whose sufferance they serve. Thus, from an economic standpoint, the dependence of in-house counsel is indistinguishable from that of other corporate managers or senior executives who also owe their livelihoods, career goals and satisfaction to a single organizational employer. 876 P.2d at 491.

The pressure to conform to corporate misconduct at the expense of one's entire livelihood, therefore, presents some risk that ethical standards could be disregarded. Like other non-lawyer employees, an in-house lawyer is dependent upon the corporation for his or her sole income, benefits, and pensions; the lawyer is often governed by the corporation's personnel policies and employees' handbooks; and the lawyer is subject to raises and promotions as determined by the corporation. In addition, the lawyer's hours of employment and nature of work are usually determined by the corporation. To the extent that these realities are ignored, the analysis here cannot hope to present an accurate picture of modern in-house practice.

---

[7] [n. 2] For example, courts have permitted in-house lawyers to sue for age and race discrimination in violation of federal law, *Stinneford v. Spiegel Inc.*, 845 F. Supp. 1243, 1245–47 (N.D. Ill. 1994); *Golightly-Howell v. Oil, Chem. & Atomic Workers Int'l Union*, 806 F. Supp. 921, 924 (D. Colo. 1992); to sue for protections under a state "whistleblower" statute, *Parker v. M & T Chems., Inc.*, 566 A.2d 215, 220 (N.J. Super. Ct. App. Div. 1989); to sue for breach of express and implied employment contracts, *Chyten v. Lawrence & Howell Invs.*, 18 Cal. App. 4th 618 (1993); *Nordling v. Northern State Power Co.*, 478 N.W.2d 498, 502 (Minn. 1991); and to sue based on implied covenants of good faith and fair dealing, *Golightly-Howell*, 806 F. Supp. at 924.

[8] [n. 3] Model Rule 5.5(b) imposes a similar mandatory duty: "A lawyer shall not . . . assist a person who is not a member of the bar in the performance of activity that constitutes the unauthorized practice of law."

We also reject *Balla*'s reasoning that recognition of a retaliatory discharge action under these circumstances would have a chilling effect upon the attorney-client relationship and would impair the trust between an attorney and his or her client. This rationale appears to be premised on one key assumption: the employer desires to act contrary to public policy and expects the lawyer to further that conduct in violation of the lawyer's ethical duties. We are simply unwilling to presume that employers as a class operate with so nefarious a motive, and we recognize that when employers seek legal advice from in-house counsel, they usually do so with the intent to comply with the law.

Moreover, employers of in-house counsel should be aware that the lawyer is bound by the Code of Professional Responsibility, and that the lawyer may ethically reveal client confidences and secrets in many cases. Therefore, with respect to the employer's willingness to seek the advice of the lawyer for legally questionable conduct, the nature of the relationship should not be further diminished by the remote possibility of a retaliatory discharge suit. In fact, "there should be no discernible impact on the attorney-client relationship [by recognition of a retaliatory discharge action], unless the employer expects his counsel to blindly follow his mandate in contravention of the lawyer's ethical duty." *See* Elliot M. Lonker, General Dynamics v. Superior Court: *One Giant Step Forward for In-House Counsel or One Small Step Back to the Status Quo?*, 31 Cal. W. L. Rev. 277, 298 n.139 (1995). Therefore, we conclude that little, if any, adverse effect upon the attorney-client relationship will occur if we recognize an action for discharge in violation of public policy.

Finally, we reject *Balla*'s assertion that allowing damages as a remedy for retaliatory discharge would have the effect of shifting to the employer the costs of in-house counsel's adherence to the ethics rules. The very purpose of permitting a claim for retaliatory discharge in violation of public policy is to encourage employers to refrain from conduct that is injurious to the public interest. Because retaliatory discharge actions recognize that it is the *employer* who is attempting to circumvent clear expressions of public policy, basic principles of equity all but demand that the costs associated with such conduct also be borne by the employer.

Indeed, permitting the employer to shift the costs of adhering to public policy from itself to an employee—irrespective of whether the employee is also a lawyer—strikes us as an inherently improper balance "between the employment-at-will doctrine and rights granted employees under well-defined expressions of public policy." *See Stein*, 945 S.W.2d at 717 (Tenn. 1997). If anything, the "public interest is better served [when] in-house counsel's resolve to comply with ethical and statutorily mandated duties is strengthened by providing judicial recourse when an employer's demands are in direct and unequivocal conflict with those duties." *Stewart*, 653 N.E.2d at 167.

In summary, we find unpersuasive the rationales set forth by *Balla* and other cases which equate the employment opportunities of in-house counsel with those of a lawyer possessing a larger client base. While in-house counsel may be a lawyer, we must further recognize that he or she is also an employee of the corporation, with all of the attendant benefits and responsibilities. Therefore, we hold that a lawyer may generally bring a claim for retaliatory discharge when the lawyer is discharged for abiding by the ethics rules as established by this Court.

. . . [W]hile the special relationship between a lawyer and a client does not categorically prohibit in-house counsel from bringing a retaliatory discharge action, other courts have held that it necessarily shapes the contours of the action when the plaintiff was employed as in-house counsel. For example, the courts in *General Dynamics* and *Stewart* held that a lawyer could pursue a retaliatory discharge claim, but only if the lawyer could do so without breaching the duty of confidentiality. *See General Dynamics*, 876 P.2d at 504; *Stewart*, 653 N.E.2d at 167–68. Indeed, the California Supreme Court went so far as to forewarn lawyers that those who revealed confidential information in a retaliatory discharge suit, without a basis for doing so under the ethics rules, would be subject to disciplinary proceedings. *General Dynamics*, 876 P.2d at 504.

Since 1970, lawyers in this state have been subject to the Tennessee Code of Professional Responsibility, and, at least with respect to the ethical duty of confidentiality, our Code is similar to the ethical provisions relied upon in *General Dynamics* and *Stewart*. The Disciplinary Rules generally require that a lawyer not knowingly reveal the confidences or secrets of a client. *See* Tenn. Sup. Ct. R. 8, DR 4-101(B)(1). However, this rule is subject to some limited exceptions, including when the client consents, when compelled by law or court order, or when necessary to prevent the client from committing a crime. *See* DR 4-101(C). A lawyer may also reveal client confidences and secrets as a defensive measure against "accusations of wrongful conduct," though no exception permits a lawyer to reveal client confidences or secrets "offensively" to establish a claim against a client, except in fee-collection disputes. *Id.*

If we perceive any shortcomings in the holdings of *General Dynamics* and *Stewart*, it is that they largely take away with one hand what they appear to give with the other. Although the courts in these cases gave in-house counsel an important right of action, their respective admonitions about preserving client confidentiality appear to stop just short of halting most of these actions at the courthouse door. With little imagination, one could envision cases involving important issues of public concern being denied relief merely because the wrongdoer is protected by the lawyer's duty of confidentiality. Therefore, given that courts have recognized retaliatory discharge actions in order to protect the public interest, this potentially severe limitation strikes us as a curious, if not largely ineffective, measure to achieve that goal.

However, some courts following versions of the Model Rules of Professional Conduct have reached different conclusions concerning a lawyer's ability to use confidential information in a retaliatory discharge action. Unlike Disciplinary Rule 4-101(C), Model Rule 1.6(b)(2) permits a lawyer to reveal "information relating to the representation of a client" when the lawyer reasonably believes such information is necessary "to establish *a claim or defense* on behalf of the lawyer in a controversy between the lawyer and the client . . . ." (emphasis added). Although some commentators have asserted that this provision merely permits lawyers to use confidential information in fee-collection disputes as under the Model Code, the plain language of the Model Rule is clearly more broad than these authorities would presume. In fact, at least one state supreme court has held that this language permits in-house counsel to reveal confidential information in a retaliatory discharge suit, at least to the extent reasonably necessary to establish the claim. *See* Burkhart, 5 P.3d at 1041 (stating that a lawyer "does not forfeit his rights simply because to prove them he must utilize confidential information. Nor does the client gain a right to cheat the lawyer by imparting confidences to him." (citation omitted)); *see also* Oregon State Bar Legal Ethics Comm., Formal Op. 1994-136 (stating that the "plain language" of a provision similar to Model Rule 1.6(b)(2) "permits disclosure [of client confidences and secrets] to establish a wrongful discharge claim" to the extent reasonably necessary to do so).

We agree with the approach taken by the Model Rules, and pursuant to our inherent authority to regulate and govern the practice of law in this state, we hereby expressly adopt a new provision in Disciplinary Rule 4-101(C) to permit in-house counsel to reveal the confidences and secrets of a client when the lawyer reasonably believes that such information is necessary to establish a claim or defense on behalf of the lawyer in a controversy between the lawyer and the client. This exception parallels the language of Model Rule of Professional Conduct 1.6(b)(2), and we perceive the adoption of a similar standard to be essential in protecting the ability of in-house counsel to effectively assert an action for discharge in violation of public policy. Nevertheless, while in-house counsel may ethically disclose such information to the extent necessary to establish the claim, we emphasize that in-house counsel "must make every effort practicable to avoid unnecessary disclosure of [client confidences and secrets], to limit disclosure to those having the need to know it, and to obtain protective orders or make other arrangements minimizing the risk of disclosure." Model Rule 1.6 Comment 19.

. . . [T]he plaintiff argues that the ethical rules relating to the unauthorized practice of law—such as Disciplinary Rule 3-101(A), which places upon lawyers a mandatory ethical duty "not [to] aid a non-lawyer in the unauthorized practice of law"—are for the protection of the public interest and may serve as the basis for a retaliatory discharge action. We agree. It cannot seriously be questioned that many of the duties imposed upon lawyers by the Tennessee Code of Professional Responsibility represent a clear and definitive statement of public policy. . . .

Although we need not conclude today that every provision of the Code of Professional Responsibility reflects an important *public* policy, there can be no doubt that the public has a substantial interest in preventing the unauthorized practice of law. As this Court has acknowledged, "the purpose of regulations governing the unauthorized practice of law is . . . to serve the public right to protection against unlearned and unskilled advice in matters relating to the science of the law." *See Burson*, 909 S.W.2d at 777. As such, we find here the existence of a clear public policy evidenced by the ethical duty not to aid in the unauthorized practice of law.

To be clear, although the plaintiff was not under a *mandatory* ethical duty to report Ms. Davis's alleged unauthorized practice of law to the Board of Law Examiners, she certainly possessed a *permissive* duty to report Ms. Davis's conduct. Ethical Consideration 1-3 is clear that "although lawyers should not become self-appointed investigators or judges of applicants for admission, they should report to proper officials all unfavorable information they possess relating to the character or other qualifications of applicants." As such, given the clear expression of this permissive duty, combined with the clear expression of public policy in Disciplinary Rule 3-101(A), we hold that the complaint has sufficiently alleged the existence of a clear public policy evidenced by an unambiguous provision of the Tennessee Code of Professional Responsibility. . . .

In summary, we hold that in-house counsel may bring a common-law action of retaliatory discharge resulting from counsel's compliance with a provision of the Code of Professional Responsibility that represents a clear and definitive statement of public policy. We also hold that the complaint in this case, which alleges discharge for reporting the unauthorized practice of law, states a claim for relief. . . .

NOTES

1. **The Attorney-Employee.** Should the fact that attorneys are subject to special ethical obligations mean that they are entitled to more or less protection than the ordinary employee? The *Balla* court thought the fact that Roger Balla was an attorney meant he should not have a claim for wrongful discharge. In contrast, the California Supreme Court thought that attorneys have a *stronger* claim to protection under the public policy exception:

> Lawyers are given wide professional license in part because of ethical restraints on their discretion designed to further (or at least not endanger) the public weal . . . These standards are in turn linked by their nature and goals to important values affecting the public interest at large. . . . [B]ecause their professional work is by definition affected with a public interest, in-house attorneys are even more liable to conflicts between corporate goals and professional norms than their nonattorney colleagues . . . [and] have, if anything, an *even more* powerful claim to judicial protection than their nonprofessional colleagues.

General Dynamics Corp. v. Rose, 876 P.2d 487, 498 (Cal. 1994).

Although *Balla* was an early leading case, the majority of courts which have addressed the issue since then permit in-house attorneys to bring retaliatory discharge claims. *See Heckman v. Zurich Holding Co.*, 242 F.R.D. 606 (D. Kan. 2007).

Does permitting in-house counsel to sue for wrongful discharge undermine the attorney-client relationship? The court in *Crews* rebuts each of the reasons articulated in *Balla* for not allowing such a claim—are you convinced? Or have the courts been too quick to dismiss the concerns raised by the *Balla* court? Can you think of any complications that may arise when in-house counsel are permitted to sue their employer/clients?

2. **Mandatory vs. Permissive Disclosures.** The *Balla* court relied on attorneys' mandatory obligation to reveal information that threatens serious bodily injury under the Illinois Code of Professional Responsibility. A majority of states, however, follow the Model Rules, which state that "a lawyer *may* reveal information relating to the representation of a client to the extent the lawyer reasonably believes necessary to prevent reasonably certain death or substantial bodily harm." MODEL

RULES OF PROF'L CONDUCT R. 1.6(b)(1) (emphasis added). Should it make any difference if the relevant rule of professional conduct provides for mandatory or permissive disclosure of client wrong-doing? Should it matter whether the alleged wrong-doing involves financial improprieties or a breach of professional ethics rather than threats to health and safety?

3. Difficulties of Proof. In wrongful discharge cases involving attorney-employees, the Rules of Professional Conduct are relevant not only to the question whether a public policy is implicated, but also how any subsequent litigation is conducted, because of an attorney's continuing obligation to preserve client confidences.

The Supreme Judicial Court of Massachusetts emphasized these concerns in defining the scope of a wrongful discharge action brought by in-house counsel. *GTE Products Corp. v. Stewart*, 653 N.E.2d 161 (Mass. 1995). It held that such a claim would be recognized only if "it depends on (1) explicit and unequivocal statutory norms (2) which embody policies of importance to the public at large in the circumstances of the particular case, and (3) the claim can be proved without any violation of the attorney's obligation to respect client confidences and secrets." *Id.* at 167. As discussed in *Crews*, the ability to prove such a claim without violating an attorney's ethical duties of confidentiality depends in part on whether a state has adopted the Model Code ("A lawyer may reveal . . . confidences or secrets necessary to establish or collect his fee or to defend himself . . . against an accusation of wrongful conduct." Rule 4-101(C)) or the Model Rules ("A lawyer may reveal information relating to the representation of a client to the extent the lawyer reasonably believes necessary . . . to establish a claim or defense on behalf of the lawyer in a controversy between the lawyer and the client." Rule 1.6(b)(3)).

In addition, trial courts have a number of tools at their disposal to limit the public disclosure of client confidences in a wrongful discharge suit:

> [T]he trial courts can and should apply an array of ad hoc measures from their equitable arsenal designed to permit the attorney plaintiff to attempt to make the necessary proof while protecting from disclosure client confidences subject to the privilege. The use of sealing and protective orders, limited admissibility of evidence, orders restricting the use of testimony in successive proceedings, and, where appropriate, in camera proceedings, are but some of a number of measures that might usefully be explored by the trial courts as circumstances warrant. We are confident that by taking an aggressive managerial role, judges can minimize the dangers to the legitimate privilege interests the trial of such cases may present.

General Dynamics, 876 P.2d at 504.

F.   REVISITING THE PRESUMPTION OF AT-WILL EMPLOYMENT

As explored in this chapter and the previous chapter, contemporary doctrine has softened the impact of the at-will rule by recognizing a number of routes by which the presumption of at-will employment may be avoided. Nevertheless, scholars and commentators have been critical of the rule, arguing that it is unduly harsh and unfair to employees, while others defend the rule as necessary to protect employers' interests and their ability to respond to rapidly changing business conditions. In this section, we consider the policy arguments for and against the at-will rule and the alternatives to an at-will presumption.

One argument in defense of the at-will rule is that it represents the most efficient arrangement across a broad array of employment relationships. Defenders of the rule point out that it is merely a default rule, one that the parties can contract around, and yet, at-will employment arrangements are commonly observed in the real world. Is the prevalence of at-will employment contracts the result of an efficient contracting process? Or not? Consider the following arguments:

Richard A. Epstein, *In Defense of the Contract at Will*
51 U. Chi. L. Rev. 947, 954–57, 963–70, 672–74 (1984)

. . . It is simply incredible to postulate that either employers or employees, motivated as they are by self-interest, would enter routinely into a transaction that leaves them worse off than they were before, or even worse off than their next best alternative.

From this perspective, then, the task is to explain how and why the at-will contracting arrangement (in sharp contrast to slavery) typically works to the mutual advantage of the parties. . . .

1. *Monitoring Behavior.* . . . In all too many cases, the firm must contend with the recurrent problem of employee theft and with the related problems of unauthorized use of firm equipment and employee kickback arrangements. . . . [T]he proper concerns of the firm are not limited to obvious forms of criminal misconduct. The employee on a fixed wage can, at the margin, capture only a portion of the gain from his labor, and therefore has a tendency to reduce output. . . . Internal auditors may help control some forms of abuse, and simple observation by coworkers may well monitor employee activities. . . . Promotions, bonuses, and wages are also critical in shaping the level of employee performance. But the carrot cannot be used to the exclusion of the stick. In order to maintain internal discipline, the firm may have to resort to sanctions against individual employees. It is far easier to use those powers that can be unilaterally exercised: to fire, to demote, to withhold wages, or to reprimand. These devices can visit very powerful losses upon individual employees without the need to resort to legal action, and they permit the firm to monitor employee performance continually in order to identify both strong and weak workers and to compensate them accordingly. . . .

[T]he contract at will also contains powerful limitations on employers' abuses of power. . . . [T]he worker can quit whenever the net value of the employment contract turns negative. As with the employer's power to fire or demote, the threat to quit (or at a lower level to come late or leave early) is one that can be exercised without resort to litigation. Furthermore, that threat turns out to be most effective when the employer's opportunistic behavior is the greatest because the situation is one in which the worker has least to lose. . . .

2. *Reputational Losses.* Another reason why employees are often willing to enter into at-will employment contracts stems from the asymmetry of reputational losses. Any party who cheats may well obtain a bad reputation that will induce others to avoid dealing with him. The size of these losses tends to differ systematically between employers and employees—to the advantage of the employee. Thus in the usual situation there are many workers and a single employer. The disparity in number is apt to be greatest in large industrial concerns, where the at-will contract is commonly, if mistakenly, thought to be most unsatisfactory because of the supposed inequality of bargaining power. The employer who decides to act for bad reason or no reason at all may not face any legal liability under the classical common law rule. But he faces very powerful adverse economic consequences. If coworkers perceive the dismissal as arbitrary, they will take fresh stock of their own prospects, for they can no longer be certain that their faithful performance will ensure their security and advancement. The uncertain prospects created by arbitrary employer behavior is functionally indistinguishable from a reduction in wages unilaterally imposed by the employer. At the margin some workers will look elsewhere, and typically the best workers will have the greatest opportunities. By the same token the large employer has more to gain if he dismisses undesirable employees, for this ordinarily acts as an implicit increase in wages to the other employees, who are no longer burdened with uncooperative or obtuse coworkers. . . .

3. *Risk Diversification and Imperfect Information.* . . . Ordinarily, employees cannot work more than one, or perhaps two, jobs at the same time. Thereafter the level of performance falls dramatically, so that diversification brings in its wake a low return on labor. The contract at will is designed in part to offset the concentration of individual investment in a single job by allowing diversification among employers over time. The employee is not locked into an unfortunate contract if he finds better opportunities elsewhere or if he detects some weakness in the internal structure of the firm. . . .

The contract at will is also a sensible private adaptation to the problem of imperfect information over time. . . . The at-will contract . . . allows both sides to take a wait-and-see attitude to their relationship so that new and more accurate choices can be made on the strength of improved information. ("You can start Tuesday and we'll see how the job works out" is a highly intelligent response to uncertainty.) . . .

4. *Administrative Costs.* There is one last way in which the contract at will has an enormous advantage over its rivals. It is very cheap to administer. Any effort to use a for-cause rule will in principle allow all, or at least a substantial fraction of, dismissals to generate litigation. Because motive will be a critical element in these cases, the chances of either side obtaining summary judgment will be negligible. Similarly, the broad modern rules of discovery will allow exploration into every aspect of the employment relation. Indeed, a little imagination will allow the plaintiff's lawyer to delve into the general employment policies of the firm, the

treatment of similar cases, and a review of the individual file. The employer for his part will be able to examine every aspect of the employee's performance and personal life in order to bolster the case for dismissal. . . .

The reason why these contracts at will are effective is precisely that the employer must always pay an implicit price when he exercises his right to fire. He no longer has the right to compel the employee's service, as the employee can enter the market to find another job. The costs of the employer's decision therefore are borne in large measure by the employer himself, creating an implicit system of coinsurance between employer and employee against employer abuse. Nor, it must be stressed, are the costs to the employer light. It is true that employees who work within a firm acquire specific knowledge about its operation and upon dismissal can transfer only a portion of that knowledge to the new job. Nonetheless, the problem is roughly symmetrical, as the employer must find, select, and train a replacement worker who may not turn out to be better than the first employee. Workers are not fungible, and sorting them out may be difficult: resumes can be misleading, if not fraudulent; references may be only too eager to unload an unsuitable employee; training is expensive; and the new worker may not like the job or may be forced to move out of town. In any case, firms must bear the costs of voluntary turnover by workers who quit, which gives them a frequent reminder of the need to avoid self-inflicted losses. The institutional stability of employment contracts at will can now be explained in part by their legal fragility. The right to fire is exercised only infrequently because the threat of firing is effective. . . .

Pauline T. Kim, *Bargaining with Imperfect Information: A Study of Worker Perceptions of Legal Protection in an At-Will World*
83 Cornell L. Rev. 105, 115–19 (1997)

For its defenders, the prevalence of the at-will rule in the real world weighs heavily in their conclusion that it represents an efficient arrangement. . . . [T]he simplest explanation for the prevalence of the at-will contract across businesses, regions, and circumstances is that it represents "the 'efficient' solution as between employers and employees." After all, the common-law rule merely establishes a default presumption; the parties remain free to contract around it if they desire. That they rarely do so is taken as evidence that at-will contracts not only are what employers and employees want, but that they represent the most efficient arrangement as well.

A number of critics assail this conclusion, challenging the assumption that market outcomes necessarily reflect an efficient result. In their view, the nearly total absence of job-security guarantees in the nonunion sector does not so much reflect the desires of the parties as it evidences systematic market failure. Pointing to the prevalence of just-cause provisions in collectively bargained agreements, the critics argue that nonunion workers are unlikely to have such vastly different preferences from their union counterparts that they would neither desire, nor be willing to pay for, a job security guarantee. In diagnosing this market failure, they identify the following likely defects in the bargaining process that lead to the under-production of just-cause guarantees. . . .

Imperfect Information. One possible explanation for the failure of individual employment contracts to provide for job security is that employees go into the job search process with inadequate information. A number of commentators suggest that employees misapprehend the degree of job security that legal rules afford. If workers erroneously believe that the law already protects them from unjust discharge, they will not seek guarantees of job security from their employer. Moreover, even if they correctly understand the legal rules, they may be unable to assess accurately a prospective employer's personnel policies, or to obtain meaningful information as to the actual risk of dismissal they might face with a given firm. Any of these information failures is likely to render employees unable to bargain meaningfully over the issue of job security.

Of course, employer and employee rarely negotiate individual employment contracts in a formal sense. Outside of the collective bargaining context, employer and employee do not sit down face to face and dicker over a long list of employment terms and conditions. Rather, bargaining supposedly takes place implicitly: by offering varying compensation packages, employers compete with one another to attract the best employees. Under this model, if employees value job security, they would accept lower wages, or some other reduction in benefits, in order to obtain the desired term. Once again, however, the efficiency of implicit bargaining rests on the assumption that employees have the information necessary to make meaningful comparisons of the compensation packages offered by different employers regarding the issue of job security. Thus, the possibility of widespread information failure undermines confidence in the efficiency of the contracting process, whether bargaining occurs explicitly or implicitly.

Employees' inaccurate assessment of risk. Even if workers have accurate information, they may be unable to rationally process the information they *do* have about the risk of discharge. Some hypothesize that the natural psychological tendency to discount the likelihood of low-probability bad events leads employees to undervalue just-cause protections. The tendency to underestimate not only the likelihood, but also the *costs* of job loss, exacerbates this undervaluation. Although temporary wage loss might adequately measure the costs of termination early in one's career, the same is not true for late-career discharges. Typically, wages, benefits, and opportunities within a firm all increase with seniority, such that the loss of one's job after many years of service entails far more than a mere loss of wages. Moreover, "endowment effects"—the tendency of individuals to value what they have more than identical things they might obtain—suggest that workers will value their *own* jobs more highly than any calculation of their tangible benefits might suggest. These effects are compounded by the social significance attached to one's job in this society, and likely result in employees seriously underestimating, when initially entering an employment relationship, the consequences of a job loss years down the road.

Employers' misperceptions of costs. Some commentators suggest that a similar misperception of risk mars decisionmaking on the employer's side as well. While employees underestimate the risks and costs of suffering an unjust dismissal, employers likely overestimate the costs of wrongful-discharge litigation. Moreover, employers may fail to recognize the benefits of offering just-cause protections. Greater employee loyalty, together with improved hiring and supervisory practices, might prove more profitable in the long run than relying on the threat of discharge.

Signaling Problems. Informational asymmetries inherent in the employment contracting process may create signaling problems which further interfere with efficient bargaining over the issue of job security. When entering an employment contract, employees know about the future quality of their work and their likelihood of shirking, and employers know whether they intend to abide by basic fairness norms in handling future discipline and termination. In the absence of a means to verify the claims of the other side, however, neither side is likely to raise the issue of job security. On the one hand, the employee is unlikely to express a desire for just-cause protection, out of fear that the employer will perceive her as a shirker. On the other hand, the employer will hesitate to announce its willingness to offer a just-cause term in exchange for a wage discount, fearing that it will attract a greater proportion of employees who are likely to shirk.

Public Goods. Other critics theorize that just-cause provisions are under-produced in individual employment contracts because such provisions are "public goods." They argue that just-cause protections are collective in nature because once an employer creates the administrative and adjudicatory mechanisms necessary to support such a term, it would likely be extended to all its employees. While the benefit to employees collectively might well exceed the costs of instituting such protections on a firm-wide basis, individual employees will have an incentive to understate the value they place on a just-cause term in order to position themselves as free riders. Thus, the combination of strategic behavior and informational barriers will likely result in the under-production of contractual guarantees of job security for nonunion employees.

NOTES

1. **Efficiency Arguments.** Do you think the operation of the labor market can be relied upon to provide the optimal level of job security for employees? How would you judge what level of job security is "optimal"?

2. **Employee Misperceptions.** Based on surveys of hundreds of workers, Pauline Kim has documented widespread misunderstanding of the at-will default rule among employees. *See* Pauline T. Kim, *Norms, Learning, and Law: Exploring the Influences on Workers' Legal Knowledge*, 1999 U. ILL. L. REV. 447 (1999); Pauline T. Kim, *Bargaining with Imperfect Information: A Study of Worker Perceptions of Legal Protection in an At-Will World*, 83 CORNELL L. REV. 105 (1997). Contrary to the presumption of at-will employment, the survey data suggest that employees systematically overestimate their legal rights, apparently believing that they have something akin to just cause protections when in fact they can be dismissed at will. Moreover, her survey research found that these beliefs are remarkably resistant to change. Even when told that the employer's manual contained a disclaimer reserving the right to discharge employees "with or without cause," nearly three-quarters of the respondents persisted in believing that a discharge without cause was unlawful.

These basic findings have been confirmed in several other studies. *See, e.g.,* Ian H. Eliasoph, *Know Your (Lack of) Rights: Reexamining the Causes and Effects of*

Phantom Employment Rights, 12 EMP. RTS & EMP. POL'Y J. 197 (2009) (citing several studies documenting that workers overestimate their rights); Jesse Rudy, *What They Don't Know Won't Hurt Them: Defending Employment-At-Will in Light of Findings That Employees Believe They Possess Just Cause Protection*, 23 BERKELEY J. EMP. & LAB. L. 307 (2002) (replicating and confirming results of Kim's study). What do you think accounts for employee misperceptions of their legal rights and the persistence of these beliefs? Do employees confuse fairness norms with legal protections? Do the numerous sources of employment regulation lead workers to overestimate the protections they provide? Or are employees simply rationally ignorant of the at-will rule because arbitrary discharges are rare? *See* Eliasoph, *supra* and Rudy, *supra*, discussing competing explanations for these findings.

3. **Penalty Defaults.** If employees believe they have greater legal protection of their job security than they in fact have under an at-will presumption, is that misunderstanding relevant to the choice of the default rule? What alternatives are there to the at-will presumption and what would be the costs of adopting them? Under standard economic theory, default terms should be set based on what most contracting parties would want in order to avoid imposing on them the costs of contracting around an undesirable rule. An alternative theory of default rules suggests that under certain circumstances, the default term should be one that the parties would *not* want, thereby forcing them to bargain over the issue. *See* Ian Ayres & Robert Gertner, *Filling Gaps in Incomplete Contracts: An Economic Theory of Default Rules*, 99 YALE L.J. 87 (1989). Such "penalty default" rules are appropriate when one party has information that the other does not, and the party with superior information can capture a greater portion of the gains from contracting by not revealing the information. Sharing the information might increase the contract's overall value, but the party with the information will not disclose it in order to preserve its own potential gains. In such situations, a penalty default rule may be more efficient, because it will force the party with superior information to share it, thereby increasing the overall value of the contract. Is employment contracting an area in which penalty defaults would be appropriate? *See* Samuel Issacharoff, *Contracting for Employment: The Limited Return of the Common Law*, 74 TEX. L. REV. 1783, 1793 (1996) (arguing that employment is "a prime arena" for the use of penalty default rules because informational asymmetries, disparities of bargaining power and cognitive limitations interfere with efficient bargaining).

4. **Reversing the Presumption.** In light of evidence that employees misperceive their legal protection, some scholars have proposed reversing the presumption, such that employers would be prohibited from firing without cause unless they specifically contracted otherwise. *See, e.g.*, Cass R. Sunstein, *Switching the Default Rule*, 77 N.Y.U. L. REV. 106 (2002); Pauline T. Kim, *Bargaining with Imperfect Information: A Study of Worker Perceptions of Legal Protection in an At-Will World*, 83 CORNELL L. REV. 105 (1997). Is such a rule likely to make a significant practical difference in the level of job security afforded individual employees? Are there other reasons for making the switch? Consider the arguments of Cynthia Estlund:

 . . . A weak "for-cause" default would make little difference in actual contracting practices, because most employers already act as if the default is "for cause," and disclaim it; and it would not close the gap between employee beliefs and legal reality because most employees do not give credence to a standard at-will disclaimer.

A stronger default, in the form of a waivable legal right to for-cause protection with relatively stringent requirements for knowing waiver, holds greater promise. Employees who are asked to waive their for-cause rights "knowingly" still might have no real choice in the matter. But if the standard for waiver is high enough to ensure that employees actually know what they are and are not getting, it would force the employer to make a choice between the benefits of employees' belief that they enjoy legal job security and the benefits of employment at will. . . .

As long as employees know exactly what they are getting *before* they make any investment in the job, and as long as labor markets are reasonably competitive, employees can "vote with their feet" for more or less job security. And if employees accept a job with less job security than they prefer, employers presumably will pay a price in terms of employee morale and commitment. . . .

What this adds up to is an affirmative argument for allowing employers to secure a waiver of litigable for-cause rights as a condition of employment. . . . [if the threat of litigation] can be traded up front as a condition of employment, it may afford systemic leverage on behalf of employees. It may induce employers to offer a more accessible, speedy, and efficient alternative regime for determining the fairness of discharge (perhaps, for example, some kind of arbitration process). . . . [This argument] assumes that an improved internal system of job security entails additional costs; that a combination of economic and psychological factors will make it practically necessary to extend the system to the workforce as a whole; and that the investment will not be worthwhile unless the workforce as a whole can be made to trade off their litigable for-cause rights in advance. The assumption is, in other words, that internal guarantees of job security are "public goods" within the workplace, and are subject to the standard collective-action problems of holdouts and free riders.

That suggests that what is actually needed is an effective mechanism of collective employee voice so as to enable genuine bargaining over job security. Collective employee voice in the workplace offers, in my view, a better solution to the problems discussed in this Essay, and to many other problems of workplace governance. But this Essay seeks a solution for the vast majority of workplaces that are nonunion and currently governed by employment at will. It suggests that, within a modestly reconstructed legal regime aimed at insuring employee knowledge of their rights, even a one-sided solution to the collective-action problem—allowing employers to bar holdouts and free riders by enforcing a workforce-wide deal on basic job security—may work significant improvements in the nature of that deal.

Cynthia L. Estlund, *How Wrong Are Employees About Their Rights, and Why Does It Matter?*, 77 N.Y.U. L. Rev. 6, 7–8, 25–26 (2002).

5. The Limits of Contract. Current doctrine emphasizes the contractual nature of the employment relationship, but is it appropriate to view the employment relationship primarily in contractual terms? Are there any problems with doing so?

Consider Samuel Issacharoff's description of the employment contracting process:

> In some ways, the hiring stage is like a first date. . . . While some dates may develop into romance and even marriage, it is hardly far-fetched to anticipate difficulties with a discussion of potential divorce and child-custody arrangements on the first date.

> The inherent difficulty in discussing end-term arrangements at the point of initial courtship is compounded by the general presumption of bargaining inequality for all but the most select employees. To stretch the dating metaphor one step further, the hiring stage is most like a first date between a polygamist and a monogamist. The employer has entered into a number of contemporaneous courtships such that there is a diversification of the risk associated with any individual affair. By contrast, the employee in a stable working relationship is restricted to faithful monogamy. . . . The employer is protected against employee shirking not only by the capacity to discharge any particular employee, but by the diminution of the consequences of any individual shirking in a broader pool of employees. By contrast, the employee's decision to accept one primary employment forecloses the ability to earn service credits with other employers.

Samuel Issacharoff, *Contracting for Employment: The Limited Return of the Common Law*, 74 TEX. L. REV. 1783, 1795 (1996).

As Issacharoff suggests, the employment relationship differs significantly from the classical paradigm of two independent, self-interested parties bargaining over the terms of their relationship to their mutual advantage. Except for high-level employees, very little negotiation generally occurs between employer and employee over the terms and conditions of employment. The parties rarely mention much about the details of employment beyond the basic outlines of the job to be performed and the wages paid. Little or no discussion occurs about such issues as the future prospects of the company, its long-term business plans as they bear on the employee's job, what specific aspects of performance will be expected of the employee over time, or on what terms the parties contemplate ending the relationship. To what extent does the law recognize and respond to the informality of the employment contract? Do you think the law adequately takes account of the ways in which employment differs from the standard commercial contract?

Are there ways other than contract of conceptualizing the employment relationship? Consider the following:

> [J]ust as the employer has invested capital in the business, so the employee has invested years of his working life, accumulating seniority, accruing pension rights, and developing skills that may or may not be salable to another employer. And, just as the employer's interest in the protection of his capital investment is entitled to consideration in our interpretation of

the [National Labor Relations] Act, so too is the employee's interest in the protection of his livelihood.

Ozark Trailers, Inc., 161 N.L.R.B. 561, 566 (1966). What difference would it make to think of the employment in terms of a property interest? For a discussion of this question, see Jack M. Beermann & Joseph William Singer, *Baseline Questions in Legal Reasoning: The Example of Property in Jobs*, 23 GA. L. REV. 911 (1989)

6. Alternative Approaches. In 1987, the Montana legislature passed the Wrongful Discharge from Employment Act (WDEA), which requires employers to have "good cause" for dismissal, and preempts all other common law claims for wrongful discharge. The statute permits an employee to recover lost wages and fringe benefits (less amounts for mitigation) for up to a maximum of four years from the date of discharge. Punitive damages are not allowed unless the employee shows "by clear and convincing evidence that the employer engaged in actual fraud or actual malice in the discharge of the employee." Passage of the bill followed a couple of high-profile cases in which discharged employees were awarded million dollar jury verdicts against their former employers based on claims of tortious breach of the implied covenant of good faith and fair dealing.

In 1991, the National Conference of Commissioners on Uniform State Laws approved a Model Employment Termination Act (META) for potential adoption by the states. Like the Montana statute, it attempted to balance employee and employer interests by limiting discharge of covered employees to "good cause" dismissals only, while restricting the remedies available to wrongfully terminated employees and encouraging resolution of disputes through arbitration or other alternative dispute resolution mechanisms. In doing so, it sought to address what was viewed as the twin deficiencies of the common law system: inadequate protection for most employees, and the risk of infrequent but extremely costly wrongful termination verdicts for employers. *See* Theodore J. St. Antoine, *The Making of the Model Employment Termination Act*, 69 WASH. L. REV. 361, 364–65 (1994). Despite the efforts of the NCCUSL, no state has yet adopted a statute modeled on META.

What would be the advantages to a state passing legislation along the lines of the Montana statute or META? The disadvantages? Who is likely to support such legislation? What should be the policy of unions be toward such legislation?

One of the arguments often made in support of "just cause" legislation is that such standards are common throughout the world. For example, in an early article arguing for a statutory response, Clyde Summers pointed out that the United States is "one of the few industrial countries that does not provide general legal protection against unjust dismissals." Clyde W. Summers, *Individual Protection Against Unjust Dismissal: Time for a Statute*, 62 VA. L. REV. 481, 508 (1976). Although it is true that many other countries recognize and protect employment security rights, the degree of protection afforded individual employees varies quite a bit depending upon the details of the law. *See* Samuel Estreicher, *Unjust Dismissal Laws: Some Cautionary Notes*, 33 AM. J. COMP. L. 310 (1985). Scholars have also raised concerns about the negative incentive effects created by just cause dismissal laws in other countries, suggesting that employees who are insulated from the consequences of their actions are likely to shirk, and that employers faced with restrictive dismissal laws may be disinclined to increase their hiring. *See, e.g.,* Samuel Issacharoff, *Contracting for Employment: The Limited Return of the Common Law,* 74 TEX. L. REV. 1783, 1809 (1996).

Chapter 5

COLLECTIVE JOB SECURITY

Suppose an employer decides to close an entire business, a store, a plant or a department, resulting in collective job loss. In this area, too, the background rule of employment at will has powerful sway. Employer prerogative to determine the future direction, profitability, and workforce necessary to operate a business is assumed in law. Accordingly, protection of worker job security at the collective level is limited. Three possible bases for legal claims by workers exist: (1) common law claims based in contract, property, and tort; (2) the notice provisions of the Worker Adjustment Retraining and Notice Act of 1988; and (3) the National Labor Relations Act's prohibition on retaliatory partial closings in the context of a union organizing drive and (in the unionized workforce) its requirement that the employer bargain over decisions affecting working conditions, including job security. Parts A through C of this chapter examine these bases for challenge. Part D provides a brief overview of the unemployment insurance system, the structural stopgap for temporary interruptions in income caused by job loss.

A. COMMON LAW CONTRACT, PROPERTY, AND TORT CLAIMS

Consider the following "hypothetical" fact scenario based on the case that follows it here, *Local 1330, United Steelworkers of America v. United States Steel Corporation.*

Kent Greenfield, *The Unjustified Absence of Federal Fraud Protection in the Labor Market*
107 YALE L.J. 715, 717–19, 734–35 (1997)

Imagine a steel company struggling to stay afloat against strong national and international competition. The company has an outdated production facility in Youngstown, Ohio, and faces two related problems: the need for an infusion of capital to upgrade the facility and the need to maintain employee morale and productivity. A company official meets with people who are interested in making an equity investment in the company. One potential investor asks whether the company is currently profitable and whether the company plans to stay in business for the long term. The official answers, "The company has been profitable, and there are no plans for shutting down our operation." The investors make a sizable equity contribution. Later that day, the official meets with the employees of the Youngstown facility. Employees considering job offers at a new plant down the street ask whether the facility is currently profitable and whether the company plans to keep the plant operating for the long term. The official answers, "The

241

Youngstown facility has been profitable, and there are no plans for shutting down our operation." The employees decline the job offers elsewhere and continue working at the Youngstown facility.

Now assume that the answers to both questions were lies. The official knew that neither the company nor the plant was profitable and that plans were in the works to shut down the plant and liquidate the company. The official lied to the potential investors in order to gain a capital infusion to satisfy other creditors holding short-term obligations. The official lied to the workers to keep them working diligently while the company went through its death throes. The company does eventually shut down, and the securities held by the investors lose a significant portion of their value while the workers lose their jobs.

Both the capital investors and the workers have suffered damage because of the official's lies. Can they do anything about it? For the capital investors, the answer is a resounding yes. Federal law offers significant protection against fraud in the capital market. In this hypothetical, the capital investors would likely have a claim against the official and the company under several provisions of federal law, including section 10(b) of the 1934 Securities Exchange Act and the Securities Exchange Commission's Rule 10b-5. The workers, however, are not the beneficiaries of any federal law protecting them from such fraud in the labor market and would be left without a federal cause of action against the company or the official. . . .

This hypothetical is derived from an actual case arising from the closing of two United States Steel facilities in Youngstown in the late 1970s and early 1980s. The corporation had operated two large steel mills in Youngstown since the turn of the century. In the fall of 1977, the workers in these mills and the Youngstown community generally were worried about rumors that the two factories were to be closed. These rumors were not groundless. In later litigation, U.S. Steel itself introduced exhibits of never-mailed letters dated August 25, 1977, announcing the closing of both plants.

Nonetheless, management answered the rumors by assuring employees that shutdowns were not definite and stated on several occasions that the plants could be saved if the workers improved productivity. "Hotline" telephones were strategically placed in the two plants so that employees could listen to prerecorded messages from management. The first such message told the workers that there were "no immediate plans to permanently shut down" either factory and that the mills' "continued operation" was "absolutely dependent upon their being profit-makers." Randall Walthius, an agent of U.S. Steel, told the press that there were studies under way "aimed at making the Youngstown facilities profitable" and that it would be "on the basis of the plants' profitability that they will continue to operate."

The steelworkers responded to these representations as the company must have hoped: They improved productivity and cut costs. In April 1978, plant superintendent William Kirwan stated on the hotline that his plant had made a profit during the previous month, thus showing that the goal of profitability was "attainable." Kirwan told the press later that month that the company would "be doing business here for some time to come." In both May and June 1978, Kirwan made similar profitability reports. By the end of 1978, Kirwan was able to record a statement on the hotline recounting the year's successes: "[E]arly in 1978 we initiated significant changes in our operations in order to make Youngstown Works profitable and once again a viable plant. . . . [W]e have attained our 1978 goal which was 'survival' and now we embark on the 1979 goal which is 'revival.'"

The company also made representations to the general public that the plants had righted themselves. For example, in a letter to the editor of the Wall Street Journal published in April 1979, company management boasted that a "complete turn-around has been achieved at Youngstown in the past year." The letter asserted that a report that the Youngstown plants were eroding corporate profits was "nonsense" and "fiction." These assurances continued throughout 1979. Indeed, the Chairman of the Board of U.S. Steel, David Roderick, emphasized in mid-June that, "[s]imply stated, we have no plans for shutting down our Youngstown operation."

The employees appeared to rely on the company's representations. They improved their productivity, allowed management to adjust seniority policy to save money, and waived grievances when management combined some jobs. Moreover, individual employees depended on the company's representations to make important personal decisions. One employee, Frank Georges, bought a new house on November 27, 1979, the day the Board of Directors of U.S. Steel met in New York and voted to close both Youngstown plants. The decision would put 3500 employees out of work. Georges heard the news as he was driving home from the bank. . . .

Like investors, workers contribute an essential input to companies' creation of wealth through the production of goods and services. Also like investors, workers have a difficult time acquiring and evaluating the information necessary for them to decide whether and how they should make their contribution. Like investors who have to evaluate factors including the complexity of financial documents, market risk, and expected returns, workers have to analyze the financial strength of employers, market risk, working conditions, benefits, wages, termination policies, promotion practices, grievance procedures, and hours. Moreover, the decisions workers make in choosing employers tend to have long-term implications, probably to a greater extent than for investors choosing among investment vehicles. Unlike investors, however, workers are not protected by a federal statute comparable to those protecting capital investors. No generally applicable federal protection exists, even for statements that would seemingly be at the core of antifraud protection.

LOCAL 1330, UNITED STEEL WORKERS OF AMERICA v. UNITED STATES STEEL CORP.
United States Court of Appeals for the Sixth Circuit
631 F.2d 1264 (1980)

EDWARDS, CHIEF JUDGE.

This appeal represents a cry for help from steelworkers and townspeople in the City of Youngstown, Ohio who are distressed by the prospective impact upon their lives and their city of the closing of two large steel mills. These two mills were built and have been operated by the United States Steel Corporation since the turn of the century. The Ohio Works began producing in 1901; the McDonald Works in 1918. The District Court which heard this cause of action found that as of the notice of closing, the two plants employed 3,500 employees.

The leading plaintiffs are two labor organizations, Locals 1330 and 1307 of the United Steel Workers of America. This union has had a collective bargaining contract with the United States Steel Corporation for many years. These local unions represent production and maintenance employees at the Ohio and McDonald Works, respectively.

In the background of this litigation is the obsolescence of the two plants concerned, occasioned both by the age of the facilities and machinery involved and by the changes in technology and marketing in steel making in the years intervening since the early nineteen hundreds.

For all of the years United States Steel has been operating in Youngstown, it has been a dominant factor in the lives of its thousands of employees and their families, and in the life of the city itself. The contemplated abrupt departure of United States Steel from Youngstown will, of course, have direct impact on 3,500 workers and their families. It will doubtless mean a devastating blow to them, to the business community and to the City of Youngstown itself. While we cannot read the future of Youngstown from this record, what the record does indicate clearly is that we deal with an economic tragedy of major proportion to Youngstown and Ohio's Mahoning Valley. As the District Judge who heard this case put the matter:

> Everything that has happened in the Mahoning Valley has been happen-
> ing for many years because of steel. Schools have been built, roads have
> been built. Expansion that has taken place is because of steel. And to
> accommodate that industry, lives and destinies of the inhabitants of that
> community were based and planned on the basis of that institution: Steel.

In the face of this tragedy, the steel worker local unions, the Congressman from this district, and the Attorney General of Ohio have sued United States Steel Corporation, asking the federal courts to order the United States Steel Corporation to keep the two plants at issue in operation. Alternatively, if they could not legally prevail on that issue, they have sought intervention of the courts by injunction to require the United States Steel Corporation to sell the two plants to the plaintiffs under an as yet tentative plan of purchase and operation by a community corporation and to restrain the piecemeal sale or dismantling of the plants until such a proposal could be brought to fruition.

Defendant United States Steel Corporation answered plaintiffs' complaints, claiming that the plants were unprofitable and could not be made otherwise due to obsolescence and change in technology, markets, and transportation. The company also asserts an absolute right to make a business decision to discharge its former employees and abandon Youngstown. It states that there is no law in either the State of Ohio or the United States of America which provides either legal or equitable remedy for plaintiffs.

The District Judge, after originally restraining the corporation from ceasing operations as it had announced it would, and after advancing the case for prompt hearing, entered a formal opinion holding that the plants had become unprofitable and denying all relief. We believe the dispositive paragraphs of a lengthy opinion entered by the District Judge are the following:

This Court has spent many hours searching for a way to cut to the heart of the economic reality that obsolescence and market forces demand the close of the Mahoning Valley plants, and yet the lives of 3500 workers and their families and the supporting Youngstown community cannot be dismissed as inconsequential. United States Steel should not be permitted to leave the Youngstown area devastated after drawing from the lifeblood of the community for so many years.

Unfortunately, the mechanism to reach this ideal settlement, to recognize this new property right, is not now in existence in the code of laws of our nation.

This Court is mindful of the efforts taken by the workers to increase productivity, and has applauded these efforts in the preceding paragraphs. In view of the fact, however, that this Court has found that no contract or enforceable promise was entered into by the company and that, additionally, there is clear evidence to support the company's decision that the plants were not profitable, the various acts of fore-bearance taken by the plaintiffs do not give them the basis for relief against defendant.

Plaintiffs-appellants claim that certain of the District Judge's findings of fact are clearly erroneous, that he has misconstrued federal and state contract law, and that he failed to grant a hearing on their antitrust claims.

With this introduction, we turn to the legal issues presented by this appeal. . . . The primary issue in this case is a claim on the part of the steel worker plaintiffs that United States Steel made proposals to the plaintiffs and/or the membership of the plaintiffs to the general effect that if the workers at the two steel plants concerned put forth their best efforts in terms of productivity and thereby rendered the two plants "profitable," the plants would then not be closed. It is clear that this claimed contract does not rest upon any formal written document, either authorized or signed by the parties to this lawsuit. . . .

As noted above, the steelworkers have a formal collective bargaining contract with the U.S. Steel Corporation. In this record there is no indication that there ever was any formal negotiation or amendment of that contract in relation to the issues of this case. Further, there is no indication in this record that the contract alleged in this complaint could be the subject for arbitration under [any provision of the parties' collective bargaining agreement].

The collective bargaining agreement applicable in this period also contains three sections which management asserts bear directly upon its claim of unilateral right to close any plant. These provisions are two rather general paragraphs on page 15 of the contract entitled "Management" which recite as follows:

SECTION 3 MANAGEMENT

The Company retains the exclusive rights to manage the business and plants and to direct the working forces. The Company, in the exercise of its rights, shall observe the provisions of this Agreement.

The rights to manage the business and plants and to direct the working forces include the right to hire, suspend or discharge for proper cause, or transfer and the right to relieve employees from duty because of lack of work or for other legitimate reasons.

. . . .

We are unable to construe any claims set forth in the instant litigation as being based upon any language contained in this collective bargaining agreement. Indeed, plaintiffs make no claim in this case that the United States Steel Corporation has violated . . . the collective bargaining agreement. . . .

Appellants' principal argument in this appeal is, however, that the District Court should have found a contract based upon the equitable doctrine of promissory estoppel, which contract is enforceable in the federal courts under § 301 of the National Labor Relations Act.

PROMISSORY ESTOPPEL

The doctrine of promissory estoppel recognizes the possibility of the formation of a contract by action or forbearance on the part of a second party, based upon a promise made by the first party under circumstances where the actions or forbearance of the second party should reasonably have been expected to produce the detrimental results to the second party which they did produce. Restatement (Second) of Contracts § 90 (1932).

Thus, appellants' contract claim depends essentially upon oral statements and newspaper releases concerning the efforts of the company to secure increased productivity by enlisting the help of the workers of the plant and upon the employee responses thereto. The representations as set forth in the steelworkers' complaint include many oral statements made over the "hotline" employed by management in the plants to advise U.S. Steel employees of company policy. They began in the Fall of 1977 in the midst of much public speculation that the Ohio and McDonald works at Youngstown were to be closed. . . . [The court summarized evidence adduced at trial, including statements made by executives at U.S. Steel].

The opposite side of the contract bargain alleged by plaintiffs consists of performance claimed by plaintiffs to have been induced by the sort of promises recited above and actions taken by them "in detrimental reliance" upon said promises. . . . [Here the court included examples of individual employee reliance on U.S. Steel's representations].

Based on these allegations, appellant steelworkers make this fundamental assertion which is the heart of the contract claim:

> 13. Defendant's promise, and the detrimental reliance thereon of Locals 1330, 1307, 3073, and 3072, and of their members gave rise to a contract between Defendant and Locals 1330, 1307, 3073, and 3072, and their members, that the Ohio and McDonald Works would be kept open if they became profitable.

They also assert that "The Ohio and McDonald works would become profitable."

As we read this lengthy record, and as the District Judge read it, it does not contain any factual dispute over the allegations as to company statements or the responsive actions of steelworkers in relation thereto. It is beyond argument that the local management of U.S. Steel's Youngstown plants engaged in a major campaign to enlist employee participation in an all-out effort to make these two plants profitable in order to prevent their being closed. It is equally obvious that the employees responded wholeheartedly.

The District Judge, however, rejected the promissory estoppel contract theory on three grounds. The first ground was that none of the statements made by officers and employees of the company constituted a definite promise to continue operation of the plants if they did become profitable. The second ground was that the statements relied upon by plaintiffs were made by employees and public relations officers of the company and not by company officers. The third ground was a finding of fact that "The condition precedent of the alleged contract and promise—profitability of the Youngstown facilities—was never fulfilled, and the actions in contract and for detrimental reliance cannot be found for plaintiffs." . . .

Our examination of this record offers no ground for our holding that this finding of fact is "clearly erroneous." *See* Fed. R. Civ. P. 52(a). . . .

[With regard to profitability, the district court concluded]:

> This Court is loath to exchange its own view of the parameters of profitability for that of the corporation. It is clear that there is little argument as to the production figures for the Youngstown mills—the controversy surrounds the interpretation of those figures. Plaintiffs read the figures in light of a gross profit margin analysis of minimum profitability. Defendant sees capital expenditure, fixed costs and technical obsolescence as essential ingredients of the notion of profitability. Perhaps if this Court were being asked to interpret the word "profit" in a written contract between plaintiffs and defendant, some choice would have to be made. Given the oral nature of the alleged promises in the case at bar and the obvious ambiguity of the statements made, this Court finds that there is a very reasonable basis on which it can be said that Youngstown facilities were not profitable. Further, plaintiffs have made no showing of bad faith on the part of the Board of Directors in the Board's determination of profitability, nor have they given any grounds to suggest that defendant's definition of profitability is an unrealistic or unreasonable one. The condition precedent of the alleged contract and promise—profitability of the Youngstown facilities—was never fulfilled, and the actions in contract and for detrimental reliance cannot be found for plaintiffs.

. . . .

We believe that this record demonstrates without significant dispute that the profitability issue in the case depends in large part upon definition. The plaintiffs wish to employ the direct costs of operating the two plants, compared to the total selling price of their products. The difference, they contend, is "profit." This formula would eliminate such charges as corporate purchasing and sales expense allocable to the Youngstown plants, and allocable corporate management expenses including, but not limited to marketing, engineering, auditing, accounting, advertising. Obviously, any multiplant corporation could quickly go bankrupt if such a definition of profit was employed generally and over any period of time.

Plaintiffs-appellants point out, however, that this version of Youngstown profitability was employed by the Youngstown management in setting a goal for its employees and in statements which described achieving that goal. The standard of Restatement (Second) of Contracts § 90, upon which plaintiffs-appellants rely, however, is one of reasonable expectability of the "promise" detrimentally relied upon. The District Judge did not find, nor can we, that reliance upon a promise to keep these plants open on the basis of coverage of plant fixed costs was within reasonable expectability. We cannot hold that the District Judge erred legally or was "clearly erroneous" in his fact finding when he held that the "promise" to keep the plants open had to be read in the context of normal corporate profit accounting and that profitability had not been achieved.

Complete analysis of plaintiffs-appellants' promissory estoppel claims against the background of the collective bargaining agreement and Section 301 of the National Labor Relations Act would be a formidable task. We decline to undertake it, however, since even if we decided those issues favorably to plaintiffs, we would nonetheless be forced to decide the contract claim adversely to them because of failure to prove profitability.

THE COMMUNITY PROPERTY CLAIM

At a pretrial hearing of this case on February 28, 1980, the District Judge made a statement at some length about the relationship between the parties to this case and the public interest involved therein. He said:

> Everything that has happened in the Mahoning Valley has been happening for many years because of steel. Schools have been built, roads have been built. Expansion that has taken place is because of steel. And to accommodate that industry, lives and destinies of the inhabitants of that community were based and planned on the basis of that institution: Steel.

> We are talking about an institution, a large corporate institution that is virtually the reason for the existence of that segment of this nation (Youngstown). Without it, that segment of this nation perhaps suffers, instantly and severely. Whether it becomes a ghost town or not, I don't know. I am not aware of its capability for adapting.

> But what has happened over the years between U.S. Steel, Youngstown and the inhabitants? Hasn't something come out of that relationship, something that out of which—not reaching for a case on property law or a series of cases but looking at the law as a whole, the Constitution, the whole body of law, not only contract law, but tort, corporations, agency, negotiable instruments—taking a look at the whole body of American law and then sitting back and reflecting on what it seeks to do, and that is to adjust human relationships in keeping with the whole spirit and foundation of the American system of law, to preserve property rights.

It would seem to me that when we take a look at the whole body of American law and the principles we attempt to come out with—and although a legislature has not pronounced any laws with respect to such a property right, that is not to suggest that there will not be a need for such a law in the future dealing with similar situations—it seems to me that a property right has arisen from this lengthy, long-established relationship between United States Steel, the steel industry as an institution, the community in Youngstown, the people in Mahoning County and the Mahoning Valley in having given and devoted their lives to this industry. Perhaps not a property right to the extent that can be remedied by compelling U.S. Steel to remain in Youngstown. But I think the law can recognize the property right to the extent that U.S. Steel cannot leave that Mahoning Valley and the Youngstown area in a state of waste, that it cannot completely abandon its obligation to that community, because certain vested rights have arisen out of this long relationship and institution.

Subsequently thereto, steelworkers' complaint was amended, realleging the first cause of action, paragraphs 1–49, claiming pendent jurisdiction over claims arising out of the laws of the State of Ohio and asserting as follows:

52. A property right has arisen from the long-established relation between the community of the 19th Congressional District and Plaintiffs, on the one hand, and Defendant on the other hand, which this Court can enforce.

53. This right, in the nature of an easement, requires that Defendant:

a. Assist in the preservation of the institution of steel in that community;

b. Figure into its cost of withdrawing and closing the Ohio and McDonald Works the cost of rehabilitating the community and the workers;

c. Be restrained from leaving the Mahoning Valley in a state of waste and from abandoning its obligation to that community.

This court has examined these allegations with care and with great sympathy for the community interest reflected therein. Our problem in dealing with plaintiffs' fourth cause of action is one of authority. Neither in brief nor oral argument have plaintiffs pointed to any constitutional provision contained in either the Constitution of the United States or the Constitution of the State of Ohio, nor any law enacted by the United States Congress or the Legislature of Ohio, nor any case decided by the courts of either of these jurisdictions which would convey authority to this court to require the United States Steel Corporation to continue operations in Youngstown which its officers and Board of Directors had decided to discontinue on the basis of unprofitability. . . .

[The court then discussed an earlier Sixth Circuit case, *Charland v. Norge Division, Borg-Warner Corp.*, 407 F.2d 1062 (6th Cir.), cert. denied, 395 U.S. 927 (1969), involving a claim by an individual worker who lost his job due to a plant relocation after 30 years of employment, in which he alleged an unconstitutional deprivation of his property rights in his job.] This court's response to Charland's claims bears repetition here:

> Article V of the Constitution, of course, makes no mention of employment. But it (and the Fourteenth Amendment) does prohibit deprivation of property without due process of law. Thus appellant's assumption submits the fundamental question of whether or not there is a legally recognizable property right in a job which has been held for something approaching a lifetime.

> The claim presented by this appellant brings sharply into focus such problems as unemployment crises, the mobility of capital, technological change and the right of an industrial owner to go out of business. *See Textile Workers Union of America v. Darlington Manufacturing Co.*, 380 U.S. 263 (1965). Thus far federal law has sought to protect the human values to which appellant calls our attention by means of such legislation as unemployment compensation, 42 U.S.C. §§ 1400–1400v (1964), and social security laws, 42 U.S.C. ch. 7 (1964), as amended, (Supp. III, 1965–67). These statutes afford limited financial protection to the individual worker, but they assume his loss of employment.

> Whatever the future may bring, neither by statute nor by court decision has appellant's claimed property right been recognized to date in this country. . . .

The problem of plant closing and plant removal from one section of the country to another is by no means new in American history. The former mill towns of New England, with their empty textile factory buildings, are monuments to the migration of textile manufacturers to the South, without hindrance from the Congress of the United States, from the legislatures of the states concerned, or, for that matter, from the courts of the land.

In the view of this court, formulation of public policy on the great issues involved in plant closings and removals is clearly the responsibility of the legislatures of the states or of the Congress of the United States. . . .

We find no legal basis for judicial relief.

NOTES

1. **Shareholders' Rights vs. Workers' Rights.** As Greenfield points out, capital investors receive protection against corporate fraud in the capital market, but workers do not. Why does the law provide such inconsistent treatment of shareholders and workers?

2. **Reasons for Closing the Mills.** Should it matter why the company decided to close the steel mills? U.S. Steel argued that the mills were closed because they had become unprofitable, largely as a result of foreign competition. The plaintiff unions argued that the mills' unprofitability resulted from U.S. Steel's failure to reinvest in them and to modernize the plants. U.S. Steel thus made a business decision to disinvest in the Youngstown plants and to shift its capital either to new plants in nonunion regions of the country or to other industries (oil, cement,

chemicals, and fertilizer production) that might yield higher rates of profit. U.S. Steel's decision was not solely a matter of labor costs; concern about the costs of required changes to equipment in order to comply with environmental laws was a part of the equation as well. Was its decision to divert capital toward nonunion sectors actionable? On what theory? What about its decision to diversify its investments?

An Indiana steel mill followed a very different path in response to the competitive pressures of globalization. Built by Bethlehem Steel in the 1960s as a supplier to Detroit's automobile manufacturing industry, the Burns Harbor mill provided 90% of the tax revenue for the town of 1200. Its unionized workers enjoyed relatively high wages and benefits during the 1970s, 1980s, and early 1990s, but its high labor costs, pressure from foreign competitors, and the declining auto industry ultimately caused its bankruptcy in 2002. In 2005, Luxembourg-based ArcelorMittal purchased the mill and found that corporate decisions not to invest in infrastructure and training programs had rendered the mill's equipment hopelessly out of date; its workers were still relying on pencil and paper to calculate the proper mix of iron ore, coking coal, and limestone for each batch of steel. Initially, ArcelorMittal planned to lay off 2,444 workers at Burns Harbor. After union negotiations, 500 workers left voluntarily, 900 agreed to work 32-hour weeks, and no further layoffs were made. ArcelorMittal invested $150 million in capital improvements and "twinned" the mill with a hypermodern mill in Belgium. U.S. engineers and managers were flown to Belgium to learn how to run a more efficient and profitable mill, and the two mills were then benchmarked against each other. Burns Harbor now enjoys record output, thanks to labor-saving technology that has cut the number of workers needed in half, and new training programs that prepared longtime workers to deploy computerized systems. The remaining workers, represented by the Steelworkers' Union, averaged $80,000 per year in wages and benefits in 2011, up 14% from 2007. John W. Miller, *Indiana Steel Mill Revived with Lessons from Abroad*, WALL ST. J., May 21, 2012, at A1, A2.

3. The Aftermath: The Community Impact of the Mill Closings. The plaintiffs ultimately abandoned their effort to purchase the business as a going concern, and in 1982 U.S. Steel imploded two of the larger plants, which was covered in dramatic form in major newspapers throughout the country.[*]

---

[*] Reprinted from the Vindicator, © The Vindicator Printing Company, 2002.

The plaintiffs did eventually manage to purchase one of the smaller plants through a lease agreement, and the company was renamed McDonald Steel. McDonald Steel began operations in 1981 with 75 nonunion employees working at about half their previous wage rate. The company specialized in making high-quality hot-rolled steel in special bars and shapes, and the company became profitable by the second quarter of 1982. By 1988 the company employed 150 workers and had annual sales of nearly $20 million. In 1994 the company formed an employee stock ownership plan (ESOP) that would provide the workers with a 30% interest in the company. In 1997, somewhat ironically, an unsuccessful union organizing drive occurred at the plant.

Meanwhile, nationwide employment in the steel industry dropped from more than 400,000 in 1977 to less than 150,000 by 1987. The Mahoning Valley, and particularly Youngstown and Pittsburgh, absorbed the brunt of the losses: Youngstown lost 10,000 jobs in steel alone between 1977 and 1980, and Pittsburgh lost 68,000 jobs in steel between 1982 and 1987. Overall, the city of Youngstown lost about a third of its population and continues to have one of the highest unemployment rates in the state. *See* Staughton Lynd, *The Genesis of the Idea of a Community Right to Industrial Property in Youngstown and Pittsburgh, 1977–1987*, 74 J. Am. Hist. 926, 926–27 & n.2 (1987).

Thirty-five years after the *Local 1330, United Steel Workers* decision, the population of Youngstown continues to diminish: it has lost 60% of its population over the last half-century as a result of the decline of the steel industry, and only a single large steel mill remains. After decades of seeking other big employers to replace steel, including prisons, city planners "accept[ed] the inevitable," and instituted a redevelopment plan known as "controlled shrinkage." Under this plan, the city targeted the most severe blight for demolition (abandoned buildings were torn down, unused streets were dug up to recreate green spaces, sidewalks were removed and street lights were taken down), reduced infrastructure supporting more sparsely-populated areas labeled as transitional, and reallocated resources to repair and develop more stable neighborhoods. Timothy Aeppel, *As Its Population Declines, Youngstown Thinks Small*, WALL ST. J., May 3, 2007, at A1, A15. This unconventional plan flies in the face of the more typical growth-promoting strategies favored by most cities seeking more jobs, more taxpayers, and more revenue. Controlled shrinkage is now being considered by several other Midwestern cities affected by population losses in the wake of the decline of a single industry in which the city's employment had been heavily concentrated, including Muncie, Indiana, and Flint, Michigan, both former strongholds of the auto industry. *See, e.g.*, David Streitfeld, *An Effort to Save Flint, Mich., by Shrinking It*, N.Y. TIMES, Apr. 21, 2009, at A12 (discussing controlled shrinkage efforts in Flint, Michigan and other cities). For a critical analysis of controlled shrinkage and its impact on localities, see James Rhodes & John Russo, *Shrinking 'Smart'? Urban Redevelopment and Shrinkage in Youngstown, Ohio*, 34 URBAN GEOG. No. 3, 305 (2013).

Is controlled shrinkage tantamount to giving up? Or is it, as one urban planner put it, simply about "managing change"? *See* Aeppel, *supra*, at A15. Would the aftermath for the community have been different if the court had ruled the other way in *Local 1330*? If so, in what ways—and for how long?

4. The Community Property Claim. The plaintiffs asserted two theories upon which relief might have been granted: a contract theory and a community property right. The community property theory was suggested by the district court judge, Thomas D. Lambros, when he granted a preliminary injunction before trial to prevent the mills from closing. The sympathy that Judge Lambros—and later the Sixth Circuit—felt for the plaintiffs was palpable. Why did the courts refuse to grant a remedy at law? Did they have a choice?

Consider Joseph Singer's analysis of the interests at stake here:

> Despite his tentative conclusion that the company should have a continuing legal obligation to the community, Judge Lambros decided that no precedent for such a property right existed and that he lacked the power to create one. He reached this conclusion even though he had earlier defended the power of judges to recognize or create a new property right when social conditions and values had changed to warrant it. He saw the issue as a divergence of the company's moral and legal obligations. This disjunction existed because the federal court lacked the legal authority to change state property law to conform to the dictates of morality. . . .

> The courts should have recognized the workers' property rights arising out of their relationship with the company. Such a new legally protected interest would place obligations on the company toward the workers and the community to alleviate the social costs of its decision to close the plant. Protection of this reliance interest could take a variety of forms: It could grant the workers the right to buy the plant from the company for its fair market value; it could require the company to review possible modernization proposals to determine the feasibility and profitability of updating the plant; it could give workers access to information held by the company regarding operation of the facility; it could impose obligations on the company to make severance payments to workers and tax payments to the

municipality to protect them until new businesses could be established in the community; it could require the company to assist in finding a purchaser for the plant; it could mean other things as well. The goal should be to identify flexible remedies that are appropriate to protect the workers' reliance interests.

Moreover, contrary to the conclusions of the judges in this case, precedent for the creation of property rights of the kind asserted by the union does exist. . . . [T]he legal system contains a variety of doctrines—in torts, property, contracts, family law and in legislative modifications of those common law doctrines—that recognize the sharing or shifting of various property interests in situations that should be viewed as analogous to plant closings. . . .

[T]he judges in the *United Steel Workers* case failed to find these precedents and principles in the rules in force because they asked the wrong questions. They wrongly defined the issue as a search for the "owner" of the property. They then assumed that, in the absence of specific doctrinal exceptions to the contrary, owners are allowed to do whatever they want with their property. This approach is seriously misleading: Property rights are more often shared than unitary, and rights to use and dispose of property are never absolute. Moreover, this approach takes our attention away from the relations of mutual dependence that develop within industrial enterprises and between those enterprises and the communities in which they are situated. Legitimate reliance on such relationships constitutes a central aspect of our social and economic life—so central that numerous rules in force protect reliance on those relationships. Although both the district court and the court of appeals sympathetically noted the legitimate interests of the workers and the community, and the long term relationships that had developed between U.S. Steel, the workers and the community, the courts deemed those interests irrelevant in defining property entitlements. Consideration of competing interests in access to resources and past reliance on relationships granting such access should be a central component of any legal determination of how to allocate lawful power over those resources. . . .

Staughton Lynd [counsel to the steelworkers] reports that at a community meeting in Youngstown, Ohio, concerning a threatened plant closing, a steelworker cried out, "Those are our jobs!" Another worker answered him, "But it's their mill." I want to argue that people who think this way are wrong. In part, I mean to emphasize that "Who owns the mill?" is a hard, not an easy, question to answer; I also mean to call attention to the fact that even if it is "their mill," they do not necessarily have the legal power to use it in a way that destroys a community. But I mean something more fundamental than either of these things. I want to argue that phrasing the problem as "identifying the owner" is fundamentally wrong. It is simply not the right question. To assume that we can know who property owners are, and to assume that once we have identified them their rights follow as a matter of course, is to assume what needs to be decided. . . .

We ask who the owner is because we need to resolve a specific question of how to allocate control of resources among all the parties with legally protected interests in access to those resources. Can the company blow up the plant when the workers want to buy it? To answer this question by looking for the owner is like asking how may angels can dance on the head of a pin. It is a species of conceptualism; to say the company can blow up the plant because it owns it states a conclusion rather than a premise. It does not give us a reason to allocate rights between the workers and the company in this way. Both the workers and the managers have legal rights of access to the plant that arise from their relationships with each other and with others. The real issue is how to allocate those entitlements among the managers, the shareholders and the workers. We decide who wins the dispute on grounds of policy and morality, and then we call that person the owner. . . .

Judge Lambros believed that he would infringe upon private freedom by recognizing the community property claim. Yet by not recognizing it, he also infringed upon private freedom—the freedom of the workers to rely on a long-standing relationship with U.S. Steel. Judge Lambros felt that he would be acting tyrannically by imposing his will on private actors; so he authorized some private actors (the management of the corporation) to impose their will on thousands of other persons. . . .

Judge Lambros also believed he would be acting tyrannically by making new law and taking on a task properly left to elected officials in the legislature. Yet in ruling for the company, he effectively made law anyway. The workers claimed that they had presented Judge Lambros with a case of first impression; no workers had ever made the community property claim before, and Judge Lambros recognized that the factual situation was different from any previously addressed by any court in the country. He had to define the allocation of property rights between the company and the workers. It was impossible for the court not to recognize a property right. It had no choice but to grant a property right either to the company or to the workers. He ruled in favor of the company, confirming its claimed property rights and denying the workers' claim. How did he defer to the legislature? The legislature had not spoken on this new question. Nor had any court.

I can think of several reasons why Judge Lambros would understand a ruling for the company as deference to the legislature. First, he knew that a ruling for the workers would be understood as a substantial change in the law and would be controversial. Second, ruling for the company confirmed the existing social practice in which companies have exercised more or less dictatorial control over plant closing decisions. Third, ruling for the company confirmed the existing distribution of power and wealth in the marketplace. None of these reasons seems related to the goal of deference to the legislature. The only way they can be equated with deference is if we assume that the legislature, when faced with any new case, would choose to ratify the existing distribution of power in society. But this assumption is unwarranted. It is politically biased, moreover, toward the status quo. This construction of the proper institutional roles of the courts and the legislature is not neutral. It teaches judges a normative lesson: In cases of first impression, you fulfill your proper institutional role in a democracy only if you further concentrate property rights in the hands of those who already own property. . . . It is not neutral for judges to use their substantial power to reinforce private hierarchy. Of course, this is an explicitly political definition of the judge's proper institutional role. Yet it is no more political than the traditional definition; the traditional definition merely hides its political bent by defining as restraint the active creation and perpetuation of bastions of private privilege.

Joseph William Singer, *The Reliance Interest in Property*, 40 STAN. L. REV. 611, 620–22, 637–38, 745–47 (1988).

    5.   The Family Law Origins of the Community Property Claim. Although the "community property" claim was the more radical of the two claims asserted, it was not without precedent in the law. Indeed, the term is borrowed from the family property law of the nine states that apply community property principles to characterize and divide property at divorce. The bulk of the remaining states have adopted equitable distribution systems that characterize property earned during marriage as "marital" property, divisible at divorce (regardless of title), and apply equitable principles to its division. The premise of both systems is that marriage is a partnership. Accordingly, the law recognizes the mutual dependence of the parties and their expectation that the relationship will continue and creates property rights from it. Should the employment relation be treated differently? If so, is it because the marriage contract is "till death do us part" while the employment contract is at will? Does the widespread availability of no-fault, unilateral divorce alter our assumption that property rights arise out of a marital partnership? Why, then, should employment at will lead to a different result in the employment relation?

    6.   The Contract Claim. Some scholars have argued that the case was wrongly decided on the contract claim as well. What value should contract law place on promoting trust as a public good? Is trust particularly important in the employment context? Why or why not? *See* Daniel A. Farber & John H. Matheson, *Beyond Promissory Estoppel: Contract Law and the "Invisible Handshake,"* 52 U. CHI. L. REV. 903 (1985) (suggesting that employers and workers have a mutual interest in promoting trust and loyalty because of their corresponding investments in the relationship and their interests in productivity). Does the law's refusal to redress employer breaches of trust injure society as a whole?

    7.   Equitable Grounds for Relief. One other trial court found an equitable basis for relief in a plant closing context. In *Charter Township of Ypsilanti v. General Motors Corp.*, 8 I.E.R. Cas. (BNA) 385 (Mich. Cir. Ct. 1993), a Michigan trial court ruled that GM's decision to close its Willow Run plant and to transfer its automotive assembly operations to Texas supported an action for breach of promissory estoppel by the township of Ypsilanti. The court recited promises made to the township by GM to maintain operations at the Willow Run plant in exchange for twelve years' worth of property tax abatements, and granted injunctive relief to the plaintiffs. Noting the "terrible injustice" that would be wrought by a failure to act, the trial court said:

> Each judge who dons this robe assumes the awesome, and lonely, respon-
> sibility to make decisions about justice, and injustice, which will dramati-
> cally affect the way people are forced to live their lives. . . . There would be
> a gross inequity and patent unfairness if General Motors, having lulled the
> people of the Ypsilanti area into giving up millions of tax dollars which they
> so desperately need to educate their children and provide basic govern-
> mental services, is allowed to simply decide that it will desert 4500 workers
> and their families because it thinks it can make these same cars a little
> cheaper somewhere else. Perhaps another judge in another court would not
> feel moved by that injustice and would labor to find a legal rationalization
> to allow such conduct. But in this Court it is my responsibility to make that
> decision. My conscience will not allow this injustice to happen.

Id. The case was reversed on appeal. *Charter Township of Ypsilanti v. General
Motors Corp.*, 506 N.W.2d 556 (Mich. Ct. App. 1993). The appellate court characterized GM's statements to the township as "hyperbole and puffery" rather than
promises justifying reliance and cited *Local 1330, United Steel Workers* in support
of its conclusion.

    8. **A Role for Unions?** Would proactive participation by workers in decisions
affecting the plant be a better strategy than reacting after the fact to news of an
impending shutdown? One might think that worker representation and collective
bargaining could have averted the situation at U.S. Steel. However, the management rights clause in the collective bargaining agreement (quoted in the case
excerpt above) reserved to the company the exclusive right to make decisions about
the future direction of the enterprise—including decisions about capital investment,
modernization, plant location, and plant closings. And the union had agreed to a
no-strike clause, so the workers were hamstrung in their ability to respond to
management's disinvestment strategy. Such clauses are standard in labor contracts,
with very few exceptions. Why? Staughton Lynd, who represented the workers in
the litigation, has been very critical of the model of American unionism that
produced such labor contracts. *See* Staughton Lynd, *Local 1330 v. U.S. Steel
(1977–1980), in* AMERICAN LABOR STRUGGLES AND LAW HISTORIES 367, 369–71 (Kenneth
M. Casebeer ed., 2011). The cases covered in Section C of this chapter address the
law governing collective bargaining in more detail.

    Might the presence of a union in the workplace actually undermine employees'
rights? In *Ackers v. Celestica Corp.*, 2007 U.S. Dist. LEXIS 24400 (S.D. Ohio Mar.
21, 2007), several employees brought state law claims of fraud and fraudulent
inducement in violation of public policy against their former employer, Lucent
Technologies, and Celestica Corporation, the eventual purchaser of Lucent's
business. The employees alleged that Lucent had promised to work with Celestica
and the union during the transition period surrounding sale of the business to
provide continued employment for Lucent employees based in Columbus, Ohio.
They complained that Celestica "repeatedly assured, represented and promised"
them during bargaining sessions that they would keep their jobs with Celestica for
at least five years, during which time Celestica would endeavor to build the
production and service aspects of the business in Columbus. In exchange for these
assurances, plaintiffs agreed to reductions in their hourly wages and made other
contract concessions, ultimately ratifying a five-year collective bargaining agree-

ment with Celestica. Celestica then reassigned employees from its other facilities to Columbus to learn the methods used there, and then announced a corporate restructuring that led to layoffs in Columbus and a relocation of manufacturing processes to Canada. The Columbus facility closed less than one year after plaintiffs ratified the collective bargaining agreement with Celestica.

The court ruled that the employees' state law claims were preempted by the NLRA. The court applied the broad NLRA preemption doctrine laid out in *San Diego Building Trades Council v. Garmon*, 359 U.S. 236 (1959), which established that the NLRB, not the courts, has exclusive primary jurisdiction to regulate conduct that is potentially governed by or, in the Court's words, "arguably subject to" the NLRA—even if it is not yet clear that the NLRA in fact covers the asserted conduct. The plaintiffs had alleged that Lucent and Celestica failed to bargain in good faith with the plaintiffs' union over the effects of the sale of the company, inducing them to ratify a collective bargaining agreement to which they would not otherwise have assented. As "artfully pleaded unfair labor practices charges," plaintiffs' claims were arguably governed by the NLRA. Thus, only the NLRB had jurisdiction to hear them. *Ackers*, 2007 U.S. Dist. LEXIS 24400, at *16. Indeed, the court noted that the employees had filed unfair labor practice charges arising out of the same conduct, and suggested that while the filing of such charges was not "dispositive of the issue nor a necessary prerequisite to a finding of preemption," it nonetheless bolstered the court's conclusion that the claims were preempted. *Id.* at *24. The decision was affirmed on appeal by the Sixth Circuit. *Ackers v. Celestica Corp.*, 2008 U.S. App. LEXIS 8862 (6th Cir. Apr. 17, 2008).

On the other hand, the Fifth Circuit ruled that fraudulent inducement claims brought by former employees of DuPont against the company were not preempted by the NLRA. The employees claimed that DuPont made fraudulent representations to them, inducing them to accept employment with a "spin-off" company which it promised that it would not sell—and then subsequently sold. The plaintiffs sought compensation for lost wages and reduced pension benefits. The court reasoned that the gravamen of plaintiffs' claims was the affirmative representation made to them individually to induce them to accept employment, which did not concern the relationship between the company and the union; thus, federal labor policy was not implicated. Nor did the NLRA require bargaining with the union over Dupont's initial decision to sell the business. Accordingly, the plaintiffs were permitted to proceed with their state fraud claims. *Sawyer v. E.I. DuPont de Nemours & Co.*, 517 F.3d 785 (5th Cir. 2008). The plaintiffs won the battle but lost the war, however; the district court ultimately granted summary judgment to the employer, reasoning that having opted to proceed outside the collective bargaining context, the workers were at-will employees, and Texas law barred their fraud claims based on loss of employment. After seeking advice on state law from the Texas Supreme Court, the Fifth Circuit affirmed. 754 F.3d 313 (5th Cir. 2014).

Why were the plaintiffs anxious to frame their claims as state tort claims in *Ackers* and *Sawyer*, rather than as unfair labor practices? Recall that plaintiffs can obtain jury trials and seek compensatory and punitive damages on state tort claims; by contrast, unfair labor practices are remedied by the National Labor Relations Board, which can order only equitable remedies such as reinstatement (not applicable here since the facility had closed) and backpay—no damages are available. Thus, the *Ackers* plaintiffs would have to establish the level of wages and benefits that they would have received under a labor contract negotiated without the taint of the false representations of the company. The NLRB has historically been hostile to such claims because they are both speculative and inconsistent with the policy of the NLRA, which requires that the parties negotiate their own contract rather than the Board writing one for them. *See, e.g., Ex-Cell-O Corp.*, 185 N.L.R.B. 107, 110 (1970) (refusing to issue a remedial order including financial reparations for bad faith refusal to bargain where the remedy would "retroactively . . . impose financial liability upon an employer flowing from a presumed contractual agreement").

9. Fraudulent Misrepresentation Claims. Some courts have allowed individuals who can show specific damage resulting from employer misrepresentations made during the hiring process to recover on tort grounds. *See, e.g., Meade v. Cedarapids, Inc.*, 164 F.3d 1218 (9th Cir. 1999) (permitting plaintiff workers who gave up other jobs or declined other job offers to accept jobs at the El-Jay plant in Eugene, Oregon to proceed with fraudulent misrepresentation claims when the plant closed shortly after they began work; plaintiffs were told during the hiring process that El-Jay was "ramping up," that the company's future "looked great," and that its growth was a "long-term situation"). Why should only some workers affected by a plant closing decision possess actionable claims for relief? Should recently hired workers have stronger claims than long-term employees?

Surprisingly, individual plaintiffs enjoy a fairly high success rate in cases involving fraudulent inducement at the hiring stage. Richard Perna conducted a survey of court decisions issued between 1990 and 2002 involving such claims and found a 41% plaintiff success rate despite the relatively high burden of proof that plaintiffs must meet in order to prevail. Plaintiffs in cases alleging fraud as to job security, which present the most direct clash with the employment at will doctrine, were somewhat less likely to be successful than those in other types of cases. *See* Richard P. Perna, *Deceitful Employers: Common Law Fraud as a Mechanism to Remedy Intentional Employer Misrepresentation in Hiring*, 41 WILLAMETTE L. REV. 233, 240–49 (2005).

Fraud claims are far less successful when framed as a collective harm, though, even where the facts seem stark. For example, in *Campbell v. PMI Food Equipment Group, Inc.*, 509 F.3d 776 (6th Cir. 2007), the company decided to close its food equipment and parts repair facility in Dayton, Ohio due to the facility's age and inefficiency. In December 1994, PMI informed the 66 hourly workers at its Dayton facility who were covered by a collective bargaining contract that it would lay off a few workers at a time. The company then negotiated a 10-year tax abatement agreement in exchange for its decision to open a new facility in Piqua, Ohio. During the negotiations with local officials, the company falsely stated that it was considering moving its operation to Kentucky if the tax abatement deal was not granted in Piqua. The agreement was approved in January 1995. In July 1995 the company informed the Dayton facility workers that they would all be terminated in eight days, and then closed the plant just three days later. Meanwhile, PMI retained all 32 salaried employees at its Dayton plant and relocated them to its new facility, and filled the hourly positions with workers supplied by a temporary employment agency. The hourly workers brought suit asserting that the tax abatement agreement violated their due process and equal protection rights under the U.S. and Ohio Constitutions, fraud claims on behalf of themselves as taxpayers, and a WARN Act claim, among others. After a nine-year delay, the district court eventually ruled against the plaintiffs on all but the WARN Act claim (which the company settled), and by the time the case reached the Sixth Circuit the tax abatement agreement had expired. The Sixth Circuit dismissed the plaintiffs' claims on the basis that they were moot or that the plaintiffs lacked standing. *Id.* at 781–83.

10. **Litigation as Consciousness-Raising.** What role does litigation play in educating the public and in altering social norms? Staughton Lynd was lead counsel for the steelworkers in the *U.S. Steel* litigation. He has suggested that one of the most noteworthy results of the *Local 1330* litigation was the foundation laid for questioning the cultural norm that the private ownership and management of property creates only private rights. Observing that economic hardship makes people more receptive to new ideas, he pointed out that the collapse of the steel industries and the accompanying social distress led a normally conservative local populace to embrace the idea that a community property right arises from a long-standing relationship between a company and a community and to formulate the demand for the government to utilize its power of eminent domain to acquire the industrial facilities when the corporations no longer wished to operate them. The *Local 1330* lawsuit was thus an "act of resistance" that was important as a part of a larger struggle: It "sharpen[ed] issues and provide[d] opportunities to stimulate debate in the community," "compelled the top executives of U.S. Steel to come to Youngstown and to confront the community they had wronged," and made it "possible to obtain essential information [through the discovery process]." Staughton Lynd, The Fight Against Shutdowns: Youngstown's Steel Mill Closings 187–89 (1982).

Jules Lobel has expanded on this point, observing that unsuccessful test cases can inspire political action:

> Traditional public interest litigation relies on political action to create a favorable climate for court victory and to implement that victory. Politics is thus a necessary predicate to the courtroom drama. In many losing efforts, however, the relationship is reversed: the primary point of the cases is to inspire political action. Litigation may serve to legitimate a political movement, to publicize the issues raised by that movement, and perhaps to spur political action. These cases thus illustrate the role of law not merely in adjudicating disputes between parties, but also in educating the public.
> . . .
> The fundamental significance of these aspirational cases lies not in their inversion of the roles of law and politics, but in their radically different view of the meaning and nature of law. They represent a prophetic vision of law, stemming from the Old Testament prophets such as Amos who viewed justice as "a fighting challenge, a restless drive." To understand this genre of litigation one must regard law as a process of struggle rather than a collection of substantive rules or "mere norm[s]." Law, under this view, arises from the clash between the state seeking to enforce its rules and the

activist communities seeking to create, extend, or preserve an alternative vision of justice.

The key prophetic legal symbol is not the traditional scales of justice, connoting the calm, detached, and neutral balancing of legal principles, but Amos's imagery of a turbulent, cascading river. The prophetic vision is dynamic; it is not a stagnant snapshot of present normative principles. The mobility of this vision allows law to move towards an imagined ideal. As Robert Cover put it, law links "a concept of a reality to an imagined alternative". . . .

Jules Lobel, *Losers, Fools & Prophets: Justice as Struggle*, 80 CORNELL L. REV. 1331, 1332–33 (1995).

The *Local 1330* litigation and other similar struggles of the 1970s and 80s provided the political impetus for the Worker Adjustment Retraining and Notification Act of 1988.

B. WORKER ADJUSTMENT AND RETRAINING NOTIFICATION ACT

1. The Statute

In 1988 Congress passed the Worker Adjustment and Retraining Notification Act (WARN), 29 U.S.C. §§ 2101–2109. The Act requires employers with 100 or more full-time employees to provide notification of plant closings and mass layoffs involving 50 or more workers at a single worksite to workers, unions, and affected state agencies 60 days in advance and authorizes the Department of Labor to promulgate regulations clarifying its applicability. The regulations explain:

req. of WARN

> Advance notice provides workers and their families some transition time to adjust to the prospective loss of employment, to seek and obtain alternative jobs and, if necessary, to enter skill training or retraining that will allow these workers to successfully compete in the job market. WARN also provides for notice to State dislocated worker units so that dislocated worker assistance can be promptly provided.

purpose

20 C.F.R. § 639.1(a). The notice period may be reduced or in some cases eliminated where the employer can establish that providing notice at an earlier point would have interfered with good faith efforts by the employer to obtain infusions of capital or new business necessary to avoid or postpone the closing, or where the closing was caused by unforeseeable business circumstances or natural disasters. Reductions in penalties are also available where the employer establishes that it made good faith efforts to comply with the Act. The statute is enforced through civil actions initiated by employees, their representatives (unions), or the municipality in which the employer's operation is located; the Department of Labor has no enforcement role. Available remedies include backpay, benefits, civil fines for failure to notify the appropriate unit of local government, and attorneys' fees.

notice period

penalties

Although WARN has been far from revolutionary in its impact, it is nonetheless significant. To understand this, consider what workers, state officials, and the larger *anecdote*

community lose when notice of a mass closing or layoff is not provided. When Sprint announced the closing of its Tualatin, Oregon call center, it provided one day's advance notice to the 102 employees impacted. Workers were told that they could return the next day, monitored by a security guard, to collect their belongings. The local news media reported damage to credit ratings for those who had purchased cars, furniture, land, or houses during the preceding two months; lack of opportunity for state officials, who provide referrals and labor market information to dislocated workers, to reach workers on site; and ultimately, lengthier periods of unemployment and lower pay on average for workers who located new positions. Brent Hunsberger, *Laid off Without Notice*, THE OREGONIAN, July 14, 2002, at 20. Scholarly studies confirm that advance notice of plant closings is generally associated with lower unemployment and poverty rates three years later and lower usage of social welfare services. *See* Richard W. McHugh, *Fair Warning or Foul? An Analysis of the Worker Adjustment and Retraining Notification (WARN) Act in Practice*, 14 BERKELEY J. EMP. & LAB. L. 1, 63–64 (1993) (summarizing studies). What impact might WARN have had if it had been in effect in the Youngstown U.S. Steel closing situation?

other countries

The United States is committed to a notice-and-layoff system. Other countries have tried different approaches. The Chinese government encourages employers to retain employees at lower wages—or even no wages (in the case of commission-based work)—to "diminish the shock to workers, confine industrial action to within factory gates and defuse public anger." In exchange, the government offers employers tax relief and relaxation of applicable regulatory regimes. *See* James T. Areddy, *China Mediates Job Disputes in Effort to Pacify Workers*, WALL ST. J., Jan. 26, 2009. The Netherlands, Germany and Austria rely on "short work" programs that keep people in their jobs during financial downturns but reduce the number of hours that they work; the government subsidizes the workers for a time-limited period (for example, six months in the Netherlands) by paying them the wages lost due to reduction in their hours. *See* Adam Cohen, *A Dutch Formula Holds Down Joblessness*, WALL ST. J., Dec. 28, 2009. What is the philosophy behind these governmental policy approaches? Thinking back to our discussion of the meaning of work in Chapter 1, what if any benefits might employment that is essentially in name only (such as the Chinese system) offer for workers? What are the pros and cons of the Dutch system? Would either be feasible in the United States? Why do you think that the United States has adopted a notice system rather than a system that is focused on keeping people in their jobs until a recovery can take hold?

2. Enforcement and Compliance Issues

The recession that began in 2007 ensured the continuing relevance of WARN. *See* Ianthe Jeanne Dugan, *Companies, Workers Tangle over Law to Curb Layoffs*, WALL ST. J., July 6, 2009 (reporting that employment attorneys saw their WARN Act caseloads triple over the preceding year). According to the most recent study of the Act by the Government Accountability Office (GAO), 24% of all mass layoffs and plant closings between 1998 and 2002 were subject to WARN's notification requirements. In 2001, however, covered employers provided notice in only 36% of the mass layoffs and plant closings subject to the Act; and of that number, only 68% of the notices conformed to the Act's 60-day period. *See* GAO-03-1003, The Worker

Adjustment and Retraining Notification Act, Sept. 19, 2003. The GAO believes that at least some of the compliance gap is attributable to difficulty applying the WARN calculations (layoff thresholds in particular) because the Department of Labor, state agencies, and employer groups report numerous inquiries from both employers and employees about the Act's applicability. The GAO recommended that the Secretary of Labor make educational materials available to employees and employers to assist them in understanding the regulations.

Additional problems arise from the statute's enforcement mechanisms. WARN Act notification requirements are enforced solely through civil actions brought by employees, their bargaining agents, or on rare occasions by the local municipality where the company is based (most municipalities are loathe to sue employers for WARN Act violations because of the political repercussions of driving business away). Nonunionized employees are less likely to be aware of their rights, and it can be difficult to persuade private attorneys to take the cases because of the limited remedies available (up to 60 days' backpay and benefits, reduced by each day the employer gave notice if less than 60 days' notice was afforded, and, for prevailing parties, reasonable attorneys' fees). Consequently, labor unions have played a significant enforcement role. In 1996, the Supreme Court ruled unanimously that unions have standing under WARN to sue for damages on behalf of their members. *UFCW Local 751 v. Brown Group, Inc.*, 517 U.S. 544 (1996). In a private sector workforce where union density is low, is some additional enforcement mechanism necessary? Should the remedial provisions of WARN be altered by increasing financial penalties to make cases more attractive to plaintiffs' attorneys? In 2012, supporters offered an amendment to expand the Labor Department's authority to enforce WARN, providing for double back pay as a remedy, reducing the mass layoff trigger from 50 workers to 25, increasing coverage to include employers with 75 or more employees, and lengthening the notice period to 90 days. Derrick Cain, *Sen. Sherrod Brown Offers Bill to Bolster Law Requiring Employee Notice of 'Mass Layoffs,'* DAILY LAB. REP. (BNA) No. 118, June 19, 2012. The bill did not pass.

Section 2105 of the Act explicitly authorizes state regulation of plant closings and layoffs. About half of the states have enacted WARN equivalents. Some states have broadened WARN Act coverage, typically either by expanding employer coverage by WARN to smaller employers (California, for example, applies its state WARN statute to employers of 75 or more employees), lengthening the notification period, or lowering the affected employee mass layoff and closing thresholds. *See, e.g.,* CAL. LAB. CODE § 1400 *et seq.* The recent economic downturn motivated a few states that had not previously enacted such legislation to do so. *See, e.g., Iowa Governor Signs Bill Requiring Employers to Notify Workers of Layoffs*, DAILY LAB. REP. (BNA) No. 55, Mar. 24, 2010 (describing Iowa legislation that covers small employers and layoffs involving fewer workers); *New York Issues Emergency Rules for State WARN Act Passed in 2008*, DAILY LAB. REP. (BNA) No. 21, Feb. 4, 2009 (discussing New York's WARN Act, which provides for longer notice periods and lower affected employee thresholds).

3. Statutory Interpretation Issues

WARN section 2101 provides:

(a) Definitions

As used in this chapter—

(1) the term "employer" means any business enterprise that employs—

    (A) 100 or more employees, excluding part-time employees; or

    (B) 100 or more employees who in the aggregate work at least 4,000 hours per week (exclusive of hours of overtime);

(2) the term "plant closing" means the permanent or temporary shutdown of a single site of employment, or one or more facilities or operating units within a single site of employment, if the shutdown results in an employment loss at the single site of employment during any 30-day period for 50 or more employees excluding any part-time employees;

(3) the term "mass layoff" means a reduction in force which—

    (A) is not the result of a plant closing; and

    (B) results in an employment loss at the single site of employment during any 30-day period for—

        (i) (I) at least 33 percent of the employees (excluding any part-time employees); and

            (II) at least 50 employees (excluding any part-time employees); or

        (ii) at least 500 employees (excluding any part-time employees);

. . . .

(5) the term "affected employees" means employees who may reasonably be expected to experience an employment loss as a consequence of a proposed plant closing or mass layoff by their employer;

(6) subject to subsection (b) of this section [reproduced in this text in Note 4, following *Ellis v. DHL Express, Inc.*], the term "employment loss" means

    (A) an employment termination, other than a discharge for cause, voluntary departure, or retirement,

    (B) a layoff exceeding 6 months, or

    (C) a reduction in hours of work of more than 50 percent during each month of any 6-month period. . . .

. . . .

(8) the term "part-time employee" means an employee who is engaged for an average of fewer than 20 hours per week or who has been employed for fewer than 6 of the 12 months preceding the date on which notice is required. . . .

29 U.S.C. § 2101.

———————

A great deal of litigation has ensued over interpretation of these definitional provisions in the Act. In 2007, the Toledo Blade Newspaper conducted a survey of 226 WARN lawsuits filed since 1989. According to its data, employees prevailed in 52.2% of the cases and employers prevailed in 47.8%. James Drew & Steve Eder, *Without Warning: Flaws, Loopholes, Deny Employees Protection Mandated by WARN Act*, TOLEDO BLADE, July 15, 2007. Cases often turn on whether ambiguities in the statute excuse the employer's failure to give notice, particularly layoffs conducted in sequential waves of under 50 employees per layoff, which do not trigger WARN's provisions, or layoffs spread across multiple plant sites, so that the site-specific tally of employees affected does not reach the WARN Act threshold. *See id.; see also* Steve Lohr, *Piecemeal Layoffs Avoid Warning Laws*, N.Y. TIMES, Mar. 5, 2009 (discussing IBM layoffs involving thousands of workers to which WARN's notice provisions are not applicable).

lawsuit data

The exceptions to the Act's notice obligation have also generated significant litigation. Section 2102 provides:

(a) **Notice to employees, State dislocated worker units, and local governments**

An employer shall not order a plant closing or mass layoff until the end of a 60-day period after the employer serves written notice of such an order—

(1) to each representative of the affected employees as of the time of the notice or, if there is no such representative, to each affected employee; and

(2) to the State or entity designated by the State . . . and the chief elected official of the unit of local government within which such closing or layoff is to occur. . . .

(b) **Reduction of Notification Period**

(1) An employer may order the shutdown of a single site of employment before the conclusion of the 60-day period if as of the time that notice would have been required the employer was actively seeking capital or business which, if obtained, would have enabled the employer to avoid or postpone the shutdown and the employer reasonably and in good faith believed that giving the notice required would have precluded the employer from obtaining the needed capital or business.

(2) (A) An employer may order a plant closing or mass layoff before the conclusion of the 60-day period if the closing or mass layoff is caused by business circumstances that were not reasonably foreseeable as of the time that notice would have been required.

(B) No notice under this chapter shall be required if the plant closing or mass layoff is due to any form of natural disaster, such as a flood, earthquake, or the drought currently ravaging the farmlands of the United States.

(3) An employer relying on this subsection shall give as much notice as is practicable and at that time shall give a brief statement of the basis for reducing the notification period. . . .

. . . .

(d) **Determinations with respect to employment loss**

For purposes of this section, in determining whether a plant closing or mass layoff has occurred or will occur, employment losses for two or more groups at a single site of employment, each of which is less than the minimum number of employees specified in section 2101 (a)(2) or (3) of this title but which in the aggregate exceed that minimum number, and which occur within any 90-day period shall be considered to be a plant closing or mass layoff unless the employer demonstrates that the employment losses are the result of separate and distinct actions and causes and are not an attempt by the employer to evade the requirements of this chapter.

29 U.S.C. § 2102.

The following cases and notes focus on the parameters of the exceptions to the employer's obligation to provide timely notice: the "good faith" exception, the "business circumstances" exception, and the "faltering company" exception; and the issues raised by the Act's "bright line" numerical thresholds and time frames.

CHILDRESS v. DARBY LUMBER, INC.
United States Court of Appeals for the Ninth Circuit
357 F.3d 1000 (2004)

ILLSTON, DISTRICT JUDGE [sitting by designation].

Darby Lumber and Bob Russell Construction, Inc. appeal the district court's grant of summary judgment in favor of Sharon Childress and other former employees in their action alleging violations of the Worker Adjustment and Retraining Notification (WARN) Act, 29 U.S.C. §§ 2101–09. At issue is whether the district court erred in: 1) concluding that Darby Lumber and Bob Russell Construction constituted a single employer for purposes of the WARN Act; 2) concluding that the companies were not exempt from the WARN Act's sixty-day notice requirement . . . for mass layoffs; 3) deciding various discovery disputes; and 4) awarding attorney's fees. We conclude that the district court was not in error, and therefore affirm its ruling in full. . . .

DLI [Darby Lumber, Inc.] operated as a lumber mill and manufactured, marketed, and sold finished lumber. . . .

On September 24, 1998, Larry Guerrero, the general manager of the DLI mill, placed a written statement in the paychecks of all DLI employees, advising them of the financial difficulties of the company, and informing them that there would be a "major layoff." On September 25, 1998, DLI shut down the mill, and all mill employees were laid off. The planer operation at the mill continued to operate for several weeks thereafter, but was then shut down, and all of those employees were laid off. . . .

On February 8, 1999 this suit was filed by former DLI employees, alleging violations of the WARN Act, which requires a sixty-day notice of layoffs in certain situations. The WARN Act requires employers of 100 or more fulltime employees to give at least sixty days advance notice of a plant closing if the shutdown results in an employment loss at a single employment site during any thirty-day period for fifty or more employees (excluding any part-time employees). *Id.* Appellants . . . claimed that . . . the affirmative defenses of "faltering company," "unforeseeable business circumstances," and/or "good faith" applied and would preclude application of the WARN Act. . . .

[handwritten: Er claimed defenses]

. . . The district court [found] that neither the good faith, business circumstances, nor faltering company exceptions applied. The district court then found that Darby Lumber would still be liable even if some of the exceptions applied, because its notice was inadequate. In subsequent orders, the Court granted plaintiffs' motion for attorney's fees in the amount of $123,033.44 and ordered defendants to pay damages to plaintiffs in the amount of $60,345.45, which was sixty work days of wages/benefits lost to the individual plaintiffs from the layoff date of September 25, 1998, minus any days worked. . . .

[handwritten: dist. ct. said N/A to defenses]

The purpose of the WARN Act is to provide:

> protection to workers, their families and communities by requiring employers to provide notification 60 calendar days in advance of plant closings and mass layoffs. Advance notice provides workers and their families some transition time to adjust to the prospective loss of employment, to seek and obtain alternative jobs and, if necessary, to enter skill training or retraining that will allow these workers to successfully compete in the job market.

[handwritten: purpose of WARN]

20 C.F.R. § 639.1. Employers with 100 or more full-time employees are barred from ordering a plant closing or mass layoff "until the end of a 60-day period after the employer serves written notice of such an order to each representative of the affected employees as of the time of the notice or, if there is no such representative at that time, to each affected employee." 29 U.S.C. § 2101(a), 2102(a)(1).

. . . .

[Whether the employer's actions affect a sufficient number of employees to meet the definition of a plant closing or mass layoff] are calculated from the "snap-shot" date of the last date upon which the notice would be required to be given, in this case, July 27, 1998, sixty days before September 25, 1998, the date of the layoff. *See* 20 C.F.R. § 639.5(a)(2). On July 27, 1998, DLI and BRC [Bob Russell Construction] had more than 100 employees combined, while alone, each company had fewer than 100 employees. . . . [The court found that DLI and BRC shared common ownership, direction, and had interdependent operations, and that they operated as a single employer for purposes of the WARN Act.]

[handwritten: snap shot date]

Appellants contend that they were exempt from the WARN Act's sixty day notice requirement for layoffs under either the "good faith" exception, the "business circumstances" exception or the "faltering company" exception, and that the district court erred in not allowing these defenses to go to a jury.

A. Good faith exception

The WARN Act provides:

> If an employer which has violated this Act proves to the satisfaction of the court that the act or omission that violated this chapter was in good faith and that the employer had reasonable grounds for believing that the act or omission was not a violation of this chapter the court may, in its discretion, reduce the amount of the liability or penalty provided for in this section.

29 U.S.C. § 2104(a)(4). Appellants claim that this defense should have gone to a jury, and that the district court's decision to dismiss it at the summary judgment stage was reversible error.

However, as the district court recognized, good faith is an affirmative defense as to which defendants have the burden of proof, and in this case they failed to raise triable issues as to several elements of the defense. As the district court stated:

> The good faith defense requires a showing by the employer of a subjective intent to comply with the Act as well as evidence of objective reasonableness by the employer in applying the Act. *In re James way Corp.*, 235 B.R. 329, 345 (S.D.N.Y.1999). If there is not a material fact issue concerning one or both of these factors, good faith can be a matter appropriate for summary judgment. *Id.* Under the good faith exception, the employer must establish that it had "an honest intention to ascertain and follow the dictates of the [statute]" and that it had "reasonable grounds for believing that [its] conduct complie[d] with the [statute]." *Local 246 Utility Workers Union of America v. Southern California Edison Company*, 83 F.3d 292, 298 (9th Cir.1996).

Childress, No. CV-99-M-DWM (D.Mont. Jan. 4, 2001) (order granting summary judgment) (alterations in original).

Appellants failed to provide facts to establish that they had an honest intention to ascertain and follow the dictates of the WARN Act or that they had reasonable grounds for believing that their conduct complied with it. Appellants did provide evidence that they had little or no knowledge of the Act and that Russell did not want to close the DLI mill. That information tends to show that defendants were ignorant of the WARN Act; it does not, however, show that they had an honest intention to follow it, or that they had grounds for believing that they were in compliance with it. Mere ignorance of the WARN Act is not enough to establish the good faith exception. The district court was correct in finding that the good faith exception to the WARN Act did not apply.

B. Business circumstances exception

The WARN Act's sixty-day notice requirements do not apply "if the closing or mass layoff is caused by business circumstances that were not reasonably foreseeable as of the time that notice would have been required." 29 U.S.C. § 2102(b)(2)(A). The Code of Federal Regulations gives guidance on what types of business circumstances will be considered "not reasonably foreseeable":

> (1) An important indicator of a business circumstance that is not reasonably foreseeable is that the circumstance is caused by some sudden, dramatic, and unexpected action or condition outside the employer's control. A principal client's sudden and unexpected termination of a major contract with the employer, a strike at a major supplier of the employer, and an unanticipated and dramatic major economic downturn might each be considered a business circumstance that is not reasonably foreseeable. A government ordered closing of an employment site that occurs without prior notice also may be an unforeseeable business circumstance.

> (2) The test for determining when business circumstances are not reasonably foreseeable focuses on an employer's business judgment. The employer must exercise such commercially reasonable business judgment as would a similarly situated employer in predicting the demands of its particular market. The employer is not required, however, to accurately predict general economic conditions that also may affect demand for its products or services.

20 C.F.R. § 639.9(b)(1)–(2).

Appellants point to the decision by U.S. Bank on September 7, 1998, refusing to rewrite DLI's credit, as the sudden and unforeseeable event that caused the shutdown of the mill. However, appellants' own response to a discovery request stated:

> The closure of the plant and layoffs in September 1998 was occasioned by losses to the company which could not be sustained any longer. These losses were a function of the depressed lumber market, increased cost of raw materials, operational difficulty in the startup of a new planer, and factors effected by the price of raw materials and finished goods beyond the control of Darby Lumber, Inc. In turn, raw materials and finished goods markets and prices were effected by the general economic downturn in Pacific rim countries, influences by NAFTA, and significantly influenced by environmental pressure to halt sales of forest service timber.

This statement makes it evident that the plant closure was not caused solely by the decision of U.S. Bank, but was caused by a variety of factors which accumulated over time, making the closure foreseeable. Indeed, as the district court noted, while U.S. Bank decided not to rewrite DLI's loans on September 7, 1998, the company did not actually lose its credit with the bank until November 1998, a month following the mass layoff.

Appellants failed to meet their burden of showing that the business circumstances exception applies in this case. Accordingly, we affirm the district court's finding that the business circumstances exception did not apply.

C. Faltering company exception

The Code of Federal Regulations, at 20 C.F.R. § 639.9(a), outlines the require-ments for the faltering company exception. It first notes that the exception "applies to plant closings but not to mass layoffs and should be narrowly construed." *Id.* It goes on to provide that the exception generally allows for reduced notice to employees where (1) the employer was actively seeking capital at the time that sixty-day notice would have been required; (2) there was a realistic opportunity to obtain the financing sought; (3) the financing would have been sufficient, if obtained, to enable the employer to keep the facility open for a reasonable period of time; and most critically here:

> (4) The employer reasonably and in good faith . . . believed that giving the required notice would have precluded the employer from obtaining the needed capital or business. The employer must be able to objectively demonstrate that it reasonably thought that a potential customer or source of financing would have been unwilling to provide the new business or capital if notice were given, that is, if the employees, customers, or the public were aware that the facility, operating unit, or site might have to close. This condition may be satisfied if the employer can show that the financing or business source would not choose to do business with a troubled company or with a company whose workforce would be looking for other jobs.

Id. § 639.9(a)(4).

Appellants seek to qualify for this "faltering company" exception because they were in the process of seeking a line of credit from U.S. Bank. However, even assuming that there was a realistic opportunity to obtain such financing, and that the financing, if obtained, would have enabled them to avoid or postpone the closure of the mill, appellants provided no evidence that they reasonably and in good faith believed that giving the sixty-day notice to their employees during the negotiations with U.S. Bank would have precluded them from obtaining the credit from the bank. The district court's ruling that the faltering company exception does not apply in this case was not in error, and is hereby affirmed. . . .

This Court AFFIRMS the rulings of the district court in full.

NOTES

1.   **The Unforeseeable Business Conditions Defense**. In *Childress*, the Ninth Circuit rejected the company's argument that the unforeseeable business circum-stance was U.S. Bank's refusal to rewrite the company's credit, occasioning the mill's shutdown. The court emphasized instead events within the company's control that had occurred earlier in time (the cumulative effect of financial losses that led to the denial of credit). Other courts have analyzed similar situations differently, focusing on the last event in the chain and relieving employers of their WARN Act liability. For example, in *United Steel Workers Local 2660 v. U.S. Steel Corp.*, 683 F.3d 882 (8th Cir. 2012), the court ruled that a sharp fall-off in demand for steel occasioned by the economic downturn of 2008 constituted unforeseeable business

circumstances that justified an exception to the 60-day notice requirement. Although the economic downturn had begun months earlier and was well-known to the company, it was the sudden decline in the demand for steel that made it foreseeable that the previous operational approach would not be sufficient to combat the economic circumstances. Thus, the company was excused from WARN Act obligations where it had provided only one week's notice to more than 300 employees after learning of a massive drop in customer orders in the last quarter of 2008. *Id.* at 888–89. Similarly, in *Roquet v. Arthur Andersen LLP*, 398 F.3d 585 (7th Cir. 2005), the court pinpointed the Justice Department's decision to indict accounting firm Arthur Andersen for destroying documents relating to its audit of the troubled company Enron as the point at which the company's closing became foreseeable, despite prior negative publicity stemming from the SEC's subpoena of Enron-related documents and the known possibility of client defection. The court held that the layoff was not probable until the company had lost business or been indicted, and that Arthur Andersen had acted reasonably by attempting to negotiate with the government until it was forced to turn to layoffs in the face of a public indictment. *Id.* at 589. Nor did Arthur Andersen's long awareness of its own misconduct prior to the investigation mean that the indictment was inherently foreseeable at earlier junctures, since the Justice Department's decision to indict the company as an entity was unprecedented. *Id.* at 590.

The question whether the employer exercised "such commercially reasonable business judgment as would a similarly situated employer," 20 C.F.R. § 639.9(b)(2) (2004) requires a case-by-case examination of the facts with an industry-specific focus, which has produced varying results. *Compare Gross v. Hale-Halsell*, 554 F.3d 870 (10th Cir. 2009) (finding grocery warehouse distribution center shutdown unforeseeable where closing was attributable to loss of largest and long-time (31-year) customer, despite problems in filling customer's orders over preceding two years) and *Hotel Employees and Restaurant Employees International Union Local 54 v. Elsinore Shore Associates,* 173 F.3d 175 (3d Cir. 1999) (finding casino shutdown unforeseeable where government agency refused to renew its license due to casino's ongoing financial difficulties, because commission had never before refused to renew a casino license) with *Pena v. American Meat Packing Corp.*, 362 F.3d 418 (7th Cir. 2004) (finding triable issue of fact existed as to whether closing of hog processing plant was foreseeable and denying summary judgment where USDA inspectors issued a significant number of noncompliance records for failure to comply with USDA standards, requiring the company to destroy meat and make significant expenditures for repairs to capital facilities).

An important prerequisite to use of the unforeseeable business conditions defense is that the employer must "give as much notice as is practicable," and the notice must be specific, including "a brief statement of the basis for reducing the notification period." WARN Act § 2102(b)(3). Thus, an employer that gives no notice at all cannot assert the unforeseeable business conditions defense; the defense serves only to reduce the notice period, not eliminate it entirely. *Sides v. Macon Cty. Greyhound Park, Inc.*, 725 F.3d 1276, 1285 (11th Cir. 2013).

2.   **Class-Based Distinctions.** The WARN Act applies to all employees, regardless of occupation or social class. In a recent highly publicized case stemming from the collapse of the New York-based law firm Dewey & LeBoeuf, which at its zenith

employed more than 1400 lawyers in 26 domestic and foreign offices, the bankruptcy court permitted 550 employees (lawyers and staff) to move forward with federal and state WARN Act claims against Dewey's bankruptcy estate. *In Re Dewey & LeBoeuf, LLP*, 507 B.R. 522 (U.S. Bankr. Ct., S.D.N.Y. 2014). Dewey's downfall resulted from indictments of key partners for securities fraud, grand larceny, and falsifying business records relating to fraudulent accounting practices that they engaged in to live up to the terms of credit extended to the firm by banks. Jennifer Smith & Ashby Jones, *Fallen Law Firm's Leaders Are Charged with Fraud*, WALL ST. J., Mar. 6, 2014. Disclosure of the criminal investigation by the Manhattan district attorney's office blocked the firm's efforts to arrange further financing of its operation or a merger with another firm. Notice to employees was sent on May 10, 2012, a mere five days before the firm filed for bankruptcy.

What difference, if any, should it make that the plaintiffs in *U.S. Steel* and *Childress* were blue-collar workers and the plaintiffs in *Dewey & LeBoeuf* were white-collar and pink-collar workers? Are the interests at stake any different? Should the nature of the business, the level of the workers' skills, and their likely re-employability affect our analysis of the company's obligations to warn its employees of an impending closing or to provide stop-gap protections against wage and job loss? Which group of workers benefits more from WARN Act notice?

Steven Willborn argues that American law reflects a profound faith in markets to protect workers, particularly against job and wage loss; the law steps in only where the market is not adequate to the task. *See* Steven L. Willborn, *Workers in Troubled Firms: When Are (Should) They Be Protected?*, 7 U. PA. J. LAB. & EMP. L. 35, 50 (2004). Thus, if a worker can easily replace a lost job, legal protection is unnecessary; if an equivalent job cannot readily be found, the law should step in. *Id.* Willborn defends market protections as superior to the law because they create incentives for workers to focus their attention forward, to firms where they have a future, rather than backward, to firms that are distressed, and because they foster firm flexibility and incentivize job creation by reducing legal entitlements of incumbent employees, ultimately benefiting displaced workers by expanding the number of replacement jobs available. At some point, for some workers, however, the risk levels become unacceptable. *Id.* at 52–53. What does this market analysis suggest about how workers' skill levels, reemployability and class status should impact interpretations of WARN?

ELLIS v. DHL EXPRESS, INC.
United States Court of Appeals for the Seventh Circuit
633 F.3d 522 (2011)

TINDER, CIRCUIT JUDGE.

Package delivery service DHL Express and its German parent company, Deutsche Post AG, publicly announced on November 10, 2008, that they would stop offering U.S. domestic shipping on January 30, 2009. This announcement effectively sounded the death knell for five of DHL's six Chicagoland facilities, which handled domestic parcels almost exclusively and had been shedding jobs since August. The union that represented the drivers and clerical workers at those facilities, the

International Brotherhood of Teamsters Local 705, immediately began talks with DHL to negotiate severance agreements for its members. (The collective bargaining agreements that covered the workers did not provide for severance benefits.) The negotiations were successful and on December 5, 2008, yielded a severance agreement for each bargaining unit, the drivers and the office workers. The agreements became operative on December 9, 2008, when DHL's representative signed them. Whether DHL violated the Worker Adjustment and Retraining Notification (WARN) Act, 29 U.S.C. §§ 2101–2109, in reaching and implementing these agreements is the principal question before us in this appeal.

The agreements contained a number of different severance benefits packages. The first was available to up to 325 of DHL's full-time drivers. Drivers who opted (and qualified on seniority grounds) for this package would receive ten weeks of pay and benefits. Drivers had little time to decide whether to participate in this plan; they were simultaneously required to complete a job rebid form on which they had to indicate by the close of business on December 11, 2008, not only their future shift preferences but also whether they had signed up for the ten-week plan. The other severance packages Local 705 negotiated provided four rather than ten weeks of pay and benefits but were otherwise substantially similar to the ten-week plan. There were no limits placed upon the number of workers who could enroll in the four-week plans, though one of the packages for each bargaining unit was aimed exclusively at individuals who had already been laid off (these packages provided no benefits), and the others were aimed at workers who remained on staff. Drivers and already-laid-off office workers were given until December 22, 2008, to decide whether they wanted to participate in the four-week plans. Employed office workers appear to have been given until January 18, 2009, to make their decisions.

Workers who accepted any of the Local 705-negotiated severance packages signed the following "General Waiver and Release":

> For and in consideration of the receipt of the Severance Payment and other benefits provided in the Effects Bargaining Agreement (which I acknowledge are payments and benefits beyond anything to which I am already or otherwise entitled), I hereby waive, release and discharge DHL Express (USA), Inc., its parent corporation, subsidiaries, related corporations and affiliates, their successors and assigns, and their shareholders, officers, directors, employees and agents (hereinafter together the "Company"), and the Teamsters Local Union No. 705, affiliated with the International Brotherhood of Teamsters (hereinafter the "Union") from any and all actions, causes of action, demands, claims or liabilities (whether known or unknown) arising out of my employment or the termination of my employment by the Company, including but not limited to any claims under any federal, state, or local law concerning employment rights or employment discrimination of any type, including the National Labor Relations Act, the Illinois Worker Adjustment and Retraining Notification Act, the Federal Worker Adjustment and Retraining Notification (WARN) Act, and laws involving claims of discrimination based on race, sex, religion, national origin, disability, veteran's status, union activity, marital status, retaliation, harassment or other protected categories, claims for breach of any implied or express employment contracts or covenants, claims for wrongful termi-

nation, public policy violations, defamation, emotional distress or other common law torts, or claims under any Collective Bargaining Agreement, Supplemental Agreement, Memorandum of Understanding (MOU), or any other agreement between the Company and the Union. I further understand that by accepting the Severance Payment, I am giving up my employment relationship with the Company, including any recall rights and seniority. . . .

I acknowledge that I have been and am in this document advised in writing to consult an attorney before executing this General Release and that the foregoing shall operate as a general release and as a promise not to sue, and that I have read and understand this General Release. I acknowledge I have received seven (7) days to consider this General Release before signing it, and I understand that I have seven (7) days to revoke it after I sign it.

A total of 506 workers (some of them were members of Automobile Mechanics Union Local 701, which negotiated its own similar four-week plan) signed a release and resigned their employment in exchange for either four or ten weeks of severance pay and benefits. Three hundred nineteen drivers took the ten-week plan, while 187 workers participated in one of the three four-week plans.

Workers who did not participate in one of the union-negotiated severance plans did not receive any severance pay from DHL. Those individuals instead retained their seniority status and recall rights, as well as the right to bring legal claims against DHL and its parent, Deutsche Post. John Ellis and Timothy Price, the named plaintiffs in this putative class action, were DHL drivers and Local 705 members who did not participate in the union-negotiated plans. Ellis, who was laid off days before the discontinuation of domestic shipping was announced, and Price, who was laid off on January 9, 2009, instead filed suit, alleging that DHL and its parent Deutsche Post failed to comply with the WARN Act, which requires certain businesses contemplating "plant closings" or "mass layoffs" to inform workers of these impending events at least sixty days in advance. Ellis and Price sought back pay and benefits. *See* 29 U.S.C. § 2104. They also sought to represent a class of former DHL employees who had been represented by Local 705, but the district court terminated as moot their motion to certify a class after granting in full DHL's motion for summary judgment. *See Muro v. Target Corp.*, 580 F.3d 485, 494 (7th Cir. 2009).

The district court provided three interrelated bases for its grant of summary judgment, all of which led it to the conclusion that the WARN Act was not applicable here. First, the district court concluded that the DHL layoffs could not constitute a "plant closing" as defined in 29 U.S.C. § 2101(a)(2) because the five Chicagoland facilities could not together be considered a "single site of employment," and Price and Ellis failed to put forth allegations sufficient to raise a genuine issue of material fact as to whether a "plant closing" occurred at any of the individual facilities. Second, the district court concluded that the layoffs could not constitute a "mass layoff" as defined in 29 U.S.C. § 2101(a)(3) because the employment losses at the five facilities (considered collectively for the sake of argument) did not reach the requisite critical mass of 33% of the full-time work-force during the relevant statutory time period. Finally, the district court determined that Ellis and Price failed to raise a genuine issue of material fact regarding the voluntariness of the union-negotiated severance agreements, fatally undermining their contention that the workers who left DHL pursuant to those agreements should be counted as involuntarily separated for WARN Act purposes. *See* 29 U.S.C. § 2101(a)(6); 54 Fed. Reg. 16042, 16048 (Apr. 20, 1989). The district court recognized that the DHL workers had to make a tough choice in the face of daunting economic circumstances, but concluded that there was no evidence that they signed the severance agreements involuntarily. Because it found that the bases for its grant of summary judgment in favor of DHL applied equally to Deutsche Post, against whom Ellis and Price levied identical claims, the district court sua sponte granted summary judgment in favor of Deutsche Post as well and terminated the case. Ellis and Price appeal the grants of summary judgment.

. . . .

The WARN Act requires "employers" (defined as businesses with 100 or more full-time employees, 29 U.S.C. § 2101(a)(1)) to provide employees with written notice of impending "plant closings" or "mass layoffs" at least sixty days prior to the closing or layoffs. 29 U.S.C. § 2102. The WARN Act does not apply—and the employer need not provide advance notice to any of its workers—if the shutdown of a plant does not result in an employment loss of at least 50 full-time employees at a single site of employment, 29 U.S.C. § 2101(a)(2), or the layoffs do not affect at least 33% of full-time employees, 29 U.S.C. § 2101(a)(3). Despite the lack of practical distinction between eliminating 49 or 50 full-time jobs, or between laying off 32% or 33% of a work-force in a thirty-day period, the numerical thresholds in the WARN Act are immutable. *See Phason v. Meridian Rail Corp.*, 479 F.3d 527, 530 (7th Cir. 2007) ("The [WARN Act] draws a lot of bright lines; it is really nothing *but* lines. . . . None of these distinctions is inevitable; all are arbitrary. But using sharp lines makes the Act easier to administer."). If an employer crosses one of them without providing affected employees the requisite notice, it is liable to provide "each aggrieved employee" with back pay and benefits for each day that the WARN Act was violated. 29 U.S.C. § 2104. That is why the 506 departures pursuant to the union-negotiated severance agreements are crucial here: if those workers are counted in the total number of affected employees, DHL may have overstepped one of WARN's lines. If they are not counted, however, DHL is in the clear; Ellis and Price explicitly conceded this point twice at oral argument. We therefore begin and end our analysis by examining the voluntariness issue, as it is dispositive. *See Spivey*, 622 F.3d at 822.

The WARN Act excludes "voluntary departure[s]" from its definition of "employment loss[es]" that trigger its notification requirements. 29 U.S.C. § 2101(a)(6). The WARN Act does not provide a definition of "voluntary," though it authorizes the Secretary of Labor to issue "such regulations as may be necessary to carry out this chapter." 29 U.S.C. § 2107(a). Before enacting the regulations currently codified at 20 C.F.R. §§ 639.1–639.10, the Secretary in the Federal Register addressed public comments. *See* 54 Fed. Reg. 16042 (Apr. 20, 1989). In doing so, the Secretary clarified the Department of Labor's position on "what constitutes a 'voluntary departure.'" *Id.* at 16048. . . .

The Secretary explained that "incentive programs, including incentive retirement programs and voluntary layoffs" should typically be considered voluntary departures within the meaning of the WARN Act so long as the circumstances surrounding them comport with traditional legal notions of voluntariness. 54 Fed. Reg. at 16048. That is, "a worker's resignation or retirement may be found to not be voluntary if the employer has created a hostile or intolerable work environment or has applied other forms of pressure or coercion which forced the employee to quit or resign," or "where a worker was unduly pressured to accept the program." *Id.* The Secretary expressly disagreed with the proposition that "a worker who, after the announcement of a plant closing or mass layoff, decides to leave early has necessarily been constructively discharged or quit 'involuntarily.'" *Id.* In other words, worker participation in incentive programs is generally considered voluntary unless the employer improperly induced workers to leave their jobs, either by creating a hostile or intolerable work environment or by applying other forms of undue pressure or coercion.

We have not previously addressed the issue of voluntariness in the WARN Act context, though we have considered the voluntariness of early retirement offers. In that analogous context, we explained,

> The "voluntariness" question . . . turns on such things as: did the person receive information about what would happen in response to the choice? was the choice free from fraud or other misconduct? did the person have an opportunity to say no? A very short period to make a complex choice may show that the person could not digest the information necessary to the decision. This would show that the offer of information was illusory and there was no informed choice. But when the employee has time to consult spouse and financial adviser, the fact that he still found the decision hard cannot be decisive. *Henn v. Nat'l Geographic Soc'y*, 819 F.2d 824, 828–29 (7th Cir. 1987).

The arguments raised by Ellis and Price echo these very concerns. Ellis and Price contend that the resignations, particularly those of the already-laid-off workers, cannot be considered voluntary because the employees resigned against a backdrop of extreme economic uncertainty and pressure exerted by DHL. They emphasize that the drivers were simultaneously presented with the severance agreements and the job rebid forms, which in their view rendered any choice they had about signing up for one of the severance packages a Hobson's choice at best. They also contend that the 319 drivers who accepted the ten-week plan had inadequate time to make their decisions. With respect to the already-laid-off workers who accepted the four-week packages aimed at them, Ellis and Price assert that their resignations could not possibly have been voluntary because they did not have jobs to resign from.

While we recognize the unenviable positions in which DHL's Chicagoland workers found themselves, we are unpersuaded by these arguments and cannot conclude on the evidence before us that the workers who accepted the union-negotiated severance packages did so involuntarily. The affidavits of former DHL employees that Ellis and Price present paint a wrenching picture of a difficult decision that had to be made quickly. But they do not demonstrate that the workers were given incomplete information, or that DHL somehow strong-armed them into signing the release forms and accepting the severance packages against their will. (Indeed, Ellis and Price expressly disclaim any arguments that DHL harassed workers or created a hostile work environment to induce them to resign.) To the contrary, several affiants testified that their managers declined to discuss the options with them. *Cf. Henn*, 819 F.2d at 829 (observing that employer's unwillingness to advise potential early retirees whether to accept an early retirement offer was probably due to a desire to "avoid charges of placing undue pressure on the employees"). The severance agreements and the General Waiver and Release were both negotiated by Local 705 with the workers' interests in mind, and were written unambiguously in plain English. The General Waiver and Release also expressly advised workers to consult an attorney before signing, as did a letter that Local 705 sent to the already-laid-off workers.

We appreciate that two business days may not have been an expansive window in which to fully discuss matters with an attorney. *But see Joe v. First Bank Sys., Inc.*, 202 F.3d 1067, 1070 (8th Cir. 2000) (noting that a WARN Act plaintiff "presented no meaningful proof of duress" which was "not surprising since [he] had the release for two or three days and discussed it with his attorney"). Yet "the need to make a decision in a short time, under pressure, is an unusual definition of 'involuntary.'" *Henn*, 819 F.2d at 828. Indeed, many criminal defendants must decide whether to sign take-it-or-leave-it plea agreements; "the need to act in haste does not make the plea 'involuntary' if the defendant knows and accepts the terms of the offer." *Id*. Of course, criminal defendants are afforded procedural safeguards to ensure that their decisions truly are voluntary. *See Fed. R. Crim. P. 11*. The workers here were not required to have their decisions evaluated by an impartial judge, but neither is there any evidence that DHL denied them the opportunity to educate themselves about their options or to discuss the terms of the offers with their families, friends, financial advisors, or attorneys. Moreover, the workers who were considering the ten-week package had not two days but nine in which to do so; the General Waiver and Release gave workers seven days after accepting a severance package in which to reconsider and revoke their acceptance. That the workers had to decide whether to take the bird in the hand—the severance packages—or the bird in the bush—the right to retain their seniority rank, remain on the recall rolls for three years, and pursue claims against DHL—in a short period of time does not render their decisions involuntary. Nor does the fact that neither bird was particularly attractive.

Ellis and Price's final argument about the voluntariness of the departures—that the already-laid-off workers could not leave DHL voluntarily because they had no jobs to leave from—gets them no further. Their position presupposes that the already-laid-off workers lost their attachment to DHL the moment they were laid off. The record shows, and Ellis and Price acknowledged at oral argument, that laid-off workers retained their hard-earned seniority status and recall rights with DHL for up to three years. If the laid-off workers elected to sign the General Waiver and Release in exchange for the severance package, they gave up those potentially valuable rights and fully cut their ties with DHL. They may not have been walking away from specific positions, but they were electing to end their relationships with DHL rather than waiting around for three years to see if new opportunities came to fruition.

In offering its workers the olive branch of severance pay, DHL was hedging its bets against WARN Act liability. Employers are permitted to "gamble" that enough workers accept their proffered incentive packages to absolve them from potential WARN Act liability, 54 Fed. Reg. at 16043, and DHL successfully tossed the dice here. Ellis and Price are in effect asking us to prohibit such behavior, but we cannot rewrite the WARN Act. We likewise decline their invitation to treat the WARN Act less like the notification procedure that it is and more like the universally applicable Fair Labor Standards Act and Older Workers Benefit Protection Act that it is not. That is, we maintain our previous stance that WARN Act claims can be waived as part of a voluntarily signed general release. *See Hardy v. Chi. Hous. Auth.*, 189 F. App'x. 510, 512 (7th Cir. 2006).

. . . .

The district court's grant of summary judgment in favor of both defendants is *Affirmed.*

NOTES

1. **Waivers of WARN Act Rights.** The court found that the workers' WARN Act waivers were voluntary. Why? Is the court's analogy to early retirement offers persuasive? What about the analogy to criminal defendants deciding whether to accept plea agreements?

The Ninth Circuit took a different approach to voluntariness in *Collins v. Gee West Seattle LLC*, 631 F.3d 1001 (9th Cir. 2011). The court ruled that workers who stopped reporting to work in response to their employer's announcement that the business would close in less than two weeks were entitled to prevail on their WARN Act claim. The court found that they had suffered an employment loss for purposes of the statute because their decision to depart before the company's closure was not voluntary but instead a consequence of the closure. The court characterized the employer's argument that the workers' departure was voluntary as inconsistent with WARN's purpose and goals; accepting it would allow the employer to escape responsibility for a situation that it had created: the urgent need to find new employment. *Id.* at 1007.

How much difference did it make to the Seventh Circuit's decision that the workers were represented by a union? The court reasoned that the union's involvement ensured the voluntariness of the waivers; note also that the existence of the collective bargaining agreement created seniority and recall rights that undercut the plaintiffs' argument that they had no jobs to voluntarily leave. Would the waivers have been enforceable if the workers had not been represented by a union and if their interests in job security had not been protected by the collective bargaining agreement? If so, does this mean that workers who suffer a mass layoff are better off without a union?

2. **Public Policy Considerations.** Is the only purpose of WARN to protect employees' individual rights to notice and compensation for a specified period of time? Are there public policy considerations beyond voluntariness that should bear on the waivability of WARN Act rights?

3.   Bright Lines. Having concluded that the waivers were voluntary, the *Ellis* court rigidly applied the Act's numerical thresholds and found that the layoff did not trigger WARN Act obligations. The court cited *Phason v. Meridian Rail Corp.*, 479 F.3d 527 (7th Cir. 2007), in which the employer urged the court to look through the form of a sale transaction to the business realities of the situation and not apply the "bright line" standards in the Act mechanically. The Seventh Circuit's full response was as follows:

> The statute draws a lot of bright lines; it is really nothing *but* lines. It applies, for example, only if the employer has 100 or more workers; one worker fewer and the Act drops out, though as a practical matter 99 and 100 are identical—and from any given employee's perspective it matters little how many others worked at the same plant. An "employment loss" occurs only when 50 or more workers lose their jobs; again one fewer and the Act drops out, even though the difference between 49 and 50 is not economically significant to a given worker.

>   . . . .

> None of these distinctions is inevitable; all are arbitrary. But using sharp lines makes the Act easier to administer. Bright lines must be enforced consistently or they won't work. If employees can lose because of a difference between 99 and 100 workers that seems inconsequential, employers likewise must lose when what seems like an inconsequential difference (the closing date [of the business followed by a subsequent sale]) comes out the employees' way. . . .

Id. at 530. Do you agree that WARN is "nothing but [bright] lines"? What are the advantages and disadvantages of bright lines in statutes? What do the WARN Act cases tell us about whether the lines are really so bright? Can you think of a way to draft a statute providing for notice in plant closing and mass layoff situations that would not rely upon bright lines?

4.   Which Employment Losses Trigger WARN Act Obligations? The loss of a job may take a variety of forms, and not all of them trigger WARN Act obligations for the employer. For example, should the sale of a business impose WARN notice requirements on the seller? Section 2101(b)(1) provides:

> In the case of a sale of part or all of an employer's business, the seller shall be responsible for providing notice for any plant closing or mass layoff . . . up to and including the effective date of the sale. After the effective date of the sale of part or all of an employer's business, the purchaser shall be responsible for providing notice for any plant closing or mass layoff. . . . Notwithstanding any other provision of this chapter, any person who is an employee of the seller (other than a part-time employee) as of the effective date of the sale shall be considered an employee of the purchaser immediately after the effective date of the sale.

Most courts have ruled that the seller need not give a WARN notice as long as the business is sold as a going concern, i.e., the buyer rehires nearly all of the seller's former employees and the business never ceases to operate. *See, e.g., Smullin v. Mity Enters., Inc.*, 420 F.3d 836 (8th Cir. 2005) (no mass layoff where business was sold as a going concern, buyer rehired all but 24 of the predecessor's employees and continued operations the next day). On the other hand, an employment loss that occurs *after* the date of sale—as, for example, where the purchasing entity refuses to rehire the employees of the purchased business or if there is a delay between the date of the business closing and the subsequent sale—triggers WARN Act notification requirements for the *buyer* of the business: The WARN Act obligations simply skip from seller to buyer. *See* 29 U.S.C. § 2101(b); *see Phason v. Meridian Rail Corp., supra* (finding that a business closure followed by formalization of the sale of the company one week later triggered WARN Act notification obligations for the buyer even though the buyer ultimately rehired all but 40–45 of the predecessor's employees).

Pinning down the date of the employment loss can also be tricky. This was the issue in the much-publicized 2003 demise of the Brobeck, Phleger & Harrison law firm. A few days prior to the mass layoff of Brobeck employees in conjunction with bankruptcy proceedings, Morgan, Lewis & Bockius absorbed 57 of the 170 former Brobeck partners, hired 100 former Brobeck associates and 150 former Brobeck staff members, emphasized lawyer continuity in its press relations, rented the office space that Brobeck had vacated, and purchased its furniture, equipment, and a license to use its Intranet structure and document management system. The laid-off Brobeck employees sued both firms, alleging WARN violations. A district court judge denied Morgan Lewis' motion for summary judgment, finding that a triable issue of fact existed as to whether Morgan Lewis had purchased part of the Brobeck business and consequently triggered its WARN Act notification obligations as a purchaser to the employees who were not hired and received no advance notice. *McCaffrey v. Brobeck, Phleger & Harrison*, 20 I.E.R. Cas. (BNA) 1706 (N.D. Cal. 2004).

The district court subsequently granted Morgan Lewis's motion for summary judgment in *McCaffrey v. Brobeck, Phleger & Harrison*. The court reaffirmed its original ruling that Morgan Lewis was a purchaser of Brobeck and therefore a sale had occurred, triggering WARN Act obligations. However, it found that the seller (Brobeck) remained responsible for giving notice of the impending layoffs until the effective date of the sale, which was stipulated in the Purchase and Transition Agreement. *McCaffrey v. Brobeck, Phleger & Harrison*, 2005 U.S. Dist. LEXIS 40327 (N.D. Calif. 2005). Unfortunately for the former employees, Brobeck filed for Chapter 11 reorganization and the bankruptcy was converted to an involuntary Chapter 7 proceeding shortly thereafter. DAILY LAB. REP. (BNA) No. 93, May 16, 2005.

Suppose that an employer hires temporary workers to replace union workers who are out on strike, and then fires the temporary workers once the labor dispute is settled. Does the discharge of the temporary workers qualify as a mass layoff generating WARN Act obligations for the employer? In *Sanders v. Kohler Co.*, 641 F.3d 290 (8th Cir. 2011), the court held that the replacement workers who must give up their jobs to allow reinstated strikers to return to work do not count as part of the total number of employee layoffs that must occur in order to meet WARN Act thresholds. The Eighth Circuit reasoned that the statute's reference to a "reduction in force" in section 2101(a)(3) when defining "mass layoff" requires a net loss in the number of employees. *Id.* at 294.

5. Pay or Play? Could an employer avoid WARN Act liability by simply closing
its business and placing its employees on paid leave for 60 days? Yes, said the
Fourth Circuit in *Long v. Dunlop Sports Group, Inc.*, 506 F.3d 299 (4th Cir. 2007),
because in that event the employees have not suffered an unanticipated employment
loss for purposes of the statute. The pay and benefits provided must fully
compensate employees for their losses, however.

Rachel Arnow-Richman has proposed a pay-or-play system in which all
employers—not just those covered by WARN who engage in a mass layoff—would
be required to provide advance warning of termination to individual employees or,
at the employer's election, pay terminated workers their salary and benefits for a
specified period. Rachel Arnow-Richman, *Just Notice: Re-reforming Employment
At Will*, 58 UCLA L. REV. 1, 7 (2010). She explains:

> Such an approach would extend to all terminated workers the protection
> currently afforded only to those affected by a plant closing or mass layoff
> under the federal WARN Act. . . . [E]mployers would be obliged to provide
> severance pay in lieu of notice in the event that they are unable to foresee,
> or choose not to announce, the need for termination. In this way, pay-or-
> play would serve primarily as a source of income replacement that
> terminated workers would be obligated to exhaust before becoming eligible
> for unemployment benefits. Importantly, the rights of terminated workers
> would not be dependent on the employer's reason for terminating. Absent
> serious misconduct, employers would be obligated to provide notice or
> severance irrespective of the reason for termination.

Id. Would such a system be desirable?

C. COLLECTIVE JOB SECURITY UNDER THE NATIONAL LABOR RELATIONS ACT

In addition to common law claims and WARN Act violations, plant closings
resulting in collective job loss may also impinge upon the collective rights protected
by the NLRA. Section 7 of the NLRA protects employees' rights to form, join, or
assist labor organizations; to bargain collectively through representatives of their
choosing; and to engage in other concerted activity for purposes of collective
bargaining or other mutual aid or protection. Section 8(a)(1) makes it an unfair
labor practice for an employer to "interfere with, restrain, or coerce employees"
who are exercising rights under § 7. Section 8(a)(3) makes it an unfair labor practice
for an employer to discriminate "in regard to hire or tenure of employment or any
term or condition of employment to encourage or discourage membership in any
labor organization." Section 8(a)(5) makes it an unfair labor practice for an employer
to refuse to bargain collectively with the majority representative of its employees.
Charges may be filed with the National Labor Relations Board under §§ 8(a)(1), (3),
or (5); equitable remedies are available.

Plant closings may violate the NLRA in several ways. The three most common
involve situations where the employer closes the plant or a part thereof in response
to a union organizing campaign, potentially violating §§ 8(a)(1) and 8(a)(3); situations where the employer threatens to close the plant in an effort to discourage

union organizing activity or as part of an anti-union campaign during a union organizing drive, implicating §§ 8(a)(1) and 8(a)(3); or in an already unionized workforce, situations where an employer shifts work to another operation without first bargaining with the union in violation of its § 8(a)(5) duty to bargain or if there is a labor contract, in violation of a provision barring such contracting out.

1. Union Organizing Drives

Suppose that an employer believes that unionization will increase labor costs and render its operation unprofitable. May the employer shut down its business in response to a union organizing drive? The employment relation is fundamentally cabined by its common law master-servant origins, which visualize the employment relation "as a dominant-servient relation rather than one of mutual rights and obligations." Clyde W. Summers, *Employment at Will in the United States: The Divine Right of Employers*, 3 U. PA. J. L. & EMP. L. 65, 78 (2000). Thus, "[t]he employer, as owner of the enterprise, is viewed as owning the job with a property right to control the job and the worker who fills it." *Id.* Employers have the unquestioned right to manage and control their businesses. Did enactment of the NLRA, with its protection of workers' rights to organize and collectively bargain with their employers, alter this vision of the employment relation?

TEXTILE WORKERS UNION v. DARLINGTON MANUFACTURING CO.
United States Supreme Court
380 U.S. 263 (1965)

MR. JUSTICE HARLAN delivered the opinion of the Court [JUSTICES STEWART and GOLDBERG took no part in the decision].

We here review judgments of the Court of Appeals setting aside and refusing to enforce an order of the National Labor Relations Board which found respondent Darlington guilty of an unfair labor practice by reason of having permanently closed its plant following petitioner union's election as the bargaining representative of Darlington's employees.

Darlington Manufacturing Company was a South Carolina corporation operating one textile mill. A majority of Darlington's stock was held by Deering Milliken, a New York 'selling house' marketing textiles produced by others. Deering Milliken in turn was controlled by Roger Milliken, president of Darlington, and by other members of the Milliken family. The National Labor Relations Board found that the Milliken family, through Deering Milliken, operated 17 textile manufacturers, including Darlington, whose products manufactured in 27 different mills, were marketed through Deering Milliken.

In March 1956 petitioner Textile Workers Union initiated an organizational campaign at Darlington which the company resisted vigorously in various ways, including threats to close the mill if the union won a representation election.[1] On

---

[1] [n. 3] The Board found that Darlington had interrogated employees and threatened to close the mill

September 6, 1956, the union won an election by a narrow margin. When Roger Milliken was advised of the union victory, he decided to call a meeting of the Darlington board of directors to consider closing the mill. Mr. Milliken testified before the Labor Board:

> "I felt that as a result of the campaign that had been conducted and the promises and statements made in these letters that had been distributed [favoring unionization], that if before we had had some hope, possible hope of achieving competitive [costs] . . . by taking advantage of new machinery that was being put in, that this hope had diminished as a result of the election because a majority of the employees had voted in favor of the union . . . ." (R. 457.)

The board of directors met on September 12 and voted to liquidate the corporation, action which was approved by the stockholders on October 17. The plant ceased operations entirely in November, and all plant machinery and equipment were sold piecemeal at auction in December.

The union filed charges with the Labor Board claiming that Darlington had violated §§ 8(a)(1) and (3) of the National Labor Relations Act by closing its plant, and § 8(a)(5) by refusing to bargain with the union after the election. The Board, by a divided vote, found that Darlington had been closed because of the antiunion animus of Roger Milliken, and held that to be a violation of § 8(a)(3). The Board also found Darlington to be part of a single integrated employer group controlled by the Milliken family through Deering Milliken; therefore Deering Milliken could be held liable for the unfair labor practices of Darlington. Alternatively, since Darlington was a part of the Deering Milliken enterprise, Deering Milliken had violated the Act by closing part of its business for a discriminatory purpose. The Board ordered back pay for all Darlington employees until they obtained substantially equivalent work or were put on preferential hiring lists at the other Deering Milliken mills. Respondent Deering Milliken was ordered to bargain with the union in regard to details of compliance with the Board order. 139 N.L.R.B. 241.

On review, the Court of Appeals, sitting en banc, set aside the order and denied enforcement by a divided vote. 325 F.2d 682. The Court of Appeals held that even accepting arguendo the Board's determination that Deering Milliken had the status of a single employer, a company has the absolute right to close out a part or all of its business regardless of antiunion motives. The court therefore did not review the Board's finding that Deering Milliken was a single integrated employer. We granted certiorari to consider the important questions involved. We hold that so far as the Labor Relations Act is concerned, an employer has the absolute right to terminate his entire business for any reason he pleases, but disagree with the Court of Appeals that such right includes the ability to close part of a business no matter what the reason. We conclude that the cause must be remanded to the Board for further proceedings. . . .

---

if the union won the election. After the decision to liquidate was made (see infra), Darlington employees were told that the decision to close was caused by the election, and they were encouraged to sign a petition disavowing the union. These practices were held to violate § 8(a)(1) of the National Labor Relations Act, . . . and that part of the Board decision is not challenged here.

I.

We consider first the argument, advanced by the petitioner union . . . that an employer may not go completely out of business without running afoul of the Labor Relations Act if such action is prompted by a desire to avoid unionization. Given the Board's findings on the issue of motive, acceptance of this contention would carry the day for the Board's conclusion that the closing of this plant was an unfair labor practice, even on the assumption that Darlington is to be regarded as an independent unrelated employer. A proposition that a single businessman cannot choose to go out of business if he wants to would represent such a startling innovation that it should not be entertained without the clearest manifestation of legislative intent or unequivocal judicial precedent so construing the Labor Relations Act. We find neither.

So far as legislative manifestation is concerned, it is sufficient to say that there is not the slightest indication in the history of the Wagner Act or of the Taft-Hartley Act that Congress envisaged any such result under either statute.

As for judicial precedent, the Board recognized that '[t]here is no decided case directly dispositive of Darlington's claim that it had an absolute right to close its mill, irrespective of motive.' 139 N.L.R.B., at 250. . . . The courts of appeals have generally assumed that a complete cessation of business will remove an employer from future coverage by the Act. Thus the Court of Appeals said in these cases: The Act 'does not compel a person to become or remain an employee. It does not compel one to become or remain an employer. Either may withdraw from that status with immunity, so long as the obligations of any employment contract have been met.' 325 F.2d at 685. . . .

The AFL-CIO suggests in its amicus brief that Darlington's action was similar to a discriminatory lockout, which is prohibited 'because designed to frustrate organizational efforts, to destroy or undermine bargaining representation, or to evade the duty to bargain.' One of the purposes of the Labor Relations Act is to prohibit the discriminatory use of economic weapons in an effort to obtain future benefits. The discriminatory lockout designed to destroy a union, like a 'runaway shop,' is a lever which has been used to discourage collective employee activities in the future. But a complete liquidation of a business yields no such future benefit for the employer, if the termination is bona fide. It may be motivated more by spite against the union than by business reasons, but it is not the type of discrimination which is prohibited by the Act. The personal satisfaction that such an employer may derive from standing on his beliefs and the mere possibility that other employers will follow his example are surely too remote to be considered dangers at which the labor statutes were aimed. Although employees may be prohibited from engaging in a strike under certain conditions, no one would consider it a violation of the Act for the same employees to quit their employment en masse, even if motivated by a desire to ruin the employer. The very permanence of such action would negate any future economic benefit to the employees. The employer's right to go out of business is no different.

We are not presented here with the case of a 'runaway shop,' whereby Darlington would transfer its work to another plant or open a new plant in another locality to replace its closed plant. Nor are we concerned with a shutdown where the employees, by renouncing the union, could cause the plant to reopen. Such cases would involve discriminatory employer action for the purpose of obtaining some benefit in the future from the employees in the future. We hold here only that when an employer closes his entire business, even if the liquidation is motivated by vindictiveness toward the union, such action is not an unfair labor practice. . . .[2]

NOTE

Complete Closings Versus Partial Closings. In later segments of the opinion, the Court nonetheless found that an employer could violate § 8(a)(3) of the Act if the closing was not a closing of the entire business operation—which would end the employer-employee relationship altogether—but was instead a partial closing designed to afford the employer leverage for discouraging the exercise of § 7 rights among the remaining employees at operations under the business owners' common control. The Court ruled that a partial closing would violate § 8(a)(3) if "motivated by a purpose to chill unionism in any of the remaining plants of the single employer and if the employer may reasonably have foreseen that such closing would likely have that effect," and remanded the case to the Board for factual findings. On remand, the trial examiner found that there was not sufficient evidence of a purpose to chill unionism at the other plants or a foreseeable chilling effect. The Board disagreed, concluding that the record did indicate an illegal "purpose" and "foreseeable effect" of closing on unionization efforts at other plants. *Darlington Mfg. Co.*, 165 N.L.R.B. 1074 (1967), *enforced*, 397 F.2d 760 (4th Cir.), *cert. denied*, 393 U.S. 1023 (1968). In so ruling, the Board relied upon evidence that Roger Milliken made speeches to business and government leaders in South Carolina prior to the union organizing drive at Darlington, in which he described unionism as a threat to the Southern industrial community. He advocated preserving cooperative management-labor relations (by which he evidently meant a nonunion shop) "at all costs." In addition, Milliken sent managers at other Deering Milliken mills reprints of a trade magazine article entitled "Darlington Situation Becomes Object Lesson to All Concerned," and urged them to initiate a public relations campaign concerning the risks of unionism. News of the Darlington closing was disseminated rapidly through the other Deering Milliken plants. From this evidence the Board deduced both purpose and effect.

---

[2] [n. 20] Nothing we have said in this opinion would justify an employer's interfering with employee organizational activities by threatening to close his plant, as distinguished from announcing a decision to close already reached by the board of directors or other management authority empowered to make such a decision. We recognize that this safeguard does not wholly remove the possibility that our holding may result in some deterrent effect on organizational activities independent of that arising from the closing itself. An employer may be encouraged to make a definitive decision to close on the theory that its mere announcement before a representation election will discourage the employees from voting for the union, and thus his decision may not have to be implemented. Such a possibility is not likely to occur, however, except in a marginal business; a solidly successful employer is not apt to hazard the possibility that the employees will call his bluff by voting to organize. We see no practical way of eliminating this possible consequence of our holding short of allowing the Board to order an employer who chooses so to gamble with his employees not to carry out his announced intention to close. We do not consider the matter of sufficient significance in the overall labor-management relations picture to require or justify a decision different from the one we have made.

2. Threats to Close in Response to Union Organizing Activity

May the employer tell the employees of its intent to close if a union is voted in? Does it matter whether the employer is telling the truth or bluffing? In footnote 20 of the *Darlington* opinion, the Court adverted to the possibility that some employers might be encouraged to tell the workers that it plans to close if a union is voted in, whether or not this is in fact the case. At the time, the Court considered this an unlikely and relatively insignificant scenario, an assumption which was soon revealed as erroneous.

NLRB v. Gissel Packing Co., 395 U.S. 575 (1969). An employer facing a union organizing drive sought to persuade employees not to support the union. The company president referenced a lengthy strike over failed labor contract negotiations that had occurred over a decade earlier and ended when the company reopened without a union contract, which he claimed " 'almost put our company out of business.' " *Id.* at 587. He expressed concern that employees would forget the " 'lessons of the past,' " and pointed out that "the Company was still on 'thin ice' financially, that the Union's 'only weapon is to strike,' " and that a strike " 'could lead to the closing of the plant,' since the parent company had ample manufacturing facilities elsewhere." *Id.* at 588. He also observed that " 'because of their age and the limited usefulness of their skills outside their craft, the employees might not be able to find re-employment if they lost their jobs as a result of a strike.' " *Id.* Finally, he "warned those who did not believe that the plant could go out of business to 'look around Holyoke and see a lot of them out of business.' " *Id.* In the two or three week period preceding the election, the president prepared and distributed a pamphlet captioned: " 'Do you want another 13-week strike?' "and predicting that the union would be likely to call a strike and close the plant. Two days prior to the election, the Company distributed a pamphlet entitled: " 'Let's Look at the Record,' " which purported to be "an obituary of companies in the Holyoke-Springfield, Massachusetts area that had allegedly gone out of business because of union demands, eliminating some 3,500 jobs; the first page carried a large cartoon showing the preparation of a grave for the Sinclair Company and other headstones containing the names of other plants allegedly victimized by the unions." *Id.* Finally, "the day before the election, the president made another personal appeal to his employees to reject the Union. He repeated that the Company's financial condition was precarious; that a possible strike would jeopardize the continued operation of the plant; and that age and lack of education would make re-employment difficult." The union lost the election. *Id.* at 588–89.

The Court ruled that although the First Amendment and § 8(c) protect the employer's right to speak to its employees, the context of the labor relations setting and the need to give full effect to the employees' § 7 rights to organize a union necessitated a balancing of interests. The Court explained:

> [A]ny balancing of those rights must take into account the economic dependence of the employees on their employers, and the necessary tendency of the former, because of that relationship, to pick up intended implications of the latter that might be more readily dismissed by a more

disinterested ear. Stating these obvious principles is but another way of recognizing that what is basically at stake is the establishment of a nonpermanent, limited relationship between the employer, his economically dependent employee and his union agent, not the election of legislators or the enactment of legislation whereby that relationship is ultimately defined and where the independent voter may be freer to listen more objectively and employers as a class freer to talk.

Id. at 617–18. The Court established the following rule:

[A]n employer is free to communicate to his employees any of his general views about unionism or any of his specific views about a particular union, so long as the communications do not contain a "threat of reprisal or force or promise of benefit." He may even make a prediction as to the precise effects he believes unionization will have on his company. In such a case, however, the prediction must be carefully phrased on the basis of objective fact to convey an employer's belief as to demonstrably probable consequences beyond his control or to convey a management decision already arrived at to close the plant in case of unionization. *See Textile Workers v. Darlington Mfg. Co.*, 380 U.S. 263, 274, n. 20 (1965). If there is any implication that an employer may or may not take action solely on his own initiative for reasons unrelated to economic necessities and known only to him, the statement is no longer a reasonable prediction based on available facts but a threat of retaliation based on misrepresentation and coercion, and as such without the protection of the First Amendment. . . . [A]n employer is free only to tell "what he reasonably believes will be the likely economic consequences of unionization that are outside his control" and not "threats of economic reprisal to be taken solely on his own volition." . . .

Id. at 618–19.

NOTE

The Prevalence of Threats to Close. The *Gissel* rule that threats to close are prohibited but predictions as to the economic consequences of unionization that are beyond the employer's control are permissible has proved very difficult to administer and has furnished the basis for many unfair labor practice charges. Employer threats to close all or part of a plant are one of the most common strategies utilized in modern anti-union campaigns. The most frequently cited study found that 57% of all employers made threats to shut down or move their businesses in response to union organizing activity. *See* Kate Bronfenbrenner, *No Holds Barred: The Intensification of Employer Opposition to Organizing* 1–2 (Econ. Pol'y Inst., Briefing Paper No. 235, 2009). The threat rate is even higher—68%—where the industry is mobile and the threat is therefore most credible (industries such as manufacturing, communication, and wholesale/distribution). *See* Kate Bronfenbrenner, *Uneasy Terrain: The Impact of Capital Mobility on Workers, Wages, and Union Organizing*, Report to the U.S. Trade Deficit Review Commission, Sept. 6, 2000. The 2000 study also found that threats of plant closing are extremely effective: unions win 38% of elections where plant closing threats are made, compared with 51% when threats are not made.

Interestingly, threats were unrelated to the financial condition of the company, with threats just as likely to occur from businesses in stable financial condition as from those on the edge of bankruptcy. Employers followed through on the threats in fewer than 3% of the campaigns where threats were made; most threats were motivated primarily by anti-union hostility. *Id.*

3. Plant Closings Where the Workforce Is Already Unionized

What, if any, role should unions play in the decision whether to close a plant? Does it matter why the employer is considering closing the operation? Must an already unionized, financially troubled employer consult with its union to attempt to reduce labor costs and avoid employment losses? Though the Court at first seemed inclined to treat the unionized employees and the employer as partners in the operation of the business, it later reaffirmed its understanding of the employer as the owner of the business and the employees as "junior partners" in the enterprise.

In *Fibreboard Paper Products Corp. v. NLRB*, 379 U.S. 203 (1964), the Court ruled that a unionized employer was obligated to bargain with the union representing its employees prior to making decisions to contract out work being performed by employees in the bargaining unit in an effort to effect labor cost savings. The Court enforced the Labor Board's order requiring the employer to "reinstitute the maintenance operation previously performed by the employees represented by the Union, to reinstate the employees to their former or substantially equivalent positions with back pay computed from the date of the Board's supplemental decision, and to fulfill its statutory obligation to bargain." *Id.* at 208. The Court reasoned:

> Industrial experience is not only reflective of the interests of labor and management in the subject matter but is also indicative of the amenability of such subjects to the collective bargaining process. Experience illustrates that contracting out in one form or another has been brought, widely and successfully, within the collective bargaining framework. Provisions relating to contracting out exist in numerous collective bargaining agreements, and "(c)ontracting out work is the basis of many grievances; and that type of claim is grist in the mills of the arbitrators." . . .

> While "the Act does not encourage a party to engage in fruitless marathon discussions at the expense of frank statement and support of his position," it at least demands that the issue be submitted to the mediatory influence of collective negotiations. As the Court of Appeals pointed out, "[i]t is not necessary that it be likely or probable that the union will yield or supply a feasible solution but rather that the union be afforded an opportunity to meet management's legitimate complaints that its maintenance was unduly costly."

Id. at 211–12, 214.

Concurring Justices Stewart, Douglas, and Harlan emphasized the limits of the Court's decision:

The question posed is whether the particular decision sought to be made unilaterally by the employer in this case is a subject of mandatory collective bargaining within the statutory phrase "terms and conditions of employment." That is all the Court decides. The Court most assuredly does not decide that every managerial decision which necessarily terminates an individual's employment is subject to the duty to bargain. Nor does the Court decide that subcontracting decisions are as a general matter subject to that duty. The Court holds no more than that this employer's decision to subcontract this work, involving "the replacement of employees in the existing bargaining unit with those of an independent contractor to do the same work under similar conditions of employment," is subject to the duty to bargain collectively. . . .

While employment security has thus properly been recognized in various circumstances as a condition of employment, it surely does not follow that every decision which may affect job security is a subject of compulsory collective bargaining. Many decisions made by management affect the job security of employees. Decisions concerning the volume and kind of advertising expenditures, product design, the manner of financing, and sales, all may bear upon the security of the workers' jobs. Yet it is hardly conceivable that such decisions so involve "conditions of employment" that they must be negotiated with the employees' bargaining representative.

Id. at 218, 233.

During the recessionary era of the 1980s, the Court adopted Justice Stewart's vision of the NLRA as continuing the common law tradition of the dominant-servient relation, ruling that the NLRA did not impair employer property rights to manage and control the operation and direction of the business unfettered by obligations to bargain with the union. In *First National Maintenance Corp. v. NLRB*, 452 U.S. 666 (1981), the Court refused to require a unionized employer to bargain over its decision to terminate a contract with a customer (Greenpark) even though the decision necessitated job loss for the employees who performed work pursuant to that contract. The employer's only obligation under the NLRA was to bargain with the union over the *effects* of the decision to close its business. The Court explained:

[I]n establishing what issues must be submitted to the process of bargaining, Congress had no expectation that the elected union representative would become an equal partner in the running of the business enterprise in which the union's members are employed. Despite the deliberate open-endedness of the statutory language, there is an undeniable limit to the subjects about which bargaining must take place. . . .

Some management decisions, such as choice of advertising and promotion, product type and design, and financing arrangements, have only an indirect and attenuated impact on the employment relationship. *See Fibreboard*, 379 U.S., at 223 (STEWART, J., concurring). Other management decisions, such as the order of succession of layoffs and recalls, production quotas, and work rules, are almost exclusively "an aspect of the relationship" between employer and employee. . . . The present case concerns a third type of management decision, one that had a direct impact on employment, since jobs were inexorably eliminated by the termination, but had as its focus only the economic profitability of the contract with Greenpark, a concern under these facts wholly apart from the employment relationship. This decision, involving a change in the scope and direction of the enterprise, is akin to the decision whether to be in business at all, "not in [itself] primarily about conditions of employment, though the effect of the decision may be necessarily to terminate employment." Fibreboard, 379 U.S., at 223 (STEWART, J., concurring). Cf. Textile Workers v. Darlington Co., 380 U.S. 263, 268 (1965) ("an employer has the absolute right to terminate his entire business for any reason he pleases"). At the same time, this decision touches on a matter of central and pressing concern to the union and its member employees: the possibility of continued employment and the retention of the employees' very jobs. . . .

Management must be free from the constraints of the bargaining process to the extent essential for the running of a profitable business. It also must have some degree of certainty beforehand as to when it may proceed to reach decisions without fear of later evaluations labeling its conduct an unfair labor practice. Congress did not explicitly state what issues of mutual concern to union and management it intended to exclude from mandatory bargaining. Nonetheless, in view of an employer's need for unencumbered decision-making, bargaining over management decisions that have a substantial impact on the continued availability of employment should be required only if the benefit, for labor-management relations and the collective-bargaining process, outweighs the burden placed on the conduct of the business. . . .

We conclude that the harm likely to be done to an employer's need to operate freely in deciding whether to shut down part of its business purely for economic reasons outweighs the incremental benefit that might be gained through the union's participation in making the decision. . . .

Id. at 676–79, 686. Dissenting Justices Brennan and Marshall criticized the Court's analysis as "one-sided," noting that such a vision of the employment relation was not congruent with the expressed philosophy of the NLRA: " 'to foster in a neutral manner' a system for resolution of these serious, two-sided controversies." Id. at 689–90.

Finally, where a collective bargaining agreement contains provisions that limit the employer's rights to close or to subcontract out work, the agreement itself can furnish the basis for injunctive relief or a damage award in a breach of contract action by the union against the employer. In Local 461, International Union of Electrical, Radio & Machine Workers v. Singer Co., 540 F. Supp. 442 (D.N.J. 1982), the court ruled in favor of the union on its Labor Management Relations Act § 301 claim against Singer for breach of the labor contract. Singer had announced its plan to close a sewing machine manufacturing plant in New Jersey. The union that represented the workers at the plant brought an action in federal district court for breach of the collective bargaining agreement, in which Singer had promised to invest $2 million to restructure the plant in exchange for union "give-backs" (agreements by the union to relinquish benefits it had obtained in previous contracts and to alter incentive standards to increase productivity) and to use its best efforts to obtain government contracts which would facilitate keeping the plant open. Although the court refused the union's request for an injunction restraining Singer from closing the plant, it did award the plaintiffs monetary damages measured by the value of the union "give-backs" or the $2 million that Singer promised to invest but did not, whichever was greater. *Id.* at 450. The court cited *First National Maintenance Corp. v. NLRB* in support of its conclusion that the company had not relinquished its right to determine whether to close parts of its business for economic reasons. *Id.* at 448. Absent express waiver, management retains the right to discontinue operations. *Id.*

Similarly, in *District Lodge 26, Int'l Ass'n of Machinists & Aerospace Workers v. United Techs. Corp.*, 610 F.3d 44 (2d Cir. 2010), the Second Circuit affirmed a district court order granting the union injunctive relief where the company had breached a provision in a letter of agreement incorporated into its collective bargaining contract with the union in which it promised to make "every reasonable effort" to preserve work within the bargaining unit. The court's order barred the company from implementing a planned shutdown of the facilities covered by the labor contract until the expiration of the labor agreement—but not beyond it. The same limitation was applied by the Seventh Circuit in *UAW v. ZF Boge Elastmetall LLC*, 649 F.3d 641 (7th Cir. 2011), where union members agreed to concessions (freezing their pension plan and reducing working hours) in order to make the plant more competitive and avoid plant closures: absent an explicit provision to that effect, the agreement did not extend beyond the term of the labor contract.

NOTES

1. **The Decline of Unions and the Rise of Collective Job Insecurity.** What role should unions or alternative vehicles for employee representation play in protecting employee job security? In the following excerpt, Charles Craver suggests that the decline in union density is responsible for the collective job insecurity that has become the modern cultural norm. Craver argues that the broader public interest demands legislative action to protect worker voice. He recommends the adoption of federal legislation mandating the creation of worker participation programs parallel to those used in Germany, France, the Netherlands, and Sweden (known as works councils) to substitute for unions and implementation of a more cooperative approach in which employee representatives would possess "consultation rights" on matters of employee interest, enforceable via injunctive relief in the federal courts, but no rights to collectively bargain or to strike:

> Over the past ten to fifteen years, downsizing has become an organizational mantra for many corporate leaders, resulting in the layoff of millions of American workers. Some of these firm reductions have been required by economic exigencies and/or changing consumer demands. When true business factors dictate employer restructuring, it would be irresponsible to argue in favor of the continued employment of superfluous workers. Such an approach would jeopardize the continued viability of the company and the future positions of the other employees. This reality does not mean,

however, that worker interests should be ignored when these decisions are being made. Board members and CEOs should be legally obligated to consider non-layoff cost-reduction options before they decide to implement significant reductions. Even when layoffs are necessary, firm officials should be required to soften the impact of these reductions on the affected personnel. Retraining and relocation possibilities should be explored to determine whether loyal employees could be transferred to other useful positions. Severance packages could cushion the adverse consequences for individuals who must actually lose their jobs. . . .

The contemporary corporation is no longer a wholly private entity that primarily affects a limited group of shareholders, customers, employees, and the contiguous community. Large domestic and transnational enterprises have a "profound effect on the lives of a variety of groups not traditionally within the corporate law structure." By expanding the fiduciary duties of corporate leaders to at least include those most directly affected by fundamental company changes, Congress or state legislatures could greatly enhance the public interest. When wholly selfish decisions are made that ignore appropriate constituent interests, legal liability should be imposed.

Charles B. Craver, *The American Worker: Junior Partner in Success and Senior Partner in Failure*, 37 U.S.F. L. REV. 587, 587–90, 620–21 (2003). Do you agree? Will establishing vehicles for worker voice and mandating consultation be effective, or is a more radical restructuring of property rights in the employment context required? We discuss works councils and other employee representation mechanisms further in Chapter 15.

2. Union Efficacy in Protecting Workers Impacted by Mass Layoffs in an Economic Downturn. Are unionized workers any better off than nonunion workers in an economic downturn of global proportions? Consider the following scenario. On December 3, 2008 unionized workers at Republic Windows & Doors in Chicago were notified that the business would close down on December 5th. The company cited cancellation of its line of credit due to cash flow problems, and "limited options for sales in the stalled residential construction market." The union assisted workers in filing a WARN Act charge and also filed unfair labor practice charges with the National Labor Relations Board, arguing that the company had closed the factory and relocated the work to a newly formed operation in Iowa in order to avoid its collective bargaining commitments. Meanwhile, the workers staged a six-day sit-in at the factory in an attempt to pressure the company into reopening the plant and paying compensation due them under the WARN Act. Although Republic did not reopen the plant, the sit-in is credited with leading the Bank of America and JP Morgan Chase to make credit commitments that enabled Republic to fully compensate the workers for wages owed under the WARN Act, avoiding litigation and its attendant costs and delays. *See Republic Windows Workers' Union Files ULP Charges over Firm's Failure to Bargain*, DAILY LAB. REP. (BNA) No. 3, Jan. 7, 2009, at A-9. The presence of a union clearly facilitated organization of the sit-in that obtained publicity that ultimately led to a successful resolution of the workers' WARN Act claims, but it did not protect workers from the plant closure itself. The story had a happy ending for the workers, however: the union was later able to negotiate an arrangement with the new purchaser of the former Republic Windows and Doors plant, a company called Serious Materials, to rehire the laid-off workers to produce energy-efficient building materials at the old plant. *See Biden Comes to Town*, Chicago Trib., Apr. 28, 2009, at 10.

The experience of unionized workers in the auto industry has also been instructive on the efficacy of unions in turbulent economic times. The government conditioned the receipt of bailout monies for troubled automobile manufacturers upon renegotiation of the manufacturers' labor contracts, with significant concessions required of the United Auto Workers Union on behalf of the workers. While nearly all commentators agree that this was essential in order to prevent collapse of the American automobile manufacturing industry, the renegotiation requirement raises serious questions about the continuing viability of the collective bargaining model in industries dependent upon government aid and thus, subject to government controls. *See* Stephen Labaton & David M. Herszenhorn, *White House Ready to Aid Auto Industry*, N.Y. Times, Dec. 12, 2008.

3. **Communal Rights vs. Individual Rights.** American law is premised on the language of individual rights, which are "owned" by individuals. The NLRA, specifically § 7, seeks to protect communal rights. If given full effect at law, communal rights would yield a society structured very differently than our present system. Consider the following ruminations by Staughton Lynd, lawyer for the plaintiffs in the *Local 1330, United Steel Workers* case in Section A:

> [T]he conventional view implicitly assumes that the supply of rights is finite, and thus that "right" is a scarce commodity. In this view the assertion of one person's right is likely to impinge on and diminish the rights of others. . . . If we desire a society in which we share life as a common creation and genuinely care for each other's needs, then this rhetoric, which pictures us as separated owners of our respective bundles of rights, stands as an obstacle. . . .

> I suggest that the right of workers "to engage in concerted activities for . . . mutual aid or protection" now guaranteed by federal labor law is an example of a communal right. More than any other institution in capitalist society, the labor movement is based on communal values. Its central historical experience is solidarity, the banding together of individual workers who are alone too weak to protect themselves. Thus, there has arisen the value expressed by the phrase, "an injury to one is an injury to all." . . .

> This distinctive experience of solidarity, underlying the right to engage in concerted activity, has three unusual attributes. First, the well-being of the individual and the well-being of the group are not experienced as antagonistic. . . . Second, the group of those who work together—the informal work group, the department, the local union, the class—is often experienced as a reality in itself. . . . I do not scratch your back only because one day I may need you to scratch mine. Labor solidarity is more than an updated version of the social contract through which each individual undertakes to assist others for the advancement of his or her own interest.

In a family, when I as son, husband, or father, express love toward you, I do not do so in order to assure myself of love in return. I do not help my son in order to be able to claim assistance from him when I am old; I do it because he and I are in the world together; we are one flesh. Similarly in a workplace, persons who work together form families-at-work. When you and I are working together, and the foreman suddenly discharges you, and I find myself putting down my tools or stopping my machine before I have had time to think—why do I do this? Is it not because, as I actually experience the event, your discharge does not happen only to you but also happens to *us*? . . .

The right to engage in concerted activity for mutual aid or protection is the paradigm communal right. Neither a narrowly individual nor a merely collective right, it is a right derived from the actual character of working-class solidarity and accordingly a right that foreshadows a society in which group life and individual self-realization mutually reinforce each other.

Staughton Lynd, *Communal Rights*, 62 TEX. L. REV. 1417, 1423–30 (1984). What difference would recognition of communal rights make in the plant closing context? Does Lynd's description of NLRA rights as "communal" rights unique at law help to explain the uneasy fit between labor law and the evolving system of employment law rights as individual rights?

4. A Role for Law in Market Restructuring? The larger question is whether the law can or should play any role in curbing the economic restructuring of the labor market. Where entire sectors of the economy are disappearing due to technology or are being outsourced to other countries where the work can be done more cheaply or efficiently, is it desirable for law to intervene to protect against job losses occasioned by those shifts? What if the effect of those shifts is to eliminate the middle class? Will intervention impair the ability of the U.S. to compete at a global level? *See* Brad Plummer, *Here's Where Middle-Class Jobs Are Vanishing the Fastest*, WASH. POST, Aug. 27, 2013 (charting drop in manufacturing, construction, and other blue collar trades that featured relatively high pay and benefits, and linking it to the decline in the middle class); *see generally* WORKING AND LIVING IN THE SHADOW OF ECONOMIC FRAGILITY (MARION CRAIN & MICHAEL SHERRADEN eds., 2014) (analyzing causes of economic insecurity for working families and arguing for market intervention through law and policy reform).

D. THE UNEMPLOYMENT INSURANCE SYSTEM

The structural response to job loss for economic reasons in the United States is the unemployment insurance system (UI). Unemployment insurance was introduced in response to the rampant unemployment of the Great Depression. Title III of the Social Security Act of 1935, 42 U.S.C. §§ 501–504, and the companion Federal Unemployment Tax Act ("FUTA") established a joint state and federal unemployment insurance program that provides workers with up to 26 weeks of partial wage replacement in qualifying job loss situations. Federally funded supplemental benefits are made available in periods of national recession through emergency unemployment compensation programs (the most recent of these was effective from July 2008 to January 2014). Financed by a payroll tax levied on employers and linked to a firm-level experience rating based on the employer's history of layoffs, the system aims to encourage employers to provide more stable employment and provides a stopgap for employees who possess some attachment to the workforce (as opposed to transient or temporary workers), who lose jobs through no fault of their own, and who actively seek and remain available for work. U.S. Dep't of Labor, *Unemployment Compensation: Federal-State Partnership* 1–2, 11–12 (April 2014). The system is administered at the state level; eligibility requirements and the amount of unemployment insurance benefits to which an employee is entitled vary from state to state.

Once an individual is deemed eligible to receive UI benefits, the amount he or she is entitled to receive will vary depending upon the worker's income level. Most states use a "base period" consisting of earnings during the first four of the last five quarters as a basis for calculating benefits and as a rough proxy for workforce attachment. A worker earning the minimum during the base period could be eligible for as little as $30–40 dollars a week. *See, e.g.,* CAL. UNEMP. INS. CODE 1281(c)(3) (listing California's minimum benefit amount of $40); 43 PA. CONST. STAT. ANN. § 804(e)(1) (listing Pennsylvania's minimum benefit amount of $35). States replace, on average, 50% of a worker's pre-unemployment earnings, up to a limit of the average weekly wage in the state. In almost all states, workers can collect "extended benefits" beyond the standard 26 week period for up to 13 additional weeks during periods of high unemployment (many states automatically extend the benefit period once unemployment rates in the state reach specified levels). U.S. Dep't of Labor, *Unemployment Compensation: Federal-State Partnership* 2, 12.

As you read the following excerpt and notes describing the purpose and function of the UI system, consider whether it is responsive to the challenges faced by cities like Youngstown or to the larger societal dilemma of entire industries that fail.

Gillian Lester, *The Unemployment Insurance and Wealth Redistribution*
49 UCLA L. REV. 335, 341–43 (2001)

[Unemployment insurance] was designed to help workers maintain an accustomed standard of living. UI was intended to smooth workers' income over time, assuming it would be difficult or impossible to borrow against future earnings to maintain income stability or to save during periods of unemployment. Because then, as now, few American workers had significant savings or income from sources other than wages, UI would be an important way to reduce the hardship of wage interruption. In contrast to general relief (welfare), a worker would not have to wait until savings and resources were exhausted before being eligible for a cash payment. Although UI benefits would only partially replace wages, they would still reduce the net depletion of personal resources (as well as unpaid bills, cutbacks on spending, new debt, and so on) caused by unemployment.

Although UI was designed as a poverty-fighting device, it was not intended as a form of aid to poor Americans per se. Insofar as eligibility required no proof of the threat of imminent poverty—the system is not means-tested—it recognized the pure harm of downward mobility. Further still, much of the rhetoric surrounding passage of the legislation, albeit partly driven by political expediency, augured that

purpose of UI

UI would preserve the dignity of working people who lost their jobs by distinguishing them from welfare recipients. In addition, because a worker had to lose his job without fault in order to claim benefits, receiving UI would not, in theory, signify a failure of personal responsibility.

Unemployment insurance was also very much part of a broader program of Keynesian demand stabilization: Injecting money into the economy through unemployment benefits would stimulate the economy during recessions by minimizing troughs in consumer spending, thus slowing the progress of economic downturns. Employers would be deterred from laying off workers through firm-level experience rating, and labor supply would be stimulated directly through public sector job creation, training subsidies, relocation subsidies, and the like.

Finally, the program was intended to optimize workers' ability to find jobs that fully utilize their skills and experience, thus preventing skill erosion and tapping labor power as fully as possible. While the payment of a weekly benefit might delay a recipient's return to work, the reason for that delay would not necessarily be because the worker preferred leisure, even at a reduced income, to work. The delay would also, in theory, give him an opportunity to engage in a more rigorous job search. Rather than having to take the first job that came along just in order to make ends meet, the worker could hold out for a job better matched to his skills and training. Optimizing job matches upon reemployment would also, in theory, minimize career interruptions. Moreover, UI made it easier for at least short-term laid off workers to remain in the area in the event that rehiring would be possible upon recovery. Productivity gains through workforce retention were seen to offset the concomitant dampening of worker mobility.

In essence, then, the United States' system of public provision, that is, the social safety net, was structured as a two-tiered system: UI was designed for workers with stable labor market attachment, without regard to their means, and welfare was designed for workers lacking attachment, and it was based on means.

NOTES

1. **Unemployment Insurance vs. Welfare.** What is the significance of the dichotomy between need-based aid (welfare) and non-need-based aid (UI)? Consider Kenneth Casebeer's explanation of the ideology that drove the creation of the unemployment insurance program:

> Unemployment compensation was to be a limited benefit; it applied only to certain people, under prescribed circumstances, for a limited period of time. Its beneficiaries were deserving because they had a history of employment, were willing to work, and were not to blame for their current joblessness. Unemployment insurance was to be distinguished from public relief or the dole; the benefits were earned entitlements because the money paid out during times of idleness had been specifically set aside for that purpose during times of employment. Finally, the right to the benefit, because it was earned, vested at a time a worker became unemployed. The government applied no means test and the worker made no showing of need.

Kenneth M. Casebeer, *Unemployment Insurance: American Social Wage, Labor Organization, and Legal Ideology*, 35 B.C. L. REV. 259, 313–14 (1994). Despite the fact that most workers in a sense "earn" UI coverage during the periods in which they are employed, only 38% of unemployed workers actually collect benefits. U.S. Department of Labor, *Unemployment Insurance Data Summary, First Quarter 2014*, *available at* http://ows.doleta.gov/unemploy/content/data_stats/datasum14/DataSum_2014_1.pdf. Why do you think that might be?

2. **The Workforce Attachment Requirement for Eligibility.** Unemployment insurance targets workers with a stable attachment to the workforce; these workers are understood as having "earned" the benefits through some minimum level of prior workforce participation. States use either an income threshold or an hours worked threshold to filter out workers who possess a weak labor market affiliation. New entrants to the workforce, intermittent workers, and workers with very low wages or hours tend to be excluded. *See* Lester, *supra*, at 346–47. Under California law, for example, a worker must have earned at least $1,300 dollars in one of the calendar quarters of the base period, or earned at least $900 dollars in one of the first four of the last five calendar quarters and a total of $1,125 over those quarters. *See* CAL. UNEMP. INS. CODE §§ 1275, 1281. In other states, an employee might need to earn a higher or lower threshold amount, or have been employed in a certain number of quarters of the base period in order to be eligible for UI. *See* U.S. Dep't of Labor, *Comparison of State Unemployment Laws* Ch. 3, at 5–7 (2014), *available at* http://workforcesecurity.doleta.gov/unemploy/comparison2014.asp.

3. **Good Cause for Separation from Employment.** Employees who leave their jobs voluntarily, without work-related "good cause" or who are discharged for misconduct are not eligible for UI benefits. Gillian Lester explains how the good cause determination is made under most state laws:

> In contrast to the employer-centered construction of good cause in wrongful termination law, good cause for purposes of UI eligibility focuses on the employee, asking whether the separation is truly involuntary. The standard notion of good cause is a reason "related to" or "attributable to" work (which typically means the result of an employer's layoff decision, hazardous working conditions, a transfer to unsuitable work, or a unilateral change of working conditions such as wages or hours by the employer). Most states also recognize a limited range of additional reasons, which might variously include sexual harassment, domestic violence, compulsory retirement, leaving to accept other work (but the new job unexpectedly falls through), illness, and joining the armed forces. Workers who voluntarily leave their employment without good cause must typically work some period of time in order to restore eligibility. Misconduct will disqualify a worker as well. Misconduct must generally be "willful" (or result from persistent negligence). Examples include violations of company rules, insubordination, refusal to perform assigned work, impermissible absences, and testing positive for drug use. Inability to perform the requirements of the job generally does not disqualify a worker.

Id. at 350.

What about personal or family reasons that are not related to work? In most states, workers who quit their jobs because of family-related obligations (caring for an elder parent or ill spouse, having and caring for children, moving to follow a spouse's job, etc.) will be deemed to have quit voluntarily, for personal rather than work-related reasons—and thus will be ineligible for UI benefits. *Id.* at 350–51; *see* U.S. Dep't of Labor, *Comparison of State Unemployment Laws*, Ch. 5, at 2–9 (2014), *available at* http://workforcesecurity.doleta.gov/unemploy/comparison2014.asp.

State standards differ significantly on what constitutes "cause," however, and an increasing number of states provide greater protection for employees. The Assistance for Unemployed Workers and Struggling Families Act, part of the American Recovery and Reinvestment Act of 2009, Pub. L. 111-5, established an incentive system for states that make certain changes and improvements to their UI systems. Among other things, the incentive payments encourage states to amend eligibility requirements so that individuals who must leave work for "compelling family reasons," such as an illness in the family, domestic abuse, or sexual assault, can still qualify for benefits. *Id.* at § 1103(f)(3)(B). A number of states responded with reforms. *See* Nat'l Employment Law Project, *Federal Stimulus Funding Produces Unprecedented Wave of State Unemployment Insurance Reforms* 6 (Dec. 2, 2009).

4. Availability for Work. Recall that in order to remain UI eligible, a worker must actively seek suitable re-employment and must remain available for work. But what is "suitable" work? States utilize various criteria to evaluate job suitability, including compatibility with the claimant's prior experience, training, and earnings, the job's distance from the claimant's home; the prospects for securing work of that type in the locality; and the length of unemployment. Typically, it is work with equivalent wages, hours, or working conditions to the job that was lost or to similar jobs in the locality (i.e., the employee need not accept a substantially less favorable employment circumstance or move to another locale to find work). Claimants must register at regional offices and document their searches.

5. Low Wage and Part-Time Workers. Studies by the Government Accountability Office reveal that low-wage workers are at least twice as likely to be unemployed as their higher-wage counterparts, yet they are half as likely to receive UI benefits. *See* Gov't Accountability Office, GAO Rep. No. 12-408, *Unemployment Insurance: Economic Circumstances of Individuals Who Exhausted Benefits*, at 10 (Feb. 17, 2012); Gov't Accountability Office, GAO Rep. No. 07-1243T, *Unemployment Insurance: Receipt of Benefits Has Declined, with Continued Disparities for Low-Wage and Part-Time Workers*, at 6–7 (Sept. 19, 2007). What accounts for this disparity? First, lower-wage workers lacking specialized skills are likely more fungible, and the industries in which lower-wage workers are employed are more sensitive to economic fluctuations. Indeed, 32.8% of unemployed low-wage workers in the earlier GAO study came from retail trades, compared to only 12.8% for higher-wage workers. GAO Rep. No. 07-1243T, *Unemployment Insurance: Receipt of Benefits Has Declined, supra*, at 8. These factors account for their higher unemployment rates. Second, lower-wage workers are less likely to meet the state law eligibility rules, including earnings thresholds (particularly if they are part-time) and reasons for separating from work (particularly family care obligations that negate eligibility). *Id.* at 11. Third, lower-wage workers are likely to have lower levels of education, are less likely to be represented by a union and thus are less likely to be aware of their rights to claim UI and equipped to navigate the system. *Id.* at 4, 11. Finally, many states do not consider individuals eligible for UI benefits if they are only available for part-time employment. *Id.* at 12. Such persons are counted as unemployed for purposes of the unemployment rate statistics, however, since the Bureau of Labor Statistics makes no distinction between full- and part-time workers when computing the unemployment rate. The Assistance for Unemployed Workers and Struggling Families Act erected incentives designed to encourage states to ease access to benefits for part-time workers. *See* Pub. L. 111-5 at § 1103(f)(3)(A).

6.   **Short-Time Compensation.** In an effort to help businesses struggling as a result of the recent recession to stay open and avoid displacing workers, in 2012 the Department of Labor began promoting short-time compensation programs at the state level to support work-sharing practices. Work-sharing is a strategy in which an employer facing reduced demand for its product or dealing with significantly reduced profits reduces operating costs by cutting work hours for an entire group of employees rather than laying off some and maintaining others on a full-time basis. Short-time compensation extends partial unemployment compensation benefits to those whose hours are reduced from full-time to part-time on the same job. Benefits are payable for hours of work lost as a proportion of the benefit amount that would have been due for a full week, within an hours-reduction range of 10% to 60%. States whose short-time compensation programs conform to standards established by the Department of Labor are eligible for federal funding pursuant to the Middle Class Tax Relief and Job Creation Act of 2012, Pub. L. 112-96, 126 Stat. 156. By 2014, 28 states offered short-time compensation. U.S. Dep't of Labor, *Unemployment Compensation: Federal-State Partnership* 1–2, 11–12 (April 2014). Short-time compensation programs are modeled on "short work" programs that were in place in some European countries including the Netherlands, Germany, and Austria and which helped them to weather the recession; scholars and activists had been calling for reform of U.S. laws to support such programs. *See* Marion Crain, *Work Matters*, 19 KAN. J. L. & PUB. POL'Y 365, 377–79 (2010); Neil Ridley, *Work Sharing—An Alternative to Layoffs for Tough Times*, CENTER FOR LAW AND SOCIAL POLICY, Mar. 26, 2009, *available at* http://www.clasp.org/admin/site/publications/files/0481.pdf.

7.   **The "Great" Recession, Unemployment Rates, and Rising Long-Term Unemployment.** The recent economic recession sent unemployment rates skyrocketing from 4.7 % at the end of 2007 to 10% by the end of 2009. Rates fell gradually over the next several years to around 6% in 2014. U.S. Department of Labor, Bureau of Labor Statistics, *available at* http://data.bls.gov/timeseries/LNS14000000. Unemployment rates in many states—particularly those in the Midwest which were hardest hit by the decline of the manufacturing sector—were considerably higher at the worst point in the recession and continue to be elevated. *See* Bureau of Labor Statistics, *Regional and State Employment and Unemployment—November 2009*, USDL-09-1535 (Dec. 18, 2009), at 2, 5 (reporting unemployment rate of 14.7 % for Michigan in 2009); Bureau of Labor Statistics, *Local Area Unemployment Statistics*, *available at* http://www.bls.gov/web/laus/laumstrk.htm (reporting unemployment rate of 7.7% for Michigan by 2014). The

recession was also especially hard for those at the bottom of the income strata, who suffered unemployment rates that rivaled or exceeded those of the Great Depression. *See* Andrew Sum *et al., Labor Underutilization Problems of U.S. Workers Across Household Income Groups at the End of the Great Recession: A Truly Great Depression Among the Nation's Low Income Workers Amidst Full Employment Among the Most Affluent,* Center for Labor Market Studies, Northeastern University, Feb. 2010, at 8, *available at* http://www.clms.neu.edu/publication/documents/Labor_Underutilization_Problems_of_U.pdf (reporting that unemployment rate during the fourth quarter of 2009 was 30.8 % for households with income of under $12,500, 19.1% for households with earnings between $12,500 and $20,000, compared with rate of 3.2% for those earning $150,000 or more and 4% for those earning between $100,000 and $150,000). Younger workers ages 16–24 were also hard-hit, with the jobless rate for them soaring to 19% in 2009. Larry Swisher, *Youth Faring Poorly in Job Market, as Older Workers Delay Retirement,* DAILY LAB. REP. (BNA) No. 146, July 29, 2011.

A "hallmark" of the recent recession and the nation's recovery has been an increase in long-term unemployment, defined as those searching for work for greater than six months. Joint Economic Committee, *Long-Term Unemployment in the United States,* (April 2013), *available at* http://www.jec.senate.gov/public/?a=Files.Serve&File_id=ee31ad2d-5eb0-4f60-a852-87a27d559457. In July 2014, the U.S. Bureau of Labor Statistics estimated that 9.7 million persons were unemployed; of those workers, almost one-third, 3.2 million, had been jobless for more than 27 weeks. News Release, U.S. Bureau of Labor Statistics, *The Employment Situation—July 2014, available at* http://www.bls.gov/news.release/pdf/empsit.pdf. The current UI system assumes that most people will experience short-term unemployment. Is UI an adequate response when unemployment rates remain high for extended periods of time? When an industry disappears due to mechanization of processes formerly performed by workers? When entire industries are outsourced to other countries? What other relief or programs might assist the unemployed and their families, who are only eligible to receive a fraction of their former income through the UI system? *See* Nelson D. Schwartz, *Jobless and Staying That Way,* N.Y. TIMES, Aug. 8, 2010 (raising these questions and noting proposals for government investment in infrastructure projects to put people to work and stimulate demand, and for expanded job training programs).

8. **Job Training Programs for Long-Term Unemployed.** A few states have experimented with programs that supplement the UI system with on-the-job training for unemployed workers who receive UI benefits. For example, the "Georgia Works" program gives individuals the option of participating in an eight-week training period with an employer. The employer pays nothing; the worker receives a small stipend from the state plus workers' compensation coverage. The training program is designed to help unemployed workers develop skills that might assist them in finding new employment, and to give workers the opportunity to cultivate a relationship with an employer who might offer them employment after the training period, although there is no obligation for the employer to hire the trainee. In the first six years of its existence, the program grew rapidly and appeared to be quite successful: about 35% of the unemployed workers who completed the eight-week training period were offered a job by the employer

with whom they trained. Due to a change in administration at the Georgia Department of Labor, the program was reduced in size and scope. Julie M. Whittaker, *Expediting the Return to Work: Approaches in the Unemployment Compensation Program* at 27–28, May 1, 2013 (Congressional Research Service Report No. 7-5700), *available at* www.http://fas.org/sgp/crs/misc/R43044.pdf. President Obama proposed a similar program at the federal level in the American Jobs Act of 2011. The so-called "Bridge to Work" program would have encouraged other states to develop training programs aimed at the long-term unemployed. *See* Gayle Cinquegrani, *Union Seeks Audit of Georgia Works Program That Is Model for Obama's Jobs Proposal*, DAILY LAB. REP. (BNA) No. 177, Sept. 13, 2011. Though the Act did not pass, Congress did make available funding for demonstration projects in 10 states pursuant to the Middle Class Tax Relief and Job Creation Act of 2012, and the Department of Labor issued guidelines for these projects. *U.S. Department of Labor Announces Opportunity for States to Develop Innovative Demonstrations of Reemployment Strategies*, April 19, 2012, *available at* http://www.dol.gov/opa/media/press/eta/ETA20120769.htm.

On the one hand, it seems this type of program would help unemployed workers develop new skills and obtain references which might assist them in finding new employment. On the other hand, however, participating in such a program might detract from an individual's employment search and the program itself might discourage employers from hiring paid workers. Do these types of programs truly help the unemployed, or just provide a source of free labor for employers?

9. **Discrimination on the Basis of Unemployed Status.** In 2010, anecdotal evidence began to surface that employers were preferring currently employed applicants over unemployed applicants. Seth Katsuya Endo, *Neither Panacea, Placebo, nor Poison: Examining the Rise of Anti-Unemployment Discrimination Laws*, 33 PACE L. REV. 1007, 1010–11 (2013). Responding to public outcry over this phenomenon, states and cities moved to pass legislation prohibiting discrimination on the basis of employment status. President Obama proposed legislation at the federal level modeled on Title VII as part of The American Jobs Act of 2011, but it did not pass. Whittaker, *supra*, at 24. What beliefs about the long-term unemployed might result in discrimination on this basis? Should the law intervene to prohibit this form of discrimination, given that it is not immutable? If so, what public interests would justify doing so?

10. **Risk-Spreading, the Free Market and Employment at Will.** Like other forms of insurance, UI is a risk-spreading/pooling device. UI reduces the risk of economic insecurity for individuals by spreading it across a pool that includes all workers and employers. Should other workers (and employers) bear the costs of risks associated with individual workers' lack of skills or job choices that render them more vulnerable to job loss? Should other workers (and employers) bear the costs associated with work/family conflicts that result in job loss for some workers? On what justification(s)? Should UI be used as a vehicle for wealth redistribution? *See* Lester, *supra*, at 373–93 (arguing that UI is a "clumsy vehicle" for redistributing wealth to the working poor or alleviating the burdens of family care, and urging consideration of more direct tools such as tax and transfer programs).

Who benefits by avoiding risk through the UI system? Casebeer argues that UI primarily benefits employers by relieving them of the burden of durational contracts to secure a skilled workforce; instead, employers can lay off and later recall workers without having to train new employees. UI covers the employee during the layoff and ensures for the employer an available reserve labor pool, subsidized by employees still working at the firm. Casebeer, *supra*, at 324–26. Do you agree? Doesn't UI also benefit the employee who is later rehired by the same employer by insuring against the need to retrain or relocate? Consider the relationship between UI and employment at will: does UI reinforce or undermine the premises of employment at will? Who is more "free" to exercise the power to exit the employment relationship against the backdrop of UI benefits: the employer to discharge or the employee to quit?

Chapter 6

EMPLOYEE MOBILITY

One traditional justification for the employment-at-will rule is that employees are free to leave their employer at any time. But that is not always the case, and increasingly, employers are seeking to limit employee mobility through covenants not to compete (also known as non-competes, non-competition agreements and restrictive covenants), trade secret enforcement actions, and obligations that arise under the duty of loyalty. Employers justify these restrictions as necessary to protect their investments in their employees, and in their business practices. These restrictions, however, often conflict with a judicial reluctance to force employees to work for particular employers. As you may have studied in Contracts, absent highly unusual circumstances, courts generally will not require employees to continue working for an employer, though they may prevent that employee from working for other employers, leaving the employee with the option of not working or remaining with their current employer. *See Lumley v. Wagner*, 42 Eng. Rep. 687 (Ch. 1852) (prohibiting opera singer from working for another company while under contract).

In recent years, restrictions on employee mobility have acquired additional complexity as employees typically move among employers more frequently than they once did. As a general matter, restrictions on employee mobility are of considerably less importance when employees have long-term careers with a single [*more mobility expectation*] employer. With long-term stable employment no longer the dominant model, employees increasingly expect to be able to take their services to a higher bidder or one who offers greater opportunities. Indeed, Professor Katherine Stone has suggested that this expected mobility is part of what she terms a new "psychological contract" in the modern labor market, where employers offer training and enhanced skills to employees in lieu of long-term employment. *See* Katherine V. W. Stone, *The New Psychological Contract: Implications of the Changing Workplace for Labor & Employment Law*, 48 UCLA L. Rev. 519 (2001). Part of that implicit contract includes an understanding that employees will be able to take their training and skills to other employers.

The shift in employee and employer expectations discussed by Professor Stone represents another effect of the decline in unions. In union workplaces, the union often provides training through apprenticeships and other forms, and this training, which frequently produces highly skilled workers, is one reason some employers prefer to hire union employees.

As you will see in the cases below, training plays an important role in efforts to justify restrictions on employee mobility. Economists tend to divide training into two broad categories: general training that provides skills that will be useful for a number of employers and specific training, or training that will be valuable to the particular employer but does not generally have broad value in the labor market.

See GARY BECKER, HUMAN CAPITAL 19–26 (2d ed. 1975). Within this schema, employees are generally thought implicitly to pay for general training in the form of lower wages, while employers pay for specific training because they will be the primary beneficiaries of that training. Of course, much of the training employers provide will enhance both general and specific skills so it is often difficult to determine the true beneficiary of the training. Nevertheless, the theory has been influential in assessing restrictive covenants and other post-employment obligations. For an excellent discussion of the relation between training and restrictive covenants see Gillian Lester, *Restrictive Covenants, Employee Training, and the Limits of Transaction-Cost Analysis*, 76 IND. L.J. 49 (2001).

In addition, employers often seek to protect their investments through restrictions on employee mobility. These investments may include tangible assets such as customers or trade secrets or they might involve the general good will of the business. As you will see as we work through this Chapter, there are a number of competing interests at stake and courts often seek to balance those interests in diverse ways. This is also an area where jurisdictions can vary in their approach: some jurisdictions maintain what was a historical aversion to restrictive covenants and thus scrutinize those agreements carefully to ensure they are serving a legitimate purpose in a narrow way, while other courts limit trade secret protection in favor of creating incentives for employers and employees to negotiate a restrictive covenant. These jurisdictional differences will allow you to consider some of the advantages to a contractual relationship (restrictive covenant) compared to a common law or statutory protection such as trade secrets or the duty of loyalty.

This chapter will explore the existing law that governs covenants not to compete and the way in which trade secrets law has developed to impose significant limitations on employees who have access to important secret information. The chapter will also take up the related topics of the duty of loyalty that attaches to the employee-employer relationship and employee inventions (who owns them).

A. COVENANTS NOT TO COMPETE

HOPPER v. ALL PET ANIMAL CLINIC, INC.
Supreme Court of Wyoming
861 P.2d 531 (1993)

TAYLOR, JUSTICE.

These consolidated appeals test the enforceability of a covenant not to compete which was included in an employment contract. The district court found that the covenant imposed reasonable geographic and durational limits necessary to protect the employers' businesses and enjoined a veterinarian from practicing small animal medicine for three years within a five mile radius of the city limits of Laramie, Wyoming. . . . The veterinarian appeals from the decision to enforce the terms of the covenant. . . .

We hold that the covenant's three year duration imposed an unreasonable restraint of trade permitting only partial enforcement of a portion of that term of the covenant. We affirm the district court's conclusions of law that the remaining terms of the covenant were reasonable. . . .

I. Facts.

Following her graduation from Colorado State University, Dr. Glenna Hopper (Dr. Hopper) began working part-time as a veterinarian at the All Pet Animal Clinic, Inc. (All Pet) in July of 1988. All Pet specialized in the care of small animals; mostly domesticated dogs and cats, and those exotic animals maintained as household pets. Dr. Hopper practiced under the guidance and direction of the President of All Pet, Dr. Robert Bruce Johnson (Dr. Johnson).

Dr. Johnson, on behalf of All Pet, offered Dr. Hopper full-time employment in February of 1989. The oral offer included a specified salary and potential for bonus earnings as well as other terms of employment. According to Dr. Johnson, he conditioned the offer on Dr. Hopper's acceptance of a covenant not to compete, the specific details of which were not discussed at the time. Dr. Hopper commenced full-time employment with All Pet under the oral agreement in March of 1989 and relocated to Laramie. . . .

A written Employment Agreement incorporating the terms of the oral agreement was finally executed by the parties on December 11, 1989. Ancillary to the provisions for employment, the agreement detailed the terms of a covenant not to compete:

> 12. This agreement may be terminated by either party upon 30 days' notice to the other party. Upon termination, Dr. Hopper agrees that she will not practice small animal medicine for a period of three years from the date of termination within 5 miles of the corporate limits of the City of Laramie, Wyoming. Dr. Hopper agrees that the duration and geographic scope of that limitation is reasonable.

The agreement was antedated to be effective to March 3, 1989.

The parties executed an Addendum To Agreement on June 1, 1990. The addendum provided that All Pet and a newly acquired corporate entity, Alpine Animal Hospital, Inc. (Alpine), also located in Laramie, would share in Dr. Hopper's professional services. As the President of All Pet and Alpine, Dr. Johnson agreed, in the addendum, to raise Dr. Hopper's salary. The bonus provision of the original agreement was eliminated. Except as modified, the other terms of the March 3, 1989 employment agreement, including the covenant not to compete, were reaffirmed and Dr. Hopper continued her employment.

One year later, reacting to a rumor that Dr. Hopper was investigating the purchase of a veterinary practice in Laramie, Dr. Johnson asked his attorney to prepare a letter which was presented to Dr. Hopper. The letter, dated June 17, 1991, stated:

> I have learned that you are considering leaving us to take over the small animal part of Dr. Meeboer's practice in Laramie.

When we negotiated the terms of your employment, we agreed that you could leave upon 30 days' notice, but that you would not practice small animal medicine within five miles of Laramie for a three-year period. We do not have any non-competition agreement for large-animal medicine, which therefore does not enter into the picture.

I am willing to release you from the non-competition agreement in return for a cash buy-out. I have worked back from the proportion of the income of All-Pet and Alpine which you contribute and have decided that a reasonable figure would be $40,000.00, to compensate the practice for the loss of business which will happen if you practice small-animal medicine elsewhere in Laramie.

If you are willing to approach the problem in the way I suggest, please let me know and I will have the appropriate paperwork taken care of.

Sincerely,

[Signed]

R. Bruce Johnson, D.V.M.

Dr. Hopper responded to the letter by denying that she was going to purchase Dr. Meeboer's practice. Dr. Hopper told Dr. Johnson that the Employment Agreement was not worth the paper it was written on and that she could do anything she wanted to do. Dr. Johnson terminated Dr. Hopper's employment and informed her to consider the 30-day notice as having been given. An unsigned, handwritten note from Dr. Johnson to Dr. Hopper, dated June 18, 1991, affirmed the termination and notice. . . .

Subsequently, Dr. Hopper purchased Gem City Veterinary Clinic (Gem City), the practice of Dr. Melanie Manning. Beginning on July 15, 1991, Dr. Hopper operated Gem City, in violation of the covenant not to compete, within the City of Laramie and with a practice including large and small animals. Under Dr. Hopper's guidance, Gem City's client list grew from 368 at the time she purchased the practice to approximately 950 at the time of trial. A comparison of client lists disclosed that 187 clients served by Dr. Hopper at Gem City were also clients of All Pet or Alpine. Some of these shared clients received permissible large animal services from Dr. Hopper. Overall, the small animal work contributed from fifty-one to fifty-two percent of Dr. Hopper's gross income at Gem City.

All Pet and Alpine filed a complaint against Dr. Hopper on November 15, 1991 seeking injunctive relief and damages for breach of the covenant not to compete contained in the Employment Agreement. Notably, All Pet and Alpine did not seek a temporary injunction to restrict Dr. Hopper's practice and possibly mitigate damages during the pendency of the proceeding. Trial was conducted on September 28, 1992.

The district court, in its Findings of Fact, Conclusions of law and Judgment, determined that the covenant not to compete was enforceable as a matter of law and contained reasonable durational and geographic limits necessary to protect All Pet's and Alpine's special interests. The special interests found by the district court included: special influence over and direct contact with All Pet's and Alpine's clients;

access to client files; access to pricing policies; and instruction in practice development. Dr. Hopper was enjoined from practicing small animal medicine within five miles of the corporate limits of the City of Laramie for a period of three years from July 18, 1991. The district court found that the amount of damages suffered by All Pet and Alpine was speculative and not proven by a preponderance of the evidence. . . .

II. Discussion.

The common law policy against contracts in restraint of trade is one of the oldest and most firmly established. *Restatement (Second) of Contracts* §§ 185–188 (1981) (Introductory Note at 35). The traditional disfavor of such restraints means covenants not to compete are construed against the party seeking to enforce them. Commercial Bankers Life Ins. Co. of America v. Smith, 516 N.E.2d 110, 112 (Ind. App. 1987). The initial burden is on the employer to prove the covenant is reasonable and has a fair relation to, and is necessary for, the business interests for which protection is sought. Tench v. Weaver, 374 P.2d 27, 29 (Wyo. 1962).

Two principles, the freedom to contract and the freedom to work, conflict when courts test the enforceability of covenants not to compete. Ridley v. Krout, 180 P.2d 124, 128 (Wyo. 1947). There is general recognition that while an employer may seek protection from improper and unfair competition of a former employee, the employer is not entitled to protection against ordinary competition. *See, e.g., Duffner v. Alberty*, 718 S.W.2d 111, 112 (Ark. 1986). The enforceability of a covenant not to compete depends upon a finding that the proper balance exists between the competing interests of the employer and the employee. *See Restatement (Second) of Agency* § 393 cmt. e (1958) (noting that without a covenant not to compete, an agent, employee, can compete with a principal despite past employment and can begin preparations for future competition, such as purchasing a competitive business, before leaving present employment).

Wyoming adopted a rule of reason inquiry from the Restatement of Contracts testing the validity of a covenant not to compete. Ridley, 180 P.2d at 127. The present formulation of the rule of reason is contained in Restatement (Second) of Contracts, supra, § 188:

> (1) A promise to refrain from competition that imposes a restraint that is ancillary to an otherwise valid transaction or relationship is unreasonably in restraint of trade if
>
>> (a) the restraint is greater than is needed to protect the promisee's legitimate interest, or
>>
>> (b) the promisee's need is outweighed by the hardship to the promisor and the likely injury to the public. . . .

See also Restatement (Second) of Contracts, supra, §§ 186–187. An often quoted reformulation of the rule of reason inquiry states that "[a] restraint is reasonable only if it (1) is no greater than is required for the protection of the employer, (2) does not impose undue hardship on the employee, and (3) is not injurious to the public." Harlan M. Blake, *Employee Agreements Not to Compete*, 73 Harv. L. Rev. 625, 648–49 (1960).

A valid and enforceable covenant not to compete requires a showing that the covenant is: (1) in writing; (2) part of a contract of employment; (3) based on reasonable consideration; (4) reasonable in durational and geographical limitations; and (5) not against public policy. A.E.P. Industries, Inc. v. McClure, 302 S.E.2d 754, 760 (N.C. 1983). The reasonableness of a covenant not to compete is assessed based upon the facts of the particular case and a review of all of the circumstances. . . .

Wyoming has previously recognized that the legitimate interests of the employer, covenantee, which may be protected from competition include: (a) the employer's trade secrets which have been communicated to the employee during the course of employment; (b) confidential information communicated by the employer to the employee, but not involving trade secrets, such as information on a unique business method; and (c) special influence by the employee obtained during the course of employment over the employer's customers. Ridley, 180 P.2d at 129.

The enforceability of a covenant not to compete using the rule of reason analysis depends upon a determination, as a matter of law, that the promise not to compete is ancillary to the existence of an otherwise valid transaction or relationship. Restatement (Second) of Contracts, supra, § 187. If, for example, the contract of employment containing the covenant not to compete fails for lack of consideration, adhesion or other contractual excuse, the covenant is without effect. Reddy v. Community Health Foundation of Man, 298 S.E.2d 906, 915 (W. Va. 1982). . . . [The Court went on to find that although the initial written contract was not supported by consideration, the salary increase included as part of the revised agreement constituted adequate consideration to support the covenant.]

The contract permitted either Dr. Hopper or her corporate employers to terminate her employment with notice. The agreement did not state a length of employment and it permitted termination at will. Without more, the terms present the potential for an unreasonable restraint of trade. For example, if an employer hired an employee at will, obtained a covenant not to compete, and then terminated the employee, without cause, to arbitrarily restrict competition, we believe such conduct would constitute bad faith. Simple justice requires that a termination by the employer of an at will employee be in good faith if a covenant not to compete is to be enforced. Dutch Maid Bakeries, 131 P.2d 630, 635–36 (Wyo. 1942).

Under the present facts, we cannot say that the termination of Dr. Hopper occurred in bad faith. Trial testimony presented evidence of increasing tension prior to termination in the professional relationship between Dr. Johnson and Dr. Hopper. This tension, however, did not appear to result in the termination. The notice of termination was given after Dr. Hopper was confronted about her negotiations to purchase a competitive practice and after Dr. Hopper had termed the employment contract worthless. We cannot find in these facts a bad faith termination which would provide a reason to depart from the district court's finding that the contract of employment was valid. With the determination that as a matter of law the covenant is ancillary to a valid employment relationship, we turn to the rule of reason inquiry.

Employers are entitled to protect their business from the detrimental impact of competition by employees who, but for their employment, would not have had the ability to gain a special influence over clients or customers. Ridley, 180 P.2d at 131. . . . [At the same time] "It is true that an employee's aptitude, skill, dexterity, manual and mental ability and other subjective knowledge obtained in the course of employment are not property of the employer which the employer can, in absence of a contractual right, prohibit the employee from taking with him at the termination of employment." Beckman v. Cox Broadcasting Corp., 296 S.E.2d 566 (Ga. 1982). . . .

. . . Dr. Hopper moved to Laramie upon completion of her degree prior to any significant professional contact with the community. Her introduction to All Pet's and Alpine's clients, client files, pricing policies, and practice development techniques provided information which exceeded the skills she brought to her employment. While she was a licensed and trained veterinarian when she accepted employment, the additional exposure to clients and knowledge of clinic operations her employers shared with her had a monetary value for which the employers are entitled to reasonable protection from irreparable harm. See Reddy, 298 S.E.2d at 912–14. The proven loss of 187 of All Pet's and Alpine's clients to Dr. Hopper's new practice sufficiently demonstrated actual harm from unfair competition. . . .

All parties to this litigation devoted extensive research to evaluations of the reasonableness of various covenants not to compete from different authorities. However, we find precedent from our own or from other jurisdictions to be of limited value in considering the reasonableness of limits contained in a specific covenant not to compete. See Specter & Finkin, supra, § 8.03 at 454–55. . . . We believe the reasonableness of individual limitations contained in a specific covenant not to compete must be assessed based upon the facts of that proceeding. Ridley, 180 P.2d at 131.

Useful legal principles do emerge from a survey of relevant authorities and may certainly be applied to decisions about the reasonableness of the type of activity, geographic, and durational limitations. Testing the reasonableness of the type of activity limitation provides an opportunity for the court to consider the broader public policy implications of a covenant not to compete. Tench, 374 P.2d at 29. The decision of the Court of Appeals of Ohio in Williams v. Hobbs, 460 N.E.2d 287 (1983) explains. The Williams court determined that enforcing a covenant not to compete restricting a radiologist's uncommon specialty practice would violate public policy because the community would be deprived of a unique skill. Id. at 290. In addition, the court held the type of activity limitation was unreasonable because it created an undue hardship on the physician where there were only a limited number of osteopathic hospitals available to practice his specialty. Id. . . .

Enforcement of the practice restrictions Dr. Hopper accepted as part of her covenant not to compete does not create an unreasonable restraint of trade. While the specific terms of the covenant failed to define the practice of small animal medicine, the parties' trade usage provided a conforming standard of domesticated dogs and cats along with exotic animals maintained as household pets. As a veterinarian licensed to practice in Wyoming, Dr. Hopper was therefore permitted to earn a living in her chosen profession without relocating by practicing large animal medicine, a significant area of practice in this state. The restriction on the type of activity contained in the covenant was sufficiently limited to avoid undue hardship to Dr. Hopper while protecting the special interests of All Pet and Alpine.

In addition, as a professional, Dr. Hopper certainly realized the implications of agreeing to the terms of the covenant. While she may have doubted either her employers desires to enforce the terms or the legality of the covenant, her actions in establishing a small animal practice violated the promise she made. In equity, she comes before the court with unclean hands. If Dr. Hopper sought to challenge the enforceability of the covenant, her proper remedy was to seek a declaratory judgment. WYO. STAT. § 1-37-103 (1988).

The public will not suffer injury from enforcement of the covenant. Dr. Hopper's services at All Pet and Alpine were primarily to provide relief for the full-time veterinarians at those clinics. In addition to dividing her time between the clinics, she covered when others had days off or, on a rotating basis, on weekends. While Dr. Hopper provided competent care to All Pet's and Alpine's clients, her services there were neither unique nor uncommon. Furthermore, the services which Dr. Hopper provided in her new practice to small animal clients were available at several other veterinary clinics within Laramie. Evidence did not challenge the public's ability to receive complete and satisfactory service from these other sources. Dr. Hopper's short term unavailability resulting from enforcement of a reasonable restraint against unfair competition is unlikely, as a matter of law, to produce injury to the public.

Reasonable geographic restraints are generally limited to the area in which the former employee actually worked or from which clients were drawn. Brewer v. Tracy, 253 N.W.2d 319, 322 (Neb. 1977). When the business serves a limited geographic area, as opposed to statewide or nationwide, courts have upheld geographic limits which are coextensive with the area in which the employer conducts business. Torrence v. Hewitt Associates, 493 N.E.2d 74, 78 (Ill. App. 1986). A broad geographic restriction may be reasonable when it is coupled with a specific activity restriction within an industry or business which has an inherently limited client base. System Concepts, Inc. v. Dixon, 669 P.2d 421, 427 (Utah 1983).

The geographical limit contained in the covenant not to compete restricts Dr. Hopper from practicing within a five mile radius of the corporate limits of Laramie. As a matter of law, this limit is reasonable in this circumstance. The evidence presented at trial indicated that the clients of All Pet and Alpine were located throughout the county. Despite Wyoming's rural character, the five mile restriction effectively limited unfair competition without presenting an undue hardship. Dr. Hopper could, for example, have opened a practice at other locations within the county.

A durational limitation should be reasonably related to the legitimate interest which the employer is seeking to protect. Restatement (Second) of Contracts, supra, § 188 cmt. b.

> In determining whether a restraint extends for a longer period of time than necessary to protect the employer, the court must determine how much time is needed for the risk of injury to be reasonably moderated. When the

restraint is for the purpose of protecting customer relationships, its duration is reasonable only if it is no longer than necessary for the employer to put a new [individual] on the job and for the new employee to have a reasonable opportunity to demonstrate his [or her] effectiveness to the customers. . . .

Blake, 73 HARV. L. REV. at 677 (footnote omitted).

The evidence at trial focused on the durational requirement in attempting to establish the three year term as being necessary to diffuse the potential loss of clients from All Pet and Alpine to Dr. Hopper. Dr. Charles Sink, a licensed veterinarian, testified as an expert on behalf of All Pet and Alpine and indicated that in Wyoming, his experience correlated with national studies that disclosed about 70% of clients visit a clinic more than once per year. The remaining 30% of the clients use the clinic at least one time per year. Dr. Johnson estimated that at All Pet and Alpine, the average client seeks veterinarian services one and one-half times a year. . . .

We are unable to find a reasonable relationship between the three year durational requirement and the protection of All Pet's and Alpine's special interests. . . . Based on figures of client visits, a replacement veterinarian at All Pet and Alpine would be able to effectively demonstrate his or her own professionalism to virtually all of the clinics' clients within a one year durational limit.

A one year durational limit sufficiently secures All Pet's and Alpine's interests in pricing policies and practice development information. Pricing policies at All Pet and Alpine were changed yearly . . . to reflect changes in material and service costs provided by the clinics as well as new procedures. Practice development information, especially in a learned profession, loses its value quickly as technological change occurs and new reference material become available. We hold, as a matter of law, that enforcement of a one year durational limit is reasonable and sufficiently protects the interests of All Pet and Alpine without violating public policy.

Under the formulation of the rule of reason inquiry adopted by Wyoming from the first *Restatement of Contracts*, the unreasonableness of any non-divisible term of a covenant not to compete made the entire covenant unenforceable. Restatement of Contracts, supra, § 518. . . . Restatement (Second) of Contracts, supra, § 184, which we now adopt, . . . permits enforcement of a narrower term which is reasonable in a covenant not to compete. . . . The position adopted in Restatement (Second) of Contracts, supra, § 184 does not permit the court to add to the terms of the covenant. *Id.* at § 184 cmt. b.

We believe the ability to narrow the term of a covenant not to compete and enforce a reasonable restraint permits public policy to be served in the most effective manner. Businesses function through the efforts of dedicated employees who provide the services and build the products desired by customers. Both the employer and the employee invest in success by expressing a commitment to one another in the form of a reasonable covenant not to compete. For the employer, this commitment may mean providing the employee with access to trade secrets, customer contacts or special training. These assets of the business are entitled to protection. For the employee, who covenants as part of a bargained for exchange, the covenant provides notice of the limits both parties have accepted in their relationship. The employee benefits during his tenure with the employer by his or her greater importance to the organization as a result of the exposure to the trade secrets, customer contacts or special training. When the employer-employee relationship terminates, a reasonable covenant not to compete then avoids unfair competition by the employee against the former employer and the specter, which no court would enforce, of specific performance of the employment agreement. When the parties agree to terms of a covenant, one of which is too broad, the court is permitted to enforce a narrower term which effectuates these public policy goals without arbitrarily invalidating the entire agreement between the parties and creating an uncertain business environment. . . .

Enforcement of a one year durational term, along with the other terms of the covenant not to compete, is reasonable in light of the circumstances of this case. Public policy is fairly served by this restraint on unfair competition by Dr. Hopper. All Pet and Alpine established irreparable harm from the loss of clients to unfair competition which entitled them to injunctive relief. While the terms of the covenant, as enforced, restrict Dr. Hopper's practice for a limited time, she will suffer no undue hardship from compliance with her bargained for promise. . . .

III. Conclusion.

A well-drafted covenant not to compete preserves a careful and necessary economic balance in our society. While there are many layers to the employer-employee relationship, preventing unfair competition from employees who misuse trade secrets or special influence over customers serves public policy. Tempering the balance is the need to protect employees from unfair restraints on competition which defeat broad policy goals in favor of small business and individual advancement. Courts, in reviewing covenants not to compete, must consider these policy implications in assessing the reasonableness of the restraint as it applies to both employer and employee.

Affirmed as modified and remanded for issuance of a judgment in conformity herewith.

[The dissenting opinion of JUSTICE CARDINE is omitted.]

NOTES

1.   **Scope of Review.** What is the court's rationale for scrutinizing the covenant not to compete so carefully? Is there any indication that Dr. Hopper entered into the agreement unknowingly or that she was coerced into signing the agreement? Why shouldn't basic contract law provide adequate protection for her?

2.   **Policy Justifications.** Assume Dr. Hopper provided better services cheaper than her former employer, why should the public be denied those services? Is it that she never would have had access to the clients without her previous employer? Or perhaps she has an unfair advantage as a result of lower start-up costs once she has made the initial contacts? But what if she is just a better veterinarian, how should

that factor into the analysis? Along these lines, what does the court identify as the rationale for the restrictive covenant?

3. **Blue-Pencil Rule.** In *Hopper*, the court rewrote the term of the contract to what it determined to be a reasonable length of time. As the court notes, historically courts were reluctant to rewrite contracts but instead would find them unenforceable if any part of the contract were unenforceable. Today, most courts follow the "blue-pencil" approach of the *Hopper* court, though there remain a few holdouts. *See Lapolla Indust. v. Hess*, 750 S.E.2d 467, 473 (Ga. Ct. App. 2013) (Georgia will not "blue pencil" an otherwise unenforceable non-compete agreement); *CAE Vanguard, Inc. v. Newman*, 518 N.W.2d 652, 655–56 (Neb. 1994) (refusing to allow reformation because it was "tantamount to the construction of a private agreement").

4. **Remedies.** Non-compete agreements are contracts and contract remedies are typically available when a breach is established. However, the most common remedy is one of specific enforcement so that the employee will be enjoined from moving to a new competitor consistent with the terms of the agreement. In *Hopper*, the plaintiff did not seek a preliminary injunction but instead was seeking damages for the loss of clients. How would those damages be measured? What would be the relevance of the offer that All Pet made to Hopper that she could buy herself out of the restrictive covenant for $40,000?

5. **Modern Approaches to Covenants.** As noted in the *Hopper* case, courts have traditionally been reluctant to enforce covenants not to compete because of a concern that they impose a restraint on trade, thus potentially injuring the public, while also depriving an employee of the freedom to control her own labor. A number of courts, however, are now more receptive to enforcing non-compete agreements for reasons reflected in the following excerpt from a dissenting opinion by Chief Judge Richard Posner of the Seventh Circuit Court of Appeals. After noting that Illinois law, which the court was applying, was "hostile to covenants not to compete found in employment contracts," Judge Posner went on to consider the basis for such hostility:

> There is no longer any good reason for such hostility, though it is nothing either new or limited to Illinois. The English common law called such covenants "restraints of trade" and refused to enforce them unless they were adjudged "reasonable" in time and geographical scope. The original rationale had nothing to do with restraint of trade in its modern, antitrust sense. It was paternalism in a culture of poverty, restricted employment, and an exiguous social safety net. The fear behind it was that workers would be tricked into agreeing to covenants that would, if enforced, propel them into destitution. . . .

> Later, however, the focus of concern shifted to whether a covenant not to compete might have anticompetitive consequences, since the covenant would eliminate the covenantor as a potential competitor of the covenantee within the area covered by, and during the term of, the covenant. . . . At the same time that the concerns behind judicial hostility to covenants not to compete have waned, recognition of their social value has grown. The clearest case for such a covenant is where the employee's work gives him

access to the employer's trade secrets. The employer could include in the employment contract a clause forbidding the employee to take any of the employer's trade secrets with him when he left the employment. . . . Such clauses are difficult to enforce, however, as it is often difficult to determine whether the former employee is using his former employer's trade secrets or using either ideas of his own invention or ideas that are in the public domain. A covenant not to compete is much easier to enforce, and to the extent enforced prevents the employee, during the time and within the geographical scope of the covenant, from using his former employer's trade secrets.

A related function of such a covenant is to protect the employer's investment in the employee's "human capital," or earning capacity. The employer may give the employee training that the employee could use to compete against the employer. If covenants not to compete are forbidden, the employer will pay a lower wage, in effect charging the employee for the training. There is no reason why the law should prefer this method of protecting the employer's investment to a covenant not to compete.

I can see no reason in today's America for judicial hostility to covenants not to compete. It is possible to imagine situations in which the device might be abused, but the doctrines of fraud, duress, and unconscionability are available to deal with such situations. A covenant's reasonableness in terms of duration and geographical scope is merely a consideration bearing on such defenses. . . .

Outsource Int'l, Inc. v. Barton & Barton's Staffing Solutions, Inc., 192 F.3d 662 (7th Cir. 1999) (POSNER, J., dissenting) (citations omitted). Which approach makes more sense today? Even though many courts have altered their traditional hostility, a number of courts continue to view non-compete agreements with suspicion, subjecting them to close scrutiny. *See, e.g., Goodman v. N.Y. Oncology Hematology, P.C.*, 101 A.D.3d 1524, 1525 (N.Y. App. Div. 2012) ("Agreements restricting an individual's right to work or compete are not favored and thus are strictly construed."); *Coats v. Heat Wagons, Inc.*, 942 N.E.2d 905, 913 (Ind. Ct. App. 2011) ("Indiana courts strongly disfavor as restraints of trade covenants not to compete in employment contracts."); *Wriggs v. Junkermier, Clark, Campanella*, 265 P.3d 646, 649 (Mont. 2011) ("Montana law strongly disfavors covenants not to compete."); *Star Direct, Inc. v. Dal Pra*, 767 N.W.2d 898, 905 (Wis. 2009) ("Restrictive covenants in Wisconsin are *prima facie* suspect as restraints of trade that are disfavored at law, and must withstand close scrutiny as to their reasonableness.").

From an economic point of view, an employer might argue that it paid the employee more in wages in return for a non-compete clause because of the value such a clause adds to the employment relationship. How should that concern be factored into whether the agreement is enforceable? Might this depend on what the employer is purchasing, or what interests it is seeking to protect? Another frequently asserted rationale is that an employer is more likely to expose an employee to trade secrets under the restriction of a covenant not to compete, and that employees benefit by such exposure. How should this consideration be factored into the analysis on the validity of an agreement? How does an employee benefit by such exposure?

6.   Protectable Interests. As the court notes in *Hopper*, a restrictive covenant will only be valid to the extent it seeks to protect a legitimate interest. It is not, for example, legitimate for an employer to use a restrictive covenant as a way of keeping a good employee or protecting itself from ordinary competition. Rather, the employer must seek to protect what courts deem a legitimate interest, frequently information of a confidential nature or a trade secret. The recently promulgated THIRD RESTATEMENT OF EMPLOYMENT LAW defines as protectable interests: (1) trade secrets or confidential information; (2) customer relationships; (3) investment in the employee's reputation in the market; and (4) purchase of a business owned by the employee. THIRD RESTATEMENT OF EMPLOYMENT LAW, § 8.07(b) (2014).

In addition to these specific interests, a common protectable interest involves what might be defined as the company's good will, in the form of the company's reputation and its customers, and often, its reputation with its customers. The First Circuit Court of Appeals recently noted, "In the employment context, restrictive covenants are meant to afford the original employer bargained-for-protection of its accrued good will." *Corporate Techs., Inc. v. Harnett*, 731 F.3d 6, 11 (1st Cir. 2013). One court has defined good will in terms of customers as the "competitive advantage gained for an employer through personal contacts between employee and customer when the products offered by competitors are similar." *Coates v. Heat Wagons, Inc.*, 942 N.E.2d 905, 913 (Ind. Ct. App. 2011). What role did this interest play in *Hopper* and the court's determination of the proper duration of the non-compete agreement? How should a court determine whether an employer is seeking to protect its good will or simply trying to protect itself from competition? The Illinois Supreme Court has stated that in determining whether an employer has a legitimate protectable interest, courts should focus on "the totality of circumstances" including whether the customer relationships are "near permanent" or whether they are more transitory, and whether the employee has acquired confidential information through her employment. *See Reliable Fire Equip. Co. v. Arredondo*, 965 N.E.2d 393, 403 (Ill. 2011).

Customers or clients are an important part of a firm's good will, and employers often seek to restrain their former employees from soliciting customers when they move to a new position. Sometimes these provisions are part of a non-compete agreement, although they are also frequently found in separate agreements. The Missouri Supreme Court recently reviewed a non-solicitation agreement that prohibited contact with any of the firm's customer "regardless of prior contacts" during the employee's employment. *Whelan Sec. Co. v. Kennebrew*, 379 S.W.3d 835 (Mo. 2012). In reviewing the agreement, the Court noted that, "An employer has a legitimate interest in customer contacts to the extent it seeks to protect against the influence an employee acquires over his employee's customers through personal contact" during the term of employment. *Id.* at 842. The Court narrowed the agreement so that it applied only to the departing employee's actual prior customers and not prospective customers. *Id.* at 845. At the same time, the Court upheld the employee's two-year fifty mile non-compete agreement. *Id.* at 847.

7. Covenants in a Mobile Labor Market. The evolving nature of the labor market where employees change jobs frequently while employers increasingly engage in national and international competition has had important and diverse effects on the law defining what constitutes reasonable restraints. As discussed in the *Hopper* case, courts typically assess the reasonableness of the agreement by reviewing (1) the purpose of the agreement; (2) the geographical restriction and the (3) length of time. The latter two factors are directly related to the purpose of the agreement in that the length and scope of the agreement must be necessary to further its legitimate purpose.

In order to adapt to changing economic and employment settings, courts have recently allowed more variation in the duration and geographical reach of a covenant. Traditionally courts required well-defined geographical limitations and were often less concerned about the length of the agreement. *See, e.g., Karpinski v. Ingrasci*, 268 N.E.2d 751 (N.Y. 1971) (upholding five-county geographical limitation with no time limit). Increasingly, that emphasis has been reversed as courts are willing to uphold national or worldwide restrictions for companies that do business nationally or internationally but typically require short durations. In dealing with a national market, one court explained, "a geographical restriction on the covenants would render them nullities." *Natsource LLC v. Paribello*, 151 F. Supp. 2d 465, 471 (S.D.N.Y. 2001) (upholding restriction on 120-day solicitation on clients for broker). *See also Env. Servs. v. Carter*, 9 So. 3d 1258, 1264 (Fla. Dist. Ct. App. 2009) (upholding covenant with no geographical restriction); *Ackerman v. Kimball Int'l, Inc.*, 652 N.E.2d 507 (Ind. 1995) (same). The proper duration of a covenant will typically depend on the time needed to protect the employer's legitimate interest. For businesses that have operations on the internet, that can result in a very short life span. In *EarthWeb, Inc. v. Schlack*, the court refused to enforce a one-year covenant, explaining, "[T]his court finds that the one-year duration of EarthWeb's restrictive covenant is too long given the dynamic nature of this industry, its lack of geographical borders, and Schlack's former cutting-edge position with EarthWeb where his success depended on keeping abreast of daily challenges in content on the internet." 71 F. Supp. 2d 299, 313 (S.D.N.Y. 1999), *remanded by* 205 F.3d 1322 (2d Cir. 2000) (requesting an explanation from the District Court for its decision to deny EarthWeb's motion to enjoin Schlack from revealing EarthWeb's trade secrets), *aff'd*, 2000 U.S. App. LEXIS 11446 (2d Cir. May 18, 2000) .When there are fixed geographical limitations, courts frequently uphold longer terms, and covenants that last one or two years are often deemed reasonable. *See ACAS Acquistions v. Hobert*, 923 A.2d 1076, 1088 (N.H. 2007) (upholding two-year term as necessary to protect customers and to establish replacements). It is worth emphasizing that courts vary widely on what they consider reasonable agreements. *See, e.g., Avalon Legal Info. Serv. v. Keating*, 110 So. 3d 75, 82 (Fla. Dist. Ct. App. 2013) (upholding a restrictive covenant with a three-year duration and no geographical limitation); *Coleman v. Retina Consultants*, 687 S.E.2d 457 (Ga. 2009) (absence of geographical limitation renders covenant void); *Universal Engraving, Inc. v. Duarte*, 519 F. Supp. 2d 1140 (D. Kan. 2007) (blue-penciling time limit from five to two-years in an agreement without geographical restriction).

8. **The Proliferation of Restrictive Covenants.** Over the course of the last decade, there has been a sharp increase in the prevalence of restrictive covenants for a wide range of jobs. Professor Charles Sullivan has observed that, "In the past, only the most valuable employees, often those under individual contracts, were subject to noncompetition clauses. Today, however, many at-will employees are also subject to such restrictions." Charles A. Sullivan, *The Puzzling Persistence of Unenforceable Contract Terms*, 70 OHIO ST. L.J. 1127, 1149 (2009). This trend was picked up by the national news media, which recently reported that non-competes have been imposed on a wide variety of jobs, including summer camp counselors, hair stylists, lawn maintenance workers and yoga instructors. *See* Steven Greenhouse, *Non-compete Clauses Increasingly Pop Up in Array of Jobs*, N.Y. TIMES, June 8, 2014, at B1. How should the nature of the job factor into a court's analysis? Consider that the vast majority of non-compete agreements will never be litigated, and most employees will assume they are valid and comply with their restrictions. This is likely to be particularly true of low-level employees who will not have the resources to litigate a claim or who will be moving to a job where the new employer will neither fund nor support the litigation. Does Judge Posner's analysis from the *Outsource Int'l* case referenced in note 5 above have the same force with low-level employees? In *National Employment Serv. Corp v. Olsten Staffing Service., Inc.*, 761 A.2d 401 (N.H. 2000), the Supreme Court of New Hampshire considered the validity of restrictive covenants signed by employees of a temporary employment agency, National Employment Service, that prevented the workers from accepting employment with a client company for 90 days after termination with the temporary company. The client, a light manufacturing company, switched temporary agencies to Olsten Staffing Service and many of the temporary employees also sought to switch from National Employment to Olsten so that they could maintain their employment. National sued to enforce the restrictive covenants, but the Court found that there was no legitimate rationale to permit the restrictions. The Court explained:

> In this case, the sole "employer interest" articulated by National is the retention of employees for a sufficient period to enable it to recoup costs associated with "recruiting, interviewing, checking references, qualifying, insuring, and placing" its employees. All businesses, however, incur expenses in recruiting and hiring employees. National does not allege that the restrictive covenant was necessary to prevent its employees from appropriating the company's confidential information, trade secrets, or goodwill. Its employees were light industrial laborers who were not in a position to appropriate the company's goodwill and were without access to sensitive information. Post-employment restrictions on such employees would be contrary to public policy and would impose an undue hardship, particularly for at-will employees who could be discharged at any time. Thus, we hold that although there may be valid reasons for restrictive covenants, the mere cost associated with recruiting and hiring employees is not a legitimate interest protectable by a restrictive covenant in an employment contract.

Id. at 405.

Employers have also sought to recoup training costs through contractual agreements that require employees to pay back the costs of training if they do not work for a certain period of time. Courts typically uphold these agreements so long as the employer's training costs are properly documented, the time period of expected employment is reasonable, and the employee knowingly entered into the agreement. *See Suburban Air Freight, Inc. v. Aust*, 636 N.W.2d 629 (Neb. 2001) (upholding requirement that employee reimburse employer for costs of pilot training when he failed to work for the agreed upon one-year period); *City of Pembroke v. Hagin*, 391 S.E.2d 465 (Ga. Ct. App. 1990) (upholding agreement requiring police officer to reimburse city for costs of training when he failed to complete one year of employment). These agreements may also be held invalid under state statutory law regulating wage payment systems, or because the agreements are unreasonable penalty clauses designed to prevent the employee from leaving rather than to compensate the employer for its training costs. *See Newsom v. Global Data Sys., Inc.*, 107 So. 3d 781, 789 (La. Ct. App. 2012) (holding employment contract provision requiring employees to reimburse company for education and training expenses violated public policy because employees had no choice but to participate in training to remain employed); *Sands Appliance Servs., Inc. v. Wilson*, 615 N.W.2d 241 (Mich. 2000) (finding contract requiring employee to pay $50 per week for training costs invalid under state statutory law); *Med + Plus Neck & Back Pain Ctr. v. Noffsinger*, 726 N.E.2d 687 (Ill. App. Ct. 2000) (invalidating $50,000 promissory note as unrelated to employer's training costs).

9. Enforcing Agreements After an Employee Is Terminated. The *Hopper* court noted that its analysis might be different if Hopper had been terminated in bad faith. Courts vary in their approach to employees who leave involuntarily. Some courts refuse to enforce a non-compete when an employee is terminated without cause. *See, e.g., Outside Television, Inc. v. Murin*, 977 F. Supp. 2d 1, 31 (D. Me. 2013) ("Provided that employment in the broadcasting industry is terminated without the employee's fault, Maine favors protecting the employee's freedom to engage in further employment without restriction."); *Arakelian v. Omnicare, Inc.*, 735 F. Supp. 2d 22, 41 (S.D.N.Y. 2010) ("Enforcing a noncompetition provision when the employee has been discharged without cause would be unconscionable because it would destroy the mutuality of obligation on which a covenant not to compete is based."). Many other courts do not explore the reason why the employee left her employment but instead focus on the language of the covenant. *See, e.g., Fulford v. Drawdy Bros. Constr.*, 903 So. 2d 1007 (Fla. Dist. Ct. App. 2005) (upholding covenant even though employee claimed he was fired to avoid paying him a bonus); *Safety-Kleen Sys., Inc., v. Hennkens*, 301 F.3d 931 (8th Cir. 2002) (upholding non-compete agreement under Missouri law despite employee's claim that he was fired without cause). Relatedly, some courts have begun to scrutinize the agreements carefully to determine if there was adequate consideration, and a recent Illinois Appellate Court held that two years of continuous employment was necessary "to constitute adequate consideration in support of a restrictive covenant" even when the employee had resigned. *See Fifield v. Premier Dealer Servs.*, 993 N.E.2d 938, 943 (Ill. App. Ct. 2013). Other courts continue to follow the traditional notion that continued employment can constitute adequate consideration for at-will employees. *See Lucht's Concrete Pumping, Inc. v. Horner*, 255 P.3d 1058, 1061 (Colo. 2011).

10. Professionals. Many courts apply different rules of interpretation to restrictive covenants for professionals, such as doctors, because of a concern that depriving communities of professionals may adversely affect the public interest. *See Valley Med. Specialists v. Farber*, 982 P.2d 1277 (Ariz. 1999) (invalidating doctor's restrictive covenant because it interferes with the doctor-patient relationship). As courts have become more permissive in upholding agreements generally, they have also begun to be more willing to uphold non-compete agreements among doctors so long as a community is not deprived of important medical services. *See, e.g., Emerick v. Cardiac Study Ctr.*, 286 P.3d 689, 694 (Wash. Ct. App. 2012); *Central Indiana Podiatry v. Krueger*, 882 N.E.2d 723 (Ind. 2008); *Mohanty v. St. John Heart Clinic, S.C.*, 866 N.E.2d 85 (Ill. 2006).

Restrictive covenants among attorneys are generally prohibited. *See*, e.g., *Cohen v. Lord, Day & Lord*, 550 N.E.2d 410 (N.Y. 1989). The Arizona Supreme Court, however, has upheld a provision in a law firm's partnership agreement that required a departing partner who intended to practice within the firm's geographic area to tender his equity back to the partnership without compensation. *See Fearnow v. Ridenour et al.*, 138 P.3d 723 (Ariz. 2006). The court found that the agreement did not run afoul of the Arizona Rules of Professional Conduct and should be subject to a traditional reasonableness analysis applicable to restrictive covenants. Outside of the attorney context, courts have taken varying approaches to what are often defined as penalty clauses, some analyzing them as restrictive covenants, others as simply contracts, while still others find them per se invalid. For a discussion of the varying approaches to financial penalty clauses *see Deming v. Nationwide Mut. Ins.*, 905 A.2d 623 (Conn. 2006).

Professional entertainers, on the other hand, are often held strictly to their contractual commitments. The Indiana Court of Appeals has found a radio station had a protectable interest in an on-the-air personality even though it had fired him because the station had devoted substantial resources to creating his personality. Nevertheless, the court denied the request for preliminary injunction because the station had failed to demonstrate specific damages or that its remedies at law were inadequate. *Pathfinder Commc'n Corp. v. Macy*, 795 N.E.2d 1103 (Ind. Ct. App. 2003). What might be the basis for applying different levels of scrutiny depending on the job that is at issue?

11. California's Prohibition on Covenants. California has long prohibited the use of restrictive covenants. *See* CALIF. BUS. & PROF. CODE § 16600; *see also Edwards v. Arthur Anderson LLP*, 189 P.3d 285 (Cal. 2008) (reiterating state's broad prohibition). A number of other states, including Alabama, Colorado, Hawaii, North Dakota, and Oklahoma, have similar restrictions, though the statutes often make various exceptions in the case of partnerships or to protect trade secrets. Many scholars have suggested that California's prohibition on restrictive covenants has fueled much of the ingenuity in its high-tech community. Professor Ronald Gilson, for example, has argued that California's legal regulation of restrictive covenants best explains the triumph of Silicon Valley as the dominant technology region over the competing area in Massachusetts known as Route 128 where restrictive covenants are enforced. *See* Ronald J. Gilson, *The Legal Infrastructure of High Technology Industrial Districts: Silicon Valley, Route 128, and Covenants Not to Compete*, 74 N.Y.U. L. REV. 575 (1999). While acknowledging the importance of

California's statutory prohibition, Professor Alan Hyde suggests the rise of Silicon Valley is better explained by a pervasive culture that accepts employee mobility as both inevitable and desirable. He writes:

> Silicon Valley . . . owes its existence to the reticence of employers to enforce their rights under trade secrets law. Start-ups are the strength of the Valley. Most start-ups are founded by employees of existing firms. Sometimes the start-up will compete directly with the founders' former firm. Examples are the many firms making knock-offs of Intel and other chips. Sometimes the start-up will make products, software or hardware, designed to be compatible with the products of the former firm. In either of these homey examples . . . the start-up will make use of some piece of information that is a trade secret of the former employer.

ALAN HYDE, WORKING IN SILICON VALLEY 31 (2003). As many of the companies have grown, their practices have also changed. A high-profile class action lawsuit has accused several of the largest companies, including Apple, Google, Adobe, and Intel, of impermissibly agreeing not to hire each other's employees, what has been referred to as an anti-poaching pact among the companies. The district court judge overseeing the case recently rejected a $324 million settlement suggesting the amount was too low for the 64,000 member class. *See* David Streitfield, *Court Rejects Deal on Hiring in Silicon Valley*, N.Y. TIMES, Aug. 8, 2014, at B1.

B. TRADE SECRETS

1. Protecting Trade Secrets

SATURN SYSTEMS v. MILITARE
Colorado Court of Appeals
252 P.3d 516 (2011)

JUDGE LOEB.

PH

Defendant, Delbert J. Militare, appeals the judgment entered after a bench trial in favor of plaintiff, Saturn Systems, Inc., on its claims of misappropriation of trade secrets . . . . We affirm and remand with directions.

I. Background and Procedural History

Saturn

Saturn is a debt collection agency that offers numerous types of debt collection services, including recovery of commercial, consumer, medical, government, and retail accounts, both domestically and abroad. According to testimony at trial, since its founding in 1997, Saturn has provided its services to over 1,600 clients, for whom it has processed and helped collect over 120,000 debts.

Evidence at trial showed that Saturn spent significant time and money to develop a proprietary website to provide its clients access to its database of client and debtor information. Thus, Saturn assigns each client a unique username and password that can be used to log in to the website and view real-time information related to that client's account. For example, a client can view a "status report" for its account, which summarizes Saturn's debt recovery to date and tells the client how many pre-purchased debt collection accounts it has available to designate to debtors in default so that Saturn can initiate collection activities. A client can also view the "debtor notes" for its debtors that have entered Saturn's "hardcore" collection phase. Saturn uses the "debtor notes" component of its website to record pending collection efforts, settlement negotiations, and all known personal information for a debtor, such as addresses, bank accounts, and employment history. Because of the confidential nature of the information that can be accessed via its website, Saturn only releases the usernames and passwords to the client and, if needed, to the sales agent assigned to that client's account.

On January 13, 2003, Saturn hired Militare for a sales agent position. The parties entered into a written sales agent agreement (Agreement) that outlined their respective roles. In that regard, Militare agreed to . . . sell Saturn's services, receive funds on Saturn's behalf, and make sales presentations to prospective clients. Additionally, Militare agreed to provide ongoing customer care to the clients that he signed up for Saturn's services. In return, Saturn agreed to pay Militare a commission on each sale that he made. As a Saturn sales agent, Militare was provided access to and was taught how to use the confidential database on the Saturn website.

Saturn terminated the Agreement with Militare approximately two years later by proper written notice. The effective date of the termination was January 18, 2005. Shortly thereafter, on January 31, 2005, Militare accepted a position with CB Solutions, LLC, a Texas-based company and a direct competitor of Saturn. In March 2005, while working for CB Solutions, Militare personally visited Premier Members Federal Credit Union, a longtime Saturn client that still had unused pre-purchased debt collection accounts available with Saturn. Militare admitted at trial that he contacted Premier on behalf of CB Solutions to win the Premier account. Although the parties disputed the details of Militare's visit, the record indicates that Premier contacted Saturn shortly after the visit to request a new password for its Saturn account.

Upon learning of Militare's visit to Premier, in early April 2005, Saturn retained David Travis, a computer and website specialist, to investigate suspected unauthorized access of Saturn's website by Militare. Travis's investigation confirmed Saturn's suspicions. According to Travis, Militare repeatedly accessed fifteen client accounts, including the debtor notes associated with those accounts, subsequent to his termination from Saturn. Travis found that in doing so, Militare reviewed a total of seventy-two privileged and confidential Saturn web pages.

On May 6, 2005, Saturn filed its complaint in this action, alleging claims of misappropriation of trade secrets and breach of contract and seeking damages and injunctive relief. The parties submitted cross-motions for summary judgment, which were denied, and the case was then tried to the court on September 11 and 12, 2007.

On October 31, 2007, the court entered a written order of judgment in Saturn's favor, finding Militare liable for misappropriation of Saturn's trade secrets . . . .

The court awarded Saturn $525 in damages for the cost of Travis's investigation as well as attorney fees and costs under the fee-shifting provision of the Agreement. After briefing by the parties on the amount of attorney fees and costs, the court entered an order on January 3, 2008, awarding Saturn $70,619.03 in attorney fees and $2,482.04 in costs. Militare timely appealed from the court's October 31, 2007 judgment and the January 3, 2008 attorney fees order . . . .

III. Misappropriation of Trade Secrets

Militare contends the trial court erred by finding that he misappropriated Saturn's trade secrets because there was insufficient evidence to show that (1) Saturn possessed valid trade secrets, and (2) Militare misappropriated Saturn's trade secrets. We reject these contentions in turn.

A. Trade Secrets Finding

First, Militare contends there is insufficient evidence to support the trial court's finding that the client and debtor information contained within Saturn's proprietary website database qualifies as trade secrets under Colorado law. We disagree.

What constitutes a trade secret is a question of fact for the trial court. *Network Telecomms., Inc. v. Boor-Crepeau*, 790 P.2d 901, 902 (Colo. App. 1990). Accordingly, if the court's trade secret determination is supported by the record, we will not disturb it on appeal. *See Page*, 197 Colo. at 313, 592 P.2d at 796.

The Colorado Uniform Trade Secrets Act (UTSA), defines a trade secret as:

> [T]he whole or any portion or phase of any scientific or technical information, design, process, procedure, formula, improvement, confidential business or financial information, listing of names, addresses, or telephone numbers, or other information relating to any business or profession which is secret and of value. § 7-74-102(4), C.R.S. 2010.

Colorado courts may consider several factors to make the factual determination of whether a trade secret exists under this statutory definition, including: (1) the extent to which the information is known outside the business; (2) the extent to which it is known to those inside the business, such as the employees; (3) the precautions taken by the holder of the trade secret to guard the secrecy of the information; (4) the savings effected and the value to the holder in having the information as against competitors; (5) the amount of effort or money expended in obtaining and developing the information; and (6) the amount of time and expense it would take for others to acquire and duplicate the information. *Network Telecomms., Inc.*, 790 P.2d at 903.

The UTSA further provides: "To be a "trade secret" the owner thereof must have taken measures to prevent the secret from becoming available to persons other than those selected by the owner to have access thereto for limited purposes." § 7-74-102(4). Thus, prior divisions of this court have held that "the alleged secret must be the subject of efforts that are reasonable under the circumstances to maintain its secrecy," but that "[e]xtreme and unduly expensive procedures need not be taken." *Colo. Supply Co. v. Stewart*, 797 P.2d 1303, 1306 (Colo. App. 1990). Reasonable efforts have been held to include advising employees of the existence of a trade secret, limiting access to a trade secret on a "need to know" basis, and controlling plant access. *Id.*

[handwritten: examples of reas. efforts]

Here, the trial court found that Saturn's client and debtor information stored within its proprietary database qualified as trade secrets under Colorado law because: (1) the information is confidential and not known outside of the business, either by competitors or the general public; (2) the real-time information is available only through the use of a client's username and password; (3) access to Saturn's database is strictly limited on a "need to know" basis; and (4) Saturn has taken reasonable efforts to maintain the secrecy of the information stored within its database.

[handwritten: trial ct]

The record supports the trial court's findings. Saturn's president testified that the specific information contained within its "status reports" and "debtor notes" is highly valuable to it and to competitors. For example, the testimony established that a competitor could use its knowledge of a client's available pre-purchased accounts and of the amount of debt recovered to date to develop a competitive marketing strategy exactly when that client was ripe for renewal with Saturn. Likewise, the testimony established that a competitor could use the highly detailed information contained within Saturn's debtor notes to usurp sales opportunities.

Further, Saturn's president described the security precautions that Saturn has taken to protect its proprietary information, including a password-protected and encrypted website and a policy of limited access. There was also testimony about the significant amount of money spent by Saturn to develop and maintain its database of information . . . .

We are not persuaded by Militare's contention that because Saturn did not present evidence of the exact data and figures allegedly misappropriated by Militare from its database, Saturn did not carry its burden to prove the existence of valid trade secrets. Given the dynamic nature of the information stored within Saturn's database, it was not necessary for Saturn to produce the exact client and debtor information accessed by Militare. Nor, in our view, would it be practical to impose such a burden on the owner of trade secrets, where, as here, the confidential information is constantly being updated in real time. Saturn produced evidence of the specific types of confidential information stored in its database, with sufficient particularity to identify the existence of its claimed trade secrets. As discussed above, the trial court properly relied on Saturn's evidence to determine that Saturn possessed valid trade secrets as defined by the UTSA and well-established Colorado case law.

[handwritten: ct unpersuaded by Militaire]

B. Misappropriation Finding *[handwritten: - yes]*

[handwritten: whether the TS was misappropriated]

Militare also contends there is insufficient evidence to support the trial court's finding that Militare misappropriated Saturn's trade secrets . . . .

Under the UTSA, "misappropriation" is defined in pertinent part as the "[a]cquisition of a trade secret of another by a person who knows or has reason to know that the trade secret was acquired by improper means." § 7-74-102(2)(a), C.R.S. 2010. "Improper means includes theft, bribery, misrepresentation, breach or inducement of a breach of a duty to maintain secrecy, or espionage through electronic or other means." *Id.* at § 7-74-102(1), C.R.S. 2010. As a prior division of this court observed, "[t]here is no requirement in Colorado's [UTSA] that there be actual use or commercial implementation of the misappropriated trade secret for damages to accrue. Misappropriation consists only of the improper disclosure or acquisition of the trade secret." *Sonoco Prods. Co. v. Johnson*, 23 P.3d 1287, 1290 (Colo. App. 2001).

Here, the trial court found that Militare "knowingly misappropriated numerous trade secrets belonging to Saturn" at the time of his termination and that "subsequent to that termination, [he] repeatedly accessed the Saturn website to review and update privileged information, without permission . . . caus[ing] injury to [Saturn]." The court further concluded that Militare "knowingly used improper means in order to use Saturn's trade secrets for his benefit." . . .

At trial, Militare testified that he "viewed" the restricted areas of Saturn's website subsequent to his termination, but that he did not "utilize" or "print" any information. For the purposes of a misappropriation inquiry under the UTSA, it is irrelevant whether Militare actually used Saturn's client and debtor information to compete against Saturn, or actually disclosed the information to others. *See* § 7-74-102(2); *Sonoco Prods. Co.*, 23 P.3d at 1290. Thus, because there is ample evidence in the record that Militare knowingly acquired password-protected information by improper means, we will not disturb the court's misappropriation finding on appeal.

NOTES

1. **Trade Secrets vs. Restrictive Covenants.** As illustrated by this case, restrictive covenants and trade secrets law can both be used to protect the same or similar information. What advantages do you see in one approach over the other? The *Militare* case reflects a recent trend in trade secrets cases where a former employee moves to a competitor and seeks to take with him information—often involving customers—from the prior position. The case, however, is atypical, in the damages remedy where Saturn Systems recovered only the cost of the search to determine whether Militare had accessed the database, as well as statutory attorney's fees. Damages in trade secrets cases are discussed further in note 6 below.

2. **Uniform Trade Secrets Act.** Trade secret law developed under the common law, but 48 states (Massachusetts and New York are the outliers) have adopted some form of the Uniform Trade Secrets Act. Although there are variations among states, the similarities are far more pronounced, and the vast majority of states have adopted the same broad definition of trade secrets. When one thinks of trade secrets, something like the formula for Coca-Cola is likely to come to mind, but a trade secret can be anything that meets the statutory test. As indicated in *Saturn Systems* and discussed in the note 4, customer lists are a common form of trade secrets. Pricing information can also be protected. *See LeJeune v. Coin Acceptors, Inc.*, 849 A.2d 451 (Md. 2004) (finding that pricing information could provide competitor economic advantage and therefore properly treated as trade secret). Strategic elements of a business plan have also been protected as a trade secret. *See*

Lydall, Inc. v. Ruschmeyer, 919 A.2d 421, 424 (Conn. 2007). One court has found that the entire business process, rather than any specific component, was a trade secret. *See Elm City Cheese Co. v. Federico*, 752 A.2d 1037, 1049 (Conn. 1999) (finding that specialty cheese maker's entire "business method" was protectable as a trade secret); *see also Altavion, Inc. v. Konica Minolta Sys. Lab, Inc.*, 226 Cal. App. 4th 26, 56–57 (2014) (algorithms, source code and design concepts for barcodes were trade secrets); *Harvey Barnett, Inc. v. Shidler*, 338 F.3d 1125 (10th Cir. 2003) (applying Colorado law to find that infant swimming program was trade secret), *rev'd on other grounds*, 2006 U.S. App. LEXIS 21078 (10th Cir. Aug. 15, 2006).

The critical question in many trade secret disputes is not whether the information at issue can be a trade secret, but whether the information was readily ascertainable or whether the employer took sufficient steps to guard its secrecy. *See Lehman v. Dow Jones & Co.*, 783 F.2d 285, 298 (2d Cir. 1986) (noting that the most important consideration is whether information was kept secret). A common means of establishing an intent to preserve secrecy is to require a confidentiality agreement for the employees. *See, e.g., Dionne v. Southeast Foam Converting & Packaging, Inc.*, 397 S.E.2d 110, 112 (Va. 1990) (noting that the presence of a confidentiality agreement can be sufficient to establish secrecy). Other methods include the existence of passcodes or passwords for sensitive information, and restrictions on public disclosures of confidential information. *See Finkel v. Cashman Prof'l, Inc.*, 270 P.3d 1259, 1264 (Nev. 2012) (company limited access to customer information to four employees); *Tyson Foods, Inc. v. ConAgra, Inc.*, 79 S.W.3d 326, 330 (Ark. 2002) (discussing ways in which secrecy can be demonstrated and holding that a confidentiality agreement is not required). If the information can be "ascertained" by means such as reverse engineering, it often will not qualify for trade secret protection. *See Marshall v. Gipson Steel, Inc.*, 806 So. 2d 266 (Miss. 2002) (where software could be derived by reverse engineering it was not a trade secret). Information will generally not be defined as a trade secret if it could be obtained by proper means even if it was not. *See First Express Grp., Inc. v. Easter*, 840 N.W.2d 465, 475 (Neb. 2013) (crop insurance customers). Why do you think this is true? Little Caesar's pizza has recently sued several of its former franchise owners for misappropriating the company's secrets regarding how to produce inexpensive pizza. How do you think this claim should be determined?

3.   **The Misappropriation Element**. To run afoul of the trade secrets laws, an individual must "misappropriate" the secrets but this issue rarely turns out to be a key component of most litigation. Why do you think that is? One reason why the "misappropriation" element is rarely at issue is because the secrecy element to define a trade secret—namely whether the employer took sufficient steps to protect the confidentiality of the information—largely duplicates the misappropriation element. If the employer took sufficient steps, then the employee generally will not have the authority to use the information. In a case that involved the question of whether a treasure map was a trade secret (it was), the court provided the following definition of misappropriation: "The elements of a claim for misappropriation of a trade secret are (1) the trade secret existed; (2) the trade secret was acquired through breach of a confidential relationship or was discovered by improper means; (3) the defendant used the trade secret without authorization; and (4) the plaintiff suffered damages." *Lamont v. Vaquillas Energy Lopeno Ltd.*, 421 S.W.3d 198, 210

(Tex. App. 2013). As noted in the *Militare* case, some courts permit a claim based on the acquisition, rather than the use of a trade secret, which is particularly relevant when the plaintiff is seeking injunctive relief. The Florida Trade Secrets statute provides: "[T]he acquisition, disclosure and/or use of the information to the disadvantage of the owner of the trade secret." FLA. STAT. § 688.002(2).

4. **Customer Lists**. Disputes over customer lists generate a substantial amount of trade secret litigation. It is well settled that customer lists can be trade secrets to the extent the employer has taken steps to protect their identities and the information is not publicly available. *See Dicks v. Jensen*, 768 A.2d 1279 (Vt. 2001). Interpreting Colorado law, one court has noted that in evaluating whether information has been kept secret requires determining if "the owner . . . [has] taken measures to prevent the secret from becoming available to persons other than those selected by the owner to have access thereto for limited purposes." *Harvey Barnett, Inc. v. Shidler*, 338 F.3d 1125, 1129 (10th Cir. 2003). The difficulty of protecting customer information, which can often be obtained from public sources, is one reason why restrictive covenants may be preferred as a way of protecting a customer base. Many employees have their customers or customer lists memorized, and courts have had to grapple with the question of whether the fact the list is memorized, as opposed to tangible, makes a difference. The majority of courts have found that it does not make a difference. As one court explained, "[T]he determination of whether a client list constitutes a trade secret . . . does not depend on whether it has been memorized by a former employee." *Al Minor & Assocs. v. Martin*, 881 N.E.2d 850, 855 (Ohio 2008) (following the majority rule).

5. **Trade Secrets vs. Patents**. There is often an overlap between protection afforded under trade secret law and what could be available under patent protection—though many trade secrets may not qualify for patent protection. One court has recently commented on the connection:

> The Uniform Trade Secrets Act operates in conjunction with patent law to protect developers and legitimate users of new commercial ideas and technology. A key difference between a trade secret and a patent is that the latter is open to public inspection, while the former is maintained in secrecy: "A patent owner acquires a time limited monopoly over the patented technology, and patent infringement can occur through the use of that technology by any means. The owner of a trade secret, on the other hand, is protected only against improper appropriation of the secret and subsequent use of a secret wrongly acquired. An owner of a trade secret may forgo resort to patent protection, but this choice risks the loss of the secret by voluntary use and disclosure or through legitimate, good faith means, such as reverse engineering." *Evans v. General Motors Corp., 976 A.2d 84, 51 Conn. Supp. 44, 55–56 (2007).*

Trade secrets are not protected against independent invention. Instead, the law of trade secrets recognizes that private parties invest extensive sums of money in certain information that loses its value when published to the world at large. Based on this logic, trade secret law creates a property right that is defined by the extent to which the owner of the secret protects that interest from disclosure to others. In doing so, the law allows the trade secret owner to reap the fruits of its labor and protects the owner's moral entitlement to these fruits. Trade secret law encourages the development and exploitation of lesser or different inventions than might be accorded protection under the patent laws, but which still play an important part in technological and scientific advancement. Without trade secret protection, organized scientific and technological research could become fragmented, and society as a whole could suffer. By restricting the acquisition, use, and disclosure of another's valuable, proprietary information by improper means, trade secret law minimizes the inevitable cost to the basic decency of society when one steals from another.

Progressive Prods., Inc. v. Swatz, 258 P.3d 969, 954 (Kan. 2011). The *Progressive Products* case involved a claim of misappropriation of trade secrets for a formula and mixing process of a ceramic backing that was used to coat pipes. The plaintiffs had developed the ceramic backing mix by obtaining ingredients from other available products, and with some assistance from the University of Pittsburgh. The defendants later left to start their own company, modifying the product created by Progressive. The court found that the formula for the product was protected as a trade secret because the company had sought to conceal the ingredients from third parties, including customers, and had told the employees that the product ingredients were confidential. However, the court went on to conclude that the pricing and the mixing process were publicly available and thus not protected as trade secrets.

other case

6. Damages. In the vast majority of trade secrets claims, the primary relief sought is an injunction to prevent the use of the information. In appropriate cases, damages are also available, though it can be difficult to determine the appropriate damages. The Texas Court of Appeals recently explained:

injunction

> Damages in trade secret cases can take a variety of forms. The methods used to calculate damages include the value of the plaintiff's lost actual profits from the use of the secret; the defendant's actual profits from the use of the secret; the value that a reasonably prudent investor would have paid for the trade secret; the development costs the defendant avoided by the misappropriation; and a reasonable royalty.

calc damages

Southwestern Energy Prod. Co. v. Berry-Helfand, 411 S.W.3d 581, 609 (Tex. App. 2013). Consider the *Militare* case—the court awarded damages for the cost of the search to determine the trade secret breach (and awarded attorneys' fees under the non-solicitation agreement). But what other damages might have been available? The lost profits to the plaintiff might be measured by a loss of business, and the same would be true if the court were to award the profits the defendant made on the trade secrets. As may be apparent, the damages resemble contract damages more than tort damages, and punitive damages are typically not available other than for egregious violations.

7. Advising Employers. What advice would you offer to an employer who wanted to know how best to protect its trade secrets? Covenants not to compete are often thought to be a superior means of enforcement because they offer greater certainty for employers. In one case involving efforts to restrict an employee from working for a competitor—in any capacity, anywhere in the United States for one year—the Fourth Circuit held that there had been no trade secret misappropriation but that the covenant not to compete was valid. The Court noted, "It will often be difficult, if not impossible, to prove that a competing employee has misappropriated trade secret information belonging to his former employer." *Comprehensive Tech. Int'l v. Software Artisans, Inc.*, 3 F.3d 730, 739 (4th Cir.) (citation omitted), *vacated on settlement*, 1993 U.S. App. LEXIS 28601 (4th Cir. Sept. 30, 1993). Other employers prefer to rely on trade secrets law. SAS, the largest privately held software company in the world, requires all of its employees to sign agreements that they will not disclose company secrets, but they do not use non-compete agreements. Their general counsel explained, "It kind of runs counter to our culture. . . . We only want people here who want to be here." Nancy Rivera Brooks, *Putting a Leash on Employees*, L.A. TIMES, Sept. 5, 1999, at C1.

2. Inevitable Disclosure

PEPSICO, INC. v. REDMOND
United States Court of Appeals for the Seventh Circuit
54 F.3d 1262 (1995)

FLAUM, CIRCUIT JUDGE.

Plaintiff PepsiCo, Inc., sought a preliminary injunction against defendants William Redmond and the Quaker Oats Company to prevent Redmond, a former PepsiCo employee, from divulging PepsiCo trade secrets and confidential information in his new job with Quaker and from assuming any duties with Quaker relating to beverage pricing, marketing, and distribution. The district court agreed with PepsiCo and granted the injunction. We now affirm that decision.

I.

The facts of this case lay against a backdrop of fierce beverage-industry competition between Quaker and PepsiCo, especially in "sports drinks" and "new age drinks." Quaker's sports drink, "Gatorade," is the dominant brand in its market niche. PepsiCo introduced its Gatorade rival, "All Sport," in March and April of 1994, but sales of All Sport lag far behind those of Gatorade. Quaker also has the lead in the new-age-drink category. Although PepsiCo has entered the market through joint ventures with the Thomas J. Lipton Company and Ocean Spray Cranberries, Inc., Quaker purchased Snapple Beverage Corp., a large new-age-drink maker, in late 1994. PepsiCo's products have about half of Snapple's market share. Both companies see 1995 as an important year for their products: PepsiCo has developed extensive plans to increase its market presence, while Quaker is trying to solidify its lead by integrating Gatorade and Snapple distribution. Meanwhile, PepsiCo and Quaker each face strong competition from Coca Cola Co., which has its own sports drink, "PowerAde," and which introduced its own Snapple-rival, "Fruitopia," in 1994, as well as from independent beverage producers. William Redmond, Jr., worked for PepsiCo in its Pepsi-Cola North America division ("PCNA") from 1984 to 1994. Redmond became the General Manager of the Northern California Business Unit in June, 1993, and was promoted one year later to General Manager of the business unit covering all of California, a unit having annual revenues of more than 500 million dollars and representing twenty percent of PCNA's profit for all of the United States.

Redmond's relatively high-level position at PCNA gave him access to inside information and trade secrets. Redmond, like other PepsiCo management employees, had signed a confidentiality agreement with PepsiCo. That agreement stated in relevant part that he

> would not disclose at any time, to anyone other than officers or employees of [PepsiCo], or make use of, confidential information relating to the *confidentiality agreement* business of [PepsiCo] . . . obtained while in the employ of [PepsiCo], which shall not be generally known or available to the public or recognized as standard practices.

Donald Uzzi, who had left PepsiCo in the beginning of 1994 to become the head of Quaker's Gatorade division, began courting Redmond for Quaker in May, 1994. Redmond met in Chicago with Quaker officers in August, 1994, and on October 20, 1994, Quaker, through Uzzi, offered Redmond the position of Vice President—On *Redmond* Premise Sales for Gatorade. Redmond did not then accept the offer but continued *Quaker* to negotiate for more money. Throughout this time, Redmond kept his dealings with Quaker secret from his employers at PCNA.

On November 8, 1994, Uzzi extended Redmond a written offer for the position of Vice President—Field Operations for Gatorade and Redmond accepted. Later that same day, Redmond called William Bensyl, the Senior Vice President of Human Resources for PCNA, and told him that he had an offer from Quaker to become the Chief Operating Officer of the combined Gatorade and Snapple company but had not yet accepted it. Redmond also asked whether he should, in light of the offer, carry out his plans to make calls upon certain PCNA customers. Bensyl told Redmond to make the visits.

Redmond also misstated his situation to a number of his PCNA colleagues, *misstating* including Craig Weatherup, PCNA's President and Chief Executive Officer, and *situation* Brenda Barnes, PCNA's Chief Operating Officer and Redmond's immediate superior. As with Bensyl, Redmond told them that he had been offered the position of Chief Operating Officer at Gatorade and that he was leaning "60/40" in favor of accepting the new position.

On November 10, 1994, Redmond met with Barnes and told her that he had decided to accept the Quaker offer and was resigning from PCNA. Barnes immediately took Redmond to Bensyl, who told Redmond that PepsiCo was considering legal action against him.

True to its word, PepsiCo filed this diversity suit on November 16, 1994, seeking *action* a temporary restraining order to enjoin Redmond from assuming his duties at Quaker and to prevent him from disclosing trade secrets or confidential information to his new employer. . . .

From November 23, 1994, to December 1, 1994, the district court conducted a preliminary injunction hearing. . . . At the hearing, PepsiCo offered evidence of a number of trade secrets and confidential information it desired protected and to *PH* which Redmond was privy. First, it identified PCNA's "Strategic Plan," an annually revised document that contains PCNA's plans to compete, its financial goals, and its strategies for manufacturing, production, marketing, packaging, and distribution for the coming three years. Strategic Plans are developed by Weatherup and his staff with input from PCNA's general managers, including Redmond, and are considered highly confidential. The Strategic Plan derives much of its value from the fact that it is secret and competitors cannot anticipate PCNA's next moves. PCNA managers received the most recent Strategic Plan at a meeting in July, 1994, a meeting Redmond attended. PCNA also presented information at the meeting regarding its plans for Lipton ready-to-drink teas and for All Sport for 1995 and beyond, including new flavors and package sizes.

Second, PepsiCo pointed to PCNA's Annual Operating Plan ("AOP") as a trade secret. The AOP is a national plan for a given year and guides PCNA's financial goals, marketing plans, promotional event calendars, growth expectations, and operational changes in that year. The AOP, which is implemented by PCNA unit General Managers, including Redmond, contains specific information regarding all PCNA initiatives for the forthcoming year. The AOP bears a label that reads "Private and Confidential—Do Not Reproduce" and is considered highly confidential by PCNA managers.

In particular, the AOP contains important and sensitive information about "pricing architecture"—how PCNA prices its products in the marketplace. Pricing architecture covers both a national pricing approach and specific price points for given areas. . . . As with other information contained in the AOP, pricing architecture is highly confidential and would be extremely valuable to a competitor. Knowing PCNA's pricing architecture would allow a competitor to anticipate PCNA's pricing moves and underbid PCNA strategically whenever and wherever the competitor so desired. PepsiCo introduced evidence that Redmond had detailed knowledge of PCNA's pricing architecture and . . . , as the General Manager for California, would have been responsible for implementing the pricing architecture guidelines for his business unit. . . .

Having shown Redmond's intimate knowledge of PCNA's plans for 1995, PepsiCo argued that Redmond would inevitably disclose that information to Quaker in his new position, at which he would have substantial input as to Gatorade and Snapple pricing, costs, margins, distribution systems, products, packaging and marketing, and could give Quaker an unfair advantage in its upcoming skirmishes with PepsiCo. Redmond and Quaker countered that Redmond's primary initial duties at Quaker as Vice President—Field Operations would be to integrate Gatorade and Snapple distribution and then to manage that distribution as well as the promotion, marketing and sales of these products. Redmond asserted that the integration would be conducted according to a pre-existing plan and that his special knowledge of PCNA strategies would be irrelevant. . . . The defendants also pointed out that Redmond had signed a confidentiality agreement with Quaker preventing him from disclosing "any confidential information belonging to others," as well as the Quaker Code of Ethics, which prohibits employees from engaging in "illegal or improper acts to acquire a competitor's trade secrets." Redmond additionally promised at the hearing that should he be faced with a situation at Quaker that might involve the use or disclosure of PCNA information, he would seek advice from Quaker's in-house counsel and would refrain from making the decision. . . .

On December 15, 1994, the district court issued an order enjoining Redmond from assuming his position at Quaker through May, 1995, and permanently from using or disclosing any PCNA trade secrets or confidential information. . . . This appeal followed.

II.

. . . The Illinois Trade Secrets Act ("ITSA"), which governs the trade secret issues in this case, provides that a court may enjoin the "actual or threatened misappropriation" of a trade secret. 765 ILCS 1065/3(a). A party seeking an injunction must therefore prove both the existence of a trade secret and the misappropriation. The defendants' appeal focuses solely on misappropriation; although the defendants only reluctantly refer to PepsiCo's marketing and distribution plans as trade secrets, they do not seriously contest that this information falls under the ITSA.

The question of threatened or inevitable misappropriation in this case lies at the heart of a basic tension in trade secret law. Trade secret law serves to protect "standards of commercial morality" and "encourage[ ] invention and innovation" while maintaining "the public interest in having free and open competition in the manufacture and sale of unpatented goods." 2 Jager, supra, § IL.03 at IL-12. Yet that same law should not prevent workers from pursuing their livelihoods when they leave their current positions. American Can Co. v. Mansukhani, 742 F.2d 314, 329 (7th Cir. 1984). . . . This tension is particularly exacerbated when a plaintiff sues to prevent not the actual misappropriation of trade secrets but the mere threat that it will occur. . . .

PepsiCo presented substantial evidence at the preliminary injunction hearing that Redmond possessed extensive and intimate knowledge about PCNA's strategic goals for 1995 in sports drinks and new age drinks. The district court concluded on the basis of that presentation that unless Redmond possessed an uncanny ability to compartmentalize information, he would necessarily be making decisions about Gatorade and Snapple by relying on his knowledge of PCNA trade secrets. It is not the "general skills and knowledge acquired during his tenure with" PepsiCo that PepsiCo seeks to keep from falling into Quaker's hands, but rather "the particularized plans or processes developed by [PCNA] and disclosed to him while the employer-employee relationship existed, which are unknown to others in the industry and which give the employer an advantage over his competitors." Amp, Inc. v. Fleishacker, 823 F.2d 1199, 1203 (7th Cir. 1987).

Admittedly, PepsiCo has not brought a traditional trade secret case, in which a former employee has knowledge of a special manufacturing process or customer list and can give a competitor an unfair advantage by transferring the technology or customers to that competitor. See, e.g., Glenayre Electronics, Ltd. v. Sandahl, 830 F. Supp. 1149 (C.D. Ill. 1993) (preliminary injunction sought to prevent use of trade secrets regarding pager technology). PepsiCo has not contended that Quaker has stolen the All Sport formula or its list of distributors. Rather PepsiCo has asserted that Redmond cannot help but rely on PCNA trade secrets as he helps plot Gatorade and Snapple's new course, and that these secrets will enable Quaker to achieve a substantial advantage by knowing exactly how PCNA will price, distribute, and market its sports drinks and new age drinks and being able to respond strategically. This type of trade secret problem may arise less often, but it nevertheless falls within the realm of trade secret protection under the present circumstances.

Quaker and Redmond assert that they have not and do not intend to use whatever confidential information Redmond has by virtue of his former employment. They point out that Redmond has already signed an agreement with Quaker not to disclose any trade secrets or confidential information gleaned from his earlier employment. They also note with regard to distribution systems that even if Quaker wanted to steal information about PCNA's distribution plans, they would be completely useless in attempting to integrate the Gatorade and Snapple beverage lines.

The defendants' arguments fall somewhat short of the mark. Again, the danger of misappropriation in the present case is not that Quaker threatens to use PCNA's secrets to create distribution systems or coopt PCNA's advertising and marketing ideas. Rather, PepsiCo believes that Quaker, unfairly armed with knowledge of PCNA's plans, will be able to anticipate its distribution, packaging, pricing, and marketing moves. Redmond and Quaker even concede that Redmond might be faced with a decision that could be influenced by certain confidential information that he obtained while at PepsiCo. In other words, PepsiCo finds itself in the position of a coach, one of whose players has left, playbook in hand, to join the opposing team before the big game. . . .

The district court also concluded from the evidence that Uzzi's actions in hiring Redmond and Redmond's actions in pursuing and accepting his new job demonstrated a lack of candor on their part and proof of their willingness to misuse PCNA trade secrets, findings Quaker and Redmond vigorously challenge. The court expressly found that:

> Redmond's lack of forthrightness on some occasions, and out and out lies on others, in the period between the time he accepted the position with defendant Quaker and when he informed plaintiff that he had accepted that position leads the court to conclude that defendant Redmond could not be trusted to act with the necessary sensitivity and good faith under the circumstances in which the only practical verification that he was not using plaintiff's secrets would be defendant Redmond's word to that effect.

The facts of the case do not ineluctably dictate the district court's conclusion. Redmond's ambiguous behavior toward his PepsiCo superiors might have been nothing more than an attempt to gain leverage in employment negotiations. The discrepancy between Redmond's and Uzzi's comprehension of what Redmond's job would entail may well have been a simple misunderstanding. The court also pointed out that Quaker, through Uzzi, seemed to express an unnatural interest in hiring PCNA employees: all three of the people interviewed for the position Redmond ultimately accepted worked at PCNA. Uzzi may well have focused on recruiting PCNA employees because he knew they were good and not because of their confidential knowledge. Nonetheless, the district court, after listening to the witnesses, determined otherwise. That conclusion was not an abuse of discretion.

Thus, when we couple the demonstrated inevitability that Redmond would rely on PCNA trade secrets in his new job at Quaker with the district court's reluctance to believe that Redmond would refrain from disclosing these secrets in his new position (or that Quaker would ensure Redmond did not disclose them), we conclude that the district court correctly decided that PepsiCo demonstrated a likelihood of success on its statutory claim of trade secret misappropriation . . . .

For the foregoing reasons, we affirm the district court's order enjoining Redmond from assuming his responsibilities at Quaker through May, 1995, and preventing him forever from disclosing PCNA trade secrets and confidential information.

Affirmed.

NOTES

1. **Relevant Factors.** What was the relevance of his confidentiality agreement? What do you think are the most significant factors for why the court upheld the injunction? Redmond had been a long-time employee; do you think that mattered to the court?

2. **Remedies.** How does the relief granted to PepsiCo differ from what might have been available through a covenant not to compete, which Redmond did not have? Injunctive relief is also available to enforce non-compete agreements, as are traditional contractual remedies, including the damages the employer incurred as a result of the breach of the agreement.

3. **Policy Justifications.** What is the justification for the inevitable disclosure doctrine? In applying the doctrine, one court quipped, "A trade secret once lost is, of course, lost forever." *FMC Corp. v. Taiwan Tainan Giant Indus. Co.*, 730 F.2d 61, 63 (2d Cir. 1984). Not only might the information be lost once it is revealed, but without the inevitable disclosure doctrine, employers might seek to hide information from their employees, or underinvest in their development and consequently, underinvest in innovation. Does that seem like a real threat? How might it apply to Redmond's situation?

Another problem that arises in this area is that for a long-term employee like Redmond, his services may be most valuable to another competitor. This is particularly true for someone like Redmond who has devoted his career to a particular industry. One court has taken what amounts to judicial notice of this fact:

> There was ample evidence that the reason Nihon Kohdren hired Plant was to obtain access to his intimate knowledge of Astro-Med's business. Viewing the evidence in the light most favorable to the verdict, it is a logical inference that a competitor who hires away a rival valued employer with access to inside information has done so in order to use that information to compete with the rival, and it is an equally logical inference that once Plant became a Nishon Kohdren employee, he sought to justify its hiring decision by revealing and using [that] information. . . .

Astro-Meds. Inc., v. Nihon Kohdren, 591 F.3d 1, 39 (1st Cir. 2009). Does that analysis seem convincing? If so, does that mean a high-level employee, or an employee with trade secrets, should never be permitted to move to a competitor? To avoid this problem, courts are increasingly rejecting the inevitable disclosure doctrine or requiring actual proof of threatened disclosure in order to obtain injunctive relief. *See Janus Et Cie v. Kahnke*, 2013 U.S. Dist. LEXIS 139686 (S.D.N.Y. Aug. 28, 2013) (need proof of actual misappropriation so as to avoid creating an implied restrictive covenant); *Pellerin v. Honeywell Int'l*, 877 F. Supp. 2d 983, 989 (S.D. Cal. 2012) ("California does not recognize the inevitable disclosure doctrine."); *Del Monte Fresh, Prod. Co. v. Dole Food Co.*, 148 F. Supp. 2d 1326, 1338 (S.D. Fla. 2001) (requiring actual proof of threatened disclosure in move of a scientist who worked on pineapple production from Del Monte to Dole Foods). Some courts, however, adhere to the doctrine but look for active concealment or steps by the employee that indicate theft. For example, in a case similar to *Redmond* where the employee was moving from a large baking company to Hostess, the court noted that the employee had failed to inform his employer of his intended move and had downloaded files just before he left. Under those circumstances, the court upheld a preliminary injunction under the inevitable disclosure doctrine. *See Bimbo Bakeries USA, Inc. v. Botticella*, 613 F.3d 102, 114 (3d Cir. 2010).

4. **Who Pays?** Assuming Redmond was out of work for six months, who should pay for that time period? Should he have to absorb the cost as a consequence of his work with PepsiCo, or should PepsiCo pay his salary? In England, the practice—known as "garden leave"—is that the company pays the employee's full salary and benefits during the time that he is restrained from working for a competitor. *See* Note, *Garden Leave: A Possible Solution to the Uncertain Enforceability of Restrictive Employment Covenants*, 102 COLUM. L. REV. 2291 (2002). Increasingly, employers are including a provision in restrictive covenants that require them to pay an employee's salary if they elect to enforce the agreement, and at least one court has noted this practice favorably in upholding an agreement. *See Estee Lauder Cos. v. Batra*, 430 F. Supp. 2d 158 (S.D.N.Y. 2006) (the contract provided, "During the period in which you are subject to the non-competition restrictions of paragraph 4, the Company will continue to pay your last regular salary at the company."). Without such a provision, an employee can suffer significant harm if she is enjoined from moving to a new employer. One court, in denying a preliminary injunction, noted: "The damage to Mr. Johnson's career [he was 58 at the time] and the risk that he will be sentenced to an early retirement, especially during these volatile times, cannot be underestimated." *IBM Corp. v. Johnson*, 629 F. Supp. 2d 321, 337 (S.D.N.Y. 2009), *aff'd*, 2009 U.S. App. LEXIS 23233 (2d Cir. Oct. 22, 2009); *see also* Cynthia L. Estlund, *Between Rights and Contract: Arbitration Agreements and Non-Compete Covenants as a Hybrid Form of Employment Law*, 155 U. PA. L. REV. 379 (2006) (advocating that employers be required to pay for the period a covenant is in place so as to ensure employers rely on the agreements only when they are valuable). Some employers have instituted a slightly different form of "garden leave" by requiring their employees to provide a certain amount of notice (up to six months) before they leave their position. During the notice period, the employee is paid her salary but generally relieved of her duties (allowed to work in the garden so to speak). Several courts have recently expressed concern that such a policy essentially compels the employee to continue working for her employer and have indicated a reluctance to enforce such agreements. *See Smiths Grp. PLC v.*

Frisbie, 2013 U.S. Dist. LEXIS 9445 (D. Minn. Jan. 24, 2013) (denying preliminary injunction on a contract that required six months' notice before resigning); *Bear, Stearns & Co. v. Sharon*, 550 F. Supp. 2d 174, 178 (D. Mass. 2008) (denying preliminary injunction because failure to show irreparable harm on a 90-day notice contract).

5. **A Collective Approach.** Trade secret law has been described as a curious amalgam of property, torts and contracts. *See* Robert G. Bone, *A New Look at Trade Secret Law: Doctrine in Search of Justification*, 86 CALIF. L. REV. 241 (1998). The secrets themselves are typically treated as the property of their employer; but there is a tort element to the claim in that there must be a "misappropriation," and contractual elements often come in to play whether through explicit agreements like the confidentiality agreement at issue in *PepsiCo* or through implicit agreements. Professor Bone advocates narrowing the focus of the law to its contractual basis. Another approach advocated by Nathan Newman is to incorporate a "collective" element to the bargaining process. He argues:

> . . . [B]ecause trade secrets are not typically the product of individual effort by any employee but result from the collaboration of many workers dependent upon one another, a better model for governing trade secrets would be through a collective bargaining system. Such a system would balance the collective interest of employees in their individual liberty to change jobs when needed and in preserving their collective investments of time and firm-specific human capital in any particular company. As well, such a collective bargaining system would better reflect society's interest in incentives for the production of intellectual property and its interest in the wide dissemination of ideas and skills. . . .

> Traditional economic theory had seen the choice for employees as either to continue marketing their particular set of skills to their present employer or to seek an alternative firm which might price them at a higher level. Even under traditional models ignoring innovation, this choice rarely if ever was costless, since there are usually high costs for leaving one's present employer for an exactly equivalent job. This basic dichotomy has been used to explain the traditional reasons why workers preferred an enhanced "voice" in the workplace through unions, over the "exit" option of threatening to quit. Such a collective voice was needed, in this view, to make up for the bargaining advantage employers had over employees due to the costs of switching jobs.

> When trade secrets and innovation are integrated into these models, the failure of employment markets and the need for collective bargaining become even clearer. Because much of the value of a worker's skills may be linked to firm-specific trade secrets, a worker's present employer has significant leverage over that worker. Since any "exit" from the firm threatens to "strip them naked" mentally of any skills they have learned, or created, on the job, they have much less to offer the next employer. It is only collective bargaining through unions at their present employers that is likely to compensate workers for this legally-enforced failure of the employment market to fully value their skills when switching employers. As

well, collective bargaining allows employees as a group to claim a fair share of the "quasi-rents" generated by the employer through its competitive advantage due to enforced trade secret protection . . . .

The main reform suggested by the analysis of this article is for unions and other advocates to argue for legislation requiring that any trade secret be declared invalid unless fair compensation has been negotiated collectively with employees involved in developing them. There is an opening for labor advocates to force "team" advocates to argue why management should receive the benefits of innovation in the trade secrets framework without a channel for workers to demand fair compensation. The very focus on group involvement in the process of innovation highlights the limits of both traditional intellectual property doctrine and individual contract traditions in the workplace. Labor advocates need to press on the point that the collective nature of process-innovation in the workplace just emphasizes why both compensation for the generation of innovation and the acceptable limits on worker freedom make sense only through collective bargaining negotiations.

Nathan Newman, *Trade Secrets and Collective Bargaining: A Solution to Resolving Tensions in the Economics of the Workplace*, 6 EMPL. RTS. & EMPLOY. POL'Y J. 1 (2002). Do these proposals make sense to you? What should the relation be between restrictive covenants and trade secrets?

C. THE DUTY OF LOYALTY

AUGAT, INC. v. AEGIS, INC.
Supreme Judicial Court of Massachusetts
565 N.E.2d 415 (1991)

WILKINS, J.

The plaintiff Isotronics, Inc. (Isotronics), a subsidiary of the plaintiff Augat, Inc. (Augat), manufactures high reliability metal microcircuit packages used to house electronic circuits. The individual defendant (Scherer) was one of three stockholders who sold Isotronics to Augat in 1975. He continued to work for Isotronics until 1980, served next as an Augat vice president, and then acted as a consultant to Augat until April, 1983. In May, 1984, one month after his agreement not to compete with Isotronics expired, Scherer formed the defendant Aegis, Inc., intending to manufacture high reliability metal and ceramic microcircuit packages. Scherer then communicated with Jay Greenspan, who was vice president and general manager of Isotronics, offering him employment and an equity interest in Aegis. Greenspan, an able and energetic manager, held a position of trust and confidence in Isotronics and was primarily responsible for Isotronics's success in becoming the dominant force in the metal packaging industry. Greenspan was not happy at Isotronics. In 1983, he had explored the possibility of forming his own company, but had been unable to obtain financing. At that time, Greenspan had discussed his plan with four Isotronics employees who held important senior managerial positions. Greenspan told Scherer that these senior managers had been interested in Greenspan's 1983 plan. In May or June, 1984, Greenspan and Scherer approached these four men, and over the next several months had meetings with them, separately and collectively, and on occasion also with prospective investors in Aegis. Three of these four men subsequently left Isotronics and went directly to work for Aegis. One major ground for the plaintiffs' claims against the defendants is that, in secretly seeking to obtain the services of key Isotronics managers, they knowingly joined in Greenspan's breach of his duty to Isotronics. That breach, the plaintiffs assert, in time led to a disruption of Isotronics when all those managers left Isotronics within a period of approximately two months.

In the summer of 1984, Scherer devoted his efforts to obtaining financing for Aegis. Greenspan and three of the managers who had been on Greenspan's prospective list in 1983 were committed to work for Aegis, if Aegis could be funded. The existence of the prospective management team was the most important factor in the view of the venture capitalists. . . .

Scherer sent his business plan to potential investors late in July, 1984. Greenspan delivered a letter of resignation on August 1, 1984, not stating any specific date for his departure. He made no mention then, or at any other time, of the possible departure of those key managers with whom he and Scherer had been talking or of other Isotronics personnel with whom Greenspan had been talking about joining Aegis. The prospective management team of Aegis met early in September and agreed on their relative shares of ownership of Aegis stock. Greenspan left Isotronics on September 27. On October 9, Aegis received a commitment letter for an investment of $4,300,000. The transaction was concluded on November 6. Aegis then entered the metal packaging business, not producing its first packages until May, 1985.

Augat and Isotronics brought this action in April, 1985, advancing various claims against the defendants. After extensive discovery and other pretrial activity and the bifurcation for trial of the liability and damages portions of the case, the matter was tried in June and July, 1988, before a judge without a jury, during twenty-four trial days. In August, 1989, the judge filed his findings of fact and rulings of law. . . . The judge . . . . ruled that Greenspan violated his duty of loyalty when, while still an Isotronics employee, he secretly solicited key managerial employees to join Aegis once it was funded. We uphold this ruling. . . .

We agree with the plaintiffs that the defendants are liable for Greenspan's breach of his duty of loyalty to Isotronics in not protecting Isotronics's interests against the loss of key employees to Aegis. Greenspan, as a vice president and general manager of Isotronics from 1981 to September 27, 1984, ran all aspects of Isotronics under the general supervision of the president of Augat, who was also the president of Isotronics. Greenspan was responsible for staffing and for hiring necessary replacements for any employees who might leave Isotronics. He regarded his duties to include maintaining at least one "backup" employee for each managerial position.

While Greenspan was still general manager of Isotronics he and Scherer solicited several important Isotronics employees to join Aegis if and when it were to be financed. Among those solicited, who later left Isotronics and went directly to work at Aegis, were: the vice president for marketing and sales, who left Isotronics on November 11, 1984; the new product design manager, Isotronics's most experienced engineer in the technology of making metal packages, who left on November 30, 1984; the manufacturing manager for Isotronics, who left on January 7, 1985; and Isotronics's engineering manager, who left on January 4, 1985. . . .

An at-will employee may properly plan to go into competition with his employer and may take active steps to do so while still employed. See Meehan v. Shaughnessy, 404 Mass. 419, 435 (1989). Such an employee has no general duty to disclose his plans to his employer, and generally he may secretly join other employees in the endeavor without violating any duty to his employer. *Id.* at 12 n.20. The general policy considerations are that at-will employees should be allowed to change employers freely and competition should be encouraged. See Maryland Metals, Inc. v. Metzner, 282 Md. 31, 47–48 (1978). If an employer wishes to restrict the post-employment competitive activities of a key employee, it may seek that goal through a non-competition agreement. See All Stainless, Inc. v. Colby, 364 Mass. 773, 778 (1974). The plaintiffs did not do so in this case.

There are, however, certain limitations on the conduct of an employee who plans to compete with his employer. He may not appropriate his employer's trade secrets. See Eastern Marble Products Corp. v. Roman Marble, Inc., 372 Mass. 835, 838–842 (1977). He may not solicit his employer's customers while still working for his employer, and he may not carry away certain information, such as lists of customers (New England Overall Co., Inc. v. Woltmann, 343 Mass. 69, 77 [1961]). Of course, such a person may not act for his future interests at the expense of his employer by using the employer's funds or employees for personal gain or by a course of conduct designed to hurt the employer.

The special circumstance of this case, distinguishing it from the typical case of improper employee conduct leading to competition with a former employer, is that there is but one significant breach of duty. It is important but substantially isolated. The defendants did not knowingly participate in any breach of duty by an Isotronics employee in any respect except in joining with Greenspan in soliciting the future employment of important employees. . . . The employees other than Greenspan committed no breach of duty. There is no showing that the key employees who left Isotronics for Aegis joined together to destroy Isotronics. If Scherer and Aegis had solicited the employees of Isotronics without the involvement of Greenspan prior to his departure from Isotronics, there would be no liability here.

The principle that, before he terminates his employment, a top managerial employee may not solicit the departure of employees to work for a competitor has been applied in various situations. The rule is most clearly applicable if the supervisor-manager, as a corporate pied piper, leads all his employer's employees away, thus destroying the employer's entire business. See Barden Cream & Milk Co. v. Mooney, [305 Mass. 545, 546 (1940)] (managers' solicitation of all employer's drivers, at-will employees, to join competitor simultaneously is a breach of duty). Although Greenspan's solicitation was directed only at certain key managerial personnel, his duty to maintain at least adequate managerial personnel forbade him, while still general manager of Isotronics, from seeking to draw key managers away to a competitor. See American Republic Ins. Co. v. Union Fidelity Life Ins. Co., 470 F.2d 820, 824 (9th Cir. 1972) (area manager's solicitation of insurance salesmen to join him in leaving plaintiff's employment to join competitor violated duty of loyalty). The rule we express for the purposes of this case applies only to a general manager who, while still employed, secretly solicits key managerial employees to leave their employment to join the general manager in a competitive enterprise. Greenspan admitted that he put his loyalties to the people who were to go to Aegis ahead of his obligations as an officer of Isotronics.

The defendants argue that the plaintiffs failed to show that their wrongdoing caused any loss to the plaintiffs. In the liability portion of a bifurcated trial, the plaintiff must show that the defendant's breach of duty caused some harm for which the law provides redress because there can be no liability in the absence of causation. The judge's findings on causation are sparse and, of course, are not focused on the consequences of the breach of duty that we have identified in this opinion. We have considered the evidence and conclude that the plaintiffs have shown that the departure of the key employees whom Greenspan solicited caused some disruption of Isotronics.

Def arg.

The plaintiffs' damages relate to negative effects on operating results that would not have occurred but for the departure of the key managerial employees. Because there is no finding or showing that Aegis would not have been financed if these key employees were not to work for it, and Aegis did not sell any products until well into 1985, the plaintiffs' damages are not to be measured by Aegis's profits. The plaintiffs must prove that losses that Isotronics sustained would not have occurred but for Greenspan's breach of his duty of loyalty. These would be losses that were caused by problems arising from the departure to Aegis of key managerial employees who were approached by Greenspan while he and they were still employed by Isotronics, provided that the losses were caused by events occurring before Isotronics reasonably should have replaced the departed managerial employees with competent people. See BBF, Inc. v. Germanium Power Devices Corp., 13 Mass. App. Ct. 166, 173 (1982). . . .

damages

The case is remanded to the Superior Court for proceedings consistent with this opinion.

So ordered.

NOTES

1. **Permissible Actions.** What did Greenspan do wrong in the case? What could he have done to recruit the employees? The court suggests that its holding is limited to managerial employees; from the case, can you determine what duties are owed by lower-level employees? The law varies regarding which employees owe a duty to their employer, and the scope of the duty often differs for higher and lower-level employees. *See, e.g., Alpha Schl. Bus. Co. v. Wagner*, 910 N.E.2d 1134, 1150 (Ill. App. Ct. 2009) (under Illinois law the duty of loyalty only applies to corporate officers); *Houng Que, Inc. v. Luu*, 150 Cal. App. 4th 400, 413 (2007) (noting that an employee breaches a duty whenever she "takes action that is inimical to the best interests of the employer"). The duty of executives is often referred to as a fiduciary duty and is distinct from the duty of loyalty. *See, e.g., Western Blue Print Co. v. Roberts*, 367 S.W.3d 7, 12 (Mo. 2012) ("Missouri law is clear that officers and directors of public

and closely held corporations are fiduciaries because they occupy positions of the highest trust and confidence and are required to exercise the utmost good faith when using the powers conferred upon them to both the corporation and their shareholders."). Several courts have gone further and declined to find a duty of loyalty for at-will employees. *See Dalton v. Camp*, 548 S.E.2d 704 (N.C. 2001) (no independent duty of loyalty for at-will employees who are not fiduciaries); *Physician Specialists in Anesthesia, P.C. v. Wildmon*, 521 S.E.2d 358, 362 (Ga. Ct. App. 1999) ("Allowing an employer to sue an at-will employee for breach of loyalty when our law allows an employer to terminate an at-will employee for 'any or no reason' would create an unjust advantage for employers.").

2.   **Duty of Loyalty vs. Trade Secrets.** The duty of loyalty cause of action offers a third means of restricting employee mobility. Does the duty of loyalty tort offer more protection to employers than trade secrets law? The New Jersey Supreme Court has also imposed a duty on employees not to take information relating to customers even if the information was not protected under trade secrets law. The court noted, "An employee's duty of loyalty to his or her employer goes beyond refraining from privately soliciting the employer's customers while still employed. The duty of loyalty prohibits the employee from taking affirmative steps to injure the employer's business." *Lamorte Burns & Co. v. Walters*, 770 A.2d 1158, 1169–70 (N.J. 2001).

3.   **Clients.** Soliciting clients also frequently leads to claims for a breach of the duty of loyalty. Like employees, absent a contractual agreement clients are free to take their business elsewhere. As a result, many courts draw the line between solicitation of clients and announcing one's new business to those clients, with the latter treated as a permissible action. *See, e.g., McCallister Co. v. Kastella*, 825 P.2d 980 (Ariz. Ct. App. 1992) (finding that a letter notifying clients of new business without soliciting those clients was a permissible employment practice for employee). In interpreting a non-solicitation agreement, the First Circuit Court of Appeals recently noted that a targeted email by a departing employee may go too far: "While we do not question the rights of parties to make public announcements of changes in employment, 'targeted mailings' of former customers may cross the line into impermissible solicitation." *Corporate Techs., Inc. v. Harnett*, 731 F.3d 6, 12 (1st Cir. 2013) (interpreting Mass. Law).

4.   **Remedies.** As noted earlier, an important difference among the various avenues for protecting information post-employment are the available remedies. In the case of a breach of the duty of loyalty, the common remedy is a disgorgement of the profits the defendant obtained as a result of the breach. *See Eckard Brandes, Inc. v. Riley*, 338 F.3d 1082 (9th Cir. 2003), *cert. denied*, 541 U.S. 1009 (2004). In other words, the defendant would have to turn over to the plaintiff its wrongfully earned profits. In *Augat*, the Massachusetts Supreme Judicial Court found that the defendant's profits were not the proper measure; but instead it required the plaintiffs to prove their lost profits that were attributable to the breach. What is the difference between these two standards? Punitive damages may also be available for serious cases of misconduct. Under trade secrets law, the preferred remedy is injunctive relief, would injunctive relief be appropriate for a duty of loyalty claim?

In a case that drew national attention, a Chief Executive Officer was required to forfeit all of the compensation he received during his period of disloyalty. In *Astra USA, Inc. v. Bildman*, 914 N.E.2d 36 (Mass. 2009), the executive was fired after a news story reported he had engaged in a pattern of sexual harassment that had resulted in a number of settlements and reputational damage to the company. Interpreting New York law, the Massachusetts Supreme Court noted, "The law of New York requires the disloyal employee to forfeit his compensation [even] if he otherwise performed valuable services for the principal." *Id.* at 47. The court also noted that other jurisdictions, including Massachusetts, take into account the value the employee might have rendered, and ultimately the court upheld the $1 million jury verdict awarded to Astra as the reasonable valuation of his compensation during his approximately five years of disloyalty.

5. Employer Practices and Loyalty. Ken Matheny and Marion Crain argue that the employment-at-will rule largely undermines efforts to create employee loyalty, and suggest that employers ought to revise their employment practices as a way of engendering more employee loyalty. They write:

> The survival of the employment-at-will doctrine into the twenty-first century is one of the central paradoxes of American capitalism. Employee loyalty is more important now than it has ever been. The growing service sector demands a high level of commitment to the employer's goals because of the difficulty of directly supervising and monitoring employee activities in the service sector. Employee loyalty is doubly significant because customer loyalty (and hence, profitability) increases proportionally in relation to employee loyalty. A one-sided psychological contract unilaterally imposed by management is unlikely to elicit the loyalty required in a post-Taylorist workplace where direct monitoring of employee performance is difficult.

> Most employers do not enjoy the sort of employee attachment that they need to prosper. In a recent survey of 36,000 American workers and just under 4,400 Canadian workers, Towers Perrin found that a substantial majority of workers (sixty-four percent, or approximately two-thirds of the group surveyed) are only moderately "engaged" in their workplaces. Only seventeen percent of employees are highly engaged . . . [and] nineteen percent are disengaged (unenthusiastic and "checked out"). An earlier Towers Perrin study probed even deeper, focusing on the emotional connection that workers feel to their work, and seeking to identify the factors that contribute to emotional investment—loyalty—as distinguished from a more intellectual engagement in the work. Those who are emotionally engaged are dedicated at the level of the heart (as opposed to the mind) and feel attachment to the firm (as opposed to ties to their occupation or to their individual careers). Disturbingly, the study results indicated that the majority of workers, fifty-five percent, display either negative or intensely negative feelings toward their work. . . .

> This data suggests that the triumph of exit in the at-will state has become dysfunctional. Worker turnover is higher where workers are only moderately engaged or disengaged, increasing training costs and resulting

in losses of human capital and knowledge to the firm. Worker productivity is directly linked to engagement: highly engaged workers devote discretionary effort to their jobs, improving the organization's financial performance (particularly in service businesses, where customer service determines profitability); hence, a culture that undermines morale undermines productivity. Finally, negative worker attitudes can influence employee morale at the institutional level, spreading like a virus to workers who were previously moderately or highly engaged.

Employers have sought to elicit commitment through a combination of monitoring, financial incentives, and peer pressure. Others have instituted incentive or positive reinforcement programs which communicate the firm's gratitude and dependence on the workers' efforts. However, these strategies have not been sufficient to overcome the disengagement created by the unidirectional loyalty norms operating on the employment relation and the at-will rule's commitment to the role of exit. . . .

We suggest that engendering worker loyalty by providing some measure of job security and avenues for voice in workplace decision-making is a superior strategy because it invests workers in the firm. Survey results support this approach: workers rated employer care and concern for employees along with opportunities for growth and career development as the top motivators for employee loyalty, outstripping financial compensation and contractual barriers to exit. . . . Thus, key factors likely to build worker engagement include a demonstrated interest by the company in employees' well-being, evidenced by honest communication and a two-way dialogue; a sense of control by workers over their work environment and the flow and pace of work; challenging work; accountability for performance and opportunities for development and advancement; and a feeling of shared destiny that creates a community at the workplace. . . .

The studies of worker loyalty referenced above have confirmed that the presence of vehicles for employee voice and participation are a major factor in building the foundation for worker loyalty. Affording workers the opportunity to have input into and control over their work increases investment not only in the jobs/occupations, but to the firm. By stimulating employee interest in the work, the firm reaps the benefits of increased willingness to invest discretionary effort and improved morale, even when the employees so engaged are doing more work than others in terms of volume.

These are not new insights. The essence of loyalty is not exit, but voice. Rather than quitting when she is dissatisfied, the loyal employee voices her discontent. Mechanisms furthering participatory democracy in the workplace have long been thought to counteract feelings of alienation and apathy. Indeed, this was the goal of the Wagner Act—the protection of unionization and adoption of collective bargaining would enhance worker participation and promote democracy in the workplace. . . . Unionization and collective bargaining have not, however, proven to be the solution to these problems. Union affiliation correlates negatively with measures of employee satisfaction and loyalty. Perhaps it is time to consider new structures to foster worker voice and participation.

Ken Matheny & Marion Crain, *Disloyal Workers and the "Un-American" Labor Law*, 82 N.C. L. REV. 1705, 1740–50 (2004). As a way of restructuring the workplace "to give more priority to voice and loyalty than to exit," the authors suggest changing the default rule of employment-at-will to one of discharge for good cause, and allowing alternative modes of employee representation such as identity caucuses, worker councils and interest arbitration as a way of fostering an independent employee voice in the workplace. *Id.* at 1755–57. Does this analysis seem persuasive to you? If so, why don't more employers alter their workplace practices as a means of creating loyalty rather than imposing various restrictions on their employees?

6. Tortious Interference with a Contract. When individuals, typically former employees but not always, recruit employees and clients they are frequently the subject of a claim for tortious interference with a contract. While only an employee owes a duty of loyalty to the employer, third parties can be sued when they cause existing contracts to be breached. Some courts have allowed the tort even when a third-party seeks to recruit an at-will employee. *See, e.g., Huff v. Swartz*, 606 N.W.2d 461 (Neb. 2000) (discussing other jurisdictions and allowing a claim against a co-employee so long as the person was not acting in the interest of the employer). In *Reeves v. Hanlon*, 95 P.3d 513 (Cal. 2004), the California Supreme Court explored the contours of the claim in the context of attorneys who left a law partnership and sought to take files and clients with them. The court explained:

> To prevail on a cause of action for intentional interference with contractual relations, a plaintiff must plead and prove (1) the existence of a valid contract between the plaintiff and a third party; (2) the defendant's knowledge of that contract; (3) the defendant's intentional acts designed to induce a breach or disruption of the contractual relationship; (4) actual breach or disruption of the contractual relationship; and (5) resulting damage. To establish the claim, the plaintiff need not prove that a defendant acted with the primary purpose of disrupting the contract, but must show the defendant's knowledge that the interference was certain or substantially certain to occur as a result of his or her action.

Id. at 1148 (citations omitted). The *Hanlon* case involved at-will employees, and in order to preserve the freedom implicit in such a relationship the court added the requirement to recover for interference in an at-will relationship the employer must establish that the third party engaged in "an independently wrongful act." *Id.* To carve out run-of-the-mill solicitation of employee cases, many courts have imposed heightened requirements of proof to establish a tortious interference claim. *See Lockheed Martin Corp. v. Aatlas Commerce, Inc.*, 283 A.D.2d 801, 803 (N.Y. App. Div. 2001) (plaintiff must prove defendant engaged in "very serious misconduct"); *Daley v. Wellpoint Health Networks, Inc.*, 146 F. Supp. 2d 92, 104 (D. Mass. 2001) (requiring actual malice under Massachusetts law).

PROBLEM AND THOUGHTS FOR THE FUTURE

As we noted at the beginning of this Chapter, there has been a substantial increase in the use of non-compete agreements and a similar growth in trade secrets litigation, both of which have led to serious concerns among employee advocates regarding restraints on employee mobility. Two scholars recently reviewed the developments from what they called an "ethical" viewpoint and concluded that: (1) non-compete agreements should be limited to those in possession of proprietary business information; (2) the inevitable disclosure rule should only apply when actual disclosure is threatened; and (3) garden leave policies best protect the interests of employers and employees. Norman D. Bishara & Michelle Westermann, *The Law and Ethics of Restrictions on Employee's Post-Employment Mobility*, 49 Am. Bus. L.J. 1 (2012). Consider those issues, and issues raised throughout this Chapter, as you work through the following problem:

Matthew Fields worked at one of the largest fireworks companies in the United States where he was employed as a pyrotechnician and ran the fireworks shows. In his job, he had contact with customers, and also had access to pricing information. The company he was employed with was a family-owned business that specifically advertised Fields as a skilled pyrotechnician, and it paid for his certification and training. During his employment, Fields signed a two-year non-compete agreement that prohibited him from working with a competitor or soliciting clients. The family that had owned the company sold it to a large company, and shortly thereafter Fields decided to leave to work for a direct competitor. The company then sued Fields for breaching his restrictive covenant; misappropriation of trade secrets, and breach of his duty of loyalty, and it sued the new employer for tortious interference with a contract.

Based on those facts, what would the employer have to prove in order to enforce the non-compete agreement? How about on the misappropriation of trade secrets? In the new job, Fields had little or no client contact and primarily was responsible for putting on the fireworks shows. If you represented the employer, what would be your strongest argument? What about if you represented the employee? A slightly different question, in this scenario, how do you think a court should rule, and why? In thinking about the future direction of the law, and how you might advise employees and employers, consider a recent decision by the Virginia Supreme Court. The case involved a restrictive covenant for a pest control employee that prevented him from working for a competitor that the court held was overbroad because it did not serve a permissible purpose. The employer responded that the Court had upheld the identical provision two decades earlier to which the Court observed that it had "refined" its application of the law and that the provision was now impermissibly overbroad. *See Home Paramount Pest Control Cos. v. Shaffer*, 718 S.E.2d 762, 770 (Va. 2011).

D. EMPLOYEE INVENTIONS

The final section of this chapter focuses on the question of who owns inventions created by employees. Although questions relating to employee inventions do not necessarily involve restraints on employee mobility, they raise related questions of who owns the product of the employee's labor where the employer contributes to the creation of the project. Many inventions are patented, and patent law frequently plays a role in determining ownership. Moreover, in workplaces where patentable ideas or inventions are likely to be created, many employers require their employees to sign specific contracts governing the ownership of any resulting patents (typically fully assigning the rights to the employer or providing for some form of joint ownership). As indicated by the case that follows, disputes can arise when there is no explicit contract.

WOMMACK v. DURHAM PECAN CO.
United States Court of Appeals for the Fifth Circuit
715 F.2d 962 (1983)

Gee, Circuit Judge.

This patent infringement action has been brought by the inventor of a patented process against his former employer requesting reasonable royalties for the employer's use of the process in his plant. The employer admits that he used the process and he neither contests the validity of plaintiff's patent nor asserts any right to receive assignment of the patent arising from the contract of employment. Instead, the employer claims he had acquired a shop right or implied license to use the process and he therefore owes plaintiff nothing. We agree with the employer's position and affirm the district court's dismissal.

Facts

The following representation of the facts is not contested by the parties. The story is one of an amicable and mutually beneficial employer-employee relationship turned sour. The employer is the Durham Pecan Company of Comanche, Texas. Since 1965, Durham has been in the business of processing pecans. Its operations include shelling the pecans, separating the pecan pieces into various gradations of size and packaging and selling the final product. The employee is Malcolm Wommack. In 1970, Wommack was hired by Durham as a general laborer in its pecan processing plant. His duties included unloading trucks, sweeping floors and moving supplies. His initial salary was $1.80 an hour, and, as might be expected from the nature of his employment, there were no agreements regarding any inventions he might produce.

And yet Wommack proved more curious and clever than expected. The process he ultimately patented indicates that he took a special interest in at least one aspect of pecan processing: the separation of worms from the shelled pecan pieces. The worm-like larvae of the pecan weevil found in pecans hatch there from eggs laid in the pecan shell while still on the tree. If the pecans are to be successfully marketed, these worms must be removed from the shelled pecan pieces. This is one of the stages of pecan processing performed by Durham.

For years Durham employees handpicked the worms from the shelled pecan pieces. The task was made difficult by the fact that the worms were the same color as the pecans. The ability of the handpickers to distinguish visually between the worms and the pecans was improved when, in 1973, Durham began using an ultraviolet (UV) light on its worm table. When illuminated by UV light, the worms and the pecan meat (inside of pecan exposed when broken) fluoresce while the pecan skin (outside of pecan separated from shell) does not. While this process improved the identification of the worms, it solved only part of the problem; it still was difficult for the handpickers to distinguish between the worms and the pecan meat, both of which fluoresced.

Such was the state of the art of worm picking in pecan processing when Wommack conceived his process. On roughly January 25, 1975, Wommack discovered that yellow food coloring blocked the fluorescence produced by the UV light. Working in his home, he conducted some simple experiments using his own equipment and materials. The resulting process required simply that the shelled pecan pieces be soaked in a weak solution of yellow food coloring and then dried. Because the yellow food coloring adhered to, or was absorbed by, the pecan pieces and not by the worms, the UV light now caused only the worms to fluoresce.

On February 17, 1975, Wommack took the precaution of mailing to himself in a certified letter a complete description of the process he had developed. On the same day, Wommack informed his employer, W. M. Durham, who is also co-owner of Durham, that he had developed an improved method of distinguishing the worms from the pecans. Later that evening Mr. Durham accepted his employee's invitation and visited Wommack's home to observe a demonstration. After viewing some treated pecans under a black light, Mr. Durham concluded, "the meats were—had been dulled in color, the white sides were not as prominent, and yet the worms still fluoresced very well." . . .

It is unclear what, if anything, transpired between February and May of 1975, but during the first week of May, Mr. Durham and Wommack again discussed the process and Wommack explained that the dulling of the pecan meats had been produced by yellow food coloring. Later that week, Durham received and began experimenting with a UV sorting machine. . . . After the machine was installed and several tests were run with uncolored pecan pieces, Mr. Durham asked Wommack if he could use Wommack's process. Wommack said, "Yes." In only a few hours, Wommack and another Durham employee were able to bring Wommack's homespun process to commercial application in the Durham plant.

When Wommack agreed to permit Durham to use his process, it also was agreed that Durham would loan to Wommack various pieces of sorting equipment for Wommack's home experiments. Several Durham employees transported this equipment to Wommack's house. Based on his personal experiments and on the experience acquired by use of the process in the Durham plant, Wommack prepared a patent application. The application described in detail the process as it was then being used by Durham, including diagrams of Durham's processing operations and equipment. On December 15, 1975, Wommack filed the application in his own name and at his own expense. He showed the application to Mr. Durham sometime during this month.

On January 26, 1976, Wommack was fired,[1] at which point the relationship

---

[1] [n. 3] Mr. Durham testified that the decision to fire was based on personal differences between Wommack and several other Durham employees.

between Wommack and his former employer disintegrated rapidly. In February 1976, Wommack wrote a letter to Mr. Durham explaining, among other things, "since I have been let go from your Company, the word agreement that you could use my process in your plant, is no longer valid. We need a signed agreement on the use of my process." Mr. Durham promptly responded by explaining his position, "[the process] was all yours. That all I wanted was the right to use this in my plant and you agreed to this." In July of that year, Wommack demanded that if Durham continued to use the process without a signed agreement, he would take the matter to court. Durham continued using the process until sometime in July 1979. This action was brought on November 7, 1979.

This case was submitted to a jury . . . [and] [t]he jury found the essential elements of patent infringement, all of which are no longer, and many of which were never, contested by defendant. . . . Nevertheless, the district court found in favor of defendant based on the finding . . . that defendant had acquired a shop right. Because a shop right, also referred to as an implied license, is a complete defense to infringement, plaintiff's claim was dismissed.

Shop Right or Implied License

That an invention was conceived or developed while the inventor was employed by another does not alone give the employer any right in the invention. The employer must show that a mutual understanding existed between the inventor and his employer that the inventor was employed to exercise his inventive faculties for the employer's benefit. If the employer proves this, he acquires ownership of the patent. Durham, however, makes no such claim. Wommack was hired as a general laborer at $1.80 an hour.

Alternatively, if the employee was not hired to invent, the employer may establish a shop right. As commonly stated, a shop right will be found where the employer shows that the invention was developed by his employee during the employer's time or with the assistance of the employer's property or labor. A shop right permits the employer to use the subject of the patent for his own purposes, but not to sell or prohibit others from using it. The inventor retains a valid patent. This circuit has explained the shop right rule in the following manner:

> The classic shop rights doctrine ordains that when an employee makes and reduces to practice an invention on his employer's time, using his employer's tools and the services of other employees, the employer is the recipient of an implied nonexclusive, royalty-free license.

Hobbs v. United States, 376 F.2d 488, 494 (5th Cir.1967).

Appellant places particular weight on the language in this and other cases indicating that the invention be "reduce[d] to practice" with the employer's assistance. Although it is unclear precisely what the court in *Hobbs* intended by using this term in the shop right context, reduced to practice has a specific meaning in other patent law contexts. . . .

An invention begins when the idea is conceived in the inventor's mind. Its development may proceed to actual use, but it need not for the idea to be patentable.

For this, the idea simply must be reduced to practice . . . [so as] . . . "to demonstrate that the device as it exists possesses sufficient utility to justify a patent, i.e., that the invention is suitable for its intended purpose." Stearns v. Beckman Instruments, Inc., 669 F.2d 1095, 1099 (5th Cir.1982). Yet, reduction to practice does not require that the device embodying the invention be mechanically perfect or in a commercially marketable form. Kardulas v. Florida Machine Products Co., 438 F.2d 1118, 1121 (5th Cir. 1971).

For the purposes of patentability, therefore, reduction to practice marks a distinct point of time in the development of a novel idea. In the shop right context, *Hobbs* tells us that "when an employee makes and reduces to practice an invention" with the assistance of his employer, the employer acquires a right to use. Appellant reads this to imply that if the employer's assistance does not contribute to the reduction to practice of an idea—for example, if Wommack had reduced his idea to practice before obtaining Durham's assistance—the employer cannot obtain a shop right.

This reading of the shop right rule apparently guided the trial of this case and its argument on appeal. It is, however, erroneous. The employer's assistance in the reduction to practice of an idea is not necessary to his obtaining a shop right in the invention. An employee may reduce his idea to practice on his own time before showing his invention to his employer, and nevertheless subsequent employer-employee cooperation on the invention may be sufficient to confer a shop right upon the employer. In fact, the principal consideration in the shop right determination is not the employer's assistance, but the employee's consent.

. . . This circuit has explained that the finding of a shop right involves two principal considerations:

> First, it seems only fair that when an employee has used his employer's time and equipment to make an invention, the employer should be able to use the device without paying a royalty. Second, under the doctrine of estoppel if an employee encourages his employer to use an invention, and then stands by and allows him to construct and operate the new device without making any claim for compensation or royalties, it would not be equitable to allow the employee later to assert a claim for royalties or other compensation.

Hobbs, 376 F.2d at 495 (*citing Gill*).

A court therefore must conduct more than merely a quantitative analysis of how much of the employer's assistance was contributed to the process or during exactly what stage of development it was rendered. The assistance of the employer "is important only as furnishing an item of evidence tending to show that the patentee consented to and encouraged [his employer] in making use of his devices." *Id.* . . .

As we have demonstrated above, an idea may pass through several stages as it develops from inventor's conception to ultimate commercial use. The law has identified a particular intermediary stage as marking its reduction to practice. While this stage is critical for purposes of patentability, it is not for the shop right determination. The district court therefore was correct in . . . finding that Durham's property and employees assisted in "putting [the process] into . . .

practical use" and "develop[ing] or put[ting it] into practical form"—to support its finding that Durham assisted in the development of the process. . . . [This] . . . finding [is] supported by the uncontradicted evidence that Wommack conceived, experimented with and perhaps reduced to practice his process without Durham's assistance, and that Durham's resources were used to develop the process further, ultimately to a commercially useable form.

It must be recalled that the employer's assistance "is important only as furnishing an item of evidence tending to show that the patentee consented to and encouraged [his employer] in making use of his device." Gill, 160 U.S. at 435. The estoppel, arising from the patentee's consent, is the "ultimate fact to be proved." *Id.* Such consent may be proven in more than one way:

> The most conclusive evidence of such consent is an express agreement or license, . . . but it may also be shown by parol testimony, or by conduct on the part of the patentee proving acquiescence on his part in the use of his invention. The fact that he made use of the time and tools of his employer, put at his service for the purpose, raises either an inference that the work was done for the benefit of such employer, or an implication of bad faith on the patentee's part in claiming the fruits of labor which technically he had no right to enlist in his service.

Id. In the present case, the special verdicts, supported by the uncontradicted evidence, permit only one reasonable inference: Wommack consented to his employer's use in return for Durham's assistance in developing his process to commercial use.

First, we have the evidence of Wommack's objective conduct. Wommack invited Mr. Durham to his house to demonstrate his process. Later, he permitted Durham to adapt its processing operations to accommodate his process. Principally through his efforts, Durham succeeded in reducing his process to commercial application. In addition, Wommack accepted the loan of Durham's equipment in order to conduct his home experiments and relied heavily upon the experience acquired in the Durham plant when preparing his patent application. Wommack permitted Durham to use his process for a full year without any claim for compensation.

If Wommack's objective conduct were the only evidence of consent available in this case, we nevertheless would be persuaded to infer a shop right. Such conduct is sufficient to permit the inference that the work performed in the Durham plant was done for Durham's benefit. A shop right has often been found where the employee merely makes use of his employer's property or labor to develop his process. Such conduct can provide sufficient evidence of consent. *See Gill*, 160 U.S. at 429–34. In the present case, however, we have more direct evidence of consent: Wommack's verbal agreement that Durham could use his process. . . .

The uncontradicted evidence in this case permits the inference that behind Wommack's express consent was an implicit exchange of consideration. When Wommack first consented to and assisted in Durham's use of his process, he had nothing more than an idea he hoped to patent and sell. The patentability of the process, the manner in which it would be applied in a processing plant and the profitability of such application was uncertain. Yet, the exchange of benefits was certain. Wommack received the opportunity to test his process commercially and to use Durham's equipment in his home for his own experiments. Wommack benefitted from this experience in preparing his patent application; he also may have hoped that proven commercial success in the Durham plant would facilitate the sale of his process to other plants. Durham offered this assistance, at its own risk, with the only possible hope that it would be permitted the continued use of that process. . . .

We therefore affirm the dismissal of plaintiff's action for infringement.

Affirmed.

NOTES

1. **Justifications.** What is the basis for providing the employer with an irrevocable license to the invention? As discussed in *Wommack*, there are two different approaches: (1) implied contract and (2) equitable estoppel, both of which relate to the use of the employer's resources to assist in the development of the project. In general, regardless of the specific approach, "the end result is often the same." *McElmurry v. Arkansas Power & Light Co.*, 995 F.2d 1576, 1581 (Fed. Cir. 1993). In *Wommack*, the company ultimately determined that the invention was too costly for the limited results it produced and abandoned its use shortly before the litigation began. With this in mind, why did the parties continue to litigate?

2. **Evolution of the Law on Employee Inventions.** According to Catherine Fisk, the law on employee inventions has shifted over time from an emphasis on the property rights of employee-inventors to the property rights of employers. *See* Catherine L. Fisk, *Removing the "Fuel of Interest" from the "Fire of Genius": Law and the Employee-Inventor, 1830–1930*, 65 U. CHI. L. REV. 1127 (1998). In the early 19th century, employees typically owned their inventions, even those created in the workplace, but later in the century employers acquired a license to use the product, what is now defined as a shop right. During the first half of the 20th century, courts began to ask whether the employee was hired to invent, and if so, the invention was determined to be the property of the owner. *See United States v. Dubilier Condenser Corp.*, 289 U.S. 178 (1933) ("One employed to make an invention, who succeeds during his term of service in accomplishing that task, is bound to assign to his employer any patent obtained."), *decision amended*, 289 U.S. 706 (1933). Today, Professor Fisk concludes, "Courts are much more willing to find that an employee was hired specifically to invent and to find that an employer is entitled to a shop right based on the relation between the employment and the invention." *Id.* at 132.

The turn to employer ownership has been justified as necessary to encourage adequate employer investments. If employees owned the inventions, they might seek to hold-up employers with exorbitant requests for payments on their projects, and the fear of such actions might also render employers reluctant to invest sufficiently in research and development. *See* Robert P. Merges, *The Law and Economics of Employee Inventions*, 13 HARV. J. LAW & TECH. 1, 20–30 (1999). Professor Merges argues that the prospect of employee mobility ensures the relationship remains fair: "[A]n employee is in general free to leave a firm, develop an inchoate concept, and enjoy full ownership of the resulting invention. Thus, employee mobility continues to be an important policy informing both trade secret law and the law of ex-employee invention ownership." *Id.* at 51. Does this seem consistent with the law of trade secrets? What other connections do you see between trade secret law and the law of employee inventions?

Chapter 7

DIGNITARY INTERESTS

The employment relationship is sometimes described purely in terms of an economic exchange: the worker trades her labor for wages and other forms of compensation. Labor, however, is not merely another commodity that can be freely bought and sold on the market, because labor is inseparable from the laborer. The conditions under which work occurs impact not just the labor performed but the individual who performs it. Thus, employees have an interest in the conditions under which they labor that extends beyond the amount of compensation they receive.

Focusing attention on employees *as persons* highlights their interest in protecting individual dignity and autonomy. Employment, however, necessarily entails relinquishing some measure of personal autonomy to the authority of the employer who controls the production process. Although this authority need not undermine respect for the individual, the employer that seeks to maximize the efficiency of its business operations may sometimes exercise its authority in ways that the employee views as abusive or degrading. Thus, employees have challenged employers' surveillance practices and the imposition of drug and polygraph tests as unduly intrusive, and have complained of abusive treatment at the hands of supervisors. Recent technological innovations, such as those that permit employers to monitor their employees' email, internet usage and exact physical location at all times, have further heightened conflict over the legitimate scope of employer oversight. This tension between the employer's desire to control the workplace and the employee's desire for respect as an individual raises questions of whether and when the law should step in to ensure that employer authority does not trench too deeply on the dignity and autonomy of employees.

Er's desire to control workplac vs. EEs' desire for respect

From a neoclassical economic perspective, employees' dignitary interests raise no particular concerns. Rather, the conditions of work affecting these interests are seen as appropriately determined by the market, like any other aspect of the employment relationship. An alternative view sees individual dignitary interests as too fundamental to rely on private bargaining for their protection. If viewed purely as a matter of contract, "the individual worker becomes vulnerable to economic forces in the market where the collectivized economic power of the employer enables it to treat the worker as an object to be used, not a human being entitled to dignity, respect, individuality and autonomy." Clyde W. Summers, *Individualism, Collectivism and Autonomy in American Labor Law*, 5 EMP. RTS. & EMPLOY. POL'Y J. 453, 487 (2001). Summers further argues that the legal response has been inadequate:

> [N]either the courts nor the legislatures have reflectively sought to balance or accommodate [employees' and employers'] competing interests.

Instead, they give conclusive or dominant weight to the employer's interests. This invites the question why, in the employment relation, the complex of personal interests of autonomy have been given so little weight by the law in a society that prides itself on individual rights. In part, it may be that the individual's interest in autonomy is so intangible, abstract and indefinite that it is too elusive to weigh, while the employer's interest in efficiency and production is tangible and visibly substantial so that its weight is obvious. But the relative weight given to these two interests may be indicative that today in our society we are more concerned with increased production than enhancement of human worth; that what we see in the law is a reflection of ourselves; that despite our declarations of individualism, we secretly prefer products to personal autonomy.

Id. at 488. Any attempt to protect employees' dignitary interests directly, however, runs up against the at-will rule. Because employers retain the ultimate power of discharge in most non-union workplaces, individual employees resist employer incursions only at the risk of losing their jobs. Nevertheless, several sources of law potentially offer protection of employee dignitary interests even under an at-will regime.

The materials in this chapter consider a variety of dignitary interests and the extent to which the law protects them. These dignitary interests are closely related, even overlapping—for example, using a monitoring device to collect information about an employee could be characterized as an invasion of privacy, or as an infringement of employee autonomy, and its use might cause unwarranted emotional harm. Despite the potential for overlap, it is useful to conceptualize the distinct types of dignitary interests that may be at stake in order to understand how the law responds. In Part A, we first consider employees' interests in avoiding emotional harm. Part B canvasses a number of different sources of protection of employees' privacy, while Part C focuses in particular in employees' interest in avoiding employer scrutiny of their off-duty conduct, whether or not that conduct occurs in private. Part D considers a number of testing, screening and monitoring practices that might infringe on employees' dignitary interests. Finally, Part E reviews the legal protections for employees' interests in their reputations. In reading these materials, you should consider when employer actions threaten legitimate employee interests, and whether and how the law should respond.

A. AVOIDING EMOTIONAL HARM

Employees sometimes assert that unjustified, abusive treatment in the workplace has caused them mental suffering. In extreme cases, their suffering may be so severe as to cause psychological or physical symptoms. When the employer's action satisfies the elements of wrongful discharge in violation of public policy or certain statutory claims, the employee may be able to recover damages for emotional distress suffered as a result. But what about instances of abusive employer behavior that cause mental suffering, but do not fall into an established exception to the at-will rule?

Most states recognize a tort of intentional infliction of emotional distress, or tort of outrage, that allows plaintiffs to recover damages when a defendant's extreme conduct causes mental anguish, even in the absence of proof that the defendant breached an independent legal duty. The tort is not intended to redress "mere insults, indignities, threats, annoyances, petty oppressions, or other trivialities." RESTATEMENT (SECOND) OF TORTS § 46 (1977). Rather, liability is reserved for those instances in which the defendant's conduct "has been so outrageous in character, and so extreme in degree, as to go beyond all possible bounds of decency, and to be regarded as atrocious, and utterly intolerable in a civilized community. . . . Generally, the case is one in which a recitation of the facts to an average member of the community would lead him to exclaim, 'Outrageous!' " *Id.* cmt d. The following cases explore how this standard is applied in the employment setting.

WORNICK CO. v. CASAS
Supreme Court of Texas
856 S.W.2d 732 (1993)

PHILLIPS, CHIEF JUSTICE.

. . . Diana Casas was employed by Right Away Foods Corporation ("RAFCO"), a wholly owned subsidiary of Wornick Company, from December 1979 until her discharge on April 22, 1986. Casas was assigned to RAFCO's "M.R.E." (Meals Ready to Eat) division, which assembled military rations for sale to the United States Department of Defense. Casas was hired as personnel manager for the M.R.E. division, and at the time of her discharge served as its director of human resources. Casas' firing was sudden and unexpected. She was approached by her supervisor, Valerie Hutchins Woerner, in the hall at the RAFCO offices at approximately 3:45 p.m. and asked to come to Woerner's office. There, Woerner said that she had some "bad news," that Casas was being terminated. No one else was present at this meeting and the office door was closed. The reasons given by Woerner were that Casas had been disloyal to the company, had exhibited a bad attitude by "snapping at people," and had failed to perform certain assigned tasks. Prior to this time, however, Casas had received favorable job-performance reviews, and she believed that RAFCO fired her to prevent her from revealing information to government auditors concerning unethical practices of RAFCO employees. Woerner refused Casas' request for further explanation and told her to leave the property immediately. Although Woerner appeared nervous, her demeanor was normal, and she did not raise her voice. The entire meeting lasted only about four minutes.

Upon leaving Woerner's office, Casas was approached by a security guard, who explained that he was to escort her off the premises. . . . Casas and the security guard then proceeded to Casas' office, where Joe Sepulveda, the security supervisor, was waiting. Sepulveda, who had been on vacation, told Casas that Woerner had called him at home to come escort Casas off the property. Sepulveda was "uneasy" with the situation. He gave her a box in which to pack her belongings. Another person then came to the office and told Sepulveda that Woerner wanted Casas off the property within five minutes. They then walked to Casas' car, with Sepulveda carrying Casas' box. Sepulveda placed the box in the car, and, shortly after 4:30 p.m., Casas drove away. Neither Sepulveda nor the original security guard were rude or offensive in any way. It was standard company procedure for security guards to escort terminated hourly employees off the property, but not terminated salaried employees such as Casas. . . .

Casas subsequently sued RAFCO, the Wornick Company [and] Woerner. . . . The sole issue before us is whether a genuine issue of material fact exists regarding each element of Casas' claim for intentional infliction of emotional distress.

We recently recognized the tort of intentional infliction of emotional distress, adopting the elements set forth in Restatement (Second) of Torts § 46 (1965). *Twyman v. Twyman*, 855 S.W.2d 619 (Tex.1993). To recover under this tort, the plaintiff must prove that 1) the defendant acted intentionally or recklessly, 2) the conduct was "extreme and outrageous," 3) the actions of the defendant caused the plaintiff emotional distress, and 4) the resulting emotional distress was severe. *Id.* at 621.

We conclude that the summary judgment evidence conclusively establishes that RAFCO's conduct was not "outrageous," an essential element of the intentional infliction tort. Outrageous conduct is that which "[goes] beyond all possible bounds of decency, and to be regarded as atrocious, and utterly intolerable in a civilized community." Restatement § 46, cmt. d. "It is for the court to determine, in the first instance, whether the defendant's conduct may reasonably be regarded as so extreme and outrageous as to permit recovery. . . ." *Id.*, cmt. h.

Subject to certain narrow exceptions, employees in Texas may be terminated at will and without cause. *Sabine Pilot Service, Inc. v. Hauck*, 687 S.W.2d 733, 734 (Tex.1985). The trial court and court of appeals rejected Casas' contentions that her firing fell within exceptions to the employment-at-will doctrine, and Casas has not challenged those findings here. RAFCO therefore acted within its legal rights in discharging Casas. Therefore, the fact of discharge itself as a matter of law cannot constitute outrageous behavior.

Casas argues, however, that even if the firing was not outrageous, the *manner* in which she was fired was outrageous. We have previously observed that there may be instances where a termination is accompanied by outrageous behavior. *See Diamond Shamrock Refining and Marketing Co. v. Mendez*, 844 S.W.2d 198, 202 (Tex.1992). In this case, however, the record conclusively establishes that RAFCO's conduct fell short of the requisite level of outrageousness.

. . . Woerner required Casas to leave the premises immediately and directed security guards to escort her, actions which could reasonably be expected to cause humiliation. In exercising its rights as an employer-at-will, however, RAFCO's conduct as a matter of law did not "exceed all possible bounds of decency" and was not "utterly intolerable in a civilized community." . . . . Even accepting Casas' contention that she was fired because she possessed incriminating information, this does not constitute an existing exception to the employment-at-will doctrine under *Sabine Pilot*, and Casas does not argue for extending the *Sabine Pilot* exception to such conduct. RAFCO, therefore, was exercising its legal rights, which legally cannot constitute outrageous conduct. . . .

Termination of an employee is never pleasant, especially for the employee. But if we accept Casas' arguments in this case, employers would be subjected to a potential jury trial in connection with virtually every discharge, and "there would be *slippery slope* little left of the employment-at-will doctrine." *Mendez*, 844 S.W.2d at 202.

We conclude that the conduct of RAFCO in this case was, as a matter of law, not outrageous. . . .

HECHT, JUSTICE, concurring.   *concurrence*

Two months ago this Court recognized for the first time a tort of intentional infliction of emotional distress. *Twyman v. Twyman*, 855 S.W.2d 619 (Tex.1993). This tort allows recovery of money damages for severe emotional distress caused by another's extreme and outrageous conduct if that conduct is intentional or reckless. There are, however, no legal standards by which judges and juries can distinguish conduct which is extreme and outrageous from conduct which is not. And because outrageousness is entirely in the eye of the beholder, it can neither be proved nor disproved by evidence. Liability under this tort depends upon whether a jury, trial court or appellate court, as the case may be, is offended by the particular circumstances of the case before it. This case, the first in which the Court attempts to decide what is extreme and outrageous conduct, demonstrates the impossibility of the effort. . . .

The truth of the matter is that Wornick's conduct was not outrageous simply because most of the Members of this Court, Casas' court of last resort, are not sufficiently offended by it. If they were, the result would be different. If Casas were permitted to present her case to a jury, it is not at all unlikely that she would prevail, not because her case has more merit to it than this Court sees, but because jurors might well have different views about what is outrageous. Twelve employers would probably agree with this Court; twelve recently terminated employees might not. . . . With the tort of intentional infliction of emotional distress, the Court embarks on what I predict will be an endless wandering over a sea of factual circumstances, meandering this way and that, blown about by bias and inclination, and guided by nothing steadier than the personal preferences of the helmsmen, who change with every watch. . . .

[The concurring opinion of JUSTICE DOGGETT is omitted.]

I think its consistent. The tort of IIED will likely only prevail when they're discharging EE w/ disrespect, extreme circ.

NOTES

1. **Discipline and Discharge.** As part of managing their workforce, employers sometimes need to discipline or even discharge employees, and these adverse actions will inevitably cause those employees to experience emotional distress. Not only are such actions unavoidable, but the law gives employers the legal right to discharge employees without cause in the absence of a contract to the contrary. Is recognition of the tort of intentional infliction of emotional distress in the employment setting consistent with at-will employment, or does it entail an end-run around the at-will rule?

2. **"A Sea of Factual Circumstances."** The concurrence in *Wornick* complains about the lack of a clear standard for identifying extreme and outrageous conduct.

Consider the following cases:

yes

Plaintiff's claim that employer retaliated against him because of complaints about violations of nuclear safety regulations by launching a sham investigation, terminating his employment and then intentionally filing a false charge against him with a federal regulatory agency is sufficient to state a claim for intentional infliction of emotional distress. *Kassem v. Washington Hosp. Ctr.*, 513 F.3d 251 (D.C. Cir. 2008).

no

It was not outrageous for an employer to discharge employees without notice and then escort them from the premises in front of other employees. *Toth v. Square D. Co.*, 712 F. Supp. 1231 (D.S.C. 1989).

no

Allegations that plaintiff's supervisors subjected her to public discussion and ridicule concerning her pregnancy and medical restrictions; that one supervisor stated her intent to make plaintiff's life miserable; and that employer subjected her to such onerous work conditions that she quit her job are insufficient to meet legal standard for outrageous conduct. *Merfeld v. Warren County Health Servs.*, 597 F. Supp. 2d 942 (S.D. Iowa 2009).

no

Firing plaintiff after almost ten years of employment was not extreme and outrageous even though the discharge occurred in the middle of the work day, plaintiff was asked to leave without returning to his own office and almost all of the defendant's other employees knew about the discharge within minutes. *Lapidus v. New York City Chapter of New York State Ass'n for Retarded Children, Inc.*, 504 N.Y.S.2d 629 (N.Y. App. Div. 1986).

yes

Plaintiff properly alleged cause of action for intentional infliction of emotional distress where employer made the plaintiff the target of a federal investigation in order to cover up its own misconduct. *Russ v. TRW, Inc.*, 570 N.E.2d 1076 (Ohio 1991).

yes

Allegations that a supervisor informed waitresses at a meeting that "there was some stealing going on" and that he would fire them in alphabetical order, beginning with the plaintiff, until the thief was discovered, state a claim for outrageous conduct. *Agis v. Howard Johnson Co.*, 355 N.E.2d 315 (D. Mass. 1976).

examples of outrageous

Based on these case descriptions, does it appear that the standard for outrageous conduct is consistently applied? Does any pattern emerge as to what types of conduct are outrageous?

BODEWIG v. K-MART, INC.

Court of Appeals of Oregon
635 P.2d 657 (1981)

BUTTLER, PRESIDING JUDGE.

In this tort action for outrageous conduct, plaintiff seeks damages against her former employer, K-Mart, and a K-Mart customer, Mrs. Golden. Both defendants moved for summary judgment, which the trial court granted. Plaintiff appeals from the resulting final judgments entered. We reverse and remand.

. . . On the evening of March 29, 1979, plaintiff was working as a part-time checker at K-Mart. Defendant Golden entered plaintiff's checkout lane and plaintiff began to ring up Golden's purchases on the cash register. When plaintiff called out the price on a package of curtains, Golden told plaintiff the price was incorrect because the curtains were on sale. Plaintiff called a domestics department clerk for a price check. That clerk told plaintiff the curtains in question were not on sale. Upon hearing this, Golden left her merchandise on plaintiff's counter and returned with the clerk to the domestics department to find the "sale" curtains.

After Golden left, plaintiff moved Golden's merchandise to the service counter, voided the register slip containing the partial listing of Golden's items and began to check out other customers. Three to ten minutes later, Golden returned to plaintiff's checkstand, where another customer was being served. Golden "looked around" that customer and asked what plaintiff had done with her money. When plaintiff replied, "What money?," Golden said that she had left four five-dollar bills on top of the merchandise she was purchasing before she left with the domestics clerk. Plaintiff told Golden she had not seen any money. Golden continued in a loud, abrupt voice to demand her money from plaintiff and caused a general commotion. Customers and store personnel in the area began to look on curiously.

The K-Mart manager, who had been observing the incident from a nearby service desk, walked over to plaintiff's counter. After a short discussion with Golden, he walked up to plaintiff, pulled out her jacket pockets, looked inside and found nothing. Then he, plaintiff and two or three other store employees conducted a general search of the area for the money. When this effort proved fruitless, the manager explained there was nothing more he could do except check out plaintiff's register. Golden said, "Well, do it." The manager and an assistant manager locked plaintiff's register and took the till and the register receipt to the cash cage. While the register was being checked, Golden continued to glare at plaintiff while plaintiff checked out customers at another register. The register balanced perfectly. When the manager so advised Golden, Golden replied that she still believed plaintiff took her money and continued to "cause commotion" and glare at plaintiff. A further general search of the surrounding area was conducted without success. Golden still would not leave; another employee was trying to calm her down.

The manager then told plaintiff to accompany a female assistant manager into the women's public restroom for the purpose of disrobing in order to prove to Golden that she did not have the money. As plaintiff and the assistant manager walked to the restroom, the manager asked Golden if she wanted to watch the search; Golden replied: "You had better believe I do, it is my money." In the restroom, plaintiff took off all her clothes except her underwear while Golden and the assistant manager watched closely. When plaintiff asked Golden if she needed to take off more, Golden replied that it was not necessary because she could see through plaintiff's underwear anyway.

Plaintiff put on her clothes and started to leave the restroom when the assistant manager asked Golden how much money she had in her purse. Golden replied that she did not know the exact amount, but thought she had between five and six hundred dollars. She did not attempt to count it at that time.

Plaintiff then returned to her check stand. Golden followed plaintiff to the counter and continued to glare at her as she worked. Finally, the manager told Golden nothing more could be done for her, and after more loud protestations, Golden left the store.

Upon arriving home, Golden counted the money in her purse. She had $560. She called plaintiff's mother, whom she knew casually, and related the entire incident to her, stating that she had told K-Mart that plaintiff had taken her money. She described the strip search to plaintiff's mother and stated that when she was asked if she wanted to watch the strip, she responded, "Damn right." The mother expressed concern that plaintiff would lose her job; Golden said she would call the store and ask them not to let her go. Golden did make that call. After the conversation with Golden, plaintiff's mother, father and sister went to K-Mart to see if plaintiff was all right and to take her home.

Plaintiff returned to work the next day and was told that the keys to the cash register were lost and she was to work on a register with another employee. That procedure is known as "piggy-backing," and plaintiff had been told three months earlier that the store would no longer "piggy-back" checkers. Plaintiff believed the store was monitoring her by the "piggy-back" procedure; she quit at the end of her scheduled shift that day.

. . . K-Mart contends that the trial court properly granted its motion, because the facts presented do not constitute outrageous conduct as a matter of law. Its principal argument is that plaintiff consented to the strip search, either expressly as its manager stated, or tacitly by not expressly objecting. Plaintiff stated, variously, that she was told or asked by the manager to disrobe, but, whether asked or told, she did not consider that she had a choice. She thought she would lose her job if she refused, and she needed the job. The issue of lack of consent to that search is an issue of fact, but whether it is an issue of material fact depends upon whether, assuming plaintiff's version to be true, the facts are sufficient to submit the case to the jury on the outrageous conduct theory.

. . . There are at least two versions of the tort [of outrageous conduct]. One . . . involves intentional conduct, the very purpose of which is to inflict psychological and emotional distress on the plaintiff. The other is represented by *Rockhill v. Pollard*, 485 P.2d 28 (1971), where the wrongful purpose was lacking, but "the tortious element can be found in the breach of some obligation, statutory or otherwise, that attaches to defendant's relationship to plaintiff . . ." 600 P.2d 398. . . .

Neither the Supreme Court nor this court has been presented with the question of whether the employer-employee relationship falls into that special category. This court, however, has treated the landlord-tenant relationship as a "prime consideration" in evaluating the defendant's conduct. *Fitzpatrick v. Robbins*, 626 P.2d 910 (1981). We reached that conclusion because landlords were in a position of authority with respect to tenants and could affect the tenants' interest in the quiet enjoyment of their leasehold. An employer has even more authority over an employee, who, by the nature of the relationship, is subject to the direction and control of the employer and may be discharged for any or no reason, absent an agreement restricting that authority. Clearly, that relationship is not an arm's length one between strangers. Accordingly, we conclude that the relationship between plaintiff and K-Mart was a special relationship, based on which liability may be imposed if K-Mart's conduct, though not deliberately aimed at causing emotional distress, was such that a jury might find it to be beyond the limits of social toleration and reckless of the conduct's predictable effects on plaintiff.

We conclude that a jury could find that the K-Mart manager, a 32-year-old male in charge of the entire store, after concluding that plaintiff did not take the customer's money, put her through the degrading and humiliating experience of submitting to a strip search in order to satisfy the customer, who was not only acting unreasonably, but was creating a commotion in the store; that the manager's conduct exceeded the bounds of social toleration and was in reckless disregard of its predictable effects on plaintiff.

Because there was no special relationship between plaintiff and Golden, the evidence must be such that a jury could find Golden's conduct not only socially intolerable, but that it was deliberately aimed at causing plaintiff emotional distress. Golden contends the evidence does not permit those findings, because she was merely trying to get her money back from plaintiff. . . .

We conclude that the facts, viewed most favorably to plaintiff, would permit a jury to find that Golden's entire course of conduct was intended to embarrass and humiliate plaintiff in order to coerce her into giving Golden $20, whether rightfully hers or not; that Golden did not know how much money she had in her purse, variously stated to be between $300 and $600, made no effort to determine if she was, in fact, missing four five dollar bills until she returned home, at which time she found she was mistaken; that Golden's insistence on a check of plaintiff's cash register, her insistence that plaintiff still had her money after the register checked out perfectly, her eager participation in the strip search of plaintiff and her continuing to stare angrily at plaintiff over an extended period, even after all efforts to find her money failed, would permit a jury to find Golden's conduct deliberately calculated to cause plaintiff emotional distress and exceeded the bounds of social toleration.

A jury could also find in Golden's favor, but the mere fact that her stated ultimate objective was to get her money back is not sufficient to defeat plaintiff's claim. . . . There are lawful (socially tolerable) ways to collect money from another, and there are unlawful (socially intolerable) ways to do so.

Common to her claims against both defendants is the requirement that plaintiff prove that she suffered severe emotional distress. If the facts presented are believed, plaintiff suffered shock, humiliation and embarrassment, suffering that was not merely transient. Plaintiff characterized herself as a shy, modest person, and said that she had two or three sleepless nights, cried a lot and still gets nervous and upset when she thinks about the incident. Concededly, this element of the tort has been, and still is, troublesome to courts. K-Mart contends there is no objective evidence of the distress, such as medical, economic or social problems. In *Rockhill v. Pollard, supra*, plaintiff became nervous and suffered from sleeplessness and a loss of appetite over a period of about two years. The court said: ". . . Defendant belittles these symptoms, but it is the distress which must be severe, not the physical manifestations. . . ." 485 P.2d 28.

Defendant Golden contends that the purpose of requiring proof of severe emotional distress is to guard against fraudulent or frivolous claims and that some degree of transient and trivial distress is a part of the price of living among people. Here, however, it is not unreasonable to expect that a shy, modest, young woman put in plaintiff's position would suffer the effects she claims to have suffered from the incident, and that her distress was more than that which a person might be reasonably expected to pay as the price of living among people.

We cannot say as a matter of law that plaintiff's evidence of severe emotional distress is insufficient to go to a jury. Because neither defendant was entitled to judgment as a matter of law, neither motion for summary judgment should have been granted. The judgment for each of the defendants is reversed. The case is remanded for trial.

HOLLOMON v. KEADLE
Supreme Court of Arkansas
931 S.W.2d 413 (1996)

ROAF, JUSTICE.

This case involves a claim for the tort of outrage brought by Appellant Mary Hollomon against her former employer, Dr. W.R. Keadle. Hollomon alleges that Keadle repeatedly insulted her and subjected her to veiled threats of bodily harm. The trial court found that Hollomon's allegations were insufficient as a matter of law to state a claim for the tort of outrage. . . . We affirm.

Mary Hollomon worked for Dr. Keadle, a sixty-eight-year-old physician, for approximately two years before she voluntarily left his employ. Hollomon alleges that during her employment, Keadle repeatedly cursed her and referred to her with offensive terms, such as "white nigger," "slut," "whore," and "the ignorance of Glenwood, Arkansas." Hollomon contends that Keadle frequently made, in her presence, degrading remarks about women such as: "women should be at home, not working, and if they are out there working they are whores and prostitutes . . . only whores and prostitutes work" and "any time a woman wears rings [other than wedding rings], she is a whore and a slut." In addition, Hollomon claims that Keadle frequently directed profanity at her in front of patients and other employees. In her deposition, Hollomon stated that she became aware that Keadle was a "grouch" by the second day of her employment with him and that he constantly yelled and cursed and used the "F" word almost every day. She stated that he cursed and belittled his wife and other women in his office.

According to Hollomon's deposition, Keadle also told her that he had connections with the mob in California and could pay one of his schizophrenic patients $500.00 to "take care of" anyone he chose. As an example of these "connections," Hollomon stated that Keadle told her that one of his former female employees "supposedly" died in an automobile accident in California. Finally, Hollomon states that Keadle told her that he carried a gun and that he had recently pulled the gun on a patient who angered him. Hollomon asserts that Keadle told her these stories to intimidate her and to suggest that he would have her killed if she quit or caused trouble.

why she didn't quit

symptoms

Hollomon contends that she did not resign earlier because she feared Keadle would have her killed. In addition, Hollomon asserts that her status as a single parent and her dire financial condition, of which Keadle was aware, prevented her from leaving the job. Hollomon claims that Keadle's comments caused her stomach problems, loss of sleep, loss of self-esteem, anxiety attacks, and embarrassment. In her deposition, Hollomon stated that she told Jim Butler, a counselor, about the constant ridicule by Keadle but admitted that she did not go to his office or seek counseling services from him. She further stated that Keadle's cursing upset her stomach and that Keadle and a Dr. Jansen gave her medication for her stomach problems. After two years and three months of working for Keadle, Hollomon alleges that she resigned because of his cursing. In his deposition, Keadle denied all of Hollomon's allegations. . . .

[Plaintiff] asserts that the trial court erred by holding that the facts she alleged did not support a cause of action for the tort of outrage or intentional infliction of emotional distress. We have said that to succeed on a tort of outrage claim, the plaintiff must prove: 1) the defendant intended to inflict emotional distress or knew or should have known that emotional distress was the likely result of his conduct; 2) the conduct was extreme and outrageous, and was utterly intolerable in a civilized community; 3) the defendant's conduct was the cause of the plaintiff's distress; and 4) the plaintiff's emotional distress sustained by the plaintiff was so severe that no reasonable person could be expected to endure it. . . .

[In *Tandy Corp. v. Bone*, 678 S.W.2d 312 (Ark. 1984),] we stated that:

> [w]e have taken a somewhat strict approach to this cause of action. Recognition of this new tort should not and does not open the doors of the courts to every slight insult or indignity one must endure in life. For example, abrasive profanity alone is not sufficient reason to have a cause of action.

Bone was the manager of a Radio Shack store who was questioned by his employer in the course of an investigation into thefts which took place at his store. Bone testified that he was questioned throughout an entire day, and was cursed and threatened by Tandy's security personnel. He further alleged that he was twice refused permission to take a tranquilizer which had been prescribed to him by a psychiatrist for three years. It was the latter testimony by Bone which concerned this court, and we stated that:

> The conduct on the part of the employer that does give us difficulty is the undisputed evidence that Bone was obviously undergoing a good deal of stress, requested his Valium or medication, and was denied that privilege. *The employer was on notice at that point that Bone may not have been a person of ordinary temperament, able to endure a stressful situation such as he was placed in without injury. . . . We emphasize that the notice to the employer of Bone's condition is the only basis for a jury question of extreme outrage.*

Tandy, 678 S.W.2d at 316. (Emphasis added.)

Because of the holding in *Tandy*, we do not reach the question of whether Keadle's conduct was "extreme and outrageous" and "utterly intolerable in a civilized community." . . . We conclude that Hollomon, unlike Bone, has failed to establish that her employer was made aware that she was "not a person of ordinary temperament" or that she was "peculiarly susceptible to emotional distress by reason of some physical or mental condition or peculiarity." *See* Restatement (Second) of Torts § 46, cmt. f. In her brief filed in response to Keadle's motion for summary judgment, Hollomon asserted that she was "assured that Keadle's actions would cease." She does not state in her abstract who assured her of this or whether she notified Keadle of any mental or physical condition which would make her peculiarly susceptible to stress. Although she claims that her status as a single parent caused her to remain in Keadle's employment for over two years, we cannot say that this status is in any respect unique, or that it constitutes a physical or mental condition necessary under our holding in *Tandy, supra* . . . .

[In reversing plaintiff's outrage claim in *City of Green Forest v. Morse*, 873 S.W.2d 155 (1994),] we said:

> We have consistently taken a narrow view in recognizing claims for the tort of outrage that arise out of the discharge of an employee. The reason is that an employer must be given considerable latitude in dealing with employees, and at the same time, an employee will frequently feel considerable insult when discharged.

. . . Although Hollomon was not discharged, nor does she claim that she was constructively discharged, we have consistently stated that we will take a strict view in recognizing a claim for the tort of outrage in employment relationship situations. The rationale for doing so holds true whether the employee bringing such a claim has been discharged or resigns. Here, Hollomon knew by the second day of her employment with Keadle that he was a singularly unpleasant man given to constantly yelling and cursing, yet she remained in his employment for more than two years. In *Tandy, supra*, we said that "abrasive profanity alone is not sufficient reason to bring a cause of action." Absent a showing that the employer had knowledge that the employee was "peculiarly susceptible to emotional distress by reasons of some physical or mental condition or peculiarity" and "proceeds in the face of such knowledge," we do not depart from that position. *See* Restatement (Second) of Torts § 46 . . . .

Affirmed.

NOTES

1. The Employment Setting. The *Bodewig* and *Hollomon* opinions both suggest that the fact that an employment relationship existed should impact how a claim of intentional infliction of emotional distress is evaluated. How do their approaches differ from one another? What difference *should* the employment setting make when determining the "outrageousness" of a defendant's actions?

The Supreme Court in Oregon later clarified the standard for establishing a claim of intentional infliction of emotional distress and the meaning of its earlier decision in *Rockhill v. Pollard*, 485 P.2d 28 (Or. 1971), a case relied on by the court in *Bodewig*. In *McGanty v. Staudenraus*, 901 P.2d 841 (Or. 1995), the court explained that *Rockhill* had reaffirmed Oregon's recognition of the tort of intentional infliction of emotional distress as defined in the Restatement (Second) of Torts. It further held that the existence of a special relationship was relevant, *not* to determining the requisite level of intent, but "in deciding what behavior may be found to be extreme or outrageous." *Id.* at 850, *quoting Rockhill*, 485 P.2d 28. Thus, the nature of the relationship between the parties helps to determine "what the bounds of socially acceptable behavior were," *id.* at 851. Regardless of the relationship, however, the "intent" element is satisfied if the defendant acted with the desire to inflict severe emotional distress or "knows that such distress is certain, or substantially certain, to result from his conduct." *Id.* at 853, *quoting* RESTATEMENT (SECOND) OF TORTS § 46 (1965).

Like the Oregon courts, a number of courts have found that the existence of the employment relationship is relevant to the outrageousness inquiry, following the Restatement position that "[t]he extreme and outrageous character of the conduct may arise from an abuse by the actor of a position, or a relation with the other, which gives him actual or apparent authority over the other, or power to affect his interests." RESTATEMENT (SECOND) OF TORTS § 46, cmt. e (1965). *See, e.g., Napreljac v. John Q. Hammons Hotels, Inc.*, 461 F. Supp. 2d 981 (S.D. Iowa 2006).

2. "Ordinary" Abuse. Regina Austin has criticized the manner in which courts have applied the tort of intentional infliction of emotional distress in the workplace to reach only highly unusual, extraordinary forms of abuse, dismissing lesser or more common forms of abuse as "trivial". *See* Regina Austin, *Employer Abuse, Worker Resistance, and the Tort of Intentional Infliction of Emotional Distress*, 41 STAN. L. REV. 1 (1988). She argues for a "structural analysis" that would recognize that abuse at the hands of supervisors is "sufficiently concrete, widespread, systemic, destructive, and avoidable to warrant political and judicial reform." A legal response is warranted, in her view, because workplace abuse "facilitates the exploitation of politically and economically unorganized workers by accentuating their wage dependency" and compounds race and sex discrimination.

David C. Yamada has similarly criticized the law as inadequate to redress workplace bullying which can cause serious psychological harm. He asserts that "[e]specially in the context of the workplace, where not only a worker's emotional well-being, but also her source of income, benefits, and perhaps a career are on the line, [the IIED standard for extreme and outrageous conduct] is an excessively high threshold for legal intervention." David C. Yamada, *Workplace Bullying and American Employment Law: A Ten-Year Progress Report and Assessment*, 32 COMP. LAB. LAW & POL'Y 251, 257 (2010). Yamada has drafted a model statute that would create a cause of action for employees who are "subjected to malicious, harmful workplace bullying." *Id.* at 259.

Can or should the law step in to redress forms of employer abuse short of "extreme and outrageous" conduct? Should the common law tort be extended to reach lower level forms of abuse? Or would a legislative solution be more desirable or effective? If an employer acts in a systematically abusive way, should the entire group of affected employees—for example, a whole work group or division—be allowed to bring a collective claim against the employer? Would a class action be an appropriate vehicle for raising claims of systematic abuse?

3. Employee Susceptibility to Emotional Distress. Commentary in the Restatement (Second) of Torts suggests that outrageousness may arise from a defendant's action in the face of knowledge that the plaintiff is "peculiarly susceptible to emotional distress, by reason of some physical or mental condition." RESTATEMENT (SECOND) OF TORTS § 46 cmt. f (1965). Did the *Hollomon* court apply the doctrine consistently with the Restatement comment? *See* David C. Yamada, *The Phenomenon of "Workplace Bullying" and the Need for Status-Blind Hostile Work Environment Protection*, 88 GEO. L.J. 475, 497 (2000) (arguing that *Hollomon* "twisted the intentional infliction of emotional distress doctrine out of shape" by requiring defendant's prior knowledge of plaintiff's unusual sensitivity, rather than seeing such a factor as contributing to outrageousness). Does the approach of the *Hollomon* court suggest that in Arkansas only employees with unusual susceptibility to emotional distress can meet the elements of intentional infliction of emotional distress? For another case interpreting the Restatement comment regarding plaintiff susceptibility to emotional distress, see *Kroger v. Willgruber*, 920 S.W.2d 61 (Ky. 1996) (upholding liability where employer exerted pressure on fired employee to sign a release even though employer knew about his "precarious emotional health").

4. Bias and Harassment. Because the requirement of "outrageousness" is so vague, applying it to particular factual situations allows implicit cultural assumptions to come into play. Consider the case of *Wilson v. Monarch Paper Co.*, 939 F.2d 1138 (5th Cir. 1991), in which a high-level executive with 30 years of experience in the paper business was demoted to warehouse supervisor. In his new position, Wilson was assigned to sweep the warehouse and clean up after employees in the cafeteria. In upholding a jury verdict for Wilson on his claim of intentional infliction of emotional distress, the Fifth Circuit stated,

> [W]e find it difficult to conceive a workplace scenario more painful and embarrassing than an executive, indeed a vice-president and the assistant to the president, being subjected before his fellow employees to the most menial janitorial services and duties of cleaning up after entry level employees: the steep downhill push to total humiliation was complete.

Id. at 1145.

Pairing *Wilson* with *Bodewig* raises the following question: "[W]hy is strip-searching humiliating to a 'shy, modest, young woman' working as a K-Mart cashier, but not to a prison guard? Why is working as a janitor humiliating to an executive, but not to a janitor?" Catherine L. Fisk, *Humiliation at Work*, 8 WM. & MARY J. WOMEN & LAW 73, 89 (2001). Should courts and juries take into account the gender, class and race of plaintiffs in deciding their claims?

What about situations in which the allegedly outrageous behavior involves harassment explicitly based on the employee's race or sex? As we will see in Chapter 9, *infra*, federal and state anti-discrimination laws make racial and sexual harassment in the workplace actionable. However, victims of race and sex harassment often bring claims of intentional infliction of emotional distress in addition to their statutory claims. In assessing the common law tort claim, some courts have found that the racial and sexual nature of the harassment *itself* contributes to its outrageousness, *see, e.g., Taylor v. Metzger*, 706 A.2d 685 (N.J. 1998) (finding that a single incident involving employer's use of the racial epithet "jungle bunny" was sufficiently outrageous because it conjured up an entire history of racial discrimination), while other courts appear to demand something *more* than the level of harassment actionable under anti-discrimination laws before finding tort liability for intentional infliction of emotional distress, *see, e.g., Hoy v. Angelone*, 720 A.2d 745 (Pa. 1998) (holding that actionable sexual harassment alone does not rise to the level of outrageousness necessary for a claim of intentional infliction of emotional distress).

    5. Other Hurdles. In addition to the difficulty of establishing the outrageousness of defendant's actions, employee claims of intentional infliction of emotional distress also sometimes founder on the requirement that the resulting emotional distress be severe. *See, e.g., Merfeld v. Warren Cnty. Health Srvs.*, 597 F. Supp. 2d 942 (S.D. Iowa 2009) (holding allegations that plaintiff was an "emotional basket case" and "cried every day" insufficient to establish "severe or extreme emotional distress"); *Abdul-Malik v. AirTran Airways, Inc.*, 678 S.E. 2d 555 (Ga. Ct. App. 2009) (finding no evidence of severe emotional distress given that plaintiff could not sleep and eventually gained 15 pounds, but did not take medication or seek professional help). While in *Bodewig*, the plaintiff's allegation that she "had two or three sleepless nights, cried a lot and still gets nervous and upset when she thinks about the incident" was sufficient to avoid summary judgment, other courts expressly require expert testimony to establish the severity of the emotional distress. *See, e.g., Comstock v. Consumers Mkts., Inc.*, 953 F. Supp. 1096 (W.D. Mo. 1996) (requiring expert testimony to establish that plaintiff suffered "medically diagnosable" or "medically significant" emotional distress).

    Another hurdle for plaintiffs suing for intentional infliction of emotional distress may be proving that the employer is liable for the acts of an abusive supervisor. Liability of the employing entity may turn on whether the court views the outrageous conduct as falling within the scope of the supervisor's employment. *Compare Sofia v. McWilliams*, 2003 U.S. Dist. LEXIS 5622 (E.D. Pa. Mar. 31, 2003) (finding no employer liability for intentional infliction of emotional distress on the grounds that the supervisor's sexually harassing conduct was beyond the scope of his employment), *with GTE Southwest, Inc. v. Bruce*, 998 S.W.2d 605 (Tex. 1998) (holding that a supervisor's on-going and repeated abusive behaviors involved conduct within the scope of his position as supervisor).

    6. Alternatives to Tort Law? Are individual tort claims the best way to protect employees against workplace abuse? Dennis Duffy argues that the tort of intentional infliction of emotional distress "represents a false promise to employees that minimal standards of social decency and justice in the workplace will be enforced." Dennis P. Duffy, *Intentional Infliction of Emotional Distress and Employment at Will: The Case Against "Tortification" of Labor and Employment Law*, 74 B.U. L. Rev. 387, 422 (1994). He argues that the lack of a clear standard for liability, workers' limited access to lawyers, and the backward-looking focus of the individual lawsuit mean that tort litigation "does nothing to change the balance of power in the workplace." *Id.* at 423–24. A better alternative, he suggests, is "the collective vision of the Wagner Act." *Id.* at 424.

To the extent that it counter-balances the inherent inequality of the employment relationship, collective bargaining by workers should tend to curb extreme cases of employer abuse. More concretely, most collective bargaining agreements establish a grievance arbitration system through which individual workers can raise concerns about working conditions, including abusive treatment by supervisors or co-workers. Such grievance procedures offer workers an affordable and relatively quick process—one in which they may receive assistance from the union—for seeking resolution of relatively minor workplace problems, as well as "outrageous" ones. The reality, however, is that the vast majority of employees are not currently represented by unions.

Given the small proportion of unionized workplaces, is David Yamada correct that "the right of every worker to be treated with a minimal degree of dignity is so basic that it should not be dependent upon collective action for its existence and enforcement"? *See* David C. Yamada, *The Phenomenon of "Workplace Bullying" and the Need for Status-Blind Hostile Work Environment Protection*, 88 GEO. L.J. 475, 521 (2000). Or do you agree with Duffy that recognition of tort theories like intentional infliction of emotional distress "could retard political collective efforts to empower workers . . . [by giving them] a false sense of security about the available legal arsenal in the event of adverse action by their employers"? *See* Duffy, *supra* at 425.

B. PRIVACY

With the proliferation of new technologies that permit employers to investigate, surveille, test and monitor their workforces, employees have increasingly raised concerns about intrusions by employers on their privacy. Although many consider privacy interests to be fundamental, defining their precise contours has proven difficult. Part of the difficulty arises because the concept of privacy is ill defined. The term has been invoked to protect widely varying interests such as avoiding intrusion on physical spaces, protecting against the seizure of personal effects, insuring bodily integrity, shielding certain communications and preventing the disclosure of personal information. And privacy is closely entwined with the interest in autonomy. Sometimes privacy is defined in terms of preserving individual autonomy to make certain choices free from unwarranted interference. At other times, the two interests are viewed as entirely distinct, with privacy concerned with shielding against intrusion or disclosure, while autonomy is viewed as freedom from interference regardless of whether the activity is open to public view. In this chapter, we assume a distinction between the two issues, focusing first in this section on employee privacy claims and in the next on the extent to which employees are protected against employer interference with their off-duty activities.

The inquiry into employees' privacy rights is complicated by the existence of the employment relationship. The fact that an alleged violation occurs between parties to an employment contract, rather than by the government or a stranger, raises questions about how employees' asserted interests should be weighed given legitimate employer concerns about promoting safety and productivity of the workplace, and protecting valuable business information.

Determining the sources of law relevant to protecting employee privacy is not simple either. Numerous sources of law potentially impact employees' claims, from constitutional provisions that speak in broadly aspirational terms to highly specific statutes regulating the details of how particular types of tests may be administered and used. For example, the Federal Employee Polygraph Protection Act of 1988, 29 U.S.C. § 2001 et seq. prohibits employer use of lie detector tests except under certain narrowly defined circumstances. Dozens of state statutes regulate the details of when and under what conditions employers may conduct polygraph testing, drug testing and electronic monitoring and surveillance. *See* Matthew W. Finkin, Privacy in Employment Law (4th ed. 2013) (compiling state statutes regulating employee privacy). Despite their sheer number, these laws are often quite narrow in scope. Because no single source of law comprehensively addresses privacy concerns, protection of employee privacy interests is fragmentary and often ad hoc. Rather than survey the multitude of specific statutes regulating particular types of intrusions, this section focuses on sources of law that offer broad principles for understanding and evaluating claims of privacy. For public sector employees, those principles are rooted in constitutional provisions; in the private sector, they are derived from common law doctrine, statutory protections, or, in the case of unionized employees, a body of arbitral law. We explore these sources of law in the first three subsections below. The fourth subsection considers the issues posed by application of these legal frameworks to electronic communication in the workplace.

1. Constitutional Protection for Public Employees

O'CONNOR v. ORTEGA
United States Supreme Court
480 U.S. 709 (1987)

Justice O'Connor announced the judgment of the Court and delivered an opinion in which the Chief Justice, Justice White, and Justice Powell join.

. . . Dr. Magno Ortega, a physician and psychiatrist, held the position of Chief of Professional Education at Napa State Hospital (Hospital) for 17 years, until his dismissal from that position in 1981. As Chief of Professional Education, Dr. Ortega had primary responsibility for training young physicians in psychiatric residency programs. . . . [In July 1981, Dr. Ortega was placed on administrative leave pending an investigation by Hospital officials, including Dennis O'Connor, Executive Director of the Hospital. The investigation involved allegations that Dr. Ortega coerced resident physicians into donating money for a computer, and that he sexually harassed two female hospital employees. His employment was terminated on September 22, 1981. During the investigation, a decision was made to enter Dr. Ortega's office.] The specific reason for the entry into Dr. Ortega's office is unclear from the record. The petitioners claim that the search was conducted to secure state property. Initially, petitioners contended that such a search was pursuant to a Hospital policy of conducting a routine inventory of state property in the office of a terminated employee. At the time of the search, however, the Hospital had not yet terminated Dr. Ortega's employment; Dr. Ortega was still on administrative leave. Apparently, there was no policy of inventorying the offices of those on administrative leave. Before the search had been initiated, however, petitioners had become aware that Dr. Ortega had taken the computer to his home. Dr. Ortega contends that the purpose of the search was to secure evidence for use against him in administrative disciplinary proceedings.

what they seized

The resulting search of Dr. Ortega's office was quite thorough. The investigators entered the office a number of times and seized several items from Dr. Ortega's desk and file cabinets, including a Valentine's Day card, a photograph, and a book of poetry all sent to Dr. Ortega by a former resident physician. These items were later used in a proceeding before a hearing officer of the California State Personnel Board to impeach the credibility of the former resident, who testified on Dr. Ortega's behalf. The investigators also seized billing documentation of one of Dr. Ortega's private patients under the California Medicaid program. The investigators did not otherwise separate Dr. Ortega's property from state property because, as one investigator testified, "[t]rying to sort State from non-State, it was too much to do, so I gave it up and boxed it up." Thus, no formal inventory of the property in the office was ever made. Instead, all the papers in Dr. Ortega's office were merely placed in boxes, and put in storage for Dr. Ortega to retrieve.

I

Dr. Ortega commenced this action against petitioners in Federal District Court under 42 U.S.C. § 1983, alleging that the search of his office violated the Fourth Amendment. . . . [The district court granted defendants' motion for summary judgment. The Court of Appeals reversed in part, holding that a grant of partial summary judgment for Dr. Ortega was justified on the issue of liability for an unlawful search.] *PH*

The strictures of the Fourth Amendment, applied to the States through the Fourteenth Amendment, have been applied to the conduct of governmental officials in various civil activities. *New Jersey v. T.L.O.*, 469 U.S. 325, 334–335 (1985). . . . Searches and seizures by government employers or supervisors of the private property of their employees, therefore, are subject to the restraints of the Fourth Amendment.

The Fourth Amendment protects the "right of the people to be secure in their persons, houses, papers, and effects, against unreasonable searches and seizures. . . ." Our cases establish that Dr. Ortega's Fourth Amendment rights are implicated only if the conduct of the Hospital officials at issue in this case infringed "an expectation of privacy that society is prepared to consider reasonable." *United States v. Jacobsen*, 466 U.S. 109, 113 (1984). We have no talisman that determines in all cases those privacy expectations that society is prepared to accept as reasonable. Instead, "the Court has given weight to such factors as the intention of the Framers of the Fourth Amendment, the uses to which the individual has put a location, and our societal understanding that certain areas deserve the most scrupulous protection from government invasion." *Oliver v. United States*, 466 U.S. 170, 178 (1984) (citations omitted).

Because the reasonableness of an expectation of privacy, as well as the appropriate standard for a search, is understood to differ according to context, it is essential first to delineate the boundaries of the workplace context. The workplace includes those areas and items that are related to work and are generally within the employer's control. At a hospital, for example, the hallways, cafeteria, offices, desks, and file cabinets, among other areas, are all part of the workplace. These areas remain part of the workplace context even if the employee has placed personal items in them, such as a photograph placed in a desk or a letter posted on an employee bulletin board.

Not everything that passes through the confines of the business address can be considered part of the workplace context, however. An employee may bring closed luggage to the office prior to leaving on a trip, or a handbag or briefcase each workday. While whatever expectation of privacy the employee has in the existence and the outward appearance of the luggage is affected by its presence in the workplace, the employee's expectation of privacy in the *contents* of the luggage is not affected in the same way. The appropriate standard for a workplace search does not necessarily apply to a piece of closed personal luggage, a handbag or a briefcase that happens to be within the employer's business address.

Within the workplace context, this Court has recognized that employees may have a reasonable expectation of privacy against intrusions by police. As with the expectation of privacy in one's home, such an expectation in one's place of work is "based upon societal expectations that have deep roots in the history of the Amendment." *Oliver v. United States, supra*, 466 U.S., at 178, n. 8. . . .

Given the societal expectations of privacy in one's place of work . . . we reject the contention made by the Solicitor General and petitioners that public employees can never have a reasonable expectation of privacy in their place of work. Individuals do not lose Fourth Amendment rights merely because they work for the government instead of a private employer. The operational realities of the workplace, however, may make *some* employees' expectations of privacy unreasonable when an intrusion is by a supervisor rather than a law enforcement official. Public employees' expectations of privacy in their offices, desks, and file cabinets, like similar expectations of employees in the private sector, may be reduced by virtue of actual office practices and procedures, or by legitimate regulation. . . . The employee's expectation of privacy must be assessed in the context of the employment relation. An office is seldom a private enclave free from entry by supervisors, other employees, and business and personal invitees. Instead, in many cases offices are continually entered by fellow employees and other visitors during the workday for conferences, consultations, and other work-related visits. . . . [S]ome government offices may be so open to fellow employees or the public that no expectation of privacy is reasonable. . . . Given the great variety of work environments in the public sector, the question whether an employee has a reasonable expectation of privacy must be addressed on a case-by-case basis.

. . . [Five of the Justices concluded that Dr. Ortega had a reasonable expectation of privacy in his office, while four Justices would have remanded for the District Court to determine this issue in light of actual practices at the Hospital.] But regardless of any legitimate right of access the Hospital staff may have had to the office as such . . . [t]he undisputed evidence discloses that Dr. Ortega did not share his desk or file cabinets with any other employees. Dr. Ortega had occupied the office for 17 years and he kept materials in his office, which included personal correspondence, medical files, correspondence from private patients unconnected to the Hospital, personal financial records, teaching aids and notes, and personal gifts and mementos. The files on physicians in residency training were kept outside Dr. Ortega's office. Indeed, the only items found by the investigators were apparently personal items because, with the exception of the items seized for use in the administrative hearings, all the papers and effects found in the office were simply placed in boxes and made available to Dr. Ortega. Finally, we note that there was no evidence that the Hospital had established any reasonable regulation or policy discouraging employees such as Dr. Ortega from storing personal papers and effects in their desks or file cabinets, although the absence of such a policy does not create an expectation of privacy where it would not otherwise exist.

On the basis of this undisputed evidence . . . Dr. Ortega had a reasonable expectation of privacy at least in his desk and file cabinets. . . .

[Having found that the Fourth Amendment applies to searches by public employers,] we must determine the appropriate standard of reasonableness applicable to the search. A determination of the standard of reasonableness applicable to a particular class of searches requires "balanc[ing] the nature and quality of the intrusion on the individual's Fourth Amendment interests against the importance of the governmental interests alleged to justify the intrusion." *United States v. Place*, 462 U.S. 696, 703 (1983). In the case of searches conducted by a public employer, we must balance the invasion of the employees' legitimate expectations of privacy against the government's need for supervision, control, and the efficient operation of the workplace. . . .

[The Court held that it would be unreasonable to impose a warrant requirement before public employers could undertake work-related searches. It next considered whether probable cause was required for public employers' searches of their employees' offices.]

The governmental interest justifying work-related intrusions by public employers is the efficient and proper operation of the workplace. Government agencies provide myriad services to the public, and the work of these agencies would suffer if employers were required to have probable cause before they entered an employee's desk for the purpose of finding a file or piece of office correspondence. Indeed, it is difficult to give the concept of probable cause, rooted as it is in the criminal investigatory context, much meaning when the purpose of a search is to retrieve a file for work-related reasons. Similarly, the concept of probable cause has little meaning for a routine inventory conducted by public employers for the purpose of securing state property. To ensure the efficient and proper operation of the agency, therefore, public employers must be given wide latitude to enter employee offices for work-related, noninvestigatory reasons.

We come to a similar conclusion for searches conducted pursuant to an investigation of work-related employee misconduct. . . . Public employers have an interest in ensuring that their agencies operate in an effective and efficient manner, and the work of these agencies inevitably suffers from the inefficiency, incompetence, mismanagement, or other work-related misfeasance of its employees. Indeed, in many cases, public employees are entrusted with tremendous responsibility, and the consequences of their misconduct or incompetence to both the agency and the public interest can be severe. In contrast to law enforcement officials, therefore, public employers are not enforcers of the criminal law; instead, public employers have a direct and overriding interest in ensuring that the work of the agency is conducted in a proper and efficient manner. In our view, therefore, a probable cause requirement for searches of the type at issue here would impose intolerable burdens on public employers. The delay in correcting the employee misconduct caused by the need for probable cause rather than reasonable suspicion will be translated into tangible and often irreparable damage to the agency's work, and ultimately to the public interest. . . .

Balanced against the substantial government interests in the efficient and proper operation of the workplace are the privacy interests of government employees in their place of work which, while not insubstantial, are far less than those found at home or in some other contexts. . . . Government offices are provided to employees for the sole purpose of facilitating the work of an agency. The employee may avoid exposing personal belongings at work by simply leaving them at home.

In sum, we conclude that the "special needs, beyond the normal need for law enforcement make the . . . probable-cause requirement impracticable," *New Jersey v. T.L.O.*, 469 U.S., at 351 (Blackmun, J., concurring in judgment), for legitimate work-related, noninvestigatory intrusions as well as investigations of work-related misconduct. A standard of reasonableness will neither unduly burden the efforts of government employers to ensure the efficient and proper operation of the workplace, nor authorize arbitrary intrusions upon the privacy of public employees. We hold, therefore, that public employer intrusions on the constitutionally protected privacy interests of government employees for noninvestigatory, work-related purposes, as well as for investigations of work-related misconduct, should be judged by the standard of reasonableness under all the circumstances. Under this reasonableness standard, both the inception and the scope of the intrusion must be reasonable:

> "Determining the reasonableness of any search involves a twofold inquiry: first, one must consider 'whether the . . . action was justified at its inception,' *Terry v. Ohio*, 392 U.S. [1], at 20 (1968); second, one must determine whether the search as actually conducted 'was reasonably related in scope to the circumstances which justified the interference in the first place,' *ibid.*" *New Jersey v. T.L.O., supra*, at 341.

Ordinarily, a search of an employee's office by a supervisor will be "justified at its inception" when there are reasonable grounds for suspecting that the search will turn up evidence that the employee is guilty of work-related misconduct, or that the search is necessary for a noninvestigatory work-related purpose such as to retrieve a needed file. Because petitioners had an "individualized suspicion" of misconduct by Dr. Ortega, we need not decide whether individualized suspicion is an essential element of the standard of reasonableness that we adopt today. See *New Jersey v. T.L.O., supra*, at 342, n. 8. The search will be permissible in its scope when "the measures adopted are reasonably related to the objectives of the search and not excessively intrusive in light of . . . the nature of the [misconduct]." 469 U.S., at 342.

[The Court then remanded the case for the District Court to determine the justification for the search, and to evaluate its reasonableness in both its inception and its scope.]

Justice Scalia, concurring in the judgment.

. . . [I]n my view, one's personal office is constitutionally protected against warrantless intrusions by the police, even though employer and co-workers are not excluded . . . . There is no reason why this determination that a legitimate expectation of privacy exists should be affected by the fact that the government, rather than a private entity, is the employer. Constitutional protection against *unreasonable* searches by the government does not disappear merely because the government has the right to make reasonable intrusions in its capacity as employer . . . . I would hold, therefore, that the offices of government employees, and *a fortiori* the drawers and files within those offices, are covered by Fourth Amendment protections as a general matter . . . .

The case turns, therefore, on whether the Fourth Amendment was violated—i.e., whether the governmental intrusion was reasonable. It is here that the government's status as employer, and the employment-related character of the search, become relevant. While as a general rule warrantless searches are *per se* unreasonable, we have recognized exceptions when "special needs, beyond the normal need for law enforcement, make the warrant and probable-cause requirement impracticable . . . ." *New Jersey v. T.L.O.*, 469 U.S. 325, 351, 105 S. Ct. 733, 749, 83 L. Ed. 2d 720 (Blackmun, J., concurring in judgment). Such "special needs" are present in the context of government employment. The government, like any other employer, needs frequent and convenient access to its desks, offices, and file cabinets for work-related purposes. I would hold that government searches to retrieve work-related materials or to investigate violations of workplace rules—searches of the sort that are regarded as reasonable and normal in the private-employer context—do not violate the Fourth Amendment. Because the conflicting and incomplete evidence in the present case could not conceivably support summary judgment that the search did not have such a validating purpose, I agree with the plurality that the decision must be reversed and remanded.

[The opinion of Justice Blackmun, dissenting, is omitted.]

NOTES

1. Government as Employer. The Fourth Amendment traditionally restrains the government's activities when enforcing criminal laws or acting in its regulatory capacity. It comes into play in this case only because Ortega worked for a government employer. Are the concerns that animate the Fourth Amendment relevant when the government acts in its role as an employer, rather than law enforcer? To put the question differently, why should government employers be restrained by constitutional norms protecting privacy in ways that private employers are not?

What does Justice Scalia think about this question? Does the test that he offers differ materially from the test articulated by Justice O'Connor's plurality? If so, which is the better test? For many years following the decision in *O'Connor*, the lower courts largely treated the plurality opinion as controlling, but the Supreme Court's decision in *City of Ontario v. Quon*, 560 U.S. 746 (2010), reproduced in section 4 below, pointed out that a majority of the Justices in *O'Connor* had not agreed on the appropriate test and that Justice Scalia had proposed a different approach from the plurality. To the extent that courts have analyzed cases using both the plurality's and Justice Scalia's frameworks, they have largely reached the same outcome. *See, e.g., Quon*, 560 U.S. at 757.

2.   **Reasonable Expectations of Privacy.** A crucial issue in evaluating Ortega's claim is whether or not he had a reasonable expectation of privacy in his office, desk and file cabinets. What factors does the Court suggest are relevant in determining whether an expectation of privacy should be recognized as legitimate? Why are "actual office practices" relevant to this inquiry? Would there be any problem with relying solely on actual practices to determine when a legitimate expectation of privacy exists?

Courts have found that employees may have legitimate expectations of privacy in cases involving activities such as the monitoring of personal communications, *see, e.g., Narducci v. Moore*, 572 F.3d 313 (7th Cir. 2009) (recording of personal phone calls), or intrusions on physical privacy, *see, e.g, Doe v. Luzerne County*, 660 F.3d 169 (3d Cir. 2011) (videotaping of partially nude officer during decontamination); *Rosario v. United States*, 538 F. Supp. 2d 480 (D.P.R. 2008) (video surveillance of locker-break room). On the other hand, employee expectations of privacy can be reduced when the government employer has given notice of the intrusion, *see, e.g., United States v. Simons*, 206 F.3d 392 (4th Cir. 2000) (concluding no reasonable expectation of privacy in computer files given employer's policy that internet use would be audited and monitored for non-business use); *American Postal Workers Union v. United States Postal Serv.*, 871 F.2d 556, 560 (6th Cir.1989) (finding no reasonable expectation of privacy in lockers in light of policies notifying employees of locker inspections). It is less clear whether notice can negate employees' expectations of privacy altogether, even in situations where strong social norms would support such a claim (e.g., in the case of bodily privacy) and there is no strong government justification for the intrusion.

3.   **Separating Work and Private Life**. One could argue that the lack of privacy protections at work is not a matter of concern, because employees can respond to reduced expectations of privacy in the workplace by maintaining a rigid separation between their work life and their personal lives. In his dissent in *O'Connor v. Ortega*, Justice Blackman rejects such a possibility as illusory, asserting that

> [T]he reality of work in modern time, whether done by public or private employees, reveals why a public employee's expectation of privacy in the workplace should be carefully safeguarded and not lightly set aside. It is, unfortunately, all too true that the workplace has become another home for most working Americans. Many employees spend the better part of their days and much of their evenings at work. . . . Consequently, an employee's private life must intersect with the workplace, for example, when the employee takes advantage of work or lunch breaks to make personal telephone calls, to attend to personal business, or to receive personal visitors in the office. As a result, the tidy distinctions . . . between the workplace and professional affairs, on the one hand, and personal posses-sions and private activities, on the other, do not exist in reality. Not all of an

> employee's private possessions will stay in his or her briefcase or handbag. Thus, the plurality's remark that the "employee may avoid exposing personal belongings at work by simply leaving them at home," reveals on the part of the Members of the plurality a certain insensitivity to the "operational realities of the workplace," they so value.

480 U.S. at 739. The line between personal and professional life has become even more difficult to discern with the rapidly expanding use of new technologies. In subsection 4 below we will explore the challenges to privacy law posed by expanding use of email, texting and social media.

4. Constitutional Protection for Confidential Information and Personal Autonomy. In addition to the privacy protections against unreasonable searches and seizures afforded by the Fourth Amendment, the Fourteenth Amendment's "concept of ordered liberty" has been interpreted to protect two types of privacy interests: "One is the individual interest in avoiding disclosure of personal matters, and another is the interest in independence in making certain kinds of important decisions." *Whalen v. Roe*, 429 U.S. 589, 599 (1977).

Public employees have raised constitutional challenges when a government employer seeks access to sensitive personal information such as medical or financial records. *See, e.g., Denius v. Dunlap*, 209 F.3d 944 (7th Cir. 2000) (finding infringement of a public employee's right of privacy where the employer required employee to sign a release permitting it to review personal medical records and confidential financial information without any justification for seeking the information and in the absence of safeguards against misuse). The right of confidentiality, however, is not absolute, but must be balanced against the government's interest in disclosure. *See Fraternal Order of Police v. Philadelphia*, 812 F.2d 105 (3d Cir. 1987) (holding that a flexible balancing test should be applied to public employees' claims that required disclosures violated their privacy interest in avoiding disclosure of confidential information).

The U.S. Supreme Court decided a case involving a claim by employees of a government contractor that parts of a government-required background investigation violated their constitutional right to avoid disclosure of personal matters. *Nat'l Aeronautics and Space Admin. v. Nelson*, 131 S. Ct. 746 (2011). A Ninth Circuit panel had granted a preliminary injunction against the background investigations, finding that there were serious questions as to whether a broad, open-ended inquiry seeking *"any* adverse information" from third parties violated the employees' informational privacy rights. *Nelson v. Nat'l Aeronautics & Space Admin.*, 530 F.3d 865, 881 (9th Cir. 2008). The panel also found that the balance of hardships tipped sharply in favor of the plaintiffs "who face a stark choice—either violation of their constitutional rights or loss of their jobs." *Id.*

Noting that only two cases, decided more than 30 years earlier, had "referred broadly" to such a constitutional privacy interest, the Supreme Court "assume[d], without deciding" that the Constitution protects informational privacy. 131 S. Ct. at 751. Even assuming that such a right exists, the Court held that the challenged background checks would not violate that right because "[t]he Government's interests as employer and proprietor in managing its internal operations" combined with existing statutory protections against dissemination of the information satisfied any such constitutional right. *Id.* Justices Scalia and Thomas concurred in the judgment, but wrote separately to emphasize that in their view "[a] federal constitutional right to 'informational privacy' does not exist." *Id.* at 764.

The *Nelson* decision raises some uncertainty about the status of a constitutionally protected right of informational privacy in general. But even if such a right exists, the Court's opinion makes clear that the employment context is highly relevant to evaluating any such claim, noting that "the Government has a much freer hand in dealing 'with citizen employees than it does when it brings its sovereign power to bear on citizens at large.' " *Id.* at 757–58 (citing *Enquist v. Oregon Dept. of Agriculture*, 553 U.S. 591, 598 (2008)).

Public employees have also asserted constitutional privacy claims under the "autonomy" prong—with mixed success—to challenge decisions by their employers based on their off-duty relationships. *Compare Thorne v. El Segundo*, 726 F.2d 459 (9th Cir. 1983) (holding that police department's refusal to hire plaintiff based in part on a past, private sexual relationship violated her constitutional rights of privacy and free association), *with Mercure v. Van Buren*, 81 F. Supp. 2d 814 (E.D. Mich. 2000) (rejecting constitutional privacy claim by police officer fired for having an affair with the estranged wife of a fellow officer on the grounds that adultery is not constitutionally protected).

2.   Common Law Protections for Private Employees

Because the Constitution only constrains state actors, the privacy protections grounded in the Fourth and Fourteenth Amendments do not directly apply to private sector employers. Constitutional jurisprudence has certainly influenced views about the privacy rights of private sector employees, and it is not unusual to find courts citing public employee cases when confronted with the privacy claims of private employees. Nevertheless, these cases do not provide direct precedent, and employees in the private sector generally must rely on the common law to protect their privacy interests, unless some statutory provision specifically makes a particular intrusion unlawful.

Common law protections against invasions of privacy by private actors crystallized relatively recently. Over the course of the 20th century, common law courts increasingly found actionable certain invasions of privacy. The term "privacy," however, was ambiguous, invoked to protect a variety of distinct interests. In 1977, the Restatement of Torts attempted to impose some order on the cases by identifying four forms of invasion of privacy that had "clearly become crystallized and generally been held actionable" at that time. RESTATEMENT (SECOND) OF TORTS § 652A cmt. c (1977). According to the Restatement typology, the right of privacy may be invaded by:

1) unreasonable intrusion upon the seclusion of another . . . ; or

2) appropriation of the other's name or likeness . . . ; or

3) unreasonable publicity given to the other's private life . . . ; or

4) publicity that unreasonably places the other in a false light before the public. . . .

Id. at § 652A(2).

Of these, the first and third types of invasions are the most likely to be brought in the employment setting. Employees occasionally bring claims based on the fourth category, the "false light" tort, but this cause of action is more closely connected with defamation, with its focus on reputational harm. Claims of "appropriation" rarely have application in the employment context. The next several cases examine how the common law torts of "intrusion upon seclusion" and "publicity given to another's private life" apply to claims that arise in the workplace.

a. Intrusion on Seclusion

K-MART CORP. STORE NO. 7441 v. TROTTI
Court of Appeals of Texas
677 S.W.2d 632 (1984)

BULLOCK, JUSTICE.

K-Mart Corporation appeals from a judgment awarding the appellee, Trotti, $8,000.00 in actual damages and $100,000.00 in exemplary damages for invasion of privacy.

We reverse and remand.

The appellee was an employee in the hosiery department at the appellants' store number 7441. Her supervisors had never indicated any dissatisfaction with her work nor any suspicion of her honesty.

The appellants provided their employees with lockers for the storage of personal effects during working hours. There was no assignment of any given locker to any individual employee. The employees could, on request, receive locks for the lockers from the appellants, and if the appellants provided the lock to an employee they would keep either a copy of the lock's combination or a master key for padlocks. Testimony indicated that there was some problem in providing a sufficient number of locks to employees, and, as a result, the store's administrative personnel permitted employees to purchase and use their own locks on the lockers, but in these instances, the appellants did not require the employee to provide the manager with either a combination or duplicate key. The appellee, with appellants' knowledge, used one of these lockers and provided her own combination lock.

On October 31, 1981, the appellee placed her purse in her locker when she arrived for work. She testified that she snapped the lock closed and then pulled on it to make sure it was locked. When she returned to her locker during her afternoon break, she discovered the lock hanging open. Searching through her locker, the appellee further discovered her personal items in her purse in considerable disorder. Nothing was missing from either the locker or the purse. The store manager testified that, in the company of three junior administrators at the store, he had that afternoon searched the lockers because of a suspicion raised by the appellants' security personnel that an unidentified employee, not the appellee, had stolen a watch. The manager and his assistants were also searching for missing price-marking guns. The appellee further testified that, as she left the employee's locker area after discovering her locker open, she heard the manager suggest to his assistants, "Let's get busy again." The manager testified that none of the parties searched through employees' personal effects.

The appellee approached the manager later that day and asked if he had searched employees' lockers and/or her purse. The manager initially denied either kind of search and maintained this denial for approximately one month. At that time, the manager then admitted having searched the employees' lockers and further mentioned that they had, in fact, searched the appellee's purse, later saying that he meant that they had searched only her locker and not her purse.

The manager testified that during the initial hiring interviews, all prospective employees received verbal notification from personnel supervisors that it was the appellants' policy to conduct ingress-egress searches of employees and also to conduct unannounced searches of lockers. A personnel supervisor and an assistant manager, however, testified that, although locker searches did regularly occur, the personnel supervisors did not apprise prospective employees of this policy. . . .

Er policy inconsiste[n] [handwritten margin note]

The fundamental and basic right to be left alone constitutes the essence of the right to privacy.

> The right of privacy has been defined as the right of an individual to be left alone, to live a life of seclusion, to be free from unwarranted publicity.

rt to privacy [handwritten margin note]

Billings v. Atkinson, 489 S.W.2d 858, 859 (Tex.1973). This right to privacy is so important that the United States Supreme Court has repeatedly deemed it to stem implicitly from the Bill of Rights. Our State courts have long recognized a civil cause of action for the invasion of the right to privacy and have defined such an invasion in many ways: As an intentional intrusion upon the solitude or seclusion of another that is highly offensive to a reasonable person, and as the right to be free from the wrongful intrusion into one's private activities in such manner as to outrage or cause mental suffering, shame or humiliation to a person of ordinary sensibilities.

The appellants requested the trial court to define an "invasion of privacy" as "the intentional intrusion upon the solitude or seclusion of another that is highly offensive to a reasonable person." . . . The court refused to include the part of the requested instruction, ". . . that is highly offensive to a reasonable person." The appellants argue that this refusal constituted an abuse of discretion . . . The appellee alleges that the record establishes that the intrusion was highly offensive as a matter of law, and that, therefore, the instruction was unnecessary . . . .

requested def of invasion of priv. [handwritten margin note]

We disagree with the appellee's contention. The record does indicate the appellee's outrage upon discovering the appellants' activities but fails to demonstrate that there could be no dispute as to the severity of the offensiveness of the intrusion, thereby making it impossible for us to conclude that the facts established the disputed portion of the instruction as a matter of law.

Moreover, we note that the result of accepting this contention would be to raise the legal theory of invasion of privacy from the realm of intentional torts into the sphere of strict liability. It would make any wrongful intrusion actionable, requiring a plaintiff to establish merely that the intrusion occurred and that the plaintiff did not consent to it. Because of the stern form of liability which already stems from an invasion of privacy, discussed, *infra*, accepting a definition of invasion of privacy which lacked a standard of high offensiveness would result in fundamentally unfair assessments against defendants who offended unreasonably sensitive plaintiffs, but whose transgressions would not realistically fill either an ordinary person or the general society with any sense of outrage. A business executive, for example, could find himself liable for entering an associate's office without express permission; so could a beautician who opened a co-worker's drawer in order to find some supplies needed for a customer.

We hold that the element of a highly offensive intrusion is a fundamental part of the definition of an invasion of privacy. . . . [S]ince we are ordering a new trial, we find it appropriate to examine the sufficiency of the evidence supporting the jury's finding. . . .

The lockers undisputably were the appellants' property, and in their unlocked state, a jury could reasonably infer that those lockers were subject to legitimate, reasonable searches by the appellants. This would also be true where the employee used a lock provided by the appellants, because in retaining the lock's combination or master key, it could be inferred that the appellants manifested an interest both in maintaining control over the locker and in conducting legitimate, reasonable searches. Where, as in the instant case, however, the employee purchases and uses his own lock on the lockers, with the employer's knowledge, the fact finder is justified in concluding that the employee manifested, and the employer recognized, an expectation that the locker and its contents would be free from intrusion and interference.

In the present case, there is evidence that the appellee locked the locker with her own lock; that when the appellee returned from a break, the lock was lying open; that upon searching her locker, the appellee discovered that someone had rifled her purse; that the appellants' managerial personnel initially denied making the search but subsequently admitted searching her locker and her purse. We find this is far more evidence than a "mere scintilla," and we hold that there is some evidence to support the jury's finding.

As to the "insufficiency" point, after examining the record as a whole, we find it indicates all of the above. The appellee remembers having locked the locker and having seen the lock closed before starting work that day. The record indicates that the searching personnel denied having gone through any employee's purses, yet nothing in the record directly challenges the appellee's testimony as to the disruption of her personal effects inside her purse, and, therefore, the jury could make a reasonable inference that the managerial personnel had, in fact, gone through her personal effects. The record also establishes that other employees knew these searches were going on. The store manager testified that all employees received notification of these sporadic searches during their hiring interviews; however, two administrators, including a former personnel supervisor, denied that employees ever received this notification. We hold that the weight of the evidence indicates that the appellants' employees came upon a locker with a lock provided by an employee, disregarded the appellee's demonstration of her expectation of privacy, opened and searched the locker, and probably opened and searched her purse as well; and, in so holding, we consider it is immaterial whether the appellee actually securely locked her locker or not. It is sufficient that an employee in this situation, by having placed a lock on the locker at the employee's own expense and with the appellants' consent, has demonstrated a legitimate expectation to a right of privacy in both the locker itself and those personal effects within it . . . .

The basis of a cause of action for invasion of privacy is that the defendant has violated the plaintiff's rights to be left alone. This intrusion itself is actionable, and the plaintiff can receive at least nominal damages for that actionable intrusion without demonstrating physical detriment. The appellants' improper intrusion of an area where the appellee had manifested an expectation of privacy alone raised her right to recover. . . .

The judgment is reversed, and the case is remanded for new trial.

NOTES

1. **Expectations of Privacy**. What factors led the court to conclude that Trotti's expectation of privacy in her locker and its contents was legitimate? Would its conclusion change if the locker searches had been clearly announced beforehand? What if such searches were conducted routinely? Matthew Finkin has argued that making the legitimacy of privacy rights contingent on business practices offers little real protection for employee privacy:

> [T]o the extent the reasonableness of the legitimate expectation of privacy is determined on objective grounds, it would rest upon employer policies, practices, or assurances in the matter only in the absence of which would the judgment have to turn to external norms. As others have noted, this bids fair to eviscerate any claim to privacy at all. For example, it is unsurprising that a lawyer would advise employers to minimize liability for workplace searches by, among other things, distributing a search policy to employees, posting signs about the workplace reminding them of their being subject to search, and, periodically, actually performing searches ostensibly for no reason other than to show that it is done.

Matthew W. Finkin, *Employee Privacy, American Values, and the Law*, 72 CHI.-KENT L. REV. 221, 226 (1996).

Is there any limit on how far an employer can reduce its employees' expectations of privacy through its policies and practices? On the other hand, can employer promises and practices create expectations of privacy that would not exist otherwise? *See Rulon-Miller v. Int'l Bus. Mach. Corp.*, 162 Cal. App. 3d 241 (1984) (upholding jury verdict for employee fired for a dating relationship, on the grounds that the discharge violated the employer's express policy that disciplinary actions would not be based on employees' outside activities that had no impact on job performance).

2. **Offensive Intrusions**. The court in *Trotti* holds that the requirement that an intrusion be "highly offensive to a reasonable person" is an essential element of the tort of invasion of privacy. What reasons exist for protecting against only "highly

offensive" intrusions? How does the standard under the common law tort compare with constitutional privacy protections?

Finkin criticizes the "highly offensive" standard on the grounds that the law should protect against not just "the occasional outrageous intrusion by a manager off on a frolic," but also situations in which "an employer acts in a systematically invasive fashion in what it takes to be a legitimate business interest." Finkin, *supra*, 72 CHI.-KENT L. REV. at 229. Such an approach would require employers to show a specific business need to justify any invasive intrusion, not just those meeting the "highly offensive" threshold. In a separate article, he contrasts the strong deference to employers shown by common law courts in the United States with the more robust legal protections afforded employee privacy and autonomy in continental Europe, and, in particular, Germany. *See* Matthew W. Finkin, *Menschenbild: The Conception of the Employee as a Person in Western Law*, 23 COMP. LAB. L & POL'Y J. 577 (2002).

3. **The Market Argument.** Given that a contractual relationship exists between employer and employee, is a cause of action to protect employee privacy necessary? Why not rely on the bargaining between employer and employee to achieve the optimal level of privacy in the workplace?

Consider the following argument: If employees truly value their personal privacy, then they should be willing to work at a lower wage for an employer who respects those interests. Conversely, the employer who routinely disrespects fundamental privacy interests will have to pay higher wages to attract employees. The rational employer will only infringe on its employees' privacy to the extent that these incursions improve the overall productivity of the firm. Thus, a well-functioning labor market will produce an optimal level of protection—that is, privacy will be respected to the extent that employees actually value those rights more highly than employers value the freedom to invade their workers' privacy.

One set of objections to the traditional market argument questions whether the labor market will actually operate in this way. As discussed in connection with the at-will rule above, employees' lack of accurate information, cognitive biases, signaling problems and other barriers to negotiation may interfere with efficient bargaining over workplace conditions, such that privacy interests are insufficiently protected, at least when workers contract with the employer on an individual basis. The extent to which collective bargaining better protects employees' privacy interests remains an open question. As we will discuss in subsection B. 3., *infra*, in the union setting employers may be required to bargain over privacy issues that directly impact the working environment. In other areas, such as protecting employees' off-duty conduct, a body of arbitral law restricts employers' ability to rely on such conduct as a basis for termination where employees are protected by a "just cause" provision. On the other hand, the opposition of unions did little to slow the drive to impose routine drug testing in certain workplaces, although their presence arguably influenced the procedural protections available to workers who were disciplined after a positive test result.

Under what conditions can the market be expected to restrain unjustified invasions of employee privacy? When do you think you would be *least* likely to see employee privacy respected? Even assuming that the labor market operates efficiently with respect to employee privacy interests, are there any arguments that the law still has a role to play in protecting employee privacy?

4.   Protected Privacy Interests. The invasion of privacy tort articulated in the Restatement of Torts has been recognized in one form or another by a majority of states, and employees are generally permitted to bring invasion of privacy claims. Because the common law tort of invasion of privacy speaks in terms of "solitude" or "seclusion," the tort fits most comfortably in cases challenging employer activities such as entering an employee's home or hotel room without permission, *Wal-Mart Stores, Inc. v. Lee*, 74 S.W.3d 634 (Ark. 2002) (home); *Sowards v. Norbar, Inc.*, 605 N.E.2d 468 (Ohio Ct. App. 1992) (hotel room); or surreptitiously observing employees in traditionally private spaces such as a restroom. *See, e.g., Koeppel v. Speirs*, 808 N.W.2d 177 (Iowa 2011); *Johnson v. Allen*, 613 S.E.2d 657 (Ga. 2005).

Because of the nature of the employment relationship, however, such claims do not often prevail. Courts frequently find that employees have a reduced expectation of privacy in the workplace. *See, e.g., Terrell v. Rowsey*, 647 N.E.2d 662 (Ind. Ct. App. 1995) (finding plaintiff had a diminished privacy interest in his car when parked on employer's property during working hours); *O'Bryan v. KTIV Television*, 868 F. Supp. 1146 (N.D. Iowa 1994) (holding plaintiff did not have a reasonable expectation of privacy that employer would not search his desk or office area for work-related documents). Employee privacy claims are also defeated when courts find that the employer's intrusion was justified for business reasons, *see, e.g., Terrell*, 647 N.E.2d at 667 (vehicle search reasonable in light of employer's rule against drinking on company property and its interest in providing a safe workplace), or that the employee consented to the intrusion.

5.   Restating Employee Privacy Rights. Employees' common law privacy rights have traditionally been based on the general invasion of privacy tort set out in the Restatement of Torts and reproduced at the beginning of this subsection. The recently adopted Restatement of Employment Law specifically addresses privacy rights in the context of the employee-employer relationship. The Restatement preserves the basic structure of the common law privacy tort, stating that "An employer is subject to liability for a wrongful intrusion upon an employee's protected privacy interest if the intrusion would be highly offensive to a reasonable person under the circumstances." RESTATEMENT (THIRD) OF EMPLOYMENT LAW § 7.06(a) (Proposed Final Draft, April 18, 2014). It further states that the intrusion is highly offensive "if the nature, manner, and scope of the intrusion upon the employee's protected privacy interest are clearly unreasonable when judged against the employer's legitimate business interests or public interests in effecting the intrusion," § 7.06(b), and thereby explicitly connects judgments about the offensiveness of the intrusion to the employer's business justification.

The Restatement of Employment Law also goes beyond the Restatement of Torts version of the invasion of privacy tort by trying to identify the situations in which a legitimate employee interest is at stake. It provides:

   (a)   An employee has a protected privacy interest against employer intrusion upon:

      (1)   the employee's physical person, bodily functions, and personal possessions; and

(2) physical and electronic locations, including employer-provided locations, in which the employee has a reasonable expectation of privacy.

(b) An employee has a reasonable expectation in the privacy of a physical or electronic work location provided by the employer if:

(1) the employer has provided express notice that the location or aspects of the locations are private for employees; or

(2) the employer has acted in a manner that treats the location or aspects of the location as private for employees, the type of location is customarily treated as private for employees, and the employee has made reasonable efforts to keep the location private.

(c) An employer intrudes upon an employee's protected privacy interest under this Section by such means as an examination, search, or surveillance.

RESTATEMENT (THIRD) OF EMPLOYMENT LAW § 7.03 (Proposed Final Draft, April 18, 2014) (cross-references omitted).

What does the new Restatement of Employment Law add to the understanding of the common law tort of invasion of privacy? Do you think its description of an employee's "protected privacy interest" accurately captures the areas of concern for employees? What are the advantages and disadvantages of the Restatement of Employment Law's approach over the simple statement of the claim under the Restatement of Torts?

6. Information Gathering By Employers. The Restatement of Employment Law also suggests that employees have an interest in avoiding the forced disclosure or collection of information of a personal nature by their employer when such information is not necessary for business reasons. §§ 7.02(b) and 7.04. These types of interests were also sometimes protected under the "intrusion on seclusion" tort, but the new Restatement expressly recognizes that employees have an interest in avoiding disclosure of sensitive information, such as sexual information or health information. An example of the type of case decided under the invasion of privacy tort is *Johnson v. K-Mart Corp.*, 723 N.E.2d 1192 (Ill. App. Ct. 2000), in which the court recognized a claim for intrusion upon seclusion where private investigators hired to investigate concerns about theft and vandalism compiled information about employees' family problems, health problems, sex lives, and future work plans, and reported this "extremely personal information" to K-Mart management. Similarly, in *Phillips v. Smalley Maint. Servs.*, 435 So. 2d 705 (Ala. 1983), the plaintiff brought an intrusion upon seclusion claim against her employer based upon his intrusive sexual demands, including repeated inquiries into her sexual relationship with her husband. However, courts often hold that employers have a legitimate interest in obtaining certain types of sensitive information. *See, e.g., Fletcher v. Price Chopper Food of Trumann Inc.*, 220 F.3d 871 (8th Cir. 2000) (holding that employer's legitimate need to know about employee's staph infection trumped her right to privacy).

Apart from the common law, a patchwork of federal and state laws also limit an employer's ability to collect certain specific types of information. For example, the Fair Credit Reporting Act, 15 U.S.C. §§ 1681–1681T, restricts the use of consumer credit information for employment purposes, and the federal Genetic Information

Nondiscrimination Act restricts an employer's ability to access genetic information about its employees or their family members. *See* 42 U.S.C. § 2000ff-1(b). The Americans with Disabilities Act limits employers' ability to require medical examinations or make inquiries regarding an employee's disability. *See* 42 U.S.C. § 12112 (forbidding employers from requiring job applicants to undergo medical exams prior to receiving an offer and limiting the scope and circumstances of medical exams and inquiries post offer). In addition, anti-discrimination laws are sometimes interpreted to forbid certain types of pre-employment inquiries, such as questions regarding an applicant's membership in a protected class. *See e.g.*, CAL. CODE REGS. tit. 2, § 7287.3, subd. (b)(1) (stating that inquiries that identify an individual on the basis of religious creed are unlawful under state anti-discrimination law).

7.   Privacy Rights vs. At-Will Employment. Even though the *Trotti* case arose in the workplace setting, her claims involved a fairly straightforward application of the common law privacy tort. She alleged that her employer had acted in a way that constituted an unlawful invasion of privacy, and the principal harm she complained of was the invasion itself. Suppose, however, that an at-will employee learns that her employer plans some action that she believes will violate her privacy. At that point, she could (a) submit to the invasive search or testing procedure and sue later for invasion of privacy; (b) go to court immediately to seek injunctive relief barring the alleged invasion of privacy; or (c) object to the employer's plans, be fired, and sue for wrongful discharge after the fact. Do you see any difficulties with each of these options? As these questions suggest, recognition of employee privacy rights is often in tension with the at-will rule.

In *Jennings v. Minco Technology Labs, Inc.*, 765 S.W.2d 497 (Tex. App. 1989), the plaintiff, upon learning of her employer's plan to begin conducting random urinalysis drug testing of its employees, went to court seeking an injunction to block implementation of the plan on the grounds that it would violate the employees' common-law right of privacy. The Texas Court of Appeals rejected her claim, noting that because she was an at-will employee, the company could impose modifications to the employment at any time. Moreover, it reasoned that "Jennings's employer threatens no *unlawful* invasion of any employee's privacy interest" because the drug testing would only occur if the employee consented. 765 S.W.2d at 502. The court held that the common law right of privacy could not be used offensively to enlarge her contractual rights as an at-will employee. What if, instead of seeking an injunction, an employee simply refuses to submit to a drug test that she believes violates her privacy rights? Would the common law afford any protection?

The court in *Luck v. Southern Pacific Transportation, Co.*, 218 Cal. App. 3d 1 (1990) rejected the possibility that a plaintiff fired for resisting an invasion of privacy could sue for wrongful discharge in violation of public policy. It reasoned as follows:

> . . . A termination that is against public policy must affect a duty which inures to the benefit of the public at large rather than to a particular employer or employee. . . . The right to privacy is, by its very name, a private right, not a public one. The parties could have lawfully agreed that Luck would submit to urinalysis without violating any public interest. Such

an agreement between Luck and Southern Pacific would not have been against public policy. Therefore . . . there was no violation of *public* policy.

Id. at 28. Judge Poché dissented from this portion of the majority opinion, arguing that the California constitution, which explicitly lists privacy as an "inalienable right" in its Preamble, could provid the basis for a public policy tort claim:

> [I]t is the task of constitutions by their very nature to enunciate high public policy rather than to simply regulate conduct between private individuals . . . . Unless we accept the perfectly logical and defensible position that inalienable personal rights inure by their very nature to the benefit of all Californians and thus to the public benefit, we accord no practical protection to the very rights given the greatest deference by our Constitution. . . .

Id. at 33.

Other courts have found that privacy rights can provide a public policy basis for a wrongful discharge claim. For example, the Alaska Supreme Court held:

> Alaska law clearly evidences strong support for the public interest in employee privacy. First, state statutes support the policy that there are private sectors of employee's lives not subject to direct scrutiny by their employers [citing examples of statutes regulating polygraphs and forbidding inquiry into topics such as race or religion] . . .

> Second, . . . Alaska's constitution contains a right to privacy clause. While we have held . . . that this clause does not proscribe the private action at issue, it can be viewed by this court as evidence of a public policy supporting privacy. . . .

> Third, there exists a common law right to privacy. . . . Thus, the citizens' right to be protected against unwarranted intrusions into their private lives has been recognized in the law of Alaska. The constitution protects against governmental intrusion, statutes protect against employer intrusion, and the common law protects against intrusions by other private persons. As a result, there is sufficient evidence to support the conclusion that there exists a public policy protecting spheres of employee conduct into which employers may not intrude. . . .

Luedtke v. Nabors Alaska Drilling, Inc., 768 P.2d 1123 (Alaska 1989). *See also Hellanbrand v. Nat'l Waste Assocs.*, 2008 Conn. Super. LEXIS 249 (Jan. 30, 2008) (permitting claim for wrongful discharge in violation of public policy based on the right to privacy where employee alleged she was fired after refusing her employer's demand to inspect her private cellphone records).

Such an approach raises several issues. First, is protecting privacy a value articulated in an accepted source of public policy? Should the courts look to constitutional provisions as sources of public policy? Do constitutional provisions protecting privacy articulate important public policies relevant to the workplace? Second, is it incoherent to talk about "privacy" as a matter of "public policy"? "Private" and "public" are often spoken of as oppositional categories. Is there any way in which individual claims of privacy protection can be understood as affecting the public? What effect would widespread recognition of employee privacy as a protected public policy have? *See* Pauline T. Kim, *Privacy Rights, Public Policy, and the Employment Relationship*, 57 Ohio St. L.J. 671 (1996) (arguing for recognizing common law privacy rights as a basis for the public policy tort).

The Restatement of Employment Law adopts the position that an employer that discharges an employee "for refusing to consent to a wrongful employer intrusion upon a protected employee privacy interest" is liable for wrongful discharge in violation of public policy. Restatement (Third) of Employment Law § 7.07 (Proposed Final Draft, April 18, 2014). It reasons that "[t]he purposes of the public-policy cause of action are furthered because the refusing employee is empowered to protect her personal interests and at the same time to resist an employer policy likely adversely to affect other employees and to impair the public interest as well." § 7.07 cmt. b. Such a claim is only viable, however, if the employee can show that the employer's demands, if carried out, would constitute a wrongful intrusion on an employee's protected privacy interest as defined in the chapter. § 7.07 cmt. c.

b.   Publicity to Private Life

BORQUEZ v. ROBERT C. OZER, P.C.
Colorado Court of Appeals
923 P.2d 166 (1996)

Opinion by Judge Taubman.

In this action for wrongful discharge based on sexual orientation and invasion of privacy, defendants, Robert C. Ozer, P.C., d/b/a Ozer and Mullen, P.C. (the Ozer law firm) and Robert C. Ozer (Ozer), individually, appeal from the judgment entered upon a jury verdict against them and in favor of plaintiff, Robert Borquez.

. . . Borquez was discharged from his position as an associate with the Ozer law firm within a week after his disclosure to Ozer that he was gay, that his companion was in the hospital, and that his companion had just been diagnosed with Acquired Immune Deficiency Syndrome (AIDS).

Borquez was hired by the Ozer law firm as an associate in May 1990. He did not disclose his sexual orientation to Ozer or to anyone else at the firm. Also, because he was concerned about Ozer's acknowledged dislike of homosexuals, he kept his personal life confidential.

Borquez was well-respected, liked, and performed capably as an attorney with the firm. He was awarded three merit raises in his salary, including one just eleven days before he was fired.

On February 19, 1992, Borquez learned for the first time that his companion had been diagnosed with AIDS. Upset by that news and having been advised by his physician that he should be tested immediately for AIDS, Borquez concluded that he could not represent a client effectively in a deposition that afternoon, nor could he participate in an arbitration hearing the following day.

In an effort to locate another attorney to handle the deposition and the hearing,

Borquez discussed the matter with Ozer and disclosed facts about his personal life including his sexual orientation, his homosexual relationship, and his need for immediate AIDS testing. Borquez asked Ozer to keep this information confidential, but Ozer made no reply. However, Ozer agreed to handle the deposition and hearing.

Shortly thereafter, Ozer told his wife, who is another shareholder in the firm, and others of Borquez' disclosures. Within two days, all employees and shareholders in the firm had learned about Borquez' personal life and his need for AIDS testing.

Two days later, Ozer met with Borquez and told him that he had not agreed to keep the disclosures confidential. Ozer also made derogatory comments about people with AIDS.

Five days later, on February 26, Ozer fired Borquez. The reason for the firing was a significant disputed issue at trial, with defendants maintaining that it had been for economic reasons. Those economic reasons stemmed from a pending bankruptcy which had been filed by the Ozer law firm in August 1991.

Indeed, on February 17, 1992, two days before Borquez' disclosure, Ozer had met with his bankruptcy attorney and, according to Ozer, had then decided that, in order to cut costs, Borquez and another lawyer would be laid off. According to Ozer, Borquez was scheduled to be laid off during the month of February. Following Borquez' disclosures, the shareholders of the firm discussed whether to follow through with their plan to discharge Borquez, recognizing that such discharge might result in litigation against the law firm. According to defendants' evidence, faced with the need to pare costs because of the pending bankruptcy, the shareholders decided to follow through with their plan to discharge Borquez.

[Borquez then sued, alleging wrongful dismissal under a Denver ordinance and a Colorado statute, and invasion of privacy for public disclosure of private facts. The jury found for Borquez on both the wrongful discharge and the invasion of privacy claims. The Court first discussed the wrongful discharge claim, then turned to the invasion of privacy tort.] . . .

Defendants also contend that, because Colorado has not formally recognized the tort of invasion of privacy in the form of "unreasonable publicity given to the life of another," no cause of action exists for such a claim. Again, we disagree. . . .

Although no Colorado court has specifically recognized an invasion of privacy action for unreasonable publicity given to the private life of another, as outlined in Restatement (Second) of Torts § 652D (1976), more than 30 jurisdictions have done so. We conclude that Restatement § 652D provides sufficient authority for resolution of the issues before us. . . .

Restatement (Second) of Torts § 652D (1976) provides:

> One who gives publicity to a matter concerning the private life of another is subject to liability to the other for invasion of privacy, if the matter publicized is of a kind that (a) would be highly offensive to a reasonable person, and (b) is not of legitimate concern to the public.

Critical to this particular claim of invasion of privacy is that the disclosure concerns the "private" life of the plaintiff and that it would be highly offensive to a reasonable person. Restatement (Second) of Torts § 652D comment b (1976) further explains that:

> Every individual has some phases of his life and his activities and some facts about himself that he does not expose to the public eye, but keeps entirely to himself or at most reveals only to his family or to close personal friends. Sexual relations, for example, are normally entirely private matters, as are . . . disgraceful or humiliating illnesses.

Here, the information regarding Borquez' sexual conduct and, in particular, his exposure to the HIV virus, clearly constitutes a "private" matter as defined by the Restatement. . . . Further, as both courts and commentators have noted, the disclosure of this information would be highly objectionable to a reasonable person because a strong stigma still attaches to both homosexuality and AIDS.

In addition, the information disclosed was not a matter of legitimate concern to the public. The facts about Borquez' health and private life were inherently private, as discussed above. Also, public health reports and records relating to individuals diagnosed with AIDS, HIV-related illness, or HIV infection are "strictly confidential information" and may be disclosed only under narrowly specified circumstances. *See* § 25-4-1404(1), C.R.S. (1995 Cum. Supp.). The information concerning Borquez' health and possible HIV infection was therefore not of legitimate public concern. . . .

However, for there to be a supportable claim under Restatement § 652D, there must also be "publicity" of the private facts. According to the Restatement, publicity occurs when a matter is communicated to the public at large, or to so many persons that the matter must be regarded as substantially certain to become one of public knowledge. *See* Restatement (Second) of Torts § 652D comment a (1976). [The Court of Appeals concluded that this element was satisfied.] . . .

Ozer asserts that whatever information was disseminated about Borquez' sexual orientation and HIV status was authorized by consent or qualified privilege. In effect, Ozer contends that Borquez "waived" his right to bring this action for public disclosure of private facts by telling Ozer about his personal situation.

The protection afforded an individual's right to privacy may be waived "to whatever degree and in whatever connection a man's life has ceased to be private." *Cabaniss v. Hipsley*, 151 S.E.2d 496, 502 (1966). However, the scope of the waiver is related to and limited by the actions on which the waiver is based. More specifically: "[The right of privacy] may be waived for one purpose and still asserted for another; it may be waived in behalf of one class and retained as against another class." *Pavesich v. New England Life Insurance Co.*, 50 S.E. 68, 72 (1905).

Here, it is undisputed that Borquez informed Ozer of his circumstances *only* because he felt that it was necessary in relation to his responsibilities at work. Additionally, the record reveals that Borquez went to great measures to keep his sexual orientation private and, upon disclosure to Ozer, expressly requested the information be kept confidential. Although Ozer did not promise to keep this personal information about Borquez private, evidence was presented to the jury indicating that Borquez did not consent to further disclosure regarding his sexual orientation.

Thus, Borquez expressly limited the scope of his waiver to Ozer and Ozer's subsequent disclosures went beyond the scope specified by Borquez, in terms of both audience and purpose. Hence, we reject defendants' contention that by informing Ozer, Borquez waived his right to privacy and made the facts of his personal life and medical condition public as a matter of law.

Further, the jury was instructed that defendants had a qualified privilege to communicate information regarding Borquez' sexual orientation to "officers and employees relating to the status and conduct of an employee and that information was of common interest to them for health and professional reasons." The jury was also instructed that the privilege did not protect the defendants if they abused it by, *inter alia*, communicating such information "primarily for purposes other than the protection of the interest for which the privilege was given."

Although the shareholders of the law firm had a qualified privilege to discuss information regarding Borquez' sexual orientation among themselves, particularly in light of their asserted recent decision to discharge him because of the pending bankruptcy, there was evidence presented to the jury that defendants abused that privilege by communicating the information to others at the firm who did not have a legitimate reason to learn this information. Accordingly, the jury was properly instructed regarding defendant's affirmative defense of privilege and, based upon conflicting evidence, rejected it.

Viewing the evidence in the light most favorable to the jury verdict, we conclude that there was sufficient evidence to support it. . . .

METZGER, J., concurs.

[The opinion of PLANK, J., concurring in part and dissenting in part is omitted.]

NOTES

1. **Private Information.** A threshold inquiry in a case alleging public disclosure of private facts is whether the matters disclosed are in fact private. The court in *Borquez* easily concluded that both the plaintiff's homosexuality and his exposure to HIV were "private" matters entitled to be protected from disclosure. Other public disclosure claims have failed, however, on the grounds that the information disclosed is not "private." *See, e.g., Dancy v. Fina Oil & Chem. Co.*, 3 F. Supp. 2d 737 (E.D. Tex. 1997) (finding no invasion of privacy based on employer's publication of a list of employees with excessive absences because the facts disclosed were not private); *Chisolm v. Foothill Capital Corp.*, 3 F. Supp. 2d 925 (N.D. Ill. 1998) (statement that the plaintiff's relationship with her current husband overlapped with his previous marriage is not a private fact where the relationship was openly acknowledged and the date of his divorce was a matter of public record).

How should courts decide which facts are sufficiently private to warrant protection from disclosure by the tort? Should extreme embarrassment on the part of the employee be sufficient to establish the private nature of the information? Is the behavior of the plaintiff regarding the allegedly private facts relevant in any way to this inquiry? *See* RESTATEMENT (SECOND) OF TORTS, § 652D cmt. b (stating that action for disclosure of private facts will not lie where the fact allegedly publicized is one that the plaintiff leaves open to the public eye).

The issue of unwarranted disclosures of private information has become more pressing as employers increasingly have access to highly personal information about their employees. The disclosure prong of the privacy tort, however, does not limit what types of information an employer may gather about its employees although, as discussed above, the "intrusion or seclusion" tort, as well as some state and federal statutes, places some restrictions on employer gathering of private information.

2. Who Is the Public? One of the elements of the public disclosure tort requires that "publicity" is given to private facts. In instructing the jury, the trial court in *Borquez* had used the term "published" rather than "publicized," telling the jury that in order for the plaintiff to recover, it must find that the defendants "published" a matter concerning plaintiff's private life. On appeal, the defendant had argued that the jury instructions were erroneous as a matter of law, because the term "published" is associated with defamation law and requires only a communication to a third party, rather than "publicity" to the public at large. Thus, it argued, the term "published" erroneously set a lower threshold for liability than the requirement of "publicity."

The Court of Appeals thought the language used was harmless error because Ozer had in fact communicated Borquez's private information to a "public" with whom he had a special relationship. The court explained:

> Some courts . . . have recognized the need for flexibility in the application of the Restatement's theory to permit recovery for particularly egregious conduct. These courts have held the general rule not applicable to a claim of invasion of privacy where a special relationship exists between the plaintiff and the "public" to whom the information is disclosed. *See Miller v. Motorola*, 560 N.E.2d 900 (special relationship exists between an employee, whose supervisor disclosed information about her mastectomy, and her fellow employees); *Beaumont v. Brown*, 257 N.W.2d 522 (1977) (special relationship exists between the Army Reserve office and a reservist who was the subject of a derogatory letter from his employer).

> Communication to the general public has not been required by some courts because disclosure to those persons with whom the plaintiff has a special relationship may be just as devastating as disclosure to many. In *Beaumont v. Brown, supra*, 257 N.W.2d at 531, the court explained:

>> Communication of embarrassing facts about an individual to a public not concerned with that individual and with whom the individual is not concerned obviously is not a serious interference with plaintiff's right to privacy, although it might be "unnecessary" or "unreasonable." An invasion of a plaintiff's right to privacy is important if it exposes private facts to a public whose knowledge of those facts would be

embarrassing to the plaintiff. Such a public might be the general public if the person were a public figure, or a particular public such as fellow employees, club members, church members, family, or neighbors if the person were not a public figure.

Accordingly, we hold that it is appropriate to recognize the tort of invasion of privacy in the form of unreasonable publicity given to the private life of another in the circumstances of this case where private information was unreasonably disseminated to fellow employees who had no legitimate interest therein. . . .

Here, Borquez' companion's medical condition and Borquez' at-risk status were disclosed to all employees of the firm, including shareholders, associates, and support staff. Borquez' coworkers are a "public" with whom he has a special relationship and to whom disclosure of his sexual orientation and possible HIV infection could prove particularly embarrassing.

Borquez, 923 P.2d at 173–74.

The Colorado Supreme Court reversed the Court of Appeals on the adequacy of the jury instructions, explaining that

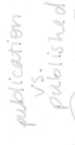

Public disclosure connotes publicity, and the term "publicity" is distinct from the term "publication." *See* Restatement (Second) of Torts § 652D cmt. a (1976). The term "publicity" requires communication to the public in general or to a large number of persons rather than to just one individual or a few. In contrast, the term "publication," as it is applied in defamation claims, "is a word of art, which includes any communication by the defendant to a third person." Restatement (Second) of Torts § 652D cmt. a (1976). . . . [B]ecause the terms "publication" and "publicity" are not interchangeable, we hold that the trial court's instruction was erroneous.

Robert C. Ozer, P.C. v. Borquez, 940 P.2d 371, 379 (Colo. 1997).

Based on this error in instructing the jury, the Colorado Supreme Court remanded the case for a new trial. In doing so, it did not address the Court of Appeal's finding that Borquez's co-workers constituted a "public" with whom he had a "special relationship," satisfying the publicity requirement. The Colorado Supreme Court, however, did state that "the facts and circumstances of a particular case must be taken into consideration in determining whether the disclosure was sufficiently public so as to support a claim for invasion of privacy," *Id.* at 378, *citing Kinsey v. Macur*, 107 Cal. App. 3d 265, 270 (1980), in which the court held that the defendant's dissemination of copies of a letter to only 20 people constituted public disclosure.

Should the existence of a "special relationship" with the audience affect the publicity requirement? What role is played by the requirement of disclosure to "the public"? Some courts have found that the disclosure of private facts to even a small group of co-workers can satisfy the element of publicity because of the existence of a "special relationship." *See, e.g., Karch v. BayBank FSB*, 794 A.2d 763, 774 (N.H. 2002); *Johnson v. K-Mart Corp.*, 723 N.E.2d 1192 (Ill. App. Ct. 2000). Many others, however, have interpreted the "publicity" element to require communication to the public at large and have found that disclosing private facts to a group of co-workers is insufficient. *See, e.g., Beyene v. Hilton Hotels Corp.*, 815 F. Supp. 2d 235 (D.D.C. 2011); *Williams v. Wicomico County Bd. of Educ.*, 836 F. Supp. 2d 387 (D. Md. 2011).

3. Collective Approaches to Protecting Employee Privacy.

Many employer uses of investigatory tools or surveillance to detect workplace wrongdoing or impediments to productivity impact all workers in the workplace. Does the law provide any basis for a collective challenge to these practices?

The labor laws are potentially applicable to both nonunion and union workplaces in such situations. First, employer surveillance will violate NLRA § 8(a)(1) (prohibiting interference with employees' § 7 rights to organize, bargain, or utilize economic pressure) if the surveillance tends to discourage employees' exercise of those rights, particularly the right to organize a union. In the days prior to the enactment of the NLRA, employers often used labor spies to infiltrate labor unions and report on the "ringleaders," who were then discharged and blacklisted. Section 8(a)(1) was intended to protect workers against these practices, and it applies as well to more technologically advanced methods of surveillance, including videotaping. *See, e.g., Snap-On Tools, Inc.*, 342 N.L.R.B. 5 (2004) (employer videotaping of worker handbilling was prohibited surveillance). Where employers use the information obtained through surveillance to punish or discharge the union activists, § 8(a)(3) (prohibiting discrimination that tends to discourage union affiliation) will also be violated.

Second, where there is a union in place, the Labor Board has concluded that a wide variety of employer investigative tools used to detect employee misconduct are mandatory subjects of bargaining: they have the potential to affect the continued employment of employees through discipline up to and including discharge, and are outside the employer's exclusive prerogative to manage and control the workplace. Accordingly, the employer who utilizes such tools without first bargaining with the union to impasse violates § 8(a)(5) of the NLRA, imposing a duty to bargain in good faith over wages, hours, and terms and conditions of employment. *See, e.g., Lockheed Shipbuilding Co.*, 273 N.L.R.B. 171 (1984) (employee physical examinations are mandatory subject of bargaining); *Austin-Berryhill, Inc.*, 246 N.L.R.B. 1139 (1979) (polygraph testing is mandatory subject of bargaining); *Johnson-Bateman Co.*, 295 N.L.R.B. 180 (1989) (drug testing of current employees is mandatory subject of bargaining); *but see Star-Tribune*, 295 N.L.R.B. 543 (1989) (drug testing of applicants is not mandatory subject of bargaining). The following materials offer further insight into the basis for NLRA protection of collective employee dignity and privacy interests and its significance.

COLGATE-PALMOLIVE CO. AND LOCAL 15, INTERNATIONAL CHEMICAL WORKERS UNION
National Labor Relations Board
323 N.L.R.B. 515 (1997)

By William B Gould IV, Chairman.

[In 1994, a Colgate-Palmolive employee was cleaning the restrooms when he noticed a surveillance camera located in the air vent and angled toward him. He brought it to the attention of the union steward, and the union thereafter contacted management. The human resources director explained that the company was investigating theft and had placed a camera in the employee restroom on the advice of legal counsel. The company immediately removed the camera. The union, asserting that cameras had also been seen in the employees' fitness center, filed a grievance. At the grievance hearing management took the position that it had the absolute right to install internal surveillance cameras when it suspects theft or impairment of its property rights. It admitted that since 1982 it had utilized cameras located in plain view to survey the plant premises, and that since 1990 it had also used hidden cameras both inside and outside to investigate theft or other suspected misconduct in the plant. The union demanded bargaining, and the company did not respond. The union then filed unfair labor practice charges alleging violations of §§ 8(a)(1) and 8(a)(5).]

. . . The [administrative law] judge found that the issue of the Respondent's installation and use of hidden surveillance cameras in the workplace is a mandatory subject of bargaining, and that the Union has a statutory right to bargain over the installation and continued use of these surveillance cameras. We agree.

In *Ford Motor Co. v. N.L.R.B.* [441 U.S. 488 (1979)], the Supreme Court described mandatory subjects of bargaining as such matters that are "plainly germane to the 'working environment'" and "not among those 'managerial decisions, which lie at the core of entrepreneurial control.'" As the judge found, the installation of surveillance cameras is both germane to the working environment, and outside the scope of managerial decisions lying at the core of entrepreneurial control.

As to the first factor—germane to the working environment—the installation of surveillance cameras is analogous to physical examinations, drug/alcohol testing requirements, and polygraph testing, all of which the Board has found to be mandatory subjects of bargaining. They are all investigatory tools or methods used by an employer to ascertain whether any of its employees has engaged in misconduct.

The Respondent implemented the installation and use of surveillance cameras because of an increase in workplace theft and other suspected employee misconduct in the facility, such as reports of employees sleeping instead of working. The Respondent acknowledges that employees caught involved in theft and/ or other misconduct are subject to discipline, including discharge. Accordingly, the installation and use of surveillance cameras has the potential to affect the continued employment of employees whose actions are being monitored.

Further, as the judge finds, the use of surveillance cameras in the restroom and fitness center raises privacy concerns which add to the potential effect upon employees. We agree that these areas are part of the work environment and that the use of hidden cameras in these areas raises privacy concerns which impinged upon the employees' working conditions. The use of cameras in these or similar circumstances is unquestionably germane to the working environment.

With regard to the second criterion, we agree with the judge that the decision is not a managerial decision that lies at the core of entrepreneurial control. In discussing this issue in *Ford Motor Co.*, *supra*, the Court relied on Justice Stewart's concurring opinion in *Fibreboard Corp.*, in which he states that "decisions concerning the commitment of investment capital and the basic scope of the enterprise are not in themselves primarily about conditions of employment, . . . those management decisions which are fundamental to the basic direction of a corporate enterprise or which impinge only indirectly upon employment security should be excluded from that area."

The installation and use of surveillance cameras in the workplace are not among that class of managerial decisions that lie at the core of entrepreneurial control. The use of surveillance cameras is not entrepreneurial in character, is not fundamental to the basic direction of the enterprise, and impinges directly upon employment security. It is a change in the Respondent's methods used to reduce workplace theft or detect other suspected employee misconduct with serious implications for its employees' job security, which in no way touches on the discretionary "core of entrepreneurial control."[1]

What we say here today, of course, has no bearing upon the content of any agreement or arrangement that may emerge from collective bargaining. Nor does it address the employer's establishment of practices on the subject matter subsequent to having bargained to impasse. It is the duty to bargain and only the duty to bargain that is involved here.[2] . . .

Accordingly, we affirm the judge's finding that the Union has the statutory right to engage in collective bargaining over the installation and continued use of surveillance cameras, including the circumstances under which the cameras will be

---

[1] [n. 10] 221 N.L.R.B. at 676. The Respondent urges that bargaining before a hidden camera is actually installed would defeat the very purpose of the camera. The very existence of secret cameras, however, is a term and condition of employment, and is thus a legitimate concern for the employees' bargaining representative. Thus, the placing of cameras, and the extent to which they will be secret or hidden, if at all, is a proper subject of negotiations between the Respondent and the Union. Concededly, the Respondent also has a legitimate concern. However, bargaining about hidden cameras can embrace a host of matters other than mere location. And, even as to location, mutual accommodations can and should be negotiated. The vice in the instant case was the Respondent's refusal to bargain.

[2] [n. 11] In its brief, the Respondent relies on *First National Maintenance Corp. v. N.L.R.B.*, 452 U.S. 666 (1981), to argue that the burden placed on the Company's ability to run its business is not outweighed by the benefits of bargaining regarding the installation of surveillance cameras in the workplace. However, as we have already found, the Respondent's decision to install surveillance cameras does not involve a change in the basic direction or scope of its business. Rather, it is the type of management decision that is "almost exclusively 'an aspect of the relationship' " between the employer and employees and, as to such decisions, there is an obligation to bargain. *Id.* at 677. The decision to install surveillance cameras is, therefore, not subject to the balancing test urged by the Respondent.

activated, the general areas in which they may be placed, and how affected employees will be disciplined if improper conduct is observed. We also affirm the judge's conclusion that the Respondent's failure and refusal to bargain with the Union after its bargaining demand letter of August 16, 1994, violated Section 8(a)(1) and (5) of the Act. . . . [The Board then ordered the Company to bargain with the union over the installation and use of surveillance cameras, and to post notices to employees stating that the Board had found an unfair labor practice and informing the employees of their bargaining rights.]

NOTES

1. **The Basis for Collective Employee Rights.** Is the basis for protection of employee bargaining rights in cases arising under NLRA § 8(a)(5) rooted in concern for employee privacy rights or in employee job security? To answer this question, consider what significance the placement of the hidden cameras had in *Colgate-Palmolive*. Restrooms are areas traditionally understood as private. This fact seems intuitively important, but how critical was the location of the surveillance to the Board's decision? The Board subsequently applied the *Colgate-Palmolive* analysis to another case involving hidden surveillance cameras, this time installed in an office file cabinet in an effort to discover who was using a manager's office at night to make long distance telephone calls. The company fired the wrongdoer, and the union filed a grievance over his termination. The union sought information about hidden surveillance cameras from the company, citing *Colgate-Palmolive*. The company refused, taking the position that disclosing the location of the cameras would defeat the company's purpose. The Board rejected the argument, relying on *Colgate-Palmolive*, and ordered the company to provide the information, which was part of its bargaining obligation. The Seventh Circuit enforced the Board's order. *See Nat'l Steel Corp.*, 335 N.L.R.B. 747 (2001), *enforced*, 324 F.3d 928 (7th Cir. 2003). And in a case involving surveillance even further removed from areas considered private, the Board applied the same rule where surveillance cameras were hidden in a rooftop location where employees performed work and took breaks. In *Brewers & Maltsters, Local No. 6 v. NLRB*, 414 F.3d 36 (D.C. Cir. 2005), the employer sought to limit *Colgate-Palmolive* to situations involving employee privacy concerns such as those raised by surveillance in restrooms and fitness rooms. The Board rejected the argument and the D.C. Circuit agreed, explaining that privacy considerations in the use of hidden surveillance measures were secondary; the primary focus was on whether the surveillance occurred in the working environment and had implications for the continued employment of employees whose actions were monitored. *Id.* at 44.

2. **Accommodating Employer Managerial Interests and Employee Dignity Interests.** The court in *National Steel Corp.* deferred to the Board's accommodation of conflicting managerial and employee interests in *Colgate-Palmolive*, reasoning that the imposition of a bargaining obligation did not mandate the outcome of negotiations, nor did it "make any suggestion that National Steel must yield any prerogatives, other than yielding the right to proceed exclusive of consultation with the union." If consultation is all that is required, why did the company resist, undoubtedly incurring substantial legal fees challenging the Board's order?

3. The Relationship Between Just Cause Protection and Worker Privacy Rights. Related issues have arisen in contexts where employers have unilaterally issued rules impacting upon unionized workers' privacy or autonomy and, potentially, job security, because workers who violate the rules may be subject to discipline or discharge. An employer that discharges or disciplines an employee on the basis of information discovered through the use of unilaterally promulgated work rules that are mandatory subjects of bargaining will likely face a challenge under the typical collective bargaining agreement's protection against discipline or discharge without "just cause." Pursuant to the contract, the employer will be required to negotiate with the union at various steps in the contractually specified grievance process, and to arbitrate if a satisfactory resolution is not reached. One basis for challenging a discharge is lack of industrial due process. Industrial due process is understood to require adequate notice of workplace rules, compliance with progressive discipline, equitable treatment relative to other rule violators, substantive reasonableness of rules, that misconduct be job-related, and that the penalty imposed be proportional to the work rule violation. The employer's use of investigatory techniques or application of rules that have not been bargained over previously or contractually established will strengthen the due process challenge.

4. Collective vs. Individual Claims. What difference does it make whether employee privacy claims are framed in collective or individual terms? To put the question differently, how does the involvement of a union affect how employee privacy concerns are raised? Pauline Kim explored these questions by examining the history of legal challenges to employer drug testing policies in the 1980s and 1990s. Unions played a crucial role in bringing most of the early workforce-wide injunctive challenges to employment drug testing; however their role changed over time:

> [T]he types of court cases with union involvement appears to have shifted from high profile suits challenging the legitimacy of government and employer policies to defending the rights of individual workers subjected to such policies. While likely reflecting a rational response on the part of unions to signals from the courts, this shift in emphasis transformed the discourse surrounding challenges to workplace drug testing. The early workforce-wide cases spoke in terms of basic human dignity and fundamental rights, asking what types of interests were sufficiently weighty to justify burdening these important rights. By contrast, the later cases hardly speak at all in terms of privacy or dignity. Rather, they focus on compliance with procedural safeguards and the protection of the material interests, for example jobs and wages, of their members. Workers who felt aggrieved because of the *manner* in which a test was administered, or by the intrusiveness of the test itself, could not recover damages for dignitary harms, and those who suffered no tangible job loss were essentially remediless under the collective bargaining system. Thus, although the presence of a union undoubtedly insured that its members received procedural protections they otherwise might not have had and likely worked to check the worst abuses, collective resistance to mandatory drug testing became routinized over time, focusing on consistent application of

the rules, rather than on protecting the dignitary and privacy interests of workers.

What about an individual rights model for protecting employee privacy? [I]ndividual litigants, in the absence of a union, are less likely to bring suit seeking workforce-wide relief. In addition, individual litigants are unlikely to seek any sort of *prospective* relief. The vast majority of individual suits involve after-the-fact challenges to a workplace drug testing policy. . . . Although the cost-benefit calculus of litigation may look more attractive to the individual worker after termination, raising the policy and dignitary concerns that motivate resistance to workplace drug testing is significantly more difficult in after-the-fact challenges. Despite the very real possibility that chemical testing of urine will produce false positives, the worker fired for failing a drug test suffers from an implicit presumption of guilt. . . . The worker fired for refusing to submit to drug testing also faces difficulties. Although not tainted by a positive test result, her resistance to taking the test naturally raises questions about her motivation. . . . Despite these difficulties, an individual rights approach to protecting employee privacy has at least one distinct advantage over collective challenges, at least under the current legal regime for collective bargaining. The individual privacy claim, asserting tort theories or violation of constitutional rights, brings with it the possibility of significant damages. . . . Judging from published court opinions, individual privacy claims rarely succeed; nevertheless, the threat of legal liability for invasion of employee privacy may more effectively discourage unreasonably intrusive testing practices than the risks posed by individual grievances under a collective bargaining regime that offers no remedy for dignitary harm.

Pauline T. Kim, *Collective and Individual Approaches to Protecting Employee Privacy: The Experience with Workplace Drug Testing*, 66 LA. L. REV. 1009, 1029–31 (2006).

4. Privacy of Electronic Communications

As discussed in the last several sections, the source and nature of legal protection of employee privacy interests varies depending upon whether the workplace is public or private, union or nonunion. Regardless of the type of workplace, however, the rapidly expanding use of new technologies on the job has raised challenging new questions about how to balance employee privacy with employers' interests in using these technologies to improve productivity and security.

One recurring area of conflict has been over the extent to which employers are permitted to access their employees' electronic communications, such as emails, text messages, or social media communications. The legal basis for challenging such employer actions varies depending upon the circumstances, and in this subsection we will explore the ways in which different sources of law might provide some protection for employees' privacy in their electronic communications. Underlying all of these cases, however, is a common question—namely, whether and to what extent do employees have a reasonable expectation of privacy in their electronic communications? In the next case, the Supreme Court confronted this question in the context of employer provided text pagers:

a. Constitutional Law

CITY OF ONTARIO v. QUON
United States Supreme Court
560 U.S. 746 (2010)

JUSTICE KENNEDY delivered the opinion of the Court.

[Jeff Quon was employed by the Ontario Police Department (OPD) as a police sergeant and member of OPD's Special Weapons and Tactics (SWAT) Team. The City issued pagers to Quon and other SWAT team members in order to help them mobilize and respond to emergency situations. Each pager was allotted a limited number of characters sent or received each month. Usage in excess of that amount would result in an additional fee. The City had a "Computer Usage, Internet and E-Mail Policy" which specified that the City "reserves the right to monitor and log all network activity including e-mail and Internet use, with or without notice. Users should have no expectation of privacy or confidentiality when using these re-sources." Quon signed a statement acknowledging that he had read and understood the Computer Policy.]

Although the Computer Policy did not cover text messages by its explicit terms, the City made clear to employees, including Quon, that the City would treat text messages the same way as it treated e-mails. At an April 18, 2002, staff meeting at which Quon was present, Lieutenant Steven Duke, the OPD officer responsible for the City's contract with [the wireless service provider], told officers that messages sent on the pagers "are considered e-mail messages. This means that [text] messages would fall under the City's policy as public information and [would be] eligible for auditing." Duke's comments were put in writing in a memorandum sent on April 29, 2002, by [the Chief of the Ontario Police Department, Lloyd] Scharf to Quon and other City personnel.

Within the first or second billing cycle after the pagers were distributed, Quon exceeded his monthly text message character allotment. Duke told Quon about the overage, and reminded him that messages sent on the pagers were "considered e-mail and could be audited." Duke said, however, that "it was not his intent to audit [an] employee's text messages to see if the overage [was] due to work related transmissions." Duke suggested that Quon could reimburse the City for the overage fee rather than have Duke audit the messages. Quon wrote a check to the City for the overage. Duke offered the same arrangement to other employees who incurred overage fees.

Over the next few months, Quon exceeded his character limit three or four times. Each time he reimbursed the City. Quon and another officer again incurred overage fees for their pager usage in August 2002 . . . . Scharf decided to determine whether the existing character limit was too low . . . . Duke reviewed the transcripts [of text messages sent in August and September by Quon and the other officer who had exceeded the character allowance] and discovered that many of the messages sent and received on Quon's pager were not work related, and some were sexually explicit. Duke reported his findings to Scharf, who, along with Quon's immediate supervisor, reviewed the transcripts himself. After his review, Scharf referred the matter to OPD's internal affairs division for an investigation into whether Quon was violating OPD rules by pursuing personal matters while on duty.

The officer in charge of the internal affairs review was Sergeant Patrick McMahon. Before conducting a review, McMahon used Quon's work schedule to redact the transcripts in order to eliminate any messages Quon sent while off duty. He then reviewed the content of the messages Quon sent during work hours. McMahon's report noted that Quon sent or received 456 messages during work hours in the month of August 2002, of which no more than 57 were work related; he sent as many as 80 messages during a single day at work; and on an average workday, Quon sent or received 28 messages, of which only 3 were related to police business. The report concluded that Quon had violated OPD rules. Quon was allegedly disciplined.

. . . . [Quon filed suit alleging] that petitioners violated [his] Fourth Amendment rights . . . by obtaining and reviewing the transcript of [his] pager messages . . . .

[The parties disagree] over whether Quon had a reasonable expectation of privacy . . . . The Court must proceed with care when considering the whole concept of privacy expectations in communications made on electronic equipment owned by a government employer. The judiciary risks error by elaborating too fully on the Fourth Amendment implications of emerging technology before its role in society has become clear. *See, e.g., Olmstead v. United States*, 277 U.S. 438 (1928), overruled by *Katz v. United States*, 389 U.S. 347, 353 (1967). In *Katz*, the Court relied on its own knowledge and experience to conclude that there is a reasonable expectation of privacy in a telephone booth. *See id.*, at 360–361 (Harlan, J., concurring). It is not so clear that courts at present are on so sure a ground. Prudence counsels caution before the facts in the instant case are used to establish far-reaching premises that define the existence, and extent, of privacy expectations enjoyed by employees when using employer-provided communication devices.

Rapid changes in the dynamics of communication and information transmission are evident not just in the technology itself but in what society accepts as proper behavior. As one *amici* brief notes, many employers expect or at least tolerate personal use of such equipment by employees because it often increases worker efficiency. Another *amicus* points out that the law is beginning to respond to these developments, as some States have recently passed statutes requiring employers to notify employees when monitoring their electronic communications. At present, it is uncertain how workplace norms, and the law's treatment of them, will evolve.

[Even if the Court follows the *O'Connor* plurality's approach,] the Court would have difficulty predicting how employees' privacy expectations will be shaped by those changes or the degree to which society will be prepared to recognize those expectations as reasonable. Cell phone and text message communications are so pervasive that some persons may consider them to be essential means or necessary instruments for self-expression, even self-identification. That might strengthen the case for an expectation of privacy. On the other hand, the ubiquity of those devices has made them generally affordable, so one could counter that employees who need cell phones or similar devices for personal matters can purchase and pay for their own. And employer policies concerning communications will of course shape the reasonable expectations of their employees, especially to the extent that such policies are clearly communicated.

A broad holding concerning employees' privacy expectations vis-à-vis employer-provided technological equipment might have implications for future cases that cannot be predicted. It is preferable to dispose of this case on narrower grounds. For present purposes we assume . . . Quon had a reasonable expectation of privacy in the text messages sent on the pager provided to him by the City . . . .

narrow

Even if Quon had a reasonable expectation of privacy in his text messages, petitioners did not necessarily violate the Fourth Amendment by obtaining and reviewing the transcripts . . . .

Under the approach of the *O'Connor* plurality, when conducted for a "noninvestigatory, work-related purpos[e]" or for the "investigatio[n] of work-related misconduct," a government employer's warrantless search is reasonable if it is " 'justified at its inception' " and if " 'the measures adopted are reasonably related to the objectives of the search and not excessively intrusive in light of' " the circumstances giving rise to the search. 480 U.S., at 725–726. The search here satisfied the standard of the *O'Connor* plurality and was reasonable under that approach.

rule

The search was justified at its inception because there were "reasonable grounds for suspecting that the search [was] necessary for a noninvestigatory work-related purpose." *Id.*, at 726. As a jury found, Chief Scharf ordered the search in order to determine whether the character limit on the City's contract with Arch Wireless was sufficient to meet the City's needs. . . . The City and OPD had a legitimate interest in ensuring that employees were not being forced to pay out of their own pockets for work-related expenses, or on the other hand that the City was not paying for extensive personal communications.

As for the scope of the search, reviewing the transcripts was reasonable because it was an efficient and expedient way to determine whether Quon's overages were the result of work-related messaging or personal use. The review was also not " 'excessively intrusive.' " *O'Connor, supra*, at 726 (plurality opinion). Although Quon had gone over his monthly allotment a number of times, OPD requested transcripts for only the months of August and September 2002. While it may have been reasonable as well for OPD to review transcripts of all the months in which Quon exceeded his allowance, it was certainly reasonable for OPD to review messages for just two months in order to obtain a large enough sample to decide whether the character limits were efficacious. And it is worth noting that during his internal affairs investigation, McMahon redacted all messages Quon sent while off duty, a measure which reduced the intrusiveness of any further review of the transcripts.

Furthermore, and again on the assumption that Quon had a reasonable expectation of privacy in the contents of his messages, the extent of an expectation is relevant to assessing whether the search was too intrusive. Even if he could assume some level of privacy would inhere in his messages, it would not have been reasonable for Quon to conclude that his messages were in all circumstances immune from scrutiny. Quon was told that his messages were subject to auditing. As a law enforcement officer, he would or should have known that his actions were likely to come under legal scrutiny, and that this might entail an analysis of his on-the-job communications. Under the circumstances, a reasonable employee would be aware that sound management principles might require the audit of messages to determine whether the pager was being appropriately used. Given that the City issued the pagers to Quon and other SWAT Team members in order to help them more quickly respond to crises—and given that Quon had received no assurances of privacy—Quon could have anticipated that it might be necessary for the City to audit pager messages to assess the SWAT Team's performance in particular emergency situations.

From OPD's perspective, the fact that Quon likely had only a limited privacy expectation, with boundaries that we need not here explore, lessened the risk that the review would intrude on highly private details of Quon's life. OPD's audit of messages on Quon's employer-provided pager was not nearly as intrusive as a search of his personal e-mail account or pager, or a wiretap on his home phone line, would have been. That the search did reveal intimate details of Quon's life does not make it unreasonable, for under the circumstances a reasonable employer would not expect that such a review would intrude on such matters. The search was permissible in its scope.

The Court of Appeals erred in finding the search unreasonable. It pointed to a "host of simple ways to verify the efficacy of the 25,000 character limit . . . without intruding on [respondents'] Fourth Amendment rights." 529 F.3d, at 909 . . . . This approach was inconsistent with controlling precedents. This Court has "repeatedly refused to declare that only the 'least intrusive' search practicable can be reasonable under the Fourth Amendment." *Vernonia, supra,* at 663. That rationale "could raise insuperable barriers to the exercise of virtually all search-and-seizure powers," *United States v. Martinez-Fuerte,* 428 U.S. 543, 557, n. 12 (1976), because "judges engaged in *post hoc* evaluations of government conduct can almost always imagine some alternative means by which the objectives of the government might have been accomplished." *Skinner,* 489 U.S., at 629, n. 9 . . . . Even assuming there were ways that OPD could have performed the search that would have been less intrusive, it does not follow that the search as conducted was unreasonable . . . .

Because the search was motivated by a legitimate work-related purpose, and because it was not excessive in scope, the search was reasonable under the approach of the *O'Connor* plurality. 480 U.S., at 726. For these same reasons—that the employer had a legitimate reason for the search, and that the search was not excessively intrusive in light of that justification—the Court also concludes that the search would be "regarded as reasonable and normal in the private-employer context" and would satisfy the approach of Justice Scalia's concurrence. *Id.* at 732. The search was reasonable, and the Court of Appeals erred by holding to the contrary. Petitioners did not violate Quon's Fourth Amendment rights . . . .

[The opinion of JUSTICE STEVENS, concurring on this judgment, is omitted]

[The opinion of JUSTICE SCALIA, concurring in part and concurring in the judgment, is omitted]

NOTES

1. **Reasonable in Scope?** The Ninth Circuit had a different view of the reasonableness of the scope of the search in *Quon*. It wrote:

> A search is reasonable "at its inception" if there are "reasonable grounds for suspecting . . . that the search is necessary for a noninvestigatory work-related purpose such as to retrieve a needed file." *O'Connor*, 480 U.S. at 726. Here, the purpose was to ensure that officers were not being required to pay for work-related expenses. This is a legitimate work-related rationale, as the district court acknowledged.
>
> However, the search was not reasonable in scope. As *O'Connor* makes clear, a search is reasonable in scope "when the measures adopted are reasonably related to the objectives of the search and not excessively intrusive in light of . . . the nature of the [misconduct]." *Id.* Thus, "if less intrusive methods were feasible, or if the depth of the inquiry or extent of the seizure exceeded that necessary for the government's legitimate purposes . . . the search would be unreasonable . . ." *Schowengerdt* [*v. General Dynamics Corp.*], 823 F.2d [1328,] 1336 [(9th Cir. 1987)]. . . . There were a host of simple ways to verify the efficacy of the 25,000 character limit (if that, indeed, was the intended purpose) without intruding on Appellants' Fourth Amendment rights. For example, the Department could have warned Quon that for the month of September he was forbidden from using his pager for personal communications, and that the contents of all of his messages would be reviewed to ensure the pager was used only for work-related purposes during that time frame. Alternatively, if the Department wanted to review past usage, it could have asked Quon to count the characters himself, or asked him to redact personal messages and grant permission to the Department to review the redacted transcript. . . . Instead, the Department opted to review the contents of all the messages, work-related and personal, without the consent of Quon or the remaining Appellants. This was excessively intrusive in light of the noninvestigatory object of the search, and because Appellants had a reasonable expectation of privacy in those messages, the search violated their Fourth Amendment rights.

Quon, 529 F.3d at 908–09. How did the Supreme Court respond to this reasoning? Which approach do you think is most consistent with Justice O'Connor's plurality opinion in *O'Connor v. Ortega*?

In *Quon*, the Supreme Court pointed out that the *O'Connor* court "did disagree on the proper analytical framework for Fourth Amendment claims against government employers." 560 U.S. at 576. It did not attempt to resolve the difference between the plurality and Justice Scalia in *O'Connor*, but instead analyzed the case using both tests and reached the same conclusion under each.

2. **New Technologies and the Fourth Amendment.** Determining how the Fourth Amendment's prohibition of unreasonable searches and seizures applies to new technologies like email and text messages can be difficult. Although the Supreme Court avoided this question in *Quon*, it has begun to address it in the criminal context. In *United States v. Jones*, 132 S. Ct. 945 (2012), it ruled that attaching a GPS device to a vehicle to monitor its movements continuously over several weeks constitutes a search under the Fourth Amendment. The Court however was divided in its reasoning, with several Justices emphasizing the physical nature of the intrusion, and others focused on the reasonableness of the defendant's expectation of privacy in his movements over an extended period of time. More recently, the Court found that individuals have significant privacy interests in their cell phones. Cell phones contain vast amounts of data, information that constitutes "a digital record of nearly every aspect of their lives—from the mundane to the intimate." *Riley v. California*, 134 S. Ct. 2473, 2490 (2014). Because of the significant privacy interests at stake, the Court concluded that the Fourth Amendment ordinarily requires police to obtain a warrant before searching a cell phone seized incident to an arrest. *Id.*

Should the Justices in *Quon* have squarely confronted the question whether Officer Quon had a reasonable expectation of privacy in his text messages? If so, how should it have answered that question? Although the Supreme Court in *Quon* declined to provide an answer, other courts have considered cases involving private sector employees asserting claims of privacy in their electronic communications.

b. Reasonable Expectations of Privacy

Many of the earliest cases arising in the private sector involved employer monitoring or accessing of employees' work email accounts. When email systems were relatively new, users often thought of their accounts as private because they were provided with a password to access them, even though the system was created by the employer and typically resided on the employer's computers. Employees then objected when they found out that they could be disciplined or discharged for communications made over these accounts that they believed to be private.

For example, in *Smyth v. Pillsbury Co.*, 914 F. Supp. 97 (E.D. Pa. 1996), the plaintiff alleged that he was wrongfully discharged when his employer fired him after discovering several "inappropriate and unprofessional" emails that he had sent over the company's email system to his supervisor. Those emails allegedly suggested "kill[ing] the backstabbing bastards" in referring to management, and called a planned holiday party the "Jim Jones Koolaid affair." 914 F. Supp. at 98, n.1. The defendant had repeatedly assured employees that email communications were confidential and privileged and would not be intercepted and used as grounds for discipline or discharge. Nevertheless, sometime after the plaintiff sent those emails, they were accessed by the employer and became the basis for his termination. The plaintiff sued, alleging wrongful discharge in violation of public policy, locating the public policy in the common law tort of intrusion upon seclusion.

The court in *Smyth* rejected the plaintiff's claim, concluding that "we do not find a reasonable expectation of privacy in e-mail communications voluntarily made by an employee to his supervisor over the company e-mail system notwithstanding any assurances that such communications would not be intercepted by management." *Id.* at 101. The court emphasized that the plaintiff had not been required to disclose any personal information about himself. Rather, he had "voluntarily communicated the alleged unprofessional comments over the company e-mail system. We find no privacy interests in such communications." *Id.* The court further argued that "even if we found that an employee had a reasonable expectation of privacy in the contents of his e-mail communications over the company e-mail system, we do not find that a reasonable person would consider the defendant's interception of these communications to be a substantial and highly offensive invasion of his privacy." *Id.*

Like *Smyth*, cases raising privacy claims in an employee's work email generally have not succeeded. *See, e.g., Garrity v. John Hancock Mutual Life Ins. Co.*, 18 IER Cases 981 (D. Mass. 2002) (holding that plaintiff employees had no reasonable expectation of privacy in their work email); *McLaren v. Microsoft Corp.*, 1999 Texas App. LEXIS 4103 (May 28, 1999) (same). In many cases, the existence of an employer policy stating that employees have no expectation of privacy in their work email has been sufficient to defeat any such expectation. *See, e.g, Thygeson v. U.S. Bancorp*, 2004 U.S. Dist. LEXIS 18863 (D. Or. Sept. 15, 2004) (finding no reasonable expectation of privacy when employer has an explicit policy banning personal use of office computers and permitting monitoring).

Although courts were initially quite skeptical of employees' privacy claims in electronic communications at work, that attitude has shifted as technology and common practices evolved. Workers increasingly have personal accounts, including web-based email accounts or social media accounts, and they may access them at work using either employer-owned equipment or their own devices. The next case considers what happens when an employee accesses one of those accounts on an employer-owned computer.

STENGART v. LOVING CARE AGENCY, INC.
Supreme Court of New Jersey
990 A.2d 650 (2010)

CHIEF JUSTICE RABNER delivered of the opinion of the Court.

In the past twenty years, businesses and private citizens alike have embraced the use of computers, electronic communication devices, the Internet, and e-mail. As those and other forms of technology evolve, the line separating business from personal activities can easily blur.

In the modern workplace, for example, occasional, personal use of the Internet is commonplace. Yet that simple act can raise complex issues about an employer's monitoring of the workplace and an employee's reasonable expectation of privacy . . . .

Loving Care provides home-care nursing and health services. Stengart began working for Loving Care in 1994 and, over time, was promoted to Executive Director of Nursing. The company provided her with a laptop computer to conduct company business. From that laptop, Stengart could send e-mails using her company e-mail address; she could also access the Internet and visit websites through Loving Care's server. Unbeknownst to Stengart, certain browser software in place automatically made a copy of each web page she viewed, which was then saved on the computer's hard drive in a "cache" folder of temporary Internet files. Unless deleted and overwritten with new data, those temporary Internet files remained on the hard drive.

On several days in December 2007, Stengart used her laptop to access a personal, password-protected e-mail account on Yahoo's website, through which she communicated with her attorney about her situation at work. She never saved her Yahoo ID or password on the company laptop.

Not long after, Stengart left her employment with Loving Care and returned the laptop. On February 7, 2008, she filed the pending complaint [alleging employment discrimination].

In an effort to preserve electronic evidence for discovery, in or around April 2008, Loving Care hired experts to create a forensic image of the laptop's hard drive. Among the items retrieved were temporary Internet files containing the contents of seven or eight e-mails Stengart had exchanged with her lawyer via her Yahoo account.[3] . . . [Loving Care's attorneys reviewed the e-mails and used information culled from them in the course of discovery. When Stengart's lawyers learned that defense counsel had copies of their e-mail communications with plaintiff, they sought the return of the originals and all copies of the e-mails and moved to disqualify defense counsel as a sanction for violating the attorney-client privilege.]

A legend appears at the bottom of the e-mails that Stengart's lawyer sent [warning readers that the e-mail was confidential and might contain a privileged attorney-client communication.]

. . . Loving Care and its counsel relied on an Administrative and Office Staff Employee Handbook that they maintain contains the company's Electronic Communication policy (Policy) [to argue that its employees have no expectation of privacy in their use of company computers.]

The proffered Policy states, in relevant part:

> The company reserves and will exercise the right to review, audit, intercept, access, and disclose all matters on the company's media systems and services at any time, with or without notice . . . .

> E-mail and voice mail messages, internet use and communication and computer files are considered part of the company's business and client records. Such communications are not to be considered private or personal to any individual employee.

---

[3] [n. 1] The record does not specify how many of the e-mails were sent or received during work hours. Loving Care asserts that the e-mails in question were exchanged during work hours through the company's server. However, counsel for Stengart represented at oral argument that four of the e-mails were transmitted or accessed during non-work hours—three on a weekend and one on a holiday. It is unclear, and ultimately not relevant, whether Stengart was at the office when she sent or reviewed them.

The principal purpose of electronic mail (*e-mail*) is for company business communications. Occasional personal use is permitted; however, the system should not be used to solicit for outside business ventures, charitable organizations, or for any political or religious purpose, unless authorized by the Director of Human Resources.

The Policy also specifically prohibits "[c]ertain uses of the e-mail system" including sending inappropriate sexual, discriminatory, or harassing messages, chain letters, "[m]essages in violation of government laws," or messages relating to job searches, business activities unrelated to Loving Care, or political activities. The Policy concludes with the following warning: "Abuse of the electronic communications system may result in disciplinary action up to and including separation of employment." . . .

It is not clear from [the Policy's] language whether the use of personal, password-protected, web-based e-mail accounts via company equipment is covered. The Policy uses general language to refer to its "media systems and services" but does not define those terms. Elsewhere, the Policy prohibits certain uses of "the e-mail system," which appears to be a reference to company e-mail accounts. The Policy does not address personal accounts at all. In other words, employees do not have express notice that messages sent or received on a personal, web-based e-mail account are subject to monitoring if company equipment is used to access the account.

The Policy also does not warn employees that the contents of such e-mails are stored on a hard drive and can be forensically retrieved and read by Loving Care.

The Policy goes on to declare that e-mails "are not to be considered private or personal to any individual employee." In the very next point, the Policy acknowledges that "[o]ccasional personal use [of e-mail] is permitted." As written, the Policy creates ambiguity about whether personal e-mail use is company or private property . . . .

According to some courts, employees appear to have a lesser expectation of privacy when they communicate with an attorney using a company e-mail system as compared to a personal, web-based account like the one used here. *See, e.g., Smyth v. Pillsbury Co.,* 914 F. Supp. 97, 100–01 (E.D. Pa. 1996) (finding no reasonable expectation of privacy in unprofessional e-mails sent to supervisor through internal corporate e-mail system); *Scott v. Beth Israel Med. Ctr., Inc.,* 17 *Misc.* 3d 934, 847 *N.Y.S.*2d 436, 441–43 (N.Y. Sup. Ct. 2007) (finding no expectation of confidentiality when company e-mail used to send attorney-client messages). *But see Convertino v. U.S. Dep't of Justice,* 674 *F. Supp.* 2d 97, 110 (D.D.C. 2009) (finding reasonable expectation of privacy in attorney-client e-mails sent via employer's e-mail system). As a result, courts might treat e-mails transmitted via an employer's e-mail account differently than they would web-based e-mails sent on the same company computer.

Courts have also found that the existence of a clear company policy banning personal e-mails can also diminish the reasonableness of an employee's claim to privacy in e-mail messages with his or her attorney. We recognize that a zero-tolerance policy can be unworkable and unwelcome in today's dynamic and mobile workforce and do not seek to encourage that approach in any way.

The location of the company's computer may also be a relevant consideration. In *Curto v. Medical World Communications, Inc.*, 99 Fair Empl. Prac. Cas. (BNA) 298 (E.D.N.Y. May 15, 2006), for example, an employee working from a home office sent e-mails to her attorney on a company laptop via her personal AOL account. *Id.* at 301. Those messages did not go through the company's servers but were nonetheless retrievable. *Ibid.* Notwithstanding a company policy banning personal use, the trial court found that the e-mails were privileged. *Id.* at 305 . . . .

Applying the above considerations to the facts before us, we find that Stengart had a reasonable expectation of privacy in the e-mails she exchanged with her attorney on Loving Care's laptop.

Stengart plainly took steps to protect the privacy of those e-mails and shield them from her employer. She used a personal, password-protected e-mail account instead of her company e-mail address and did not save the account's password on her computer. In other words, she had a subjective expectation of privacy in messages to and from her lawyer discussing the subject of a future lawsuit.

In light of the language of the Policy and the attorney-client nature of the communications, her expectation of privacy was also objectively reasonable. As noted earlier, the Policy does not address the use of personal, web-based e-mail accounts accessed through company equipment. It does not address personal accounts at all. Nor does it warn employees that the contents of e-mails sent via personal accounts can be forensically retrieved and read by the company. Indeed, in acknowledging that occasional personal use of e-mail is permitted, the Policy created doubt about whether those e-mails are company or private property.

Moreover, the e-mails are not illegal or inappropriate material stored on Loving Care's equipment, which might harm the company in some way. They are conversations between a lawyer and client about confidential legal matters, which are historically cloaked in privacy. Our system strives to keep private the very type of conversations that took place here in order to foster probing and honest exchanges.

In addition, the e-mails bear a standard hallmark of attorney-client messages. They warn the reader directly that the e-mails are personal, confidential, and may be attorney-client communications. While a pro forma warning at the end of an e-mail might not, on its own, protect a communication, other facts present here raise additional privacy concerns.

Under all of the circumstances, we find that Stengart could reasonably expect that e-mails she exchanged with her attorney on her personal, password-protected, web-based e-mail account, accessed on a company laptop, would remain private.

It follows that the attorney-client privilege protects those e-mails. In reaching that conclusion, we necessarily reject Loving Care's claim that the attorney-client privilege either did not attach or was waived . . . . Specifically, Loving Care contends that Stengart effectively brought a third person into the conversation from the start—watching over her shoulder—and thereby forfeited any claim to confidentiality in her communications. We disagree.

. . . The Policy did not give Stengart, or a reasonable person in her position, cause to anticipate that Loving Care would be peering over her shoulder as she opened e-mails from her lawyer on her personal, password-protected Yahoo account. The language of the Policy, the method of transmittal that Stengart selected, and the warning on the e-mails themselves all support that conclusion. . . . Stengart took reasonable steps to keep discussions with her attorney confidential: she elected not to use the company e-mail system and relied on a personal, password-protected, web-based account instead. She also did not save the password on her laptop or share it in some other way with Loving Care.

As to whether Stengart knowingly disclosed the e-mails, she certified that she is unsophisticated in the use of computers and did not know that Loving Care could read communications sent on her Yahoo account. Use of a company laptop alone does not establish that knowledge. Nor does the Policy fill in that gap. Under the circumstances, we do not find either a knowing or reckless waiver.

Our conclusion that Stengart had an expectation of privacy in e-mails with her lawyer does not mean that employers cannot monitor or regulate the use of workplace computers. Companies can adopt lawful policies relating to computer use to protect the assets, reputation, and productivity of a business and to ensure compliance with legitimate corporate policies. And employers can enforce such policies. They may discipline employees and, when appropriate, terminate them, for violating proper workplace rules that are not inconsistent with a clear mandate of public policy. For example, an employee who spends long stretches of the workday getting personal, confidential legal advice from a private lawyer may be disciplined for violating a policy permitting only occasional personal use of the Internet. But employers have no need or basis to read the specific *contents* of personal, privileged, attorney-client communications in order to enforce corporate policy. Because of the important public policy concerns underlying the attorney-client privilege, even a more clearly written company manual—that is, a policy that banned all personal computer use and provided unambiguous notice that an employer could retrieve and read an employee's attorney-client communications, if accessed on a personal, password-protected e-mail account using the company's computer system—would not be enforceable.

[The Court then decided that the defendant violated a New Jersey rule of professional conduct by failing to immediately notify plaintiff's counsel or seek court permission to read the e-mails once it realized that they were attorney-client communications. The Court remanded the case to determine what sanctions were appropriate.]

NOTES

1. **Expectations of Privacy.** In the early cases like *Smyth*, courts generally rejected employees' claims of privacy in email sent on a company-owned system. Why is the outcome in *Stengart* different? What specific facts led the court to conclude that Stengart had a reasonable expectation of privacy in her email?

Note that Stengart's privacy claim did not involve a claim for damages for the invasion of her privacy, but rather arose in the context of a discovery battle in her lawsuit alleging discrimination. Thus, the court did not need to analyze whether her claim of privacy satisfied the standards for liability under the common law invasion of privacy tort or some other source of law. Instead, it asked whether she had a reasonable expectation of privacy sufficient to sustain her claim that her communications were protected by the attorney-client privilege.

Using similar reasoning, other courts have permitted claims for invasion of privacy when an employer read emails on an employee's personal email account, even if the employee accessed the account at work or through employer provided equipment. *See, e.g.*, *Mintz v. Mark Bartelstein & Assoc.*, 906 F. Supp. 2d 1017 (C.D. Cal. 2012) (granting summary judgment for plaintiff on his invasion of privacy claim under the California constitution based on former employer's accessing his personal email account without permission); *Fischer v. Mt. Olive Lutheran Church*, 207 F. Supp. 2d 914 (W.D. Wis. 2002) (denying defendants' summary judgment motion on a common law invasion of privacy claim based on employer's accessing of plaintiff's personal email account).

2. **Employer Policies.** In *Stengart*, the employer had a policy reserving the right to review all electronic communications. How are employer policies relevant to determining whether an employee's privacy was invaded? Why was the policy in Stengart's case not determinative of the outcome? Suppose the employer has a very clear policy that any electronic communication that occurs on employer owned equipment or passes through the employer's server can be read. Should that policy be decisive? Are there any problems with relying solely on an employer's formal policies to determine whether an employee has a reasonable expectation of privacy?

3. **Employee Interests.** What interests do employees have in maintaining the privacy of their electronic communications? In *Stengart* the court put significant emphasis on the importance of the attorney-client privilege. Does an employee's interest in privacy depend upon the content of the communication sought to be protected? What if the emails recovered by Stengart's former employer were not privileged attorney-client communications, but emails to her boyfriend complaining about her supervisors? Would her privacy have been invaded in that case? In other words, is it the sensitive content of the communications that gives rise to privacy concerns, or are there other privacy interests at stake?

One might question whether it makes any difference what rules are chosen so long as employees know what they are. If it is clear that email messages in the workplace setting are not protected communications, then employees can protect confidential communications simply by not using email to transmit sensitive information. *See* Michael Selmi, *Privacy for the Working Class: Public Work and Private Lives*, 66 LA. L. REV. 1035 (2006) (arguing that employees should avoid using employer equipment for personal use during work, but that their activities off-duty should be protected from employer scrutiny). Other commentators disagree, arguing that the effect of technology is to blur the line between work and personal life, making it more difficult to shield purely private matters from the workplace. *See, e.g.*, Patricia Sanchez Abril, Avner Levin, & Alissa Del Riego, *Blurred Boundaries: Social Media Privacy and the Twenty-First Century Employee*, 49 AM. BUS. L.J. 63, 64 (2012); Robert Sprague, *Invasion of the Social Networks: Blurring the Line Between Personal Life and the Employment Relationship*, 50 U. LOUISVILLE L. REV. 1 (2011). Could employees neatly segregate work and personal aspects of their communications and their lives if they wanted to do so? Are there any costs of failing to protect the privacy of employees' electronic communications at work? *See* Pauline T. Kim, *Electronic Privacy and Employee Speech*, 87 CHI-KENT L. REV. 901 (2012) (arguing that employer monitoring of electronic communications may discourage certain types of valuable workplace speech, such as collective speech or whistleblowing speech that the law otherwise protects and encourages).

4.   **Employer Interests.** Employers assert a number of interests in accessing and monitoring their employees' electronic communications. Among other things, employers worry about lost productivity, the disclosure of trade secrets, liability for sexual or racial harassment and unauthorized use of property. These concerns led one federal court of appeals to comment that "the abuse of access to workplace computers is so common (workers being prone to use them as media of gossip, titillation, and other entertainment and distraction) that reserving a right of inspection is so far from being unreasonable that the failure to do so might well be thought irresponsible." *Muick v. Glenayre Elecs.*, 280 F.3d 741, 743 (7th Cir. 2002). Do you agree? Would you advise an employer to have a "zero tolerance" policy that makes it clear that *no* personal use of workplace computers is ever permitted? Are there any downsides to having such a policy?

Although employers have some legitimate business reasons for engaging in electronic monitoring and surveillance, the law also affects their incentives for doing so. To the extent that employers fear liability for sexual or racial harassment based on electronic communications, they have an incentive to monitor their employees. The legal standard for liability, however, requires that the conduct must be "severe or pervasive"; isolated or sporadic incidents will not give rise to liability. Although purportedly intended to avoid liability for harassment, employer monitoring practices may go far beyond what the law requires. Dennis Nolan points out that employers may do more monitoring than required to avoid liability, because of the relative liability risks. Employers fear the substantial costs involved in losing a sexual harassment lawsuit, or even having to defend against such a claim. By contrast, the risk of liability for monitoring employees' electronic communications is far less. As Nolan explains, "[a]bsent a legal counterweight to sexual or racial harassment suits, it is safer for employers to err on the side of intrusion and restriction than on the side of toleration; to do the former is almost costless; to do the latter could be expensive." Dennis R. Nolan, *Privacy and Profitability in the Technological Workplace*, 24 J. LAB. RES. 209, 210–20 (2003).

5.   **BYOD.** The early litigation over employees' electronic privacy typically dealt with communications taking place on employer-provided equipment. New issues are emerging with the increase in BYOD ("bring your own device") work arrangements. With the growth of mobile computing, employees often purchase their own personal smartphones or tablets which they then use to access work files or email. Some employers have even encouraged or required employees to provide their own devices as a way to save on equipment costs. This mingling of work and personal functions on employee-owned devices creates both opportunities and challenges for employers.

Employers may welcome the BYOD trend to the extent that it increases workers' productivity and reduces costs. However, it also raises risks that confidential data or valuable business information, including trade secrets, may be compromised, either inadvertently or intentionally. A company's efforts to secure its proprietary information may conflict with employees' interests or expectations regarding control over their devices or personal information stored on them. For example, an employer may wish to search the contents of an employee's smartphone upon termination of employment to ensure that it contains no confidential information, but doing so may intrude on her privacy by subjecting her personal emails, texts, photos, and web activity to scrutiny. Similarly, an employee's interest in preserving personal content may conflict with an employer's desire to remotely "wipe" a phone that has been lost or stolen in order to protect sensitive data.

There is very little legal authority directly addressing BYOD situations, although numerous laws are potentially relevant. Depending upon the industry and the type of business, data privacy, anti-discrimination law, financial reporting, consumer protection and other laws may impose obligations on firms to control how their employees use mobile computing devices. At the same time, employees may try to rely on common law or statutory privacy rights to resist employer control over their devices. Contract law and trade secret laws may also affect the respective rights of employers and employees. Finally, the growing use of BYOD situations further blurs the boundaries of the workplace, raising questions about when time spent on personal devices is compensable work time under wage and hour laws.

Given all these legal complications, should employers require that their employees use only company-owned devices to conduct company business? Or should employers take advantage of the cost-savings opportunity and encourage BYOD arrangements? Should the decision turn on the type of business the employer is engaged in or on some other factors? If an employer permits employees to BYOD, should it have a policy regarding the use of those devices? What should such a policy say?

c.   Statutory Protections.

In addition to constitutional rights and common law claims, employees seeking to protect the privacy of their electronic communications have also relied on statutory authority. The federal Electronic Communications Privacy Act of 1986 (ECPA), 18 U.S.C. § 2510 *et seq.*, which amended the Omnibus Crime Control and Safe Streets Act, would appear to provide some privacy protections for electronic communications, but its application to the employment context has been somewhat limited and uncertain.

Title I of the statute, which provides for criminal and civil sanctions for anyone who "intentionally intercepts . . . any wire, oral, or electronic communication," 18 U.S.C. § 2511(1)(a), has proven largely inapplicable to employers accessing their employees' email or other electronic communications. Because this provision of the ECPA forbids an "intercept," most courts have concluded that a violation only occurs when a message is seized during transmission and that therefore the provision does not apply to the retrieval of messages after they have been delivered to the recipient's inbox. *See, e.g., Fraser v. Nationwide Mut. Ins. Co.*, 352 F.3d 107,

113 (3d Cir. 2004) (holding that an insurance agent had no claim under the ECPA when the insurance company searched its file server on which all of his email messages were stored because there was no "intercept"); *Konop v. Hawaiian Airlines, Inc.*, 302 F.3d 868 (9th Cir. 2002) (concluding that employer's unauthorized access of employee's secure website did not violate Title I because the communication must be acquired during transmission, not while in electronic storage, to be an unlawful "intercept").

Title II of the ECPA, also referred to as the Stored Communications Act (SCA), prohibits unauthorized access to stored electronic communications and has proven more relevant. Its operative provisions state:

> (a) Offense.—Except as provided in subsection (c) of this section whoever—
>
>> (1) intentionally accesses without authorization a facility through which an electronic communication service is provided; or
>>
>> (2) intentionally exceeds an authorization to access that facility;
>
> and thereby obtains, alters, or prevents authorized access to a wire or electronic communication while it is in electronic storage in such system shall be punished as provided in subsection (b) of this section.

18 U.S.C.A. § 2701.

Elsewhere the statute defines *electronic storage* as "(A) any temporary, intermediate storage of a wire or electronic communication incidental to the electronic transmission thereof; and (B) any storage of such communication by an electronic communication service for purposes of backup protection of such communication . . ." 18 U.S.C. §§ 2510(17).

The statute has been widely criticized as difficult to interpret and out of touch with current technology. Nevertheless, employees have relied on its provisions, with some success, to challenge the legality of their employers' accessing their personal electronic communications. The following case explores some of the possibilities and challenges for employees bringing claims under the SCA.

Pure Power Boot Camp v. Warrior Fitness Boot Camp, 587 F. Supp. 2d 548 (S.D.N.Y. 2008). Pure Power Boot Camp (PPBC) sued its former employees, Alexander Fell and Ruben Belliard, who left to form a competing business. The company alleged that the defendants had stolen trade secrets, breached their fiduciary duties and infringed on PPBC's trademarks. During the course of the discovery, the defendants learned that the owner of PPBC, Lauren Brenner, had accessed three of Fell's personal email accounts after he was no longer working there. She was able to do so because Fell had accessed one of his private email accounts from a computer at work, and it had stored his username and password. Using the same password, she accessed all three of his personal email accounts and recovered a couple of dozen emails discussing his efforts to set up his competing business. When PPBC sought to use these emails as evidence, Fell argued that the company should be precluded from doing so because it had obtained the emails in violation of the Electronic Communications Privacy Act and the Stored Communications Privacy Act.

The court in *Pure Power Boot Camp* first followed the weight of authority by holding that an "intercept" under the ECPA must occur contemporaneously with transmission. It concluded that Brenner did not "intercept" Fell's emails and therefore Title I of the ECPA did not apply. The court then considered the applicability of Title II, the Stored Communications Act:

> . . . [A] person violates the SCA if she accesses an electronic communication service, *or* obtains an electronic communication while it is still in electronic storage, without authorization. . . .
>
> The majority of courts which have addressed the issue have determined that e-mail stored on an electronic communication service provider's systems after it has been delivered, as opposed to e-mail stored on a personal computer, is a stored communication subject to the SCA. . . .
>
> In this case, Brenner obtained Fell's username and password to his Hotmail account because he left that information stored on [PPBC's] computers. She then used that information to go into his Hotmail account, and read and printed his e-mails. Some of those e-mails may have been read by Fell while he was at work, but there is no evidence indicating which e-mails he may have viewed on [PPBC's] computers, and there is no evidence that the e-mails were downloaded onto PPBC's computers. At most, only e-mails dated prior to his last day of work could have been viewed by him and thus potentially stored on the company's systems.
>
> In any event, Brenner did not use an examination of PPBC's computer's memory to determine what Fell accessed at work. Instead, she logged directly onto Microsoft's Hotmail system where the e-mails were stored, and viewed and printed them directly off of Hotmail's system. She accessed Fell's other accounts in the same manner, and there is no evidence indicating that Fell accessed his Gmail or [Warrior Fitness Boot Camp] accounts at any time while he worked at PPBC. By Plaintiffs' own admission, Brenner obtained the username and password for the Gmail account from Fell's Hotmail account, and made a "lucky guess" that Fell would use the same password for all three accounts, including his WFBC account.
>
> Thus, Brenner accessed three separate electronic communication services, and she obtained Fell's e-mails while they were in storage on those service providers' systems. Either of those actions, if done without authorization, would be a violation of the SCA.

587 F. Supp. 2d at 555–56. Having decided that the SCA applied, the court then confronted the question whether what Brenner had done constituted access "without authorization."

> [PPBC argues] that Brenner was authorized to view and print Fell's e-mails, and assert two theories in support of this position. First, [PPBC claims] that PPBC's e-mail policy put Fell on notice that his e-mails could be viewed by Brenner, and thus he had no expectation of privacy in his Hotmail account. Second, [PPBC argues] that even if he had an expectation of privacy, Fell, by leaving his username and password on PPBC's

computers, gave Brenner implied consent to access his accounts . . . .

As an initial matter, [PPBC's] position is not supported by [its] policy. PPBC's e-mail policy—the basis of [its] consent defense—is, by its own terms, limited to "Company equipment." The reservation of rights is explicitly limited to "any matter stored in, created on, received from, or sent through [PPBC's] system." Therefore, it could not apply to e-mails on systems maintained by outside entities such as Microsoft or Google. In addition, there is no evidence that the e-mails in issue were created on, sent through, or received from PPBC's computers. Moreover, [PPBC's] position makes no distinction between the Hotmail account Fell accessed while at work, and the other accounts, which by all appearances were never accessed by Fell at work, and may not even have existed until after he left PPBC's employ.

[PPBC's] position—that Brenner was authorized to access Fell's e-mails on his personal e-mail service providers' systems through his implied consent—also has no support in the law . . . .

This is not . . . a case where an employee was using an employer's computer or e-mail system, and then claimed that the e-mails contained on the employer's computers are private. Here, the employee—Fell—did not store any of the communications which his former employer now seeks to use against him on the employer's computers, servers, or systems; nor were they sent from or received on the company e-mail system or computer. These e-mails were located on, and accessed from, third-party communication service provider systems. There is not even an implication that Fell's personal e-mail accounts were used for PPBC work, or that PPBC paid or supported Fell's maintenance of those accounts. Furthermore, there is nothing in the PPBC policy that even suggests that if an employee simply views a single, personal e-mail from a third party e-mail provider, over PPBC computers, then all of the his personal e-mails on whatever personal e-mail accounts he uses, would be subject to inspection. In short, this case is distinguishable from those cases which hold that employees have no expectation of privacy in e-mails sent from or received and stored on the employer's computers.

Here, Fell had a subjective belief that his personal e-mail accounts, stored on third-party computer systems, protected (albeit ineffectively) by passwords, would be private. That expectation of privacy was also reasonable, as nothing in PPBC's policy suggests that it could extend beyond [PPBC's] own systems, and beyond the employment relationship . . . .

There is no sound basis to argue that Fell, by inadvertently leaving his Hotmail password accessible, was thereby authorizing access to all of his Hotmail e-mails, no less the e-mails in his two other accounts. If he had left a key to his house on the front desk at PPBC, one could not reasonably argue that he was giving consent to whoever found the key, to use it to enter his house and rummage through his belongings. And, to take the analogy a step further, had the person rummaging through the belongings in Fell's house found the key to Fell's country house, could that be taken as authorization to search his country house[?] We think not. The Court rejects the notion that carelessness equals consent.

Implied consent, at a minimum, requires clear notice that one's conduct may result in a search being conducted of areas which the person has been warned are subject to search . . . . In this case, Fell only had notice that PPBC's computers could be searched for evidence of personal e-mail use, not that his Hotmail, Gmail, or WFBC e-mail accounts would also be searched. He was also never given the opportunity to refuse Brenner any authorization to search his e-mails. At most, one could argue that Fell [had] consented to Brenner viewing his password. But he did not consent to her [ ] using it. Absent clear knowledge of the extent of what could be searched, and the opportunity to refuse or withdraw his consent, the Court rejects [PPBC's] argument that Fell gave implied consent to Brenner to search his Hotmail account simply by leaving his password on her computer.

Even less sustainable is the proposition that correctly "guessing" a person's password, as Brenner did, amounts to authorization to access all accounts which use that password. Were that the case, computer hackers across the country could escape liability for breaking into computer systems by correctly "guessing" the codes and passwords of their victims. This absurd result stands in direct conflict with the entire purpose of the SCA and basic principles of privacy.

Id. at 559–62. The court found that Brenner had wrongfully obtained Fell's emails in a manner that arguably violated the SCA. On the other hand, it also recognized that Fell and Belliard were accused of theft of trade secrets and breach of fiduciary duties. Because the case had not yet been decided on the merits, it was possible that Fell and Belliard had "unclean hands." Balancing these considerations, the court concluded that Pure Power Boot Camp should be precluded from using the emails in its litigation against its former employees, but might be allowed to use them for impeachment purposes.

NOTES

1. **Statutory Applications.** Like *Stengart, Pure Power Boot Camp* addressed the issue of the privacy protections for employees' personal email accounts in the context of a discovery dispute rather than a claim for damages brought by the former employee. Nevertheless, its discussion of the ECPA and SCA is fairly typical. As discussed above, most courts agree that Title I of the ECPA requires an intercept contemporaneous with transmission and therefore it does not apply when an employer accesses stored email messages. And, as in *Pure Power*, courts have been more likely to find that the SCA applies where an employer has accessed an employee's personal email account maintained by a third party service provider.

For example, the court in *Lazette v. Kulmatycki*, 949 F. Supp. 2d 748 (N.D. Ohio 2013) allowed the plaintiff's SCA claim to proceed where her former employer had accessed her personal email account. The complaint alleged that after terminating her employment, the plaintiff returned her company-issued blackberry to her former supervisor, who used it to access her personal g-mail account and to read some 48,000 emails over the next 18 months. *See also Fischer v. Mt. Olive Lutheran Church, Inc.*, 207 F. Supp. 2d 914, 926 (2002) (denying summary judgment on SCA claim to employer who accessed plaintiff's web-based Hotmail account); *Van Alstyne v. Elec. Scriptorium, Ltd.*, 560 F.3d 199 (4th Cir. 2009) (reporting jury verdict in favor of former employee on her claim that employer's accessing of her personal email account violated the SCA).

An important exception to liability under the SCA exempts the seizure of electronic communications by the person or entity providing the service. Thus, to the extent that an employer accesses messages on an electronic communications service that it provides, such as a company email system, its actions are likely exempted from the prohibitions of the SCA. *See, e.g., Fraser v. Nationwide Mut. Ins. Co.*, 352 F.3d 107, 115 (3d Cir. 2004) (holding that because insurance agent's email was stored on insurance company's email system, the search of his email falls within exception for provider of service).

In addition to the federal ECPA and SCA, a number of states also have statutes regulating access to electronic communications. Those statutes are largely similar to the federal statutes, but depending upon the details of the legislation, they may provide more or less protection.

2. Authorization. As seen in *Pure Power*, one of the key issues that arises when applying the SCA is whether an employer has "authorization" to access an employee's electronic communications. How did the former employer in *Pure Power* try to make the case that it did have authorization to read Fell's emails? Why didn't that argument work? If the company had a clear policy from the outset stating employees have no expectation of privacy in any communications occurring over the employer's computer system and Fell was aware of the policy, would Brenner's access to Fell's email have been "authorized"? What if the policy explicitly included the contents of any and all accounts accessed through the employer's email system?

In *Lazette*, the court rejected the argument that the fact that the company owned the Blackberry and that the plaintiff had used it to access her personal email account meant that she had "authorized" her former employer to access her emails. *Lazette v. Kulmatycki*, 949 F. Supp. 2d 748 (N.D. Ohio 2013). The court noted that the employee thought she had closed her account on the phone and that "[n]egligence . . . is not the same as approval, much less authorization. There is a difference between someone who fails to leave the door locked when going out and one who leaves it open knowing someone [will] be stopping by." *Id.* at 757. The court further argued, that "even knowledge of the capability of monitoring alone cannot be considered implied consent." *Id.* at 757 (citation omitted).

3. Other Issues of Statutory Interpretation. In addition to determining whether access is "authorized," courts have faced other questions of statutory interpretation when applying the Stored Communications Act. When a personal device like a smartphone or laptop is used to access an email service like Yahoo or Gmail, the courts have had to decide what is a "facility through which an electronic communication service is provided," 18 U.S.C. § 2701(a)(1), and whether email that has been opened, but not yet deleted is in "electronic storage" for purposes of the SCA. 18 U.S.C. § 2701(a)(2). *See, e.g., Lazette v. Kulmatycki*, 949 F. Supp. 2d 748 (N.D. Ohio 2013) (finding that emails that were accessed before being opened were in electronic storage, while those accessed after being opened were not). The courts have not always agreed on the answers to these questions, which turn on details of the underlying technology and difficult questions of statutory interpretation. A full discussion of these issues is beyond the scope of this text. Nevertheless, it is important to keep in mind that the SCA applies in many contexts beyond the workplace, and how courts interpret its terms in those other settings will impact the extent to which the statute provides a basis for employees' privacy claims.

d. Social Media

The explosive growth in social media has raised new privacy concerns. With many employees now posting detailed and sometimes highly personal information on Facebook and other social media sites, several distinct sets of questions have emerged. Should employers be restricted from gathering information about applicants from Facebook, Twitter and other social media sites? Should they be able to discipline their employees for what they post on these sites? And are employers entitled to require their employees to give them access to these sites by providing their personal passwords?

In recent years, many employers have conducted internet checks, including review of publicly available postings on social networking sites, to evaluate job applicants. A simple Google search can bring up large amounts of information about an individual—and about individuals who share the same name—captured from public databases, websites, Facebook and Twitter posts, and other sites. Currently, very little law has developed specifically to regulate the gathering and use of information from these sources by employers. However, other laws restricting the types of information employers may collect and use will also apply to information collected from the internet. For example, accessing personal information revealed on Facebook may run afoul of prohibitions on inquiries into an applicant's protected class status under anti-discrimination laws, *see, e.g.*, CAL. CODE REGS. tit. 2, § 72873, subd. (b)(1), or raise an inference of discrimination, as when an adverse personnel action follows the discovery through a social networking site that an employee is pregnant. Other laws, such as the Fair Credit Reporting Act, 15 U.S.C. §§ 1681–1681t, and the Genetic Information Nondiscrimination Act, 42 U.S.C. § 2000ff-1(b), regulate the acquisition and use of certain types of sensitive personal information for employment purposes and should apply to information collected from online sources as well. *See, e.g.*, Edward Wyatt, *U.S. Penalizes Online Company in Sale of Personal Data*, N.Y. TIMES, June 12, 2012.

What about after employees are hired? Employers may have some legitimate interests in knowing about their employees' off-duty communications, such as preventing co-worker harassment, or protecting trade secrets or other confidential business information from disclosure or misuse. Third party vendors now offer software that can monitor current employees' activities on sites like Facebook and LinkedIn and report the results to employers. *See, e.g.*, Kristin Samuelson, *Should I be worried about Spokeo.com?*, CHI. TRIBUNE, May 28, 2010; Joshua Brustein, *Keeping a Closer Eye on Employees' Social Networking*, N.Y. TIMES, Mar. 26, 2010. Does such monitoring by employers violate employees' rights?

Consider, first, the common law invasion of privacy tort. It applies only when the area intruded upon is "secluded," a condition unlikely to pertain to information available on an unrestricted social media site. But what if the information is on a password protected site? Or the employee has established privacy settings such that her Facebook posts are only available to those she has accepted as "friends"? What if she has dozens of Facebook friends? Hundreds?

In *Ehling v. Monmouth-Ocean Hosp. Service Corp.*, 872 F. Supp. 2d 369 (D.N.J. 2012), the plaintiff, a registered nurse and paramedic, sued her employer when she was discharged because of comments she made on Facebook. Her privacy settings permitted only "friends" to see her postings, and many of her co-workers, but no managers, were among her friends. After a white supremacist shot and killed a guard at the Holocaust Museum in D.C., Ehling posted a comment about the paramedics who had saved the life of the shooter: "1. WHAT WERE YOU THINKING? and 2. This was your opportunity to really make a difference! WTF!!!!" A supervisor asked one of the plaintiff's co-workers and Facebook friends to access his account in the supervisor's presence in order to see what the plaintiff had posted. Noting that case law is underdeveloped in this area, the court found that plaintiff stated a "plausible claim for invasion of privacy" because she had actively taken steps to restrict access to her posts by the public and allowed her to proceed with her common law privacy tort claim. Do you think that accessing an employee's Facebook page under these circumstances constitutes an intrusion of seclusion that is highly offensive to a reasonable person?

The SCA also provides some protection for restricted social networking sites. For example, in *Pietrylo v. Hillstone Rest. Grp.*, 2008 U.S. Dist. LEXIS 108834 (D.N.J. July 25, 2008), two employees who worked as servers at the employer's restaurant were fired after managers read their postings on a private MySpace group. The two employees had created the private group for the restaurant's employees for the purpose of "vent[ing] about any BS we deal with out [sic] work without any outside eyes spying in on us. This group is entirely private, and can only be joined by invitation." Postings on the site included sexual remarks about management and customers, jokes about the specifications established for customer service and quality, and references to violence and illegal drug use. The employer accessed the site, and a factual dispute arose over whether the employee who had provided the password had done so voluntarily. Because there was a dispute as to whether the managers had accessed the postings "with authorization," the court denied summary judgment for the employer on the SCA claim. A jury ultimately found a violation of the SCA and awarded damages. *See Pietrylo v. Hillstone Rest. Grp.*, 2009 U.S. Dist. LEXIS 88702 (D.N.J. Sep. 25, 2009). *See also Konop*, 302 F.3d at 880 (reversing summary judgment on SCA claim for employer who accessed employee's password protected website).

Employers might try to avoid uncertainty about whether they have "authorization" by asking applicants or employees to turn over their social media passwords. After several reports about employers doing just that, lawmakers responded. In May of 2012, Maryland became the first state to adopt a law prohibiting employers from asking employees or applicants to reveal passwords to their social media accounts. *See* 2012 Bill Text Md. S.B. 433, *modifying* Md. Code Ann., Lab. & Empl. § 3-712 (LexisNexis 2012) (effective Oct. 1, 2012). Other states soon followed suit, and as of mid-2014 a dozen states had passed laws restricting employer access to employees' or applicants' social media accounts. Christine Lyon & Melissa Crespo, *Employer Access to Employee Social Media: Applicant Screening, 'Friend' Requests and Workplace Investigations*, DAILY LAB. REP. (BNA) (April 4, 2014). While these bills limit access to password-protected content, they generally do not prohibit supervisors or managers from seeking to "friend" their subordinates, nor do they prevent an employer from monitoring publicly available posts by its employees. Do these practices raise similar privacy concerns?

Although the common law and the SCA may sometimes protect restricted-access postings, employers remain largely free to make judgments about employees based on their publicly-available online activities. They can, and do, discipline and terminate employees for comments posted on online that are deemed unprofessional, inappropriate or damaging to the employers' reputation. There is, however, one significant exception to employers' prerogative to scrutinize publicly-available posts, and it concerns employer policies or disciplinary actions that interfere with concerted activity protected under the National Labor Relations Act. Suppose, for example, that employees post comments on social media sites about work-related matters. The employer may feel it has a strong interest in monitoring and preventing negative comments about coworkers, supervisors or work policies that are made on-line; however, these comments may be exactly the type of discussion protected because of their connection to collective action. In Chapter 8, we will discuss the protections available under the NLRA for these types of activities.

C. OFF-DUTY CONDUCT AND ASSOCIATIONS

In addition to concerns about unwarranted intrusions or the collection of confidential information, employees also have an interest in autonomy—that is, in maintaining a certain degree of freedom in their choices about how to live their lives. Autonomy concerns are sometimes characterized as a type of privacy interest; at other times, they are viewed as involving distinct claims, albeit closely related to concerns about privacy. The Supreme Court has written that the Constitution protects two types of privacy interests: "One is the individual interest in avoiding disclosure of personal matters, and another is the interest in independence in making certain kinds of important decisions." *Whalen v. Roe*, 429 U.S. 589, 599 (1977). The common law tort of invasion of privacy, however, is defined in a way that limits its protection for individual autonomy. Recall that the Restatement (Second) of Torts defines privacy in terms of an "unreasonable intrusion upon the seclusion" of another. RESTATEMENT (SECOND) OF TORTS § 652A (1977). This definition makes the traditional privacy tort ill-suited to address employees' interests in maintaining some independence and freedom in how they live their lives away from work, such as in their off-duty conduct and associations.

Matthew Finkin has criticized the common law definition of privacy, which he argues, "acknowledges no element of autonomy". Matthew W. Finkin, *Employee Privacy, American Values, and the Law*, 72 CHI.-KENT L. REV. 221, 224 (1996). He argues that privacy and autonomy are closely connected:

> The [interest in freedom from intrusion] might also be expressed in terms
> of autonomy, in one's right of informational self-determination, and the

[interest in autonomy] might also be framed in terms of intrusion, in not having one's activities minded by another. Both are implicated in the modern employment relationship: To be an employee is to be in the hands of an organization that seeks to exact an enormous amount of personal information irrespective of the employee's deep desire. To be an employee is to be enmeshed in a hierarchical structure of subordination that is quite at odds with any claim of individual autonomy even over arguably private spheres of endeavor. Thus, the question of privacy is one of degree: how much information should an employer be allowed to collect and how much control should it be allowed to exert?

Id. at 223.

The same technological developments that have increased conflict over privacy at work may also provide employers with a wealth of information about their employees' off-duty activities. For example, employer-provided vehicles and cell phones containing global positioning system (GPS) technology may supply information about an employee's whereabouts, not only while working, but during breaks and off-duty as well. And the growing use of blogs and social networking sites may make it easy for employers to learn about their employees' activities and associations during non-working hours. To what extent do employers have legitimate interests in regulating their employees' off-duty conduct? To what extent do employees have interests in avoiding employer control or discipline based on how they spend their time away from work?

The notion of privacy, understood in the traditional sense, is an awkward fit for exploring these questions, because very often the activity that the employer wants to regulate—for example, employee blogging, volunteering, engaging in recreational activities—is publicly known or performed in public. Thus, these interests are perhaps better understood as autonomy interests, but, as discussed above, the common law tort of invasion of privacy does not really speak to autonomy. Some of these interests, such as employees' freedom to engage in certain types of speech, may be protected by specific statutory provisions, as we will explore in the next chapter. But what about employees' interests in freedom from interference with their activities outside of work more generally?

The new Restatement of Employment Law treats employees' interests in personal autonomy as a distinct topic from privacy. Sections 7.01–7.07 deal with employees' right "not to be subjected to wrongful employer intrusions upon their protected employee privacy interests," while section 7.08 addresses their "interests in personal autonomy outside of the employment relationship." According to the Restatement, such interests include engaging in lawful off-duty conduct, and holding or expressing "political, moral, ethical, religious or other personal beliefs" outside of work. RESTATEMENT (THIRD) OF EMPLOYMENT LAW § 7.08(a) (Proposed Final Draft, April 18, 2014). However, the Restatement's formulation of protection of autonomy interests is subject to important qualifications:

. . . .

(b) Unless the employer and employee agree otherwise, an employer is subject to liability for intruding upon an employee's personal autonomy interests if the employer discharges the employee because of the employee's exercise of a personal autonomy interest . . .

(c) The employer is not liable under § 7.08(b) if it can prove that it had a reasonable good-faith belief that the employee's exercise of her or his autonomy interest interfered with the employer's legitimate business interests, including its orderly operations and reputation in the marketplace.

Id. at § 7.08(b) and (c). Do you think these provisions appropriately balance employer and employee interests in this area? Are employers' legitimate interests adequately taken into account by a reasonable good-faith standard? How effective is the protection for employee autonomy interests given that employer liability for intruding is a default rule that can be contracted around?

The just cause provisions found in most collective bargaining agreements generally require some kind of nexus to a legitimate employer interest before an employee can be discharged. Thus, union employees fired for their off-duty conduct can challenge their dismissals on the grounds that their activities had no bearing on their job performance or the workplace. However, for the non-union employee, finding a legal basis for challenging such a dismissal will be difficult if the employer has made clear that the employment is at will.

Apart from the common law, a handful of statutes protect off-duty conduct or associations incidentally—for example, an employer cannot take adverse action against an employee because of his or her association with someone with a disability under the Americans with Disabilities Act. 42 U.S.C. § 12112(b)(4). In addition, a few states have passed statutes that protect employees for retaliation based on their off-duty activities. As seen in the following case, even such statutes may be of limited reach.

McCAVITT v. SWISS REINSURANCE AMERICA CORP.
United States Court of Appeals for the Second Circuit
237 F.3d 166 (2001)

PER CURIAM:

. . . On November 30, 1999, the plaintiff, Jess D. McCavitt, brought suit against the defendant, Swiss Reinsurance America Corporation ("Swiss Re") . . . alleg[ing] that he was hired . . . in 1996, and that by January 1999, he was a Swiss Re officer whose performance was highly regarded by his superiors.

According to the complaint, "[s]ince 1999, plaintiff has been involved in a personal relationship with Diane Butler [also a Swiss Re officer]. . . . Plaintiff and Ms. Butler dated and spent time together after working hours." (At oral argument before us, the plaintiff through counsel confirmed that by "personal relationship" and "dated," the plaintiff meant that the plaintiff and Ms. Butler were romantically involved with one another.) The complaint alleges that even though "[t]he personal relationship between plaintiff and Ms. Butler has had no repercussions whatever for the professional responsibilities or accomplishments of either" and "Swiss Re . . .

has no written anti-fraternization or anti-nepotism policy," the plaintiff was passed over for promotion and then discharged from employment largely because of their dating.

The plaintiff asserts that his termination violated New York Labor Law § 201-d, which states in pertinent part:

> 2. Unless otherwise provided by law, it shall be unlawful for any employer or employment agency to refuse to hire, employ or license, or to discharge from employment or otherwise discriminate against an individual in compensation, promotion or terms, conditions or privileges of employment because of: . . . .

> c. an individual's legal recreational activities outside work hours, off of the employer's premises and without use of the employer's equipment or other property.

Id., § 201-d(2). The statute defines "recreational activities" as:

> any lawful, leisure-time activity, for which the employee receives no compensation and which is generally engaged in for recreational purposes, including but not limited to sports, games, hobbies, exercise, reading and the viewing of television, movies and similar material.

Id., § 201-d(1)(b).

On February 14, 2000, Swiss Re filed a motion to dismiss pursuant to Fed. R. Civ. P. 12(b)(6), arguing that romantic dating is not a protected "recreational activit[y]" under § 201-d. [The district court granted the motion.]

Although the New York Court of Appeals has never addressed this issue, the Appellate Division of the New York Supreme Court, Third Department, has. In *State v. Wal-Mart Stores, Inc.*, 207 A.D.2d 150 (3d Dep't 1995), that court held, albeit over a dissenting opinion, that romantic dating is not a protected "recreational activity." The district court considered itself bound by *Wal-Mart* because it was not "highly likely that the highest state court would reach a different conclusion." In reaching this conclusion, the district court relied in part on the principle that under New York law, "absent a Constitutionally impermissible purpose, a statutory proscription, or an express limitation in the individual contract of employment, an employer's right at any time to terminate an employment at will remains unimpaired." *Id.* (quoting *Murphy v. American Home Products Corp.*, 448 N.E.2d 86, 91 (1983)). The court reviewed the legislative history of the statute, but found it to be inconclusive. The district court also applied the cannon of statutory construction known as *noscitur a sociis*,[4] "to prevent the concept of 'dating' from being regarded as within a statutory definition of recreational activities including sports, games, hobbies, exercise, reading and the viewing of television, movies and similar material." *Id.* . . . .

Having reviewed de novo the district court's decision to dismiss the complaint for failure to state a cause of action, we affirm the court's judgment substantially for the

---

[4] [n. 2] "A canon of construction holding that the meaning of an unclear word or phrase should be determined by the words immediately surrounding it." *Black's Law Dictionary* 1084 (7th Ed. 1999).

reasons set forth in its opinion. We agree with the district court that our decision in this case is governed by the Third Department's decision in *Wal-Mart*. As the district court noted, we "are bound . . . to apply [New York state] law as interpreted by New York's intermediate appellate courts . . . unless we find persuasive evidence that the New York Court of Appeals, which has not ruled on this issue, would reach a different conclusion." We, like the district court, find no persuasive evidence— nothing in logic, the language of § 201-d, its legislative history, or New York state case law—that leads us to conclude that the New York Court of Appeals would hold that romantic dating is a "recreational activity" under New York Labor Law § 201-d(1)(b) contrary to the holding of *Wal-Mart*. . . .

The judgment of the district court is affirmed.

McLAUGHLIN, CIRCUIT JUDGE, concurring:

Sister Mary Lauretta, a Roman Catholic nun, once counseled:

To be successful, the first thing to do is fall in love with your work.

She should, of course, now have to add:

Just don't fall in love *at* work.

Although I concur in my colleagues' decision, I do so grudgingly. We have been unable to find in the record before us persuasive evidence that the New York Court of Appeals would reach a conclusion different from that reached by the Appellate Division, Third Department, in *Wal-Mart*. I harbor the hope that, if given the chance, it would.

On the record before us, it appears that Jess McCavitt and Diane Butler, both unmarried, committed no crime (either religious or secular), and their relationship (the romantic aspect of which was explored solely outside the office, during non-working hours) adversely affected neither their job performance nor the business interests of Swiss Re.

Ms. Butler, however, made one fatal mistake—she told Swiss Re's Senior Vice President of Human Resources (who apparently serves as the Senior Vice President of *Employee Relations* as well), that she was involved in a personal relationship with Mr. McCavitt. Immediately, what had been nobody's business became everybody's business. And, as it is no secret that is known by three, Mr. McCavitt's relationship with Swiss Re came to an abrupt end.

Concededly, New York continues to adhere to the common-law rule of employment-at-will. Major incursions, however, have been made into that hoary doctrine, not the least of which is N.Y. Labor Law § 201-d, barring employers from firing workers because of "legal recreational activities outside work hours, off of [sic] the employer's premises and without use of the employer's equipment or other property." Not especially enlightening is the statute's definition of recreational activities as "any lawful, leisure-time activity . . . which is generally engaged in for recreational purposes, including, but not limited to sports, games, hobbies, exercises, reading and the viewing of television, movies and similar material."

Romance has a distinctly distinguished history of originating in office contacts. It is one of the most clichéd of movie plots—see notably the Katharine Hepburn and Gig Young (or, if you prefer, Spencer Tracy) roles in the holiday classic "Desk Set." As Justice Frankfurter observed, "[T]here comes a point where this Court should not be ignorant as judges of what we know as men." *Watts v. Indiana*, 338 U.S. 49, 52 (1949).

I fully endorse the reasoning of Justice Paul J. Yesawich, a most learned and distinguished member of the Appellate Division, Third Department, who wrote in his dissent in *Wal-Mart*:

> In my view, given the fact that the Legislature's primary intent in enacting Labor Law § 201-d was to curtail employers' ability to discriminate on the basis of activities that are pursued outside of work hours, and that have no bearing on one's ability to perform one's job, and concomitantly to guarantee employees a certain degree of freedom to conduct their lives as they please during nonworking hours, the narrow interpretation adopted by the majority is indefensible.

207 A.D.2d at 153. Nevertheless, I agree with my colleagues that we are bound by the majority opinion in *Wal-Mart*.

If, when deciding to protect "recreational activities," the Legislature saw fit to protect an employee's right to engage in such historically revered activities as riding a motorcycle and hang-gliding, it certainly should have extended protection to the pursuit of a romantic relationship with whomever an employee chooses—even a fellow, unmarried employee—outside the office, during non-working hours. This is compellingly so in today's society, where ostracizing anyone associated with one's office from the acceptable dating pool would doom the majority of the population to the life of a Trappist monk.

It is repugnant to our most basic ideals in a free society that an employer can destroy an individual's livelihood on the basis of whom he is courting, without first having to establish that the employee's relationship is adversely affecting the employer's business interests. Lest our faith in this free society be dampened, it is my sincerest hope that, if given the chance, the New York Court of Appeals will find that the necessary protection lies within N.Y. Labor Law § 201-d. If not, may the State Legislature amend the statute accordingly.

NOTES

1. **"Recreational Activities."** The court's decision in *McCavitt* turns on a question of statutory interpretation: is "romantic dating" a "recreational activity" within the meaning of the New York statute? Is there any good policy reason to forbid employers from discharging employees because of hobbies they pursue or sports that they play, but not because of their dating relationships? Which activities are more fundamental to individual identity? Why do you think the court resists a broader reading of the New York statute?

Do you think blogging, or posting information and pictures about oneself on social media sites like Facebook and Instagram should be considered "recreational activities"? Does it matter whether the subject of an employee blog or Facebook posting is about the workplace? Or whether the particular employer is identified? What about participation in virtual games like World of Warcraft? Would it infringe an employee's rights if an employer based its personnel decisions on an employee's off-duty, virtual conduct in an online game like World of Warcraft?

Keep in mind that these questions are only relevant because New York has a statute that protects an individual's "legal recreational activities." In addition to New York, only a couple of other states have statutes protecting employees from discrimination based on their off-duty activities, *see* N.D. CENT. CODE § 14-02.4-03; COLO. REV. STAT. § 24-34-402.5. Beyond these limited statutory protections, however, employees have very few protections against adverse employment actions taken because of their lawful, off-duty activities or associations. Thus, in the absence of a protective statute, courts have rejected claims by employees alleging that they were discharged for such activities as attending law school at night, *Scroghan v. Kraftco Corp.*, 551 S.W.2d 811 (Ky. Ct. App. 1977), or volunteering for the AIDS Foundation. *Brunner v. Al Attar*, 786 S.W.2d 784 (Tex. App. 1990).

2. Regulating Workplace Romance. *McCavitt* offers no information about the employer's justification for discharging the plaintiff. Assuming that McCavitt's job performance was "highly regarded" as he alleges, what reasons might the employer have for terminating him? Do employers have legitimate interests in regulating or forbidding office romance?

In *Barbee v. Household Automotive Finance Corp.*, 113 Cal. App. 4th 525 (2003), the court rejected the plaintiff's claim that his termination for dating a subordinate employee violated his privacy rights. Although the court acknowledged that California's constitutional right of privacy restrains private actors, including private employers, it held that Barbee did not have a reasonable expectation of privacy in pursuing an intimate relationship with a subordinate. Citing other cases that approved restrictions on intimate relationships between co-workers, it argued that employers have legitimate interests in "avoiding conflicts of interest between work-related and family-related obligations; reducing favoritism or even the appearance of favoritism; [and] preventing family conflicts from affecting the workplace." *Id.* at 411 (*quoting Parks v. City of Warner Robins*, 43 F.3d 609 (11th Cir. 1995)). In addition, the court found that managerial-subordinate relationships "present issues of potential sexual harassment." *Id.*

Do these concerns justify forbidding all workplace romances, or only those between certain employees? Are there costs to enforcing strict anti-fraternization rules in the workplace? *See* Vicki Schultz, *The Sanitized Workplace*, 112 YALE L.J. 2061 (2003), which is discussed in Chapter 9.

3. Off-Duty Relationships. Suppose that McCavitt had been fired, not for dating a co-worker, but for dating someone who was not a Swiss Reinsurance employee. Because the court's decision turned on whether dating relationships were included in the statutory definition, McCavitt still would not have been protected under its interpretation of the New York statute. But what about the common law? Do any of the limits on an employer's power to discharge discussed in Chapters 3 and 4, *supra*, protect the off-duty relationships of employees?

In *Rulon-Miller v. International Business Machines Corp.*, 162 Cal. App. 3d 241 (1984), the court considered the common law claims of an employee discharged because of a dating relationship with the employee of a competitor. The plaintiff, Virginia Rulon-Miller, started working for IBM in 1967 as a receptionist. While working, she attended night school to earn her baccalaureate degree. Later, she enrolled in and completed various IBM training programs. Over the years she was promoted numerous times until she was named a marketing manager in 1978. The court described the events leading to her termination as follows:

> IBM knew about respondent's relationship with Matt Blum well before her appointment as a manager. Respondent met Blum in 1976 when he was an account manager for IBM. That they were dating was widely known within the organization. In 1977 Blum left IBM to join QYX, an IBM competitor, and was transferred to Philadelphia. When Blum returned to San Francisco in the summer of 1978, IBM personnel were aware that he and respondent began dating again. This seemed to present no problems to respondent's superiors, as Callahan [Rulon-Miller's supervisor] confirmed when she was promoted to manager. Respondent testified: "Somewhat in passing, Phil said: I heard the other day you were dating Matt Blum, and I said: Oh. And he said, I don't have any problem with that. You're my number one pick. I just want to assure you that you are my selection." The relationship with Blum was also known to Regional Manager Gary Nelson who agreed with Callahan. Neither Callahan nor Nelson raised any issue of conflict of interest because of the Blum relationship.

> Respondent flourished in her management position, and the company, apparently grateful for her efforts, gave her a $4,000 merit raise in 1979 and told her that she was doing a good job. A week later, her manager, Phillip Callahan, left a message that he wanted to see her.

> When she walked into Callahan's office he confronted her with the question of whether she was *dating* Matt Blum. She wondered at the relevance of the inquiry and he said the dating constituted a "conflict of interest," and told her to stop dating Blum or lose her job and said she had a "couple of days to a week" to think about it.

> The next day Callahan called her in again, told her "he had made up her mind for her," and when she protested, dismissed her.

Id. at 528. Rulon-Miller sued IBM, alleging wrongful discharge and intentional infliction of emotional distress, and a jury returned a verdict of $100,000 in compensatory and $200,000 in punitive damages. The California Court of Appeal upheld the verdict. Addressing the plaintiff's wrongful discharge claim, it wrote:

> When Callahan questioned her relationship with Blum, respondent invoked her right to privacy in her personal life relying on existing IBM policies. A threshold inquiry is thus presented whether respondent could reasonably rely on those policies for job protection. Any conflicting action by the company would be wrongful in that it would constitute a violation of her contract rights. . . . The covenant of good faith and fair dealing embraces a number of rights, obligations, and considerations implicit in

contractual relations and certain other relationships. At least two of those considerations are relevant herein. The duty of fair dealing by an employer is, simply stated, a requirement that like cases be treated alike. Implied in this, of course, is that the company, if it has rules and regulations, apply those rules and regulations to its employees as well as affording its employees their protection. . . . [I]f an employee has the right in an employment contract (as distinct from an implied covenant), the courts have routinely given her the benefit of that contract. (Rest.2d Contracts, § 81; 1A Corbin on Contracts (1963) § 152, pp. 13–17.) Thus, the fair dealing portion of the covenant of good faith and fair dealing is at least the right of an employee to the benefit of rules and regulations adopted for his or her protection.

In this case, there is a close question of whether those rules or regulations permit IBM to inquire into the purely personal life of the employee. If so, an attendant question is whether such a policy was applied consistently, particularly as between men and women. The distinction is important because the right of privacy, a constitutional right in California (*City and County of San Francisco v. Superior Court* (1981) 125 Cal.App.3d 879, 883[, 178 Cal. Rptr. 435]), could be implicated by the IBM inquiry. Much of the testimony below concerned what those policies were. The evidence was conflicting on the meaning of certain IBM policies. We observe ambiguity in the application but not in the intent. The "Watson Memo" (so called because it was signed by a former chairman of IBM) provided as follows:

"To All IBM Managers:

"The line that separates an individual's on-the-job business life from his other life as a private citizen is at times well-defined and at other times indistinct. But the line does exist, and you and I, as managers in IBM, must be able to recognize that line.

"I have seen instances where managers took disciplinary measures against employees for actions or conduct that are not rightfully the company's concern. These managers usually justified their decisions by citing their personal code of ethics and morals or by quoting some fragment of company policy that seemed to support their position. Both arguments proved unjust on close examination. What we need, in every case, is balanced judgment which weighs the needs of the business and the rights of the individual.

"Our primary objective as IBM managers is to further the business of this company by leading our people properly and measuring quantity and quality of work and effectiveness on the job against clearly set standards of responsibility and compensation. This is performance— and performance is, in the final analysis, the one thing that the company can insist on from everyone.

"We have concern with an employee's off-the-job behavior only when it reduces his ability to perform regular job assignments, interferes with the job performance of other employees, or if his outside behavior affects the reputation of the company in a major way. When on-the-job performance is acceptable, I can think of few situations in which outside activities could result in disciplinary action or dismissal.

"When such situations do come to your attention, you should seek the advice and counsel of the next appropriate level of management and the personnel department in determining what action—if any—is called for. Action should be taken only when a legitimate interest of the company is injured or jeopardized. Furthermore the damage must be clear beyond reasonable doubt and not based on hasty decisions about what one person might think is good for the company.

"IBM's first basic belief is respect for the individual, and the essence of this belief is a strict regard for his right to personal privacy. This idea should never be compromised easily or quickly.

"/s/ Tom Watson, Jr."

It is clear that this company policy insures to the employee both the right of privacy and the right to hold a job even though "off-the-job behavior" might not be approved of by the employee's manager. . . .

Callahan based his action against respondent on a "conflict of interest." But the record shows that IBM did not interpret this policy to prohibit a romantic relationship. Callahan admitted that there was no company rule or policy requiring an employee to terminate friendships with fellow employees who leave and join competitors.[5] Gary Nelson, Callahan's superior, also confirmed that IBM had no policy against employees socializing with competitors. . . .

We observe that while respondent was successful, her primary job did not give her access to sensitive information which could have been useful to competitors. She was, after all, a seller of typewriters and office equipment. Respondent's brief makes much of the concession by IBM that there was no evidence whatever that respondent had given any information or help to IBM's competitor QYX. It really is no concession at all; she did not have the information or help to give.

Id. at 529–30.

Rulon-Miller suggests that employee privacy rights may arise through contract. In practice, however, such claims are rarely brought. Few companies have policies like IBM's that explicitly promise employees protection against unwarranted interference with their off-the-job behavior. Moreover, because the California Supreme Court narrowed the application of the implied covenant of good faith and fair dealing in *Foley v. Interactive Data Corp.*, 765 P.2d 373 (Cal. 1988), it is doubtful that the *Rulon-Miller* court's reliance on that claim is still sound. In the absence of explicit employer promises to respect employee privacy, the claims of workers

---

[5] [n. 4] An interesting side issue to this point is that Blum continued to play on an IBM softball team while working for QYX.

discharged in situations similar to Rulon-Miller's have not fared so well. For example, in *Salazar v. Furr's, Inc.*, 629 F. Supp. 1403 (D.N.M. 1986), the court rejected the wrongful discharge claim of a supermarket employee terminated because her husband worked for a competing supermarket. *See also Miller v. Fairfield Communities, Inc.*, 382 S.E.2d 16 (S.C. Ct. App. 1989) (rejecting wrongful discharge claim of a man who was told that his continued employment depended upon his wife resigning from her job with another company).

And even though marriage has been recognized as a fundamental right under the federal constitution, courts have rejected claims by employees asserting that they lost their jobs because of the decision to get married. *See, e.g., Delmonte v. Laidlaw Envtl. Servs.*, 46 F. Supp. 2d 89 (D. Mass. 1999); *Karren v. Far West Fed. Sav.*, 717 P.2d 1271 (Or. Ct. App. 1986).

D.　TESTING, SCREENING, AND MONITORING

Employers have always used a variety of methods to screen, select and supervise their employees. In recent years, however, the technology available to employers to accomplish these goals has expanded rapidly. Some have argued that these new technologies threaten privacy or other fundamental employee interests. In this section, we briefly canvass several of the major areas which have provoked controversy.

1.　Genetic Testing

In 2008, Congress passed the Genetic Information Nondiscrimination Act (GINA) in order to "fully protect the public from discrimination and allay their concerns about the potential for discrimination, thereby allowing individuals to take advantage of genetic testing, technologies, research and new therapies." Genetic Information Nondiscrimination Act of 2008, Pub. L. 110–233, § 2, 122 STAT. 881. GINA's substantive provisions aim to eliminate the use of genetic information in decision-making by health insurers and employers. Title I amends several federal statutes that regulate the provision of health insurance and the privacy of medical information in order to restrict the use of genetic information in setting premiums or determining eligibility for benefits. Title II addresses the use of genetic information by employers.

Although little systematic evidence existed that genetic testing was being used to discriminate, some research suggested that patients were avoiding genetic testing that could improve their medical care out of fear that the results might be used against them by employers and insurers. These fears, and the resulting reluctance to consent to genetic testing, not only compromised medical care, they also hampered research into the genetic basis for disease and its treatment. In addition, the growing availability and falling costs of genetic testing raised concerns that employers and insurers might rely on genetic information, burdening the autonomy of individuals by foreclosing opportunities on the basis of their latent genetic characteristics. *See* Pauline T. Kim, *Genetic Discrimination, Genetic Privacy: Rethinking Employee Protections for a Brave New Workplace*, 96 Nw. U. L. REV. 1497, 1533–36 (2002).

Although GINA is framed as a nondiscrimination statute, many of its substantive provisions are directed at protecting the privacy of an individual's genetic information. The nondiscrimination provisions of Title II of GINA are modeled on the prohibition against discrimination based on race, color, religion, sex or national original in Title VII of the Civil Rights Act of 1964. More specifically, GINA makes it unlawful for an employer:

(1) to fail or refuse to hire, or to discharge, any employee, or otherwise to discriminate against any employee with respect to the compensation, terms, conditions, or privileges of employment of the employee, because of genetic information with respect to the employee; or

(2) to limit, segregate, or classify the employees of the employer in any way that would deprive or tend to deprive any employee of employment opportunities or otherwise adversely affect the status of the employee as an employee, because of genetic information with respect to the employee.

42 U.S.C. § 2000ff-1(a). GINA also invokes the same remedies and enforcement mechanisms used for claims of discrimination under Title VII of the Civil Rights Act of 1964. 42 U.S.C. § 2000ff-6.

The statute defines "genetic information" as "information about—(i) [an] individual's genetic tests, (ii) the genetic tests of family members of such individual, and (iii) the manifestation of a disease or disorder in family members of such individual." 42 U.S.C. § 2000ff(4)(A). The term also includes information that an individual has requested or received genetic counseling or education or has undergone genetic testing. 42 U.S.C. § 2000ff(4)(B). A "genetic test" is further defined to mean "an analysis of human DNA, RNA, chromosomes, proteins, or metabolites, that detects genotypes, mutations, or chromosomal changes," but does not include "an analysis of proteins or metabolites that does not detect genotypes, mutations, or chromosomal changes." 42 U.S.C. § 2000ff(7).

In addition to the basic nondiscrimination provisions, GINA also seeks to protect the privacy of employees' genetic information. Thus, it also prohibits an employer from requesting, requiring, or purchasing genetic information with respect to an employee or a family member of the employee. 42 U.S.C. § 2000ff-1(b). This prohibition, however, is subject to a number of exceptions. 42 U.S.C. §§ 2000ff-1(b)(1)–2000ff-1(b)(6). For example, acquisition of genetic information is not unlawful if an employer offers a wellness program that includes genetic services, so long as the employee voluntarily participates and any individually identifiable information is not disclosed to the employer. Similarly, no violation occurs if the employer acquires genetic information when requesting medical information in order to comply with federal or state family and medical leave laws, or when the employer undertakes genetic monitoring to determine the effects of exposure to toxic substances in the workplace, as long as such monitoring complies with certain requirements. 42 U.S.C. §§ 2000ff-1(b)(2)–2000ff-1(b)(5).

The potentially most expansive exceptions exempt an employer from liability when it "inadvertently requests or requires family medical history of the employee or family member of the employee," 42 U.S.C. § 2000ff-1(b)(1), or where the information is acquired from "documents that are commercially and publicly available (including newspapers, magazines, periodicals, and books, but not including medical databases or court records) that include family medical history." 42 U.S.C. § 2000ff-1(b)(4). The former exception is the so-called "water-cooler" exception, intended to protect the employer who learns, for example, of a genetically-based disease suffered by an employee's family member, through casual conversation. The latter exception reflects the pervasiveness of genetic information in a myriad of information sources.

Even if an employer acquires genetic information under any of the exceptions, it must maintain the confidentiality of the information, 42 U.S.C. § 2000ff-5(a), and may not rely upon it to make employment decisions. 42 U.S.C. § 2000ff-1(a). However, once genetic information is known by an employer, preventing it from influencing personnel decisions and proving when it has influenced these decisions may be nearly impossible. See *Kim, supra*, 96 Nw. U. L. REV. at 1524–32 (2002). Because GINA prohibits discrimination only on the basis of genetic information, it appears to apply only to individuals who are asymptomatic—that is, those whose genes put them at increased risk of developing certain diseases. Once those genes are expressed, employers are permitted to use "medical information that is not genetic information about a manifested disease, disorder, or pathological condition . . . that has or may have a genetic basis." 42 U.S.C. § 2000ff-9.

The number of exceptions and the difficulty in defining them highlight the significant challenges in prohibiting employer acquisition and use of genetic information. Most individuals who have health insurance are covered through their employers. In addition, federal laws like the Americans with Disabilities Act and the Family and Medical Leave Act permit or require employees to share certain types of medical information with their employers. However, genetic information is not easily separable from non-genetic medical information as a conceptual matter, and in fact, most medical records currently include both types of information. Mark Rothstein has argued that the statute is "based on a scientifically dubious dichotomy between genetic and non-genetic information, tests, and disorders . . . [V]irtually all human disease has both genetic and environmental components." Mark A. Rothstein, *GINA, the ADA, and Genetic Discrimination in Employment*, 36 J.L. MED. & ETHICS 837, 839 (2008). Moreover, the fact that the statute protects only genetic information, but not information about physiological changes that may result from an individual's genetic makeup creates significant gaps in coverage. As technological advances increasingly permit detection of subtle physiological changes, the line between using genetic information and non-genetic medical information will become more and more difficult to police.

In the years since GINA was passed, relatively little litigation has occurred under the statute. The EEOC receives far fewer charges of genetic discrimination than, for example, race or sex discrimination, U.S EQUAL EMP'T OPPORTUNITY COMM'R, *Charge Statistics*, http://www.eeoc.gov/eeoc/statistics/enforcement/charges.cfm, and in 2013, it settled the first lawsuit it ever filed under the statute. U.S EQUAL EMP'T OPPORTUNITY COMM'R, *Fabricut to Pay $50,000 to Settle EEOC Disability and Genetic Information Discrimination Lawsuit*, http://www.eeoc.gov/eeoc/ newsroom/release/5-7-13b.cfm. The case, against Fabricut, Inc., alleged that the company violated GINA when it asked for an applicant's family medical history—a type of genetic information under the statute—during a post-offer medical examination. In addition to paying a monetary award, the company agreed to comply with the statute and to take specified actions to prevent further discrimination. Although there have been few high profile cases under GINA, the statute has created compliance challenges for employers in handling employees' medical information acquired through pre-employment testing or when dealing with requests for medical leave or reasonable accommodation of a disability.

2.   Drug Testing

Much of the law of employee privacy developed in the 1980s and 1990s in the context of challenges to drug testing. In the 1980s, the federal government's focus on eradicating illegal drug use joined with technological advances making drug testing more affordable and accessible to produce an explosion in workplace drug testing programs—and in litigation challenging them. Public employees invoked their constitutional rights, asserting that drug testing violates the Fourth Amendment's prohibition on unreasonable searches and seizures. These constitutional challenges eventually reached the Supreme Court which decided a pair of employee drug testing cases in 1989.

In the first case, *Skinner v. Railway Labor Executives' Association,* 489 U.S. 602 (1989), unions representing railroad workers challenged regulations promulgated by the Federal Railroad Administration which mandated blood and urine testing for alcohol and illegal drugs upon the occurrence of certain accidents. In considering the Fourth Amendment challenge, the Supreme Court first assessed the Fourth Amendment interests implicated by the tests:

> The initial detention necessary to procure the evidence may be a seizure of the person, if the detention amounts to a meaningful interference with his freedom of movement. Obtaining and examining the evidence may also be a search, if doing so infringes an expectation of privacy that society is prepared to recognize as reasonable.
>
> We have long held that a "compelled intrusio[n] into the body for blood to be analyzed for alcohol content" must be deemed a Fourth Amendment search. See *Schmerber v. California,* 384 U.S. 757, 767–68 (1966). . . . The ensuing chemical analysis of the sample to obtain physiological data is a further invasion of the tested employee's privacy interests. . . .
>
> Unlike the blood-testing procedure . . . collecting and testing urine samples do not entail a surgical intrusion into the body. It is not disputed, however, that chemical analysis of urine, like that of blood, can reveal a host of private medical facts about an employee, including whether he or she is epileptic, pregnant, or diabetic. Nor can it be disputed that the process of collecting the sample to be tested, which may in some cases involve visual or aural monitoring of the act of urination, itself implicates privacy interests.

Id. at 616–17.

Although concluding that blood and urine tests are "searches" for purposes of the Fourth Amendment, the Court went on to hold that the usual requirements of a warrant on probable cause or individualized suspicion were not necessary for the searches at issue to be "reasonable." Reasoning that "the expectations of privacy of [railroad employees covered by the regulations] are diminished by reason of their participation in an industry that is regulated pervasively to ensure safety," *id.* at 627, the Court found those privacy interests were outweighed by the government's compelling interest in ensuring safety. It noted that the "[e]mployees subject to the tests discharge duties fraught with such risks of injury to others that even a momentary lapse of attention can have disastrous consequences." *Id.* at 628. The Court thus concluded that the blood and urine tests were reasonable under the Fourth Amendment.

Justice Marshall, joined by Justice Brennan, dissented, complaining that the majority had "trivialized" the intrusions on worker privacy, while blindly accepting the Government's assertion that testing would effectively achieve its purposes of deterring drug use and ascertaining the cause of accidents. *Id.* at 652.

National Treasury Employees Union v. Von Raab, 489 U.S. 656 (1989), decided the same day, involved a challenge to the United States Customs Service's requirement that three categories of employees—those directly involved in drug interdiction, those that carry firearms while on the job, and those that handle "classified" materials—submit to drug tests. *Id.* at 660–61. Weighing the government's asserted interest in deterring drug use and preventing the promotion of drug users to certain positions, five members of the Court concluded that the government's need to conduct the tests without any individualized suspicion of drug use outweighed the employees' privacy interests for the first two categories of employees. *Id.* at 668. It then remanded the case for the lower court to assess the reasonableness of the testing program as applied to the third category of employees, stating that the record before it was insufficient to determine whether all of the employment positions included were in fact likely to have access to sensitive information. *Id.* at 677–78.

Justice Scalia, who had joined the majority in upholding drug testing of the railway employees in *Skinner*, dissented in *Von Raab*, complaining that the Customs Service had not shown any evidence that drug use was a problem among its employees, or that any harm was likely. "In my view," wrote Scalia, "the Customs Service rules are a kind of immolation of privacy and human dignity in symbolic opposition to drug use." *Id.* at 681.

Skinner and *Von Raab* established the basic framework for evaluating drug testing programs administered by public employers. Under this framework, drug testing is typically upheld for employees holding safety-sensitive jobs, *see, e.g., Krieg v. Seybold*, 481 F.3d 512 (7th Cir. 2007) (rejecting Fourth Amendment challenge to random drug testing of employee who regularly drove a one ton dump truck and other heavy vehicles because the job was safety-sensitive); however, policies that are overly broad and unconnected to a compelling government interest may not survive scrutiny under the Fourth Amendment. *See, e.g., National Fed'n of Fed. Emp's v. Vilsack*, 681 F.3d 483, (D.C. Cir. 2012) (reversing summary judgment for employer on employees' claim that random drug testing of all Job Corps Center staff without regard to job duties violates their Fourth Amendment rights); *AFSCME v. Scott*, 717 F.3d 851 (11th Cir. 2013) (remanding a case challenging an executive order requiring random drug testing of all state employees in Florida and instructing district court to determine for each type of job whether random drug testing would be unconstitutional).

The Fourth Amendment prohibition of unreasonable searches and seizures generally does not restrain private actors. A narrow exception applies Fourth *private* Amendment restrictions to a private party that is essentially acting as an *sector* instrument or agent of the government. *See Skinner*, 489 U.S. at 614. For the vast majority of private sector workers, however, the Fourth Amendment offers no basis for challenging workplace drug testing. Private employees have therefore turned primarily to the common law to oppose employer drug testing; however, these cases *C L* have had limited success, often because the courts found that the employees had no reasonable expectation of privacy or that the testing was not "highly offensive."

In addition to the common law, statutes in over half the states regulate the use of drug testing in employment. Most of these focus on providing various procedural protections, such as giving employees notice of the testing, insuring the integrity of samples or permitting confirmatory tests. Only a few states, however, place any substantive limitations on employer drug testing, such as limiting testing to safety sensitive jobs. *See, e.g.*, MONT. CODE ANN. §§ 39-2-205 to 211. Some state statutes encourage employer drug testing, by limiting the liability of employers who conduct their testing in compliance with the statute's procedural requirements, or permitting employers who implement testing programs to receive discounts on their workers' compensation premiums. *See, e.g.*, ALA. CODE § 25-5-51; GA. CODE ANN. § 34-9-17.

NOTES

1.   **Privacy Interests.** The Court in *Skinner* identified several distinct Fourth Amendment interests implicated by blood and urine tests. Depending upon how the testing is conducted, other privacy interests may be at stake as well. Urinalysis involves testing a subject's urine for the presence of drug metabolites, rather than the illegal drugs themselves. Drug metabolites may be present in the urine for many days after exposure, depending upon the drug. Thus, urinalysis testing potentially provides a peek into an employee's off-duty activities, even if he or she is never actually impaired during working hours. *See* Mark A. Rothstein, *Drug Testing in the Workplace: The Challenge to Employment Relations and Employment Law*, 63 CHI.-KENT L. REV. 683, 695 (1987).

In addition, screening tests may sometimes misidentify metabolites of legal substances as metabolites of illegal drugs. *Id.* at 697–98. For this reason, test subjects are typically asked to complete a questionnaire identifying over-the-counter or prescription medications to avoid mistakenly attributing a positive screen to illegal drug use. Independent of the chemical testing, these questionnaires may involve the disclosure of personal medical information.

2.   **Bargaining over Drug Testing.** The drug testing challenge in *Skinner* was brought by the union that represents railway workers. Although the union in that case raised a Fourth Amendment claim, the Court's decision had ramifications for the role of collective bargaining in determining how drug testing programs are

implemented in the railway industry. The drug testing regulations promulgated by the Federal Railroad Administration (FRA) stated that they supersede "any provision of a collective bargaining agreement," *see Skinner*, 489 U.S. at 615, and that railroads could not bargain away the authority to perform testing. *Id.* By upholding the regulations at issue, the Court in *Skinner* appeared to approve the FRA's policy of removing the issue of drug testing and how it would be implemented from the collective bargaining table. Marion Crain has argued that direct government intervention in the workplace, like the FRA regulations on drug testing, discourages labor and management from voluntarily negotiating effective prevention programs and undermines the collective bargaining system. *See* Marion Crain, *Expanded Employee Drug-Detection Programs and the Public Good: Big Brother at the Bargaining Table*, 64 N.Y.U. L. REV. 1286, 1343–44 (1989). Although such intervention in the case of drug testing has been justified by public safety concerns, Crain argues that those concerns can be entrusted to the collective bargaining process because both workers and management have genuine and immediate interests in preventing accidents. *Id.* at 1343.

3.   **Legalization.** The legalization of marijuana for medical and recreational use by a number of states raises new issues related to drug testing in the workplace. For example, Connecticut's statute permits medical use of marijuana and prohibits an employer from discriminating against an employee who is a qualifying medical user of the drug. CONN. GEN. STAT. § 21a-408p. However, the law also permits an employer "to prohibit the use of intoxicating substances during work hours" and "to discipline an employee who is under the influence of intoxicating substances during work hours." *Id.* One challenge confronting employers is how to establish that an employee is "under the influence." Traditional forms of drug testing that rely on the analysis of bodily fluids reveal past exposure to certain substances, but cannot accurately determine current impairment. In the case of marijuana in particular, the metabolite indicating exposure to the drug may be present in an individual's urine for several weeks, long past the period of active impairment. *See* Stacy A. Hickox, *Drug Testing of Medical Marijuana Users in the Workplace: An Inaccurate Test of Impairment*, 29 HOFSTRA LAB. & EMP. L.J. 273, 301 (2012). Some state statutes have attempted to address the limits of chemical testing directly. Delaware's medical marijuana statute, for example, prohibits employers from discriminating against a qualified user solely on the basis of a positive drug test for marijuana metabolites or components. DEL. CODE ANN. tit. 16 § 4905A. In other states that permit medical uses of marijuana, the statutes contain no protections against job loss for qualified users. Should they?

Colorado and Washington have passed laws legalizing the recreational use of marijuana. COLO. CONST. Art. 18, § 16; REV. CODE WASH. § 69.50.101 *et seq*. Should the passage of those laws change the way in which courts apply the balancing test set out in *Skinner* and *Von Raab*? Or are the employees' and employers' interests no different than before? Unlike most states, Colorado has a statute that protects employees against discharge because of their "legal recreational activities" off-duty. COLO. REV. STAT. § 24-34-402.5. That statute might have protected employees against discharge for recreational marijuana use except that the legalization law also specifically preserved employers' rights to have policies restricting the use of marijuana by employees. COLO. REV. STAT. § 8-73-108(IX.5) (2013).

4. **Applicants vs. Employees.** Are the privacy interests of applicants the same as those of current employees? In *Baughman v. Wal-Mart Stores, Inc.*, 592 S.E.2d 824 (W. Va. 2003), the Supreme Court of Appeals of West Virginia, concluded that they are not. The court in an earlier case had held that the employer's interest in drug testing outweighs the employee's right of privacy only where "specific heightened safety concerns or well-grounded individualized suspicion is present." *Id.* at 827. Nevertheless, it rejected the plaintiff's suit challenging Wal-Mart's requirement that applicants provide a urine sample prior to being hired, finding that a person clearly has a lower expectation of privacy in the pre-employment context. *Id.*; *see also Loder v. City of Glendale*, 927 P.2d 1200 (Cal. 1997) (holding that employer drug testing is a less significant invasion of privacy of applicants than current employees).

3. Monitoring and Data Analytics

In subsection B.4, *supra*, we considered the extent to which employer monitoring of employees' electronic communications might threaten their privacy. Other forms of employer monitoring, however, focus on employees' work activity and productivity levels. These forms of monitoring do not really raise privacy concerns, as few would question the right of an employer to observe and supervise the activities of its workers, or its legitimate interest in knowing where its employees are during working hours and how they are spending their time. Rather, this type of employer monitoring raises questions about whether there are or should be any limits on the employer's ability to monitor and control work performance. In an earlier era, craft workers fought to maintain control over their hours and the pace of the production process, and employees continue to argue that having some measure of control over their work lives is essential to maintaining a sense of identity and personal dignity.

On the other hand, employers argue that they have a legitimate interest in managing and directing the business entity. Recent innovations have made available a broad variety of technological devices that can monitor and record employee activity far more comprehensively than was possible through visual observation by a supervisor. For example, software programs can record the number of keystrokes made by a computer operator, or the number and length of every phone call placed or received by customer service personnel. Radio frequency identification (RFID) can be used to track and record the exact location of an employee in a building throughout the day. And the capacity of computers to process and store immense amounts of information means that this type of monitoring not only produces and records detailed information of an employee's activities and whereabouts during the work day, but it can also be used to reward or discipline employees, or to impose production goals and quotas. Employers offer a number of justifications for using monitoring and tracking technologies, such as the interest in increasing productivity, protecting the companies' physical and intellectual property, providing adequate security, preventing employees' illegal activities and avoiding legal liability.

reasons for monitoring

Opposition to workplace monitoring has focused on the detrimental effects on employees. Employee advocates argue that these monitoring technologies are degrading and dehumanizing and that they lower employee morale, leading to increased employee turnover. In addition, some research has suggested that workplace monitoring of clerical workers causes physical and emotional health problems. One study found that monitored workers suffered a higher incidence of headaches, backaches, wrist pain and fatigue, as well as increased incidence of depression and anxiety. Another study found that "heavily monitored clerical workers 'exhibited a greater degree of stress, depression, anxiety, instability, fatigue and anger.' " Julie A. Flanagan, Note, *Restricting Electronic Monitoring in the Private Workplace*, 43 DUKE L.J. 1256, 1263–64 (1994).

Unions have tried to capitalize on discontent over these types of monitoring practices, engaging in public education, lobbying and advocacy on behalf of workers subject to these forms of monitoring. *See* William A. Herbert & Amelia K. Tuminaro, *The Impact of Emerging Technologies in the Workplace: Who's Watching the Man (Who's Watching Me)*, 25 HOFSTRA LAB. & EMPLOY. L.J. 355, 357 (2008); Sewell Chan, *New Scanners for Tracking City Workers*, N.Y. TIMES, Jan. 23, 2007. In addition, in some unionized workplaces, use of monitoring technologies has led to demands for bargaining over their introduction, or challenges to their use for disciplining workers. *Id.* Aside from collective bargaining over employer monitoring practices, several states have passed laws regulating employer use of monitoring or surveillance devices, for example, by prohibiting employers from monitoring phone or electronic communications without consent or prior notice. *See* MATTHEW W. FINKIN, PRIVACY IN EMPLOYMENT LAW 1076–89 (4th ed. 2013) (summarizing state statutes addressing electronic monitoring and surveillance by employers).

The amount of data collected about employees is growing exponentially, making possible not only simple monitoring like counting key strokes or phone calls, but also sophisticated data analysis of which characteristics make workers most effective. The result is an emerging field of "workforce analytics," which involves the application of the techniques of data analytics to decisions regarding the hiring, managing and promoting of employees. For an extended discussion of "what happens when Big Data meets human resources," see Don Peck, *They're Watching You at Work*, THE ATLANTIC (Nov. 20, 2013). In one example discussed in the article, electronic badges worn by employees collected data about all of their interactions throughout the day, including "information about formal and informal conversations: their length; the tone of voice and gestures of the people involved; how much those people talk, listen, and interrupt; the degree to which they demonstrate empathy and extroversion; and more." *Id.* The data generated was then used to determine what characteristics are associated with successful or unsuccessful employees; who is most productive; who is an effective team leader; and the like. In another example, employees were asked to play a video game for twenty minutes, generating hundreds of data points about things such as how they made decisions, how long they hesitated before acting, and how quickly they learned from experience. These data points were then used to develop a profile of the most effective employees. *Id.*

The use of data analytics to manage personnel is too new to know its impact on the law, but it will likely raise challenging questions for work law in the future. Should these developments be encouraged, tolerated or regulated? Perhaps they will offer a way to bypass subjective decision-making that too often enables unconscious bias to operate. Perhaps they will offer metrics to determine whether an employee truly has a performance problem or whether the reasons given for a discharge are actually a cover for a retaliatory motive. Perhaps data analytics will offer information that can empower employees by identifying their strengths and giving them tools for improving their performance. On the other hand, maybe "people analytics" will introduce new forms of bias or operate in a way that merely reproduces existing biases. Maybe they will encourage employers to further encroach on employee privacy in an effort to collect more data and build better models, or will further decrease workers' sense of autonomy and increase their levels of stress. It is too early to know which of these possibilities will be realized, however much will depend upon how the new techniques are deployed and whether any constraints are placed on their use.

E. REPUTATION

Employees have a strong interest in avoiding harm to their reputations. In addition to causing humiliation or embarrassment, statements that impugn an individual's character or abilities can cause real economic damage, limiting the willingness of co-workers or prospective employers to deal with her. Because employers exercise authority and supervision over the work of their employees, they wield a great deal of power to affect employee reputations. Employees' interests in avoiding negative assessments by their employers, however, run directly counter to the interests of employers in facilitating accurate and honest assessments about both current and prospective employees in order to inform their personnel decisions. The common law tort of defamation, as applied in the employment context, attempts to balance these competing interests.

ZINDA v. LOUISIANA PACIFIC CORP.
Supreme Court of Wisconsin
440 N.W.2d 548 (1989)

Bablitch, Justice.

Allan D. "Rick" Zinda (Zinda) brought both a defamation and invasion of privacy action against his former employer, Louisiana Pacific Corporation (Louisiana Pacific), based on a statement concerning his discharge which was published in a company newsletter. . . .

The essential facts are undisputed. Approximately two years prior to his employment with Louisiana Pacific, Zinda was injured as a result of falling through "waferboard" on the roof of a garage he was constructing at his home. Zinda sustained numerous injuries, including a broken rib, a broken bone in the back, and a broken heel.

In connection with his application for employment with Louisiana Pacific in 1983, Zinda completed a standard application form as well as a medical history form. In the "personal health history" portion of the medical form, Zinda provided the following answers:

Upper Back Trouble—No.
Middle Back Trouble—No.
Low Back Trouble—No.
Back Injury or Disability—No.
Fracture or Broken Bone—No.
Back X-ray—No.

In explaining a "yes" answer regarding previous hospitalizations and surgery, Zinda wrote: "[W]hen I was 15 years old for Hay Fever, Tonsil, Appendits [sic], and fall off roof." Later, during a pre-employment interview, Zinda clarified that he had previously fallen off a roof and broken some bones including his ribs and a heel, but that he had no present problems. Zinda signed both forms acknowledging that all answers were true and that any false statements or misrepresentations would result in immediate discharge, regardless of when such facts were discovered.

Approximately one year later, Zinda filed a products liability action against Louisiana Pacific, alleging that it negligently manufactured the "waferboard" involved in his fall off the roof. The complaint asserted that Zinda had suffered permanent disabilities as a result of the injuries, and sought substantial compensatory and punitive damages.

The complaint was served on the personnel manager of the Louisiana Pacific plant who compared the allegations against the answers Zinda gave on his application forms. Apparently concluding that Zinda had intentionally withheld adverse information concerning his physical condition, the personnel manager notified Zinda that his employment was suspended pending an investigation into possible fraud regarding his employment forms. Approximately three weeks later, Louisiana Pacific terminated Zinda's employment.

Subsequently, Louisiana Pacific published a notice regarding Zinda's termination on the seventh page of the plant newspaper, the "Waferboard Press," under the following heading: "Comings and Goings." [The paper then described recent changes in personnel at the company in a list which contained the date of the change, the name of the affected employee, the nature of the change, such as "hire" or "terminate" and the reason for the change. Included on the list was a line for Zinda that read:

"5/29/84 Terminate Al Zinda Falsification of Emp. forms."]

Approximately 160 copies of the newsletter were distributed to employees by placement in the lunchroom. Employees were not restricted from taking the newsletter home, and employees regularly took the newsletters out of the workplace. Testimony indicates that a copy reached the local hospital, where Zinda's wife worked, and two of her co-workers read the reference to Zinda's termination.

Zinda amended his complaint to include allegations of defamation, invasion of privacy, and wrongful discharge. Louisiana Pacific answered, raising conditional privilege as a defense, asserting that it had no liability for good faith communications to employees concerning the reasons for the discharge of another employee.

The circuit court granted summary judgment dismissing Zinda's claim for wrongful discharge. Zinda then voluntarily dismissed the products liability claim.

The defamation and invasion of privacy claims were tried to a jury. . . . Regarding the defamation and invasion of privacy claims, the trial court refused without explanation to submit Louisiana Pacific's requested instruction on conditional privilege.

The jury returned a verdict awarding $50,000.00 for defamation as well as $50,000.00 for invasion of privacy. . . .

Louisiana Pacific appealed, arguing that it was entitled to the instruction on conditional privilege. . . .

We turn first to the issue of liability for defamation. We conclude that the information published in the company newsletter was conditionally privileged as a communication of common interest concerning the employer-employee relationship. We further conclude that although the privilege may be lost if abused, a jury question was presented in this case as to whether the information was excessively published.

A communication is defamatory if it tends to harm the reputation of another so as to lower him in the estimation of the community or deter third persons from associating or dealing with him. If the statements are capable of a nondefamatory as well as a defamatory meaning, then a jury question is presented as to how the statement was understood by its recipients.

However, not all defamations are actionable. Some defamations fall within a class of conduct which the law terms privileged. The defense of privilege has developed under the public policy that certain conduct which would otherwise be actionable may escape liability because the defendant is acting in furtherance of some interest of societal importance, which is entitled to protection even at the expense of uncompensated harm to the plaintiff.

Privileged defamations may be either absolute or conditional. Absolute privileges give complete protection without any inquiry into the defendant's motives. This privilege has been extended to judicial officers, legislative proceedings, and to certain governmental executive officers.

The arguments in this case, however, are concerned only with conditional privilege. In the area of conditional privilege, we have endorsed the language of the Restatement of Torts. The Restatement recognizes the existence of a conditional privilege in a number of different situations. Among these are statements made on a subject matter in which the person making the statement and the person to whom it is made have a legitimate common interest.

Section 596 of the Restatement (Second) of Torts defines the "common interest" privilege:

> An occasion makes a publication conditionally privileged if the circumstances lead any one of several persons having a common interest in a particular subject matter correctly or reasonably to believe that there is information that another sharing the common interest is entitled to know.

The common interest privilege is based on the policy that one is entitled to learn from his associates what is being done in a matter in which he or she has an interest in common. Thus, defamatory statements are privileged which are made in furtherance of common property, business, or professional interests. The Restatement extends such privilege to "partners, fellow officers of a corporation for profit, fellow shareholders, and fellow servants. . . ." *See Id.*, Comment d. at 597.

The common interest privilege is particularly germane to the employer-employee relationship. We have applied a conditional privilege to various communications between employers and persons having a common interest in the employee's conduct. For instance, in *Hett v. Ploetz*, 121 N.W.2d 270 (1963), a defamatory letter of reference from an ex-employer to a prospective employer was held to be entitled to a conditional privilege. We stated that the prospective employer has an interest in receiving information concerning the character and qualifications of the former employee, and the ex-employer has an interest in giving such information in good faith to insure that he may receive an honest evaluation when he hires new employees.

Similarly, in *Johnson v. Rudolph Wurlitzer Co.*, 222 N.W. 451, 454 (1928), we held that a conditional privilege applied to defamatory statements by a store manager to other employees in the office about an alleged embezzlement involving a fellow employee. We stated that because of their employment, the employees had a common interest in discovering the source of the shortage that was being investigated.

We conclude that the common interest privilege attaches to the employer-employee relationship in this case. Employees have a legitimate interest in knowing the reasons a fellow employee was discharged. Conversely, an employer has an interest in maintaining morale and quieting rumors which may disrupt business. Here, Louisiana Pacific's personnel manager testified that at the time of Zinda's termination, the plant had been going through a rather extensive retooling and reprocessing. During that time, normal crews had been broken apart and there were prevailing rumors that Louisiana Pacific was laying off employees. The company believed for this reason that it would be the best policy to immediately suppress rumors by being completely honest concerning employees who were no longer with the company.

Moreover, we conclude that truthfulness and integrity in the employment application process is an important common interest. An employer who asks questions such as those involved here is entitled to receive an honest answer, and reasonable communication in a plant newsletter concerning terminations for misrepresentations discourages other employees from engaging in similar conduct. In addition, the employees have an interest in knowing how the rules are enforced, and the type of conduct that may result in their discharge from employment. Accordingly, Louisiana Pacific's communication to its employees concerning Zinda's discharge was entitled to a conditional privilege.

However, conditional privilege is not absolute and may be forfeited if the privilege is abused. The Restatement (Second) of Torts lists five conditions which may constitute an abuse of the privilege, and the occurrence of any one causes the loss of the privilege. The privilege may be abused: (1) because of the defendant's knowledge or reckless disregard as to the falsity of the defamatory matter; (2) because the defamatory matter is published for some purpose other than that for which the particular privilege is given; (3) because the publication is made to some person not reasonably believed to be necessary for the accomplishment of the purpose of the particular privilege; (4) because the publication includes defamatory matter not reasonably believed to be necessary to accomplish the purpose for which the occasion is privileged; or (5) the publication includes unprivileged matter as well as privileged matter.

Zinda insists that any privilege which may have existed in this case was abused as a matter of law by excessive publication under condition (3). Essentially, Zinda argues that Louisiana Pacific made no attempt to restrict the publication to persons with a common interest in his termination. Zinda alludes to testimony elicited on cross-examination which purportedly indicates that the personnel manager had knowledge that employees routinely took the newsletters home. Furthermore, Zinda asserts that the content of the newsletter encouraged its removal from the plant.

We disagree that Louisiana Pacific abused its privilege as a matter of law. The question whether a conditional privilege has been abused is a factual question for the jury, unless the facts are such that only one conclusion can be reasonably drawn.

Contrary to Zinda's insistence, the evidence alluded to does not necessarily lead to the conclusion that Louisiana Pacific excessively published the statement concerning Zinda's discharge. Once it is determined by the court that the defamatory communication was made on an occasion of conditional privilege, the burden shifts to the plaintiff to affirmatively prove abuse. Here, despite allegations of widespread distribution throughout the community, Zinda's proof at trial was limited to the testimony of two unprivileged women who read the reference to Zinda's termination at the hospital where his wife worked.

An employer is entitled to use a method of publication that involves an incidental communication to persons not within the scope of the privilege. Often the only practical means of communicating defamatory information involves a probability or even a certainty that it will reach persons whose knowledge of it is of no value in accomplishing the purpose for which the privilege is given.

As previously discussed, Louisiana Pacific had an interest in informing each and every one of its employees about the subject of Zinda's discharge. We cannot as a matter of law consider the communication in this case an unreasonable means to accomplish this purpose. Testimony indicates that the company attempted to correlate the number of copies printed to the number of employees in the plant. These copies were circulated only in the lunchroom, over the course of several days, so that every workshift would have an opportunity to read the newsletter. Thus, despite the company's alleged knowledge that employees often took the newsletter home, a jury could conclude that the great bulk of its readers had a direct and legitimate interest in the information regarding Zinda's termination, and that the outside communication was reasonably believed to be necessary to communicate the privileged information. Accordingly, the privilege was not abused as a matter of law, and it was error to refuse the requested instruction.

[The court then held that although credible evidence supported Zinda's claim of invasion of privacy for public disclosure of private facts, conditional privilege was also a defense to that claim.]

We conclude that Zinda's proof at trial does not demonstrate an abuse of the privilege as a matter of law, but is rather a question of fact to be determined by the jury. . . .

Accordingly, we reverse the decision of the court of appeals on the issue of liability and remand for a new trial concerning both the defamation and the invasion of privacy claims. On retrial, the trial court should instruct the jury that Louisiana Pacific's newsletter was issued on an occasion of conditional privilege. The court should then instruct the jury that liability on either claim cannot be established without proof of the abuse of the conditional privilege. . . .

NOTES

1. **The Restatement Definition.** The Restatement of Torts contains the following definition:

To create liability for defamation there must be:

   (a)   a false and defamatory statement concerning another;

   (b)   an unprivileged publication to a third party;

   (c)   fault amounting at least to negligence on the part of the publisher; and

   (d)   either actionability of the statement irrespective of special harm or the existence of special harm caused by the publication.

RESTATEMENT (SECOND) OF TORTS § 558 (1977). As in *Zinda*, most courts recognize a conditional privilege—also called a qualified privilege—in the employment context. Because the showing required to overcome the privilege—abuse of the privilege or malice—is usually more demanding than a negligence standard, the third element does not often play a significant role in employment cases. Similarly, the fourth element does not figure in to every employment case because some courts presume the existence of harm where the defamatory statement imputes "unfitness" for one's business or profession. *See, e.g., Gibson v. Phillip Morris, Inc.*, 685 N.E.2d 638 (Ill. App. Ct. 1997).

2. **Intracorporate Communications.** Some courts hold that statements made by one employee to another employed by the same company do not meet the element of "publication" for purposes of defamation law. *See, e.g., Starr v. Pearle Vision, Inc.*, 54 F.3d 1548 (10th Cir. 1995). This approach amounts to granting an exception to defamation law for intracorporate communications. The court in *Hagebak v. Stone*, 61 P.3d 201 (N.M. Ct. App. 2002), considered the rationale behind such a rule, and analyzed the policy choice confronting courts:

The intracorporate communication exception derives from agency theory. A corporation can act only through its agents or employees. Under agency theory, employees acting on behalf of the corporation are "not third persons vis-à-vis the corporation." *Hayes v. Wal-Mart Stores, Inc.*, 953 F. Supp. 1334, 1340 (M.D. Ala. 1996) (*quoting Nelson v. Lapeyrouse Grain Corp.*, 534 So. 2d 1085, 1093 (Ala. 1988)). Accordingly, an intracorporate communication between employees or agents is not considered "published" because the corporation, in effect, is merely " 'communicating with itself.' " *Starr* [*v. Pearle Vision, Inc.*], 54 F.3d at 1553.

The exception finds some support in public policy. To make an informed decision, corporations need to communicate internally in a free and candid manner. The possibility of litigation may make employees less willing to come forward with truthful statements about sensitive corporate matters. A chilling effect on employee communication may impede a corporation's ability to investigate important subjects like alleged employee misconduct. As a result, the corporation may be less likely to take necessary corrective action, even if in the best interests of the corporation, its shareholders, and the public.

On the other hand, a number of jurisdictions have rejected the intracorporate communication exception. . . . They disagree . . . that corporations require what amounts to an absolute privilege barring all defamation lawsuits. They prefer, instead, a qualified privilege that precludes lawsuits if the defamatory statements are made in good faith. . . .

Qualified privilege applies when a statement is made in good faith during the discharge of a public or private duty. Qualified privilege allows the fact finder to "balance the competing interests at stake: shielding corporate officers when they act in good faith in furtherance of corporate goals, but withdrawing that protection if they use corporate power simply to serve their own, personal ends." *Ettenson v. Burke*, 17 P.3d 440 [(N.M. Ct. App. 2001)]. . . .

This split among the authorities implies a policy choice. The absolute exception protects intracorporate communications from resulting litigation, but at a huge cost. False statements knowingly made, even malicious lies disseminated with devastating effect on one's reputation, are all protected on an equal plane with statements innocently made in the best interest of the corporation. . . . Thus, one flaw in the intracorporate communication exception is that it can be overinclusive.

The qualified privilege approach, on the other hand, recognizes that "damage to one's reputation within a corporate community may be just as devastating as that effected by defamation spread to the outside." *Luttrell* [*v. United Tel. Sys., Inc.*], 683 P.2d [1291,] 1294 [(Kan. Ct. App. 1989)]. Although corporate officers may be the embodiment of a corporation, they "remain individuals with distinct personalities and opinions, which opinions may be affected just as surely as those of other employees by the spread of injurious falsehoods. It is this evil that the law of defamation is designed to remedy." *Pirre* [*v. Printing Devs. Inc.*], 468 F. Supp. [1028,] 1041 [(S.D.N.Y. 1979)]. As one federal court analogized, "if a truck negligently driven by a corporate employee ran over another employee or officer of the same corporation, no court would dismiss a claim against the corporate employer on the theory that the corporation had merely injured itself." *Id.* at 1042 n.18. Thus, the qualified-privilege approach provides protection for victims of defamatory statements, but again there is a cost. The mere fact of ongoing litigation over the privilege—the fact-finding process of determining whether statements were made in good faith—may itself have a chilling effect on free expression. Thus, one flaw in the qualified-privilege approach is that it can be underinclusive. . . .

Unlike speech involving public figures, which implicates the interests of the public and raises important constitutional issues, intracorporate speech primarily concerns private interests in corporate efficiency. When purely private interests are at stake, rather than issues of public concern, well-balanced policy considerations mitigate in favor of preserving some remedy for the individual injured in his reputation.

Id. at 204–7.

3. **False and Defamatory.** In order to be actionable, a statement must be both "false and defamatory." The opinion in *Zinda* does not address the issue of whether the company's statement was in fact false. Although a plaintiff must prove that the defendant published a defamatory statement, truth is an affirmative defense on which the defendant bears the burden of proof. The question of the truth of an allegedly defamatory statement is generally an issue to be decided by the jury.

As stated by the court in *Zinda*, a defamatory communication is one that "tends so to harm the reputation of another as to lower him in the estimation of the community or to deter third parties from associating or dealing with him." RESTATEMENT (SECOND) OF TORTS § 559 (1977). What was the allegedly defamatory statement made about Zinda? Does it meet the Restatement definition?

Some statements, such as those accusing a plaintiff of "falsification" or "dishonesty" are clearly defamatory in that they tend to harm one's reputation. In other cases, the defamatory nature of a statement is less clear. Should a supervisor's statement that an employee "did not follow up on assignments" or "could not get along with her co-workers" be considered defamatory? *See Anderson v. Vanden Dorpel*, 667 N.E.2d 1296 (Ill. 1996) (holding that these statements could be innocently construed and thus did not constitute defamation per se). *Cf. Elbeshbeshy v. Franklin Inst.*, 618 F. Supp. 170 (E.D. Pa. 1985) (finding statement that plaintiff was terminated for "lack of cooperation" could be defamatory). What if a supervisor gives an employee a performance rating of "2" on a 1 to 7 point scale, where a "2" was defined as "rarely met expectations"? *Landers v. Nat'l R.R. Passenger Corp.*, 345 F.3d 669 (8th Cir. 2003) (implying that a "2" rating could be defamatory, but finding the rating to be protected by qualified privilege). Suppose an employer tells potential employers that there is pending litigation between the former employee and the company? *Walker v. Braes Feed Ingredients, Inc.*, 2003 U.S. Dist. LEXIS 6873 (N.D. Ill. Apr. 23, 2003) (not defamatory).

4. **False Light Tort.** The "false light tort," one of the four commonly recognized types of common law invasion of privacy torts, is as much concerned with protecting reputation as "privacy" in the traditional sense. As described in the RESTATEMENT (SECOND) OF TORTS:

One who gives publicity to a matter concerning another that places the other before the public in a false light is subject to liability to the other for invasion of his privacy, if (a) the false light in which the other was placed would be highly offensive to a reasonable person, and (b) the actor has knowledge of or acted in reckless disregard as to the falsity of the publicized matter and the false light in which the other would be placed.

RESTATEMENT (SECOND) OF TORTS § 652E (1977).

Although both defamation and the false light tort require a false communication to others that damages the plaintiff, the precise elements differ somewhat. Defamation requires a statement harmful to a person's reputation, while the false light tort asks whether the communication would be "highly offensive to a reasonable person." Defamation requires publication, a term of art which indicates communication to a least one other person, while liability for the false light tort requires that the matter be published to the public generally, or to a large number of persons. Another difference is that defamation aims to protect against damage to one's reputation, while the false light tort seeks compensation for "the mental distress from having been exposed to public view." *Castleberry v. Boeing Co.*, 880 F. Supp. 1435 (D. Kan. 1995). For both torts, however, truth and privilege are defenses.

CHAMBERS v. AMERICAN TRANS AIR, INC.
Court of Appeals of Indiana
577 N.E.2d 612 (1991)

RUCKER, JUDGE.

Becky Chambers filed suit for defamation against her former employer, American Trans Air, Inc., and two former supervisors, Laura Knowles and John Piburn. The trial court entered summary judgment against Chambers and she appeals. The sole issue presented for our review is whether the trial court erred in granting summary judgment in favor of American Trans Air, Inc., Laura Knowles and John Piburn. Finding no error, we affirm.

I.

Chambers was employed by American Trans Air, Inc. (ATA) from October 1982 to July 1987. During part of that time Knowles was Chambers' supervisor and Piburn was Knowles' supervisor.

Chambers resigned from ATA after a dispute over working conditions. She then sought new employment. When asked by prospective employers the names of her supervisors at ATA, Chambers named Knowles and Piburn as references. Chambers began experiencing difficulty in finding new employment and the pattern of responses Chambers was receiving from prospective employers led her to become suspicious of the ATA references.

In an effort to determine the nature of the references ATA was providing prospective employers, Chambers instructed her mother to call ATA, represent herself as a prospective employer and ask to speak with Chambers' supervisors. Chambers was aware of ATA policy that inquiries concerning former employees should be directed to the company's personnel department. However, Chambers' instructions to her mother were tailored to avoid having the inquiries forwarded to personnel.

Chambers' mother was able to speak with Knowles and to ask specific questions concerning Chambers. In response Knowles made the following statements: "could work without supervision on occasion," "did not get along well with other employees," and "was somewhat dependable."

At Chambers' request, Chambers' boyfriend also called ATA, represented himself as a prospective employer and spoke to Piburn. In response to specific questions posed to him Piburn replied that Chambers: "does not work good with other people," "is a trouble maker," "was not an accomplished planner," and "would not be a good person to rehire."

Chambers brought this action against ATA, Knowles and Piburn, alleging that the foregoing statements were defamatory. Chambers contends the defendants have similarly defamed her with prospective employers. However, there is no evidence indicating any prospective employers of Chambers spoke to Knowles or Piburn or contacted ATA for a reference.

ATA, Knowles, and Piburn moved for summary judgment advancing various theories including lack of publication, consent, and qualified privilege. The trial court determined that as a matter of law there was no publication of the statements of Knowles and Piburn and entered summary judgment against Chambers. . . .

III.

Qualified privilege is a defense to a defamation action and it applies to "communication made in good faith on any subject matter in which the party making the communication has an interest or in reference to which he has a duty, either public or private, either legal, moral, or social, if made to a person having a corresponding interest or duty." *Elliott v. Roach* (1980), 409 N.E.2d 661, 672 *quoting* 18 I.L.E. *Libel and Slander* § 52 at 475 (1959). The privilege arises out of the necessity for full and unrestricted communication on matters in which the parties have a common interest or duty.

Whether a statement is protected by a qualified privilege is a matter of law, unless facts giving rise to the privilege are in dispute. This court has held that various communications are protected as privileged, including those between employers and employees, business partners, members of fraternal organizations, creditors and credit agencies. We have not, however, had occasion to determine whether a qualified privilege exists regarding a former employer's statements given to a prospective employer concerning a former employee. We now hold that it does.

As a general rule an employee reference given by a former employer to a prospective employer is clothed with the mantle of a qualified privilege. *See* Prosser & Keaton, *Torts*, Ch. 19, § 115, at 827 (5th ed. 1984); 50 Am.Jur.2d, *Libel & Slander* § 273, at 791 (1970). A former employer has an interest in open communications with a prospective employer regarding a former employee's work characteristics. Without the protection of the privilege, employers might be reluctant to give sincere yet critical responses to requests for an appraisal of a prospective employee's qualifications.

We agree with the viewpoint of the foregoing authorities and find them consistent with our existing case law. There is a self-evident social utility in free and open communications between former and prospective employers concerning an employee reference. Accordingly, we hold that such communications are protected by a qualified privilege.

In the case before us, both Knowles and Piburn were under the impression they were communicating with a prospective employer of Chambers. Their responses to specific questions represented appraisals of Chambers' employment qualifications. The communications under these circumstances are entitled to the protection of a qualified privilege.

[margin note: spec here:]

However, a statement otherwise protected by the doctrine of qualified privilege may lose its privileged character upon a showing of abuse, namely: (1) The communicator was primarily motivated by ill will in making the statement; (2) there was excessive publication of the defamatory statement; or (3) the statement is made without belief or grounds for belief in its truth. . . .

[margin note: abuse of priv.]

Chambers does not argue the alleged defamatory statements were excessively published. Rather, she contends that Knowles' statements were primarily motivated by ill will. In support of her contention Chambers directs our attention to deposition testimony which indicates there was an ATA policy which provided that all calls from prospective employers were to be directed to the ATA personnel department; that Knowles was aware of the policy; Knowles did not direct the inquiry from Chambers' mother to personnel and therefore, according to Chambers, Knowles lost any qualified privilege by "stepping outside the scope of the privilege." We are not persuaded. . . .

[margin note: chamber arg for abuse: ill will]

[margin note: ct disagree]

We cannot agree Knowles abused the protection afforded by a qualified privilege in responding to inquiries from Chambers' mother rather than directing those inquiries to personnel.

In further support of her claim that Knowles' statements were primarily motivated by ill will Chambers asserts Knowles did not like her and was jealous of her because Chambers was unmarried; that Knowles was rude and "nasty" to her, as evidenced by incidents in which Knowles jerked paperwork out of her hand and snapped her fingers at Chambers in a peremptory fashion; and that Knowles generally talked about people behind their backs and that Knowles talked "down" to Chambers in a tone that she did not use with other workers at ATA.

[margin note: evid]

To the extent the foregoing constitutes admissible evidence at all, at most Chambers has merely shown that while she was employed at ATA animosity existed between her and Knowles. That is not enough to overcome the defense of qualified privilege. The animosity must provide the underlying basis for the otherwise privileged statement.

[margin note: resp.]

Chambers presented no material facts to the trial court showing Knowles' alleged defamatory statements were primarily motivated by feelings of ill will.

IV.

Next, Chambers argues the statements of Knowles and Piburn were made without belief or grounds for belief in their truthfulness. "Lack of grounds for belief" has been equated to reckless disregard for the truth. In support of her claim Chambers points to her deposition and the deposition of Knowles which in summary indicate: Chambers' work habits while employed at ATA were satisfactory; there were employees whose overall performance was superior to Chambers, but Knowles did not observe that Chambers was slower or made more mistakes than the others; the group in which Chambers worked had a problem with deadlines, but Knowles could not specify the precise nature of the problem; Chambers had difficulty in getting along with co-workers, but Knowles got along as well with Chambers as she did with other employees; Knowles did not perceive that Chambers had any more difficulty getting along with her than did any other employee.

The thrust of Chambers' argument is that the allegedly defamatory statements of Knowles and Piburn did not reflect an honest evaluation of Chambers' work performance. However the relevant inquiry here is whether the statements of Knowles and Piburn lost the protection of a qualified privilege. Chambers has not presented sufficient evidence to demonstrate that either Knowles or Piburn uttered the alleged defamatory statements with reckless disregard for the truth.

Judgment affirmed.

NOTES

1.   **Employer Reference Practices.** In recent years, employers have become increasingly reluctant to provide references for former employees, citing a fear of defamation lawsuits. Although most employers ask for references, considering them a valuable source of information about prospective hires, many are also unwilling to share information—particularly negative information—about their former employees. Recent surveys have found that substantial numbers of companies have policies prohibiting the release of any information about former employees beyond verification of the dates of their employment and job title.

Ramona L. Paetzold and Steven L. Willborn question whether employers' refusal to provide references is rational in light of the actual risk that they will pay a substantial judgment on a defamation claim. Ramona L. Paetzold & Steven L. Willborn, *Employer (Ir)rationality and the Demise of Employment References*, 30 AM. BUS. L. J. 123 (1992). They collected all reported employment defamation cases in two time periods—1965–70 and 1985–90—which bracket the time in which employers shifted toward policies of providing limited or no employment references. Based on a comparison of the cases in the two time periods, they conclude that "the relative frequency of such litigation probably has not increased, that defamation law still privileged employers so that (former) employees seldom win any award, and that the size of awards has declined over time." *Id.* at 124. Thus, they argue that "the recent trend of not issuing informative employment references is either irrational, or rational but based on highly biased perceptions" of the risk of defamation liability. *Id.* at 141.

Are employer "no comment" policies irrational? How much can an analysis of published decisions in defamation cases tell us about the actual costs of defamation litigation for employers? How would a "rational" employer weigh the costs and benefits of providing employment references?

2. "Immunity" Statutes. Concerned about employers' unwillingness to provide references for their former employees, a number of state legislatures passed "job reference immunity" laws in the 1990s. Consider two fairly typical laws:

Maine: Employment Reference Immunity

An employer who discloses information about a former employee's job performance or work record to a prospective employer is presumed to be acting in good faith and, unless lack of good faith is shown by clear and convincing evidence, is immune from civil liability for such disclosure or its consequences. Clear and convincing evidence of lack of good faith means evidence that clearly shows the knowing disclosure, with malicious intent, of false or deliberately misleading information. This section is supplemental to and not in derogation of any claims available to the former employee that exist under state law and any protections that are already afforded employers under state law.

ME. REV. STAT. ANN. TIT. 26 § 598.

Tennessee: Disclosure of Employee's Job Performance

Any employer that, upon request by a prospective employer or a current or former employee, provides truthful, fair and unbiased information about a current or former employee's job performance is presumed to be acting in good faith and is granted a qualified immunity for the disclosure and the consequences of the disclosure. The presumption of good faith is rebuttable upon a showing by a preponderance of the evidence that the information disclosed was:

(1) Knowingly false;

(2) Deliberately misleading;

(3) Disclosed for a malicious purpose;

(4) Disclosed in reckless disregard for its falsity or defamatory nature; or

(5) Violative of the current or former employee's civil rights pursuant to current employment discrimination laws.

TENN. CODE ANN. § 50-1-105.

What sort of immunity do these statutes provide employers? How significantly do they differ from existing common law standards?

After surveying the thirty-six state immunity statutes adopted as of 2000, Markita Cooper concludes that the statutes "have little, if any, impact on employers' practices or the advice given by the lawyers and human resource professionals who counsel employers." Markita D. Cooper, *Job Reference Immunity Statutes: Preva-*

lent but Irrelevant, 11 CORNELL J. L. & PUB. POL'Y 1, 65 (2001). Some of the statutes appear to impose a higher evidentiary burden on plaintiffs than common law standards. Although a higher burden may help employers obtain summary judgment in defamation cases, Cooper argues that "the lingering threat of being sued—even with the protection of statutory qualified immunity—may keep many employers tied to 'name, rank and serial number' policies." *Id.* at 60.

3. Labor Market Effects. J. Hoult Verkerke points out that lack of information creates three related inefficiencies in the labor market: mismatching, churning and scarring. *See* J. Hoult Verkerke, *Legal Regulation of Employment Reference Practices*, 65 U. CHI. L. REV. 115 (1998). "Mismatching" results when the lack of accurate information leads employers to hire workers in jobs for which they are not suited, reducing productivity. In extreme cases, a mismatch between a job and worker can have disastrous consequences, such as accidents or harm to vulnerable third parties like patients or children. "Churning" is unproductive employee turnover when mismatched employees return to the labor market, either through a quit or discharge, but the lack of accurate references makes it unlikely that their new job search will produce a better match. Churning is costly to both employers who incur hiring and training costs, as well as to employees and society as a whole. "Scarring" occurs when employers, relying on imperfect labor market signals, or even false negative information, refuse to hire someone who would be a productive employee. *Id.* at 138–149.

Verkerke argues that:

> Mismatching, churning, and scarring interact with one another in complex ways, and neither regulatory measures nor market forces can produce an efficient full-information equilibrium. . . . Falsely negative references cause scarring, and no market mechanism adequately internalizes the resulting costs to employees. Thus, defamation law serves the important role of ensuring that employers take adequate precautions against providing falsely negative references. The conditional privilege encourages employers to provide a larger quantity of references. However . . . lawmakers face substantial uncertainty about the extent of protection that optimally balances the quantity and quality of available information. Both disclosure obligations and a tort of wrongful referral create difficult enforcement problems. . . . These more aggressive regulatory cures for the activity-level problem and for falsely positive references may well be worse than the disease.

Id. at 177.

These inter-related difficulties, according to Verkerke, explain the lack of any significant change in the law, despite the commonplace complaints that current defamation law results in too few employment references.

4. Reference Pools. Can technology help to overcome the problem of a lack of accurate employer references in the job market? Consider the following proposal by Kenneth G. Dau-Schmidt:

> The shared information the employers could enjoy from a universal system of references poses a classic public-good problem. Why should an employer

give a reference and take any risk of defamation liability when he cannot compel other employers to give him references, and thus gets nothing in return?

> The solution is for states to encourage employers to use the new information technology to create reference pools which all participating employers can access with the permission of job applicants. Once established, employers would see benefits from participating and giving job references because they would be sure of receiving useful employee references in return. . . . The state laws that would be necessary would be laws that allow such pools to punish members who do not cooperate or who supply inadequate information, laws to prevent the abuse of such power, and laws to make it clear that exchanges of information within the reference pool should be treated the same as exchanges within a single firm for the purposes of defamation liability. Under such an arrangement, area employers would become like one or several big employers for the purposes of sharing information on employees' job performance. State law could also add a right on the part of the employee to view his employment file on record with the reference pool and to correct any erroneous information . . . [similar to rights under the Fair Credit Reporting Act]. In the interests of providing full and accurate information, the review and correction procedure could allow for arbitration of the disputed facts so that prospective employers are not just left with two conflicting accounts of an employee's departure from a firm when deciding whether to hire the prospective employee.

Kenneth G. Dau-Schmidt, *Employment in the New Age of Trade and Technology: Implications for Labor and Employment Law*, 76 IND. L.J. 1, 16–17 (2001).

Would such a system solve the problem of lack of employer references? Do you foresee any difficulties with such a system?

Like employers, employees have an interest in gathering accurate information about prospective employers. As discussed earlier, employees' lack of information may interfere with their ability to assess the risks entailed by a particular job, and therefore, to bargain over, or at least to value accurately, such factors as job security, privacy intrusions or health and safety risks. Could the solution proposed by Dau-Schmidt work both ways?

> If a state wanted to further empower employees, it could also maintain Internet accessible pools of employee experiences with employers, governed by the law of defamation, or it could foster the development of such employer reference pools by unions, with the grant of a qualified privilege against defamation to unions.

Id. at 17.

5. **Liability for Positive References.** Employers concerned about defamation liability might err in the other direction, providing unjustifiably positive references about a former employee. Factually inaccurate, but positive references, have no harmful impact on an employee's reputation, but in rare circumstances may cause harm to others. In *Randi W. v. Muroc Joint Unified School District*, 929 P.2d 582

(Cal. 1997), a school district "unreservedly recommended" a former employee, despite its knowledge that numerous charges of sexual improprieties had been made against him. Another school, relying on the recommendation, hired the employee, who later sexually assaulted a student. In a suit by the student against the school district that had recommended the employee, the California Supreme Court held that "[a]lthough policy considerations dictate that ordinarily a recommending employer should not be held accountable to third persons for failing to disclose negative information regarding a former employee, nonetheless liability may be imposed if, as alleged here, the recommendation letter amounts to an *affirmative misrepresentation* presenting a foreseeable and substantial risk of physical harm to a third person." *Id.* at 584.

The theory of liability in *Randi W.* has not yet been widely accepted, and its practical impact may be limited, because it imposes liability only if an employer makes an *affirmative* misrepresentation that raises a *substantial risk of physical harm* to others. Employers with knowledge of an employee's past behavior that raises a risk of physical harm to others could avoid liability either by revealing all relevant information, or giving a "no comment" reference that makes no affirmative representation about the employee's qualifications. *Id.* at 589.

If recognizing such a tort claim will discourage employers from providing references, should the courts reject such claims? In *Passmore v. Multi-Management Services, Inc.*, 810 N.E.2d 1022 (Ind. 2004), the Supreme Court of Indiana recognized the tort of intentional misrepresentation in the context of employment references, but declined to permit claims for liability based on negligent references. It reasoned that

> [D]eclaring employers liable for negligence in providing employment references will lead universally to employer reluctance to provide any information other than name, rank, and serial number. Only those employers dull-witted enough to issue free-wheeling assessments without calling their lawyers would supply any but the most rudimentary information. A legal policy that discourages providing assessments to subsequent employers will not make for safer nursing homes, or other safe workplaces, for that matter. We therefore decline to adopt [the tort of negligent misrepresentation] as it applies to employment references.

Id. at 1028.

The Court of Appeals of New Mexico viewed the matter differently when it adopted the theory of negligent misrepresentation in the context of employment references:

> We acknowledge that, at the margins, the common-law duty we recognize in this opinion may discourage some employment referrals. But that impact should be minimal. The duty not to misrepresent applies only in cases of foreseeable physical harm. The vast majority of cases will involve pejorative information in the hands of an employer that does not create a risk of foreseeable physical harm and accordingly does not implicate this duty to disclose. When physical harm by the employee is foreseeable, the employer who discloses will be protected against defamation by the qualified

privilege. However, even if some overly cautious employers are deterred unnecessarily from volunteering helpful information and elect to remain silent, we determine that silence may be preferable under these circumstances. . . . In the face of silence from a former employer, the prospective employer can still conduct its own investigation; silence renders the employer no worse off. In contrast, the prospective employer who is misled may relax its own guard; it may not investigate as thoroughly, and may end up worse off than if it had received no information at all. On balance, therefore, the policy gains of imposing a duty not to misrepresent under these limited circumstances outweigh the potential consequences of inhibiting employer disclosure.

Davis v. Board of County Commissioners, 987 P.2d 1172, 1182 (N.M. Ct. App. 1999).

6.   Self-publication. Ordinarily, a defamatory statement must be "published"— that is, communicated to a third person—in order to be actionable. Some courts, however, have found that the publication requirement may be satisfied if the plaintiff was compelled to repeat a defamatory statement to another, even though the defendant did not communicate it to anyone other than the plaintiff. For example, in *Theisen v. Covenant Medical Center, Inc.*, 636 N.W. 2d 74 (Iowa 2001), the Iowa Supreme Court recognized this "self-publication" doctrine in situations where the subject is under "strong compulsion" to repeat the allegedly defamatory statement. *Id.* at 83.

> The [doctrine] rests on the concept of foreseeability—if the person making the statement can reasonably foresee that the person defamed will be compelled to repeat the defamatory statement to a third party, "there is a strong causal link between the originator's actions and the harm caused to the defamed person, and . . . this causal connection makes the imposition of liability reasonable." 50 Am.Jur.2d Libel and Slander § 242, at 501 (1995). Such forseeability is especially apparent in employment situations because an employee will ordinarily seek new employment after being terminated for alleged wrongdoing.

Id. at 83. The court then held that, like the communication between former and prospective employers, an employer's communications to its employee of the reason for discharge is protected by a qualified privilege.

The self-publication doctrine has not been widely accepted by the states. Decisions by the Minnesota and Colorado State Supreme Courts recognizing the doctrine were followed by legislation limiting or eliminating the doctrine altogether. *See* Colo. Rev. Stat. Ann. § 13-25-125.5 (1997); Minn. Stat. Ann. § 181.933 (1993). Other state courts have simply rejected the doctrine outright. *See, e.g., White v. Blue Cross & Blue Shield of Mass. Inc.*, 809 N.E.2d 1034 (Mass. 2004) (rejecting doctrine of compelled self-publication on the grounds that such a doctrine would have an "unpredictable effect on at-will employment" and stifle workplace communication).

Chapter 8

EMPLOYEE VOICE

Closely related to dignitary interests are employees' interests in "voice"—that is, the ability to speak out without fear of reprisal from their employer. The individual employee may value "voice" because speaking out on issues she deems important is a form of self-expression, or is crucial to her self-realization. Employees as a group may value "voice" because collective speech is a necessary precursor to collective action, either through formal unionization or more informal group action. Given the individual employee's vulnerability to discharge, collective speech may be the only effective avenue by which to affect workplace conditions.

Employees' interests in voice, however, run directly up against the employer's interest in controlling its property and the details of the production process. The traditional hierarchical view of the workplace would leave no place for employee voice. In this view, the employer, as owner of the plant or office, has the right to control the activities that occur there. The employee has no legitimate claim to free speech on the employer's property. The workplace is for work, not self-expression.

In this Chapter we explore how the law balances these competing interests. We begin in Section A by discussing what interests employees have in being able to speak freely. We then consider the potential sources of legal protection for employee voice—and their limits. Section B explores the extent of protection afforded by the Constitution for speech by government workers, while Section C considers whether the common law can provide comparable protections to private sector employees. In part D, we examine statutory protections for employee speech, with a particular focus on the two most significant federal statutes in the area—the whistleblower provisions of the Sarbanes-Oxley Act and the Dodd-Frank Act. Finally, Part E explores the extent to which the National Labor Relations Act may restrict employers' ability to punish employee speech when it is collective in nature, even in the absence of a union.

A. EMPLOYEE INTERESTS IN VOICE

Cynthia Estlund suggests several reasons that we should care about employees' speech rights. First, speech has an "intrinsic value" in that it fosters individual self-realization and fulfilment and promotes individual autonomy. Cynthia L. Estlund, *Free Speech and Due Process in the Workplace*, 71 IND. L.J. 101, 106 (1995–96). Second, free speech should be valued to the extent that it promotes "informed self-governance" within the workplace. *Id.* at 107. Although the ideal of workplace democracy is highly contested, employee participation in workplace governance is valuable both as an intrinsic good and for instrumental reasons. Employees generally express greater job satisfaction when they have a voice in workplace decisions. Moreover, as Estlund argues, cooperation between workers and management is a "crucial prerequisite to a high-performance economy," and "cooperation, in turn, requires mechanisms for fostering employee 'voice' in the workplace." *Id.* at 109. Third, employee speech "may provide information to the public about how private firms operate with regard to working conditions, product safety, environmental practices, and other matters in which the society has a well-established regulatory interest." *Id.* at 111. Such speech informs the public and policy-makers about the wisdom or effectiveness of government efforts to regulate workplace conditions.

In the following excerpt, Estlund further argues that the workplace—and employee speech at the workplace—plays a unique and crucial role in strengthening our democratic institutions.

Cynthia L. Estlund, *Working Together: The Workplace, Civil Society, and the Law*
89 Geo. L.J. 1, 51–55, 96 (2000)

One of the things that is supposed to take place in a democratic civil society is political deliberation and public discourse, which have come to occupy an increasingly central place in democratic theory. . . . Where, if at all, do ordinary citizens participate in public discourse? In particular, do the millions of conversations that take place at work among coworkers count as a form of public discourse or deliberation?

If the question were simply where citizens converse with each other about shared concerns, social issues, and public affairs, one would have to conclude that the workplace is a leading site of public discourse. People practice skills of deliberation at work—they communicate their views, listen to others, compromise, and often participate in making decisions. They learn and do those things, in part, through the communication that is part of performing the job. They also communicate about other workplace issues—matters of shared concern among workers who share terms and conditions of employment. Some of those workplace concerns have grown into major national policy issues such as health care coverage and costs, the minimum wage, family and medical leave, affirmative action, and workplace discrimination and harassment. But citizens also discuss public issues that have nothing to do with the workplace. Studies show that, among those with whom individuals discuss matters of importance, including politics, coworkers figure as frequently as spouses, and more often than any other category of nonrelatives.

At least if we are concerned about the participation of ordinary citizens, and especially if we value face-to-face discussions that reach across boundaries of family and neighborhood, we should regard the workplace as a significant deliberative forum. For it is clear that citizens deliberate with each other at work far more than in the fabled public square, and far more than through voluntary civic organizations. . . .

Deliberation is said to lead to better decisions, decisions that better approximate "the public good," or at least better accommodate the varying interests and values of a diverse public. . . . Through the process of deliberation, the citizens discover shared concerns and conflicts, and may come to understand and empathize with others who have different interests, experiences, and beliefs. As a result, they form political opinions and preferences that are more informed by and take greater account of the interests and experiences of others. . . . The sharing and interaction of these individual opinions and preferences creates a public opinion that, while not unitary, is more truly public than a simple aggregation of private, self-regarding preferences. . . . [C]ertain features of workplace discourse give it a distinctive role in the process of preference and opinion formation in a diverse democratic society.

First, conversations among coworkers are less private, less particularistic, and in that sense more public than conversations among family members and close friends. Because people neither choose nor grow up among their coworkers, the norms of workplace discourse may be closer to the norms of public discourse than are the norms of discourse among family and close friends. Most workplace discourse occupies an important intermediate point on the spectrum from the most particularistic to the most public. It is more public than conversations within families or voluntary associations that are based on shared identity or views, yet less public than self-conscious interventions in political decisionmaking. Perhaps in part for this reason, communication across these "weak ties" helps to weave private views and experiences into something more like "public opinion."

Second, and relatedly, conversations among coworkers are more likely to cross lines of social division, such as racial, ethnic, or cultural identity, than are conversations with family and nonwork friends. The importance of dialogue across group lines has gained some attention from the deliberative democrats. But the workplace adds a crucial element: the workplace fosters face-to-face conversation among people who have *both* different experiences, perspectives, and opinions *and* a reason to care about and get along with one another. The social science research . . . offers some empirical basis for the notion that the convergence of diversity and common ground that is found in the workplace (and almost exclusively there) is particularly likely to challenge individual preconceptions, biases, and ignorance about others. . . .

[M]any readers may rebel at the very idea that private economic firms have a role in democratic society and self-governance, and that the law has any business assigning or monitoring such a role. "The workplace is for work," it is said, not for political discourse or the cultivation of civic virtues or social bonds.

It is certainly fair to question efforts to use the workplace in the pursuit of societal and political ends, although we have a long tradition of doing just that. Moreover, efforts to use the workplace for noneconomic ends may run headlong into legitimate considerations of efficiency and productivity that are inescapable in discussions of workplace governance. . . .

Still, the claim that "the workplace is for work" calls for a response. Fortunately, the workplace is for much more than work. It is a locus of associational life and of human connections without which a diverse democratic society cannot flourish. And it is an institution that has proven amenable to reform through legal intervention. As we ponder the state of civil society, we should recognize and work to realize the civic potential that lies in the daily experience of working together.

NOTE

The Workplace as an Institution. Do you agree with Estlund's description of the functions the workplace as an institution plays in our society? If one were to accept her description, what types of employee speech should be protected given these functions? Which of these would trench most deeply on management prerogatives? Are any other values served by protecting employee speech rights? *See* CYNTHIA ESTLUND, WORKING TOGETHER: HOW WORKPLACE BONDS STRENGTHEN A DIVERSE DEMOCRACY (2003), for an elaboration of the argument that the workplace plays a crucial role in promoting deliberative democracy.

B. CONSTITUTIONAL PROTECTIONS

The First Amendment to the United States Constitution expressly protects freedom of speech, constraining the government from acting in ways that burden the right of individual citizens to speak. When a government employer acts to suppress or punish the speech of its employees, however, it acts in two capacities: as sovereign and as an employer. Should the constitutional concerns that animate the First Amendment mean that public employees enjoy the same speech rights as any other citizen? Or does the government's interest *as an employer* in managing its workplace defeat any claim of free speech rights by public employees? This section considers the First Amendment speech rights of public employees.

Pickering v. Board of Education, 391 U.S. 563 (1968). In *Pickering*, the United States Supreme Court laid out the basic framework for addressing the First Amendment claims of public employees. The plaintiff in that case, Marvin Pickering, was a schoolteacher who was dismissed after writing a letter to a local newspaper in connection with a proposed school bond issue. The letter criticized the Board of Education for its handling of prior bond issue proposals and its allocation of funds between athletic and educational programs. Pickering challenged his dismissal, claiming that his writing the letter was protected by the First and Fourteenth Amendments. In holding that Pickering's rights to freedom of speech were violated by his firing, the Supreme Court wrote:

> To the extent that [the decision by the Illinois Supreme Court rejecting Pickering's claim] may be read to suggest that teachers may constitution-ally be compelled to relinquish the First Amendment rights they would otherwise enjoy as citizens to comment on matters of public interest in connection with the operation of the public schools in which they work, it proceeds on a premise that has been unequivocally rejected in numerous prior decisions of this Court. E.g., *Wieman v. Updegraff*, 344 U.S. 183 (1952); *Shelton v. Tucker*, 364 U.S. 479 (1960); *Keyishian v. Board of Regents*, 385 U.S. 589 (1967). "[T]he theory that public employment which may be denied altogether may be subjected to any conditions, regardless of how unreasonable, has been uniformly rejected." *Keyishian v. Board of Regents*, 385 U.S. 589, 605–606 (1967). At the same time it cannot be gainsaid that the State has interests as an employer in regulating the speech of its employees that differ significantly from those it possesses in connection with regulation of the speech of the citizenry in general. The

problem in any case is to arrive at a balance between the interests of the teacher, as a citizen, in commenting upon matters of public concern and the interest of the State, as an employer, in promoting the efficiency of the public services it performs through its employees. . . .

[T]he question whether a school system requires additional funds is a matter of legitimate public concern on which the judgment of the school administration, including the School Board, cannot, in a society that leaves such questions to popular vote, be taken as conclusive. On such a question free and open debate is vital to informed decisionmaking by the electorate. Teachers are, as a class, the members of a community most likely to have informed and definite opinions as to how funds allotted to the operations of the schools should be spent. Accordingly, it is essential that they be able to speak out freely on such questions without fear of retaliatory dismissal. . . .

[I]t is apparent that the threat of dismissal from public employment is [ ] a potent means of inhibiting speech. . . . [I]n a case such as the present one, in which the fact of employment is only tangentially and insubstantially involved in the subject matter of the public communication made by a teacher, we conclude that it is necessary to regard the teacher as the member of the general public he seeks to be.

391 U.S. at 568, 571–72, 574.

Although the Court cautioned that "we do not deem it either appropriate or feasible to attempt to lay down a general standard against which all such statements may be judged," it indicated some of the factors it thought relevant in reaching the conclusion that it did in *Pickering*:

[Pickering's] statements are in no way directed towards any person with whom appellant would normally be in contact in the course of his daily work as a teacher. Thus no question of maintaining either discipline by immediate superiors or harmony among coworkers is presented here. Appellant's employment relationships with the Board and, to a somewhat lesser extent, with the superintendent are not the kind of close working relationships for which it can persuasively be claimed that personal loyalty and confidence are necessary to their proper functioning. Accordingly, to the extent that the Board's position here can be taken to suggest that even comments on matters of public concern that are substantially correct . . . may furnish grounds for dismissal if they are sufficiently critical in tone, we unequivocally reject it.[1]

---

[1] [n. 3] It is possible to conceive of some positions in public employment in which the need for confidentiality is so great that even completely correct public statements might furnish a permissible ground for dismissal. Likewise, positions in public employment in which the relationship between superior and subordinate is of such a personal and intimate nature that certain forms of public criticism of the superior by the subordinate would seriously undermine the effectiveness of the working relationship between them can also be imagined. We intimate no views as to how we would resolve any specific instances of such situations, but merely note that significantly different considerations would be involved in such cases.

Id. at 569–70. Finding it "essential" that teachers feel free to speak out on issues such as how a school district spends its funds, the Court concluded that the interests of the school administration in limiting Pickering's speech were outweighed by his interest in speaking on a matter of public concern.

Pickering established the basic framework for analyzing the free speech claims of government employees under the First Amendment by creating a balancing test that weighs the employee's and employer's interests. Over time, the Supreme Court has moved away from an open-ended balancing test, incorporating additional steps into the analysis. Consider how the next two cases, *Connick v. Myers* and *Garcetti v. Ceballos* add to the original *Pickering* analysis. Do these cases clarify the original balancing test? Or change it?

CONNICK v. MYERS
United States Supreme Court
461 U.S. 138 (1983)

JUSTICE WHITE delivered the opinion of the Court.

The respondent, Sheila Myers, was employed as an Assistant District Attorney in New Orleans for five and a half years. She served at the pleasure of petitioner Harry Connick, the District Attorney for Orleans Parish. During this period Myers competently performed her responsibilities of trying criminal cases.

In the early part of October, 1980, Myers was informed that she would be transferred to prosecute cases in a different section of the criminal court. Myers was strongly opposed to the proposed transfer and expressed her view to several of her supervisors, including Connick. Despite her objections, on October 6 Myers was notified that she was being transferred. Myers again spoke with Dennis Waldron, one of the first assistant district attorneys, expressing her reluctance to accept the transfer. A number of other office matters were discussed and Myers later testified that, in response to Waldron's suggestion that her concerns were not shared by others in the office, she informed him that she would do some research on the matter.

That night Myers prepared a questionnaire soliciting the views of her fellow staff members concerning office transfer policy, office morale, the need for a grievance committee, the level of confidence in supervisors, and whether employees felt pressured to work in political campaigns. Early the following morning, Myers typed and copied the questionnaire. She also met with Connick who urged her to accept the transfer. She said she would "consider" it. Connick then left the office. Myers then distributed the questionnaire to 15 assistant district attorneys. Shortly after noon, Dennis Waldron learned that Myers was distributing the survey. He immediately phoned Connick and informed him that Myers was creating a "mini-insurrection" within the office. Connick returned to the office and told Myers that she was being terminated because of her refusal to accept the transfer. She was also told that her distribution of the questionnaire was considered an act of insubordination. Connick particularly objected to the question which inquired whether employees "had confidence in and would rely on the word" of various superiors in the office, and to a question concerning pressure to work in political campaigns which he felt would be damaging if discovered by the press.

Myers filed suit under 42 U.S.C. § 1983, contending that her employment was wrongfully terminated because she had exercised her constitutionally-protected right of free speech. The District Court agreed, ordered Myers reinstated, and awarded backpay, damages, and attorney's fees. 507 F. Supp. 752 (E.D.La.1981). The District Court found that although Connick informed Myers that she was being fired because of her refusal to accept a transfer, the facts showed that the questionnaire was the real reason for her termination. The court then proceeded to hold that Myers' questionnaire involved matters of public concern and that the state had not "clearly demonstrated" that the survey "substantially interfered" with the operations of the District Attorney's office. [The Court of Appeals for the Fifth Circuit affirmed.]

. . . .

The District Court got off on the wrong foot in this case by initially finding that, "[t]aken as a whole, the issues presented in the questionnaire relate to the effective functioning of the District Attorney's Office and are matters of public importance and concern." 507 F. Supp., at 758. Connick contends at the outset that no balancing of interests is required in this case because Myers' questionnaire concerned only internal office matters and that such speech is not upon a matter of "public concern," as the term was used in *Pickering*. Although we do not agree that Myers' communication in this case was wholly without First Amendment protection, there is much force to Connick's submission. The repeated emphasis in *Pickering* on the right of a public employee "as a citizen, in commenting upon matters of public concern," was not accidental. This language, reiterated in all of *Pickering*'s progeny, reflects both the historical evolvement of the rights of public employees, and the common sense realization that government offices could not function if every employment decision became a constitutional matter. . . .

In . . . the precedents in which *Pickering* is rooted, the invalidated statutes and actions sought to suppress the rights of public employees to participate in public affairs. The issue was whether government employees could be prevented or "chilled" by the fear of discharge from joining political parties and other associations that certain public officials might find "subversive." The explanation for the Constitution's special concern with threats to the right of citizens to participate in political affairs is no mystery. The First Amendment "was fashioned to assure unfettered interchange of ideas for the bringing about of political and social changes desired by the people." *Roth v. United States*, 354 U.S. 476, 484 (1957). "[S]peech concerning public affairs is more than self-expression; it is the essence of self-government." *Garrison v. Louisiana*, 379 U.S. 64, 74–75, (1964). Accordingly, the Court has frequently reaffirmed that speech on public issues occupies the "highest rung of the hierarchy of First Amendment values," and is entitled to special protection. *NAACP v. Claiborne Hardware Co.*, [458 U.S. 886, 913] (1982); *Carey v. Brown*, 447 U.S. 455, 467 (1980).

. . . [I]f Myers' questionnaire cannot be fairly characterized as constituting speech on a matter of public concern, it is unnecessary for us to scrutinize the reasons for her discharge. When employee expression cannot be fairly considered as relating to any matter of political, social, or other concern to the community, government officials should enjoy wide latitude in managing their offices, without intrusive oversight by the judiciary in the name of the First Amendment. . . .

We hold . . . that when a public employee speaks not as a citizen upon matters of public concern, but instead as an employee upon matters only of personal interest, absent the most unusual circumstances, a federal court is not the appropriate forum in which to review the wisdom of a personnel decision taken by a public agency allegedly in reaction to the employee's behavior. Our responsibility is to ensure that citizens are not deprived of fundamental rights by virtue of working for the government; this does not require a grant of immunity for employee grievances not afforded by the First Amendment to those who do not work for the state.

Whether an employee's speech addresses a matter of public concern must be determined by the content, form, and context of a given statement, as revealed by the whole record. In this case, with but one exception, the questions posed by Myers to her coworkers do not fall under the rubric of matters of "public concern." We view the questions pertaining to the confidence and trust that Myers' coworkers possess in various supervisors, the level of office morale, and the need for a grievance committee as mere extensions of Myers' dispute over her transfer to another section of the criminal court. Unlike the dissent, we do not believe these questions are of public import in evaluating the performance of the District Attorney as an elected official. Myers did not seek to inform the public that the District Attorney's office was not discharging its governmental responsibilities in the investigation and prosecution of criminal cases. Nor did Myers seek to bring to light actual or potential wrongdoing or breach of public trust on the part of Connick and others. Indeed, the questionnaire, if released to the public, would convey no information at all other than the fact that a single employee is upset with the status quo. While discipline and morale in the workplace are related to an agency's efficient performance of its duties, the focus of Myers' questions is not to evaluate the performance of the office but rather to gather ammunition for another round of controversy with her superiors. These questions reflect one employee's dissatisfaction with a transfer and an attempt to turn that displeasure into a cause célèbre.

To presume that all matters which transpire within a government office are of public concern would mean that virtually every remark—and certainly every criticism directed at a public official—would plant the seed of a constitutional case. While as a matter of good judgment, public officials should be receptive to constructive criticism offered by their employees, the First Amendment does not require a public office to be run as a roundtable for employee complaints over internal office affairs.

One question in Myers' questionnaire, however, does touch upon a matter of public concern. Question 11 inquires if assistant district attorneys "ever feel pressured to work in political campaigns on behalf of office supported candidates." We have recently noted that official pressure upon employees to work for political candidates not of the worker's own choice constitutes a coercion of belief in violation of fundamental constitutional rights. *Branti v. Finkel*, 445 U.S. 507, 515–516, (1980); *Elrod v. Burns*, 427 U.S. 347, (1976). . . .

Because one of the questions in Myers' survey touched upon a matter of public concern, and contributed to her discharge we must determine whether Connick was justified in discharging Myers. . . . *Pickering* unmistakably states . . . that the state's burden in justifying a particular discharge varies depending upon the nature of the employee's expression. Although such particularized balancing is difficult, the courts must reach the most appropriate possible balance of the competing interests.

burden for discharge

. . . We agree with the District Court that there is no demonstration here that the questionnaire impeded Myers' ability to perform her responsibilities. The District Court was also correct to recognize that "it is important to the efficient and successful operation of the District Attorney's office for Assistants to maintain close working relationships with their superiors." 507 F. Supp., at 759. Connick's judgment, and apparently also that of his first assistant Dennis Waldron, who characterized Myers' actions as causing a "mini-insurrection", was that Myers' questionnaire was an act of insubordination which interfered with working relationships. When close working relationships are essential to fulfilling public responsibilities, a wide degree of deference to the employer's judgment is appropriate. Furthermore, we do not see the necessity for an employer to allow events to unfold to the extent that the disruption of the office and the destruction of working relationships is manifest before taking action. We caution that a stronger showing may be necessary if the employee's speech more substantially involved matters of public concern. . . .

factors to consider w/ discharge

Also relevant is the manner, time, and place in which the questionnaire was distributed. . . . Here the questionnaire was prepared, and distributed at the office; the manner of distribution required not only Myers to leave her work but for others to do the same in order that the questionnaire be completed. Although some latitude in when official work is performed is to be allowed when professional employees are involved, and Myers did not violate announced office policy, the fact that Myers, unlike Pickering, exercised her rights to speech at the office supports Connick's fears that the functioning of his office was endangered.

context

Finally, the context in which the dispute arose is also significant. This is not a case where an employee, out of purely academic interest, circulated a questionnaire so as to obtain useful research. Myers acknowledges that it is no coincidence that the questionnaire followed upon the heels of the transfer notice. When employee speech concerning office policy arises from an employment dispute concerning the very application of that policy to the speaker, additional weight must be given to the supervisor's view that the employee has threatened the authority of the employer to run the office. . . .

Myers' questionnaire touched upon matters of public concern in only a most limited sense; her survey, in our view, is most accurately characterized as an employee grievance concerning internal office policy. The limited First Amendment interest involved here does not require that Connick tolerate action which he reasonably believed would disrupt the office, undermine his authority, and destroy close working relationships. Myers' discharge therefore did not offend the First Amendment. . . .

Reversed.

JUSTICE BRENNAN, with whom JUSTICE MARSHALL, JUSTICE BLACKMUN, and JUSTICE STEVENS join, dissenting.

. . . The balancing test articulated in *Pickering* comes into play only when a public employee's speech implicates the government's interests as an employer. When public employees engage in expression unrelated to their employment while away from the work place, their First Amendment rights are, of course, no different from those of the general public. Thus, whether a public employee's speech addresses a matter of public concern is relevant to the constitutional inquiry only when the statements at issue—by virtue of their content or the context in which they were made—may have an adverse impact on the government's ability to perform its duties efficiently.[2]

The Court's decision today is flawed in three respects. First, the Court distorts the balancing analysis required under *Pickering* by suggesting that one factor, the context in which a statement is made, is to be weighed *twice*—first in determining whether an employee's speech addresses a matter of public concern and then in deciding whether the statement adversely affected the government's interest as an employer. Second, in concluding that the effect of respondent's personnel policies on employee morale and the work performance of the District Attorney's Office is not a matter of public concern, the Court impermissibly narrows the class of subjects on which public employees may speak out without fear of retaliatory dismissal. Third, the Court misapplies the *Pickering* balancing test in holding that Myers could constitutionally be dismissed for circulating a questionnaire addressed to at least one subject that *was* "a matter of interest to the community," in the absence of evidence that her conduct disrupted the efficient functioning of the District Attorney's Office.

. . . The standard announced by the Court suggests that the manner and context in which a statement is made must be weighed on *both* sides of the *Pickering* balance. It is beyond dispute that how and where a public employee expresses his views are relevant in the second half of the *Pickering* inquiry—determining whether the employee's speech adversely affects the government's interests as an employer. . . . But the fact that a public employee has chosen to express his views in private has nothing whatsoever to do with the first half of the *Pickering* calculus—whether those views relate to a matter of public concern. . . . [W]hether a particular statement by a public employee is addressed to a subject of public concern does not depend on where it was said or why. The First Amendment affords special protection to speech that may inform public debate about how our society is to be governed—regardless of whether it actually becomes the subject of a public controversy. . . .

---

[2] [n. 1] Although the Court's opinion states that "if Myers' questionnaire cannot be fairly characterized as constituting speech on a matter of public concern, it is unnecessary for us to scrutinize the reasons for her discharge," I do not understand it to imply that a governmental employee's First Amendment rights outside the employment context are limited to speech on matters of public concern. To the extent that the Court's opinion may be read to suggest that the dismissal of a public employee for speech unrelated to a subject of public interest does not implicate First Amendment interests, I disagree, because our cases establish that public employees enjoy the full range of First Amendment rights guaranteed to members of the general public. Under the balancing test articulated in *Pickering*, however, the government's burden to justify such a dismissal may be lighter.

. . . I would hold that Myers' questionnaire addressed matters of public concern because it discussed subjects that could reasonably be expected to be of interest to persons seeking to develop informed opinions about the manner in which the Orleans Parish District Attorney, an elected official charged with managing a vital governmental agency, discharges his responsibilities. The questionnaire sought primarily to obtain information about the impact of the recent transfers on morale in the District Attorney's Office. It is beyond doubt that personnel decisions that adversely affect discipline and morale may ultimately impair an agency's efficient performance of its duties. Because I believe the First Amendment protects the right of public employees to discuss such matters so that the public may be better informed about how their elected officials fulfill their responsibilities, I would affirm the District Court's conclusion that the questionnaire related to matters of public importance and concern. . . .

public concern [handwritten margin note]

Although the Court finds most of Myers' questionnaire unrelated to matters of public interest, it does hold that one question—asking whether Assistants felt pressured to work in political campaigns on behalf of office-supported candidates—addressed a matter of public importance and concern. The Court also recognizes that this determination of public interest must weigh heavily in the balancing of competing interests required by *Pickering.* Having gone that far however, the Court misapplies the *Pickering* test and holds—against our previous authorities—that a public employer's mere apprehension that speech will be disruptive justifies suppression of that speech when all the objective evidence suggests that those fears are essentially unfounded. . . .

Such extreme deference to the employer's judgment is not appropriate when public employees voice critical views concerning the operations of the agency for which they work. Although an employer's determination that an employee's statements have undermined essential working relationships must be carefully weighed in the *Pickering* balance, we must bear in mind that "the threat of dismissal from public employment is . . . a potent means of inhibiting speech." Pickering, *supra*, at 574. If the employer's judgment is to be controlling, public employees will not speak out when what they have to say is critical of their supervisors. In order to protect public employees' First Amendment right to voice critical views on issues of public importance, the courts must make their own appraisal of the effects of the speech in question. . . .

NOTES

1. **Competing Interests.** What values underlie the First Amendment? To what extent are these values threatened by a government employer using its dismissal power in retaliation for employee speech? What competing interests does the government employer have in regulating employee speech? In *Pickering*, should the fact that the dismissed employee was a teacher speaking out about education entitle him to more or less protection?

2. **Matters of Public Concern.** *Connick* added a gloss to the *Pickering* balancing test, creating a threshold requirement that public employees first show that their speech was on "a matter of public concern" when invoking the First Amendment to challenge their dismissal from public employment. The addition of

a threshold test in *Connick* means that courts are given the task of determining whether particular employee speech is on a matter of public concern—and therefore protected—or not. In *Connick*, the majority and the dissent reached very different conclusions about the nature of Myers' speech. How do their respective approaches to analyzing this question differ, and how do they lead them to their differing conclusions? Should it matter whether the public has taken an interest in the subject? *See Connick*, 461 U.S. at 160 n.2 (Brennan, J., dissenting) (arguing that Myers' statements were matters of public concern because the internal operations of the DA's office were often the subject of local news stories).

The Court in *Connick* distinguished speech on matters of public concern from "employee complaints over internal office affairs." Does that mean that all employee speech regarding internal office matters will be unprotected? A number of lower courts have said no. *See, e.g., LeFande v. District of Columbia*, 613 F.3d 1155, 1161 (D.C. Cir. 2010) ("we reject the proposition that a personnel matter per se cannot be a matter of public concern, even if it may seriously affect the public welfare.") If speech about workplace matters is sometimes protected, how should a court determine when that speech is about a matter of public concern and not a purely private grievance? What if an employee speaks as a representative of a union? Or an association of employees raises a group complaint? *See, e.g., Cromer v. Brown*, 88 F.3d 1315 (4th Cir. 1996) (finding that complaint from association of African-American officers regarding allegations of systemic racial discrimination addressed matters of public concern). Is speech undertaken by or on behalf of a group of employees more likely to be on a matter of public concern?

The fact that the speech occurred at work is not dispositive either. Consider the case of Ardith McPherson, a probationary clerical employee in a local sheriff's office, who was fired for comments she made at work. *Rankin v. McPherson*, 483 U.S. 378 (1987). After hearing of an assassination attempt on President Reagan's life in 1981, she remarked, "If they go for him again, I hope they get him." McPherson's comments were made in a private conversation with her boyfriend in a room to which the public did not have access. She clearly did not intend her remark to inform public debate, nor did she even realize that it would be heard by anyone other than her boyfriend; nevertheless, the Court held that it was speech on a matter of public concern because it was made in the context of a conversation critical of the President's policies. *Id.* at 386. Finding no evidence that her statement interfered with the efficient functioning of the office, the Court upheld her First Amendment challenge to her dismissal. *Id.* at 388–89. In dissent, Justice Scalia complained that law enforcement employees should not be permitted to "ride with the cops and cheer for the robbers." *Id.* at 394. He argued that McPherson's statement, far from addressing matters of public concern, was "only one step removed from statements that we have previously held entitled to no First Amendment protection"—statements such as threats of violence, "fighting words" and epithets or personal abuse. *Id.* at 397–98. Do you agree that McPherson's speech was more deserving of protection than Sheila Myers'? Should it matter that McPherson's speech occurred in a private conversation?

3. **Off-Duty Speech.** The framework established in *Pickering* and *Connick* is motivated by concerns for the efficiency of the government workplace. But what about cases in which a public employee alleges that he was retaliated against for

speech that occurred off-duty and is unconnected with internal workplace matters? Suppose, for example, that a clerical employee in a state's Department of Motor Vehicles is fired because her supervisor learns that she is an activist in the anti-abortion movement, a position with which he disagrees? What if the discharge is motivated not by the employee's political activism, but rather participation in an artistic performance that he finds distasteful?

Because *Connick* required that speech be on a matter of public concern in order to be protected by the First Amendment, courts sometimes stretch to fit particular speech within the meaning of "public concern." For example, in *Berger v. Battaglia*, 779 F.2d 992 (4th Cir. 1985), the Court of Appeals held that a police officer's off-duty impersonation of Al Jolson in blackface was protected by the First Amendment. The court interpreted *Connick*'s "public concern" test as designed "to identify a narrow spectrum of employee speech that is not entitled even to qualified protection [rather than to] set outer limits on all that is." *Id.* at 998. Accordingly, because the plaintiff's speech was not "a private personnel grievance" of purely "personal concern," it was entitled to qualified protection under the *Pickering* balancing test.

However, the United States Supreme Court later explained that "public concern is something that is a subject of legitimate news interest; that is, a subject of general interest and of value and concern to the public at the time of publication." *City of San Diego v. Roe*, 543 U.S. 77, 83–84 (2004). The case involved a challenge by a police officer terminated because of his performance in and sale of sexually explicit videos. The Court found that the plaintiff's expression did not qualify as speech on a matter of public concern, and that *Pickering* balancing therefore did not come into play. *Id.* at 526.

Should the sorts of public employee speech and expression at issue in *Berger* and *Roe* be protected from employer retaliation? If so, is protection warranted because the speech is on matters of public concern or for some other reason? Conversely, if the plaintiffs in *Berger* and *Roe* do not warrant protection, is that because there are no First Amendment interests at stake? Or is it because the government's interest as an employer changes the equation?

4. **"Liking" as Speech.** Cases such as *Berger* and *Roe* are likely to arise with increasing frequency because of the spread of social media. As more and more people rely on social media as a means of communication and self-expression, employers are more likely to learn about their employees' activities and non-work related views and may be tempted to take action in response to their employees' off-duty expression. As discussed in Chapter 7, *supra*, depending upon the circumstances, an employee may be able to challenge her employer's actions in accessing or monitoring her online communications. However, if the communication is intended to be public, no privacy claims will lie. Instead, public employees may allege that any adverse action their government employer takes because of their online activities violates their First Amendment rights. For example, in a recent case, an employee of a sheriff's office alleged that he was retaliated against after he "liked" the campaign page of a rival candidate for sheriff on Facebook. The Fourth Circuit held that "liking" a page on Facebook was a form of speech protected by the First Amendment. *Bland v. Roberts*, 730 F.3d 368 (4th Cir. 2013).

5. Loyalty or Voice? The *Pickering/Connick* test requires balancing the interests of the public employee in speaking against "the interest of the State, as an employer, in promoting the efficiency of the public services it performs through its employees." 461 U.S. at 140. Both Pickering and Connick were fired because of speech critical of their government employers. Marion Crain and Ken Matheny argue that the public employee speech cases reflect the influence of "the traditional master-servant image of the employment relation borrowed from the common law, in which management is entitled to demand loyalty from its employees." Ken Matheny & Marion Crain, *Disloyal Workers and the "Un-American" Labor Law*, 82 N.C. L. REV. 1735 (2004). The result, they argue, is that the notion of employees' duty of loyalty drives the analysis in these cases at the expense of the constitutional value placed on exercising "voice."

6. Political Expression. The Court in *Connick* found that the question whether assistant district attorneys ever felt pressure to work on political campaigns did touch on a matter of public concern, citing its earlier decisions in *Elrod v. Burns*, 427 U.S. 347 (1976), and *Branti v. Finkel*, 445 U.S. 507 (1980). Those cases involved First Amendment challenges to patronage practices, by which newly elected officials would replace incumbent employees with members or supporters of their own political party. The Supreme Court has explained the rationale behind its political patronage cases:

> In Elrod, *supra*, we decided that a newly elected Democratic sheriff could not constitutionally engage in the patronage practice of replacing certain office staff with members of his own party "when the existing employees lack or fail to obtain requisite support from, or fail to affiliate with, that party." [*Elrod v. Burns*], 427 U.S., at 351, 373 (plurality opinion), and 375 (Stewart, J., joined by Blackmun, J., concurring in judgment). The plurality explained that conditioning public employment on the provision of support for the favored political party "unquestionably inhibits protected belief and association." *Id.*, at 359. It reasoned that conditioning employment on political activity pressures employees to pledge political allegiance to a party with which they prefer not to associate, to work for the election of political candidates they do not support, and to contribute money to be used to further policies with which they do not agree. The latter, the plurality noted, had been recognized by this Court as "tantamount to coerced belief." *Id.*, 427 U.S., at 355 (citing *Buckley v. Valeo*, 424 U.S. 1 (1976)). At the same time, employees are constrained from joining, working for or contributing to the political party and candidates of their own choice. Elrod, *supra*, 427 U.S., at 355–356. "[P]olitical belief and association constitute the core of those activities protected by the First Amendment,"
>
> . . . .
>
> The plurality acknowledged that a government has a significant interest in ensuring that it has effective and efficient employees. It expressed doubt, however, that "mere difference of political persuasion motivates poor performance" and concluded that, in any case, the government can ensure employee effectiveness and efficiency through the less drastic means of discharging staff members whose work is inadequate. 427 U.S., at 365–366. The plurality also found that a government can meet its need for politically

loyal employees to implement its policies by the less intrusive measure of dismissing, on political grounds, only those employees in policymaking positions. *Id.*, at 367. . . . Patronage, it explained, "can result in the entrenchment of one or a few parties to the exclusion of others" and "is a very effective impediment to the associational and speech freedoms which are essential to a meaningful system of democratic government." *Id.*, at 368–370.

Rutan v. Republican Party, 497 U.S. 62, 68–70 (1990).

Rutan involved a similar challenge to certain employment practices instituted by Governor James Thompson of Illinois in the 1980s. By executive order, Governor Thompson imposed a hiring freeze for all state government positions under his control—approximately 60,000 positions—and required that his office approve any "exceptions." These practices effectively created a patronage system that limited hiring, promotions, transfers and recalls after layoffs to individuals supported by the Republican Party. Finding that "there are deprivations less harsh than dismissal that nevertheless press state employees and applicants to conform their beliefs and associations to some state-selected orthodoxy," *id.* at 75, the Court concluded that the challenged practices violated the First Amendment.

Although non policy-making government employees are protected under the First Amendment against patronage practices that might otherwise coerce their political beliefs and associations, many of these same employees have limited rights of political expression because of their government jobs. The Hatch Act, 5 U.S.C. §§ 7321–7326, prohibits covered federal employees from engaging in specified forms of partisan political activity, such as soliciting political contributions or being candidates for public office in partisan elections. 5 U.S.C. § 7323(a)(2), (3). The Supreme Court upheld the constitutionality of an even stricter version of the Act against a First Amendment challenge, finding that the restrictions were justified by "the obviously important interests sought to be served," including ensuring that employment and advancement were based on merit, not politics, and avoiding the appearance of partisan administration of the laws. *U.S. Civil Serv. Comm'n v. Nat'l Ass'n of Letter Carriers*, 413 U.S. 548, 564–66 (1973). The Hatch Act also places restrictions on the political activities of state and local employees employed in connection with federally financed programs. 5 U.S.C. §§ 1501–08. In addition, the states have legislation similar to the Hatch Act that restricts the political activities of state employees. The Supreme Court has also upheld the constitutionality of such state statutes. *See Broadrick v. Oklahoma*, 413 U.S. 601 (1973). On the other hand, legislation may not broadly prohibit government employees' non-partisan speech and expressive activity. *See United States v. National Treasury Employees Union*, 513 U.S. 454 (1995) (holding that statute prohibiting federal employees from receiving honoraria for speeches and articles unduly burdened their First Amendment right).

   7. Statutory Protections for Public Employees. Because Sheila Myers "served at the pleasure" of the District Attorney, she had no established expectation of continued employment, making her the public sector equivalent of an at-will employee. Although her employer was not required to have cause to fire her, it could not do so for a reason that violated her constitutional rights. Many public employees, however, are also covered by civil service laws that protect certain categories of public employees from discharge without cause. Because civil service laws typically provide some sort of procedure for challenging dismissals, as well as substantive protections limiting the grounds for which an employee may be discharged, they indirectly protect public employee speech rights by requiring that discharges be justified by legitimate work-related reasons.

GARCETTI v. CEBALLOS
United States Supreme Court
547 U.S. 410 (2006)

JUSTICE KENNEDY delivered the opinion of the Court.

I

Respondent Richard Ceballos has been employed since 1989 as a deputy district attorney for the Los Angeles County District Attorney's Office. During the period relevant to this case, Ceballos was a calendar deputy in the office's Pomona branch, and in this capacity he exercised certain supervisory responsibilities over other lawyers. In February 2000, a defense attorney contacted Ceballos about a pending criminal case. The defense attorney said there were inaccuracies in an affidavit used to obtain a critical search warrant. . . . After examining the affidavit and visiting the location it described, Ceballos determined the affidavit contained serious misrepresentations. . . . He relayed his findings to his supervisors, petitioners Carol Najera and Frank Sundstedt, and followed up by preparing a disposition memorandum. The memo explained Ceballos' concerns and recommended dismissal of the case. . . . Based on Ceballos' statements, a meeting was held to discuss the affidavit. Attendees included Ceballos, Sundstedt, and Najera, as well as the warrant affiant and other employees from the sheriff's department. The meeting allegedly became heated, with one lieutenant sharply criticizing Ceballos for his handling of the case.

Despite Ceballos' concerns, Sundstedt decided to proceed with the prosecution, pending disposition of the defense motion [challenging the warrant]. . . . [T]he trial court rejected the challenge to the warrant.

Ceballos claims that in the aftermath of these events he was subjected to a series of retaliatory employment actions. The actions included reassignment from his calendar deputy position to a trial deputy position, transfer to another courthouse, and denial of a promotion. . . . Ceballos sued in the United States District Court for the Central District of California. . . . He alleged petitioners violated the First and Fourteenth Amendments by retaliating against him based on his memo [recommending dismissal of the case]. . . .

[T]he District Court granted [summary judgment for defendants]. . . . Noting that Ceballos wrote his memo pursuant to his employment duties, the court concluded he was not entitled to First Amendment protection for the memo's contents. . . . The Court of Appeals for the Ninth Circuit reversed. . . . [It] determined that Ceballos' memo, which recited what he thought to be governmental

misconduct, was "inherently a matter of public concern." . . . Having concluded that *PH*
Ceballos' memo satisfied the public-concern requirement, the Court of Appeals
proceeded to balance Ceballos' interest in his speech against his supervisors'
interest in responding to it. The court struck the balance in Ceballos' favor, noting
that petitioners "failed even to suggest disruption or inefficiency in the workings of
the District Attorney's Office" as a result of the memo. . . . We granted certiorari,
and we now reverse.

II

gov't Ers

 . . . When a citizen enters government service, the citizen by necessity must
accept certain limitations on his or her freedom. *See, e.g., Waters v. Churchill*, 511
U.S. 661, 671 (1994) (plurality opinion) ("[T]he government as employer indeed has
far broader powers than does the government as sovereign"). Government employers, like private employers, need a significant degree of control over their
employees' words and actions; without it, there would be little chance for the
efficient provision of public services. Public employees, moreover, often occupy
trusted positions in society. When they speak out, they can express views that
contravene governmental policies or impair the proper performance of governmental functions.

At the same time, the Court has recognized that a citizen who works for the
government is nonetheless a citizen. The First Amendment limits the ability of a
public employer to leverage the employment relationship to restrict, incidentally or
intentionally, the liberties employees enjoy in their capacities as private citizens. So
long as employees are speaking as citizens about matters of public concern, they
must face only those speech restrictions that are necessary for their employers to
operate efficiently and effectively.

PP

The Court's employee-speech jurisprudence protects, of course, the constitutional rights of public employees. Yet the First Amendment interests at stake
extend beyond the individual speaker. The Court has acknowledged the importance
of promoting the public's interest in receiving the well-informed views of government employees engaging in civic discussion. . . . The Court's approach acknowledged the necessity for informed, vibrant dialogue in a democratic society. . . . *See,
e.g., San Diego v. Roe*, 543 U.S. 77, 82 (2004) *(per curiam)* ("Were [public
employees] not able to speak on [the operation of their employers], the community
would be deprived of informed opinions on important public issues. The interest at
stake is as much the public's interest in receiving informed opinion as it is the
employee's own right to disseminate it"). . . .

III

here

 . . . Respondent Ceballos believed the affidavit used to obtain a search warrant
contained serious misrepresentations. He conveyed his opinion and recommendation in a memo to his supervisor. That Ceballos expressed his views inside his office,
rather than publicly, is not dispositive. Employees in some cases may receive First
Amendment protection for expressions made at work. *See, e.g., Givhan v. Western
Line Consol. School Dist.*, 439 U.S. 410 (1979). . . . The memo concerned the

subject matter of Ceballos' employment, but this, too, is nondispositive. The First Amendment protects some expressions related to the speaker's job. . . . The controlling factor in Ceballos' case is that his expressions were made pursuant to his duties as a calendar deputy. That consideration—the fact that Ceballos spoke as a prosecutor fulfilling a responsibility to advise his supervisor about how best to proceed with a pending case—distinguishes Ceballos' case from those in which the First Amendment provides protection against discipline. We hold that when public employees make statements pursuant to their official duties, the employees are not speaking as citizens for First Amendment purposes, and the Constitution does not insulate their communications from employer discipline.

Ceballos wrote his disposition memo because that is part of what he, as a calendar deputy, was employed to do. It is immaterial whether he experienced some personal gratification from writing the memo; his First Amendment rights do not depend on his job satisfaction. The significant point is that the memo was written pursuant to Ceballos' official duties. Restricting speech that owes its existence to a public employee's professional responsibilities does not infringe any liberties the employee might have enjoyed as a private citizen. It simply reflects the exercise of employer control over what the employer itself has commissioned or created. . . .

Ceballos did not act as a citizen when he went about conducting his daily professional activities, such as supervising attorneys, investigating charges, and preparing filings. In the same way he did not speak as a citizen by writing a memo that addressed the proper disposition of a pending criminal case. When he went to work and performed the tasks he was paid to perform, Ceballos acted as a government employee. The fact that his duties sometimes required him to speak or write does not mean his supervisors were prohibited from evaluating his performance.

This result is consistent with our precedents' attention to the potential societal value of employee speech. Refusing to recognize First Amendment claims based on government employees' work product does not prevent them from participating in public debate. The employees retain the prospect of constitutional protection for their contributions to the civic discourse. This prospect of protection, however, does not invest them with a right to perform their jobs however they see fit.

Our holding likewise is supported by the emphasis of our precedents on affording government employers sufficient discretion to manage their operations. Employers have heightened interests in controlling speech made by an employee in his or her professional capacity. Official communications have official consequences, creating a need for substantive consistency and clarity. Supervisors must ensure that their employees' official communications are accurate, demonstrate sound judgment, and promote the employer's mission. Ceballos' memo is illustrative. It demanded the attention of his supervisors and led to a heated meeting with employees from the sheriff's department. If Ceballos' superiors thought his memo was inflammatory or misguided, they had the authority to take proper corrective action.

Ceballos' proposed contrary rule, adopted by the Court of Appeals, would commit state and federal courts to a new, permanent, and intrusive role, mandating judicial oversight of communications between and among government employees and their superiors in the course of official business. . . . When an employee speaks as a

Ceballos proposed rule

citizen addressing a matter of public concern, the First Amendment requires a delicate balancing of the competing interests surrounding the speech and its consequences. When, however, the employee is simply performing his or her job duties, there is no warrant for a similar degree of scrutiny. . . .

. . . Employees who make public statements outside the course of performing their official duties retain some possibility of First Amendment protection because that is the kind of activity engaged in by citizens who do not work for the government. The same goes for writing a letter to a local newspaper, or discussing politics with a co-worker. When a public employee speaks pursuant to employment responsibilities, however, there is no relevant analogue to speech by citizens who are not government employees.

. . . We reject . . . the suggestion that employers can restrict employees' rights by creating excessively broad job descriptions. The proper inquiry is a practical one. Formal job descriptions often bear little resemblance to the duties an employee actually is expected to perform, and the listing of a given task in an employee's written job description is neither necessary nor sufficient to demonstrate that conducting the task is within the scope of the employee's professional duties for First Amendment purposes. . . .

IV

Exposing governmental inefficiency and misconduct is a matter of considerable significance. As the Court noted in *Connick*, public employers should, "as a matter of good judgment," be "receptive to constructive criticism offered by their employees." 461 U.S., at 149. The dictates of sound judgment are reinforced by the powerful network of legislative enactments—such as whistle-blower protection laws and labor codes—available to those who seek to expose wrongdoing. Cases involving government attorneys implicate additional safeguards in the form of, for example, rules of conduct and constitutional obligations apart from the First Amendment. *See, e.g.*, CAL. RULE PROF. CONDUCT 5-110 (2005) ("A member in government service shall not institute or cause to be instituted criminal charges when the member knows or should know that the charges are not supported by probable cause"); *Brady v. Maryland*, 373 U.S. 83 (1963). These imperatives, as well as obligations arising from any other applicable constitutional provisions and mandates of the criminal and civil laws, protect employees and provide checks on supervisors who would order unlawful or otherwise inappropriate actions. . . .

The judgment of the Court of Appeals is reversed, and the case is remanded for proceedings consistent with this opinion.

[The opinion of JUSTICE STEVENS, dissenting, is omitted.]

JUSTICE SOUTER, with whom JUSTICE STEVENS and JUSTICE GINSBURG join, dissenting.

. . . Open speech by a private citizen on a matter of public importance lies at the heart of expression subject to protection by the First Amendment. At the other extreme, a statement by a government employee complaining about nothing beyond treatment under personnel rules raises no greater claim to constitutional protection against retaliatory response than the remarks of a private employee. See *Connick v. Myers*, 461 U.S. 138, 147 (1983). In between these points lies a public employee's speech unwelcome to the government but on a significant public issue. Such an employee speaking as a citizen, that is, with a citizen's interest, is protected from reprisal unless the statements are too damaging to the government's capacity to conduct public business to be justified by any individual or public benefit thought to flow from the statements. . . .

This significant, albeit qualified, protection of public employees who irritate the government is understood to flow from the First Amendment, in part, because a government paycheck does nothing to eliminate the value to an individual of speaking on public matters, and there is no good reason for categorically discounting a speaker's interest in commenting on a matter of public concern just because the government employs him. Still, the First Amendment safeguard rests on something more, being the value to the public of receiving the opinions and information that a public employee may disclose. "Government employees are often in the best position to know what ails the agencies for which they work." *Waters v. Churchill*, 511 U.S. 661, 674 (1994).

. . . In *Givhan v. Western Line Consol. School Dist.*, 439 U.S. 410 (1979) we followed *Pickering* when a teacher was fired for complaining to a superior about the racial composition of the school's administrative, cafeteria, and library staffs. . . . The difference between a case like *Givhan* and this one is that the subject of Ceballos's speech fell within the scope of his job responsibilities, whereas choosing personnel was not what the teacher was hired to do. The effect of the majority's constitutional line between these two cases, then, is that a *Givhan* schoolteacher is protected when complaining to the principal about hiring policy, but a school personnel officer would not be if he protested that the principal disapproved of hiring minority job applicants. This is an odd place to draw a distinction[3]. . . .

. . . The need for [*Pickering* balancing] hardly disappears when an employee speaks on matters his job requires him to address; rather, it seems obvious that the individual and public value of such speech is no less, and may well be greater, when the employee speaks pursuant to his duties in addressing a subject he knows intimately for the very reason that it falls within his duties.[4]

As for the importance of such speech to the individual, it stands to reason that a citizen may well place a very high value on a right to speak on the public issues he decides to make the subject of his work day after day. . . . Would anyone deny that

---

[3] [n. 1] It seems stranger still in light of the majority's concession of some First Amendment protection when a public employee repeats statements made pursuant to his duties but in a separate, public forum or in a letter to a newspaper.

[4] [n. 2] I am pessimistic enough to expect that one response to the Court's holding will be moves by government employers to expand stated job descriptions to include more official duties and so exclude even some currently protectable speech from First Amendment purview. . . . The majority's response, that the enquiry to determine duties is a "practical one," does not alleviate this concern. It sets out a standard that will not discourage government employers from setting duties expansively, but will engender litigation to decide which stated duties were actual and which were merely formal.

a prosecutor like Richard Ceballos may claim the interest of any citizen in speaking out against a rogue law enforcement officer, simply because his job requires him to express a judgment about the officer's performance? (But the majority says the First Amendment gives Ceballos no protection, even if his judgment in this case was sound and appropriately expressed.)

. . . .

[Our recognition in *Pickering*] "that public employees are often the members of the community who are likely to have informed opinions as to the operations of their public employers, operations which are of substantial concern to the public," . . . is not a whit less true when an employee's job duties require him to speak about such things: when, for example, a public auditor speaks on his discovery of embezzlement of public funds, when a building inspector makes an obligatory report of an attempt to bribe him, or when a law enforcement officer expressly balks at a superior's order to violate constitutional rights he is sworn to protect. (The majority, however, places all these speakers beyond the reach of First Amendment protection against retaliation.)

Nothing, then, accountable on the individual and public side of the *Pickering* balance changes when an employee speaks "pursuant" to public duties. On the side of the government employer, however, something is different, and to this extent, I agree with the majority of the Court. The majority is rightly concerned that the employee who speaks out on matters subject to comment in doing his own work has the greater leverage to create office uproars and fracture the government's authority to set policy to be carried out coherently through the ranks. . . .

But why do the majority's concerns, which we all share, require categorical exclusion of First Amendment protection against any official retaliation for things said on the job? Is it not possible to respect the unchallenged individual and public interests in the speech through a *Pickering* balance without drawing the strange line I mentioned before? This is, to be sure, a matter of judgment, but the judgment has to account for the undoubted value of speech to those, and by those, whose specific public job responsibilities bring them face to face with wrongdoing and incompetence in government, who refuse to avert their eyes and shut their mouths. And it has to account for the need actually to disrupt government if its officials are corrupt or dangerously incompetent. . . .

. . . [T]he extent of the government's legitimate authority over subjects of speech required by a public job can be recognized in advance by setting in effect a minimum heft for comments with any claim to outweigh it. Thus, the risks to the government are great enough for us to hold from the outset that an employee commenting on subjects in the course of duties should not prevail on balance unless he speaks on a matter of unusual importance and satisfies high standards of responsibility in the way he does it. . . . [O]nly comment on official dishonesty, deliberately unconstitutional action, other serious wrongdoing, or threats to health and safety can weigh out in an employee's favor. . . .

[T]he majority's position comes with no guarantee against factbound litigation over whether a public employee's statements were made "pursuant to . . . official duties." In fact, the majority invites such litigation by describing the enquiry as a "practical one," apparently based on the totality of employment circumstances. . . .

. . . [The majority also argues] that the First Amendment has little or no work to do here owing to an assertedly comprehensive complement of state and national statutes protecting government whistle-blowers from vindictive bosses. . . . [T]he combined variants of statutory whistle-blower definitions and protections add up to a patchwork, not a showing that worries may be remitted to legislatures for relief. Some state statutes protect all government workers, including the employees of municipalities and other subdivisions; others stop at state employees. Some limit protection to employees who tell their bosses before they speak out; others forbid bosses from imposing any requirement to warn. As for the federal Whistleblower Protection Act of 1989, 5 U.S.C. § 1213 *et seq.*, [it has been interpreted in ways that significantly limit its protections of federal government employee whistleblowers.]

[The dissenting opinion of JUSTICE BREYER is omitted.]

NOTES

1. **Speaking as an Employee vs. Speaking as a Citizen**. Do you agree with the Court that it makes a difference, as a matter of Constitutional right, whether a public employee was punished for speaking as an employee as opposed to speaking as a citizen? Are the two types of speech mutually exclusive? For example, does the fact that a public auditor's job involves reporting on government accounting practices mean that she cannot also be acting as a citizen when she speaks up about financial wrongdoing that she has uncovered? Given that a great deal now rides on the distinction between speech as an employee and speech as a citizen, consider whether the Court has created incentives for public employers or employees to change what they do.

2. **A Revised Test**. The lower federal courts have interpreted *Garcetti* as creating an additional test that must be met before applying the *Pickering* balancing test. As the Fifth Circuit wrote, *Garcetti* "added a threshold layer to the *Pickering* balancing test" which focuses on the role of the speaker at the time the speech was made. *Williams v. Dallas Indep. Sch. Dist.*, 480 F.3d 689 (5th Cir. 2007). As that court wrote, "[e]ven if the speech is of great social importance, it is not protected by the First Amendment so long as it was made pursuant to the worker's official duties." *Id.* On the other hand, even if the employee's speech was not part of her official job duties and was made "as a citizen," it must still meet the *Connick* "public concern" test before the *Pickering* balancing test will be applied. After *Garcetti* and *Connick*, the lower courts have created multi-part tests for analyzing when a public employees' speech is protected. The Third Circuit, for example, has stated that First Amendment protections apply when "(1) in making [the statement], the employee spoke as a citizen; (2) the statement involved a matter of public concern, and (3) the government employer did not have 'an adequate justification for treating the employee differently from any other member of the general public' as a result of the statement he made." *Hill v. Borough of Kutztown*, 455 F.3d 225, 241–42 (3d Cir. 2006).

3. **Scope of Job Duties**. How should a court determine whether a public employee's speech falls within her job responsibilities or not? What guidance does *Garcetti* offer on this question? As anticipated, a great deal of litigation now focuses on whether particular speech was citizen speech or employee speech. Some courts have defined job duties broadly, finding speech unprotected when it is related to an employee's responsibilities, even though not part of the official job description, *see, e.g., Green v. Bd. of County Commr's*, 472 F.3d 794, 800–01 (10th Cir. 2007), while others have read job duties narrowly, for example, finding an employee's report of police corruption protected despite a general rule requiring all officers to report rule violations to their superior officers. *See, e.g., Taylor v. Freetown*, 479 F. Supp. 2d 227 (D. Mass. 2007).

Some courts have attempted to articulate tests or guidelines to help determine the scope of a public employee's job duties. In *Dahlia v. Rodriguez*, 735 F.3d 1060 (9th Cir. 2013), the Ninth Circuit set out some "guiding principles." It noted, first, that speech made outside the chain of command is unlikely to be speech pursuant to job duties. Similarly, speech that raises "broad concerns about corruption or systemic abuse" is unlikely to fall within the job duties of an average public employee. And finally, speech that is in direct contravention of a supervisor's orders will often fall outside the speaker's job responsibilities. *Id.* at 1074–75. The Second Circuit offered a different approach, suggesting that if "there is no relevant civilian analogue" to a public employee's speech, the speech was likely made pursuant to the employee's job duties. *Weintraub v. Bd of Educ.*, 593 F.3d 196, 203 (2d Cir. 2010). *See also Jackler v. Byrne*, 658 F.3d 225 (2d Cir. 2011). The D.C. Circuit rejected the converse of this approach, arguing that "[a] test that allows a First Amendment retaliation claim to proceed whenever the government employee can identify a civilian analogue is about as useful as a mosquito net made of chicken wire: All official speech, viewed at a sufficient level of abstraction, has a civilian analogue." *Bowie v. Maddox*, 653 F.3d 45, 48 (D.C. Cir. 2011).

How *should* courts determine whether speech is made pursuant to a public employee's job duties? Do any of the tests suggested above help make that determination? Can you think of other tests that would identify where the line should be drawn? Or is this necessarily a fact-intensive inquiry not amenable to clearly articulable tests?

4. **External Complaints**. One way courts have distinguished citizen speech from employee speech is by considering *to whom* the speech was made. For example, in *Freitag v. Ayers*, 468 F.3d 528 (9th Cir. 2006), the Ninth Circuit found a female prison guard's complaints of sexual harassment by male prisoners were *not* protected when made to her superiors, but *were* protected when made to a state investigator and in a letter to a state senator. *Freitag*, 468 F.3d at 545–46.

Does the *Garcetti* decision encourage public employees to report their allegations of government wrongful discharge to an outside agency or the press rather than to their agency superiors? Does it make sense to provide such an incentive because public employee speech outside the workplace, particularly to the press, deserves more protection? Or does such speech deserve less protection because of its greater disruptive potential?

In *Andrew v. Clark*, 561 F.3d 261 (4th Cir. 2009), the Fourth Circuit allowed a police officer to proceed with his case alleging retaliation after he wrote a memo criticizing how the Department handled an incident involving lethal force and then provided the memo to a local newspaper. One of the judges suggested that speech to the press was particularly worthy of protection:

> To throw out this citizen who took his concerns to the press on a motion to dismiss would have profound adverse effects on accountability in government. . . . [T]he First Amendment should never countenance the gamble that informed scrutiny of the workings of government will be left to wither on the vine. That scrutiny is impossible without some assistance from inside sources such as [plaintiff]. Indeed it may be more important than ever that such sources carry the story to the reporter, because there are, sad to say, fewer shoeleather journalists to ferret the story out.
>
> . . . [A]s the state grows more layered and impacts lives more profoundly, it seems inimical to First Amendment principles to treat too summarily those who bring, often at some personal risk, its operations into public view. It is vital to the health of our polity that the functioning of the ever more complex and powerful machinery of government not become democracy's dark lagoon.

Id. at 272–73 (J. Wilkinson, concurring).

5.   Duty to Speak. Should it matter that Ceballos had a duty to speak as he did? Prosecutors are constitutionally required to preserve and share with the defense any exculpatory evidence in their possession. *Brady v. Maryland*, 373 U.S. 83 (1963). In addition, California Rules of Professional Conduct forbid an attorney from instituting criminal charges that he or she knows are not supported by probable cause. Cal. Rule Prof. Conduct 5-110. Which way does the existence of these professional and constitutional duties cut? Do they make Ceballos's speech more worthy of protection? Or do they alleviate the need for a constitutional remedy?

Justice Breyer, whose dissent is omitted above, did not join Justice Souter's dissent, which he felt gave insufficient weight to the serious managerial and administrative concerns raised by First Amendment challenges based on speech encompassed within a public employee's official duties. Nevertheless, he thought that in Ceballos's case, the fact that his speech was subject to professional and constitutional obligations constituted special circumstances that "justify First Amendment review." 547 U.S. at 446 (Breyer, J., dissenting).

What about when a public employee alleges he was retaliated against for testifying truthfully, given that all citizens have an obligation to give truthful testimony? In *Reilly v. City of Atlantic City*, 532 F.3d 216 (3d Cir. 2008), a police officer alleged that he was retaliated against for testifying for the prosecution at a police corruption trial. The Third Circuit noted that "all citizens owe an independent duty to society to testify in court proceedings," *id.* at 229, and that in-court testimony plays a "fundamental role" in our society. *Id.* at 230. It then argued that "[w]hen a government employee testifies truthfully [at trial], s/he is not 'simply performing his or her job duties.' *Garcetti*, 547 U.S. at 423; rather, the employee is acting as a citizen and is bound by the dictates of the court and the rules of evidence." *Id.* at 231. Thus, the plaintiff's trial testimony, even though part of his official duties in the corruption investigation, was "citizen speech" and therefore protected by the First Amendment.

In a recent case, *Lane v. Franks*, 134 S. Ct. 2369 (2014), the Supreme Court similarly held that the court testimony of a public employee was protected by the First Amendment. The Court emphasized that witnesses owe an important obligation to the court and to society to tell the truth when testifying and called sworn testimony in court "a quintessential example of speech as a citizen." It held that "the mere fact that a citizen's speech concerns information acquired by virtue of his public employment does not transform that speech into employee—rather than citizen—speech." *Id.* at 2379. In *Lane*, however, there was no dispute that the plaintiff's testimony, while concerning matters learned on the job, was not part of his ordinary job duties and therefore, did not fall within the *Garcetti* rule. Thus, while recognizing the special status of trial testimony as a form of "citizen speech," the decision in *Lane* did not resolve the question whether the First Amendment protects trial testimony that *is* part of a public employee's ordinary duties—for example, when police officers or laboratory technicians testify as a routine part of their jobs. Would protection of such speech under the First Amendment be consistent with *Garcetti*? Should it be protected? If so, how?

6. **Speech and Whistleblowing.** The majority in *Garcetti* asserts that public employees like Richard Ceballos will be adequately protected by existing whistle-blower protections. However, as suggested by Justice Souter in his dissent, statutory whistleblower protections—even for public employees—offer only a patchwork of protection. *See* DANIEL P. WESTMAN & NANCY M. MODESITT, WHISTLE-BLOWING: THE LAW OF RETALIATORY DISCHARGE 67 (2d ed. 2004 & Supp. 2013). Whether or not a particular employee is covered depends upon such factors as the type of government employer (federal, state, or local), the type of employment, what state the employee works in, the type of violation reported and to whom the complaint was made.

Apart from the adequacy of existing whistleblower protections for public employees, this case raises the question whether Ceballos' claim and those like it are better analyzed in terms of free speech or whistleblowing. In other words, was Ceballos a classic whistleblower attempting to expose wrongdoing who just happened to be a government employee? Or are the values that animate the First Amendment also at stake? To put the question differently, does Ceballos' claim raise constitutional concerns properly adjudicated by the courts? Or is striking the appropriate balance between employee, employer, and public interests in exposing wrongdoing best left to the legislature? Does the fact that the legislature *could* choose to protect speech like Ceballos's diminish the need for constitutional protection?

7. **Academic Freedom.** In his dissent in *Garcetti*, Justice Souter raised a concern that the majority opinion might be applied in a way that imperiled academic freedom, given that public university professors "necessarily speak and write 'pursuant to . . . official duties.'" 547 U.S. at 438 (Souter, J., dissenting). Recognizing that "there is some argument that expression related to academic scholarship

or classroom instruction implicates additional constitutional interests," the majority left open the question whether its holding applied to "speech related to scholarship or teaching." *Id.* at 425.

Should a university professor's decisions regarding how and what to teach in the classroom, her scholarly publications or her statements on matters of public debate be considered "official duty speech" that is not protected by the First Amendment since she is hired to teach and publish? Or do concerns about academic freedom call for a different rule in the academic context? To what extent do public universities have legitimate interests in controlling what and how its faculty teach and write? The Courts of Appeals are split on the issue of whether *Garcetti* applies to university professors. *Compare Demers v. Austin*, 746 F.3d 402 (9th Cir. 2014) (holding that *Garcetti* does not apply to teaching and academic writing that are part of the "official duties" of a university professor) *and Adams v. Trustees of the Univ. of North Carolina-Wilmington*, 640 F.3d 550 (4th Cir. 2011) (refusing to apply *Garcetti* to the academic work of a public university faculty member) *with Renken v. Gregory*, 541 F.3d 769 (7th Cir. 2008) (holding that professor's criticism of use of grant funds was not protected because they were part of his official duties).

C. THE COMMON LAW

The First Amendment restrains state actors, prohibiting them from infringing on individual rights of speech and expression. As we saw in the last section, that broad restraint on government power also applies to public employers, albeit in a form modified to take into account the competing interests of the government when acting in its capacity as an employer. What about employee speech in the private sector? Except in certain narrowly defined circumstances, the constitution does not apply to non-state actors. Are the values underlying the First Amendment nevertheless relevant in the private sector workplace? And if so, are they worthy of legal protection? Consider the following contrasting pair of cases:

NOVOSEL v. NATIONWIDE INSURANCE CO.
United States Court of Appeals, Third Circuit
721 F.2d 894 (1983)

Adams, Circuit Judge.

Novosel was an employee of Nationwide from December 1966 until November 18, 1981. He had steadily advanced through the company's ranks in a career unmarred by reprimands or disciplinary action. At the time his employment was terminated, he was a district claims manager and one of three candidates for the position of division claims manager.

In late October 1981, a memorandum was circulated through Nationwide's offices soliciting the participation of all employees in an effort to lobby the Pennsylvania House of Representatives. Specifically, employees were instructed to clip, copy, and obtain signatures on coupons bearing the insignia of the Pennsylvania Committee for No-Fault Reform. This Committee was actively supporting the passage of House Bill 1285, the "No-Fault Reform Act," then before the state legislature.

The allegations of the complaint charge that the sole reason for Novosel's discharge was his refusal to participate in the lobbying effort and his privately stated opposition to the company's political stand. Novosel contends that the discharge for refusing to lobby the state legislature on the employer's behalf constituted the tort of wrongful discharge on the grounds it was willful, arbitrary, malicious and in bad faith, and that it was contrary to public policy. . . . [The district court granted Nationwide's motion to dismiss.] . . .

The circumstances of the discharge presented by Novosel fall squarely within the range of activity embraced by the emerging tort case law. As one commentator has written:

> The factual pattern alleged in these cases seldom varies. The employee objects to work that the employee believes is violative of state or federal law or otherwise improper; the employee protests to his employer that the work should not be performed; the employee expresses his intention not to assist the employer in the furtherance of such work and/or engages in "self-help" activity outside the work place to halt the work; and the employer discharges the employee for refusal to work or incompatibility with management.

Olsen, *Wrongful Discharge Claims Raised By At Will Employees: A New Legal Concern for Employers*, 32 LAB. L.J. 265, 276 (1981). In a landmark opinion, the Pennsylvania Supreme Court acknowledged that such a situation could give rise to a legal cause of action:

> It may be granted that there are areas of an employee's life in which his employer has no legitimate interest. An intrusion into one of these areas by virtue of the employer's power of discharge might plausibly give rise to a cause of action, particularly where some recognized facet of public policy is threatened. The notion that substantive due process elevates an employer's privilege of hiring and discharging his employees to an absolute constitutional right has long since been discredited.

Geary v. United States Steel Corp., 319 A.2d 174, 180 (1974). Under the particular facts of *Geary*, the court held:

> this case does not require us to define in comprehensive fashion the perimeters of this privilege [to employ-at-will], and we decline to do so. We hold only that where the complaint itself discloses a plausible and legitimate reason for terminating an at-will employment relationship and no clear mandate of public policy is violated thereby, an employee at will has no right of action against his employer for wrongful discharge.

319 A.2d at 180. . . .

Applying the logic of *Geary*, we find that Pennsylvania law permits a cause of action for wrongful discharge where the employment termination abridges a significant and recognized public policy. The district court did not consider the question whether an averment of discharge for refusing to support the employer's lobbying efforts is sufficiently violative of such public policy as to state a cause of action. . . . Given that there are no statutory remedies available in the present case and taking into consideration the importance of the political and associational freedoms of the federal and state Constitutions, the absence of a statutory declaration of public policy would appear to be no bar to the existence of a cause of action. Accordingly, a cognizable expression of public policy may be derived in this case from either the First Amendment of the United States Constitution or Article I, Section 7 of the Pennsylvania Constitution.[5]

The key question in considering the tort claim is therefore whether a discharge for disagreement with the employer's legislative agenda or a refusal to lobby the state legislature on the employer's behalf sufficiently implicate a recognized facet of public policy. The definition of a "clearly mandated public policy" as one that "strikes at the heart of a citizen's social right, duties and responsibilities," set forth in *Palmateer v. International Harvester Co.*, 421 N.E.2d 876 (1981), appears to provide a workable standard for the tort action. While no Pennsylvania law directly addresses the public policy question at bar, the protection of an employee's freedom of political expression would appear to involve no less compelling a societal interest than the fulfillment of jury service or the filing of a workers' compensation claim.

An extensive case law has developed concerning the protection of constitutional rights, particularly First Amendment rights, of government employees. As the Supreme Court has commented, "[f]or most of this century, the unchallenged dogma was that a public employee had no right to object to conditions placed upon the terms of employment—including those which restricted the exercise of constitutional rights." *Connick v. Myers*, 461 U.S. 138 (1983). The Court in *Connick*, however, also observed the constitutional repudiation of this dogma: "[f]or at least 15 years, it has been settled that a state cannot condition public employment on a basis that infringes the employee's constitutionally protected interest in freedom of expression." *Id.* at [142], *citing Branti v. Finkel*, 445 U.S. 507, 515–516 (1980); *Perry v. Sindermann*, 408 U.S. 593, 597 (1972); *Pickering v. Board of Education*, 391 U.S. 563 (1968); *Keyishian v. Board of Regents*, 385 U.S. 589, 605–606 (1967). "If there is any fixed star in our constitutional constellation, it is that no official, high or petty, can prescribe what shall be orthodox in politics, nationalism, religion, or other matters of opinion or force citizens to confess by word or act their faith therein." *Board of Education v. Barnette*, 319 U.S. 624, 642 (1943). Thus, there can no longer be any doubt that speech on public issues "has always rested on the highest rung of the hierarchy of First Amendment values." *NAACP v. Claiborne Hardware Co.*, 458 U.S. 886 (1982), *quoting Carey v. Brown*, 447 U.S. 455, 467 (1980).[6]

In striking down the use of patronage appointments for federal government employees, the Court further noted that one of its goals was to insure that "employees themselves are to be sufficiently free from improper influences." *CSC v. Letter Carriers*, 413 U.S. 548 (1973). It was not, however, simply the abuse of state authority over public employees that fueled the Court's concern over patronage political appointments; no less central is the fear that the political process would be

---

[5] [n. 6] The relevant portion of Article I, Section 7 of the Pennsylvania Constitution states: The free communication of thoughts and opinions is one of the invaluable rights of man, and every citizen may freely speak, write and print on any subject, being responsible for the abuse of that liberty.

[6] [n. 7] Nor can there be any doubt that the right to petition or not petition the legislature is incorporated within protected speech on public issues . . . .

irremediably distorted. If employers such as federal, state or municipal governments are allowed coercive control of the scope and direction of employee political activities, it is argued, their influence will be geometrically enhanced at the expense of both the individual rights of the employees and the ability of the lone political actor to be effectively heard.

Although Novosel is not a government employee, the public employee cases do not confine themselves to the narrow question of state action. Rather, these cases suggest that an important public policy is in fact implicated wherever the power to hire and fire is utilized to dictate the terms of employee political activities. In dealing with public employees, the cause of action arises directly from the Constitution rather than from common law developments. The protection of important political freedoms, however, goes well beyond the question whether the threat comes from state or private bodies. The inquiry before us is whether the concern for the rights of political expression and association which animated the public employee cases is sufficient to state a public policy under Pennsylvania law. While there are no Pennsylvania cases squarely on this point, we believe that the clear direction of the opinions promulgated by the state's courts suggests that this question be answered in the affirmative.

Having concluded thereby that an important public policy is at stake, we now hold that Novosel's allegations state a claim within the ambit of *Geary* in that Novosel's complaint discloses no plausible and legitimate reason for terminating his employment, and his discharge violates a clear mandate of public policy. The Pennsylvania Supreme Court's rulings . . . are thus interpreted to extend to a non-constitutional claim where a corporation conditions employment upon political subordination. This is not the first judicial recognition of the relationship between economic power and the political process:

> the special status of corporations has placed them in a position to control vast amounts of economic power which may, if not regulated, dominate not only the economy but also the very heart of our democracy, the electoral process. . . . [The desired end] is not one of equalizing the resources of opposing candidates or opposing positions, but rather of preventing institutions which have been permitted to amass wealth as a result of special advantages extended by the State for certain economic purposes from using that wealth to acquire an unfair advantage in the political process. . . .

First National Bank of Boston v. Bellotti, 435 U.S. 765, 809 (1978) (White, J., dissenting).[7]

---

[7] [n. 9] The district court relies heavily upon the majority opinion in *Bellotti* to support the proposition that so long as an employer's actions were "in furtherance of its normal and ordinary business interests," its political activities are beyond court scrutiny. By extending constitutional protection to corporate political activity, the district court precludes any common law tort claim. In our view, this reliance on *Bellotti* obscures the fact that there are two distinct issues present here: 1) whether a corporation may engage in the type of lobbying demonstrated by defendant; and 2) whether the economic power of such corporations (in this case the power to discharge) may be utilized to coerce individual employee assistance to the corporate political agenda. Although *Bellotti* does find that corporate speech is entitled to First Amendment protection, the opinion does not stand for the proposition that corporations in the

. . . [O]n remand the district court should employ the four part inquiry
. . . derived from *Connick* and *Pickering:*

1. Whether, because of the speech, the employer is prevented from efficiently carrying out its responsibilities;

2. Whether the speech impairs the employee's ability to carry out his own responsibilities;

3. Whether the speech interferes with essential and close working relationships;

4. Whether the manner, time and place in which the speech occurs interferes with business operations. . . .

The judgment and order of the district court will be vacated and the case remanded for discovery and further proceedings consistent with this opinion.

STATEMENT OF JUDGE BECKER SUR THE DENIAL
OF THE PETITION FOR REHEARING

. . . I have three major problems with the panel opinion.

First, the opinion ignores the state action requirement of first amendment jurisprudence, particularly by its repeated, and, in my view, inappropriate citation of public employee cases, and by its implicit assumption that a public policy against government interference with free speech may be readily extended to private actors in voluntary association with another, *see, e.g., Hudgens v. NLRB*, 424 U.S. 507 (1976). Second, the opinion could be read to suggest that an explicit contractual provision authorizing an employer to dismiss a lobbyist for failure to undertake lobbying might be unenforceable or subject to a balancing test. Third, the opinion fails to consider other public policy interests, such as the economic interests of the public in efficient corporate performance, the first amendment interests of corporations, *see First National Bank of Boston v. Bellotti*, 435 U.S. 765 (1978), and the legitimate interests of a corporation in commanding the loyalty of its employees to pursue its economic well being.

I therefore dissent from the denial of rehearing.

EDMONDSON v. SHEARER LUMBER PRODUCTS
Supreme Court of Idaho
75 P.3d 733 (2003)

WALTERS, JUSTICE

Michael Edmondson was employed by Shearer Lumber Products for twenty-two years at the company's Elk City mill. In 1999, he became a salaried employee and on his most recent performance review, he received a rating of "very good." However, on February 15, 2000, the plant manager, David Paisley, following

---

political arena can neither do any wrong nor be regulated. *See, e.g., Buckley v. Valeo*, 424 U.S. 1 (1976); Federal Corrupt Practices Act, 2 U.S.C. § 441(b) (1976).

directions from his superiors fired Edmondson, by reading a statement that informed Edmondson: "Because of your continued involvement in activities that are harmful to the long term interests of Shearer Lumber Products, we are terminating your employment immediately."

It was well known at Shearer Lumber that Edmondson was extensively involved in the community and regularly attended public meetings concerning matters of public interest and concern, such that he was recognized with the Idaho GEM Citizen Award by then Governor Batt. In January of 2000, Edmondson attended a public meeting of a group known as Save Elk City. One of the leaders of the group was the resource manager at Shearer Lumber, Dick Wilhite, who at the group meetings encouraged public support for the proposal that Save Elk City had submitted to the Federal Lands Task Force Working Group for consideration as to how best to manage the Nez Perce National Forest. Edmondson attended the group meetings, but he made no comments on the group's proposal. Nor did he discuss his opinions regarding the Save Elk City proposal at work with other employees.

Shearer Lumber did not openly campaign for the Save Elk City proposal, but Edmondson later learned from Wilhite that the proposal submitted in the name of Save Elk City was the project of Shearer Lumber's owner, Dick Bennett. At that time, Wilhite and Edmondson discussed the various outstanding proposals that might be competing for the Task Force's recommendation to the State Land Board, but Edmondson did not declare a preference for any of the proposals.

Shearer Lumber obtained information that Edmondson had attended meetings of the Task Force, had contacted someone in the administration of the Task Force, and was opposed to the collaborative project that Shearer had sponsored and submitted on behalf of the Save Elk City group. Edmondson was twice called into meetings at Shearer Lumber, where he claimed he was subjected to intimidation and pressure from Wilhite, Paisley, and John Bennett, Shearer's general manager. It was made clear that Edmondson was *not* to form any opinions on or make any statements to the Federal Lands Task Force. In effect, Edmondson was warned that any opposition to the collaborative project that was contrary to Shearer's interest would lead to serious consequences. Edmondson was informed at the February 2, 2000, meeting that Shearer Lumber wanted all of its employees to support the projects the mill was involved in, if they wanted to avoid serious consequences that would result if the project was derailed or negatively impacted.

John Bennett testified in his deposition that the reason Edmondson was terminated was that Edmondson was opposing the project that Shearer Lumber Products supported, in direct conflict with the company's goals that could ultimately jeopardize a Task Force decision favorable to Shearer's interests. Bennett also attributed to Edmondson contact with the Task Force administration, although it was Edmondson's wife, Jamie, who had made inquiries to the Task Force. . . .

Edmondson brought an action against Shearer Lumber for wrongful termination of employment. . . . The district court awarded summary judgment to Shearer, holding that Edmondson's allegations did not fall within the limited public policy exception recognized in Idaho. . . .

Edmondson argues that summary judgment was improperly granted because issues of material fact exist that must be resolved by a jury, such as which meetings he attended, which proposal he endorsed, and which of his actions constituted the "continued involvement in activities harmful to the long term interests of Shearer." No dispute of fact is "material," however, unless it relates to an issue that is disclosed by the pleadings. The tendered factual issues as to the reasons for Edmondson's discharge are not material to Edmondson's claims because, as the district court held, Edmondson was an at-will employee, who could be terminated by his employer at any time for any reason without creating liability. . . .

In Idaho, the only general exception to the employment at-will doctrine is that an employer may be liable for wrongful discharge when the motivation for discharge contravenes public policy. The purpose of the exception is to balance the competing interests of society, the employer, and the employee in light of modern business experience. *Crea v. FMC Corp.*, 16 P.3d 272, 275 (2000). . . .

Courts have recognized that public policy expressed in the constitution and the statutes of the state may serve as a basis for finding an exception to the employment at-will doctrine. The First Amendment prohibits the government from restraining or abridging freedom of speech and assembly. Article I, § 9 of the Idaho Constitution also guarantees the right of free speech: "Every person may freely speak, write and publish on all subjects, being responsible for the abuse of that liberty." Article I, § 10 of the Idaho Constitution guarantees the right of freedom of association: "The people shall have the right to assemble in a peaceful manner, to consult for their common good; to instruct their representatives, and to petition the legislature for the redress of grievances." The First Amendment and Article I, §§ 9 and 10 of the Idaho Constitution do not apply to alleged restrictions imposed by private parties, however.

Edmondson maintains that he was wrongfully terminated because he exercised his constitutionally protected rights of free speech and association. He argues that the public policy at issue prohibits restrictions on free speech and association. He relies on *Gardner v. Evans*, 719 P.2d 1185 (1986) and *Lubcke v. Boise City/Ada County Housing Authority*, 860 P.2d 653 (1993), which followed the two-step analysis of *Connick v. Myers*, 461 U.S. 138 (1983), in determining initially whether the speech involves a matter of public concern and, if so, applying a balancing test. These cases, however, all deal with governmental restrictions on free speech and associative rights of employees of public agencies, which are inapplicable in the private employment context in which Edmondson worked. The prevailing view among those courts addressing the issue in the private sector is that state or federal constitutional free speech cannot, in the absence of state action, be the basis of a public policy exception in wrongful discharge claims. . . .

Finally, Edmondson urges that public policy is implicated wherever the power to hire and fire is utilized to dictate the terms of an employee's political activities and associations, relying on *Novosel v. Nationwide Ins. Co.*, 721 F.2d 894, 900 (3rd Cir. 1983). . . . We . . . decline to extend Idaho's public policy exception through the adoption of *Novosel*.

Accordingly, we hold that an employee does not have a cause of action against a private sector employer who terminates the employee because of the exercise of the employee's constitutional right of free speech. . . .

JUSTICE KIDWELL, dissenting.

I wholeheartedly support the presumption that employment in Idaho is "at-will" unless otherwise provided. Unlike the majority, however, I would hold that there is a narrow, but important, public policy exception to the at-will presumption for certain exercises of one's first amendment rights. Therefore, I respectfully dissent. . . .

I believe that statutes are not the only place in which one may find public policy. Indeed, one may find the most significant public policies in this state and our nation in the Idaho Constitution and the Constitution of the United States. Thus, I would hold that certain constitutional public policies deserve protection and vindication through the public policy exception to at-will employment even in the absence of a statutory enactment.

One such policy that deserves protection in the at-will employment context is the policy of encouraging participation and debate regarding issues of public concern. The Idaho Constitution makes clear that "[a]ll political power is inherent in the people. Government is instituted for their benefit, and they have the right to alter, reform, or abolish the same whenever they may deem it necessary. . . ." Idaho Constitution Art. 1, § 2. In order to exercise the political power inherent in the people, the Idaho and United States constitutions endow individuals with the liberty to speak freely and participate in vigorous public debate. United States Constitution, Amend. 1; Idaho Constitution Art. 1, § 9. Allowing employers to terminate employment based on an individual's association and speech regarding public issues that may have little or nothing in connection with the employer's business, invites employers to squelch the association, speech, and debate so necessary to our system of government. This is particularly true in the context of the myriad of small Idaho communities with only one or two prominent employers. Thus, I would hold it against public policy to discharge an employee for constitutionally-protected political speech or activities regarding a matter of public concern, provided that such speech or activity does not interfere with the employee's job performance or the business of the employer.

. . . It is my opinion that even absent a state action, a very narrowly drawn public policy exception to the employment at-will doctrine should apply. That narrowly drawn exception would require a two-step analysis. First, did the at-will employee's speech impact the employer's business in *any* manner? If so, was the employee terminated because of his or her speech? The free speech public policy exception would apply to at-will employment in the case where the employee's speech does not impact the employer's business and the employee was terminated for the speech. . . .

In this case, the evidence in the record clearly creates genuine issues of material fact regarding whether Edmondson was terminated for political speech or activities regarding a matter of public concern. Further, the record shows genuine issues regarding whether Edmondson's speech and activities interfered with his job performance or the business of his employer. On these grounds, I would vacate summary judgment and remand this matter for further proceedings.

NOTES

1. **Uncertain Authority.** *Novosel* and *Edmondson* represent two contrasting
approaches to the question of whether a wrongful discharge in violation of public
policy tort claim can be based on the free speech rights guaranteed by the First
Amendment or an analogous state constitutional provision. In *Novosel*, however, a
federal district court sitting in a diversity case decided a question of Pennsylvania
state law. Because the Pennsylvania courts had not yet decided the precise question
presented, the *Novosel* opinion entailed a prediction by the federal court of the
likely development of state law. Subsequent cases have cast doubt on whether
Novosel accurately represents Pennsylvania law. Although the Pennsylvania Supreme Court has not expressly repudiated the holding in *Novosel*, it indicated in
several later cases that the public policy exception in Pennsylvania is quite narrow.
See McLaughlin v. Gastrointestinal Specialists, Inc., 750 A.2d 283, 314 (Pa. 2000)
(stating that exceptions to at-will employment should be found "only in the most
limited of circumstances where the termination implicates a clear mandate of public
policy in this Commonwealth"). *Cf. Borse v. Piece Goods Shop, Inc.*, 963 F.2d 611,
618, 620 (3d Cir. 1992) (rejecting the argument that a constitutional argument may
never serve as a source of public policy in Pennsylvania wrongful discharge actions,
but recognizing that the clear trend indicates that Pennsylvania courts would be
highly unlikely to extend *Novosel*).

Regardless of its status in Pennsylvania, the *Novosel* decision has proven
controversial. A number of courts, including the Idaho Supreme Court in *Edmondson*, have rejected its reasoning, holding that constitutional guarantees of free
speech do not restrict the actions of non-governmental entities. *See, e.g., McGarvey
v. Key Prop. Mgmt. LLC*, 211 P.3d 503 (Wyo. 2009) (holding that speech made at
work on employer's private property is not protected under Wyoming's constitutional right to free speech); *Petrovski v. Federal Express Corp.*, 210 F. Supp. 2d 943
(N.D. Ohio 2002) (concluding that Ohio courts would not find state or federal
constitutional free speech rights to be the basis for a public policy exception in
wrongful discharge claims in the absence of state action); *Prysak v. R.L. Polk Co.*,
483 N.W.2d 629 (Mich. Ct. App. 1992) (rejecting plaintiff's claim that his discharge
in retaliation for his speech violated public policy on the grounds that the federal
and Michigan constitutional provisions guaranteeing free speech are limited to
protecting against state action).

Several other courts appear to endorse the rationale of *Novosel. See Emerick v.
Kuhn*, 737 A.2d 456 (Conn. App. Ct. 1999) (stating that if plaintiff had properly
asserted a violation of his First Amendment free speech rights, he could properly
allege a cause of action for wrongful termination; however, in this case, his speech
at management sponsored programs was not constitutionally protected); *Carl v.
Children's Hosp.*, 702 A.2d 159, 182–84 (D.C. 1997) (Schwelb, J., concurring)
(common law courts may recognize an exception to at-will employment that
affirmatively promotes the values protected by the First Amendment). Consistent
with the holding and reasoning in *Novosel*, the New Mexico Supreme Court
permitted a former production supervisor's wrongful discharge claim to proceed to

trial based on his allegations that he was fired for declining to participate in his employer's lobbying efforts and objecting to the company's unauthorized use of his name in a letter to a Senator. *Chavez v. Manville Prods. Corp.*, 777 P.2d 371 (N.M. 1989).

In other cases, courts have rejected wrongful discharge claims alleging employer retaliation for employee speech without reaching the issue of whether the First Amendment can provide the basis for a public policy claim. These cases turned instead on the nature of the employee speech at issue, and the threat it posed to the employer's legitimate interests. *See, e.g., Wiegand v. Motiva Enters.*, 295 F. Supp. 2d 465 (D.N.J. 2003) (holding that even if wrongful discharge claim can be based on First Amendment, public policy is not violated by employer terminating an employee with extensive contact with the public because of his side business selling racist music and hate paraphernalia over the internet); *Korb v. Raytheon Corp.*, 574 N.E.2d 370 (Mass. 1991) (finding no public policy prohibiting employer from discharging plaintiff, who was hired as a lobbyist, after he publicly expressed views in direct conflict with the employer's economic interests); *Schultz v. Industrial Coils, Inc.*, 373 N.W.2d 74 (Wis. Ct. App. 1985) (stating that "we do not hold that interference with an employee's right to freedom of speech or expression may never form the basis for a cause of action," only that the termination of plaintiff's employment for publishing derogatory comments about his employer did not violate public policy).

2. **The First Amendment as Public Policy.** Comparing the reasoning of *Novosel* and *Edmondson*, which opinion do you think has the better argument? Should common law courts look to the First Amendment and analogous state constitutional guarantees as sources of public policy? Most courts that reject the First Amendment as a source of public policy do so on the grounds that the Constitution only applies to state action. Although the wording of the free speech guarantees in many state constitutions differs from the First Amendment, most state courts have followed the federal courts in directly applying state constitutional guarantees only where there is state action. The plaintiffs in *Novosel* and *Edmondson*, however, did not argue that constitutional guarantees of freedom of speech applied directly to their employers, but that they provided a source of public policy for recognizing an exception to the at-will rule. Is there any difference between applying constitutional constraints directly to private employers and doing so by locating a public policy exception rooted in constitutional sources?

Consider the different methods by which courts have identified public policy exceptions to the at-will rule. Are federal and state constitutional provisions, as well as statutes, authoritative declarations of important public values? Do discharges in retaliation for employee speech have third-party effects? Would a contract in which an employee agreed to support whatever political position the employer dictated be void as against public policy?

3. **Speech and Association.** The First Amendment's protection encompasses not only the right to speak, but also the right to avoid endorsing speech with which one disagrees and the right to associate with others to pursue shared goals. In those states that do not recognize the First Amendment as a source of public policy, employees may lawfully be dismissed not only based on their speech on public

issues, but also because they refuse to participate in employer-sponsored speech with which they disagree, *see, e.g., Drake v. Cheyenne Newspapers, Inc.*, 891 P.2d 80 (Wyo. 1995) (rejecting wrongful discharge claims of managers fired for refusing to wear anti-union buttons as requested by employer), or because of their off-duty political activities or associations with others. *See, e.g., Shovelin v. Cent. N.M. Elec. Coop., Inc.*, 850 P.2d 996 (N.M. 1993) (rejecting wrongful discharge claim of employee terminated for being elected mayor); *Brunner v. Al Attar*, 786 S.W.2d 784 (Tex. App. 1990) (rejecting wrongful discharge claim of employee fired for performing volunteer work at a local AIDS Foundation).

Although the common law provides little protection, nearly half the states specifically forbid employer interference with employees' right to vote. *See* MATTHEW W. FINKIN, PRIVACY IN EMPLOYMENT LAW 505 n.93 (4th ed. 2009). In addition, several states have passed statutes that prohibit employers from requiring employees to attend an employer-sponsored meeting when the purpose of the meeting is to communicate the employers' religious or political opinions. *See, e.g.*, N.J. STAT. ANN. SEC. 34:19-9 to -11; OR. REV. STAT. ANN. SEC. 659.785; WIS. STAT. ANN. SEC. 111.32, 111.321. Employers have argued that such a prohibition violates their First Amendment speech rights and is preempted by the NLRA to the extent that it prevents them from holding mandatory meetings to express their views about unionization. Supporters of such legislation assert that workers have a right not to be required to hear communications about political or religious views with which they disagree and cite the example of an employer accused of holding mandatory meetings about political issues and candidates prior to a presidential election. *See* Susan J. McGolrick, *Business Groups Bring Legal Challenge to Oregon Statute on Mandatory Meetings*, DAILY LAB. REP. (BNA) No. 145, (Dec. 24, 2009).

Should employees have the right to avoid association with views with which they disagree? Should they be protected from being forced to hear the views of an employer on political or religious matters unrelated to their work? Or does legislation that forbids such communications unduly infringe on the employer's speech and associational interests?

4. Social Media and Employee Voice. New forms of electronic communication are creating challenges for employers and employees alike when they seek to take advantage of these new media. Employees today are increasingly likely to use social media to express their opinions regarding matters ranging from the mundane and personal to the geo-political. What happens when those forms of self-expression relate to workplace matters? What if they are unrelated to an employee's job, but are deemed offensive to the employer? What if the employer believes they are harmful to the firm's reputation in the market?

Early examples of conflict involved employees' off-duty postings that displeased their employers. For example, a former Google employee was fired for blogging about the company's employee orientation process, while a Delta flight attendant lost her job after she posted a picture of herself posing suggestively in her Delta uniform. *See* Matt Villano, *Blogging the Hand That Feeds You*, N.Y. TIMES, Sept. 27, 2006, *available at* http://www.nytimes.com/2006/09/27/technology/circuits/27peril. html?pagewanted=all&_r=0. If the online communications have nothing to do with an employee's job, the conflict can be understood as instances of employer regulation of off-duty conduct, implicating the privacy and autonomy concerns explored in Chapter 7. Employers, however, typically claim that their employees' online communications have the potential to harm their interests in some way. For example, a company may assert a strong interest in controlling its brand, or protecting business information or its reputation, and therefore seek to control employees' off-duty speech. Are these legitimate employer interests that trump employees' rights of self-expression? Or should there be limits to when employer interests can justify controlling employee use of social media? We explore one such legal limit in subsection E., *infra*, namely the National Labor Relations Act's prohibition on retaliation for concerted activity which likely protects some discussion of shared workplace concerns on Facebook and other social media sites.

On the other hand, social media is also a tool that is increasingly being used by firms to enhance their business. They view blogs and networking sites as opportunities for communicating with customers, as well as useful tools for internal discussion. For example, IBM encourages the use of external social-networking sites and "looks to employees throughout the company to 'be the brand' through their use of social-networking tools." *See Social Networking Tools Carry Risks; Policies Can Protect Firms, Commenters Say*, DAILY LAB. REP. (BNA) No. 242, Dec. 21, 2009. Such widespread use of social-networking tools may be good for marketing, but it also creates risks for employers. With so many employees communicating publicly about a company and its products, employers risk being held responsible if employees' blogs or posts run afoul of copyright, privacy, defamation or consumer fraud laws, in addition to the traditional concerns about the loss of trade secrets or product disparagement. As a result, some companies have begun to promulgate written policies about blogging, or require that their employees undergo training on the appropriate use of social media. *Id.* In addition, disputes may arise over who has the rights to access an account or who owns a list of contacts after an employee leaves the firm. *See, e.g.*, Jeff John Roberts, *New York Times Editor to Take 75,000 Twitter Followers out the Door with Him*, GIGAOM (Jan. 24, 2013), http://gigaom.com/2013/01/24/new-york-times-editor-to-take-75000-twitter-followers-out-the-door-with-him/.

Do you think these new forms of online communication expand the opportunities for employee voice? Will they encourage the types of employee speech that promote public interests, as discussed at the beginning of this chapter? Or will they lead to greater employer efforts to control employee speech? Does the power of these new media strengthen employers' claims that they have legitimate business interests in controlling their employees' speech in a wide variety of settings?

D. STATUTORY PROTECTIONS FOR EMPLOYEE SPEECH

As we saw in the last two sections, constitutional rights and common law doctrines offer some, albeit limited, protection to employees against discipline or discharge because of their speech. Under the First Amendment, protection extends only to a public employee's speech as a citizen on a matter of public concern. And the common law doctrine of wrongful discharge in violation of public policy has only been applied in a handful of cases to protect a private employee's expressive freedom. Although courts have been reluctant to step in, legislatures at both the state and federal level have become increasingly active in creating statutory protections. Unlike the First Amendment and the common law—which offered at least the potential for protecting a broad range of employee speech—many statutory enactments are quite narrow, protecting employees only when they engage in certain specified types of speech. In this section, we explore these statutory protections, beginning with state laws that protect political speech and then discussing whistleblower protections which have grown in number and significance in recent years. We then focus on the most significant of these, the whistleblower protections enacted as part of the Sarbanes-Oxley Act and the Dodd-Frank Act.

1. State Statutory Protection for Speech and Political Activity

Several states have enacted statutes that broadly protect private employees from retaliation for their speech or political activity. Connecticut's statute provides the broadest protection:

> Any employer, including the state and any instrumentality or political subdivision thereof, who subjects any employee to discipline or discharge on account of the exercise by such employee of rights guaranteed by the first amendment to the United States Constitution or section 3, 4 or 14 of article first of the Constitution of the state, provided such activity does not substantially or materially interfere with the employee's bona fide job performance or the working relationship between the employee and the employer, shall be liable to such employee for damages caused by such discipline or discharge, including punitive damages, and for reasonable attorney's fees as part of the costs of any such action for damages. If the court determines that such action for damages was brought without substantial justification, the court may award costs and reasonable attorney's fees to the employer.

CONN. GEN. STAT. § 31-51q.

The Supreme Court of Connecticut has held that this provision applies to both public and private employers. *Cotto v. United Technologies Corp.*, 738 A.2d 623 (Conn. 1999). In order for § 31-51q to apply, however, "the speech at issue must be constitutionally protected" and thus, private employees' speech claims are analyzed under the Supreme Court's First Amendment precedents, including *Garcetti* which limits protection to speech that is not part of an employee's job duties. *Schumann v. Dianon Systems, Inc.*, 43 A.3d 111 (Conn. 2012).

Several other states, such as California, more narrowly protect employees' right to participate in political activities, *see, e.g.*, CAL. LABOR CODE §§ 1101, 1102, or bar discrimination based on "political opinions." *See* N.M. STAT. ANN. § 1-20-13. Eugene Volokh has conducted a comprehensive survey of state statutes that protect private employees' rights to speech and to engage in political activity free from employer interference. *See* Eugene Volokh, *Private Employees' Speech and Political Activity: Statutory Protection Against Employer Retaliation*, 16 TEX. REV. L. & POL. 295

(2012). In addition to collecting and describing these protections, Volokh questions the wisdom of these types of statutes:

> First, employers may have a legitimate interest in not associating themselves with people whose views they despise. Second, employees are hired to advance the employer's interests, not to undermine it. When an employee's speech or political activity sufficiently alienates coworkers, customers, or political figures, an employer may reasonably claim a right to sever his connection to the employee.

Id. at 301. Do employers have a legitimate interest in controlling the speech and political activity of their employees? Or do employees' interests in free expression justify restrictions on a private employer's ability to decide who they will employ? If so, how should the law strike the appropriate balance between the competing interests?

When states have recognized employees' interests in speech and political activity, those rights have sometimes come into conflict with other important public policy goals. For example, in *Nelson v. McClatchey Newspapers*, 936 P.2d 1123 (Wash. 1997), a reporter alleged that she was retaliated against by her employer because of her off-duty advocacy for abortion rights and gay rights in violation of a Washington state statute that forbids discrimination against an employee for engaging in political activities. The Supreme Court of Washington found that although the statute clearly applied to her case, it was unconstitutional as applied to her employer, a newspaper publisher, because it conflicted with the employer's First Amendment right to determine the content of its publication, which includes as an integral component maintaining its credibility through conflict-of-interest policies. *Id.* at 1128–29.

Another such conflict may arise when employees invoke speech rights to protect expression that others find discriminatory or harassing. Consider the following factual situation:

Beginning in January 2000, a conflict developed among South Carolinians over whether to remove the Confederate battle flag from atop their state capitol dome. This conflict became "a burning issue in the State of South Carolina," marking a "period of intense national scrutiny and public debate." The flag had first been raised over the capitol during the years leading up to the passage of federal civil rights legislation in the 1960s, and given this historical context, the decision to fly the flag over the capitol was widely understood as a defiant act opposing the national pressure to desegregate. Although the State of South Carolina eventually capitulated in its fight against civil rights, the Confederate flag continued to fly over the capitol.

In the context of this controversy, Matthew Dixon, a mechanic employed by Coburg Dairy, Inc., placed two Confederate battle flag stickers on his tool box. An African-American co-worker, Leroy Garner, complained that he found the stickers racially offensive and believed that they violated Coburg's policy against racial harassment. In an attempt to resolve the dispute, Coburg offered to buy Dixon a new, unadorned tool box, allowing him to keep his previously decorated box for home use. When Dixon refused, Coburg fired him on September 5, 2000, on the ground that he had violated the company's anti-harassment policy. Another co-worker who also had a Confederate battle flag on his toolbox agreed to remove it and continued to work at Coburg.

These facts are adapted from a real case heard by the Fourth Circuit Court of Appeal. *Dixon v. Coburg Dairy, Inc.*, 330 F.3d 250 (4th Cir. 2003), *rev'd en banc*, 369 F.3d 811 (4th Cir. 2004). A South Carolina statute makes it "unlawful to discharge a citizen from employment because of the exercise of *political* rights and privileges guaranteed under the Constitution of the United States" or because of an individual's political opinions. S.C. CODE ANN. § 16-17-560 (2002). Dixon sued under the statute, alleging that Coburg had violated his constitutional right to free speech, thereby violating the state statute. Although the Fourth Circuit, sitting *en banc*, eventually found that it lacked jurisdiction and remanded the case to state court, the appellate panel that initially heard the case ruled in favor of the employer. Noting the legitimate concern that failure to respond could expose the company to liability for racial harassment, the panel concluded that Coburg had not discharged Dixon because of his political views, but had "merely insisted that he voice those viewpoints in a manner that would be less likely to goad one of his co-workers into an emotional confrontation." 330 F.3d at 264.

Was Dixon discharged because of his political opinions or how he expressed them? How should Dixon's speech rights under the South Carolina statute be reconciled with the important public policies embodied in state and federal anti-discrimination laws? Suppose Dixon had attended a pro-Confederate flag rally—would he be protected against discharge under the South Carolina statute? What if Dixon were a public employee? Would he have a claim under *Pickering* and *Connick*? For a thoughtful analysis of the competing interests in a situation like *Dixon*, see Cynthia L. Estlund, *Freedom of Expression in the Workplace and the Problem of Discriminatory Harassment*, 75 TEX. L. REV. 687 (1997).

2. Statutory Protections Against Retaliation

Statutes creating substantive employment rights have typically included a form of speech protection—namely, prohibitions on employer retaliation for complaining about violation of those rights. For example, the NLRA includes a provision that prohibits discharging workers for filing charges alleging a violation of the statute. 29 U.S.C.A. § 158(a)(4). Similarly, other statutes that establish employment rights, such as Title VII or OSHA, also include prohibitions on retaliation against employees who complain about discrimination or unsafe working conditions. *See, e.g.*, 42 U.S.C.A. § 2000e–3(a); 29 U.S.C.A. § 660(c). These types of protections recognize that enforcement of substantive employment rights depends upon employees' ability to speak up freely. If they can be retaliated against for asserting those rights, the statutory guarantees will be undermined.

In addition to employment-specific statutes, laws with a broader purpose may contain provisions forbidding retaliation against those who report violations. For example, a law aimed at preventing child abuse might prohibit retaliating against someone who reports such abuse. *See, e.g.*, CONN. GEN. STAT. ANN. § 17a-101e; N.D. CENT. CODE § 50-25.1-09.1. Similarly, federal statutes directed at goals such as improving railroad or aviation safety also protect those who report violations of the standards they establish. *See, e.g.*, Federal Railroad Safety Act, 49 U.S.C. § 20109; Wendell H. Ford Aviation Investment and Reform Act, 49 U.S.C. § 42121. In these statutes, the anti-retaliation provisions are intended to ensure compliance with other policies, not to encourage whistleblowing per se. Thus, the protections apply only when the employee has made a report falling within the particular subject matter of the statute.

Up until the mid-1970s, no laws broadly protected employees who objected to or reported wrongdoing from retaliation. Since then, general whistleblower protections have become common. As discussed in Chapter 4 above, the common law doctrine of wrongful discharge in violation of public policy can encompass some claims that an employee was terminated for reporting illegal or harmful conduct by an employer. However, the extent of common law protections for whistleblowers varies greatly depending upon how a state's courts have defined the contours of the public policy exception.

During the same time period when courts were developing wrongful discharge doctrines, state legislatures began to enact general whistleblower statutes. When doing so, legislatures confronted questions about what particular circumstances and types of reports should be protected. For example, should only certain types of employees be protected? Only government employees? Or all workers? And what level of proof that an actual violation occurred should be required? Is the employee's good faith belief enough? Should the belief be objectively reasonable as well? Or must the plaintiff show that illegality actually occurred? What types of violations must be shown? Any violation of law, or only those that pose an imminent threat to the public or only specifically listed violations? And should employees be required to first report alleged wrong-doing internally? If they are fired before making a complaint to an external agency, are they still protected?

The statutes that resulted answered these questions in a variety of ways, such that whether or not an employee is protected will depend upon the type of employee, the alleged violation and the precise factual circumstances of the whistleblowing. According to lists compiled by Daniel P. Westman and Nancy M. Modesitt, nearly every state has a statute protecting public employees for engaging in at least some forms of whistleblowing, whereas less than half the states provide similarly broad protection to private sector workers. DANIEL P. WESTMAN & NANCY M. MODESITT, WHISTLEBLOWING: THE LAW OF RETALIATORY DISCHARGE (2d ed. 2004 & Supp. 2013) (listing state statutes providing protections for employee whistleblowers). In addition to being more common, state statutes protecting public employees generally have broader coverage, protecting not only reports of all kinds of legal violations, but also allegations of waste and mismanagement. *Id.* at 80. In contrast, among the statutes providing general whistleblower protection to private sector employees, "there is little consensus . . . [regarding issues] such as the scope of protected complaints, the strength of remedies available, and overlap with other sources of whistleblower protection." *Id.* at 78–79.

To some extent, the uneven protection afforded by state whistleblower statutes mirrored the uncertainty of common law courts in defining the contours of the public policy tort. In particular, recall that courts have been reluctant to permit claims by private employees who report internal problems with corporate management, on the grounds that such cases raise "purely private concerns." Thus, for many years non-governmental employees who complained of financial wrongdoing by their employers received little protection from retaliation. All that began to change with the passage of the Sarbanes-Oxley Act in 2002.

3.   Whistleblower Protections of the Sarbanes-Oxley Act

Beginning with the collapse of Enron in 2001, a series of accounting scandals resulted in corporate failures, billions of dollars of shareholder losses, and massive layoffs. These events highlighted the significant public losses suffered as a result of private financial wrongdoing. In addition, they raised questions about how such extensive accounting irregularities and outright fraud could go on undetected for years. Public attention focused on the role of whistleblowers and the question whether employees with knowledge of the corporate frauds could have stopped or exposed these fraudulent practices.

Among the witnesses who testified before Congress in the wake of Enron's collapse was Sherron Watkins, a former Enron Vice-President, who had warned the company's chairman about extensive accounting improprieties. After raising these concerns internally, she had been "reassigned from her executive suite to a starkly furnished office 33 floors below and relegated to performing make-work tasks." Kathleen F. Brickey, *From Enron to WorldCom and Beyond: Life and Crime After Sarbanes-Oxley*, 81 WASH. U.L.Q. 357, 363 (2003). Enron's outside counsel had advised the firm—accurately—that Texas law did not prohibit retaliatory actions taken against corporate whistleblowers. *Id.* Although the Texas Supreme Court had recognized the public policy exception to the at-will rule, it construed it narrowly to apply only when an employee was discharged "for the sole reason that the employee refused to perform an illegal act that carried criminal penalties." *Sabine Pilot Service, Inc. v. Hauck*, 687 S.W.2d 733 (Tex. 2006). Thus, Watkins' reports of financial irregularities were not protected.

After hearings about Enron's collapse and other corporate failures, Congress responded by passing the Sarbanes-Oxley Act of 2002. Many of the statute's provisions are focused on ensuring accountability by public companies by, for example, requiring increased disclosures, strengthening the role of independent audit committees, and creating new rules to improve internal controls and reduce conflicts of interest. *See* Larry E. Ribstein, *Market v. Regulatory Responses to Corporate Fraud: A Critique of the Sarbanes-Oxley Act of 2002*, 28 J. CORP. L. 2 (2002). Significantly for employment law, however, the statute also enacted important new protections for whistleblowers.

The key whistleblower provisions of the Sarbanes-Oxley Act (SOX) are found in Section 806(a) of the Act (codified at 18 U.S.C. § 1514A), which prohibits regulated companies from retaliating against employees who report certain types of corporate wrongdoing. More specifically, the statute prohibits retaliation against employees who report alleged violations of several listed statutes—namely, those relating to mail fraud, wire fraud, bank fraud and securities fraud, and the rules and regulations of the Securities and Exchange Commission. Thus, the statute does not provide generalized protection for whistleblowers; rather, employees seeking protection under the statute have to show that their activities are covered by the statutory language. As we shall see, what exactly that requires is a matter of some dispute in the courts. In addition, controversy has arisen over exactly which employees are entitled to protection, an issue addressed by the Supreme Court in *Lawson v. FMR*, below.

The relevant part of Sarbanes-Oxley, as amended, provides the following:

(a) [No company regulated by the Securities Exchange Act of 1934, its subsidiary or affiliate, or nationally recognized statistical rating organization,] or any officer, employee, contractor, subcontractor, or agent of such company or nationally recognized statistical rating organization, may discharge, demote, suspend, threaten, harass, or in any other manner discriminate against an employee in the terms and conditions of employment because of any lawful act done by the employee—

(1) to provide information, cause information to be provided, or otherwise assist in an investigation regarding any conduct which the employee reasonably believes constitutes a violation of section 1341 [mail fraud], 1343 [wire fraud], 1344 [bank fraud], or 1348 [securities fraud], any rule or regulation of the Securities and Exchange Commission, or any provision of Federal law relating to fraud against shareholders, when the information or assistance is provided to or the investigation is conducted by—

(A) a Federal regulatory or law enforcement agency;

(B) any Member of Congress or any committee of Congress; or

(C) a person with supervisory authority over the employee (or such other person working for the employer who has the authority to investigate, discover, or terminate misconduct); or

(2) to file, cause to be filed, testify, participate in, or otherwise assist in a proceeding filed or about to be filed (with any knowledge of the employer) relating to an alleged violation of section 1341, 1343, 1344, or 1348, any rule or regulation of the Securities and Exchange Commission, or any provision of Federal law relating to fraud against shareholders.

Sarbanes-Oxley Act of 2002, 18 U.S.C. § 1514A(a).

Employees who believe they have been retaliated against in violation of this section can file a complaint with the Secretary of Labor. 18 U.S.C. § 1514A(b). The Secretary has delegated the responsibility of receiving and investigating these complaints to the Occupational Safety and Health Administration ("OSHA") which already had authority to investigate employee claims of retaliation for reporting violations under the Occupational Safety and Health Act and a handful of other federal statutes regulating areas such as trucking, aviation and the environment. Upon receiving a complaint, OSHA conducts an investigation and issues written findings regarding the retaliation claim. The findings become the final order of the Department of Labor unless a party requests further review from an Administrative Law Judge. ALJs conduct de novo hearings and their decisions can be appealed to the Department of Labor's Administrative Review Board (ARB). ARB decisions can be appealed to a federal circuit court of appeals.

Aggrieved employees cannot sue directly in federal court under Sarbanes-Oxley's whistleblower provisions unless they file a complaint with OSHA within a certain period of time (within 90 days of the date of the violation under the initial version of the statute; now 180 days after amendment), and the Secretary of Labor does not issue a final decision within 180 days of the filing of the complaint. 18 U.S.C. § 1514A(b)(1). If these administrative prerequisites are met, the claim will be heard *de novo* in the federal court.

According to the statutory language, an employee who prevails under § 1514A is entitled to "all relief necessary to make the employee whole," including reinstatement, backpay and "compensation for any special damages sustained as a result of the discrimination, including litigation costs, expert witness fees, and reasonable attorney fees." § 1514A(c). The lower courts have been divided about whether this language authorizes damages for noneconomic losses such as harm to reputation or emotional damages. *Compare Hanna v. WCI Cmtys., Inc.*, 348 F. Supp. 2d 1332, 1333–34 (S.D. Fla. 2004) (allowing "damages for reputational injury that diminishes plaintiff's future earning capacity"), *with Walton v. Nova Info. Sys.*, 514 F. Supp. 2d 1031, 1035 (E.D. Tenn. 2007) (rejecting non-pecuniary damages such as injury to reputation, mental and physical distress, or punitive damages), and *Schmidt v. Levi Strauss Co.*, 621 F. Supp. 2d 796, 803 (N.D. Cal. 2008) (finding § 1514A does not permit compensatory or special damages). The Tenth Circuit, however, recently upheld an award that included damages for emotional pain and suffering, mental anguish, embarrassment and humiliation. *Lockheed Martin Corp. v. Administrative Review Bd.*, 717 F.3d 1121 (10th Cir. 2013).

Unlike many statutes creating employment rights, Sarbanes-Oxley specifically addressed the question of preclusion, stating that "Nothing in this section shall be deemed to diminish the rights, privileges, or remedies of any employee under any Federal or State law, or under any collective bargaining agreement." 18 U.S.C. § 1514A(d).

Scholars and commentators initially heralded Sarbanes-Oxley's whistleblower provisions as a significant change in the law, one that established systematic protections for corporate whistleblowers. In the years immediately after its passage, experience under the statute did not match these high expectations; only a tiny fraction of employees succeeded on their whistleblower claims in the administrative process. *See* Richard Moberly, *Unfulfilled Expectations: An Empirical Analysis of Why Sarbanes-Oxley Whistleblowers Rarely Win*, 49 WM. & MARY L. REV. 65 (2007) (finding that in the first three years after the statute was enacted, OSHA's initial investigations found in favor of complaining employees only 3.6% of the time, and when appealed, administrative law judges ruled in favor of employees in only 6.5% of cases); Richard Moberly, *Sarbanes-Oxley's Whistleblower Provisions—Ten Years Later*, 64 S.C. L. REV. 1, 28–29 (2012) (reporting that employees prevailed in only 1.8% of the cases OSHA decided in a nearly six-year period).

With the financial crisis of 2008 and ensuing recession, public attention again focused on how to prevent corporate wrong-doing. In response, Congress passed the Dodd-Frank Wall Street Reform and Consumer Protection Act of 2010, which among other things, strengthened Sarbanes-Oxley Act's protections for corporate whistleblowers. Dodd-Frank amended Sarbanes-Oxley in a number of ways—for example, by extending the period of time to file a whistleblower complaint with OSHA from 90 days after the violation occurs to 180 days after the violation or the date on which the employee became aware of the violation. 18 U.S.C. § 1514A(b)(2)(D). In addition, Dodd-Frank created a right to jury trial in Sarbanes-Oxley whistleblower actions, § 1514A(b)(2)(E), and added a provision barring predispute agreements to arbitrate these claims. § 1514A(e). Finally, Dodd-Frank created new whistleblower incentives and protections going far beyond those provided in Sarbanes-Oxley. We will consider the new protections enacted by Dodd-Frank in the next subsection, but we first explore the whistleblower protections afforded by the Sarbanes-Oxley Act and some of the interpretative difficulties that have arisen under the statute.

a.   Who Is Protected?

LAWSON v. FMR LLC
United States Supreme Court
134 S. Ct. 1158 (2014)

JUSTICE GINSBURG delivered the opinion of the Court.

To safeguard investors in public companies and restore trust in the financial markets following the collapse of Enron Corporation, Congress enacted the Sarbanes-Oxley Act of 2002. A provision of the Act, 18 U.S.C. § 1514A, protects whistleblowers. Section 1514A, at the time here relevant, instructed:

> "No [public] company . . . , or any officer, employee, contractor, sub-contractor, or agent of such company, may discharge, demote, suspend, threaten, harass, or in any other manner discriminate against an employee in the terms and conditions of employment because of [whistleblowing or other protected activity]." § 1514A(a) (2006 ed.).

This case concerns the definition of the protected class: Does § 1514A shield only those employed by the public company itself, or does it shield as well employees of privately held contractors and subcontractors—for example, investment advisers, law firms, accounting enterprises—who perform work for the public company?

We hold . . . that the provision shelters employees of private contractors and subcontractors, just as it shelters employees of the public company served by the contractors and subcontractors.

I.

A.

The Sarbanes-Oxley Act of 2002 (Sarbanes-Oxley or Act) aims to "prevent and punish corporate and criminal fraud, protect the victims of such fraud, preserve evidence of such fraud, and hold wrongdoers accountable for their actions." S. Rep. No. 107-146, p. 2 (2002) (hereinafter S. Rep.). Of particular concern to Congress was abundant evidence that Enron had succeeded in perpetuating its massive share-holder fraud in large part due to a "corporate code of silence"; that code, Congress found, "discourage[d] employees from reporting fraudulent behavior not only to the proper authorities, such as the FBI and the SEC, but even internally." *Id.*, at 4–5 (internal quotation marks omitted). When employees of Enron and its accounting firm, Arthur Andersen, attempted to report corporate misconduct, Congress learned, they faced retaliation, including discharge. As outside counsel advised company officials at the time, Enron's efforts to "quiet" whistleblowers generally were not proscribed under then-existing law. *Id.*, at 5, 10. Congress identified the lack of whistleblower protection as "a significant deficiency" in the law, for in complex securities fraud investigations, employees "are [often] the only firsthand witnesses to the fraud." *Id.*, at 10.

Section 806 of Sarbanes-Oxley, [codified at 18 U.S.C. § 1514A,] addresses this concern. . . .

B.

Petitioners Jackie Hosang Lawson and Jonathan M. Zang (plaintiffs) separately initiated proceedings under § 1514A against their former employers [collectively referred to as FMR, LLC], privately held companies that provide advisory and management services to the Fidelity family of mutual funds. The Fidelity funds are not parties to either case; as is common in the mutual fund industry, the Fidelity funds themselves have no employees. Instead, they contract with investment advisers like respondents to handle their day-to-day operations, which include making investment decisions, preparing reports for shareholders, and filing reports with the Securities and Exchange Commission (SEC).

Lawson worked for FMR for 14 years, eventually serving as a Senior Director of Finance. She alleges that, after she raised concerns about certain cost accounting methodologies, believing that they overstated expenses associated with operating the mutual funds, she suffered a series of adverse actions, ultimately amounting to constructive discharge. Zang was employed by FMR for eight years, most recently as a portfolio manager for several of the funds. He alleges that he was fired in retaliation for raising concerns about inaccuracies in a draft SEC registration statement concerning certain Fidelity funds. . . . Lawson and Zang each filed suit in the U.S. District Court for the District of Massachusetts.

FMR moved to dismiss the suits . . . . FMR is privately held, and maintained that § 1514A protects only employees of public companies—*i.e.*, companies that either have "a class of securities registered under section 12 of the Securities Exchange Act of 1934," or that are "required to file reports under section 15(d)" of that Act. § 1514A(a) . . . . [T]he District Court . . . denied the dismissal motions . . . . [A] divided panel of the First Circuit reversed. 670 F.3d 61 (2012). . . .

II.

A.

In determining the meaning of a statutory provision, "we look first to its language, giving the words used their ordinary meaning." *Moskal v. United States*, 498 U.S. 103, 108 (1990). As Judge Thompson observed in her dissent from the Court of Appeals' judgment, "boiling [§ 1514A(a)] down to its relevant syntactic elements, it provides that 'no . . . contractor . . . may discharge . . . an employee.' " 670 F.3d, at 84 (quoting § 1514A(a)). The ordinary meaning of "an employee" in this proscription is the contractor's own employee.

FMR's interpretation of the text requires insertion of "of a public company" after "an employee." But where Congress meant "an employee of a public company," it said so: With respect to the actors governed by § 1514A, the provision's interdictions run to the officers, employees, contractors, subcontractors, and agents "of such company," *i.e.*, a public company. § 1514A(a) . . . . In contrast, nothing in § 1514A's language confines the class of employees protected to those of a designated employer. Absent any textual qualification, we presume the operative language means what it appears to mean: A contractor may not retaliate against its own employee for engaging in protected whistleblowing activity.

Section 1514A's application to contractor employees is confirmed when we enlarge our view from the term "an employee" to the provision as a whole. The prohibited retaliatory measures enumerated in § 1514A(a)—discharge, demotion, suspension, threats, harassment, or discrimination in the terms and conditions of employment—are commonly actions an employer takes against its *own* employees. Contractors are not ordinarily positioned to take adverse actions against employees of the public company with whom they contract.

FMR urges that Congress included contractors in § 1514A's list of governed actors simply to prevent public companies from avoiding liability by employing contractors to effectuate retaliatory discharges. FMR describes such a contractor as an "ax-wielding specialist," illustrated by George Clooney's character in the movie Up in the Air. As portrayed by Clooney, an ax-wielding specialist is a contractor engaged only as the bearer of the bad news that the employee has been fired; he plays no role in deciding who to terminate. If the company employing the ax-wielder chose the recipients of the bad tidings for retaliatory reasons, the § 1514A claim would properly be directed at the company. Hiring the ax-wielder would not insulate the company from liability. Moreover, we see no indication that retaliatory ax-wielding specialists are the real-world problem that prompted Congress to add contractors to § 1514A . . . .

Regarding remedies, § 1514A(c)(2) states that a successful claimant shall be entitled to "reinstatement with the same seniority status that the employee would have had, but for the discrimination," as well as "the amount of back pay, with interest." As the Solicitor General, for the United States as *amicus curiae*, observed, "It is difficult, if not impossible, to see how a contractor or subcontractor could provide those remedies to an employee of a public company." The most sensible reading of § 1514A's numerous references to an employer-employee relationship between the respondent and the claimant is that the provision's protections run between contractors and their own employees.

Remarkably, the dissent attributes to Congress a strange design. Under the dissent's "narrower" construction, a public company's contractor may not retaliate against a public company's employees, academic here because the public company has no employees. According to the dissent, this coverage is necessary to prevent "a gaping hole" that would allow public companies to "evade § 1514A simply by hiring a contractor to engage in the very retaliatory acts that an officer or employee could not." This cannot be right—even if Congress had omitted any reference to contractors, subcontractors, or agents in § 1514A, the remaining language surely would prohibit a public company from directing someone else to engage in retaliatory conduct against the public company's employees; hiring an ax-wielder to announce an employee's demotion does not change the fact that the public company is the entity commanding the demotion. Under the dissent's reading of § 1514A, the inclusion of contractors as covered employers does no more than make the contractor secondarily liable for complying with such marching orders—hardly a hole at all.

There would be a huge hole, on the other hand, were the dissent's view of § 1514A's reach to prevail: Contractors' employees would be disarmed; they would be vulnerable to retaliation by their employers for blowing the whistle on a scheme to defraud the public company's investors, even a scheme engineered entirely by the contractor. Not only would mutual fund advisers and managers escape § 1514A's control. Legions of accountants and lawyers would be denied § 1514A's protections. Instead of indulging in fanciful visions of whistleblowing babysitters and the like, the dissent might pause to consider whether a Congress, prompted by the Enron debacle, would exclude from whistleblower protection countless professionals equipped to bring fraud on investors to a halt.

B.

. . . FMR urges that "an employee" must be read to refer exclusively to public company employees to avoid the absurd result of extending protection to the personal employees of company officers and employees, *e.g.*, their housekeepers or gardeners. . . . If, as we hold, "an employee" includes employees of contractors, then grammatically, the term also includes employees of public company officers and employees. Nothing suggests Congress' attention was drawn to the curiosity its drafting produced. The issue, however, is likely more theoretical than real. Few housekeepers or gardeners, we suspect, are likely to come upon and comprehend evidence of their employer's complicity in fraud. In any event, FMR's point is outweighed by the compelling arguments opposing FMR's contention that "an employee" refers simply and only to public company employees . . . .

III.

A.

Our textual analysis of § 1514A fits the provision's purpose. It is common ground that Congress installed whistleblower protection in the Sarbanes-Oxley Act as one means to ward off another Enron debacle. S. Rep., at 2–11. And, as the ARB observed in *Spinner v. David Landau & Assoc., LLC*, No. 10-111 etc., ALJ No. 2010-SOX-029 (May 31, 2012), "Congress plainly recognized that outside professionals—accountants, law firms, contractors, agents, and the like—were complicit in, if not integral to, the shareholder fraud and subsequent cover-up [Enron] officers . . . perpetrated." Indeed, the Senate Report demonstrates that Congress was as focused on the role of Enron's outside contractors in facilitating the fraud as it was on the actions of Enron's own officers. See, *e.g.*, S. Rep., at 3 (fraud "occurred with extensive participation and structuring advice from Arthur Andersen . . . which was simultaneously serving as both consultant and independent auditor for Enron"); *id.*, at 4 ("professionals from accounting firms, law firms and business consulting firms, who were paid millions to advise Enron on these practices, assured others that Enron was a solid investment") . . .

Also clear from the legislative record is Congress' understanding that outside professionals bear significant responsibility for reporting fraud by the public companies with whom they contract, and that fear of retaliation was the primary deterrent to such reporting by the employees of Enron's contractors. Congressional investigators discovered ample evidence of contractors demoting or discharging employees they have engaged who jeopardized the contractor's business relationship with Enron by objecting to Enron's financial practices . . . . Emphasizing the importance of outside professionals as "gatekeepers who detect and deter fraud," the Senate Report concludes: "Congress must reconsider the incentive system that has been set up that encourages accountants and lawyers who come across fraud in their work to remain silent." From this legislative history, one can safely conclude that Congress enacted § 1514A aiming to encourage whistleblowing by contractor employees who suspect fraud involving the public companies with whom they work.

FMR argues that Congress addressed its concerns about the role of outside accountants and lawyers in facilitating Enron's wrongdoing, not in § 1514A, but exclusively in other provisions of Sarbanes-Oxley "*directly* regulat[ing] accountants and lawyers." In particular, FMR points to sections of the Act requiring accountants and lawyers for public companies to investigate and report misconduct, or risk being banned from further practice before the SEC. *Id.* at 41 (citing 15 U.S.C. §§ 7215(c)(4), 7245). These requirements, however, indicate why Congress would have wanted to extend § 1514A's coverage to the many lawyers and accountants who perform outside work for public companies. Although lawyers and accountants are subject to extensive regulations and sanctions throughout Sarbanes-Oxley, no provision of the Act other than § 1514A affords them protection from retaliation by their employers for complying with the Act's reporting requirements.[8] In short, we

---

[8] [n.14] The dissent suggests that the Public Company Accounting Oversight Board's and the SEC's authority to sanction unprofessional conduct by accountants and lawyers, respectively, "could well

cannot countenance the position advanced by FMR and the dissent that Congress intended to leave these professionals vulnerable to discharge or other retaliatory action for complying with the law.

B.

Our reading of § 1514A avoids insulating the entire mutual fund industry from § 1514A, as FMR's and the dissent's "narrower construction" would do. As companies "required to file reports under section 15(d) of the Securities Exchange Act of 1934," 18 U.S.C. § 1514A(a), mutual funds unquestionably are governed by § 1514A. . . . Virtually all mutual funds are structured so that they have no employees of their own; they are managed, instead, by independent investment advisers. . . .

C.

. . . The dissent's fears that household employees and others, on learning of today's decision, will be prompted to pursue retaliation claims, and that OSHA will find them meritorious under § 1514A, seem to us unwarranted. If we are wrong, however, Congress can easily fix the problem by amending § 1514A explicitly to remove personal employees of public company officers and employees from the provision's reach. But it would thwart Congress' dominant aim if contractors were taken off the hook for retaliating against their whistleblowing employees, just to avoid the unlikely prospect that babysitters, nannies, gardeners, and the like will flood OSHA with § 1514A complaints. . . .

Plaintiffs' allegations fall squarely within Congress' aim in enacting § 1514A. Lawson alleges that she was constructively discharged for reporting accounting practices that overstated expenses associated with managing certain Fidelity mutual funds. This alleged fraud directly implicates the funds' shareholders: "By inflating its expenses, and thus understating its profits, [FMR] could potentially increase the fees it would earn from the mutual funds, fees ultimately paid by the shareholders of those funds." Zang alleges that he was fired for expressing concerns about inaccuracies in a draft registration statement FMR prepared for the SEC on behalf of certain Fidelity funds. The potential impact on shareholders of false or misleading registration statements needs no elaboration . . . .

---

provide" a disincentive to retaliate against other accountants and lawyers. The possibility of such sanctions, however, is cold comfort to the accountant or lawyer who loses her job in retaliation for her efforts to comply with the Act's requirements if, as the dissent would have it, § 1514A does not enable her to seek reinstatement or backpay.

[The concurring opinion of JUSTICE SCALIA, with whom JUSTICE THOMAS joins, is omitted.]

JUSTICE SOTOMAYOR, with whom JUSTICE KENNEDY and JUSTICE ALITO join, dissenting.

. . . The Court's interpretation gives § 1514A a stunning reach. As interpreted today, the Sarbanes-Oxley Act authorizes a babysitter to bring a federal case against his employer—a parent who happens to work at the local Walmart (a public company)—if the parent stops employing the babysitter after he expresses concern that the parent's teenage son may have participated in an Internet purchase fraud. And it opens the door to a cause of action against a small business that contracts to clean the local Starbucks (a public company) if an employee is demoted after reporting that another nonpublic company client has mailed the cleaning company a fraudulent invoice.

Congress was of course free to create this kind of sweeping regime that subjects a multitude of individuals and private businesses to litigation over fraud reports that have no connection to, or impact on, the interests of public company shareholders. But because nothing in the text, context, or purpose of the Sarbanes-Oxley Act suggests that Congress actually wanted to do so, I respectfully dissent.

. . . [Section] 1514A(a) . . . provides that "[n]o [public] company . . . or any officer, employee, contractor, subcontractor, or agent of such company . . . may discharge, demote, suspend, threaten, harass, or in any other manner discriminate against an employee." The provision thus does not speak only (or even primarily) to "contractors." It speaks to public companies, and then includes a list of five types of representatives that companies hire to carry out their business: "officer[s], employee[s], contractor[s], subcontractor[s], [and] agent[s]." . . . [T]he Government and petitioners readily concede that § 1514A is meant to bar two of the enumerated representatives—"officer[s]" and "employee[s]"—from retaliating against other employees of the public company, as opposed to their own babysitters and housekeepers. . . . And if § 1514A prohibits an "officer" or "employee" of a public company from retaliating against only the public company's own employees, then as the majority points out, the same should be true "grammatically" of contractors, subcontractors, and agents as well. . . .

Statutory context confirms that Congress intended § 1514A to apply only to employees of public companies. To start, the Sarbanes-Oxley Act as a whole evinces a clear focus on public companies. Congress stated in the Act's preamble that its objective was to "protect investors by improving the accuracy and reliability of corporate disclosures made pursuant to the securities laws," disclosures that public companies alone must file. . . .

[I]t must be noted that § 1514A protects the reporting of a variety of frauds—not only securities fraud, but also mail, wire, and bank fraud. By interpreting a statute that already protects an expansive class of conduct also to cover a large class of employees, today's opinion threatens to subject private companies to a costly new front of employment litigation. Congress almost certainly did not intend the statute to have that reach. . . .

* * * *

The Court's interpretation of § 1514A undeniably serves a laudatory purpose. By covering employees of every officer, employee, and contractor of every public company, the majority's interpretation extends § 1514A's protections to the outside lawyers and accountants who could have helped prevent the Enron fraud.

But that is not the statute Congress wrote. Congress envisioned a system in which public company employees would be covered by § 1514A, and in which outside lawyers, investment advisers, and accountants would be regulated by the SEC and PCAOB. Congress did not envision a system in which employees of other private businesses—such as cleaning and construction company workers who have little interaction with investor-related activities and who are thus ill suited to assist in detecting fraud against shareholders—would fall within § 1514A. Nor, needless to say, did it envision § 1514A applying to the household employees of millions of individuals who happen to work for public companies—housekeepers, gardeners, and babysitters who are also poorly positioned to prevent fraud against public company investors . . . . The Court's decision upsets the balance struck by Congress. Fortunately, just as Congress has added further protections to the system it originally designed when necessary, so too may Congress now respond to limit the far-reaching implications of the Court's interpretation.[9]

NOTES

1. **Who Is Protected?** In deciding *Lawson*, the Supreme Court resolved an emerging split in authority regarding which employees are protected under the whistleblower provision of Sarbanes-Oxley. *Compare Lawson v. FMR, LLC*, 670 F.3d 61 (1st Cir. 2012) *with Spinner v. David Landau & Assoc., LLC*, No. 10-111 etc., ALJ No. 2010-SOX-029 (May 31, 2012). The First Circuit had held that Lawson and Zang were not protected from retaliation under Sarbanes-Oxley because they were not employees of a publicly-held company, even though their employer contracted with such a company. Over a strong dissent, a majority of the Supreme Court reversed, reading the statute to encompass claims by employees who work for contractors of public companies.

How do the majority and the dissent reach such different conclusions in their interpretation of the scope of Sarbanes-Oxley's whistleblower protections? Which reading do you think is most consistent with the text of the statute? With the purposes behind it? Both the majority and the dissent point to the dire consequences that will result if their interpretation does not prevail. What consequences does each side fear and which pose the greatest risk from a policy standpoint? Do you think Congress anticipated any of these risks when drafting the statute?

2. **Regulating the Professions.** As the opinions in *Lawson* note, Sarbanes-Oxley did far more than create whistleblower protections. One of the other things it did was to strengthen direct regulation by the Public Company Accounting

---

[9] [n.12] Congress could, for example, limit § 1514A to contractor employees in only those professions that can assist in detecting fraud on public company shareholders, or it could restrict the fraud reports that trigger whistleblower protection to those that implicate the interests of public company investors.

Oversight Board and the Securities and Exchange Commission of the accountants and lawyers who advise public companies. *See, e.g.*, 15 U.S.C § 7215 (providing for investigation and discipline of registered public accounting firms); 15 U.S.C. § 7245 (requiring SEC to issue rules creating standards of professional conduct for attorneys appearing and practicing before the Commission to protect the public and investors). Pursuant to the latter section, the SEC adopted new rules of professional conduct that require attorneys who become aware of "evidence of a material violation" of securities law, breach of fiduciary duty, or similar violations to report them "up the ladder" of corporate authority to the Chief Legal Officer or Chief Executive Officer. 17 C.F.R. § 205.3. If such reporting does not result in an "appropriate response" from the corporation, covered attorneys are required to report the violation to the company's audit committee, another committee of independent directors, or the full board of directors. *Id.*

In the view of the dissenting justices, these provisions indicate that Congress made a choice to impose a duty directly on the outside accountants and attorneys who advise public firms to report wrongdoing, while excluding them from § 1514A's whistleblower protections. The majority, on the other hand, believed that imposing professional obligations without legal protection from retaliation was insufficient to adequately incentivize accountants and lawyers to blow the whistle. This disagreement echoes the debate covered in Chapter 4 over whether in-house attorneys should be permitted to sue for wrongful discharge in violation of public policy, or whether the ethical rules governing attorneys are sufficient to ensure that they act in the public interest when they learn of employer wrongdoing.

3.   **A Congressional Fix.** Because the issue in *Lawson* is a matter of statutory construction, Congress can step in and alter the scope of § 1514A protections if it disagrees with the Court. Should it do so? If you were on a committee drafting a proposed amendment to § 1514A after *Lawson*, what language would you add to make clear which employees are intended to be protected?

* * * *

Lawson illustrates how ambiguity in the text of Sarbanes-Oxley created uncertainty about which employees Congress intended to protect. Additional questions have arisen regarding the scope of activities protected as whistleblowing under the statute. The following materials explore that question.

b.   What Is Protected Activity?

WIEST v. LYNCH
United States Court of Appeals for the Third Circuit
710 F.3d 121 (2013)

VANASKIE, CIRCUIT JUDGE.

Appellant Jeffrey Wiest brought an action under the whistleblower protection provisions set forth in Section 806 of the Sarbanes-Oxley Act ("SOX"), 18 U.S.C. § 1514A . . . [against] Tyco Electronics Corporation . . . . The District Court granted Tyco's Motion to Dismiss . . . . According to the Complaint, Wiest worked for approximately thirty-one years in Tyco's accounting department until his termination in April 2010. For Wiest's last ten years of employment, his office was under "a high level of audit scrutiny" due to the well-known corporate scandal involving its former parent company, Tyco International, and its CEO, Dennis Kozlowski. Around 2007, Wiest "established a pattern of rejecting and questioning expenses" that failed to satisfy accounting standards or securities and tax laws.

In mid-2008, Wiest refused to process a payment and sent an email to his supervisor regarding an event that Tyco intended to hold at the Atlantis Resort in the Bahamas, which was similar to a corporate party under Kozlowski's management that had drawn significant criticism. Expenses for the $350,000 Atlantis event included "Mermaid Greeters" and "Costumed Pirates/Wenches" at a cost of $3,000; a "Tattoo Artist (includes tattoos)" and "Limbo" and "Fire" at a cost of $2,350; chair decorations at a cost of $2,500; and hotel room rentals ranging from $475 to $1,000 per night. In an email to his supervisor, Wiest expressed his belief that the costs were inappropriately charged entirely as advertising expenses. He asserted that the costs needed to be detailed and charged as income to attending employees because the employees were bringing guests, and the expenses needed to "be reviewed for potential disallowance by a taxing authority based on excessive/ extravagant spend [sic] levels." Following Wiest's email, Tyco's management determined that the five-day event included only a single one-and-one-half hour business meeting. As a result, they determined that processing the payment "would have resulted in a misstatement of accounting records and a fraudulent tax deduction," and that Tyco needed to treat the event as income for attending employees. Tyco decided to proceed with the event and to compensate the attendees for the additional tax liability by increasing (i.e., "grossing-up") their bonuses.

Also in mid-2008, Wiest received a request to process a payment of $218,000 for a conference at the Venetian Resort in Las Vegas, Nevada. The request lacked both sufficient documentation for tax purposes and proper approval pursuant to Tyco's "delegation of authority." Additionally, the request included inaccurate accounting and tax treatment information. At Wiest's direction, one of his subordinates sent an email to the Tyco employee who submitted the request, explaining that the accounts payable department could not process the request until it had received an agenda and business purpose for the event, correct accounting treatment for various expenses, and approval pursuant to Tyco's delegation of authority. The tax department eventually concluded that the conference served a business purpose, and the accounts payable department subsequently allowed the payment.

In late 2008, Wiest was presented with a request for approval of a conference at the Wintergreen Resort in Virginia in the amount of $335,000. Like the Venetian Resort request, the Wintergreen expense request lacked both sufficient documentation and proper approval from Tyco's CEO. Wiest emailed his supervisor, explaining that he believed Tyco's internal policies required that the CEO be notified about the transaction. To the best of Wiest knowledge, Tyco processed the payment without the CEO's approval, in violation of Tyco's internal policies. . . .

Wiest alleges that Tyco became frustrated with his persistence in following proper accounting procedures. In September 2009, two human resources employees met with Wiest and informed him that he was under investigation for incorrectly reporting the receipt of two basketball game tickets in August 2009, for having a relationship with a coworker ten years earlier, and for allegedly making sexually-oriented comments to co-workers. After Wiest learned of the investigation, his health declined and he went on medical leave. Seven months later, Tyco terminated his employment . . . .

On July 7, 2010, Wiest sued the Tyco Defendants, asserting that his discharge was in retaliation for his reports of improper expenditures, in violation of Section 806 of SOX. . . .

SOX Section 806 prohibits publicly traded companies and their employees from retaliating against an employee who

> provide[s] information, cause[s] information to be provided, or otherwise assist[s] in an investigation regarding any conduct which the employee reasonably believes constitutes a violation of section 1341 [mail fraud], 1343 [wire, radio, or television fraud], 1344 [bank fraud], or 1348 [securities and commodities fraud], any rule or regulation of the Securities and Exchange Commission, or any provision of Federal law relating to fraud against shareholders, when the information is provided to or the investigation is conducted by . . . a person with supervisory authority over the employee (or such other person working for the employer who has the authority to investigate, discover, or terminate misconduct). . . .

18 U.S.C. § 1514A. To establish a prima facie case for a Section 806 claim, the employee must allege that he or she (1) "engaged in a protected activity;" (2) "[t]he respondent knew or suspected that the employee engaged in the protected activity;" (3) "[t]he employee suffered an adverse action;" and (4) "[t]he circumstances were sufficient to raise the inference that the protected activity was a contributing factor in the adverse action." 29 C.F.R. § 1980.104(e)(2)(i)–(iv). . . .

Focusing on the "protected activity" prong . . . the District Court invoked the ARB's opinion in *Platone* [*In the Matter of Platone v. FLYI, Inc.*, ARB 04-154, (ARB Sept. 29, 2006), *aff'd* 548 F.3d 322 (4th Cir. 2008)] and concluded that "[f]or a communication to be protected, it must 'definitively and specifically' relate to one of the statutes or rules listed in" Section 806. [The District Court also cited several Court of Appeals cases which followed *Platone*'s "definitive and specific" standard. Concluding that Wiest's complaint failed to meet this standard, the District Court dismissed the complaint.]

In *Sylvester* [*In the Matter of Sylvester v. Parexel Int'l LLC*, ARB 07-123, (ARB May 25, 2011) (en banc)], however, the ARB abandoned the "definitive and specific" standard announced in *Platone* [because that case had inappropriately relied on cases under a different statute protecting whistleblowers in the nuclear energy industry.] Moreover, the ARB determined that the definitive and specific standard potentially conflicts with the statutory language of Section 806, which prohibits retaliation against employees for reporting information that he or she *reasonably believes* violates SOX. Id. . . .

[The court followed the ARB's opinion in *Sylvester* in rejecting the "definitive and specific" standard and held that in order to show a "reasonable belief,"] an employee must establish not only a subjective, good faith belief that his or her employer violated a provision listed in SOX, but also that his or her belief was objectively reasonable. A belief is objectively reasonable when a reasonable person with the same training and experience as the employee would believe that the conduct implicated in the employee's communication could rise to the level of a violation of one of the enumerated provisions in Section 806.

The Dissent contends that we have adopted an internally inconsistent test by recognizing that an employee must have an objectively reasonable belief of a violation of one of the listed federal laws but not a reasonable belief that each element of a listed anti-fraud law is satisfied. We perceive no inconsistency because we do not think Congress intended such a formalistic approach to the question of whether an employee has engaged in "protected activity." . . . [The employee who identifies conduct "within the ample bounds of the anti-fraud laws"] should not be unprotected from reprisal because she did not have access to information sufficient to form an objectively reasonable belief that there was an intent to defraud or the information communicated to her supervisor was material to a shareholder's investment decision. "Congress chose statutory language which ensures that 'an employee's reasonable but mistaken belief that an employer engaged in conduct that constitutes a violation of one of the six enumerated categories [set forth in § 806] is protected.'" *Van Asdale*, 577 F.3d at 1001 (quoting *Allen* [*v. Admin Review Board*, 514 F.3d 468, at 477 (5th Cir. 2008)]. An employee's lack of knowledge of certain facts that pertain to an element of one of the anti-fraud laws would be relevant to, but not dispositive of, whether the employee did have an objectively reasonable belief that a listed anti-fraud law had been violated. . . .

[We also disagree with the District Court's conclusion] that to constitute protected activity, the information contained within an employee's communication must implicate "a reasonable belief of an *existing* violation." . . . Section 806 protects an employee's communication about a violation that has not yet occurred "as long as the employee reasonably believes that the violation is likely to happen." *Sylvester*, [2011 DOLSOX LEXIS 39]. [This interpretation is] reasonable given the statute's purpose to combat corporate wrongdoing. . . . It would frustrate that purpose to require an employee, who knows that a violation is imminent, to wait for the actual violation to occur when an earlier report possibly could have prevented it.

Contrary to our dissenting colleague's assertion, we are not "ignor[ing] the need for a whistleblower's employer to actually perceive that a whistle has been blown." We agree with the Dissent that, in order for an employer to "know or suspect that the whistleblower-plaintiff is engaged in protected conduct . . . the plaintiff's intra-corporate communications [must] relate in an understandable way to one of the stated provisions of federal law [in § 806]." (*Id.*) But the whistleblower's communication need not ring the bell on each element of one of the stated provisions of federal law to support an inference that the employer knew or suspected that the plaintiff was blowing the whistle on conduct that may fall within the ample reach of the anti-fraud laws listed in § 806. To hold that an employer could not have suspected that the plaintiff was engaged in protected activity because the communication did not recite facts showing an objectively reasonable belief in the satisfaction of each element of one of the listed anti-fraud provisions would eviscerate § 806. An employee may not have access to information necessary to form a judgment on certain elements of a generic fraud claim, such as scienter or materiality, and yet have knowledge of facts sufficient to alert the employer to fraudulent conduct. When an employee communicates these facts to a supervisor, the employer has a sufficient basis to suspect that the employee is protected against reprisal for communicating that information.

Moreover, whether an employee's communication is indeed "protected activity" under § 806 is distinct from whether the employer had reason to suspect that the communication was protected. To show that the communication is protected, the employee must have both a subjective and an objective belief that the conduct that is the subject of the communication relates to an existing or prospective violation of one of the federal laws referenced in § 806. The communication itself need not reveal all the facts that would cause a reasonable person with the whistleblower's training and background to conclude that a referenced federal law has been or will be violated. That determination should be based upon all the attendant circumstances, and not be limited to the facts conveyed by a whistleblower to the employer. If the communication itself had to convey facts sufficient to support an objectively reasonable belief of a violation of one of the referenced laws, Congress would not have imposed liability upon an employer who merely "suspected" that the communication is protected from reprisal . . . .

The Complaint alleges that Wiest refused to process a payment for and questioned the legitimacy of an extravagant event to be held at the Atlantis Resort. In particular, in a June 3, 2008 email to his supervisor, Wiest explained, among other concerns, that "[a]s submitted, the costs are charged entirely to advertising expense which seems inappropriate and does not address the issue of breaking out the meals and entertainment portions which we feel would fall into the 50% deductibility classification for tax purposes." The Complaint also alleges that Wiest, like many others, was aware of a similar event held during Kozlowski's tenure. Wiest's email to his supervisor expressed his concerns about Tyco treating the costs of the event as business expenses and his belief that certain costs should be treated as income for the guests. Because of his communication, a review of the expenses revealed that if Tyco had processed the transaction as originally submitted, it "would have resulted in a misstatement of accounting records and a fraudulent tax deduction . . . ."

These facts are sufficient to support a plausible inference that Wiest reasonably believed that Tyco's conduct would violate one of the provisions in Section 806 because he foresaw a potentially fraudulent tax deduction and misstatement of accounting records if he did not bring that information to the attention of his supervisors . . . . A reasonable person in Wiest's position who had seen the expense request for the extravagant Atlantis event could have believed that treating the Atlantis event as a business expense violated a provision of Section 806, especially given the scrutiny Tyco received during the Tyco International scandal under Kozlowski . . . . [W]e reverse the District Court's dismissal Order with respect to Wiest's communications relating to the Atlantis event.

Wiest also alleges that he directed an expense request for an event at the Venetian Resort to be held while the tax department evaluated the business purpose of the event and until his department received proper documentation and accounting treatment. After receiving a revised agenda, the tax department eventually approved the event as a business expense. . . . [W]e conclude that, objectively, a reasonable person in Wiest's position would not have believed that the expense request that initially lacked a detailed agenda and breakdown of expenses would constitute a violation of one of the provisions listed in Section 806. Therefore, we affirm the District's dismissal Order with respect to Wiest's communications relating to the Venetian event.

Regarding the $355,000 event that took place at the Wintergreen Resort, Wiest alleges that the initial invoice lacked sufficient documentation and accounting breakdowns. In addition, Wiest alleges that a planned attendee of the event had approved the request instead of Defendant Thomas Lynch, the CEO, as required by Tyco's delegation of authority. . . . [I]t is plausible that a reasonable person in Wiest's position could have believed that the event's approval by an attendee of the event, who would therefore directly benefit from that approval, instead of by the CEO as required by internal control procedures, may have violated one of the provisions contained in Section 806.[10] Therefore, we reverse the District Court's dismissal Order with respect to Wiest's communications relating to the Wintergreen event. . . .

In sum, we hold that the reasonable belief test is the appropriate standard with which to analyze the communications that Wiest contends constitute "protected activity." As explained in *Sylvester*, that standard requires that an employee's communication reflect a subjective and objectively reasonable belief that his employer's conduct constitutes a violation of an enumerated provision in Section 806. The District Court erred in dismissing Wiest's Complaint by employing the "definitive and specific" standard . . . and by requiring that his or her communication reference an *existing* violation. . . .

JORDAN, CIRCUIT JUDGE, Dissenting.

. . . Whistleblower statutes like SOX § 806 seek to protect people who have the courage to stand against institutional pressures and say plainly, "what you are doing here is wrong"—not wrong in some abstract or philosophical way, but wrong in the particular way identified in the statute at issue. . . . [Protected conduct is defined] by reference to four federal fraud statutes, SEC rules and regulations, and other federal law that is circumscribed as "relating to fraud against shareholders." . . . Thus, general allegations of misconduct by corporate officers, even if that misconduct relates to financial matters, are not sufficient to state a § 806 claim. *See Day*, 555 F.3d at 56–57 (noting that "violations of 'general accounting principles' "

---

[10] [n.6] The Dissent questions whether unauthorized expenditures for the Wintergreen Resort event could support a claim under one of the anti-fraud laws listed in § 806. Approval authorities exist to ensure that large expenditures are undertaken for appropriate business purposes. Expenditures for which required approvals have not been obtained raise the specter that they are not undertaken for an appropriate business purpose. Once again, such expenditures could plunder corporate assets for the benefit of those attending lavish events, masking personal income. We believe that the Complaint alleges sufficient facts to plausibly support an inference that Wiest had an objectively reasonable belief that the absence of the CEO's authorization for the Wintergreen Resort Event was part of a fraudulent scheme.

do not constitute "shareholder fraud" that gives rise to SOX-protected activity).

The second element of a SOX retaliation claim [i.e. that the employer knew or suspected that the employee engaged in the protected activity] confirms that conclusion. It is difficult to see how a defendant, such as a whistleblower's supervisor, can know or suspect that the whistleblower-plaintiff is engaged in protected conduct if the plaintiff's intra-corporate communications do not relate in an understandable way to one of the stated provisions of federal law. What matters is not what is locked inside the plaintiff's mind or how the plaintiff may later describe his actions; it is what is communicated to the employer that counts. Both the Department of Labor's Administrative Review Board ("ARB") and the Majority effectively bypass that element of a SOX retaliation claim and concentrate their focus on the complainant's frame of mind and after-the-fact spin. In doing so, they ignore the need for a whistleblower's employer to actually perceive that a whistle has been blown. . . .

Pre-*Sylvester* case law from federal courts made it clear that "[t]he reasonableness of [a SOX complainant's] belief for purposes of § [806] must be measured against the basic elements of the laws specified in the statute." *Day*, 555 F.3d at 55. Logically, that ought still to be the case. Section 806 references identifiable pieces of positive law. They are not mere generalities and they do not open the door to whistleblower relief to anyone with vague feelings of unease or even specific discomfort with something other than that which is identified in § 806. Particularly pertinent here, " '[f]raud' itself has defined legal meanings and is not, in the context of SOX, a colloquial term." *Id.* Section 806 thus requires a SOX whistleblower to demonstrate that he has done more than criticize undesirable corporate conduct. He is required to demonstrate that his protected communication concerned a "violation" of one of the listed statutes or of an SEC rule or regulation or other Federal law relating to fraud on shareholders. A violation can only be said to "relat[e] to . . . fraud against shareholders" if it manifests at least some of the elements of fraud as defined in the securities context, such as falsity, scienter, and materiality.

In this case, the application of a test of objective reasonableness that looks to the elements of securities fraud shows Wiest's allegedly protected communications for what they are: a bookkeeper's sensible inquiries about proper accounting for expenses, not allegations of fraud. Wiest's statements about the Atlantis Resort Event prove the point. The Majority concludes that "[a] reasonable person in Wiest's position who had seen the expense request for the extravagant Atlantis event could have believed that treating the Atlantis event as a business expense may have violated a provision of Section 806 . . . ." A fair question is "which one?" Wiest does not claim that he reasonably believed that "extravagance" or the possible reporting of employee expenses as advertising expenses constituted mail fraud, wire fraud, or bank fraud. He alleges rather that, "if Tyco had processed the transaction as originally submitted, it 'would have resulted in a misstatement of accounting records and a fraudulent tax deduction.' " That would seem to point to a violation of 18 U.S.C. § 1348, which involves fraud in connection with a sale of securities, or of a "rule or regulation of the Securities and Exchange Commission, or any provision of Federal law relating to fraud against shareholders." 18 U.S.C. § 1514A(a)(1). However, Wiest's communication with Tyco about the Atlantis Event contains none of the elements of a securities fraud. In particular, it contains no hint of falsity but rather suggests that an accounting judgment was faulty and needed to be corrected, which it was.

The supposed connection between Wiest's communications regarding the Wintergreen Resort Event and a violation of a statute or regulation referenced in § 806 is even more strained. . . . Unlike his allegations concerning the Atlantis Resort Event, Wiest does not claim that expenses from that event were not recorded correctly, nor does he allege that any public financial disclosure was at issue. As a result, it is impossible to identify a securities fraud. . . .

Given the present record, two final observations should be made about the Majority's application of the objective reasonableness standard. First, even *Sylvester* acknowledged that objective reasonableness "is evaluated based on the knowledge available to a reasonable person in the same factual circumstances with the same training and experience as the aggrieved employee." 32 IER Cases at 507 (quoting *Harp*, 558 F.3d at 723) (internal quotation marks omitted). When an employee is a licensed CPA, and thus able to distinguish between violations of accounting rules and violations of SEC rules or regulations, a failure to do so tends to show his asserted belief that a violation of the latter has occurred to be less than objectively reasonable. Wiest is a trained accountant who had more than thirty years experience in Tyco's accounting department, which, as the Majority points out, had been under "a high level of audit scrutiny" for the last decade. The Majority itself observes that Wiest had knowledge of both "accounting standards . . . and securities and tax laws." Therefore, Wiest should be held to a "higher [objective reasonableness] standard" than someone of "limited education." *Sylvester*, 32 IER Cases at 507 (citing *Parexel Int'l Corp. v. Feliciano*, 28 IER Cases 820, [2008 U.S. Dist. LEXIS 98195], (E.D. Pa. 2008)). Since his allegedly protected communications do not meet even an objective standard geared to the general public, they certainly do not meet a heightened standard applicable to someone of his training and experience.

Second, as the ARB acknowledged in *Sylvester*, "many of the laws listed in § [806] of SOX contain materiality requirements," and "[i]t may well be that a complainant's complaint concerns such a trivial matter that he or she did not engage in protected activity under Section 806." 32 IER Cases at 512. For that grudging acknowledgement of a materiality requirement to be consistent with existing law concerning fraud against shareholders, a SOX complainant must believe that there is "a substantial likelihood that the disclosure of the omitted fact would have been viewed by the reasonable investor as having significantly altered the 'total mix' of information made available." *Basic, Inc. v. Levinson*, 485 U.S. 224, 231–32, (1988) (quoting *TSC Indus., Inc. v. Northway, Inc.*, 426 U.S. 438, 449 (1976) (internal quotation marks omitted)); *see also TSC Indus.*, 426 U.S. at 448 (acknowledging that certain information concerning corporate developments is of "dubious significance"). Wiest's allegedly protected communications concerned transactions with no financial impact on Tyco, or internal control practices that are not financial in nature and are not reported to shareholders. The subjects of Wiest's communications were not material, and contrary to the Majority's conclusion, those communications do not demonstrate an objectively reasonable belief that a shareholder fraud was being threatened.

The essence of Wiest's assertion that the conduct he found objectionable "relates to" fraud against shareholders for purposes of § 806 is, as his attorney put it to the District Court, that "every time you improperly allocate money to something that is improper, you are affecting the value of the company, and the value of the company is determined by individuals who buy and sell stock." That sweeping statement, which even the attorney attempted to walk back at oral argument before us, underscores the flaw in the Majority's approach to post-*Sylvester* objective reasonableness. If it is unnecessary to measure a SOX complainant's reasonable belief against at least some of the elements of securities fraud, like materiality, then virtually any internal questioning of an accounting mistake or a judgment call turns the questioner into a SOX whistleblower, and that cannot be right . . . .

NOTES

1. **A Notorious Defendant.** The defendant employer in *Wiest* is Tyco Electronics Corp., one of three companies created from the breakup of Tyco International, a conglomerate that came to symbolize corporate excesses in the 1990s. Tyco International's chief executive, Dennis Kozlowski, and his chief lieutenant, Mark Swartz, were convicted in 2005 on charges of fraud, conspiracy, and grand larceny for stealing millions of dollars in unauthorized bonuses, abusing the company's loan program, and artificially inflating the value of the company's stock in order to reap greater profits for themselves. Andrew Ross Sorkin, *Ex-Chief and Aide Guilty of Looting Millions at Tyco*, N.Y. TIMES, June 18, 2005. Evidence at the trial revealed that Kozlowski had used Tyco money to support a lavish lifestyle, including furnishing his Manhattan apartment with items such as a $6,000 shower curtain and a $15,000 umbrella stand, and to help pay for a $2 million party in Sardinia featuring toga-clad servers for his wife's birthday. Mark Maremont & Laurie P. Cohen, *Tyco Spent Millions for Benefit of Kozlowski, Its Former CEO*, WALL ST. J., Aug. 7, 2002. In 2007, Tyco International settled several investor class-actions for nearly $3 billion. Floyd Norris, *Tyco to Pay $3 Billion to Settle Investor Lawsuits*, N.Y. TIMES, May 16, 2007.

Wiest's case alleging SOX violations against Tyco Electronics Corp. is based on events which occurred long after Kozlowski had left the company and after Tyco International had split into three different companies. Do you think the history of financial scandal surrounding Tyco International influenced the outcome in this case? What are the elements for establishing a prima facie case of retaliation under SOX? Is Tyco's corporate history relevant to any of those elements?

2. **Reasonable Belief.** In order to be protected as a whistleblower, a plaintiff must show that she reported conduct that she "reasonably believe[d]" constitutes a violation of one of the laws listed in § 1514A. How does the *Wiest* court interpret the "reasonably believes" language in § 1514A? In its view, what factual showing will be sufficient to satisfy this requirement? What standard would the dissent require for showing the objective reasonableness of a plaintiff's belief? Which interpretation is most consistent with the purposes behind the Sarbanes-Oxley whistleblower provisions? Should the types of reports made by Wiest be protected against retaliation, or does that stretch the protections of SOX beyond what Congress intended?

A split in authority has emerged regarding what is required to show a "reasonable belief" satisfying the element that the plaintiff engaged in a protected activity. Several courts of appeals have insisted that "an employee must show that his communications to his employer 'definitively and specifically relate[d]' to one of the [listed] laws . . . ." *Welch v. Chao*, 536 F.3d 269, 275 (4th Cir. 2008). *See also Platone v. U.S. Dep't of Labor*, 548 F.3d 322 (4th Cir. 2008); *Allen v. Admin Review Board*, 514 F.3d 468 (5th Cir. 2008) (requiring employees' reasonable belief that reported behavior satisfied each element of securities fraud).

In *Day v. Staples*, 555 F.3d 42 (1st Cir. 2009), for example, the First Circuit upheld summary judgment for the employer, concluding that the plaintiff did not have an objectively reasonable belief that one of the laws listed in § 1514A had been violated. The plaintiff alleged that he was retaliated against for complaining that some of his employer's policies and practices for handling customer returns resulted in the "manipulat[ion][of] accounting data in an unlawful manner that had negative financial ramifications for Staples," which "defrauded Staples' shareholders" and violated the Staples Code of Ethics. *Id.* at 45. According to the court,

> The reasonableness of Day's belief for purposes of § 1514A must be measured against the basic elements of the laws specified in the statute. "Fraud" itself has defined legal meanings and is not, in the context of SOX, a colloquial term . . . . Wire or mail fraud is "broader than the common law definition [of fraud]" but also emphasizes the deceit requirement. *Ed Peters Jewelry Co.*, 215 F.3d at 192. To have an objectively reasonable belief there has been shareholder fraud, the complaining employee's theory of such fraud must at least approximate the basic elements of a claim of securities fraud . . . . Securities fraud under section 10(b) and Rule 10b-5 requires: "(1) a material misrepresentation or omission; (2) scienter; (3) connection with the purchase or sale of a security; (4) reliance; (5) economic loss; and (6) loss causation." *Ezra Charitable Trust v. Tyco Int'l, Ltd.*, 466 F.3d 1, 6 (1st Cir. 2006). The employee need not reference a specific statute, or prove actual harm, but he must have an objectively reasonable belief that the company intentionally misrepresented or omitted certain facts to investors, which were material and which risked loss.

Day, 555 F.3d at 56.

Wiest is notable because it is the first appellate decision to follow the ARB's *Sylvester* decision, cited in the opinion, in rejecting the "definitively and specifically" standard. A number of other lower courts have followed suit, while others have held to the "definitively and specifically" standard, deepening the split over how to interpret this requirement of a Sarbanes-Oxley whistleblower claim.

3. Protected Activity. Sarbanes-Oxley does not protect all types of whistle-blowing, only those that involve reporting information "regarding any conduct which the employee reasonably believes constitutes a violation of section 1341 [mail fraud], 1343 [wire fraud], 1344 [bank fraud], or 1348 [securities fraud], any rule or regulation of the Securities and Exchange Commission, or any provision of Federal law relating to fraud against shareholders." 18 U.S.C. § 1514A(a)(1). Some decisions have insisted that the alleged wrongdoing relate to *shareholder* fraud—that is, the reported fraud must be "of a type that would be adverse to investors' interests." *In* *the Matter of Platone v. FLYi, Inc.*, DOLSOX LEXIS 105, at *29 (Sept. 29, 2006), *aff'd*, *Platone v. U.S. Dep't of Labor*, 548 F.3d 322 (4th Cir. 2008). In this view, general allegations of corporate fraud that do not impact shareholders directly are insufficient.

In *Lockheed Martin Corp. v. ARB*, 717 F.3d 1121 (10th Cir. 2013), the Tenth Circuit rejected the argument that violations of § 1514A must involve complaints of shareholder fraud. The plaintiff in that case, Andrea Brown, complained that her supervisor, the Vice President of Communications, had developed sexual relationships with several soldiers participating in a "pen pal" program run by Lockheed and was using company funds to purchase gifts and to pay for limousines and hotel rooms in which to entertain soldiers. Following her complaints, Brown alleged that she lost her title, office and supervisory responsibilities and was left in a continuing state of uncertainty as to whether she would still have a job with the company.

In the administrative hearing on her Sarbanes-Oxley claim, the ALJ concluded that Brown reasonably believed that her supervisor had committed mail or wire fraud, but failed to establish a reasonable belief that shareholder fraud occurred. In appealing the administrative ruling, Lockheed argued that employee reports of mail and wire fraud that do not relate to fraud against shareholders are not protected under Sarbanes-Oxley. The Tenth Circuit disagreed, holding that "[t]he plain, unambiguous text of § 1514A(a)(1) establishes six categories of employer conduct against which an employee is protected from retaliation for reporting: violations of 18 U.S.C. § 1341 (mail fraud), § 1343 (wire fraud), § 1344 (bank fraud), § 1348 (securities fraud), any rule or regulation of the SEC, or any provision of Federal law relating to fraud against shareholders." *Id.* at 1130. It rejected Lockheed's argument that the phrase "relating to fraud against shareholders" modified each of the enumerated protected activities, and held that "the proper interpretation of § 1514A(a) gives each phrase distinct meaning" such that a claimant reporting mail fraud, wire fraud or bank fraud need not show that those violations related to fraud against shareholders in order to be protected.

4. Complaints to Whom? In drafting Sarbanes-Oxley, Congress chose to extend its protections to cover both external complaints to certain governmental bodies and internal complaints to a supervisor. Reports of corporate wrongdoing to the press, however, are not protected. *See Tides v. Boeing Co.*, 644 F.3d 809, 815 (9th Cir. 2011) (rejecting employees' argument that their disclosures about improper auditing practices to the news media might eventually cause information to be provided to government agencies or Congress and therefore should be protected under Sarbanes-Oxley). Why do you think Congress limited protection of external complaints only to federal regulatory and law enforcement agencies and Congress? Is such a limitation justified?

5. A Contributing Factor. *Wiest* sets out the elements of a prima facie case for a whistleblower claim under Sarbanes-Oxley, but never reached the question of causation. Is the plaintiff's burden of proving that retaliation was "a contributing factor" under the fourth element higher or lower than in other employment cases? Some courts have suggested that the standard under Sarbanes-Oxley is more lenient than under other employment statutes. For example, the Tenth Circuit in *Lockheed Martin Corp. v. Administrative Review Bd.*, 717 F.3d 1121 (10th Cir.

2013) stated that the "contributing factor" element is "broad and forgiving," *id.* at 1136, and that "a contributing factor" means "any factor, which alone or in connection with other factors, tends to affect in any way the outcome of the decision." *Id.* (*quoting Klopfenstein v. PCC Flow Technologies Holdings*, 2006 DOL Ad. Rev. Bd. LEXIS 50, at *18 (May 31, 2006)).

In the absence of "smoking-gun" evidence, plaintiffs often rely upon temporal proximity to establish the fourth element of a prima facie case, similar to the way plaintiffs alleging retaliation for objecting to discrimination often try to prove a causal link between their complaints and adverse personnel actions. If adverse personnel actions follow closely after an employee's protected activity, it may be taken as circumstantial evidence of causation. Although the burden imposed by the "contributing factor" test may be "rather light," the plaintiff still must show "by a preponderance of evidence that the activities tended to affect his termination in at least some way." *Feldman v. Law Enforcement Assocs., Corp.*, 752 F.3d 339, 348 (4th Cir. 2014). Thus, in *Feldman*, the Fourth Circuit dismissed the SOX claim of a plaintiff who had a long history of antagonism with his superiors predating his complaints, whose termination occurred roughly twenty months after his protected complaints and who was fired immediately following events in which he was insubordinate. *Id.*

If a plaintiff is able to show that the protected activity was a contributing factor, the employer can avoid liability only if it shows "by clear and convincing evidence" that it would have taken the same action in the absence of the protected activity. *See Lockheed*, 717 F.3d at 1130 n.3; *Welch*, 536 F.3d at 275. This standard clearly places a greater burden on the employer than the usual "preponderance of the evidence" standard used in other types of employment cases. Under Title VII, for example, once a plaintiff has shown that unlawful discrimination was a motivating factor in an employment decision, the defendant, in order to avoid liability for damages, need only show by a preponderance of the evidence that it would have made the same decision absent the discriminatory motive. *See, e.g., Byrd v. Ill. Dep't of Pub. Health*, 423 F.3d 696, 709 (7th Cir. 2005) (approving a preponderance of the evidence standard for defendant seeking to avoid liability for damages in mixed motive case). For a discussion of "mixed motive" cases under Title VII, see Chapter 9.

4. Whistleblower Provisions of the Dodd-Frank Act

Despite Sarbanes-Oxley's purpose to prevent corporate wrongdoing and stabilize financial markets, another financial crisis unfolded beginning in the late 2000s. Lehman Brothers, a global financial institution, declared bankruptcy, and many others were on the brink of collapse. The U.S. government spent billions to bail out failing financial institutions, stock values plunged, and the global economy went into recession. Once again, lawmakers attempted to respond to the root causes of the financial instability through legislation, passing the Dodd-Frank Wall Street Reform and Consumer Protection Act of 2010, 15 U.S.C. § 78u-6. Like Sarbanes-Oxley, many of Dodd-Frank's provisions directly regulate covered entities in an effort to promote accountability and improve oversight of financial markets. In addition, the Act also seeks to increase whistleblowing by those who have inside knowledge of corporate wrong-doing.

As discussed in section 3 above, the Dodd-Frank Act does so in part by amending and strengthening the anti-retaliation provisions of Sarbanes-Oxley in several ways. In addition, it expands coverage by creating new anti-retaliation protections to reach a broader array of potential whistleblowers. More specifically, Dodd-Frank enacted new provisions prohibiting retaliation against whistleblowers who report information to the Securities and Exchange Commission (SEC), to the Commodity Futures Trading Commission (CFTC), 7 U.S.C. § 26(h), and to the newly created Bureau of Consumer Financial Protection, 12 U.S.C. § 5567(a), about violations of law that each agency enforces.

But Dodd-Frank goes beyond prohibiting retaliation, seeking to incentivize those with information about corporate wrong-doing to come forward by offering "whistleblower bounties". These provisions affirmatively encourage whistleblowers to report certain forms of corporate wrongdoing by offering substantial monetary awards to those who provide information leading to successful government enforcement actions. 17 C.F.R. § 240.21F-3; 7 U.S.C. § 26(b).

Because the Dodd-Frank Act is still a relatively new statute, it is not entirely clear how it will affect rights in the workplace, and many legal ambiguities remain to be resolved by the courts and enforcement agencies. In the subsections that follow, we focus on two of the most significant controversies surrounding the statute's whistleblower protections that have emerged to date: questions surrounding implementation of the bounty provisions and uncertainty about how Dodd-Frank's anti-retaliation provisions interact with those of the Sarbanes-Oxley Act.

a. The Bounty Provisions

Immediately following passage of the Dodd-Frank Act, the most discussed and most controversial of the whistleblower protections were the "bounty provisions." Financial bounties have been used in other contexts to incentivize the reporting of wrongdoing, most notably under the False Claims Act, 31 U.S.C. § 3729 *et seq.*, which offers an award to individuals who successfully pursue claims against private parties who have defrauded the federal government. Along similar lines, the Dodd-Frank Act seeks "to motivate those with inside knowledge to come forward and assist the Government to identify and prosecute persons who have violated securities laws and recover money for victims of financial fraud." S. REP. No. 111-176, at 110 (2009).

The relevant provisions in Dodd-Frank state that the SEC "shall pay an award or awards" to whistleblowers who "voluntarily provided original information to the Commission" if that information leads to a successful enforcement action resulting in the recovery of sanctions exceeding one million dollars. 15 U.S.C. § 78u-6(b). The amount of the awards will range between 10 and 30% of the monetary sanctions collected, with the exact amount to be determined at the discretion of the SEC. *Id.* Similar provisions elsewhere in the Dodd-Frank Act offer monetary awards to individuals who provide information regarding violations of the Commodities Exchange Act to the Commodity Futures Trading Commission (CFTC), 7 U.S.C. § 26(b).

The section that sets out the criteria for receiving a monetary award from the SEC defines a whistleblower as "any individual who provides, or two or more individuals acting jointly who provide, information relating to a violation of the securities laws to the Commission . . . ." 15 U.S.C. § 78u-6(a)(6). Thus, the statute is clear that an individual must provide information *to the SEC* in order to be eligible for a monetary award, but it says nothing about how an employee's eligibility is affected by her decision to utilize or bypass an employer's internal compliance program.

One of the things that Sarbanes-Oxley did was to encourage firms to create internal compliance programs. Specifically, it required public companies to establish procedures for receiving internal complaints about accounting or auditing matters. Pursuant to those provisions, companies implemented or further developed programs intended to promote compliance with financial regulations. These programs typically provide mechanisms for employees to report concerns about fraud or other corporate wrongdoing internally so that a company can investigate and respond appropriately to any violations. One of the concerns raised about the Dodd-Frank bounty provisions was that they would over-incentivize employees to go directly to the SEC, thereby undermining firms' efforts to voluntarily comply with the law by detecting and preventing violations on their own. Because of these concerns, numerous comments were submitted during the SEC's rulemaking process arguing that the agency's implementing regulations should require employees to report any concerns to a company's internal compliance program before going to the SEC in order to be eligible for a monetary award. Stephen Joyce & Lawrence E. Dubé, *SEC Whistleblower Proposal Draws Mixed Comments on Role of Internal Programs*, 9 WORKPLACE L. REP. (BNA) No. 27, Jan. 7, 2011. Whistleblower advocates argued the opposite, pointing out that corporate compliance programs have failed in numerous instances. They contended that requiring employees to report internally first would have a chilling effect on whistleblowers fearful of employer retaliation. *Id.*

The final regulations issued by the SEC in 2011 sought to balance these concerns. They do not require whistleblowers to report internally before taking their concerns to the SEC; however, they seek in various ways to encourage employees to do so. For example, an employee who provides original information to an internal compliance program will also be considered a whistleblower eligible for an award if the company later provides the information or the results of a subsequent investigation to the SEC. § 240.21F-4. In addition, participation in internal compliance systems is one of the factors listed in the regulations as relevant to increase the amount of an award. § 240.21F-6.

As noted above, the bounty provisions were quite controversial when first enacted. Richard Moberly praised the "bounty model" for encouraging whistleblowing by focusing attention on the alleged corporate misconduct (rather than a subsequent personnel action), by compensating whistleblowers for their risk and by directing disclosures to external regulators who can act on the information. *See* Richard Moberly, *Sarbanes-Oxley's Whistleblower Provisions—Ten Years Later*, 64 S.C. L. REV. 1 (2012). Other commentators have been more critical, arguing that the bounty provisions of Dodd-Frank do not go far enough to incentivize effective whistleblowing, *see* Geoffrey Christopher Rapp, *Mutiny by the Bounties? The*

Attempt to Reform Wall Street by the New Whistleblower Provisions of the Dodd-Frank Act, 2012 B.Y.U. L. Rev. 73 (arguing for bounties in cases producing less than $1 million and for allowing whistleblowers to bring actions independent of the SEC), or conversely, that the bounty provisions go too far and will impose significant costs on employers and regulators. *See* Jenny Lee, *Corporate Corruption and the New Gold Mine: How the Dodd-Frank Act Overincentivizes Whistleblowing*, 77 Brook. L. Rev. 303, 339 (2011) (asserting that the Dodd-Frank Act overincentivizes whistleblowing); Dave Ebersole, *Blowing the Whistle on the Dodd-Frank Whistleblower Provisions*, 6 Ohio St. Enterpren. Bus. L.J. 123, 174 (2011) (arguing that the bounty provisions impose costs on businesses and agencies, but provide uncertain benefits to society).

The SEC's bounty program started in August of 2011, and the number of tips received has steadily increased since then. The SEC's Office of the Whistleblower reported that in fiscal year 2013, it received more than 3,000 tips and complaints from all 50 states and over 50 foreign jurisdictions. *SEC Whistle-Blower Report for FY 2013 Shows Bounty Program's Gradual Expansion*, Daily Lab. Rep. (BNA) No. 223, Nov. 18, 2013. The highest award was reported to be for $14 million, *id.*, and a total of eight whistleblowers had received awards through the SEC's bounty program by the summer of 2014. *SEC Awards More than $875,000 to Be Split Between Two Whistle-Blowers*, 12 Corp. Accountability Rep. (BNA) No. 23, June 6, 2014. SEC Chairman Mary Jo White has praised the program, saying that it has "had a big impact on our investigations by providing us with high quality, meaningful tips," while a skeptic has cautioned that it remains to be seen whether the resulting cases justify the resources that must be devoted to culling through and evaluating the tips. Phyllis Diamond, *SEC Announces $1.4M Award to Whistle-Blower*, 45 Sec. Reg. & L. Rep. (BNA) No. 1823, Oct. 7, 2013.

b.   The Interaction Between Dodd-Frank and Sarbanes-Oxley

In addition to creating the bounty provision described above, Section 922 of the Dodd-Frank Act amended the Securities Exchange Act of 1934 to add a new-anti-retaliation provision. The relevant provision reads:

(A) . . . No employer may discharge, demote, suspend, threaten, harass, directly or indirectly, or in any other manner discriminate against a whistleblower in the terms and conditions of employment because of any lawful act done by the whistleblower—

(i) in providing information to the [Securities and Exchange] Commission in accordance with this section;

(ii) in initiating, testifying in, or assisting in any investigation or judicial or administrative action of the Commission based upon or related to such information; or

(iii) in making disclosures that are required or protected under the Sarbanes-Oxley Act of 2002 (15 U.S.C. 7201 et seq.), the Securities Exchange Act of 1934 (15 U.S.C. 78a et seq.), including section 10A(m) of such Act (15 U.S.C. 78f(m)), section 1513(e) of title 18, United

States Code, and any other law, rule, or regulation subject to the jurisdiction of the Commission.

15 U.S.C. § 78u-6(h)(1)(A). The section further provides that an individual alleging violation of this provision may sue in federal district court.

Controversy has arisen over exactly what activities qualify for whistleblower protection under this provision of Dodd-Frank. Recall that another section of 922 defines a whistleblower as "any individual who provides, or two or more individuals acting jointly who provide, information relating to a violation of the securities laws to the Commission . . . ." § 78u-6(a)(6). This definition clearly applies to the bounty provisions, and only individuals who have reported information to the SEC are eligible to receive a monetary award. Less clear is how this definition was meant to interact with the protected activities listed in the anti-retaliation section reproduced above.

While the protected activities listed in subsections (i) and (ii) are consistent with the narrow definition of a whistleblower as someone who provides information to the SEC, subsection (iii) lists protected acts that do not necessarily involve reporting to the SEC. For example, subsection (iii) protects "making disclosures that are required or protected under the Sarbanes-Oxley Act of 2002." As discussed in section 3 above, Sarbanes-Oxley protects an employee from reprisal for reports to a supervisor and some government agencies other than the SEC.

Thus, there is an apparent tension in the statute: the definition section seems to require that a whistleblower provide information to the SEC in order to be protected, while the list of protected activities in § 78u-6(h)(1)(A) encompasses some disclosures *not* made to the SEC, but protected under section 806 of the Sarbanes-Oxley Act, 18 U.S.C. § 1514A(a), or the other laws listed in subsection (iii). This ambiguity regarding whether a report to the SEC is necessary led one of the first courts to address the issue to conclude that a plaintiff must show that "he *either* provided information to the SEC, *or* that his disclosures fell under the four categories listed in 15 U.S.C. § 78u-6(h)(1)(A)(iii)." *Egan v. TradingScreen, Inc.,* 2011 U.S. Dist. LEXIS 47713, at *19 (S.D.N.Y. May 4, 2011) (emphasis added).

Since then, most district courts have read the statute in the same way as *Egan*, and the SEC's regulations are consistent with this reading. However one circuit court, the Fifth Circuit, sharply departed from this interpretation, holding in *Asadi v. G.E. Energy,* 720 F.3d 620 (5th Cir. 2013) that a whistleblower was protected from retaliation under Dodd-Frank *only* if she had provided information to the SEC. Even though *Asadi* was the first circuit court decision on the issue, other district courts have continued to follow an interpretation allowing plaintiffs to pursue claims under Dodd-Frank even if they did not report to the SEC, so long as they engaged in one of the activities listed in subsection (iii) of the anti-retaliation section. *See, e.g., Bussing v. COR Clearing, LLC,* 2014 U.S. Dist. LEXIS 69461 at *35.

How this issue is resolved matters, because under the broader interpretation, the Dodd-Frank Act offers coverage that partially overlaps with the whistleblower protections of Sarbanes-Oxley. That overlap is significant, because Dodd-Frank offers a quite different enforcement scheme, allowing a complainant to go directly to federal court without first filing with OSHA. In addition, the Dodd-Frank anti-retaliation provisions may be brought within six years after the date of the violation or three years after the date the violation becomes known (but no more than 10 years after the date of the violation), 15 U.S.C. § 78u-6(h)(1)(B)(iii), a period far longer than the 180-day limit for filing a Sarbanes-Oxley claim. Dodd-Frank also provides different remedies, entitling a successful plaintiff to two times the amount of back pay owed, plus interest, as well as litigation costs and attorneys' fees. § 78u-6(h)(1)(C).

The debate over the scope of Dodd-Frank's anti-retaliation provisions once again raises the issue whether only external reporting should be protected or whether internal reports warrant protection as well. If employers want to encourage their employees to report internally first before going to the SEC, which rule should they prefer? Can you think of reasons they might nevertheless prefer the rule in the *Asadi* case?

E. COLLECTIVE VOICE PROTECTIONS—THE NLRA

As we have seen, individual employees in the private sector do not possess First Amendment rights to freedom of speech or association vis-à-vis their employers. The absence of state action and the employer's rights to control its property and manage its business afford the employer authority to silence speech that does not, in its view, enhance productivity. Exceptions to this rule exist only in jurisdictions that permit wrongful discharge in violation of public policy claims *and* recognize the First Amendment or parallel state constitutional speech protections as sufficiently well-defined public policy to support them, in jurisdictions that afford statutory protection for certain types of speech (political speech for example) or where the speech falls within the ambit of federal or state whistleblower protection. Some very common types of worker speech do not fall into these categories. Consider, for example, speech concerning workplace policies or complaints about how one is treated—matters of "personal concern"—fall outside the categories of speech protection afforded private sector workers. Is there any other basis for protecting such speech?

Where employee speech concerns matters that pertain to workplace issues that are traditional areas of collective bargaining—wages, hours, and working conditions—workplace speech may be protected under § 7 of the National Labor Relations Act whether or not there is a union in the picture. In order for the speech to receive protection, it must be either for the purpose of organizing a union through which to engage in collective bargaining, or "concerted" and for "mutual aid or protection." Section 7 provides:

> Employees shall have the right to self-organization . . . to bargain collectively through representatives of their own choosing, and to engage in other concerted activities for the purpose of collective bargaining or other mutual aid or protection. . . .

Discharges or discipline of employees who engage in protected concerted activities—including speech—may be challenged under NLRA § 8(a)(1) as unfair labor practices. In *Connick v. Myers*, the NLRA was not applicable because Sheila Myers was a public sector employee to whom the NLRA's protections were not available. *See* NLRA § 2(2), 29 U.S.C. § 152(2) (excluding federal and state governments from definition of covered employers under the Act). Had Myers been a private sector employee or a state employee covered by public sector bargaining law, however, her actions in preparing and distributing the questionnaire regarding office transfer policy, morale, and the need for a grievance committee—which ultimately created a "mini-insurrection" in the office—would have been protected concerted activity because she was seeking to involve her coworkers in a dialogue about working conditions that might lead to a union organizing effort, other concerted protest, or collective bargaining. (It is possible that she might have been excluded from the Act's coverage as a supervisory or managerial employee, although we would need additional facts about her job duties to ascertain this. *See* § 2(3), 29 U.S.C. § 152(3) (excluding supervisory employees from coverage); *NLRB v. Yeshiva Univ.*, 444 U.S. 672 (1980) (holding that faculty at a private university were excluded from coverage because they were managerial employees who played a significant role in formulating and implementing university policy). Nevertheless, some public sector statutes provide coverage to supervisors and managers.)

Several cases in this chapter explain the basis for protection of concerted activity, including speech, under § 7. As we shall see, such protection has been extended to concerted activity that occurs on social media. And employer policies that ban such speech or that employees might reasonably understand as doing so may be unlawful, as well. Before turning to the specifics of protections afforded to workers—as well as limitations on those protections stemming from employers' property rights to manage and control their businesses—it is useful to consider what Congress intended when it enacted § 7. As the excerpt below makes clear, the NLRA has a voice-protection function as well as a market-power-enhancing function. Does the statute amount to a private sector constitution for the workplace? Or is its reach more limited?

1. The Voice-Protection Function of NLRA § 7

Clyde W. Summers, *The Privatization of Personal Freedoms and Enrichment of Democracy: Some Lessons from Labor Law*
1986 U. ILL. L. REV. 689, 697–98, 701

National labor policy, as articulated by Congress, was rooted in the first amendment right of freedom of association; Congress acted to protect that right because the courts had failed to do so. That fundamental right, declared Congress, could not be bartered away by private contract; promises could not be extracted empowering one party to restrict free exercise of the right by another [referencing the Norris-LaGuardia Act's ban on "yellow-dog" contracts, which condition employment upon an employee's promise not to join, become, or remain a member of a labor union]. Congress instructed the courts to interpret the statute so as to recognize the right of free association, and not to enforce contracts denying that right. Courts were not to use their powers to enable property or contract rights to control free exercise of this personal freedom.

Congress's second and major step was the Wagner Act of 1935 [subsequently codified as the National Labor Relations Act]. . . . [S]ection 1 declared the national policy to be "protecting the exercise by workers of full freedom of association, self-organization, and designation of representatives of their own choosing." Section 7, the heart of the Act, stated in constitutional tones, "Employees shall have the right to self-organization, to form, join, or assist labor organizations, [and] to bargain collectively through representatives of their own choosing." Congress protected these rights, rooted in the first amendment, against private action, against encroachments by employers exercising private power. Section 8 made it an unfair labor practice for an employer "to interfere, restrain or coerce employees in the exercise of the rights guaranteed by § 7." This included dominating or interfering with their association, or discriminating in employment because of their exercise of associational rights. Congress brought the first amendment to private employment.

Freedom of association was statutorily protected not solely for its own sake; it was protected as a necessary precondition to the broader statutory purpose of "encouraging the practice and procedure of collective bargaining." The most obvious function of collective bargaining was of course its market function, to provide a better balance of bargaining power. The workers' economic weakness in individual bargaining, when confronted with the collective economic power of the employer, produced socially unacceptable results. The inequality of the individual labor market was to be remedied by creating a collective labor market, a bargaining with collectives on both sides. A market, so constructed, would not guarantee socially desired outcomes but would leave market forces free to produce socially acceptable results.

Collective bargaining, however, was conceived as much more than a market mechanism; it was prized as a process for extending constitutional values by bringing "an element of democracy into the government of industry." . . .

. . . Freedom of association and the closely-linked freedom of expression are protected against employer restraints because such freedoms are preconditions to the declared national policy of encouraging collective bargaining, and collective bargaining is to be encouraged because it promotes the constitutional values of democratic decision-making and due process at the workplace. This reminder is crucially important because preoccupation with the economic function of labor law too often causes the constitutional values to be overlooked or not recognized. The National Labor Relations Act is too often viewed solely as striking a balance between union and employers rather than as a statute primarily protecting the personal freedoms of individual employees and extending democratic procedures to industrial life. . . .

2. Balancing Employer Rights to Manage and Control the Business Against Employees' § 7 Rights

Summers observes that a core function of labor law was to extend constitutional values into the workplace, particularly the First Amendment values of freedom of speech and freedom of association. Yet obviously the workplace is for work, not for self-expression. Employers have legitimate concerns about productivity, and their capital investment in the business surely affords them some right to manage and control the workplace. To what degree should employers' private property rights be required to yield to public democratic values? Must employers tolerate interference with productivity goals in furtherance of social policy agendas such as promoting workers' right to unionize? Clearly employees have § 7 rights to discuss traditional subjects of collective bargaining—wages, hours, and conditions of employment—but may they do so in the workplace? During working hours (breaks, rest periods)? On working time (while "on-the-clock")? On employer-provided equipment, such as company email systems?

In *Republic Aviation Corp. v. NLRB*, 324 U.S. 793 (1945), the employer disciplined and/or discharged several workers for distributing union literature, soliciting union membership, and wearing union steward buttons during nonworking time on plant premises in violation of the employer's no-solicitation rules. The Court agreed with the Board that such restrictions on employee organizing activity during non-working time should be "presumed to be an unreasonable impediment to self-organization" in the absence of special circumstances, such as a demonstration that the solicitation interfered with production, safety, or discipline in the workplace. *Id.* at 804 n.10. The Court held that enforcement of the no-solicitation rule violated § 8(a)(1). Thus, employers can prohibit union solicitation by employees during working time, but absent special circumstances (such as, for example, the risk of customer confusion on the sales floor of a retail store or interference with patient care in a hospital), they may not prohibit solicitation during working hours—breaks, rest periods, or before and after work.

Many employees, however, will have no knowledge of their NLRA rights. Does § 7 encompass a right of access for outside organizers to the employer's property? In a series of cases interpreting § 7, the Labor Board and the Court were required to balance employees' rights to organize and to have access to information from labor organizations to assist them in organizing, against employers' property rights to manage and control their businesses and to exclude outsiders from access to employer property.

In *NLRB v. Babcock & Wilcox Co.*, 351 U.S. 105 (1956), the employer refused to allow nonemployee union organizers access to the company-owned parking lot to distribute union literature. The Board found that the parking lot was the only "safe and practicable" place for distribution of the leaflets, and ordered the employer to admit the union organizers, subject only to reasonable rules "in the interest of plant efficiency and discipline." *Id.* at 107–08. The Court overturned the Board, explaining that nonemployees enjoyed only derivative rights under § 7; accordingly, their rights were required to yield to the employer's property rights as long as there were other channels of communication available, such as home visits, telephones, letters, or advertised meetings.

More recently, in *Lechmere, Inc. v. NLRB*, 502 U.S. 527 (1992), the Court held that union organizers were not entitled to trespass on the employer's parking lot where the store was located in a strip mall shopping center and the only access to the parking lot was a publicly owned grassy strip separating the parking lot from the highway. The Court explained that the accommodation required between employees' and employers' rights is accomplished so long as nonemployee organizers have "reasonable" access to employees outside the employer's property. Only where access is "infeasible"—a "rare" case where "employees . . . by virtue of their employment, are isolated from the ordinary flow of information that characterizes our society"—will a balancing of employer property rights against employee rights to organize be required. *Id.* at 540.

In another line of cases, the Board determined that an employer who exploits its property rights by conducting anti-union campaigns through captive audience speeches during working hours is not obligated to make its premises available to the union for purposes of equal time to reply. *See Livingston Shirt Co.*, 107 N.L.R.B. 400 (1953).

How does employee access to outside union organizers relate to the voice-enhancing and market-power-enhancing functions of § 7? How should the appropriate balance between the competing interests be struck? Consider the following analysis and proposal by Cynthia Estlund.

Cynthia L. Estlund, *Labor, Property, and Sovereignty* *After* Lechmere
46 STAN. L. REV. 305, 326–27, 330–32, 308 (1994)

According to the Court, no section 7 right is directly impacted when an employer excludes union organizers [from its physical property]. "By its plain terms, . . . the NLRA confers rights only on employees, not on unions or their nonemployee organizers." Organizers' sole claim to access under the plain terms of the NLRA . . . derives from the rights of their audience to learn the benefits of unionization from others. . . .

. . . [W]e must consider not only the interests of Lechmere's unorganized employees, but the interests of the union's members at other workplaces as well.

The economic theory of unionism, which the framers of the Wagner Act largely adopted, recognized that the effectiveness of collective bargaining depends on a union's ability to organize across employer lines. Unions expend resources not only to help unorganized workers improve their own working conditions, but also to enhance the bargaining power of current members; for the presence of a large nonunion sector in the relevant labor market constrains the leverage that organized employees can exert. Union organizing is thus an exercise not in altruism but in solidarity—in making common cause with others "for mutual aid or protection." . . .

. . . The *Lechmere* Court assumed that only the rights of the unorganized workers were at stake; from that vantage point, the majority described union organizing as merely "inform[ing] the employees about the union's organizational efforts." Based on that understanding, the Court held that exclusion of organizers from the workplace would rarely interfere with the rights at stake. The majority reasoned that "direct contact . . . is not a necessary element of 'reasonably effective' communication," and that "signs or advertising also may suffice." Indeed, *Lechmere* suggested that alternatives to access will almost always be adequate to justify excluding organizers from employer property, except in the rare case of "employees who, by virtue of their employment, are isolated from the ordinary flow of information that characterizes our society."

This reasoning reflects a basic misunderstanding of the nature of union organizing. Deciding to support a union is unlike a simple decision whether to purchase a pair of pants, for example, or even a more complex decision whether to vote for a particular candidate in a political election. Deciding to support a union may have serious immediate consequences for an employee's wages, benefits, and daily job conditions; that decision may also entail a significant risk of discharge or other employer retaliation. Union organizing therefore requires more than merely "inform[ing] the employees about the union's organization efforts," as *Lechmere* assumed. Union organizing is in part a concerted attempt to persuade a majority of employees in a bargaining unit that they will be better off with union representation than without it and that the benefits will outweigh the risks of supporting the union. It is also an effort to form a cohesive group capable of collective decisionmaking and activity. This understanding of organizing activity leads to a different conclusion from that of the *Lechmere* majority: Sustained face-to-face contact with employees is crucial in realizing the section 7 right to organize.

Such face-to-face contact is very difficult to arrange outside of the workplace. The majority in *Lechmere* alluded to the union's "success in contacting a substantial percentage of [employees] directly, via mailings, phone calls, and home visits." Yet the union failed to gather the names and addresses for 80 percent of the targeted workforce through such means. In any event, the ability to contact employees at their homes does not make workplace contact unnecessary. Home visits are costly and difficult and unnecessarily invade employees' privacy. Even if home visits provided a viable alternative in *Babcock*, in which most of the employees lived near their workplace, home visits should not have been considered a viable option in *Lechmere*, nor do they provide a viable alternative for reaching employees in the majority of workplaces today.

Moreover, the very nature of unionization requires communication with employees in the workplace. For while the decision to support a union is in one sense an individual decision, protected from coercion and expressed by secret vote, it is ultimately a decision to trust the group and act collectively. The workplace thus serves as a unique forum for discussions about unionization because it is the one place where all employees, including those undecided about unionization and those unlikely to attend a union meeting elsewhere, necessarily gather as a group. It was these considerations that prompted the Court in *Republic Aviation* to approve the Board's view that the workplace is the "very . . . place uniquely appropriate and almost solely available" to employees for discussing unionization. . . .

Lechmere reflects both an impoverished conception of section 7 rights and an overbroad, undifferentiated vision of employer property rights. In *Lechmere*, the employer asserted a bare right to exclude others, unadorned by any specific claim that the union activity interfered with production, services, security, or other business functions. The court allowed this naked property right to trump the substantial statutory interests of organized employees in spreading information about and seeking support for unionization, and of unorganized employees in receiving that information. *Lechmere* essentially recognized an employer's right to exclude others not only for "good reasons," but for "bad reasons" or for no reason at all. This broad right to exclude confers sovereignty over others beyond what any legitimate business interest would warrant.

NOTES

1. **Property Rights vs. Organizing Rights.** Estlund suggests that the current "balance" between employer property rights and employees' rights to have access to union organizers on employer property affords insufficient weight to the employees' § 7 rights. She proposes the following test (drawn from the *Republic Aviation* standard applicable to workplace organizing by employees) instead:

> *Republic Aviation . . .* contains the germ of a principle that could and should be extended to the full range of conflicts between employers' right to exclude others and the rights that section 7 provides to labor. That principle is straightforward: When an employer seeks to prohibit activity that is otherwise protected by section 7 by asserting its right to private property, the employer must first demonstrate "good reasons" for excluding the protected participants. In short, I argue that courts should always require the employer to show that the speakers' presence or activity would actually interfere with continuing production, the delivery of services, physical safety or security of individuals on the premises, or to provide other substantial functional justifications.
>
> Not all reasons for exclusion should be considered "good reasons" under the NLRA. For example, employers may wish to exclude union speakers because of a perfectly rational desire to stop employees and customers from hearing and heeding the union's message. But an employer can hardly justify its interference with labor activity based solely on a desire to inhibit the communication of messages protected by section 7, for that is literally what the Act prohibits. In many cases, an employer will simply have nothing to balance against employees' federal statutory rights, because the employer's interest in exclusion will stand unsupported by any substantial functional justification independent of a mere desire to frustrate the competing interests embodied in section 7. In other cases, of course, there will be substantial interests on both sides of the ledger—interests that are not facially incompatible but that nonetheless conflict. In those cases, some "accommodation" is necessary. But the proper accommodation should not be between section 7 rights and "property rights"; it should be between section 7 rights and the particular legitimate employer interests underlying the specific claim of property rights in a given situation. Accordingly, my proposed principle would drastically confine the class of cases in which it is appropriate or necessary to engage in balancing in the first place, and would help bring order and clarity to the balancing of rights that is still required.

Cynthia L. Estlund, *Labor, Property, and Sovereignty After* Lechmere, 46 STAN. L. REV. 305, 309–10 (1994). Would this balancing test be superior to the test adopted in *Lechmere*?

2. **Employer Property Rights in a High-Tech World.** Suppose that an employer maintains a rule against using its internal email system for non-job related communications and solicitations. Would such a rule violate section 7, or would the employer's interest in protecting the property rights in its email systems justify the rule? In *Register-Guard*, 351 N.L.R.B. 1110 (2007), the Board concluded

that the employer's property rights outweigh the employees' section 7 interests even where the rule is applied to ban emails by employees advocating union organizing, so long as the rule (and its application) does not discriminate along section 7 lines. Thus, the employer could permit charitable solicitations but not allow non-charitable solicitations, but could not permit anti-union emails but prohibit prounion emails. The dissenting members accused the majority of ignoring the ways in which email has revolutionized business and personal communications and being the "Rip Van Winkle" of administrative agencies because of its failure to craft a sensible doctrine for the technological age. *Id.* at 1122. On appeal, however, the D.C. Circuit concluded that the employer had applied its neutral ban on email solicitation selectively in violation of NLRA § 8(a)(3) by disciplining an employee for sending a union-related solicitation email while tolerating other employees' personal solicitations for baby showers, dog-walking services, party invitations, and the like via email. The court observed that neither the company's written policy nor its explanation in the warning issued to the disciplined employee distinguished between individual and organizational solicitations; the employer's rationale was a "post hoc invention" developed after the Board's General Counsel issued a complaint. *Guard Publ'g Co. v. NLRB*, 571 F.3d 53, 61 (D.C. Cir. 2009). On remand, the Board accepted the court's ruling as the law of the case. *Register-Guard*, 357 N.L.R.B. No. 27 (2011).

The decision in *Register-Guard* was controversial. Email and electronic communications have become entrenched as a means for employee discourse in the modern age, transforming the ways in which workplace communication occurs. In *Purple Communications, Inc.*, 361 N.L.R.B. No. 126 (2014), the Board recognized that "[e]mpirical evidence demonstrates that email has become such a significant conduit for employees' communications with one another that it is effectively a new 'natural gathering place.'" The Board went on to overrule *Register-Guard* and apply its *Republic Aviation* standard to email. Thus, employees with access to employers' email systems may use them during nonworking time for statutorily protected communications about organizing or for other concerted activity, unless the employer can demonstrate special circumstances justifying a restriction in order to maintain production and discipline. Appellate wrangling is likely to follow. Can you think of arguments to distinguish email from other forms of access? Where should the balance be struck between employer property rights and employee section 7 rights?

3. The Hallmark of Property Rights: The Right to Exclude. Can any act of balancing between employee and employer interests appropriately respect the employer's right to control its own property? Consider the following:

> The central mistake of the statute as construed is that it introduces any balancing test at all. Any balancing under the Act, however reasonable, quite clearly cuts back upon the absolute power to exclude that is the hallmark of any system of private property. It is wholly incorrect to treat as coercive any action by an employer that works to the economic detriment of union members. The real question is whether a firm should be required to provide an in-kind subsidy to a union regarded as antithetical to its prosperity, and perhaps to its survival. Employers need not make cash contributions to unions; why must they make contributions in kind?

Richard A. Epstein, *A Common Law for Labor Relations: A Critique of the New Deal Labor Legislation*, 92 YALE L.J. 1357, 1388–89 (1983).

   4.   Employers' Rights to Demand Employee Loyalty. As we saw in Chapter 6 (Employee Mobility), employees owe a duty of loyalty to their employers. Indeed, the Court has noted in a labor context that "[t]here is no more elemental cause for discharge of an employee than disloyalty to his employer." *NLRB v. IBEW Local 1129 (Jefferson Standard Broadcasting Co.)*, 346 U.S. 464, 472 (1953) (finding that certain employee actions are unprotected under the NLRA because they are disloyal). Is union organizing itself fundamentally disloyal? After all, one of the goals of most union organizing campaigns is to diminish the share of the company's profits that are allocated to the company's owners, and to distribute them instead to the workers. Thus, union organizing trenches upon employer property rights in another sense beyond physical trespass: If successful, it impairs employers' rights to control the proceeds of their capital investments. Can the Act's protection of concerted activity be reconciled with the duty of loyalty owed by employees to their employers?

   The Court was forced to confront this dilemma directly in a case involving union "salting," a practice in which union organizers apply for and obtain jobs with employers in order to organize employees from the inside, and so take advantage of the greater access available to employee-organizers under *Republic Aviation*. An employer's refusal to hire or decision to discharge a "salt" provokes unfair labor practice charges under § 8(a)(1) (interfering with the rights of employees to organize) and § 8(a)(3) (discrimination on the basis of union affiliation). In *NLRB v. Town & Country Elec.*, 516 U.S. 85 (1995), the Supreme Court ruled unanimously that an employer commits an unfair labor practice if it refuses to hire or terminates a union organizer upon learning of his or her union affiliation. Paid union organizers are "employees" under the NLRA, said the Court, relying on § 226 of the RESTATEMENT (SECOND) OF AGENCY which provides that a person may serve two masters, as long as service to one does not entail abandonment of services to the other. *Id.* at 94–95. The Court analogized to the practice of moonlighting, a permissible activity, and added that since union organizing activities are protected under § 7 (whereas moonlighting is not), the argument that union organizing activity performed on non-work time would be grounds for refusal to hire or termination had no force. *Id.* at 95. To the employer's argument that union salts are likely to act adversely to the company's interest by engaging in disloyal acts that undermine the firm's interests, the Court responded that absent specific proof, disloyalty will not be presumed. If a union organizer in fact engages in disloyal acts, the employer may discharge her without liability under the Act. *Id.* at 96–97.

   Is this analysis satisfactory? Should employers be required to countenance "Trojan Horses" in their workplaces? Must they tolerate "the presence of union members and activists—in the eyes of most employers, dangerous traitors intent upon subverting the employer's rule—on their property and in their employ"? *See* Cynthia L. Estlund, *Working Together: The Workplace, Civil Society, and the Law*, 89 GEO. L.J. 1, 75 (2000). If so, can you think of a better justification than the one offered by the Court in *Town & Country*?

3. NLRA § 7 Rights in the NonUnion Workplace

You may be surprised to learn that the NLRA applies to the nonunion workplace, even in the absence of union organizing activity. If so, you are not alone: most employers, most workers, and many employment lawyers likely suffer from the same misapprehension. Nonetheless, the NLRA does not condition § 7 rights on the presence of a union; it declares a right to engage in concerted activity "for the purpose of collective bargaining or other mutual aid or protection." NLRA § 7, 29 U.S.C. § 157. Why did Congress choose to accord such broad protection to concerted activity? Charles Morris explains:

> [C]oncerted conduct in which employees engage for "mutual aid or protection" may not necessarily be intended to achieve union organization, at least not deliberately or initially. In some situations the involved employees will have no present or foreseeable desire to organize into a union; in other cases they may have such a desire; and in some situations such a desire might eventually develop. Such nexus between unstructured concerted activity and more formalized union activity is central to the legislative intent embedded in Section 7. Congress thus intended by the broad language of the provision to encourage a flexible and relatively unstructured process. Hence, it should follow that unrepresented, and usually ill-informed, employees ought not to be required to act at their peril when they begin informal joint discussions, for they may not yet be "looking toward group action." But given the opportunity, group action—be it mild or assertive—might in time evolve from that rudimentary process.
>
> In the early organizational stages of the process that Section 7 describes, employees need not be consciously aware that they are engaged in a concerted act. They need only be involved in an act of association, speech, or petition ("petition," in workplace terminology, being essentially the presentation of a grievance) that reasonably relates to "wages, hours, [or] other terms and conditions of employment."

Charles J. Morris, *NLRB Protection in the NonUnion Workplace: A Glimpse at a General Theory of § 7 Conduct*, 137 U. PA. L. REV. 1673, 1701 (1989).

Often the impulse to act collectively stems from informal conversations between co-workers about compensation, benefits, or working conditions. The word "union" may never be mentioned. To what degree may the employer seek to nip such impulses in the bud by disciplining or discharging the ringleader(s)? Should it make a difference whether the conversations and actions occur in person, on the employer's email system, or on social media platforms visible to the public? The following cases explore these questions.

NLRB v. WASHINGTON ALUMINUM CO.
United States Supreme Court
370 U.S. 9 (1962)

MR. JUSTICE BLACK delivered the opinion of the Court.

The Court of Appeals for the Fourth Circuit . . . refused to enforce an order of the National Labor Relations Board directing the respondent Washington Aluminum Company to reinstate and make whole seven employees whom the company had discharged for leaving their work in the machine shop without permission on claims that the shop was too cold to work in. Because that decision raises important questions affecting the proper administration of the National Labor Relations Act, we granted certiorari.

The Board's order, as shown by the record and its findings, rested upon these facts and circumstances. The respondent company is engaged in the fabrication of aluminum products in Baltimore, Maryland, a business having interstate aspects that subject it to regulation under the National Labor Relations Act. The machine shop in which the seven discharged employees worked was not insulated and had a number of doors to the outside that had to be opened frequently. An oil furnace located in an adjoining building was the chief source of heat for the shop, although there were two gas-fired space heaters that contributed heat to a lesser extent. The heat produced by these units was not always satisfactory and, even prior to the day of the walkout involved here, several of the eight machinists who made up the day shift at the shop had complained from time to time to the company's foreman "over the cold working conditions."

January 5, 1959, was an extraordinarily cold day for Baltimore, with unusually high winds and a low temperature of 11 degrees followed by a high of 22. When the employees on the day shift came to work that morning, they found the shop bitterly cold, due not only to the unusually harsh weather, but also to the fact that the large oil furnace had broken down the night before and had not as yet been put back into operation. As the workers gathered in the shop just before the starting hour of 7:30, one of them, a Mr. Caron, went into the office of Mr. Jarvis, the foreman, hoping to warm himself but, instead, found the foreman's quarters as uncomfortable as the rest of the shop. As Caron and Jarvis sat in Jarvis' office discussing how bitingly cold the building was, some of the other machinists walked by the office window "huddled" together in a fashion that caused Jarvis to exclaim that "if those fellows had any guts at all, they would go home." When the starting buzzer sounded a few moments later, Caron walked back to his working place in the shop and found all the other machinists "huddled there, shaking a little, cold." Caron then said to these workers, ". . . Dave [Jarvis] told me if we had any guts, we would go home. . . . I am going home, it is too damned cold to work." Caron asked the other workers what they were going to do and, after some discussion among themselves, they decided to leave with him. One of these workers, testifying before the Board, summarized their entire discussion this way: "And we had all got together and thought it would be a good idea to go home; maybe we could get some heat brought into the plant that way." As they started to leave, Jarvis approached and persuaded one of the workers to remain at the job. But Caron and the other six workers on the day shift left practically in a body in a matter of minutes after the 7:30 buzzer.

When the company's general foreman arrived between 7:45 and 8 that morning, Jarvis promptly informed him that all but one of the employees had left because the shop was too cold. The company's president came in at approximately 8:20 a.m. and, upon learning of the walkout, immediately said to the foreman, ". . . if they have all gone, we are going to terminate them." After discussion "at great length" between the general foreman and the company president as to what might be the effect of the walkout on employee discipline and plant production, the president formalized his discharge of the workers who had walked out by giving orders at 9 a.m. that the affected workers should be notified about their discharge immediately, either by telephone, telegram or personally. This was done.

On these facts the Board found that the conduct of the workers was a concerted activity to protest the company's failure to supply adequate heat in its machine shop, that such conduct is protected under the provision of § 7 of the National Labor Relations Act which guarantees that "Employees shall have the right . . . to engage in . . . concerted activities for the purpose of collective bargaining or other mutual aid or protection," and that the discharge of these workers by the company amounted to an unfair labor practice under § 8(a)(1) of the Act, which forbids employers "to interfere with, restrain, or coerce employees in the exercise of the rights guaranteed in § 7." Acting under the authority of § 10(c) of the Act, which provides that when an employer has been guilty of an unfair labor practice the Board can "take such affirmative action including reinstatement of employees with or without back pay, as will effectuate the policies of this Act," the Board then ordered the company to reinstate the discharged workers to their previous positions and to make them whole for losses resulting from what the Board found to have been the unlawful termination of their employment.

In denying enforcement of this order, the majority of the Court of Appeals took the position that because the workers simply "summarily left their place of employment" without affording the company an "opportunity to avoid the work stoppage by granting a concession to a demand," their walkout did not amount to a concerted activity protected by § 7 of the Act. On this basis, they held that there was no justification for the conduct of the workers in violating the established rules of the plant by leaving their jobs without permission and that the Board had therefore exceeded its power in issuing the order involved here because § 10(c) declares that the Board shall not require reinstatement or back pay for an employee whom an employer has suspended or discharged "for cause."

We cannot agree that employees necessarily lose their right to engage in concerted activities under § 7 merely because they do not present a specific demand upon their employer to remedy a condition they find objectionable. The language of § 7 is broad enough to protect concerted activities whether they take place before, after, or at the same time such a demand is made. To compel the Board to interpret and apply that language in the restricted fashion suggested by the respondent here would only tend to frustrate the policy of the Act to protect the right of workers to act together to better their working conditions. Indeed, as indicated by this very case, such an interpretation of § 7 might place burdens upon employees so great that it would effectively nullify the right to engage in concerted activities which that protects. The seven employees here were part of a small group of employees who were wholly unorganized. They had no bargaining representative and, in fact, no representative of any kind to present their grievances to their employer. Under these circumstances, they had to speak for themselves as best they could. As pointed out above, prior to the day they left the shop, several of them had repeatedly complained to company officials about the cold working conditions in the shop. These had been more or less spontaneous individual pleas, unsupported by any threat of concerted protest, to which the company apparently gave little consideration and which it now says the Board should have treated as nothing more than "the same sort of gripes as the gripes made about the heat in the summertime." The bitter cold of January 5, however, finally brought these workers' individual complaints into concert so that some more effective action could be considered. Having no bargaining representative and no established procedure by which they could take full advantage of their unanimity of opinion in negotiations with the company, the men took the most direct course to let the company know that they wanted a warmer place in which to work. So, after talking among themselves, they walked out together in the hope that this action might spotlight their complaint and bring about some improvement in what they considered to be the "miserable" conditions of their employment. This we think was enough to justify the Board's holding that they were not required to make any more specific demand than they did to be entitled to the protection of § 7.

Although the company contends to the contrary, we think that the walkout involved here did grow out of a "labor dispute" within the plain meaning of the definition of that term in § 2(9) of the Act, which declares that it includes "any controversy concerning terms, tenure or *conditions of employment.* . . ." The findings of the Board, which are supported by substantial evidence and which were not disturbed below, show a running dispute between the machine shop employees and the company over the heating of the shop on cold days—a dispute which culminated in the decision of the employees to act concertedly in an effort to force the company to improve that condition of their employment. The fact that the company was already making every effort to repair the furnace and bring heat into the shop that morning does not change the nature of the controversy that caused the walkout. At the very most, that fact might tend to indicate that the conduct of the men in leaving was unnecessary and unwise, and it has long been settled that the reasonableness of workers' decisions to engage in concerted activity is irrelevant to the determination of whether a labor dispute exists or not. Moreover, the evidence here shows that the conduct of these workers was far from unjustified under the circumstances. The company's own foreman expressed the opinion that the shop was so cold that the men should go home. . . .

Nor can we accept the company's contention that because it admittedly had an established plant rule which forbade employees to leave their work without permission of the foreman, there was justifiable "cause" for discharging these employees, wholly separate and apart from any concerted activities in which they engaged in protest against the poorly heated plant. § 10(c) of the Act does authorize an employer to discharge employees for "cause" and our cases have long recognized this right on the part of an employer. But this, of course, cannot mean that an employer is at liberty to punish a man by discharging him for engaging in concerted activities which § 7 of the Act protects. And the plant rule in question here purports to permit the company to do just that for it would prohibit even the most plainly protected kinds of concerted work stoppages until and unless the permission of the company's foreman was obtained.

It is of course true that § 7 does not protect all concerted activities, but that aspect of the section is not involved in this case. The activities engaged in here do not fall within the normal categories of unprotected concerted activities such as those that are unlawful, violent or in breach of contract. Nor can they be brought under this Court's more recent pronouncement which denied the protection of § 7 to activities characterized as "indefensible" because they were there found to show a disloyalty to the workers' employer which this Court deemed unnecessary to carry on the workers' legitimate concerted activities. The activities of these seven employees cannot be classified as "indefensible" by any recognized standard of conduct. Indeed, concerted activities by employees for the purpose of trying to protect themselves from working conditions as uncomfortable as the testimony and Board findings showed them to be in this case are unquestionably activities to correct conditions which modern labor-management legislation treats as too bad to have to be tolerated in a humane and civilized society like ours.

We hold therefore that the Board correctly interpreted and applied the Act to the circumstances of this case and it was error for the Court of Appeals to refuse to enforce its order. The judgment of the Court of Appeals is reversed and the cause is remanded to that court with directions to enforce the order in its entirety.

Reversed and remanded.

TIMEKEEPING SYSTEMS, INC.
National Labor Relations Board
323 N.L.R.B. 244 (1997)

By CHAIRMAN GOULD, MEMBERS BROWNING and FOX.

On November 12, 1996, Administrative Law Judge Bernard Ries issued the attached decision. . . . The Board has considered the decision and the record in light of the exceptions and briefs, and has decided to affirm the judge's rulings, findings, and conclusions and to adopt the recommended Order as modified.

Bernard Ries, Administrative Law Judge. . . . The sole issue presented is whether Respondent discharged Lawrence Leinweber on December 5, 1995, because of his protected concerted activities and therefore violated Section 8(a)(1) of the Act. . . .

Respondent is a small Cleveland, Ohio company which manufactures data collection products. The chief operational officer of Respondent is Barry Markwitz. . . . Larry Leinweber, the Charging Party, 1 of about 23 employees located in two buildings, was hired by Respondent in April 1995 as a "software engineer" who prepared computer programs.

On December 1, Markwitz sent a message to all of Respondent's employees by electronic mail ("e-mail") regarding "proposed plans" for an incentive based bonus system (as to which employees were told to "reply with your comments or stop by to see me. A response to this is required.") and changes in vacation policy ("Your comments are welcome, but not required"). The incorporated memorandum regarding the proposed vacation policy changes, which are our only concern here, stated prefatorily, "Please give me your comments (send me an email or stop in and talk to me) by Tuesday, 12/5." The particular suggested policy changes in which we are interested were to close the offices on December 23 and reopen on January 2 and to adjust the number of paid days off over a 5-year period, the effect of which, Markwitz asserted, was that the employees "actually get more days off each year, compared to our present system."

Markwitz received a number of employee responses regarding his vacation proposals, including one on December 1, by e-mail, from Leinweber. Leinweber's response demonstrated that, in fact, the change referred to above would result in the same number of vacation days per year, and less flexibility as to their use. On December 4, Leinweber, having checked his calculations over the weekend, discovered a minor error, and notified Markwitz by e-mail.

Markwitz did not reply to Leinweber's communications. On December 5, Tom Dutton, a member of the engineering team, sent an e-mail to Markwitz, with copies to other engineering team members (which would include Leinweber), reading, "In response to the proposed vacation plan, I have only one word, GREAT!" Promptly, Leinweber, according to his credible testimony, sent an e-mail to Dutton telling him that the proposed policy did not, in fact, redound to the advantage of the employees.

Also on December 5, Leinweber sent a lengthy e-mail message to all employees, including Markwitz. The message spelled out in detail Leinweber's calculations regarding the result of the proposed vacation policy change. It contained, as well, some flippant and rather grating language.

The salutation was "Greetings Fellow Traveler." In his initial remarks, Leinweber wrote, "The closing statement in Barry's memo: 'The effect of this is that you actually get more days off each year, compared to our present system,' will be proven false." This declaration is reiterated in the final thought of the memo: "Thus, the closing statement in Barry's memo . . . is proven false." The paragraph preceding that statement reads, "Assuming anyone actually cares about the company and being productive on the job, if Christmas falls on Tuesday or Wednesday (sic) as it will in 1996 and 1997, respectively, two work weeks of one and two days each will be produced by the proposed plan, and I wouldn't expect these to be any more productive than the fragmented weeks that they replace." In closing, Leinweber asked that the recipient "please send errata to the (sic) Larry."

Also on December 5, after reading the e-mail message from Leinweber, Dutton e-mailed again to Markwitz, and also the engineering team (as shown on the e-mail address), saying in part, "After reading Larry's e-mail(s) of this date[,] I realized I had made a mistake in calculating the vacation days and wish to change my comment from 'GREAT' to 'Not so Great' on the proposed vacation policy." Dutton also noted in his message that the proposals had "generated more e-mail than any other plan in the company."

At the hearing, Markwitz at first admitted that he was "angry that Mr.

Leinweber sent his e-mail messages to all employees." He prepared on December 5 a memorandum to Leinweber which was conveyed to him by the engineering team leader. The memo stated that Markwitz was "saddened and disappointed" by Leinweber's e-mail, which was "inappropriate and intentionally provocative" and beneath "someone as talented and intelligent as you are." Markwitz then wrote:

> Our employment manual states: "Certain actions or types of behavior may result in immediate dismissal. These include, but are not limited to: Failure to treat others with courtesy and respect."

Markwitz went on to "direct" Leinweber to write him, by 5 p.m. that day: "In light of the above, why this e-mail message was inappropriate. How sending an e-mail message like this hurts the company. How this matter should have been handled."

Markwitz continued: "If your response is acceptable to me, you will post it by e-mail today to those who received your other message. If you decline to do so, or if your response is unacceptable to me, your employment will be terminated immediately. Otherwise, your employment will continue on a probationary basis for six months, during which time your employment may be terminated at any time and for any reason. Larry, I am very disappointed in you."

At the hearing, Markwitz testified that what upset him about the document was its "tone": it was a "slap in the face" of employees with good attitudes and a "personal attack" upon him. [Leinweber was discharged after he failed to draft an acceptable response. The reasons given for his termination were "failure to treat others with courtesy and respect," and "failure to follow instructions or to perform assigned work"]. . . .

In *Meyers I* [Meyers Industries, 268 N.L.R.B. 493 (1984), *remanded sub nom. Prill v. N.L.R.B.*, 755 F.2d 941 (D.C. Cir. 1985)], the Board stated the principles applicable to an alleged discharge for protected concerted activity under Section 8(a)(1) of the Act, and *Meyers II* [Meyers Industries, 281 N.L.R.B. 882 (1986), *aff'd sub nom.* Prill v. N.L.R.B., 835 F.2d 1481 (D.C. Cir. 1987)], did not purport to change those principles:

> Once the activity is found to be concerted, an 8(a)(1) violation will be found if, in addition, the employer knew of the concerted nature of the employee's activity, the concerted activity was protected by the Act, and the adverse employment action at issue (e.g., discharge) was motivated by the employee's protected concerted activity.

Leinweber's e-mailings clearly constituted "concerted" activity as that term has been defined by case law. While *Meyers II* stated that the Board was "fully embracing" the rule in Mushroom Transportation Co. v. N.L.R.B., 330 F.2d 683 (3d Cir. 1964), in which the court held that "mere talk" could be found to be protected Section 7 activity only when it is "looking toward group action," id. at 685, the Board has thereafter repeatedly held that "the object of inducing group action need not be express. For instance, 'it is obvious that higher wages are a frequent objective of organizational activity, and discussions about wages are necessary to further that goal.' Jeannette Corp. v. N.L.R.B., 532 F.2d 916, 918 (3d Cir. 1976)."

Plainly, in communicating with his fellow employees, Leinweber was attempting to correct any misimpression of the vacation proposal, such as Dutton's, and to arouse support for his own decision to oppose the proposal. Leinweber credibly testified that his purpose in circulating the e-mail was "because I understood everybody didn't understand and that they needed help in making an informed decision." While his "object of inducing group action [was not] express," it is manifest from the record. . . .

Contrary to Respondent's contention on brief, this is a case of concerted activity for the "purpose of mutual aid or protection," as required by Section 7 of the Act. Leinweber's effort to incite the other employees to help him preserve a vacation policy which he believed best served his interests, and perhaps the interests of other employees, unquestionably qualified his communication as being in pursuit of "mutual aid or protection." While the court in New River Industries, Inc. v. N.L.R.B., 945 F.2d 1290 (4th Cir. 1991), may have thought, contrary to the Board, that a sarcastic letter was, in Respondent's words, intended "merely to belittle management," here there is no doubt that Leinweber had a specific objective in mind for which he hoped to elicit "mutual aid." . . .

While I have found that Markwitz was principally aggrieved by the tenor of Leinweber's e-mail and its perceived personal denigration of Markwitz, his December 9 message to employees establishes as well that a component of his anger was caused by the fact that Leinweber had attempted to enlist other employees in his cause. Although the law of "protected concerted activity" does not require the General Counsel to prove that the employer has disciplined an employee because he/she has engaged in concerted activity, but rather only requires that the employer knows that the conduct being disciplined is concerted, the evidence here shows that the concertedness of Leinweber's conduct also very likely infected Markwitz's decision to discharge.[11] In considering the other elements of a prima facie protected concerted activity case, as outlined in Meyer I, supra, there is obviously no question that Markwitz was aware of the concerted activity, nor any doubt that it played the principal role in Leinweber's discharge.

The final question raised by the Respondent is whether Leinweber's December 5 message was "protected." Some concerted conduct can be expressed in so intolerable a manner as to lose the protection of Section 7. N.L.R.B. v. Thor Power Tool Co., 351 F.2d 584, 587 (7th Cir. 1965). While the legal description of the sort of behavior which withdraws the protection of the Act from concerted activity has varied, Dreis & Krump Mfg. Co. Inc. v. N.L.R.B., 544 F.2d 320, 329 (7th Cir. 1976) . . . has often been spotlighted for its statement of the test:

> [C]ommunications occurring during the course of otherwise protected activity remain likewise protected unless found to be "so violent or of such serious character as to render the employee unfit for further service."

---

[11] [n. 11] I note that Respondent's employee manual lists as a ground for discharge "Discussing your rate of pay or your compensation arrangement with another employee." This would normally constitute an unfair labor practice, *see, e.g., Radisson Plaza Minneapolis*, 307 N.L.R.B. 94 (1992); Heck's, Inc., 293 N.L.R.B. 1111, 1113 (1989). However, the complaint contains no such allegation and the General Counsel has not, on brief, sought a finding based on this statement. I shall therefore not address the matter further.

In applying the foregoing or similar standards the Board has invoked a forfeiture of the protection of the Act only in cases where the concerted behavior has been truly insubordinate or disruptive of the work process. It has generally been the Board's position that unpleasantries uttered in the course of otherwise protected concerted activity do not strip away the Act's protection. In Postal Service, 241 N.L.R.B. 389 (1979), a letter characterizing acting supervisors as "a-holes" was not beyond the pale. In Harris Corp., 269 N.L.R.B. 733 (1984), a letter describing management with such words as "hypocritical," "despotic," and "tyrannical" was not disqualifying, despite its "boorish, ill-bred, and hostile tone." Id. at 738. In Churchill's Restaurant, 276 N.L.R.B. 775 (1985), where an employer discharged an employee who, he believed, was saying that the employer was "prejudiced," which the latter considered an "insult," the remarks were held not "so offensive as to threaten plant discipline," id. at 777 fn. 11. A statement to other employees that the chief executive officer was a "cheap son of a bitch" was considered to be protected concerted activity in Groves Truck & Trailer, 281 N.L.R.B. 1194, 1195 (1986).

The question of the protected nature of Leinweber's activity is controlled by the latter line of precedents. It is clear from Markwitz's correspondence and testimony that his ultimate decision to discharge Leinweber was based on two aspects of Leinweber's conduct. The major reason was the tone of the letter and the specific remarks about Markwitz. As I have noted previously, it is also evident that Markwitz was displeased by the fact that Leinweber had communicated the message to the other employees, and that concern entwined with and aggravated, in Markwitz's mind, the first reaction.

Markwitz, like any other employer, wants a friction free working environment. But, as the court of appeals pointed out in Thor Power Tool, *supra*, Section 7 activity may acceptably be accompanied by some "impropriety." And, in Dreis & Krump Mfg. Co., *supra*, the Court of Appeals laid down the rather stiff test of whether the questioned activity is "of such serious character as to render the employee unfit for further service." Surely, the words and phrases used by Leinweber in his message were not that egregious. The Leinweber message has arrogant overtones, but the language is less assaultive than the "boorish, ill-bred, and hostile" wording found not [sic] be disqualifying in Harris Corp., *supra*. Indeed, Markwitz was prepared to retain Leinweber if he would submit some sort of apology, which he failed to do. I find that the message itself was not couched in language sufficiently serious to warrant divestment of Section 7 protection. . . .

[The judge dismissed the company's argument that Leinweber "took over" the email system and wasted a great deal of employee time as employees read and digested the contents of his email, noting that the employer permitted its workers to post simple e-mails to one another, to make personal telephone calls, and to spend de minimis amounts of working time on nonwork pursuits; the judge determined that Leinweber's message "could not have taken . . . more than a few minutes to digest." Nor did the email hold company management up to "ridicule and embarrassment" within the meaning of *N.L.R.B. v. Electrical Workers IBEW Local 1229 (Jefferson Standard)*, 346 U.S. 464 (1953), which ruled that public disparagement of a company product amounted to unprotected disloyalty; no public disparagement occurred here.]

Finally, although unnecessarily, I address Respondent's contention that "[i]t would be wrong to saddle Respondent for many years into the future with the burden of a reinstated employee the likes of Leinweber." Leinweber is, I concede, a rather unusual person, perhaps one of the new breed of cyberspace pioneers who are attracting public attention, and at the same time—how else can I say it—a bit of a wise guy. Still, in his December 5 e-mail, Markwitz described Leinweber as "talented and intelligent," and he was willing to retain Leinweber after receipt of the offending message if Leinweber would publicly apologize. Markwitz also implored employee Heather Hudson on December 5 to urge Leinweber to write the apology because "he did not want to fire him." I do not gather from this that Markwitz would be totally distraught if he had to rehire Leinweber. In any event, Markwitz's feelings must take second place to the dictates of the statute; the employer who was called a "cheap son-of-a-bitch" by an employee in Groves Truck & Trailer, *supra*, was probably not entirely pleased either. [The judge ordered that Leinweber be reinstated with back pay and that the company post a notice informing the employees of the result of the case and promising not to violate the NLRA in the future.]

NOTES

1. **Requirements for Protection Under § 7.** Employee activity is protected under § 7 whether conducted in a union or nonunion workplace if: (1) it is "concerted"—involving two or more employees, or one employee acting on the authority of other employees or seeking to enlist their support in a common endeavor; (2) it is for "mutual aid"—relates to wages, hours, or terms and conditions of employment, broadly interpreted; and (3) it is "protected"—i.e., neither disloyal, indefensible, violent, unlawful, or in breach of contract.

Although *Washington Aluminum* and *Timekeeping Systems* primarily involved the first issue, the other two requirements have been important issues in other cases. In *Eastex, Inc. v. NLRB*, 437 U.S. 556 (1978), the Court ruled that the employer's ban on distribution of union literature opposing a right-to-work law and advocating for higher minimum wage laws violated the NLRA. The Court reasoned that even though the changes advocated were at the legislative and administrative level, the communications sought to improve workers' lot "as employees," and thus were "for mutual aid or protection." *Id.* at 566–67. The Court did note, however, that at some point the relationship between the subject matter of the communication and the employees' workplace interests becomes "so attenuated that an activity cannot fairly be deemed within the 'mutual aid or protection' clause." *Id.* at 568.

In *NLRB v. IBEW Local 1129 (Jefferson Standard Broadcasting Co.)*, 346 U.S. 464 (1953), the Court found that television technicians who distributed handbills criticizing their TV station-employer for refusing to purchase equipment needed to put on live programs and suggesting that the station was treating the city as "second-class" were engaged in a "sharp, public disparaging attack upon the quality of the Company's business product and its business policies, in a manner reasonably calculated to harm the Company's reputation and reduce its income," an act so disloyal that their discharges were justified. *Id.* at 471–72. The Court relied heavily on the fact that the employees' attack on the company's product was divorced from complaints about wages or working conditions; the handbill made no reference to a labor dispute, and did not disclose that the employees sought public support for the purpose of extracting a concession from the employer. *Id.* at 475–77.

Determining whether conduct is so indefensible and disloyal that it loses section 7 protection has proved challenging, since union organizing activity is often adverse to the employer's economic interests and frequently disrupts the workplace, with potential impacts on employee morale and customer perceptions. In *Timekeeping Systems*, the Board found Leinweber's tone in his emails not so offensive that it should lose protection under section 7. As the Board observed in *Dreis & Krump Mfg., Inc.*, 221 N.L.R.B. 309, 315 (1975), cited in *Timekeeping Systems*, "the language of the shop is not the language of 'polite society.' " Why not? Why shouldn't speech about union organizing and complaints about pay, benefits and working conditions be held to standards of decorum and civility? Should it matter whether the speech occurs in the presence of coworkers? Of customers?

In *Triple Play Sports Bar & Grille*, 361 N.L.R.B. No. 31 (2014), the Board applied *Jefferson Standard* to a dialogue between employees on Facebook in which other Facebook friends (non-employees) also participated. The conversation involved complaints over the employer's calculation of tax withholding, and was characterized by expletives and comments that the bar owners were so incompetent that they "couldn't even do the tax paperwork correctly" and that someone should do the owners "a favor" and purchase the business from them. *Id.* at *7. The Board found the comments protected, distinguishing *Jefferson Standard*: the comments in *Triple Play* clearly disclosed the existence of a labor dispute; they were not directed at the general public but were on an employee's personal Facebook page; and they did not disparage the employer's products or services. *Id.* at *22–*24. Here is a sampling of the original posting and the comments:

JAMIE LAFRANCE   [former Triple Play employee]: Maybe someone should do the owners of Triple Play a favor and buy it from them. They can't even do the tax paperwork correctly!!! Now I OWE money . . . Wtf!!!!

KEN DESANTIS   (a Facebook "friend" . . . and a customer): "You owe them money . . . that's fucked up."

DANIELLE MARIE PARENT   (Triple Play employee): "I FUCKING OWE MONEY TOO!"

LAFRANCE: "The state. Not Triple Play. I would never give that place a penny of my money. Ralph [DelBuono] fucked up the paperwork . . . as per usual."

DESANTIS: "yeah I really dont go to that place anymore."

LAFRANCE: "It's all Ralph's fault. He didn't do the paperwork right. I'm calling the labor board to look into it bc he still owes me about 2000 in paychecks."

. . . .

LAFRANCE: "We shouldn't have to pay it. It's every employee there that its happening to."

DESANTIS: "you better get that money . . . thats bullshit if thats the case im sure he did it to other people too."

PARENT: "Let me know what the board says because I owe $ 323 and ive never owed."

LAFRANCE: "I'm already getting my 2000 after writing to the labor board and them investigating but now I find out he fucked up my taxes and I owe the state a bunch. Grrr."

PARENT: "I mentioned it to him and he said that we should want to owe."

LAFRANCE: "Hahahaha he's such a shady little man. He prolly pocketed it all from all our paychecks. I've never owed a penny in my life till I worked for him. Thank goodness I got outta there."

JILLIAN SANZONE   [Triple Play employee]: "I owe too. Such an asshole."

PARENT: "yeah me neither, i told him we will be discussing it at the meeting."

SARAH BAUMBACH   (Triple Play employee): "I have never had to owe money at any jobs . . . i hope i wont have to at TP . . . probably will have to seeing as everyone else does!"

LAFRANCE: "Well discuss good bc I won't be there to hear it. And let me know what his excuse is;)."

JONATHAN FEELEY   (a Facebook "friend" of LaFrance's and customer) : "And ther way to expensive."

Do you agree that this type of dialogue should be protected?

2. Greater Levels of Protection for Concerted Activity in Union Workplaces. In a unionized workplace where a collective bargaining agreement exists, a single employee acting alone in furtherance of rights protected under the collective bargaining agreement will be deemed to be acting "concertedly" for mutual aid or protection because his or her act is a continuation of the ongoing process of employee concerted action that produced the labor agreement. This is so even where the employee does not explicitly reference the collective bargaining agreement in his or her protest. *NLRB v. City Disposal Systems*, 465 U.S. 822 (1984) (ruling that truck driver discharged for refusing to drive a truck that he honestly and reasonably believed had faulty brakes was engaged in protected concerted activity). Thus, unionized employees receive broader protection under § 7 than do nonunion employees. Does this make sense? Unionized employees have the right to challenge ("grieve") violations of the labor contract through the arbitration provisions in the contract, and to obtain relief from discipline administered in violation of the contract. Why, then, should they also be entitled to protection under § 7? Aren't nonunion workers actually in greater need of protection because their organizing efforts are in an inchoate, fragile stage?

Is a single employee's invocation of statutory rights conferred by employment statutes (such as the right to receive minimum wages or overtime pay under the Fair Labor Standards Act, or the right to safe working conditions conferred by the Occupational Safety and Health Act) "concerted" activity where the employer policy challenged affects many workers? One might argue that the same rationale that led the Court to conclude that a single unionized employee's invocation of contractual rights was protected concerted activity should apply to a single worker's effort to enforce rights conferred in an employment statute. The Board rejected this argument in *Meyers II*, which was subsequently affirmed by the D.C. Circuit in *Prill v. NLRB*, 835 F.2d 1481 (D.C. Cir. 1987): Any concerted activity in the lobbying process that led to the passage of the employment legislation would have only an "attenuated" link to the workplace assertion of individual rights, unlike assertions of contractual rights by individual workers in unionized workplaces where the contract clauses were produced by union organizing and collective action. Thus, unless explicitly authorized by other workers, invocations of statutory rights are not protected concerted activity under NLRA § 7. (As discussed in section C, above, complaining workers are sometimes protected under the anti-retaliation provisions of those statutes, although some courts may require the formal filing of such complaints as a condition for extending protection.)

Employment legislation is said to confer individual rights, not collective rights. Suppose that the employee files a collective action for enforcement, would that satisfy the requirement that the activity be concerted? *See 200 E. 81st Rest. Corp.*, 2014 NLRB LEXIS 306 (N.L.R.B. Apr. 29, 2014) (finding that individual employee engaged in protected concerted activity when he filed a collective action under the FLSA, even though the employee was the only named plaintiff and no other employees had yet joined the litigation, because the employer was on notice that the activity was group-based). What difference does this make, if the employee can bring a claim under the anti-retaliation provisions of the FLSA anyhow?

3. Refusals to Work Under Hazardous Conditions. The *Washington Aluminum* employees refused to work in response to very onerous working conditions, but there was no allegation that the conditions were hazardous. Suppose that employees perceive a working condition that poses a hazard, and refuse to work until it is abated. Regulations promulgated under the Occupational Safety and Health Act authorize employee refusals to perform unsafe work if the fear of serious injury or death is objectively reasonable. *See Whirlpool Corp. v. Marshall*, 445 U.S. 1 (1980), discussed in Chapter 13 (Health and Safety), *infra*. NLRA § 7 provides even broader protection for concerted refusals to work, protecting refusals predicated on a genuine fear of harm, even if objectively unreasonable. *See NLRB v. Modern Carpet Indus.*, 611 F.2d 811 (10th Cir. 1979).

4. The Employer's Property Interest in Continuing the Operation of Its Business. *Washington Aluminum* makes it clear that an employer cannot discharge employees who walk off the job to protest wages or working conditions. Must an employer let its business stand idle while the employees engage in a protected work stoppage? No, said the Supreme Court in an early case. In *NLRB v. Mackay Radio & Telegraph Co.*, 304 U.S. 333 (1938), the Court held that while employers may not discharge striking employees, they may replace them in order to carry on the business. In *dicta*, the Court explained that the replacement workers may be "permanent" if necessary in order to recruit workers to take the places of those who have walked off the job, and if the employer itself has not committed any unfair labor practice. However, striking workers who subsequently express the desire to return to work must be reinstated as positions become available. Is the distinction between being discharged and being "permanently replaced" one that most employees are likely to find meaningful?

4. NLRA § 7 Rights on Social Media

In a series of cases decided over the last several years, the Board has made it clear that NLRA section 7 rights apply to communications between employees on social media, whether on- or off-duty. Protection is limited by the usual rules applicable to NLRA section 7 activity: it must be concerted; it must pertain to wages, hours, or terms and conditions of employment; and it must not be disloyal, indefensible, violent, or in breach of contract. A sampling of representative cases follows.

HISPANICS UNITED OF BUFFALO, INC.
359 N.L.R.B. No. 37 (2012)

By MARK GASTON PEARCE, CHAIRMAN.

At issue in this case is whether the Respondent violated Section 8(a)(1) of the Act by discharging five employees for Facebook comments they wrote in response to a coworker's criticisms of their job performance. Although the employees' mode of communicating their workplace concerns might be novel, we agree with the judge that the appropriate analytical framework for resolving their discharge allegations has long been settled under *Meyers Industries* [268 N.L.R.B. 493 (1983)] and its progeny. Applying *Meyers*, we agree with the judge that the Respondent violated 8(a)(1) by discharging the five employees.

The relevant facts are as follows. Marianna Cole-Rivera and Lydia Cruz-Moore were coworkers employed by the Respondent to assist victims of domestic violence. The two employees frequently communicated with each other by phone and text message during the workday and after hours. According to Cole-Rivera's credited testimony, Cruz-Moore often criticized other employees during these communications, particularly housing department employees who, Cruz-Moore asserted, did not provide timely and adequate assistance to clients. Other employees similarly testified that Cruz-Moore spoke critically to them about their work habits and those of other employees.

This "criticism" issue escalated on Saturday, October 9, 2010, a nonworkday, when Cole-Rivera received a text message from Cruz-Moore stating that the latter intended to discuss her concerns regarding employee performance with Executive Director Lourdes Iglesias. Cole-Rivera sent Cruz-Moore a responsive text questioning whether she really "wanted Lourdes to know . . . how u feel we don't do our job . . . ." From her home, and using her own personal computer, Cole-Rivera then posted the following message on her Facebook page:

> Lydia Cruz, a coworker feels that we don't help our clients enough at [Respondent]. I about had it! My fellow coworkers how do u feel?

Four off-duty employees—Damicela Rodriguez, Ludimar Rodriguez, Yaritza Campos, and Carlos Ortiz—responded by posting messages, via their personal computers, on Cole-Rivera's Facebook page; the employees' responses generally objected to the assertion that their work performance was substandard.

Cruz-Moore also responded, demanding that Cole-Rivera "stop with ur lies about me." She then complained to Iglesias about the Facebook comments, stating that she had been slandered and defamed. At Iglesias' request, Cruz-Moore printed all the Facebook comments and had the printout delivered to Iglesias. On October 12, the first workday after the Facebook postings, Iglesias discharged Cole-Rivera and her four coworkers, stating that their remarks constituted "bullying and harassment" of a coworker and violated the Respondent's "zero tolerance" policy prohibiting such conduct.

. . . .

The Board first defined concerted activity in *Meyers I* as that which is "engaged in with or on the authority of other employees, and not solely by and on behalf of the employee himself." 268 N.L.R.B. at 497. In *Meyers II*, the Board expanded this definition to include those "circumstances where individual employees seek to initiate or to induce or to prepare for group action, as well as individual employees bringing truly group complaints to the attention of management." 281 N.L.R.B. at 887.

Applying these principles, as the [administrative law] judge did, there should be no question that the activity engaged in by the five employees was concerted for the "purpose of mutual aid or protection" as required by Section 7. As set forth in her initial Facebook post, Cole-Rivera alerted fellow employees of another employee's complaint that they "don't help our clients enough," stated that she "about had it" with the complaints, and solicited her coworkers' views about this criticism. By responding to this solicitation with comments of protest, Cole-Rivera's four coworkers made common cause with her, and, together, their actions were concerted within the definition of *Meyers I*, because they were undertaken "with . . . other employees." 268 N.L.R.B. at 497. The actions of the five employees were also concerted under the expanded definition of *Meyers II*, because, as the judge found, they "were taking a first step towards taking group action to defend themselves against the accusations they could reasonably believe Cruz-Moore was going to make to management."

Our dissenting colleague contends that the employees' Facebook discussions about Cruz-Moore's criticisms were not undertaken for the purpose of their "mutual aid and protection." Specifically, he states that a group action defense to Cruz-Moore's criticisms could not have been intended because Cole-Rivera failed to tell her coworkers that Cruz-Moore was going to voice her criticisms to Iglesias. We disagree.

In *Relco Locomotives, Inc.*, 358 N.L.R.B. No. 37, slip op. at 17 (2012), the Board reiterated established precedent that the "object or goal of initiating, inducing or preparing for group action does not have to be stated explicitly when employees communicate," citing *Whittaker Corp.*, 289 N.L.R.B. 933, 933 (1988). Even absent an express announcement about the object of an employee's activity, "a concerted objective may be inferred from a variety of circumstances in which employees might discuss or seek to address concerns about working conditions . . . ." *Id.* Relying on this authority, the Board in *Relco* found unlawful the discharge of two employees for discussing among themselves and other employees their "concern" about the rumored discharge of a fellow employee. Notwithstanding that the two never "talk[ed] specifically about working together to address their concerns about [the employee's] termination," the Board adopted the judge's finding that they "engaged in concerted activities when they communicated with other employees about their concern . . . [and i]t matter[ed] not that [they] had not yet taken their concerns to management—their discussions with coworkers were indispensable initial steps along the way to possible group action" *Id.*, slip op. at 17.

Here, too, Cole-Rivera's Facebook communication with her fellow employees, immediately after learning that Cruz-Moore planned to complain about her coworkers to Iglesias, had the clear "mutual aid" objective of preparing her coworkers for a group defense to those complaints. Contrary to our colleague, Cole-Rivera was not required under *Relco* to discuss this object with coworkers or tell them it was made necessary by Cruz-Moore's impending visit with Iglesias. Her "mutual aid" object of preparing her coworkers for group action was implicitly manifest from the surrounding circumstances. *Timekeeping Systems, Inc.*, 323 N.L.R.B. 244, 248 (1997).

As to the third element of the violation, whether the employees' concerted activity was protected, we find that the Facebook comments here fall well within the Act's protection. The Board has long held that Section 7 protects employee discussions about their job performance, and the Facebook comments plainly centered on that subject. As discussed, the employees were directly responding to allegations they were providing substandard service to the Respondent's clients. Given the negative impact such criticisms could have on their employment, the five employees were clearly engaged in protected activity in mutual aid of each other's defense to those criticisms.

The Respondent does not argue that the employees' comments were unprotected because they were made via Facebook. To the contrary, the Respondent asserts that, "regardless of where the comments and actions of the five terminated at-will employees took place, the result herein would have been the same." According to the Respondent, it was privileged to discharge the five employees because their comments constituted unprotected harassment and bullying of Cruz-Moore, in violation of its "zero tolerance" policy. The judge rejected this argument, and so do we.

First, as the judge found, the Facebook comments cannot reasonably be construed as a form of harassment or bullying within the meaning of the Respondent's policy.[12] Second, even assuming that the policy covered the comments, the Respondent could not lawfully apply its policy "without reference to Board law." *Consolidated Diesel Co.*, 332 N.L.R.B. 1019, 1020 (2000), *enforced*, 263 F.3d 345 (4th Cir. 2011). As the Board explained in *Consolidated Diesel*, "legitimate managerial concerns to prevent harassment do not justify policies that discourage the free exercise of Section 7 rights by subjecting employees to . . . discipline on the basis

---

[12] [n. 13] As found by the judge, there was no evidence that any of the five employees harassed Cruz-Moore by their comments, or that any purported harassment was covered by the zero tolerance policy, which refers to "race, color, sex, religion, national origin, age, disability, veteran status, or other prohibited basis."

of the subjective reactions of others to their protected activity." *Id.* Here, as in *Consolidated Diesel*, the Respondent applied its harassment policy to the discharged employees based solely on Cruz-Moore's subjective claim (in a text message) that she felt offended by the Facebook comments. As the United States Court of Appeals for the Fourth Circuit noted in enforcing the Board's decision, "[s]uch a wholly subjective notion of harassment is unknown to the Act," 263 F.3d 354, and discipline imposed on this basis violates Section 8(a)(1).

In sum, because we have found that the Facebook postings were concerted and protected, and because it is undisputed that the Respondent discharged the five employees based solely on their postings, we conclude that the discharges violated Section 8(a)(1).

[The Board adopted the order of the administrative law judge, requiring the employer to reinstate the discharged employees and make them whole for loss of pay and benefits].

NOTES

1. **Section 7 Rights in Facebook Postings.** Should it make any difference whether protected communications occur on a social networking site or blog, as opposed to an email system maintained by the employer, as in *Timekeeping Systems*? Is it relevant whether the communication occurs on or off duty? Are the interests at stake different from those implicated in email communications? Are they different from the interests in conversations around the water-cooler or in the coffee room?

At one level, *Hispanics United* is an unexceptional application of § 7 to a situation where an employee explicitly sought responses from coworkers to speech concerning working conditions. But the application of § 7 rights in the social media context attracted a great deal of media attention because of the potential breadth of its impact in the nonunion workplace. As a result, employees became more aware of their rights. Note also the clear evidentiary record and timeline established by postings in social media cases, which make proof of violations far easier than had been the case with conversations around the water-cooler.

2. **"Liking" a Facebook Status as Protected Concerted Activity.** The question soon arose as to what degree of activity was actually required for § 7 protection. For example, if an employee responds to another's Facebook post critical of the employer by "liking" that comment or status, would this amount to sufficiently meaningful participation to receive protection under the Act? The Board ruled that it does in *Triple Play Sports Bar & Grille*, 361 N.L.R.B. No. 31 (2014), at least where it is part of an ongoing conversation concerning a dispute about pay or working conditions.

5. Employer Policies Restricting Collective Employee Speech

Recall that the purpose of NLRA § 7 rights is to protect free association and free expression among employees as preconditions to encouraging union organizing and collective bargaining. Employer work rules and policies that restrict dialogue about wages or working conditions may chill that speech if employees perceive them as applying to section 7 protected activities, and for this reason the Board has developed a test that has been applied to invalidate a wide variety of work rules that are neutral on their face and may seem quite innocuous to those not acquainted with the application of section 7 rights in nonunion workplaces.

The following case deals with social media postings, and provides a useful review of the principles discussed in section 4, above. It also explains the application of section 7 to workplace policies.

KARL KNAUZ MOTORS, INC.
358 N.L.R.B. No. 164 (2012)

[The Administrative Law Judge provided the following description of the facts.]

JOEL B. BIBLOWITZ, ALJ.

The Respondent operates a BMW dealership in Lake Bluff, Illinois, called the facility, selling new BMW automobiles, as well as used cars. The Respondent also owns an adjoining dealership that sells Land Rover automobiles . . . . Becker began working at the Land Rover dealership in 1998; he transferred to the Respondent's BMW facility in July 2004, where he was employed until his termination on June 22. His immediate supervisor at the facility was Phillip Ceraulo, the general sales manager; Peter Giannini and Robert Graziano were the sales director and sales manager at the facility, and Barry Taylor was the vice president and general manager.

. . . .

The event that precipitated the situation here was an Ultimate Driving Event, at times called the Event, held on June 9 to introduce a redesigned BMW 5 Series automobile. Everybody considered this to be a significant event, especially because the BMW Series 5 automobile is their "bread and butter" product . . . .

Becker testified that about a day or two prior to the Ultimate Driving Event, all the sales people met with Ceraulo in his office to discuss the event. In addition to Becker, the other sales people were Greg Larsen, Fadwa Charnidski, Steve Rayburn, Chad Holland, Howard Krause, and Dave Benck. Ceraulo told them about the Event and what was expected of them. He told them that for food, they were going to have a hot dog cart serving the clients, in addition to cookies and chips. He testified that the sales people rolled their eyes "in amazement" and he told Ceraulo, "I can't believe we're not doing more for this event." Larsen said the same thing and added: "This is a major launch of a new product and . . . we just don't understand what the thought is behind it." Ceraulo responded: "This is not a food event." After the meeting the sales people spoke more about it and Larsen told him that at the Mercedes Benz dealership they served hors d'oeuvres with servers. Becker also testified that Larsen said, "we're the bread and butter store in the auto park and we're going to get the hot dog cart." As to why this was important, Becker testified:

> Everything in life is perception. BMW [is] a luxury brand and . . . what I've talked about with all my co-workers was the fact that what they were going to do for this event was absolutely not up to par with the image of the brand, the ultimate driving machine, a luxury brand. And we were concerned about the fact that it would . . . affect our commissions, especially in the sense that it would affect . . . how the dealership looks and, how it's presented . . . when somebody walks into our dealership . . . it's a beautiful auto park . . . it's a beautiful place . . . and if you walk in and you sit down and your waiter serves you a happy meal from McDonald's. The two just don't mix . . . we were very concerned about the fact . . . that it could potentially affect our bottom line.

. . . .

On the day of the Event, there was the hot dog cart (with hot dogs), bags of Doritos, cookies and bowls of apples and oranges. Becker took pictures of the sales people holding hot dogs, water and Doritos and told them that he was going to post the pictures on his Facebook page.

As stated above, the Respondent also owns a Land Rover dealership located adjacent to the facility. On June 14 an accident occurred at that dealership. A salesperson was showing a customer a car and allowed the customer's 13-year-old son to sit in the driver's seat of the car while the salesperson was in the passenger seat, apparently, with the door open. The customer's son must have stepped on the gas pedal and the car drove down a small embankment, drove over the foot of the customer into an adjacent pond, and the salesperson was thrown into the water (but was unharmed, otherwise).

Becker was told of the Land Rover incident and could see it from the facility. He got his camera and took pictures of the car in the pond. On June 14, he posted comments and pictures of the Ultimate Driving Event of June 9, as well as the Land Rover accident of June 14 on his Facebook page.[13] The Event pages are entitled: "BMW 2011 5 Series Soiree." On the first page, Becker wrote:

> I was happy to see that Knauz went "All Out" for the most important launch of a new BMW in years . . . the new 5 series. A car that will generate tens in millions of dollars in revenues for Knauz over the next few years. The small 8 oz bags of chips, and the $ 2.00 cookie plate from Sam's Club, and the semi fresh apples and oranges were such a nice touch . . . but to top it all off . . . the Hot Dog Cart. Where our clients could attain a[n] over cooked wiener and a stale bun.

---

[13] [n. 3] At the time, Becker had approximately 95 Facebook "Friends" 15 or 16 of whom were employed by the Respondent, who would be able to access his Facebook account. He testified that, at the time, his "Privacy Settings" allowed access, as well, to "friends of Friends," so that they could also see his postings.

Underneath were comments by relatives and friends of Becker, followed by Becker's responses . . . .

On June 14, Becker also posted the pictures of the Land Rover accident, as well as comments, on his Facebook page. The caption is "This is your car: This is your car on drugs." The first picture shows the car, the front part of which was in the pond, with the salesperson with a blanket around her sitting next to a woman, and a young boy holding his head. Becker wrote:

> This is what happens when a sales Person sitting in the front passenger seat (Former Sales Person, actually) allows a 13 year old boy to get behind the wheel of a 6000 lb. truck built and designed to pretty much drive over anything. The kid drives over his father's foot and into the pond in all about 4 seconds and destroys a $ 50,000 truck. OOOPS!

There are a number of comments on the first page, one of which was from an employee of the Respondent in the warranty department, stating: "How did I miss all the fun stuff?" On the second page, under the photo of the car in the pond, Becker wrote: "I love this one . . . The kid's pulling his hair out . . . Du, what did I do? Oh no, is Mom gonna give me a time out?" Below, there were comments from two of Respondent's employees. Counsel for the [Board] also introduced in evidence a Facebook page of Casey Felling, a service advisor employed by the Respondent, containing Becker's picture of the car in the pond with Felling's comment: "Finally, some action at our Land Rover store."

By the next day, the Respondent's representatives had learned of, and had been given copies of, Becker's Facebook postings for the BMW Event and the Land Rover accident. As a result, Ceraulo asked Becker to remove the postings, which he did, and Taylor decided that he wanted to meet with Becker on the following day to discuss the postings.

On June 16, at Taylor's request, Becker met with Taylor, Giannini and Ceraulo in a conference room at the facility. Becker testified that Taylor had the Facebook postings of the BMW Event and the Land Rover accident in his hand and tossed them to him and asked, "What were you thinking?" Becker responded that it was his Facebook page and his friends: "It's none of your business." Taylor asked, "That's what you're going to claim?" and Becker said, "That's exactly what I'm going to claim." Taylor again asked what he was thinking and Becker said that he wasn't thinking anything. Taylor said that they received calls from other dealers and that he thoroughly embarrassed all management and "all of your coworkers and everybody that works at BMW." . . .

[The employer terminated Becker. The Administrative Law Judge found that Becker was terminated solely for his post on the Land Rover incident.]

. . . I find that Becker's posting of the Land Rover accident on his Facebook account was neither protected nor concerted activit[y] . . . . It was posted solely by Becker, apparently as a lark, without any discussion with any other employee of the Respondent, and had no connection to any of the employees' terms and conditions of employment. It is so obviously unprotected that it is unnecessary to discuss whether the mocking tone of the posting further affects the nature of the posting.

[The Administrative Law Judge concluded that Becker's discharge did not violate section 7. The employer maintained a Courtesy Rule, however, which represented an independent violation of the Act. The NLRB's decision, discussing the Courtesy Rule, follows.]

* * * *

BY MARK GASTON PEARCE, CHAIRMAN.

The [administrative law] judge found that the Respondent, which owned and operated a BMW dealership, violated Section 8(a)(1) of the Act by maintaining a rule in its employee handbook stating:

> (b) Courtesy: Courtesy is the responsibility of every employee. Everyone is expected to be courteous, polite and friendly to our customers, vendors and suppliers, as well as to their fellow employees. No one should be disrespectful or use profanity or any other language which injures the image or reputation of the Dealership.

For the following reasons, we agree with the judge's finding.

An employer violates Section 8(a)(1) when it maintains a work rule that reasonably tends to chill employees in the exercise of their Section 7 rights. *Lafayette Park Hotel*, 326 N.L.R.B. 824, 825 (1998), *enfd*. 203 F.3d 52, 340 (D.C. Cir. 1999). If the rule explicitly restricts Section 7 rights, it is unlawful. *Lutheran Heritage Village-Livonia*, 343 N.L.R.B. 646, 646 (2004). If it does not, the violation is dependent upon a showing of one of the following: (1) employees would reasonably construe the language to prohibit Section 7 activity; (2) the rule was promulgated in response to union activity; or (3) the rule has been applied to restrict the exercise of Section 7 rights. Id. at 647.

We find the "Courtesy" rule unlawful because employees would reasonably construe its broad prohibition against "disrespectful" conduct and "language which injures the image or reputation of the Dealership" as encompassing Section 7 activity, such as employees' protected statements—whether to coworkers, supervisors, managers, or third parties who deal with the Respondent—that object to their working conditions and seek the support of others in improving them. First, there is nothing in the rule, or anywhere else in the employee handbook, that would reasonably suggest to employees that employee communications protected by Section 7 of the Act are excluded from the rule's broad reach. *See generally Costco Wholesale Corp.*, 358 N.L.R.B. No. 106 (2012) (finding unlawful the maintenance of a rule prohibiting statements posted electronically that "damage the Company . . . or damage any person's reputation"). Second, an employee reading this rule would reasonably assume that the Respondent would regard statements of protest or criticism as "disrespectful" or "injur[ious] [to] the image or reputation of the Dealership." Cf. *NLRB v. Gissel Packing Co.*, 395 U.S. 575 (1969) (in evaluating employer statements alleged to violate Sec. 8(a)(1), "assessment of the precise scope of employer expression . . . must be made in the context of its labor relations setting" and "must take into account the economic dependence of the employees on their employers"). As we recently observed:

> Board law is settled that ambiguous employer rules—rules that reasonably could be read to have a coercive meaning—are construed against the employer. This principle follows from the Act's goal of preventing employees from being chilled in the exercise of their Section 7 rights[,] whether or not that is the intent of the employer . . . .

Flex Frac Logistics, LLC, 358 N.L.R.B. No. 127, slip op. at 2 (2012).

Our dissenting colleague contends that we have read the crucial phrases of the rule out of context. In support, he argues that the first section of the rule, encouraging "courteous, polite, and friendly" behavior, clearly establishes that the rule is nothing more than a "commonsense behavioral guideline for employees." If the rule only contained the first section, we might agree.[14] By going further than just providing the positive, aspirational language of the first section, the rule conveys a more complicated message to employees. The second section of the rule is in sharp contrast to the first, specifically proscribing certain types of conduct and statements. A reasonable employee who wishes to avoid discipline or discharge will surely pay careful attention and exercise caution when he is told what lines he may not safely cross at work.

. . . .

In other words, compliance with the first sentence of the rule is no assurance against sanctions under the second sentence of the rule. Reasonable employees would believe that even "courteous, polite, and friendly" expressions of disagreement with the Respondent's employment practices or terms and conditions of employment risk being deemed "disrespectful" or damaging to the Respondent's image or reputation. Thus, . . . the second sentence of the rule proscribes not a manner of speaking, but the content of employee speech—content that would damage the Respondent's reputation. . . . A reasonable employee . . . would believe that such a communication would expose him or her to sanctions under the Respondent's rule.

For these reasons, we affirm the judge's finding that the Respondent's maintenance of this rule violates Section 8(a)(1).

[The Board ordered the employer to rescind the Courtesy Rule in its employee handbook and to furnish all employees with an insert that notified them of the rule's rescission. However, it did not order Becker reinstated because it agreed with the administrative law judge that Becker's unprotected post concerning the Land Rover incident was the sole reason for his discharge; it did not reach the question whether his posting about the hot dog cart was protected concerted activity.]

---

[14] [n. 5] *See, e.g., Costco Wholesale Corp., supra*, in which the Board adopted the judge's dismissal of the complaint allegation that the employer violated Sec. 8(a)(1) by maintaining a different rule requiring employees to use "appropriate business decorum" in communication with others. Unlike the rule in this case, the rule there contained no prohibition on employee statements or conduct that would reasonably apply to protected activity.

NOTES

1. **Section 7 Protection for Becker's Postings.** Becker made two posts that are relevant for section 7 purposes: the post about the Land Rover incident, and the post about the hot dog cart. The Board accepted the Administrative Law Judge's determination that Becker's post regarding the Land Rover incident was unprotected, and that Becker was discharged solely as a result of this post. The ALJ had observed that the Land Rover post was "so obviously unprotected that it is unnecessary to discuss whether the mocking tone of the posting further affects the nature of the posting." 358 N.L.R.B. No. 164, at *47–*48. Why? Do you agree?

If Becker had not posted comments about the Land Rover incident and had only posted about the hot dog cart, would he have been entitled to reinstatement? Was the hot dog cart post concerted? For mutual aid or protection? Should its tone deprive the activity of protection?

2. **Speech Interests or Privacy Interests?** When Becker was called in to meet with his supervisors subsequent to his postings, did he immediately assert his section 7 rights to engage his coworkers in speech critical of working conditions? Or did he see this as a violation of his privacy interests? Would he have been able to assert a claim for violation of his privacy rights under any of the theories we discussed in Chapter 7?

3. **Workplace Civility and Professionalism Policies.** As *Karl Knauz* illustrates, employer policies such as broadly worded "courtesy rules" that might chill employee criticism or speech relating to wages or working conditions are vulnerable to challenges under section 8(a)(1). Is the analysis laid out in *Karl Knauz* helpful in distinguishing lawful from unlawful rules, or is it too subjective? Why does the Board accord so much deference to what an employee reading the rule might (reasonably) perceive? The Board quotes language from the Supreme Court's decision in *NLRB v. Gissel Packing Co.*, 395 U.S. 575 (1969), to the effect that employer expression must be assessed "in the context of its labor relations setting" and "must take into account the economic dependence of the employees on their employers." What do you think the Court and Board were alluding to?

Other common workplace policies that might violate section 8(a)(1) because employees might reasonably understand them as prohibiting conversation critical of the company, its supervisors, and working conditions include anti-disparagement rules, rules barring negativity or requiring employees to represent the employer in a positive and professional manner in the community, and no-gossip policies. *See Dish Network*, 359 N.L.R.B. No. 108 (2012) (policy forbidding employees from making "disparaging or defamatory comments" about the company on social media sites violated § 8(a)(1)); *Hills & Dales General Hosp.*, 360 N.L.R.B. No. 70 (2014) (policy banning "negativity" and requiring employees to represent the employer in the community "in a positive and professional manner in every opportunity" violated § 8(a)(1)); *The Room-Store*, 357 N.L.R.B. No. 143 (2011) (employees would reasonably construe rule prohibiting "[a]ny type of negative energy or attitudes" to include protected activity given employer's repeated warnings not to talk negatively about the employer's pay practices); *Laurus Tech. Institute*, 360 N.L.R.B. No. 133 (2014) ("no-gossip" policy that prohibited employees from participating in or instigating gossip about the company, fellow employees or customers violated

§ 8(a)(1)). Also unlawful are policies that require employees to obtain prior authorization from management before speaking about the employer to government agencies or the media, because employees might understand them as barring conversations with NLRB field agents or undercutting efforts to mobilize public support for concerted actions. *Dish Network, supra.*

On the other hand, company policies that advance legitimate employer business interests such as preventing disclosure of trade secrets, prohibiting harassment, bullying, discrimination, or retaliation do not violate the NLRA, particularly if they provide specific illustrations of prohibited acts and it is clear from the context that they are not designed to quell NLRA-protected activity. Similarly, rules that are closely linked to an accepted and specific business purpose such as customer service are likely to be upheld, such as those prohibiting "[i]nsubordination to a manager or lack of respect and cooperation with fellow employees or guests," "displaying a negative attitude that is disruptive to other staff or has a negative impact on guests" or "any other behavior which the Company believes represents an actual or potential threat to the smooth operation, goodwill, or profitability of its business." Taken in context, employees would understand these rules to ban only unprotected conduct harmful to the employer's legitimate business concerns. *Copper River of Boiling Springs, LLC*, 360 N.L.R.B. No. 60 (2014). Can you distinguish the rule in *Copper River* from the courtesy policy in *Karl Knauz*?

Finally, the Board has indicated that inclusion of "savings" clauses making it explicit that nothing in the rule is intended to prohibit employees from engaging in union activities or protected concerted activities or from exercising their rights under the NLRA, will be given considerable weight in evaluating the rule. On the other hand, if the employer has a history of displaying anti-union animus or the rule was adopted in response to union organizing activity, the Board is more likely to find that the rule violates section 8(a)(1). In short, savings clauses are effective where they serve to limit and clarify the scope of workplace rules, but they will not insulate the policy from scrutiny. The overriding question is still whether employees would reasonably understand the rule, as modified by the savings clause, as restricting their exercise of section 7 rights. *First Transit, Inc.*, 360 N.L.R.B. No. 72 (2014).

4. Confidentiality Policies. Employer policies that prohibit employees from sharing or disseminating "confidential information," such as names, addresses, telephone numbers, and email addresses, or locations of customer work sites may also infringe on section 7 rights. Why? Such rules can be perceived as undermining employees' ability to discuss wages and working conditions with one another or with outsiders, including union organizers, and make it more difficult for workers to communicate with one another (consider, for example, their importance to a union seeking to reach workers in order to organize them). If they contain no limiting language linking the types of confidential information to particular business purposes, they are construed against the employer and violate § 8(a)(1). *Flex Frac Logistics, LLC*, 358 N.L.R.B. No. 127 (2012), *enforced*, 746 F.3d 205 (5th Cir. 2014) (personnel information and documents); *Prof'l Elec. Contractors of Conn., Inc.*, 2014 NLRB LEXIS 427 (N.L.R.B. June 4, 2014) (locations of customers' job sites).

Further, any confidentiality policy that could reasonably be understood by employees as blocking discussion of wages is problematic. In *Flex Frac Logistics, supra*, the employer maintained a confidentiality clause that provided as follows:

Confidential Information

Employees deal with and have access to information that must stay within the Organization. Confidential Information includes, but is not limited to, information that is related to: our customers, suppliers, distributors; Silver Eagle Logistics LLC organization management and marketing processes, plans and ideas, processes and plans, our financial information, including costs, prices; current and future business plans, our computer and software systems and processes; personnel information and documents, and our logos, and art work. No employee is permitted to share this Confidential Information outside the organization, or to remove or make copies of any Silver Eagle Logistics LLC records, reports or documents in any form, without prior management approval. Disclosure of Confidential Information could lead to termination, as well as other possible legal action.

Id. at 207. The Fifth Circuit enforced the Board's ruling that the confidentiality clause violated section 8(a)(1) because even though it did not mention employee compensation, it referenced "financial information, including costs," which employees would reasonably understand to include wages, blocking discussion of employee pay with union organizers.

5. Pay Secrecy Policies. Approximately 60% of private sector employers have adopted pay secrecy rules explicitly barring employees from discussing wages or compensation with coworkers. Kevin P. McGowan, *Griffin Discusses Section 10(j) Emphasis, Top Labor Issues in the Courts and NLRB*, DAILY LAB. REP. (BNA) No. 110, June 9, 2014 (referencing 2011 report by the Institute for Women's Policy Research, *available at* http://www.iwpr.org/publications/pubs/pay-secrecy-and-wage-discrimination). Indeed, *Timekeeping Systems* involved such a provision in the employee handbook. As the ALJ observed in footnote 11, such prohibitions are inconsistent with the exercise of § 7 rights under the NLRA because they interfere with communication between employees on one of the most common bases for union organizing: wages. *See also MCPc, Inc.*, 360 N.L.R.B. No. 39 (2014) (discussion of wages is a traditional subject of organizing and falls within the zone of § 7 protection).

Recall that damages are not available to remedy NLRA violations (although the employer may be ordered to reinstate employees discharged pursuant to an unlawful policy, and pay backpay). The Board's order in *Karl Knauz* required only that the company rescind the disputed language and provide employees with handbook inserts substituting lawful language or notifying them of the rescission of the unlawful rule, which is also the usual remedy where pay confidentiality policies are challenged. The Board also typically requires the employer to post a remedial notice. With no exposure to damages at stake, why do employers fight so hard to defend their policies?

Leonard Bierman and Rafael Gely argue that formal pay secrecy rules legitimate, clarify and disseminate social norms of silence concerning relative rates of pay. *See* Leonard Bierman & Rafael Gely, *"Love, Sex, and Politics? Sure. Salary? No Way": Workplace Social Norms and the Law*, 25 BERKELEY J. EMP. & LAB. L. 167

(2004). Why is silence about worker pay so important to employers? What impact might pay secrecy rules have on wage levels and worker mobility? On union organizing? On enforcement of other statutory rights such as prohibitions on sex-and race-based wage discrimination? *See generally* Matthew A. Edwards, *The Law and Social Norms of Pay Secrecy*, 26 BERKELEY J. EMP. & LAB. L. 41 (2005).

The significance of pay confidentiality norms in employment cases was graphically illustrated in *Ledbetter v. Goodyear Tire & Rubber Co.*, 550 U.S. 618 (2007). Lilly Ledbetter worked as an area manager at a Goodyear Tire plant in Alabama for 19 years. She brought a sex discrimination claim on a disparate treatment theory under Title VII and the Equal Pay Act of 1963, arguing that sex discriminatory evaluations early in her career negatively impacted her pay throughout the course of her employment. The issue before the Court was whether her pay discrimination claim was time-barred for all but the last 180 days prior to the filing of her EEOC claim. The Court held that it was, significantly limiting her recovery. The Court rejected Ledbetter's argument that pay discrimination is particularly difficult for an employee to detect compared with other forms of discrimination, saying "[w]e are not in a position to evaluate Ledbetter's policy arguments." *Id.* at 642. A vigorous dissent by Justice Ginsburg, joined by Justices Stevens, Souter and Breyer, argued that pay disparities often go unnoticed for a period both because they occur in small increments and because comparative pay information is typically kept secret. *Id.* at 645 (Ginsburg, J., dissenting). The dissent noted the common norm of pay confidentiality, citing the Bierman & Gely article discussed above, and argued for a rule that would reflect "[t]he realities of the workplace." *Id.* at 649.

Two weeks later, Ledbetter testified before Congress in favor of a bill to overturn the result in her case. She explained that although she had begun to suspect that she might be earning less than the male managers, Goodyear's pay secrecy policy meant that she had no "hard evidence" of the pay disparity until someone left an anonymous document in her mailbox at work that showed the comparative earnings of managers at the plant. Testimony of Lilly Ledbetter Before the Committee on Education and Labor, U.S. House of Representatives, on the Amendment of Title VII, June 12, 2007. Congress responded by enacting the Lilly Ledbetter Fair Pay Act of 2009 which overturned the result in *Ledbetter*, amending § 706(e) of Title VII to clarify that "an unlawful employment practice occurs, with respect to discrimination in compensation in violation of this title . . . each time wages, benefits, or other compensation is paid." Pub. L. 111-2, § 3 (2009).

Ledbetter's testimony about the difficulties of finding out about discriminatory pay practices that affected her also provided ammunition for worker advocacy groups and scholars who were pressing state legislatures to enact "wage transparency" laws designed to restrict the ability of employers to discipline or discharge employees for comparing or discussing salaries with one another. *See* Michael Starr & Christine Wagner, *Wage Transparency Laws*, NAT'L L.J., Nov. 24, 2008 (discussing legislation enacted in Colorado, California and Michigan); Sarah Lyons, *Why the Law Should Intervene to Disrupt Pay-Secrecy Norms: Analyzing the Lilly Ledbetter Fair Pay Act Through the Lens of Social Norms*, 46 COLUM. J. L. & SOC. PROBS. 361 (2013). Such legislation is very likely preempted by the NLRA, which preempts state common law claims or statutes that challenge or regulate conduct that is "arguably protected or arguably prohibited" by the NLRA because of the risk that a uniform national labor policy could be frustrated by state efforts to exert control. *See id.; San Diego Building Trades Council v. Garmon*, 359 U.S. 263 (1959).

Part Three

FREEDOM FROM DISCRIMINATION VERSUS FLEXIBILITY

Labor markets have long been rife with discrimination of all kinds, and in this part we will concentrate on the federal antidiscrimination laws that have significantly shaped the workplace over the last five decades. In exploring the antidiscrimination laws, it is worth noting that these laws impose significant restrictions on the employment-at-will rule, and it is also important to keep in mind that until 1964 discrimination was lawful under federal law, and even today, there is no comprehensive federal prohibition on discrimination based on sexual orientation or identity. The chapter will begin with an introduction, and then explore important doctrinal and policy issues.

Chapter 9

EMPLOYMENT DISCRIMINATION LAW

A. INTRODUCTION

Many of the central issues that arise in the workplace involve questions of discrimination, and the various antidiscrimination statutes that govern the workplace generate an enormous amount of litigation. In some ways, the antidiscrimination model, which emphasizes individual rights related to one's status, has replaced the collective rights model embodied in the National Labor Relations Act as the prevailing mode of workplace regulation. There is, to be sure, a collective component to the antidiscrimination statutes in the form of class action lawsuits but most such claims involve only a segment of the workforce rather than its totality, and far more individual claims are filed than class claims.

There are a large number of antidiscrimination statutes that apply to the workforce. The primary federal statutes are (1) Title VII of the Civil Rights Act of 1964 ("Title VII"), which prohibits discrimination on the basis of race, sex, national origin, religion, and color; (2) the Americans With Disabilities Act ("ADA"), which prohibits discrimination on the basis of disability and requires employers to offer reasonable accommodations to disabled individuals; and (3) the Age Discrimination in Employment Act ("ADEA"), which prohibits discrimination against employees who are 40 years old or older. A statute that originated in the Reconstruction Era, known as Section 1981 (42 U.S.C. § 1981) prohibits discrimination in contracting on the basis of race and national origin, and this statute can be used for many cases of employment discrimination.

The most recent federal statute, the Family and Medical Leave Act ("FMLA"), is not technically an antidiscrimination statute because it does not prohibit discrimination based on status but instead permits certain employees to take unpaid leave for the birth or adoption of a child or for certain illnesses. However, a central purpose of the FMLA was to help break down gender stereotypes and to ease the burden many women encounter in seeking to balance their work and family lives, and for that reason we will discuss the FMLA in this chapter. One notable absence of antidiscrimination coverage in the federal context is sexual orientation—no federal statute currently proscribes employment discrimination based on gender identity or sexual orientation. A number of states (21 as of 2014)[1] and many localities, however, prohibit discrimination based on sexual orientation and gender identity. A proposed law, known as the Employment Nondiscrimination Act, that would extend current federal antidiscrimination law to include prohibitions on

---

[1] A map of the states can be found at https://www.aclu.org/maps/non-discrimination-laws-state-state-information-map.

discrimination based on sexual orientation and gender identity has been introduced in Congress on multiple occasions but no action has yet been taken on the legislation.

The law of employment discrimination is notoriously complex and often the subject of a separate law school course. It is not our intent to cover all of the details of the law but instead we want to provide an overview that will explain how cases are proved, and discuss various issues that arise with some regularity in the course of the litigation.

Title VII has been the most influential of the antidiscrimination statutes and many of the other statutes borrow directly from the law that has developed around Title VII. As you may know, the Civil Rights Act of 1964, of which Title VII was an important part, was the subject of the longest Congressional filibuster in history, and now 50 years later continues to hold onto that record. In honor of the Act's fiftieth anniversary, a number of books have been published recounting the history of its passage. For one such recounting see CLAY RISEN, THE BILL OF THE CENTURY: THE EPIC BATTLE FOR THE CIVIL RIGHTS ACT (2014). Prior to the passage of Title VII, it was legal—at least under federal law—for employers to discriminate on the basis of race, sex, national origin and religion, and many employers did so. Many unions also had exclusionary policies despite their duty to represent all employees. The basic antidiscrimination principle of Title VII is contained in section 703(a)(1), which in pertinent part reads:

> It shall be an unlawful employment practice for an employer . . . to fail or refuse to hire or to discharge any individual, or otherwise to discriminate against any individual with respect to his compensation, terms, conditions, or privileges of employment, because of such individual's race, color, religion, sex, or national origin. . . .

42 U.S.C. § 2000e-2(a)(1).

When originally passed, Title VII did not apply to state or local governments, but the statute was amended to include governmental entities in 1972. The statute has also been amended several times since, the most significant of which was the passage of the Civil Rights Act of 1991, which was a statute that substantially modified Title VII and in the process overturned seven Supreme Court decisions. For the purposes of the materials that follow, two changes from the 1991 Act were particularly important. Originally, Title VII did not provide for jury trials or damages but instead cases were tried before a judge and plaintiffs were limited to equitable relief, typically lost wages, a job, seniority rights, and perhaps an injunction. One reason for the lack of a damages remedy in the original statute was that in 1964 there was a strong sentiment that plaintiffs would not be able to obtain a fair trial before southern juries. However, by 1991, that presumption had been replaced to a significant degree by a perception that plaintiffs had a very difficult time prevailing before judges. As a result, the Civil Rights Act of 1991 provided for jury trials and damages for claims of intentional discrimination. The damage remedies are capped at a maximum of $300,000 for employers that have more than 500 employees, with lower damages depending on the size of the employer. (The damage provisions of Title VII are located in a separate statute, 42 U.S.C. § 1981a.) Neither jury trials nor damages are available for claims based on a disparate impact theory—a theory that does not require proof of intent. Another important change brought about by the Civil Rights Act of 1991 was to codify the disparate impact theory in what is now section 42 U.S.C. § 2000e-2(k) of Title VII. Previously the disparate impact theory had been a matter of statutory interpretation but was not specifically mentioned in the statute. *See Griggs v. Duke Power Co.*, discussed *infra* at section C.

In addition to the Civil Rights Act of 1991, Congress has also passed important amendments to the Americans With Disabilities Act. As was true with the 1991 Act, the ADA amendments were designed to overturn or modify a series of restrictive Supreme Court decisions. Those Amendments—awkwardly named the Americans With Disabilities Act Amendments Act of 2008 and commonly referred to as the ADAAA—were not retroactive and cases interpreting the statute are only now arising in the appellate courts. The ADA, and the Amendments, are discussed in section E of this Chapter.

Most employment discrimination claims must initially be filed with a federal agency, the Equal Employment Opportunity Commission ("EEOC"), before a court action can be initiated. Title VII, the ADA, and the ADEA all require that employees file their claims with the EEOC generally within 180 days from the date of the discriminatory act, although if the employee files with the equivalent state agency, then the claim can be filed within 300 days. Most states now have such agencies so the general deadline for filing an administrative claim is within 300 days. Based on statistics for the years 2010–14, the EEOC receives more than 90,000 administrative claims a year, with claims based on race constituting the largest group of claims followed by sex, disability, age, national origin and religion. Retaliation claims, among all of the statutes, now constitute the largest single category of administrative claim. Once a claim is filed with the EEOC, the agency will typically investigate the allegations, though it may also seek to conciliate a claim without any significant investigation. If a claim is successfully conciliated or mediated, then it will effectively be settled. If an investigation is conducted, the agency will issue a determination whether discrimination occurred, what is known as a cause determination (there was discrimination) or a no-cause determination (no discrimination occurred).

As noted, a charge of discrimination typically must be filed within either 300 or 180 days from the date the discrimination occurred but it is not always easy to tell when that period begins, or ends. For example, several years ago, a controversy arose over when a claim for salary discrimination commences—when the discriminatory salary, or raise, decision is made or every time the individual receives a pay check based on the discriminatory salary decision. In *Ledbetter v. Goodyear Tire & Rubber Co.*, 550 U.S. 618 (2007), the Supreme Court held that the time to file a charge for pay discrimination commences when the decision is made. The Court's decision proved highly controversial because many individuals may not know the decision was discriminatory until later in their career and the Court's decision was altered by the Lilly Ledbetter Fair Pay Act of 2009, which was the first piece of legislation signed into law by President Obama. The Act states that a discriminatory act occurs when the salary decision is adopted, or when the individual is subjected to or affected by the pay decision. *See* Pub. L. No. 111-2, 123 Stat. 5 (2009), *amending* 42 U.S.C. 2000e-5(e) (2006). As a result, an individual can now file a claim within 300 (or 180) days of receiving a paycheck that is lower than it would be absent the discriminatory decision. The Act also explicitly limits an individual's remedy to two years of lost pay (known as back pay) from the date the charge is filed, in addition to whatever punitive and compensatory damages she might be able to prove.

The EEOC's investigation of a charge does not necessarily terminate the claim, regardless of the ultimate finding. If the agency finds cause, then it will seek to conciliate the claim, and if it is unable to do so, the agency will generally file a lawsuit on behalf of the person who filed the claim ("claimant"). The individual has a right to intervene in the action, with or without an attorney, but the EEOC files the complaint on behalf of the EEOC and does not formally represent the claimant, but instead represents the agency. (If the defendant is a state agency, the EEOC transfers the cause finding to the Civil Rights Division of the United States Department of Justice, which will then decide whether to prosecute the claim.) On the other hand, if the agency issues a no-cause determination, then it will also issue a Notice of Right-to-Sue to the claimant, who may then choose to file a lawsuit in federal court without the assistance of the EEOC. An individual may also choose to bypass the investigation process by requesting a Notice of Right-to-Sue one hundred eighty (180) days after the claim was initially filed, and the EEOC must issue the Notice, which then entitles the claimant to proceed to federal court. In this way, although the filing of a claim is mandatory, the EEOC cannot deprive an individual of her right to file a lawsuit in federal court.

The original hope of the proponents of the Civil Rights Act of 1964 was that most claims would be settled informally through the administrative process, and in fact, most of the claims are resolved through that process without resort to federal court litigation. In any given year, a majority of the claims are resolved through no-cause determinations; only between 5–10% of the determinations issued by the agency are findings that discrimination did occur. (The statistics are available on the EEOC's website, www.eeoc.gov.) Including various settlements, only about 20% of the claims filed with the EEOC result in a favorable agency determination. In addition to processing administrative complaints, the EEOC also issues regulations, and guidance to employers on cases and statutory changes. For Title VII, the EEOC does not follow the rule-making procedures mandated by the Administrative Procedure Act so its regulations are not due any particular deference by courts, and you will see in the cases that follow that courts, and the Supreme Court in particular, will defer to the EEOC's regulations on some occasions while ignoring them on others.

There is an important exception to the administrative process. For claims filed under Section 1981 involving race and national origin discrimination, there is no administrative process, and neither the tight time limitations that govern filings with the EEOC nor the damage caps applicable to Title VII and the ADA are applicable. Section 1981, called such because the statute is found at 42 U.S.C. § 1981, prohibits discrimination in contracting which has been interpreted to include employment contracts even in an employment-at-will setting where no formal contract exists. *See Walker v. Abbott Labs.*, 340 F.3d 471, 478 (7th Cir. 2003) (holding that an at-will relationship was "sufficiently contractual" to proceed under section 1981). Section 1981, however, only applies to claims of intentional discrimination. *See Gen. Bldg. Contractors Ass'n v. Pennsylvania*, 458 U.S. 375 (1982). Otherwise, much of the law applicable to Title VII also applies to Section 1981. As a practical matter, any intentional discrimination claim for discrimination based on race and national origin should likely include a claim under Section 1981.

The antidiscrimination statutes differ in their scope. Title VII and the ADA apply to employers that have 15 or more employees, while the ADEA applies to employers that have 20 or more employees, and the FMLA only applies to employers with 50 or more employees. The Supreme Court has also held that Congress exceeded its statutory powers when it applied the ADA and the ADEA to state employers. *See Bd. of Trustees v. Garrett*, 531 U.S. 356 (2001) (ADA); *Kimel v. Florida Bd. of Regents*, 528 U.S. 62 (2000) (ADEA). As a result, state agencies are immune from damage suits brought by private individuals, although the federal government can still bring such suits and individuals may also sue for injunctive relief. Sovereign immunity extends only to arms of the state so most local and regional agencies are still subject to suit. *See Savage v. Glendale Union High School Dist.*, 343 F.3d 1036 (9th Cir. 2003), *cert. denied*, 541 U.S. 1009 (2004) (holding that the school board not entitled to immunity from ADA suit); *Williams v. Dallas Area Rapid Transit*, 242 F.3d 315 (5th Cir. 2001) (holding that a regional government is not an "arm of the state" and therefore not entitled to immunity from ADEA suit). In contrast to the ADA and the ADEA, the Supreme Court has upheld the FMLA as applied to state governments. *See Nevada Dep't of Human Res. v. Hibbs*, 538 U.S. 721 (2003).

The following cases and discussion are intended to provide an overview to antidiscrimination law and also to raise questions about what it means to discriminate as well as our societal commitment to eradicate discrimination in the workplace.

B. CLAIMS OF INTENTIONAL DISCRIMINATION: THE DISPARATE TREATMENT MODEL

1. Individual Claims of Intentional Discrimination

Most claims filed under the antidiscrimination statutes involve claims of intentional discrimination, what are also known as disparate treatment claims. These claims can take one of three forms: (1) individual treatment claim based on direct evidence; (2) individual claim based on circumstantial evidence; (3) class action claims typically based on circumstantial evidence. By far, the largest category of claim involves those based on circumstantial evidence, and the Supreme Court has created different standards of proof depending on whether the underlying evidence is labeled as circumstantial or direct. It is therefore first necessary to explore the difference in meaning between the two kinds of evidence.

There is not always a hard and fast distinction between direct and circumstantial evidence. Direct evidence is defined as evidence that does not require the finder of fact to draw an inference of discrimination; in other words, the evidence, by itself, establishes an intent to discriminate. As one court has explained, "A remark by a decisionmaker, in order to be direct evidence . . . , must show a specific link between a discriminatory bias and the adverse employment action, sufficient to support a finding by a reasonable fact-finder that the bias motivated the action." *Torgerson v. City of Rochester*, 643 F.3d 1031, 1045–46 (8th Cir. 2011) (en banc), *cert. denied*, 132 S. Ct. 513 (2011); *see also Johnson v. Kroger Co.*, 319 F.3d 858, 865 (6th Cir. 2003) ("[D]irect evidence of discrimination does not require a factfinder to draw any inferences in order to conclude that the challenged employment action was motivated at least in part by prejudice against members of the protected group."). Today such cases are relatively rare, though they can still arise particularly in cases involving age or sex discrimination. In the age discrimination context, perhaps because employers are not as sensitized to age-based discrimination as they are for other forms of discrimination, employers occasionally explicitly state that they want to hire younger employees, or that a particular individual is "too old" to do his job. *See Wilson v. Cox*, 753 F.3d 244, 248 (D.C. Cir. 2014) (commenting that a security guard at an Air Force retirement home "didn't come here to work, you came here to retire" constituted direct evidence); *Van Voorhis v. Hillsborough Cnty Bd. of Comm'rs*, 512 F.3d 1296, 1300 (11th Cir. 2008) (commenting that the company did not "want to hire an old pilot" constituted direct evidence). While direct evidence arises most frequently in age discrimination cases, it is by no means restricted to such cases. For example, in a case involving a doctor of Asian-Indian ethnicity, for example, was asked during an interview, "Being an older, foreign-born physician, how comfortable do you feel dealing with young white American women?" *Sanghvi v. St. Catherine's Hosp., Inc.*, 258 F.3d 570, 574 (7th Cir. 2001), *cert. denied*, 534 U.S. 114 (2002) (finding that the statement was direct evidence of racial discrimination); *see also Gold v. FedEx Freight E., Inc. (In re Rodriguez)*, 487 F.3d 1001, 1008 (6th Cir. 2007) (finding that supervisor's comments regarding Latino employee's accent and speech pattern constituted direct evidence). Similarly, disability cases may include direct evidence of discrimination often because the employer believes the individual is not capable of performing the job, an assumption the law requires the employer to establish in a particular case. *See Hoffman v. Caterpillar, Inc.*, 256 F.3d 568, 574 (7th Cir. 2001) (plaintiff was denied training on high-speed scanner because she only had one hand). But the point noted above must be reiterated: cases of direct evidence are relatively rare, and most cases involve proof of discrimination through circumstantial evidence.

The significance of the direct evidence distinction comes in the applicable proof structures. In cases that involve direct evidence of discrimination, where the evidence is causally linked to the disputed employment action, the burden shifts to the defendant to establish one of the available defenses and the plaintiff need offer nothing more to establish a *prima facie* case of discrimination. *See Trans World Airlines, Inc. v. Thurston*, 469 U.S. 111, 121 (1984). Those defenses include allowing the employer to establish that it would have made the same decision absent the discriminatory statements, a model of proof that is known as a mixed motives model because the employer is said to have more than one motive, some of which may have been legitimate. *See Price Waterhouse v. Hopkins*, 490 U.S. 228 (1989) (establishing the mixed-motives model), *superseded by statute*, Civil Rights Act of 1991, 105 Stat. 1075 (codified at 42 U.S.C. § 2000e-2(m)). This model of proof, which is not restricted to cases of direct evidence, will be discussed in more detail shortly. Another available defense, to be discussed in section 3.b. *infra*, allows the employer to establish that age, gender, national origin or religion was a bona fide occupational qualification ("BFOQ")—in other words, that age or one of the other categories (but not race) was an essential requirement for performance of the job. We will return to these issues later on, but now want to explore the more common method of proving discrimination through circumstantial evidence.

McDONNELL DOUGLAS CORP. v. GREEN
United States Supreme Court
411 U.S. 792 (1973)

Mr. Justice Powell delivered the opinion of the Court.

The case before us raises significant questions as to the proper order and nature of proof in actions under Title VII of the Civil Rights Act of 1964, 78 Stat. 253, 42 U.S.C. § 2000e et seq. Petitioner, McDonnell Douglas Corp., is an aerospace and aircraft manufacturer headquartered in St. Louis, Missouri, where it employs over 30,000 people. Respondent, a black citizen of St. Louis, worked for petitioner as a mechanic and laboratory technician from 1956 until August 28, 1964 when he was laid off in the course of a general reduction in petitioner's work force.

Respondent, a long-time activist in the civil rights movement, protested vigorously that his discharge and the general hiring practices of petitioner were racially motivated. As part of this protest, respondent and other members of the Congress on Racial Equality illegally stalled their cars on the main roads leading to petitioner's plant for the purpose of blocking access to it at the time of the morning shift change. The District Judge described the plan for, and respondent's participation in, the "stall-in" as follows:

> . . . "Acting under the 'stall in' plan, plaintiff [respondent in the present action] drove his car onto Brown Road, a McDonnell access road, at approximately 7:00 a. m., at the start of the morning rush hour. Plaintiff was aware of the traffic problems that would result. He stopped his car with the intent to block traffic. The police arrived shortly and requested plaintiff to move his car. He refused to move his car voluntarily. Plaintiff's car was towed away by the police, and he was arrested for obstructing traffic. Plaintiff pleaded guilty to the charge of obstructing traffic and was fined." 318 F. Supp. 846, 849.

On July 2, 1965, a "lock-in" took place wherein a chain and padlock were placed on the front door of a building to prevent the occupants, certain of petitioner's employees, from leaving. Though respondent apparently knew beforehand of the "lock-in," the full extent of his involvement remains uncertain. . . .

Some three weeks following the "lock-in," on July 25, 1965, petitioner publicly advertised for qualified mechanics, respondent's trade, and respondent promptly applied for re-employment. Petitioner turned down respondent, basing its rejection on respondent's participation in the "stall-in" and "lock-in." . . .

II

The critical issue before us concerns the order and allocation of proof in a private, non-class action challenging employment discrimination. The language of Title VII makes plain the purpose of Congress to assure equality of employment opportunities and to eliminate those discriminatory practices and devices which have fostered racially stratified job environments to the disadvantage of minority citizens. Griggs v. Duke Power Co., 401 U.S. 424, 429 (1971). As noted in *Griggs:*

> "Congress did not intend by Title VII, however, to guarantee a job to every person regardless of qualifications. In short, the Act does not command that any person be hired simply because he was formerly the subject of discrimination, or because he is a member of a minority group. Discriminatory preference for any group, minority or majority, is precisely and only what Congress has proscribed. What is required by Congress is the removal of artificial, arbitrary, and unnecessary barriers to employment when the barriers operate invidiously to discriminate on the basis of racial or other impermissible classification." *Id.*, at 430–431.

There are societal as well as personal interests on both sides of this equation. The broad, overriding interest, shared by employer, employee, and consumer, is efficient and trustworthy workmanship assured through fair and racially neutral employment and personnel decisions. In the implementation of such decisions, it is abundantly clear that Title VII tolerates no racial discrimination, subtle or otherwise.

In this case respondent, the complainant below, charges that he was denied employment "because of his involvement in civil rights activities" and "because of his race and color." Petitioner denied discrimination of any kind, asserting that its failure to re-employ respondent was based upon and justified by his participation in the unlawful conduct against it. Thus, the issue at the trial on remand is framed by those opposing factual contentions. . . .

The complainant in a Title VII trial must carry the initial burden under the statute of establishing a prima facie case of racial discrimination. This may be done by showing (i) that he belongs to a racial minority; (ii) that he applied and was qualified for a job for which the employer was seeking applicants; (iii) that, despite his qualifications, he was rejected; and (iv) that, after his rejection, the position remained open and the employer continued to seek applicants from persons of complainant's qualifications. In the instant case, we agree with the Court of Appeals that respondent proved a prima facie case. Petitioner sought mechanics, respondent's trade, and continued to do so after respondent's rejection. Petitioner, moreover, does not dispute respondent's qualifications and acknowledges that his past work performance in petitioner's employ was "satisfactory."

The burden then must shift to the employer to articulate some legitimate, nondiscriminatory reason for the employee's rejection. We need not attempt in the instant case to detail every matter which fairly could be recognized as a reasonable basis for a refusal to hire. Here petitioner has assigned respondent's participation in unlawful conduct against it as the cause for his rejection. We think that this suffices to discharge petitioner's burden of proof at this stage and to meet respondent's prima facie case of discrimination. . . . Respondent admittedly had taken part in a carefully planned "stall-in," designed to tie up access to and egress from petitioner's plant at a peak traffic hour. Nothing in Title VII compels an employer to absolve and rehire one who has engaged in such deliberate, unlawful activity against it. . . .

Petitioner's reason for rejection thus suffices to meet the prima facie case, but the inquiry must not end here. While Title VII does not, without more, compel rehiring of respondent, neither does it permit petitioner to use respondent's conduct as a pretext for the sort of discrimination prohibited by § 703(a)(1). On remand, respondent must, as the Court of Appeals recognized, be afforded a fair opportunity to show that petitioner's stated reason for respondent's rejection was in fact pretext. Especially relevant to such a showing would be evidence that white employees involved in acts against petitioner of comparable seriousness to the "stall-in" were nevertheless retained or rehired. Petitioner may justifiably refuse to rehire one who was engaged in unlawful, disruptive acts against it, but only if this criterion is applied alike to members of all races.

Other evidence that may be relevant to any showing of pretext includes facts as to the petitioner's treatment of respondent during his prior term of employment; petitioner's reaction, if any, to respondent's legitimate civil rights activities; and petitioner's general policy and practice with respect to minority employment. On the latter point, statistics as to petitioner's employment policy and practice may be helpful to a determination of whether petitioner's refusal to rehire respondent in this case conformed to a general pattern of discrimination against blacks. In short, on the retrial respondent must be given a full and fair opportunity to demonstrate by competent evidence that the presumptively valid reasons for his rejection were in fact a coverup for a racially discriminatory decision. . . .

III

In sum, respondent should have been allowed to pursue his claim under § 703(a)(1). If the evidence on retrial is substantially in accord with that before us in this case, we think that respondent carried his burden of establishing a prima facie case of racial discrimination and that petitioner successfully rebutted that case. But this does not end the matter. On retrial, respondent must be afforded a fair opportunity to demonstrate that petitioner's assigned reason for refusing to re-employ was a pretext or discriminatory in its application. If the District Judge so finds, he must order a prompt and appropriate remedy. In the absence of such a finding, petitioner's refusal to rehire must stand.

The judgment is vacated and the cause is hereby remanded to the District Court for further proceedings consistent with this opinion.

NOTES

1. **Explaining the Proof Structure.** The proof structure announced in *McDonnell Douglas* continues to guide discrimination claims now more than 40 years later, and is generally referred to as the *McDonnell Douglas* structure. One of the most interesting aspects of the opinion is that the Court did not explain why the

prima facie case raises an inference of discrimination. A few years later the Court elaborated on the rationale behind the proof structure:

> A prima facie case under *McDonnell Douglas* raises an inference of discrimination only because we presume these acts, if otherwise unexplained, are more likely than not based on the consideration of impermissible factors. And we are willing to presume this largely because we know from our experience that more often than not people do not act in a totally arbitrary manner, without any underlying reasons, especially in a business setting. Thus, when all legitimate reasons for rejecting an applicant have been eliminated as possible reasons for the employer's actions, it is more likely than not the employer, who we generally assume acts only with *some* reason, based his decision on an impermissible consideration such as race.

Furnco Constr. Corp. v. Waters, 438 U.S. 567 (1978).

2. **The Meaning of a *Prima Facie* Case.** Does the Court's explanation in *Furnco* clarify the basis for the *prima facie* case? How would you characterize the Court's statement? One way of interpreting this statement would be to suggest that the *prima facie* case eliminates the two most common reasons an employer does not hire an applicant—the employee is not qualified or no job was available—and at the same time injects another common reason for workplace actions, the employee's race. Does this perspective seem consistent with the theory described in *McDonnell Douglas*, and is it consistent with the more contemporary cases, such as the *Hicks* case discussed below?

3. **Percy Green**. The plaintiff, Percy Green, had been a long-time civil rights activist who regularly participated in protests in the St. Louis area, including protesting at the home of the Chairman of the Board of Directors for McDonnell Douglas. The event that triggered the now famous case was a "stall in" where several cars blocked traffic leading to the plant for about 10 minutes. For a discussion of the protests and the significance of the case see David Benjamin Oppenheimer, McDonnell Douglas Corp. v. Green *Revisited: Why Non-Violence Civil Disobedience Should Be Protected from Retaliation by Title VII*, 34 COLUM. HUMAN RTS. L. REV. 635, 638–40 (2003).

ST. MARY'S HONOR CENTER v. HICKS
United States Supreme Court
509 U.S. 502 (1993)

JUSTICE SCALIA delivered the opinion of the Court.

We granted certiorari to determine whether, in a suit against an employer alleging intentional racial discrimination in violation of § 703(a)(1) of Title VII of the Civil Rights Act of 1964, 42 U.S.C. § 2000e-2(a)(1), the trier of fact's rejection of the employer's asserted reasons for its actions mandates a finding for the plaintiff.

I

Petitioner St. Mary's Honor Center (St. Mary's) is a halfway house operated by the Missouri Department of Corrections and Human Resources (MDCHR). Respondent Melvin Hicks, a black man, was hired as a correctional officer at St. Mary's in August 1978 and was promoted to shift commander, one of six supervisory positions, in February 1980.

In 1983 MDCHR conducted an investigation of the administration of St. Mary's, which resulted in extensive supervisory changes in January 1984. Respondent retained his position, but John Powell became the new chief of custody (respondent's immediate supervisor) and petitioner Steve Long the new superintendent. Prior to these personnel changes respondent had enjoyed a satisfactory employment record, but soon thereafter became the subject of repeated, and increasingly severe, disciplinary actions. He was suspended for five days for violations of institutional rules by his subordinates on March 3, 1984. He received a letter of reprimand for alleged failure to conduct an adequate investigation of a brawl between inmates that occurred during his shift on March 21. He was later demoted from shift commander to correctional officer for his failure to ensure that his subordinates entered their use of a St. Mary's vehicle into the official logbook on March 19, 1984. Finally, on June 7, 1984, he was discharged for threatening Powell during an exchange of heated words on April 19.

Respondent brought this suit in the United States District Court for the Eastern District of Missouri, alleging that petitioner St. Mary's violated § 703(a)(1) of Title VII of the Civil Rights Act of 1964, 42 U.S.C. § 2000e-2(a)(1), and that petitioner Long violated 42 U.S.C. § 1983, by demoting and then discharging him because of his race. After a full bench trial, the District Court found for petitioners. 756 F. Supp. 1244 (ED Mo. 1991). The United States Court of Appeals for the Eighth Circuit reversed and remanded, 970 F.2d 487 (1992), and we granted certiorari, 506 U.S. 1042 (1993).

II

Section 703(a)(1) of Title VII of the Civil Rights Act of 1964 provides in relevant part:

"It shall be an unlawful employment practice for an employer—

"(1) . . . to discharge any individual, or otherwise to discriminate against any individual with respect to his compensation, terms, conditions, or privileges of employment, because of such individual's race. . . ." 42 U.S.C. § 2000e-2(a).

With the goal of "progressively . . . sharpening the inquiry into the elusive factual question of intentional discrimination," Texas Dept. of Community Affairs v. Burdine, 450 U.S. 248, 255, n. 8 (1981), our opinion in McDonnell Douglas Corp. v. Green, 411 U.S. 792 (1973), established an allocation of the burden of production and an order for the presentation of proof in Title VII discriminatory-treatment cases. The plaintiff in such a case . . . must first establish, by a preponderance of the evidence, a "prima facie" case of racial discrimination. Burdine, supra, at 252–253.

Petitioners do not challenge the District Court's finding that respondent satisfied the minimal requirements of such a prima facie case by proving (1) that he is black, (2) that he was qualified for the position of shift commander, (3) that he was demoted from that position and ultimately discharged, and (4) that the position remained open and was ultimately filled by a white man. 756 F. Supp. at 1249–1250.

Under the *McDonnell Douglas* scheme, "establishment of the prima facie case in effect creates a presumption that the employer unlawfully discriminated against the employee." Burdine, supra, at 254. To establish a "presumption" is to say that a finding of the predicate fact (here, the prima facie case) produces "a required conclusion in the absence of explanation" (here, the finding of unlawful discrimination). 1 D. Louisell & C. Mueller, Federal Evidence § 67, p. 536 (1977). Thus, the *McDonnell Douglas* presumption places upon the defendant the burden of producing an explanation to rebut the prima facie case—i.e., the burden of "producing evidence" that the adverse employment actions were taken "for a legitimate, nondiscriminatory reason." Burdine, 450 U.S. at 254. "The defendant must clearly set forth, through the introduction of admissible evidence," reasons for its actions which, *if believed by the trier of fact*, would support a finding that unlawful discrimination was not the cause of the employment action. *Id.*, at 254–255, and n. 8. It is important to note, however, that although the *McDonnell Douglas* presumption shifts the burden of *production* to the defendant, "the ultimate burden of persuading the trier of fact that the defendant intentionally discriminated against the plaintiff remains at all times with the plaintiff." 450 U.S. at 253. . . .

Respondent does not challenge the District Court's finding that petitioners sustained their burden of production by introducing evidence of two legitimate, nondiscriminatory reasons for their actions: the severity and the accumulation of rules violations committed by respondent. Our cases make clear that at that point the shifted burden of production became irrelevant: "If the defendant carries this burden of production, the presumption raised by the prima facie case is rebutted," Burdine, 450 U.S. at 255, and "drops from the case," *id.*, at 255, n. 10. The plaintiff then has "the full and fair opportunity to demonstrate," through presentation of his own case and through cross-examination of the defendant's witnesses, "that the proffered reason was not the true reason for the employment decision," *id.*, at 256, and that race was. . . .

The District Court, acting as trier of fact in this bench trial, found that the reasons petitioners gave were not the real reasons for respondent's demotion and discharge. It found that respondent was the only supervisor disciplined for violations committed by his subordinates; that similar and even more serious violations committed by respondent's co-workers were either disregarded or treated more leniently; and that Powell manufactured the final verbal confrontation in order to provoke respondent into threatening him. 756 F. Supp. at 1250–1251. It nonetheless held that respondent had failed to carry his ultimate burden of proving that *his race* was the determining factor in petitioners' decision first to demote and then to dismiss him.[2] In short, the District Court concluded that "although

---

[2] [n. 3] Various considerations led it to this conclusion, including the fact that two blacks sat on the disciplinary review board that recommended disciplining respondent, that respondent's black subordinates who actually committed the violations were not disciplined, and that "the number of black

[respondent] has proven the existence of a crusade to terminate him, he has not proven that the crusade was racially rather than personally motivated." *Id.*, at 1252.

The Court of Appeals set this determination aside on the ground that "once [respondent] proved all of [petitioner's] proffered reasons for the adverse employment actions to be pretextual, [respondent] was entitled to judgment as a matter of law." 970 F.2d at 492. The Court of Appeals reasoned:

> "Because all of defendants' proffered reasons were discredited, defendants were in a position of having offered no legitimate reason for their actions. In other words, defendants were in no better position than if they had remained silent, offering no rebuttal to an established inference that they had unlawfully discriminated against plaintiff on the basis of his race." *Ibid.*

That is not so. By producing *evidence* (whether ultimately persuasive or not) of nondiscriminatory reasons, petitioners sustained their burden of production, and thus placed themselves in a "better position than if they had remained silent."

In the nature of things, the determination that a defendant has met its burden of production (and has thus rebutted any legal presumption of intentional discrimination) can involve no credibility assessment. For the burden-of-production determination necessarily *precedes* the credibility-assessment stage. At the close of the defendant's case, the court is asked to decide whether an issue of fact remains for the trier of fact to determine. None does if, on the evidence presented, (1) any rational person would have to find the existence of facts constituting a prima facie case, and (2) the defendant has failed to meet its burden of production—*i. e.*, has failed to introduce evidence which, *taken as true*, would *permit* the conclusion that there was a nondiscriminatory reason for the adverse action. In that event, the court must award judgment to the plaintiff as a matter of law. . . . If the defendant has failed to sustain its burden but reasonable minds could *differ* as to whether a preponderance of the evidence establishes the facts of a prima facie case, then a question of fact *does* remain, which the trier of fact will be called upon to answer.

If, on the other hand, the defendant has succeeded in carrying its burden of production, the *McDonnell Douglas* framework—with its presumptions and burdens—is no longer relevant. . . . The presumption, having fulfilled its role of forcing the defendant to come forward with some response, simply drops out of the picture. Burdine, 450 U.S. at 255. The defendant's "production" having been made, the trier of fact proceeds to decide the ultimate question: whether plaintiff has proved "that the defendant intentionally discriminated against [him]" because of his race, *id.*, at 253. The factfinder's disbelief of the reasons put forward by the defendant (particularly if disbelief is accompanied by a suspicion of mendacity) may, together with the elements of the prima facie case, suffice to show intentional discrimination. Thus, rejection of the defendant's proffered reasons will *permit* the trier of fact to infer the ultimate fact of intentional discrimination, and the Court of Appeals was correct when it noted that, upon such rejection, "no additional proof of discrimination is *required*," 970 F.2d at 493 (emphasis added). But the Court of Appeals' holding that rejection of the defendant's proffered reasons *compels* judgment for the plaintiff disregards the fundamental principle . . . that a

---

employees at St. Mary's remained constant." 756 F. Supp. at 1252.

presumption does not shift the burden of proof, and ignores our repeated admonition that the Title VII plaintiff at all times bears the "ultimate burden of persuasion." *See, e. g., Postal Service Bd. of Governors v. Aikens*, 460 U.S. 711, 716, (1983).

III

Only one unfamiliar with our case law will be upset by the dissent's alarum that we are today setting aside "settled precedent," . . . "two decades of stable law in this Court," "a framework carefully crafted in precedents as old as 20 years," *post*, at 540 . . . . Here (in the context of the now-permissible jury trials for Title VII causes of action) is what the dissent asserts we have held to be a proper assessment of liability for violation of this law: Assume that 40% of a business' work force are members of a particular minority group, a group which comprises only 10% of the relevant labor market. An applicant, who is a member of that group, applies for an opening for which he is minimally qualified, but is rejected by a hiring officer of that *same minority group*, and the search to fill the opening continues. The rejected applicant files suit for racial discrimination under Title VII, and before the suit comes to trial, the supervisor who conducted the company's hiring is fired. Under *McDonnell Douglas*, the plaintiff has a prima facie case, see 411 U.S. at 802, and under the dissent's interpretation of our law not only must the company come forward with some explanation for the refusal to hire (which it will have to try to confirm out of the mouth of its now antagonistic former employee), but the jury must be instructed that, if they find that explanation to be *incorrect*, they must assess damages against the company, *whether or not they believe the company was guilty of racial discrimination*. The disproportionate minority makeup of the company's work force and the fact that its hiring officer was of the same minority group as the plaintiff will be irrelevant, because the plaintiff's case can be proved "indirectly by showing that the employer's proffered explanation is unworthy of credence." 450 U.S. at 256. Surely nothing short of inescapable prior *holdings* (the dissent does not pretend there are any) should make one assume that this is the law we have created. . . .

IV

We turn, finally, to the dire practical consequences that the respondents and the dissent claim our decision today will produce. What appears to trouble the dissent more than anything is that, in its view, our rule is adopted "for the benefit of employers who have been found to have given false evidence in a court of law," whom we "favor" by "exempting them from responsibility for lies." As we shall explain, our rule in no way gives special favor to those employers whose evidence is disbelieved. But initially we must point out that there is no justification for assuming . . . that those employers whose evidence is disbelieved are perjurers and liars. Even if these were typically cases in which an individual defendant's sworn assertion regarding a physical occurrence was pitted against an individual plaintiff's sworn assertion regarding the same physical occurrence, surely it would be imprudent to call the party whose assertion is (by a mere preponderance of the evidence) disbelieved, a perjurer and a liar. And in these Title VII cases, the defendant is ordinarily *not* an individual but a company, which must rely upon the statement of an employee—often a relatively low-level employee—as to the central fact; and that central fact is *not* a physical occurrence, but rather that employee's state of mind. To say that the company which in good faith introduces such testimony, or even the testifying employee himself, becomes a liar and a perjurer when the testimony is not believed, is nothing short of absurd.

Undoubtedly some employers (or at least their employees) will be lying. But even if we could readily identify these perjurers, what an extraordinary notion, that we "exempt them from responsibility for their lies" unless we enter Title VII judgments for the plaintiffs! Title VII is not a cause of action for perjury; we have other civil and criminal remedies for that. . . .

The dissent repeatedly raises a procedural objection that is impressive only to one who mistakes the basic nature of the *McDonnell Douglas* procedure. It asserts that . . . [t]he plaintiff cannot be expected to refute "reasons not articulated by the employer, but discerned in the record by the factfinder." He should not "be saddled with the tremendous disadvantage of having to confront, not the defined task of proving the employer's stated reasons to be false, but the amorphous requirement of disproving all possible nondiscriminatory reasons that a factfinder might find lurking in the record." . . . These statements imply that the employer's "proffered explanation," his "stated reasons," his "articulated reasons," somehow exist *apart from the record*—in some pleading, or perhaps in some formal, nontestimonial statement made on behalf of the defendant to the factfinder. ("Your honor, pursuant to *McDonnell Douglas* the defendant hereby formally asserts, as *its* reason for the dismissal at issue here, incompetence of the employee.") Of course it does not work like that. . . . [T]he defendant's "articulated reasons" *themselves* are to be found "lurking in the record." . . . Finally, respondent argues that it "would be particularly ill-advised" for us to come forth with the holding we pronounce today "just as Congress has provided a right to jury trials in Title VII" cases. *See* § 102 of the Civil Rights Act of 1991, 42 U.S.C. § 1981a(c). We think quite the opposite is true. Clarity regarding the requisite elements of proof becomes all the more important when a jury must be instructed concerning them, and when detailed factual findings by the trial court will not be available upon review.

. . . .

We reaffirm today what we said in *Aikens*:

"The question facing triers of fact in discrimination cases is both sensitive and difficult. The prohibitions against discrimination contained in the Civil Rights Act of 1964 reflect an important national policy. There will seldom be 'eyewitness' testimony as to the employer's mental processes. But none of this means that trial courts or reviewing courts should treat discrimination differently from other ultimate questions of fact. Nor should they make their inquiry even more difficult by applying legal rules which were devised to govern 'the basic allocation of burdens and order of presentation of proof,' Burdine, 450 U.S. at 252, in deciding this ultimate question." 460 U.S. at 716.

The judgment of the Court of Appeals is reversed, and the case is remanded for further proceedings consistent with this opinion.

It is so ordered.

JUSTICE SOUTER, with whom JUSTICE WHITE, JUSTICE BLACKMUN, and JUSTICE STEVENS join, dissenting.

Twenty years ago, in McDonnell Douglas Corp. v. Green, 411 U.S. 792 (1973), this Court unanimously prescribed a "sensible, orderly way to evaluate the evidence" in a Title VII disparate-treatment case, giving both plaintiff and defendant fair opportunities to litigate "in light of common experience as it bears on the critical question of discrimination." Furnco Constr. Corp. v. Waters, 438 U.S. 567, 577 (1978). . . .

We adopted th[e] three-step [*McDonnell Douglas* framework] to implement, in an orderly fashion, "the language of Title VII," which "makes plain the purpose of Congress to assure equality of employment opportunities and to eliminate those discriminatory practices and devices which have fostered racially stratified job environments to the disadvantage of minority citizens." 411 U.S. at 800. Because "Title VII tolerates no racial discrimination, subtle or otherwise," *id.*, at 801, we devised a framework that would allow both plaintiffs and the courts to deal effectively with employment discrimination revealed only through circumstantial evidence. *See* Aikens, supra, at 716 ("There will seldom be 'eyewitness' testimony as to the employer's mental processes"). . . .

The Court today decides to abandon the settled law that sets out this structure for trying disparate-treatment Title VII cases, only to adopt a scheme that will be unfair to plaintiffs, unworkable in practice, and inexplicable in forgiving employers who present false evidence in court. Under the majority's scheme, once the employer succeeds in meeting its burden of production, "the *McDonnell Douglas* framework . . . is no longer relevant." Whereas we said in *Burdine* that if the employer carries its burden of production, "the factual inquiry proceeds to a new level of specificity," 450 U.S. at 255, the Court now holds that the further enquiry is wide open, not limited at all by the scope of the employer's proffered explanation. . . . We have repeatedly identified the compelling reason for limiting the factual issues in the final stage of a *McDonnell Douglas* case as "the requirement that the plaintiff be afforded a full and fair opportunity to demonstrate pretext." 450 U.S. at 258 (internal quotation marks omitted). . . . The majority fails to explain how the plaintiff, under its scheme, will ever have a "full and fair opportunity" to demonstrate that reasons not articulated by the employer, but discerned in the record by the factfinder, are also unworthy of credence. The Court thus transforms the employer's burden of production from a device used to provide notice and promote fairness into a misleading and potentially useless ritual.

The majority's scheme greatly disfavors Title VII plaintiffs without the good luck to have direct evidence of discriminatory intent. The Court repeats the truism that the plaintiff has the "ultimate burden" of proving discrimination, without ever facing the practical question of how the plaintiff without such direct evidence can meet this burden. *Burdine* provides the answer, telling us that such a plaintiff may succeed in meeting his ultimate burden of proving discrimination "indirectly by showing that the employer's proffered explanation is unworthy of credence." 450 U.S. at 256. The possibility of some practical procedure for addressing what *Burdine* calls indirect proof is crucial to the success of most Title VII claims, for the simple reason that employers who discriminate are not likely to announce their discriminatory motive. And yet, under the majority's scheme, a victim of discrimination lacking direct evidence will now be saddled with the tremendous disadvantage of having to confront, not the defined task of proving the employer's stated reasons to be false, but the amorphous requirement of disproving all possible nondiscriminatory reasons that a factfinder might find lurking in the record. . . .

The Court fails to explain, moreover, under either interpretation of its holding, why proof that the employer's articulated reasons are "unpersuasive, or even obviously contrived," *ante*, at 524, falls short. . . . By telling the factfinder to keep digging in cases where the plaintiff's proof of pretext turns on showing the employer's reasons to be unworthy of credence, the majority rejects the very point of the *McDonnell Douglas* rule requiring the scope of the factual enquiry to be limited, albeit in a manner chosen by the employer. What is more, the Court is throwing out the rule for the benefit of employers who have been found to have given false evidence in a court of law. There is simply no justification for favoring these employers by exempting them from responsibility for lies. It may indeed be true that such employers have nondiscriminatory reasons for their actions, but ones so shameful that they wish to conceal them. One can understand human frailty and the natural desire to conceal it, however, without finding in it a justification to dispense with an orderly procedure for getting at "the elusive factual question of intentional discrimination." Burdine, 450 U.S. at 255, n. 8.

With no justification in the employer's favor, the consequences to actual and potential Title VII litigants stand out sharply. To the extent that workers like Melvin Hicks decide not to sue, given the uncertainties they would face under the majority's scheme, the legislative purpose in adopting Title VII will be frustrated. To the extent such workers nevertheless decide to press forward, the result will likely be wasted time, effort, and money for all concerned. Under the scheme announced today, any conceivable explanation for the employer's actions that might be suggested by the evidence, however unrelated to the employer's articulated reasons, must be addressed by a plaintiff who does not wish to risk losing. . . . [P]retrial discovery will become more extensive and wide ranging (if the plaintiff can afford it), for a much wider set of facts could prove to be both relevant and important at trial. The majority's scheme, therefore, will promote longer trials and more pretrial discovery, threatening increased expense and delay in Title VII litigation for both plaintiffs and defendants, and increased burdens on the judiciary.

. . . The enhancement of a Title VII plaintiff's burden wrought by the Court's opinion is exemplified in this case. Melvin Hicks was denied any opportunity, much less a full and fair one, to demonstrate that the supposedly nondiscriminatory explanation for his demotion and termination, the personal animosity of his immediate supervisor, was unworthy of credence. In fact, the District Court did not find that personal animosity (which it failed to recognize might be racially motivated) was the true reason for the actions St. Mary's took; it adduced this reason simply as a possibility in explaining that Hicks had failed to prove "that the crusade [to terminate him] was racially rather than personally motivated." 756 F.

Supp. 1244, 1252 (ED Mo. 1991). It is hardly surprising that Hicks failed to prove anything about this supposed personal crusade, since St. Mary's never articulated such an explanation for Hicks's discharge, and since the person who allegedly conducted this crusade denied at trial any personal difficulties between himself and Hicks. . . . Whether Melvin Hicks wins or loses on remand, many plaintiffs in a like position will surely lose under the scheme adopted by the Court today, unless they possess both prescience and resources beyond what this Court has previously required Title VII litigants to employ.

Because I see no reason why Title VII interpretation should be driven by concern for employers who are too ashamed to be honest in court, at the expense of victims of discrimination who do not happen to have direct evidence of discriminatory intent, I respectfully dissent.

NOTES

1.   **Understanding *Hicks*.** There were two important aspects to the *Hicks* case. One involved an interpretation of the Court's own past precedent, in particular whether based on that precedent a plaintiff could prevail by establishing "pretext" or whether it was necessary to establish "pretext for discrimination." The majority and dissent engaged in a spirited reading of that precedent, a fair reading of which suggests that the Court had not previously focused on the distinction between the two phrases and no definitive answer was to be found among the precedent. The second aspect of the case involved what the proof structure ought to allow—whether proof of pretext should result in a mandatory finding of discrimination as suggested by the dissent. On this point, which side do you think was more persuasive, and why? What was at stake?

2.   **Justice Scalia's Hypothetical.** In his majority opinion, Justice Scalia suggests that one reason to adopt a permissive rather than a mandatory inference of discrimination involves the situation where an employer is forced to justify its decision after "the supervisor who conducted the company's hiring is fired." A more extreme example might be what would happen if the relevant employment records had been destroyed in a fire? If you were arguing the case, how would you respond to that question? If the Court had adopted a mandatory inference, could an employer be held liable because its records were destroyed in a fire? What about his hypothetical about the "fired supervisor"—how might you address that issue at the oral argument (or in a brief)?

3.   ***Hicks* on Remand.** If you were advising Hicks or his lawyers on remand, what would you suggest he try to do to establish discrimination? What other evidence could Hicks offer? Is the dissent correct that unless he could offer "direct evidence" he was likely to lose?

On remand, the case took a predictable but unusual twist. The Court of Appeals initially remanded the case to the district court for further consideration, and the district court simply reaffirmed its earlier decision that Hicks had failed to establish that racial discrimination, rather than personal animosity, explained the actions against him. The plaintiff appealed, and on appeal the defendant changed its position, or as the Court of Appeals explained: "[D]efendants' counsel now abandons the rule violations explanation (even though Long himself does not) and astutely embraces 'personal animosity' as the justification for defendants' actions. Defendants now argue that Powell's personal animosity toward plaintiff is 'the lawful reason for [plaintiff's] discharge.' " *Hicks v. St. Mary's Honor Ctr.*, 90 F.3d 285, 291 (8th Cir. 1996). In light of this turn of events, the Court of Appeals summarily affirmed the judgment for the defendants. *Id.* Does the experience on remand support either the majority or the dissent in *Hicks*? Given that the defendants had previously disclaimed that it, or any of its agents, had any personal animosity towards Hicks, was Hicks afforded a "full and fair opportunity" to establish his claim?

4. **Jury Trials.** As the Supreme Court notes, *Hicks* was decided under the law in place prior to the 1991 Amendments to Title VII that provided for jury trials. In a jury trial, the practical implications of *Hicks* are in the instructions a court would give to the jury. How might those instructions be phrased? The jury is not likely to be told anything about the *McDonnell Douglas* model, but that model serves primarily to help narrow the issues during pretrial discovery and on summary judgment. As a result, what is the significance of *Hicks* for a jury trial?

5. **The Pretext-Plus Model.** In his dissenting opinion, Justice Souter suggests that the Supreme Court effectively requires a plaintiff to prove more than pretext, what is also known as pretext-plus. This was a model of proof developed in some of the appellate courts prior to the *Hicks* decision and which required plaintiffs to offer some evidence beyond pretext in order to survive a motion for summary judgment. *See, e.g., Bienkowski v. Am. Airlines, Inc.*, 851 F.2d 1503, 1508 (5th Cir. 1988) (plaintiff must show more than that the employer's decision was unsupported by the facts or unjustified). Some of the development in the lower courts had to do with a particular misconception of the meaning of pretext. Prior to *Hicks*, some lower courts defined pretext to include a situation where the employer was factually wrong on the merits. For example, in one case the plaintiff was a body-builder who, according to his employer, occasionally called in sick to attend body building competitions. On one occasion, after the plaintiff had been denied leave to attend a competition, the plaintiff called in sick complaining of an ankle injury that prevented him from working, and the plaintiff was subsequently fired. At the trial, the plaintiff proved that he was, in fact, injured, and the district court accepted that as proof of pretext and ordered judgment for the plaintiff. The Seventh Circuit Court of Appeals reversed noting: "If [an employer] honestly explain[s] the reasons behind [its] decision, but the decision was ill-informed or ill-considered, [its] explanation is not a 'pretext'." *Pollard v. Rea Magnet Wire Co.*, 824 F.2d 557, 559 (7th Cir. 1987), *cert. denied*, 484 U.S. 977 (1987). The factual scenario in *Pollard* is, as the Court of Appeals rightly held, something different from pretext, but the issue raised by the *Pollard* case seemed to influence a number of lower courts that sought to erect a barrier to plaintiffs with a weak *prima facie* case.

6. ***Reeves v. Sanderson Plumbing.*** Justice Souter's claim that *Hicks* required proof beyond pretext was effectively laid to rest several years later. In *Reeves v. Sanderson Plumbing Products, Inc.*, 530 U.S. 133 (2000), the Supreme Court reiterated its holding from *Hicks* that proof of pretext may, but need not, suffice to prove discrimination. The Court explained:

Proof that the defendant's explanation is unworthy of credence is simply one form of circumstantial evidence that is probative of intentional discrimination, and it may be quite persuasive. In appropriate circumstances, the trier of fact can reasonably infer from the falsity of the explanation that the employer is dissembling to cover up a discriminatory purpose. Such an inference is consistent with the general principle of evidence law that the factfinder is entitled to consider a party's dishonesty about a material fact as "affirmative evidence of guilt." Wright v. West, 505 U.S. 277, 296 (1992). Moreover, once the employer's justification has been eliminated, discrimination may well be the most likely alternative explanation, especially since the employer is in the best position to put forth the actual reason for its decision. Thus, a plaintiff's prima facie case, combined with sufficient evidence to find that the employer's asserted justification is false, may permit the trier of fact to conclude that the employer unlawfully discriminated.

This is not to say that such a showing by the plaintiff will always be adequate to sustain a jury's finding of liability. Certainly there will be instances where, although the plaintiff has established a prima facie case and set forth sufficient evidence to reject the defendant's explanation, no rational factfinder could conclude that the action was discriminatory. For instance, an employer would be entitled to judgment as a matter of law if the record conclusively revealed some other, nondiscriminatory reason for the employer's decision, or if the plaintiff created only a weak issue of fact as to whether the employer's reason was untrue and there was abundant and uncontroverted independent evidence that no discrimination had occurred. . . .

Whether judgment as a matter of law is appropriate in any particular case will depend on a number of factors. Those include the strength of the plaintiff's prima facie case, the probative value of the proof that the employer's explanation is false, and any other evidence that supports the employer's case and that properly may be considered on a motion for judgment as a matter of law. For purposes of this case, we need not—and could not—resolve all of the circumstances in which such factors would entitle an employer to judgment as a matter of law. It suffices to say that, because a prima facie case and sufficient evidence to reject the employer's explanation may permit a finding of liability, the Court of Appeals erred in proceeding from the premise that a plaintiff must always introduce additional, independent evidence of discrimination.

Reeves, 530 U.S. at 147–49.

7. The Importance of "Similarly Situated" Individuals. As noted in *Hicks*, many claims of discrimination are proved by establishing that other similarly situated individuals were treated differently. Many courts look carefully at whether the plaintiff is able to identify a similarly situated individual, though circuits vary on how the issue is considered. For example, several courts have established the identification of a similarly situated individual as a fourth element of the prima facie case. *See. e.g., Adams v. Wal-Mart Stores, Inc.*, 324 F.3d 935, 939 (7th Cir. 2003) (requiring, as part of the *prima facie* case, that the plaintiff establish that "a similarly situated person outside the protected class was treated better."). Because plaintiffs challenging a hiring decision will usually not have access to comparative information before discovery, the requirement is not applied to a hiring claim, but it is imposed in other contexts. *See, e.g., White v. Baxter Healthcare Corp.*, 533 F.3d 381 (6th Cir. 2008), *cert. denied*, 556 U.S. 1235 (2009) (promotion). Rather than creating a fourth element of the *prima facie* case, other courts have held that establishing a "similarly situated" comparator is one means of proving discrimination, but is not a required element of proof. For example, the Second Circuit lists as a fourth element that the plaintiff has introduced evidence "that the adverse employment action occurred under circumstances giving rise to an inference of discriminatory intent." *Holcomb v. Iona Coll.*, 521 F.3d 130, 138 (2d Cir. 2008). Under that standard, the identification of a similarly situated individual is one way to provide such evidence. *See Tr. v. Gate Gourmet Inc.*, 683 F.3d 1249, 1255–56 (11th Cir. 2012) (noting that plaintiff's failure to name a comparator did not "doom" her case but was instead relevant to whether she proved pretext). Which approach seems most consistent with the requirements established in *McDonnell Douglas* and *Hicks*?

When courts require plaintiffs to identify a similarly situated individual as part of a prima facie case, it can pose a significant barrier to surviving summary judgment. A common standard to determine whether a comparator is "similarly situated" is that developed in the Seventh Circuit: "In order for an individual to be similarly situated to the plaintiff, the plaintiff must show that the individual is directly comparable to her in all material respects." *Burks v. Wisconsin Dep't of Transp.*, 464 F.3d 744, 751 (7th Cir. 2006). The court went on to note that this required the same supervisor, the same job duties, experience, performance, and whatever other relevant factors were at issue. *Id.* The Fifth Circuit has specifically required that the plaintiff identify a similar employee who worked "under nearly identical circumstances." *Love v. Kansas City S. Ry.*, 574 F.3d 253, 259–60 (5th Cir. 2009). These standards can be difficult to satisfy. To give one recent, and perhaps extreme, example, the Eighth Circuit upheld summary judgment granted for an employer where an employee at a nursing home who had been charged with misconduct failed to identify "other employees who were not Pentecostal, female, or disabled [who] were accused of the exact or similar behavior as she was." *Evance v. Trumann Health Servs., LLC*, 719 F.3d 673, 678 (8th Cir. 2013). As several scholars have noted, the imposition of a rigorous requirement of identifying a similarly situated individual has led to a surge in dismissals for failure to establish a prima facie case, which at one time was seen as a relatively easy burden to meet. For discussions and critiques of the importance of comparators in establishing pretext see Suzanne B. Goldberg, *Discrimination by Comparison*, 120 Yale L.J. 728 (2011); Charles A. Sullivan, *The Phoenix from the Ash: Proving Discrimination by Comparators*, 60 Ala. L. Rev. 191 (2009).

8. **The Continuing Relevance of *McDonnell Douglas*.** The *McDonnell Douglas* framework was created in the early 1970s, and perhaps one of the reasons that courts have been struggling with it more recently is that the framework has lost its force. As discussed earlier, the rationale behind the framework was an underlying belief that discrimination was a frequent rationale for employment decisions. Is that

rationale still pertinent today? Although the *Hicks* decision has been the subject of extensive criticism, Deborah Malamud has defended the decision on the grounds that it represents a proper approach to the modern workplace where decisions are not easily understood as the product of simple or single motives, but more commonly involve mixed motives, many of which are not necessarily rational in the way that *McDonnell Douglas* assumes. *See* Deborah Malamud, *The Last Minuet: Disparate Treatment After* Hicks, 93 MICH. L. REV. 2229 (1995). Malamud suggests that the *McDonnell Douglas* framework should be abandoned in favor of relying on a mixed motives framework developed by the Supreme Court in *Price Waterhouse vs. Hopkins*, discussed *infra*. In contrast, Michael Selmi suggests that Malamud follows the *Hicks* majority in seeking to protect employers against unfounded judgments of discrimination at the expense of deserving plaintiffs. *See* Michael Selmi, *Proving Intentional Discrimination: The Reality of Supreme Court Rhetoric*, 86 GEO. L.J. 279, 330–34 (1998). Selmi contends that whenever courts draw lines such as they did in *Hicks*, a certain number of errors will inevitably result, so that by allowing juries to treat pretext as discretionary rather than mandatory proof of discrimination, some deserving plaintiffs will lose out, whereas a mandatory inference would lead to some deserving defendants ending up with erroneous judgments. With this in mind, how should a court draw the line, and what factors should a court take into account in doing so?

9. Other Proof Issues. The *Hicks* case represents the Supreme Court's most definitive treatment regarding the inferences courts should draw from circumstantial evidence but lower courts have fashioned a number of other principles. For example, a number of courts have created what is known as a "same-actor" presumption where there is a presumption of non-discrimination where the same person who made the hiring decision was also responsible for the termination or promotion decision. *See, e.g., Grady v. Affiliated Cent., Inc.*, 130 F.3d 553, 560 (2d Cir. 1997) ("When the same actor hires a person and then fires that same person it is difficult to impute to her an invidious motivation that would be inconsistent with the decision to hire"). It, is, however, just an inference a jury might draw. As the Seventh Circuit has explained, "The 'common actor' or 'same actor' inference is a reasonable inference that may be argued to the jury, but it is not a conclusive presumption that applies as a matter of law." *Perez v. Thorntons, Inc.*, 731 F.3d 699, 709 (7th Cir. 2013) (quotations and citations omitted); *see also EEOC v. Boeing Co.*, 577 F.3d 1044 (9th Cir. 2009) (evaluating weight of evidence supporting same-actor inference).

Another issue that arises in many trials is whether evidence of discrimination against other employees within the company can be admitted in a trial brought by an individual plaintiff. The Supreme Court has addressed this question in the context of an age discrimination lawsuit where the plaintiff sought to introduce testimony of five employees regarding their alleged discriminatory treatment. In a unanimous decision, the Supreme Court held that "evidence of discrimination by other supervisors" is neither automatically excluded nor automatically admissible, but instead must meet the relevance test generally applicable to evidentiary issues. *See Sprint/United Mgmt. Co. v. Mendelsohn*, 552 U.S. 379 (2008). Because the court of appeals had concluded on its own that the evidence was relevant, the Supreme Court vacated the judgment and remanded so the district court could determine whether the evidence was relevant. How should the district court make this determination? What factors should the court take into account?

2.   The Mixed-Motives Proof Structure

DESERT PALACE, INC. v. COSTA
United States Supreme Court
539 U.S. 90 (2003)

JUSTICE THOMAS delivered the opinion of the Court.

The question before us in this case is whether a plaintiff must present direct evidence of discrimination in order to obtain a mixed-motive instruction under Title VII of the Civil Rights Act of 1964, as amended by the Civil Rights Act of 1991 (1991 Act). We hold that direct evidence is not required.

I

A

Since 1964, Title VII has made it an "unlawful employment practice for an employer . . . to discriminate against any individual . . . , *because of* such individual's race, color, religion, sex, or national origin." 42 U.S.C. § 2000e-2(a)(1) (emphasis added). In Price Waterhouse v. Hopkins, 490 U.S. 228 (1989), the Court considered whether an employment decision is made "because of" sex in a "mixed-motive" case, i.e., where both legitimate and illegitimate reasons motivated the decision. The Court concluded that, under § 2000e-2(a)(1), an employer could "avoid a finding of liability . . . by proving that it would have made the same decision even if it had not allowed gender to play such a role." *Id.*, at 244. The Court was divided, however, over the predicate question of when the burden of proof may be shifted to an employer to prove the affirmative defense.

Justice Brennan, writing for a plurality of four Justices, would have held that "when a plaintiff . . . proves that her gender played a *motivating* part in an employment decision, the defendant may avoid a finding of liability only by proving by a preponderance of the evidence that it would have made the same decision even if it had not taken the plaintiff's gender into account." *Id.*, at 258 (emphasis added). The plurality did not, however, "suggest a limitation on the possible ways of proving that [gender] stereotyping played a motivating role in an employment decision." *Id.*, at 251–252.

Justice White and Justice O'Connor both concurred in the judgment. Justice White . . . would have shifted the burden to the employer only when a plaintiff "showed that the unlawful motive was a *substantial* factor in the adverse employment action." Price Waterhouse, supra, at 259. Justice O'Connor, like Justice White, would have required the plaintiff to show that an illegitimate consideration was a "substantial factor" in the employment decision. 490 U.S., at 276. But, under Justice O'Connor's view, "the burden on the issue of causation" would shift to the employer only where "a disparate treatment plaintiff [could] show by *direct evidence* that an illegitimate criterion was a substantial factor in the decision." *Ibid.* (emphasis added).

Two years after *Price Waterhouse*, Congress passed the 1991 Act "in large part [as] a response to a series of decisions of this Court interpreting the Civil Rights Acts of 1866 and 1964." Landgraf v. USI Film Products, 511 U.S. 244, 250 (1994). In particular, § 107 of the 1991 Act, which is at issue in this case, "responded" to *Price Waterhouse* by "setting forth standards applicable in 'mixed motive' cases" in two new statutory provisions. 511 U.S., at 251. The first establishes an alternative for proving that an "unlawful employment practice" has occurred:

> " 'Except as otherwise provided in this subchapter, an unlawful employment practice is established when the complaining party demonstrates that race, color, religion, sex, or national origin was a motivating factor for any employment practice, even though other factors also motivated the practice.' " 42 U.S.C. § 2000e-2(m).

The second provides that, with respect to " 'a claim in which an individual proves a violation under section 2000e-2(m),' " the employer has a limited affirmative defense that does not absolve it of liability, but restricts the remedies available to a plaintiff. The available remedies include only declaratory relief, certain types of injunctive relief, and attorney's fees and costs. 42 U.S.C. § 2000e-5(g)(2)(B). In order to avail itself of the affirmative defense, the employer must "demonstrate that [it] would have taken the same action in the absence of the impermissible motivating factor." *Ibid.*

Since the passage of the 1991 Act, the Courts of Appeals have divided over whether a plaintiff must prove by direct evidence that an impermissible consideration was a "motivating factor" in an adverse employment action. *See* 42 U.S.C. § 2000e-2(m). Relying primarily on Justice O'Connor's concurrence in *Price Waterhouse*, a number of courts have held that direct evidence is required to establish liability under § 2000e-2(m). *See*, e.g., *Mohr v. Dustrol, Inc.*, 306 F.3d 636, 640–641 (CA8 2002) . . . . In the decision below, however, the Ninth Circuit concluded otherwise.

B

Petitioner Desert Palace, Inc., dba Caesar's Palace Hotel & Casino of Las Vegas, Nevada, employed respondent Catharina Costa as a warehouse worker and heavy equipment operator. Respondent was the only woman in this job and in her local Teamsters bargaining unit.

Respondent experienced a number of problems with management and her co-workers that led to an escalating series of disciplinary sanctions, including informal rebukes, a denial of privileges, and suspension. Petitioner finally terminated respondent after she was involved in a physical altercation in a warehouse elevator with fellow Teamsters member Herbert Gerber. Petitioner disciplined both employees because the facts surrounding the incident were in dispute, but Gerber, who had a clean disciplinary record, received only a 5-day suspension.

Respondent subsequently filed this lawsuit against petitioner in the United States District Court for the District of Nevada, asserting claims of sex discrimination and sexual harassment under Title VII. The District Court dismissed the sexual harassment claim, but allowed the claim for sex discrimination to go to the jury. At trial, respondent presented evidence that (1) she was singled out for "intense 'stalking' " by one of her supervisors, (2) she received harsher discipline than men for the same conduct, (3) she was treated less favorably than men in the assignment of overtime, and (4) supervisors repeatedly "stacked" her disciplinary record and "frequently used or tolerated" sex-based slurs against her. 299 F.3d 838, 845–846 (CA9 2002).

Based on this evidence, the District Court denied petitioner's motion for judgment as a matter of law, and submitted the case to the jury with instructions. . . . [T]he District Court gave the jury the following mixed-motive instruction:

> " 'You have heard evidence that the defendant's treatment of the plaintiff was motivated by the plaintiff's sex and also by other lawful reasons. If you find that the plaintiff's sex was a motivating factor in the defendant's treatment of the plaintiff, the plaintiff is entitled to your verdict, even if you find that the defendant's conduct was also motivated by a lawful reason.
>
> " 'However, if you find that the defendant's treatment of the plaintiff was motivated by both gender and lawful reasons, you must decide whether the plaintiff is entitled to damages. The plaintiff is entitled to damages unless the defendant proves by a preponderance of the evidence that the defendant would have treated plaintiff similarly even if the plaintiff's gender had played no role in the employment decision.' " *Ibid.*

Petitioner unsuccessfully objected to this instruction, claiming that respondent had failed to adduce "direct evidence" that sex was a motivating factor in her dismissal or in any of the other adverse employment actions taken against her. The jury rendered a verdict for respondent, awarding backpay, compensatory damages, and punitive damages. . . . The Court of Appeals initially vacated and remanded . . . [but] reinstated the District Court's judgment after rehearing the case en banc. 299 F.3d 838 (CA9 2002). The en banc court saw no need to decide whether Justice O'Connor's concurrence in *Price Waterhouse* controlled because it concluded that Justice O'Connor's references to "direct evidence" had been "wholly abrogated" by the 1991 Act. 299 F.3d at 850 . . . . Accordingly, the court concluded that a "plaintiff . . . may establish a violation through a preponderance of evidence (whether direct or circumstantial) that a protected characteristic played 'a motivating factor'." *Id.*, at 853–854 (footnote omitted). Based on that standard, the Court of Appeals held that respondent's evidence was sufficient to warrant a mixed-motive instruction and that a reasonable jury could have found that respondent's sex was a "motivating factor in her treatment." *Id.*, at 859. . . .

II

This case provides us with the first opportunity to consider the effects of the 1991 Act on jury instructions in mixed-motive cases. Specifically, we must decide whether a plaintiff must present direct evidence of discrimination in order to obtain a mixed-motive instruction under 42 U.S.C. § 2000e-2(m). . . .

Our precedents make clear that the starting point for our analysis is the statutory text. *See* Connecticut Nat. Bank v. Germain, 503 U.S. 249, 253–254 (1992). And where, as here, the words of the statute are unambiguous, the "judicial inquiry is complete." *Id.*, at 254. Section 2000e-2(m) unambiguously states that a plaintiff need only "demonstrate" that an employer used a forbidden consideration with respect to "any employment practice." On its face, the statute does not mention, much less require, that a plaintiff make a heightened showing through direct evidence. . . .

Moreover, Congress explicitly defined the term "demonstrates" in the 1991 Act, leaving little doubt that no special evidentiary showing is required. Title VII defines the term " 'demonstrates' " as to "meet the burdens of production and persuasion." § 2000e(m). If Congress intended the term " 'demonstrates' " to require that the "burdens of production and persuasion" be met by direct evidence or some other heightened showing, it could have made that intent clear by including language to that effect in § 2000e(m). . . .

In addition, Title VII's silence with respect to the type of evidence required in mixed-motive cases also suggests that we should not depart from the "conventional rule of civil litigation [that] generally applies in Title VII cases." Price Waterhouse, 490 U.S., at 253. That rule requires a plaintiff to prove his case "by a preponderance of the evidence," *ibid.* using "direct or circumstantial evidence," Postal Service Bd. of Governors v. Aikens, 460 U.S. 711, 714, n. 3 (1983). We have often acknowledged the utility of circumstantial evidence in discrimination cases. For instance, in Reeves v. Sanderson Plumbing Products, Inc., 530 U.S. 133 (2000), we recognized that evidence that a defendant's explanation for an employment practice is "unworthy of credence" is "one form of *circumstantial evidence* that is probative of intentional discrimination." *Id.*, at 147 (emphasis added). The reason for treating circumstantial and direct evidence alike is both clear and deep-rooted: "Circumstantial evidence is not only sufficient, but may also be more certain, satisfying and persuasive than direct evidence." Rogers v. Missouri *Pac.* R.R. Co., 352 U.S. 500, 508 n. 17 (1957). . . .

For the reasons stated above, we agree with the Court of Appeals that no heightened showing is required under § 2000e-2(m). . . . In order to obtain an instruction under § 2000e-2(m), a plaintiff need only present sufficient evidence for a reasonable jury to conclude, by a preponderance of the evidence, that "race, color, religion, sex, or national origin was a motivating factor for any employment practice." Because direct evidence of discrimination is not required in mixed-motive cases, the Court of Appeals correctly concluded that the District Court did not abuse its discretion in giving a mixed-motive instruction to the jury. Accordingly, the judgment of the Court of Appeals is affirmed.

[The concurring opinion of JUSTICE O'CONNOR is omitted.]

NOTES

1. **The Purpose of the Mixed-Motives Structure.** In many cases of discrimination, employers may have had several motives for their decision, some of which may have been discriminatory and others of which might have been nondiscriminatory or legitimate. In *Price Waterhouse v. Hopkins*, 490 U.S. 228 (1989), the Supreme Court considered how a court should evaluate cases involving mixed motives. Justice Brennan, writing for a plurality of the Court, ultimately concluded that when a plaintiff was able to establish that a discriminatory factor played a motivating role in an employer's decision, the burden shifted to the employer to establish that it would have made the same decision absent the discriminatory motive. *See id.* at 244–45. As the Supreme Court explains in *Desert Palace*, the Civil Rights Act of 1991 changed the standard so that now when a plaintiff establishes that discrimination played "a motivating" factor in the employer's decision, the plaintiff is entitled to a judgment. *See* 42 U.S.C. § 2000e-2(m). The defendant then has an opportunity to prove that it would have made the same decision absent the discriminatory motive, and if it succeeds in doing so, the plaintiff is not entitled to any relief on her claim. *See* 42 U.S.C. § 2000e-5(g). The judgment, therefore, effectively provides her with attorney's fees for prevailing on the merits and possibly injunctive relief.

2. **The Effects of *Desert Palace*.** Although, on its face, the Supreme Court's unanimous decision in *Desert Palace* was uncontroversial, it sparked a lively debate among commentators and in the lower courts regarding whether the case has altered the *McDonnell Douglas* proof structure. Traditionally, the mixed-motives structure was seen as an alternative proof structure—either one proceeded under *McDonnell Douglas* to prove pretext or one proceeded under *Price Waterhouse* to establish a mixed-motive. But now that the Supreme Court has held that circumstantial evidence can be used to prove a mixed-motives case, some have suggested that the two structures have been merged, given that circumstantial evidence is the means to prove pretext. William Corbett has succinctly summarized this position: "Once a defendant produces evidence of a legitimate, nondiscriminatory reason, the case has at least two motives at issue, and pretext analysis, with its higher standard of causation, is irrelevant." William R. Corbett, *McDonnell Douglas, 1973–2003: May You Rest in Peace?*, 6 U. PA. J. LAB. & EMP. L. 199, 213 (2003). Several courts adopted this position, allowing plaintiffs to survive summary judgment by proffering sufficient evidence to demonstrate that discrimination was a motivating factor. Other courts did not perceive any shift in the law, in part because in *Desert Palace* the Supreme Court never mentioned *McDonnell Douglas*, and it seemed highly unusual that the decision would change the landscape of employment discrimination law sub silentio.

The issue has had its greatest resonance on summary judgment. One appellate court has summarized the various approaches courts have adopted in the wake of the *Desert Palace* decision:

Since *Desert Palace*, the federal courts of appeals have, without much, if any, consideration of the issue, developed widely differing approaches to the question of how to analyze summary judgment challenges in Title VII mixed-motive cases. . . . The Eighth Circuit has explicitly held that the *McDonnell Douglas / Burdine* burden-shifting framework applies to the summary judgment analysis of mixed-motive claims after *Desert Palace*. See *Griffith v. City of Des Moines*, 387 F.3d 733, 736 (8th Cir. 2004). The Eleventh Circuit seems to have joined the Eighth Circuit in this regard. See *Burstein v. Entel, Inc.*, 137 F. App'x. 205, 209 n.8 (11th Cir. 2005) . . .

The Fifth Circuit, in contrast, has adopted a "modified *McDonnell Douglas*" approach, under which a plaintiff in a mixed-motive case can rebut the defendant's legitimate non-discriminatory reason not only through evidence of pretext (the traditional *McDonnell Douglas / Burdine* burden), but also with evidence that the defendant's proffered reason is only one of the reasons for its conduct (the mixed-motive alternative). *See Rachid v. Jack in the Box, Inc.*, 376 F.3d 305, 312 (5th Cir. 2004).

Adopting a sort of middle ground between these two positions are the Fourth and Ninth Circuits which permit a mixed-motive plaintiff to avoid a defendant's motion for summary judgment by proceeding either under the "pretext framework" of the traditional *McDonnell Douglas / Burdine* analysis or by "presenting direct or circumstantial evidence that raises a genuine issue of material fact as to whether an impermissible factor such as race motivated[, at least in part,] the adverse employment decision." *Diamond v. Colonial Life & Accident Ins. Co.*, 416 F.3d 310, 318 (4th Cir. 2005); *McGinest v. GTE Serv. Corp.*, 360 F.3d 1103, 1122 (9th Cir. 2004). The D.C. Circuit appears to have recently joined this middle ground approach. *See Fogg v. Gonzales*, 492 F.3d 447, 451 & n* (D.C. Cir. 2007) (indicating that "a plaintiff can establish an unlawful employment practice by showing that 'discrimination or retaliation played a "motivating part" or was a "substantial factor" in the employment decision' " but noting that a "plaintiff may also, of course, use evidence of pretext and the *McDonnell Douglas* framework to prove a mixed-motive case").

White v. Baxter Healthcare Corp., 533 F.3d 381, 399–400 (6th Cir. 2008), *cert. denied*, 556 U.S. 1235 (2009). The Sixth Circuit went on to consider what the appropriate standard should be:

This case now presents us with the opportunity to finally clarify how Title VII mixed-motive claims should be analyzed at the summary judgment stage. We do so by holding that the *McDonnell Douglas / Burdine* burden-shifting framework does *not* apply to the summary judgment analysis of Title VII mixed-motive claims. We likewise hold that to survive a defendant's motion for summary judgment, a Title VII plaintiff asserting a mixed-motive claim need only produce evidence sufficient to convince a jury that: (1) the defendant took an adverse employment action against the plaintiff; and (2) "race, color, religion, sex, or national origin was *a* motivating factor" for the defendant's adverse employment action. 42 U.S.C. § 2000e-2(m) (emphasis added). . . . This burden of producing some evidence in support of a mixed-motive claim is not onerous and should preclude sending the case to the jury only where the record is devoid of evidence that could reasonably be construed to support the plaintiff's claim. . . .

[The] elimination of possible legitimate reasons for the defendant's action is not needed when assessing whether trial is warranted in the mixed-motive context. In mixed-motive cases, a plaintiff can win simply by showing that the defendant's consideration of a protected characteristic "was *a* motivating factor for any employment practice, *even though other factors also motivated the practice.*" 42 U.S.C. § 2000e-2(m) (emphasis added). In order to reach a jury, the plaintiff is not required to eliminate or rebut all the possible legitimate motivations of the defendant as long as the plaintiff can demonstrate that an illegitimate discriminatory animus factored into the defendant's decision to take the adverse employment action. . . . The only question that a court need ask in determining whether the plaintiff is entitled to submit his claim to a jury in such cases is whether the plaintiff has presented "sufficient evidence for a reasonable jury to conclude, by a preponderance of the evidence, that 'race, color, religion, sex, or national origin was a motivating factor for'" the defendant's adverse employment decision.

Id. at 400–01. How does the Sixth Circuit's standard compare to that of other Circuits? What do you think should be the proper standard based on the Court's decision in *Costa*? In addition, should a plaintiff have to choose a method of proof or should the case be allowed to proceed to trial on any theory? Courts generally require plaintiffs to give notice of their intent to proceed on a mixed motives claim and that typically comes in the complaint. *See Spees v. Gen. Marine, Inc.*, 617 F.3d 380, 390 (6th Cir. 2010) (plaintiff must provide notice of mixed motives claim).

3. **The Future of the Mixed Motives Claim**. With time, the enthusiasm for the mixed motives cause of action appears to have waned, most likely due to the limited remedies available for a successful claim. The Supreme Court has also seemingly lost some of its enthusiasm for the theory as it has declined to apply the analysis from *Costa* to either age discrimination cases or retaliation claims. *See Univ. of Texas Sw. Med. Ctr. v. Nassar*, 133. S. Ct. 2517 (2013) (plaintiff may not proceed under mixed-motives framework in a Title VII retaliation case); *Gross v. FBL Fin. Servs., Inc.*, 557 U.S. 167 (2009) (holding that mixed-motives theory does not apply to the Age Discrimination statute). The standard for proving retaliation case will be taken up shortly, and Age Discrimination claims will be discussed later in this Chapter.

3. The "Cat's Paw" Theory

STAUB v. PROCTOR HOSPITAL
United States Supreme Court
131 S. Ct. 1186 (2011)

JUSTICE SCALIA delivered the opinion of the Court.

We consider the circumstances under which an employer may be held liable for employment discrimination based on the discriminatory animus of an employee who influenced, but did not make, the ultimate employment decision.

I

Petitioner Vincent Staub worked as an angiography technician for respondent Proctor Hospital until 2004, when he was fired. Staub and Proctor hotly dispute the facts surrounding the firing, but because a jury found for Staub in his claim of employment discrimination against Proctor, we describe the facts viewed in the light most favorable to him.

While employed by Proctor, Staub was a member of the United States Army Reserve, which required him to attend drill one weekend per month and to train full time for two to three weeks a year. Both Janice Mulally, Staub's immediate supervisor, and Michael Korenchuk, Mulally's supervisor, were hostile to Staub's military obligations. Mulally scheduled Staub for additional shifts without notice so that he would "pa[y] back the department for everyone else having to bend over backwards to cover [his] schedule for the Reserves." 560 F.3d 647, 652 (CA7 2009). She also informed Staub's co-worker, Leslie Sweborg, that Staub's "military duty had been a strain on th[e] department," and asked Sweborg to help her "get rid of him." *Ibid.* Korenchuk referred to Staub's military obligations as "a b[u]nch of smoking and joking and [a] waste of taxpayers['] money." *Ibid.* He was also aware that Mulally was "out to get" Staub. *Ibid.*

In January 2004, Mulally issued Staub a "Corrective Action" disciplinary warning for purportedly violating a company rule requiring him to stay in his work area whenever he was not working with a patient. The Corrective Action included a directive requiring Staub to report to Mulally or Korenchuk "when [he] ha[d] no patients and [the angio] cases [we]re complete[d]." *Id.* at 653. According to Staub, Mulally's justification for the Corrective Action was false for two reasons: First, the company rule invoked by Mulally did not exist; and second, even if it did, Staub did not violate it.

On April 2, 2004, Angie Day, Staub's co-worker, complained to Linda Buck, Proctor's vice president of human resources, and Garrett McGowan, Proctor's chief operating officer, about Staub's frequent unavailability and abruptness. McGowan directed Korenchuk and Buck to create a plan that would solve Staub's " 'availability' problems." *Id.* at 654. But three weeks later, before they had time to do so, Korenchuk informed Buck that Staub had left his desk without informing a supervisor, in violation of the January Corrective Action. Staub now contends this accusation was false: he had left Korenchuk a voice-mail notification that he was leaving his desk. Buck relied on Korenchuk's accusation, however, and after reviewing Staub's personnel file, she decided to fire him. The termination notice stated that Staub had ignored the directive issued in the January 2004 Corrective Action.

Staub challenged his firing through Proctor's grievance process, claiming that Mulally had fabricated the allegation underlying the Corrective Action out of hostility toward his military obligations. Buck did not follow up with Mulally about this claim. After discussing the matter with another personnel officer, Buck adhered to her decision.

Staub sued Proctor under the Uniformed Services Employment and Reemployment Rights Act of 1994, 38 U.S.C. § 4301 *et seq.*, claiming that his discharge was motivated by hostility to his obligations as a military reservist. His contention was not that Buck had any such hostility but that Mulally and Korenchuk did, and that their actions influenced Buck's ultimate employment decision. A jury found that Staub's "military status was a motivating factor in [Proctor's] decision to discharge him," and awarded $57,640 in damages.

The Seventh Circuit reversed . . . . The court observed that Staub had brought a "cat's paw case," meaning that he sought to hold his employer liable for the animus of a supervisor who was not charged with making the ultimate employment decision. *Id.* at 655–656.[3] It explained that under Seventh Circuit precedent, a "cat's paw" case could not succeed unless the nondecisionmaker exercised such "singular influence" over the decisionmaker that the decision to terminate was the product of "blind reliance." *Id.* at 659 . . . . The court "admit[ted] that Buck's investigation could have been more robust," since it "failed to pursue Staub's theory that Mulally fabricated the write-up." *Ibid.* But the court said that the "singular influence" rule "does not require the decisionmaker to be a paragon of independence": "It is enough that the decisionmaker is not wholly dependent on a single source of information and conducts her own investigation into the facts relevant to the decision." *Ibid.* Because the undisputed evidence established that Buck was not wholly dependent on the advice of Korenchuk and Mulally, the court held that Proctor was entitled to judgment. *Ibid.* We granted certiorari.

II

The Uniformed Services Employment and Reemployment Rights Act (USERRA) provides in relevant part as follows:

"A person who is a member of . . . or has an obligation to perform service in a uniformed service shall not be denied initial employment, reemployment, retention in employment, promotion, or any benefit of

---

[3] [n. 1] The term "cat's paw" derives from a fable conceived by Aesop, put into verse by La Fontaine in 1679, and injected into United States employment discrimination law by [Judge] Posner in 1990. See *Shager v. Upjohn Co.*, 913 F.2d 398, 405 (CA7). In the fable, a monkey induces a cat by flattery to extract roasting chestnuts from the fire. After the cat has done so, burning its paws in the process, the monkey makes off with the chestnuts and leaves the cat with nothing.

employment by an employer on the basis of that membership, . . . or obligation." 38 U.S.C. § 4311(a).

It elaborates further:

"An employer shall be considered to have engaged in actions prohibited . . . under subsection (a), if the person's membership . . . is a motivating factor in the employer's action, unless the employer can prove that the action would have been taken in the absence of such membership." § 4311(c).

The statute is very similar to Title VII . . . . The central difficulty in this case is construing the phrase "motivating factor in the employer's action." When the company official who makes the decision to take an adverse employment action is personally acting out of hostility to the employee's membership in or obligation to a uniformed service, a motivating factor obviously exists. The problem we confront arises when that official has no discriminatory animus but is influenced by previous company action that is the product of a like animus in someone else.

In approaching this question, we start from the premise that when Congress creates a federal tort it adopts the background of general tort law. *See Burlington N. & S. F. R. Co. v. United States*, 129 S. Ct. 1870 (2009). Intentional torts such as this, "as distinguished from negligent or reckless torts, . . . generally require that the actor intend 'the *consequences*' of an act, not simply the act itself." *Kawaauhau v. Geiger*, 523 U.S. 57, 61–62 (1998).

Staub contends that the fact that an unfavorable entry on the plaintiff's personnel record was caused to be put there, with discriminatory animus, by Mulally and Korenchuk, suffices to establish the tort, even if Mulally and Korenchuk did not intend to cause his dismissal. But discrimination was not part of Buck's reason for the dismissal; and while Korenchuk and Mulally acted with discriminatory animus, the act they committed—the mere making of the reports—was not a denial of "initial employment, reemployment, retention in employment, promotion, or any benefit of employment," as liability under USERRA requires. If dismissal was not the object of Mulally's and Korenchuk's reports, it may have been their result, or even their foreseeable consequence, but that is not enough to render Mulally or Korenchuk responsible.

Here, however, Staub is seeking to hold liable not Mulally and Korenchuk, but their employer. Perhaps, therefore, the discriminatory motive of one of the employer's agents (Mulally or Korenchuk) can be aggregated with the act of another agent (Buck) to impose liability on Proctor. Again we consult general principles of law, agency law, which form the background against which federal tort laws are enacted . . . . Here, however, the answer is not so clear. The Restatement of Agency suggests that the malicious mental state of one agent cannot generally be combined with the harmful action of another agent to hold the principal liable for a tort that requires both. See Restatement (Second) Agency § 275. Some of the cases involving federal torts apply that rule. See *United States v. Science Applications Int'l Corp.*, 626 F.3d 1257, 1273–1276 (CADC 2010); *Chaney v. Dreyfus Service Corp.*, 595 F.3d 219, 241 (CA5 2010) . . . . But another case involving a federal tort, and one involving a federal crime, hold to the contrary. See *United States ex rel.*

Harrison v. Westinghouse Savannah River Co., 352 F.3d 908, 918–919 (CA4 2003); *United States v. Bank of New England, N. A.*, 821 F.2d 844, 856 (CA1 1987). Ultimately, we think it unnecessary in this case to decide what the background rule of agency law may be, since the former line of authority is suggested by the governing text, which requires that discrimination be "a motivating factor" *in the adverse action*. When a decision to fire is made with no unlawful animus on the part of the firing agent, but partly on the basis of a report prompted (unbeknownst to that agent) by discrimination, discrimination might perhaps be called a "factor" or a "causal factor" in the decision; but it seems to us a considerable stretch to call it "a motivating factor."

Proctor, on the other hand, contends that the employer is not liable unless the *de facto* decisionmaker (the technical decisionmaker or the agent for whom he is the "cat's paw") is motivated by discriminatory animus. This avoids the aggregation of animus and adverse action, but it seems to us not the only application of general tort law that can do so. Animus and responsibility for the adverse action can both be attributed to the earlier agent (here, Staub's supervisors) if the adverse action is the intended consequence of that agent's discriminatory conduct. So long as the agent intends, for discriminatory reasons, that the adverse action occur, he has the scienter required to be liable under USERRA. And it is axiomatic under tort law that the exercise of judgment by the decisionmaker does not prevent the earlier agent's action (and hence the earlier agent's discriminatory animus) from being the proximate cause of the harm. Proximate cause requires only "some direct relation between the injury asserted and the injurious conduct alleged," and excludes only those "link[s] that are too remote, purely contingent, or indirect." *Hemi Group, LLC v. City of New York*, 130 S. Ct. 983 (2010). We do not think that the ultimate decisionmaker's exercise of judgment automatically renders the link to the supervisor's bias "remote" or "purely contingent." The decisionmaker's exercise of judgment is *also* a proximate cause of the employment decision, but it is common for injuries to have multiple proximate causes . . . .

Moreover, the approach urged upon us by Proctor gives an unlikely meaning to a provision designed to prevent employer discrimination. An employer's authority to reward, punish, or dismiss is often allocated among multiple agents. The one who makes the ultimate decision does so on the basis of performance assessments by other supervisors. Proctor's view would have the improbable consequence that if an employer isolates a personnel official from an employee's supervisors, vests the decision to take adverse employment actions in that official, and asks that official to review the employee's personnel file before taking the adverse action, then the employer will be effectively shielded from discriminatory acts and recommendations of supervisors that were *designed and intended* to produce the adverse action. That seems to us an implausible meaning of the text, and one that is not compelled by its words.

Proctor suggests that even if the decisionmaker's mere exercise of independent judgment does not suffice to negate the effect of the prior discrimination, at least the decisionmaker's independent investigation (and rejection) of the employee's allegations of discriminatory animus ought to do so. We decline to adopt such a hard-and-fast rule. As we have already acknowledged, the requirement that the biased supervisor's action be a causal factor of the ultimate employment action incorporates the traditional tort-law concept of proximate cause. See, *e.g., Anza v. Ideal Steel Supply Corp.*, 547 U.S. 451, 457–458 (2006). Thus, if the employer's investigation results in an adverse action for reasons unrelated to the supervisor's original biased action, then the employer will not be liable. But the supervisor's biased report may remain a causal factor if the independent investigation takes it into account without determining that the adverse action was, apart from the supervisor's recommendation, entirely justified. We are aware of no principle in tort or agency law under which an employer's mere conduct of an independent investigation has a claim-preclusive effect. Nor do we think the independent investigation somehow relieves the employer of "fault." The employer is at fault because one of its agents committed an action based on discriminatory animus that was intended to cause, and did in fact cause, an adverse employment decision.

. . . .

We therefore hold that if a supervisor performs an act motivated by antimilitary animus that is *intended* by the supervisor to cause an adverse employment action, and if that act is a proximate cause of the ultimate employment action, then the employer is liable under USERRA.

III

Applying our analysis to the facts of this case, it is clear that the Seventh Circuit's judgment must be reversed. Both Mulally and Korenchuk were acting within the scope of their employment when they took the actions that allegedly caused Buck to fire Staub . . . . As the Seventh Circuit recognized, there was evidence that Mulally's and Korenchuk's actions were motivated by hostility toward Staub's military obligations. There was also evidence that Mulally's and Korenchuk's actions were causal factors underlying Buck's decision to fire Staub. Finally, there was evidence that both Mulally and Korenchuk had the specific intent to cause Staub to be terminated. Mulally stated she was trying to "get rid of" Staub, and Korenchuk was aware that Mulally was "out to get" Staub. Moreover, Korenchuk informed Buck, Proctor's personnel officer responsible for terminating employees, of Staub's alleged noncompliance with Mulally's Corrective Action, and Buck fired Staub immediately thereafter; a reasonable jury could infer that Korenchuk intended that Staub be fired . . . .

It is less clear whether the jury's verdict should be reinstated or whether Proctor is entitled to a new trial. The jury instruction did not hew precisely to the rule we adopt today; it required only that the jury find that "military status was a motivating factor in [Proctor's] decision to discharge him." Whether the variance between the instruction and our rule was harmless error or should mandate a new trial is a matter the Seventh Circuit may consider in the first instance.

The judgment of the Seventh Circuit is reversed, and the case is remanded for further proceedings consistent with this opinion.

JUSTICE KAGAN took no part in the consideration or decision of this case.

JUSTICE ALITO'S concurring opinion, joined by JUSTICE THOMAS, is omitted.

NOTES

1. **The Court's Approach.** In *Staub*, the Court adopts—as it often does—a middle ground between the asserted positions. Why do you think it did so here? Do you think the Court adopted an appropriate standard? What problems do you anticipate that plaintiffs might have in establishing liability under the "cat's paw" theory? One of the more interesting aspects of the "cat's paw" theory, what is also known as subordinate liability, is that it took so long for the Court to address the issue. In some ways, the theory is akin to the mixed motives claim, but there is a significant difference as well, what do you think that difference is?

2. **USERRA.** The *Staub* case arose under the Uniformed Services Employment and Reemployment Rights Act (USERRA), which prohibits discrimination based on an individual's military service obligation. As the Court notes, much of the case law parallels Title VII, though one distinguishing feature is that the cases often involve direct evidence of discrimination. For example, in *Bobo v. UPS*, 665 F.3d 741 (6th Cir. 2012), the plaintiff upon notifying his supervisor of his service obligations was told that "he needed to choose between UPS and the Army," *id.* at 744, and when he later returned from his military service he was assigned three times as many drivers to train than his peers. *Id.* at 745. Why do you think these cases may involve direct evidence? Is there something about the cases that might make them different in this respect?

3. **The Cat's Paw Theory in Other Contexts.** The question whether the *Staub* case would be applied to Title VII has been answered affirmatively, often without any analysis. *See Guinares v. SuperValu, Inc.*, 674 F.3d 962, 972 (8th Cir. 2012) (applying to Title VII); *McKenna v. City of Philadelphia*, 649 F.3d 171 (3rd Cir. 2011) (applying to Title VII case with little discussion), *cert. denied*, 132 S. Ct. 1918 (2012). For an entertaining discussion of the theory and its complications, by Judge Posner, who introduced the cat's paw fable into the jurisprudence lexicon, see *Cook v. IPS Int'l Corp.*, 673 F.3d 625, 627–29 (7th Cir. 2012). Whether the *Staub* standard applies in the age discrimination context seems a more difficult question. Two Circuits have applied the standard in a modified fashion by requiring "but-for" rather than proximate causation regarding the role the subordinate played. *See Sims v. MVM, Inc.*, 704 F.3d 1327 (11th Cir. 2013); *Simmons v. Sykes Enters.*, Inc., 647 F.3d 943 (10th Cir. 2011). Based on the limited early sampling, the cases have proved difficult to establish but the reasons seem to turn on the particular facts of the cases rather than the standard the Supreme Court adopted.

4. **Retaliation Claims.** In addition to prohibiting discrimination in employment practices, Title VII, like most antidiscrimination statutes also includes prohibitions on retaliating against individuals who complain about unlawful employment practices or who participate in discrimination proceedings. Specifically, section 704(a) of Title VII makes it an unlawful employment practice to take actions against individuals who "oppose" unlawful discrimination or who "participate" in

any proceeding, and in the last decade there has been a huge increase in litigation relating to claims of retaliation, which now form the largest category of claim filed with the EEOC. During that time, the Supreme Court has addressed the scope of the antiretaliation provision in several important cases.

In *Burlington Northern & Santa Fe Railway Co. v. White*, 548 U.S. 53, 57 (2006), the question was what standard governed the determination of what constituted retaliation. In some instances, the alleged retaliation is clear—an individual files a complaint of discrimination, and is terminated or immediately transferred to a position with different job responsibilities. But other times, the alleged retaliatory acts can be more subtle, and courts are required to decide whether the acts rise to a level of retaliation sufficient to constitute unlawful discrimination under the antiretaliation provision. In *Burlington Northern*, the Court held that in order to establish a retaliatory act "a plaintiff must show that a reasonable employee would have found the challenged action materially adverse, which in this context means it might well have dissuaded a reasonable worker from making or supporting a charge of discrimination." *Id.* at 68. This standard was broader than that advocated by the employer, who had suggested that acts should be defined as retaliation only to the extent they would violate the substantive provision of Title VII. In its unanimous opinion, the Supreme Court also provided some illustrations of how the standard should be interpreted, noting specifically:

> Context matters . . . A schedule change in an employee's work schedule may make little difference to many workers, but may matter enormously to a young mother with school age children. A supervisor's refusal to invite an employee to lunch is normally trivial, a nonactionable petty slight. But to retaliate by excluding an employee from a weekly training lunch that contributes significantly to the employer's professional advancement might well deter a reasonable employee from complaining about discrimination. Hence a legal standard that speaks in general terms rather than specific prohibited acts is preferable for an act that would be immaterial in some situations is material in others.

Id. at 69. Since the Court's decision, lower courts have applied the standard articulated in *Burlington Northern* to other antidiscrimination statutes. *See, e.g., Harnes v. Level 3 Commc'ns, LLC*, 456 F.3d 1215 (10th Cir. 2006) (applying standard to the ADEA), *cert. denied*, 549 U.S. 1252 (2007); *Metzler v. Fed. Home Loan Bank*, 464 F.3d 1164 (10th Cir. 2006) (applying standard to claims under FMLA, ADA, and ADEA); *Humphris v. CBOCs W., Inc.*, 474 F.3d 387 (7th Cir. 2007) (applying standard to claim of retaliation under 42 U.S.C. § 1981), *aff'd on other grounds*, 553 U.S. 442 (2008).

As a result of the contextual standard, it is difficult to make broad judgments regarding how the antiretaliation provision is interpreted. Some themes have developed. In particular, the plaintiff must establish that she suffered a "materially adverse" employment action, one that might dissuade a reasonable person from pursuing a claim. Many courts look to determine whether the employee suffered some actual injury that results in a change in pay, responsibilities, or employment. *See, e.g., Taylor v. Solis*, 571 F.3d 1313, 1321 (D.C. Cir. 2009) (lowering a performance evaluation is not materially adverse decision unless it results in tangible harm); *Stephens v. Erickson*, 569 F.3d 779, 791 (7th Cir. 2009) (job transfer or reassignment is not materially adverse "unless it represents a *significant* alteration to the employee's duties"); *Weger v. City of Ladue*, 500 F.3d 710, 727 (8th Cir. 2007) (exclusion from work actions were not materially adverse).

But such a tangible action is not always necessary as the fundamental question is whether the employer's actions would likely deter an employee from complaining. An important aspect of the *Burlington* decision is that the Court's standard for determining when an employer's actions result in a "materially adverse" employment action is distinct from the standard for an adverse employment action in the context of a discrimination claim. This issue was recently explored by the Sixth Circuit Court of Appeals in a case where a public safety officer argued that a litany of actions by his employer led to his constructive discharge in violation of Title VII and also constituted retaliation for having filed claims with the EEOC. *See Laster v. City of Kalamazoo*, 746 F.3d 714 (6th Cir. 2014). The Court found that the actions did not rise to the level of constructive discharge and thus dismissed his discrimination claim, but that the very same actions may be construed as "materially adverse" under the retaliation doctrine. The court began its analysis on the retaliation claim by noting that the "materially adverse" standard is "less onerous" than the standard for establishing an adverse employment action as a discrimination claim. *Id.* at 731. The court went on to conclude that the alleged actions might reasonably dissuade an employee from filing a claim:

> Facing heightened scrutiny, receiving frequent reprimands for breaking selectively enforced policies, being disciplined more harshly than similarly situated peers, and forced to attend a pre-determination hearing based on unfounded allegations of wrongdoing might well have dissuaded a reasonable person from making or supporting a claim of discrimination.

Id. at 732. This case provides a good example of a circumstance where an employer's actions might not be sufficient to force one to quit, and thus fail to constitute constructive discharge, but are sufficient to dissuade someone from bringing forth complaints. *See Rivera v. Rochester Genessee Reg'l. Transp. Auth.*, 743 F.3d 11, 26 (2d Cir. 2012) (statements that plaintiff "could lose his job" for filing discrimination complaints constituted materially adverse action).

In addition to establishing that the employer's actions rise to the level of retaliation, an employee must also establish a causal link between the action and some protected activity. Timing often proves important, and while courts have generally not created bright lines, it is generally the case that the closer the time between the protected act (i.e., a complaint) and the employer's retaliation, the more likely a court is to identify the necessary causal link. *See. e.g., Jones v. Bernanke*, 557 F.3d 670, 677 (D.C. Cir. 2009) (noting that "temporal proximity between protected EEOC activity and adverse action can support an inference of causation when the two events are very close in time"). The Supreme Court has cautioned that actions within three or four months will usually not be sufficient to raise a causal question based on "mere temporal proximity." *Clark Cnty. Sch. Dist. v. Breeden*, 532 U.S. 268, 274 (2001). There are, however, exceptions, and if an employee is able to explain why an inference of retaliation is permissible despite the passage of time, courts will generally allow a case to go forward. For example, in a recent case, the plaintiff argued that her demotion was in retaliation for sexual harassment charges she had filed three years earlier. The district court's conclusion that the passage of time was fatal to her claim was reversed by the Court of Appeals, which explained: "We reiterate what we have said consistently and repeatedly in retaliation cases stretching back more than a decade: a long time interval between protected activity and adverse employment action may weaken but does not conclusively bar an inference of retaliation." *Malin v. Hospira, Inc.*, 2014 U.S. App. LEXIS 15243 (7th Cir. Aug. 7, 2014). The court noted that additional circumstantial evidence supported the link between the two events.

Most claims of retaliation arise after the employee has filed a complaint, either formally or informally, but other cases arise when an individual might be assisting another with a complaint. The Supreme Court unanimously held that the protections of section 704(a) extend to an employee who participates in an internal investigation even if that individual did not initiate a complaint. *See Crawford v. Metro. Gov't of Nashville & Davidson Cnty., Tennessee*, 555 U.S. 271 (2009). The Supreme Court has also considered a circumstance where rather than fire the employee who files a complaint with the EEOC, the employer fires the employee's fiancé. The Court unanimously held the employee who originally filed the charges could pursue a retaliation claim because firing one's fiancé is the kind of activity that would likely dissuade an employee from pursuing a discrimination complaint. *See Thompson v. N. Am. Stainless, LP*, 562 U.S. 170 (2011). These cases are generally referred to as "third-party" retaliation claims.

The Elusive Nature of Discrimination

This section explores intentional discrimination and how an intent to discriminate can be established through circumstantial evidence. In other words, these are cases in which there is no direct evidence of discrimination—no confession so to speak—and the issue of intent must be inferred from the evidence. The *McDonnell Douglas* structure helps get at this question, but as the Supreme Court stated in *Hicks*, the ultimate question is whether the acts in question can be explained as intentional discrimination.

When the law talks about intent, it often does so with different meanings in mind. For example, an intent to discriminate might be equated with animus or hatred, with a clear and unequivocal desire to treat a person differently because of his or her race, gender, disability etc. Under Title VII, and other statutes governing workplace discrimination, that is not what the law means by intent, indeed, courts have repeatedly stated that an intent to discriminate does not necessarily include animus. *See EEOC v. Joe's Stone Crab*, 220 F.3d 1263 (11th Cir. 2000). Another possibility would be to equate intent with motive, that the actor's motive was to discriminate. But the law also does not require proof of motive. Rather, when it comes to intent under Title VII, the law focuses on disparate treatment, establishing that the plaintiff was treated differently because of his race, gender, etc. For a discussion of this meaning of intent in antidiscrimination law, see Michael Selmi, *Proving Intentional Discrimination: The Reality of Supreme Court Rhetoric*, 86 GEO. L.J. 280, 286–91(1997). This is why it can be so important for plaintiffs to produce comparators as a way to establish an intent to discriminate because the comparators are relevant to establishing whether the plaintiff was treated differently.

Proving discrimination has become increasingly difficult as we move farther away from an era of overt racism or sexism, and when discriminatory behavior becomes increasingly subtle, and often unconscious, in nature. Linda Hamilton Krieger has written extensively about the changing nature of discrimination, and the way in which discrimination can have unconscious origins to the point that the actor may be unaware of his or her intent. *See* Linda Hamilton Krieger, *The Content of Our Categories: A Cognitive Bias Approach to Discrimination and Equal Employment Opportunity*, 47 STAN L. REV. 1161 (1995). In some ways, this may sound inconsistent with the emphasis on intent under Title VII but it is consistent with the focus on disparate treatment. By the same measure, unconscious or subtle discrimination is often far more difficult to prove. Given that much discrimination has become more subtle in nature, you should consider how the doctrine might adapt to that change. How might the law take into account these changes? Should, for example, jury instructions be offered on the nature of contemporary discrimination? One law professor has suggested that, because "unconscious" discrimination cannot easily be controlled, the law should not hold employers liable for unconscious discrimination. *See* Amy L. Wax, *Discrimination as Accident*, 74 IND. L.J. 1129 (1999). Does that perspective make sense to you? Are there things employers can do to limit discrimination, even discrimination that is subtle in nature? How do the theories of "mixed-motives" or the "cat's paw" relate to claims of subtle discrimination?

Over the last decade, within legal scholarship, the emphasis has moved from a focus on "unconscious" discrimination to what is increasingly defined as "implicit bias." Although the concept shares much in common with unconscious bias, it is based on recent empirical evidence arising from social psychology that has documented the widespread presence of implicit bias among individuals. The most common form of evidence is a study called the Implicit Association Test ("IAT"), which is an online test individuals can take that measures the strength of certain associations. (*You can access it at* https://implict.harvard.edu.) The test has been widely used and studied and the results consistently demonstrate that individuals associate African Americans with negative qualities, and other tests have demonstrated preferences, or more positive associations, with young over old and heterosexual over gay and lesbian individuals. *See, e.g.*, Christine Jolls & Cass Sunstein, *The Law of Implicit Bias*, 94 CALIF. L. REV. 969 (2006). These, and other studies, help to explain the source of bias even among individuals who do not appear to be biased or who explicitly disclaim any biased opinions. For a comprehensive discussion of implicit bias see Jerry Kang *et al.*, *Implicit Bias in the Courtroom*, 59 UCLA L. REV. 1124 (2012). It should be noted that the studies are controversial, and many question whether the results—which are produced in very quick judgments— translate into actual behavior. *See, e.g.*, Gregory Mitchell & Philip E. Tetlock, *Antidiscrimination Law & the Perils of Mindreading*, 67 OHIO ST. L.J. 1023 (2006). How might the concept of implicit or unconscious bias have played a role in the *Hicks* case? What about *Desert Palace*? Might it alter how courts should define discrimination?

Another problem that lurks in the area is that defining discrimination can often be a matter of one's perspective and life experiences so that certain actions may have meaning to African Americans, Latinos or other groups, even when it would not have a similar meaning for whites. As one court has noted, "Racially motivated comments or actions may appear innocent or only mildly offensive to one who is not a member of the targeted group, but in reality be intolerably abusive or threatening when understood from the perspective of a plaintiff who is a member of the targeted group." *McGinest v. GTE Serv. Corp.*, 360 F.3d 1103, 1116 (9th Cir. 2004). Studies continually show that African Americans and whites differ with regards to the extent to which discrimination continues to be a strong force in American life. *See, e.g.*, Lawrence D. Bobo, *et al.*, *Through the Eyes of Black America*, Public Perspectives, May/June 2001, 13 at 15 (noting that in a recent survey "One third of whites said that African Americans had already achieved equality, while fewer than one in ten blacks held such a view."). *See also* Russell K. Robinson, *Perceptual Segregation*, 108 COLUM. L. REV. 1093 (2008) (exploring the importance of perception in defining discrimination). Given that discrimination has become more subtle, and that there is often a substantial difference in perspectives, discrimination has become not just more difficult to prove but more difficult to define.

As a way of understanding the complexities of proving discrimination today, consider the following case study:

Lawrence Mungin was an African-American Harvard trained lawyer who specialized in bankruptcy law. Upon graduation from law school, Mr. Mungin went to work for a large New York firm, but moved to a Houston firm shortly thereafter, and then to a Washington, D.C. branch office of a large Atlanta firm. When that office began to experience financial difficulties, Mungin began looking for new work and with the help of a head hunter quickly landed a position at the D.C. branch office of a Chicago firm. The branch office was operated by a powerful partner with an insurance practice who was interested in adding a bankruptcy lawyer to assist some of his existing clients. The head hunter also specifically stressed that Mungin was a "minority" and the law firm that hired him, Katten Muchin, was eager to add minority lawyers to its staff.

After Mungin joined the firm, the office began to encounter significant problems and one of the other bankruptcy attorneys (a partner) left for another firm shortly after Mungin arrived. Mungin was thus left with little work to do, and although he sought to develop some of his own clients, his efforts were not very successful.

Mungin then sought help from the Chicago office where he was not well known. Mungin was also at a point in his career when he was eligible for partnership but no one in the firm had thought to consider him, and indeed, Mungin discovered that he had never received an annual review. Mungin also discovered that white attorneys who were less senior than him were being paid more than he was. After telling Mungin that he had "fallen through the cracks," the firm sought to correct those issues by providing him with a raise and a review of his work, although the review did not offer much substantive comment on the quality of his work in part because few attorneys had worked with him. Shortly thereafter, the main partner of the Washington, D.C. office left the firm, leaving only a handful of attorneys behind.

The firm then offered to allow Mungin to transfer to its New York office which Mungin found unattractive because the office had no other bankruptcy lawyers. The firm then lowered Mungin's billing rate to that of a first-year associate and sent him equivalent work. Mungin ultimately quit and sued the firm for racial discrimination.

Mungin claimed that the firm's treatment of him constituted unlawful discrimination in the salary that he was paid, the failure to provide him with a performance evaluation, the failure to mentor him and to offer him opportunities to develop his skills sufficiently. Part of the theory developed by his attorneys was that he was hired to be a "token minority," and once hired he was effectively neglected. In response, the firm contended that the issues Mr. Mungin encountered were the result of poor management rather than racial discrimination. It contended that a number of other associates had also not received timely performance evaluations, and that Mungin's salary was largely a reflection of his status as a lateral attorney. The firm also explained that it lowered his billing rate as a way to help him obtain work.

A Washington, D.C. jury found in favor of Mungin and returned a verdict for $1.5 million. The U.S. Court of Appeals for the D.C. Circuit reversed the decision, concluding that no reasonable jury could have found racial discrimination on the trial record. While all of the members of the appellate panel found that Mungin had not established that he was constructively discharged, one judge dissented on the basis that the question of discrimination was properly submitted to the jury. *See Mungin v. Katten Muchin & Zavis*, 116 F.3d 1549 (D.C. Cir. 1997) and Edwards, J., dissenting. Based on the discussion above, do you believe Mungin was the victim of racial discrimination? What more evidence or information would you want to know? Mungin's case has been chronicled in the book, written by his college roommate, PAUL BARRETT, THE GOOD BLACK: A TRUE STORY OF RACE IN AMERICA (1999). For a thorough and excellent review of the book and the issues raised by the case, see David B. Wilkins, *The Good Black: A True Story of Race in America*, 112 HARV. L. REV. 1924 (1999) (book review).

4. Intentional Discrimination Class Claims: Pattern or Practice and the BFOQ

Although most claims pursued under Title VII and the other antidiscrimination statutes are individual claims, the statutes also provide for class actions, and there is a considerable amount of law involving class claims. These claims can be broadly divided into three classifications: (1) pattern or practice claims; (2) claims that are defended under the statutory affirmative defense known as the "BFOQ" or a bona fide occupational qualification; and (3) disparate impact claims. We will take up the first two of these classifications in this section, and discuss the disparate impact theory in the following section.

a. Pattern or Practice Claims

Section 707 of Title VII permits claims that are designed to demonstrate that the employer is engaging in a pattern or practice of discrimination. The Supreme Court has defined this claim as one where discrimination is demonstrated to be "the standard operating procedure—the regular rather than the unusual practice." *Int'l Bhd. of Teamsters v. United States*, 431 U.S. 324, 336 (1977).

In general, these claims are proved through a combination of statistical and anecdotal evidence from individuals who were affected by the employer's practices. Statistics, however, are central to proving the claims, and statistics are used to establish an employer's intent to discriminate.

For example, in the *Teamsters* case, the United States, acting as a plaintiff in the case, alleged a pattern of discrimination against African Americans and Latinos in the hiring practices for line drivers. The plaintiffs demonstrated that the company had more than 6,000 employees, 5% of whom were African Americans and 4% were Latinos. However, when it came to the more lucrative job of line drivers, only eight of the drivers (0.4%) were African Americans with 5 (0.3%) Latinos, and all of the African-American line drivers were hired after the lawsuit had been filed. It was also demonstrated that approximately 80% of the African Americans and Latino employees held lower paying jobs in city operations and serviceman positions, while 39% of white employees held these positions. These statistics could be used, the Court held, to demonstrate that the employer had engaged in an intentional pattern or practice of discrimination. The Court noted further that "like any other kind of evidence, [statistics] may be rebutted." *Id.* at 340. In the *Teamsters* case, it was asserted that a nondiscriminatory hiring process would have produced a similar number of African American and Latino drivers when compared to white line drivers. In other words, if 60% of the white employees held jobs as line drivers, one would expect that 60% of the African American and Latino employees would be line drivers, unless the employer offers an excuse, or defense, to challenge that expectation.

Why would these statistics create an inference of discrimination? The rationale has to do with establishing an appropriate measure for statistical proof so that the statistics create an inference that the observed pattern of employment could not have occurred by chance but was likely the product of some deliberate action. In order to make this proof, courts typically require the plaintiffs to establish their *prima facie* case by showing a statistically significant disparity attributable to the challenged practice. *See Hazelwood Sch. Dist. v. United States*, 433 U.S. 299, 307–08 (1977). In the social sciences, the common measure of statistical significance is two standard deviations, a measure courts have generally adopted as well. What this means is that if the disparity is more than two standard deviations from what would be expected, then a court can eliminate chance as having caused the disparity, and the focus then becomes on the defenses the employer has available to it to rebut the statistics. (This method of proof is very similar to what is used in disparate impact cases and is discussed further in section C in this chapter.)

Once a plaintiff establishes a statistically significant disparity, the employer can seek to rebut the statistics in various ways. A common method of rebutting the statistics is to suggest that the group challenging the practice was not qualified or interested in the jobs. In the *Teamsters* case, the employer might argue that African American and Latino employees did not have the necessary qualifications to be line drivers, and were in this respect less qualified than white employees for the positions. It is important to highlight the comparative nature of the rebuttal—it would not be sufficient to show that most or many African Americans were not qualified, what is at issue is showing that the groups (African Americans vs. whites in the example) differ in some material respects. Additionally, the employer would have to show that the existing number of line drivers was reasonably proportionate to the number of qualified African American and Latino employees. The focus on qualified individuals is also relevant to the plaintiffs' *prima facie* case, as it is generally the plaintiffs' burden to establish the appropriate measure for assessing whether the employer's practices have led to a statistically significant disparity. This measure will often be based on what is known as "applicant flow" data—a measure that seeks to compare the percentage of applicants that are African American or some other protected group with the number of individuals who are ultimately hired.

The Supreme Court's doctrine with respect to pattern or practice cases is found primarily in the *Teamsters* and *Hazelwood* cases discussed above, even though these cases are now nearly forty years old. However, the last decade has seen a steady stream of pattern or practice cases involving race and sex discrimination, including high profile cases against Texaco and Coca-Cola for race discrimination, and Home Depot and Wal-Mart for sex discrimination. These cases are premised on the same assumptions that arose in *Teamsters*, namely that the employer's practices result in a statistically significant disparity in its workforce. For example, in the class action claim against Home Depot, the plaintiffs alleged that women were typically assigned to positions working a cash register, whereas men were more commonly assigned to positions working on the sales floor, and the plaintiffs argued further that most promotional positions required sales floor experience. Although the case settled before trial, the company defended its practices by arguing that women generally were not interested in positions working on the sales floor, and they lacked experience in the construction trade industry which was important for the floor positions.

The next case involves a nationwide class action alleging a pattern and practice of sex discrimination at Wal-Mart. The lawsuit was originally filed in 2001, and class certification was granted in 2004 after a lengthy District Court hearing. The class certification decision was then followed by a lengthy appeal process, including an en banc hearing in the Ninth Circuit Court of Appeals. The result was that by the time the case reached the Supreme Court, it had been pending for nearly 10 years but remained at the class certification stage. The Supreme Court granted *certiorari* to determine whether the class had been properly certified pursuant to Rule 23 of the Federal Rules of Civil Procedure. Much of the case discussion involves the particular demands of Rule 23, and we have edited out most of the Civil Procedure discussion so as to focus on the nature of the class pattern or practice claims that were brought against Wal-Mart. There were two different questions addressed by the Supreme Court. First, and what the focus of the excerpted opinion below involves, was whether there was sufficient "commonality" or common questions to justify class treatment under the basic provision of Rule 23(a). There was also a question whether, assuming the case could satisfy the requirements of 23(a), it would have to meet the requirements of 23(b)(2) or 23(b)(3) in order to proceed as a class. Historically, employment discrimination class actions that sought primarily injunctive relief were certified under section 23(b)(2), which has the advantage for plaintiffs that no notice is required to be provided to potential class members and the class is mandatory in nature. On the other hand, if a class is certified under Rule 23(b)(3), the type of class action usually required when a case is primarily about money damages, the class representatives must provide notice and an opportunity to opt out to all potential class members. In a case that involved as many as one million potential class members, the notice and opt out requirements could prove significant obstacles to pursuing the case as a class. Ultimately, the Supreme Court held that class actions like those brought against Wal-Mart must proceed under Rule 23(b)(3), and the Court by a 5-4 margin also held that the class was improperly certified because the claims lacked commonality. This latter issue is addressed below while the 23(b)(2) vs. 23(b)(3) discussion will be deferred to other relevant courses.

WAL-MART STORES, INC., v. DUKES
United States Supreme Court
131 S. Ct. 2541 (2011)

JUSTICE SCALIA delivered the opinion of the Court.

We are presented with one of the most expansive class actions ever. The District Court and the Court of Appeals approved the certification of a class comprising about one and a half million plaintiffs, current and former female employees of petitioner Wal-Mart who allege that the discretion exercised by their local supervisors over pay and promotion matters violates Title VII by discriminating against women. In addition to injunctive and declaratory relief, the plaintiffs seek an award of backpay. We consider whether the certification of the plaintiff class was consistent with Federal Rules of Civil Procedure 23(a) and (b)(2).

I

A

Petitioner Wal-Mart is the Nation's largest private employer. It operates four types of retail stores throughout the country: Discount Stores, Supercenters, Neighborhood Markets, and Sam's Clubs. Those stores are divided into seven nationwide divisions, which in turn comprise 41 regions of 80 to 85 stores apiece. Each store has between 40 and 53 separate departments and 80 to 500 staff positions. In all, Wal-Mart operates approximately 3,400 stores and employs more than one million people.

Pay and promotion decisions at Wal-Mart are generally committed to local managers' broad discretion, which is exercised "in a largely subjective manner." 222 F.R.D. 137, 145 (N.D. Cal. 2004). Local store managers may increase the wages of hourly employees (within limits) with only limited corporate oversight. As for salaried employees, such as store managers and their deputies, higher corporate authorities have discretion to set their pay within preestablished ranges.

Promotions work in a similar fashion. Wal-Mart permits store managers to apply their own subjective criteria when selecting candidates as "support managers," which is the first step on the path to management. Admission to Wal-Mart's management training program, however, does require that a candidate meet certain objective criteria, including an above-average performance rating, at least one year's tenure in the applicant's current position, and a willingness to relocate. But except for those requirements, regional and district managers have discretion to use their own judgment when selecting candidates for management training. Promotion to higher office—e.g., assistant manager, co-manager, or store manager—is similarly at the discretion of the employee's superiors after prescribed objective factors are satisfied.

B

The named plaintiffs in this lawsuit, representing the 1.5 million members of the certified class, are three current or former Wal-Mart employees who allege that the company discriminated against them on the basis of their sex by denying them equal pay or promotions, in violation of Title VII of the Civil Rights Act of 1964, as amended, 42 U.S.C. § 2000e–1 *et seq.*

Betty Dukes began working at a Pittsburgh, California, Wal-Mart in 1994. She started as a cashier, but later sought and received a promotion to customer service manager. After a series of disciplinary violations, however, Dukes was demoted back to cashier and then to greeter. Dukes concedes she violated company policy, but contends that the disciplinary actions were in fact retaliation for invoking internal complaint procedures and that male employees have not been disciplined for similar infractions. Dukes also claims two male greeters in the Pittsburgh store are paid more than she is.

Christine Kwapnoski has worked at Sam's Club stores in Missouri and California for most of her adult life. She has held a number of positions, including a supervisory position. She claims that a male manager yelled at her frequently and screamed at female employees, but not at men. The manager in question "told her to 'doll up,' to wear some makeup, and to dress a little better." App. 1003a.

The final named plaintiff, Edith Arana, worked at a Wal-Mart store in Duarte, California, from 1995 to 2001. In 2000, she approached the store manager on more than one occasion about management training, but was brushed off. Arana concluded she was being denied opportunity for advancement because of her sex. She initiated internal complaint procedures, whereupon she was told to apply directly to the district manager if she thought her store manager was being unfair. Arana, however, decided against that and never applied for management training again. In 2001, she was fired for failure to comply with Wal-Mart's timekeeping policy.

These plaintiffs, respondents here, do not allege that Wal-Mart has any express corporate policy against the advancement of women. Rather, they claim that their local managers' discretion over pay and promotions is exercised disproportionately in favor of men, leading to an unlawful disparate impact on female employees, see 42 U.S.C. § 2000e-2(k). And, respondents say, because Wal-Mart is aware of this effect, its refusal to cabin its managers' authority amounts to disparate treatment, see § 2000e-2(a). Their complaint seeks injunctive and declaratory relief, punitive damages, and backpay. It does not ask for compensatory damages.

Importantly for our purposes, respondents claim that the discrimination to which they have been subjected is common to *all* Wal-Mart's female employees. The basic theory of their case is that a strong and uniform "corporate culture" permits bias against women to infect, perhaps subconsciously, the discretionary decisionmaking of each one of Wal-Mart's thousands of managers—thereby making every woman at the company the victim of one common discriminatory practice. Respondents therefore wish to litigate the Title VII claims of all female employees at Wal-Mart's stores in a nationwide class action.

C

Class certification is governed by Federal Rule of Civil Procedure 23. Under Rule 23(a), the party seeking certification must demonstrate, first, that:

"(1) the class is so numerous that joinder of all members is impracticable,

(2) there are questions of law or fact common to the class,

(3) the claims or defenses of the representative parties are typical of the claims or defenses of the class, and

(4) the representative parties will fairly and adequately protect the interests of the class" (paragraph breaks added)."

Second, the proposed class must satisfy at least one of the three requirements listed in Rule 23(b) [further discussion of the requirements of 23(b) is omitted].

. . . [R]espondents moved the District Court to certify a plaintiff class consisting of "[a]ll women employed at any Wal-Mart domestic retail store at any time since December 26, 1998, who have been or may be subjected to Wal-Mart's challenged pay and management track promotions policies and practices." 222 F.R.D., at 141–142. As evidence that there were indeed "questions of law or fact common to" all the women of Wal-Mart . . . respondents relied chiefly on three forms of proof: statistical evidence about pay and promotion disparities between men and women at the company, anecdotal reports of discrimination from about 120 of Wal-Mart's female employees, and the testimony of a sociologist, Dr. William Bielby, who conducted a "social framework analysis" of Wal-Mart's "culture" and personnel practices, and concluded that the company was "vulnerable" to gender discrimination. 603 F.3d 571, 601 (CA9 2010) (en banc).

Wal-Mart . . . offered its own countervailing statistical and other proof. . . . With one limitation not relevant here, the District Court granted respondents' motion and certified their proposed class. . . .

II

The class action is "an exception to the usual rule that litigation is conducted by and on behalf of the individual named parties only." *Califano v. Yamasaki*, 442 U.S. 682, 700–701 (1979). In order to justify a departure from that rule, "a class representative must be part of the class and possess the same interest and suffer the same injury as the class members." *East Tex. Motor Freight Sys., Inc. v. Rodriguez*, 431 U.S. 395, 403 (1977). . . . The Rule's four requirements—numerosity, commonality, typicality, and adequate representation—"effectively 'limit the class claims to those fairly encompassed by the named plaintiff's claims.' " *General Tel. Co. of Southwest v. Falcon*, 457 U.S. 147, 156 (1982).

A

The crux of this case is commonality—the rule requiring a plaintiff to show that "there are questions of law or fact common to the class." Rule 23(a)(2). . . . Commonality requires the plaintiff to demonstrate that the class members "have suffered the same injury," *Falcon, supra*, at 157. This does not mean merely that they have all suffered a violation of the same provision of law. Title VII, for example, can be violated in many ways—by intentional discrimination, or by hiring and promotion criteria that result in disparate impact, and by the use of these practices on the part of many different superiors in a single company. Quite obviously, the mere claim by employees of the same company that they have suffered a Title VII injury, or even a disparate-impact Title VII injury, gives no cause to believe that all their claims can productively be litigated at once. Their claims must depend upon a common contention—for example, the assertion of discriminatory bias on the part of the same supervisor. That common contention, moreover, must be of such a nature that it is capable of classwide resolution—which means that determination of its truth or falsity will resolve an issue that is central to the validity of each one of the claims in one stroke.

Rule 23 does not set forth a mere pleading standard. A party seeking class certification must affirmatively demonstrate his compliance with the Rule—that is, he must be prepared to prove that there are *in fact* sufficiently numerous parties, common questions of law or fact, etc. We recognized in *Falcon* that "sometimes it may be necessary for the court to probe behind the pleadings before coming to rest on the certification question," 457 U.S., at 160, and that certification is proper only if "the trial court is satisfied, after a rigorous analysis, that the prerequisites of Rule 23(a) have been satisfied," *id.* at 161. Frequently that "rigorous analysis" will entail some overlap with the merits of the plaintiff's underlying claim. That cannot be helped . . . .

In this case, proof of commonality necessarily overlaps with respondents' merits contention that Wal-Mart engages in a *pattern or practice* of discrimination.[4] . . .

---

[4] [n. 7] In a pattern-or-practice case, the plaintiff tries to "establish by a preponderance of the evidence that . . . discrimination was the company's standard operating procedure[,] the regular rather than the unusual practice." *Teamsters* v. *United States*, 431 U.S. 324, 358 (1977). If he succeeds, that showing will support a rebuttable inference that all class members were victims of the discriminatory practice, and will justify "an award of prospective relief," such as "an injunctive order against the

Here respondents wish to sue about literally millions of employment decisions at once. Without some glue holding the alleged *reasons* for all those decisions together, it will be impossible to say that examination of all the class members' claims for relief will produce a common answer to the crucial question *why was I disfavored.*

B

This Court's opinion in *Falcon* describes how the commonality issue must be approached . . . . explaining:

> "Conceptually, there is a wide gap between (a) an individual's claim that he has been denied a promotion [or higher pay] on discriminatory grounds, and his otherwise unsupported allegation that the company has a policy of discrimination, and (b) the existence of a class of persons who have suffered the same injury as that individual, such that the individual's claim and the class claim will share common questions of law or fact and that the individual's claim will be typical of the class claims." Id. at 157–158.

Falcon suggested two ways in which that conceptual gap might be bridged. First, if the employer "used a biased testing procedure . . . ." Id. at 159, n. 15. Second, "[s]ignificant proof that an employer operated under a general policy of discrimination conceivably could justify a class of both applicants and employees if the discrimination manifested itself in hiring and promotion practices in the same general fashion, such as through entirely subjective decisionmaking processes." *Ibid.* We think that statement precisely describes respondents' burden in this case. The first manner of bridging the gap obviously has no application here; Wal-Mart has no testing procedure or other companywide evaluation method that can be charged with bias. The whole point of permitting discretionary decisionmaking is to avoid evaluating employees under a common standard.

The second manner of bridging the gap requires "significant proof" that Wal-Mart "operated under a general policy of discrimination." That is entirely absent here. Wal-Mart's announced policy forbids sex discrimination, and as the District Court recognized the company imposes penalties for denials of equal employment opportunity, 222 F.R.D., at 154. The only evidence of a "general policy of discrimination" respondents produced was the testimony of Dr. William Bielby, their sociological expert. Relying on "social framework" analysis, Bielby testified that Wal-Mart has a "strong corporate culture," that makes it " 'vulnerable' " to "gender bias." Id. at 152. He could not, however, "determine with any specificity how regularly stereotypes play a meaningful role in employment decisions at Wal-Mart. At his deposition . . . Dr. Bielby conceded that he could not calculate whether 0.5 percent or 95 percent of the employment decisions at Wal-Mart might be determined by stereotyped thinking." 222 F.R.D. 189, 192 (N.D. Cal. 2004). The parties dispute whether Bielby's testimony even met the standards for the admission of expert testimony under Federal Rule of Evidence 702 and our *Daubert* case, see *Daubert v. Merrell Dow Pharmaceuticals, Inc.*, 509 U.S. 579. The District Court concluded that *Daubert* did not apply to expert testimony at the certification stage of class-action proceedings. 222 F.R.D., at 191. We doubt that is so, but even if

continuation of the discriminatory practice." *Teamsters, supra,* at 361.

properly considered, Bielby's testimony does nothing to advance respondents' case. "[W]hether 0.5 percent or 95 percent of the employment decisions at Wal-Mart might be determined by stereotyped thinking" is the essential question on which respondents' theory of commonality depends. If Bielby admittedly has no answer to that question, we can safely disregard what he has to say. It is worlds away from "significant proof" that Wal-Mart "operated under a general policy of discrimination."

C

The only corporate policy that the plaintiffs' evidence convincingly establishes is Wal-Mart's "policy" of *allowing discretion* by local supervisors over employment matters. On its face, of course, that is just the opposite of a uniform employment practice that would provide the commonality needed for a class action; it is a policy *against having* uniform employment practices. It is also a very common and presumptively reasonable way of doing business—one that we have said "should itself raise no inference of discriminatory conduct," *Watson v. Fort Worth Bank & Trust*, 487 U.S. 977, 990 (1988).

To be sure, we have recognized that, "in appropriate cases," giving discretion to lower-level supervisors can be the basis of Title VII liability under a disparate-impact theory—since "an employer's undisciplined system of subjective decision-making [can have] precisely the same effects as a system pervaded by impermissible intentional discrimination." Id. at 990–991. But the recognition that this type of Title VII claim "can" exist does not lead to the conclusion that every employee in a company using a system of discretion has such a claim in common. To the contrary, left to their own devices most managers in any corporation—and surely most managers in a corporation that forbids sex discrimination—would select sex-neutral, performance-based criteria for hiring and promotion that produce no actionable disparity at all. Others may choose to reward various attributes that produce disparate impact—such as scores on general aptitude tests or educational achievements, see *Griggs v. Duke Power Co.*, 401 U.S. 424, 431–432 (1971). And still other managers may be guilty of intentional discrimination that produces a sex-based disparity. In such a company, demonstrating the invalidity of one manager's use of discretion will do nothing to demonstrate the invalidity of another's. A party seeking to certify a nationwide class will be unable to show that all the employees' Title VII claims will in fact depend on the answers to common questions.

Respondents have not identified a common mode of exercising discretion that pervades the entire company—aside from their reliance on Dr. Bielby's social frameworks analysis that we have rejected. In a company of Wal-Mart's size and geographical scope, it is quite unbelievable that all managers would exercise their discretion in a common way without some common direction. Respondents attempt to make that showing by means of statistical and anecdotal evidence, but their evidence falls well short.

The statistical evidence consists primarily of regression analyses performed by Dr. Richard Drogin, a statistician, and Dr. Marc Bendick, a labor economist. Drogin conducted his analysis region-by-region, comparing the number of women promoted into management positions with the percentage of women in the available pool of hourly workers. After considering regional and national data, Drogin concluded that "there are statistically significant disparities between men and women at Wal-Mart . . . [and] these disparities . . . can be explained only by gender discrimination." 603 F.3d, at 604. Bendick compared workforce data from Wal-Mart and competitive retailers and concluded that Wal-Mart "promotes a lower percentage of women than its competitors." *Ibid.*

Even if they are taken at face value, these studies are insufficient to establish that respondents' theory can be proved on a classwide basis . . . . As Judge Ikuta observed in her dissent, "[i]nformation about disparities at the regional and national level does not establish the existence of disparities at individual stores, let alone raise the inference that a company-wide policy of discrimination is implemented by discretionary decisions at the store and district level." 603 F.3d, at 637. A regional pay disparity, for example, may be attributable to only a small set of Wal-Mart stores, and cannot by itself establish the uniform, store-by-store disparity upon which the plaintiffs' theory of commonality depends.

There is another, more fundamental, respect in which respondents' statistical proof fails. Even if it established (as it does not) a pay or promotion pattern that differs from the nationwide figures or the regional figures in *all* of Wal-Mart's 3,400 stores, that would still not demonstrate that commonality of issue exists. Some managers will claim that the availability of women, or qualified women, or interested women, in their stores' area does not mirror the national or regional statistics. And almost all of them will claim to have been applying some sex-neutral, performance-based criteria—whose nature and effects will differ from store to store. In the landmark case of ours which held that giving discretion to lower-level supervisors can be the basis of Title VII liability under a disparate-impact theory, the plurality opinion *conditioned* that holding on the corollary that merely proving that the discretionary system has produced a racial or sexual disparity *is not enough*. "[T]he plaintiff must begin by identifying the specific employment practice that is challenged." *Watson*, 487 U.S., at 994; accord, *Wards Cove Packing Co. v. Atonio*, 490 U.S. 642, 656 (1989) (approving that statement), superseded by statute on other grounds, 42 U.S.C. § 2000e-2(k). That is all the more necessary when a class of plaintiffs is sought to be certified. Other than the bare existence of delegated discretion, respondents have identified no "specific employment practice"—much less one that ties all their 1.5 million claims together. Merely showing that Wal-Mart's policy of discretion has produced an overall sex-based disparity does not suffice.

Respondents' anecdotal evidence suffers from the same defects, and in addition is too weak to raise any inference that all the individual, discretionary personnel decisions are discriminatory. In *Teamsters v. United States*, 431 U.S. 324 (1977), in addition to substantial statistical evidence of company-wide discrimination, the Government (as plaintiff) produced about 40 specific accounts of racial discrimination from particular individuals. See *id.* at 338. That number was significant because the company involved had only 6,472 employees, of whom 571 were minorities, *id.* at 337, and the class itself consisted of around 334 persons, *United States v. T.I.M.E.-D. C.*, Inc., 517 F.2d 299, 308 (CA5 1975), overruled on other grounds, *Teamsters, supra*. The 40 anecdotes thus represented roughly one account for every eight members of the class . . . . Here, by contrast, respondents filed some 120 affidavits reporting experiences of discrimination—about 1 for every 12,500 class members—relating to only some 235 out of Wal-Mart's 3,400 stores. 603 F.3d, at 634 (Ikuta, J., dissenting). More than half of these reports are concentrated in only six States (Alabama, California, Florida, Missouri, Texas, and Wisconsin); half of all States have only one or two anecdotes; and 14 States have no anecdotes about Wal-Mart's operations at all. *Id.* at 634–635, and n. 10. Even if every single one of these accounts is true, that would not demonstrate that the entire company "operate[s] under a general policy of discrimination," *Falcon, supra,* at 159, n. 15. . . .

In sum, we agree with Chief Judge Kozinski that the members of the class:

> "held a multitude of different jobs, at different levels of Wal-Mart's hierarchy, for variable lengths of time, in 3,400 stores, sprinkled across 50 states, with a kaleidoscope of supervisors (male and female), subject to a variety of regional policies that all differed . . . . Some thrived while others did poorly. They have little in common but their sex and this lawsuit." 603 F.3d, at 652 (dissenting opinion).

. . . .

The judgment of the Court of Appeals is reversed.

JUSTICE GINSBURG, with whom JUSTICE BREYER, JUSTICE SOTOMAYOR, and JUSTICE KAGAN join, concurring in part and dissenting in part.

. . . Rule 23(a)(2) establishes a preliminary requirement for maintaining a class action: "[T]here are questions of law or fact common to the class." The Rule "does not require that all questions of law or fact raised in the litigation be common," 1 H. Newberg & A. Conte, Newberg on Class Actions § 3.10, pp. 3-48 to 3-49 (3d ed. 1992); indeed, "[e]ven a single question of law or fact common to the members of the class will satisfy the commonality requirement," Nagareda, *The Preexistence Principle and the Structure of the Class Action,* 103 COLUM. L. REV. 149, 176, n. 110 (2003).

The District Court, recognizing that "one significant issue common to the class may be sufficient to warrant certification," 222 F.R.D. 137, 145 (N.D. Cal. 2004), found that the plaintiffs easily met that test. . . .

The District Court certified a class of "[a]ll women employed at any Wal-Mart domestic retail store at any time since December 26, 1998." 222 F.R.D., at 141–143 (internal quotation marks omitted). The named plaintiffs, led by Betty Dukes, propose to litigate, on behalf of the class, allegations that Wal-Mart discriminates on the basis of gender in pay and promotions. They allege that the company "[r]eli[es] on gender stereotypes in making employment decisions such as . . . promotion[s] [and] pay." App. 55a. Wal-Mart permits those prejudices to infect personnel decisions, the plaintiffs contend, by leaving pay and promotions in the hands of "a nearly all male managerial workforce" using "arbitrary and subjective criteria." *Ibid.* Further alleged barriers to the advancement of female employees include the company's requirement, "as a condition of promotion to management jobs, that employees be willing to relocate." *Id.* at 56a. Absent instruction otherwise, there is a risk that managers will act on the familiar assumption that women, because of their services to husband and children, are less mobile than men. *See* Dept. of Labor, *Federal Glass Ceiling Commission, Good for Business: Making Full Use of the Nation's Human Capital* 151 (1995).

Women fill 70 percent of the hourly jobs in the retailer's stores but make up only "33 percent of management employees." 222 F.R.D., at 146. "[T]he higher one looks in the organization the lower the percentage of women." Id. at 155. The plaintiffs' "largely uncontested descriptive statistics" also show that women working in the company's stores "are paid less than men in every region" and "that the salary gap widens over time even for men and women hired into the same jobs at the same time." *Ibid.*

The District Court identified "systems for . . . promoting in-store employees" that were "sufficiently similar across regions and stores" to conclude that "the manner in which these systems affect the class raises issues that are common to all class members." 222 F.R.D., at 149. The selection of employees for promotion to in-store management "is fairly characterized as a 'tap on the shoulder' process," in which managers have discretion about whose shoulders to tap. Id. at 148. Vacancies are not regularly posted; from among those employees satisfying minimum qualifications, managers choose whom to promote on the basis of their own subjective impressions. *Ibid.*

Wal-Mart's compensation policies also operate uniformly across stores, the District Court found. The retailer leaves open a $2 band for every position's hourly pay rate. Wal-Mart provides no standards or criteria for setting wages within that band, and thus does nothing to counter unconscious bias on the part of supervisors. See *id.* at 146–147.

Wal-Mart's supervisors do not make their discretionary decisions in a vacuum. The District Court reviewed means Wal-Mart used to maintain a "carefully constructed . . . corporate culture," such as frequent meetings to reinforce the common way of thinking, regular transfers of managers between stores to ensure uniformity throughout the company, monitoring of stores "on a close and constant basis," and "Wal-Mart TV," "broadcas[t] . . . into all stores." Id. at 151–153.

The plaintiffs' evidence, including class members' tales of their own experiences, suggests that gender bias suffused Wal-Mart's company culture. Among illustrations, senior management often refer to female associates as "little Janie Qs." Plaintiffs' Motion for Class Certification in No. 3:01-CV-02252-CRB (ND Cal.), Doc. 99, p. 13. One manager told an employee that "[m]en are here to make a career and women aren't." 222 F.R.D., at 166. A committee of female Wal-Mart executives concluded that "[s]tereotypes limit the opportunities offered to women." Plaintiffs' Motion for Class Certification in No. 3:01-CV-02252-CRB (ND Cal.), Doc. 99, at 16.

Finally, the plaintiffs presented an expert's appraisal to show that the pay and promotions disparities at Wal-Mart "can be explained only by gender discrimination and not by . . . neutral variables." 222 F.R.D., at 155. Using regression analyses, their expert, Richard Drogin, controlled for factors including, *inter alia*, job performance, length of time with the company, and the store where an employee worked. *Id.* at 159. The results, the District Court found, were sufficient to raise an "inference of discrimination." *Id.* at 155–160.

The District Court's identification of a common question, whether Wal-Mart's pay and promotions policies gave rise to unlawful discrimination, was hardly infirm. The practice of delegating to supervisors large discretion to make personnel decisions, uncontrolled by formal standards, has long been known to have the potential to produce disparate effects. Managers, like all humankind, may be prey to biases of which they are unaware.[5] The risk of discrimination is heightened when those managers are predominantly of one sex, and are steeped in a corporate culture that perpetuates gender stereotypes.

. . . The plaintiffs' allegations state claims of gender discrimination in the form of biased decisionmaking in both pay and promotions. The evidence reviewed by the District Court adequately demonstrated that resolving those claims would necessitate examination of particular policies and practices alleged to affect, adversely and globally, women employed at Wal-Mart's stores. Rule 23(a)(2), setting a necessary but not a sufficient criterion for class-action certification, demands nothing further.

. . . .

Wal-Mart's delegation of discretion over pay and promotions is a policy uniform throughout all stores. The very nature of discretion is that people will exercise it in various ways. A system of delegated discretion, *Watson* held, is a practice actionable under Title VII when it produces discriminatory outcomes. 487 U.S., at 990–991. A finding that Wal-Mart's pay and promotions practices in fact violate the law would be the first step in the usual order of proof for plaintiffs seeking individual remedies for company-wide discrimination. *Teamsters v. United States*, 431 U.S. 324, 359 (1977). That each individual employee's unique circumstances will ultimately determine whether she is entitled to backpay or damages, § 2000e-5(g)(2)(A) (barring backpay if a plaintiff "was refused . . . advancement . . . for any reason other than discrimination"), should not factor into the Rule 23(a)(2) determination.

NOTES

1. **Class Certification**. Although the *Wal-Mart* case was decided on a Motion relating to class certification, there was considerable discussion regarding how a pattern and practice case might be proved. What message might you draw from the case regarding the proof the Supreme Court might require to establish a pattern and practice claim? Do you think the Court's view of the merits of the underlying claims influenced its decision? If so, is there something in the opinion you can point

---

[5] [n. 6] An example vividly illustrates how subjective decisionmaking can be a vehicle for discrimination. Performing in symphony orchestras was long a male preserve. Goldin and Rouse, *Orchestrating Impartiality: The Impact of "Blind" Auditions on Female Musicians*, 90 AM. ECON. REV. 715, 715–716 (2000). In the 1970's orchestras began hiring musicians through auditions open to all comers. *Id.* at 716. Reviewers were to judge applicants solely on their musical abilities, yet subconscious bias led some reviewers to disfavor women. Orchestras that permitted reviewers to see the applicants hired far fewer female musicians than orchestras that conducted blind auditions, in which candidates played behind opaque screens. *Id.* at 738.

to that reflects the Court's views? One thing seems clear, the Court made it more difficult to certify a pattern and practice claim as a class action. For a discussion of the class certification implications, see Melissa Hart, *Civil Rights and Systemic Wrongs*, 32 BERKELEY J. EMP. & LAB. L. 455 (2011).

2. The Effect on Pattern or Practice Claims. It is difficult to predict the ultimate effect of the *Wal-Mart* decision on employment discrimination cases. The Fourth Circuit, for example, recently reversed a district court's decision denying leave to amend a class action complaint base on the lower court's "erroneous" reading of the Wal-Mart decision. *See Scott v. Family Dollar Stores*, 733 F.3d 105 (4th Cir. 2014), *cert. denied*, 134 S. Ct. 2871 (2014). Nevertheless, given the Court's relatively hostile treatment of the plaintiffs' evidence, the decision may force plaintiffs' attorneys to create more distinctive cases, ones that offer a clear theory that is applicable to the defendants' practices. One problem with the case the *Wal-Mart* plaintiffs offered is that it had a fairly generic quality to it, and relied, perhaps excessively, on the power of statistics to establish discrimination. In light of the Court's decision in *Wal-Mart*, Michael Selmi has observed: "[I]t now appears that plaintiffs must demonstrate that the employer's actions—actions for which the employer is blameworthy—caused the imbalance or underrepresentation, a determination that will typically require proof beyond statistics, no matter how powerful the statistical analysis might be." Michael Selmi, *Theorizing Systemic Disparate Treatment After Wal-Mart v. Dukes*, 32 BERKELEY J. EMP. & LABOR L. 477, 479 (2011). The size of the *Wal-Mart* case was obviously problematic in a number of respects. As a result, the attorneys who represented the plaintiffs in the original litigation have filed a series of smaller regional cases. To date, the class allegations raised in most of the cases have been dismissed. *See Dukes v. Wal-Mart Stores, Inc.*, 964 F. Supp. 2d 1115 (N.D. Cal. 2013) (smaller class dismissed); *Love v. Wal-Mart Stores*, 2013 U.S. Dist. LEXIS 143234 (S.D. Fla. Sept. 23, 2013); *Phipps v. Wal-Mart Stores*, 925 F. Supp. 2d 875 (M.D. Tenn. 2013).

3. Social Framework Evidence. In its decision, the Supreme Court was quite critical of the plaintiff's "social framework" evidence. This kind of evidence has been controversial but it has also played an important role in establishing patterns of discrimination that may not be tied to a single actor or even a group of individual actors. Although sociologists provide the social framework testimony, the term derives its meaning from the legal actions and is not a term that is used within sociology. In its most basic sense, social framework evidence provides a framework to explain how systemic discrimination permeates institutional organizations and workplaces. In the *Wal-Mart* case, the evidence focused primarily on how subjective employment practices can lead to discriminatory results based on stereotypical notions of who might make the best manager or based on the presumed conflicts women's schedules might present. The difficulty with applying the evidence to a particular workplace is that the framework itself is generic in nature—it explains research findings but does not involve any analysis or investigation of a particular workplace, other than to say that a workplace, like Wal-Mart's, has the characteristics that can lead to discrimination based on the research findings. This led to the plaintiffs' expert's admission that he was unable to say more than that Wal-Mart's system was "vulnerable" to discrimination and was unable to quantify just how vulnerable it might have been. For a discussion of social framework evidence and its limitations, see Melissa Hart & Paul M. Secunda, *A Matter of Social Framework Evidence in Employment Discrimination Class Actions*, 78 FORDHAM L. REV. 37 (2009) (discussing importance of social framework evidence to establishing systemic discrimination) and Gregory Mitchell, Laurens Walker & John Monahan, *Beyond Context: Social Facts as Case-Specific Evidence*, 60 EMORY L.J. 1109 (2011) (criticizing introduction of social framework evidence). The Supreme Court's criticism of the social framework evidence offered by the plaintiffs is likely to restrict this kind of evidence in future cases. How else might a plaintiff go about establishing discrimination based on subjective practices across an organization? What about in the case of Wal-Mart, what do you think might have helped persuade the Court that there were common questions to link the class claims?

b.　The BFOQ Defense

Pattern or practice cases require proof of intent through circumstantial evidence, but there is another kind of class claim that generally does not require proof of intent at all. In these cases, the employer's practice is facially discriminatory in that it treats women, or others such as the aged, differently and there is no question that the employer has an intent to discriminate. For example, in an early case of this nature, the Alabama prison system refused to hire women to work in contact positions in male prisons. *See Dothard v. Rawlinson*, 433 U.S. 321 (1977). Here there was no question that the employer was treating women differently, the question was whether the practice could be defended consistent with Title VII.

Under Title VII, an employer can defend a classification based on sex, national origin, religion or age, by establishing that the classification is a bona fide occupational qualification ("BFOQ"). *See* 42 U.S.C. § 2000e-2(c). In essence, this defense allows an employer to determine that sex, or one of the other classifications, is reasonably necessary to the efficient operation of the business so that women would be unable to perform the job properly. The Supreme Court has always read this defense narrowly, and it is generally quite difficult for an employer to prevail on the defense.

For example, in *UAW v. Johnson Controls, Inc.*, 499 U.S. 187 (1991), the Supreme Court considered whether it was permissible for an employer that manufactured batteries to exclude women who were capable of having children from positions that involved high levels of exposure to lead. The Court found that the policy was facially discriminatory even though it did not apply to all women. *Id.* at 197. ("The policy excludes women with childbearing capacity from lead-exposed jobs and so creates a facial classification based on gender.") In general, singling out women due to pregnancy or potential pregnancy constitutes sex discrimination under Title VII (an issue discussed further in Chapter 10.) As a result, the policy could only be justified under the narrow BFOQ defense, and here the Court rejected the employer's concern for protecting the health of the fetus as unrelated to the employers' business interests. The Court concluded: *Id.* at 206.

> [T]he language of both the BFOQ provision and the PDA [Pregnancy Discrimination Act] which amended it, as well as the legislative history and the case law, prohibit an employer from discriminating against a woman because of her capacity to become pregnant unless her reproductive

potential prevents her from performing the duties of her job.

Id. at 206.

In *Johnson Controls*, the Court specifically stated that "[t]he BFOQ defense is written narrowly, and this Court has read it narrowly," *id.* at 201, and courts have generally been reluctant to permit employers to justify their policies as reasonably necessary to the essence of the business. One of the Court's first cases on the defense involved an exclusion of women from working in male prisons in Alabama where they would have contact with the inmates. *See Dothard v. Rawlinson*, 433 U.S. 321 (1977). In *Dothard*, the Court ultimately upheld the exclusion as a BFOQ at least in significant part because of the nature of the prisons where sex offenders were housed in the general population, and the prison documented that female correctional officers would likely be at risk of assault from these and other inmates. *Id.* at 335. How can this situation be distinguished from *Johnson Controls*? Is it that the nature of the enterprise in the prison context is to protect the third party, namely the inmates? Despite the outcome in *Dothard*, courts have typically invalidated broad exclusions of women from working in male prisons when accommodations could be made in job assignments to protect legitimate inmate privacy concerns. *See Gunther v. Iowa State Men*'s Reformatory, 612 F.2d 1079 (8th Cir. 1980); *Hardin v. Stynchcomb*, 691 F.2d 1364 (11th Cir. 1982); *United States v. Gregory*, 818 F.2d 1114 (4th Cir. 1987). Despite the history of litigation over gender-specific assignments, correctional facilities continue to impose restrictions, and under certain circumstances those restrictions can be upheld to the extent the facility offers a substantial justification. *Compare Henry v. Milwaukee County*, 539 F.3d 573 (7th Cir. 2008) (holding that the County had failed to justify sex-specific assignments in a juvenile detention facility) *with Everson v. Michigan Dept. of Corrections*, 391 F.3d 737 (6th Cir. 2004), *cert. denied*, 546 U.S. 825 (2005) (upholding ban on male officers in female prisons following widespread sexual abuse of female prisoners by male officers). *But see Ambat v. City and County of San Francisco*, 757 F.3d 1017 (9th Cir. 2014) (reversing grant of summary judgment for county and remanding for further determination whether a prohibition of male deputies supervising female inmates satisfies BFOQ standard).

Some of the other cases that have succeeded under a BFOQ affirmative defense have involved privacy of third parties or where gender assignments were seen as necessary to further particular treatment. *See Healey v. Southwood Psychiatric Hosp.*, 78 F.3d 128 (3d Cir. 1996) (upholding sex-based assignments for hospital that treated abused patients); *Backus v. Baptist Medical Center*, 510 F. Supp. 1191 (E.D. Ark. 1981), *vacated as moot*, 671 F.2d 1100 (8th Cir. 1982) (upholding exclusion of male nurses from labor and delivery room).

One of the most well-known cases involving a BFOQ defense concerned Southwest Airline's attempt to hire only women as flight attendants in order to present an image of the "love airline" as a way of appealing to its male clientele. In *Wilson v. Southwest Airlines Co.*, 517 F. Supp. 292 (N.D. Tex. 1981), the district court rejected Southwest's defense, concluding that sex was not essential to the company's primary business of transporting "passengers safely and quickly." *Id.* at 302. The court explained, "[S]ex does not become a BFOQ merely because an employer chooses to exploit female sexuality as a marketing tool, or to better insure profitability." *Id.* at 303. The court also rejected Southwest's claim that the essence of its business was "to make a profit" (*id.* at 302 n.25) reaffirming the notion that it is not a defense to a claim under Title VII that discrimination is profitable or cheaper than a nondiscriminatory policy would be.

The BFOQ defense has also arisen in age discrimination cases. In *Western Air Lines v. Criswell*, 472 U.S. 400 (1985), the Supreme Court considered an airline's rule that required flight engineers to retire at age 60. Flight engineers are the third officer in the cockpit, and pursuant to a rule promulgated by the Federal Aviation Administration, pilots were required to retire at age 60, and the airline sought to extend that rule to flight engineers. In the context of an age discrimination challenge, the Court articulated two distinct ways in which an employer might justify its rule as a BFOQ: (1) by establishing a factual basis "for believing that all, or substantially all, [persons over the age qualification] would be unable to perform safely and efficiently the duties of the job involved," *Id.* at 414, or (2) by establishing "age was a legitimate proxy for the safety-related job qualifications by proving it is 'impossible' or 'highly impractical' to deal with older employees on an individualized basis," *Id.* The Court held that the airline had failed to satisfy either standard.

C.   DISPARATE IMPACT CLAIMS AND THEIR RELATION TO OTHER THEORIES OF DISCRIMINATION

GRIGGS v. DUKE POWER CO.
United States Supreme Court
401 U.S. 424 (1971)

MR. CHIEF JUSTICE BURGER delivered the opinion of the Court.

We granted the writ in this case to resolve the question whether an employer is prohibited by the Civil Rights Act of 1964, Title VII, from requiring a high school education or passing of a standardized general intelligence test as a condition of employment in or transfer to jobs when (a) neither standard is shown to be significantly related to successful job performance, (b) both requirements operate to disqualify Negroes at a substantially higher rate than white applicants, and (c) the jobs in question formerly had been filled only by white employees as part of a longstanding practice of giving preference to whites.

Congress provided, in Title VII of the Civil Rights Act of 1964, for class actions for enforcement of provisions of the Act and this proceeding was brought by a group of incumbent Negro employees against Duke Power Company. All the petitioners are employed at the Company's Dan River Steam Station, a power generating facility located at Draper, North Carolina. At the time this action was instituted, the Company had 95 employees at the Dan River Station, 14 of whom were Negroes; 13 of these are petitioners here.

The District Court found that prior to July 2, 1965, the effective date of the Civil Rights Act of 1964, the Company openly discriminated on the basis of race in the hiring and assigning of employees at its Dan River plant. The plant was organized into five operating departments: (1) Labor, (2) Coal Handling, (3) Operations, (4)

Maintenance, and (5) Laboratory and Test. Negroes were employed only in the Labor Department where the highest paying jobs paid less than the lowest paying jobs in the other four "operating" departments in which only whites were employed. Promotions were normally made within each department on the basis of job seniority. Transferees into a department usually began in the lowest position.

In 1955 the Company instituted a policy of requiring a high school education for initial assignment to any department except Labor, and for transfer from the Coal Handling to any "inside" department (Operations, Maintenance, or Laboratory). When the Company abandoned its policy of restricting Negroes to the Labor Department in 1965, completion of high school also was made a prerequisite to transfer from Labor to any other department. From the time the high school requirement was instituted to the time of trial, however, white employees hired before the time of the high school education requirement continued to perform satisfactorily and achieve promotions in the "operating" departments. Findings on this score are not challenged.

The Company added a further requirement for new employees on July 2, 1965, the date on which Title VII became effective. To qualify for placement in any but the Labor Department it became necessary to register satisfactory scores on two professionally prepared aptitude tests, as well as to have a high school education. Completion of high school alone continued to render employees eligible for transfer to the four desirable departments from which Negroes had been excluded if the incumbent had been employed prior to the time of the new requirement. In September 1965 the Company began to permit incumbent employees who lacked a high school education to qualify for transfer from Labor or Coal Handling to an "inside" job by passing two tests—the Wonderlic Personnel Test, which purports to measure general intelligence, and the Bennett Mechanical Comprehension Test. Neither was directed or intended to measure the ability to learn to perform a particular job or category of jobs. The requisite scores used for both initial hiring and transfer approximated the national median for high school graduates.

The District Court had found that while the Company previously followed a policy of overt racial discrimination in a period prior to the Act, such conduct had ceased. The District Court also concluded that Title VII was intended to be prospective only and, consequently, the impact of prior inequities was beyond the reach of corrective action authorized by the Act.

The Court of Appeals was confronted with a question of first impression, as are we, concerning the meaning of Title VII. After careful analysis a majority of that court concluded that a subjective test of the employer's intent should govern, particularly in a close case, and that in this case there was no showing of a discriminatory purpose in the adoption of the diploma and test requirements. On this basis, the Court of Appeals concluded there was no violation of the Act. . . . In so doing, the Court of Appeals rejected the claim that because these two requirements operated to render ineligible a markedly disproportionate number of Negroes, they were unlawful under Title VII unless shown to be job related. We granted the writ on these claims. 399 U.S. 926.

The objective of Congress in the enactment of Title VII is plain from the language of the statute. It was to achieve equality of employment opportunities and remove barriers that have operated in the past to favor an identifiable group of white employees over other employees. Under the Act, practices, procedures, or tests neutral on their face, and even neutral in terms of intent, cannot be maintained if they operate to "freeze" the status quo of prior discriminatory employment practices.

The Court of Appeals' opinion, and the partial dissent, agreed that, on the record in the present case, "whites register far better on the Company's alternative requirements" than Negroes.[6] 420 F.2d 1225, 1239 n. 6. This consequence would appear to be directly traceable to race. Basic intelligence must have the means of articulation to manifest itself fairly in a testing process. Because they are Negroes, petitioners have long received inferior education in segregated schools and this Court expressly recognized these differences in Gaston County v. United States, 395 U.S. 285 (1969). There, because of the inferior education received by Negroes in North Carolina, this Court barred the institution of a literacy test for voter registration on the ground that the test would abridge the right to vote indirectly on account of race. Congress did not intend by Title VII, however, to guarantee a job to every person regardless of qualifications. In short, the Act does not command that any person be hired simply because he was formerly the subject of discrimination, or because he is a member of a minority group. Discriminatory preference for any group, minority or majority, is precisely and only what Congress has proscribed. What is required by Congress is the removal of artificial, arbitrary, and unnecessary barriers to employment when the barriers operate invidiously to discriminate on the basis of racial or other impermissible classification.

Congress has now provided that tests or criteria for employment or promotion may not provide equality of opportunity merely in the sense of the fabled offer of milk to the stork and the fox. On the contrary, Congress has now required that the posture and condition of the job-seeker be taken into account. It has—to resort again to the fable—provided that the vessel in which the milk is proffered be one all seekers can use. The Act proscribes not only overt discrimination but also practices that are fair in form, but discriminatory in operation. The touchstone is business necessity. If an employment practice which operates to exclude Negroes cannot be shown to be related to job performance, the practice is prohibited.

On the record before us, neither the high school completion requirement nor the general intelligence test is shown to bear a demonstrable relationship to successful performance of the jobs for which it was used. Both were adopted, as the Court of Appeals noted, without meaningful study of their relationship to job-performance ability. Rather, a vice president of the Company testified, the requirements were instituted on the Company's judgment that they generally would improve the overall quality of the work force.

---

[6] [n. 6] In North Carolina, 1960 census statistics show that, while 34% of white males had completed high school, only 12% of Negro males had done so. U.S. Bureau of the Census, U.S. Census of Population: 1960, Vol. 1, Characteristics of the Population, pt. 35, Table 47. Similarly, with respect to standardized tests, the EEOC in one case found that use of a battery of tests, including the Wonderlic and Bennett tests used by the Company in the instant case, resulted in 58% of whites passing the tests, as compared with only 6% of the blacks. Decision of EEOC, CCH Empl. Prac. Guide, para. 17,304.53 (Dec. 2, 1966). See also Decision of EEOC 70-552, CCH Empl. Prac. Guide, para. 6139 (Feb. 19, 1970).

The evidence, however, shows that employees who have not completed high school or taken the tests have continued to perform satisfactorily and make progress in departments for which the high school and test criteria are now used. The promotion record of present employees who would not be able to meet the new criteria thus suggests the possibility that the requirements may not be needed even for the limited purpose of preserving the avowed policy of advancement within the Company. In the context of this case, it is unnecessary to reach the question whether testing requirements that take into account capability for the next succeeding position or related future promotion might be utilized upon a showing that such long-range requirements fulfill a genuine business need. In the present case the Company has made no such showing.

The Court of Appeals held that the Company had adopted the diploma and test requirements without any "intention to discriminate against Negro employees." 420 F.2d, at 1232. We do not suggest that either the District Court or the Court of Appeals erred in examining the employer's intent; but good intent or absence of discriminatory intent does not redeem employment procedures or testing mechanisms that operate as "built-in headwinds" for minority groups and are unrelated to measuring job capability.

The Company's lack of discriminatory intent is suggested by special efforts to help the undereducated employees through Company financing of two-thirds the cost of tuition for high school training. But Congress directed the thrust of the Act to the *consequences* of employment practices, not simply the motivation. More than that, Congress has placed on the employer the burden of showing that any given requirement must have a manifest relationship to the employment in question.

The facts of this case demonstrate the inadequacy of broad and general testing devices as well as the infirmity of using diplomas or degrees as fixed measures of capability. History is filled with examples of men and women who rendered highly effective performance without the conventional badges of accomplishment in terms of certificates, diplomas, or degrees. Diplomas and tests are useful servants, but Congress has mandated the commonsense proposition that they are not to become masters of reality.

The Company contends that its general intelligence tests are specifically permitted by § 703(h) of the Act. That section authorizes the use of "any professionally developed ability test" that is not "designed, intended *or used* to discriminate because of race . . . ." (Emphasis added.)

The Equal Employment Opportunity Commission, having enforcement responsibility, has issued guidelines interpreting § 703(h) to permit only the use of job-related tests. The administrative interpretation of the Act by the enforcing agency is entitled to great deference. See, *e. g., United States v. City of Chicago,* 400 U.S. 8 (1970). Since the Act and its legislative history support the Commission's construction, this affords good reason to treat the guidelines as expressing the will of Congress.

Section 703(h) was not contained in the House version of the Civil Rights Act but was added in the Senate during extended debate. For a period, debate revolved around claims that the bill as proposed would prohibit all testing and force employers to hire unqualified persons simply because they were part of a group formerly subject to job discrimination.[7] Proponents of Title VII sought throughout the debate to assure the critics that the Act would have no effect on job-related tests. . . . Despite these assurances, Senator Tower of Texas introduced an amendment authorizing "professionally developed ability tests." Proponents of Title VII opposed the amendment because, as written, it would permit an employer to give any test, "whether it was a good test or not, so long as it was professionally designed. Discrimination could actually exist under the guise of compliance with the statute." 110 Cong. Rec. 13504 (remarks of Sen. Case).

The amendment was defeated and two days later Senator Tower offered a substitute amendment which was adopted verbatim and is now the testing provision of § 703(h). Speaking for the supporters of Title VII, Senator Humphrey, who had vigorously opposed the first amendment, endorsed the substitute amendment, stating: "Senators on both sides of the aisle who were deeply interested in Title VII have examined the text of this amendment and have found it to be in accord with the intent and purpose of that title." 110 Cong. Rec. 13724. The amendment was then adopted. From the sum of the legislative history relevant in this case, the conclusion is inescapable that the EEOC's construction of § 703(h) to require that employment tests be job related comports with congressional intent.

Nothing in the Act precludes the use of testing or measuring procedures; obviously they are useful. What Congress has forbidden is giving these devices and mechanisms controlling force unless they are demonstrably a reasonable measure of job performance. Congress has not commanded that the less qualified be preferred over the better qualified simply because of minority origins. Far from disparaging job qualifications as such, Congress has made such qualifications the controlling factor, so that race, religion, nationality, and sex become irrelevant. What Congress has commanded is that any tests used must measure the person for the job and not the person in the abstract.

The judgment of the Court of Appeals is, as to that portion of the judgment appealed from, reversed.

MR. JUSTICE BRENNAN took no part in the consideration or decision of this case.

NOTES

1. **Understanding *Griggs*.** The *Griggs* case was a landmark decision that has had an influence on the law that is difficult to overestimate. What was the Court's rationale for permitting disparate impact challenges? It seems clear that the language of Title VII did not mandate a disparate impact cause of action, and

---

[7] [n. 10] The congressional discussion was prompted by the decision of a hearing examiner for the Illinois Fair Employment Commission in *Myart v. Motorola Co.* (The decision is reprinted at 110 Cong. Rec. 5662.) That case suggested that standardized tests on which whites performed better than Negroes could never be used. The decision was taken to mean that such tests could never be justified even if the needs of the business required them. A number of Senators feared that Title VII might produce a similar result. See remarks of Senators Ervin, 110 Cong. Rec. 5614–5616; Smathers, *id.*, at 5999–6000; Holland, *id.*, at 7012–7013; Hill, *id.*, at 8447 . . . .

arguably, the Tower Amendment the Court discusses in its opinion was intended to insulate professionally developed tests from legal challenges. *See* Michael Evan Gold, Griggs, *Folly: An Essay on the Theory, Problems, and Origin of the Adverse Impact Definition of Employment Discrimination and a Recommendation for Reform*, 7 INDUS. REL. L.J. 429 (1985). In its opinion, the Court also notes that African Americans were disadvantaged by the inferior education the state of North Carolina had provided, but should an employer be held responsible for that deficient education or be required to remedy it?

2. *Griggs* as a Form of Intentional Discrimination. One scholar has suggested that although the disparate impact theory does not require proof of intent, it is actually a means of proving intentional discrimination that is simply too difficult to prove through the traditional methods of proof. *See* George Rutherglen, *Disparate Impact Under Title VII: An Objective Theory of Discrimination*, 73 VA. L. REV. 1297 (1987). The *Griggs* case itself offers some support for this theory given that some of the employer's new qualifications were implemented on the day Title VII became effective, although the employer explained this curious fact by noting that only at that point did it become necessary to ensure that all of its employees were qualified for the positions, given that African Americans had generally received less and inferior education but had previously been excluded from most skilled jobs. You should consider this argument as you explore the cases discussed in the following notes, in particular, how the disparate impact theory might be used to uncover covert intentional discrimination.

3. The Disparate Impact Proof Structure. Most commonly, disparate impact claims involve class claims, and they are also most commonly used to challenge objective employment practices such as written examinations. As discussed in this note, the standard established in *Griggs* has been elaborated upon in a number of cases, and ultimately was codified in Title VII through the Civil Rights Act of 1991.

The test announced in *Griggs* was that an employment practice that had a substantial adverse impact against a protected group must be justified by business necessity, and the Court has subsequently defined what constitutes a substantial adverse impact and business necessity.

(A) **Substantial adverse impact.** Not just any adverse impact will suffice to state a claim under the disparate impact theory, but that impact must be substantial. How the impact will be measured will depend on the nature of the claim. When the class involves applicants who believe they were disadvantaged by a particular employment practice, their success rate on the practice is typically measured against the success rate of the majority group. For example, assume a group of African Americans file a claim challenging the use of a written test as a prerequisite for a particular job, and assume further that African Americans perform less well on the test than white applicants. Whether the test had a disparate impact against African Americans would depend on the differential success rates between whites and African Americans. If 80% of white applicants passed the test but only 10% of African Americans did so, then it is likely a substantial disparate impact could be shown. Another way of assessing disparate impact is by assuming that in a non-discriminatory setting, African Americans would obtain jobs proportionate to their representation in the applicant pool so that if African Americans constituted

30% of the applicant pool, one would expect that 30% of the hires (more or less) would be African Americans.

These are the basic principles behind defining adverse impact but how the actual calculations are made can become quite complex, particularly if there is not a ready measure available such as the applicant flow measure discussed above. If, for example, few women apply for a job because they know that they would not be hired, it can be difficult to determine what the appropriate measure of adverse impact ought to be. Courts generally define a statistically significant impact as the equivalent of two standard deviations, which is the measure used in the social sciences to indicate statistical significance. A standard deviation is a measure of the deviation around a mean, and it indicates the likelihood that the observed results occurred by chance. If the results are more than two standard deviations from what was expected, then it is highly unlikely that the observed figure occurred by chance. *See, e.g., Smith v. Xerox Corp.*, 196 F.3d 358, 366 (2d Cir. 1999) ("If an obtained result varies from the expected result by two standard deviations, there is only about a 5% probability that the variance is due to chance. Courts generally consider this level of statistical significance to warrant an inference of discrimination.").

(B) **Business Necessity.** Establishing a substantial adverse impact is only the first step in the proof structure. Once adverse impact is proved, then the burden of proof shifts to the employer to justify its practice as "job-related and consistent with business necessity." 42 U.S.C. § 2000e-(k)(1). This language comes from the Civil Rights Act of 1991, and was intended to codify the standard that existed prior to the Supreme Court decision in *Wards Cove Packing Co. v. Atonio*, 490 U.S. 642 (1989). The *Wards Cove* case was controversial in that, with respect to the business necessity test, the Supreme Court held that the burden of proof belonged to the plaintiff; in other words, the plaintiff had to establish that the employer's practice could not be justified under the business necessity test. This was seen by Congress as a substantial change in the law, and Congress reacted quickly to return the burden of proof to the employer. It is also worth noting that prior to the Civil Rights Act of 1991, the disparate impact standard was based on a judicial interpretation of Title VII without a clear statutory basis, and there was some sense that the *Wards Cove* case signaled an intent by the Court to scale back, or perhaps even eliminate the disparate impact standard altogether. Accordingly, many in Congress saw the codification of adverse impact as a critical means of preserving the theory.

Although the statute makes clear that the employer now has the burden to justify its practice, it is far less clear what the employer must do in order to satisfy that burden. The statute itself has an unusual provision that precludes courts from looking at legislative history to discern what the standard means, other than one particular memorandum which indicates that the statute was "intended to restore the law" to its state the day before the *Wards Cove* case was decided. *See* § 105(b), Civil Rights Act of 1991, Pub. L. 102-166. There is no consensus, however, on what the law was prior to *Wards Cove*, and the few courts that have sought to interpret the provision have interpreted it in various ways. Many disparate impact challenges involve tests of one kind or another, written tests or frequently physical agility tests, and the United States, through the EEOC and the Justice Department, has developed technical standards for determining when such tests are valid, and therefore might satisfy the statutory standards. Without going into the technical requirements for validating tests, we can describe what these validation efforts are designed to do. (For a discussion of the various standards, see *Gillespie v. Wisconsin*, 771 F.2d 1035 (7th Cir. 1985), *cert. denied*, 474 U.S. 1083. In many instances, the test will seek to replicate the content of the job and determine who is qualified to perform the job based on its content. The classic example is a typing test designed to measure typing skills necessary for a job. Written examinations may also assess basic knowledge that is necessary to perform a job.

Alternatively, an employer such as a police department might seek to determine what makes its current officers successful, and it may devise a testing measure based on how incumbent employees perform. For example, an employer might offer a written test to its current employees, and then correlate the scores on the test with some other measure of job performance, such as supervisor ratings, to determine if the officers who perform best on the test are also those who perform best on the job. Regardless of the method of validation, the employer is seeking to determine whether the test is providing important, or valuable, information about who is likely to be a successful employee.

Tests can also be used as a qualifying examination so that those who pass a certain threshold might move on to a further stage in the process, or it is even possible that an employer might hire by lottery from those who achieve some defined minimum test score. Other tests may be used to hire, or promote, individuals based on how they perform on the test; in other words, individuals might be hired or promoted in rank order of their scores. In general, it is more difficult to validate a test if it is to be used for rank order purposes because most tests do not provide information that would reliably be able to distinguish among individuals who have scores that are only marginally different from each other. *See Guardians Ass'n of New York Police Dep't v. Civil Service Comm'n*, 630 F.2d 79, 101–02 (2d Cir. 1980) (use of test scores must be validated for their reliability), *cert. denied*, 452 U.S. 940 (1981). A third method is for employers to choose employees (or to promote employees) from a band of scores that are considered to be statistically equivalent to one another to avoid the problems that can come in making fine distinctions among scores. *See Officers for Justice v. Civil Serv. Comm'n*, 979 F.2d 721 (9th Cir. 1992) (upholding the use of banding as a measure to reduce adverse impact), *cert. denied*, 507 U.S. 1004 (1993). Under this method, individuals whose scores fall within a defined range, say between 90–95, would be treated the same, rather than treating a score of 95 as demonstrably better than a score of 90 (or 94).

Much of the case law regarding the justification of objective practices arose during the 1970s, when there were many challenges to written examinations, particularly those used by police and fire departments. For those who are interested, two of the most influential cases are *Guardians Association of New York Police Department, and Association Against Discrimination in Employment, Inc. v. City of Bridgeport*, 647 F.2d 256 (2d Cir. 1981). Both of these cases were brought by associations of African-American officers, and the association typically split off from the union that was in place to bargain for the police officers. This is one example in which groups have formed within a workplace based on identity in order to assert their interests when they thought the union was not adequately representing them.

There have been many fewer cases interpreting the standard established by the 1991 Civil Rights Act, but one case gives a good idea of the standard courts are using to determine whether employment practices can satisfy the statutory test. The case involved female applicants for positions with the Transit Authority in Pennsylvania who complained about having to pass a running requirement in order to be hired as a transit police officer. Applicants for the position were required to run 1.5 miles in 12 minutes, and that standard had a substantial adverse impact against female applicants. *See Lanning v. SEPTA*, 181 F.3d 478 (3d Cir. 1999). Initially, the appellate court held that a cutoff score that had a disparate impact must be demonstrated to measure the minimum, as opposed to some optimal, necessary qualification. *See id.* at 481. The case was then remanded to the district court to determine whether the test, which was designed to measure aerobic capacity the department believed was necessary to be a successful transit officer, was intended to measure minimum qualifications. Following further consideration by the district court, the Court of Appeals upheld the use of the test and its cutoff point. *See Lanning v. SEPTA*, 308 F.3d 286 (3d Cir. 2002). The court concluded that there was a significant correlation between arrest rates and being a successful police officer, and arrest rates were further correlated with having a certain aerobic capacity that was necessary to ensure an officer could chase a fleeing suspect. *Id.* at 290. The court accepted the proof even though it was very rare that officers would actually have to chase a suspect down. Yet, because public safety was at issue the court applied a slightly less rigorous standard than it might have if public safety were not involved. *Id.* at 292. The court also rejected the plaintiffs' argument that the cutoff score should be rejected because the employer had not demonstrated that all of the applicants who fell below that score could not be successful officers. All that was necessary, the court said, was establishing that there was a significant correlation between the targeted aerobic capacity and success on the job. *Id.* at 291–92. Finally, the court noted that since many women were able to pass the test once they trained for it, the applicants should be held responsible for not having trained prior to taking the test. *Id.* at 292–93. If you were representing the plaintiffs, how might you respond to this latter point?

(C) **Alternative Employment Practices.** Even if an employer is able to demonstrate that its test or employment practice is job-related and consistent with business necessity, a plaintiff can still prevail in a case by showing that there are alternative employment practices that would serve the employer's needs with less adverse impact and the defendant refuses to adopt the practice. *See* 42 U.S.C. § 2000e-2(k)(1)(A)(i). This "third-prong" of the disparate impact inquiry was first established in the case of *Albemarle Paper Co. v. Moody*, 422 U.S. 405, 425 (1975), but it has remained underdeveloped in the cases. In the context of examinations, one possible alternative would be to change the scoring mechanism, either to lower the cutoff point or to alter how the test results are used. One court has held that the proposed alternative must be demonstrated to be equally valid, noting in the particular case involving a challenge to a sergeant's promotional examination, "Without any evidence that the officers' alternative of increasing merit promotions would lead to a workforce substantially equally qualified, we cannot accept the officers' alternative as equally valid." *Allen v. City of Chicago*, 351 F.3d 306, 314 (7th Cir. 2003).

4. Subjective Employment Practices. The standards just discussed involve objective tests, but the Supreme Court has held that subjective employment practices (such as interviews) can be challenged under the disparate impact theory. *See Watson v. Fort Worth Bank & Trust*, 487 U.S. 977 (1988). Despite the Supreme Court's ruling, successful challenges to subjective employment practices are quite rare. Why might that be? Relatedly, the law is less clear on how subjective practices ought to be validated so as to satisfy the "job related and consistent with business necessity" test since there often is not an objective measure by which to judge the practices.

5. Recent Disparate Impact Challenges. Since the passage of the Civil Rights Act of 1991, the volume of disparate impact litigation has decreased rather dramatically. One reason for this development has already been touched on— because damages are available for disparate treatment claims but not for disparate impact claims, plaintiffs have a clear incentive to proceed under a disparate treatment theory whenever possible. Many of the recent cases involve issues that have long been staples of the disparate impact theory. *See, e.g., M.O.C.H.A. Soc'y, Inc. v. City of Buffalo*, 689 F.3d 263 (2d Cir. 2012) (dismissing challenge to promotional fire examination); *Franklin v. Local 2 of the Sheet Metal Workers Int'l Ass'n*, 565 F.3d 508, 516–21 (8th Cir. 2009) (unsuccessful disparate impact challenge to a union referral policy brought by African-American workers); *El v. SEPTA*, 479 F.3d 232 (3d Cir. 2007) (unsuccessful disparate impact challenge to defendants' policy of excluding individuals with felony convictions from transit driver positions brought by African-American driver-trainee). The examination to certify the competency of teachers in New York City was also recently invalidated because the examination failed to emphasize tasks that were important to teaching. *See Gulino v. Bd. of Educ. of the City Sch. Dist. of NY*, 907 F. Supp. 2d 492 (S.D.N.Y. 2012), *aff'd*, 2014 U.S. App. LEXIS 2070 (2d Cir. Feb. 4, 2014). A group of plaintiffs have also challenged the City of Boston's police department's practice of using hair samples to test for drug use, and the First Circuit Court of Appeals recently found that the practice had an adverse impact on African-American officers. *See Jones v. City of Boston*, 752 F.3d 38, 52 (1st Cir. 2014). The court did not address whether the practice could be justified under the business necessity test, what would the defendants have to show to satisfy that test? The plaintiffs' contention was not that drug use was irrelevant but that the practice was inaccurate. Does that argument fit within the disparate impact theory?

Although private lawsuits based on disparate impact claims have declined substantially, the Equal Employment Opportunity Commission has recently begun a litigation campaign that has challenged various employer policies under the disparate impact theory. The agency has emphasized two areas in particular: (1) credit history checks as part of an application process and (2) employer's policies that prohibit employment of those with felony convictions. The cases are still few in number and so far they have been unsuccessful primarily because of difficulties involving data or establishing the existence of a policy. *See, e.g., EEOC v. Kaplan Higher Educ. Corp.*, 748 F.3d 749 (6th Cir. 2014) (upholding exclusion of expert testimony that sought to determine the race of applicants in connection with challenge to employer's use of credit history checks); *EEOC v. Peoplemark, Inc.*, 732 F.3d 584 (6th Cir. 2013) (upholding attorneys' fee award against the EEOC after it was determined that the employer did not have a company policy that refused to employ individuals with felony convictions); *EEOC v. Freeman*, 961 F. Supp. 2d 783 (D. Md. 2013) (granting summary judgment to defendant in EEOC's challenge to credit background checks for failure to establish disparate impact). In order to prove disparate impact on a challenge to an employer's use of credit history, what would a plaintiff need to establish? What about on a criminal conviction policy? Would it matter what the nature of the conviction was? It is worth noting that a number of states, and many local jurisdictions, have adopted what are known as "Ban the Box" laws, which generally prohibit employers from taking into account criminal backgrounds in their hiring practices. The laws often have many exceptions and are gaining momentum. *See, e.g.*, Jeffrey Stinson, *More States, Cities "Ban the Box" in Hiring: Criminal Pasts Have Disrupted Hiring*, Buff. News, June 17, 2014, at A8.

6. **Disparate Impact and Affirmative Action.** The disparate impact theory has frequently been seen as tied to the controversy that surrounds affirmative action. Many commentators have suggested that employers are likely to engage in "quota" hiring to avoid disparate impact lawsuits. *See, e.g.*, Kingsley Browne, *The Civil Rights Act of 1991: A "Quota Bill"; A Codification of* Griggs, *A Partial Return to Wards Cove, or All of the Above?*, 43 Case Wes. Res. L. Rev. 287, 379–83 (1993) (suggesting that employers impose quotas to avoid disparate impact lawsuits). How does this relate to the theory that underlies the disparate impact theory? Does this argument suggest that disparate impact cases are easy to win, or just expensive to litigate?

In a related context, the Supreme Court has held that employers may not defend against an adverse impact challenge by relying on their "bottom-line" numbers. In *Connecticut v. Teal*, 457 U.S. 440 (1982), plaintiffs challenged a promotional test that had an adverse impact against African-American candidates, and the employer argued that it had compensated for the adverse impact by other means so that ultimately African Americans were promoted in a nondiscriminatory manner. The Supreme Court, however, held that the "bottom-line" statistics were not relevant to the question whether the test had an adverse impact and was job-related, noting that "Congress never intended to give an employer license to discriminate against some employees . . . merely because he favorably treats other members of the employees group." *Id.* at 455.

7. **The *Ricci* Case.** The City of New Haven administered promotional examinations for Lieutenant and Captain positions within the fire department, and the written examinations had significant adverse impact against African American and Latino firefighters. Based on statutory requirements and the collective bargaining agreement, the City was required to select from the top-three scores for each position, and if it had done so, none or very few African Americans or Latinos would have been promoted. The City then decided not to use the test results and a group of white firefighters, and one Latino, sued the City claiming that the decision not to use the test results constituted intentional discrimination in violation of Title VII. When the case reached the Supreme Court, the primary question was whether an employer could take voluntary actions to address the adverse impact of an administered examination. In a 5-4 decision that gained national attention, the Supreme Court held that the City's actions violated Title VII given that the test had

not been demonstrated to be invalid. Because the City had failed to determine whether the test was consistent with business necessity, the Court found that the City had engaged in impermissible intentional discrimination because it was acting out of a concern with the racial distribution of the test results. *See Ricci v. DeStefano*, 557 U.S. 557 (2009). For a variety of reasons, it is not clear what implications the *Ricci* case might have for disparate impact theory given that the Court did not directly alter any aspect of the law. One likely result is that when a test has adverse impact, an employer may be required to wait until the affected group sues—rather than acting voluntarily—before it can take steps to address the adverse impact.

The case has had an interesting subsequent history. Following the Supreme Court's decision in *Ricci*, the City certified the test results and made promotions. Michael Briscoe, an African-American firefighter who had taken the Lieutenant's test, then filed a disparate impact challenge to the use of the test, specifically identifying the 60/40 weighting of the written test to the oral examination as having caused disparate impact. The District Court initially dismissed the case as foreclosed by the *Ricci* decision but the Second Circuit Court of Appeals reversed, holding instead that the City was required to defend the test against the disparate impact challenge. *See Briscoe v. City of New Haven*, 654 F.3d 200 (2d Cir. 2011), *cert. denied*, 132 S. Ct. 2741 (2012). Here one can see the difficult position the city was placed in: it was sued when it sought to voluntarily address the disparate impact and it was later sued for the test's disparate impact. On remand, the District Court held that the 60/40 weighting, which received considerable attention in the Supreme Court proceeding, was not the cause of the disparate impact—changing the weights would not have altered the number of African Americans who would have been promoted (three of 16 promotions ultimately went to African Americans), though changing the weighting likely would have meant that Mr. Briscoe would have been promoted instead of one of the other African-American candidates. The court, however, noted that the disparate impact theory is not concerned with the individual results of the examination but only the disparate effects on a group and therefore dismissed the challenge. *See Briscoe v. City of New Haven*, 967 F. Supp. 2d 563 (D. Conn. 2013).

D. SEXUAL HARASSMENT LAW

It is common today to think of sexual harassment as a form of employment discrimination but that was not always the case. It was not until 1986 that the Supreme Court recognized sexual harassment as constituting a form of sex discrimination prohibited by Title VII. *See Meritor Sav. Bank, FSB v. Vinson*, 477 U.S. 57 (1986). In *Meritor Savings*, the Supreme Court identified two forms of sexual harassment. The first is known as "quid pro quo" harassment, which occurs when sex becomes a condition of employment. There tends to be less litigation involving this form of harassment, in large part because when this form of harassment arises employers are apt to settle any such credible claims. The second form of harassment is known as a "hostile work environment," which is now the more prevalent and well-known form of harassment. In *Meritor Savings*, the Court stated that "[f]or sexual harassment to be actionable, it must be sufficiently severe or pervasive to alter the conditions of [the victim's] employment and create an abusive working environment." *Id.* at 67.

Following *Meritor*, the Court has decided two other cases involving the definition of a hostile working environment. In *Harris v. Forklift Systems, Inc.*, 510 U.S. 17 (1993), a unanimous Court held that a plaintiff need not demonstrate that she had suffered "severe psychological injury" in order to establish a hostile environment claim. *Id.* at 22. The Court went on to note that whether behavior rises to a level that violates Title VII "can be determined only by looking at all the circumstances. These may include the frequency of the discriminatory conduct; its severity; whether it is physically threatening or humiliating, or a mere offensive utterance; and whether it unreasonably interferes with an employee's work performance." *Id.* at 23. Finally, the Court stated in passing that the circumstances should be viewed through the standard of a reasonable person. *Id.*

Several years later, in another unanimous decision, the Supreme Court held that same-sex harassment was cognizable under Title VII, concluding that, "We see no justification in the statutory language or our precedents for a categorical rule excluding same-sex harassment claims from the coverage of Title VII." *Oncale v. Sundowner Offshore Servs., Inc.*, 523 U.S. 75 (1998).

In context of sexual harassment claims, a considerable amount of the litigation has involved two particular issues (1) when a hostile working environment is created and (2) when an employer should be held liable for the actions of its employees, in particular its supervisors. These two issues are addressed below.

1.   The Hostile Working Environment Theory

BILLINGS v. TOWN OF GRAFTON
United States Court of Appeals for the First
515 F.3d 39 (2008)

HOWARD, CIRCUIT JUDGE.

Nancy M. Billings, the former secretary to the Town Administrator for Grafton, Massachusetts, appeals from the entry of summary judgment in favor of the Administrator, the Town, and its Board of Selectmen on her claims of a hostile work environment and retaliation in violation of Title VII of the Civil Rights Act of 1964, 42 U.S.C. §§ 2000e-2(a)(1), 2000e-3(a) (2003), and its state law analog. . . . The district court ruled, as a matter of law, that (1) the Town Administrator's alleged staring at Billings's breasts did not make her workplace atmosphere hostile, (2) her transfer to another secretarial position within the Town, among other things, after she complained of the Administrator's behavior did not amount to a materially adverse employment action. . . . We find error in these rulings, and vacate the decision in large part and remand for further proceedings.

I

. . . Billings began working as the secretary to the Grafton Town Administrator, Russell J. Connor, Jr., in September 1999. A few months into the job, Billings began to notice that Connor was looking at her chest during their conversations. According to Billings, Connor would "make eye contact, and then his eyes would shift down to [her] chest. It was always the same." Connor would then stare for approximately five seconds, or what "seem[ed] like a long time" to Billings.

In response, Billings avoided being alone with Connor, and held a piece of paper in front of her chest while walking through the office. Connor once stared at Billings so many times in the first half-hour of her workday that she went home to change out of the sweater she was wearing before returning. On that same day, Billings formally complained about the incident to the Town's sexual harassment officer, Nancy Hazen, who worked with both Billings and Connor in the Office of the Grafton Board of Selectmen, as the Board's secretary. Hazen had previously heard accounts of similar behavior on Connor's part. . . .

Billings's formal complaint reached the Board of Selectmen, which instructed her to contact an attorney at the Town's law firm. Billings, along with the two clerks who had previously mentioned Connor's staring to Hazen, told the attorney that Connor "was leering at [their] chests, and that it was occurring frequently and that it wasn't stopping, and [they] wanted it to stop." Hazen, for her part, started keeping a written record of Billings's reports of Connor's staring at her chest. Hazen noted four separate incidents in one two-week span in the early spring of 2001, including one where Billings "stormed out of [Connor's] office slamming papers saying 'He did it again.'" On a separate occasion, Connor told the tax collector's clerk that Billings was "under the desk" where Connor was sitting when he was asked her whereabouts. Connor, who quickly added that he was "kidding," later acknowledged that his comment could have been taken to suggest that Billings was under the desk performing oral sex, though he denied having meant it that way. But Billings, who soon learned of Connor's remark from the clerk, found it offensive.

Billings noticed that Connor's staring became less frequent after the Town's attorney reported to the Board of Selectmen regarding her inquiry into Billings's complaint, decreasing from a number of times each day to "a couple of times a week." But the staring returned to its former frequency after a few weeks. That August, after calling Billings into his office and closing the door, Connor accused her of trying to embarrass and humiliate him by asking questions at a Board of Selectmen meeting about his appointment of a new public works director, Roger Hammond. Billings came to see this as retaliation for making the sexual harassment complaint; one of the Selectmen had recently disclosed to Connor that Billings was the complainant. After this disclosure, Billings noticed that Connor began avoiding her around the office and using written notes and "grunts" to communicate.

Billings reported a number of additional instances of Connor's staring at her chest in the late fall of 2001. In November, she informed the Board of Selectmen "that the conduct has not stopped" and asked the Board for a "formal investigation." The Board instructed the Town's labor lawyer to look into this claim, but Billings refused to participate in the investigation out of a concern that the lawyer's representation of the Town would bias the lawyer in its favor. The lawyer thus did not interview Billings, and also did not interview any of the other women who had previously said Connor had stared at their chests. Based on interviews with Connor and two members of the Board of Selectmen, the lawyer found that Connor had not stared at Billings's chest, but that he simply "does not maintain eye contact when conversing with others." The lawyer concluded, in a report prepared for the Board, that "Billings' allegations of sexual harassment cannot be sustained."

Just before the report was submitted, Billings pressed her allegations by filing a charge of discrimination against Connor and the Town with both the Equal Employment Opportunity Commission and the Massachusetts Commission Against Discrimination ("MCAD"). . . .

By the end of 2002, the [EEOC] had issued Billings a notice of her right to sue, and Billings had filed a complaint against Connor and the Town in U.S. District Court. Billings later informed the Board of Selectmen via letter "that the behavior of Mr. Connor leering at my chest has not ceased and has continued to date," alleging eleven separate examples of such conduct between January 3, 2003, and March 19, 2003. This time, the Board hired an outside attorney, Judith Loitherstein, to investigate the incidents referenced in Billings's most recent letter. Less than two weeks after learning of that letter, Connor provided Billings with two typed memoranda criticizing her failure to follow particular instructions he had given her. . . .

While interviewing Connor as part of her investigation, Loitherstein "noticed that his eyes frequently darted down and then back up again," but that she "did not get the impression that he was staring at [her] chest"—he looked in some other direction "just as frequently." This led Loitherstein to wonder "whether his eye movement is the result of a physical condition, a nervous condition, or some other reason" besides "sexual intent." After learning of these musings, Connor visited an ophthalmologist, who diagnosed him with "alternating intermittent exotropia"—"a condition in which one eye or the other will lose fixation and drift outward as one looks at him."

* * * *

. . . [T]he Town and Connor moved for summary judgment on Billings's complaint, which included claims of a hostile work environment and retaliation in violation of Title VII . . . against both defendants, and a common law claim of intentional infliction of emotional distress against Connor. Billings opposed the motion and cross-moved to amend her complaint to make additional allegations in support of her retaliation claim. . . .

The district court granted summary judgment for the Town and Connor on the hostile environment and intentional infliction of emotional distress claims, ruling that "the alleged harassing conduct here is insufficient as a matter of law to create an objectively hostile work environment because it is not sufficiently severe or pervasive." . . . [Editors note: The remaining discussion of the retaliation claim has been omitted.]

II

Billings challenges the entry of summary judgment against her on her claims of a hostile work environment and retaliation. . . .

A

Title VII's ban on employment practices that "discriminate against any individual with respect to his . . . terms, conditions, or privileges of employment, because of such individual's . . . sex," 42 U.S.C. § 2000e-2(a)(1), extends to sex-based discrimination that creates a hostile or abusive work environment. Meritor Sav. Bank, FSB v. Vinson, 477 U.S. 57, 66 (1986). This sort of discrimination is generally referred to as "sexual harassment," but "not all workplace conduct that may be described as 'harassment' affects a 'term, condition, or privilege' of employment within the meaning of Title VII . . . ; [f]or sexual harassment to be actionable, it must be sufficiently severe or pervasive 'to alter the conditions of [the victim's] employment and create an abusive working environment'." Meritor, 477 U.S. at 67 (quoting Henson v. City of Dundee, 682 F.2d 897, 904 (11th Cir. 1982)); see also Harris v. Forklift Sys., Inc., 510 U.S. 17, 21 (1993).

To give rise to a sexual harassment claim, "a sexually objectionable environment must be both objectively and subjectively offensive, one that a reasonable person would find hostile or abusive, and one that the victim in fact did perceive to be so." Faragher v. City of Boca Raton, 524 U.S. 775, 787 (1998). The district court ruled that, though Billings "subjectively experienced" Connor's staring as abusive, it nevertheless did not create a hostile environment in the objective sense—in essence, that a reasonable person in Billings's position would disagree with her subjective assessment. We do not think that the summary judgment record permits that conclusion as a matter of law.

The point at which a work environment becomes hostile or abusive does not depend on any "mathematically precise test." Harris, 510 U.S. at 22. Instead, "the objective severity of harassment should be judged from the perspective of a reasonable person in the plaintiff's position, considering 'all the circumstances.'" Oncale v. Sundowner Offshore Servs., Inc., 523 U.S. 75, 81 (1998) (quoting Harris, 510 U.S. at 23). These circumstances "may include the frequency of the discriminatory conduct; its severity; whether it is physically threatening or humiliating, or a mere offensive utterance; and whether it unreasonably interferes with an employee's work performance," but are by no means limited to them, and "no single factor is required." Harris, 510 U.S. at 23.

While the district court properly articulated this standard, we think it applied the standard in too rigid a manner. In particular, we think the court's analysis placed undue weight on the fact—undisputed though it was—that Connor's alleged behavior did not include touching, sexual advances, or "overtly sexual comments to or about her." As we have just explained, the hostility vel non of a workplace does not depend on any particular kind of conduct; indeed, "[a] worker need not be propositioned, touched offensively, or harassed by sexual innuendo in order to have been sexually harassed." Quick v. Donaldson Co., 90 F.3d 1372, 1379 (8th Cir. 1996); see also Smith v. First Union Nat'l Bank, 202 F.3d 234, 242 (4th Cir. 2000) (reversing summary judgment for defendant on hostile environment claim, despite absence of touching, propositioning, or ogling, because "a woman's work environment can be hostile even if she is not subjected to sexual advances or propositions").

Of course, behavior like fondling, come-ons, and lewd remarks is often the stuff of hostile environment claims, including several previously upheld by this Court. *See*, e.g., Marrero v. Goya of P.R., Inc., 304 F.3d 7, 19–20 (1st Cir. 2002) ("sexual remarks and innuendos," including "a sexual invitation," as well as "unwelcome physical touching"); Hernandez-Loring v. Universidad Metropolitana, 233 F.3d 49, 55–56 (1st Cir. 2000) (repeated requests for dates and use of suggestive language); White v. N.H. Dep't of Corr., 221 F.3d 254, 260–61 (1st Cir. 2000) (commonplace "sexual conversations and jokes," including at the plaintiff's expense, coupled with disparate treatment). In ruling that Billings could not succeed on such a claim as a matter of law, the district court relied on these cases, reasoning that "the record is devoid of the types of behavior that marked the presence of a hostile work environment" in those cases. But, as we have said, no particular "types of behavior" are essential to a hostile environment claim.

Each of these cases simply held that, based on the evidence presented, a reasonable jury could have found the harassment sufficiently severe or pervasive to constitute a hostile environment as a matter of law. Marrero, 304 F.3d at 20 . . . Thus, while they serve as instructive examples of actionable sexual harassment, they do not suggest that harassing conduct of a different kind or lesser degree will necessarily fall short of that standard. . . .

The highly fact-specific nature of a hostile environment claim tends to make it difficult to draw meaningful contrasts between one case and another for purposes of distinguishing between sufficiently and insufficiently abusive behavior. Conduct that amounts to sexual harassment under one set of circumstances may, in a different context, equate with the sort of "merely offensive" behavior that lies beyond the purview of Title VII, and vice versa. *See Marrero*, 304 F.3d at 18–19. . . .

By like token, we disagree with the district court's reasoning that Connor's alleged behavior did not constitute sexual harassment as a matter of law because it was "similar in terms of degree" to the conduct we considered in Lee-Crespo v. Schering-Plough Del Caribe Inc., 354 F.3d 34 (1st Cir. 2003), where we upheld summary judgment for the employer because the employee failed to prove she was subjected to a hostile work environment that was severe or pervasive. In *Lee-Crespo*, the plaintiff's supervisor "bothered [her] with meddlesome and prying questions about her personal life and made comments about her appearance and behavior," *id.* at 38, manifesting "a disregard for professional courtesy and a penchant for inquiring about the personal affairs of other workers (both male and female)." *Id.* at 46. We held that this conduct—which we characterized as "a supervisor's unprofessional managerial approach and accompanying efforts to assert her authority"—was simply "not the focus of the discrimination laws." *Id.* at 47.

Connor's complained-of behavior, however, does not lend itself to the same characterization. As the district court recognized, "for a male supervisor to stare repeatedly at a female subordinate's breasts . . . is inappropriate and offensive," not merely "unprofessional." Thus Connor's alleged staring is fundamentally different from the intrusive questions and comments at issue in *Lee-Crespo*. Furthermore, to the extent that actions so different in kind lend themselves to any comparison "in terms of degree," we believe that the degree of harassment allegedly experienced by Billings in this case exceeds that allegedly experienced by the plaintiff in *Lee-Crespo*. There, applying the *Harris* factors, we reasoned that "the complained of conduct was episodic, but not so frequent as to become pervasive; was never severe; was never physically threatening (though occasionally discomforting or mildly humiliating); and significantly, was never . . . an impediment to [the plaintiff's] work performance." 354 F.3d at 46. We cannot make the same determinations about Connor's behavior here, particularly where the record permits competing conclusions about the frequency and intensity of Connor's alleged conduct.

Billings, for example, describes her interactions with Connor as "stares" "about five seconds long", while Loitherstein concluded, based on her interviews with both Billings and Connor, that his eyes simply "darted" downward for no more than two or three seconds at a time. As the district court noted, "[t]he evidence regarding the frequency of Connor's alleged staring is somewhat incomplete," but Billings testified "that [i]t happened a lot." When we resolve these and the other factual disputes in the record in favor of Billings, we cannot definitively say, as the district court did, that Connor's conduct was not sufficiently severe or pervasive to allow a jury to find in favor of Billings on her hostile environment claim. As we have observed, the hostile environment "question is commonly one of degree—both as to severity and pervasiveness—to be resolved by the trier of fact on the basis of inferences drawn 'from a broad array of circumstantial and often conflicting evidence.' " Gorski v. N.H. Dep't of Corr., 290 F.3d 466, 474 (1st Cir. 2002) (quoting Lipsett v. Univ. of Puerto Rico, 864 F.2d 881, 895 (1st Cir. 1998)). We see this case as no exception.

We do not mean, of course, that hostile environment cases inevitably raise issues that cannot be resolved by summary judgment, which remains "an appropriate vehicle for policing the baseline for hostile environment claims" Pomales v. Celulares Telefonica, Inc., 447 F.3d 79, 83 (1st Cir. 2006). And we accept, as a general proposition, that not every such claim premised on staring or leering in the workplace automatically presents a question for the jury. We hold simply that the record in this case does not permit the ruling, as a matter of law, that the circumstances of Billings's employment did not add up to a hostile environment.

Taken in the light most favorable to Billings, the evidence depicts a supervisor who regularly stared at her breasts for much of the two and a half years they worked together. Thus, the alleged harassment did not consist merely of the sort of "isolated incidents" that ordinarily "will not amount to discriminatory changes in the terms and conditions of employment." Faragher, 524 U.S. at 788. Other women who worked for the Town also said Connor had subjected them to similar behavior, which they, too, found objectionable. *See Hernandez-Loring*, 233 F.3d at 55 n.4 ("Evidence of the harassment of third parties can help to prove a legally cognizable claim of a hostile environment."). Furthermore, Billings did not stand silent in the face of her alleged treatment, but repeatedly complained to both Hazen and the Board of Selectmen.

Based on these and other aspects of Billings's response to Connor's alleged staring, we disagree with the defendants that no reasonable jury could conclude that the staring unreasonably interfered with her work performance or altered the terms and conditions of her employment as a matter of law. As the defendants emphasize, Billings did testify that she was able to continue performing her duties notwithstanding the complained-of behavior: as she put it, "I mean, I could sit and type a letter, yes." She added, however, that "every time I needed to talk to him, I had to make sure I was carrying something in front of me so that he wouldn't look at me. I just had to be careful with what I wore in the morning, be careful with what I said." The fact that Billings managed to get her work done despite these measures is by no means fatal to her hostile environment claim. *See Dey v. Colt Constr. & Dev. Co.*, 28 F.3d 1446, 1454 (7th Cir. 1994) ("[T]he mention in *Harris* of an unreasonable interference with work performance was not intended to penalize the employee who possesses the dedication and fortitude to complete her assigned tasks even in the face of offensive and abusive sexual [harassment] from one of her superiors.").

The defendants also maintain that, whatever the effect of Connor's behavior on Billings in the subjective sense or on her workplace in the objective sense, it did not amount to "sexual harassment" under Title VII because it was not "of a sexual nature." We cannot reasonably accept, however, that a man's repeated staring at a woman's breasts is to be ordinarily understood as anything other than sexual. In arguing to the contrary in this case, the defendants rely on Connor's eye condition, coupled with the fact that others who worked with him "did not sense any sexual intent underlying" his "failure to maintain eye contact." While this might have some bearing on whether Connor's staring created an objectively hostile work environment, it does not mean that the staring cannot support such a claim as a matter of law, because "harassing conduct need not be motivated by sexual desire to support an inference of discrimination on the basis of sex." Oncale, 523 U.S. at 80. In any event, the defendants' innocent explanation for Connor's behavior is certainly not the only reasonable view of the evidence. Because that evidence, in its entirety, does not foreclose a finding that Billings experienced a hostile work environment, the district court should not have entered summary judgment against her on that claim.

III

For the foregoing reasons, we vacate the district court's entry of summary judgment for the defendants on Billings's hostile environment claims, and remand them for further consideration consistent with this opinion. . . .

NOTES

1. **On Remand.** How do you think the case should proceed on remand? Do you think the facts alleged should constitute a hostile working environment, why or why not? How would you go about proving the existence (or lack) of such a claim?

2. **Origins of the Theory.** The hostile environment theory originally arose in the context of race and national origin claims, and remains available for all of the various protected categories, although claims for sexual harassment far outdistance all of the other categories. Also influential in the development of the theory was the work of CATHARINE MACKINNON, THE SEXUAL HARASSMENT OF WORKING WOMEN (1978),

in which she advocated treating sexual harassment as a form of sex discrimination under Title VII and much of what MacKinnon advocated the Court ultimately adopted as the contours of the hostile work environment claim.

3. **The Elements of a Hostile Environment Claim.** In summary fashion, to establish a claim of hostile work environment the plaintiff must show that the conduct was "unwelcome," and that it was sufficiently severe and pervasive so as to constitute a hostile working environment. The plaintiff must also establish a basis for holding the employer liable, an issue that is addressed in the next case. The requirement that the conduct must be "unwelcome" has received a substantial amount of scholarly criticism because it requires the plaintiff to prove that she did not do something to invite the harassment. Susan Estrich contends: "Unwelcomeness has emerged as the doctrinal stepchild of the rape standards of consent and resistance, and shares virtually all of their problems." Susan Estrich, *Sex at Work*, 42 STAN. L. REV. 813, 827 (1991). While this remains a possibility, the law has developed in such a way as to diminish the importance of the "unwelcomeness" inquiry. In one case, the plaintiff had done nude photographs for a motorcycle magazine, and when those pictures found their way into the workplace and led to significant harassing behavior, the plaintiff filed a complaint alleging she was forced to work in a hostile environment. The employer argued that because she had posed for the photographs, she could not later argue that the workplace behavior was "unwelcome," a position the Court of Appeals soundly rejected distinguishing between activities she chose to engage in outside of the workplace and the behavior she had to endure on the job. *See Burns v. McGregor Elec.* Indus, *Corp.*, 989 F.2d 959 (8th Cir. 1993). When the issue of unwelcomeness arises today, it tends to be in cases where the plaintiff participated in sexual banter or sexual pranks, rather than in cases concerning whether the plaintiff's actions invited harassment. *See, e.g., Scusa v. Nestle U.S.A. Co.*, 181 F.3d 958 (8th Cir. 1999) (finding conduct was not unwelcome when plaintiff engaged in behavior similar to that which she complained about including use of profanity and off-color jokes); *Reed v. Shepard*, 939 F.2d 484, 486–87 (7th Cir. 1991) (holding that no sexual harassment had been established where plaintiff had participated and instigated some of the "repulsive" workplace behavior). What do you think might account for this change in the way "unwelcome" is interpreted (if it is a change)? The above cases may still be problematic in that they may overlook reasons why a woman might have participated in the workplace behavior, such as a felt need to get along with co-workers or a hope that participation may help end the conduct. *See* Marion Crain, *Women, Labor Unions & Hostile Environment Sexual Harassment: The Untold Story*, 4 TEX. J. WOMEN & LAW 9, 22–23 (1995) (discussing some of the reasons women may go along with or participate in horseplay or sexual banter, including means of avoidance, defusion or negotiation).

4. **Sexual Conduct.** As discussed in *Billings*, hostile environment cases can be broadly defined to include two types of cases: (1) those involving conduct of a sexual nature, touching, propositions, etc. and (2) behavior that is not necessarily sexual in nature but that is demeaning or offensive in a way that renders the conditions for women different from men's. In general, courts have an easier time finding the existence of a hostile environment when the case involves conduct of a sexual nature than when such behavior is not at issue in the case. *See* Vicki Schultz, *Reconcep-*

tualizing Sexual Harassment, 107 YALE L.J. 1683 (1998) (arguing that courts focus too much on sexual conduct and frequently ignore behavior that is designed to reinforce male workplace norms). Based on a survey of published federal court decisions, Ann Juliano and Stewart Schwab concluded that cases that involved behavior of a sexual nature had a far higher success rate than cases where such behavior was absent. *See* Ann Juliano & Stewart J. Schwab, *The Sweep of Sexual Harassment Cases*, 86 CORNELL L. REV. 548 (2001). However, as indicated in *Billings*, courts are increasingly recognizing that cases that do not involve touching or other sexual behavior can still rise to the level of a hostile working environment. This has been particularly true with more recent cases. *See, e.g., Waldo v. Consumers Energy Co.*, 726 F.3d 802, 806 (6th Cir. 2013) (workplace that was permeated with demeaning and ostracizing comments towards women constituted hostile environment); *Passnanti v. Cook County*, 689 F.3d 655, 665 (7th Cir. 2012) (finding that Supervisor's pervasive "use of the term 'bitch' to address and demean [the plaintiff] was based on her sex."); *Tali v. Brigham & Women's Hosp.*, 656 F.3d 33, 39–40 (1st Cir. 2011) (repeated demeaning comments to plaintiff, who was a spinal neurosurgeon, by her supervisor and co-worker created a hostile working environment). Similarly, courts have also permitted claims by individuals who complain about a degrading environment even if they are not the targets of the comments. *See, e.g., Gallagher v. C.H. Robinson Worldwide, Inc.*, 567 F.3d 263, 271 (6th Cir. 2009) ("[E]ven though members of both sexes were exposed to the offensive conduct . . . , considering the nature of the patently degrading and anti-female nature of the harassment, it stands to reason that women would suffer, as a result of the exposure, greater disadvantage in the terms and conditions of their employment than men."); *EEOC v. Cent. Wholesalers, Inc.*, 573 F.3d 167, 175 (4th Cir. 2009) (EEOC established hostile working environment based on degrading language and presence of pornography in the workplace). What do you think accounts for this shift?

The move away from purely sexual conduct as forming the basis of a hostile environment has raised concerns among employers and others that the workplace might be subjected to heavy regulation. The Supreme Court sought to allay these concerns in its decision in *Oncale* acknowledging that same-sex harassment can violate Title VII. Writing for the Court, Justice Scalia observed:

> Respondents and their *amici* contend that recognizing liability for same-sex harassment will transform Title VII into a general civility code for the American workplace. But that risk is no greater for same-sex than for opposite-sex harassment, and is adequately met by careful attention to the requirements of the statute. Title VII does not prohibit all verbal or physical harassment in the workplace; it is directed only at *"discrimination . . . because of . . . sex."* We have never held that workplace harassment, even harassment between men and women, is automatically discrimination because of sex merely because the words used have sexual content or connotations. "The critical issue, Title VII's text indicates, is whether members of one sex are exposed to disadvantageous terms or conditions of employment to which members of the other sex are not exposed." Harris, 510 U.S. at 25 (Ginsburg, J., concurring).

Courts and juries have found the inference of discrimination easy to draw in most male-female sexual harassment situations, because the challenged conduct typically involves explicit or implicit proposals of sexual activity; it is reasonable to assume those proposals would not have been made to someone of the same sex. The same chain of inference would be available to a plaintiff alleging same-sex harassment, if there were credible evidence that the harasser was homosexual. But harassing conduct need not be motivated by sexual desire to support an inference of discrimination on the basis of sex. A trier of fact might reasonably find such discrimination, for example, if a female victim is harassed in such sex-specific and derogatory terms by another woman as to make it clear that the harasser is motivated by general hostility to the presence of women in the workplace. A same-sex harassment plaintiff may also, of course, offer direct comparative evidence about how the alleged harasser treated members of both sexes in a mixed-sex workplace. Whatever evidentiary route the plaintiff chooses to follow, he or she must always prove that the conduct at issue was not merely tinged with offensive sexual connotations, but actually constituted "*discrimination* . . . because of . . . sex."

And there is another requirement that prevents Title VII from expanding into a general civility code: As we emphasized in *Meritor* and *Harris*, the statute does not reach genuine but innocuous differences in the ways men and women routinely interact with members of the same sex and of the opposite sex. The prohibition of harassment on the basis of sex requires neither asexuality nor androgyny in the workplace; it forbids only behavior so objectively offensive as to alter the "conditions" of the victim's employment. "Conduct that is not severe or pervasive enough to create an objectively hostile or abusive work environment—an environment that a reasonable person would find hostile or abusive—is beyond Title VII's purview." Harris, 510 U.S. at 21. We have always regarded that requirement as crucial, and as sufficient to ensure that courts and juries do not mistake ordinary socializing in the workplace—such as male-on-male horseplay or intersexual flirtation—for discriminatory "conditions of employment."

We have emphasized, moreover, that the objective severity of harassment should be judged from the perspective of a reasonable person in the plaintiff's position, considering "all the circumstances." Harris, supra, at 23. In same-sex (as in all) harassment cases, that inquiry requires careful consideration of the social context in which particular behavior occurs and is experienced by its target. A professional football player's working environment is not severely or pervasively abusive, for example, if the coach smacks him on the buttocks as he heads onto the field—even if the same behavior would reasonably be experienced as abusive by the coach's secretary (male or female) back at the office. The real social impact of workplace behavior often depends on a constellation of surrounding circumstances, expectations, and relationships which are not fully captured by a simple recitation of the words used or the physical acts performed. Common sense, and an appropriate sensitivity to social context, will enable courts and juries to distinguish between simple teasing or roughhousing among members of the same sex, and conduct which a reasonable person in the plaintiff's position would find severely hostile or abusive.

Id. at 80–82

5. Perspective: Reasonable Woman vs. Reasonable Person. One of the issues that has long complicated questions relating to sexual harassment is that men and women frequently have different perspectives on what constitutes sexual harassment, and on what behavior in the workplace might be appropriate. As a result of these different experiences, a number of feminist scholars advocated that a hostile working environment ought to be assessed from the perspective of a reasonable woman. *See* Nancy S. Ehrenreich, *Pluralist Myths and Powerless Men: The Ideology of Reasonableness in Sexual Harassment Law*, 99 YALE L.J. 1177 (1990). In an important case, the Ninth Circuit Court of Appeals applied such a standard, explaining its rationale as follows:

> If we only examined whether a reasonable person would engage in allegedly harassing conduct, we would run the risk of reinforcing the prevailing level of discrimination. Harassers could continue to harass merely because a particular discriminatory practice was common, and victims of harassment would have no remedy. . . . A complete understanding of the victim's view requires, among other things, an analysis of the different perspectives of men and women. Conduct that many men consider unobjectionable may offend many women. *See*, e.g., *Lipsett v. Univ. of Puerto Rico*, 864 F.2d 881, 898 (1st Cir. 1988) ("A male supervisor might believe, for example, that it is legitimate for him to tell a female subordinate that she has a 'great figure' or 'nice legs.' The female subordinate may find such comments offensive."). We realize that there is a broad range of viewpoints among women as a group, but we believe that many women share common concerns which men do not necessarily share. For example, because women are disproportionately victims of rape and sexual assault, women have a stronger incentive to be concerned with sexual behavior. Women who are victims of mild forms of sexual harassment may understandably worry whether a harasser's conduct is merely a prelude to violent sexual assault. Men, who are rarely victims of sexual assault, may view sexual conduct in a vacuum without a full appreciation of the social setting or the underlying threat of violence that a woman may perceive. We adopt the perspective of a reasonable woman primarily because we believe that a sex-blind reasonable person standard tends to be male-biased and tends to systematically ignore the experiences of women. The reasonable woman standard does not establish a higher level of protection for women than men. . . . Instead, a gender-conscious examination of sexual harassment enables women to participate in the workplace on an equal footing with men.

Ellison v. Brady, 924 F.2d 872, 878–81 (9th Cir. 1991). In *Harris*, and more clearly in *Oncale*, the Supreme Court stated that whether a hostile environment exists ought to be measured under a reasonable person test, though it also indicated that it was important to consider all of the circumstances, which may include the plaintiff's gender. In the *Harris* case, the defendant called several of its female employees to testify that they were not offended by their bosses' behavior. How would that evidence be relevant under a reasonable person test? What about a reasonable woman test? Under either test, how would you explain to a jury the relevance of perspective and experience in evaluating the claim? There is some evidence that the divide between men and women on what constitutes sexual harassment is closing. *See* Theresa M. Beiner, *Let the Jury Decide: The Gap Between What Judges and Reasonable People Believe Is Sexually Harassing*, 75 S. CAL. L. REV. 791, 846 (2002) (discussing an "increasing consensus—even among men and women—about what constitutes harassment in the workplace"). Assuming a consensus is developing, how ought that factor into a court's consideration of what constitutes a hostile environment? For an excellent discussion, including an empirical analysis, of the role perspective plays in hostile environment claims see V. Blair Druhan, *Severe and Pervasive: An Analysis of Who, What, and Where Matters When Determining Sexual Harassment*, 66 VAND. L. REV. 355 (2013).

6. **Sex-Stereotyping Theory.** Prior to the Supreme Court's decision in *Oncale*, the question of whether same-sex harassment could be pursued under Title VII caused considerable confusion in the lower courts. One reason for the confusion was that some courts equated the concept with discrimination based on sexual orientation, a classification that Title VII does not include. Indeed, when an individual is the subject of harassment because of his or her sexual orientation, courts have generally determined that such harassment falls outside the scope of Title VII's protection. For example, in *Spearman v. Ford Motor Co.*, 231 F.3d 1080 (7th Cir. 2000), the court ruled against the plaintiff because the harassment that he complained about, including sexually explicit graffiti and vulgar insults, was directed at his apparent homosexuality rather than his sex. More recently, courts have developed a theory known as "sex-stereotyping," that has provided some protection to individuals who do not fit gender norms. These cases are not cases strictly about discrimination based on one's sexual orientation but instead turn on the fact that an employee is being discriminated against because he or she does not conform to an employer's definition of a particular gender norm.

The Sixth Circuit, for example, has decided a series of interesting cases, including one involving a transsexual who was a lieutenant in a Fire Department. Once the Fire Department became aware that the lieutenant was a transsexual, they sought to drive him out of the department and eventually succeeded. He later filed suit and the Sixth Circuit allowed his sexual stereotyping claim to go forward based on his "failure to conform to sex stereotypes of how a man should look and behave." *Smith v. City of Salem*, 378 F.3d 566 (6th Cir. 2004); *see also Barnes v. City of Cincinnati*, 401 F.3d 729 (6th Cir. 2005) (upholding jury verdict based on sexual stereotyping for police sergeant who was a preoperative transsexual who sometimes came "to work with makeup or lipstick on his face"), *cert. denied*, 546 U.S. 1003 (2005). The Ninth Circuit applied the theory in a case involving a plaintiff who alleged that he had been repeatedly harassed because he was gay, with much of the behavior involving groping and physical conduct of a sexual nature. A plurality of the en banc court determined that the plaintiff's sexual identity was irrelevant to whether he was being harassed "because of sex," noting that, "In none of those cases has a court denied relief because the victim was, or might have been, a lesbian.

The sexual orientation of the victim was simply irrelevant. If sexual orientation is irrelevant for a female victim, we see no reason why it is not also irrelevant for a male victim." *Rene v. MGM Grand Hotel, Inc.*, 305 F.3d 1061, 1065 (9th Cir. 2002) (plurality *en banc* opinion), *cert. denied*, 538 U.S. 922 (2003). Most recently, The Fifth Circuit, sitting en banc, applied the theory of gender stereotyping to a case where an ironworker on an all-male construction crew was subjected to verbal and physical harassment because he "did not conform to [his supervisor's] view of how a man should act," which the court further defined as constituting discrimination because of sex. *EEOC v. Boh Bros. Constr. Co.*, 731 F.3d 444, 453 (5th Cir. 2013).

2.   Employer Liability

BURLINGTON INDUSTRIES, INC. v. ELLERTH
United States Supreme Court
524 U.S. 742 (1998)

JUSTICE KENNEDY delivered the opinion of the Court.

We decide whether, under Title VII of the Civil Rights Act of 1964, 78 STAT. 253, as amended, 42 U.S.C. § 2000e et seq., an employee who refuses the unwelcome and threatening sexual advances of a supervisor, yet suffers no adverse, tangible job consequences, can recover against the employer without showing the employer is negligent or otherwise at fault for the supervisor's actions.

I

. . . From March 1993 until May 1994, Ellerth worked as a salesperson in one of Burlington's divisions in Chicago, Illinois. During her employment, she alleges, she was subjected to constant sexual harassment by her supervisor, one Ted Slowik. In the hierarchy of Burlington's management structure, Slowik was a mid-level manager. Burlington has eight divisions, employing more than 22,000 people in some 50 plants around the United States. Slowik was a vice president in one of five business units within one of the divisions. He had authority to make hiring and promotion decisions subject to the approval of his supervisor, who signed the paperwork. See 912 F. Supp. 1101, 1119, n. 14 (ND Ill. 1996). According to Slowik's supervisor, his position was "not considered an upper-level management position," and he was "not amongst the decision-making or policy-making hierarchy." *Ibid.* Slowik was not Ellerth's immediate supervisor. Ellerth worked in a two-person office in Chicago, and she answered to her office colleague, who in turn answered to Slowik in New York.

Against a background of repeated boorish and offensive remarks and gestures which Slowik allegedly made, Ellerth places particular emphasis on three alleged incidents where Slowik's comments could be construed as threats to deny her tangible job benefits. In the summer of 1993, while on a business trip, Slowik invited Ellerth to the hotel lounge, an invitation Ellerth felt compelled to accept because Slowik was her boss. App. 155. When Ellerth gave no encouragement to remarks Slowik made about her breasts, he told her to "loosen up" and warned, "you know,

Kim, I could make your life very hard or very easy at Burlington." *Id.* at 156.

In March 1994, when Ellerth was being considered for a promotion, Slowik expressed reservations during the promotion interview because she was not "loose enough." *Id.* at 159. The comment was followed by his reaching over and rubbing her knee. *Ibid.* Ellerth did receive the promotion; but when Slowik called to announce it, he told Ellerth, "you're gonna be out there with men who work in factories, and they certainly like women with pretty butts/legs." *Id.* at 159–160.

In May 1994, Ellerth called Slowik, asking permission to insert a customer's logo into a fabric sample. Slowik responded, "I don't have time for you right now, Kim—unless you want to tell me what you're wearing." *Id.* at 78. Ellerth told Slowik she had to go and ended the call. *Ibid.* A day or two later, Ellerth called Slowik to ask permission again. This time he denied her request, but added something along the lines of, "are you wearing shorter skirts yet, Kim, because it would make your job a whole heck of a lot easier." *Id.* at 79.

A short time later, Ellerth's immediate supervisor cautioned her about returning telephone calls to customers in a prompt fashion. 912 F. Supp. at 1109. In response, Ellerth quit. She faxed a letter giving reasons unrelated to the alleged sexual harassment we have described. *Ibid.* About three weeks later, however, she sent a letter explaining she quit because of Slowik's behavior. *Ibid.* During her tenure at Burlington, Ellerth did not inform anyone in authority about Slowik's conduct, despite knowing Burlington had a policy against sexual harassment. *Ibid.* In fact, she chose not to inform her immediate supervisor (not Slowik) because " 'it would be his duty as my supervisor to report any incidents of sexual harassment.' " *Ibid.* On one occasion, she told Slowik a comment he made was inappropriate. *Ibid.*

. . . The District Court granted summary judgment to Burlington. The Court found Slowik's behavior, as described by Ellerth, severe and pervasive enough to create a hostile work environment, but found Burlington neither knew nor should have known about the conduct. . . . The Court of Appeals en banc reversed in a decision which produced eight separate opinions and no consensus for a controlling rationale. . . .

II

At the outset, we assume an important proposition yet to be established before a trier of fact. It is a premise assumed as well, in explicit or implicit terms, in the various opinions by the judges of the Court of Appeals. The premise is: a trier of fact could find in Slowik's remarks numerous threats to retaliate against Ellerth if she denied some sexual liberties. The threats, however, were not carried out or fulfilled. Cases based on threats which are carried out are referred to often as *quid pro quo* cases, as distinct from bothersome attentions or sexual remarks that are sufficiently severe or pervasive to create a hostile work environment. The terms *quid pro quo* and hostile work environment are helpful, perhaps, in making a rough demarcation between cases in which threats are carried out and those where they are not or are absent altogether, but beyond this are of limited utility. . . .

"*Quid pro quo*" and "hostile work environment" do not appear in the statutory text. The terms appeared first in the academic literature, see C. MacKinnon, Sexual

Harassment of Working Women (1979); found their way into decisions of the Courts of Appeals, *see*, e.g., Henson v. Dundee, 682 F.2d 897, 909 (CA11 1982); and were mentioned in this Court's decision in Meritor Savings Bank, FSB v. Vinson, 477 U.S. 57 (1986).

In *Meritor*, the terms served a specific and limited purpose. There we considered whether the conduct in question constituted discrimination in the terms or conditions of employment in violation of Title VII. We assumed, and with adequate reason, that if an employer demanded sexual favors from an employee in return for a job benefit, discrimination with respect to terms or conditions of employment was explicit. Less obvious was whether an employer's sexually demeaning behavior altered terms or conditions of employment in violation of Title VII. We distinguished between *quid pro quo* claims and hostile environment claims, see 477 U.S. at 65, and said both were cognizable under Title VII, though the latter requires harassment that is severe or pervasive. *Ibid.* The principal significance of the distinction is to instruct that Title VII is violated by either explicit or constructive alterations in the terms or conditions of employment and to explain the latter must be severe or pervasive. The distinction was not discussed for its bearing upon an employer's liability for an employee's discrimination. On this question *Meritor* held, with no further specifics, that agency principles controlled. *Id.*, at 72.

Nevertheless, as use of the terms grew in the wake of *Meritor*, they acquired their own significance. The standard of employer responsibility turned on which type of harassment occurred. If the plaintiff established a *quid pro quo* claim, the Courts of Appeals held, the employer was subject to vicarious liability. See, e.g., Davis v. Sioux City, 115 F.3d 1365, 1367 (CA8 1997). The rule encouraged Title VII plaintiffs to state their claims as *quid pro quo* claims, which in turn put expansive pressure on the definition. The equivalence of the *quid pro quo* label and vicarious liability is illustrated by this case. The question presented on certiorari is whether Ellerth can state a claim of *quid pro quo* harassment; but the issue of real concern to the parties is whether Burlington has vicarious liability for Slowik's alleged misconduct, rather than liability limited to its own negligence. . . .

We do not suggest the terms *quid pro quo* and hostile work environment are irrelevant to Title VII litigation. To the extent they illustrate the distinction between cases involving a threat which is carried out and offensive conduct in general, the terms are relevant when there is a threshold question whether a plaintiff can prove discrimination in violation of Title VII. When a plaintiff proves that a tangible employment action resulted from a refusal to submit to a supervisor's sexual demands, he or she establishes that the employment decision itself constitutes a change in the terms and conditions of employment that is actionable under Title VII. For any sexual harassment preceding the employment decision to be actionable, however, the conduct must be severe or pervasive. Because Ellerth's claim involves only unfulfilled threats, it should be categorized as a hostile work environment claim which requires a showing of severe or pervasive conduct. For purposes of this case, we accept the District Court's finding that the alleged conduct was severe or pervasive. The case before us involves numerous alleged threats, and we express no opinion as to whether a single unfulfilled threat is sufficient to constitute discrimination in the terms or conditions of employment.

When we assume discrimination can be proved, however, the factors we discuss below, and not the categories *quid pro quo* and hostile work environment, will be controlling on the issue of vicarious liability. That is the question we must resolve.

III

We must decide, then, whether an employer has vicarious liability when a supervisor creates a hostile work environment by making explicit threats to alter a subordinate's terms or conditions of employment, based on sex, but does not fulfill the threat. We turn to principles of agency law, for the term "employer" is defined under Title VII to include "agents." 42 U.S.C. § 2000e(b); see Meritor, supra, at 72. In express terms, Congress has directed federal courts to interpret Title VII based on agency principles. . . .

As *Meritor* acknowledged, the Restatement (Second) of Agency (1957) (hereinafter Restatement), is a useful beginning point for a discussion of general agency principles. 477 U.S. at 72. Since our decision in *Meritor*, federal courts have explored agency principles, and we find useful instruction in their decisions, noting that "common-law principles may not be transferable in all their particulars to Title VII." *Ibid.* . . .

A

Section 219(1) of the Restatement sets out a central principle of agency law:

> "A master is subject to liability for the torts of his servants committed while acting in the scope of their employment."

An employer may be liable for both negligent and intentional torts committed by an employee within the scope of his or her employment. Sexual harassment under Title VII presupposes intentional conduct. While early decisions absolved employers of liability for the intentional torts of their employees, the law now imposes liability where the employee's "purpose, however misguided, is wholly or in part to further the master's business." W. Keeton, D. Dobbs, R. Keeton, & D. Owen, Prosser and Keeton on Law of Torts § 70, p. 505 (5th ed. 1984) (hereinafter Prosser and Keeton on Torts). In applying scope of employment principles to intentional torts, however, it is accepted that "it is less likely that a willful tort will properly be held to be in the course of employment and that the liability of the master for such torts will naturally be more limited." F. Mechem, Outlines of the Law of Agency § 394, p. 266 (P. Mechem 4th ed., 1952). The Restatement defines conduct, including an intentional tort, to be within the scope of employment when "actuated, at least in part, by a purpose to serve the [employer]," even if it is forbidden by the employer. Restatement §§ 228(1)(c), 230. For example, when a salesperson lies to a customer to make a sale, the tortious conduct is within the scope of employment because it benefits the employer by increasing sales, even though it may violate the employer's policies. See Prosser and Keeton on Torts § 70, at 505–506.

As Courts of Appeals have recognized, a supervisor acting out of gender-based animus or a desire to fulfill sexual urges may not be actuated by a purpose to serve the employer. *See*, e.g., Torres v. Pisano, 116 F.3d 625, 634, n. 10 (CA2 1997). The harassing supervisor often acts for personal motives, motives unrelated and even antithetical to the objectives of the employer. . . .

The general rule is that sexual harassment by a supervisor is not conduct within the scope of employment.

B

Scope of employment does not define the only basis for employer liability under agency principles. In limited circumstances, agency principles impose liability on employers even where employees commit torts outside the scope of employment. The principles are set forth in the much-cited § 219(2) of the Restatement:

"(2) A master is not subject to liability for the torts of his servants acting outside the scope of their employment, unless:

"(a) the master intended the conduct or the consequences, or

"(b) the master was negligent or reckless, or

"(c) the conduct violated a non-delegable duty of the master, or

"(d) the servant purported to act or to speak on behalf of the principal and there was reliance upon apparent authority, or he was aided in accomplishing the tort by the existence of the agency relation."

. . . Subsection (a) addresses direct liability, where the employer acts with tortious intent, and indirect liability, where the agent's high rank in the company makes him or her the employer's alter ego. None of the parties contend Slowik's rank imputes liability under this principle. There is no contention, furthermore, that a nondelegable duty is involved. See § 219(2)(c). So, for our purposes here, subsections (a) and (c) can be put aside.

Subsections (b) and (d) are possible grounds for imposing employer liability on account of a supervisor's acts and must be considered. Under subsection (b), an employer is liable when the tort is attributable to the employer's own negligence. § 219(2)(b). Thus, although a supervisor's sexual harassment is outside the scope of employment because the conduct was for personal motives, an employer can be liable, nonetheless, where its own negligence is a cause of the harassment. An employer is negligent with respect to sexual harassment if it knew or should have known about the conduct and failed to stop it. Negligence sets a minimum standard for employer liability under Title VII; but Ellerth seeks to invoke the more stringent standard of vicarious liability.

Subsection 219(2)(d) concerns vicarious liability for intentional torts committed by an employee when the employee uses apparent authority (the apparent authority standard), or when the employee "was aided in accomplishing the tort by the existence of the agency relation" (the aided in the agency relation standard). *Ibid.* As other federal decisions have done in discussing vicarious liability for supervisor harassment, e.g., Henson v. Dundee, 682 F.2d 897, 909 (CA11 1982), we begin with § 219(2)(d).

C

As a general rule, apparent authority is relevant where the agent purports to exercise a power which he or she does not have, as distinct from where the agent threatens to misuse actual power. In the usual case, a supervisor's harassment involves misuse of actual power, not the false impression of its existence. Apparent authority analysis therefore is inappropriate in this context. . . . When a party seeks to impose vicarious liability based on an agent's misuse of delegated authority, the Restatement's aided in the agency relation rule, rather than the apparent authority rule, appears to be the appropriate form of analysis.

D

We turn to the aided in the agency relation standard. In a sense, most workplace tortfeasors are aided in accomplishing their tortious objective by the existence of the agency relation: Proximity and regular contact may afford a captive pool of potential victims. Were this to satisfy the aided in the agency relation standard, an employer would be subject to vicarious liability not only for all supervisor harassment, but also for all co-worker harassment, a result enforced by neither the EEOC nor any court of appeals to have considered the issue. *See*, e.g., Blankenship v. Parke Care Centers, Inc., 123 F.3d 868, 872 (CA6 1997), cert. denied, 522 U.S. 1110 (1998) (sex discrimination); see also *29* CFR 1604.11(d) (1997) ("knows or should have known" standard of liability for cases of harassment between "fellow employees"). The aided in the agency relation standard, therefore, requires the existence of something more than the employment relation itself.

At the outset, we can identify a class of cases where, beyond question, more than the mere existence of the employment relation aids in commission of the harassment: when a supervisor takes a tangible employment action against the subordinate. Every Federal Court of Appeals to have considered the question has found vicarious liability when a discriminatory act results in a tangible employment action. In *Meritor*, we acknowledged this consensus. See 477 U.S. at 70–71 ("The courts have consistently held employers liable for the discriminatory discharges of employees by supervisory personnel, whether or not the employer knew, or should have known, or approved of the supervisor's actions"). Although few courts have elaborated how agency principles support this rule, we think it reflects a correct application of the aided in the agency relation standard.

In the context of this case, a tangible employment action would have taken the form of a denial of a raise or a promotion. The concept of a tangible employment action appears in numerous cases in the Courts of Appeals discussing claims involving race, age, and national origin discrimination, as well as sex discrimination. Without endorsing the specific results of those decisions, we think it prudent to import the concept of a tangible employment action for resolution of the vicarious liability issue we consider here. A tangible employment action constitutes a significant change in employment status, such as hiring, firing, failing to promote, reassignment with significantly different responsibilities, or a decision causing a significant change in benefits. Compare Crady v. Liberty Nat. Bank & Trust Co. of Ind., 993 F.2d 132, 136 (CA7 1993) ("A materially adverse change might be indicated by a termination of employment, a demotion evidenced by a decrease in wage or salary, a less distinguished title, a material loss of benefits, significantly diminished material responsibilities, or other indices that might be unique to a particular situation"), with Flaherty v. Gas Research Institute, 31 F.3d 451, 456 (CA7 1994) (a "bruised ego" is not enough); Kocsis v. Multi-Care Management, Inc., 97 F.3d 876, 887 (CA6 1996) (demotion without change in pay, benefits, duties, or prestige insufficient) and Harlston v. McDonnell Douglas Corp., 37 F.3d 379, 382 (CA8 1994) (reassignment to more inconvenient job insufficient).

When a supervisor makes a tangible employment decision, there is assurance the injury could not have been inflicted absent the agency relation. A tangible employment action in most cases inflicts direct economic harm. As a general proposition, only a supervisor, or other person acting with the authority of the company, can cause this sort of injury. A co-worker can break a co-worker's arm as easily as a supervisor, and anyone who has regular contact with an employee can inflict psychological injuries by his or her offensive conduct. But one co-worker (absent some elaborate scheme) cannot dock another's pay, nor can one co-worker demote another. Tangible employment actions fall within the special province of the supervisor. The supervisor has been empowered by the company as a distinct class of agent to make economic decisions affecting other employees under his or her control.

Tangible employment actions are the means by which the supervisor brings the official power of the enterprise to bear on subordinates. A tangible employment decision requires an official act of the enterprise, a company act. The decision in most cases is documented in official company records, and may be subject to review by higher level supervisors. The supervisor often must obtain the imprimatur of the enterprise and use its internal processes. . . .

For these reasons, a tangible employment action taken by the supervisor becomes for Title VII purposes the act of the employer. Whatever the exact contours of the aided in the agency relation standard, its requirements will always be met when a supervisor takes a tangible employment action against a subordinate. . . .

Whether the agency relation aids in commission of supervisor harassment which does not culminate in a tangible employment action is less obvious.

Application of the standard is made difficult by its malleable terminology, which can be read to either expand or limit liability in the context of supervisor harassment. On the one hand, a supervisor's power and authority invests his or her harassing conduct with a particular threatening character, and in this sense, a supervisor always is aided by the agency relation. On the other hand, there are acts of harassment a supervisor might commit which might be the same acts a co-employee would commit, and there may be some circumstances where the supervisor's status makes little difference.

It is this tension which, we think, has caused so much confusion among the Courts of Appeals which have sought to apply the aided in the agency relation standard to Title VII cases. The aided in the agency relation standard, however, is a developing feature of agency law, and we hesitate to render a definitive explanation of our understanding of the standard in an area where other important considerations must affect our judgment. In particular, we are bound by our holding in *Meritor* that agency principles constrain the imposition of vicarious liability in cases of supervisory harassment. See Meritor, supra, at 72. Congress has not altered *Meritor*'s rule even though it has made significant amendments to Title VII in the interim.

Although *Meritor* suggested the limitation on employer liability stemmed from agency principles, the Court acknowledged other considerations might be relevant as well. For example, Title VII is designed to encourage the creation of antiharassment policies and effective grievance mechanisms. Were employer liability to depend in part on an employer's effort to create such procedures, it would effect Congress' intention to promote conciliation rather than litigation in the Title VII context, see EEOC v. Shell Oil Co., 466 U.S. 54, 77 (1984), and the EEOC's policy of encouraging the development of grievance procedures. See EEOC Policy Guidance on Sexual Harassment, 8 BNA FEP Manual 405:6699 (Mar. 19, 1990). To the extent limiting employer liability could encourage employees to report harassing conduct before it becomes severe or pervasive, it would also serve Title VII's deterrent purpose. As we have observed, Title VII borrows from tort law the avoidable consequences doctrine, see Ford Motor Co. v. EEOC, 458 U.S. 219, 231, n. 15 (1982), and the considerations which animate that doctrine would also support the limitation of employer liability in certain circumstances.

In order to accommodate the agency principles of vicarious liability for harm caused by misuse of supervisory authority, as well as Title VII's equally basic policies of encouraging forethought by employers and saving action by objecting employees, we adopt the following holding in this case and in *Faragher v. Boca Raton*, also decided today. An employer is subject to vicarious liability to a victimized employee for an actionable hostile environment created by a supervisor with immediate (or successively higher) authority over the employee. When no tangible employment action is taken, a defending employer may raise an affirmative defense to liability or damages, subject to proof by a preponderance of the evidence, see Fed. Rule Civ. Proc. 8(c). The defense comprises two necessary elements: (a) that the employer exercised reasonable care to prevent and correct promptly any sexually harassing behavior, and (b) that the plaintiff employee unreasonably failed to take advantage of any preventive or corrective opportunities provided by the employer or to avoid harm otherwise. While proof that an employer had promulgated an anti-harassment policy with complaint procedure is not necessary in every instance as a matter of law, the need for a stated policy suitable to the employment circumstances may appropriately be addressed in any case when litigating the first element of the defense. And while proof that an employee failed to fulfill the corresponding obligation of reasonable care to avoid harm is not limited to showing any unreasonable failure to use any complaint procedure provided by the employer, a demonstration of such failure will normally suffice to satisfy the employer's burden under the second element of the defense. No affirmative defense is available, however, when the supervisor's harassment culminates in a tangible employment action, such as discharge, demotion, or undesirable reassignment.

IV

Relying on existing case law which held out the promise of vicarious liability for all *quid pro quo* claims, Ellerth focused all her attention in the Court of Appeals on proving her claim fit within that category. Given our explanation that the labels *quid pro quo* and hostile work environment are not controlling for purposes of establishing employer liability, Ellerth should have an adequate opportunity to prove she has a claim for which Burlington is liable. . . .

For these reasons, we will affirm the judgment of the Court of Appeals, reversing the grant of summary judgment against Ellerth. On remand, the District Court will have the opportunity to decide whether it would be appropriate to allow Ellerth to amend her pleading or supplement her discovery.

The judgment of the Court of Appeals is affirmed.

[The opinion of JUSTICE GINSBURG, concurring in the judgment, is omitted.]

JUSTICE THOMAS, with whom JUSTICE SCALIA joins, dissenting.

The Court today manufactures a rule that employers are vicariously liable if supervisors create a sexually hostile work environment, subject to an affirmative defense that the Court barely attempts to define. This rule applies even if the employer has a policy against sexual harassment, the employee knows about that policy, and the employee never informs anyone in a position of authority about the supervisor's conduct. . . . An employer should be liable if, and only if, the plaintiff proves that the employer was negligent in permitting the supervisor's conduct to occur.

I

. . . When a supervisor inflicts an adverse employment consequence upon an employee who has rebuffed his advances, the supervisor exercises the specific authority granted to him by his company. His acts, therefore, are the company's acts and are properly chargeable to it. See 123 F.3d 490, 514 (1997) (Posner, C.J., dissenting). If a supervisor creates a hostile work environment, however, he does not act for the employer. As the Court concedes, a supervisor's creation of a hostile work environment is neither within the scope of his employment, nor part of his apparent authority. Indeed, a hostile work environment is antithetical to the interest of the employer. In such circumstances, an employer should be liable only if it has been negligent. That is, liability should attach only if the employer either knew, or in the exercise of reasonable care should have known, about the hostile work environment and failed to take remedial action.

Sexual harassment is simply not something that employers can wholly prevent without taking extraordinary measures—constant video and audio surveillance, for example—that would revolutionize the workplace in a manner incompatible with a free society. See 123 F.3d 490, 513 (POSNER, C.J., dissenting). Indeed, such measures could not even detect incidents of harassment such as the comments Slowick allegedly made to respondent in a hotel bar. The most that employers can be charged with, therefore, is a duty to act reasonably under the circumstances. . . .

Under a negligence standard, Burlington cannot be held liable for Slowick's conduct. Although respondent alleged a hostile work environment, she never contended that Burlington had been negligent in permitting the harassment to occur, and there is no question that Burlington acted reasonably under the circumstances. The company had a policy against sexual harassment, and respondent admitted that she was aware of the policy but nonetheless failed to tell anyone with authority over Slowick about his behavior. Burlington therefore cannot be charged with knowledge of Slowick's alleged harassment or with a failure to exercise reasonable care in not knowing about it.

II

Rejecting a negligence standard, the Court instead imposes a rule of vicarious employer liability, subject to a vague affirmative defense, for the acts of supervisors who wield no delegated authority in creating a hostile work environment. This rule is a whole-cloth creation. . . . [A]lthough the Court implies that it has found guidance in both precedent and statute . . . its holding is a product of willful policymaking, pure and simple. The only agency principle that justifies imposing employer liability in this context is the principle that a master will be liable for a servant's torts if the master was negligent or reckless in permitting them to occur; and as noted, under a negligence standard, Burlington cannot be held liable.

The Court's decision is also in considerable tension with our holding in *Meritor* that employers are not strictly liable for a supervisor's sexual harassment. See Meritor Savings Bank, FSB v. Vinson, supra, at 72. Although the Court recognizes an affirmative defense—based solely on its divination of Title VII's *gestalt*, it provides shockingly little guidance about how employers can actually avoid vicarious liability. . . . Moreover, employers will be liable notwithstanding the affirmative defense, *even though they acted reasonably*, so long as the plaintiff in question fulfilled *her* duty of reasonable care to avoid harm. See *ibid.* In practice, therefore, employer liability very well may be the rule. But as the Court acknowledges, this is the one result that it is clear Congress did *not* intend. See Meritor Savings Bank, FSB v. Vinson, 477 U.S. at 72.

The Court's holding does guarantee one result: There will be more and more litigation to clarify applicable legal rules in an area in which both practitioners and the courts have long been begging for guidance. It thus truly boggles the mind that the Court can claim that its holding will effect "Congress' intention to promote conciliation rather than litigation in the Title VII context." *Ante*, at 19. . . .

NOTES

1. **The Rationale Behind the Affirmative Defense.** The Court's decision in *Burlington Industries* has antecedents in the Court's *Meritor Savings* decision, but no appellate court had adopted the affirmative defense established in *Burlington*, giving some credence to the dissent's view that it was created out of "whole cloth." What purpose(s) was the Court seeking to further through the affirmative defense?

What difference would the negligence standard advocated by Justice Thomas in dissent have made, not just in the particular case, but in terms of establishing liability more broadly? On remand, how should Ellerth's claim be evaluated?

2. The *Faragher* Decision. On the same day as the Court's decision in *Burlington Industries*, the Court issued a separate decision in another sexual harassment case involving an employer's liability for supervisor harassment. The two cases were indistinguishable in their holding, although their reasoning varied somewhat. Writing for the Court in *Faragher v. City of Boca Raton*, 524 U.S. 775 (1998), Justice Souter elaborated on the rationale for the affirmative defense:

> This composite defense would, we think, implement the statute sensibly, for reasons that are not hard to fathom. Although Title VII seeks "to make persons whole for injuries suffered on account of unlawful employment discrimination," *Albemarle Paper Co. v. Moody*, 422 U.S. 405, 418 (1975), its "primary objective," like that of any statute meant to influence primary conduct, is not to provide redress but to avoid harm. *Id.*, at 417. As long ago as 1980, the Equal Employment Opportunity Commission (EEOC), charged with the enforcement of Title VII, adopted regulations advising employers to "take all steps necessary to prevent sexual harassment from occurring, such as . . . informing employees of their right to raise and how to raise the issue of harassment." 29 CFR § 1604.11(f) (1997), and in 1990 the Commission issued a policy statement enjoining employers to establish a complaint procedure "designed to encourage victims of harassment to come forward [without requiring] a victim to complain first to the offending supervisor." EEOC Policy Guidance on Sexual Harassment, 8 FEP Manual 405:6699 (Mar. 19, 1990) (internal quotation marks omitted). It would therefore implement clear statutory policy and complement the Government's Title VII enforcement efforts to recognize the employer's affirmative obligation to prevent violations and give credit here to employers who make reasonable efforts to discharge their duty.

> The requirement to show that the employee has failed in a coordinate duty to avoid or mitigate harm reflects an equally obvious policy imported from the general theory of damages, that a victim has a duty "to use such means as are reasonable under the circumstances to avoid or minimize the damages" that result from violations of the statute. *Ford Motor Co. v. EEOC*, 458 U.S. 219, 231, n. 15 (1982). An employer may, for example, have provided a proven, effective mechanism for reporting and resolving complaints of sexual harassment, available to the employee without undue risk or expense. If the plaintiff unreasonably failed to avail herself of the employer's preventive or remedial apparatus, she should not recover damages that could have been avoided if she had done so. If the victim could have avoided harm, no liability should be found against the employer who had taken reasonable care, and if damages could reasonably have been mitigated no award against a liable employer should reward a plaintiff for what her own efforts could have avoided.

Id. at 805–07.

3. Who Is a Supervisor? The liability standard established in *Burlington Industries* only applies to supervisor harassment, which leads to the question of how a supervisor might be defined. The Supreme Court recently took up the question of who is a supervisor for purposes of vicarious liability and adopted a narrow definition that had previously been adopted by the Seventh Circuit. In *Vance v. Ball State University*, 133 S. Ct. 2434 (2013), a divided court held: "[A]n employee is a 'supervisor' for purposes of vicarious liability under Title VII if he or she is empowered by the employer to take tangible employment actions against the victim." *Id.* at 2439. In so holding the Court rejected what it described as a more "nebulous" standard that would have included as supervisors those who had an ability to control the daily work lives of employees. *See id.* at 2448 and *id.* at 2459 (Ginsburg, J., dissenting) (suggesting the definition of supervisor should include those with the "power to direct subordinates' day-to-day work activities.").

4. Tangible Employment Actions. The initial question in assessing an employer's liability for harassment committed by a supervisor is whether a tangible employment action has occurred. As the Court explained in *Burlington Industries*, common examples of tangible employment actions are demotions, firings, denial of a promotion, and changes in salary or benefits. But what if there was no detrimental change in conditions because the plaintiff submitted to the supervisor's requests? Traditionally, such a situation has been defined as quid pro quo harassment for which the employer is strictly liable. *See Karibian v. Columbia Univ.*, 14 F.3d 773, 778 (2d Cir. 1994). Courts have applied the same rationale after *Burlington Industries*, noting that submitting to sexual requests as a condition of retaining employment constitutes a tangible employment action. *See Jin v. Metro. Life Ins. Co.*, 310 F.3d 84 (2d Cir. 2002). To hold otherwise, the court explained, would be to "punish employees who submit because, for example, they desperately need the income to make house payments, or because a sick spouse or child depends on their health benefits." *Id.* at 99. The court noted further that an "employee who is coerced into satisfying a supervisor's sexual demands to keep her job may suffer a greater injury than the employee who is able to refuse those demands." *Id.*

An issue that has generated substantial controversy is whether a constructive discharge amounts to a change in a tangible employment action so as to deny the employer the affirmative defense. The appellate courts split on the matter, and the Supreme Court resolved the issue by holding that the affirmative defense is unavailable to the extent the plaintiff alleges that an "official act" underlies the constructive discharge. *See Pennsylvania State Police v. Suders*, 542 U.S. 129 (2004). To explain its holding, the Court turned to two appellate court decisions:

> We note, finally, two recent Court of Appeals decisions that indicate how the "official act" (or "tangible employment action") criterion should play out when constructive discharge is alleged. . . . In Reed v. MBNA Marketing Systems, Inc., 333 F.3d 27 (1st Cir. 2003), the plaintiff claimed a constructive discharge based on her supervisor's repeated sexual comments and an incident in which he sexually assaulted her. The First Circuit held that the alleged wrongdoing did not preclude the employer from asserting the *Ellerth/Faragher* affirmative defense. As the court explained in *Reed*, the supervisor's behavior involved no official actions. . . . [T]he supervisor's conduct in *Reed* "was exceedingly unofficial and involved no direct exercise

of company authority"; indeed, it was "exactly the kind of wholly unathorized conduct for which the affirmative defense was designed," ibid. In contrast, in Robinson v. Sappington, 351 F.3d 317 (7th Cir. 2003), after the plaintiff complained that she was sexually harassed by the judge for whom she worked, the presiding judge decided to transfer her to another judge, but told her that her first six months [in the new post] probably would be "hell," and that it was in her "best interest to resign." Id., at 324. The Seventh Circuit held that the employer was precluded from asserting the affirmative defense to the plaintiff's constructive discharge claim. The Robinson plaintiff's decision to resign, the court explained, "resulted, at least in part, from [the presiding judge's] official action in transferring" her to a judge who resisted placing her on his staff. Id., at 337.

Pennsylvania State Police, 542 U.S. at 150.

5.   **The Scope of the Affirmative Defense.** Where the affirmative defense is available, both prongs must be satisfied. In determining whether the employer satisfies the first prong, namely whether the employer has a reasonable mechanism in place to prevent and remedy harassment, courts typically require an effective sexual harassment policy that has been distributed to all employees. See Helm v. Kansas, 656 F.3d 1277, 1286 (10th Cir. 2011). Training for management level employees is now common but not required to demonstrate that an effective policy is in place. Id. One important facet of any effective policy is that it provide for clear channels to report harassment, and that alternative channels be identified when the person committing the harassment is also the one to whom the harassment should be reported. See EEOC v. V.& J. Foods, Inc., 507 F.3d 575 (7th Cir. 2007) (holding that employer's policy was too vague and confusing particularly since many of the employees were teenagers); Madray v. Publix Supermarkets, Inc., 208 F.3d 1290, 1299 (11th Cir. 2000), cert. denied, 531 U.S. 926 (2000) (disseminating a sexual harassment policy is "fundamental" and it must offer alternative reporting channels).

The second prong—when a plaintiff has "unreasonably" failed to avail herself of the employer's policy—has led to more interpretive difficulties, and recently there has been a subtle but important shift in the law. There are typically two different situations: one where an employee fails to complain at all, in other words, fails to avail herself of the policy. The other scenario is when an employee delays in filing a claim. In the way the law has developed, courts strictly apply this prong of the defense and often focus on the employer's remedial actions, even though that is not technically part of the second prong of the defense, which focuses on the reasonableness of the employee's acts. Indeed, a strict reading of the affirmative defense would suggest that the employer's remedial actions are not relevant to the second prong at all but that is not how lower courts have interpreted the law. To give one example, the Eighth Circuit recently upheld the affirmative defense when an employee waited eight months to complain out of a fear of retaliation. The court, as has been true of most courts, rejected a generalized fear of retaliation as excusing the delayed filing and specifically noted, "As soon as Crawford reported the harassment, BNSF took prompt and effective action in investigating the complaint, putting the [alleged harasser] on administrative leave, and terminating him less than two weeks later." Crawford v. BNSF Railway Co., 665 F.3d 978, 985 (8th Cir.

2012), *cert denied*, 133 S. Ct. 144 (2012); *see also Crockett v. Mission Hosp., Inc.*, 717 F.3d 348, 357 (4th Cir. 2013) (focusing on the employer's "prompt and reasonable care" to hold that employee's failure to file formal complaint, even though employer had knowledge of the claim, was unreasonable). Should the employer's response to a complaint be a factor in whether the affirmative defense should be successful? What are the reasons for and against taking into account the response? This trend in the law for courts to implicitly take into account the employer's action has been recently documented by an empirical study that reviewed appeals from the grants of summary judgments. After reviewing the cases through a careful statistical analysis, the authors concluded that "employees who do not suffer a tangible loss will recover only if the employer did not exercise reasonable care to prevent harassment, and if reported, the employer did not respond well." Zev J. Eigen, David Sherwyn, & Nicholas Menillo, *When Rules Are Meant to Be Broken*, forthcoming NORTHWESTERN LAW REVIEW (2014).

As a practical matter, the way courts have incorporated an employer's response is by rejecting most explanations for why an individual either failed to file a complaint or delayed in filing. General and unexplained delays in reporting have typically failed to satisfy the plaintiff's reporting requirement. *See Baldwin v. BlueCross/Blue Shield of Alabama*, 480 F.3d 1287, 1307 (11th Cir. 2007) (unexplained three-month delay in reporting deemed unreasonable), *cert. denied*, 552 U.S. 991 (2007); *Gawley v. Indiana Univ.*, 276 F.3d 301, 312 (7th Cir. 2001) (waiting seven months to file formal complaint "unreasonable"). An unsubstantiated fear of retaliation will also not likely excuse a failure to report harassment. *See Adams v. O'Reilly Auto., Inc.*, 538 F.3d 926, 932 (8th Cir. 2008). Courts have responded in similar fashion when the plaintiff asserts a general belief that the employer would not do anything about the harassment, and thus considered reporting the behavior to be futile. *See Debord v. Mercy Health Sys.*, 737 F.3d 642, 655 (10th Cir. 2013) ("A failure to report harassment cannot be excused merely because the accuser believes the report will be futile."), *cert. denied*, 134 S. Ct. 2664 (2014). The employee must be able to articulate why she felt the filing would, in fact, prove futile. *Id. See also Thornton v. Fed. Express Corp.*, 530 F.3d 451, 457 (6th Cir. 2008) (generalized fear of retaliation does not excuse failure to file a complaint). When the employee is able to offer a specific explanation, courts are far more likely to find her actions reasonable. In one case, the court found that an employee's failure to report harassment was reasonable because the contact person for filing the report was a friend of the supervisor who was the focus of the complaint, witnesses had failed to report the harassment, the union told her it would be "extremely difficult and quite delicate" to get involved, and there was a significant age difference between the employee and the supervisor who was accused of harassment. *See Monteagudo v. Asociación de Empleados del Estado Libre Asociado*, 554 F.3d 164 (1st Cir. 2009), *cert. denied*, 558 U.S. 821 (2009); *see also Craig v. M&O Agencies, Inc.*, 496 F.3d 1047 (9th Cir. 2007) (19-day delay in filing complaint not unreasonable). Taking this line of cases and the development of the law into account, how would you counsel an employee who seeks your advice about how to address ongoing workplace harassment? What about if you represented an employer who came to you seeking advice regarding what the law required?

6. Other Forms of Harassment. We have been focusing on hostile environment perpetrated by supervisors, but there are three other forms of sexual harassment that should be noted. First, as discussed in the principal cases, sexual harassment can take the form of quid pro quo harassment, which is generally defined as a situation when the employer conditions employment on acceding to a sexual demand. *See Burlington Industries*, 524 U.S. at 723 (defining quid pro quo harassment as when "an employer demands sexual favors from an employee in return for a job benefit."). In the case of quid pro quo harassment, an employer is held strictly liable and quid pro quo harassment can only be committed by a supervisor with decisionmaking authority. In light of the Supreme Court's decision in *Burlington Industries*, whether conduct is treated as quid pro quo or hostile environment harassment is of significantly less importance given that the employer's liability is determined by agency principles rather than the particular label that is applied to the conduct. *See Jin v. Metro. Live Ins. Co.*, 310 F.3d 84, 91 (2d Cir. 2002) (discussing change in the law effected by *Burlington Industries*).

Co-worker harassment poses different issues, and as discussed in *Burlington Industries*, the standard for employer liability differs as well. When a hostile environment is created by co-workers, the standard for employer liability is one of negligence—whether the employer "knew or should have known of the harassment and failed to take prompt remedial action." *See Green v. Franklin Nat'l Bank*, 459 F.3d 903, 910 (8th Cir. 2006).

Finally, a number of courts have recognized claims for harassment perpetrated by customers or other third parties. In cases of customer harassment, courts apply the negligence standard applicable in co-worker cases, but they do so with a more stringent eye so that the duties of employers are lessened because they have less control over their customers than they do their employees. *See Lockard v. Pizza Hut*, 162 F.3d 1062 (10th Cir. 1998) (applying the standard for co-worker harassment to case of customer harassment). A Corrections Department was also found liable for failing to address a hostile environment created by male inmates perpetrated against female correctional officers. *See Beckford v. Dep't of Corr.*, 605 F.3d 951 (11th Cir. 2010).

7. Evaluating Sexual Harassment Law. The law governing sexual harassment in the workplace has come a long way since its inception in the late 1970s, so much so that many are now questioning whether it has gone too far. Feminist legal scholar Vicki Schultz has argued that the law has created an atmosphere that seeks to drive all sex-related interactions out of the workplace. She writes:

> In the name of preventing sexual harassment, employers increasingly ban or discourage employee romance, chilling intimacy and solidarity among employees of both a sexual and nonsexual variety. Many companies are punishing employees for behavior that does not meet the legal definition of sex harassment, costing many workers their jobs and undercutting their ability to express themselves and create their own cultures and sexual norms. Women are encouraged to translate—and perhaps even to understand—broader forms of discrimination and managerial abuse as sexual harms. Perhaps most disturbingly, managers sometimes invoke sex harassment law as a pretext for firing people on discriminatory or

> otherwise suspect grounds, and employees use it to legitimate their bias against coworkers of a different race, sexual orientation, or class whose sexuality threatens or offends them.

Vicki Schultz, *The Sanitized Workplace*, 112 YALE L.J. 2061, 2191 (2003). Is it possible that the law has gone too far? Although there are very few cases that hold an employer liable for offensive jokes, or comments about a woman's clothes, employers may want to excise all such comments from the workplace as a way of protecting themselves from liability. Does the affirmative defense create such incentives? Another way of perceiving the changes is that the workplace has also eradicated lots of behavior that was deeply offensive to women even though it was also common workplace behavior, and in this respect, even assuming the law has moved significantly towards sanitizing the workplace, there would remain a question whether the workplace is now a more hospitable place for women. Is this perhaps a way of defining a workable balance, one that may find a proper equilibrium in time but that may need to swing more broadly for awhile in order to change the existing norms?

The affirmative defense established in *Burlington Industries* has also generated considerable controversy, in part because many perceive that the balance has shifted to blaming women who fail to complain in a timely fashion. For a personal account of a law professor who reported harassment while a Professor of Finance see Anne Lawton, *Between Scylla & Charybdis: The Perils of Reporting Sexual Harassment*, 9 U. PA. J. L. 603 (2007). Although Lawton prevailed on her claim, she contends that requiring women to report harassment frequently leads to retaliation, in effect exchanging one problem for another. *See also* L. Camille Hebert, *Why Don't "Reasonable Women" Complain About Sexual Harassment?* 82 IND. L.J. 711 (2007) (advocating that courts should consider a women's perspective in determining whether the failure to report was reasonable). In the area of sexual harassment, what should the law's objective be?

E. DISABILITY DISCRIMINATION: THE AMERICANS WITH DISABILITIES ACT

The Americans With Disabilities Act ("ADA") was passed in 1990, and has generated a substantial amount of litigation, controversy and recent amendments. Prior to the passage of the ADA, there was a predecessor act called the Rehabilitation Act of 1973 ("Rehabilitation Act") that applied to federal contractors and the federal government, and still does. Although there was not nearly as much law developed under the Rehabilitation Act, the law that existed under the Act substantially influenced the development of the ADA, and courts often use the two statutes interchangeably.

At least three public policies supported the passage of the ADA. First, Congress sought to prohibit discrimination against the disabled, and it relied on a broad, and comprehensive definition of disability to further that interest. Second, Congress sought to eradicate the persistent stereotypes that operated against the disabled, particularly with respect to the abilities of the disabled. Much of the legislative history is devoted to explaining how employers, and society more generally, frequently misperceived the abilities of those with disabilities. This particular concern is directly encompassed in the statutory prohibition on discriminating against individuals who are "regarded as" disabled. *See* Michelle A. Travis, *Leveling the Playing Field or Stacking the Deck? The "Unfair Advantage" Critique of Perceived Disability Claims*, 78 N.C. L. Rev. 901, 903–05 (2000) (discussing legislative history). Third, there was a public welfare concern insofar as many individuals who were disabled but unable to find work were receiving federal disability payments, and because of the belief that many of these individuals were capable of working, there was a Congressional desire to reduce the public welfare burden by employing those who would otherwise receive public assistance. *See* Samuel R. Bagenstos, *The Americans With Disabilities Act as Welfare Reform*, 44 Wm. & Mary L. Rev. 921 (2003) (discussing public welfare aspect of the ADA).

1. Defining Disability

The ADA defines discrimination in a way that is quite different from the prohibitions contained within Title VII. The ADA provides that "no covered entity shall discriminate against a qualified individual with a disability because of the disability of such individual . . . ." 42 U.S.C. § 12112(a). The ADA further defines "qualified individual with a disability" as

> an individual with a disability who, with or without reasonable accommodation, can perform the essential functions of the employment position that such individual holds or desires.

42 U.S.C. § 12111(8). The statute also provides three different ways of establishing that one is disabled. A plaintiff may show that he is disabled within the meaning of the ADA by establishing that: (A) he is physically or mentally impaired such that he is substantially limited in one or more major life activity; (B) he has a record of such an impairment; or (C) that he is regarded as having such an impairment. 42 U.S.C. § 12102(2).

As noted above, the statute generated a tremendous amount of litigation and many courts, including most importantly the Supreme Court, interpreted the statute narrowly, particularly when it came to defining disability. The Supreme Court's most controversial case was *Sutton v. United Airlines, Inc.*, 527 U.S. 471 (1999), where the plaintiffs, twin sisters with poor eyesight, challenged United Airline's vision requirement for pilot positions. The plaintiffs argued that their eyesight rendered them disabled under the terms of the statute, even though when they wore glasses their vision was fine. The primary issue before the Court was in determining whether the plaintiffs were disabled and entitled to protection under the ADA, they should be assessed in their mitigated or unmitigated condition— whether their glasses should be taken into account. In a 7-2 decision, the Court held that individuals should be assessed in their mitigated condition, which as a practical matter meant that the Suttons were not disabled since their glasses corrected their condition.

The Suttons also argued that if they were not disabled under the terms of the statute, then they were being "regarded as" disabled since the employer considered their eyesight to be disqualifying for pilot positions. The Supreme Court, however, rejected their claim holding instead that an employee was only "regarded as disabled" to the extent that the employer considered them disabled from a broad class of jobs, a standard that is very difficult to meet. *Id.* at 492.

Although the Sutton case generated the most controversy, the Supreme Court decided two other cases during the same Term that likewise narrowed the scope of the statute. In *Toyota Motor Mfg. v. Williams*, 534, U.S. 184 (2002), the plaintiff worked on an assembly line for Toyota Motors and sought an accommodation for her carpel tunnel syndrome which limited her in many of the manual activities required by her job, even though she was still able to perform many of the manual activities that were part of her everyday life, such as brushing her teeth, bathing and various household chores. The Supreme Court defined the standard that should be applied to such a case. Noting that the statute should be "interpreted strictly to create a demanding standard for qualifying as disabled," *id.* at 197, the Court went on to hold that where a plaintiff alleges she is substantially limited in the major life activity of performing manual tasks, the question is whether the plaintiff is limited in activities that are of "central importance to most people's daily lives." *Id.* at 198. It is not sufficient, the Court held, for the plaintiff to establish that she is substantially limited in performing manual tasks that are associated with a particular job. *Id.* at 201.

Both of these cases substantially limited the scope of the statute, and the *Sutton* case in particular had the effect of excluding certain conditions that had originally prompted the passage of the ADA. For example, the sponsor of the bill in the House, Tony Coehlo, suffered from epilepsy, and the discrimination he had faced during his life was one of the motivating factors for him to help fashion the bill. But because epilepsy can often be treated with medication, those who suffer from epilepsy were often determined not to be disabled. *See, e.g., Nese v. Julian Nordic Constr. Co.*, 405 F.3d 638, 639 (7th Cir.), *cert. denied*, 546 U.S. 1003 (2005); *Brunke v. Goodyear Tire & Rubber Co.*, 344 F.3d 819 (8th Cir. 2003). Individuals who suffered from depression or diabetes were also frequently determined not to be disabled. *See, e.g., Ristrom v. Abestos Workers Local 34 Joint Apprentice Comm.*, 370 F.3d 763, 772 (8th Cir. 2004); *Swanson v. Univ. of Cincinnati*, 268 F.3d 307 (6th Cir. 2001). The *Toyota* case also led both to some unusual inquiries, such as whether hugging was a major life activity, and led to the denial of coverage to many individuals. *See, e.g., Nuzum v. Ozark Auto. Distribs., Inc.*, 432 F.3d 839, 846 (8th Cir. 2005) (considering but not deciding whether hugging was a major life activity); *Guzman-Rosario v. UPS, Inc.*, 397 F.3d 6, 10–11 (1st Cir. 2005) (plaintiff's ovarian cysts did not interfere with daily activities).

As a result of these and other developments, Congress passed the ADA Amendments Act of 2008. The primary purpose of the Act is to "reinstate[e] a broad scope of protection to be available under the ADA," and the findings and purposes section specifically references the Supreme Court's decisions in *Sutton* and *Toyota Motor* as incorrectly narrowing the scope of the statute. *See* Sec. 2(b)(1–5), 42 U.S.C. § 12101. The 2008 Amendments did not change the basic definition of disability but instead altered the meanings of some of the terms.

The statute specifically alters the definition of "major life activities" by including specific conditions that qualify, including internal bodily functions, which had created some controversy under the prior statute. 42 U.S.C. § 12102(2). Perhaps most importantly, the statute also excludes "the ameliorative effects of mitigating measures" in determining whether someone is disabled. 42 U.S.C. § 12102(4)(E). The statute, however, specifically notes that "ordinary eyeglasses or contact lenses" should generally be considered. The statute also redefines the "regarded as" prong to mean that a person is regarded as disabled if "the individual establishes that he or she has been subjected to an action prohibited under this Act because of an actual or perceived physical or mental impairment whether or not the impairment limits or is perceived to limit a major life activity." 42 U.S.C. § 12102(3)(A).

The statute went into effect in January 2009 but courts uniformly held that the statute did not apply retroactively. In other words, the prior statute governed all claims that arose prior to January 2009. For a variety of reasons, cases only began to appear in the Courts of Appeals under the Amendments beginning in 2014, though in many cases courts do not identify whether the case is being determined under the pre or post-Amendments Act (and in many instances, it does not matter). The next case, and the accompanying notes provide some indication of how the law is likely to be interpreted moving forward. For a thorough discussion of the Amendments with a particular focus on how they were designed to alter the law see Alex. B. Long, *Introducing the New and Improved Americans With Disabilities Act: Assessing the ADA Amendments Act of 2008*, 103 N.W. U. L. REV. COLLOQUY 217 (2008). One issue that has not been changed by the Amendments and is worth noting, is that individuals who are HIV-positive, but who do not have AIDs, have been defined as disabled for purposes of the ADA, and the Rehabilitation Act. *See Bragdon v. Abbott*, 524 U.S. 624 (1998).

WEAVING v. CITY OF HILLSBORO
United States Court of Appeals for the Ninth Circuit
763 F.3d 1106 (2014)

W. FLETCHER, CIRCUIT JUDGE:

We must decide whether, consistent with the Americans with Disabilities Act ("ADA"), an employer properly terminated an employee who had recurring interpersonal problems with his colleagues that were attributable to attention deficit hyperactivity disorder ("ADHD"). Plaintiff Matthew Weaving worked for the Hillsboro Police Department ("HPD") in Oregon from 2006 to 2009. HPD terminated Weaving's employment in 2009 following severe interpersonal problems between Weaving and other HPD employees. Weaving contends that these interpersonal problems resulted from his ADHD. After his discharge, Weaving brought suit under the ADA. He contended that he was disabled because his ADHD substantially limited his ability to engage in two major life activities: working and interacting with others. He claimed that HPD had discharged him because of his disabilities in violation of the ADA.

The jury returned a general verdict for Weaving, finding that he was disabled and that the City of Hillsboro ("the City") had discharged him because of his disability. The City moved for judgment as a matter of law. It also moved for a new trial on the ground of improper jury instructions. The district court denied both motions, and the City appealed.

We reverse. We hold as a matter of law that the jury could not have found that ADHD substantially limited Weaving's ability to work or to interact with others within the meaning of the ADA.

I. Background

The evidence presented at trial showed the following. In 1973, Weaving, then six years old, was diagnosed with "hyperkinetic activity," known today as ADHD. His pediatrician prescribed medication. Weaving stopped taking medication at age twelve because, as his mother explained to him, he seemed to have outgrown the symptoms of ADHD. He continued, however, to experience interpersonal problems throughout childhood and adolescence.

Weaving joined the Beaverton Police Department ("BPD") in Oregon as a police officer in July 1995. During the application process, he passed a battery of tests, including psychological and medical evaluations. Because he believed ADHD no longer affected him, Weaving did not disclose or discuss his childhood diagnosis and medication. Weaving's evaluations during his employment at BPD described him as "[a]loof, abrasive, too outspoken at inappropriate times," "forcefully outspoken," "disgruntled," and "intimidating," but also stated that he "works well with co-workers" and was "friendly, helpful and hard working." Some of his supervisors noted that he "[h]ad difficulty working in a team environment."

In 2001, while employed by BPD, Weaving became a narcotics detective on an interagency team. He was removed from the team less than a year later because of "personality conflicts" with another officer. While still employed by BPD, due to ongoing difficulties with colleagues Weaving left the interagency narcotics team to join an FBI task force. Weaving later learned that an FBI agent had complained to BPD about "communication issues" with him. . . .

Weaving was hired by HPD in 2006. During the application process, Weaving disclosed what he described as the "intermittent interpersonal communication issues" he experienced at BPD. HPD offered Weaving provisional employment, contingent upon passing a psychological evaluation. Weaving disclosed his childhood history of ADHD but did not believe at that time that ADHD continued to affect him.

Weaving's first-year evaluation at HPD was generally positive. His supervisor, Lt. Jim Kelly, praised his experience and knowledge. Lt. Kelly wrote that he had seen Weaving conduct all his investigations in a "thorough, professional, and conscientious manner." Lt. Kelly noted that "[a] few members of the Department have the misconception that Weaving is arrogant," but that neither he nor members of Weaving's patrol team had found this to be the case.

Weaving applied for a promotion to sergeant in 2007. The application process included a "psychological leadership assessment," conducted by an off-site psychologist. Weaving did not mention ADHD during the application process because he believed he had outgrown it. The psychologist provided a six-page report in which he described Weaving as having a profile similar to individuals who "tend to be dominant in interpersonal relationships." He described Weaving as "socially interactive" and engaging in "cooperative and outgoing" relationships with others. . . .

Weaving was promoted to sergeant in April 2007. In his annual evaluation, covering the period from May 2007 through April 2008, Lt. Kelly wrote that Weaving's interactions with the public were professional and that he displayed empathy toward members of the public. Lt. Kelly wrote that Weaving's communication style ("[d]irectness") came across to officers as "arrogant" and inspired fear, but that he personally did not have difficulties with Weaving. Lt. Kelly wrote that Weaving was aware of his communication issues and seemed willing to try new approaches.

Weaving's interpersonal difficulties continued after Lt. Kelly's 2008 evaluation. One subordinate testified at trial that he found Weaving's responses to his questions "demeaning." Another subordinate testified that Weaving's responses to questions were "intimidating," making him "feel stupid and small." . . . In addition, Weaving referred to some HPD officers in a derogatory fashion, calling them "salad eaters," rather than "meat eaters" or "warriors," to imply that the officers were weak. He also criticized the language skills of a newly hired Latino officer who did not speak English as his first language.

In March 2009, Weaving issued a several-page disciplinary letter to a subordinate who had driven a marked police vehicle through a surveillance area. At the time of the incident, Weaving had verbally rebuked the officer over the open radio. The officer believed the letter was a disproportionate response to what he had done. He filed a grievance against Weaving with the City Human Resources Department. On April 7, 2009, the City placed Weaving on paid administrative leave pending investigation of the grievance.

Weaving testified that, while he was on leave, it occurred to him that some of his interpersonal difficulties at HPD might have been due to ADHD. He met with a mental health nurse practitioner who prescribed him a low dose of medication and referred him to Dr. Gary Monkarsh, a clinical psychologist. Dr. Monkarsh concluded that Weaving suffered from adult ADHD. Dr. Monkarsh testified at trial that people with ADHD "have a hard time understanding their emotions, the emotions of others, the ability to regulate one's emotions and the emotions of others, the ability to empathize with others." He also testified that someone with Weaving's characteristics "could be an excellent police officer."

On May 7, 2009, Dr. Monkarsh sent a letter to the HPD Police Chief stating that he had diagnosed Weaving as having ADHD. A day later, Weaving wrote to the City Human Resources director informing her of Dr. Monkarsh's diagnosis and attaching his letter to the Police Chief. He wrote:

> My Psychologist . . . has advised me that he is confident that with sustained treatment I will eliminate communication issues that currently are being considered adverse to the work environment of the Hillsboro Police Department (HPD). . . .

Weaving requested "all reasonable accommodations," including reinstatement to his position as an active-duty sergeant.

On June 16, 2009, Lt. Richard Goerling wrote a memorandum summarizing the findings of the investigation of the grievance against Weaving. The investigation, conducted while Weaving was on leave, included interviews of 28 HPD employees. Lt. Goerling concluded that Weaving had "creat[ed] and foster[ed] a hostile work environment for his subordinates and peers; in particular, he has been described in terms such as tyrannical, unapproachable, non-communicative, belittling, demeaning, threatening, intimidating, arrogant and vindictive." He wrote, "In the short time Weaving has been employed at HPD, he has demonstrated time and again unacceptable interpersonal communication that suggests he does not possess adequate emotional intelligence to successfully work in a team environment, much less lead a team of police officers."

On Lt. Goerling's recommendation, the City conducted an independent medical evaluation and evaluated Weaving's fitness for duty. Two doctors found Weaving fit for duty despite his ADHD diagnosis. On November 24, 2009, the Deputy Chief of Police sent Weaving, through his attorney, a sixteen-page letter advising him of the City's intention to terminate his employment "unless you persuade me otherwise." The letter described in detail Weaving's interpersonal problems and their effect on HPD. After a hearing, the City terminated Weaving's employment effective December 11, 2009.

Weaving sued the City in federal district court under the ADA. He alleged that (1) the City fired him because he had an impairment that limited his ability to work or interact with others, and (2) the City fired him because it regarded him as disabled. The case was tried to a jury. The City moved for judgment as a matter of law at the close of Weaving's case-in-chief. The district court denied the motion. The City renewed its motion at the close of all evidence. The district court again denied the motion . . . .

The jury returned a verdict for Weaving, finding him disabled under the ADA. It found that the City had terminated him because of his disability. The jury awarded Weaving $75,000 in damages. The district court awarded $232,143 in back pay, $330,807 in front pay, and $139,712 in attorney's fees. The district court refused Weaving's request for reinstatement because of "hostility and antagonism between" Weaving and HPD.

The City filed a renewed motion for judgment as matter of law based on insufficient evidence to support the verdict, as well as a motion for a new trial based on an allegedly erroneous jury instruction. The district court denied both motions. The City timely appealed.

We reverse the denial of the motion for judgment as a matter of law. We do not reach the denial of the motion for a new trial . . . .

II. Discussion

The ADA forbids discrimination against a "qualified individual on the basis of disability." 42 U.S.C. § 12112(a). A disability is "a physical or mental impairment that substantially limits one or more major life activities of [the] individual [who claims the disability]," or "a record of such an impairment," or "being regarded as having such an impairment." Id. § 12102(1). The ADA provides a nonexhaustive list of "major life activities." Such activities include "caring for oneself, performing manual tasks, seeing, hearing, eating, sleeping, walking, standing, lifting, bending, speaking, breathing, learning, reading, concentrating, thinking, communicating, and working." Id. § 12102(2)(A).

A 2008 amendment to the ADA provides, "The definition of disability in this chapter shall be construed in favor of broad coverage of individuals under this chapter, to the maximum extent permitted by the terms of this chapter." Id. § 12102(4)(A). "The term 'substantially limits' shall be interpreted consistently with the findings and purposes of the ADA Amendments Act of 2008." Id. § 12102(4)(B). Those findings and purposes specifically express Congress's view that prior Supreme Court and lower court cases, as well as Equal Employment Opportunity Commission ("EEOC") regulations, had given "substantially limits" an unduly narrow construction. ADA Amendments Act of 2008, § 2(a)(4)–(8), Pub. L. No. 110-325. "An impairment that substantially limits one major life activity need not limit other major life activities in order to be considered a disability." 42 U.S.C. § 12102(4)(C). According to post-2008 regulations promulgated by the EEOC,

> An impairment is a disability . . . if it substantially limits the ability of an individual to perform a major life activity as compared to most people in the general population. An impairment need not prevent, or significantly or severely restrict, the individual from performing a major life activity in order to be considered substantially limiting.

29 C.F.R. § 1630.2(j)(1)(ii). Determining whether an impairment is substantially limiting "requires an individualized assessment." Id. § 1630.2(j)(1)(iv).

Weaving contends that the evidence at trial shows that he is substantially limited in the major life activities of working and of interacting with others. We take these two activities in turn.

A. Working

The ADA specifically lists working as a major life activity. See 42 U.S.C. § 12012(2)(A). Under our pre-2008 case law, in order to show a substantial limitation on his ability to work, a plaintiff had to establish that his impairment precluded working not only at a particular job, but also a class of jobs or a broad range of jobs in various classes. See Sutton v. United Air Lines, Inc., 527 U.S. 471, 491(1999); Holihan v. Lucky Stores, Inc., 87 F.3d 362, 366 (9th Cir. 1996). The plaintiff had to present specific evidence about relevant labor markets in order to avoid summary judgment on a claim that he was substantially limited in his ability to work. Thornton v. McClatchy Newspapers, Inc., 261 F.3d 789, 795 (9th Cir. 2001).

The 2008 amendments to the ADA relaxed the standard for determining whether a plaintiff is substantially limited in engaging in a major life activity, but Weaving cannot satisfy even the lower standard under current law. The record does not contain substantial evidence showing that Weaving was limited in his ability to work compared to "most people in the general population." See 29 C.F.R. § 1630.2(j)(1)(ii).

On the contrary, there is evidence showing that Weaving was in many respects a skilled police officer. Dr. Monkarsh and Weaving both testified that Weaving had developed compensatory mechanisms that helped him overcome ADHD's impediments and succeed in his career. Weaving's supervisors recognized his knowledge and technical competence and selected him for high-level assignments. In 2007, before receiving any treatment for adult ADHD, he was promoted to sergeant. In 2009, a psychologist and a physician/psychiatrist both deemed Weaving fit for duty as a police officer . . . .

B. Interacting with Others

Weaving also argues that he is disabled because his ADHD substantially limits his ability to interact with others. Unlike many of our sister circuits, we have specifically recognized interacting with others as a major life activity. *Cf. Bodenstab v. Cnty. of Cook*, 569 F.3d 651, 656 (7th Cir. 2009) (assuming, without deciding, that interacting with others is a major life activity); *Heisler v. Metro. Council*, 339 F.3d 622, 628 (8th Cir. 2003) (same); *Steele v. Thiokol Corp.*, 241 F.3d 1248, 1255 (10th Cir. 2001) (same); *Soileau v. Guilford of Me., Inc.*, 105 F.3d 12, 15 (1st Cir. 1997) (assuming, "*dubitante*, that a colorable claim may be made that 'ability to get along with others' is or may be . . . a major life activity under the ADA").

We wrote in *McAlindin v. County of San Diego*, 192 F.3d 1226 (9th Cir. 1999), that "[b]ecause interacting with others is an essential, regular function, like walking and breathing, it easily falls within the definition of 'major life activity.' " *Id.* at 1234. There was evidence in *McAlindin* that the plaintiff suffered from panic attacks, "fear reaction[s]," and "communicative paralysis," which caused him to stay at home for at least twenty hours per day. *Id.* at 1235. We held that this evidence was enough to defeat the defendant's motion for summary judgment. *Id.* at 1235–36. However, we cautioned:

> Recognizing interacting with others as a major life activity of course does not mean that any cantankerous person will be deemed substantially limited in a major life activity. Mere trouble getting along with coworkers is not sufficient to show a substantial limitation . . . .

> In addition, the limitation must be severe . . . . We hold that a plaintiff must show that his "relations with others were characterized on a regular basis by severe problems, for example, consistently high levels of hostility, social withdrawal, or failure to communicate when necessary."

Id. at 1235. In *Head v. Glacier Northwest, Inc.*, 413 F.3d 1053 (9th Cir. 2005), we held that a plaintiff who "avoid[ed] crowds, stores, large family gatherings, and even doctor's appointments," and who did not leave the house for weeks after losing his job, had offered sufficient evidence of disability to survive summary judgment. *Id.* at 1060–61.

The evidence in this case differs starkly from that in *McAlindin* and *Head*. The plaintiffs in those cases were so severely impaired that they were essentially housebound. McAlindin's doctor described him as "barely functional," and there was evidence that he "suffer[ed] from a total inability to communicate at times." *McAlindin*, 192 F.3d at 1235. Head avoided contact with others, even members of his family, and had difficulty even carrying on conversations over the telephone. *Head*, 413 F.3d at 1061.

The evidence at trial showed that Weaving has experienced recurring interpersonal problems throughout his professional life. Those problems have had significant repercussions on his career as a police officer, resulting, most recently, in the termination of his employment with HPD. But Weaving's interpersonal problems do not amount to a substantial impairment of his ability to interact with others within the meaning of the ADA. Weaving's ADHD may well have limited his ability to *get along* with others. But that is not the same as a substantial limitation on the ability to *interact* with others.

In contrast to the plaintiffs in *McAlindin* and *Head*, Weaving was able to engage in normal social interactions. His interpersonal problems existed almost exclusively in his interactions with his peers and subordinates. He had little, if any, difficulty comporting himself appropriately with his supervisors . . . .

As we wrote in *McAlindin*, a "cantankerous person" who has "[m]ere trouble getting along with coworkers" is not disabled under the ADA. 192 F.3d at 1235. One who is able to communicate with others, though his communications may at times be offensive, "inappropriate, ineffective, or unsuccessful," is not substantially limited in his ability to interact with others within the meaning of the ADA. *Jacques*, 386 F.3d 192, 203 (2d Cir. 2004). To hold otherwise would be to expose to potential ADA liability employers who take adverse employment actions against ill-tempered employees who create a hostile workplace environment for their colleagues.

III. Conclusion

Based on the evidence presented in this case, no reasonable jury could have found Weaving disabled under the ADA. His ADHD did not substantially limit either his ability to work or to interact with others. The district court erred in denying the City's motion for judgment as a matter of law.

CALLAHAN, CIRCUIT JUDGE, dissenting:

A jury of Matthew Weaving's peers sat in a courtroom for four days. They observed and listened to his coworkers, his supervisors, his doctors, his wife, as well as Weaving, himself. After being properly instructed on the law of our circuit, they dutifully studied the evidence and deliberated for eight hours over the course of two days. They found that Weaving was disabled and that the City of Hillsboro fired him because of his disability in violation of the Americans with Disabilities Act ("ADA").

Now on appeal, the majority decides that it knows better. It reweighs the evidence on a cold record and issues its own diagnosis: Weaving isn't disabled, he's just a jerk. Therefore, the City was free to fire him. In the course of doing so, the majority usurps the jury's role and guts our controlling circuit precedent, *McAlindin v. County of San Diego*, 192 F.3d 1226 (9th Cir. 1999). Instead of following *McAlindin*, as it was bound to do, the majority abrogates *McAlindin sub silentio* and replaces our circuit's standards with those announced in another circuit's patently incompatible decision, *Jacques v. DiMarzio, Inc.*, 386 F.3d 192 (2d Cir. 2004). I cannot concur.

I

The majority selectively reviews the evidence to cast Weaving in an unsympathetic light. But there are two sides to every story and the one that the jury heard was more nuanced than the majority acknowledges.

The evidence showed that Weaving was diagnosed with ADHD as a child but had been led to believe that he had "outgrown" his symptoms. As an adult, Weaving had a strong dedication to police work, and initially "was a strong performer" as a patrol officer who was promoted to sergeant over several others. However, he had difficulty in his jobs both at the Beaverton Police Department and the Hillsboro Police Department ("HPD"), particularly once he was promoted beyond patrolman. In particular, his coworkers said that: they would avoid interactions with him; he would engage in lengthy lectures in response to simple questions; he would send impulsive emails; he would "beat a dead horse"; he was "socially retarded"; he made them feel intimidated and demeaned; he lacked any awareness of the reactions of others; and that he was hard to approach.

Lieutenant Richard Goerling's investigation was critical to the City's decision to terminate Weaving. Goerling found that Weaving had difficulty interacting with subordinates, peers, supervisors, and informants throughout his career. Among other things, Goerling concluded that Weaving refused to accept responsibility for his behavior. Goerling also repeatedly suggested that Weaving was a bully and intimidated his coworkers. At trial, however, Goerling *admitted* on the stand that he was *biased* against Weaving and that his report contained numerous inaccuracies and omissions in what were represented as interviewees' direct quotations. Additionally, *none* of the City's witnesses actually suggested that Weaving had bullied or intentionally intimidated his coworkers.

Deputy Chief Chris Skinner adopted Goerling's characterization of Weaving as a "bully" and suggested that he was "hostile" in his letter advising Weaving of the City's decision to terminate Weaving's employment. Despite the fact that Weaving was found "fit for duty," Skinner concluded that Weaving was critically deficient in the area of emotional intelligence. At trial, Skinner testified that Weaving's lack of emotional intelligence was the "foundation" of his decision. Skinner recognized that Weaving said that he had ADHD, but suggested that Weaving's recent diagnosis was inconsistent with his earlier statements indicating that he had outgrown his symptoms and found that it did not substantially limit him in any major life activity, including work as a law enforcement officer . . . .

At trial, Weaving explained that although he was aware that he had a history of childhood problems with ADHD, he initially did not believe that he was affected by it as an adult and also "didn't want to be stigmatized as a police officer with a mental disorder." Weaving's treating psychologist, Dr. Gary Monkarsh, testified that Weaving displayed "one of the clearest examples of adult ADHD I've ever encountered in my clinical practice in 25 years." Dr. Monkarsh's testimony suggested that much of Weaving's problematic behavior was attributable to his

ADHD, and that it could be successfully treated with medication and therapy. Among other things, Weaving had been able to improve his weak emotional intelligence—a common symptom of those suffering from ADHD—through therapy. Dr. Monkarsh elaborated that there is a "big difference" between someone who is simply "a jerk" and someone who has ADHD.

Driven by his love of his profession, Weaving had been able to become a successful police officer by developing compensatory mechanisms, such as calendaring systems, that allowed him to prioritize his tasks and overcome some of the effects of his disability, like slow processing speed. Nonetheless, Weaving was "unable to self-regulate" some of the other symptoms of ADHD without therapy, including impulsiveness, "not seeming to listen when spoken to, . . . interrupting others, . . . difficulty waiting his turn, blurting out comments without having emotional intelligence, [and lack of] awareness of the effect that that communication would have on his other workers at the police department." ADHD thus impaired Weaving's major life activities, including his "work." Dr. Monkarsh also indicated that although Weaving's ability to articulate sounds was not impaired, his communication was impaired because of his lack of ability to speak with emotional intelligence.

* * * *

The jury found that Weaving had proven that he had a disability under the ADA, that the City failed to reasonably accommodate his disability, and that the City discharged him because of it. Nonetheless, the jury found that Weaving had not proven that he was regarded as having a disability. The district court subsequently awarded equitable relief in the form of significant back and front pay in light of Weaving's inability to find other employment and the court's finding that Weaving would not be rehired in law enforcement.

* * * *

III

A

. . . There was sufficient evidence to support the verdict based on Weaving's ADHD substantially limiting his ability to interact with others. However characterized, the gist of Weaving's primary claim all along has been that he suffered from the type of impairment that we recognized in *McAlindin v. County of San Diego*, 192 F.3d 1226, 1234–35 (9th Cir. 1999). In *McAlindin*, the plaintiff contended that he suffered from anxiety and panic disorders that would cause him to become "incapacitated" and force him to lie down "at least once a month." *Id.* at 1230–31, 1241. Among other things, during one stress-induced incident that precipitated his taking leave from work, he became agitated, accusatory, and shouted at a supervisor. *Id.* at 1231.

We reversed the district court's grant of summary judgment on the plaintiff's

ADA claim. *Id.* at 1230. We recognized that a plaintiff with an "interacting with others" impairment could prevail "[b]ecause interacting with others is an essential, regular function, like walking and breathing." *Id.* at 1234. Thus, we held that a plaintiff could prevail where he showed "that his 'relations with others were characterized on a regular basis by severe problems, for example, consistently high levels of hostility, social withdrawal, or failure to communicate when necessary.' " *McAlindin*, 192 F.3d at 1235. Summary judgment was inappropriate on the plaintiff's claim because the evidence indicated that he "suffer[ed] from a total inability to communicate at times, in addition to a more subtle impairment in engaging in meaningful discussion." *Id.* at 1235–36. We emphasized that the plaintiff's claims were supported by "clinical findings" and "medical evaluations." *Id.* at 1235 . . . .

In contrast, in *Jacques v. DiMarzio, Inc.*, 386 F.3d 192, 200–04 (2d Cir. 2004), the Second Circuit *vacated* a jury verdict based on an instruction that tracked the *McAlindin* standard. It held that in order to satisfy the standard for an "interacting with others" impairment, a plaintiff must establish that "the impairment severely limits the plaintiff's ability to connect with others, i.e., to initiate contact with other people and respond to them, or to go among other people—at the most basic level of these activities." *Id.* at 203 (emphasis omitted). The court elaborated: "The standard is not satisfied by a plaintiff whose basic ability to communicate with others is not substantially limited but whose communication is inappropriate, ineffective, or unsuccessful." *Id.* . . . The court went on to suggest—as the dissent in *McAlindin* did—that the "Ninth Circuit approach" would frustrate "the maintenance of a civil workplace environment" by exposing employers to the risk of litigating hostile work environment claims by "unpleasant" employees. *Id.* at 203.

The majority distinguishes *McAlindin* . . . by claiming that Weaving was "able to engage in normal social interactions" and that the plaintiffs in those cases "were essentially housebound." Then, relying on the *Jacques* standard and channeling the *McAlindin* dissent, it holds that those who are capable of communicating but whose communications may be "inappropriate, ineffective, or unsuccessful" cannot prevail under the ADA because otherwise, employers would be exposed to liability in the form of actions by "ill-tempered employees who create a hostile workplace environment for their colleagues."

We, however, are compelled to construe the evidence in favor of the jury's verdict. Here, the evidence showed that Weaving was well beyond being merely cantankerous or troublesome. To the contrary, he had problems in his interactions with just about everyone throughout his career in law enforcement. Not only was he unable to engage in meaningful communication on a regular basis, but his ADHD made him seem unapproachable to his coworkers, thus completely precluding some interactions . . . . His doctors explained that his disability caused the severe lack of emotional intelligence that the City invoked when it fired him—he was not simply being "a jerk" who refused to control himself. The jury outright rejected the City's opposing argument that Weaving was not disabled.

Weaving's relations with others were undoubtedly characterized on a regular basis by severe problems including "high levels of hostility," "failure to communicate when necessary" due to his perceived unapproachability, and a constant inability to engage in "meaningful discussion." *See McAlindin*, 192 F.3d at 1235. That is sufficient to satisfy *McAlindin*, which by its own terms, did not limit relief to the "housebound." Consequently, under the law of our circuit, the jury was entitled to conclude that Weaving's ADHD substantially limited his ability to interact with others.

IV

Not all disabilities are obvious. To a casual observer, Matthew Weaving may not appear to be disabled. But that doesn't give a panel of appellate judges license to brush away the contrary medical evidence and jury findings. Mental disabilities that cause socially unacceptable behavior are less obvious than physical disabilities, but the Americans with Disabilities Act protects those suffering from either form of disability equally.

The majority may not like Matthew Weaving—or at least the picture of him that it paints based on a cold record. But the outcomes of our disabled litigants' cases should not turn solely on the amount of sympathy they inspire. The law protects the disabled, not the likeable. Because the majority has gutted our controlling precedent and substituted its own factual findings for that of the jury, I respectfully dissent.

NOTES

1. **Evaluating *Weaving*.** In the case you see several conflicts arise in the way the judges approach the statute. What do you think divides the court? Is it a difference with respect to the deference a jury is due? Or might it be their approach to defining disability? Why do you think the majority—in an opinion written by a judge who is widely considered to be a liberal judge who was appointed by President Clinton—would see this as an appropriate case to overturn a jury verdict? What kind of evidence would someone like Weaving need in the future to establish that his difficult interpersonal behavior was the product of a disability, or is the dissent correct that the court has essentially determined that difficulty interacting with others cannot be defined as a disability within the Ninth Circuit?

2. **The 2008 Amendments.** As noted previously, although the statute was passed in 2008, cases are only now finding their way into the appellate courts. It is difficult to draw any conclusions because of the limited number of cases but it appears that some courts are interpreting the statute more broadly at least with respect to the question of who is disabled. *See Mazzeo v. Color Resolution Int'l, Inc.*, 746 F.3d 1264 (11th Cir. 2014) (interpreting the new mandate of the ADAAA to find that an employee with a herniated disc that required surgery stated a prima facie case of disability); *Summers v. Altarum Inst., Corp.*, 740 F.3d 325 (4th Cir. 2014) (holding that temporary disabilities suffered as a result of an injury are included in the amended definition of a disability.) A court also recently interpreted the Amendments to encompass episodic conditions, such as an "episode of a blood-pressure spike." *Gogos v. AMS Mech. Sys.*, 737 F.3d 1170, 1174 (7th Cir. 2013).

One goal of the 2008 Amendments was to shift the legal analysis away from whether someone is disabled and towards the individual's ability to perform the job.

Indeed, based on some of the early cases decided under the 2008 Amendments, particularly at the district court level, it appears that courts are focusing much less on whether an individual is "disabled" under the terms of the statute and instead concentrating on whether the individual is qualified to perform the essential functions of the job. For example, in *Blackard v. Livingston Parish Sewer District*, 2014 U.S. Dist. LEXIS 5490 (M.D. La. Jan. 15, 2014), the court did not analyze whether the plaintiff was disabled but instead concluded that his inability to show up for work on time rendered him unqualified to meet the "essential function" of regular attendance. These cases are, in essence, effectively cases that involve accommodations questions, and will be discussed in the next case and accompanying notes, but some courts fail to address the issue of accommodation and simply conclude that the person is not qualified for the position in question. *See Mobley v. Miami Valley Hosp., Inc.*, 2014 U.S. Dist. LEXIS 77968 (S.D. Ohio June 9, 2014) (court accepts that plaintiff is disabled under the amendments but his request to permanently restructure position to make it a light-duty job was deemed not reasonable). This shift away from disability status and towards the question of whether the plaintiff is qualified for the position in question is consistent with the findings of a recent article that surveyed early court decisions under the 2008 Amendments. *See* Stephen F. Befort, *An Empirical Examination of Case Outcomes Under the ADA Amendments Act*, 70 WASH. & LEE. L. REV. 2027 (2013). Befort found that under the ADA Amendments plaintiffs were surviving summary judgment at a higher rate than previously on the question of whether they were disabled but that employers were now frequently prevailing on the question of whether those plaintiffs were qualified for their positions. *Id.* at 2070–71.

3. **"Regarded As" Disabled**. The 2008 Amendments specifically loosened the Supreme Court's interpretation of the "regarded as" prong and there was initially some sense that more disability cases would turn on whether the employee was "regarded as" disabled rather than actually disabled. But, to date, this shift has not occurred and there have been very few regarded as claims under the Amendments. Even before the Supreme Court's restrictive interpretation of that phrase, courts struggled to give meaning to the concept that someone was being "regarded as" disabled. As one court explained, a plaintiff cannot state a claim under the "regarded as prong of the ADA . . . simply by alleging that the employer believes some physical condition such as height, weight, or hair color, renders the plaintiff disabled. Rather, the plaintiff must allege that the employer believed, however erroneously, that the plaintiff suffered from an 'impairment' that if it truly existed would be covered under the statute[] and that the employer discriminated against the plaintiff on that basis." *Francis v. City of Meriden*, 129 F.3d 281, 285 (2d Cir. 1997); *see also Deas v. River West*, 152 F.3d 471 (5th Cir. 1998) (plaintiff was not regarded as disabled based on his epilepsy), *cert. denied*, 527 U.S. 1044 (1999); *Olson v. Dubuque Cmty. Sch. Dist.*, 137 F.3d 609 (8th Cir. 1998) (fact that defendant was aware of plaintiff's depression not sufficient to establish employer regarded her as disabled). There were, however, some successful claims that are likely to provide a model for the regarded as claims under the broader definition. In *Heyman v. Queens Village Committee for Mental Health*, 198 F.3d 68 (2d Cir. 1999), the plaintiff was diagnosed with lymphoma but his condition was not disabling. However, another employee had died of lymphoma and the employer feared that Heyman's condition "would render him unable to complete his tasks," which the

court found to satisfy the regarded as prong. *Id.* at 73. One of the likely reasons why there has not been a significant increase in "regarded as" claims as a result of the Amendments is that those Amendments make it clear that no reasonable accommodation is necessary for such claims, and most individuals bringing disability claims seek some form of accommodation.

2. The Duty to Accommodate

US AIRWAYS, INC. v. BARNETT
United States Supreme Court
535 U.S. 391 (2002)

JUSTICE BREYER delivered the opinion of the Court.

The Americans with Disabilities Act of 1990 (ADA or Act) prohibits an employer from discriminating against an "individual with a disability" who, with "reasonable accommodation," can perform the essential functions of the job. §§ 12112(a) and (b) (1994 ed.). This case, arising in the context of summary judgment, asks us how the Act resolves a potential conflict between: (1) the interests of a disabled worker who seeks assignment to a particular position as a "reasonable accommodation," and (2) the interests of other workers with superior rights to bid for the job under an employer's seniority system. In such a case, does the accommodation demand trump the seniority system?

In our view, the seniority system will prevail in the run of cases. As we interpret the statute, to show that a requested accommodation conflicts with the rules of a seniority system is ordinarily to show that the accommodation is not "reasonable." Hence such a showing will entitle an employer/defendant to summary judgment on the question—unless there is more. The plaintiff remains free to present evidence of special circumstances that make "reasonable" a seniority rule exception in the particular case. And such a showing will defeat the employer's demand for summary judgment. Fed. Rule Civ. Proc. 56(e).

I

In 1990, Robert Barnett, the plaintiff and respondent here, injured his back while working in a cargo-handling position at petitioner US Airways, Inc. He invoked seniority rights and transferred to a less physically demanding mailroom position. Under US Airways' seniority system, that position, like others, periodically became open to seniority-based employee bidding. In 1992, Barnett learned that at least two employees senior to him intended to bid for the mailroom job. He asked US Airways to accommodate his disability-imposed limitations by making an exception that would allow him to remain in the mailroom. After permitting Barnett to continue his mailroom work for five months while it considered the matter, US Airways eventually decided not to make an exception. And Barnett lost his job.

Barnett then brought this ADA suit claiming, among other things, that he was an "individual with a disability" capable of performing the essential functions of the mailroom job, that the mailroom job amounted to a "reasonable accommodation" of his disability, and that US Airways, in refusing to assign him the job, unlawfully discriminated against him. US Airways moved for summary judgment . . . contending that its "well-established" seniority system granted other employees the right to obtain the mailroom position.

The District Court found that the undisputed facts about seniority warranted summary judgment in US Airways' favor. The Act says that an employer who fails to make "reasonable accommodations to the known physical or mental limitations of an [employee] with a disability" discriminates *"unless"* the employer "can demonstrate that the accommodation would impose an *undue hardship* on the operation of [its] business." 42 U.S.C. § 12112(b)(5)(A) (emphasis added). The court said:

> "The uncontroverted evidence shows that the USAir seniority system has been in place for 'decades' and governs over 14,000 USAir Agents. Moreover, seniority policies such as the one at issue in this case are common to the airline industry. Given this context, it seems clear that the USAir employees were justified in relying upon the policy. As such, any significant alteration of that policy would result in undue hardship to both the company and its non-disabled employees." App. to Pet. for Cert. 96a.

An en banc panel of the United States Court of Appeals for the Ninth Circuit reversed. It said that the presence of a seniority system is merely "a factor in the undue hardship analysis." 228 F.3d 1105, 1120 (2000). And it held that "[a] case-by-case fact intensive analysis is required to determine whether any particular reassignment would constitute an undue hardship to the employer." *Ibid.* . . . The Circuits have reached different conclusions about the legal significance of a seniority system. Compare 228 F.3d at 1120, with EEOC v. Sara Lee Corp., 237 F.3d 349, 354 (CA4 2001). We agreed to answer US Airways' question.

II

In answering the question presented, we must consider the following statutory provisions. First, the ADA says that an employer may not "discriminate against a qualified individual with a disability." 42 U.S.C. § 12112(a). Second, the ADA says that a "qualified" individual includes "an individual with a disability who, *with* or without *reasonable accommodation*, can perform the essential functions of" review the relevant "employment position." § 12111(8) (emphasis added). Third, the ADA says that "discrimination" includes an employer's *"not making reasonable accommodations* to the known physical or mental limitations of an otherwise qualified . . . employee, *unless* [the employer] can demonstrate that the accommodation would impose an *undue hardship* on the operation of [its] business." § 12112(b)(5)(A) (emphasis added). Fourth, the ADA says that the term " 'reasonable accommodation' may include . . . reassignment to a vacant position." § 12111(9)(B).

The parties interpret this statutory language as applied to seniority systems in radically different ways. In US Airways' view, the fact that an accommodation would violate the rules of a seniority system always shows that the accommodation is not a "reasonable" one. In Barnett's polar opposite view, a seniority system violation never shows that an accommodation sought is not a "reasonable" one. Barnett concedes that a violation of seniority rules might help to show that the accommodation will work "undue" employer "hardship," but that is a matter for an employer to demonstrate case by case. We shall initially consider the parties' main legal arguments in support of these conflicting positions.

A

US Airways' claim that a seniority system virtually always trumps a conflicting accommodation demand rests primarily upon its view of how the Act treats workplace "preferences." Insofar as a requested accommodation violates a disability-neutral workplace rule, such as a seniority rule, it grants the employee with a disability treatment that other workers could not receive. Yet the Act, US Airways says, seeks only "equal" treatment for those with disabilities. *See, e.g.*, 42 U.S.C. § 12101(a)(9). It does not, it contends, require an employer to grant preferential treatment. Hence it does not require the employer to grant a request that, in violating a disability-neutral rule, would provide a preference.

While linguistically logical, this argument fails to recognize what the Act specifies, namely, that preferences will sometimes prove necessary to achieve the Act's basic equal opportunity goal. The Act requires preferences in the form of "reasonable accommodations" that are needed for those with disabilities to obtain the *same* workplace opportunities that those without disabilities automatically enjoy. By definition any special "accommodation" requires the employer to treat an employee with a disability differently, *i.e.*, preferentially. And the fact that the difference in treatment violates an employer's disability-neutral rule cannot by itself place the accommodation beyond the Act's potential reach.

Were that not so, the "reasonable accommodation" provision could not accomplish its intended objective. Neutral office assignment rules would automatically prevent the accommodation of an employee whose disability-imposed limitations require him to work on the ground floor. Neutral "break-from-work" rules would automatically prevent the accommodation of an individual who needs additional breaks from work, perhaps to permit medical visits. Neutral furniture budget rules would automatically prevent the accommodation of an individual who needs a different kind of chair or desk. Many employers will have neutral rules governing the kinds of actions most needed to reasonably accommodate a worker with a disability. See 42 U.S.C. § 12111(9)(b) (setting forth examples such as "job restructuring," "part-time or modified work schedules," "acquisition or modification of equipment or devices," "and other similar accommodations"). Yet Congress, while providing such examples, said nothing suggesting that the presence of such neutral rules would create an automatic exemption. . . . The simple fact that an accommodation would provide a "preference"—in the sense that it would permit the worker with a disability to violate a rule that others must obey—cannot, *in and of itself*, automatically show that the accommodation is not "reasonable." . . .

B

Barnett argues that the statutory words "reasonable accommodation" mean only "effective accommodation," authorizing a court to consider the requested accommodation's ability to meet an individual's disability-related needs, and nothing more.

On this view, a seniority rule violation, having nothing to do with the accommodation's effectiveness, has nothing to do with its "reasonableness." It might, at most, help to prove an "undue hardship on the operation of the business." But, he adds, that is a matter that the statute requires the employer to demonstrate, case by case. . . . Barnett adds that any other view would make the words "reasonable accommodation" and "undue hardship" virtual mirror images—creating redundancy in the statute. . . .

These arguments do not persuade us that Barnett's legal interpretation of "reasonable" is correct. For one thing, in ordinary English the word "reasonable" does not mean "effective." It is the word "accommodation," not the word "reasonable," that conveys the need for effectiveness. An *ineffective* "modification" or "adjustment" will not *accommodate* a disabled individual's limitations. Nor does an ordinary English meaning of the term "reasonable accommodation" make of it a simple, redundant mirror image of the term "undue hardship." The statute refers to an "undue hardship on the operation of the business." 42 U.S.C. § 12112(b)(5)(A). Yet a demand for an effective accommodation could prove unreasonable because of its impact, not on business operations, but on fellow employees—say because it will lead to dismissals, relocations, or modification of employee benefits to which an employer, looking at the matter from the perspective of the business itself, may be relatively indifferent.

Neither does the statute's primary purpose require Barnett's special reading. The statute seeks to diminish or to eliminate the stereotypical thought processes, the thoughtless actions, and the hostile reactions that far too often bar those with disabilities from participating fully in the Nation's life, including the workplace. See generally §§ 12101(a) and (b). These objectives demand unprejudiced thought and reasonable responsive reaction on the part of employers and fellow workers alike. They will sometimes require affirmative conduct to promote entry of disabled people into the workforce. They do not, however, demand action beyond the realm of the reasonable. . . .

III

The question in the present case focuses on the relationship between seniority systems and the plaintiff's need to show that an "accommodation" seems reasonable on its face, i.e., ordinarily or in the run of cases. We must assume that the plaintiff, an employee, is an "individual with a disability." He has requested assignment to a mailroom position as a "reasonable accommodation." We also assume that normally such a request would be reasonable within the meaning of the statute, were it not for one circumstance, namely, that the assignment would violate the rules of a seniority system. See § 12111(9) ("reasonable accommodation" may include "reassignment to a vacant position"). Does that circumstance mean that the proposed accommodation is not a "reasonable" one?

In our view, the answer to this question ordinarily is "yes." The statute does not require proof on a case-by-case basis that a seniority system should prevail. That is because it would not be reasonable in the run of cases that the assignment in question trump the rules of a seniority system. To the contrary, it will ordinarily be unreasonable for the assignment to prevail.

A

Several factors support our conclusion that a proposed accommodation will not be reasonable in the run of cases. Analogous case law supports this conclusion, for it has recognized the importance of seniority to employee-management relations. This Court has held that, in the context of a Title VII religious discrimination case, an employer need not adapt to an employee's special worship schedule as a "reasonable accommodation" where doing so would conflict with the seniority rights of other employees. Trans World Airlines, Inc. v. Hardison, 432 U.S. 63, 79–80 (1977). The lower courts have unanimously found that collectively bargained seniority trumps the need for reasonable accommodation in the context of the linguistically similar Rehabilitation Act. See Eckles v. Consolidated Rail Corp., 94 F.3d 1041, 1047–1048 (CA7 1996) (collecting cases). . . . All these cases discuss *collectively bargained* seniority systems, not systems (like the present system) which are unilaterally imposed by management. But the relevant seniority system advantages, and related difficulties that result from violations of seniority rules, are not limited to collectively bargained systems.

For one thing, the typical seniority system provides important employee benefits by creating, and fulfilling, employee expectations of fair, uniform treatment. These benefits include "job security and an opportunity for steady and predictable advancement based on objective standards." Brief for Petitioner 32. They include "an element of due process," limiting "unfairness in personnel decisions." Gersuny, Origins of Seniority Provisions in Collective Bargaining, 33 LAB. L. J. 518, 519 (1982). And they consequently encourage employees to invest in the employing company, accepting "less than their value to the firm early in their careers" in return for greater benefits in later years. J. Baron & D. Kreps, Strategic Human Resources: Frameworks for General Managers 288 (1999).

Most important for present purposes, to require the typical employer to show more than the existence of a seniority system might well undermine the employees' expectations of consistent, uniform treatment—expectations upon which the seniority system's benefits depend. That is because such a rule would substitute a complex case-specific "accommodation" decision made by management for the more uniform, impersonal operation of seniority rules. Such management decision making, with its inevitable discretionary elements, would involve a matter of the greatest importance to employees, namely, layoffs; it would take place outside, as well as inside, the confines of a court case; and it might well take place fairly often. We can find nothing in the statute that suggests Congress intended to undermine seniority systems in this way. And we consequently conclude that the employer's showing of violation of the rules of a seniority system is by itself ordinarily sufficient.

B

The plaintiff (here the employee) nonetheless remains free to show that special circumstances warrant a finding that, despite the presence of a seniority system (which the ADA may not trump in the run of cases), the requested "accommodation" is "reasonable" on the particular facts. That is because special circumstances might alter the important expectations described above. The plaintiff might show, for example, that the employer, having retained the right to change the seniority system unilaterally, exercises that right fairly frequently, reducing employee expectations that the system will be followed—to the point where one more departure, needed to accommodate an individual with a disability, will not likely make a difference. The plaintiff might show that the system already contains exceptions such that, in the circumstances, one further exception is unlikely to matter. We do not mean these examples to exhaust the kinds of showings that a plaintiff might make. But we do mean to say that the plaintiff must bear the burden of showing special circumstances that make an exception from the seniority system reasonable in the particular case. . . .

IV

In its question presented, US Airways asked us whether the ADA requires an employer to assign a disabled employee to a particular position even though another employee is entitled to that position under the employer's "established seniority system." We answer that *ordinarily* the ADA does not require that assignment. Hence, a showing that the assignment would violate the rules of a seniority system warrants summary judgment for the employer—unless there is more. The plaintiff must present evidence of that "more," namely, special circumstances surrounding the particular case that demonstrate the assignment is nonetheless reasonable.

Because the lower courts took a different view of the matter, and because neither party has had an opportunity to seek summary judgment in accordance with the principles we set forth here, we vacate the Court of Appeals' judgment and remand the case for further proceedings consistent with this opinion.

[The concurring opinions of JUSTICE STEVENS and JUSTICE O'CONNOR are omitted.]

JUSTICE SCALIA, with whom JUSTICE THOMAS joins, dissenting.

The question presented asks whether the "reasonable accommodation" mandate of the Americans with Disabilities Act of 1990 (ADA or Act) requires reassignment of a disabled employee to a position that "another employee is entitled to hold . . . under the employer's bona fide and established seniority system." Indulging its penchant for eschewing clear rules that might avoid litigation, *see*, e.g., Kansas v. Crane, 534 U.S. 407, 423(2002) (SCALIA, J., dissenting) . . . the Court answers "maybe." . . .

The principal defect of today's opinion, however, goes well beyond the uncertainty it produces regarding the relationship between the ADA and the infinite variety of seniority systems. The conclusion that any seniority system can ever be overridden is merely one consequence of a mistaken interpretation of the ADA that makes all employment rules and practices—even those which (like a seniority system) pose no *distinctive* obstacle to the disabled—subject to suspension when that is (in a court's view) a "reasonable" means of enabling a disabled employee to keep his job. That is a far cry from what I believe the accommodation provision of the ADA requires: the suspension (within reason) of those employment rules and practices *that the employee's disability prevents him from observing.*

. . . [T]he Act says . . . an employer may not "discriminate against a qualified individual with a disability *because of the disability* of such individual." 42 U.S.C. 12112(a) (1994 ed.) (emphasis added). It further provides that discrimination includes "not making reasonable accommodations *to the known physical or mental limitations* of an otherwise qualified individual with a disability." § 12112(b)(5)(A) (emphasis added).

Read together, these provisions order employers to modify or remove (within reason) policies and practices that burden a disabled person "because of [his] disability." In other words, the ADA eliminates workplace barriers only if a disability prevents an employee from overcoming them—those barriers that would not be barriers *but for* the employee's disability. These include, for example, work stations that cannot accept the employee's wheelchair, or an assembly-line practice that requires long periods of standing. But they do not include rules and practices that bear no more heavily upon the disabled employee than upon others—even though an exemption from such a rule or practice might in a sense "make up for" the employee's disability. It is not a required accommodation, for example, to pay a disabled employee more than others at his grade level—even if that increment is earmarked for massage or physical therapy that would enable the employee to work with as little physical discomfort as his co-workers. That would be "accommodating" the disabled employee, but it would not be "making . . . accommodation *to the known physical or mental limitations*" of the employee, § 12112(b)(5)(A), because it would not eliminate any workplace practice that constitutes an obstacle because of his disability.

So also with exemption from a seniority system, which burdens the disabled and nondisabled alike. In particular cases, seniority rules may have a harsher effect upon the disabled employee than upon his co-workers. If the disabled employee is physically capable of performing only one task in the workplace, seniority rules may be, for him, the difference between employment and unemployment. But that does not make the seniority system a disability-related obstacle, any more than harsher impact upon the more needy disabled employee renders the salary system a disability-related obstacle. When one departs from this understanding, the ADA's accommodation provision becomes a standardless grab bag—leaving it to the courts to decide which workplace preferences (higher salary, longer vacations, reassignment to positions to which others are entitled) can be deemed "reasonable" to "make up for" the particular employee's disability. . . .

Because the Court's opinion leaves the question whether a seniority system must be disregarded in order to accommodate a disabled employee in a state of uncertainty that can be resolved only by constant litigation; and because it adopts an interpretation of the ADA that incorrectly subjects all employer rules and practices to the requirement of reasonable accommodation; I respectfully dissent.

JUSTICE SOUTER, with whom JUSTICE GINSBURG joins, dissenting.

"Reassignment to a vacant position," 42 U.S.C. § 12111(9) (1994 ed.), is one way an employer may "reasonably accommodate" disabled employees under the Americans with Disabilities Act of 1990, 42 U.S.C. § 12101 et seq. (1994 ed. and Supp. V). The Court today holds that a request for reassignment will nonetheless most likely be unreasonable when it would violate the terms of a seniority system imposed by an employer. Although I concur in the Court's appreciation of the value and importance of seniority systems, I do not believe my hand is free to accept the majority's result and therefore respectfully dissent.

Nothing in the ADA insulates seniority rules from the "reasonable accommodation" requirement, in marked contrast to Title VII of the Civil Rights Act of 1964 and the Age Discrimination in Employment Act of 1967, each of which has an explicit protection for seniority. See 42 U.S.C. § 2000e-2(h) (1994 ed.) ("Notwithstanding any other provision of this subchapter, it shall not be an unlawful employment practice for an employer to [provide different benefits to employees] pursuant to a bona fide seniority . . . system. . . ."); 29 U.S.C. § 623(f) (1994 ed.) ("It shall not be unlawful for an employer . . . to take any action otherwise prohibited [under previous sections] . . . to observe the terms of a bona fide seniority system [except for involuntary retirement] . . ."). Because Congress modeled several of the ADA's provisions on Title VII, its failure to replicate Title VII's exemption for seniority systems leaves the statute ambiguous, albeit with more than a hint that seniority rules do not inevitably carry the day.

In any event, the statute's legislative history resolves the ambiguity. The Committee Reports from both the House of Representatives and the Senate explain that seniority protections contained in a collective-bargaining agreement should not amount to more than "a factor" when it comes to deciding whether some accommodation at odds with the seniority rules is "reasonable" nevertheless. H. R. Rep. No. 101-485, pt. 2, p. 63 (1990), (existence of collectively bargained protections for seniority "would not be determinative" on the issue whether an accommodation was reasonable); S. Rep. No. 101–116, p. 32 (1989) (a collective-bargaining agreement assigning jobs based on seniority "may be considered as a factor in determining" whether an accommodation is reasonable). . . .

Because an unilaterally-imposed seniority system enjoys no special protection under the ADA, a consideration of facts peculiar to this very case is needed to gauge whether Barnett has carried the burden of showing his proposed accommodation to be a "reasonable" one despite the policy in force at US Airways. The majority describes this as a burden to show the accommodation is "plausible" or "feasible," ante, at 10, and I believe Barnett has met it. . . .

In fact, it is hard to see the seniority scheme here as any match for Barnett's ADA requests, since US Airways apparently took pains to ensure that its seniority rules raised no great expectations. In its policy statement, US Airways said that "the Agent Personnel Policy Guide is not intended to be a contract" and that "US Air reserves the right to change any and all of the stated policies and procedures in this Guide at any time, without advanced notice." Lodging of Respondent 2 (emphasis in original). While I will skip any state-by-state analysis of the legal treatment of employee handbooks (a source of many lawyers' fees) it is safe to say that the contract law of a number of jurisdictions would treat this disclaimer as fatal to any claim an employee might make to enforce the seniority policy over an employer's contrary decision. . . .

With US Airways itself insisting that its seniority system was noncontractual and modifiable at will, there is no reason to think that Barnett's accommodation would have resulted in anything more than minimal disruption to US Airways's operations, if that. Barnett has shown his requested accommodation to be "reasonable," and the burden ought to shift to US Airways if it wishes to claim that, in spite of surface appearances, violation of the seniority scheme would have worked an undue hardship. I would therefore affirm the Ninth Circuit.

NOTES

1. **Extending *Barnett*.** In *Barnett*, the Court seeks to strike a balance between the need of those who are disabled and other employees as reflected in the seniority provisions. Should the *Barnett* case be limited to cases involving seniority, or should it also apply to other neutral employment rules? Does the *Barnett* case offer any guidance on this question? On the merits, should seniority rules be permitted to trump accommodation requests or needs?

2. **Preferential Assignments.** The *Barnett* case also offers some guidelines for how courts interpret the accommodation requirement, particularly with respect to assignment cases. One issue that has been litigated extensively is whether an employer is obligated to assign a person with a disability to a position over a more qualified individual who is not disabled. Courts have split on the question. Some courts have held that a disabled employee "has a right in fact" to an available reassignment and "not just to be consider[ed]" in the process. *Smith v. Midland Brake, Inc.*, 180 F.3d 1154 (10th Cir. 1999) (*en banc*). Other courts have held that an employer has no duty to reassign a disabled employee when other more qualified candidates are available. *See Huber v. Wal-Mart Stores, Inc.*, 486 F.3d 480, 483 (8th Cir. 2007), *cert. dismissed*, 552 U.S. 1136 (2008)). Which of these two positions is more consistent with the statutory command of reasonable accommodation? Which is more consistent with *Barnett*?

3. **Qualified Individual and Essential Functions.** The basic concept of the ADA is that it is impermissible for an employer to discriminate against a qualified individual with a disability, and qualified is further defined as someone who is capable of performing the essential functions of the job with, or without, a reasonable accommodation. As a result, a question that arises with frequency is whether a particular job function is essential, and whether there is an accommodation that might enable an individual to perform those essential functions. An accommodation request that has arisen in the cases perhaps more than any other is a flexible schedule that might include coming to work late or an ability not to report to work. Courts have generally rejected such claims, concluding instead that "a regular and reliable level of attendance is a necessary element of most jobs." *Tyndall v. Nat'l Educ. Centers*, 31 F.3d 209, 213 (4th Cir. 1994); *see also Colon-Fontanez v. Municipality of San Juan*, 660 F.3d 17, 33 (1st Cir. 2011) ("This court—as well as the majority of circuit courts—has recognized that attendance is an essential function of any job.") . In *EEOC v. Yellow Freight Systems, Inc.*, 253 F.3d 943 (7th Cir. 2001) (*en banc*), the Court held that a plaintiff with AIDS-related cancer was not entitled to an unlimited number of sick days that would have allowed him to work when he was able. The employer had previously afforded the plaintiff a 90-day leave of absence, and the court concluded that the plaintiff was not a qualified individual because he was unable to perform the essential functions of the

job without regular attendance. *See also Moore v. Payless Shoe Source, Inc.*, 139 F.3d 1210, 1213 (8th Cir. 1998) ("An employee who is unable to come to work on a regular basis [is] unable to satisfy any of the functions of the job in question, much less the essential functions . . ."), *aff'd*, 187 F.3d 845 (8th Cir. 1999), *cert. denied*, 528 U.S. 1050 (1999). One problem with attendance issues is that what most employees seek is an open-ended schedule to deal with complications that arise from a disability but such an arrangement poses particular difficulties for employers who are unable to plan in advance. *See Semper v. Providence St. Vincent Med. Ctr.*, 675 F.3d 1233, 1240 (9th Cir. 2012) (rejecting as unreasonable an open-ended schedule that would allow the employee to set her own hours).

A related requested accommodation is the right to work at home but just as courts have been reluctant to allow prolonged absences from work, courts have also generally been hesitant to order a right to work at home as a reasonable accommodation. The Seventh Circuit has noted, "The reason working at home is rarely a reasonable accommodation is because most jobs require the kind of teamwork, personal interaction, and supervision that simply cannot be had in a home office situation." *Rauen v. United States Tobacco Mfg.*, 319 F.3d 891, 896 (7th Cir. 2003). Although courts have been careful not to create a per se rule against home work as an accommodation, most of the cases have determined that office interaction and supervision were essential functions of the job. *See Robert v. Bd. of Cnty. Comm'rs*, 691 F.3d 1211, 127 n.2 (10th Cir. 2012) (finding that site visits were an essential function of the job and therefore working at home was not a reasonable accommodation); *Mason v. Avaya Commc'ns, Inc.*, 357 F.3d 1114 (10th Cir. 2004) (denying service coordinator who suffered from post-traumatic stress disorder accommodation of working at home).

A recent and noteworthy case took a different approach. In *EEOC v. Ford Motor Co.*, 752 F.3d 634 (6th Cir. 2014), *rh'g en banc granted* (Aug. 29, 2014), the court considered whether a telecommuting arrangement could be a reasonable accommodation for an employee who suffered from irritable bowel syndrome. The court began its analysis by casting doubt on the wisdom of prior case law, including from its own circuit:

> When we first developed the principle that attendance is an essential requirement of most jobs, technology was such that the workplace and an employer's brick-and-mortar location were synonymous. However, as technology has advanced in the intervening decades, and an ever greater number of employers and employees utilize remote work arrangements, attendance at the workplace can no longer be assumed to mean attendance at the employer's physical location.

Id. at 641. The court went on to explain that whether a particular accommodation is reasonable involves a "fact-specific" inquiry and even suggested that a requirement of "teamwork" may not justify physical attendance: "We are not persuaded that positions that require a great deal of teamwork are inherently unsuitable to telecommuting arrangements." *Id.* at 642. The court remanded the case to the district court to perform a proper fact-specific inquiry, and that remand produced a spirited dissent. *See id.* at 649 (McKeague, J., dissenting). Why do you think courts are generally reluctant to see telecommuting or flexible attendance policies as reasonable accommodations? Do you think courts should reconsider their assumptions in light of changed workplace conditions, as suggested by the *EEOC v. Ford Motor* case? How do you think the case should be decided on rehearing?

4. Other Accommodations. Often employees seek a change in schedule, such as part-time work, which courts have been reluctant to order as a reasonable accommodation. *See, e.g., Terrell v. USAir*, 132 F.3d 621 (11th Cir. 1998) (employer had no duty to create part-time work). While restructuring a job to eliminate non-essential functions is presumptively valid under the terms of the statute, courts have held it unnecessary for employers to eliminate essential functions of the job. *See Hennagir v. Utah Dep't of Corr.*, 587 F.3d 1255, 1264 (10th Cir. 2009) (finding that an employer is not required to accommodate a disabled worker by modifying or eliminating an essential function of the job.) Courts have also generally found it unreasonable to require other employees to perform essential functions for a disabled employees who are unable to do so. In *Majors v. G.E. Electrical Co.*, 714 F.3d 527 (9th Cir. 2013), an employee who was unable to lift more than twenty pounds sought to have other employees do the lifting as a reasonable accommodation. The court, however, rejected that suggestion, noting, "To have another employee perform a position's essential function and to a certain extent perform the job for the employee is not a reasonable accommodation." *Id.* at 534.

5. The Cost Defense. Many of the accommodations just discussed do not involve easily identifiable monetary costs, although they typically all have some costs associated with them. In contrast, the reasonableness of some accommodations will turn on their costs, particularly in the case of the need for changed workspace, readers for blind individuals, or assistants to help with job tasks. Importantly, the fact that an accommodation may be costly does not mean it is unreasonable; rather, courts take into account many factors to determine whether the costs are so high as to be unreasonable. The statute also provides employers with an affirmative defense when costs are so substantial that they would pose an undue hardship for the particular employer. *See* 42 U.S.C. § 12112(b)(5)(A). There is an overlap between these two provisions but as one court has explained:

> [D]etermining whether a proposed accommodation is 'reasonable' requires a factual determination of reasonableness . . . untethered to the defendant employer's particularized situation. Once a determination is made that a proposed accommodation is, in a sense, 'generally' reasonable, the defendant employer then bears the burden of showing that the accommodation imposes an undue hardship upon it, given the employer's specific situation.

Monette v. Elec. Data Sys., 90 F.3d 1173, 1183 n.10 (6th Cir. 1996), *abrogated by Lewis v. Humboldt Acquisition Corp.*, 681 F.3d 312 (6th Cir. 2012).

Although the potential costs of workplace accommodations was one of the fears employers expressed in their opposition to the ADA, there have been a surprising dearth of cases discussing whether specific costs are unreasonable or would impose an undue hardship. One reason for this is that the cost issue is often dealt with implicitly, such as in the cases involving a request to work at home or for reassignment. These cases rarely turn on the specific costs of the accommodation but they do discuss their effect on an employer's workforce, including in relation to employee productivity.

A leading case for how courts should assess costs in the context of the duty to accommodate is *Vande Zande v. State of Wisconsin*, 44 F.3d 538 (7th Cir. 1995), in which the court, in an opinion written by Judge Posner, evaluated the requests of a paraplegic employee. Some of the plaintiff's requests involved restructuring the workplace, such as lowering a sink, to allow her the same access to facilities as other non-disabled employees. The court determined that the reasonableness of the costs must be balanced against the benefits that they would bring and that "the cost could not be disproportionate to the benefit." *Id.* at 542. The court further held that even though the costs to lower the sink were not high ($150) particularly for a state employer, that it was unnecessary for the employer to do so because the accommodation would not have directly affected her "ability to work or her comfort level" and the employer did not have a duty to equalize the working conditions. *Id.* at 546. The court also stated that the plaintiff had the burden to establish that the costs were reasonable. *Id.* at 543 ("The employee must show that the accommodation is reasonable in the sense both of efficacious and proportional to costs."). Although a number of other courts have adopted the cost/benefit approach to defining reasonable, others have held that it is the employer's burden to demonstrate that an accommodation would be unduly expensive. *See Borkowski v. Valley Cent. Sch. Dist.*, 63 F.3d 131 (2d Cir. 1995) (remanding for further findings on whether a school district had to provide a teacher's aide as a reasonable accommodation). *See also Reed v. La Page Bakeries, Inc.*, 244 F.3d 254, 258 (1st Cir. 2001) (noting that the Third, Eighth, and Tenth Circuit follow *Borkowski*).

6. An Interactive Process. One of the requirements of the ADA is that an employer engage in an interactive process with a disabled employee to determine what might be a reasonable accommodation. Courts, however, have concluded that an employer is not required to provide an employee's preferred accommodation, all that is required is that the employer offer a reasonable accommodation. *See Jakubowski v. Christ Hosp., Inc.*, 627 F.3d 195, 203 (6th Cir. 2010) ("When an employer offers a reasonable . . . accommodation, the employee cannot demand a different accommodation."), *cert. denied*, 131 S. Ct. 3071 (2011). Employees have, with some regularity, sought to hold employers liable for failing to engage in an interactive process but courts have uniformly held that "there is no separate cause of action for a failure of [the] interactive process." *Bunn v. Khoury Bros.*, 753 F.3d 676, 683 (7th Cir. 2014). Courts may, however, require an employer to make an individualized assessment of an individual rather than relying on assumptions about the capability of a disabled individual. *See Keith v. Cnty. of Oakland*, 703 F.3d 918 (6th Cir. 2013) (requiring an individualized assessment of whether a deaf lifeguard was capable of performing the essential functions of the job with or without an accommodation).

7. Academic Commentary on the ADA. The material in this section introduces you to the complexity and controversies surrounding the ADA. Many academic commentators have been highly critical of the Supreme Court's interpretations of the ADA prior to the 2008 Amendments. Cheryl Anderson captures much of the critical commentary when she notes that "courts are making normative distinctions between persons with different disabilities based on their perceptions of whether the individual is someone the ADA was intended to cover . . ." Cheryl L. Anderson, *"Deserving Disabilities": Why the Definition of Disability Under the Americans*

With Disabilities Act Should Be Revised to Eliminate the Substantial Limitation Requirement, 65 Mo. L. Rev. 83, 84 (2000). Others have suggested that the Supreme Court was imposing its own normative vision of what the Act ought to cover. *See* Michael Ashley Stein, *Foreword: Disability and Identity*, 44 Wm. & Mary L. Rev. 907, 908 (2003) ("The Court has zealously taken on a gatekeeping role, ensuring that only those individuals with disabilities 'worthy' of the appellation be afforded . . . protection."). Samuel Bagenstos, while acknowledging that the Court has imposed a particular vision on the scope of the statute, argues that the open-endedness of the statutory language "demands value judgments." Samuel R. Bagenstos, *Subordination, Stigma & "Disability,"* 86 Va. L. Rev. 397, 401 (2000). Bagenstos' own normative vision would be for courts to focus their attention on those who are stigmatized and in a subordinated status as a result of their disability. *See generally* Samuel R. Bagenstos, Law and the Contradictions of the Disability Rights Movement (2009).

Regardless of the reason, it is clear that ADA plaintiffs fared rather poorly in courts under the pre-Amendment law. In a comprehensive survey of both appellate and trial court decisions, Ruth Colker found what she described as "startling trends in judicial outcomes." She explained, "Defendants prevailed in 448 of 475 cases (94%) at the trial court level and in 376 of 448 instances (84%) in which plaintiffs appealed these adverse judgments." Ruth Colker, *The Americans with Disabilities Act: A Windfall for Defendants*, 34 Harv. C.R.-C.L. L. Rev. 99, 107–08 (1999). These figures are particularly revealing because they are substantially lower than the success rates of other employment discrimination claims, which tend to have a success rate of between 30–50% depending on the class of claim.

What do you think accounts for the lower success rate? Might it be a process by which a new statute develops so that many marginal claims arise early on and are defeated by courts that are not eager to expand an already expansive statute? Could it be different perceptions relating to discrimination against those with disabilities? Might it have something to do with the nature of the ADA, which includes a broad redistributive component in addition to its nondiscrimination mandate? *See* Samuel Issacharoff & Justin Nelson, *Discrimination With a Difference: Can Employment Discrimination Law Accommodate the Americans With Disabilities Act?* 79 N.C. L. Rev. 307 (2001) (arguing that the courts' interpretations can be understood against the broad redistributive mandate of the ADA). There is a question, however, just how different the ADA is in its redistributive focus. Christine Jolls has noted that Title VII imposes similar costs through the disparate impact theory and also through the lack of a cost defense so that, under Title VII, employers are frequently required to change practices that have proved profitable. *See* Christine Jolls, *Antidiscrimination and Accommodation*, 115 Harv. L. Rev. 642 (2001). From what you have read, is the ADA a different kind of statute than Title VII? Do you think that explains some of the differences in outcomes in the cases?

More recent commentary has focused on how the 2008 Amendments are likely to be interpreted. As noted previously, in a survey of early cases, Steven Befort found that employees fared better on the preliminary question whether the employee was disabled but that other hurdles, such as whether someone was qualified for the position or whether a reasonable accommodation was available, made disability claims still difficult to succeed on. *See* Stephen F. Befort, *An Empirical Analysis of*

Case Outcomes Under the ADA Amendments Act, 70 WASH. & LEE L. REV. 2027 (2013). In an ambitious recent article, a group of authors have argued that the law should move beyond the question of disability and towards a broader approach to accommodation so that the focus would be on the effectiveness of an accommodation request, regardless of one's disability status. *See* Michael Ashley Stein, *et al.*, *Accommodating Every Body*, 81 U. CHI. L. REV. 689 (2014). *See also* Nicole Buonocore Porter, *Martinizing Title I of the Americans With Disabilities Act*, 47 GA. L. REV. 527 (2013) (arguing for an expansion of the accommodation mandate so that it would be deemed reasonable to shift responsibilities to other employees when doing so does not impose a significant burden).

F. CONTEMPORARY WORKPLACE ISSUES

1. Age Discrimination

The Age Discrimination in Employment Act ("ADEA") was passed in 1967, and has been amended on a number of occasions since then. When it was originally passed, the statute protected individuals between the ages of 40 and 70 from discrimination, but over time the upper age limit was eliminated (with a few exceptions). As a result, the ADEA generally protects all individuals aged 40 and over from discrimination in employment. *See* 28 U.S.C. § 631(a).

There has been a recent surge of interest under the ADEA for a variety of reasons. One purely demographic reason is that the population is getting older, and the share of the workforce aged 55 or older has grown substantially over the last decade. The Bureau of Labor Statistics reports that, "From 1992 to 2002, the share of the labor force for those aged 55 and over increased from 11.8 percent to 14.3 percent. In 2012, their share of the labor force increased to 20.9 percent and is now projected to increase to 25.6 percent by 2022." U.S. Bureau of Labor Statistics, Share of Labor Force Projected to Rise for People Age 55 and Over and Fall for Younger Age Groups, *available at* http://www.bls.gov/opub/ted/2014/ted. Not just is the population growing older but workers are staying in the labor force longer, sometimes because they may not have adequate resources to fund their retirement but also because older workers today have more education and less demanding jobs physically than their cohorts from a generation or so ago. *See, e.g.*, Gary Burtless, *Is an Aging Workforce Less Productive?*, BROOKINGS UP FRONT, June 10, 2013 (discussing the aging of the workforce and concluding that productivity has not declined as a result of an older workforce). The aging of the workforce has been reflected in a substantial increase in charges filed with the EEOC relating to age discrimination, rising from 16,585 to 21,396 between 2005 and 2013. (The statistics are available at eeoc.gov/eeoc/statistics/enforcement/adea.cfm.)

Much of the case law—for example, with respect to proving pretext—is the same under the ADEA as it is for Title VII, and this section will focus on where the laws deviate. The ADEA differs from Title VII in several significant respects. First, the ADEA has always provided for jury trials, and it also has a different remedial scheme. The ADEA borrows the remedial scheme from the Fair Labor Standards Act, which provides for liquidated damages in the amount of the backpay award for willful violations. 29 U.S.C. § 626 (b). In other words, if a successful plaintiff in an

ADEA case recovered $100,000 in back (or front) pay, then she would be entitled to another $100,000 if she proved that the discrimination was willful, which means that the employer either knew or showed reckless disregard for the matter of whether its conduct was prohibited by the statute. *See Hazen Paper Co. v. Biggins*, 507 U.S. 604, 607 (1993). Two other important doctrinal differences have also recently emerged. In *Gross v. FBL Fin. Servs., Inc.*, 557 U.S. 167 (2009), the Supreme Court held that Title VII's mixed-motive structure does not apply to age discrimination cases, and more specifically noted that the burden of persuasion never shifts to the defendant but instead the burden is the same as "in any other ADEA disparate-treatment action. A plaintiff must prove by a preponderance of the evidence (which may be direct or circumstantial) that age was the 'but-for' cause of the challenged employer decision." *Id.* at 179. As a result, the mixed-motives framework is not available for age discrimination cases.

The second doctrinal change relates to the disparate impact theory. For many years, lower courts were divided on the question of whether the disparate impact theory was available for age discrimination claims, and the Supreme Court resolved that dispute by holding that the ADEA includes a disparate impact component. *Smith v. Jackson*, 544 U.S. 228 (2005). However, the Court did not borrow the existing Title VII standard for the business necessity test but instead noted that "the scope of the disparate-impact liability under ADEA is narrower than under Title VII." *Id.* at 240. One reason for this, the Court added, is that "age, unlike race or other classifications protected by Title VII, not uncommonly has relevance to an individual's capacity to engage in certain types of employment." *Id.* The Court went on, "Moreover, intentional discrimination on the basis of age has not occurred at the same levels as discrimination against those protected by Title VII." *Id.* As a result, the Court determined that it was appropriate to hold employers to a lower burden necessary to justify their practices that have a disparate impact on age, and the Court chose a "reasonableness" standard, premised largely on a provision of the statute that permits employment practices that are based on reasonable factors other than age. The Court went on to apply the reasonableness standard to uphold the practice challenged in *Smith*, namely the city's decision to provide higher salary raises to officers with less seniority in order "to make them competitive with comparable positions in the market." *Id.* at 242.

There are also many similarities between the ADEA and Title VII. Individuals must first file a charge of discrimination with the EEOC before pursuing a claim in court, and much of the case law developed under Title VII applies to the ADEA. This is particularly true for claims of intentional discrimination, and age discrimination claims have proved influential in establishing the governing principles for proving intentional discrimination. *See Reeves v. Sanderson Plumbing Prods., Inc.*, 530 U.S. 133 (2000) (age discrimination case discussed in section B.1, *supra*). One important variation is that the Supreme Court has held that it does not violate the ADEA for an employer to make decisions based on factors that are correlated with age, such as the time one's pension would vest. *See Hazen Paper Co. v. Biggins*, 507 U.S. 604 (1993). In *Hazen Paper*, the Court held that it would not be a violation of the ADEA for an employer to terminate an employee to keep him from obtaining his pension, even though that action would most likely affect older employees. Instead, as is true for other areas of discrimination, a plaintiff must prove that he was discriminated against because of his age, and not because of a factor that is correlated with age. The Court explained its reasoning:

Disparate treatment . . . captures the essence of what Congress sought to prohibit in the ADEA. It is the very essence of age discrimination for an older employee to be fired because the employer believes that productivity and competence decline with old age. As we explained in EEOC v. Wyoming, 460 U.S. 226 (1983), Congress' promulgation of the ADEA was prompted by its concern that older workers were being deprived of employment on the basis of inaccurate and stigmatizing stereotypes.

"Although age discrimination rarely was based on the sort of animus motivating some other forms of discrimination, it was based in large part on stereotypes unsupported by objective fact. . . . Moreover, the available empirical evidence demonstrated that arbitrary age lines were in fact generally unfounded and that, as an overall matter, the performance of older workers was at least as good as that of younger workers." *Id.*, at 231.

Thus the ADEA commands that "employers are to evaluate [older] employees . . . on their merits and not their age." Western Air Lines, Inc. v. Criswell, 472 U.S. 400, 422 (1985). The employer cannot rely on age as a proxy for an employee's remaining characteristics, such as productivity, but must instead focus on those factors directly.

When the employer's decision *is* wholly motivated by factors other than age, the problem of inaccurate and stigmatizing stereotypes disappears. This is true even if the motivating factor is correlated with age, as pension status typically is. Pension plans typically provide that an employee's accrued benefits will become nonforfeitable, or "vested," once the employee completes a certain number of years of service with the employer. See 1 J. Mamorsky, Employee Benefits Law § 5.03 (1992). On average, an older employee has had more years in the work force than a younger employee, and thus may well have accumulated more years of service with a particular employer. Yet an employee's age is analytically distinct from his years of service. An employee who is younger than 40, and therefore outside the class of older workers as defined by the ADEA . . . may have worked for a particular employer his entire career, while an older worker may have been newly hired. Because age and years of service are analytically distinct, an employer can take account of one while ignoring the other, and thus it is incorrect to say that a decision based on years of service is necessarily "age based."

. . . [A] decision by the company to fire an older employee solely because he has nine-plus years of service and therefore is "close to vesting" would not constitute discriminatory treatment on the basis of age. The prohibited stereotype ("Older employees are likely to be—") would not have figured in this decision, and the attendant stigma would not ensue. The decision would not be the result of an inaccurate and denigrating generalization about age, but would rather represent an *accurate* judgment about the employee— that he indeed is "close to vesting."

We do not mean to suggest that an employer *lawfully* could fire an employee in order to prevent his pension benefits from vesting. Such conduct is actionable under § 510 of ERISA. . . . But it would not, without more, violate the ADEA. That law requires the employer to ignore an employee's age (absent a statutory exemption or defense); it does not specify *further* characteristics that an employer must also ignore. . . . Our holding is simply that an employer does not violate the ADEA just by interfering with an older employee's pension benefits that would have vested by virtue of the employee's years of service.

Id. at 610–12; *see also Rowan v. Lockheed Martin Energy Sys.*, Inc., 360 F.3d 544 (6th Cir. 2004) (finding that the termination of two older workers was motivated by a concern that the workforce at a nuclear plant was aging did not constitute age discrimination because the firm was legitimately concerned with the future of its workforce).

As noted in the excerpt from the *Hazen Paper* case, the ADEA is much like the ADA insofar as the statute is premised on the notion that employers were making arbitrary judgments based on age that were not empirically supportable. In *Western Air Lines v. Criswell*, 472 U.S. 400, 409–12 (1985), the Court discussed the purpose behind the ADEA:

Throughout the legislative history of the ADEA, one empirical fact is repeatedly emphasized: the process of psychological and physiological degeneration · caused by aging varies with each individual. The basic research in the field of aging has established that there is a wide range of individual physical ability regardless of age. As a result, many older American workers perform at levels equal or superior to their younger colleagues.

In 1965, the Secretary of Labor reported to Congress that despite these well-established medical facts there "is persistent and widespread use of age limits in hiring that in a great many cases can be attributed only to arbitrary discrimination against older workers on the basis of age and regardless of ability." [Report, at 21, Legislative History 37.] Two years later, the President recommended that Congress enact legislation to abolish arbitrary age limits on hiring. Such limits, the President declared, have a devastating effect on the dignity of the individual and result in a staggering loss of human resources vital to the national economy. After further study, Congress responded with the enactment of the ADEA. The preamble declares that the purpose of the ADEA is "to promote employment of older persons based on their ability rather than age [and] to prohibit arbitrary age discrimination in employment." 81 Stat. 602, 29 U.S.C. § 621(b). Section 4(a)(1) makes it "unlawful for an employer . . . to fail or refuse to hire or to discharge any individual or otherwise discriminate against any individual with respect to his compensation, terms, conditions, or privileges of employment, because of such individual's age." 81 Stat. 603, 29 U.S.C. § 623(a)(1). This proscription presently applies to all persons between the ages of 40 and 70. 29 U.S.C. § 631(a). . . .

The legislative history of the 1978 Amendments to the ADEA makes quite clear that the policies and substantive provisions of the Act apply with especial force in the case of mandatory retirement provisions. The House Committee on Education and Labor reported:

> "Increasingly, it is being recognized that mandatory retirement based solely upon age is arbitrary and that chronological age alone is a poor indicator of ability to perform a job. Mandatory retirement does not take into consideration actual differing abilities and capacities. Such forced retirement can cause hardships for older persons through loss of roles and loss of income. Those older persons who wish to be re-employed have a much more difficult time finding a new job than younger persons.

> "Society, as a whole, suffers from mandatory retirement as well. As a result of mandatory retirement, skills and experience are lost from the work force resulting in reduced GNP. Such practices also add a burden to Government income maintenance programs such as social security." H. R. Rep. No. 95-527, pt. 1, p. 2 (1977), Legislative History 362. Cf. S. Rep. No. 95-493, p. 4 (1977), Legislative History 437 ("The committee believes that the arguments for retaining existing mandatory retirement policies are largely based on misconceptions rather than upon a careful analysis of the facts.")."

Id. at 409–12.

The prohibition on mandatory retirement has raised a number of issues. Economists have shown that salaries tend to increase over time with seniority while, at some point, productivity declines and fails to keep up with the salary increases so that it is not uncommon that more senior workers are being paid more than their productivity might justify. The opposite can also be true: employees tend to be underpaid early in their career as employers seek to determine which employees will be the best fit for the corporation. Thus, the higher payments later in a career effectively compensate for lower payments early on. Under this model, mandatory retirement was seen as crucial for employers to determine how best to establish wages. If an employee was to retire at age 65, the employer could then determine what the appropriate wage should be over an employee's work life. *See* Edward P. Lazear, *Why Is There Mandatory Retirement?* 87 J. POL. ECON. 1261 (1979). Without mandatory retirement, it is considerably more difficult to determine how to distribute wages over time. Employers may also have an incentive to fire an older worker once his productivity begins to trail his wage increases. In an important article, Stewart Schwab has argued that the ADEA serves to prevent opportunistic firings of older workers. He writes:

> Late-career employees face the greatest danger of opportunistic firings. At the end of their life cycle, they often earn more than their current productivity. If they do, the employer has a financial incentive to terminate them, even if it violates an implicit promise to allow the employee to reap the rewards of hard work earlier in his career. The [ADEA] provides one check against late-career opportunism. By prohibiting employers from firing workers above the age of forty because of their age, the ADEA

protects older workers from discharges based upon stereotypes that lead employers to underestimate their productivity.

Stewart J. Schwab, *Life-Cycle Justice: Accommodating Just Cause and Employment*, 92 MICH. L. REV. 8, 43 (1993). Schwab also suggests that courts generally interpret the ADEA by applying particular scrutiny to potential opportunistic firings late in one's career. The fact that federal judges enjoy life tenure may also make them particularly sensitive to stereotypes about the ability of older workers.

Although the ADEA generally prohibits mandatory retirement, it allows employers to provide retirement incentives under certain circumstances. The Older Workers Benefit Protection Act ("OWBPA") amended the ADEA in 1990 to address issues that had arisen with retirement incentives. Perhaps the most important aspect of OWBPA is that it allows employers to obtain waivers of ADEA rights from employees so long as the waivers are "knowing and voluntary." The statute also sets forth minimum conditions that, if met, will constitute a knowing and voluntary waiver and preclude workers from suing for age discrimination. *See* 29 U.S.C. § 626(f). These conditions include providing workers with notice to consult with an attorney, providing employees at least 21 days to consider their decisions and the waivers must be based on valid consideration. If the waiver is part of an early incentive program, it must include additional protections—the 21-day waiting period is increased to 45 days and the employer must provide detailed information regarding who is eligible for the plan. Additional requirements are contained in the statute. *See id.; see also Oubre v. Entergy Operations, Inc.*, 522 U.S. 422 (1998) (holding that an employee need not return consideration based on an invalid waiver if she later brings an ADEA claim).

Issues with respect to retirement and age discrimination are likely to gain new importance in the coming decades. The economic crisis that began in late 2007 disrupted the retirement plans of many employees and attendant higher unemployment also affected older workers. Indeed, there have been a surge of cases alleging age discrimination by older employees who have been laid off or removed from their positions, and in these cases the plaintiffs are often able to provide evidence of age discrimination either based on remarks (the need for "young blood") or by the implausibility of the employer's explanation. *See, e.g., Velez v. Thermo King*, 585 F.3d 441 (1st Cir. 2009) (56-year old plaintiff with 24-year career survives summary judgment in termination case); *King v. United States*, 553 F.3d 1156 (8th Cir. 2009) (claim of 54-year old who produced evidence that the agency sought "young blood" remanded for further proceedings); *Duncan v. Fleetwood Motor Homes*, 518 F.3d 486 (7th Cir. 2008) (51-year old with 20-year career who was removed from his position survived summary judgment because of employer's inconsistent explanations for its actions); *Kassner v. Second Avenue Deli.*, 496 F.3d 229 (2d Cir. 2007) (79 and 61-year-old waitresses sued for harassment and retaliation claims survive motions to dismiss).

The ADEA also has a regulatory effect on retirement plans, but those issues are discussed in Chapter 12 in the section on retirement benefits. For a comprehensive overview of the ADEA and age discrimination see Howard C. Eglit, *The Age Discrimination in Employment Act at Thirty: Where It's Been, Where It Is Today, Where It Is Going*, 31 U. RICH. L. REV. 579 (1997).

2. Diversity in the Workplace

The final topic in this chapter is one that treads across all of the previous material, namely diversity in the workplace. In many ways, Title VII was designed to create a more diverse workplace, as the original theory was that by eliminating barriers to workplace opportunity, women and minorities would flourish and obtain some form of proportional representation in the workplace. After all, if discrimination was the principal explanation for the way the workplace had been structured prior to the passage of Title VII, then prohibiting discrimination, should in time produce a more egalitarian workplace. At least that was the basic theory, and what might be the actuality is difficult to say.

You may have noticed that we have not yet discussed affirmative action and that is for two reasons. First, the affirmative action doctrine is typically discussed extensively in Constitutional Law and its principles are primarily constitutional in nature. Moreover, affirmative action doctrine has arisen primarily in the context of areas other than employment and, indeed, cases involving employment are few in number, even though affirmative action has had perhaps its greatest effect in the workplace. This is not to say that there has not been any case law development; indeed, in the mid-1980s, the Supreme Court decided two important workplace affirmative action cases.

In *Wygant v. Jackson Board of Education*, 476 U.S. 267 (1986), the Supreme Court invalidated a state affirmative action plan under the Equal Protection Clause that sought to apply affirmative action principles to lay off decisions. The case has been widely interpreted to mean that employers, even private employers, have greater leeway to engage in affirmative action in hiring than they do in layoffs. *See* Kathleen M. Sullivan, *Sins of Discrimination: Last Term's Affirmative Action Cases*, 100 HARV. L. REV. 78, 88 (1986) (noting that the Court concentrated its analysis on the effect layoffs have on workers). This interpretation is supported by the Supreme Court's other case, *Johnson v. Transportation Agency, Santa Clara County*, 480 U.S. 616 (1987), where the Court upheld a gender-based affirmative action plan that allowed the agency to select a female applicant for a promotional position over a male applicant who had scored slightly higher in a qualifying examination process so as to correct a "manifest imbalance" in the agency's workforce. Importantly, the *Johnson* case was decided under Title VII, and some have interpreted the case as suggesting that the standards for upholding an affirmative action plan under Title VII falls somewhere below the strict scrutiny required under the Fourteenth Amendment. *See* Daniel A. Farber, *The Outmoded Debate over Affirmative Action*, 82 CAL. L. REV. 893, 902 (1994) ("Under Title VII, employers may now use affirmative action to remedy a 'manifest imbalance' in their work forces so long as the plan meets some general standards of reasonableness. Because private employers are not state actors and therefore are not subject to equal protection standards, they need only meet this looser standard under Title VII."). Several courts, however, have held that the standards under Title VII are the same as under the constitution, an issue the Supreme Court has yet to resolve. *See Schurr v. Resorts Int'l Hotel, Inc.*, 196 F.3d 486, 497–98 (3d Cir. 1999) (relying on *Wygant* to invalidate affirmative action plan because it was not remedial in nature); *Hill v. Ross*, 183 F.3d 586, 588–89 (7th Cir. 1999) (using *Wygant* and

Johnson interchangeably).

As noted previously, it is not our intention to delve into the specifics of the case law, but we instead want to explore the meaning and importance of diversity in the workplace. One of the more interesting facets of affirmative action is the widespread support affirmative action policies receive within the business community. Indeed, the business community significantly aligned itself with the University of Michigan to support its affirmative action policies when they were challenged in the Supreme Court. The various amicus briefs filed by major corporations proved influential to the Supreme Court, and reinforced the importance of affirmative action for corporations. At one time, it was generally thought that businesses were opposed to affirmative action, although this assumption was never reflected in the actions of major corporations, which have long supported various efforts to diversify the workplace. For a discussion of the business community's support for affirmative action in the University of Michigan case, see Neal Devins, *Explaining Grutter v. Bollinger*, 152 U. PA. L. REV. 347, 368–70 (2003).

Businesses support affirmative action for a variety of reasons but in the last decade the predominant justification has come to be known as the "business case for diversity," where diversity is seen as good for business. Steven Ramirez summarizes the business case for diversity in the following excerpt:

> Two critical economic trends form the linchpin for the business case for diversity: demographics and globalization. First, the nation's population (and hence its labor, investor and consumer pools) is undergoing an historic change whereby the nation's minority populations are increasing rapidly, while the labor pool as a whole is stagnating. White males, therefore, constitute a decreasing percentage of key constituencies. Second, the business of America is increasingly integrated into the world economic system, meaning that American business must now deal with important constituencies (labor, investor and consumer pools) that are as multi-cultural as the world. By the year 2025, demographic experts project that the additional 72 million members of the U.S. population will include 32 million Latinos, 12 million African Americans and 7 million Asian Americans. This more diverse population pool will necessarily lead to a more diverse marketplace of consumers. Minority populations are growing in number, as well as in wealth. This wave of diverse market entrants will also be more highly educated than their parents. From 1973 to 1996, the percentage of Latinos awarded B.A. degrees grew from 6.1 to 13.4 percent for women, and from 6.6 to 12 percent for men. For African Americans the increase was from approximately 7.2 to 17.7 percent. Because these populations will expand most markedly in the key 18–24 year old range, college enrollment is expected to rise 23 percent for African Americans and 73 percent for Latinos from 1995 to 2015. Gender diversity is also on the upswing: by the year 2005 women will constitute 48 percent of the nation's workforce. Women too are attending and graduating college at dramatically higher rates. This increased population diversity will have an enormous impact upon the business environment: for example, people of color now constitute 25 percent of the nation's consumer base. . . .

Leading professional business associations have studied diversity management in great detail. For example, the Society for Human Resource
Management ("SHRM") conducted one of the most far ranging surveys on
the state of diversity initiatives in corporate America in 1998. According to
this survey top executives at 8 of 10 Fortune 500 companies found diversity
management to be an important part of business. The SHRM has shown
that embracing diversity can help firms create an attractive place for
talented employees of all backgrounds to work. . . .

Steven A. Ramirez, *Diversity and the Boardroom*, 6 STAN. J.L. BUS. & FIN. 85 (2000).
Does this argument seem compelling? How would you define what has come to be
known as "the business case for diversity"? Cynthia Estlund has succinctly defined
the concept as "the proposition that a diverse workforce is essential to serve a
diverse customer base, to gain legitimacy in the eyes of a diverse public, and to
generate workable solutions within a global economy." Cynthia L. Estlund, *Putting
Grutter to Work: Diversity, Integration, and Affirmative Action in the Workplace*,
26 BERKELEY J. EMP. & LAB. L. 1, 4 (2005).

In his article, Ramirez cites several industry surveys regarding the benefits of
diversity, but until recently there had been little critical or empirical analysis on
whether diversity makes companies more efficient or offers significant value to
employers. One major study has examined four large firms with strong commitments to diversity and found that, based on these firms, there was no evidence that
having a diverse workforce added significant value to the firms, and the authors also
concluded that there was no negative effect either. In other words, diversity proved
neutral. *See* Thomas Kochan *et al.*, *The Effects of Diversity on Business Performance: A Report of a Feasibility Study on the Diversity Research Network*, 42
Human Resource Mgt. 3 (2003). Research has also indicated that heterogeneous
groups may not be the most effective for problem-solving purposes. Devon Carbado
and G. Mitu Gulati have reviewed this literature and concluded:

> There is theoretical and empirical evidence suggesting that employers
> are motivated to pursue homogeneity: Put simply, homogeneous work-
> places facilitate trust, loyalty, and cooperative behavior. The story with
> respect to heterogeneous work teams is different. First, at an institutional
> level, heterogeneity is difficult and costly to manage. Second, the most
> cost-effective way for individual supervisors to manage heterogeneity is to
> "socialize away" outsider difference. Thus, it is more accurate to charac-
> terize this strategy as eliminating, rather than managing, heterogeneity.
> Third, even assuming that heterogeneity can be effectively managed, the
> benefits of a heterogeneous workplace are speculative, and they are
> realized primarily over the long term. . . . Studies consistently show [that]
> . . . [r]acial heterogeneity undermines trust and cooperation. Team mem-
> bers in heterogeneous teams tend not to communicate as well as team
> members in homogeneous teams. Turnover rates in heterogeneous teams
> are higher.

Devon W. Carbado & Mitu Gulati, *The Law and Economics of Critical Race Theory*,
112 YALE L.J. 1757 (2003) (book review). If a diverse workforce is not necessarily a
better workforce for the employer, why do so many employers emphasize diversity

as a core value? Does the Ramirez excerpt offer any insights? Do changing demographics explain the business community's support for affirmative action?

Assuming businesses are interested in having a diverse workforce so as to tap into an increasing consumer demand—namely that having more Latinos or African Americans might enable the company to appeal to Latino or African-American communities—would such a motive be permissible under Title VII? Recall that under Title VII, race cannot be a "BFOQ." Are there other means of justifying affirmative action that might be related to a company's business interests? Although these justifications can be problematic under the law, John Skrentny demonstrates that many employers routinely engage in just such efforts—what he calls "racial realism" which he equates with treating race as a job qualification—and that these efforts simply have not been challenged under the law. *See* John D. Skrentny, After Civil Rights: New American Racial Realism in the Workplace (2013).

Another important argument for diversity in the workplace has been advocated by Cynthia Estlund, who sees the workplace as an important facet of civil society. From this perspective, the workplace can foster important ties across racial and class divisions, and in the process promote trust and understanding. The following excerpt provides the essence of her argument:

> African-Americans' employment in professional, white-collar, and skilled blue-collar occupations has risen significantly since World War II, and particularly since the enactment of Title VII. This is especially true in public employment and among large private-sector employers that are most subject to governmental and judicial oversight in the form of federal contract requirements and large-scale litigation. As a result, people from different racial and ethnic groups increasingly work together. African-Americans have considerably more contact with whites at work than in their neighborhoods or their churches. Most white workers, too, have coworkers of another race, though most have few or no black coworkers. . . . The workplace thus offers an especially promising institutional setting for the formation of connections of social solidarity, empathy, and communication in a diverse society. It is a particularly promising incubator of connections across lines of race and ethnicity. The formation of these ties is an essential and underappreciated function of work life. . . .

> The workplace tends to bring people together from different neighborhoods and communities, with different beliefs and experiences. In part that is because the antidiscrimination laws have had a significant impact on the workplace. Since the enactment of Title VII, the workplace has become a *comparatively* integrated social environment—compared, that is, to other places in which adult citizens interact with each other. Moreover, the integration that does exist in the workplace is particularly important because it is a site of sustained, constructive, and cooperative interaction in which coworkers readily form ties of trust, solidarity, and affection. Empirical studies confirm that cooperation on common projects across racial and ethnic lines has enormous potential for improving intergroup attitudes and relations. . . .

How does the workplace stack up as a site for constructive intergroup contact? The requirement of equal status is obviously problematic within any hierarchically organized institution. Still, the workplace would seem to hold ample potential for positive interracial contact under this theory. First, as already noted, there is simply more, and more sustained, interracial contact in the workplace than elsewhere. And interracial contacts on the job—because they are ongoing and frequent—lead to "social relationships and even enduring friendships," which are the most fruitful kind of interracial contact.

But it is not just the friendship potential of workplace relations that makes it a promising source of interracial contact; it is the process of working together. A good deal of on-the-job contact, at least under the regime of equal employment law, meets the basic conditions for positive interracial contact: it is generally cooperative and directed toward shared objectives; much of it is sustained, personal, informal, and one-to-one; it is often in a context of equal status, at least in the sense that status is not determined by race; and it has the approval of managers and the society as a whole. Indeed, in the world outside the laboratory, the workplace is virtually unique in its capacity to convene individuals who would not otherwise choose to interact and to compel them to cooperate . . . .

The sheer complexity of the emerging picture is daunting. It remains true that the workplace holds more potential for constructive and productive social interaction—particularly interaction across racial and ethnic lines—than does any other social institution. It also appears that workplace practices in the leading sectors of the economy are moving in the direction of greater cooperation and less rigid hierarchy. Yet it remains true, even in the most advanced workplace organizations, that workplace interaction takes place under economic and instrumental constraints that are deeply at odds with the ideals of freedom and equality that many accounts demand in the realm of democratic civil society and civic engagement. The move toward more egalitarian organizational structures in some firms is by no means a complete answer to the problem that hierarchy and economic coercion pose for the integrative function of the workplace . . . .

Daily interaction with a relatively diverse set of coworkers creates some shared concerns—concerns about working conditions, pay and benefits, the organization of work, the quality of the work product, and the economic health of the enterprise. It also fosters communication about common interests from outside the workplace—family, current events, and the landmarks and icons of popular culture. But that daily interaction also exposes individual and group differences, even conflicts, in outlook and experience. Those differences may be muted—or they may be more safely and productively explored—in the relatively disciplined and civil environment of the workplace, and within a web of shared interests and experiences, than in the public square, but it is certain that differences will remain.

. . . Whatever mix of commonality and difference emerges from close and constructive personal interaction among individuals of different racial and ethnic groups can only improve upon the quality of public discourse and decisionmaking that would attain in the absence of these personal interactions. Yet my thesis does betray a hope for the discovery and the cultivation of commonalities, not across the whole society but within workplaces that reflect some of the diversity of the whole society. There are other spaces in the society for the cultivation of difference, of dissidence, and of distinct cultural identity; the roles of family and other intimate and expressive associations are vital and constitutionally recognized. The unique contribution of the workplace to democratic society, however, is its ability to bring individuals together without regard to those differences, and to foster ongoing cooperative relations of trust and common interests among them. We should recognize and cultivate the demonstrated capacity of citizens to rise above their differences and their biases through the experience of working together under norms of equality.

Cynthia L. Estlund, *Working Together: The Workplace, Civil Society, and the Law*, 89 GEO. L.J. 1 (2000). The excerpt from Estlund's article raises a number of interesting and important questions, many of which she considers in her article and in her book, WORKING TOGETHER (2004). Consider the following: Is the interest in fostering better racial relations also in an employer's interests, or is this more of a societal interest? What about gender, would similar arguments work for gender?

Estlund offers a particular vision of the workplace that she describes with respect to its potential, but many workplaces—even among those employers who support diversity—do not foster cooperation and trust, but instead can be divisive, particularly on racial lines. This was more true prior to Title VII when many unionized workplaces had both black and white unions, and in the 1970s, many race-specific employee groups arose within police and fire departments to support the interests of minority applicants and employees. *See* Ruben J. Garcia, *New Voices at Work: Race and Gender Identity Caucuses in the U.S. Labor Movement*, 54 HASTINGS L.J. 79, 93–113 (2002) (describing history of separate interests within unions). Tristin Green has suggested that to ensure that diversity is truly respected in the workplace—rather than leading to demands of assimilation—employers should be required to accommodate an employee's desire for group identification, particularly as it relates to appearance. *See* Tristin K. Green, *Discomfort at Work: Workplace Assimilation and the Contact Hypothesis*, 86 N.C. L. REV. 379 (2008).

Others have suggested that unions might offer a means of pulling together diverse groups, and have also cautioned against the development of identity caucuses. Molly McUsic and Michael Selmi have argued that allowing or encouraging workers to organize around identity in the workplace would likely lead to a fragmented workplace where workers would compete against each other for limited rewards, without achieving any greater power in the workplace. *See* Michael Selmi & Molly S. McUsic, *Difference and Solidarity: Unions in a Postmodern Age, in* LABOUR LAW IN AN ERA OF GLOBALIZATION 429 (J. Conaghan *et al.* eds., 2002). They emphasize that unions have the potential to foster diverse workplaces by mediating differences in the pursuit of common interests. Marion Crain and Ken Matheny have stressed the opportunity unions have to recruit from diverse groups, noting,

"Exciting new research indicates that workforce diversity presents growth opportunities for unions as Blacks and women have the highest union organizability rates." Marion Crain & Ken Matheny, *Labor's Identity Crisis*, 89 CALIF. L. REV. 1767, 1824 (2001).

The question of diversity in the workplace raises difficult and often contentious issues. What emphasis do you think should be placed on achieving a diverse workplace, and why? What rationale best explains the importance of diversity, and what means are available for achieving greater diversity? This section focuses primarily on race and ethnicity, are issues of gender or sexual orientation different in significant ways, or do they pose similar problems?

Chapter 10

CHALLENGES TO EQUALITY IN A
DIVERSIFYING WORKPLACE

The increasing diversity of the American workforce has raised new challenges to promoting equality at work. Although Title VII and the other federal statutes discussed in Chapter 9 provide the basic framework for addressing inequality, for many workers a simple prohibition against discrimination does little to insure their equal status in the workplace. The problems faced by these workers cut across legal boundaries, implicating not only anti-discrimination law, but other protective employment legislation as well. In this chapter, we consider two very different groups of workers whose growing presence in the workforce presents different types of challenges to the existing structure of work law. In section A, we focus on immigrant workers who face unique forms of discrimination, as well as the risk of exclusion from even basic forms of employment protection depending upon their immigration status. In section B, we examine the difficulty of achieving equality for workers with family-care responsibilities.

A. THE IMMIGRANT WORKFORCE

As discussed in Chapter 2, the American labor force includes a significant number of immigrant workers, the largest portion of whom are Hispanic in origin. While many immigrants from all over the world have entered the country legally, a significant number lack legal authority to work in the United States. Tighter border controls and slack demand during and following the recession somewhat reduced the flow of undocumented workers into the United States. Nevertheless, there were an estimated 11.7 million undocumented workers in the country in 2012.

Like other minorities, immigrant workers—documented and undocumented—face the risk of discrimination on the job; however, their ability to invoke the protection of the law may be complicated by their immigration status. Traditional anti-discrimination law may not reach all forms of discrimination affecting immigrant workers, and their immigration status may affect their ability to assert their rights—not only under anti-discrimination laws, but other protective labor laws as well. Employers face a complicated legal landscape as well. They must be careful not to run afoul of the prohibition on national origin discrimination. At the same time, the Immigration Reform and Control Act of 1986 (IRCA), 8 U.S.C. § 1324a, requires that they verify the employment-eligible status of every employee that they hire. Failure to do so may subject them to civil or criminal penalties. Employers have also faced private lawsuits alleging that they have knowingly hired large numbers of undocumented workers to the detriment of documented workers. In this section, we explore some of these issues confronting immigrant workers and their employers. We begin by considering in broad terms the impact of immigrant workers on the labor market.

1.   The Impact of Immigrant Labor

Frances Lee Ansley, *Rethinking Law in Globalizing Labor Markets*
1 U. PA. J. LAB. & EMP. L. 369, 388–96 (1998)

Immigrants without papers, education, or both are usually relegated to tough, low-wage sectors such as farm labor, meat and poultry processing, landscaping, tree planting, roofing and construction, day labor, and domestic service. These are the "3-D jobs" so often held by low-wage immigrants: "dirty, dangerous, and difficult." In Appalachia, they used to be held largely by poor whites. In other parts of the Southeast, it was mostly African-Americans who did this work. In the Southwest, it was often Chicanos and Chicanas. Today, in more and more communities around the Southeast, this sort of job is turning from white and black to brown. The jobs are being "re-raced" right under native-born people's startled gaze and regrouped in a system of racial categories that is itself undergoing rapid change. Nevertheless, the "Model Worker" is a useful character with a certain amount of rhetorical clout. His name is invoked in discussions about work and welfare and what young people are coming to today. He has a strong part in the morality play that accompanies the re-racing of the local labor market, and one of his primary functions is the setting up of explicit and implicit comparisons. Such racial reconfiguring is not a new phenomenon in U.S. history, of course, but for people in many communities, it is brand new in their own, and probably in their parents', lifetimes.

In addition to the influx of immigrants into low-wage sectors, there are immigrants finding places in middle and higher niches of the economy as well. From Filipina nurses to Indian moteliers, Vietnamese nail shop owners, and the foreign-born computer programmers of the Silicon Valley, immigrant entrepreneurs and professionals are becoming more commonplace in local economies.

Whether an industry is high or low, focused on computers or cucumbers, the increased presence of immigrants often coincides with at least a localized or sectoral downward pressure on wage levels and working conditions and an intensified drive to increase productivity in ways previously thought not to be tolerable. One Georgia employer enthusiastically told a newspaper reporter, "It's much more productive. You can't work side-by-side with a Mexican and do half the work. They've raised the standard." Similarly, a Georgia landscaper observed in a letter to the editor, "Unlike some Americans in this country who don't want to work, at least these guys put in blood, sweat and tears, and I like what they are doing. I'll tell you this: I'll hire a Spanish person over any of the other Americans I've had working for me."

Recently, I talked with "Manuel," a Mexican immigrant in his twenties who came illegally to Tennessee four years ago. He has worked in the local vegetable harvest and a chicken processing plant. He put it this way:

> American people have just one rhythm. You set your rhythm to work, and you don't change it. And we tend to work faster than Americans. We

know that this is not our home, that you are not going to put up with us. So we need to show you what we are worth—that we can do it as fast or better than Americans. I was working for five months at [the chicken processing plant]. I was in the stock room. I had to divide all the different processed chickens. [It was hard,] especially during the winter, when the ice was on the floor, and we had to move fast, but at the same time trying to not slip and fall. Because we were handling boxes of forty, fifty, seventy, and eighty pounds. Six. Six an hour. What we get paid is not really cheap from our point of view. How can we raise our voice if we know that we don't have papers? That we are in danger, because if you don't like me, you can call INS, you can get somebody that has some kind of pull and says, "Okay, just come and pick so many Hispanics."

American employers at earlier points in our history sometimes imported minority racial or ethnic groups in moments of labor crisis to cross picket lines and break strikes, strategically using a toxic mixture of the nativism and righteous indignation of white, native-born workers to hobble efforts at organization and collective bargaining. Today, immigrants are more likely to be used as "wage busters" and "condition busters" than as strike breakers. In some instances, the savings thus realized translate into super-profits for employers, while in others they allow an otherwise marginal enterprise barely to stay afloat. In either case, immigration policy and practice continue to be driven largely by the goals of U.S. employers. Immigrant workers are often left to bear a heavy part of the risk and to pay a heavy part of the cost of seriously deteriorated wages associated with poor working conditions. Meanwhile, the power of racial classification to divide the workforce within a given labor market and to disable the workforce from effective economic or political action remains a constant.

Caution is in order, however, regarding any easy assumptions about cause and effect. Observers of all stripes often seem to attribute what they see about the work situations and the job performance of immigrants to some personal or cultural trait that immigrant workers carry with them in the journey from third to first world. Whether the talk is of a laudable "strong work ethic" or lamentable "sweatshop conditions," immigrants are often pictured as importing something foreign into the American scene, changing the climate for good or ill.

Disturbingly, both sides often proceed as though a cost-benefit analysis oriented exclusively to the U.S. economy and public fisc adequately captures the relevant issues for the development of a good immigration policy. In a new world order so dominated by the U.S. economic agenda, this assumption appears particularly lacking in moral imagination. This characterization is too simple for several reasons. First, as a group, immigrant workers bring into their U.S. jobs and communities not only the habit of hard work, not only a situationally heightened need and desire to perform to their employers' wishes, but also traditions and experiences of collective resistance and bottom-up institution building. Despite the tremendous disincentives to immigrant organizing, there are myriad instances of immigrants doing just that, sometimes with greater militancy and creativity than their U.S.-born counterparts, and sometimes in ways that help to catalyze and animate U.S.-born collaborators and allies. Therefore, a discourse that pictures immigrant workers as the cause or carrier of deteriorated wage structures and work environments wrongly ignores immigrant activity in resisting and reforming such conditions.

NOTES

1. Immigrant Labor and Native-Born Workers. Frances Lee Ansley discusses the competitive pressure that immigrant workers' employment has on native-born workers. Why does this competitive pressure exist? If the reason is that immigrant workers are more exploitable due to their undocumented status, wouldn't one response be to ensure that they are protected by labor and employment laws equally with native-born workers? As we will see, the law's response has been ambivalent. Why do you think that might be?

As an empirical matter it is not clear whether immigrant labor negatively impacts job opportunities for native-born workers. The Immigration Policy Center issued a report in which it found that immigrants pose no threat to native-born workers where they fit into jobs that U.S.-born workers do not prefer (the "3D" jobs discussed by Ansley). Because they are not interchangeable with native-born workers, "removing immigrants would not automatically lead to job openings for natives." *See* UNTYING THE KNOT PART III (Immigration Policy Center, August 2009), *available at* www.immigrationpolicy.org. The Center for Immigration Studies, on the other hand, found that immigrant workers directly compete with native-born workers who have the lowest education levels and are employed in low skill jobs. *See* JOBS AMERICANS DON'T DO? and WORSE THAN IT SEEMS: BROADER MEASURE OF UNEMPLOYMENT SHOWS BLEAK PICTURE (Center for Immigration Studies, August 2009), *available at* www.cis.org/articles.

The "immigration equation" is more complex than these analyses might make it first appear. For example, new workers add to the supply of labor, thereby increasing competition for jobs, but they also add to the demand for labor by consuming goods and services. And the competitive effect for individual native-born workers is likely to vary depending upon how similar the immigrant workers are in terms of education and skills to the native-born population in a given region. Though a full discussion of immigration policy is beyond the scope of this text, it is impossible to ignore the influence of immigration law upon the U.S. labor market. For a good discussion of research and theory on the effect of immigrants on native-born workers, see Roger Lowenstein, *The Immigration Equation*, N.Y. TIMES, July 9, 2006, at E36.

2. "Jobs Americans Won't Do." It is often asserted that there is no conflict between native and immigrant workers, because immigrants fill "jobs Americans won't do." Jennifer Gordon looks behind this claim, arguing that it is often presented as "a natural state of affairs, reflecting only the immutable tastes of workers." Jennifer Gordon, *Tensions in Rhetoric and Reality at the Intersection of Work and Immigration*, 2 U.C. IRVINE L. REV. 125, 136 (2012). She argues that in fact employers play a significant role in shaping labor markets and that, in particular, certain types of jobs have come to be seen as immigrants' work because employers in those industries made "a concerted effort . . . to undercut unions and reduce wages and protections," *id.* at 136, and that if wages rose, non-immigrant workers would be attracted to these jobs again. *Id.* at 137. As an example, she points to the meatpacking industry, which in the mid-20th century was a largely unionized sector with relatively high paying jobs. Today, the unions are mostly gone and the jobs are characterized by low pay, poor working conditions and a significant immigrant workforce. *Id.* at 137–38.

2. Undocumented Workers

Immigrant workers who lack legal authorization to work in the United States face serious obstacles to enforcing their rights as employees. These challenges are not easily characterized as matters solely of discrimination or of working conditions, but rather they raise enforcement problems which cut across many different sources of workplace protection. Should undocumented workers be treated equally with native-born workers and legally documented workers in terms of basic employment protections? Or should the law distinguish between them in terms of the rights they are afforded?

HOFFMAN PLASTIC COMPOUNDS, INC. v. NLRB
United States Supreme Court
535 U.S. 137 (2002)

CHIEF JUSTICE REHNQUIST delivered the opinion of the Court.

The National Labor Relations Board (Board) awarded backpay to an undocumented alien who has never been legally authorized to work in the United States. We hold that such relief is foreclosed by federal immigration policy, as expressed by Congress in the Immigration Reform and Control Act of 1986 (IRCA).

Petitioner Hoffman Plastic Compounds, Inc. (petitioner or Hoffman), custom-formulates chemical compounds for businesses that manufacture pharmaceutical, construction, and household products. In May 1988, petitioner hired Jose Castro to operate various blending machines that "mix and cook" the particular formulas per customer order. Before being hired for this position, Castro presented documents that appeared to verify his authorization to work in the United States. In December 1988, the United Rubber, Cork, Linoleum, and Plastic Workers of America, AFL-CIO, began a union-organizing campaign at petitioner's production plant. Castro and several other employees supported the organizing campaign and distributed authorization cards to co-workers. In January 1989, Hoffman laid off Castro and other employees engaged in these organizing activities.

Three years later, in January 1992, respondent Board found that Hoffman unlawfully selected four employees, including Castro, for layoff "in order to rid itself of known union supporters" in violation of § 8(a)(3) of the National Labor Relations Act (NLRA). 306 N.L.R.B. 100. To remedy this violation, the Board ordered that Hoffman (1) cease and desist from further violations of the NLRA, (2) post a detailed notice to its employees regarding the remedial order, and (3) offer reinstatement and backpay to the four affected employees. Hoffman entered into a stipulation with the Board's General Counsel and agreed to abide by the Board's order.

In June 1993, the parties proceeded to a compliance hearing before an Administrative Law Judge (ALJ) to determine the amount of backpay owed to each discriminatee. On the final day of the hearing, Castro testified that he was born in Mexico and that he had never been legally admitted to, or authorized to work in, the United States. He admitted gaining employment with Hoffman only after tendering a birth certificate belonging to a friend who was born in Texas. He also admitted that he used this birth certificate to fraudulently obtain a California driver's license and a Social Security card, and to fraudulently obtain employment following his layoff by Hoffman. Neither Castro nor the Board's General Counsel offered any evidence that Castro had applied or intended to apply for legal authorization to work in the United States. Based on this testimony, the ALJ found the Board precluded from awarding Castro backpay or reinstatement as such relief would be contrary to *Sure-Tan, Inc. v. NLRB*, 467 U.S. 883 (1984), and in conflict with IRCA, which makes it unlawful for employers knowingly to hire undocumented workers or for employees to use fraudulent documents to establish employment eligibility.

In September 1998, four years after the ALJ's decision, and nine years after Castro was fired, the Board reversed with respect to backpay. Citing its earlier decision in *A.P.R.A. Fuel Oil Buyers Group, Inc.*, 320 N.L.R.B. 408 (1995), the Board determined that "the most effective way to accommodate and further the immigration policies embodied in [IRCA] is to provide the protections and remedies of the [NLRA] to undocumented workers in the same manner as to other employees." 326 N.L.R.B., at 1060. The Board thus found that Castro was entitled to $66,951 of backpay, plus interest. It calculated this backpay award from the date of Castro's termination to the date Hoffman first learned of Castro's undocumented status, a period of 4 1/2 years. A dissenting Board member would have affirmed the ALJ and denied Castro all backpay.

Hoffman filed a petition for review of the Board's order in the Court of Appeals. A panel of the Court of Appeals denied the petition for review. After rehearing the case en banc, the court again denied the petition for review and enforced the Board's order. We granted certiorari, and now reverse.

This case exemplifies the principle that the Board's discretion to select and fashion remedies for violations of the NLRA, though generally broad, is not unlimited. . . . *Sure-Tan, Inc. v. NLRB, supra*, at 902–904. Since the Board's inception, we have consistently set aside awards of reinstatement or backpay to employees found guilty of serious illegal conduct in connection with their employment. . . .

Our decision in *Sure-Tan* followed this line of cases and set aside an award closely analogous to the award challenged here. There we confronted for the first time a potential conflict between the NLRA and federal immigration policy, as then expressed in the Immigration and Nationality Act (INA), 66 Stat. 163, as amended, 8 U.S.C. § 1101 *et seq.* Two companies had unlawfully reported alien-employees to the Immigration and Naturalization Service (INS) in retaliation for union activity. Rather than face INS sanction, the employees voluntarily departed to Mexico. The Board investigated and found the companies acted in violation of §§ 8(a)(1) and (3) of the NLRA. The Board's ensuing order directed the companies to reinstate the affected workers and pay them six months' backpay.

We affirmed the Board's determination that the NLRA applied to undocumented workers, reasoning that the immigration laws "as presently written" expressed only a " 'peripheral concern' with the employment of illegal aliens." 467 U.S., at 892. "For whatever reason," Congress had not "made it a separate criminal offense" for employers to hire an illegal alien, or for an illegal alien "to accept employment after entering this country illegally." *Sure-Tan*, 467 U.S., at 892–893. Therefore, we found "no reason to conclude that application of the NLRA to employment practices affecting such aliens would necessarily conflict with the terms of the INA." *Id.*, at 893.

With respect to the Board's selection of remedies, however, we found its authority limited by federal immigration policy. For example, the Board was prohibited from effectively rewarding a violation of the immigration laws by reinstating workers not authorized to reenter the United States. *Sure-Tan*, 467 U.S., at 903. Thus, to avoid "a potential conflict with the INA," the Board's reinstatement order had to be conditioned upon proof of "the employees' legal reentry." *Ibid.* "Similarly," with respect to backpay, we stated: "[T]he employees must be deemed 'unavailable' for work (and the accrual of backpay therefore tolled) during any period when they were not lawfully entitled to be present and employed in the United States." *Ibid.* "[I]n light of the practical workings of the immigration laws," such remedial limitations were appropriate even if they led to "[t]he probable unavailability of the [NLRA's] more effective remedies." *Id.*, at 904. . . . In 1986, two years after *Sure-Tan*, Congress enacted IRCA, a comprehensive scheme prohibiting the employment of illegal aliens in the United States. § 101(a)(1), 100 STAT. 3360, 8 U.S.C. § 1324a. As we have previously noted, IRCA "forcefully" made combating the employment of illegal aliens central to "[t]he policy of immigration law." *INS v. National Center for Immigrants' Rights, Inc.*, 502 U.S. 183, 194, and n. 8 (1991). It did so by establishing an extensive "employment verification system," § 1324a(a)(1), designed to deny employment to aliens who (a) are not lawfully present in the United States, or (b) are not lawfully authorized to work in the United States, § 1324a(h)(3). This verification system is critical to the IRCA regime. To enforce it, IRCA mandates that employers verify the identity and eligibility of all new hires by examining specified documents before they begin work. § 1324a(b). If an alien applicant is unable to present the required documentation, the unauthorized alien cannot be hired. § 1324a(a)(1).

Similarly, if an employer unknowingly hires an unauthorized alien, or if the alien becomes unauthorized while employed, the employer is compelled to discharge the worker upon discovery of the worker's undocumented status. § 1324a(a)(2). Employers who violate IRCA are punished by civil fines, § 1324a(e)(4)(A), and may be subject to criminal prosecution, § 1324a(f)(1). IRCA also makes it a crime for an unauthorized alien to subvert the employer verification system by tendering fraudulent documents. § 1324c(a). It thus prohibits aliens from using or attempting to use "any forged, counterfeit, altered, or falsely made document" or "any document lawfully issued to or with respect to a person other than the possessor" for purposes of obtaining employment in the United States. §§ 1324c(a)(1)–(3). Aliens who use or attempt to use such documents are subject to fines and criminal prosecution. 18 U.S.C. § 1546(b). There is no dispute that Castro's use of false documents to obtain employment with Hoffman violated these provisions.

Under the IRCA regime, it is impossible for an undocumented alien to obtain employment in the United States without some party directly contravening explicit congressional policies. Either the undocumented alien tenders fraudulent identification, which subverts the cornerstone of IRCA's enforcement mechanism, or the employer knowingly hires the undocumented alien in direct contradiction of its IRCA obligations. The Board asks that we overlook this fact and allow it to award backpay to an illegal alien for years of work not performed, for wages that could not lawfully have been earned, and for a job obtained in the first instance by a criminal fraud. We find, however, that awarding backpay to illegal aliens runs counter to policies underlying IRCA, policies the Board has no authority to enforce or administer. Therefore, as we have consistently held in like circumstances, the award lies beyond the bounds of the Board's remedial discretion.

The Board contends that awarding limited backpay to Castro "reasonably accommodates" IRCA, because, in the Board's view, such an award is not "inconsistent" with IRCA. The Board argues that because the backpay period was closed as of the date Hoffman learned of Castro's illegal status, Hoffman could have employed Castro during the backpay period without violating IRCA. The Board further argues that while IRCA criminalized the misuse of documents, "it did not make violators ineligible for back pay awards or other compensation flowing from employment secured by the misuse of such documents." . . . What matters here, and what sinks both of the Board's claims, is that Congress has expressly made it criminally punishable for an alien to obtain employment with false documents. There is no reason to think that Congress nonetheless intended to permit backpay where but for an employer's unfair labor practices, an alien-employee would have remained in the United States illegally, and continued to work illegally, all the while successfully evading apprehension by immigration authorities. Far from "accommodating" IRCA, the Board's position, recognizing employer misconduct but discounting the misconduct of illegal alien employees, subverts it.

Indeed, awarding backpay in a case like this not only trivializes the immigration laws, it also condones and encourages future violations. The Board admits that had the INS detained Castro, or had Castro obeyed the law and departed to Mexico, Castro would have lost his right to backpay. Castro thus qualifies for the Board's award only by remaining inside the United States illegally. Similarly, Castro cannot mitigate damages, a duty our cases require, see *Sure-Tan*, 467 U.S., at 901, without triggering new IRCA violations, either by tendering false documents to employers or by finding employers willing to ignore IRCA and hire illegal workers. The Board here has failed to even consider this tension.

We therefore conclude that allowing the Board to award backpay to illegal aliens would unduly trench upon explicit statutory prohibitions critical to federal immigration policy, as expressed in IRCA. It would encourage the successful evasion of apprehension by immigration authorities, condone prior violations of the immigration laws, and encourage future violations. However broad the Board's discretion to fashion remedies when dealing only with the NLRA, it is not so unbounded as to authorize this sort of an award.

Lack of authority to award backpay does not mean that the employer gets off scot-free. The Board here has already imposed other significant sanctions against Hoffman—sanctions Hoffman does not challenge. *See supra*, at 1278–1279. These include orders that Hoffman cease and desist its violations of the NLRA, and that it conspicuously post a notice to employees setting forth their rights under the NLRA and detailing its prior unfair practices. 306 N.L.R.B., at 100–101. Hoffman will be subject to contempt proceedings should it fail to comply with these orders. We have deemed such "traditional remedies" sufficient to effectuate national labor policy regardless of whether the "spur and catalyst" of backpay accompanies them. *Sure-Tan*, 467 U.S., at 904. As we concluded in *Sure-Tan*, "in light of the practical workings of the immigration laws," any "perceived deficienc[y] in the NLRA's existing remedial arsenal" must be "addressed by congressional action," not the courts. *Id.*, at 904. In light of IRCA, this statement is even truer today.

The judgment of the Court of Appeals is reversed.

Justice Breyer, with whom Justice Stevens, Justice Souter, and Justice Ginsburg join, dissenting.

I cannot agree that the backpay award before us "runs counter to," or "trenches upon," national immigration policy (citing the Immigration Reform and Control Act of 1986 (IRCA)). As *all* the relevant agencies (including the Department of Justice) have told us, the National Labor Relations Board's limited backpay order will *not* interfere with the implementation of immigration policy. Rather, it reasonably helps to deter unlawful activity that *both* labor laws *and* immigration laws seek to prevent. Consequently, the order is lawful.

The Court does not deny that the employer in this case dismissed an employee for trying to organize a union—a crude and obvious violation of the labor laws. *See* 29 U.S.C. § 158(a)(3) (1994 ed.); *NLRB v. Transportation Management Corp.*, 462 U.S. 393, 398 (1983). And it cannot deny that the Board has especially broad discretion in choosing an appropriate remedy for addressing such violations. *NLRB v. Gissel Packing Co.*, 395 U.S. 575, 612, n. 32 (1969) (Board "draws on a fund of knowledge and expertise all its own, and its choice of remedy must therefore be given special respect by reviewing courts"). Nor can it deny that in such circumstances backpay awards serve critically important remedial purposes. Those purposes involve more than victim compensation; they also include deterrence, i.e., discouraging employers from violating the Nation's labor laws.

Without the possibility of the deterrence that backpay provides, the Board can impose only future-oriented obligations upon law-violating employers—for it has no other weapons in its remedial arsenal. And in the absence of the backpay weapon, employers could conclude that they can violate the labor laws at least once with impunity. Hence the backpay remedy is necessary; it helps make labor law enforcement credible; it makes clear that violating the labor laws will not pay.

Where in the immigration laws can the Court find a "policy" that might warrant taking from the Board this critically important remedial power? Certainly not in any statutory language. The immigration statutes say that an * * * employer may not knowingly employ an illegal alien, that an alien may not submit false documents, and that the employer must verify documentation. *See* 8 U.S.C. §§ 1324a(a)(1), 1324a(b); 18 U.S.C. § 1546(b)(1). They provide specific penalties, including criminal penalties, for violations. *Ibid.;* 8 U.S.C. §§ 1324a(e)(4), 1324a(f)(1). But the statutes' language itself does not explicitly state how a violation is to effect the enforcement of other laws, such as the labor laws. What is to happen, for example, when an employer hires, or an alien works, in violation of these provisions? Must the alien forfeit all pay earned? May the employer ignore the labor laws? More to the point, may the employer violate those laws with impunity, at least once—secure in the knowledge that the Board cannot assess a monetary penalty? The immigration statutes' language simply does not say.

Nor can the Court comfortably rest its conclusion upon the immigration laws' purposes. For one thing, the general purpose of the immigration statute's employment prohibition is to diminish the attractive force of employment, which like a "magnet" pulls illegal immigrants toward the United States. H.R.Rep. No. 99-682, pt. 1, p. 45 (1986), U.S.Code Cong. & Admin.News 1986, p. 5649. To permit the Board to award backpay could not significantly increase the strength of this magnetic force, for so speculative a future possibility could not realistically influence an individual's decision to migrate illegally. *See Patel v. Quality Inn South*, 846 F.2d 700, 704 (C.A.11 1988) (aliens enter the country "in the hope of getting a job," not gaining "the protection of our labor laws").

To *deny* the Board the power to award backpay, however, might very well increase the strength of this magnetic force. That denial lowers the cost to the employer of an initial labor law violation (provided, of course, that the only victims are illegal aliens). It thereby increases the employer's incentive to find and to hire illegal-alien employees. Were the Board forbidden to assess backpay against a *knowing* employer—a circumstance not before us today—this perverse economic incentive, which runs directly contrary to the immigration statute's basic objective, would be obvious and serious. But even if limited to cases where the employer did not know of the employee's status, the incentive may prove significant—for, as the Board has told us, the Court's rule offers employers immunity in borderline cases, thereby encouraging them to take risks, i.e., to hire with a wink and a nod those potentially unlawful aliens whose unlawful employment (given the Court's views) ultimately will lower the costs of labor law violations. The Court has recognized these considerations in stating that the labor laws must apply to illegal aliens in order to ensure that "there will be no advantage under the NLRA in preferring illegal aliens" and therefore there will be "fewer incentives for aliens themselves to enter." *Sure-Tan, supra*, at 893–894. The Court today accomplishes the precise opposite. . . .

The Court also refers to the statement in *Sure-Tan, Inc. v. NLRB*, 467 U.S., at 903, that "employees must be deemed 'unavailable' for work (and the accrual of backpay therefore tolled) during any period when they were not lawfully entitled to be present and employed in the United States." The Court, however, does not rely upon this statement as determining its conclusion. And it is right not to do so. *Sure-Tan* involved an order reinstating (with backpay) illegal aliens who had left the country and returned to Mexico. 467 U.S., at 888–889. In order to collect the backpay to which the order entitled them, the aliens would have had to reenter the country illegally. Consequently, the order itself could not have been enforced without leading to a violation of criminal law. *Id.*, at 903. Nothing in the Court's opinion suggests that the Court intended its statement to reach to circumstances different from and not at issue in *Sure-Tan*, where an order, such as the order before us, does not require the alien to engage in further illegal behavior.

Finally, the Court cannot reasonably rely upon the award's negative features taken together. The Court summarizes those negative features when it says that the Board "asks that we . . . award backpay to an illegal alien [1] for years of work not performed, [2] for wages that could not lawfully have been earned, and [3] for a job obtained in the first instance by a criminal fraud." The first of these features has little persuasive force, given the facts that (1) backpay ordinarily and necessarily is awarded to a discharged employee who may not find other work, and (2) the Board is able to tailor an alien's backpay award to avoid rewarding that alien for his legal inability to mitigate damages by obtaining lawful employment elsewhere. *See, e.g., Sure- Tan, supra,* at 901–902, n. 11, (basing backpay on "representative employee"); *A.P.R.A. Fuel,* 320 N.L.R.B., at 416 (providing backpay for reasonable period); 326 N.L.R.B., at 1062 (cutting off backpay when employer learned of unlawful status).

Neither can the remaining two features—unlawfully earned wages and criminal fraud—prove determinative, for they tell us only a small portion of the relevant story. After all, the same backpay award that compensates an employee in the circumstances the Court describes *also* requires an employer who has violated the labor laws to make a meaningful monetary payment. Considered from this equally important perspective, the award simply requires that employer to pay an employee whom the employer believed could lawfully have worked in the United States, (1) for years of work that he would have performed, (2) for a portion of the wages that he would have earned, and (3) for a job that the employee would have held—had that employer not unlawfully dismissed the employee for union organizing. In ignoring these latter features of the award, the Court undermines the public policies that underlie the Nation's labor laws.

Of course, the Court believes it is necessary to do so in order to vindicate what it sees as conflicting immigration law policies. I have explained why I believe the latter policies do not conflict. But even were I wrong, the law requires the Court to respect the Board's conclusion, rather than to substitute its own independent view of the matter for that of the Board. The Board reached its conclusion after carefully considering both labor law and immigration law. In doing so the Board has acted "with a discriminating awareness of the consequences of its action" on the immigration laws. *Burlington Truck Lines, Inc. v. United States,* 371 U.S. 156, 174 (1962). The Attorney General, charged with immigration law enforcement, has told us that the Board is right. And the Board's position is, at the least, a reasonable one. Consequently, it is lawful. *Chevron U.S.A. Inc. v. Natural Resources Defense Council, Inc.,* 467 U.S. 837, 842–843 (1984) (requiring courts to uphold reasonable agency position).

For these reasons, I respectfully dissent.

NOTES

1. **Employment as a Magnet.** Which resolution would be more likely to decrease the "magnet" effect of U.S. jobs on immigrants, a ruling that NLRA violations are remediable by back pay awards or a ruling that undocumented workers may not recover back pay? If more limited remedies are available to undocumented workers, does this make them an especially attractive labor pool for American employers? The majority in *Hoffman Plastic* argues that the lack of a

back pay award "does not mean that the employer gets off scot-free." *Id.* at 152. What other sanctions does the employer face for violating the NLRA? Are these sanctions likely to be effective in deterring labor law violations or raising the costs of hiring undocumented workers?

Catherine Fisk and Michael Wishnie ask whether, by limiting the remedies available to undocumented workers for violation of their labor law rights in order to further the purposes of the IRCA, *Hoffman Plastic* erects "two sets of rules for the twenty-first century workplace, one for citizens and legal immigrants and the other for the millions of undocumented workers in the United States." *See* Catherine L. Fisk & Michael J. Wishnie, *The Story of* Hoffman Plastic Compounds, Inc. v. NLRB: *Labor Rights Without Remedies for Undocumented Immigrants, in* LABOR LAW STORIES 399, 399 (Laura J. Cooper & Catherine L. Fisk eds., 2005). What do you think the effect of permitting "two sets of rules" will be on workers? Employers? The labor market?

2. **Legal Protection for Undocumented Workers.** A common misperception exists that non-citizens are not covered by the Constitution's protections. In fact, however, the Supreme Court held that "persons" guaranteed due process and equal protection under the Fifth and Fourteenth Amendments include both legally admitted aliens and undocumented persons. *See Plyler v. Doe*, 457 U.S. 202, 210 (1982) (undocumented aliens are covered under the Fourteenth Amendment); *Graham v. Richardson*, 403 U.S. 365, 370 (1971) (lawfully admitted aliens are covered under the Fourteenth Amendment).

Similarly, the courts have found that work law protections apply to undocumented workers. *See, e.g., EEOC v. Hacienda Hotel*, 881 F.2d 1504 (9th Cir. 1989) (affirming backpay awards for discrimination under Title VII to undocumented workers); *Rios v. Enterprise Ass'n Steamfitters Local 638*, 860 F.2d 1168 (2d Cir. 1988) (holding that undocumented workers who have remained in the country are eligible for backpay for a violation of Title VII); *In re Reyes*, 814 F.2d 168, 170 (5th Cir. 1987) (stating that "it is well established that the protections of the Fair Labor Standards Act are applicable to citizens and aliens alike and whether the alien is documented or undocumented is irrelevant"). Prior to *Hoffman Plastic*, most courts permitted undocumented workers to recover back pay along with other remedies for violation of these protective labor statutes. *Hoffman Plastic* made clear that the National Labor Relations Board could not award back pay to unauthorized immigrants. How does its holding apply when workers assert rights under other employment statutes?

The Ninth Circuit in *Rivera v. NIBCO, Inc.*, 364 F.3d 1057 (9th Cir. 2004) expressed skepticism that the holding of *Hoffman Plastic* applied in Title VII cases. More specifically, the court pointed out several significant differences between the two statutes—for example, the fact that Congress intended individual private lawsuits to play an important role in deterring employment discrimination—and concluded that "the overriding national policy against discrimination would seem likely to outweigh any bar against the payment of back wages to unlawful immigrants in Title VII cases. Thus, we seriously doubt that *Hoffman* applies in such actions." *Id.* at 1069. In contrast, a district court earlier held that *Hoffman Plastic* foreclosed back pay as a remedy for an undocumented worker subject to sexual harassment and retaliation in violation of Title VII. *Escobar v. Spartan Security Service*, 281 F. Supp. 2d 895 (S.D. Tex. 2003).

Despite the uncertainty about the availability of back pay in cases in which an undocumented worker has been terminated, courts have consistently recognized that back pay for work *already performed* is different. Thus, claims for unpaid wages under the Fair Labor Standards Act have been permitted regardless of the immigration status of the workers. In a case decided prior to *Hoffman Plastic*, the Eleventh Circuit reasoned as follows:

> We recognize the seeming anomaly of discouraging illegal immigration by allowing undocumented aliens to recover in an action under the FLSA. We doubt, however, that many illegal aliens come to this country to gain the protection of our labor laws. Rather it is the hope of getting a job—at any wage—that prompts most illegal aliens to cross our borders. By reducing the incentive to hire such workers the FLSA's coverage of undocumented aliens helps discourage illegal immigration and is thus fully consistent with the objectives of the IRCA. We therefore conclude that undocumented aliens continue to be "employees" covered by the FLSA.

Patel v. Quality Inn S., 846 F.2d 700, 705–06 (11th Cir. 1988).

After *Hoffman Plastic*, the Eleventh Circuit reconsidered the issue and reaffirmed its holding in *Patel* that undocumented workers are "employees" who may recover unpaid wages under FLSA. *See Lamonica v. Safe Hurricane Shutters, Inc.*, 711 F.3d 1299, 1306 (11th Cir. 2013). It distinguished FLSA claims from the situation in *Hoffman Plastic*, noting that the former are seeking wages for work *already performed*, whereas the plaintiff in *Hoffman Plastic* was trying to recover back pay for "being unlawfully deprived" of a job that "he could never have lawfully performed." *Id.* at 1308. Other courts have followed similar reasoning to reach the same conclusion. *See, e.g., Lucas v. Jerusalem Café*, 721 F.3d 927, 935 (8th Cir. 2013) (finding no conflict between FLSA and IRCA because "both statutes work in tandem to discourage employers from hiring unauthorized workers" and permitting undocumented workers to recover unpaid wages under FLSA); *Zavala v. Wal-Mart Stores, Inc.*, 393 F. Supp. 2d 295 (D.N.J. 2005) (holding that undocumented workers are not barred from seeking relief under the FLSA for work already performed); *Flores v. Amigon*, 233 F. Supp. 2d 462 (E.D.N.Y. 2002) (finding that *Hoffman Plastic* does not apply to claims for back wages already earned); *Liu v. Donna Karan Internat'l, Inc.*, 207 F. Supp. 2d 191 (S.D.N.Y. 2002) (same).

Using similar reasoning, some courts have found that undocumented workers are entitled to workers' compensation benefits for on-the-job injuries despite their lack of work authorization. As with the FLSA, they have found that the purposes behind both workers' compensation statutes and IRCA can best be promoted by permitting recovery. Otherwise, "employers would have a financial incentive to hire undocumented workers" because they could avoid liability for workplace injuries. *See, e.g., Staff Management v. Jiminez*, 839 N.W.2d 640 (Iowa 2013); *Dowling v. Slotnik*, 712 A.2d 396 (Conn. 1998). After *Hoffman Plastic*, however, the outcome might be different in cases where an employer could show that "suitable jobs" were available that would allow the injured worker to work, and therefore the lack of employment was due to undocumented status rather than the worker's injury. *See Jiminez*, 839

N.W.2d at 658–59 (Mansfield, J., concurring specially).

Although the issue of *Hoffman Plastic*'s reach has not been definitively resolved, the uncertainty surrounding the availability of back pay may itself reduce the incentive for undocumented workers to pursue their workplace rights. Even before *Hoffman Plastic*, these workers often hesitated to sue for labor and employment law violations out of fear that employers might retaliate by reporting them to federal immigration authorities. They may be less likely to run that risk now given the reduced likelihood of any significant recovery even if they succeed in proving that an employer violated the law.

3. **The Relevance of Immigration Status.** Another disincentive for some immigrant workers to bring claims for violation of their labor and employment rights is fear of drawing attention to their immigration status. Following the decision in *Hoffman Plastic*, employers began to aggressively seek discovery of the immigration status of plaintiffs in lawsuits brought to enforce Title VII, FLSA and other employment laws. They argued that because the decision limited the remedies available to undocumented workers, plaintiffs' immigration status was relevant to the issues in these lawsuits. The Ninth Circuit in *Rivera* discussed the concerns raised by these discovery requests:

> . . . Granting employers the right to inquire into workers' immigration status in cases like this would allow them to raise implicitly the threat of deportation and criminal prosecution every time a worker, documented or undocumented, reports illegal practices or files a Title VII action. Indeed, were we to [allow such discovery,] countless acts of illegal and reprehensible conduct would go unreported. Even documented workers may be chilled by the type of discovery at issue here. Documented workers may fear that their immigration status would be changed, or that their status would reveal the immigration problems of their family or friends; similarly, new legal residents or citizens may feel intimidated by the prospect of having their immigration history examined in a public proceeding. Any of these individuals, failing to understand the relationship between their litigation and immigration status, might choose to forego civil rights litigation.

Rivera, 364 F.3d at 1065. As a result of these concerns, a number of courts have barred such discovery. *See, e.g., id.* at 1070; *Flores*, 233 F. Supp. 2d at 464; *Liu*, 207 F. Supp. 2d at 193. After *Hoffman Plastic*, is a plaintiff's immigration status relevant to her claims under the various protective employment laws? Should discovery of that status be permitted even though the plaintiff may clearly be entitled to at least some forms of relief? Is there any way to balance employers' interests in avoiding unauthorized back pay awards with the risk of intimidating workers with valid claims?

4. **Collective vs. Individual Rights?** As Justice Rehnquist points out, Jose Castro broke the law. But so did Hoffman Plastic. Who is the bigger lawbreaker between the two? Castro was in clear violation of the IRCA. On the other hand, Hoffman Plastic's liability for an NLRA violation was also well-established. Because the NLRA protects collective rights, Hoffman Plastic's wrongful act injured not only Castro's individual rights to employment under the NLRA but also those of his

coworkers in the bargaining unit who were prevented from exercising their rights to organize a union. *See* Christopher David Ruiz Cameron, *Borderline Decisions: Hoffman Plastic Compounds, the New Bracero Program, and the Supreme Court's Role in Making Federal Labor Policy*, 51 UCLA L. REV. 1, 32 (2003).

5. The Role of Employer Knowledge of Undocumented Status. In this case, Hoffman Plastic did not know of Castro's undocumented status and was surprised to discover it at the hearing on the amount of backpay to be awarded. However, the Court did not distinguish between knowing and unknowing employers in reaching its conclusion that backpay is inappropriate. Should a different result apply if the employer can be shown to have knowledge of the worker's undocumented status? In such a case, the employer would be in violation of both the NLRA and the IRCA (which prohibits an employer from hiring or retaining employees who it knows to be without proper documentation establishing their authorization to work). *See* IRCA, 8 U.S.C. § 1324a(a). Would a different balancing of policies be warranted?

The NLRB confronted this question in *Mezonos Maven Bakery, Inc.*, 357 N.L.R.B. 47 (2011). In that case, the employer had employed several undocumented workers for periods ranging from five months to eight years without ever asking for documents to verify their work eligibility—a clear violation of the requirements of IRCA. The workers were fired after they concertedly complained about treatment by a supervisor. After a finding that the discharges constituted an unfair labor practice, an administrative judge ordered the respondent to pay back pay, distinguishing *Hoffman Plastic* on the grounds that the workers had not used fraudulent documents to obtain employment; rather, the employer had hired them knowing they were undocumented. The Board reversed, concluding that a backpay award is foreclosed by the Supreme Court's opinion in *Hoffman Plastic*. In the Board's view, the Court's opinion "evinces an intention to preclude backpay for undocumented workers regardless of the identity of the IRCA violator." *Id.* at 3. Two of the Board members concurred separately, explaining that although they were bound to follow the Supreme Court's decision in *Hoffman Plastic*, they believed that the effect of the decision is that "the [NLRA's] enforcement is undermined, employees are chilled in the exercise of their Section 7 rights, the work force is fragmented, and a vital check on workplace abuses is removed." *Id.* at 5 (Liebman and Pearce, concurring).

The question of what constitutes employer "knowledge" for purposes of IRCA liability is a difficult one. Courts generally require actual knowledge; constructive knowledge will not satisfy the knowledge element of an IRCA violation unless willful blindness can be shown. *Compare Collins Foods International, Inc. v. INS*, 948 F.2d 549 (9th Cir. 1991) (no liability where employer failed to compare the back of a social security card with the example given in the INS handbook), *with Mester Manufacturing Co. v. INS*, 879 F.2d 561 (9th Cir. 1989) (constructive knowledge found where INS notified employer that certain workers were suspected unlawful aliens and provided a list of false numbers for verification and employer continued to employ the workers and did not take corrective action). The issue is complicated further by Title VII's prohibition on national origin discrimination in hiring as well as the IRCA's prohibition on discrimination against lawfully admitted aliens because of citizenship status. Employers who question workers' national origin by requiring documentation prior to hiring risk having discrimination charges filed against them if the workers are not hired.

In spite of legal efforts to reduce the incentives for undocumented workers to enter the United States for work, they continued to do so in large numbers in the 1990s and early 2000s. Frustration with this situation led some private parties to try to utilize the federal Racketeer Influenced and Corrupt Organizations Act (RICO), 18 U.S.C. §§ 1961–68, to address the effects of undocumented immigrants in the workplace. The next case illustrates one of these efforts.

WILLIAMS v. MOHAWK INDUSTRIES, INC.
United States Court of Appeals for the Eleventh Circuit
465 F.3d 1277 (2006)

ANDERSON, HULL and GIBSON,[1] CIRCUIT JUDGES. Per Curiam.

In this case, plaintiffs-appellees Shirley Williams, Gale Pelfrey, Bonnie Jones, and Lora Sisson are current or former hourly employees of defendant-appellant Mohawk Industries, Inc. ("Mohawk"). The plaintiffs filed this class-action complaint alleging that Mohawk's widespread and knowing employment and harboring of illegal workers allowed Mohawk to reduce labor costs by depressing wages for its legal hourly employees . . . in violation of federal and state RICO statutes. [The district court denied Mohawk's 12(b)(6) motion as to the federal and state RICO claims.]

I. BACKGROUND

Mohawk is the second largest carpet and rug manufacturer in the United States and has over 30,000 employees. According to the plaintiffs, Mohawk has conspired with recruiting agencies to hire and harbor illegal workers in an effort to keep labor costs as low as possible. . . . For example, according to the plaintiffs' complaint,

> Mohawk employees have traveled to the United States Border, including areas near Brownsville, Texas, to recruit undocumented aliens that recently have entered the United States in violation of federal law. These employees and other persons have transported undocumented aliens from these border towns to North Georgia so that those aliens may procure employment at Mohawk. Mohawk has made various incentive payments to employees and other recruiters for locating workers that Mohawk eventually employs and harbors.

Furthermore, "[v]arious recruiters, including Mohawk employees, have provided housing to these illegal workers upon their arrival in North Georgia and have helped them find illegal employment with Mohawk." Additionally, Mohawk knowingly or recklessly accepts fraudulent documentation from the illegal aliens.

The plaintiffs further allege that Mohawk has concealed its efforts to hire and harbor illegal aliens by destroying documents and assisting illegal workers in

---

[1] [*] Honorable John R. Gibson, United States Circuit Judge for the Eighth Circuit, sitting by designation.

evading detection by law enforcement. According to plaintiffs' complaint, Mohawk takes steps to shield those illegal aliens from detection by, among other things, helping them evade detection during law enforcement searches and inspections at Mohawk's facilities.

According to the complaint, Mohawk's widespread and knowing employment and harboring of illegal workers has permitted Mohawk to reduce labor costs. Mohawk has done so by reducing the number of legal workers it must hire and, thereby, increasing the labor pool of legal workers from which Mohawk hires. This practice permits Mohawk to depress the wages it pays its legal hourly workers.

Finally, the plaintiffs allege that Mohawk is "able to save substantial sums of money" by paying its workers reduced wages. Furthermore, Mohawk knows that illegal workers are less likely to file worker's-compensation claims, and, therefore, Mohawk is able to save additional monies. According to the plaintiffs, these benefits constitute unjust enrichment under state law.

Mohawk filed a Rule 12(b)(6) motion to dismiss the plaintiffs' complaint for failure to state a claim. The district court determined that the plaintiffs had stated a claim under both federal and state RICO statutes . . . .

II. FEDERAL RICO CLAIMS

Pursuant to 18 U.S.C. § 1962(c), it is illegal "for any person employed by or associated with any enterprise engaged in, or the activities of which affect, interstate or foreign commerce, to conduct or participate, directly or indirectly, in the conduct of such enterprise's affairs through a pattern of racketeering activity . . . ." 18 U.S.C. § 1962(c). Thus, in order to establish a federal civil RICO violation under § 1962(c), the plaintiffs "must satisfy four elements of proof: '(1) conduct (2) of an enterprise (3) through a pattern (4) of racketeering activity.' " [citations omitted]. These requirements apply whether the RICO claim is civil or criminal in nature.

In civil cases, however, RICO plaintiffs must also satisfy the requirements of 18 U.S.C. § 1964(c). Section 1964(c) states that "[a]ny person injured in his business or property by reason of" RICO's substantive provisions has the right to "recover threefold the damages he sustains . . . ." 18 U.S.C. § 1964(c). Thus, under § 1964(c), civil RICO claimants, such as the plaintiffs here, must show (1) the requisite injury to "business or property," and (2) that such injury was "by reason of" the substantive RICO violation. We discuss each of these requirements in turn.

A. Pattern of Racketeering Activity

As mentioned above, there are four requirements under § 1962(c). Because elements (3) and (4) a pattern of racketeering activity—are easily met in this case (at least at the motion-to-dismiss stage), we address them first.

. . . .

[A "pattern of racketeering activity" requires at least two distinct, but related, acts of racketeering activity, or predicate acts.] According to 18 U.S.C. § 1961(1)(F),

" 'racketeering activity' means any act which is indictable under the Immigration and Nationality Act, section 274 (relating to bringing in and harboring certain aliens), . . . if the act indictable under such section of such Act was committed for the purpose of financial gain." In this case, the plaintiffs have alleged that the defendant has engaged in an open and ongoing pattern of violations of section 274 of the Immigration and Nationality Act. In particular, plaintiffs allege that Mohawk has violated and continues to violate: (1) 8 U.S.C. § 1324(a)(3)(A), which makes it a federal crime to "knowingly hire[] for employment at least 10 individuals with actual knowledge that the individuals are aliens" during a twelve-month period; (2) 8 U.S.C. § 1324(a)(1)(A)(iii), which makes it a federal crime to "conceal[], harbor[], or shield from detection, or attempt[] to conceal, harbor or shield from detection" aliens that have illegally entered the United States; and (3) 8 U.S.C. § 1324(a)(1)(A)(iv), which makes it a federal crime to "encourage[] or induce[] an alien to come to, enter, or reside in the United States, knowing or in reckless disregard of the fact that such coming to, entry, or residence is or will be in violation of law." According to the plaintiffs' complaint, Mohawk has committed hundreds, even thousands, of violations of federal immigration laws. Consequently, we conclude that the plaintiffs have properly alleged a "pattern of racketeering activity."

B. Conduct of an Enterprise

With regard to elements (1) and (2) of the four-part test under § 1962(c), the plaintiffs must establish "conduct of an enterprise" and that the enterprise had a common goal. . . . Furthermore, Mohawk "must participate in the operation or management of the enterprise itself." *Reves v. Ernst & Young*, 507 U.S. 170, 185 (1993).

. . . .

In this case, the plaintiffs have alleged that Mohawk and third-party temp agencies/recruiters have conspired to violate federal immigration laws, destroy documentation, and harbor illegal workers. Specifically, the plaintiffs allege that

> [e]ach recruiter is paid a fee for each worker it supplies to Mohawk, and some of those recruiters work closely with Mohawk to meet its employment need by offering a pool of illegal workers who can be dispatched to a particular Mohawk facility on short notice as the need arises. Some recruiters find workers in the Brownsville, Texas area and transport them to Georgia. Others, like TPS, have relatively formal relationships with the company in which they employ illegal workers and then loan or otherwise provide them to Mohawk for a fee. These recruiters are sometimes assisted by Mohawk employees who carry a supply of social security cards for use when a prospective or existing employee needs to assume a new identity.

Given the Rule 12(b)(6) stage of the litigation, the plaintiffs' complaint must be taken as true, and it has sufficiently alleged an "enterprise" under RICO; that is an association-in-fact between Mohawk and third-party recruiters. This Court has never required anything other than a "loose or informal" association of distinct entities. Mohawk and the third-party recruiters are distinct entities that, at least according to the complaint, are engaged in a conspiracy to bring illegal workers into this country for Mohawk's benefit. As such, the complaint sufficiently alleges an "enterprise" under RICO.

As for the common purpose, the plaintiffs' complaint alleges that "[t]he recruiters and Mohawk share the common purpose of obtaining illegal workers for employment by Mohawk." The complaint further alleges that "[e]ach recruiter is paid a fee for each worker it supplies to Mohawk" and that "Mohawk has made various incentive payments to employees and other recruiters for locating workers that Mohawk eventually employs and harbors." Furthermore, "[t]he acts of racketeering activity committed by Mohawk have the same or similar objective: the reduction of wages paid to Mohawk's hourly workforce." What is clear from the complaint is that each member of the enterprise is allegedly reaping a large economic benefit from Mohawk's employment of illegal workers.

In *United States v. Church*, 955 F.2d 688, 698 (11th Cir. 1992), this Court concluded that the common purpose of making money was sufficient under RICO. Because the complaint clearly alleges that the members of the enterprise stand to gain sufficient financial benefits from Mohawk's widespread employment and harboring of illegal workers, the plaintiffs have properly alleged a "common purpose" for the purposes of RICO.

Furthermore, Mohawk "must participate in the operation or management of the enterprise itself." *Reves*, 507 U.S. at 185. That is, Mohawk "must have some part in directing" the affairs of the enterprise. *Id.* at 179. However, the Supreme Court has cautioned that "RICO liability is not limited to those with primary responsibility for the enterprise's affairs . . . ." *Id.* In their complaint, the plaintiffs allege that "Mohawk participates in the operation and management of the affairs of the enterprise . . . ," which includes some direction over the recruiters. Whatever difficulties the plaintiffs may have in proving such an allegation, they have sufficiently alleged that Mohawk is engaged in the operation or management of the enterprise. . . .

C. Injury to "Business or Property" Interest Under RICO

As indicated above, RICO's civil-suit provision states that "[a]ny person injured in his business or property by reason of" RICO's substantive provisions has the right to "recover threefold the damages he sustains . . . ." 18 U.S.C. § 1964(c). . . . Accordingly, we must determine whether the plaintiffs have a "business or property" interest that could be injured under RICO. We need not reach whether plaintiffs have a property interest because plaintiffs clearly have alleged a business interest affected by Mohawk's alleged RICO violations.

Indeed, this case is similar to the Ninth Circuit's *Mendoza* decision [*Mendoza v. Zirkle Fruit Co.*, 301 F.3d 1163 (9th Cir. 2002)] where legally documented agricultural workers sued fruit growers under RICO alleging that the growers depressed wages by hiring illegal workers. In *Mendoza*, the defendant claimed that the employees would have to show a " 'property right' in the lost wages by showing that they were promised or contracted for higher wages." *Mendoza*, 301 F.3d at 1168 n.4. The Ninth Circuit concluded that this argument was misplaced, pointing out that the plaintiffs' claim did not implicate procedural due process. *Id.* Rather, the Ninth Circuit concluded that "what is required is precisely what the employees allege here: a legal entitlement to business relations unhampered by schemes prohibited by the RICO predicate statutes." *Id.* Given that a relationship clearly exists between plaintiff workers and their employer, Mohawk, we conclude that a similar business interest exists in this case, and that the employees' alleged injury to their business interests satisfies the business-interest requirement. Consequently, the plaintiffs have alleged a sufficient injury to a business interest to pursue their RICO claims.

D. "By Reason Of" the Substantive RICO Violations

We now turn to the "by reason of" requirement contained in § 1964(c). The "by reason of" requirement implicates two concepts: (1) a sufficiently direct injury so that a plaintiff has standing to sue; and (2) proximate cause. . . .

(i) Proximate Cause

It is well-established that RICO plaintiffs must prove proximate causation in order to recover. . . . [W]e conclude that the plaintiffs have alleged sufficient proximate cause to withstand defendant Mohawk's motion to dismiss. According to their complaint, Mohawk has hired illegal workers "[i]n an effort to keep labor costs as low as possible." Furthermore, "Mohawk's employment and harboring of large numbers of illegal workers has enabled Mohawk to depress wages and thereby pay all of its hourly employees, including legally employed workers who are members of the class, wages that are lower than they would be if Mohawk did not engage in this illegal conduct." Again, the complaint alleges that "Mohawk's widespread employment and harboring of illegal workers has substantially and unlawfully increased the supply of workers from which Mohawk makes up its hourly workforce. This unlawful expansion of the labor pool has permitted Mohawk to depress the wages that it pays all its hourly employees . . . ." The plaintiffs also allege that "[o]ne purpose and intended effect of Mohawk's widespread employment and harboring of illegal workers is to deprive Mohawk's hourly workforce of any individual or collective bargaining power" and that they "were injured by direct and proximate reason of Mohawk's illegal conduct."

Given these allegations, which we must assume are true at this Rule 12(b)(6) stage of the litigation, it is clear that the plaintiffs have alleged a sufficiently direct relation between their claimed injury and the alleged RICO violations. In short, according to the complaint, Mohawk's widespread scheme of knowingly hiring and harboring illegal workers has the purpose and direct result of depressing the wages paid to the plaintiffs. Simply put, wholesale illegal hiring depresses wages for the legal workers in north Georgia where Mohawk is located. According to plaintiffs, Mohawk's illegal conduct had a substantial and direct effect on wages that Mohawk pays to legal workers. *See DeCanas v. Bica*, 424 U.S. 351, 356–57 (1976) (explaining that "acceptance by illegal aliens of jobs on substandard terms as to wages and working conditions can seriously depress wage scales and working conditions of citizens and legally admitted aliens").[2] . . .

In response, Mohawk asserts that other economic factors contribute to the plaintiffs' wages, that illegal hiring is just one of myriad factors affecting wages, and that therefore plaintiffs have not satisfied [the] proximate-cause requirements. However, plaintiffs persuasively reply that Mohawk's argument ignores that Mohawk's conduct has grossly distorted those normal market forces by employing literally thousands of illegal, undocumented aliens at its manufacturing facilities in north Georgia, thus depriving plaintiffs of "business relations unhampered by schemes prohibited by the RICO predicate statutes." Plaintiffs submit that their complaint focuses on only what is happening in the particular narrow labor market that Mohawk dominates in north Georgia. We agree with plaintiffs that their complaint alleges a sufficiently direct injury . . . , especially given the recognition of a direct correlation between illegal hiring and lower wages. . . .

There is no more direct injured party who could bring suit. Mohawk posits the United States as the only other victim because of its interest in enforcing immigration laws. But as plaintiffs aptly point out, the United States is responsible for all federal criminal laws which includes RICO's other predicate acts. Under Mohawk's theory, the United States would arguably be the most direct victim of all RICO predicate, criminal acts. Congress, however, criminalized the employment of illegal workers in part to protect legal workers. It is consistent with civil RICO's purposes—to expand enforcement beyond federal prosecutors with limited public resources—to turn victims (here, Mohawk's legal workers) into prosecutors as private attorneys general seeking to eliminate illegal hiring activity by their own employer. *See Rotella v. Wood*, 528 U.S. 549, 557 (2000) (acknowledging that the very "object of civil RICO is . . . to turn [victims] into prosecutors, private attorneys general dedicated to eliminating racketeering activity". . . .

We also recognize that Mohawk asserts that the cause of plaintiffs' alleged harms is a set of actions (paying lower wages) "entirely distinct" from the alleged RICO violation (hiring illegal workers). We disagree. As noted earlier, it has long been recognized that hiring illegal workers on substandard wage terms depresses the wage scales of legal workers. Moreover, plaintiffs are not suing about the hiring of illegal workers on the west coast depressing the wages of legal workers on the east coast. Rather, plaintiffs' complaint is a narrow one about a single employer's— Mohawk's—hiring of thousands of illegal workers at its manufacturing facilities in north Georgia depressing the wages of legal workers of the same employer, Mohawk, at the same manufacturing facilities in the same limited geographical area. Accordingly, under the particular factual circumstances of this case, we conclude that plaintiffs' complaint satisfies the direct relationship requirement imposed by . . . the "by reason of" language in the federal RICO statute.

Our conclusion is consistent with the two other circuits to have addressed this proximate cause issue in RICO decisions involving schemes to depress wages of

---

[2] [n. 6] The Supreme Court quoted this same point in *Sure-Tan, Inc. v. NLRB*, 467 U.S. 883, 892–93 (1984) (quoting same, and adding that a "primary purpose in restricting immigration is to preserve jobs for American workers; immigrant aliens are therefore admitted to work in this country only if they 'will not adversely affect the wages and working conditions of the workers in the United States similarly employed.' " (citation omitted)).

legal workers by widespread hiring of illegal workers. *See Trollinger* [*v. Tyson Foods*, 370 F.3d 602 (6th Cir. 2004)]; *Mendoza*, 301 F.3d at 1171–72.

In *Trollinger*, the Sixth Circuit considered a situation in which former Tyson employees at a poultry processing plant sued their former employer under RICO, alleging that the use of illegal workers permitted the employer to lower wages via the collective-bargaining agreement with the union representing the employees. The Sixth Circuit, reviewing the district court's dismissal of the employees' complaint under Rule 12(b)(6), determined that "at this preliminary stage in the proceeding" it could not conclude that there was no likelihood of success on the merits. *Id.* at 619. The Sixth Circuit explained that it remained possible that the legal-worker plaintiffs might prove the following allegations in their complaint:

> (1) that Tyson hired sufficient numbers of illegal aliens to impact the legal employees' wages; (2) that each additional illegal worker hired into the bargaining unit by Tyson has a measurable impact on the bargained-for wage-scale; (3) that the illegal immigrants allegedly brought into this country through Tyson's efforts allowed Tyson not to compete with other businesses for unskilled labor; and (4) that Tyson's legal workers did not "choose" to remain at Tyson for less money than other businesses offered, but had no choice in the matter given the hiring needs of the other businesses in the area and the influx of illegal immigrants at Tyson's facilities. While Tyson's proximate-cause argument may well carry the day at the summary-judgment stage, it requires more assistance than the complaint alone provides.

> One other circuit has reached the same result on somewhat similar facts . . . *Mendoza* . . . .

Trollinger, 370 F.3d at 619.

Although the plaintiffs' evidence in this case may not ultimately prove the proximate-cause requirement, we conclude that the plaintiffs' complaint states a sufficiently direct relation between their alleged injury and Mohawk's alleged unlawful predicate acts to withstand Mohawk's motion to dismiss. Consequently, we join the Sixth and Ninth Circuits in concluding that employees such as the ones in this case have alleged sufficient proximate cause to proceed with their RICO claims.

(ii) Statutory Standing

Lastly, we address RICO's statutory standing limitation that also grows out of the "by reason of" limitation in § 1964(c). . . . [W]e must evaluate whether the plaintiffs' injury is sufficiently direct to give plaintiffs standing to sue for Mohawk's alleged RICO violations.

Both the Sixth and Ninth Circuits have expressly concluded that legal workers have sufficiently direct injuries for RICO standing in similar cases. *Trollinger*, 370 F.3d at 615–18; *Mendoza*, 301 F.3d at 1170. The Ninth Circuit's *Mendoza* decision is particularly well-reasoned and instructive on the statutory standing issue.

As mentioned earlier, the *Mendoza* plaintiffs were legal workers who claimed that the purpose and result of the defendants' scheme of hiring undocumented immigrants was to depress the wages of legally documented employees. The Ninth Circuit concluded that the plaintiffs had statutory standing because "we are unable to discern a more direct victim of the illegal conduct." *Mendoza*, 301 F.3d at 1170. The Ninth Circuit explained:

> The documented employees here do not complain of a passed-on harm. They allege that the scheme had the purpose and direct result of depressing the wages paid to them by the growers. Thus, as the district court correctly determined, "plaintiffs have stated a claim that they are the direct victims of the illegal hiring scheme."
>
>   . . . .
>
> We also note that the undocumented workers cannot "be counted on to bring suit for the law's vindication." As the district court noted, the fact that RICO specifically provides that illegal hiring is a predicate offense indicates that Congress contemplated the enforcement of the immigration laws through lawsuits like this one.

Id. (internal citations omitted). The Ninth Circuit further stated that

> the workers must be allowed to make their case through presentation of evidence, including experts who will testify about the labor market, the geographic market, and the effects of the illegal scheme. Questions regarding the relevant labor market and the growers' power within that market are exceedingly complex and best addressed by economic experts and other evidence at a later stage in the proceedings.

Id. at 1171.

Plaintiffs' complaint clearly alleges that Mohawk has engaged in widespread and knowing hiring and harboring of illegal aliens with the express purpose and direct result of lowering the wages of legal workers. For example, the complaint alleges that "[o]ne purpose and intended effect of Mohawk's widespread employment and harboring of illegal workers is to deprive Mohawk's hourly workforce of any individual or collective bargaining power." The plaintiffs also allege that "[t]he acts of racketeering activity committed by Mohawk have the same or similar objective: the reduction of wages paid to Mohawk's hourly workforce." Furthermore, the plaintiffs "were injured by direct and proximate reason of Mohawk's illegal conduct." Given this stage of the litigation, we conclude that the plaintiffs have sufficiently alleged that Mohawk's illegal conduct was aimed primarily at them. Consequently, the district court correctly denied Mohawk's 12(b)(6) motion as it relates to the plaintiffs' federal civil RICO claim.

    . . . .

[The court then addressed the plaintiffs' state law claims under the Georgia RICO statute and permitted the plaintiffs to proceed, on similar reasoning to its analysis of the federal RICO claim.]

NOTES

1. **A Private Remedy for Criminal Wrongdoing.** The RICO statute does not create new substantive liability; rather, it is a device that allows federal prosecutors and, in some cases, private parties, to allege a pattern of wrongdoing rather than focusing on a series of individual offenses. The statute was originally enacted as a tool for fighting organized crime, and it identifies a number of criminal offenses—among them immigration law violations—which can be considered "racketeering activity." Private actors are incentivized to assist with the enforcement of criminal prohibitions by the possibility of receiving treble damages, but establishing liability can be difficult, requiring the plaintiff to prove not only violation of the substantive criminal laws, but also the separate requirements for enterprise liability, private harm, causation and standing under the RICO statute.

The federal government has pursued criminal sanctions for immigration law violations under RICO. *See* Amber McKinney, *Attorneys Say RICO Immigration Lawsuits Filed by Employees, Government on the Rise*, DAILY LAB. REP. (BNA), No. 112, June 15, 2009 (reporting criminal RICO actions against employers accused of knowingly hiring undocumented workers). In addition, civil RICO cases like *Williams* have been filed against employers and recruiting agencies.

Do you think it was wise policy for Congress to include violations of the immigration laws to the list of "racketeering activities" covered by RICO? Is it a good idea to encourage private actions to combat employers' reliance on undocumented labor? Or is this an area where the federal government should have sole enforcement responsibility? What effect will the possibility of civil RICO actions have on the incentives of employers? Workers?

2. **Divergent Outcomes.** In addition to *Williams*, other circuit courts have considered whether legally documented workers can proceed on a civil RICO claim against an employer on the theory that the employer hired undocumented workers in order to lower the wages it paid to all its workers. The courts have disagreed about how to apply RICO in this context, differing, for example, on what facts are required to show "predicate acts" and whether the hiring of undocumented workers can be shown to proximately cause wage loss for others. The Seventh Circuit, in *Baker v. IBP, Inc.*, 357 F.3d 685 (7th Cir. 2004), granted a motion to dismiss, finding *inter alia* that there was no "enterprise" with a "common purpose" as required for civil RICO liability. Similarly, the Fourth Circuit dismissed a complaint on the grounds that the plaintiffs had failed to sufficiently allege violations of the "predicate acts" necessary for civil RICO liability. *Walters v. McMahen*, 684 F.3d 435 (4th Cir. 2012). In contrast, the Ninth and Sixth Circuits, in *Mendoza v. Zirkle Fruit Co.*, 301 F.3d 1163 (9th Cir. 2002) and *Trollinger v. Tyson Foods, Inc.*, 370 F.3d 602 (6th Cir. 2004) respectively, denied the defendants' 12(b)(6) motions and permitted the civil RICO claims of documented workers to proceed.

Subsequently, the *Mendoza* case settled for $1.3 million. The employer denied wrongdoing, but agreed to pay the U.S. citizen and permanent resident workers backpay for hours they had worked for the company. Michael R. Triplett, *Orchard to Pay $1.3 Million to Settle Claims It Hired Undocumented Workers to Lower Pay*, DAILY LAB. REP. (BNA) No. 15, Jan. 24, 2006. *Williams v. Mohawk Industries*, the principal case, also eventually settled. Mohawk denied any wrongdoing, but agreed to pay $18 million into a settlement fund for a class of approximately 48,000 former and current employees. As part of the settlement, Mohawk also agreed to train its employees to follow proper procedures for verifying employment eligibility when hiring workers. Amber McKinney, *Mohawk Agrees to Pay Workers $18 Million to Settle RICO Illegal Immigration Lawsuit*, DAILY LAB. REP. (BNA) No. 70, Apr. 14, 2010.

The plaintiffs in *Trollinger* did not fare as well. After remand to the district court, a plaintiff class was certified, but then the district court granted the defendant's motion for summary judgment. *Trollinger v. Tyson Foods, Inc.*, 543 F. Supp. 2d 842 (E.D. Tenn. 2008). The district court concluded that the plaintiffs had failed to produce evidence "to demonstrate the presence of at least ten unauthorized employees at any given Tyson facility" and "failed to demonstrate Tyson was harboring or concealing illegal aliens" at more than one of its facilities, thereby failing to prove the necessary "predicate acts" for a RICO violation. *Id.* at 859–60. In addition, the court found that the plaintiffs had failed to show that Tyson's violations had proximately caused their injuries. *Id.*

The Supreme Court's decisions in *Bell Atlantic Corp. v. Twombly*, 550 U.S. 544 (2007) and *Ashcroft v. Iqbal*, 556 U.S. 662 (2009), which altered traditional pleading standards for cases in federal court, have led some to ask whether cases like *Williams* or *Mendoza* would satisfy the new pleading standards articulated in these cases. The Fourth Circuit has concluded that in light of *Twombly* and *Iqbal*, the standard used in the *Mendoza* case is no longer applicable. *Walters*, 684 F.3d at 442. As a result, it dismissed a complaint very similar to the one allowed to proceed in *Mendoza*. One court has argued that suits involving RICO claims warrant a requirement that plaintiffs include specific factual pleadings in order to survive a 12(b)(6) motion. It wrote:

> A civil RICO lawsuit has vast implications for the defendants because of the specter of treble damages and the possibility of permanent reputational injury to defendants from the allegation that they are "racketeers." Courts have frequently commented on the "in terrorem" settlement value that a threat of a civil RICO claim creates.

Nichols v. Mahoney, 608 F. Supp. 2d 526, 536 (S.D.N.Y. 2009).

3. Employer Knowledge of Immigration Status. As discussed above, employer knowledge of the undocumented status of workers can be the basis for liability under the Immigration Reform and Control Act (IRCA), but it is also a critical element in RICO liability. The allegations in *Williams* pertaining to employer knowledge of and participation in recruitment of undocumented workers are not atypical. In *Baker v. IBP, Inc.*, 357 F.3d 685 (7th Cir. 2004), the court described the plaintiffs' claims as follows:

> Plaintiffs' complaint alleges, and we must assume given the case's posture, that about half of the employees at IBP's Joslin plant are aliens who cannot lawfully work in the United States—and that IBP not only knows in a statistical sense that many of its non-citizen employees lack the sort of visas that authorize working here but also can identify which ones they are, yet winks at obviously fake green cards and other spurious

credentials. IBP alerts its unauthorized employees to stay away the days when immigration officials conduct inspections. (The complaint leaves it to the imagination how IBP learns these dates.) When immigration officials do manage to catch and remove aliens not allowed to work (or be) in the United States, IBP pays "recruiters" to smuggle them back into the country and immediately re-employs them under new aliases and new bogus identification. Moreover, the complaint alleges, IBP has arrangements with immigrant-welfare organizations, such as the Chinese Mutual Aid Association based in Chicago, under which these groups refer known illegals to IBP for employment. The upshot, plaintiffs believe, is that wages at the Joslin plant are depressed by about $4 per hour compared with what IBP would have to pay if the labor force included only U.S. citizens plus aliens holding green cards.

If the allegations are true, managers at IBP have committed hundreds of felonies. . . .

357 F.3d at 686–87 (7th Cir. 2004).

When should employers be held liable for hiring undocumented workers? Should they be liable only if they have actual knowledge that a particular worker is undocumented? Or is it enough that the employer knows "in a statistical sense" that some of its employees are probably undocumented? Should employers have a duty to investigate the true immigration status of its workers? In other words, how much responsibility should employers have to check the bona fides of their employees and their documentation to work in the United States?

4. **Proximate Causation of the Claimed Injury.** In *Williams*, the Eleventh Circuit was primarily concerned with proximate causation of the claimed injury— depressed wages for documented workers. The difficulty in RICO cases is that the alleged injury is mediated by the operation of the labor market as a whole. The plaintiffs in *Williams* complained about a reduction in "individual or collective bargaining power" that led to their "voluntarily" negotiated depressed wages. *Williams*, 465 F.3d at 1292. The court agreed, finding that "wholesale illegal hiring depresses wages for the legal workers in north Georgia where Mohawk is located." *Id.* at 1289. However, the Seventh Circuit, in response to a similar claim, concluded that "things may not be so straightforward." *Baker*, 357 F.3d at 692. It wrote:

An increased supply of labor logically affects, not just the wages at IBP's Joslin plant, but wages throughout the region (if not the country). Workers can change employers (leaving IBP for higher pay elsewhere), and this process should cause equilibration throughout the labor market. Yet plaintiff's theory is not that too many aliens depress wages around Joslin; it is that IBP pays lower wages than some competitors, and *that* effect would be very hard to attribute to particular violations of [the Immigration and Naturalization Act].

Id. Not only will the effects of an employer hiring undocumented workers diffuse throughout the labor market; other factors will influence wage rates, such as demographic changes, an influx of legally authorized workers, changes in the product market, a general economic downturn, or a decline in union density. Other courts have similarly found plaintiffs' allegations or evidence of damages to be insufficient. *See, e.g., Simpson v. Sanderson Farms, Inc.*, 744 F.3d 702 (11th Cir. 2014) (holding implausible plaintiffs' allegations that the employer's reliance on fraudulent documents proximately caused their depressed wages); *Broussard-Wadkins v. Maples*, 895 F. Supp. 2d 1159 (N.D. Ala. 2012) (finding that plaintiffs had not produced admissible evidence of damages sufficient to avoid summary judgment). Can the impact of illegal hiring on the wages of a particular group of workers be separated from the larger debate over immigration policy which pertains to both documented and undocumented workers? In RICO cases, how can courts isolate the amount of the injury (degree of the reduction in wages) that is caused by the hiring of undocumented workers from other causal factors?

A lively debate has arisen among economists regarding the effect undocumented workers have on wages, particularly among low-income workers. One camp largely supports the argument of the plaintiffs in RICO cases, claiming that the addition of large numbers of low-skilled workers necessarily suppresses wages with George Borjas representing the leading voice for this position. Another group, led primarily by David Card, argues that the effects are not so pronounced, in large part because the workers have filled jobs that would otherwise have not been created, such as gardeners or some construction jobs. He notes also that the consumption of goods and services by undocumented workers expands the economy and counters some of the effect that their presence in the labor market might otherwise have. The ongoing debate is discussed in Roger Lowenstein, *The Immigration Equation*, N.Y. TIMES, July 9, 2006.

5. Who Else Is Harmed? The plaintiffs in *Williams* and most of the other leading civil RICO cases are legally documented workers. When an employer relies on a substantial number of undocumented workers to meet its labor needs is anyone else harmed? At least three other types of plaintiffs have attempted to bring civil RICO claims based on immigration law violations: local government, law-abiding employers who do not hire undocumented workers, and undocumented workers themselves. Do each of these three types of plaintiffs in fact incur harms that can be shown to be "proximately caused" by an employer's practice of hiring undocumented workers? Should they be allowed to proceed on civil RICO theories?

In *Canyon County v. Syngenta Seeds, Inc.*, 519 F.3d 969 (9th Cir. 2008), an Idaho county sued four companies with local operations, seeking civil damages under RICO for "millions of dollars for health care services and criminal justice services" it claimed to have expended for "illegal immigrants who have been employed by the defendants in violation of federal law." *Id.* at 972–73. The Ninth Circuit upheld dismissal of the County's complaint on the grounds that it was not "injured in its business or property" when it spent money for law enforcement or health services—expenses it incurs in its sovereign or quasi-sovereign capacity. *Id.* at 976. In addition, the court held that the County could not show proximate cause because the "asserted causal chain . . . is quite attenuated," *id.* at 982, pointing out that the increased cost of providing services might have resulted from a variety of factors, such as demographic changes, changes in criminal laws or public health practices, economic shifts and even improved community education and outreach. *Id.* at 98.

Competing businesses have also attempted to bring civil RICO claims based on immigration law violations, and at least one court has found that such plaintiffs may be able to prove injury proximately caused by the defendant's actions. In *Commercial Cleaning Servs., L.L.C. v. Colin Serv. Sys., Inc.*, 271 F.3d 374 (2d Cir. 2001), the plaintiff, a cleaning contractor, alleged that the defendant's bid for a cleaning contract was chosen because it was able to submit significantly lower bids in a " 'highly competitive' price-sensitive market" due to "its scheme to hire illegal immigrant workers [that] permitted it to pay well below the prevailing wage for legal workers." *Id.* at 382. The Second Circuit agreed, finding that hiring undocumented workers allowed the defendant to "take advantage of their diminished bargaining position, so as to employ a cheaper labor force and compete unfairly." *Id.* at 383.

Why don't law-abiding businesses bring suit more often? One significant hurdle is the policy of free competition protected by the antitrust laws. Nevertheless, a representative of the U.S. Business and Industry Council, an association of small and medium-sized businesses, has argued that firms that hire undocumented workers should be reined in by law, lest "[h]onest business owners . . . be placed in the difficult position of having to choose between emulating the unlawful behavior of rivals or risking the survival of their own companies." *Business Leaders Tell House Subcommittee Labor Shortages Are a Key Immigration Issue*, DAILY LAB. REP. (BNA), No. 109, June 7, 2007. The same representative added that there are larger social and public risks, as well: an influx of cheap labor in the form of undocumented workers will disincentivize corporate investment in innovative technological and labor-saving devices. Moreover, "cheap labor is really 'subsidized labor,' " since taxpayers ultimately bear the costs of health care, education, and welfare programs for workers who are unable to earn a living wage. *Id.*

Finally, undocumented workers have also attempted to bring civil RICO claims against former employers. For example, in *Zavala v. Wal-Mart Stores, Inc.*, 447 F. Supp. 2d 379 (D.N.J. 2006), a group of undocumented workers who provided janitorial services at Wal-Mart's retail stores alleged that Wal-Mart and its contractors had violated immigration laws "so they could economically exploit plaintiffs." *Id.* at 386. The district court dismissed the RICO claim on the grounds that the plaintiffs had not alleged a sufficiently direct injury to meet the proximate cause requirement, and noted that "independent and intervening causes"—namely, "the decision of the employer to employ at a particular wage, and the decision of the worker to work at that wage"—further weakened the causal connection between defendants' predicate acts and any injury to plaintiffs. *Id.* at 386. The Third Circuit affirmed the dismissal on the grounds that the plaintiffs had failed to adequately plead the "predicate acts" required for civil RICO liability. *Zavala v. Wal-Mart Stores, Inc.*, 691 F.3d 527 (2012).

Assuming that they can establish the requisite elements, should undocumented workers have standing to pursue civil RICO claims against their employers for immigration law violations? Are they harmed or benefitted by such employer practices? Even if such RICO claims are permitted, are undocumented workers likely to bring suit?

6. What Role Should a Union Play? The *Baker* case discussed above involved a RICO claim filed by unionized employees. The *Baker* court dismissed the claims for several reasons, among them the plaintiffs' failure to add the union as a party to the lawsuit:

> [The employees'] wages were set by a collective bargaining agreement . . . . This suit is at its core about the adequacy of the wages IBP pays, and . . . . it . . . does not follow that plaintiffs are entitled to represent all of the other workers. They *have* a representative—one that under the NLRA is supposed to be "exclusive" with respect to wages, see 29 U.S.C. § 159(a)—their union. Individual workers may step into the union's shoes only if it has violated its duty of fair representation. Yet the complaint does not name the union as a party and does not contend that the union neglected its duty to represent the employees' interests with respect to wages.
>
> Unless something went seriously wrong with the union's representation of the workers, IBP as the employer is not only entitled but also legally required to pay at the rates specified by the collective bargaining agreement. Without the union as a party, the litigants could not settle this suit for higher hourly pay (or back pay)—that would be a real refusal on IBP's part to bargain with its union—nor could the judge order IBP to increase its rate of pay. Yet it is only financial relief that plaintiffs seek. . . . Plaintiffs have not established the foundation for displacing the union as their representative with respect to wages. We don't say that this is impossible—for all we know, the union may be controlled by persons not authorized to work in the United States and may be pursuing a policy of expanding employment opportunities for those similarly situated—but only that plaintiffs have not tried. . . .

Baker v. IBP, Inc., 357 F.3d 685, 690–91 (7th Cir. 2004). Under the Seventh Circuit's analysis, then, to the extent that the workers complain that their wages are too low, they should work through their union to bargain for a higher wage rate. Is this strategy likely to succeed? Alternatively, the employees might either persuade the union to object to the employer's practice of hiring undocumented workers, or add the union as a defendant in a RICO civil lawsuit. Recall that unions are majority representatives and are often seeking to organize not only documented workers, but undocumented workers. Will unions be interested in bringing RICO claims? What are the risks for a union of bringing a RICO claim on behalf of documented workers? What are the benefits of doing so? If the union refuses to challenge the employer's practice of hiring undocumented workers, should it be subject to RICO liability also? Does the Seventh Circuit's approach make RICO claims more difficult to sustain in a unionized workplace than in a nonunionized workplace?

3. Language and Accent Discrimination

Regardless of their legal status, many immigrant workers identify language as a core part of their identity. Thus, unlike traditional forms of race discrimination which focus on physical appearance or skin color, these groups may experience disadvantageous treatment in the form of employer rules directed against non-

English languages, or personnel decisions focused on language abilities. Although Title VII clearly prohibits discrimination on the basis of national origin, it is less clear whether it protects against employer policies such as English-only rules that have a particular impact on immigrant workers. Is protection of language rights necessary to ensure equality? Or do employers have legitimate interests in regulating language use on the job?

MALDONADO v. CITY OF ALTUS
United States Court of Appeals for the Tenth Circuit
433 F.3d 1294 (2006)

HARTZ, CIRCUIT JUDGE.

. . . .

Plaintiffs' claims stem from the [ ] promulgation of an English-only policy [by the City of Altus, Oklahoma]. Approximately 29 City employees are Hispanic, the only significant national-origin minority group affected by the policy. All Plaintiffs are Hispanic and bilingual, each speaking fluent English and Spanish.

In the spring of 2002 the City's Street Commissioner, Defendant Holmes Willis, received a complaint that because Street Department employees were speaking Spanish, other employees could not understand what was being said on the City radio. Willis informed the City's Human Resources Director, Candy Richardson, of the complaint, and she advised Willis that he could direct his employees to speak only English when using the radio for City business. . . .

In July 2002 the City promulgated the following official policy signed by [the City Administrator, Michael] Nettles:

> To insure effective communications among and between employees and various departments of the City, to prevent misunderstandings and to promote and enhance safe work practices, *all work related and business communications during the work day shall be conducted in the English language with the exception of those circumstances where it is necessary or prudent to communicate with a citizen*, business owner, organization or criminal suspect *in his or her native language due to the person or entity's limited English language skills*. The use of the English language during work hours and while engaged in City business includes face to face communication of work orders and directions as well as communications utilizing telephones, mobile telephones, cellular telephones, radios, computer or e-mail transmissions and all written forms of communications. *If an employee or applicant for employment believes that he or she cannot understand communications due to limited English language skills, the employee is to discuss the situation with the department head* and the Human Resources Director to determine what accommodation is required and feasible. *This policy does not apply to strictly private communications between co-workers while they are on approved lunch hours or breaks or before or after work hours* while the employees are still on City property *if City property is not being used for the communication*. Further, *this*

policy does not apply to strictly private communication between an employee and a family member so long as the communications are limited in time and are not disruptive to the work environment. Employees are encouraged to be sensitive to the feelings of their fellow employees, including a possible feeling of exclusion if a co-worker cannot understand what is being said in his or her presence when a language other than English is being utilized.

Defendants state three primary reasons for adopting the policy:

1) workers and supervisors could not understand what was being said over the City's radios . . . ; 2) non-Spanish speaking employees, both before and after the adoption of the Policy, informed management that they felt uncomfortable when their co-workers were speaking in front of them in a language they could not understand because they did not know if their co-workers were speaking about them; and 3) there were safety concerns with a non-common language being used around heavy equipment.

Although the district court observed "that there was no written record of any communication problems, morale problems or safety problems resulting from the use of languages other than English prior to implementation of the policy," it noted that Willis had testified that at least one employee complained about the use of Spanish by his co-workers before implementation of the policy and other non-Spanish speaking employees subsequently made similar complaints. Those city officials who were deposed could recount no incidents of safety problems caused by the use of a language other than English, but the district court . . . . stated that "it does not seem necessary that the City await an accident before acting."

Defendants offered evidence that the restrictions in the written policy were actually relaxed to allow workers to speak Spanish during work hours and on City property if everyone present understood Spanish. But Plaintiffs offered evidence that employees were told that the restrictions went beyond the written policy and prohibited all use of Spanish if a non-Spanish speaker was present, even during breaks, lunch hours, and private telephone conversations. Plaintiff Lloyd Lopez stated in his deposition that "we were told that the only time we could speak Spanish is when two of us are in a break room by ourselves, and if anybody other than Hispanic comes in, we are to change our language." In addition he said, "We no longer can speak about anything in general in Spanish around anybody. Even if we were on the phone talking to our wives and we were having a private conversation with them and somebody happened to walk by, we were to change our language because it would offend whoever was walking by." . . . The City has not disciplined anyone for violating the English-only policy.

Plaintiffs allege . . . "that the English-only rule created a hostile environment because it pervasively—every hour of every work day—burdened, threatened and demeaned the [Plaintiffs] because of their Hispanic origin[]" [and reminded them that they are second-class and subject to rules that the Anglo employees are not subject to].

Evidence of ethnic taunting included Plaintiffs' affidavits stating that they had "personally been teased and made the subject of jokes directly because of the

English-only policy[.]" . . . Plaintiff Tommy Sanchez testified in his deposition that
. . . other employees of the City of Altus "would pull up and laugh, start saying stuff
in Spanish to us and said, 'They didn't tell us we couldn't stop. They just told you.' "
Sanchez also testified that an Altus police officer taunted him about not being
allowed to speak Spanish by saying, " 'Don't let me hear you talk Spanish.' " He
further testified that "some of the guys from the street department would . . . poke
fun out of it [the policy]" and that when he went to other departments "they would
bring it up constantly," *id.* As evidence that such taunting was not unexpected by
management, Lloyd Lopez recounted in his deposition that Street Commissioner
Willis told Ruben Rios and him that he was informing them of the English-only
policy in private because Willis had concerns about "the other guys making fun of
[them]." Plaintiffs also provided evidence that Mayor Gramling was "quoted in a
newspaper article as referring to the Spanish language as 'garbage,' " although the
Mayor claims that he used the word *garble* and was misquoted. . . .

[In addition to several other claims, the Plaintiffs brought disparate-treatment
and disparate-impact claims under Title VII, raising a hostile-work-environment
theory as part of both claims. The district court granted summary judgment in favor
of Defendants on all claims.]

[ ] Disparate-Impact Claims

. . . One might say that Plaintiffs have not been subjected to an unlawful
employment practice because they are treated identically to non-Hispanics. They
claim no discrimination with respect to their pay or benefits, their hours of work, or
their job duties. And every employee, not just Hispanics, must abide by the
English-only policy. But the Supreme Court has "repeatedly made clear that
although Title VII mentions specific employment decisions with immediate consequences, the scope of the prohibition is not limited to economic or tangible
discrimination, and that it covers more than terms and conditions in the narrow
contractual sense." *Nat'l R.R. Passenger Corp. v. Morgan*, 536 U.S. 101, 115–16
(2002). The conditions of work encompass the workplace atmosphere as well as the
more tangible elements of the job. Title VII does not tolerate, for example, a racist
or sexist work environment "that is sufficiently severe or pervasive to alter the
conditions of the victim's employment and create an abusive working environment[.]" *Harris v. Forklift Sys., Inc.*, 510 U.S. 17, 21 (1993). In their disparate-
impact claim Plaintiffs allege that the City's English-only policy has created such an
environment for Hispanic workers. Discrimination against Hispanics can be characterized as being based on either race or national origin.

To prevail on these claims, Plaintiffs need not show that the policy was created
with discriminatory intent. In the leading case on the subject, *Griggs v. Duke Power
Co.*, 401 U.S. 424, 431, (1971), the Supreme Court held that Title VII "proscribes not
only overt discrimination but also practices that are fair in form, but discriminatory
in operation." These kinds of claims, known as disparate-impact claims, "involve
employment practices that are facially neutral in their treatment of different groups
but that in fact fall more harshly on one group than another and cannot be justified
by business necessity." *Int'l Bhd. of Teamsters v. United States*, 431 U.S. 324,
335–36 n. 15, (1977). . . .

[A] plaintiff first must "demonstrate[ ] that a respondent uses a particular employment practice that causes a disparate impact on the basis of race, color, religion, sex, or national origin." 42 U.S.C. § 2000e–2(k)(1)(A)(i) . . . . If the plaintiff establishes a prima facie case, the burden then shifts to the defendant to "demonstrate that the challenged practice is job related for the position in question and consistent with business necessity." 42 U.S.C. § 2000e–2(k)(1)(A)(I).

1. Prima-facie case

The district court, relying principally on *Garcia v. Spun Steak Co.*, 998 F.2d 1480 (9th Cir.1993), concluded that Plaintiffs had "not shown that requiring them to use the English language in the workplace imposed significant, adverse effects on the terms, conditions or privileges of their employment, so as to create a prima facie case of disparate impact discrimination under Title VII." Even under *Spun Steak*, however, English-only policies are not always permissible; each case turns on its facts. 998 F.2d at 1489. Here, Plaintiffs have produced evidence that the English-only policy created a hostile atmosphere for Hispanics in their workplace. As previously set forth, all the Plaintiffs stated that they had experienced ethnic taunting as a result of the policy and that the policy made them feel like second-class citizens. . . .

Some of this evidence, as the district court pointed out, has diluted persuasive power because of the absence of specifics—who made what comment when and where. In a typical hostile-work-environment case, we might conclude that the evidence of co-worker taunting did not reach the threshold necessary for a Title VII claim.

There are, however, other considerations with respect to a *policy* that allegedly creates a hostile work environment. The policy itself, and not just the effect of the policy in evoking hostility by co-workers, may create or contribute to the hostility of the work environment. A policy requiring each employee to wear a badge noting his or her religion, for example, might well engender extreme discomfort in a reasonable employee who belongs to a minority religion, even if no co-worker utters a word on the matter. Here, the very fact that the City would forbid Hispanics from using their preferred language could reasonably be construed as an expression of hostility to Hispanics. At least that could be a reasonable inference if there was no apparent legitimate purpose for the restrictions. It would be unreasonable to take offense at a requirement that all pilots flying into an airport speak English in communications with the tower or between planes; but hostility would be a reasonable inference to draw from a requirement that an employee calling home during a work break speak only in English. The less the apparent justification for mandating English, the more reasonable it is to infer hostility toward employees whose ethnic group or nationality favors another language. For example, Plaintiffs presented evidence that the English-only policy extended beyond its written terms to include lunch hours, breaks, and even private telephone conversations, if non-Spanish-speaking co-workers were nearby. Absent a legitimate reason for such a restriction, the inference of hostility may be reasonable. . . .

It is in this context that we consider the EEOC guideline on English-only workplace rules, 29 C.F.R. § 1606.7. Under the relevant provisions of the guideline:

(1) an English-only rule that applies at all times is considered "a burdensome term and condition of employment," § 1606.7(a), presumptively constituting a Title VII violation; and (2) an English-only rule that applies only at certain times does not violate Title VII if the employer can justify the rule by showing business necessity, § 1606.7(b). The EEOC rationales for the guideline are: (1) English-only policies "may 'create an atmosphere of inferiority, isolation, and intimidation' that could make a 'discriminatory working environment,' " (quoting § 1606.7(a)); (2) "English-only rules adversely impact employees with limited or no English skills . . . by denying them a privilege enjoyed by native English speakers: the opportunity to speak at work," *id.* at 14; (3) "English-only rules create barriers to employment for employees with limited or no English skills," *id.;* (4) "English-only rules prevent bilingual employees whose first language is not English from speaking in their most effective language," *id.* at 15; and (5) "the risk of discipline and termination for violating English-only rules falls disproportionately on bilingual employees as well as persons with limited English skills," *id.* at 16.

[Although the guidelines are not controlling upon the courts,] it is enough that the EEOC, based on its expertise and experience, has consistently concluded that an English-only policy, at least when no business need for the policy is shown, is likely in itself to "create an atmosphere of inferiority, isolation, and intimidation" that constitutes a "discriminatory working environment." § 1606.7(a) . . . . We believe that these conclusions are entitled to respect, not as interpretations of the governing law, but as an indication of what a reasonable, informed person may think about the impact of an English-only work rule on minority employees, even if we might not draw the same inference. Assuming the reasonableness of the EEOC on the matter, we cannot say that on the record before us it would be unreasonable for a juror to agree that the City's English-only policy created a hostile work environment for its Hispanic employees. . . .

2. Business Necessity

As an alternative ground for granting summary judgment on the disparate-impact claim, the district court held that Defendants "offered sufficient proof of business justification." It found "that city officials had received complaints that some employees could not understand what was being said on the City's radio frequency because other employees were speaking Spanish . . . [and] that city officials received complaints from non-Spanish speaking employees who felt uncomfortable when their co-workers spoke Spanish in front of them." Based on these justifications, it concluded that "Defendants have met any burden they may have to demonstrate that the City's English-only policy was supported by an adequate business justification."

We disagree. One of Congress's stated purposes in passing the 1991 amendments to the Civil Rights Act was "to codify the concepts of 'business necessity' and 'job related' enunciated by the Supreme Court in *Griggs v. Duke Power Co.*, 401 U.S. 424 (1971), [and other Supreme Court decisions]. In *Griggs* the Supreme Court held that "Congress has placed on the employer the burden of showing that any given requirement must have a manifest relationship to the employment in question." 401 U.S. at 432. The Court stressed that "[t]he touchstone is business necessity. If an employment practice which operates to [discriminate against a protected minority] cannot be shown to be related to job performance, the practice is prohibited." *Id.* at 431.

Defendants' evidence of business necessity in this case is scant. As observed by the district court, "[T]here was no written record of any communication problems, morale problems or safety problems resulting from the use of languages other than English prior to implementation of the policy." And there was little undocumented evidence. Defendants cited only one example of an employee's complaining about the use of Spanish prior to implementation of the policy. Mr. Willis admitted that he had no knowledge of City business being disrupted or delayed because Spanish was used on the radio. In addition, "city officials who were deposed could give no specific examples of safety problems resulting from the use of languages other than English . . . ." Moreover, Plaintiffs produced evidence that the policy encompassed lunch hours, breaks, and private phone conversations; and Defendants conceded that there would be no business reason for such a restriction.

On this record we are not able to affirm summary judgment based on a business necessity for the English-only policy. A reasonable person could find from this evidence that Defendants had failed to establish a business necessity for the English-only rule.

[ ] Disparate-Treatment

1. Discrimination

. . . To prevail under a disparate-treatment theory, "a plaintiff must show, through either direct or indirect evidence, that the discrimination complained of was intentional." *EEOC v. Horizon/CMS Healthcare Corp.*, 220 F.3d 1184, 1191 (10th Cir. 2000) . . . . We have already held that there is sufficient evidence to support a finding of a hostile work environment. The issue remaining, therefore, is whether those who established the English-only policy did so with the intent to create a hostile work environment.

To begin with, the disparate impact of the English-only rule (creation of a hostile work environment) is in itself evidence of intent. As the Supreme Court stated in *International Brotherhood of Teamsters*, 431 U.S. at 335, n. 15, in a disparate-treatment case, "Proof of discriminatory motive . . . can in some situations be inferred from the mere fact of differences in treatment." *See Washington v. Davis*, 426 U.S. 229, 242, 96 S. Ct. 2040, 48 L. Ed. 2d 597 (1976) ("[A]n invidious discriminatory purpose may often be inferred from the totality of the relevant facts, including the fact, if it is true, that the law bears more heavily on one race than another.").

Here, Plaintiffs can rely on more than just that inference. First, there is evidence that management realized that the English-only policy would likely lead to taunting of Hispanic employees: Street Commissioner Willis allegedly told two Hispanic employees about the policy in private because of concern that non-Hispanic employees would tease them if they learned of it. Also, a jury could find that there were no substantial work-related reasons for the policy (particularly if it believed

Plaintiffs' evidence that the policy extended to nonwork periods), suggesting that the true reason was illegitimate. Further, the policy was adopted without prior consultation with Hispanic employees, or even prior disclosure to a consultant to the City who was conducting an investigation of alleged anti-Hispanic discrimination during the period when the English-only policy was under consideration. Finally, there is evidence that during a news interview the Mayor referred to the Spanish language as "garbage."

In our view, the record contains sufficient evidence of intent to create a hostile environment that the summary judgment on those claims must be set aside.

NOTES

1. **Disparate Impact vs. Disparate Treatment.** The plaintiffs in *Maldonado* challenged the City's English-only policy on both disparate impact and disparate treatment theories, and the Tenth Circuit denied summary judgment on both. Which theory do you think is more likely to succeed in this case? Which theory best captures the harm that the plaintiffs are complaining about? Does the mere fact that the employer instituted an English-only policy establish discriminatory intent? If not, what other proof should be necessary?

One judge has argued that

> the imposition of an English-only rule may mask intentional discrimination on the basis of national origin . . . . "language can be a potent source of racial and ethnic discrimination." Gutierrez v. Municipal Court, 861 F.2d 1187, 1192 (9th Cir. 1988) (Kozinski, J., dissenting from denial of rehearing en banc). History is replete with language conflicts that attest, not only to the crucial importance of language to its speakers, but also to the widespread tactic of using language as a surrogate for attacks on ethnic identity. [The court then referenced the harsh repression of Catalan and the Basque language in Spain under the Franco regime; the repression of Ukrainian, Georgian and Belorussian languages by the former Soviet government and the extended repression of the Kurdish language in Turkey.] As these examples reveal, the urge to repress another's language is rarely, if ever, driven by benevolent impulses.

Garcia v. Spun Steak Co., 13 F.3d 296, 298–99 (9th Cir. 1993) (J. Reinhardt, dissenting from denial of rehearing en banc).

In a later case, *Montes v. Vail Clinic, Inc.*, 497 F.3d 1160 (10th Cir. 2007), the Tenth Circuit made clear that the surrounding context is important in determining the legality of an English-only policy. The policy in that case prohibited housekeeping employees from speaking Spanish about their job duties while in the operating room of a hospital. The Tenth Circuit found the policy lawful, distinguishing its earlier decision in *Maldonado* on the grounds that in *Montes* the policy applied only at certain times, was justified by business necessity and there was no evidence of any discriminatory motive. Thus, the legality of an employer's English-only policy turns on the specific facts surrounding the adoption of the policy and its enforcement. *See, e.g., Lopez v. Flight Services & Systems, Inc.*, 881 F. Supp. 2d 431 (W.D.N.Y. 2012) (finding that one plaintiff could not show an adverse action related to the employer's English-only rule, while another raised triable issues precluding summary judgment).

2. The Impact of English-Only Rules. How did the plaintiffs in *Maldonado* establish a prima facie case that the English-only policy created a hostile environment? Apart from the testimony about teasing and taunting, would the fact that the defendant implemented an English-only policy *itself* create a hostile work environment for bilingual workers? The *Maldonado* court thought a reasonable jury could find that the City's English-only policy created a hostile work environment.

By contrast, in *Garcia v. Spun Steak*, 998 F.2d 1480 (9th Cir. 1993), cited in *Maldonado*, the Ninth Circuit expressed its skepticism that the English-only policy challenged in that case had *any* adverse effect on the bilingual plaintiffs:

> The employees argue that denying them the ability to speak Spanish on the job denies them the right to cultural expression. It cannot be gainsaid that an individual's primary language can be an important link to his ethnic culture and identity. Title VII, however, does not protect the ability of workers to express their cultural heritage at the workplace. Title VII is concerned only with disparities in the treatment of workers; it does not confer substantive privileges. *See*, e.g., *Garcia v. Gloor*, 618 F.2d 264, 269 (5th Cir. 1980), cert. denied, 449 U.S. 1113 (1981). It is axiomatic that an employee must often sacrifice individual self-expression during working hours. Just as a private employer is not required to allow other types of self-expression, there is nothing in Title VII which requires an employer to allow employees to express their cultural identity.
>
> Next, the Spanish-speaking employees argue that the English-only policy has a disparate impact on them because it deprives them of a privilege given by the employer to native-English speakers: the ability to converse on the job in the language with which they feel most comfortable. It is undisputed that Spun Steak allows its employees to converse on the job. The ability to converse—especially to make small talk—is a privilege of employment, and may in fact be a significant privilege of employment in an assembly-line job. It is inaccurate, however, to describe the privilege as broadly as the Spanish-speaking employees urge us to do.
>
> The employees have attempted to define the privilege as the ability to speak in the language of their choice. A privilege, however, is by definition given at the employer's discretion; an employer has the right to define its contours. Thus, an employer may allow employees to converse on the job, but only during certain times of the day or during the performance of certain tasks. The employer may proscribe certain topics as inappropriate during working hours or may even forbid the use of certain words, such as profanity.
>
> Here, as is its prerogative, the employer has defined the privilege narrowly. When the privilege is defined at its narrowest (as merely the ability to speak on the job), we cannot conclude that those employees fluent in both English and Spanish are adversely impacted by the policy. Because they are able to speak English, bilingual employees can engage in

conversation on the job. It is axiomatic that "the language a person who is multi-lingual elects to speak at a particular time is . . . a matter of choice." *Garcia*, 618 F.2d at 270. The bilingual employee can readily comply with the English-only rule and still enjoy the privilege of speaking on the job. "There is no disparate impact" with respect to a privilege of employment "if the rule is one that the affected employee can readily observe and nonobservance is a matter of individual preference." *Id*. . . .

The Spanish-speaking employees argue that fully bilingual employees are hampered in the enjoyment of the privilege because for them, switching from one language to another is not fully volitional. Whether a bilingual speaker can control which language is used in a given circumstance is a factual issue that cannot be resolved at the summary judgment stage. However, we fail to see the relevance of the assertion, even assuming that it can be proved. Title VII is not meant to protect against rules that merely inconvenience some employees, even if the inconvenience falls regularly on a protected class. Rather, Title VII protects against only those policies that have a significant impact. The fact that an employee may have to catch himself or herself from occasionally slipping into Spanish does not impose a burden significant enough to amount to the denial of equal opportunity. . . .

998 F.2d at 1487–88.

Judge Reinhardt disagreed, arguing:

Whether or not the employees can readily comply with a discriminatory rule is by no means the measure of whether they suffer significant adverse consequences. Some of the most objectionable discriminatory rules are the least obtrusive in terms of one's ability to comply: being required to sit in the back of a bus, for example; or being relegated during one's law school career to a portion of the classroom dedicated to one's exclusive use. *See McLaurin v. Oklahoma State Regents*, 339 U.S. 637 (1950).

13 F.3d 296, 298 (J. Reinhardt, dissenting from denial of rehearing en banc).

Who's right? If a bilingual employee can readily comply with an English-only rule in the workplace, is there no adverse impact from such a rule? How should the employer's prerogative to establish the conditions of work be weighed against any impact on the interests of bilingual workers?

3. Business Necessity. Even if plaintiffs challenging an English-only policy succeed in establishing an adverse effect, the employer may still defend its policy by showing that it was justified by business necessity. What business reasons should be considered sufficient to justify an English-only rule? Safety concerns? The importance of clear communications about the production process? What about concerns about collegiality, or about non-Spanish speaking employees feeling left out or uncomfortable? Should those be considered legitimate business reasons? Can there *ever* be a business justification for requiring that only English be spoken during breaks and in phone conversations with family or friends?

4.   Other Cases. In addition to *Garcia v. Spun Steak*, the case discussed above in note 2, a number of other cases have challenged English-only rules, with generally similar results. *See Garcia v. Gloor*, 618 F.2d 264 (5th Cir. 1980) (upholding workplace rule prohibiting speaking Spanish unless communicating with Spanish-speaking customers); *Reyes v. Pharma Chemie, Inc.*, 890 F. Supp. 2d 1147 (D. Neb. 2012) (finding that employer's English-only policy does not violate Title VII); *Pacheco v. N.Y. Presbyterian Hosp.*, 593 F. Supp. 2d 599 (S.D.N.Y. 2009) (granting summary judgment on plaintiff's disparate treatment and disparate impact claims challenging English-only policy); *Prado v. L. Luria & Son, Inc.*, 975 F. Supp. 1349 (S.D. Fla. 1997) (upholding English-only rule because speaking Spanish in the workplace is simply a matter of employee's preference). In some cases, courts have rejected challenges to English-only policies on the grounds that they are justified by legitimate business reasons. *See, e.g., Barber v. Lovelace Sandia Health Systems*, 409 F. Supp. 2d 1313 (D.N.M. 2005) (finding that employer had identified legitimate, non-discriminatory reasons for its language policy).

As discussed in *Maldonado*, the EEOC has taken the position that English-only policies must be justified by business necessity, and it has pursued a number of cases challenging such policies with some success. In *EEOC v. Premier Operator Services, Inc.*, 113 F. Supp. 2d 1066 (N.D. Tex. 2000), the district court enjoined an English-only rule that prohibited the speaking of Spanish even during the employees' lunch and breaks. *Id.* at 1074. The court also heard expert testimony

> that speaking only English is not simply a matter of preference for bilingual persons whose primary language or language of national origin is other than English. Based on the most recent and directly relevant state of research on this subject, it is evident that lapsing or switching from English to Spanish is often inadvertent and unconscious on the part of bilingual Spanish speakers such as the class members in this case.

Id. at 1074.

English-only policies have also been the subject of extensive scholarly criticism. *See*, e.g., Drucilla Cornell & William W. Bratton, *Deadweight Costs & Instrinsic Wrongs of Nativism: Economics, Freedom, and Legal Suppression of Spanish*, 84 CORNELL L. REV. 595 (1999) (arguing that English-only policies are degrading and violative of people's language rights); Juan F. Perea, *Los Olvidados: On the Making of Invisible People*, 70 N.Y.U. L. REV. 965 (1995) (contending that English-only policies contribute to the invisibility of Latinos).

B.   BALANCING WORK AND FAMILY

Balancing the demands of work and caring for a family is often seen as an issue of gender equality. This view of the issue stems from the fact that women generally perform a larger share of household labor, including child care and elder care, than men. Thus, to the extent that work and family obligations are seen as conflicting, or employers fail to accommodate workers' needs as parents or care-givers, these problems more heavily burden women workers.

Advancing gender equality has not proven to be a simple matter of prohibiting discrimination on the basis of sex. In *General Electric v. Gilbert*, 429 U.S. 125 (1976), the Supreme Court considered a challenge to General Electric's disability benefit plan, which excluded from coverage disabilities associated with pregnancy. The plaintiffs argued that this exclusion constituted sex discrimination in violation of Title VII. The Supreme Court found that the plan did not discriminate on the basis of gender, but "merely remove[d] one physical condition—pregnancy—from the list of compensable disabilities." *Id.* at 134 (citing *Geduldig v. Aiello*, 417 U.S. 484, 496–97 (1974)). It noted that although only women could get pregnant, the group of nonpregnant persons included both men and women. Given the "lack of identity between the excluded disability and gender as such," the Court concluded that excluding pregnancy from a disability-benefits plan is not gender-based discrimination. *Id.* at 135. The *General Electric* decision was greeted with a great deal of criticism, and just two years later in 1978 Congress overruled the Court's decision by passing the Pregnancy Discrimination Act (PDA), which amended Title VII to make clear that discrimination on the basis of pregnancy *is* sex discrimination. 42 U.S.C. § 2000e(k).

Then, in *California Federal Savings & Loan Ass'n v. Guerra*, 479 U.S. 272 (1987), the Supreme Court was asked to strike down a California law that required employers to provide *greater* benefits to pregnant workers than those disabled for other reasons. Specifically, the statute required unpaid leave and reinstatement for pregnancy and childbirth, but no other forms of disability. An employer challenged the California law, arguing that it violated the PDA because it treated men and women differently on the basis of pregnancy. The Supreme Court disagreed, finding that the PDA set a floor, not a ceiling, on pregnancy disability benefits. The purpose of the California law, like Title VII and the PDA, was to provide relief for working women and to end discrimination against pregnant workers, thereby promoting equal opportunity. The Court found that "[b]y 'taking pregnancy into account,' California's pregnancy disability-leave statute allows women, as well as men, to have families without losing their jobs," and therefore the California statute was not unlawful under Title VII.

As the experience with the PDA shows, the question of what constitutes "equal treatment" when men and women are differently situated is not entirely straightforward. Benefits provided on a gender neutral basis may differentially impact men and women workers. On the other hand, providing special benefits for women may undermine claims for gender equality. (At the time this book went to press, a case was pending before the Supreme Court, *Young v. UPS*, regarding the obligations of employers to provide accommodations to pregnant women.) To the extent that family responsibilities tend to burden women and men unequally in our society, any legal attempt to address work-family conflicts will raise this tension between treating men and women the same and recognizing relevant societal differences.

1. The FMLA and Gender Equality

The Family Medical Leave Act of 1993 ("FMLA") provides relief to working parents by allowing those who qualify to take unpaid leave to care for a new child, sick children, spouses or parents, or for one's own serious illness. Although the FMLA is not an antidiscrimination statute in a traditional sense, one of its primary purposes was to alleviate discriminatory barriers women encounter in the workplace. The Supreme Court in *Nevada Dept. of Human Resources v. Hibbs*, 538 U.S. 721 (2003), explained the connection between the provisions of the FMLA and Congressional efforts to promote gender equality.

NEVADA DEPT. OF HUMAN RESOURCES v. HIBBS
United States Supreme Court
538 U.S. 721 (2003)

CHIEF JUSTICE REHNQUIST delivered the opinion of the Court.

The FMLA aims to protect the right to be free from gender-based discrimination in the workplace.[3] . . . The history of the many state laws limiting women's employment opportunities is chronicled in—and, until relatively recently, was sanctioned by—this Court's own opinions. For example, in *Bradwell v. State*, 16 Wall. 130 (1873) (Illinois), and *Goesaert v. Cleary*, 335 U.S. 464, 466 (1948) (Michigan), the Court upheld state laws prohibiting women from practicing law and tending bar, respectively. State laws frequently subjected women to distinctive restrictions, terms, conditions, and benefits for those jobs they could take. In *Muller v. Oregon*, 208 U.S. 412, 419, n. 1 (1908), for example, this Court approved a state law limiting the hours that women could work for wages, and observed that 19 States had such laws at the time. Such laws were based on the related beliefs that (1) a woman is, and should remain, "the center of home and family life," *Hoyt v. Florida*, 368 U.S. 57, 62 (1961), and (2) "a proper discharge of [a woman's] maternal functions—having in view not merely her own health, but the well-being of the race—justif[ies] legislation to protect her from the greed as well as the passion of man," *Muller, supra*, at 422. . . .

Congress responded to this history [by prohibiting discrimination by the States in Title VII of the Civil Rights Act of 1964, 78 § 2000e-2(a)] . . . According to evidence that was before Congress when it enacted the FMLA, States continue to rely on invalid gender stereotypes in the employment context, specifically in the administration of leave benefits. . . .

As the FMLA's legislative record reflects, a 1990 Bureau of Labor Statistics (BLS) survey stated that 37 percent of surveyed private-sector employees were covered by maternity leave policies, while only 18 percent were covered by paternity leave policies. The corresponding numbers from a similar BLS survey the previous year were 33 percent and 16 percent, respectively. *Ibid.* While these data show an increase in the percentage of employees eligible for such leave, they also show a widening of the gender gap during the same period. Thus, stereotype-based beliefs about the allocation of family duties remained firmly rooted, and employers' reliance on them in establishing discriminatory leave policies remained widespread.

---

[3] [n. 2] The text of the Act makes this clear. Congress found that, "due to the nature of the roles of men and women in our society, the primary responsibility for family caretaking often falls on women, and such responsibility affects the working lives of women more than it affects the working lives of men." 29 U.S.C. § 2601(a)(5). In response to this finding, Congress sought "to accomplish the [Act's other] purposes . . . in a manner that . . . minimizes the potential for employment discrimination *on the basis of sex* by ensuring generally that leave is available . . . *on a gender-neutral basis[,]* and to promote the goal of equal employment opportunity for women and men (4)27" §§ 2601(b)(4) and (5) (emphasis added).

Congress also heard testimony that "[p]arental leave for fathers . . . is rare. Even . . . [w]here child-care leave policies do exist, men, *both in the public and private sectors*, receive notoriously discriminatory treatment in their requests for such leave." Joint Hearing 147 (Washington Council of Lawyers) (emphasis added). Many States offered women extended "maternity" leave that far exceeded the typical 4- to 8-week period of physical disability due to pregnancy and childbirth, but very few States granted men a parallel benefit. Fifteen States provided women up to one year of extended maternity leave, while only four provided men with the same. M. Lord & M. King, The State Reference Guide to Work-Family Programs for State Employees 30 (1991). This and other differential leave policies were not attributable to any differential physical needs of men and women, but rather to the pervasive sex-role stereotype that caring for family members is women's work.

Finally, Congress had evidence that, even where state laws and policies were not facially discriminatory, they were applied in discriminatory ways. It was aware of the "serious problems with the discretionary nature of family leave," because when "the authority to grant leave and to arrange the length of that leave rests with individual supervisors," it leaves "employees open to discretionary and possibly unequal treatment." H.R.Rep. No. 103-8, pt. 2, pp. 10–11 (1993). Testimony supported that conclusion, explaining that "[t]he lack of uniform parental and medical leave policies in the work place has created an environment where [sex] discrimination is rampant." 1987 Senate Labor Hearings, pt. 2, at 170 (testimony of Peggy Montes, Mayor's Commission on Women's Affairs, City of Chicago).

. . . [Before FMLA's enactment], seven States had childcare leave provisions that applied to women only. Indeed, Massachusetts required that notice of its leave provisions be posted only in "establishment [s] in which females are employed." These laws reinforced the very stereotypes that Congress sought to remedy through the FMLA. Second, 12 States provided their employees no family leave, beyond an initial childbirth or adoption, to care for a seriously ill child or family member. Third, many States provided no statutorily guaranteed right to family leave, offering instead only voluntary or discretionary leave programs. Three States left the amount of leave time primarily in employers' hands. Congress could reasonably conclude that such discretionary family-leave programs would do little to combat the stereotypes about the roles of male and female employees that Congress sought to eliminate. Finally, four States provided leave only through administrative regulations or personnel policies, which Congress could reasonably conclude offered significantly less firm protection than a federal law. Against the above backdrop of limited state leave policies . . . Congress was justified in enacting the FMLA as remedial legislation.[4]

The impact of the discrimination targeted by the FMLA is significant. Congress determined:

"Historically, denial or curtailment of women's employment opportunities has been traceable directly to the pervasive presumption that women are

---

[4] [n. 9] . . . The FMLA is not a "substantive entitlement program,"; Congress did not create a particular leave policy for its own sake. Rather, Congress sought to adjust family-leave policies in order to eliminate their reliance on, and perpetuation of, invalid stereotypes, and thereby dismantle persisting gender-based barriers to the hiring, retention, and promotion of women in the workplace. . . .

mothers first, and workers second. This prevailing ideology about women's roles has in turn justified discrimination against women when they are mothers or mothers-to-be." Joint Hearing 100.

⌈Stereotypes about women's domestic roles are reinforced by parallel stereotypes presuming a lack of domestic responsibilities for men⌋ Because employers continued to regard the family as the woman's domain, they often denied men similar accommodations or discouraged them from taking leave. These ⌈mutually reinforcing stereotypes created a self-fulfilling cycle of discrimination⌋ that forced women to continue to assume the role of primary family caregiver, and fostered employers' stereotypical views about women's commitment to work and their value as employees. Those perceptions, in turn, Congress reasoned, lead to subtle discrimination that may be difficult to detect on a case-by-case basis. . . .

By creating an across-the-board, routine employment benefit for all eligible employees, Congress sought to ensure that family-care leave would no longer be stigmatized as an inordinate drain on the workplace caused by female employees, and that employers could not evade leave obligations simply by hiring men. By setting a minimum standard of family leave for *all* eligible employees, irrespective of gender, the FMLA attacks the formerly state-sanctioned stereotype that only women are responsible for family caregiving, thereby reducing employers' incentives to engage in discrimination by basing hiring and promotion decisions on stereotypes. . . .

Indeed, in light of the evidence before Congress, a statute mirroring Title VII, that simply mandated gender equality in the administration of leave benefits, would not have achieved Congress' remedial object. Such a law would allow States to provide for no family leave at all. Where "[t]wo-thirds of the nonprofessional caregivers for older, chronically ill, or disabled persons are working women," H.R.Rep. No. 103-8, pt. 1, at 24; S.Rep. No. 103-3, at 7, U.S.Code Cong. & Admin.News 1993, pp. 3, 9, and state practices continue to reinforce the stereotype of women as caregivers, such a policy would exclude far more women than men from the workplace.

2. The FMLA's Provisions and Its Effects

In order to qualify for the benefits of the FMLA, employees must work more than 1,250 hours in a year, and are not eligible for leave until one year after they begin to work for the employer. In addition, the statute applies only to employers that have more than 50 employees. *See* 28 U.S.C. § 2611(2)(A) (i)–(ii). As a result of these restrictions, approximately 60% of the nation's workforce is eligible for FMLA leave. Qualified employees are entitled to take up to 12 weeks of unpaid leave for (1) the birth or adoption of a child; (2) to care for a spouse, child or parent who has a serious health condition; and (3) because of one's own serious health condition. 28 U.S.C. § 2612. Where feasible, the employee must provide 30-day notice to the employer of her planned leave, and leave relating to the birth or adoption of a child can generally not be taken intermittently but must be taken all at one time. *See* 28 U.S.C. § 2612(e) (notice provisions) and (b) (intermittent leave provisions). When the leave is unplanned, an employee must provide notice as "soon as practicable," which is typically defined as within a day or two, though

742 CHALLENGES TO EQUALITY IN A DIVERSIFYING WORKPLACE CH. 10

"extraordinary circumstances" may extend the time period for providing notice. *See* 29 C.F.R. § 825.303; *Bosley v. Cargill Meat Solutions Corp.*, 705 F.3d 777, 783 (8th Cir. 2013).

An important aspect of the legislation is that an employee is entitled to be restored to the same, or an equivalent, position after the leave is completed, and she is entitled to retain her health insurance while on leave. *See* 28 U.S.C. § 2614(a) (restoration to position) and (c) (health benefits). The employee, however, is not entitled to accrue seniority while on leave, and if the person would have lost her job even if she had not gone on leave, then the employer is not required to restore the employee to a position. *See Sabourin v. University of Utah*, 676 F.3d 950, 959 (10th Cir. 2012) (permissible to terminate employee while on FMLA leave as part of reduction in force). The statute contains other provisions, and detailed regulations promulgated by the Department of Labor, but the provisions discussed above form the core of the statute.

The FMLA establishes two substantive rights: (1) a right to take leave and (2) a right to be free from discrimination for exercising rights under the statute (an anti-retaliation provision). Both of these provisions have generated litigation, and the vast majority of claims are resolved at the administrative level through the filing of claims with the Department of Labor. With respect to the right to take leave, much of the early litigation involved what constitutes a serious health condition. Both the statute and regulations provide some guidance: a serious health condition is an "illness, injury, impairment, or physical or mental condition" that requires continuing treatment and lasts for more than three consecutive days. *See* 29 C.F.R. § 825.114(a)(2) (serious health condition defined as involving continued treatment and at least three days of incapacity); *Caskey v. Colgate-Palmolve Co.*, 535 F.3d 585 (7th Cir. 2008) (discussing regulation). Courts typically take a fact specific approach to defining a serious health condition. As one court has stated, "[W]hile the[ ] conditions in this case may not rise to the level of a 'serious medical condition' as a matter of fact (a question necessarily left for the finder of fact), they are not barred from doing so as a matter of law." *Price v. City of Fort Wayne*, 117 F.3d 1022, 1023 (7th Cir. 1997). Routine illnesses such as a cold or flu are typically not covered by the FMLA, though particularly serious instances that require medical attention can qualify for leave. *See Miller v. AT&T Corp.*, 250 F.3d 820 (4th Cir. 2001) (employee's flu defined as serious medical condition); *see also Thorson v. Gemini, Inc.*, 205 F.3d 370, 380 (8th Cir. 2000) ("While Congress may have 'expected' that minor illnesses 'normally' would not come within the definition of 'serious health condition', that does not mean that such ailments can never be FMLA 'serious health conditions.' ").

The FMLA is not necessarily designed to allow parents to handle routine illnesses of their children, and several courts have emphasized that a child must be incapacitated for more than three days and receive continued treatment for the parent to qualify for FMLA leave. *See Perry v. Jaguar of Troy*, 353 F.3d 510 (6th Cir. 2003). Efforts to amend the statute to provide parents with greater flexibility to care for ill children have failed but courts will occasionally permit claims for routine illnesses to be covered under the FMLA. *See* Katharine B. Silbaugh, *Is the Work-Family Conflict Pathological or Normal Under the FMLA? The Potential of the FMLA to Cover Ordinary Work-Family Conflicts*, 15 WASH. U. J.L. & POL'Y 193

(2004) (discussing cases involving illnesses of children).

Employees are required to provide their employers with notice regarding FMLA leave and whether an employee has provided adequate notice frequently arises in litigation. Under existing law, employers have the "responsibility to determine the applicability of the FMLA and to consider requested leave as FMLA leave." *Dotson v. Pfizer*, 558 F.3d 284, 293 (4th Cir. 2009). However, an employee must "provide [an] employer with notice sufficient to make her employer aware that her absence is due to a potentially FMLA-qualifying reason." *Cruz v. Publix Super Markets, Inc.*, 428 F.3d 1379, 1386 (11th Cir. 2005). As a result, even when the employee has a qualifying condition, failure to provide adequate notice will render the FMLA inapplicable. *See Scobey v. Nucor Steel-Arkansas*, 580 F.3d 781, 786 (8th Cir. 2009) (employee failed to notify employer that his four unexcused absences were related to his alcohol problems and depression).

When an employee alleges that she has been discriminated against for exercising her rights under the FMLA, the case proceeds much like it would under Title VII with the need to establish a *prima facie* case and ultimately the employee must prove that an adverse employment action was taken because she sought to exercise her FMLA rights. *See, e.g., Smothers v. Solvay Chems., Inc.*, 740 F.3d 530, 539–43 (10th Cir. 2014) (applying pretext model to claim that employee was terminated for using FMLA leave); *Wierman v. Casey's General Stores*, 638 F.3d 984, 999 (8th Cir. 2011) (discussing proof structure). One issue that renders FMLA retaliation claims slightly different from such claims pursued under Title VII is that an employer might terminate an employee for deficient work performance and the employee will argue that whatever deficiency existed was related to her need for FMLA leave. For example, in *Pagel v. Tin Inc.*, 695 F.3d 622 (7th Cir. 2012), the employer contended that the employee was terminated for failing to meet sales expectations and the employee countered that he failed to meet expectations because he was on FMLA leave. Courts have held that if an employee succeeds in establishing that the employer's reason was tied to FMLA leave, she can prevail on her claim. *See id.* (claim survives employer's summary judgment motion); *Clinckscale v. St. Therese of New Hope*, 701 F.3d 825 (8th Cir. 2012) (plaintiff offered sufficient evidence to establish that her performance was related to her covered anxiety issues). If an employee is unable to perform the essential functions of the job after returning from leave, the employee has no right to an accommodation or to have leave extended beyond twelve weeks. *See Demyanovich v. Cadon Plating & Coatings, L.L.C.*, 747 F.3d 419, 429 (6th Cir. 2014) (discussing employer's obligations). Finally, it remains an open question in most circuits whether the mixed-motives theory applies to claims that arise under the FMLA; to date, most courts have successfully avoided the question. *See Lichenstein v. University of Pittsburgh Med. Ctr.*, 691 F.3d 294, 302 (3d Cir. 2012) (avoiding the issue and noting conflicting authorities).

When the FMLA was originally passed, there was significant hope that the statute would ease the burdens of working parents, particularly in the context of providing leave for parents of newborn (or adopted) children. Several studies have shown that the statute has had only a limited effect, and indeed, the most frequent use of the statute has been by employees who take leave for their own illness. *See* U.S. Dept. of Labor, *Balancing the Needs of Families and Employers: The Family and Medical Leave Surveys*, 2000 Update, table 2.3 (2001) (52.4% of leave takers in 2000 took leave because of their own illnesses). According to the most recent government survey, the pattern of leave taking remains similar: 55% of leave was taken for one's own illness with another 18% of leave taken in connection with the serious health condition of another. Twenty-one percent of the leave was related to pregnancy or adoption. *See* UNITED STATES DEPARTMENT OF LABOR, FAMILY AND MEDICAL LEAVE IN 2012, *available at* www.dol.gov/asp/evaluation/fmla/fmla2012.htm. Another important aspect of the FMLA is that leave is provided to both women and men. This was done in part to avoid constitutional challenges if the leave had only been provided to women, but it was also done in the hope that the statute would encourage men to take more leave for the care of their children. This aspiration, too, at least in the context of the FMLA, has not been realized, as women take substantially more leave than men under the statute, and there is little evidence that men are taking significantly more leave than they had prior to the passage of the act. *Id.* at Exhibit 4.1.5 (noting that women are a third more likely than men to take leave).

It is not entirely clear why the FMLA has not produced more benefits to workers or change in the workplace. Part of the problem is likely attributable to the fact that FMLA leave is unpaid, and many workers are unable to afford unpaid leave. Instead, many women store up their vacation or sick leave in anticipation of the birth or adoption of a child and return to work shortly after their leave is exhausted. Some large employers also provide paid leave, often in the form of disability leave, that renders FMLA leave unnecessary. *See* Michael Selmi, *Family Leave and the Gender Wage Gap*, 78 N.C. L. REV. 707, 762 (2000) (noting that "nearly 90% of full-time employees at large firms had access to disability plans that included coverage for pregnancy."). No matter how one looks at it, the United States' legislation pales in comparison to most other industrialized countries; indeed, the United States is the only such country that does not offer some form of paid leave. *See* Tara Siegel Bernard, *In Paid Family Leave, United States Trails Most of the Globe*, N.Y. TIMES, Feb. 22, 2013, at B1 ("While the United States takes great pride in its family values, it is the only high income country that does not offer a paid leave program."). Why do you think the United States provides such limited leave? Alternatively, do you believe workers should be entitled to paid leave to care for children, either when they are first born or adopted or when they are sick?

3. The Policy Debate

Although the FMLA has generated only limited litigation, it has been in the middle of a lively and extensive debate over the ability of workers to balance the demands of work and life outside of the workplace. Much of the debate has centered on the effect women's responsibilities outside of the workplace with respect to their children have on their experiences in the workplace. Many believe that stronger leave legislation may help women better balance their competing demands, while others argue for a more fundamental restructuring of the workplace. Some of this restructuring might include more and better part-time jobs for women, more flexible work policies including greater access to telecommuting, and reduced hours. Others have expressed skepticism regarding the effect such policies might have, noting that they may, in fact, exacerbate gender inequality in the workplace to the extent that part-time jobs or other flexible work schedules become the exclusive province of women. The following two excerpts offer two perspectives on the interactions between work and family obligations and women's equality in the workplace.

Joan Williams, *Our Economy of Mothers and Others: Women and Economics Revisited*
5 J. Gender Race & Just. 411 (2002)

Today two statistics frame the way we look at women and paid work. The first is women's workforce participation, a demographic measure that documents the demise of the breadwinner/housewife model as women entered the workforce. The second is the wage gap, which measures the gap between the wages of men who work full-time against the wages of women who work fulltime. Both statistics . . . are designed to measure the extent to which women are in the labor force working shoulder to shoulder with men, as ideal workers who become employed in early adulthood, and remain employed, full-time and full-force, for forty years straight.

While the work patterns and wages of women without children are looking increasingly like those of ideal-worker men, the same is not true of mothers.

If we look at mothers during the key years of career advancement, aged twenty-five to forty-four, two out of three do not perform as ideal workers even in the minimal sense of working forty hours per week all year. What is more dramatic is that ninety-two percent work less than fifty hours per week. In an age where virtually all good jobs require full-time work, and many of the best jobs require overtime, mothers are cut out of the labor pool for many desirable jobs, blue-as well as white-collar.

Women without children earn ninety percent of the wages of men, but mothers earn only sixty percent of the wages of fathers. The "family gap" between the wages of mothers and other adults increased during the 1980s and may still be rising among the least privileged women. If we look not at women's workforce participation but at whether they perform as ideal workers along with men, what emerges is a picture of the fragile hold women have on market work in a society where nearly ninety percent of women become mothers during their working lives.

In short, a focus on wage gap and workforce participation figures tends to exaggerate the extent to which women have reached economic equality. After all, two-thirds of working women work less than forty hours per week. Therefore, the wage gap statistic comparing women who work full-time with men who work full-time grossly overestimates the extent of women's equality. Workforce participation statistics are equally misleading: consider the woman lawyer who dropped out of her legal career and ran a part-time quilt business from her home. Though she was "in the workforce," she remained firmly marginalized and economically vulnerable. We need new economic measures that document our economy of mothers and others. . . .

The problem with pinning our hopes for women's equality on a strategy of having women perform as ideal workers, as June Carbone said long ago, is that "it leaves out the small matter of who will take care of the children." The real issue is that our ideals at work do not fit with our ideals for family life. In a society with the longest hours of overtime in the industrialized world, longer even than Japan's, the ideal-worker norm clashes with our sense of what we owe to children. Fathers who work full-time work an average of forty-eight hours per week. This increases when combined with their average commutes, meaning that they may well be gone from home ten or more hours each weekday. Who among us thinks the ideal way to raise children is for both parents to be gone from nine a.m. to seven, eight or nine p.m.?

We are caught in the clash of two social ideals: the ideal-worker norm on the job, and the norm of parental care at home. This clash combines with gender performance norms that engenders in most women the desire to be a "real mother" (complete with milk, cookies, and carpool), and into most men the desire to be a "real man" (which includes performing as an ideal worker to the extent his race, class, and personality allow him to do so). The end result is that gender has proved unbending. The economy of mothers and others will not change until we redefine the ideal worker and restructure market work, and thereby, redefine our work ideals so that they are more in sync with our traditions of nurturance. The key here is family responsive policies. . . .

One approach is to change the relationship of employers and employees. We can accomplish these changes by requiring workplaces to take account of the important family work responsibilities of their employees. To do this, we need to go far beyond current "family friendly" policies and rethink how we define the ideal worker. Most large employers today have such policies, but, according to one survey, only three to five percent of workers use them. Why? The widespread perception, often true, is that workers who do so often pay a steep price. "When you work part-time or temporary," said one secretary, "they treat you differently, they don't take you serious." Many policies explicitly affect promotion, as when law firms take part-time attorneys off the partnership track, a practice that is still very common. Professional workers, who are disproportionately likely to have access to work/family benefits, also often find that "the only responsible way to work part-time is to work full-time"; they find their hours creeping up despite the fact they are being paid less, and many find themselves with less desirable work assignments to boot. . . .

What would restructured work look like if it did not carry the penalties it now does? A baseline is the principle of proportionality: proportional pay, benefits, and advancement for part-time work. This is particularly important in mandatory overtime economies that, in effect, wipe most mothers out of the labor pool for good jobs. It is also vitally important in white-collar contexts, because the "executive schedule" has sharply limited the number of women who survive in business (more than ninety-five percent of upper-level management is still men), law (eighty-seven percent of law firm partners are still men), academics (more than seventy-four percent of tenured professors are still men), and many other traditionally masculine professions. The principle of proportionality is also important in good blue-collar jobs. Such jobs tend to have a high benefit load (up to forty percent of wages), which gives employers the motivation to require long hours of existing employees rather than to hire new ones. In addition, traditionally masculine blue-collar jobs rarely have part-time tracks, and, as we have seen, mothers rarely work jobs with lots of overtime. . . . Finally, the principle of proportionality can offer significant benefits to the working poor, who often can find only part-time work, with depressed wage rates, no benefits, and no chance for advancement. . . .

To implement the principle of proportionality requires us to rethink the ways we define an ambitious, committed, valuable worker. But family responsive workplaces require other changes as well. For example, in interviews with more than three hundred women in Iowa, sociologist Jennifer Glass found that the women she spoke with, many of them working class, expressed the need for flextime so that their work hours would match with the hours of their childcare provider, as well as time off for medical appointments, child illnesses (infants average six doctor's visits a year), school plays and conferences. They also stated the need for an adequate supply of quality, affordable childcare.

Voluntary programs that persuade employers to change traditional ways of doing business hold significant promise, particularly in an age of high employment. The "business case" reflects the fact that current business practices impose steep costs on employers. Most dramatic are the costs of high attrition among mothers in full-time or overtime work, and among fathers in high-overtime environments. . . . Family responsive policies tend to reduce absenteeism. When the baby is sick, someone is going to take her to the doctor and will have to call in sick to do so. But if employees have the option of taking time off formally, through flextime or part-time, absenteeism rates fall. . . .

A final, and understudied, element of the business case for family responsive policies is the correlation between employee satisfaction, employee loyalty, and client loyalty. Employers who have effective family responsive policies in an era when employee loyalty is hard to come by find that employees who feel their family needs are being addressed can be fiercely loyal, as in the case of the moving company that experienced zero turnover when they offered telecommuting and other benefits, or the dermatology company that experienced zero turnover once it provided a twenty percent discount to the neighboring family care unit, instituted flexible work hours and provided parent education classes. Employee loyalty is important in itself because it reduces attrition and increases motivation, but it is also important for another reason: study after study has shown a correlation between retaining employees and retaining clients. . . .

Here is a radical proposition: employers should reward productivity. We should choose and promote workers based on the quality of their work product, not on the schedule they can keep. Why? In a society where schedule correlates tightly with gender, a system that systematically rewards people based on their ability to keep the schedule kept by most men, but few women, discriminates against women. . . . Note that this is gender, not sex discrimination: what is at issue is not a disadvantage that attaches to all women, but one that attaches to all caregivers. That is, men who do not conform to traditional breadwinner patterns are disadvantaged equally, indeed sometimes more, than are women. . . .

The standard approach to changing entitlements within the family in this country has been to try to change the allocation of family work between men and women. . . . [T]he strategy of shifting the allocation of family work within the household has been met with limited success. Forty years after women started bargaining for equality within the household, it is estimated that they continue to perform between sixty-six and eighty percent of the housework. We need to be more thoughtful about why women continue to perform the majority of household work, and this is where three areas of literature should prove helpful. One is the booming literature on masculinity, which can help us understand the gender pressures on men that make them resist the hydraulic pressures within individual households to share work more equally. The second is the growing literature on "gate-keeping" by women, including Naomi Cahn's important insight that mothers often refuse to let go of the sole-source supplier (primary caregiver) role because their identity as women is tied up with that particular gender performance. Finally, there is another literature that does not, but should, exist: a literature that explores the relationship of gender and class. One reason gender has proved so unbending is because gender performances play a central role in class formation. Gender performances help create class status, as when the ideology and practice of intensive mothering creates high-human-capital kids. The available cultural idioms for the performances of class are very gendered, as when families consider having the mother at home a signal of having "arrived" at middle-class status.

The most basic fact about the typically privatized, psychologized, American strategy of solving the work/family conflict by changing the allocation of family work, is that it has failed. It is time to shift attention away from women's psychology onto structural economic relations: the structure of market work and the issue of who owns what within the family.

Michael Selmi & Naomi Cahn, *Caretaking and the Contradictions of Contemporary Policy*
55 ME. L. REV. 289 (2003)

In the last several years, a rising chorus of authors . . . have urged greater societal attention to what has been labeled care work. . . . Although those who have focused on care work differ substantially in their emphases and approaches, much of the literature addresses a question that has long been central to feminist thinking, namely the devaluing of work that occurs outside of the paid labor market and the difficulties women have in balancing their home and workplace demands. . . . For most women, the quest for equal parenting has proved elusive and, indeed, women continue to perform the majority of work in the home, while failing to obtain substantial equality in the workplace in terms of wages, status, or power, much of which can be traced to their caretaking responsibilities. In addition to the frustration over the lack of progress toward equality, there is also a renewed interest in women's role as caretakers in a way that seeks to diminish the importance of gaining workplace equality by emphasizing the social importance, and the persistent devaluing, of caretaking. It is this latter emphasis in the literature that we seek to address in this essay. . . .

Our primary disagreement involves the exclusive focus on caretaking as a means of furthering women's interests, as we believe women's interests are likely to be furthered to a greater extent by providing better access and opportunities in the paid labor market, and that wage labor should not be seen as incompatible with women's caretaking responsibilities. . . . [T]he focus on care work is misleading in ways that ultimately reinforce prevailing gender stereotypes, and we also believe, emphasizing care work will ultimately lead to public policies designed to facilitate women's work in the home without substantially changing the gender dynamics of the home or the workplace, in which case it is difficult to see how these proposals benefit women.

The care work literature is misleading in several important respects. First, the literature is premised on the notion that most women are unable to balance the demands of work and family and thus are forced to choose between the two, with a further implication that women are dropping out of the workforce in significant numbers to care for their children. But, as we know, this is not an accurate picture; the majority of married women with children, even those who are very young, are in the workforce and only a relatively small percentage of women exit the workforce after having children. Nor is this a recent phenomenon: by the mid-1980s, more than half of mothers with children under two years of age were in the workforce. Even so, during the last two decades, women with children under the age of three nearly doubled their workforce participation rates, rising from 33% in 1975 to 63% in 2000. Most of these women are working full-time—only about a third of women work part-time, and the percentages of those working part-time are roughly the same for women with children and those without children.

These general figures were confirmed in a recent survey of women working more than twenty hours a week, which found substantial continued labor force attachment among women following the birth of a child. Among the survey population, only about 16% of the women failed to return to the labor force within twelve months of giving birth, a rate, the authors noted, that was comparable to nonchildbearing women. . . . Significantly, the authors found that job turnover for women was reduced most effectively by extending leave periods and reducing overtime hours rather than through flexible work practices such as part-time work. With respect to the latter, the authors concluded, "We believe that reduced work options, such as part-time work, were often accompanied by such serious reductions in autonomy, upward mobility, benefits, and pay that they did not appeal to most new mothers."

One explanation for the misleading focus on women exiting the workforce to care for their children is that it is often assumed that all of the women who are not in the paid labor force have chosen that path in order to care for their children. It is worth noting, therefore, that many women remain out of the workforce both before and after they have children, and it is not the presence of children that explains their decision. Indeed, there is a core group, which represents roughly 20% of the working-age female population, that is never in the workforce, and a smaller group of women exit the labor force for significant periods of time after having children.

. . . The high cost of child care is often said to justify women's exit from the labor force when they have children, but there is little empirical support for this argument. For example, more than 40% of child care is provided by relatives, generally at little or no cost, and this practice is particularly common among low-wage earners. A recent survey by the Census Bureau found that the average cost of care provided through institutional settings was $326 per month, certainly not an insignificant amount but generally not so high as to justify women's exit from the labor market, particularly given that only about 20% of child care is provided through institutional settings.

Moreover, whatever overtime workers are putting in tends to compensate for the lack of substantial wage gains they have obtained over the last decade. Indeed, a better balance between work and family demands could be achieved through the development of a living wage, one that would free both men and women to spend more time outside of the paid labor market, accompanied by a generous benefits plan. . . .

We do not mean to suggest that the costs of childcare are unproblematic, or that balancing the demands inside and outside of the home is easy to achieve. Obviously, the high cost of much child care substantially burdens many families and deserves serious public attention in the form of greater public subsidies. What we mean to suggest is that the costs of child care rarely cause, or justify, women to exit the labor force, nor is it the case that it is impossible to achieve some reasonable balance [between work and home life]. . . .

One reason extensive state support has not substantially improved women's equality is that gender ideologies, particularly surrounding childrearing, have remained stubbornly resistant to change, even in the face of extensive public policies designed to facilitate childrearing. The strongest predictor of whether a woman is likely to be in the labor market, before or after she has children, is her gender ideology—those women who hold traditional views about the role of women are substantially more likely to be out of the labor market than those who have more egalitarian views regarding childrearing and family income. Polls continue to demonstrate preference for maternal care. In one recent poll, more than 40% of women believed it was best for a child to have a mother at home, and a *Washington Post* poll several years ago indicated that 40% of the respondents had a nostalgic longing for the traditional model of a male breadwinner with a stay-at-home wife. Other polls purport to demonstrate greater progress on the evolution of our social norms; the percentage of respondents in a Gallup poll who indicated that preschool aged children suffered if their mother worked declined from more than 70% to 33% in the last two decades. Although this figure may appear low, it is worth noting that it is slightly higher than the number of women who remain out of the labor force. . . . Ideological expressions of a preference for maternal care, however, does not mean that women would likewise prefer to provide maternal care if that means having to leave the workforce. . . . [E]mphasizing the importance of care work to women, and its status as a public good, suggests that women do, and should, privilege care work over their paid market work. . . .

Where does this leave us? We suggest that rather than stressing the importance and value of care work, we should focus our efforts on three particular areas as a way of seeking to enhance the life choices of women. These areas are education as both a means to provide more economic choices to women and of chipping away at the prevailing gender stereotypes; restructuring the school day and school year to accommodate wage labor, rather than concentrating solely on restructuring the workplace; and finally, rethinking the ways in which workplace discrimination continues to limit women's opportunities.

Without question, education remains the strongest vehicle for increasing women's life choices, as education provides the best means out of poverty and the greatest market opportunities. Women with college degrees or beyond have a labor force participation rate of 86%, while only 55% of women without high school degrees are in the labor force. There is likewise a sharp and well documented wage premium associated with increasing education levels: women with college degrees earn approximately 45% more than women who have obtained a high school degree and about 35% more than women with some college education. . . . Women already outpace men in educational attendance and achievement, but with fewer than 30% of the population holding college degrees, there is still wide room for growth. Currently about 65% of women enter college within two years of graduating from high school, and about two-thirds of those women enter a four-year college. However, only about 30% will ultimately earn a college degree, while many others will opt for a two-year associate degree or leave without obtaining any degree at all.

Obtaining a college degree provides a particularly important advantage for women compared to their male counterparts because women face a sharply limited low-skill market, whereas among male-dominated positions there are still well-paying careers available for high school graduates, though the number of such positions is decreasing with each passing year. Again, the data are revealing: in 1999, one third of women were in jobs paying poverty-level wages compared to 20% of men, and women with less than a high school education earned $2.39 less per hour than their male counterparts. African-American and Latina women stand to benefit the most from increasing their education levels, since they tend to be concentrated in the lowest rungs of the low-wage sector and will therefore receive the strongest wage boost from obtaining higher levels of education.

Education, of course, is no guarantee of equality, and even highly-educated women continue to face workplace barriers while confronting the many difficulties of balancing their work and family demands. At the same time, enhancing the educational attainment of women remains the best means for achieving greater equality and choices, and higher levels of education are also associated with more progressive views on issues involving gender equity. . . .

As noted earlier, restructuring the workplace around parental norms occupies a central place in the care work literature. These proposals have a strong appeal on many levels though there are substantial questions regarding how they might impact women's concerns relating to power and autonomy, and whether they are in the least bit feasible. It is worth noting that many European countries have far more extensive part-time sectors, and nowhere do we find a robust part-time market in which workers are not penalized in either wages or promotional opportunities for working part-time. Equally clear, wherever an extensive part-time market has been implemented, part-time work is almost exclusively women's work.

Rather than focusing solely on restructuring the workplace, we emphasize the need for restructuring the school day to make it more compatible with fulltime work. The structure of the school day has not advanced significantly from a time when women were at home waiting their child's arrival, and indeed, the schedule still largely presumes that an adult (generally a woman) will be available by mid-afternoon to assume care of a school-aged child. To ensure efficient use of school transportation, schools often start and end at different times for different grade levels—frequently beginning very early in the morning—with corresponding ending times, and these staggered schedules make it even more difficult for parents to combine work and their children's schooling.

In terms of accommodating working parents, a school day that is longer than the workday would be the best option, although such a lengthy day may be too difficult on many children and would surely be opposed on this ground. Continuing the school day until later in the afternoon would be helpful; alternatively providing more publicly-funded after-school programs would also provide some accommodation for working parents. Publicly-financed full-day preschool and daycare would also be necessary to enable women to have a more continuous labor force attachment. . . . Moreover, extended school days would offer significant benefits to many children, particularly if the publicly provided care was of high quality. We want to emphasize, however, that the benefits these policies might provide to children are of secondary importance . . . . Although the interests of women and children are certainly not mutually exclusive . . . what is good for children will not always be good for women, and when a conflict arises, as may be the case with a longer school day, we should be attentive to policies that benefit children at the expense of women's labor force activity. . . .

NOTES

1.   **Differing Perspectives.** The two excerpts offer different perspectives on barriers women face to obtaining more workplace equality. Which do you find more persuasive, and why? Which is more appealing? Joan Williams' arguments are more fully developed in her book UNBENDING GENDER: WHY FAMILY AND WORK CONFLICT AND WHAT TO DO ABOUT IT (1999).

2.   **The Role of Men.** One important difference between the two perspectives represented in the above excerpts is who has the responsibility for reducing the burdens women currently face in seeking to achieve some balance between the demands of the home and work. On the one hand, Joan Williams emphasizes the need for employers to restructure the workplace by allowing increased flexibility and creating better part-time jobs. Selmi and Cahn, on the other hand, stress the need to restructure inequities in the family while changing social expectations of mothers. In an earlier article, Selmi wrote: "[I]f there is to be greater equality for women in the workplace, it will be necessary for men to change their behavior, both in and out of the workplace, before employers will begin to change theirs. . . . Thus, increasing workplace equality will require persuading men to behave more like women, rather than trying to induce women to behave more like men. Achieving this objective would create a new workplace norm where all employees would be expected to have and spend time with their children, and employers would adapt to that reality." Michael Selmi, *Family Leave and the Gender Wage Gap*, 78 N.C. L. REV. 708, 709 (2000). Joan Williams, and others who advocate creating more flexibility in the workplace to accommodate women's childrearing, do not necessarily disagree with this perspective, but instead emphasize the reality that women continue to be responsible for a majority of childrearing and housework.

Although men increasingly express an interest in "equal" parenting, they have been slow to translate that interest into action. Why there has not been more change in parenting roles, is not easy to say, as there are many contributing factors. Joanna Grossman has observed:

Men do not take parental leave for a variety of familiar reasons. External factors are significant. Men may "worry they'll be 'daddy-tracked.'" Employers may react to requests for paternity leave with scorn or laughter. Even self-professed family-friendly workplaces may quietly discourage paternity leave or impliedly threaten men with career damage for taking leave made available by their own policies. Men fear that taking paternity leave will lead to retaliation or the loss of professional reputation, and conduct like that alleged in *Knussman v. Maryland* reinforces those fears. In *Knussman*, a state trooper requesting paternity leave was told by his supervisor that "God made women to have babies," and unless the trooper's wife was "in a coma or dead," he could not take the leave available to primary caregivers. . . . Even where paternity leave is not overtly or covertly discouraged, it is still viewed, at the very least, as unusual. For example, when a prominent New York Times reporter took a month of paternity leave, the newspaper's honest explanation for his absence in his column space was described by another reporter as "miraculous."

Beyond the external pressures, internal or personal factors can play a role in inhibiting men from taking leave. For many men, it is not "inwardly" acceptable to take time off to care for one's children, and they may find it emasculating to take time designated as "paternity leave." The fact that men who do take leave following the birth of a child rarely classify it as paternity leave evidences this phenomenon. Leave-taking men often try to have their leave classified as vacation or personal leave, rather than paternity leave, to avoid negative reactions from the employer or even co-workers as well as having to come to terms with their own desire to be home with children.

Joanna L. Grossman, *Job Security Without Equality: The Family and Medical Leave Act of 1993*, 15 Wash. U. J.L. & POL'Y 17, 34–35 (2004); *see also* Keith Cunningham-Parmet, *Men at Work, Fathers at Home: Uncovering the Masculine Face of Caregiver Discrimination*, 24 COLUM. J. GENDER & L. 253 (2013) (arguing that masculine norms deter men from asserting their own caregiving needs). Are there other reasons that might contribute to the persistence of gendered parenting practices? Should we seek to alter the patterns? Selmi has advocated distributing governmental contracts to firms that successfully induce men to take more family leave, as one means of disrupting existing patterns. *See* Selmi, *supra*, at 775–780. Others have advocated changing social perceptions of the value of work performed in the home so that we effectively change the gap in worth and prestige of labor market work and care work or work done in the home, which is currently not compensated. *See, e.g.*, Katherine Silbaugh, *Commodification and Women's Household Labor*, 9 YALE J. LAW & FEMINISM 81 (1997) (exploring the economics of household labor and the importance of treating carework as a commodity). What might be the advantages or disadvantages of the varying strategies?

3. The Wages of Motherhood. As Williams explains in her work excerpted above, working mothers suffer a greater wage penalty than working women who do not have children. A number of scholars have sought to assess the reason for this wage penalty, and have cast doubt on some of the traditional explanations, such as that mothers do not work as hard or do not invest as much in their work. *See, e.g.*,

Michelle J. Budig & Paula England, *The Wage Penalty for Motherhood*, 66 AMER. SOCIOLOGICAL Rev. 204 (2001) (concluding that wage penalty was not the result of mothers choosing jobs that offered greater flexibility); Jane Waldfogel, *The Effect of Children on Women's Wages*, 62 AMER. SOCIOLOGICAL REV. 209 (1997) (finding that traditional human capital factors of education, training and tenure did not fully explain wage penalty suffered by mothers). One study sought to explore whether mothers in the workforce have different experiences based on their education, race or the age of their children. The authors concluded:

> We find that younger children impose a higher penalty than older children and that black and white mothers face the same penalty, patterns that are consistent with a work effort explanation. But the largest differences in the penalty arise among education groups. Although more educated women are likely to have jobs in which effort is relatively important, we find that college-educated mothers do not, in fact, face any penalty for having children. And while high school dropouts face a 3% penalty if they work when their children are infants and toddlers, they do not bear any penalty for older children. Thus high school dropouts who delay their return to the work force until their children are older bear no motherhood wage penalty at all. By contrast, high school graduates—especially those who return to work when their children are older—face persistent penalties of 4–6% up until their children enter high school.

Deborah J. Anderson, Melissa Binder & Kate Krause, *The Motherhood Wage Penalty Revisited: Experience, Heterogeneity, Work Effort and Work-Schedule Flexibility*, 56 INDUS. & LABOR REL. REV. 273, 291 (2003). Based on these empirical findings, the authors observed that it was unlikely that women's "work effort" explained the differences, but rather, "we suggest that time, and in particular time during the middle of the day, poses a binding constraint that may contribute to the motherhood penalty. High school graduates are the most likely to have jobs that require their presence during regular office hours and the least likely to gain flexibility either by finding work at other hours or by taking work home in the evening. The work-schedule flexibility model provides a compelling explanation for observed education patterns in the motherhood wage penalty." *Id.* at 293. An important study that sent out resumes that differed only by the marital status of the applicants found that non-mothers were twice as likely to be called back for interviews as were women with children. *See* Shelley J. Correll, *Stephen Bernard & In Paik, Getting a Job: Is There a Motherhood Penalty?* 112 AMER. J. of SOCIOLOGY 1297 (2007). The authors also conducted a laboratory experiment with college students that produced similar results, including significantly lower starting salaries for mothers. *Id.* at 1316–19. More recently, authors found that the motherhood pay gap attenuates some for mothers in their forties, though the authors also noted that the penalty remains high (approximately 4% per child) for mothers who have three or more children. *See* Joan R. Kahn, Javier Garcia-Manglano & Suzanne M. Bianchi, *The Motherhood Penalty at Midlife: Long-Term Effects of Children on Women's Career*, 76 J. OF MARRIAGE & FAMILY 56 (2014).

4. Stereotypes About Working Mothers

BACK v. HASTINGS ON HUDSON UNION FREE SCH. DIST.
United States Court of Appeals for the Second Circuit
365 F.3d 107 (2004)

CALABRESI, CIRCUIT JUDGE.

In 1998, Plaintiff-Appellant Elana Back was hired as a school psychologist at the Hillside Elementary School ("Hillside") on a three-year tenure track. At the end of that period, when Back came up for review, she was denied tenure and her probationary period was terminated. Back subsequently brought this lawsuit, seeking damages and injunctive relief under 42 U.S.C. § 1983 (2000). She alleged that the termination violated her constitutional right to equal protection of the laws. Defendants-Appellees contend that Back was fired because she lacked organizational and interpersonal skills. Back asserts that the real reason she was let go was that the defendants presumed that she, as a young mother, would not continue to demonstrate the necessary devotion to her job, and indeed that she could not maintain such devotion while at the same time being a good mother.

This appeal [of the district court's grant of summary judgment] thus poses an important question, one that strikes at the persistent "fault line between work and family—precisely where sex-based overgeneralization has been and remains strongest." *Nev. Dep't of Human Res. v. Hibbs*, 538 U.S. 721 (2003). It asks whether stereotyping about the qualities of mothers is a form of gender discrimination, and whether this can be determined in the absence of evidence about how the employer in question treated fathers. We answer both questions in the affirmative. . . .

A. Background

The following facts, construed as they must be in the light most favorable to the plaintiff, were adduced in the court below.

i. Back's Qualifications

As the school psychologist at Hillside Elementary School, Elana Back counseled and conducted psychological evaluations of students, prepared reports for the Committee on Special Education, assisted teachers in dealing with students who acted out in class, worked with parents on issues related to their children, and chaired the "Learning Team," a group made up of specialists and teachers which conducted intensive discussions about individual students. Defendant-Appellee Marilyn Wishnie, the Principal of Hillside, and defendant-appellee Ann Brennan, the Director of Pupil Personnel Services for the District, were Back's supervisors. They were responsible for establishing performance goals for her position, and evaluating Back's work against these standards.

In the plaintiff's first two years at Hillside, Brennan and Wishnie consistently gave her excellent evaluations. In her first annual evaluation, on a scale where the highest score was "outstanding," and the second highest score was "superior," Back was deemed "outstanding" and "superior" in almost all categories, and "average" in only one. . . .

In her second year at Hillside, Back took approximately three months of maternity leave. After she returned, she garnered another "outstanding" evaluation from Brennan, who noted that she was "very pleased with Mrs. Back's performance during her second year at Hillside." Other contemporaneous observations also resulted in strongly positive feedback, for example, that Back "demonstrated her strong social/emotional skills in her work with parents and teachers, and most especially with students," and that she was "a positive influence in many areas, and continues to extend a great deal of effort and commitment to our work." In her annual evaluation, Back received higher marks than the previous year, with more "outstandings" and no "averages." . . .

ii. Alleged Stereotyping

Back asserts that things changed dramatically as her tenure review approached. The first allegedly discriminatory comments came in spring 2000, when Back's written evaluations still indicated that she was a very strong candidate for tenure. At that time, shortly after Back had returned from maternity leave, the plaintiff claims that Brennan, (a) inquired about how she was "planning on spacing [her] offspring," (b) said " 'please do not get pregnant until I retire,' " and (c) suggested that Back "wait until [her son] was in kindergarten to have another child."

Then, a few months into Back's third year at Hillside, on December 14, 2000, Brennan allegedly told Back that she was expected to work until 4:30 p.m. every day, and asked " 'What's the big deal. You have a nanny. This is what you [have] to do to get tenure.' " Back replied that she did work these hours. And Brennan, after reportedly reassuring Back that there was no concern about her job performance, told her that Wishnie expected her to work such hours. But, always according to Back, Brennan also indicated that Back should "maybe . . . reconsider whether [Back] could be a mother and do this job which [Brennan] characterized as administrative in nature," and that Brennan and Wishnie were "concerned that, if [Back] received tenure, [she] would work only until 3:15 p.m. and did not know how [she] could possibly do this job with children."

A few days later, on January 8, 2001, Brennan allegedly told Back for the first time that she might not support Back's tenure because of what Back characterizes as minor errors that she made in a report. According to Back, shortly thereafter Principal Wishnie accused her of working only from 8:15 a.m. to 3:15 p.m. and never working during lunch. When Back disputed this, Wishnie supposedly replied that "this was not [Wishnie's] impression and . . . that she did not know how she could perform my job with little ones. She told me that she worked from 7 a.m. to 7 p.m. and that she expected the same from me. If my family was my priority, she stated, maybe this was not the job for me." A week later, both Brennan and Wishnie reportedly told Back that this was perhaps not the job or the school district for her if she had "little ones," and that it was "not possible for [her] to be a good mother and have this job." The two also allegedly remarked that it would be harder to fire Back if she had tenure, and wondered "whether my apparent commitment to my job was an act. They stated that once I obtained tenure, I would not show the same level of commitment I had shown because I had little ones at home. They expressed concerns about my child care arrangements, though these had never caused me conflict with school assignments." . . .

iii. Denial of Tenure

. . . On May 29, 2001, Brennan and Wishnie sent a formal memo to Russell informing him that they could not recommend Back for tenure. Their reasons included (a) that although their formal reports had been positive, their informal interactions with her had been less positive, (b) that there were "far too many" parents and teachers who had "serious issues" with the plaintiff and did not wish to work with her, and (c) that she had persistent difficulties with the planning and organization of her work, and with inaccuracies in her reports, and that she had not shown improvement in this area, despite warnings. . . .

On or around June 13, 2001, Wishnie and Brennan filed the first negative evaluation of Back, which gave her several "below average" marks and charged her with being inconsistent, defensive, difficult to supervise, the source of parental complaints, and inaccurate in her reports. Their evaluation, which was submitted to Russell, concluded that Back should not be granted tenure. Around the same time, several parents who had apparently complained about Back were encouraged by Russell to put their concerns in writing.

[Back was subsequently denied tenure and the grievance filed by the union was denied. She then filed suit under 42 U.S.C. § 1983, which provides a cause of action for the deprivation of constitutional rights under the color of law, and the district court granted summary judgment to the defendants. This appeal followed.]

B. Discussion

. . . Individuals have a clear right, protected by the Fourteenth Amendment, to be free from discrimination on the basis of sex in public employment. *See Davis v. Passman*, 442 U.S. 228, 234–35 (1979). To make out such a claim, the plaintiff must prove that she suffered purposeful or intentional discrimination on the basis of gender. *See Vill. of Arlington Heights v. Metro. Hous. Dev. Corp.*, 429 U.S. 252, 264–65 (1977). Discrimination based on gender, once proven, can only be tolerated if the state provides an "exceedingly persuasive justification" for the rule or practice. United States v. Virginia, 518 U.S. 515, 524 (1996) (internal quotation marks omitted). The defendants in this case have made no claim of justification; thus our inquiry revolves solely around the allegation of discrimination. . . .

To show sex discrimination, Back relies upon a *Price Waterhouse* "stereotyping" theory. Accordingly, she argues that comments made about a woman's inability to combine work and motherhood are direct evidence of such discrimination. In *Price Waterhouse*, Ann Hopkins alleged that she was denied a partnership position because the accounting firm where she worked had given credence and effect to stereotyped images of women. Price Waterhouse, 490 U.S. at 235–36. Hopkins had been called, among other things, " 'macho' " and " 'masculine,' " was told she needed " 'a course at charm school,' " and was instructed to " 'walk more femininely, talk more femininely, dress more femininely, wear make-up, have her hair styled, and wear jewelry' " if she wanted to make partner. *Id.* at 235. Six members of the Court agreed that such comments bespoke gender discrimination. *See id.* at 251 ("We are beyond the day when an employer could evaluate employees by assuming or insisting that they matched the stereotype associated with their group. . . ."); *id.* at 258 (White, J., concurring); *id.* at 272–73 (O'Connor, J., concurring) (characterizing the "failure to conform to [gender] stereotypes" as a discriminatory criterion).

It is the law, then, that "stereotyped remarks can certainly be evidence that gender played a part" in an adverse employment decision. *Id.* at 251 (italics omitted). The principle of *Price Waterhouse*, furthermore, applies as much to the supposition that a woman *will* conform to a gender stereotype (and therefore will not, for example, be dedicated to her job), as to the supposition that a woman is unqualified for a position because she does *not* conform to a gender stereotype.

The instant case, however, foregrounds a crucial question: What constitutes a "gender-based stereotype"? *Price Waterhouse* suggested that this question must be answered in the particular context in which it arises, and without undue formalization. . . . Just as "it takes no special training to discern sex stereotyping in a description of an aggressive female employee as requiring 'a course at charm school,' " Price Waterhouse, 490 U.S. at 256, so it takes no special training to discern stereotyping in the view that a woman cannot "be a good mother" and have a job that requires long hours, or in the statement that a mother who received tenure "would not show the same level of commitment [she] had shown because [she] had little ones at home." These are not the kind of "innocuous words" that we have previously held to be insufficient, as a matter of law, to provide evidence of discriminatory intent. *See Weinstock*, 224 F.3d at 45.

Moreover, the Supreme Court itself recently took judicial notice of such stereotypes. In an opinion by Chief Justice Rehnquist, the Court concluded that stereotypes of this sort were strong and pervasive enough to justify prophylactic congressional action, in the form of the Family and Medical Leave Act:

> Stereotypes about women's domestic roles are reinforced by parallel stereotypes presuming a lack of domestic responsibilities for men. Because employers continued to regard the family as the woman's domain, they often denied men similar accommodations or discouraged them from taking leave. These mutually reinforcing stereotypes created a self-fulfilling cycle of discrimination that forced women to continue to assume the role of primary family caregiver, and fostered employers' stereotypical views about women's commitment to work and their value as employees. Those perceptions, in turn, Congress reasoned, lead to subtle discrimination that may be difficult to detect on a case-by-case basis.

Nev. Dep't of Human Res. v. Hibbs, 538 U.S. 721, 736 (2003).

The defendants argue that stereotypes about pregnant women or mothers are not based upon gender, but rather, "gender plus parenthood," thereby implying that such stereotypes cannot, without comparative evidence of what was said about fathers, be presumed to be "on the basis of sex." *Hibbs* makes pellucidly clear, however, that, at least where stereotypes are considered, the notions that mothers are insufficiently devoted to work, and that work and motherhood are incompatible, are properly considered to be, themselves, gender-based. . . .

Defendants are thus wrong in their contention that Back cannot make out a claim that survives summary judgment unless she demonstrates that the defendants treated similarly situated men differently. Back has admittedly proffered no evidence about the treatment of male administrators with young children. Although her case would be stronger had she provided or alleged the existence of such evidence, there is no requirement that such evidence be adduced. . . .

Defendants also fail in their claim that they are immune from Back's allegations simply because, in the year that Back was hired, 85% of the teachers employed at Hillside were women, and 71% of these women had children. . . . [A]lthough the jury is surely allowed to consider such comparative evidence, what matters is how *Back* was treated. Furthermore, the defendants make no mention of the number of men or women in *administrative* positions, nor of the age of any of the relevant children. Both details are essential if the comparative evidence adduced by the defendants is to be given any weight. . . . As a result, stereotyping of women as caregivers can by itself and without more be evidence of an impermissible, sex-based motive. . . .

. . . Accordingly we vacate the district court's grant of summary judgment, and remand the case for trial with respect to them. . . .

NOTES

1. **Section 1983 and Title VII.** Although the *Back* case was filed under the statute 42 U.S.C. § 1983, which provides a cause of action for the deprivation of constitutional rights by state actors, the court effectively applies Title VII law, and its analysis is likely to be applicable in cases filed under Title VII.

2. **Proving Discrimination.** What would Back have to prove in order to establish discrimination on remand? How does the case relate to the previous discussion arising from the work of Williams and Selmi and Cahn?

In fact, the case proceeded to a jury trial against Wishnie and Brennan, the two individual defendants, and the jury found for the defendants, presumably concluding that Back was fired for legitimate performance-related reasons, rather than discrimination based on stereotypes about working mothers. *See Back v. Hastings-on-Hudson*, 2005 U.S. App. LEXIS 28973 (2d Cir. Dec. 28, 2005) (affirming jury verdict).

3. **Family Responsibilities Discrimination ("FRD").** The *Back* case is representative of an emerging trend of cases often labeled as involving family responsibilities discrimination ("FRD"), which has been defined as: "discrimination against employees based on their responsibilities to care for family members. It includes pregnancy discrimination, discrimination against mothers and fathers, and discrimination against workers with other family caregiving responsibilities." Joan C. Williams & Stephanie Bornstein, *The Evolution of "FRD": Family Responsibilities Discrimination & Developments in the Law of Stereotyping and Implicit Bias*, 59 HASTINGS L.J. 1311, 1313 (2008). Although the FRD label is relatively new,

the concept traces its roots to an early Title VII case that recognized what the Court termed "sex-plus" discrimination, discrimination against a subclass of women, in many instances mothers. *See Phillips v. Martin-Marietta Corp.*, 400 U.S. 542 (1971) (*per curiam*) (allowing challenge to employer's policy of refusing to accept applications from women with school-age children). The First Circuit Court of Appeals has discussed the line of cases reaching back to *Phillips* and involving current claims of women who are discriminated against because of their childcare responsibilities:

> In the simplest terms, these cases stand for the proposition that unlawful sex discrimination occurs when an employer takes an adverse job action on the assumption that a woman, because she is a woman, will neglect her job responsibilities in favor or her presumed childcare responsibilities. It is undoubtedly true that if the work performance of a woman (or a man, for that matter) actually suffers due to childcare responsibilities . . . an employer is free to respond accordingly, at least without incurring liability under Title VII. However, an employer is not free to assume that a woman, because she is a woman, will necessarily be a poor worker because of family responsibilities. The essence of Title VII in this context is that women have the right to prove their mettle in the work arena with the burden of stereotypes regarding whether they can fulfill their responsibilities.

Chadwick v. Wellpoint, 561 F.3d 38, 44–45 (1st Cir. 2009). In *Chadwick*, the court found there was sufficient evidence for a jury to infer that the plaintiff was denied a promotion because she had four young children. *Id.* at 48. *See also Lettieri v. Equant, Inc.*, 478 F.3d 640 (4th Cir. 2007) ("There is powerful evidence showing a discriminatory attitude at Equant toward female managers—particularly female managers who have children at home and commute long distances."). The EEOC has issued an important guidance on discrimination against caregivers, and the WorkLife Center at Hastings Law School tracks the developing case law. For the EEOC guidance see *EEOC Enforcement Guide: Unlawful Treatment of Workers with Caregiving Responsibilities*, No. 915.002 (2007), and the WorkLife Law project on Family Responsibilities Discrimination can be found at http://www.worklifelaw.org/FRD.html.

Part Four

GOVERNMENT INTERVENTION FOR THE PUBLIC GOOD: LEGISLATING A SAFETY NET

So far we have been concentrating on the conditions of employment—the restrictions that govern the hiring and termination of employees as well as the general conditions of one's employment. The employment relationship, however, has grown to include far more than just a paycheck for work done. Employee benefits—as well as the regulations governing worker safety and overtime pay— have become a critical aspect of work. In the United States we have historically relied upon the employment relationship to provide health insurance, pension income, as well as insurance against spells of unemployment or disabling injuries. Many employers offer substantially more benefits, including life insurance, long-term care insurance, dental insurance, mortgage assistance, gym memberships, discounted parking or automobile insurance, all of which lead employees to become more dependent on their particular job and employer. As we discussed in Part I, losing a job can mean losing one's life security, and by the same measure, not having a job can mean being deprived of many of life's essentials.

One issue we want to consider in this Part is how we have come to rely so heavily on the employment relationship to provide so many diverse social and economic functions. To take one example, discussed further below, why do we provide health insurance through employment? In our system of health insurance, the vast majority of those who are insured receive their insurance through their, or a family member's, employer, which remains true even after the passage of the Affordable Care Act ("ACA"). In most other countries, the government provides health insurance, funded through either general revenues or employment-related taxes. Similarly, pensions are publicly-funded in many other countries, while in the United States our primary means of providing pension income is through employer-sponsored pension plans. In the case of health insurance and pension plans, employers effectively obtain tax subsidies because they receive deductions for their

761

related costs and expenses, so in an indirect way these plans are funded through public funds, but they are managed and provided by private entities.

We also look to the employment relationship to relieve the government's public welfare burden. In Chapter 9, we explained that a major impetus behind the American With Disabilities Act ("ADA") was to move those who were capable of working from the public disability rolls to employer payrolls. The welfare system was likewise overhauled in the 1990s to require those receiving public support to obtain employment both as a way to ensure work opportunities were available but also as a way of reducing government financial obligations. *See* Personal Responsibility and Work Opportunity Reconciliation Act of 1996, Pub. L. No. 104-193, 110 Stat. 2105 (codified in sections of 8 U.S.C. and 42 U.S.C.). In this respect, as you work through this chapter, you should consider the question of our expectations of work: what is it that we expect from work, and why? As a policy matter, does it make sense to use the employment relationship to serve so many social needs?

Another issue raised by this chapter is how government regulation of work conditions fits in with the general employment-at-will model. In the area of employment conditions, the workplace is subjected to extensive regulation, most of it by the federal government. The Fair Labor Standards Act ("FLSA") regulates pay by establishing a minimum wage and requiring employers to provide overtime pay to many employees when they work more than 40 hours in a week. The Occupational Safety and Health Act ("OSHA") is a comprehensive regulatory scheme designed to reduce serious workplace injuries, and the Employee Retirement Income Security Act ("ERISA") regulates pensions and welfare benefit plans, and does so largely by displacing state regulation. Similarly, the Workers' Compensation system, although state operated, is a mandatory remedial scheme that provides benefits and rehabilitative services for workers injured in connection with their jobs. These statutes all ensure pervasive governmental regulation of the workplace. Yet, perhaps the most fundamental tenet of that relationship, namely the ability to retain one's job, is left largely unregulated through the preservation of the employment-at-will rule. Can these principles be reconciled?

Many have argued that governmental regulation, even as to matters as basic as worker safety or wages and hours, is unnecessary for reasons that largely reflect the arguments that have been advanced in favor of the employment-at-will relationship. For example, Kip Viscusi has suggested—more to illustrate a point than to offer a proposal—that worker safety could reliably be left to market forces. *See* W. KIP VISCUSI, FATAL TRADEOFFS 81-222 (1992). Under this theory, employers would have to pay higher wages for more dangerous workplaces, and to the extent employees preferred the higher wages to a safe workplace, an unregulated market would permit that choice. Alternatively, in a truly dangerous workplace, the wages an employer would have to pay to attract competent employees would likely exceed the cost of appropriate safety measures, thus offering incentives to create an efficiently safe workplace. As a society, we have chosen not to allow the market to determine appropriate safety levels, but how can that be distinguished from the employment-at-will relationship? The same is true with respect to the wage and hour regulation; as a society we have chosen to establish minimum and maximum standards out of concerns for creating a just and fair workplace and to ensure that those with the least ability to protect themselves—employees at the bottom rung of the employment ladder—are afforded basic governmental protections. How do we decide what those basic protections ought to be? Should workers be permitted to waive those protections? This Part will explore that question.

Employee benefits can be broadly divided into two categories: (1) mandatory and (2) discretionary. Many of the benefits employers provide are mandatory in nature, including unemployment and workers' compensation insurance and social security, both towards retirement and disability. All of these programs are funded through a combination of employee and employer taxes and are required of all employees regardless of whether they ever use the benefits. (A tenured professor, for example, still pays unemployment insurance.) Discretionary benefits include health and pension plans, as well as the other fringe benefits listed above with life insurance the most common additional benefit. The ACA changes the landscape with respect to health benefits, and as discussed later in this section, large employers will now either have to provide health insurance to their full-time employees or pay a penalty if they choose not to provide insurance. But there remains no mandatory provision for retirement, and the risks of saving for retirement have been increasingly shifted to employees. The costs of these benefits raise one further introductory issue. For economists, and most employers, benefits are treated as a form of compensation. In other words, when an employer calculates the cost of hiring an employee, that cost will include the cost of the benefits provided. If an employee receives $15 per hour as a wage, and benefits cost an additional $5 per hour, then the employer will see that employee as having a total cost of $20 per hour. There are often tradeoffs between these costs. If the costs of health insurance rise, that cost may directly influence wages, either through a wage cut or more likely by holding down a wage increase. These tradeoffs are frequently implicit rather than explicit, but there is plainly a relationship between the costs of benefits and an employee's salary.

This Part will explore some of the ways the government intervenes in the market to create a social safety net, focusing on wage and hours legislation, health and pension benefits, and worker safety. Throughout this Part we will also raise questions about reforming, or altering, the existing safety net.

Chapter 11

THE REGULATION OF WAGES AND HOURS

A central feature of the employment relationship is the exchange of labor for compensation. Understandably, then, wages and hours are core issues around which worker solidarity has been forged and workers have mobilized. Collective pressure by labor unions was instrumental in limiting oppressive working hours and ensuring a fair wage for work performed. Labor Day is one symbolic product of such pressure: Labor Day became a federal holiday in 1894 and initially represented "the only two-day weekend in an entire year for a huge segment of the working population." Scott D. Miller, *Revitalizing the FLSA*, 19 Hofstra Lab. & Emp. L.J. 1, 15 (2001). Some of the bloodiest battles revolved around workers' efforts to control their worktime, and to capture time for family, social, and leisure activities. These struggles were closely linked to concerns about unemployment and job insecurity. Fewer workers working more hours meant that many others were unemployed. Fear of joblessness in turn kept the employed in thrall to longer hours and depressed wages. Reform of the system was possible only by class-wide mobilization designed to spread employment to more workers by limiting working hours.

The Fair Labor Standards Act of 1938 ("FLSA"), enacted as part of the New Deal, sought to quell the labor unrest and to redress the rampant unemployment and poverty that characterized the Depression era by spreading work across the laboring class. The Act established a federal minimum hourly wage and imposed a financial penalty (known as the overtime premium) on employers who required employees to work more than a statutorily-imposed weekly hours norm. The linkage between wages and hours was designed to create an incentive for employers to hire more workers to work shorter hours. The Act has survived to the present day with relatively minor amendments, and its basic structure remains intact. The FLSA is the primary wage and hour statute applicable to most workers, although state wage and hour legislation (permitted under the FLSA to the extent that states impose higher standards than those established by federal law) is a powerful tool in some states. The FLSA also contains important provisions regulating oppressive child labor. Finally, it is the repository for the Equal Pay Act.

The FLSA is the paradigm minimum standards employment statute. It thus furnishes an excellent opportunity to study the effort to redress structural issues in the employment relationship legislatively rather than through collective bargaining or the common law. Moreover, wage and hour issues are among the most commonly litigated questions in modern employment law practice. They can be initiated as individual claims or as group claims under the FLSA's collective action provisions. Because employers often treat groups of employees the same with respect to wages and hours, FLSA collective wage and hour actions are potentially expensive. Plaintiffs' lawyers have pursued FLSA claims vigorously; the number of FLSA lawsuits filed increased by 514% between 1991 and 2012. Government Accountability Office, *Fair Labor Standards Act: The Department of Labor Should Develop a More Systematic Approach to Developing Its Guidance*, Report No. 14-69, at 6, Dec. 2013, *available at* http://www.gao.gov/assets/660/659772.pdf. Ninety-five percent of the FLSA cases filed in 2012 involved violations of overtime pay requirements; 32% involved violations of minimum wage laws; and 14% involved unlawful retaliation claims. *Id.* at 10. Thirty percent involved claims of "off-the-clock" work. Thirteen percent involved claims of misclassification of employees as independent contractors. *Id.* at 15–16. Fifty-eight percent were filed as individual claims, while 40% were filed as collective actions. *Id.* at 16. A thorough study of the FLSA could easily consume an entire course. Our coverage of the statute will be at a survey level, with a deeper delve into a few of the most frequently litigated areas.

A. HISTORICAL ORIGINS

Government regulation of wages and hours began in colonial times. Although the earliest regulation imposed caps on the wages of skilled workers (to prevent them from leveraging their high skills and small numbers into even-higher wages), most of the early agitation—and thus, regulation—focused on establishing limits on oppressive working hours.

Scott D. Miller, *Revitalizing the FLSA*
19 HOFSTRA LAB. & EMP. L.J. 1, 7, 10–12, 14 (2001)

. . . Maximum hours labor standards arose from the "short hours movements" of the late nineteenth and early twentieth centuries. The short hours movements were a major source of worker solidarity and growth of the United States labor movement, embracing workers' desire for personal freedom (time) from industrial order, and freedom for home life and cultural matters outside wage and job concerns. . . .

. . . .

Fighting for worker control over time (work hours and free time), labor activists and reformers argued that shorter work hours would protect public health and safety (reducing occupational injuries by reducing worker fatigue), welfare (reducing labor strife and providing workers with more time for personal, home, community, and cultural life) and morals (eradicate overwork and sweatshops).

. . . .

Serious public consideration for shorter work hours began in the United States during the close of the colonial period when journeymen sought to limit the workday to twelve or fourteen hours. Employers consistently opposed shorter work hours and traditional work habits throughout the nation's history, fearing the loss of their competitive positions within and outside the country.

By the early nineteenth century, protesting artisans, craftsmen, mechanics, and workers formed labor unions and political parties advocating a shorter hour (from ten hours to eight hours) day. This was part of a struggle against the discipline of time (symbolized by the mill clock) and the growing ethics of commercialism.

Craftspersons upheld the traditions of their trade and asserted their independence from time discipline by enforcing their stint (production quota) and work rules (rules specifying who would perform which work, how, when, and at what pace it would occur) through collective action—construction is the only major industry today where skilled workers still control their own work pace. Motivated by exhaustion, women working in textile mills joined the movement in the 1840s.

After the Civil War, the connection between wages and hours worked (the wage system) revived the question Americans thought "had been resolved by slave emancipation—the question of buying, selling, and owning human property." Wage contracts were thus viewed differently than other bargains; a free person's labor was distinct from the self, otherwise a person's sale of his/her time was analogous to wage slavery.

In 1886, Samuel Gompers (the leader of the Federation of Organized Trades and Labor Unions—the predecessor of the American Federation of Labor) called for a nationwide strike by all workers on May 1st to "achieve the shorter workweek—ten hours' pay for eight hours' work." Approximately 250,000 workers participated in what became the first general strike in the history of the international labor movement. In total, there were more than 1500 strikes and lockouts nationwide during 1886 involving over 600,000 workers, "most of them fighting for the eight-hour day." . . .

As late as 1915, "the Illinois State Federation of Labor endorsed the eight-hour day 'by any means we can get it. . . .'" The Saturday and Sunday Sabbath closing and eight-hour day initiatives advanced by Illinois barbers, garment workers, and downtown Chicago store clerks were replaced by the "one day's rest in seven movement" promoted by organized labor. The later movement also addressed concerns over unemployment. Reformers believed that the economy could spread employment to more individuals if employers scheduled more employees to work shorter hours, rather than fewer employees to work longer hours. . . .

_____

By the 1800s, states began to enact restrictions on hours of work, particularly for women, minors and those working in hazardous occupations. In 1840, the federal government established a ten-hour workday for workers at government shipyards; by 1868, it had reduced daily hours for its workforce to eight. By the early 1900s, federal enactments imposing limits on hours appeared in the maritime and railroad industries. *See* Scott D. Miller, *Revitalizing the FLSA*, 19 HOFSTRA LAB. & EMP. L. J. 1, 15–16 (2001).

The earliest state statutes were hortatory in nature, urging employer compliance but lacking enforcement provisions and allowing for individual waiver by contract. Increasingly, however, state legislatures began to enact protective labor legislation containing nonwaivable limits on work hours or minimum wage rates designed to correct market abuses. These statutes were initially denounced as offensive to both parties' freedom of contract. In *Lochner v. New York*, 198 U.S. 45 (1905), a divided Court struck down a New York state law limiting the number of hours that bakers could work per week in bakeries (the statute made it a criminal misdemeanor for an employer to require such a worker to labor for more than 60 hours per week or 10 hours per day). Distinguishing cases involving the valid exercise of the state's police power to protect health and safety, such as state legislation limiting the employment of workers to 8 hours per day in underground mines or smelting operations, the Court found that there was no justification for interfering with the liberty of person or contract in the occupation of baker. Bakers as a class were not in need of protection, and the health and safety concerns which justified limiting the hours of miners and smelting workers were not present. Thus, the law constituted an arbitrary interference with the freedom to contract as to labor. The Court concluded:

> It seems to us that the real object and purpose [of this statute] were simply to regulate the hours of labor between the master and his employees . . . in a private business, not dangerous in any degree to morals or in any real and substantial degree to the health of the employees. Under such circumstances the freedom of master and employee to contract with each other in relation to their employment, and in defining the same, cannot be prohibited or interfered with, without violating the Federal Constitution.

198 U.S. at 64.

Subsequently, the Court acknowledged states' authority to legislate minimum standards for workers' protection in a case involving women workers, *Muller v. Oregon*, 208 U.S. 412 (1908). There the Court upheld an Oregon statute limiting the employment of women in mechanical establishments, factories, or laundries to no more than ten hours per day. The Court distinguished *Lochner* on the grounds that the regulation of the working hours of women rested upon powerful justifications that did not apply to the regulation of hours of male workers. Specifically, "the physical organization of women," "her maternal functions," "the rearing and education of the children," and "the maintenance of the home" justified state intervention to protect women, whose "physical structure and . . . performance of maternal functions place her at a disadvantage in the struggle for subsistence." *Muller*, 208 U.S. at 419, 421.

Not long thereafter, however, the Court struck down a minimum wage law applicable to women and children employed in the District of Columbia, reasoning that the statute interfered with the freedom of contract guaranteed by the Fifth Amendment's due process clause. *See Adkins v. Children's* Hospital, 261 U.S. 525 (1923). The *Adkins* Court limited *Muller v. Oregon* to its historical context, noting that revolutionary changes in the intervening years had reduced the inequality of the sexes in contractual, political and civil status "almost, if not quite, to the vanishing point." *Adkins*, 261 U.S. at 553.

In *A.L.A. Schechter Poultry Corp. v. United States*, 295 U.S. 495 (1935), the Court struck down the National Industrial Recovery Act of 1933 (NIRA), which had authorized the National Recovery Administration to limit hours of work per industry to an 8-hour day, 40-hour week in order to spread work across a populace paralyzed by the economic effects of the Depression. The Court found the NIRA an unconstitutional delegation of legislative power to the executive branch. Outside the special circumstances of workers who required maximum hours protection on health and safety grounds, hopes for governmental regulation of hours appeared increasingly dim.

WEST COAST HOTEL CO. v. PARRISH
United States Supreme Court
300 U.S. 379 (1937)

Mr. Chief Justice Hughes delivered the opinion of the Court.

This case presents the question of the constitutional validity of the minimum wage law of the state of Washington.

The act, entitled "Minimum Wages for Women," authorizes the fixing of minimum wages for women and minors. It provides:

"Section 1. The welfare of the State of Washington demands that women and minors be protected from conditions of labor which have a pernicious effect on their health and morals. The State of Washington, therefore, exercising herein its police and sovereign power declares that inadequate wages and unsanitary conditions of labor exert such pernicious effect.

"Sec. 2. It shall be unlawful to employ women or minors in any industry or occupation within the State of Washington under conditions of labor detrimental to their health or morals; and it shall be unlawful to employ women workers in any industry within the State of Washington at wages which are not adequate for their maintenance. . . ."

Further provisions required the Commission to ascertain the wages and conditions of labor of women and minors within the state. Public hearings were to be held. If after investigation the Commission found that in any occupation, trade or industry the wages paid to women were "inadequate to supply them necessary cost of living and to maintain the workers in health," the Commission was empowered to call a conference of representatives of employers and employees together with disinterested persons representing the public. The conference was to recommend to the Commission, on its request, an estimate of a minimum wage adequate for the purpose above stated, and on the approval of such a recommendation it became the duty of the Commission to issue an obligatory order fixing minimum wages. . . . Special licenses were authorized for the employment of women who were "physically defective or crippled by age or otherwise," and also for apprentices, at less than the prescribed minimum wage. . . .

The appellant conducts a hotel. The appellee Elsie Parrish was employed as a chambermaid and (with her husband) brought this suit to recover the difference between the wages paid her and the minimum wage fixed pursuant to the state law. The minimum wage was $14.50 per week of 48 hours. The appellant challenged the act as repugnant to the due process clause of the Fourteenth Amendment of the Constitution of the United States. The Supreme Court of the state, reversing the trial court, sustained the statute and directed judgment for the plaintiffs. *Parrish v. West Coast Hotel Co.*, 55 P. (2d) 1083. The case is here on appeal.

The appellant relies upon the decision of this Court in *Adkins v. Children's Hospital*, 261 U.S. 525, which held invalid the District of Columbia Minimum Wage Act (40 Stat. 960) which was attacked under the due process clause of the Fifth Amendment. . . .

The Supreme Court of Washington has upheld the minimum wage statute of that state. It has decided that the statute is a reasonable exercise of the police power of the state. In reaching that conclusion, the state court has invoked principles long established by this Court in the application of the Fourteenth Amendment. The state court has refused to regard the decision in the *Adkins* case as determinative and has pointed to our decisions both before and since that case as justifying its position. We are of the opinion that this ruling of the state court demands on our part a re-examination of the *Adkins* case. The importance of the question, in which many states having similar laws are concerned, the close division by which the decision in the *Adkins* case was reached, and the economic conditions which have supervened, and in the light of which the reasonableness of the exercise of the protective power of the State must be considered, make it not only appropriate, but we think imperative, that in deciding the present case the subject should receive fresh consideration. . . .

The principle which must control our decision is not in doubt. The constitutional provision invoked is the due process clause of the Fourteenth Amendment governing the states, as the due process clause invoked in the *Adkins* case governed Congress. In each case the violation alleged by those attacking minimum wage regulation for women is deprivation of freedom of contract. What is this freedom? The Constitution does not speak of freedom of contract. It speaks of liberty and prohibits the deprivation of liberty without due process of law. In prohibiting that deprivation, the Constitution does not recognize an absolute and uncontrollable liberty. Liberty in each of its phases has its history and connotation. But the liberty safeguarded is liberty in a social organization which requires the protection of law against the evils which menace the health, safety, morals, and welfare of the people. Liberty under the Constitution is thus necessarily subject to the restraints of due process, and regulation which is reasonable in relation to its subject and is adopted in the interests of the community is due process. . . .

This power under the Constitution to restrict freedom of contract has had many illustrations. That it may be exercised in the public interest with respect to contracts between employer and employee is undeniable. Thus statutes have been sustained limiting employment in underground mines and smelters to eight hours a day (*Holden v. Hardy*, 169 U.S. 366); in requiring redemption in cash of store orders or other evidences of indebtedness issued in the payment of wages (*Knoxville Iron Co. v. Harbison*, 183 U.S. 13); . . . in prohibiting contracts limiting liability for injuries to employees (*Chicago, Burlington & Quincy R. Co. v. McGuire, supra*); in limiting hours of work of employees in manufacturing establishments (*Bunting v. Oregon*, 243 U.S. 426); and in maintaining workmen's compensation laws (*New York Central R. Co. v. White*, 243 U.S. 188; *Mountain Timber Co. v. Washington*, 243 U.S. 219). In dealing with the relation of employer and employed, the Legislature has necessarily a wide field of discretion in order that there may be suitable protection of health and safety, and that peace and good order may be promoted through regulations designed to insure wholesome conditions of work and freedom from oppression.

The point that has been strongly stressed that adult employees should be deemed competent to make their own contracts was decisively met nearly forty years ago in *Holden v. Hardy, supra*, where we pointed out the inequality in the footing of the parties. We said (Id., 169 U.S. 366, 397):

> "The legislature has also recognized the fact, which the experience of legislators in many states has corroborated, that the proprietors of these establishments and their operatives do not stand upon an equality, and that their interests are, to a certain extent, conflicting. The former naturally desire to obtain as much labor as possible from their employees, while the latter are often induced by the fear of discharge to conform to regulations which their judgment, fairly exercised, would pronounce to be detrimental to their health or strength. In other words, the proprietors lay down the rules, and the laborers are practically constrained to obey them. In such cases self-interest is often an unsafe guide, and the legislature may properly interpose its authority."

And we added that the fact "that both parties are of full age, and competent to contract, does not necessarily deprive the state of the power to interfere, where the parties do not stand upon an equality, or where the public health demands that one party to the contract shall be protected against himself." "The state still retains an interest in his welfare, however reckless he may be. The whole is no greater than the sum of all the parts, and when the individual health, safety, and welfare are sacrificed or neglected, the state must suffer."

It is manifest that this established principle is peculiarly applicable in relation to the employment of women in whose protection the state has a special interest. That phase of the subject received elaborate consideration in *Muller v. Oregon* (1908) 208 U.S. 412, where the constitutional authority of the state to limit the working hours of women was sustained. . . . We emphasized the need of protecting women against oppression despite her possession of contractual rights. . . . We concluded that the limitations which the statute there in question "places upon her contractual powers, upon her right to agree with her employer, as to the time she shall labor" were "not imposed solely for her benefit, but also largely for the benefit of all. . . ."

The minimum wage to be paid under the Washington statute is fixed after full consideration by representatives of employers, employees, and the public. It may be assumed that the minimum wage is fixed in consideration of the services that are performed in the particular occupations under normal conditions. Provision is made for special licenses at less wages in the case of women who are incapable of full service. The statement of MR. JUSTICE HOLMES in the *Adkins* case is pertinent: "This statute does not compel anybody to pay anything. It simply forbids employment at rates below those fixed as the minimum requirement of health and right living. It is safe to assume that women will not be employed at even the lowest wages allowed unless they earn them, or unless the employer's business can sustain the burden. In short the law in its character and operation is like hundreds of so-called police laws that have been up-held." 261 U.S. 525, p. 570. And CHIEF JUSTICE TAFT forcibly pointed out the consideration which is basic in a statute of this character: "Legislatures which adopt a requirement of maximum hours or minimum wages may be presumed to believe that when sweating employers are prevented from paying unduly low wages by positive law they will continue their business, abating that part of their profits, which were wrung from the necessities of their employees, and will concede the better terms required by the law, and that while in individual cases, hardship may result, the restriction will enure to the benefit of the general class of employees in whose interest the law is passed, and so to that of the community at large." *Id.*, p. 563.

We think that the views thus expressed are sound and that the decision in the *Adkins* case was a departure from the true application of the principles governing the regulation by the state of the relation of employer and employed . . .

With full recognition of the earnestness and vigor which characterize the prevailing opinion in the *Adkins* case, we find it impossible to reconcile that ruling with these well-considered declarations. What can be closer to the public interest than the health of women and their protection from unscrupulous and overreaching employers? And if the protection of women is a legitimate end of the exercise of state power, how can it be said that the requirement of the payment of a minimum wage fairly fixed in order to meet the very necessities of existence is not an admissible means to that end? The Legislature of the state was clearly entitled to consider the situation of women in employment, the fact that they are in the class receiving the least pay, that their bargaining power is relatively weak, and that they are the ready victims of those who would take advantage of their necessitous circumstances. The Legislature was entitled to adopt measures to reduce the evils of the "sweating system," the exploiting of workers at wages so low as to be insufficient to meet the bare cost of living, thus making their very helplessness the occasion of a most injurious competition. The Legislature had the right to consider that its minimum wage requirements would be an important aid in carrying out its policy of protection. The adoption of similar requirements by many states evidences a deep-seated conviction both as to the presence of the evil and as to the means adapted to check it. Legislative response to that conviction cannot be regarded as arbitrary or capricious and that is all we have to decide. Even if the wisdom of the policy be regarded as debatable and its effects uncertain, still the Legislature is entitled to its judgment.

There is an additional and compelling consideration which recent economic experience has brought into a strong light. The exploitation of a class of workers who are in an unequal position with respect to bargaining power and are thus relatively defenseless against the denial of a living wage is not only detrimental to their health and well being, but casts a direct burden for their support upon the community. What these workers lose in wages the taxpayers are called upon to pay. The bare cost of living must be met. We may take judicial notice of the unparalleled demands for relief which arose during the recent period of depression and still continue to an alarming extent despite the degree of economic recovery which has been achieved. . . . The community is not bound to provide what is in effect a subsidy for unconscionable employers. The community may direct its law-making power to correct the abuse which springs from their selfish disregard of the public interest. The argument that the legislation in question constitutes an arbitrary discrimination, because it does not extend to men, is unavailing. This Court has frequently held that the legislative authority, acting within its proper field, is not bound to extend its regulation to all cases which it might possibly reach. The Legislature "is free to recognize degrees of harm and it may confine its restrictions to those classes of cases where the need is deemed to be clearest." . . . This familiar principle has repeatedly been applied to legislation which singles out women, and particular classes of women, in the exercise of the State's protective power. Their relative need in the presence of the evil, no less than the existence of the evil itself, is a matter for the legislative judgment.

Our conclusion is that the case of *Adkins v. Children's Hospital, supra*, should be, and it is, overruled. The judgment of the Supreme Court of the state of Washington is affirmed.

NOTES

1. **The Court's "Switch In Time."** What accounts for the Court's dramatic about-face in *West Coast Hotel* from its earlier defense of freedom of contract and equality of bargaining position in *Lochner* and *Adkins*? Some theorize that *West Coast Hotel* was the Court's response to the tumultuous political period triggered when the Court struck down the NIRA in *Schechter Poultry*. Following his landslide victory in the 1936 Presidential election, President Roosevelt declared his determination to overcome judicial opposition to his New Deal legislative platform and threatened to "pack" the Court by adding up to six new judges, one for each judge who failed to retire at age 70. The *West Coast Hotel* Court's "switch in time" saved the nine justices and ensured the future constitutionality of minimum standards legislation, as well as the National Labor Relations Act. *See* Jonathan Grossman, *Fair Labor Standards Act of 1938: Maximum Struggle for a Minimum Wage*, 101 MONTHLY LAB. REV. 22 (June, 1978); *but see* Richard D. Friedman, *Switching Time and Other Thought Experiments: The Hughes Court and Constitutional Transformation*, 142 U. PA. L. REV. 1891, 1896 (1994) (arguing that the swing votes on the Court during this period—Justice Hughes and Justice Roberts—were not motivated solely by political pressure).

2. **Protective Statutes for Women as an "Entering Wedge" Strategy.** Commentators have also suggested that the Court's decision in *Muller v. Oregon*, 208 U.S. 412 (1908) (upholding Oregon law limiting the number of hours that women could work in a single day because of the state's interest in protecting women's maternal health) provided an "entering wedge" that laid the foundation for gender-neutral laws protecting all workers. Although many feminists have criticized protective labor laws for women on the ground that they reinforce gendered stereotypes, some historians argue that where the choice was between laws protecting women and no protective legislation for workers at all, gendered laws were groundbreaking.

3. **The Demise of *Lochner* and the Rise of Protective Legislation.** *West Coast Hotel* signaled the demise of the *Lochner* rationale. In subsequent cases, the Court deferred to state legislative enactments and began upholding state statutes against due process challenges. The Court's "switch in time" encouraged labor advocates to work toward a federal bill establishing fair labor standards. After a year of political struggles, the Fair Labor Standards Act (FLSA) was enacted in 1938. The Congressional declaration of policy for the FLSA listed <u>five justifications for federal protective legislation:</u>

> The Congress finds that the existence, in industries engaged in commerce or in the production of goods for commerce, of labor conditions

detrimental to the maintenance of the minimum standard of living necessary for health, efficiency, and general well-being of workers (1) causes commerce and the channels and instrumentalities of commerce to be used to spread and perpetuate such labor conditions among the workers of the several States; (2) burdens commerce and the free flow of goods in commerce; (3) constitutes an unfair method of competition in commerce; (4) leads to labor disputes burdening and obstructing commerce and the free flow of goods in commerce; and (5) interferes with the orderly and fair marketing of goods in commerce. . . .

29 U.S.C. § 202(a).

The FLSA linked minimum wages and maximum hours in a single piece of legislation. The Act established a minimum wage of 25 cents per hour for the first year it became effective, increasing to 30 cents in the second year and to 40 cents in the seventh year. Premium pay at 1.5 times the workers' regular rate of pay was required for all hours worked in excess of 44 per week (later reduced to 42 hours per week in the second year of the statute's efficacy, and to 40 hours per week in the third year and thereafter). The Act also contained child labor provisions prohibiting the interstate shipment of goods produced by businesses employing children under the age of 16 years, or under the age of 18 years in hazardous industries. The Court soon upheld the statute against a constitutional challenge in *United States v. Darby*, 312 U.S. 100 (1941), citing *West Coast Hotel.* The Court reasoned that the statute's minimum wage and maximum hours provisions were a constitutional exercise of Congress's commerce power and did not violate the Due Process clause.

4. The Goals of the Short Hours Movement. Deborah Malamud observes that the enactment of the FLSA did not accomplish all of the goals of the short hours movement:

> For well over a hundred years before the New Deal, a social movement aimed to reduce the average weekly working hours of the American worker. The movement had four major goals: improving the health of the working classes by lessening the intensity of their exposure to workplace hazards; diminishing unemployment by spreading the available work among all those customarily employed in a particular field; increasing the leisure time of the working classes to facilitate their education and full participation as citizens; and establishing working hours as a sphere of worker control over the process of industrial production. Each justification has enjoyed different degrees of acceptance over time. The first, health, characterized pre-New Deal hours regulation; the second, work-spreading, was the central policy goal of the New Deal's hours policy; the third and fourth, leisure and worker control, have never been embraced by the federal government as a reason to shorten the American working day.

Deborah C. Malamud, *Engineering the Middle Classes: Class Line-Drawing in New Deal Hours Legislation*, 96 MICH. L. REV. 2212, 2223 (1998).

What should be the relationship between a society's economic prosperity and the amount of time its citizens spend working? The shorter hours reformers believed that prosperity should be associated with a larger amount of leisure time, yielding a higher quality of life. Some have argued that the United States has endorsed precisely the opposite position. Workers in the United States lack statutory entitlement to paid holidays or vacation time, and U.S. vacation time norms are low by comparison to countries in the European Union: The U.S. averages seven paid public holidays and two to four weeks' paid vacation time, while 15 nations in the European Union average 10 public holidays and four to six weeks paid vacation. *See* Miller, *supra*, at 53. A recent study found that Americans frequently do not even take the paid time off that they do have, and identified three reasons for this pattern: some can't afford a vacation; some worry that taking a vacation might contribute to management perceiving them as replaceable; and some possess a "work martyr complex," causing them to sacrifice their personal well-being and to wear their busy-ness as a badge of honor. Caryn Freeman, *Survey Identifies 'Work Martyr Complex' as One Reason for Not Using Vacation Days*, DAILY LAB. REP. (BNA) No. 161, Aug. 20, 2014. Should employers be concerned about these patterns?

5. **The Union Role in the Struggle for Short Hours.** Although unions were historically the strongest advocates for reduced working hours, the issue has receded to the margins of the agendas of U.S. unions. Why? Marion Crain observes:

> Historically, unions were the major force advocating shorter work hours for employees. Demands for shorter hours have characterized the most dynamic periods in organized labor's history. In the 1780s, unionized male artisans and craftsmen successfully fought for a ten-hour day, which at the time must have seemed like an impossible dream. Female textile workers joined the struggle in the mid-1840s. Following the Civil War, organized labor sought an eight-hour day, and explicitly tied this request to a demand for higher pay and a family wage. By the late 1800s, increasing numbers of women in the paid labor force and the growth of the first wave of feminism made women the most innovative and committed advocates of shorter hours.

> The Depression triggered another push for hours reduction. In the 1930s, the AFL sought a legislated thirty-hour week, relying on arguments that stressed reducing unemployment by sharing available work and increasing productivity. Business resisted this proposal strenuously on the basis that it was unconstitutional and impractical. Business owners worried that full employment would deprive them of their market leverage over workers and increase labor costs. The proposal ultimately failed. Instead, the Fair Labor Standards Act was passed in 1938, setting minimum wages and promoting a forty-hour work week through overtime penalty provisions for hours worked in excess of forty per week.

> Subsequently, labor abandoned the fight, in part because it lacked a positive, compelling rationale for the hours reduction (because it was predicated on a defensive "spread-the-jobs" justification, the support for the thirty-hour work week faded when the labor market recovered during World War II). As labor increasingly accepted the capitalistic system and adopted an economic agenda that sought to obtain a larger part of the spoils for union members, it became less and less interested in obtaining a shorter

work week and more interested in obtaining higher overtime premiums and better hourly wages. Thus, within the labor movement, the historical goal of shorter hours had receded in priority. . . .

Marion Crain, *"Where Have All the Cowboys Gone?" Marriage and Breadwinning in Postindustrial Society*, 60 Ohio St. L.J. 1877, 1937–38 (1999).

B. OVERVIEW OF THE FLSA

1. Minimum Wage Provisions

Section 206 of the FLSA establishes the federal minimum wage that employers must pay their covered employees:

Every employer shall pay to each of his employees who in any workweek is engaged in commerce or in the production of goods for commerce, or is employed in an enterprise engaged in commerce or in the production of goods for commerce, wages at the following rates:

(1) except as otherwise provided in this section, not less than—

    (A) $5.85 an hour, beginning [July 24, 2007];

    (B) $6.55 an hour, beginning [July 24, 2008]; and

    (C) $7.25 an hour, beginning [July 24, 2009];

Fair Labor Standards Act of 1938, 29 U.S.C. § 206(a)(1). A subminimum youth "opportunity wage" permits employers to pay those under the age of 20 years $4.25 per hour for the first 90 consecutive calendar days of employment. Employers may not displace any employee to hire someone at the youth opportunity wage. 29 U.S.C. § 206(g).

The minimum wage is nonwaivable. According to the Supreme Court, "FLSA rights cannot be abridged by contract or otherwise waived because it would 'nullify the purposes of the statute' and thwart the legislative policies it was designed to effectuate." *See Barrentine v. Arkansas-Best Freight System*, 450 U.S. 728, 740 (1981) (ruling that employees covered by the grievance and arbitration mechanism in a collective bargaining agreement may still proceed in court on an FLSA claim; the union cannot waive the employees' FLSA rights). Is this overly paternalistic? Should workers be permitted to agree to work for less than the minimum wage? Would this question be more meaningful if contractual wage-setting occurred at a collective level rather than an individual level, either through collective bargaining or by allowing regional, local, or industry wage councils comprised of worker and employer representatives to establish minimum rates?

Calculating the minimum wage is ordinarily not difficult. Section 203(m) permits employers to credit against the minimum wage the reasonable value of board, lodging, or other facilities customarily furnished to employees. The employer may not, however, deduct the costs of purchasing, maintaining or laundering "uniforms" required as a condition of employment if the deductions would result in wages falling below the minimum.

Tipped Employees

Special rules apply to tipped employees. Employers of tipped employees who regularly receive more than $30 per month in tips may credit tips against the minimum wage owed, as long as the employees receive at least $2.13 per hour and at least the difference between that amount and the current minimum wage in tips. 29 U.S.C. § 203(m), (t). Questions concerning tipped employees arise with increasing frequency. In July 2013, the Department of Labor issued a Fact Sheet regarding the treatment of tipped employees under the FLSA. *Fact Sheet #15: Tipped Employees Under the Fair Labor Standards Act* (FLSA), *available at* http://www.dol.gov/whd/regs/compliance/whdfs15.pdf. For example, suppose that the employer requires tipped employees to perform set-up work prior to their shifts and clean-up work post-shift. Must it pay the full minimum wage during the period of time when the employees are performing this work? In a recent case, a class of more than 5,000 former and current Applebee's servers and bartenders claimed that the restaurant was paying them the tipped wage ($2.13 per hour) during periods when they were setting up the restaurant before opening and after closing, including cleaning bathrooms, sweeping the restaurant, cleaning stock rooms, and rolling silverware, tasks that do not relate to particular customers and so do not carry the potential for tips. *See Fast v. Applebee's Int'l, Inc.*, 638 F.3d 872 (8th Cir. 2011) (denying employer's motion for summary judgment), *cert. denied*, 132 S. Ct. 1094 (2012). (Following the Eighth Circuit's ruling, the case settled). The plaintiffs relied on a Department of Labor Regulation known as the "dual jobs" regulation which entitles employees to the full minimum wage ($7.25 per hour) for time spent performing a job that does not generate tips, and an interpretive DOL handbook provision that provides that if a tipped employee spends a "substantial amount of time" (defined as more than 20% of her working hours) performing related but nontipped work, the employer may not take the tip credit for that time. *See* 29 C.F.R. § 531.56(e); 1988 DOL Wage and Hour Division Field Operations Handbook.

A common practice in many restaurants is to require employees to contribute their tips to a pool, which is then split among them, usually in an effort to equalize tips across shifts or days. This practice is permissible as long as the tip pool contribution occurs only in excess of the amount taken for the tip-credit: the portion of the employee's tips that makes up the difference between the wage paid under 203(m) and the minimum wage cannot be derived from a pool. Moreover, employees cannot be required to contribute a greater percentage of their tips to a pool than is "customary and reasonable" in the locality; the Department of Labor's Wage and Hour Division targets for enforcement pool contributions greater than 15% of an employee's tips.

A number of legal issues have arisen in recent years regarding tip-pooling. For example, employees can only be required to pool tips with other employers who "customarily and regularly" receive tips because they are engaged in customer interactions (e.g., waitstaff, busboys, hosts and bartenders may share in the tip pool, but dishwashers and cooks cannot). 29 U.S.C. § 203(m); *Rubio v. Fuji Sushi & Teppani, Inc.*, 2013 U.S. Dist. LEXIS 8469 (M.D. Fla. Jan. 22, 2013) (granting summary judgment to restaurant server who challenged a tip-pool under the FLSA that included kitchen chefs, who do not engage directly with patrons and so are not customarily tipped). What about workers who have customer interaction responsibilities but who also possess managerial authority—should they be entitled to share in tip-pools?

Until recently, it seemed clear that managers and supervisors could not participate in tip-pools. However, developments under state wage and hour laws, particularly in California and New York, have generated contrary doctrine that may eventually influence interpretation of the FLSA's limitation of tip-pools to those who customarily and regularly receive tips, as well. Many of the cases have involved Starbucks. Although tip-pooling practices are widespread in the restaurant and casino industries, Starbucks has been a target in part because of its relatively flat occupational hierarchy. "Baristas" take orders, make and serve beverages, operate cash registers, clean tables, and stock products. "Shift supervisors" are primarily responsible for the same tasks as baristas, but also assign baristas to particular positions, provide them with performance feedback, and direct customer flow. "Assistant managers" likewise spend most of their time serving customers, but also assist store managers with interviewing applicants, creating shift assignments, evaluating employee performance, and hiring, firing, and disciplining others. Salaried, full-time "store managers" are responsible for the overall operation of the store, and can hire, fire, discipline, promote, transfer and schedule employees. Each store has a tip jar near the cash register, and each week the total tips are distributed among baristas and shift supervisors in proportion to hours worked. Is this the appropriate place to draw the line—baristas and shift supervisors on one side, assistant managers and store managers on the other?

In *Chau v. Starbucks*, 174 Cal. App. 4th 688 (2009), a California appeals court upheld Starbucks' tip-pooling policy. The court reasoned that the shift supervisors performed virtually the same service work as baristas and the employees worked as a team. The fact that shift supervisors also performed supervisory tasks, opened and closed the store, and were responsible for depositing money into the safe did not bar their participation; customers were unlikely to distinguish between the persons serving them when leaving tips. *Id.* at 599. Similarly, the Second Circuit upheld the practice of tip-pooling between baristas and shift supervisors, reasoning that because shift supervisors spend a majority of their time providing personal service to patrons and have no meaningful authority over baristas, they do not function as the employer's "agent" for purposes of a state law barring "the employer or his agent" from sharing in tip-pools. *Barenboim v. Starbucks Corp.*, 2013 U.S. App. LEXIS 23370 (2d Cir. Nov. 21, 2013) (unpublished). Meanwhile, a case from the First Circuit involving almost identical facts came to the opposite conclusion, relying on the plain language of Massachusetts law that prohibits participation in mandatory tip-pooling by employees who possess any level of managerial responsibility. In *Matamoros v. Starbucks Corp.*, 699 F.3d 129 (1st Cir. 2012), the court found that shift supervisors who open and close the store, account for money, ensure that baristas take their scheduled breaks, and act as the ranking employee in the absence of the store manager or assistant manager have some degree of managerial authority and thus, cannot participate in the tip-pool. *Id.* at 136.

Should Starbucks assistant managers be permitted to share in the tip-pool? What about store managers? Do these cases suggest strategies for employers looking to reduce labor costs through expanded use of tip-pools? What advice would you offer?

2. Overtime Pay Provisions

overtime [handwritten]

Section 207 of the FLSA requires that employers pay their covered employees one and one-half times their "regular rate" of pay for all hours worked in excess of forty hours in a workweek:

> Except as otherwise provided in this section, no employer shall employ any of his employees who in any workweek is engaged in commerce or in the production of goods for commerce, or is employed in an enterprise engaged in commerce or in the production of goods for commerce, for a workweek longer than forty hours unless such employee receives compensation for his employment in excess of the hours above specified at a rate not less than one and one-half times the regular rate at which he is employed.

29 U.S.C. § 207(a)(1). Contrary to popular belief, this provision does not establish a maximum number of hours that employees can work in a workweek. Instead, the overtime rate requirement for hours in excess of forty per week was designed to furnish a financial incentive for employers to limit the workweeks of individual workers to forty hours, spreading the available work across a larger group of potential workers and ultimately reducing unemployment. Stephen J. Trejo, *Does the Statutory Overtime Premium Discourage Long Workweeks?*, 56 INDUS. & LAB. REL. REV. 530, 530 (2003). [handwritten: PP]

Unless excluded because they fit into one of the exemptions discussed *infra*, section F, employees are entitled to overtime pay for hours worked in excess of 40 per week, at 1.5 times their "regular rate" of pay— *not* 1.5 times the minimum wage. The "regular rate of pay" is calculated on an hourly basis even if the employee is paid on a salary, piece rate, commission or other basis. If the employee is paid hourly, the calculation is simple: The regular rate is the hourly rate. For other employees, the regular rate must be converted to an average hourly basis. A workweek is the default unit of measurement, although exceptions exist for hospitals, other healthcare institutions, and public agencies engaged in law enforcement and fire protection, for which longer periods are specified. *See* 29 U.S.C. § 207(j), (k). Thus, an employee may work more than 8 hours in one day without triggering the overtime premium under the FLSA, although some state laws (such as those in California) may apply in this situation. [handwritten: how to calc overt pay] [handwritten: "workwee]

The regular rate is computed by dividing the employee's total weekly remuneration for a workweek by the number of hours actually worked during the week (or in the case of a salaried employee, the number of hours for which the salary is intended to compensate pursuant to the contractual arrangement between the employer and the employee). Total remuneration includes bonuses based on quantity, quality, or efficiency; commission payments; payments for meals, lodging, and other facilities; non-overtime premium payments; tip credits, and the value of awards or prizes won by employees for quality, quantity, or efficiency in their work. *See* 29 U.S.C. § 207(e). [handwritten: money paid]

Neither the minimum wage nor the overtime entitlement conferred by these sections may be waived by private agreement. Note, however, that private agreements regarding the hours that will be required as a part of job performance are relevant to computation of the regular rate for overtime purposes in the case of salaried employees. Courts generally enforce any contract regarding the computation of work hours in jobs that is "reasonable." 29 C.F.R. § 785.23; *see, e.g., Garofolo v. Donald B. Heslep Assocs., Inc.*, 405 F.3d 194 (4th Cir. 2005) (finding agreement on 40 hours per week a reasonable estimate of the hours actually worked by on-site resident managers at a storage facility).

The overtime premium presented a problem for public agencies and government employers, who often could not afford to pay it. Special rules for compensatory time off in lieu of overtime pay were developed, and these rules now have a prominent place in modern debates about whether overtime pay is the appropriate mechanism to reduce working hours. Amendments added to the FLSA in 1985 permit public employers to award compensatory time off in lieu of cash compensation for overtime, at a rate of not less than 1.5 hours for each hour of overtime. 29 U.S.C. § 207(o)(1). Public employers must meet several requirements in order to utilize comp time instead of cash for overtime. First, the employee must agree. 29 U.S.C. § 207(o)(2). The agreement may take the form of a collective bargaining agreement, an individual agreement, or in situations where employees were hired prior to the effective date of the comp time provisions (April 15, 1986), a regular prior practice will suffice. Second, the employer must permit employees who have accrued comp time to use it "within a reasonable period after making the request if the use of the compensatory time does not unduly disrupt the operations of the public agency." 29 U.S.C. § 207(o)(5). Third, the FLSA caps the maximum amount of compensatory time that can be accrued by employees at 240 hours, except that hours for public safety, emergency response, and seasonal public employees are capped at 480. 29 U.S.C. § 207(o)(3). Once the employee reaches this maximum, the employer must pay the employee cash compensation for additional overtime. The employer may also cancel or "cash out" accrued comp time by paying the employee cash compensation for the unused time. Finally, employees who leave their jobs with accrued comp time are entitled to payment of cash compensation for the overtime work.

3. The Child Labor Provisions

The FLSA regulates "oppressive child labor." Oppressive child labor is defined as a situation in which a child under 16 years is employed in any occupation by a nonparent, or where a child between 16 and 18 years of age is employed in an occupation that the Secretary of Labor has declared to be hazardous to children's health or wellbeing. 29 U.S.C. § 203(l). Three types of child labor violations are common: infractions pertaining to time of day, number of hours worked, and employment in hazardous occupations. The Secretary has promulgated regulations specifying the times and jobs in which children under 16 may work without interfering with their schooling, health, or well-being, and designating certain occupations as "hazardous." Examples of occupations currently designated as hazardous are coal mining, logging, driving motor vehicles, and operating power woodworking machines.

Child labor restrictions apply broadly, even to employers whose employees may not be subject to the Act's wage and overtime regulations. Nonetheless, the FLSA does exempt from its child labor provisions agricultural workers, actors and performers, newspaper delivery persons, evergreen wreath-makers, and children employed by parents or guardians in nonhazardous occupations. 29 U.S.C. §§ 203(l), 213(c), (d).

The most serious risks to children's health likely occur in the agricultural industry. An article in the Los Angeles Times by Victoria Riskin and Mike Farrell, co-chairs of the California Committee (South) of Human Rights Watch, highlighted some of these risks:

> Damaris was 13 years old when she began working in the broccoli and lettuce fields of Arizona. During peak season, she would often work 14 hours a day in 100-degree temperatures. For months on end she suffered frequent nosebleeds and nearly passed out on several occasions. Despite illness from exposure to dangerous pesticides, she kept on working. "It was very difficult," she told Human Rights Watch. "I just endured it."

danger agricultur work

> Between 300,000 and 800,000 children like Damaris are working as hired laborers in commercial U.S. agriculture today. These farmworker children weed cotton fields, pick lettuce and cantaloupe and climb rickety ladders in cherry and apple orchards. They often work 12 or more hours a day, sometimes beginning at 3 or 4 in the morning. They risk serious illness, including cancer and brain damage, from exposure to pesticides, and suffer high rates of injury from working with sharp tools and heavy machinery.

> Despite long and grueling days, some child farmers are paid only $2 an hour. Many of them drop out of school, too exhausted to study. Nearly half of them never graduate from high school. Lacking other options, many are relegated to a lifetime of low-wage field labor that perpetuates the cycle of farm-worker poverty through generations.

> Agriculture is the most dangerous occupation open to minors in the United States. Work-related fatalities among child farm workers are five times higher than for children working in non-agricultural jobs, and an estimated 100,000 children suffer agriculture-related injuries annually in the United States.

> The long-term effects of pesticide exposure are not yet completely known, but have been linked to cancer, brain tumors, brain damage and birth defects. Child farm workers interviewed by Human Rights Watch for a recent study described working in fields still wet with poison and being exposed to pesticide drift from spraying in nearby fields. One 16-year-old boy told us that he mixed and sprayed pesticides several times a week, but wore no mask or protective clothing because his employer told him he had nothing to worry about.

> Despite the hazards of agricultural work, current U.S. labor law allows children working in agriculture to work at younger ages and for longer hours than minors in other jobs. Surprisingly, the 14-hour days worked by a 13-year-old are not prohibited by law. Children as young as 12 can legally work unlimited hours in agriculture.

Victoria Riskin & Mike Farrell, *Profiting on the Backs of Child Laborers*, L.A. TIMES, Oct. 12, 2000, at B-11.

What is the basis for the cultural resistance to regulating child labor in agriculture? Historical arguments advanced in opposition to regulation have included the following: increased costs to an industry that relies heavily upon child labor and is a cornerstone of the American economy; farmwork is seen as wholesome and free from the "moral turpitude" that characterizes city sweatshops; parents feel that harvesting crops is a higher value than education, combined with sentiment against interfering with parental control of children; bias against furnishing educational facilities for migrant children; and enforcement difficulties. *See* Davin C. Curtiss, Note, *The Fair Labor Standards Act and Child Labor in Agriculture*, 20 IOWA J. CORP. L. 303, 306–09 (1995). Which of these rationales is persuasive today?

A vexing problem for the Secretary of Labor in enforcing the child labor provisions is learning of violations. In many circumstances, the employer, the parent and the child are unlikely to complain, and they are generally not cooperative in proving the violation. If none of these parties are concerned, who is the victim?

4. Enforcement of the FLSA

a. Basics

The FLSA is administered and enforced by the Secretary of Labor. The Secretary has delegated most of the statutory responsibilities to the Wage-Hour Division of the Department of Labor. 29 U.S.C. § 204. The FLSA can be enforced through civil actions brought either by the Secretary of Labor on behalf of aggrieved employees or by aggrieved employees themselves, or through criminal prosecutions brought by the Department of Justice.

Section 216(c) authorizes the Secretary to sue for recovery of unpaid minimum wages, overtime compensation, and an equal amount in liquidated damages. Additionally, section 216(e) authorizes the Secretary to pursue civil penalties of up to $1,100 per violation for repeated or willful violations of the minimum wage and overtime provisions. Section 212(b) of the FLSA authorizes the Secretary of Labor to enforce the child labor provisions. Section 216(e) permits recovery of up to $11,000 for each violation of the child labor provisions. Employers are liable regardless of lack of intent or willfulness with respect to the violation. *Chao v. Vidtape, Inc*, 196 F. Supp. 2d 281, 295 (E.D.N.Y. 2002). Civil penalties of up to $50,000 for each child labor violation that causes the death or serious injury of any employee under 18 are also available, and they may be doubled if the violations are willful or repeated. 29 U.S.C. § 216(e). Additionally, the Secretary can seek injunctive relief under section 217 to prevent future violations of the Act, including minimum wage, overtime, retaliation, and child labor violations. Section 217 also authorizes the Secretary to prosecute recordkeeping violations. Section 217 is equitable in nature, and therefore jury trials are unavailable and liquidated damages may not be recovered.

The Department of Labor historically utilized a complaint-driven enforcement model in which the agency launched investigations against a single employer in response to worker complaints of violations. Serious questions were raised about the efficacy of the DOL's enforcement efforts under this system. In 2008–2009, the Government Accountability Office (GAO) conducted a forensic audit of the Department of Labor's enforcement arm, the Wage and Hour Division. The audit included data mining and statistical sampling of closed cases for 2007 and an undercover investigation in which GAO investigators posed as complainants and as employers. Using fictitious scenarios involving common minimum wage, overtime, and child labor violations, the investigators initiated complaints with Wage and Hour Division offices in several states. The investigation revealed serious flaws in the Wage and Hour Division's responses, including a confusing and discouraging complaint intake process, failure to record complaints, failure to investigate, failure to use all available enforcement tools, and lengthy delays. The GAO report concluded: "This investigation clearly shows that the Department of Labor has left thousands of actual victims of wage theft who sought federal government assistance with nowhere to turn." GAO Testimony Before the House Committee on Education and Labor, House of Representatives, *Wage & Hour Division's Complaint Intake and Investigative Processes Leave Low Wage Workers Vulnerable to Wage Theft*, Mar. 25, 2009, GAO-09-458T, at 24–25. *See also* Steven Greenhouse, *Enforcement Agency Is Failing Workers, Report Says*, N.Y. Times, Mar. 25, 2009, at A16 (discussing GAO investigation and findings); Annette Bernhardt *et al.*, *Broken Laws, Unprotected Workers*, Sept. 2009, Center for Urban Economic Development, UCLA Institute for Research on Labor and Employment, and the National Employment Law Project, *available at* http://www.nelp.org/page/-/brokenlaws/BrokenLawsReport2009.pdf?nocdn=1 (reporting on survey of low wage workers in four large cities that revealed that two-thirds of the workers had suffered some form of wage violation during the preceding week, with the average worker losing 15% of her earnings).

In 2014, David Weil, the newly appointed Wage and Hour Division administrator initiated a system of targeted or strategic enforcement, in which the agency directs most of its resources at industries populated by vulnerable workers where abuses are particularly common and employees are least likely to step forward to complain. These industries include agriculture, restaurants, hotels and motels, grocery stores, residential construction, moving companies, landscaping, healthcare, janitorial, and temporary help services. Gayle Cingquegrani, *New Wage/Hour Chief Weighing Concerns of Varied Industries About Overtime Changes*, Daily Lab. Rep. (BNA) No. 109, June 6, 2014. Weil authored the blueprint for strategic enforcement in 2010 while an economics professor at Boston University, serving as the principal investigator for a report commissioned by the Wage and Hour Division. Weil contended that enforcement efforts should be focused on industries typified by "fissuring" or splintering of employment, where employees work for subcontracted or franchised entities rather than directly for the primary market actors. Weil urged the Wage and Hour Division to maximize the impact of its enforcement efforts by targeting the primary market actors and holding them responsible for the standards set by the entities with which they contract. *See* David Weil, *Improving Workplace Conditions Through Strategic Enforcement*, *available at* http://www.dol.gov/whd/resources/strategicEnforcement.pdf.

enforcement mechanism

Alternatively, an aggrieved employee can enforce the FLSA directly by bringing a suit under § 216(b) for unpaid minimum wages and overtime, as well as an equal amount in liquidated damages. Individuals may not sue for injunctive relief. A special device known as a collective action claim is available under § 216(b) for claims by multiple employees. *See infra* subsection d. Prevailing plaintiffs may recover attorneys' fees and costs. 29 U.S.C. § 216(b). However, if the Secretary of Labor initiates an action under either § 216 or 217, the aggrieved employee loses his or her right to bring an action under § 216(b). 29 U.S.C. § 216(c).

Finally, the Department of Justice may prosecute willful violations of the FLSA as criminal actions under § 216(a). Maximum sanctions prescribed by the Act are a fine of not more than $10,000 for a first violation, or fine and/or imprisonment for not more than six months for subsequent violations. 29 U.S.C. § 216(a).

b. Retaliation Complaints

cases in conflict

The FLSA contains an anti-retaliatory provision in § 215(a)(3) that prohibits employers from discriminating against or discharging an employee in retaliation for filing a complaint under the FLSA or testifying in a proceeding. Employees may enforce the Act's antiretaliation provision through a suit under § 216(b). A question arose over what constitutes "filing a complaint" for purposes of § 215(a)(3). Most federal courts had concluded that an informal, internal complaint to the employer would satisfy the complaint filing requirement. *See, e.g., Hagan v. Echostar Satellite, L.L.C.*, 529 F.3d 617 (5th Cir. 2008); *Valerio v. Putnam Associates, Inc.*, 173 F.3d 35 (1st Cir. 1999). Some had qualified this by requiring that internal complaints be in writing. *See Kasten v. Saint-Gobain Performance Plastics Corp.*, 570 F.3d 834 (7th Cir. 2009). Others, however, had held that a formal complaint to the government agency or a court was required to trigger protection. *See, e.g., Lambert v. Genesee Hospital*, 10 F.3d 46 (2d Cir. 1993). The Supreme Court resolved the circuit split in *Kasten v. Saint-Gobain Performance Plastics Corp.*, 131 S. Ct. 1325 (2011). Kasten had voiced his complaint to his shift supervisor, a human resources employee, a human resources manager, and an operations manager. *Id.* at 1329–30. The Seventh Circuit granted summary judgment in favor of Saint-Gobain, reasoning that oral complaints could not satisfy the § 215(a)(3) standard for retaliation claims. The Supreme Court ruled that oral complaints would suffice to ground a retaliation claim as long as the employer receives "fair notice that a grievance has been lodged, and does, or should, reasonably understand the matter as part of its business concerns." *Id.* at 1335. The Court explained that "functional considerations" argued in favor of its interpretation:

SCOTUS

> . . . First, an interpretation that limited the provision's coverage to written complaints would undermine the Act's basic objectives. The Act seeks to prohibit "labor conditions detrimental to the maintenance of the minimum standard of living necessary for health, efficiency, and general well-being of workers." 29 U.S.C. § 202(a). It does so in part by setting forth substantive wage, hour, and overtime standards. It relies for enforcement of these standards, not upon "continuing detailed federal supervision or inspection of payrolls," but upon "information and complaints received from employees seeking to vindicate rights claimed to have been denied." *Mitchell v. Robert De Mario Jewelry, Inc.*, 361 U.S. 288, 2929 (1960). And

its antiretaliation provision makes this enforcement scheme effective by preventing "fear of economic retaliation" from inducing workers "quietly to accept substandard conditions." *Ibid.*

Why would Congress want to limit the enforcement scheme's effectiveness by inhibiting use of the Act's complaint procedure by those who would find it difficult to reduce their complaints to writing, particularly illiterate, less educated, or overworked workers? President Franklin Roosevelt pointed out at the time that these were the workers most in need of the Act's help. *See* Message to Congress, May 24, 1937, H.R. Doc. No. 255, 75th Cong., 1st Sess., 4 (seeking a bill to help the poorest of "those who toil in factory [sic]").

. . . .

To limit the scope of the antiretaliation provision to the filing of written complaints would also take needed flexibility from those charged with the Act's enforcement. It could prevent Government agencies from using hotlines, interviews, and other oral methods of receiving complaints. And . . . it would discourage the use of desirable informal workplace grievance procedures to secure compliance with the Act. *Cf. Burlington Industries, Inc. v. Ellerth*, 524 U.S. 742, 764 (1998) (reading Title VII to encourage the development of effective grievance procedures to deter misconduct); D. MCPHERSON, C. GATES, & K. ROGERS, RESOLVING GRIEVANCES: A PRACTICAL APPROACH 38–40 (1983) (describing the significant benefits of unwritten complaints).

Id. at 1334–35. To the employer's argument that employers are entitled to receive fair notice of complaints, and its concern that it might be difficult to distinguish between a verbal complaint and an angry employee letting off steam, the Court responded:

At oral argument, the Government said that a complaint is "filed" when "a reasonable, objective person would have understood the employee" to have "put the employer on notice that [the] employee is asserting statutory rights under the [Act]." Tr. of Oral Arg. 23, 26. We agree. To fall within the scope of the antiretaliation provision, a complaint must be sufficiently clear and detailed for a reasonable employer to understand it, in light of both content and context, as an assertion of rights protected by the statute and a call for their protection. This standard can be met, however, by oral complaints, as well as by written ones.

Id. at 1336. The Court remanded the case so that the lower courts could determine whether Kasten could satisfy the FLSA's notice requirement. *Id.* at 1337. On remand, the district court concluded that Kasten had satisfied the fair notice requirement. *Kasten v. Saint-Gobain Performance Plastics Corp.*, 703 F.3d 966, 969 (7th Cir. 2012) (agreeing with district court on the notice question).

What is the significance of *Kasten*? Attorneys who represent immigrant populations hailed the Court's embrace of less formal complaints as very important for low-wage workers with limited English language skills, particularly given the complaint-based nature of FLSA enforcement and the DOL's limited resources.

Aside from the Court's apparent concern with shoring up enforcement of FLSA rights for vulnerable workers, what other factors might have influenced the Court in a pro-plaintiff direction, and do those factors have any implications for other areas of employment law, such as in the whistleblowing context? Might *Kasten* be viewed as of a piece with the Supreme Court's consistent embrace of plaintiffs' retaliation claims under Title VII? *See Thompson v. North American Stainless, LP*, 562 U.S. 170 (2011) (discussed in Chapter 9). What is it about retaliation claims that makes them so compelling? Consider also the fact that retaliation claims are by their nature individual in character—class claims are not common. Does that make a difference?

How should employers respond to *Kasten*? Many employers already encourage employees to bring complaints and comments to supervisors through open door policies or ombudsman programs. What is the significance of the Court's reference to its sexual harassment enforcement jurisprudence under Title VII and the system of "desirable informal workplace grievance procedures" that has developed in response?

Many line-drawing questions remain for the lower courts as to which complaints will afford fair notice to employers. Should all oral complaints suffice? Does it matter whether they are made inside the workplace or outside of it? What about an employee's passing remark at a cocktail party to a government official (or, if only internal complaints count, to a supervisor) concerning a Fair Labor Standards Act violation she has observed in her workplace? What about complaints which turn out to be wrong? If the employee raises the complaint in good faith, is he still protected?

Employees in states that recognize tort claims for wrongful discharge in violation of public policy may have an additional tool in the enforcement arsenal: when they are retaliated against for asserting rights under the FLSA or state wage and hour law, they may try to challenge the discharges as wrongful, pointing to the relevant legislation as evidence of the public policy offended by their discharge. Why might plaintiffs prefer to proceed on this theory rather than under the FLSA's anti-retaliation provision? Although the majority of jurisdictions hold that the statutory remedies available under the FLSA are sufficient and preempt a claim for wrongful discharge in violation of public policy, some state courts have come to different conclusions. *Compare Connor v. Schnuck Markets*, 121 F.3d 1390, 1399 (10th Cir. 1997) (dismissing retaliatory discharge claim under the public policy exception to the at-will doctrine because the FLSA provides an "adequate statutory remedy"), *with Amos v. Oakdale Knitting Co.*, 416 S.E.2d 166, 172 (N.C. 1992) (ruling that absent federal preemption or manifest state legislative intent "to supplant the common law with exclusive statutory remedies," plaintiffs fired for protesting violations of minimum wage laws may seek tort remedies for wrongful discharge in violation of public policy).

c. Defenses and Limitations on Liability

The Portal-to-Portal Act of 1947 provides a complete defense to liquidated damages for the failure to pay minimum wage or overtime if the employer can show that its violation of the FLSA was "in good faith in conformity with and in reliance on any written administrative regulation, order, ruling, approval, or interpretation" of the Wage-Hour Administrator, even if the opinion is later rescinded or invalidated. 29 U.S.C. § 259(a). Alternatively, the court may reduce or eliminate liquidated damages if it finds that the employer acted in good faith and had "reasonable grounds for believing that his act or omission was not a violation." 29 U.S.C. § 260. The employer bears a heavy burden of proof: mere ignorance, confusion about the state of the law, or conformance with industry standards will not suffice. Lisa J. Bernt, *Finding the Right Jobs for the Reasonable Person in Employment Law*, 77 UMKC L. Rev. 1, 15–16 (2008). Employers must establish that they made an honest attempt to determine the proper interpretation of the Act as applied to their situations and to comply with it. *See Reich v. Southern New England Telecommunications*, 121 F.3d 58, 70–71 (2d Cir. 1997) (employer's inquiry to Department of Labor about legality of refusing to compensate employees for mealtimes supported finding that employer did not act in good faith because employer failed to ask a question calculated to resolve the uncertainty). This defense, even if successful, does not absolve the employer from liability for unpaid minimum wages or overtime compensation. Moreover, there exists a strong preference for awarding employees double damages in § 216 actions because liquidated damages are considered compensatory rather than punitive in nature. Thus, even if the employer has shown that it acted in good faith with a reasonable belief, courts may and often do order liquidated damages. *See* G. Scott Warrick, *The FLSA's Salary Test: Impending Disaster for the American Worker and American Business*, 24 Cap. U.L. Rev. 621, 629 (1995).

The Portal-to-Portal Act of 1947 also limits employer liability by establishing a statute of limitations for FLSA claims. The statute of limitations for FLSA claims is set at two years for non-willful violations and three years for willful violations. 29 U.S.C. § 255(a). Application of the longer statute of limitations operates not only to extend the period during which timely claims may be filed, but also to expand the amount of recovery in the case of continuing violations (which are common under the FLSA). The Supreme Court ruled in *McLaughlin v. Richland Shoe Company*, 486 U.S. 128 (1988), that an FLSA violation would be deemed willful only if "the employer either knew or showed reckless disregard" for the applicable FLSA regulation. *Id.* at 133.

d.   State Wage and Hour Laws

Individual states may enact wage and hour laws that are more protective of workers' rights than the federal law. They may do so by providing for a higher minimum wage than the federal minimum wage, by extending coverage to more persons than those covered under the FLSA, by setting a lower hours threshold or higher premium for overtime pay, or by strengthening the child labor provisions. 29 U.S.C. § 218(a) expressly avoids federal preemption of such laws. By September 2014, 23 states and the District of Columbia had minimum wage rates higher than the federal rate of $7.25 per hour. *See* U.S. Dep't of Labor, *Minimum Wage Laws in the States*, Sept. 1, 2014, *available at* http://www.dol.gov/whd/minwage/america. htm.

Many states have also enacted more stringent overtime standards than the FLSA provides, whether by increasing the premium rate for overtime hours worked, decreasing the maximum hours that can be worked in a week before the premium rate must be paid, or requiring premium pay for hours worked over eight in a single workday. *See* U.S. Dep't of Labor, *Minimum Wage Laws in the States*, Sept. 1, 2014, *available at* http://www.dol.gov/whd/minwage/america.htm. Additionally, state law generally regulates the specifics of wage payment and wage collection, such as how frequently wages must be paid (monthly, weekly, etc.); limits on deductions or amounts that may be withheld from employee paychecks; and regulation of wage payment upon termination of employment, including accrued vacation pay.

e. Rule 23 Class Actions and FLSA Collective Actions

In recent years, many major employers have found themselves defendants in class actions brought under state wage and hour statutes (most states allow class action claims under Rule 23 to collect unpaid wages) or collective action cases litigated under the FLSA. These cases may be high stakes lawsuits because they involve pay for large groups of workers. The potential for big payouts and attorneys' fees, the complexity of the FLSA's provisions combined with employer neglect, the lack of an intent requirement to prove a violation, and the relative ease of collective action certification as contrasted with Rule 23 class action certification have made FLSA Collective action claims attractive to plaintiffs' lawyers. Many believe that the surge in wage and hour lawsuits over the last decade is attributable to the education of the plaintiff bar about these advantages rather than to an increase in the number of violations committed by employers. Government Accountability Office, *Fair Labor Standards Act: The Department of Labor Should Develop a More Systematic Approach to Developing Its Guidance*, Report No. 14-69, at 10–12, Dec. 2013, *available at* http://www.gao.gov/assets/660/659772.pdf. The economic crisis of 2007-09 and the increased number of laid-off workers were also contributing factors to the spike in claims. *See Id.; Report Finds Bias, ERISA Class Actions Rose in 2009, and FLSA Collective Actions 'Spiked,'* DAILY LAB. REP. (BNA) No. 8, Jan 14, 2010, at A-1.

It is important to distinguish between class actions brought pursuant to Federal Rule of Civil Procedure 23 under state wage and hour laws, and the "collective action" device available for group claims under the FLSA. In order to be certified as a class action, the named plaintiffs must satisfy a series of requirements under Rule 23. Once a class is certified, every member of the class is entitled to share in the recovery if the suit is successful, and will be bound by the result, whether or not successful, unless the individual affirmatively opts out of the class. Traditional class actions under Rule 23 are not permitted under the FLSA, 29 C.F.R. § 790.20, though they are permitted under many state wage and hour laws. Instead, the FLSA authorizes employees to bring collective actions on behalf of themselves and other similarly situated employees. 29 U.S.C. § 216(b). Collective actions require that employees opt-in to the action by filing a consent to join the suit. Only those workers who affirmatively opt-in can recover back wages through the suit or be bound by the outcome. *See generally* David Borgen & Laura L. Ho, *The Fair Labor Standards Act: Litigation of Wage and Hour Collective Actions Under the Fair Labor Standards Act*, 7 EMP. RTS. & EMPLOY. POL'Y J. 129, 130–31 (2003) (describing differences between the two types of actions).

Collective actions under the FLSA typically follow a two-step process. In the first step, the individual plaintiffs must show that the other employees they seek to represent are "similarly situated" within the meeting of FLSA section 216 (b). Generally, this threshold can be met with a rather modest factual showing and, once satisfied, notice is sent to other employees who are given the opportunity to opt-in to the lawsuit. After discovery is complete, the court conclusively determines whether the employees are in fact similarly situated such that the suit can be resolved on a collective basis. In order to satisfy this second step, the plaintiffs bear a heavier burden of showing that the members of the collective action are similarly situated. At either stage, proof of a common policy or practice resulting in wage and hour violations may be critical to showing that numerous employees can be joined in a FLSA collective action.

The "similarly situated" standard for FLSA collective actions appears similar to the commonality requirement for certifying a class under Rule 23. Thus, after the Supreme Court's decision in *Wal-Mart Stores, Inc. v. Dukes*, 131 S. Ct. 2541 (2011) (discussed *supra*, Chapter 9), employers argued that the *Dukes* standard for class certification under Rule 23 should apply to collective actions under the FLSA. Because *Dukes* made it more difficult to satisfy the commonality requirement under Rule 23, application of the standard to FLSA claims would likely result in many fewer wage and hour cases proceeding on a collective basis. So far, most courts have rejected the argument, finding that Rule 23 class actions are governed by different standards than FLSA collective actions. *See, e.g., Myles v. Prosperity Mortgage Co.*, 2012 U.S. Dist. LEXIS 75371 (D. Md. May 31, 2012) (rejecting argument and conditionally certifying class of loan officers who established they were similarly situated for FLSA purposes because they share the primary duty of selling loans and the employer had an express policy that allegedly improperly classified them as FLSA-exempt outside employees); *In re Wells Fargo Wage & Hour Empl. Practices Litig.*, 2012 U.S. Dist. LEXIS 112769 (S.D. Tex. Aug. 10, 2012) (finding Rule 23 decisions such as *Dukes* inapplicable, and conditionally certifying proposed class of home mortgage consultants who argued that they were improperly classified as FLSA-exempt).

In addition to FLSA collective actions, however, employees sometimes bring traditional opt-out class actions alleging violations of state wage and hour laws. If those class actions are brought in federal court under Rule 23, *Dukes* clearly applies. Even under the heightened commonality standard of *Dukes*, some plaintiffs have succeeded in certifying wage and hour class actions based on state law. For example, in *Wang v. Chinese Daily News, Inc.*, 709 F.3d 829 (9th Cir. 2013), the Ninth Circuit ordered a federal district court to reconsider in light of *Dukes* whether newspaper employees had satisfied class certification standards under Rule 23 in a case in which the employees had previously won a $5.1 million judgment on their FLSA and state law wage and hour claims. The district court ruled that certification was proper, finding that the plaintiffs identified common issues of law and fact and established that common issues predominated over individual questions. The case involved 200 employees working in the same location under the same supervisors subject to the same employment policies. *Wang v. Chinese Daily News*, 2014 U.S. Dist. LEXIS 59597 (C.D. Cal. Apr. 15, 2014). The Supreme Court has never addressed the standard for permitting a FLSA action to proceed on a collective basis, but in a recent case on another issue, it noted the significant differences between a Rule 23 class action and a FLSA collective action, which perhaps supports the argument that the Rule 23 commonality analysis should not apply to FLSA collective actions. *Genesis Healthcare Corp. v. Symczyk*, 133 S. Ct. 1523 (2013).

Scholars have argued that the collective action mechanism under the FLSA places workers at a distinct disadvantage relative to Rule 23 class actions. *See, e.g.*, Scott A. Moss & Nantiya Ruan, *The Second-Class Class Action: How Courts Thwart Wage Rights by Misapplying Class Action Rules*, 61 AM. U.L. REV. 523 (2012) (critiquing aggressive scrutiny applied by courts in opt-in collective action claims under the FLSA and arguing that courts should not assume the same kind of gatekeeping role on issues of commonality that they perform in Rule 23 contexts); Nantiya Ruan, *Same Law, Different Day: A Survey of the Last Thirty Years of Wage Litigation and Its Impact on Low-Wage Workers*, 30 HOFSTRA LAB. & EMP. L. J. 355 (2013) (noting importance of aggregation of wage claims to low wage workers and explaining how the FLSA's collective action provisions are far less advantageous to plaintiffs than Rule 23's class action provisions, available to plaintiffs in other civil cases). High turnover in low-waged jobs and frequent address changes among low-wage workers make it difficult to get notice of the litigation to employees. Further, it can be difficult to persuade employees to opt-in to collective actions: approximately 20% of workers opt-in to the typical collective action. Reasons for the low opt-in rate include fear of retaliation, lack of understanding of the legal system, language barriers, difficulty in contacting prospective claimants, and failure to respond to notices received in the mail. *See* Noah A. Finkel, *The Fair Labor Standards Act: State Wage-and-Hour Law Class Actions: The Real Wave of "FLSA" Litigation?*, 7 EMP. RTS. & EMPLOY. POL'Y J. 159, 162 (2003). Low opt-in rates in turn produce low damage awards, making collective actions less attractive to attorneys. These factors combine to make it difficult for most workers to enforce their rights under the FLSA. *See* Craig Becker & Paul Strauss, *Representing Low-Wage Workers in the Absence of a Class: The Peculiar Case of Section 16 of the Fair Labor Standards Act and the Underenforcement of Minimum Labor Standards*, 92 MINN. L. REV. 1317 (2008).

Labor unions are frequently behind the scenes in wage and hour group claims, as they are most likely to discover violations and to use the law to obtain leverage with employers; they sometimes bankroll the litigation for their membership. *See, e.g., Retail Stores, Former Employees Settle California Wage Claims for $15 Million*, DAILY LAB. REP. (BNA) No. 104, May 30, 2008 (discussing union investigation and bankrolling of FLSA litigation on behalf of its members); Michael R. Triplett, *Federal Judge OKs $53.3 Million Settlement with Albertsons over 'Off-the-Clock' Claims*, DAILY LAB. REP. (BNA) No. 57, Mar. 26, 2007 (reporting that union that assisted in filing off-the-clock actions against Albertson's received $6.1 million to settle other cases based on labor disputes and grievances connected to the FLSA litigation).

Some unions have tried to use collective or class action claims under wage and hour laws to mobilize workers and build a sense of solidarity on which to base a union organizing drive—or as a vehicle to demonstrate what a union can do for employees. However, two circuit courts have ruled that union funding of legal services for the filing of lawsuits under individual employment rights statutes will violate the NLRA if it occurs during a union election campaign because it is tantamount to bribing employees to support the union. *See Freund Baking Co. v. NLRB*, 165 F.3d 928 (D.C. Cir. 1999) (finding that a union-supported class action lawsuit under the California wage and hour statute impermissibly influenced the outcome of the successful union election that followed); *Nestle Ice Cream Co. v. NLRB*, 46 F.3d 578 (6th Cir. 1995) (concluding that union-financed claim against the employer under the federal Racketeer Influenced and Corrupt Organizations Act (RICO) with the potential to recover significant amounts of lost wages and punitive damages was an impermissible pre-election benefit that destroyed the possibility for a free and fair union election). Several commentators have argued that these results undermine union efficacy. *See* Catherine L. Fisk, *Union Lawyers and Employment Law*, 23 BERKELEY J. EMP. & LAB. L. 57 (2002); Michael Carlin, Note, *Are Union-Financed Legal Services Provided Prior to a Representation Election an Impermissible Grant of Benefit?: An Analysis of Nestle, Novotel, and Freund*, 79 N.C.L. REV. 551 (2001).

f. Public Sector Employment

Although the FLSA does apply to public sector employers and employees, the Supreme Court ruled in *Alden v. Maine*, 527 U.S. 706 (1999), that state employees cannot bring suit against a state in its own courts on a § 216(b) action unless the state waives its immunity. Thus, absent such a waiver, public employees must rely on the Secretary of Labor to enforce their rights with a § 216(c) action or sue under state law. *Alden* involved a group of probation officers in Maine who brought suit against the state for failure to pay them overtime as required by the FLSA. The Supreme Court held that "the States' immunity from suit is a fundamental aspect of the sovereignty they enjoyed before the Constitution's ratification and retain today except as altered by the plan of the Convention or certain constitutional Amendments." *Id.* at 713. Absent a waiver by the state, the state is subject to suit only where the national government "itself deem[s] the case of sufficient importance to take action against the State." *Id.* at 759–60.

What is the practical impact of the Court's decision in *Alden*? Although the Labor Department theoretically can enforce the rights of public sector employees under the FLSA, it lacks the resources to do so. There are approximately 4.7 million state employees in the United States. The *Alden* majority did suggest that individual employees might be able to sue state officials in their individual capacities to enforce their rights without offending state sovereignty. *Id.* at 756–57. However, the Seventh Circuit subsequently characterized such a claim as an "end run" around the Eleventh Amendment, and refused to allow it. *See Luder v. Endicott*, 253 F.3d 1020, 1025 (7th Cir. 2001). Alternatively, states may waive their immunity, either by legislative enactment or judicial decision of the states' highest court. Many states, however, have refused to do so. *See, e.g., Virginia v. Luzik*, 524 S.E.2d 871 (Va. 2000) (finding that Virginia has not waived its sovereign immunity under the FLSA).

C. THE FLSA'S PURPOSES: WEALTH REDISTRIBUTION AND WORK-SPREADING

1. The Minimum Wage Provisions

A central goal of the FLSA was to further "a minimum standard of living necessary for health, efficiency, and general well-being of workers." 29 U.S.C. § 202(a). How effective have the minimum wage provisions been in accomplishing the goal of raising the standard of living for low-income workers to an acceptable level? Do the minimum wage provisions appropriately target those workers who need assistance most? What alternative wealth redistribution mechanisms might exist?

Most American workers earn well above the minimum wage. In 2013, 58.8% of all wage and salary workers were paid on an hourly basis—a total of 75.9 million workers 16 and older. Of those, just 1.5 million were compensated at the minimum wage rate and 1.8 million had wages below the minimum; together, these represent 4.3% of all hourly-paid workers. Bureau of Labor Statistics, Department of Labor, *Characteristics of Minimum Wage Workers: 2013* (Mar. 2014), *available at* http://www.bls.gov/cps/minwage2013.pdf. The sub-minimum wage workers are predominantly food and beverage service workers, who are exempted from the minimum wage requirements as tips supplement their hourly wages.

Nevertheless, increases in the minimum wage affect not only workers whose earnings are pegged at or below the minimum wage rate, but also those earning slightly more—this is because most firms raise those wages when the minimum wage rates rise in order to preserve the wage structure of the firm. These spillover effects can be quite significant. For example, the Economic Policy Institute released projections regarding the impact of an increase to $10.10 per hour, a figure contemplated by the proposed Fair Minimum Wage Act of 2013 and subsequently endorsed by President Obama in his 2014 State of the Union Address. The EPI estimated that a raise of this magnitude would directly or indirectly raise the wages of 27.8 million workers (16.7 million would be affected directly, 11.1 would be affected indirectly). David Cooper, *Raising the Federal Minimum Wage to $10.10 Would Lift Wages for Millions and Provide a Modest Economic Boost*, Economic Policy Institute, Dec. 19, 2013, *available at* http://www.epi.org/publication/raising-federal-minimum-wage-to-1010/. The Brookings Institution released a report in 2014 concluding that a minimum wage increase would raise the wages of about 35 million workers earning up to 150% of the minimum wage. Benjamin H. Harris & Melissa S. Kearney, *The "Ripple Effect" of a Minimum Wage Increase on American Workers*, Jan. 10, 2104, *available at* http://www.brookings.edu/blogs/up-front/posts/2014/01/10-ripple-effect-of-increasing-the-minimum-wage-kearney-harris. Women and minorities benefit disproportionately from minimum wage increases because they are over-represented at the bottom of the wage market.

Many commentators argue that the minimum wage has been ineffective at accomplishing its goal of raising the standard of living. As an anti-poverty measure, the minimum wage is a blunt tool: it benefits teenagers as well as full-time workers struggling to make ends meet at the bottom of the labor market (for example, if the minimum wage were raised to $10.10 per hour, 12.5% of the workers affected would be teens). Cooper, *supra*. Moreover, the real value of the minimum wage (adjusted for inflation) has dropped significantly to 36% of the average nonsupervisory production worker's wage since the late 1960s and early 1970s, when it was about half of the average nonsupervisory production worker's wage (most studies identify its high point in 1968, when it was 53% of the average nonsupervisory production worker's wage). *Id.* Other strategies, including enhancing workers' education and skills training or using tax credits such as the earned income tax credit aimed at low-wage workers, seem more likely to raise the standard of living for those whose incomes place them at the bottom of the labor market. *See* David Neumark & William Wascher, *Minimum Wage and Low-Wage Workers: How Well Does Reality Match the Rhetoric*, 92 MINN. L. Rev. 1296, at 1312–13 (2008).

Nevertheless, the minimum wage remains a popular weapon in the arsenal of anti-poverty measures. Advocates of minimum wage legislation generally defend it on three grounds. First, workers have a moral right to a living wage, even if their individual bargaining power is inadequate to enable them to negotiate with their employer to obtain it. They point to the fact that the federal minimum wage of $7.25 per hour is below the federal poverty line for families of two (one adult, one child), assuming 52-week, 40-hour-per-week earnings. Cooper, *supra*. Second, some argue that a minimum wage enhances productivity, either by encouraging employers to hire higher-productivity workers or by pressuring low-skilled workers to increase their effort, thereby allowing businesses to absorb the higher labor costs that come with the minimum wage without reducing employment. Third, proponents believe that a minimum wage raises household income levels and stimulates consumption. *See* Neumark & Wascher, *supra*, at 1298–1302.

Would raising the minimum wage result in higher unemployment since employers would not be able to afford to hire as many workers? Would workers as a class suffer from a raise in the minimum wage? Conventional economic analysis assumed that the answer to these questions was yes. In the early 1990s, however, several studies emerged that cast significant doubt upon the validity of these assumptions. The most well-known and controversial of these studies was performed by labor economists David Card and Alan Krueger. Based on studies of the effects of increases in the state minimum wage in California, Texas, and New Jersey, Card and Krueger concluded that raising the minimum wage had no disemployment effect; indeed, their data suggested that employment levels actually increased. *See* DAVID CARD & ALAN KRUEGER, MYTH AND MEASUREMENT: THE NEW ECONOMICS OF THE MINIMUM WAGE (1995). Their results were soon criticized by other economists. The following excerpts shed further light on the resulting dialogue, which is reconstituted each time a proposal to raise the minimum wage surfaces.

Daniel Shaviro, *The Minimum Wage, the Earned Income Tax Credit, and Optimal Subsidy Policy*
64 U. CHI. L. REV. 405, 405–08, 415–17 (1997)

The minimum wage is a perennial topic of interest and controversy in American politics. Democratic Party politicians regularly call for increasing it, on grounds of progressive redistribution, economic justice, or to "make work pay." Republican Party politicians generally oppose increasing it and might even, if politically feasible, support its repeal, on the grounds that it burdens small business and causes significant job loss, particularly among young and unskilled workers. The voting public, when its fickle attention is engaged, tends to support the minimum wage. . . .

From an economically informed perspective, the political popularity of the minimum wage seems paradoxical. Most economists of all ideological persuasions have long agreed that it is self-defeating: it destroys jobs in the low-wage sector of the economy and thus hurts many of the people it is intended to help. This follows simply from the law of demand: market demand for an item generally declines as its price increases. Thus, just as a tariff reduces imports, and just as rent control decreases the supply and/or the quality of rental housing, so a legally mandated hourly wage floor reduces employment. Although a minimum wage could conceivably increase total income among low-wage workers—just as an industry cartel or monopoly could increase the industry's receipts despite reducing its output—any such increase would accrue only to those who kept their jobs, leaving the least skilled as the likely losers.

To be sure, this longstanding consensus among economists has recently been prominently challenged. David Card and Alan B. Krueger, in a 1995 book entitled Myth and Measurement: The New Economics of the Minimum Wage, argue that the traditional economic wisdom is incorrect, and that modest minimum wage hikes can actually increase low-wage employment, or at least have no significant effect on it. . . .

Now, the law of demand does not indicate how *much* any given price increase will reduce demand. Thus, it would not be absurd to claim that the job loss from retaining or increasing the minimum wage is small enough to be worth the distributional gain to low-wage workers who keep their jobs—although I [believe] that such a claim is probably mistaken. Yet the sense of paradox about widespread public support for the minimum wage returns when it is examined not merely as an isolated proposal, but as one of a range of alternative means to its most plausible ends.

In economic substance, the minimum wage is equivalent to a wage subsidy to low-wage employees, financed by a tax on low-wage employers. There are three plausible objectives that a low-wage subsidy could serve. The first is encouraging more people to regard market work as a viable long-term option, thus inducing them to develop their own employability and productivity, arguably to both their own and society's benefit. The second is reducing the tax and transfer systems' pervasive discouragement of additional work at the margin by poor individuals who are already employable. The phase-out, as a family's income rises, of social welfare benefits such as Aid to Families with Dependent Children (AFDC) and Food Stamps, combined with an array of positive federal and state taxes, often causes individuals in poor households, especially if they have children, to face the highest marginal tax rates of *any* taxpayers, sometimes exceeding 100%. The effects of 1996 welfare reform on marginal tax rates remains unclear. The third plausible objective of a low-wage subsidy is progressive wealth redistribution.

As to each rationale, the minimum wage has a strong chance of doing more harm than good. On the subsidy side, it merely does less good than one might have

HARM

expected, because it directs surprisingly little benefit to the poor households that are the preferred targets under each of the three above rationales. The relationship between low hourly wages and household poverty is extremely weak in an era when multiple-earner households are the rule. Recent estimates suggest that barely one-quarter of the benefits from the latest minimum wage increase will go to poor and near-poor households, leaving the remaining three-quarters to be divided almost evenly between middle- and upper-income households.

There is a strong prospect that the minimum wage will be affirmatively harmful, however, because it imposes a tax on low-wage employment. Taxing low-wage work is not well conceived to attract more people to seek it, or to reduce tax-and-transfer-based substitution away from it. Moreover, while the minimum wage is modestly progressive as between poor households as a group and other households—even under reasonable estimates of the likely job loss—its likely regressivity amongst poor households (the worst-off of which it probably hurts) makes it an unattractive policy tool for wealth redistribution.

Should one favor a low-wage subsidy, the obvious alternative is to finance it out of general revenues. The main such program under present law is the Earned Income Tax Credit ("EITC"), a transfer program for low-income workers that is administered through the income tax via refundable credits. Under the EITC, low-income status depends on total annual earnings and other household income, rather than on hourly wages as under the minimum wage; benefits are mainly restricted to households with children. The EITC's income-testing and reliance on general revenues make it a far better tool than the minimum wage both for making market work a more viable long-term option and for progressive redistribution. . . .

. . . Most people . . . undoubtedly think of the [minimum wage] laws as a limitation on employers, barring them from hiring people at "too low" a wage. This understanding is in fact consistent with the laws' enforcement structure: employers, rather than employees, are sanctioned for violation (in that they must make good the under-paid wages). Yet the details of enforcement do not make the minimum wage any less a constraint on both groups. Similarly, it would generally be understood that a law punishing any attorney who agreed to represent criminal defendants would burden the defendants' legal defense rights, even if they themselves were not subject to sanction for hiring an attorney.

What do we learn from construing the minimum wage as a constraint on low-wage employees (as well as employers), barring them from entering into certain contracts? Once construed this way, the notion that employees will benefit may begin to seem less intuitively plausible. Individuals are generally made worse off by denying them choices, absent the paternalistic assumption that they will choose poorly—an assumption that seems somewhat implausible when the choice they are being denied is to accept a job.

Nonetheless, low-wage employees as a group can benefit from being denied the right to accept jobs that pay less than a specified hourly rate. The ban, by applying to them collectively, in effect organizes them as a cartel. It solves the internal organizational and enforcement problems that likely would prevent their establishing, by their own unaided efforts, a cartel (such as an universal labor union) demanding a given minimum wage.

It is well known that cartels can increase their members' aggregate income, albeit by reducing output and imposing a deadweight loss on society. In the case of the minimum wage, this claim of overall group benefit appears to be empirically plausible. The pre-Card and Krueger empirical consensus among economists held that a 10% minimum wage increase would likely reduce low-wage hours worked by 1 to 3%. This implies the strong possibility of an increase in the total income of low-wage workers (along with increased leisure that could perhaps be used productively, as in housework), although there are countervailing considerations, such as the possible loss of "stepping-stone jobs" leading to better ones down the line.

Still, even if the minimum wage does boost low-wage workers' real income as a group, the internal distributional effect is likely to be quite uneven. In a classic producers' cartel, it is plausible that each participant will enjoy greater profits than it would have through competition. For this to happen with low wage employees in the setting of the minimum wage, one would have to posit that the number of jobs remained the same, with the lost output involving not overly disproportionate reductions in hours worked. In actual employment markets, where full-time work plays so large a role, it seems likely that the cartel will cost some members their jobs, leaving a mix of gainers and uncompensated losers.

To the extent that job loss is non-random, it will likely fall on those members of the cartel who have the least marketable skills—perhaps the very individuals whom altruistic supporters of the minimum wage law may have wanted to help the most. One might also be concerned about involuntariness: the losers, unless they sought a minimum wage increase through political activity, did not elect to join a cartel and take their chances. . . .

Richard B. Freeman, *What Will a 10% . . . 50% . . . 100% Increase in the Minimum Wage Do?*
48 INDUS. & LAB. REL. REV. 830, 833–34 (1995)

What factors ought we to consider as part of a "reorientation" of public discussion [on the minimum wage]? There are, in my view, five issues in assessing the policy of using the minimum wage to help low-paid workers.

1. Does the minimum wage redistribute income to low-wage workers? . . . The [Card & Krueger] book shows that modest increases in the minimum are likely to have no effect on employment. While there are researchers . . . who argue the opposite, the debate is over whether modest minimum wage increases have "no" employment effect, modest positive effects, or small negative effects. It is not about whether or not there are large negative effects.

2. Does the minimum wage divide the work force into insiders, employed permanently at the minimum, and outsiders who suffer long-term joblessness because of the minimum? In the U.S. labor market, with its high turnover, particularly in low-wage jobs, it is hard to make the case for such a division; even analysts who believe in segmented labor markets do not argue for the European insiders (employed)-outsiders (unemployed) division. . . . [L]ow and falling wages, not excessively high minimum wages or other administered wages, have reduced

employment at the bottom tier of the wage distribution.

3. Are low-wage workers low-income workers? No one who advocates the minimum wage wants to raise the pay of teenagers in upper-income families at the expense of lower-income consumers. If the result of an effective minimum wage is that Harvey Poor pays more for his hamburger so Melissa or Roderick Well-to-Do can earn more pocket money, the minimum will be redistributive, but in a regressive direction. . . . [C]urrently many workers paid around the minimum are, in fact, from low-income families: one-third of workers whose wages were affected by the 1990 and 1991 increases in the minimum came from the bottom 10% of the earnings distribution. The widening dispersion of wages has meant that more low-skill young adults earn "teenage" wages. . . .

4. How does the minimum wage fit with other economic policies? We all know that, despite the valiant efforts of the Invisible Hand, at best we live in a second-best world. The effects of the minimum wage or of any other policy must be judged in the context of numerous other policies and institutions. Many on both sides of the aisle in Congress favor Earned Income Tax Credits as a way to improve the economic well-being of low-wage workers. EITCs subsidize low-wage employers. Minimum wages "tax" those employers. The two policies would seem to complement one another. While no one has analyzed the quantitative interactions between these (and other) policies, my guess is that the minimum wage looks better in the second-best world in which we live than it does in most textbooks.

Finally, the bottom line question is:

5. At what level should we fix the minimum wage if we are to redistribute income without risking sizable job loss?

Myth and Measurement: The New Economics of the Minimum Wage [by Card and Krueger] makes a convincing case that we have overestimated the dangers of job losses and that the level of the minimum wage that does more good than harm is probably much higher than many economists have previously thought. The book shows as well as empirical economics can that 10%–20% increases in the current U.S. federal minimum will do little if any harm to employment. . . . [What about a] 100% increase in the minimum? A 200% increase? I know (sadly) that if you raise my pay to rock star levels, my employers will disemploy me, tenure and my singing talents notwithstanding. Still, if, within certain ranges, the minimum has little effect on employment, per Card and Krueger; if low wages reduce employment through supply responses . . . ; and if earnings inequality has become a major national problem, as we all recognize, policy debate should concentrate on the question, "What level of the minimum can redistribute income to low-paid workers without serious job loss?"

Brishen Rogers, *Justice at Work: Minimum Wage Laws and Social Equality*
92 TEX. L. REV. 1543, 1544–49 (2014)

In 1935, as minimum wage provisions established by President Roosevelt's National Recovery Administration came into effect, a journalist asked a New England textile worker for his reaction. The response was telling:

You can guess that the money is handy. . . . But there is something more than the money. There is knowing that the working man don't [sic] stand alone against the bosses and their smart lawyers and all their tricks. There is a government now that cares whether things [sic] is fair for us.

The sentiment remains remarkably common: low-wage workers often describe the minimum wage as a matter of respect and fairness, not just resources. President Obama has framed his push to raise the minimum wage in similar terms, calling income inequality "the defining challenge of our time" and a violation of "middle-class America's basic bargain that if you work hard, you have a chance to get ahead." The overwhelming political popularity of the minimum wage—which transcends income groups, political affiliation, and racial identity—may likewise reflect an intuitive sense that a just state will promote decent wages and decent work.

Legal academic and policy debates around the minimum wage are bloodless in comparison, focusing almost entirely on the minimum wage's efficacy at redistributing wealth. For example, law and economics scholar Daniel Shaviro has argued that the minimum wage is a perverse redistributive tool, for it not only reduces overall efficiency but also "destroys jobs in the low-wage sector of the economy and thus hurts many of the people it is intended to help." Shaviro therefore advocated repealing the minimum wage and instead assisting low-wage workers through negative income taxes or other transfers funded out of general revenues.

. . . .

Minimum wage advocates, for their part, typically respond to such critiques in several ways. Often they simply assume minimum wage laws are desirable and ask how best to ensure their enforcement. At other times, they draw on growing—yet still disputed—empirical evidence that minimum wage laws do not in fact increase unemployment. Such arguments turn what might be a question of first principles into an evidentiary contest. Other advocates appeal to the dignitary values of workplace regulations highlighted by the New England garment worker. But they have only rarely linked those values to broader theories of justice, leaving the minimum wage a bit of an academic orphan. Policy debate around the minimum wage, which has recently become more urgent due to President Obama's proposal and due to recent growth in the low-wage sector, likewise revolves around questions of unemployment.

This is a problem for minimum wage advocates. If intuitions that the minimum wage is a matter of justice are simply wrong or merely conventional, then advocates should take such critiques far more seriously. Moreover, even if minimum wage laws are here to stay, this underlying debate has implications for a host of subsidiary questions. Those include the level at which minimum wages should be set; whether particular workers deserve coverage under such laws; how much states should invest in enforcement; and which entities should be liable for violations. Lawmakers, executives, and judges often confront such questions, and the answers will differ depending on the underlying defensibility of the minimum wage itself.

To focus its analysis, and to begin to move beyond existing debates, this Article accepts for the sake of argument that minimum wage laws tend to reduce demand for low-wage labor. To be clear, this assumption may be counterfactual: there is significant evidence that past minimum wage increases have not led to job losses. But arguments based on such evidence are essentially empirical, and as Paul Samuelson once wrote, "it takes a theory to kill a theory; facts can only dent a theorist's hide." Moreover, even if minimum wages will not increase unemployment if set within traditional limits, at a certain wage rate they would undoubtedly do so. Clarifying the social goods advanced by minimum wage laws will help in assessing whether their costs are worth bearing. What is needed is a nonutilitarian defense of minimum wage laws, one that holds even if they reduce demand for low-wage labor.

This Article takes up that mantle, defending the minimum wage as a matter of justice. It builds on well-established arguments that a just state must not just redistribute resources but also ensure that "people stand in relations of equality to others." This requires combatting status inequalities that result from gender, race, and class differentiation. . . . Among other things, a society committed to social equality will seek to ensure decent work—work that enhances rather than undermines workers' self-respect and social standing.

Minimum wage laws advance this goal in several interrelated ways. First and foremost, minimum wage laws increase workers' hourly pay; this enhances workers' self-respect by improving their material lives and by increasing the social value attached to their labor. Second, minimum wage laws alter workplace power relationships. Such laws enable workers to call upon the state to protect them against certain employer demands and require employers themselves to bear duties toward workers rather than mediating all distribution through the state. These rights and duties are meaningful independent of their effects on distribution for reasons captured nicely by the textile-worker quote above. Third, minimum wage laws alter the economics of low-wage employment. They deliver additional resources to low-wage workers as a group, and they force employers and consumers to internalize some of the social costs of low-wage work.

Minimum wage laws, in short, help ensure more egalitarian work-based social structures. This analysis thus turns one common line of critique on its head: rather than a tax on low-wage work, the minimum wage can be analogized to a tax on the class and status benefits of employing or consuming the products of low-wage labor. Minimum wage laws' effects on unemployment should therefore no longer give rise to a presumption against them but rather should be seen as a collateral cost to be managed—perhaps through transfers, or perhaps through other policies that enhance employment opportunities. In fact, marginally reduced demand for extremely low-wage labor may be an affirmative good insofar as it ensures more egalitarian social relationships.

NOTES

1. **The Debate Continues.** Freeman's essay was one of several published in an issue of the Industrial & Labor Relations Review dedicated to the debate about the Krueger and Card book. For other perspectives, see Review Symposium, 48 INDUS. & LAB. REL. REV. 827–49 (1995). Card and Krueger have published a response to the critiques of their work. *See* David Card & Alan B. Krueger, *Minimum Wages and Employment: A Case Study of the Fast-Food Industry in New Jersey and Pennsylvania: Reply*, 30 AM. ECON. REV. 1397 (2001). A study by the Fiscal Policy

Institute (2004) supported Card and Krueger's findings, concluding that states that increased the minimum wage beyond the federal minimum did not experience declines in employment, and actually saw an increase in small business retail employment. *See* Fiscal Policy Institute, *State Minimum Wage and Employment in Small Business* (Apr. 20, 2004). Other studies, however, find negative effects on employment. *See, e.g.*, David Neumark & William Wascher, *Minimum Wages and Low-Wage Workers: How Well Does Reality Match the Rhetoric?*, 92 MINN. L. REV. 1296, 1313 (2008). Responding to President Obama's call for an increase in the minimum wage to $10.10, the Congressional Budget Office published a study concluding that raising the minimum wage by this amount would reduce total employment by about 500,000 jobs, equivalent to.3%. Congressional Budget Office, *The Effects of a Minimum Wage Increase on Employment and Family Income*, Feb. 18, 2014, *available at* http://www.cbo.gov/publication/44995.

As Freeman suggests, the real question may not be whether increases in the minimum wage are desirable and efficacious, but instead at what level their detrimental impact on employment outweighs their positive effect in reducing poverty among low income families. How should we determine this level? What if the disemployment effects fall most heavily on the most disadvantaged workers? *See* Harry Hutchison, *Toward a Critical Race Reformist Conception of Minimum Wage Regimes: Exploding the Power of Myth, Fantasy, and Hierarchy*, 34 HARV. J. LEGIS. 93 (1997) (suggesting that minimum wage increases result in job losses that disproportionately impact low-skilled minority workers).

Are all jobs worth saving? Why should we focus exclusively on protecting jobs (and employers) that pay minimum wage rates? Some commentators suggest that the minimum wage helps both marginal workers and efficient employers who pay higher wages by driving inefficient employers out of business. *See, e.g.*, Marc Linder, *The Minimum Wage as Industrial Policy: A Forgotten Role*, 16 J. LEGIS. 151, 155–156 (1990).

2. The Impact of a Minimum Wage Increase on Businesses. Would the impact of a minimum wage increase be spread evenly across all employers? Opponents of increases argue that small businesses would bear a disproportionate share of the costs of a higher minimum wage. Studies by economists suggest the opposite, however. When the minimum wage was raised in 1997, data showed that small businesses with fewer than 100 employees accounted for 54% of workers earning minimum wage, and overall employed 52% of the labor force. Thus, small businesses do not employ a disproportionate share of the low-waged workers who would be impacted by a rise in the minimum wage. In addition, many small businesses already pay above the current minimum wage out of concern for their employees' well-being, a sense of social responsibility to the community, and to minimize turnover and associated training and churning costs, their single biggest expense. These businesses would be helped by an increase because it would assist them in competing with larger rivals who pay employees less and can therefore discount prices on goods and services sold. *See* Gayle Cinquegrani, *Some Small Business Owners Say Paying Workers More Helps Everyone*, DAILY LAB. REP. (BNA) No. 158, Aug. 15, 2014.

3. The Political Feasibility of Minimum Wage Increases. Should the debate over raising the minimum wage rest on a "bloodless" "evidentiary contest" or on notions of fairness and justice, as Rogers suggests? Despite the lively debate among economists over the efficacy of raising the minimum wage, public opinion favors increases in the minimum wage: in a 2014 poll administered by the Pew Research Center, 73% of respondents supported an increase in the minimum wage to $10.10 per hour. *See* Pew Research Center for People & The Press, *Most See Inequality Growing, but Partisans Differ over Solutions*, Jan. 23, 2014, *available at* http://www.people-press.org/2014/01/23/most-see-inequality-growing-but-partisans-differ-over-solutions/. Neumark and Wascher suggest three explanations for the public's embrace of the minimum wage: (1) the benefits of minimum wages may be more directly observable than the costs (a decline in jobs manifested by decreased hiring rather than layoffs and the redistribution of income from one group of workers to another); (2) some constituencies, most notably labor unions, may support minimum wage increases even though their members do not directly benefit, because the increase may prompt employers to substitute higher-skilled union workers for minimum-waged workers; in addition, employers who already pay their workforces more than minimum wage have an incentive to support minimum wage increases, since this raises labor costs for their low-wage competitors; and (3) some supporters may see minimum wage policy as an issue of morality or fairness, and thus be less concerned about the inefficiencies of the minimum wage as an anti-poverty tool; for these proponents, positions taken on the minimum wage policy signal political and social concern with income inequality and the decline in the political power of workers. Neumark & Wascher, *supra*, at 1313–15. Economists remain more divided on the question, though a significant group—including seven Nobel Prize winners—also support an increase in the minimum wage. *See* Economic Policy Institute, *Over 600 Economists Sign Letter in Support of $10.10 Minimum Wage*, *available at* http://www.epi.org/minimum-wage-statement/.

4. An Alternative: Living Wage Laws. A more recent legislative innovation is the enactment of living wage laws in municipalities and towns. A living wage law establishes a local "living wage" at some standard higher than the federal and state minimum wage. The municipality or town establishes the living wage—which often includes a requirement that employers make available health benefits and other common employment benefits—after taking into account area costs of living, such as housing, transportation, clothing, health insurance, and utilities. Living wage standards may vary dramatically within a single state, and may change over time. Local governments typically guarantee the living wage to their own employees, and also to those of private sector service contractors, businesses that receive tax credits, grants, or lease public lands. *See, e.g.*, Kelly Knaub, *DeBlasio Broadens NYC's 'Living Wage' Provision*, Law 360, Sept. 30, 2014 (describing mayoral order increasing New York City's living wage provision to $13.13 per hour and extending it to commercial establishments that receive more than $1 million in city subsidies).

Living wage legislation was initiated in part as a response to the decline in the real value of both federal and state minimum wages, which lagged behind inflation and increases in the cost of living. *RUI One Corporation v. City of Berkeley*, 371 F.3d 1137, 1143 (9th Cir. 2004). The earliest legislation took the form of a local minimum wage higher than the federal minimum. In the 1960s, Baltimore, New

York City, and Washington D.C. enacted such laws, often in the absence of any statewide minimum wage. Beginning in the mid-1990s, localities began to enact new legislation targeting benefits as well as wages, and mandated wages that were above the federal or state minimum wage. *Id.* More than 120 municipalities had enacted living wage laws by July of 2011. *See* National Employment Law Project, *Local Living Wage Laws and Coverage, available at* http://www.nelp.org/page/-/Justice/2011/LocalLWLawsCoverageFINAL.pdf?nocdn=1

Increasingly, living wage laws have expanded to apply to all employers within a particular geographical area. For example, the Mayor of Seattle enacted a law raising the minimum wage to $15 per hour, applicable to all businesses operating in the city of Seattle. The wage is phased in incrementally depending upon the size of the business and whether it offers health care. Kirk Johnson, *Seattle Approves $15 Minimum Wage, Setting a New Standard for Big Cities*, N.Y. TIMES, June 2, 2014. The law was enacted in response to widespread strikes by hundreds of fast food workers in Seattle, whose efforts were supported by the Service Employees International Union (although it does not represent the workers). Jacklyn Willie, *Labor and Business Partnership a Must for $15 Seattle Minimum Wage*, Seattle Mayor Says, DAILY LAB. REP. (BNA) No. 175, Sept. 10, 2014.

Opponents of living wage laws typically make five arguments against them, many of which parallel objections to increases in the minimum wage: living wage laws (1) force small businesses and nonprofits out of business because they raise labor costs beyond tolerance; (2) drive away businesses and cause revenue losses to the local government, as well as job losses; (3) unfairly impact businesses in urban areas and undermine their ability to compete with businesses located in suburban areas not impacted by the living wage; (4) shift the tax burden from the government to private employers by elevating former welfare recipients to new tax brackets; and (5) displace unskilled and immigrant workers as those with higher education and language proficiency seek and are hired to fill living waged jobs. *See* Rachel I. Rosen, Note, *The Rise and Potential Fall of Living Wage Laws: Missouri Hotel and Motel Association v. City of St. Louis*, 21 J. L. & COM. 131, 135 (2001). Opponents are particularly critical of living wage programs applicable to all private employers of a certain size located within a defined geographical area (as contrasted with living wage laws applied to public contractors), pointing out that such broadly applicable laws are expensive and poorly targeted. Are these arguments more or less persuasive in the living wage context than they are in the federal minimum wage context?

Proponents argue that living wage laws raise disposable income for low wage workers, increase productivity, reduce costs in administering social welfare programs, and only negligibly impact employers' locational decisions. *See* ROBERT POLLIN & STEPHANIE LUCE, THE LIVING WAGE: BUILDING A FAIR ECONOMY 17, 21–22 (1998). Are these benefits worth the tradeoffs? Studies suggest that living wage programs do raise average wages for low-income employees and reduce poverty, but they may also reduce employment for the lowest-skilled workers. *Compare* Scott Adams & David Neumark, *A Decade of Living Wages: What Have We Learned?*, 1 CALIFORNIA ECON. POL'Y (Public Policy Institute of California, July 2005) (finding disemployment effect for lowest-skilled workers) *with* Arindrajit Dube *et al., The Economic Effects of a Citywide Minimum Wage*, 60 INDUS. & LAB. REL. REV. 522

(2007) (finding that San Francisco's indexed minimum wage increased worker pay in table service and fast food restaurants and compressed wage inequality but did not create detectable employment losses). In addition, the main poverty reduction effect of living wage legislation appears to stem from the spillover effect the law has on the wages of those who earn more than the minimum wage; relatively few workers are directly impacted unless the minimum wage increase is substantial (for example, Seattle's $15 hour wage). *See* Adams & Neumark, *supra.*

What are the advantages of legislating minimum wages and benefits at a local level? What the disadvantages?

2. The Overtime Pay Provisions and the "White-Collar" Exemptions

In addition to its wealth redistribution goals, the FLSA had a work-spreading goal: as a response to the Great Depression, it sought to induce employers to hire additional workers by imposing a premium on overtime (hours worked in excess of 40 per week). The choice of the overtime premium as the means to achieve the goals of work-spreading necessitated line-drawing at the upper end of the occupational hierarchy. Hourly compensation and overtime pay were seen as fundamentally incompatible with the notion of middle- or upper-class status. Further, government actors believed that so-called "white-collar" workers did not need the protection of the FLSA. Such workers typically earned salaries well above the minimum wage and were presumed to enjoy other compensatory privileges such as above-average fringe benefits and better opportunities for advancement, setting them apart from nonexempt workers entitled to overtime pay. Finally, the skilled nature of their work reduced the likelihood that work-spreading would be accomplished: the work they performed was difficult to standardize to any time frame and could not be easily spread to other workers after 40 hours in a week. Accordingly, Congress included the "white-collar exemptions"—a phrase found nowhere in the Act itself, but widely used to describe these exemptions—which excluded executive, administrative, and professional employees as well as outside salespersons from the Act's coverage. *See Defining and Delimiting the Exemptions for Executive, Administrative, Professional, Outside Sales and Computer Employees,* 69 Fed. Reg. 22,122, 22,123–22,124 (April 23, 2004). The excerpt below focuses on the first three exemptions. We will study all four in more detail *infra,* in part E.

Deborah C. Malamud, *Engineering the Middle Classes: Class Line-Drawing in New Deal Hours Legislation*
96 Mich. L. Rev. 2212, 2219–20, 2223–25, 2232, 2237, 2319–20 (1998)

. . . The New Deal legislative innovation that occasioned the . . . most sustained debate about the legal status of white-collar workers was the adoption of comprehensive wage and hour legislation. In the Fair Labor Standards Act of 1938 (FLSA), Congress exempted "executive, administrative, [and] professional" employees from the statute's requirement that employers pay their employees an overtime premium for the hours they worked beyond the statutory maximum of 40 hours per week. The FLSA's so-called "white-collar exemptions"—which are still in effect and are still the subject of controversy—arose out of a prehistory of wage and hour regulation during the period of the National Recovery Administration. . . . .

Almost all pre-New Deal legislation limiting the working hours of male workers applied only to "laborers, workmen, and mechanics." White-collar workers were not covered. There were many reasons for this restricted application of hours regulation. The most obvious was that pre-New Deal hours legislation was health-oriented, and the working conditions of white-collar workers were not as injurious to health as those of industrial workers. In addition, the two groups represented in the shorter-hours movement of the nineteenth and early twentieth century were skilled manual workers, represented through their labor unions, and unskilled industrial workers, represented by the middle-class reformers who took on their cause. White-collar workers were not organized into unions, and white-collar reformers apparently did not see their own kind as overworked.

Indeed, male white-collar workers would have found working-hours regulation contrary to their own interest. They viewed themselves as occupying entry-level positions that would lead to jobs in the upper reaches of the business class. They took it for granted that they needed to work long hours to gain the training that would advance their careers. Furthermore, they would have found shorter hours—and, worse, government intervention to secure shorter hours—inconsistent with the status they sought to maintain in their own and their employers' eyes. White-collar workers identified upwards with their bosses, not downwards with mere manual workers. Even if white-collar workers in fact needed shorter hours, their need to maintain their social status would have deterred them from seeking reform. . . .

The upward identification of lower-level white-collar workers was, as University of Chicago economist Frank William Taussig explained in 1936, crucial to the operation of the American system of class stratification. Taussig recognized five "non-competing groups," which ultimately resolved into "the two great classes of the soft handed and the hard handed." The bottom three groups, unskilled, semiskilled, and skilled manual workers, identified with one another. The next group up the ladder, the lower middle class, was made up of "clerks, bookkeepers, salesmen, small tradesmen, railway conductors, foremen, superintendents, [and] teachers in the lower grades." Taussig observed that the lower middle class identified with the top group (the "well-to-do"), and its "feeling of contempt for the manual laborers of all sorts, whether skilled or unskilled," was both central to its identity and dangerous to its economic health. The democratization of public secondary education meant that "there [was] a plethora of persons qualified to do [lower middle class] work and a consequent tendency for their wages to fall rather than to rise. The earnings of a good mechanic [were] in the United States higher than those of the average clerk." But the lower middle class failed to respond to market pressures in part because it carried the false hope that routine clerical work would someday lead to a professional or managerial job—"the alluring tho [sic] deceptive chance of a prize." . . .

It comes as no surprise, in light of these observations, that white-collar workers did not mobilize to seek government protection from long working hours. . . .

. . . [T]he notion that upper-level white-collar workers ought to be exempted from hours legislation had the commonsense quality that marks all uncontestable

lines drawn w/class

cultural propositions. But as is so often the case with seemingly uncontestable social truths, on closer examination one finds little agreement as to what had been agreed upon, or why. Who are the upper-level white-collar workers who obviously ought to be exempted from hours regulation? The terms chosen to describe them were not uniform from one assertion of this obvious point to another. Precisely what makes the exempted group different? Should the exemption include all white-collar workers? Was the logic of exclusion in fact related to collar color? Was it related to income level so that the exclusion should also apply to well-paid skilled blue-collar workers? Or was it something unique to the top tier of white-collar workers that exempted them from hours regulation? These questions were sufficiently important to reveal the conceptually difficult and contested nature of the choices government actors were required to make. . . .

If we are prepared to create a meaningful work-spreading incentive, the question of whether upper-level workers should be exempt should be reconsidered in its entirety. At least some "ordinary" work is regaining the exercise of autonomy and discretion through flexible specialization and cooperative management. At the same time, the well-publicized wave of layoffs of executive, administrative, and professional employees through corporate downsizing suggests that the use of "best practice" management techniques to control the work of upper-level employees is, to borrow a phrase, once again "taking the starch out of" upper-level white collar workers. There is good reason to suspect, then, that the trend of convergence in the work structure and working conditions of upper-level and ordinary workers continues apace. The assumption that upper-level work is (and is uniquely) noncommodified and nondivisible deserves to be freshly reexamined.

Finally, it is time to consider whether the FLSA should be shifted off of its work-spreading foundation and explicitly moved onto alternative moorings—for example, the protection, for all workers, of leisure or of their right to function simultaneously as workers, parents, and citizens. It is, in short, time to genuinely rethink the FLSA and its upper-level exemptions, not merely to "simplify" them or remake them to maximize employer "flexibility." . . .

rethink the FLSA

. . . [W]e must be cognizant of the fact that revising the FLSA will require a new wave of class line-drawing. . . . [O]vertime exemptions send working people powerful messages about their class position—a message that is reiterated with every paycheck. True, . . . government regulation does not set out to map or to alter the class system or even to send any particular messages about class. But the messages we receive are not necessarily the ones the sender sent. The class structure of contemporary American society is at least as uncertain and contested as it was in the pre-New Deal period. Any government action that draws lines on the basis of class-like criteria—income, occupation, education level, and so forth—is likely to have a significant effect on how we experience and debate the issue of class.

NOTES

1. **Class Line-Drawing.** As Malamud explains, the white-collar exemptions were ultimately an exercise in class line-drawing. The debate over where the lines should be drawn continues today as the courts struggle to define the scope of the exemptions. The regulations implementing the overtime exemptions are complex.

In 2014, President Obama instructed the Department of Labor to streamline and modernize the overtime regulations and to expand the group of workers eligible for overtime pay under the FLSA. In particular, the salary threshold for white-collar exemptions is widely perceived as too low at $455 per week, covering workers earning as little as $23,660 per year. The rulemaking process is expected to take as long as two years. Chris Opfer & Gayle Cinquegrani, *Obama Signs Memo Telling DOL to Update, Streamline White-Collar Overtime Exemption*, DAILY LAB. REP. (BNA) No. 49, Mar. 13, 2014.

2. Prestige and the White-Collar Exemptions. Malamud suggests that overtime exemptions send messages about class. What messages does the law send? Which characteristics do you think of as being associated with heightened class status? Which of them are consistent with eligibility for overtime pay?

Malamud observes that FLSA enforcement is especially difficult in the white-collar exemption area because plaintiffs must initiate and demand a categorization that, while it may yield more income in the short-term, is experienced as a loss of status in the long term. The most recent regulatory action affecting overtime pay eligibility occurred in 2004, when the Department of Labor raised pay thresholds and simplified the so-called "duties tests" so that more employees would be eligible for overtime pay. Two months after the effective date of the 2004 regulations, the Department of Labor reported that the most frequent complaint received by employers was from formerly exempt employees who were now being required to clock in and to be more accountable for their hours. These workers perceived their shift to nonexempt status as a " 'downgrade' and loss of autonomy." *DOL Says Dire Predictions on New Overtime Rule Proving Inaccurate*, DAILY LAB. REP. (BNA) No. 200, Oct. 18, 2004; *see* Kris Maher, *Changed U.S. Rules for Overtime Pay Roil the Workplace*, WALL ST. J., Sept. 7, 2004 (reporting that workers newly entitled to overtime pay experience their nonexempt status as a demotion to hourly waged work). Similarly, in *McDaniel v. Transcender LLC*, 2005 U.S. App. LEXIS 1587 (6th Cir. Jan. 31, 2005), a human resources manager sought to re-classify software developers previously classified as exempt. When she informed them that they were to be reclassified as non-exempt (and so would be eligible for overtime pay if they worked more than 40 hours per week), the employees took offense and became hostile, accusing her of viewing their work as less important than that done by exempt employees. *Id.* at *5–*11. (The manager was terminated shortly thereafter and brought a retaliation claim under the FLSA.)

A glimpse into the outlook of such workers regarding the status/hours bargain is visible in *Valerio v. Putnam Associates, Inc.*, 173 F.3d 35 (1st Cir. 1999). Elaine Valerio was hired as a receptionist/administrative assistant for a health-care consulting firm. Her duties included answering telephones, receiving packages, maintaining client files, and researching at libraries and in on-line databases. Her employer told her when she was hired that her position was exempt from the FLSA's overtime requirements. Valerio made it clear that she aspired to concentrate on the research and administration aspects of her job rather than on the receptionist duties, and subsequently enrolled in law school at night. When a dispute developed over Valerio's punctuality and performance of the receptionist part of her job, the office manager reprimanded her, making it clear that her duties

as a receptionist were a core part of her job, Valerio responded with the following
letter:

> I will repeat to you once again that I am not a receptionist. I am classified
> as an exempt, salaried employee and according to the Fair Labor Stan-
> dards Act published by the Department of Labor, a receptionist, by the
> nature of the job, not the title, cannot be an exempt employee. If you insist
> on classifying me as a receptionist, then I demand under FLSA that I be
> reclassified as non-exempt and be paid for all overtime hours worked. . . .

Id. at 38.

Nevertheless, an array of white collar workers have come forward to press claims
for overtime pay. Are workers who bring collective actions challenging their exempt
status really using the FLSA collective action as a substitute for collectively
bargaining higher wages?

3. Professional Status and Overtime Pay. The white-collar exemptions
include professionals. Is professional status fundamentally incompatible with
overtime compensation? Which aspects of professionalism are inconsistent with
overtime pay entitlement?

Lawyers are specifically covered by the white-collar exemptions as "learned
professionals," meaning that they are not entitled to overtime pay for the practice
of law. 29 C.F.R. § 541.304 (a), (d). Should attorneys performing document review on
a contract basis be considered professionals exempt from overtime pay? Suppose
that the document review is so mechanical that it could be performed by a
nonlawyer, such as a paralegal (who would be entitled to overtime pay). In *Lola v.
Skadden, Arps, Slate, Meagher & Flom, LLP*, 2014 U.S. Dist. LEXIS 130604
(S.D.N.Y. Sept. 16, 2014), the court rejected an overtime pay claim by an attorney
who worked 45 to 55 hours per week as a temporary contract employee for Skadden
reviewing documents related to multidistrict litigation. The plaintiff argued that
lawyers performing this sort of document review should not be covered by the
professional exemption because the practice of law only includes tasks requiring the
exercise of legal judgment and discretion. The court responded:

[handwritten margin notes: lawyers ~ learned professio; doc review should not be exempt]

> . . . [T]he court is not persuaded that the exercise of legal judgment and
> discretion is a *sine qua non* of legal practice. Even undisputedly legal
> services like the drafting of motion briefs and the negotiating of documents
> require the performance of tasks—checking cases to make sure quotations
> are accurately reproduced, conforming citations to the stylistic dictates of
> the *Bluebook*, ensuring that documents are free of grammatical and
> typographical errors—that require little to no legal judgment. As junior
> associates at law firms well know, these tasks are the bread and butter of
> much legal practice and essential to the competent representation of
> clients.
>
> . . . .

[handwritten margin note: ct disagree]

The Court is mindful that it appears unfair for an attorney not to receive
overtime when performing a job that a non-attorney (properly supervised)
might also perform. That result, however, is within the express contempla-

tion of 29 C.F.R. § 541.304, which extends the FLSA exemption to employees who are *both* the "holder[s] of a valid license or certificate permitting the practice of law" *and* "actually engaged in the practice thereof." 29 C.F.R. § 541.304. . . .

To the extent that this is unwise or unfair, especially in light of the employment prospects that many licensed attorneys now face, Congress and the DOL remain free to revisit the regulation to promulgate a uniform federal standard that more narrowly defines the "practice of law." Until they do so, however, the Court is constrained to apply the regulation as written. . . .

Id. at *37–*39. Should the DOL reconsider this regulation? *See Henig v. Quinn Emmanuel Urquhart & Sullivan,* 2013 U.S. Dist. LEXIS 174642, and No. 13-cv-1432, Doc. No. 45 at 5:12-7:12-20 (transcript of oral hearing) (S.D.N.Y. Dec. 11, 2013) (refusing to dismiss a similar claim by contract attorneys proceeding in a collective action under the FLSA, urging adoption of a uniform standard defining the practice of law, and suggesting that the question turn on 1) whether the individual renders legal advice to a particular client, 2) whether he holds himself out as an attorney, and 3) whether his duties require him to draw on legal knowledge and judgment). Does the *Henig* standard seem workable? Would the purposes of the overtime provisions (such as work-spreading and hours reduction) be served by adoption of such a standard?

4. The Impact of the Overtime Premium on Working Time. The FLSA's overtime pay provisions were designed to reduce working hours and spread jobs. The overtime premium did not impose a direct limit on working hours, however; instead, it gave rise to a choice. Employers and workers could exchange time for money, but the FLSA altered the bargain once the workweek extended beyond 40 hours per week. Most blue-collar workers were eager for overtime hours, which offered a route to higher pay. Employers responded by adjusting their straight-time wages downward to account for the expenses of overtime premiums. At the same time, unions' success in obtaining improved benefits through collective bargaining (health insurance, pension benefits, vacation time, etc.) soon rendered benefits costs prohibitive, creating a powerful new disincentive to work-spreading. For most employers, it was cheaper to pay the overtime premium for existing workers than it was to hire additional workers and incur associated benefits and training costs. Finally, the at-will rule supported employers' rights to mandate overtime whenever it was needed, which allowed firms to respond quickly to demand and production cycles in the economy.

Nevertheless, the overtime pay provisions were successful in establishing the 40-hour workweek as a norm. The average length of a full-time U.S. worker's workweek has not changed significantly since the 1970s—it is still approximately 8.1 hours per week, according to U.S. Department of Labor statistics based on the American Time Use Survey (*see American Time-Use Survey, 2013 Results,* June 18, 2014, *available at* http://www.bls.gov/news.release/pdf/atus.pdf). The distribution of hours across groups of workers has shifted, however. Some workers (particularly high-earning professionals) exceed the standard of 40 hours by more than a full eight-hour day. Sylvia Ann Hewlett & Carolyn Buck Luce, *Extreme Jobs: The*

Dangerous Allure of the 70-Hour Work Week, Harv. Bus. Rev., Dec. 2006, at 49, 50–51. Others are involuntarily underemployed on a part-time basis, and struggle to obtain sufficient hours to make ends meet. Susan J. Lambert, *The Limits of Voluntary Employer Action for Improving Low-Level Jobs, in* Working and Living in the Shadow of Economic Fragility 120, 124–25 (Marion Crain & Michael Sherraden eds., 2014). Do these different experiences suggest different policy responses?

What justifications might exist for legislative intervention at the high end of the income spectrum? Some high-earning employees are exempt from the overtime provisions (such as professionals), although as we shall see many workers that we might think of as middle- to upper-class white collar workers are covered. Further, the "extreme jobholders" in Hewlett and Luce's study who worked 70 hours or more per week reported that they loved their jobs and embraced the extra hours willingly; they were neither bitter nor burned out. *Id.* at 51–52. If workers desire longer hours, is there any reason to regulate? Could contractual arrangements as to hours required and pay entitlements be left to private contract?

Different considerations are at play on the low-wage end of the spectrum. The FLSA was enacted in an historical context where most low-wage workers labored for many more than 40 hours per week. Do the same concerns exist today? Many retail and service-oriented businesses have implemented cost-containment protocols such as just-in-time scheduling, which uses sophisticated software that links work hours to patterns of inventory depletion and customer demand. Under these protocols, employers post schedules for the following week with as little as one day's notice, and work hours fluctuate widely from week to week depending upon demand. Lambert, *supra*, at 125. What problems might such practices present for workers? *See* Jodi Kantor, *Working Anything but 9 to 5*, N.Y. Times, Aug. 13, 2014 (describing challenges of unpredictable scheduling and fluctuating hours for working parents, those trying to juggle multiple jobs or jobs and schooling, and those who rely upon hourly wages for basic necessities).

Some workplace scholars have suggested that a minimum work hours guarantee may be necessary to restrain these practices. *See id.* at 130–31; Gayle Cinquegrani, *Minimum Wage Hike Would Help Economy, Employers as Well as Workers, Speakers Say*, Daily Lab. Rep. (BNA) No. 224, Nov. 19, 2013 (describing arguments for minimum hours standards made by Ruth Milkman and Ann O'Leary). San Francisco became the first jurisdiction to consider such legislation. *See* Jonathan Randles, *SF Mulls Predictable Work Schedule for Retail Workers*, Law 360, Sept. 30, 2014 (discussing proposed Predictable Scheduling and Fair Treatment for Retail Workers Ordinance). A few employers have voluntarily offered a minimum hours guarantee; some unions have negotiated for such a guarantee in their collective bargaining contracts. Susan J. McGolrick, *Low-Wage Workers' Advocates Recommend Policies That Curb Erratic Work Schedules*, Daily Lab. Rep. (BNA) No. 49, Mar. 13, 2014 (describing voluntary measures at Costco and collective bargaining contract provisions at Bloomingdale's).

D. WHO IS COVERED?

Although FLSA coverage of the workforce is broad, not all employers and workers are covered. Three inquiries determine the scope of the Act's application. First, employees must be covered as individuals (engaged in commerce or in the production of goods in commerce, broadly defined) or employed by an employer that is subject to "enterprise" coverage. Second, there must exist an employment relationship: the worker must be an employee rather than an independent contractor, a student, or a volunteer, and the employer must act in the interest of an employer relative to the worker. Agents or subcontractors can be employers if they exercise sufficient control over other workers, and there can exist more than one employer under the "joint employer" doctrine. *See* 29 U.S.C. § 203(d), (e), (g). Finally, the Act exempts certain categories of employees from both the minimum wage and overtime provisions; others are exempted only from the overtime provisions but remain covered by the minimum wage provisions. We examine each of these coverage inquiries below.

1. Individual or Enterprise Coverage of Employees

1st way can be covered —

An employee is covered under the FLSA if he or she is "engaged in commerce or in the production of goods for commerce" in a given week. 29 U.S.C. §§ 206(a), 207(a)(1). Although the so-called individual coverage test has been largely supplanted by the enterprise coverage test, it is still applicable in situations where an employer does not satisfy the $500,000 annual gross volume of sales requirement of the enterprise coverage test.

Enterprise coverage extends the protection of the FLSA to all employees of an "enterprise engaged in commerce or in the production of goods for commerce," regardless of the type of work performed by individual employees. 29 U.S.C. §§ 206(a), 207(a)(1). The Act applies to all employees of an "enterprise" that has two or more employees engaged in commerce and has a gross sales or business volume of at least $500,000; or is a public agency, hospital, residential care facility or educational institution regardless of whether it meets the commerce or dollar volume tests. 29 U.S.C. §§ 203(r), (s), 29 U.S.C. §§ 206(a), 207(a). The Act explicitly exempts from enterprise coverage family-owned businesses that do not employ persons outside the immediate family. 29 U.S.C. § 203(s)(2).

exempts family business

2. The Existence of an Employment Relationship

The Act applies to those engaged in an employment relationship. This may require distinguishing "employees" from independent contractors, volunteers, prisoners, interns, and others who perform work; it also requires identification of the employer, an inquiry that can be quite complex. As we saw in Chapter 2, disputes over employment status are common, especially in a modern era of contingent, temporary and flexible employment.

The Supreme Court has commented that the FLSA defines the employment relationship "expansively" with "striking breadth." *Nationwide Mutual Ins. Co. v. Darden*, 503 U.S. 318, 326 (1992). The language of the Act itself is not very helpful, however, and the courts have been forced to interpret its very general terms. The most common disputes today revolve around whether the worker is an independent contractor, and therefore not covered by the Act, or an intern, and therefore not employed. We explore these issues further below through several cases.

The Act defines an employee as "any individual employed by an employer." 29 U.S.C. § 203(e). To "employ" means "to suffer or permit to work." 29 U.S.C. § 203(g). In *Goldberg v. Whitaker House Cooperative, Inc.*, 366 U.S. 28 (1961) the Supreme Court explained that the "economic reality" of the relationship should determine whether a worker is an employee within the meaning of the FLSA, rather than an entrepreneur or independent contractor. *Id.* at 33; *see also Brock v. Superior Care, Inc.*, 840 F.2d 1054, 1059 (2d Cir. 1988) (describing the inquiry as "whether, as a matter of economic reality, the workers depend upon someone else's business for the opportunity to render service or are in business for themselves.") The inquiry in such cases is intensely fact-specific and no single factor is determinative. Thus, courts may apply nearly identical tests to workers in similar industries and reach opposite conclusions if the key facts are different. One thing is certain: the label that the employer applies to the relationship—i.e., "employee" or "independent contractor"—is not dispositive, even where the worker accepts that designation. *See Morrison v. International Programs Consortiums*, 253 F.3d 5, 10 (D.C. Cir. 2001) ("Facile labels and subjective factors are relevant only to the extent they mirror 'economic realities' ").

An employment relationship under the FLSA also requires that the individual or company employing a covered worker fall within the Act's definition of an "employer," defined unhelpfully as those "acting directly or indirectly in the interest of an employer in relation to an employee." 29 U.S.C. § 203(d). Some of the most difficult issues have arisen in situations where more than one entity may be viewed as the employer for FLSA purposes. Under the "joint employer" doctrine, multiple entities may be mutually liable for violations of the FLSA with respect to a particular employee. The most common joint employment arrangements involve situations where two employers share or exchange employees, or where one employer is the subcontractor for another. *See* 29 C.F.R. § 791.2(b).

Courts generally utilize some version of the "economic realities" test to assess the existence of a joint employment relationship. An early and influential statement of the test appeared in *Bonnette v. California Health & Welfare Agency*, 704 F.2d 1465 (9th Cir. 1983):

> whether the alleged employer (1) had the power to hire and fire the employees, (2) supervised and controlled employee work schedules or conditions of employment, (3) determined the rate and method of payment, and (4) maintained employment records.

Id. at 1470. The court eschewed rigid application of any particular factor and looked primarily to whether the alleged employer exercised control over the nature and structure of the employment relationship and possessed economic control over the relationship. *See also Rutherford Food Corp. v. McComb*, 331 U.S. 722 (1947) (holding that determination of existence of employment relationship between meat deboners, slaughterhouse operator and labor contractors for whom deboners worked was subject to assessment on the facts as a whole; no single factor is determinative). While some courts still use the *Bonnette* test, other courts have developed multi-factor tests better tailored to confirming the existence of a joint employment relationship. *See, e.g., Zheng v. Liberty Apparel Co.*, 355 F.3d 61 (2d Cir. 2003) (criticizing district court's application of *Bonnette* factors and remanding for application of seven-factor economic realities test); *see also Barfield v. N.Y. City Health & Hospitals Corp.*, 537 F.3d 132 (2d Cir. 2008) (applying *Zheng* 7-factor test and finding that nurse employed through three different referral agencies at Bellevue Hospital was employed by the hospital for purposes of calculating liability for overtime pay, since she used hospital equipment, performed work integral to hospital's operation, she retained the same work responsibilities regardless of which agency she contracted to work for, and Bellevue controlled her schedule).

3. Exemptions from Coverage

The Act carves out exemptions from the minimum wage and overtime provisions for several categories of workers, including some who fall at the top end of the occupational hierarchy and some at the lower end of the spectrum. The "white collar exemptions" exclude those employed in an executive, administrative, or professional capacity. *See* 29 U.S.C. § 213(a)(1). Other high-end exemptions include the exemption for "outside salesmen" and computer analysts, programmers, and software engineers. *See* 29 U.S.C. §§ 213(a)(1), (17). Although these employees are exempt from both the minimum wage and overtime requirements of the Act, the practical significance of their exemption pertains primarily to overtime pay entitlement, since they are relatively highly paid. We will consider the analysis applicable to these exemptions later in this chapter.

At the lower end of the occupational hierarchy, the Act generally exempts from both minimum wage and overtime requirements employees of seasonal amusement and recreational businesses, certain employees of fishing and aquatic businesses, most agricultural workers, publishers of small newspapers, and domestic workers who perform casual babysitting or care for the disabled or aged, as well as several other categories of workers. *See* 29 U.S.C. § 213(a)(3)–(16). In addition, the FLSA exempts some workers only from the overtime provision, either because their employment is not suited to a traditional 40-hour workweek (such as employees in the transportation industry), because it is seasonal in character (such as some agricultural workers), or because it entails living on the employer's premises (such as live-in domestic workers). 29 U.S.C. § 213(b)(1)–(30).

The two most controversial of these categories involve agricultural workers and domestic service workers. Agricultural employees are exempted from both the minimum wage and overtime provisions of the FLSA if they are employed on small farms, defined as those that used less than five hundred man-days of agricultural labor during any calendar quarter; if they work on a farm owned by their immediate family; or in certain other specified situations involving hand harvest laborers paid on a piece rate basis. 29 U.S.C. § 213(a)(6)(A), (B), and (C). Other categories of agricultural employees are excluded from overtime wage entitlement only; they remain covered by the minimum wage provisions. *See, e.g.,* 29 U.S.C. §§ 213(b)(12), (13), (14), (16). In 1963, Congress passed the Farm Labor Contractor Registration Act, which was intended to extend some protections to agricultural workers, particularly migrant labor; it was replaced with the Migrant and Seasonal

Agricultural Workers' Protection Act ("AWPA") in 1983. *See* 29 U.S.C. § 1801 *et seq.* The AWPA affords farmworkers substantive rights concerning recruitment, employment, housing, and transportation, and requires employers of migrant workers to post notices of wage rates, provide pay statements and document hours and account for deductions from pay, and maintain adequate health and safety standards. It does not provide wage and hour protections, however.

What is the rationale behind the agricultural exemptions? The FLSA itself, its legislative history and its implementing regulations contain no explicit justification. Several explanations have been suggested. One view is that the agricultural exemptions were included to appease powerful opposition from agricultural industry lobby groups for large-scale farmers when the FLSA was first proposed in the 1930s. *See* Victoria Johnson, *Did Old Man McDonald Have a Farm? Holly Farms Corp. v. Labor Relations Board,* 69 U. Colo. L. Rev. 295, 308 (1998). Another possible justification is rooted in the prevailing view of the Commerce Clause at the time the FLSA was passed: it was generally understood that the Commerce Clause could not authorize federal regulation of local activity, and because agricultural activity was considered to be primarily local the legislature may have believed that it could not regulate agriculture without overstepping its constitutional authority. *See Id.* at 308–09. Still another explanation applicable to the exemptions from the overtime provisions is the seasonal nature of many forms of agricultural work and the need for rapid harvesting of crops: legislators worried that small communities would not be capable of supplying sufficient numbers of workers to avoid overtime. *Id.* at 309. Finally, some scholars have suggested that the agricultural exemptions were motivated by racism. Marc Linder explains:

> By 1938, when the FLSA became law, the [agricultural] exclusion had become routine in New Deal legislation. . . . To enact the social and economic reforms of the New Deal, President Roosevelt and his allies were forced to compromise with southern congressmen. Those congressmen negotiated with Roosevelt to obtain modifications of New Deal legislation that preserved the social and racial plantation system in the South—a system resting on the subjugation of blacks and other minorities. As a result, New Deal legislation, including the FLSA, became infected with unconstitutional racial motivation.

Marc Linder, *Farm Workers and the Fair Labor Standards Act: Racial Discrimination in the New Deal,* 65 Tex. L. Rev. 1335, 1336 (1987). Linder presents data showing that in 1940 more than 53.5% of all farm workers in the south were black. *Id.* at 1346. *See also* Jim Chen, *Of Agriculture's First Disobedience and Its Fruit,* 48 Vand. L. Rev. 1261, 1277 (1995) (observing that agriculture's "original sin" was slavery). The disproportionate impact of the agricultural exemptions on persons of color—particularly Hispanics—persists today.

Another controversial category of workers exempted from the Act at the lower end of the occupational hierarchy consists of certain domestic service workers. Congress specifically found that "the employment of persons in domestic service in households affects commerce," 29 U.S.C. § 202(a), so most domestic workers are covered under the Act, including housekeepers, cooks, gardeners, handymen, chauffeurs, and full-time babysitters and nannies. Nevertheless, the Act exempts two categories of domestic service workers from both the minimum wage and overtime provisions: (1) "casual babysitters" and (2) domestic companions "for individuals who (because of age or infirmity) are unable to care for themselves." 29 U.S.C. § 213(a)(15). In addition, domestic service employees who reside in the household where they perform services are exempted from the overtime, but not the minimum wage, provisions of the FLSA. 29 U.S.C. § 213(b)(21); 29 C.F.R. § 552.3.

The significance of the domestic service exemptions has increased dramatically as the demand for home healthcare and personal assistance workers has risen in response to demographic changes, particularly the aging of America and the shift toward home care occasioned by increased institutional health care costs. Together, personal care and home health aides constitute the second most rapidly growing occupational group, and the Bureau of Labor Statistics projects that their numbers will increase significantly. *See* Bureau of Lab. Statistics, *Employment Projections: 2012–2022, available at* http://www.bls.gov/ooh/healthcare/personal-care-aides.htm#tab-6 (2014) (estimating 49% increase for personal care aides and 48% increase for home health aides).

One of the more contested aspects of the domestic service exemptions involves domestic service workers employed by third-party agencies that contract to provide home health care aides, rehabilitation aides, or other caretakers as companions to the aged or disabled. Because the regulations define domestic service work as services performed "in or about a private home . . . of the [employer]," *see* 29 C.F.R. § 552.6, domestic workers and the unions that represent them argued that they were not exempt (i.e. that they were covered by the Act) where their employer was a third-party agency and services were performed in the home of a client. In *Long Island Care at Home v. Coke*, 551 U.S. 158 (2007), a unanimous Supreme Court deferred to the Department of Labor's interpretation of the "companionship services" exemption, which permits third-party employers or agencies to claim the domestic service exemption for their workers who perform in-home companionship services for clients such as playing cards, accompanying clients on walks or taking them to visit neighbors or family. *See* 29 C.F.R. § 552.109(a). The Court expressed concern that an opposite ruling would not only require large third party employers to pay overtime (which some had predicted would substantially increase the costs of care for the elderly and infirm), but would burden family members who do not live with the patient and choose to employ a domestic caregiver to provide care. The decision was criticized by advocates for organized labor and by scholars. *See, e.g.*, Peggie Smith, *Aging and Caring in the Home: Regulating Paid Domesticity in the Twenty-First Century*, 92 Iowa L. Rev. 1835, 1869 (2007) (arguing that the purpose of the exemption was to exclude "non-professional, non-breadwinning" individuals whose services were more akin to babysitting, and was never intended to apply to professional "third-party-employed home-care workers").

Responding to urging from President Obama, the DOL promulgated a new rule that narrows the exemption and extends minimum wage and overtime protections to most home care workers. These workers include live-in workers employed by a third party, such as a home health care agency regardless of the duties performed, and workers employed directly by the client or his or her family if they primarily perform medically-related tasks for which training is a prerequisite, or domestic duties that benefit other household members (such as preparing meals, performing housekeeping chores or doing laundry for other members). Thus, the only workers who would fall under the companionship exemption would be those employed directly by the individual or members of the household who provide fellowship and companionship. *only true exemption now* The rule was justified by findings that the majority of home care workers live near the poverty line, that they are dedicated caregivers who perform medically-related tasks for which training is a prerequisite (and thus, are distinct from casual laborers or babysitters covered by the statutory exemption), and that there is an urgent need to attract and retain more persons in the occupation as a *PP* result of increased demand for care by an aging population. The rule was originally intended to take effect on January 1, 2015 and was estimated to bring nearly 2 million home health and personal care workers within the FLSA's coverage. However, a federal district court vacated both aspects of the regulations, reasoning *but was vacated!* that the language of the statutory exemption was clear and that the DOL had exceeded its regulatory authority. *See Home Care Ass'n of America v. Weil,* No. 14-CV-967 (D.D.C. Dec. 22, 2014 & Jan. 14, 2015). For the text of the rule and related information, *see* http://www.dol.gov/whd/homecare/final_rule.pdf; Fact Sheet # 79A: Companionship Services Under the Fair Labor Standards Act (FLSA), *available at* http://www.dol.gov/whd/regs/compliance/whdfs79a.htm.

The DOL has filed an appeal. Should the court defer to this new rule? Does it matter what the cost impacts would be, or upon whom they might fall?

4. Applications

The cases in this section illustrate the difficulties of determining coverage under the FLSA in two of the most commonly litigated contexts: workers who argue that they are employees rather than independent contractors excluded from the FLSA's coverage, and interns who argue that they should be treated as employees entitled to claim the FLSA's protections.

a. Independent Contractors

In the following case, the court struggles with whether the chicken catchers at Perdue Farms are employees or independent contractors. It also confronts the questions whether their employers are the intermediary "crew leaders," Perdue, or both, and whether the workers are "agricultural employees" exempted from the Act's coverage.

HEATH v. PERDUE FARMS, INC.
United States District Court for the District of Maryland
87 F. Supp. 2d 452 (2000)

WILLIAM M. NICKERSON, U.S. DISTRICT JUDGE.

This is an action brought by over one hundred individuals employed as "chicken catchers" for processing plants owned and operated by Defendant Perdue Farms, Inc. in Salisbury, Maryland, Accomac, Virginia and Georgetown, Delaware. Plaintiffs seek to recover overtime wages to which they believe they are entitled under the Fair Labor Standards Act, 29 U.S.C. § 201 et seq. ["FLSA"], and similar provisions of the Maryland Wage and Hour Law, Md. Lab. & Emp. Code Ann. §§ 3-401 to 3-431. Presently before the Court are cross motions for summary judgment on the issue of liability. . . . Upon a review of the motions and the applicable case law, the Court determines that . . . Plaintiffs' motion for summary judgment should be granted. . . .

I. Factual Background

Perdue is a vertically integrated poultry operation which operates throughout the Delmarva region. Perdue hatches chickens in company owned hatcheries, and then ships them to independent contract farmers who raise them in accordance with Perdue's exacting specifications. Perdue, at all times, retains ownership of chickens. Once the chicks reach marketable age and size, chicken catchers travel to the contract farms, capture the chickens, and place them in cages for transport to the factory for slaughter.

Chicken catchers work in crews of approximately nine men: a crew typically consists of six catchers, one house man (who prepares the chicken houses before the catchers enter and nets the chickens), and one forklift driver, all under the supervision of a crew leader. Generally, the catchers, who collect at designated locations, are picked up by the crew leader who has retrieved a Perdue truck from the Perdue plant and has loaded the truck with necessary equipment. Most catchers ride to the farms in the Perdue crew cab because Perdue generally does not allow them to drive their own cars to the farms. The crew leaders are not allowed to vary or alter any of the instructions on the kill sheet.

The work of the catchers is physically arduous, dangerous and unpleasant. The chickens are caught by hand and stuffed into cages, which are then loaded onto Perdue trucks. Chicken catchers are paid by the piece rate, per 1000 chickens caught. The crews catch between 30,000 and 50,000 chickens each shift, and regularly work approximately 12 hours per shift for at least a five-day week; the workers do not receive overtime pay at time and one half for the hours worked over 40 hours per week.

The catchers' work, which is to deliver the raw material necessary for the operation of Perdue's poultry processing operation, is directly keyed to the work of the poultry processing plant in that the catching crews work only when a processing plant is operating; this includes working weekend and holidays depending on the slaughtering schedule at the plant. The crew leader, who is often a former chicken catcher, is presented with a contract by Perdue which specifies that the crew leader is an independent contractor and sets out the terms and conditions of the crew leader's work. None of the crew leaders have ever seriously negotiated any of the terms of their contracts or successfully challenged any of the contract provisions. The terms of the contract provide that the crew leaders will be paid on a weekly basis at a piece rate of between $28–$29 per 1000 chickens caught; this piece rate is based on the crew leader's estimated costs, and is very carefully calculated by Perdue. From this lump sum, the crew leader pays himself and the members of his crew.

The only other business expenses which the crew leaders incur are for workers' compensation insurance, bookkeeping services, and occasional expenses for personal protective equipment ["PPE"] such as dust masks, hard hats, and gloves which the crew leader purchases from the Perdue plant and provides to the catchers who choose to use the PPEs. In contrast, Perdue owns all the heavy equipment and machinery required for the chicken catching operation, including the trucks, cages, fork loaders, catching pens, nets, crew cabs, fans, hoses, and disinfectant tanks.

Perdue controls every significant aspect of the chicken catching operation. Daily "kill sheets" dictate virtually every aspect of the catchers work for the shift: the sheets instruct the crew leaders when, what time, and where to work; the order in which the chicken houses are to be entered on farms which have multiple chicken houses; how many chickens are to be stuffed into each cage; and how many loads of chickens the workers are expected to catch. The crew leaders are not allowed to vary or alter any of the instructions on the kill sheet. Throughout the shift, the Perdue live-haul manager is in constant contact with a crew leader, communicating additional instructions by way of radio in the Perdue crew cab. The Perdue live-haul manager also travels to the chicken houses at least two to three times a week to observe and critique the work, and issues letters and memoranda to the crew leaders on matters which the manager observes on these site visits.

II. Discussion

It is undisputed that Plaintiffs consistently work more than 40 hours per week and yet are not paid overtime wages. In this litigation, Perdue makes two main arguments as to why Plaintiffs are not entitled to overtime pay under the Fair Labor Standards Act. First, Perdue argues that Perdue is neither the sole nor "joint" employer of its chicken catchers. Instead, according to Perdue, Plaintiffs are the employees of the crew leaders, who are themselves independent contractors of Perdue. Second, Perdue argues that Plaintiffs qualify as "agricultural laborers," who are exempted from the overtime requirements of the FLSA. See 29 U.S.C. § 213(b)(12). . . .

A. Plaintiffs' Employment Relationship with Perdue

For Perdue to be liable for overtime violations under the FLSA or Maryland's Wage and Hour Law, the Court must find that Perdue has an employment relationship with Plaintiffs. The relevant provisions of these statutes have defined the employment relationship very broadly, consistent with the remedial purpose of the legislation. The definition of "employ" under the FLSA includes "to suffer or permit to work." 29 U.S.C. § 203(g). . . . The Supreme Court has observed of FLSA's definition of the employment relationship that "[a] broader or more comprehensive coverage of employees within the stated categories would be difficult to frame." *United States v. Rosenwasser*, 323 U.S. 360, 362 (1945). See also *Nationwide Mut. Ins. Co. v. Darden*, 503 U.S. 318, 326 (1992) (Noting that FLSA defines the employment relationship "expansively" and as having a "striking breadth").

Courts have also stressed that the label that the parties give to their relationship is not controlling. Thus, just because Perdue now[1] calls its crew leaders "independent contractors," does not exclude the crew leaders or the members of the crew from being considered employees for the purpose of the FLSA or the Maryland Wage and Hour Law. Courts look not to the label, but to the underlying "economic reality" of the relationship. *Rutherford Food v. McComb*, 331 U.S. 722 (1947).

To determine the economic reality of the relationship between workers and their putative employer, courts look at the following six factors:

1) the degree of control which the putative employer has over the manner in which the work is performed;

2) the opportunities for profit or loss dependent upon the managerial skill of the worker;

3) the putative employee's investment in equipment or material;

4) the degree of skill required for the work;

5) the permanence of the working relationship; and

6) whether the service rendered is an integral part of the putative employer's business.

Monville v. Williams, 28 Wage & Hour Cas. (BNA) 497, 501 (D. Md. 1987).[2]

Applying these factors to the undisputed facts presented makes it abundantly clear that Perdue is the employer of both the crew leaders and the chicken catchers.[3] As to the control factor, Perdue controls every aspect of the chicken

---

[1] [n. 3] Perdue itself considered the crew leaders and catchers employees of Perdue until 1991 when it switched to the current "independent contractor" system.

[2] [n. 4] These factors are considered to determine whether Perdue was the sole employer of the Plaintiffs. Plaintiffs also argue that, even were the Court to find that Perdue was not the sole employer, it is at least a "joint employer" of Plaintiffs, along with the crew leaders. The determination as to whether Perdue is a joint employer of its chicken catchers also involves a similar "economic reality," multi-factor analysis. The factors in this analysis are:

   (1) ownership of the property and facilities where the work occurred;
   (2) degree of skill required to perform the job;
   (3) investment in equipment and facilities;
   (4) permanency and exclusivity of employment;
   (5) nature and degree of control of the workers;
   (6) degree of supervision, direct and indirect, of the work;
   (7) power to determine the pay rates or the methods of payments of the workers;
   (8) the right, directly or indirectly, to hire, fire, or modify the employment conditions of the workers; and
   (9) preparation of payroll and payment of wages.

Ricketts v. Vann, 32 F.3d 71, 76 (4th Cir. 1994) (adopting this analysis from *Haywood v. Barnes*, 109 F.R.D. 568, 587 (E.D.N.C. 1986)).

Obviously, there is considerable overlap and similarity of factors between the employer and joint employer analyses. Because the Court finds that Perdue was the employer of Plaintiffs for the purposes of the FLSA and Maryland's Wage and Hour Law, the Court need not consider this alternative analysis.

[3] [n. 5] The Court will apply the analysis primarily to the crew leaders. If the crew leaders are found to be employees for the purposes of the FLSA, than the catchers are employees as well. *See Beliz v. W.H. Mcleod & Sons Packing Co.*, 765 F.2d 1317, 1327 (5th Cir. 1985) ("if the alleged contractor were held to be an employee of the farmer, it would necessarily follow that the workers were in turn the farmer's employees").

catchers' work. It controls the farms they are to go to, the order in which individual houses are to be utilized, the times the catchers are to catch, how many chickens are to be caught, and how many chickens are to be placed in each cage. Every aspect of the operation is outlined in the "Live Haul Instructional Training Manual," published by Perdue. Perdue acknowledges that it provides "constant feedback" through the crew leaders as to whether the crews are meeting Perdue's performance standards.[4]

It is also abundantly clear that the crew leaders have little opportunity to substantially increase their profit, nor do they expose themselves to much risk of loss. Crew leaders are paid at a set piece rate, a rate carefully calculated by Perdue. Perdue even pays a slightly higher piece rate to those crew leaders that have higher costs, thus assuring a consistent profit margin among the crew leaders. Furthermore, because the number of chickens to be caught is limited by Perdue, there is no occasion for extra pay or profit. Perdue comes close to conceding this point.

The lack of potential for profit or loss is closely related to the next factor, the ownership of the equipment used to catch chickens. Perdue owns virtually all of the heavy equipment and machinery required for the catching operation. It owns the crew cabs, trucks, fork lifts, cages, fans, pens and nets. Perdue is responsible for the storage, maintenance, repair, fueling, and replacement of all the major equipment. In contrast, the crew leaders' investment in equipment is limited to computers used for bookkeeping and the personal protective equipment such as gloves and masks provided to some of the catchers. The crew leaders' relative lack of capital investment in equipment is perhaps one of the strongest indicators that they are employees and not independent contractors. *See Monville*, 28 Wage & Hour Cas. (BNA) at 502 (farm labor contractor found to be employee of farmer where his only capital contribution was use of bus to transport workers).

As to the degree of skill required to catch chickens, there is little doubt that catching chickens is unskilled labor. While Perdue argues that the job must be skilled because catchers become faster with experience, that is true of most repetitive tasks, skilled or unskilled. As to the crew leaders, their position does involve certain supervision and management skills. These skills, however, are the kind of generalized management skills commonly required of a foreman or supervisor. The need for these skills does not render the crew leader position that of an independent contractor. See *Castillo v. Givens*, 704 F.2d 181 (5th Cir. 1983) (farm labor contractor who supervised workers, transported workers, kept records of laborers and hours, received weekly checks and distributed earnings to individual workers was employee of farm owner); *Monville*, 28 Wage & Hour Cas. (BNA) at 501 (crew leader with "overall supervision and control of the day-to-day activities of [farm workers]" was employee of farmer under FLSA).

The record also reveals that the crew leaders (and most of the catchers themselves) have long-standing, permanent, and exclusive relationships with Perdue. Most crew leaders have worked for Perdue for at least 10 years, some longer

Perdue control

(1)

(2)

(3)

(4)

 (5)

---

[4] [n. 6] Perdue explains that it must exercise such strict control because chickens are a perishable product, subject to the regulations of the USDA, as well as other industry standards. It makes no difference that there may be some external constraint necessitating Perdue's control, what matters is that Perdue does indeed exercise that control.

than 20 years. While Perdue makes much of the hypothetical possibility that the crew leaders could organize additional crews to work for competitors, the arduous demands of the job make that impractical and, the reality is that crew leaders work exclusively for Perdue. The same is also true for the catchers, for the most part. While a few catchers will occasionally moonlight for a competitor, or leave Perdue to go to another company, most work exclusively for Perdue, and have done so for some time.

As to the final factor, Perdue concedes that "Plaintiffs 'perform a specialized job which is integral to Perdue's business.'" Of necessity, the work of the catchers is highly coordinated with the schedule of Perdue's processing plants. Perdue depends on its catching crews for a steady supply of chickens for processing. Although geographically their work takes place outside the processing plants, the catchers' function, in a real sense, is simply part of the production line.

Using these factors to parse the economic realities of the relationship between Perdue and its crew leaders, leaves no doubt that theirs is an employer/employee relationship for the purpose of the FLSA and Maryland's Wage and Hour Law. The question then becomes, whether the nature of the work performed brings the catchers' employment within established exemptions to the statutes' overtime requirements.

B. FLSA's "Agricultural Workers" Exemption

Although Perdue continues to treat as an open question the applicability of the "agricultural laborer" exemption to the employment of chicken catchers, this Court finds that the question was effectively resolved by the Supreme Court in *Holly Farms v. N.L.R.B.*, 517 U.S. 392 (1996). *Holly Farms*, like the instant action, involved employees of a vertically-integrated poultry processor who worked in live-haul crews as chicken catchers, truck drivers, and loader operators. At issue was whether these employees were "agricultural" workers within the meaning of section 2(3) of the National Labor Relations Act ["NLRA"]. The Court held that the members of the live haul crews were not engaged in agriculture. . . .

Perdue seeks to distinguish *Holly Farms* primarily on the ground that *Holly Farms* was decided under the NLRA, and not the FLSA. This Court notes, however, as did the Supreme Court in *Holly Farms*, that "agricultural laborer" has been given the same meaning under both regulatory schemes. . . . Thus, the same analysis and considerations that led the Supreme Court to determine that chicken catchers are not agricultural laborers for the purposes of the NLRA, applies with equal force to this Court's determination as to whether they are agricultural laborers for the purpose of the FLSA. . . . The DOL, as the agency responsible for the implementation of the FLSA has consistently, since at least the early 1980s, taken the position that live-haul workers in the poultry industry are not agricultural workers and are entitled to overtime pay under the FLSA.

Furthermore, federal courts have consistently held that the *Holly Farms* decision is applicable to cases arising under the FLSA. . . . Perdue has offered no decision from any court concluding that *Holly Farms* is not controlling in a FLSA case. . . .

[The court concluded that Perdue's failure to comply with the overtime regulations in this case was reckless, and the 3-year statute of limitations applied to the workers' claim].

III. Conclusion

For the above stated reasons, the Court will grant Plaintiffs' motion for summary judgment as to liability. The Court finds that Plaintiffs are employees of Defendant Perdue for the purposes of the FLSA and Maryland's Wage and Hour Law and that no exemptions are applicable. The Court also finds that Perdue's continued failure to pay Plaintiff 's overtime was, and is, willful. . . .

NOTES

1. **Agricultural Exemption.** The *Heath* court held that the question whether the chicken catchers were exempt as agricultural workers from the FLSA's overtime provisions was controlled by the Supreme Court's decision in *Holly Farms v. NLRB*, 517 U.S. 392 (1996). Indeed, the court considered the question so clearly resolved that it extended the statute of limitations to three years, resulting in a higher backpay recovery for the workers. In *Holly Farms*, the Supreme Court had deferred to the NLRB's determination that live-haul chicken catchers at Holly Farms, a subsidiary of Tyson Foods, were covered under the NLRA. The NLRA does not contain a definition of the term "agricultural laborer," but instead incorporates the definition of agriculture found in the FLSA. *Id.* at 397. Under the FLSA, agricultural work includes various types of farming activities "performed by a farmer or on a farm as an incident to or in conjunction with such farming operations, including preparation for market, delivery to storage or to market or to carriers for transportation to market." 29 U.S.C. § 203(f). Holly Farms argued that its workers were agricultural laborers exempt from coverage because (1) they worked for a farmer and (2) they worked on a farm performing work incident to or in conjunction with farming operations. The Court found that the NLRB's conclusion that the chicken catchers were covered was reasonable because there was a disjunction between the farmer/grower's operation and the work of the live-haul crew; once the live-haul crew arrived at the farm, the grower's work was completed. Instead, the live-haul crews' work was more closely aligned with Holly Farms' processing operations. Thus, the chicken catchers were more like manufacturing workers who traditionally enjoy the protections of the NLRA than like farm workers. 517 U.S. at 403.

2. **The Joint Employer Doctrine.** In *Heath*, Perdue argued that the chicken catchers were employees of the crew leaders, who were themselves independent contractors vis-à-vis Perdue. Had this argument prevailed, Perdue would effectively have had no employees for FLSA purposes. The court found that both the crew leaders and the chicken catchers were employees of Perdue. Suppose that the court had concluded that the crew leaders were independent contractors, and that the crew leaders were employers vis-à-vis the chicken catchers. Would the existence of the crew leaders' employment relationship with the chicken catchers sever the employment relationship between Perdue and the chicken catchers? Not necessarily, observes the court in footnote 4: the crew leaders and Perdue could be joint

employers of the chicken catchers. The court did not resolve the question, considering it unnecessary.

The joint employer doctrine arises often in the agricultural context. A common practice is for farmers to hire farm laborers through "farm labor contractors" (FLCs). Under the typical FLC arrangement, farmers pay FLCs on a piece rate basis and the FLCs are then responsible for locating the workers, providing them with housing and transportation to the fields, and paying them. In this situation, most courts have held that the workers are employees of the FLC, but not the farm itself, reasoning that the FLC has day-to-day control over the work being done. *See, e.g., Martinez-Mendoza v. Champion Int'l Corp.*, 340 F.3d 1200, 1203–04, 1208–09 (11th Cir. 2003) (applying seven-factor test and finding that only the FLC was liable for wage violations to migrant workers employed to plant seedlings on the farm-manufacturer's land); *Gonzalez-Sanchez v. Int'l Paper Co.*, 346 F.3d 1017, 1021–22 (11th Cir. 2003) (refusing joint employer status and finding only FLC liable for wage violations to migrant workers employed to plant seedlings, even though the manufacturer required the workers "to wear orange visibility vests and caps" and provided an "instructional videotape . . . to demonstrate its planting specifications," because manufacturer did not exercise a sufficient degree of control over the workers to establish an employment relationship). However, some courts have held both the farm/manufacturer and the FLC liable on the joint employer theory, reasoning that migrant workers are economically dependent upon both. Joint employer liability is most likely where the farm/manufacturer exercises significant control over the workers' labor and compensation, as Perdue did in the *Heath* case. *See, e.g., Altenor v. D & S Farms*, 88 F.3d 925 (11th Cir. 1996) (finding snap-bean pickers were employees of both the growers and the FLC for FLSA and AWPA purposes; although the FLC controlled workers' day-to-day labor, the growers controlled the number of workers, supervised the precise moment at which picking would begin and assigned particular workers to particular tasks, established pay rates, and controlled the preparation of payroll and the payment of wages).

Similar issues arise in the garment industry. Garment manufacturers seeking to avoid application of the labor and employment laws as well as the overhead costs of factory maintenance contract out their in-house production of garments to "jobbers," who in turn arrange with sewing contractors to sew, press and finish garments according to patterns which the jobbers provide. *See, e.g., Zheng v. Liberty Apparel Co.*, 355 F.3d 61 (2d Cir. 2003) (discussing appropriate legal standard applicable to determine joint employer status where manufacturers hired contractors/"jobbers" to stitch and finish pieces of clothing; the plaintiff garment workers labored primarily on the manufacturer's garments, performed a line-job integral to production of the manufacturer's product, and were frequently supervised by the manufacturer's agents); *Liu v. Donna Karan Int'l, Inc.*, 6 Wage & Hour Cas. 2d (BNA) 1142 (S.D.N.Y. 2002) (finding that Chinese immigrant workers who were employed 80 hours per week for less than minimum wage in a garment factory that produced from 60–100% of the defendant designer's clothing were arguably jointly employed by Donna Karan and by the contractor/"jobber;" Donna Karan dictated the prices of garments and the production requirements, which in turn controlled the hours plaintiffs worked).

What difference does it make who is liable? FLCs are frequently undercapital- *why does it matter who is liable $*
ized and may have no assets to pay their workers, leaving workers who cannot
proceed against the farms without a remedy. *See Reyes v. Remington Hybrid Seed
Co.*, 495 F.3d 403, 409 (7th Cir. 2007) (applying joint employer doctrine where FLC
was undercapitalized and farm owner advanced funds to the FLC to pay its workers
and to secure workers' compensation insurance, supplied the tools for the job and
even paid for the portable toilets, and stating that when a farm owner hires a
"fly-by-night operator," it assumes the risk of liability). The same situation prevails
in the garment industry, with jobbers becoming insolvent and leaving workers with
no recourse against manufacturers unless the court applies the joint employer
doctrine. *See* Bruce Goldstein *et al.*, *Enforcing Fair Labor Standards in the
Modern American Sweatshop: Rediscovering the Statutory Definition of Employment*, 46 UCLA L. Rev. 983, 992–1001 (1999).

The joint employer doctrine has also cropped up with increasing frequency in the
service sector, where agencies contract to provide services on a temporary basis. In *service sector*
these cases the issue is often whether employees who contract with more than one
agency but perform work for a single entity or person are entitled to overtime pay.
See, e.g., Barfield v. N.Y. City Health & Hospitals Corp., 537 F.3d 132 (2d Cir. 2008)
(hospital found joint employer along with nursing referral agencies); *Schultz v.
Capital Int'l Security, Inc.*, 460 F.3d 595 (4th Cir. 2006) (finding personal protection
specialists assigned to guard a Saudi diplomat living in the U.S. jointly employed by
the security service that hired them and by the diplomat that they were assigned to
guard because of common control over how security would be provided). It has also
arisen in contexts where the parent company exercises considerable control over a
subsidiary. *See In re Enterprise Rent-A-Car Wage & Hour Practices Litigation*,
683 F.3d 462 (3d Cir. 2012) (finding no joint employer liability where parent
company provided administrative and human resources services and support to its
subsidiaries, including job descriptions, training guides, best practices and compensation guides, recommended salary ranges, standard performance review forms,
employee benefit plans, insurance, and technology and legal services, but none of
the services were mandatory, and parent company lacked actual control over
day-to-day supervision, job performance, working conditions, and compensation).

b.   Trainees and Interns

The percentage of college graduates undertaking internships skyrocketed
between 1981 and 1991, and the growth intensified following the 2008 recession as
students unable to find jobs sought internships. Ross Perlin, author of Intern
Nation: How to Earn Nothing and Learn Little in the Brave New Economy (2011)
characterizes internships as a "rite of passage" that is now required of the typical
college student, and estimates that 75% of students at U.S. four-year colleges and
universities will undertake at least one internship prior to graduation; 46 to 48% of
those internships are unpaid. What implications should the growth of the so-called
"intern economy" have for the FLSA? Should interns be treated as employees for
FLSA purposes?

In 2010, the Department of Labor issued guidance, establishing a six-part test
for classification of interns as employees entitled to the protections of the FLSA.
The test is drawn from a Supreme Court decision finding that a railroad trainee was

not an employee for FLSA purposes because his work "serv[ed] only his own interest." *See Walling v. Portland Terminal Co.*, 330 U.S. 148, 152 (1947). Pursuant to the DOL's guidance, laid out below, interns at for-profit companies should be treated as employees unless all six prongs of the test are satisfied:

The Test for Unpaid Interns

There are some circumstances under which individuals who participate in "for-profit" private sector internships or training programs may do so without compensation. The Supreme Court has held that the term "suffer or permit to work" cannot be interpreted so as to make a person whose work serves only his or her own interest an employee of another who provides aid or instruction. This may apply to interns who receive training for their own educational benefit if the training meets certain criteria. The determination of whether an internship or training program meets this exclusion depends upon all of the facts and circumstances of each such program.

The following six criteria must be applied when making this determination:

1. The internship, even though it includes actual operation of the facilities of the employer, is similar to training which would be given in an educational environment;

2. The internship experience is for the benefit of the intern;

3. The intern does not displace regular employees, but works under close supervision of existing staff;

4. The employer that provides the training derives no immediate advantage from the activities of the intern; and on occasion its operations may actually be impeded;

5. The intern is not necessarily entitled to a job at the conclusion of the internship; and

6. The employer and the intern understand that the intern is not entitled to wages for the time spent in the internship.

Wage and Hour Division, U.S. Dep't of Labor, Fact Sheet No. 71: *Internship Programs Under the Fair Labor Standards Act* (Apr. 2010), *available at* www.dol.gov/whd/regs/compliance/whdfs71.htm.

Since the DOL promulgated this Fact Sheet, litigation challenging the practice of unpaid internships in the for-profit sector has exploded. Litigation has been concentrated in the entertainment, film, music, fashion, journalism and publishing industries, where internships are popular because networking is particularly critical to locating jobs. Many cases have been framed as collective actions, posing significant liability concerns for the putative employers. Elite Model settled for $450,000 a collective and class action claim brought under the FLSA and New York state labor law by unpaid interns who escorted models to and from assignments, organized model portfolios, and performed miscellaneous tasks during fashion weeks that would otherwise have been done by paid employees. The interns worked more than 40-hour weeks and incurred incidental expenses such as taxi fare and meals for which they were not reimbursed. *Davenport v. Elite Model Management Corp.*, No. 1:13-cv-01061, final approval granted May 12, 2014 (S.D.N.Y.). Other pending or recently settled group claims have been asserted against Warner Music Group, Gawker Media, Conde Nast (interns at W Magazine and The New Yorker), NBC Universal (interns on MSNBC and Saturday Night Live shows), and the Charlie Rose show. Such class or collective action claims must overcome significant hurdles as we will see below, including establishing the existence of a common policy that violates the FLSA. This is particularly difficult where the corporate entity controls a number of dissimilar businesses. *See, e.g., Fraticelli v. MSG Holdings, LP*, No. 1:13-cv-06518 (S.D.N.Y. 2014) (refusing to certify FLSA collective action involving more than 500 unpaid interns in programs run by the corporate owner of Madison Square Garden, Radio City Music Hall, sports teams such as the New York Knicks and Rangers, and other entertainment businesses).

The two district court cases presented below are among the few to reach the courts and result in a reported decision, and they came to different conclusions.

GLATT v. FOX SEARCHLIGHT PICTURES INC.
United States District Court for the Southern District of New York
293 F.R.D. 516 (S.D.N.Y. 2013)

WILLIAM H. PAULEY III, U.S. DISTRICT JUDGE.

Plaintiffs Eric Glatt, Alexander Footman, Kanene Gratts, and Eden Antalik bring this putative class action under the Fair Labor Standards Act ("FLSA"), [and] New York Labor Law ("NYLL") . . . against Defendants Fox Searchlight Pictures Inc. ("Searchlight") and Fox Entertainment Group, Inc. ("FEG"). Plaintiffs contend that Searchlight and FEG violated federal and state labor laws by classifying them as unpaid interns instead of paid employees. [The parties brought cross-motions for summary judgment and plaintiff Antalik moved for class certification of her state law claims and conditional certification of her FLSA collective action.]

. . . .

BACKGROUND

The Parties

Glatt and Footman were unpaid interns who worked on production of the film *Black Swan* in New York. After production ended, Glatt took a second unpaid internship relating to *Black Swan*'s post-production. Gratts was an unpaid intern who worked on production of the film *500 Days of Summer* in California. Antalik was an unpaid intern at Searchlight's corporate offices in New York.

FEG is the parent corporation of approximately 800 subsidiaries, including co-defendant Searchlight. Searchlight produces and distributes feature films. Searchlight does not produce the films itself. Rather, it enters into Production-

Distribution-Finance Agreements ("Production Agreements") with corporations
created for the sole purpose of producing particular films.

. . . .

FEG's Internship Program

Antalik claims she was part of a "centralized unpaid internship program" in
which unpaid interns at FEG's subsidiaries were subject to a single set of policies
administered by a small team of intern recruiters. She maintains that two
employees oversaw FEG's internship program during the relevant periods and their
responsibilities included soliciting "intern request forms" from supervisors at
subsidiaries interested in hiring interns, approving those requests, screening
internship applicants, and processing interns' paperwork. According to Antalik, she
and the members of her proposed class and collective action were victims of a
common policy of using unpaid interns to perform work that required them to be
paid.

Defendants deny there was any "centralized" internship program. They argue
internships varied considerably among various FEG subsidiaries and departments,
and interns' experiences were shaped by the particular supervisors they were
matched with.

DISCUSSION

. . . .

Were Glatt and Footman "Employees" Covered by the FLSA and NYLL?

Glatt and Footman move for summary judgment holding they were "employees"
covered by the FLSA and NYLL and do not fall under the "trainee" exception
established by *Walling v. Portland Terminal Co.*, 330 U.S. 148 (1947).

In *Walling*, a case involving a railroad that held a week-long training course for
prospective brakemen, the Supreme Court determined that "trainees" were not
covered employees under the FLSA. The trainees "[did] not displace any of the
regular employees, who [did] most of the work themselves, and must stand
immediately by to supervise whatever the trainees do." *Walling*, 330 U.S. at 149–50.
The trainees' work "[did] not expedite the company business, but may, and
sometimes [did], actually impede and retard it." *Walling*, 330 U.S. at 150. The Court
held that the FLSA "cannot be interpreted so as to make a person whose work
serves only his own interest an employee of another person who gives him aid and
instruction . . . the [FLSA] was not intended to penalize [employers] for providing,
free of charge, the same kind of instruction [as a vocational school] at a place and
in a manner which would most greatly benefit the trainee." *Walling*, 330 U.S. at 153.
The Court concluded that "[a]ccepting the unchallenged findings here that the
railroads receive no 'immediate advantage' from any work done by the trainees, we
hold that they are not employees within the Act's meaning." *Walling*, 330 U.S. at
153.

A Department of Labor fact sheet helps to determine whether interns at for-profit businesses fall within this exception. *See* U.S. Dep't of Labor Fact Sheet #71 (April 2010) ("DOL Intern Fact Sheet"). The Fact Sheet notes that "[t]he Supreme Court has held that the term 'suffer or permit to work' cannot be interpreted so as to make a person whose work serves only his or her own interest an employee of another who provides aid or instruction." It enumerates six criteria for determining whether an internship may be unpaid. . . . [the court here listed the six factors from the DOL test above]. . . . "This exclusion from the definition of employment is necessarily quite narrow because the FLSA's definition of 'employ' is very broad." DOL Fact Sheet.

The Second Circuit has not addressed the "trainee" exception to the FLSA. Defendants urge that the DOL factors are not the applicable standard and that this Court should apply a "primary benefit test" by determining whether "the internship's benefits to the intern outweigh the benefits to the engaging entity."

While some Circuits have applied a "primary beneficiary" test, it has little support in *Walling*. The Supreme Court did not weigh the benefits to the trainees against those of the railroad, but relied on findings that the training program served only the trainees' interests and that the employer received "no 'immediate advantage' from any work done by the trainees." *Walling*, 330 U.S. at 153 (emphasis added).

Thus, *Walling* created a narrow exception to an expansive definition. "A broader or more comprehensive coverage of employees . . . would be difficult to frame." *United States v. Rosenwasser*, 323 U.S. 360, 362 (1945). There is "no doubt as to the Congressional intention to include all employees within the scope of the Act unless specifically excluded." Courts should be cautious in expanding the "trainee" exception established in *Walling*.

Moreover, a "primary beneficiary" test is subjective and unpredictable. Defendants' counsel argued the very same internship position might be compensable as to one intern, who took little from the experience, and not compensable as to another, who learned a lot. Under this test, an employer could never know in advance whether it would be required to pay its interns. Such a standard is unmanageable.

By contrast, the DOL factors have support in *Walling*. Because they were promulgated by the agency charged with administering the FLSA and are a reasonable application of it, they are entitled to deference.[5] *Wang v. Hearst Corp.*, F.Supp.2d, 2013 U.S. Dist. LEXIS 65869, citing *United States v. Mead Corp.*, 533 U.S. 218, 234 (2001)). No single factor is controlling; the test "requires consideration of all the circumstances." *Archie v. Grand Cent. P'ship*, 997 F. Supp. 504, 532 (S.D.N.Y. 1998); see also *Wang*, 2013 U.S. Dist. LEXIS 65869 ("[T]he prevailing

---

[5] [n.61] Defendants argue the DOL factors do not deserve deference because DOL opinion letters, which do not stem from "formal agency adjudication or notice-and-comment rulemaking, are not binding authority." Defs.' SJ Opp. Br. at 25 n.14. (quoting *Barfield*, 537 F.3d at 149). But even if not binding, "such agency letters represent 'a body of experience and informed judgment to which courts and litigants may properly resort for guidance.' " Barfield, 537 F.3d at 149 (quoting *Gualandi v. Adams*, 385 F.3d 236, 243 (2d Cir. 2004)). The DOL Intern Fact Sheet was issued in 2010, but the same six factors "have appeared in Wage and Hour Administrator opinions since at least 1967." *Reich v. Parker Fire Prot. Dist.*, 992 F.2d 1023, 1027 (10th Cir. 1993).

view is the totality of the circumstances test.").

. . . .

1. Training Similar to an Educational Environment

While classroom training is not a prerequisite, internships must provide something beyond on-the-job training that employees receive. "A training program that emphasizes the prospective employer's particular policies is nonetheless comparable to vocational school if the program teaches skills that are fungible within the industry." *Reich v. Parker Fire Prot. Dist.*, 992 F.2d 1023, 1028 (10th Cir. 1993).

Footman did not receive any formal training or education during his internship. He did not acquire any new skills aside from those specific to *Black Swan's* back office, such as how it watermarked scripts or how the photocopier or coffee maker operated. It is not enough that Footman "learned what the function of a production office was through experience." He accomplished that simply by being there, just as his paid co-workers did, and not because his internship was engineered to be more educational than a paid position.

The record for Glatt is inconclusive on this factor. Plaintiffs argue he "did not receive any training on Black Swan." But Glatt claimed only that he didn't learn much. Whether someone learned anything does not answer the question of whether training or useful knowledge was offered. As any student knows, even a classic educational environment sometimes results in surprisingly little learning.

2. Whether the Internship Experience is for the Benefit of the Intern

Undoubtedly, Glatt and Footman received some benefits from their internships, such as resume listings, job references, and an understanding of how a production office works. But those benefits were incidental to working in the office like any other employee and were not the result of internships intentionally structured to benefit them. Resume listings and job references result from any work relationship, paid or unpaid, and are not the academic or vocational training benefits envisioned by this factor.

On the other hand, Searchlight received the benefits of their unpaid work, which otherwise would have required paid employees. Even under Defendants' preferred test, the Defendants were the "primary beneficiaries" of the relationship, not Glatt and Footman.

3. Whether the Plaintiffs Displaced Regular Employees

Glatt and Footman performed routine tasks that would otherwise have been performed by regular employees. In his first internship, Glatt obtained documents for personnel files, picked up paychecks for coworkers, tracked and reconciled purchase orders and invoices, and traveled to the set to get managers' signatures. His supervisor stated that "[i]f Mr. Glatt had not performed this work, another member of my staff would have been required to work longer hours to perform it, or we would have needed a paid production assistant or another intern to do it." At his post-production internship, Glatt performed basic administrative work such as drafting cover letters, organizing filing cabinets, making photocopies, and running errands. This is work that otherwise would have been done by a paid employee.

Footman performed similar chores, including assembling office furniture, arranging travel plans, taking out trash, taking lunch orders, answering phones, watermarking scripts, and making deliveries. Again, if Footman had not performed these tasks for free, a paid employee would have been needed. When Footman went from five to three days a week, *Black Swan* hired another part-time intern.

4. *Whether Searchlight Obtained an Immediate Advantage From Plaintiffs' Work*

Searchlight does not dispute that it obtained an immediate advantage from Glatt and Footman's work. They performed tasks that would have required paid employees. There is no evidence they ever impeded work at their internships. Menial as it was, their work was essential. The fact they were beginners is irrelevant. The FLSA recognizes this by authorizing the Secretary of Labor to issue certificates allowing "learners" and "apprentices" to be paid less than minimum wage. *See* 29 U.S.C. § 214(a). "An employee is entitled to compensation for the hours he or she actually worked, whether or not someone else could have performed the duties better or in less time." *Donovan v. New Floridian Hotel, Inc.*, 676 F.2d 468, 471 n.3 (11th Cir. 1982).

5. *Whether Plaintiffs Were Entitled to a Job at the End of Their Internships*

There is no evidence Glatt or Footman were entitled to jobs at the end of their internships or thought they would be.

6. *Whether Searchlight and the Plaintiffs Understood They Were Not Entitled to Wages*

Glatt and Footman understood they would not be paid. But this factor adds little, because the FLSA does not allow employees to waive their entitlement to wages. "[T]he purposes of the Act require that it be applied even to those who would decline its protections. If an exception to the Act were carved out for employees willing to testify that they performed work 'voluntarily,' employers might be able to use superior bargaining power to coerce employees to make such assertions, or to waive their protections under the Act." *Tony & Susan Alamo Found. v. Sec'y of Labor*, 471 U.S. 290, 301 (1985). This protects more than the Plaintiffs themselves, because "[s]uch exceptions to coverage would . . . exert a general downward pressure on wages in competing businesses." *Tony & Susan Alamo Found.*, 471 U.S. at 302. It also protects businesses by preventing anticompetitive behavior. "An employer is not to be allowed to gain a competitive advantage by reason of the fact that his employees are more willing to waive [FLSA claims] than are those of his competitor." *Brooklyn Sav. Bank v. O'Neil*, 324 U.S. 697, 710 (1945).

Considering the totality of the circumstances, Glatt and Footman were classified improperly as unpaid interns and are "employees" covered by the FLSA and

NYLL. They worked as paid employees work, providing an immediate advantage to their employer and performing low-level tasks not requiring specialized training. The benefits they may have received—such as knowledge of how a production or accounting office functions or references for future jobs—are the results of simply having worked as any other employee works, not of internships designed to be uniquely educational to the interns and of little utility to the employer. They received nothing approximating the education they would receive in an academic setting or vocational school. This is a far cry from *Walling*, where trainees impeded the regular business of the employer, worked only in their own interest, and provided no advantage to the employer. Glatt and Footman do not fall within the narrow "trainee" exception to the FLSA's broad coverage. [The court then granted summary judgment for Glatt and Footman finding that they were employees covered by the FLSA and the NYLL.]

. . . .

[The court granted Antalik's motion to certify a class for the NYLL claims consisting of "[a]ll individuals who had unpaid internships in New York between September 28, 2005 and September 1, 2010 with one or more of the following divisions of FEG: Fox Filmed Entertainment, Fox Group, Fox Networks Group, and Fox Interactive Media." The court found the commonality requirement satisfied because common questions of fact and law existed on whether FEG derived immediate advantage from the interns' work, whether the interns displaced regular employees, and whether the internship program was for the benefit of interns. In particular, evidence that would answer common questions on a classwide basis included the fact that "[d]epartments at FEG companies requested interns based on their 'needs,' and they requested more when they were busier, the opposite of what one would expect if interns provided little advantage to the company and sometimes impeded its work." In addition, the court noted, "[a]n internal memo reports that because paid internships were eliminated and overtime pay and temporary employees scaled back, 'the size of our [unpaid] intern program more than doubled.' " Further, FEG's internship overseers expressed concern about the program after the DOL released its Fact Sheet, worrying about the risks of legal liability for FEG: "Antalik's supervisor . . . asked intern recruiter Aimee Hoffman '[w]hy would an office have an intern that provides no immediate advantage from said intern's activities?' Hoffman responded, 'That is the question! . . . If we give them work to benefit the company, we really should pay them . . . these DOL guidelines really make you think about whether it's worth it or not to have [an unpaid intern].' " After that, FEG altered its internship program, eventually eliminating it altogether. The court also granted Antalik's motion for conditional certification of a FLSA collective action and authorized her to send notice of the suit to other unpaid interns during the relevant time period.]

WANG v. HEARST CORP.

United States District Court for the Southern District of New York

293 F.R.D. 489 (S.D.N.Y. 2013)

HON. HAROLD BAER, JR., DISTRICT JUDGE:

Before the Court are Plaintiffs' motions for partial summary judgment under Fed. R. Civ. P. 56(a) and class certification pursuant to Fed. R. Civ. P. 23(a) and b(3). Plaintiffs previously interned at various magazines owned by Defendant Hearst Corporation ("Defendant") without pay. Plaintiffs allege that Defendant violated the minimum wage requirements, overtime provisions, and recordkeeping requirements in the Fair Labor Standards Act ("FLSA"), 29 U.S.C. §§ 201 *et seq.*, and the New York Labor Law ("NYLL") Art. 19 §§ 650 *et seq.*, and seek the certification of the following class for their claims under the NYLL: "All persons who have worked as unpaid interns at Hearst Magazines in New York between February 1, 2006 and the date of final judgment in this matter." For the reasons set forth below, Plaintiffs' motions for partial summary judgment and class certification are DENIED.

BACKGROUND

Hearst is one of the world's largest publishers of monthly magazines with 20 U.S. magazine titles and several corporate departments. Hearst is also an "employer" under the FLSA and NYLL and in addition, has had more than 3,000 interns over the past six years. . . .

Since 2008, Hearst worked to reduce costs by decreasing its headcount and expenses at the magazines as a response to the recession, and internal emails within Harper's Bazaar and Marie Claire instructed the staff to use interns rather than paid messengers to save costs. Discovery revealed that in 2008, 229 full-time employees were eliminated: 109 left due to the closure of three magazines; another 88 positions that were eliminated were middle to senior level employees; and 32 positions were entry-level.

Hearst's Human Resources Department is charged with making sure that the company's magazines and departments are in compliance with wage and hour laws, and a part of its mission was to instruct all concerned to have the interns provide "school credit letters." The primary criteria relied upon by Hearst in concluding not to pay the interns was that for the most part, they were in college and eligible to receive academic credit. This policy has been in place at least since 2006. For the most part, all magazines followed this policy. To provide some flavor, I describe below what some interns did during their internship.

Named Plaintiff Xuedan Wang worked as an intern five days a week, sometimes from 9 a.m. to 8 p.m., at the accessories department of Harper's Bazaar Magazine from August 2011 to December 2011. Wang's duties included serving as a contact between editors and public relations representatives, doing online research, cataloguing samples, maintaining the accessories closet, and doing story boards.

Named Plaintiff Erin Spencer and Opt-in Plaintiff Sarah Wheels were interns at Cosmopolitan Magazine, the former from June 1, 2010 to August 15, 2010, and the latter from May 20, 2011 to August 10, 2011. Spencer, as a bookings intern, worked four days per week from 9 a.m. to 5 or 5:30 p.m., and her duties included organizing files, holding casting calls, assisting at photo shoots, running errands, mailing magazine pages where models appear to models' agents, updating contact lists, and assisting in the fashion closet. Wheels, as an editorial intern, worked four days a week from 9:15 a.m. to 6 p.m., and her duties included responding to emails from readers, researching for articles, surveying people on the street, transcribing interviews, compiling sales statistics, locating articles in the magazine's archive, writing content, and fact-checking articles.

Opt-in Plaintiffs Elizabeth Mancini and Caitlin Leszuk were interns at Marie Claire Magazine, the former from January 2009 through June 2009 and the latter from January 11, 2010 to May 15, 2010. As a fashion intern, Mancini worked three to four days a week and arrived between 8:30 and 9 a.m. and left some time after 6 p.m., and her duties included receiving clothing ordered from photo shoots, unpacking the items and checking to make sure that everything ordered was received and not broken, photographing the items, filing invoices, and putting the items on garment racks. Leszuk, as a sales intern, worked four days a week, from 9 a.m. to 6 p.m., and she spent the majority of her time creating "edit credit" spreadsheets, which involved a line-by-line review of Marie Claire and its competitors' magazines.

Opt-in Plaintiff Matthew Wagster was an intern at Esquire from July 2009 to December 2009, where he worked three days a week from 9 a.m. to 6 p.m. As an intern in the publishing department, he ran errands, updated guest lists for events, helped prepare for events, and worked at the doors at the events.

Opt-in Plaintiff Stephanie Skorka was an intern at Redbook from September 2009 to December 2009. As a beauty intern, Skorka worked three days a week from 10 a.m. to 6 or 7 p.m., and her duties included managing the beauty closet, assisting with photo shoots, coming up with beauty story ideas, writing posts for the website, attending beauty product launches, contacting public relation firms, and selecting beauty products for potential inclusion in the magazine.

Opt-in Plaintiff Alexandra Rappaport was an intern at Seventeen from May 23, 2011 to July 26, 2011. As an intern in the fashion closet, Rappaport worked four days a week, from 9:20 a.m. to between 6:30 and 7:30 p.m., and her duties included organizing clothes, hanging them on racks, packing them, picking up and returning clothing, organizing jewelry, sending packages, copying, faxing, and responding to emails from designers.

Some interns, e.g. Spencer and Wheels, attended four, one-hour sessions of "Cosmo-U" during which the editors at Cosmopolitan talked about their careers. Leszuk received at least one MediaMath class. More importantly, all Plaintiffs understood prior to their internship that the position was unpaid, and Hearst made it clear that there was little likelihood, and certainly no guarantee, of a job at the end of their internship. The parties do not dispute that some of the duties performed by Plaintiffs were performed by paid employees. However, the parties dispute the amount of supervision provided, as well as the benefits received and the advantages that Hearst derived.

DISCUSSION

. . . .

1. Applicable Legal Standard

Plaintiffs move for partial summary judgment contending that they were "employees" under the FLSA and NYLL. The FLSA defines "employee" as "any individual employed by an employer" and the term "employ" is defined broadly to include "to suffer or permit to work." 29 U.S.C. § 203(e)(1), (g); *Zheng v. Liberty Apparel Co.* Inc., 355 F.3d 61, 66 (2d Cir. 2003). Although the term "intern" is neither defined nor provided as an exception in the FLSA, the parties do not dispute, and the Court agrees, that for this lawsuit, the Supreme Court in *Walling v. Portland Terminal Co*, 330 U.S. 148 (1947) provides, for the most part, the governing case law. In *Walling*, the Supreme Court found that trainees who worked for seven or eight days for the defendant railroad without pay during "a course of practical training" were not "employees" under the FLSA based on "the unchallenged findings [ ] that the railroads receive no 'immediate advantage' from any work done by the trainees." 330 U.S. at 153. The Court reasoned that "[t]he definition 'suffer or permit to work' was obviously not intended to stamp all persons as employees who, without any express or implied compensation agreement, might work for their own advantage on the premises of another." *Id.* at 152.

The Department of Labor ("DOL") published a fact sheet in April 2010, which puts some meat on the *Walling* bones. U.S. Dep't of Labor, "Fact Sheet # 71: Internship Programs Under The Fair Labor Standards Act," available at http://www.dol.gov/whd/regs/compliance/whdfs71.pdf ("DOL Fact Sheet #71"). [The court quoted the DOL six-factored test set out above in the Fact Sheet.] While the weight to be given to these factors is far from crystal clear, the Fact Sheet adds to the confusion with the introductory language: "whether an internship or training program meets this exclusion depends upon all of the facts and circumstances of each such program." *Id.*

Not surprisingly, the parties disagree as to the appropriate test for defining an "employee" under *Walling*. Plaintiffs urge the Court to adopt a standard of "immediate advantage," contending that the outcome in *Walling* "would have been different if the railroads had obtained an immediate advantage from the trainees. . . . When an employer obtains a direct or immediate benefit from work, it has 'suffered or permitted' work and must compensate for it." In the alternative, they argue that Hearst "must meet all of the factors" in the Department of Labor's ("DOL") six-factor test and that it has failed to do so. On the other hand, Hearst urges the Court to adopt a "balancing of the benefits test" which looks to the totality of circumstances to evaluate the "economic reality" of the relationship. As for the DOL's six-factor test, Hearst contends that no judicial deference is required and is critical of Plaintiffs' effort to apply it as "a rigid checklist." Id. at 31.

I agree with Hearst that the Supreme Court in *Walling* looked to the totality of circumstances of the training program to determine whether the plaintiffs were "employees" under the FLSA. Although the Supreme Court held in *Walling* that the men in that case were not employees because the defendant railroads received "no immediate advantage" from the trainees, 330 U.S. at 153, it does not logically follow that the reverse is true, i.e. that the presence of an "immediate advantage" alone creates an employment relationship under the FLSA. Moreover, Plaintiffs' reading of *Walling* as establishing the test for an employer-employee relationship solely based on "direct or immediate benefit" is misplaced. There is no one-dimensional test; rather, the prevailing view is the totality of circumstances test. *See Tony & Susan Alamo Found. v. Sec'y of Labor*, 471 U.S. 290, 295 (1985). To make the cheese more binding, the Second Circuit in a decision only last year echoed that view when it wrote, "whether an employer-employee relationship exists does not depend on isolated factors but rather upon the circumstances of the whole activity," and specifically noted that a key consideration in the analysis depended on "who is the primary recipient of benefits from the relationship. . . ." *Velez v. Sanchez*, 693 F.3d 308, 326, 330 (2d Cir. 2012).

All that said, I am also of the mind that the six factors in Fact Sheet #71 ought not be disregarded; rather, it suggests a framework for an analysis of the employee-employer relationship. After all, they emanate from the agency that administers the laws under which Plaintiffs brought this lawsuit. This position finds support in *United States v. Mead Corp.*, where we read "[A]n agency's interpretation may merit some deference whatever its form, given the specialized experience and broader investigations and information and given the value of uniformity in its administrative and judicial understandings of what a national law requires." 533 U.S. 218, 234 (2001) (citing *Skidmore v. Swift & Co.*, 323 U.S. 134 (1944)). . . .

2. Dispute Regarding Material Facts

Plaintiffs seek partial summary judgment based on the "immediate advantage" standard, while Hearst bases its argument on the totality of circumstances standard. This alone creates a genuine issue of fact sufficient to deny summary judgment. Further, to the extent that Plaintiffs seek partial summary judgment based on the DOL six-factor test, that branch of the motion too must be denied. A genuine dispute and material issues of fact exists, at least with respect to the first, second, third, and fourth factors. This is not a winner-take-all test, and Hearst has shown with respect to each Plaintiff that there was *some* educational training, *some* benefit to individual interns, *some* supervision, and *some* impediment to Hearst's regular operations, etc., which, if viewed in the light most favorable to the non-moving party, as it must be, supports the view that a jury could return a verdict in Hearst's favor.

[The court next considered the plaintiffs' motion for class certification, and concluded that plaintiffs had not established the "commonality" and "predominance" requirements for certification: that the case involved questions of law or fact common to the class, and that common questions predominated over individual ones. The court found that the plaintiffs had not alleged anything more than a uniform policy of unpaid internships; individual interns' job duties varied considerably within each magazine and corporate department, and so did the benefits they received. There was no uniform policy across the magazines regarding the contents of the internship, the interns' duties, training, or supervision; accordingly, the analysis under four of the six DOL factors would be individualized rather than general, and individual issues would overwhelm the common issues. The court thus denied the plaintiffs' motion for class certification on the NYLL claims.]

CONCLUSION

I have considered the parties' remaining arguments and find them to be without merit. For the foregoing reasons, Plaintiffs' motion for summary judgment regarding their status as "employees" under the FLSA and NYLL is DENIED. Plaintiffs' motion for class certification under the NYLL claims is also DENIED.

NOTES

1. **Comparing *Glatt* and *Wang*.** The *Glatt* court applied the DOL Fact Sheet criteria and concluded that the interns were employees subject to the requirements of the FLSA. The *Wang* court came to a different conclusion, refusing to grant summary judgment for the plaintiffs on the question of their employee status. What test did the *Wang* court use? How did the *Wang* court deal with the DOL's interpretation of the appropriate test for employee status? The Second Circuit certified both cases for appeal, and is expected to resolve the conflict in that circuit over what test applies to determine internship status. *Wang v. The Hearst Corp.*, No. 13-04480, 13-2616 (2d Cir. 2013).

2. **The Practical Consequences of the Class Certification Question.** Although the *Wang* plaintiffs did not prevail on their motion for summary judgment, it is conceivable that they could win at trial on the question of employee status for purposes of FLSA coverage. The real blow dealt by the *Wang* court, however, was the refusal to certify a class under the New York state labor laws: had the plaintiffs prevailed on that motion, they could have proceeded with an opt-out class action alleging violation of the New York Labor Law under Rule 23 of the Federal Rules of Civil Procedure. Without a class, would any law firm be interested in bringing these cases on behalf of individual interns? By contrast, the *Glatt* court permitted the plaintiffs' claim to move forward under both New York state law as a Rule 23 class action, and under the FLSA as a collective action, which requires similarly situated employees to opt in to the litigation. Note that the plaintiffs' lawyers must recruit other interns to opt into the FLSA action in order to maximize recovery. Will it be difficult to persuade other interns to join? Why or why not?

3. **The Primary Benefit.** Do internships primarily benefit the intern, or the employer? What do interns hope to gain from an internship? What difference should it make whether the intern receives training similar to that provided in a college or educational environment (the first factor in the DOL test)? After all, as the *Glatt* court observed, "even a classic educational environment sometimes results in surprisingly little learning." And isn't the internship valuable to interns precisely because it is *not* like the training one receives in a classroom context? What do employers gain from the arrangement? If the internship benefits both, how should a court weigh the second and fourth factors in the DOL test?

Who benefits most from an internship—a relatively class-privileged student, or a student from a less economically privileged background?

4. The Relevance of Receiving Academic Credit. In *Kaplan v. Code Blue Billing & Coding, Inc.*, 2013 U.S. App. LEXIS 1433 (11th Cir. Jan. 22, 2013) (unpublished), *cert. denied*, 134 S. Ct. 618, the Eleventh Circuit ruled that students who worked as unpaid externs as a required part of their studies (and who received academic credit for their work) were not employees covered by the FLSA. The students were enrolled in a medical billing and coding degree program, and sought minimum wage for the hours worked as externs. Applying *Walling v. Portland Terminal Co.*, discussed in *Glatt* and *Wang*, the court concluded that the DOL's six-factor test was fully consistent with *Walling* and ruled that the students received the primary benefit of the arrangement due to the academic credit awarded for their work.

Should the receipt of academic credit for an internship shield the arrangement from scrutiny under the FLSA? The *Glatt* court noted in a part of its opinion not included above that the fact that some interns received academic credit while others did not was irrelevant:

> Receipt of academic credit is of little moment. A university's decision to grant academic credit is not a determination that an unpaid internship complies with the NYLL. Universities may add additional requirements or coursework for students receiving internship credit, but the focus of the NYLL is on the requirements and training provided by the alleged employer.

Glatt, 293 F.R.D. at 536. Should colleges and universities be obligated to exercise oversight to ensure that unpaid externships are meaningful educational experiences? Should they be held jointly liable for compensation along with the putative employer if they fail to assume this oversight role? *See* Hunter Swain, *Sinking the Unpaid Externship: How Many Unpaid Externships Violate the Fair Labor Standards Act and Yield Exceptionally Broad Joint Liability*, available at http://www.kentlaw.iit.edu/Documents/Institutes%20and%20Centers/ILW/Jackson%20Louis%20Writing%20Competition/HunterSwain.pdf; Gayle Cinquegrani, *Private Sector Firms Generally Should Pay Interns at Least Minimum Wage, Lawyers Say*, DAILY LAB. REP. (BNA) No. 96, May 19, 2014. Suppose that the unpaid internship occurs during the summer months and students must pay additional tuition to receive credit for working without compensation. Is this justifiable? Ross Perlin, *Unpaid Interns, Complicit Colleges*, N.Y. TIMES, APR. 2, 2011. Should universities' career centers be held liable for simply listing unpaid internships and looking the other way to avoid acknowledging what might be FLSA violations?

5. The Intern's Choice to Work Without Pay. The last factor in the DOL's test is whether the employer and the interns understood that they would not be entitled to wages. This factor tends to cut in favor of the employer, as interns agree at the outset that they will not be paid. Why are interns nevertheless permitted to sue the employer for minimum wages and overtime pay? Shouldn't they be held to the deal they made to work without pay? Would anyone be harmed if they were?

6. Advice to Employers. What advice would you give to a for-profit company that wishes to structure an internship experience to survive scrutiny under the DOL test? Some employers have simply ended their internship programs. *See* Cara

Buckley, *Sued over Pay, Conde Nast Ends Internship Program*, N.Y. TIMES, Oct. 23, 2013. Is that a desirable result?

7. Internships at Nonprofits or Government Agencies. The DOL's six-factor test applies only to internships at for-profit companies. If the DOL's core concern is employee displacement (factor three), which is consistent with the FLSA's job-spreading goals, why should it matter whether the internship is at a for-profit or a non-profit organization? The DOL is currently considering whether its six-factor test should apply to non-profit organizations. What arguments might be made for distinguishing the two contexts? What arguments support treating them similarly? *See* Anthony J. Tucci, *Worthy Exemption? Examining How the DOL Should Apply the FLSA to Unpaid Interns at Nonprofits and Public Agencies*, 97 IOWA L. REV. 1363, 1384 (2012) (arguing that in addition to the DOL's six-part test, courts should consider whether the student "completes work that is typically associated with public-service volunteerism, [whether] the tasks comprise only a minority of the internship in a given workweek, and [whether] this work is motivated by civic or humanitarian purposes.").

Suppose that a law student interning in a for-profit law firm is assigned to work exclusively on pro bono matters that result in unbilled work. Work at a for-profit firm would ordinarily be governed by the Fact Sheet, and thus the intern might be entitled to compensation. Would her assignment to pro bono work make a difference? Suppose she wishes to obtain credit for the internship through a law school educational program. An ABA standard currently prevents a law school from granting credit toward the J.D. degree for participation in field placement programs for which the student receives compensation (The ABA recently agreed to reconsider that standard.). In response to an ABA query about the tension between ABA standards and the FLSA's requirements, the Department of Labor clarified through a letter ruling that FLSA pay requirements do not apply to internships at for-profit organizations if the interns work exclusively on pro bono matters that do not involve potential fee-generating activities, do not participate in the law firm's billable work, and the interns' work does not free up staff resources for billable work where the staff would otherwise have been deployed toward pro bono work. Under these circumstances, the law firm would not derive any immediate advantage from the students' work, and any general reputational advantage would be associated only with pro bono activities. Thus, the intern's experience would be equivalent to the educational experience the intern would receive in a law school clinical program. Finally, the intern must be a current student whose activities are monitored by the law school; this letter ruling does not apply to law school graduates. Letter from M. Patricia Smith, Solicitor, U.S. Dep't of Labor, to Laurel G. Bellows, Immediate Past President, Am. Bar. Ass'n (Sept. 12, 2013), *available at* http://www.americanbar.org/content/dam/aba/images/news/ PDF/MPS_Letter_reFLSA_091213.pdf. *See generally* Stephen A. Mazurak, *The Unpaid Intern: Liability for the Uninformed Employer*, 29 ABA J. LAB. & EMP. L. 101 (2014) (discussing these requirements); *see also* Melissa Hart, *Internships as Invisible Labor*, 18 EMP. RTS. & EMPLOY. POL'Y J. 141, 150–51 (2014) (noting pressure on law schools to offer experiential training, describing survey of law schools that permit students to perform externships, and noting that many limit their programs to externships in nonprofit or government organizations, or restrict externships at for-profit organizations to pro bono work).

What about law students who serve as unpaid judicial externs or interns? Are they trainees? Students? Employees? In *Todaro v. Township of Union*, 40 F. Supp. 2d 226 (D.N.J. 1999), the court hypothesized that it would "offend[ ] rationality" to consider such individuals covered employees entitled to a minimum wage under the FLSA and noted that the protections of the FLSA were "not intended to sweep everyone under the minimum wage umbrella." *Id.* at 230. Do you agree?

8. **Volunteers.** What is the relationship between internships at non-profit organizations and volunteers? In *Tony & Susan Alamo Foundation v. Secretary of Labor*, 471 U.S. 290 (1985), the employer was a religious foundation that operated commercial businesses staffed by "associates" who were former drug addicts and criminals. The associates received food, clothing, and shelter from the Foundation but did not receive cash wages. Although the associates denied any desire for compensation, the Court characterized them as statutory employees because of their complete dependence on the Foundation. Similarly, in *Shiloh True Light Church of Christ v. Brock*, 670 F. Supp. 158 (W.D.N.C. 1987), the court required a church that employed children in a construction vocational program to comply with the child labor provisions of the FLSA (restricting the employment of minors under the age of 18, discussed *supra* section B). The church sought to defend against the action on the grounds that enforcement of the FLSA interfered with its First Amendment right to free exercise of religion. The church asserted that the program had been established in order to instill values of "industry, hard work, pride in the job and the need to cooperate with others." The court rejected the defense, finding that the FLSA was a "reasonable, nondiscriminatory regulation" that did not violate the free exercise clause. What rationale supports application of the FLSA in these contexts?

Suppose that the employer for whom volunteer services are performed is for-profit. How should that affect the analysis? In *Hallissey v. America Online, Inc.*, 2006 U.S. Dist. LEXIS 12964 (S.D.N.Y. Mar. 10, 2006), the plaintiffs participated in AOL's "community leader" program, managing and updating message boards, moderating chat rooms, serving as "guides" to AOL subscribers, updating content on forums, and similar duties. In exchange, plaintiffs received free AOL access, discounts on AOL products, expanded space for web pages, free anti-virus software, and greater power than regular subscribers (for example, the power to "gag" members by forcing them to a five-minute "time out" if they engaged in inappropriate online conduct, or to delete or change the content of some AOL forums). Plaintiffs filed a collective action seeking unpaid minimum wage and overtime pay under the FLSA. The plaintiffs argued that they were required to undergo extensive training, to adhere to pre-set "shift" schedules, perform administrative work, submit weekly reports of hours "volunteered" and duties performed, and were subject to termination. They also claimed that the work performed was substantially the same as that performed by some paid employees, and that it was of economic benefit to AOL and integral to its business. AOL moved for summary judgment on the basis that the plaintiffs were volunteers, and therefore not covered by the Act. The district court denied AOL's motion and granted class certification for a nationwide class. 2008 U.S. Dist. LEXIS 18387 (Feb. 19, 2008). The case settled in 2009 for $15 million. Lauren Kirchner, *AOL Settled with Unpaid Volunteers for*

$15 Million, Columbia Journalism Rev., Feb. 10, 2011, *available at* http://www.cjr. org/the_news_frontier/aol_settled_with_unpaid_volunt.php?page=all&print=.

9. Connection to Precarious Labor Market. Is there a connection between the trend toward precarious labor explored in Chapter 2—including rising numbers of temporary workers, freelancers, independent contractors, and self-employed—and the rise of internships?

E.   WHAT IS COVERED WORK?

Some of the most hotly litigated questions arising under the FLSA revolve around what constitutes "work" or "compensable time" for compensation purposes under the FLSA. The Department of Labor defines compensable time as "all of the time during which an employee is on duty on the employer's premises or at a prescribed workplace, as well as all of the other time during which the employee is suffered or permitted to work for the employer." 29 C.F.R. § 553.221 (2004). However, neither the Act nor the regulations promulgated by the Department of Labor specifically define "work." The Act does contain several exclusions from "hours worked" which help to elucidate (by negative implication) the meaning of "work." *See, e.g.,* 29 U.S.C. § 203(o) (excluding time spent changing clothes or washing at the beginning or end of each workday if excluded by custom, practice, or under the terms of a collective bargaining agreement). In addition, the Portal-to-Portal Act of 1947, enacted in part to fill the gaps left by the FLSA, excludes from hours worked "activities which are preliminary to or postliminary to . . . principal . . . activities," unless made compensable by contract, custom or practice. 29 U.S.C. § 254. This leaves open many interesting and often-litigated questions, including whether "off-the clock" work, "on-call" time, meal or rest periods, training time, and travel time should be included in compensable time under the FLSA. We consider some of these issues further here.

1.   "Off-the-clock" Work

Suppose that employer work rules require employees to continue to work after punching out (for example, to continue to remain in a store after closing time until all customers exit), or the employer's productivity standards necessitate that employees take work home or perform work "off-the-clock" to meet them. Is such work compensable? The question turns on the meaning of the phrase "suffer or permit to work" in the FLSA's definition of employment.

DAVIS v. FOOD LION
United States Court of Appeals for the Fourth Circuit
792 F.2d 1274 (1986)

Chapman, Circuit Judge.

Appellant Jerry S. Davis brought this action below against appellee Food Lion, Inc., to recover overtime compensation under §§ 7(a)(1) and 16(b) of the Fair Labor Standards Act of 1938 (FLSA), 29 U.S.C. §§ 207(a)(1), 216(b) (1982). At trial the

PH

district court, sitting without a jury, found that Davis had not proved an element of his case for overtime compensation, namely, that Food Lion knew or should have known that he was working overtime hours. Accordingly, the court entered judgment for Food Lion. Davis appeals, arguing first, that the district court incorrectly required him to show Food Lion's actual or constructive knowledge of his overtime work as an element of his case, and second, that the district court committed clear error in finding that Food Lion had no such knowledge. Finding these arguments unpersuasive, we affirm.

I

facts

Jerry Davis was employed as a meat market manager with Food Lion from January 1981 to August 1983. During this period of time, he worked in two different stores, one in Eden, North Carolina, and the other in Martinsville, Virginia. As a meat market manager, Davis was an hourly employee and was required to record his working hours on a time card at the beginning and end of every work day. Davis claims that during these two and one-half years, he worked 1,414 "off-the-clock" overtime hours without compensation in violation of FLSA § 7(a)(1).

Food Lion has an established policy which prohibits employees from working unrecorded, so-called "off-the-clock," hours. Violations of this policy can result in disciplinary action ranging from verbal warnings to discharge of the offending employee. It is undisputed that Davis was aware of this well-publicized company policy. Indeed, Martinsville store manager Craig Reavis discovered Davis working off-the-clock twice, giving him a verbal warning on both occasions. In addition, Davis' immediate supervisor in the meat market division, Toby Christenberry, strongly reprimanded Davis once on an unannounced visit in July 1983 when Christenberry mistakenly believed Davis was working off-the-clock. In fact, Davis had merely punched in on the wrong side of his time card.

Davis arguing why v. he had to work off the clock

Davis contends that off-the-clock work was made necessary because of the "Effective Scheduling" system for meat market managers implemented by Food Lion in 1980. This system was designed to assist market managers in projecting the weekly volume of product to be processed and in effectively scheduling personnel. The two-part system, as implemented, allows market managers a set number of hours to complete certain fixed-time duties in the market. In addition, the system utilizes a formula to determine the number of variable hours to be allowed individual markets based upon the quantity of products being processed, wrapped, and stocked.

PH

The district court found that although Effective Scheduling was originally intended as a general time guideline for market managers, many supervisors have been using the system as a production performance standard. Thus, a market manager such as Davis is expected to "beat" Effective Scheduling by seeing that his market completes its weekly work in less time than prescribed by the scheduling plan. Davis testified that the standards set by Effective Scheduling were unattainable, and that when he failed to meet the standards, he would receive "constructive advice memos" threatening suspension or termination for substandard performance. It is Davis' contention that this high-pressured system forced him to work secretly, off-the-clock, in order to perform the weekly duties of his market.

II

The first issue is whether the district court erred by requiring Mr. Davis to prove, as an element of his case under FLSA § 7(a)(1), that Food Lion knew or should have known of his uncompensated overtime work. Appellant does not contest the proposition that employer knowledge, either actual or constructive, should play some part in the analysis of § 7(a)(1) claims. The dispute before us simply concerns whether, as a procedural matter, proof of an employer's knowledge is an element of the plaintiff/employee's case or whether lack of knowledge is an affirmative defense to be raised and proved by the employer. Upon review of the Act and the applicable case law, we find that the district court correctly required Davis to prove Food Lion's actual or constructive knowledge of his overtime work as an element of his case.

FLSA § 7(a)(1) provides that no employer shall employ any of its employees covered by the Act for a work week that is longer than forty hours unless the employee receives compensation for his overtime work at a rate at least one and one-half times his regular rate. 29 U.S.C. § 207(a)(1). Section 16(b) of the Act gives employees a cause of action against employers who have violated § 7(a)(1) and allows them to recoup the overtime wage plus liquidated damages, attorneys' fees, and costs. 29 U.S.C. § 216(b). In order to recover, an employee must prove that he worked overtime hours without compensation, and he must show the amount and extent of his overtime work as a matter of just and reasonable inference. Anderson v. Mt. Clemens Pottery Co., 328 U.S. 680, 687 (1946). This much is undisputed.

Under § 7(a)(1), however, a plaintiff must also show that he was "employed" by the defendant/employer in order to prove a violation. As defined in 29 U.S.C. § 203(g), "'Employ' includes to suffer or permit to work." The words "suffer" and "permit" as used in § 203(g) have been consistently interpreted to mean with the knowledge of the employer. Therefore, in order to prove that he is "employed" for purposes of the Act, it is necessary for a plaintiff to show that his employer had knowledge, either actual or constructive, of his overtime work. The case law uniformly supports this proposition.

We do not believe as appellant urges that the *Mt. Clemens Pottery* case requires us to reach a different result. *Mt. Clemens Pottery* was squarely directed at the issue of what evidence an employee must introduce to establish the extent of his overtime work when his employer has kept inadequate records. 328 U.S. at 687-88. Employer knowledge was not an issue in that case since the employer unquestionably knew that its time clock system was causing its employees to record less time than they were actually working. Nothing in *Mt. Clemens Pottery* or in the Act itself treats the lack of employer knowledge as an affirmative defense to be raised and proved by the employer. The Act requires the plaintiff to prove that he was "employed" by the defendant, and that means proof that the defendant knew or should have known that the plaintiff was working overtime for the employer. This element of constructive or actual knowledge is especially significant in a case such as this one, in which an employee deliberately acted in such a way to prevent his employer from acquiring knowledge of his alleged uncompensated overtime hours. *See Forrester*, 646 F.2d at 414–15.

III

The second issue is whether the district court committed clear error in its factual finding that Food Lion had no actual or constructive knowledge of Davis' off-the-clock work. Our role in reviewing factual findings of the district court is, of course, quite limited under Fed. R. Civ. P. 52(a). If the district court's account of the evidence is plausible in light of the record viewed in its entirety, then we cannot reverse. Likewise we can find no clear error if there are two permissible views of the evidence, and the district court as fact-finder chooses one over the other. 84 L. Ed. 2d at 528.

Davis' evidence focused primarily upon the proposition that Food Lion should have known of Davis' off-the-clock work because of the pressure put on market managers by the unrealistically stringent Effective Scheduling system. Richard Torrence, the author of Effective Scheduling, testified that he advised the Vice-President of Operations for Food Lion that the Effective Scheduling system, as altered for implementation by supervisors, might result in off-the-clock work by meat market managers. Torrence's original plan, based upon his own time studies had provided for more hours to complete meat market tasks than the system that was implemented. A later time study by Torrence's successor found that Food Lion's meat markets needed a twenty percent increase in hours to meet the company's processing requirements.

In addition, appellant introduced evidence of an expert, Marvin H. Agee, who had performed a comparative analysis of Food Lion's daily man-hour summaries under the Effective Scheduling system for a three-year period. Agee found that Davis' market consistently "beat" Effective Scheduling and, in fact, averaged 3.53 hours less per week than the calculated Effective Scheduling hours. Agee concluded that Food Lion's system, which he called a "planned negative variance," forced Davis and others to work off-the-clock as a common practice, recording less hours than they actually needed to complete their work.

The district court gave little weight to this expert testimony since Agee himself conceded that his analysis could just as easily have proved that the Effective Scheduling standards were in fact too lenient. In finding that Food Lion had no constructive knowledge of off-the-clock work, the district court noted that no evidence was introduced that any employee, including Davis, had ever complained to management that it was impossible to beat the standards. Indeed, although several of Davis' supervisors testified that as market managers in the past they had occasionally worked off-the-clock to make themselves look better, they also testified that off-the-clock work was not necessary to meet Effective Scheduling standards. Finally, the district court found that the company policy against off-the-clock work was fully enforced by Food Lion. As a consequence, the court noted that to accept Davis' theory of the case would mean that Food Lion should have anticipated that employees would routinely falsify their time records in violation of established company policy.

Upon review of the whole record, we cannot say that the district court's view of the evidence was implausible. The district court weighed the evidence presented by the litigants, evidence that cuts both ways, and found that Food Lion had no actual or constructive knowledge of Davis' off-the-clock work. This finding is not clearly erroneous. Since Davis did not prove that Food Lion knew or should have known of his overtime work, the district court correctly entered judgment in favor of Food Lion finding no violation of FLSA § 7(a)(1).

Affirmed.

NOTES

similar case

1. **Establishing Employer Knowledge.** In a case arising out of the same circumstances as *Davis, Pforr v. Food Lion, Inc.*, 851 F.2d 106 (4th Cir. 1988), the court explained that the plaintiff must establish employer knowledge of "off-the-clock" hours by showing a pattern or practice of employer acquiescence, so that it is reasonable to infer that the employer "suffered or permitted" the plaintiff to work off-the-clock hours. In *Pforr*, the plaintiffs claimed a combined 1350 hours of "off-the-clock" uncompensated work. Although the plaintiffs established employer knowledge of several incidents of such work, the court found this insufficient to infer employer knowledge for such a large number of overtime hours. The court remanded the case to permit the plaintiffs to make a more persuasive showing of employer acquiescence. The *Pforr* court stated that plaintiffs need not prove knowledge of each hour of "off-the-clock" work claimed. What evidence would suffice? In *Lyle v. Food Lion*, 954 F.2d 984 (4th Cir. 1992), the court found the evidence sufficient where store management gave the workers keys to the store so that they could work off-the-clock prior to regular store hours, despite an explicit policy against off-the-clock work and disciplinary measures directed at workers for violation of the policy.   *evidence of Er knowl[...]*

The *Davis* court was critical of the employees for performing "off-the-clock" work in secret. According to the court, what should the employees have done?

2. **Proving Hours Worked Off-the-Clock.** In *Davis*, the court stated that the employee must show the amount and extent of overtime as a matter of "just and reasonable inference" from the facts proved. In *Brown v. Family Dollar Stores*, 534 F.3d 593 (7th Cir. 2008), the court explained further how the burdens of proof are distributed. Normally, "a[n] employee bears the burden of proving that she performed overtime work for which she was not properly compensated." *Id.* at 594 (citing *Anderson v. Mt. Clemens Pottery Co.*, 328 U.S. 680 (1946)). However, where the employer does not maintain proper records as it is required to do under the FLSA, the burden shifts to the employer. The employee need only show that she performed work for which she was not compensated, and "produce[] sufficient evidence to show the amount and extent of that work as a matter of just and reasonable inference." *Id.* at 595. Once the employee makes this showing, the burden shifts back to the employer to produce evidence of the specific amount worked or negate the reasonableness inference.   *if Er does not maintain records*

3. **The Modern Trend in Constructive Knowledge Cases.** Some cases reflect a trend toward a more generous interpretation of the constructive knowledge of overtime work that will suffice for plaintiffs to prevail in off-the-clock cases. In *Reich v. Dep't of Conservation & Natural Resources*, 28 F.3d 1076 (11th Cir. 1994), for example, the Eleventh Circuit imposed a duty on employers to acquire knowledge through reasonable diligence, measured by the conditions prevailing in

the industry. *Id.* at 1082 (requiring Department of Conservation & Natural Resources in Alabama to "do more than to simply periodically issue admonishments [against overtime] to avoid liability under the FLSA," where it was aware that unreported overtime by fish and game officers during deer hunting season was a substantial problem). Thus, where business conditions dictate overtime, courts that adopt this standard seem more willing to impute constructive knowledge to the employer. *See, e.g., Gonzalez v. McNeil Techs., Inc.*, 2007 U.S. Dist. LEXIS 27262 (E.D. Va. Apr. 11, 2007) (finding that employer had constructive notice of overtime where its business required someone to answer the phone and greet visitors, plaintiff was the only office employee present during the lunch break, and thus plaintiff frequently worked through lunch to perform these essential job duties). On the other hand, some courts still hew quite strictly to the "knew or should have known" standard, imposing no particular duty on the employer to inquire even where the facts suggest that overtime work may be occurring. *See, e.g., Kellar v. Summit Seating, Inc.*, 664 F.3d 169 (7th Cir. 2011) (finding no liability for overtime pay where sewing manager customarily arrived 15–45 minutes early for her 5 a.m. shift and spent the time turning on lights, a compressor, reviewing schedules, gathering and distributing fabric, and distributing material to employee work stations, even though employee recorded her pre-shift work on time cards used to calculate her pay; owners did not arrive until 7–8 a.m. and never personally saw the manager working before her scheduled start time, most employees had a habit of arriving prior to their shifts to smoke, drink coffee, and socialize, and manager had never complained that her paychecks did not include overtime pay).

4. **Off-the-Clock Claims in the Restaurant Industry.** Off-the-clock claims have become increasingly common in the restaurant industry, where workers are often required to perform unpaid setup work prior to the start of their shifts. For example, employees at Outback Steakhouse filed a collective action asserting that the employer required workers to show up for work two hours before the restaurant doors open, but did not allow them to clock in until half an hour before opening. This pre-shift requirement was called "Outback Time." Dan Prochilo, *Outback Makes Employees Do Off-the-Clock Work, Suit Says*, LAW 360, Oct. 8, 2013. Similar actions have been filed against McDonald's, where workers allege that managers advise workers to arrive an hour prior to the point when they clock in, and require them to clock out for extended breaks when business falls off, putting them back on the clock only when a preset customer-to-worker ratio is achieved. *See* Susan J. McGolrick, *Class Actions Against McDonald's Allege 'Systemic' Wage Theft in Three States*, DAILY LAB. REP. (BNA) No. 49, Mar. 13, 2014.

5. **Off-the-Clock Hours Worked At Home.** Suppose that the overtime hours that the plaintiff claims are worked at home. Most courts apply the constructive notice standard to this type of work, requiring that the employer "knows or has reason to believe that work is being performed." *Holzapfel v. Town of Newburgh, NY*, 145 F.3d 516, 524 (2d Cir. 1998). However, the trend appears to be toward a more generous interpretation of constructive notice in this context. For example, in *Fletcher v. Universal Technical Inst., Inc.*, 11 Wage & Hour Cas. 2d (BNA) 1258 (M.D. Fla. 2006), the court found that the plaintiff had presented evidence sufficient to raise an inference of constructive knowledge of overtime hours worked and avoid summary judgment. The plaintiff was an instructor at a motorcycle mechanic school

and performed work such as curriculum planning and grading at home. The court mentioned the following evidence as sufficient to ground an inference of employer knowledge: employees were told not to report overtime hours; employees were told that they "would be in trouble" if they recorded overtime; the plaintiff testified that he was not able to complete the required work during scheduled working time; employees were told to work at home and the employer was aware of the fact that they did so on projects that benefitted the employer (such as curriculum overhauls and development of a grading system). *Id.* at 1264. The court explained:

> [T]he Defendants attempted to discourage instructors from working overtime by telling instructors that they should not work overtime unless it was authorized . . . However, there is evidence that instructors were told that if they did work overtime they were not to report it on their time cards. Thus, it appears that the Defendants not only had an official policy against unauthorized overtime, but they also had an unofficial policy of turning a blind eye to overtime which the instructors seemingly needed to perform in order to accomplish all the tasks associated with their jobs.
>
> . . . .
>
> This evidence supports an inference that the Defendants had, at the very least, constructive knowledge that Fletcher worked overtime for which he as not compensated, despite the fact that Fletcher apparently never reported those hours or complained to anyone in a management position about working overtime.

Id.

　　Similarly, in *Bull v. United States,* 68 Fed. Cl. 212 (2005), *aff'd*, 479 F.3d 1365 (Fed. Cir. 2007), the court found the government liable for time canine enforcement officers employed by the Department of Homeland Security, Customs and Border Protection spent laundering towels used in training drug detector dogs—including time spent waiting for laundering cycles to end. The court noted that the government did not provide access to laundry facilities while the employees were on duty, directed employees not to use commercial laundry facilities and provided special instructions for laundering the training towels, and admitted that there was never any shortage of clean towels during training sessions. Said the court, "[t]he towels did not launder themselves." *Id.* at 241. Accordingly, the government could not deny knowledge of the off-the-clock work. *See also Lewallen v. Scot County*, 724 F. Supp. 2d 893 (E.D. Tenn. 2010) (awarding overtime pay to K-9 police officer for off-the-clock time spent caring for and training his narcotics detection dog, where dog care was required, duties were primarily for the benefit of the County, and off-duty work was integral to the officer's assignment to the K-9 program).

　　Suppose that an employer embraces the use of technology to better respond to customer concerns. If it provides non-exempt employees with smart phones or other technology that makes off-the-clock work more likely, will it be liable for overtime? Suits have been filed raising the question whether time spent by non-exempt employees responding to work-related emails and calls while off-the-clock is compensable, but so far they have not resulted in a dispositive ruling. *See* Michael Sanserino, *Suits Question After Hours Demands of Email and Cellphones,*

WALL ST. J., Aug. 10, 2009, at B1 (describing complaints filed in *Agui v. T-Mobile* and *Rulli v. CB Richard Ellis, Inc.*, challenging off-the-clock time spent responding to work messages on company-issued smart phones or calls on company-issued cell phones). Does the fact that the electronic records associated with the technology may assist employees in proving hours worked factor into the analysis? *See* James M. Coleman, *DOL's Smartphone App Is a Good Reminder to Ensure FLSA Recordkeeping in Order*, DAILY LAB. REP. (BNA) No. 104, May 31, 2011 (warning employers that the DOL has made available a free smart phone app that allows employees to track their hours, tip income, commissions, etc., and automatically calculates the wages due).

6.   **Advice for Employers?** How can an employer who is serious about preventing overtime avoid liability on a constructive notice theory? Clearly, maintaining a policy against overtime work is not, by itself, sufficient. *See Devries v. Morgan Stanley & Co.*, 2014 U.S. Dist. LEXIS 15862 (S.D. Fla. Feb. 6, 2014) (certifying collective action by financial advisors claiming that they were explicitly discouraged from recording overtime while studying for required exams, notwithstanding a written corporate policy requiring accurate recordkeeping of time worked; the court noted that promulgation of a standard is not sufficient absent a sustained effort to ensure that the policies are enforced). Must the employer demonstrate that it is not mere window dressing by actually disciplining employees who violate the policy? In *Chao v. Gotham Registry, Inc.*, 514 F.3d 280 (2d Cir. 2008) the court found an employer liable for overtime where the employer had not authorized the overtime and maintained a policy against it. Gotham Registry was an employment agency that referred nurses to temporary assignments in New York area hospitals. When nurses were asked by hospital staff to work extra hours, the agency refused overtime compensation to nurses unless (1) the nurses obtained advance approval from Gotham to work overtime; and (2) the agency was able to obtain extra payment from the hospital for the overtime work after the fact. The agency did, however, pay the nurses "straight time" for overtime hours even if the hours were not pre-approved. The court held the employer liable for overtime pay for all of these hours, whether or not they were approved, citing with approval a Department of Labor regulation that imposes a duty on employers to make "every effort" to prevent the performance of undesired overtime work and makes clear that "mere promulgation of a rule against such work is not enough." *See Id.* at 288 (citing 29 C.F.R. § 785.13). The court rejected Gotham's argument that the nature of its business—essentially, Gotham functions as an employment agency—means that it has little control over the hours that nurses work The court wrote: "We recognize that Gotham does not have at its disposal all the instruments of control available to ordinary employers. That said, the law does not require Gotham to follow any particular course to forestall unwanted work, but instead to adopt all possible measures to achieve the desired result." *Id.* at 291. The court noted that the agency didn't attempt to keep a daily tally of the nurses' hours and to reassign shifts later in the week to avoid overtime, nor did it impose any adverse consequences on nurses who violated its rules. The court concluded:

> If Gotham were serious about preventing unauthorized overtime, it could discipline nurses who violate the rule. It could also entirely disavow overtime hours, announcing a policy that it does not, under any circum-

stance, employ a nurse for more than 40 hours in a week. Any hours over the limit would not be billed to the hospital and would not result in any compensation for the nurse (as opposed to the current policy of regular pay).

Id. at 291.

Do the Second Circuit's suggestions seem appealing? The concurring judge pointed out that the majority's suggestion of keeping a daily tally and reassigning shifts later in the week to avoid overtime was impractical given that many nurses worked for more than one agency. *Id.* at 295 (Jacobs, Chief Judge, concurring). This practice is apparently common in the nursing profession: in *Barfield v. New York City Health & Hospitals Corp.*, 537 F.3d 132 (2d Cir. 2008), the plaintiff worked for three different nursing referral agencies in performing work for a single hospital, and sued the hospital for overtime pay for hours worked in excess of 40 per week. The court ruled in her favor, finding the hospital a joint employer that "knew or had reason to know the total number of hours Barfield worked for them each week," *Id.* at 139, and noting that it was the hospital's own failure to maintain adequate time records which prevented it from recognizing that Barfield was working more than 40 hours per week, blocked its defense of lack of knowledge. *Id.* at 148.

2. "On-call" time

Economic pressures, the increase in women's labor market participation and concomitant work-family time conflicts, and technological advances that allow more work to be done off-site have combined to blur the boundaries between working time and nonworking time. An increasingly common arrangement requires that employees be available to work "on-call" when physically away from the workplace, so that the company can summon them on short notice. Are these employees entitled to overtime pay for periods when they are on call? Some occupations—such as emergency medical personnel and firefighters—have always been characterized by on-call requirements, and the Court early on established principles applicable to these cases. The Court ruled in 1944 that all time "spent predominantly for the employer's benefit" is compensable under the FLSA. *Armour & Co. v. Wantock,* 323 U.S. 126, 133 (1944) (holding that firefighters required to be "on-call" at a private fire house spent their time "predominantly" for the benefit of the employer, so their time was compensable under the FLSA). In a companion case the Court further specified that time spent "waiting to be engaged" is not compensable under the FLSA, but if employees are "engaged to wait" the time is compensable. *See Skidmore v. Swift & Co.*, 323 U.S. 134, 140 (1944). With the advent of technology that makes it easier for employers to stay in touch with employees who are pursuing personal and family activities while on-call (such as cell phones, paging systems, and email), the line between work time and leisure time has become increasingly difficult to draw. The courts have struggled mightily with these cases. *See* Eric Phillips, Note, *On-Call Time Under the Fair Labor Standards Act*, 95 MICH. L. REV. 2633 (1997); *see also* Loren Schwartz, Note, *Reforming the Fair Labor Standards Act: Recognizing On-Call Time as a Distinct Category of Compensable Work*, 40 U.S.F. L. REV. 217 (2005) (reviewing "on-call" cases and proposing new FLSA provisions to set minimum wage and overtime premiums specifically for on-call time).

DINGES v. SACRED HEART ST. MARY'S HOSPITALS, INC.
United States Court of Appeals for the Seventh Circuit
164 F.3d 1056 (1999)

EASTERBROOK, CIRCUIT JUDGE.

Working more than 40 hours per week draws premium pay under the Fair Labor Standards Act, 29 U.S.C. § 207. Should hours spent "on call" be treated as work? According to the Supreme Court, the answer depends on whether one has been "engaged to wait" or is "waiting to be engaged." Compare Armour & Co. v. Wantock, 323 U.S. 126 (1944), with Skidmore v. Swift & Co., 323 U.S. 134 (1944). That evocative distinction rarely decides a concrete case; on-call time readily can be characterized either way. For most purposes it is best to ask what the employee can do during on-call periods. Can the time be devoted to the ordinary activities of private life? If so, it is not "work." Even a functional approach produces close calls, however; this is one.

Sacred Heart St. Mary's Hospitals operates a hospital in rural Tomahawk, Wisconsin. The Hospital's ambulance department has two "emergency medical technicians" (EMTs) in-house during the day (and recently for an evening shift), but after hours the Hospital relies on standby crews. Two EMTs serve as the "first-out" crew and two more as the "second-out" crew, which will be called to duty if the first-out crew is in the field when the Hospital must dispatch an ambulance. An EMT on first-out status must arrive at the Hospital within 7 minutes of receiving a page. Members of the first-out crew receive $2.25 per hour of on-call time, plus pay at time-and-a-half for all hours devoted to handling a medical emergency. The Hospital credits them with at least two hours' work (and thus they receive three hours' wages) for each emergency call, even if they are back home in less—as they usually are. When calls take more than two hours, they are paid for actual time. Members of the second-out crew have 15 rather than 7 minutes to reach the Hospital. The schedule of a first-out EMT over a two-week period includes 7 days of duty at the Hospital (on 8 or 10 hour shifts) plus 7 evenings and nights of on-call time. It also has three 48-hour periods when the EMT is neither working nor on call. When the Hospital had only one shift per day of EMTs on the premises, and the on-call period correspondingly lasted 14 to 16 hours, a first-out EMT could expect to receive an average of 0.65 calls per period. Because medical emergencies sometimes occur in bunches, the probability of receiving at least one call to work during a given 14 to 16 hour period is lower, approximately one in two.

Garrett Dinges and Christine Foster asked for and were assigned first-out status. Now, in this suit, they contend that the rewards should have been even greater than those the Hospital promised and delivered—that the entire 14 to 16 hour on-call period should be treated as working time, so it would produce 21 to 24 hours' wages even if they did not receive any emergency call. Both Dinges and Foster live within 7 minutes' drive from the Hospital—indeed, the entire City of Tomahawk is within the 7-minute radius—so they can and do pass the on-call time at home or at other activities in or near the City. Plaintiffs observe that during on-call time their options are restricted:

They can't travel outside Tomahawk. Each has spent holidays at home rather than with relatives, and has been unable to attend weddings, family reunions, parties, and other events. While on call, Dinges cannot assist in operation of the family business, located 20 miles from the Hospital. Hunting, fishing, boating, camping, and other recreational activities are restricted to what is possible near the Hospital (and near a car, so that the Hospital can be reached quickly).

They cannot engage in activities such as using a power lawn mower or snowmobiling whose loud noise would prevent them from hearing a page; correspondingly they cannot attend concerts, where pagers must be turned off, or go swimming.

They are forbidden to drink alcohol.

Foster has a babysitter on hand during on-call hours, because she may be called away from her children at any time. She cannot go bike riding with the children or attend school events with them, because responding to a call would take too long.

Shopping is curtailed because retail outlets in Tomahawk are open shorter hours, and carry fewer goods, than stores in larger population centers outside the 7-minute radius from the Hospital.

The Hospital responds by emphasizing what EMTs can do during on-call hours—cook, eat, sleep, read, exercise, watch TV and movies, do housework, care for pets, family, and loved ones at home. Many things in the vicinity of home also are compatible with first-out status. For example, Foster watches her children participate in sports, attends dance recitals, and goes to restaurants and parties. Moreover, the Hospital adds, most of the things that can't be done on first-call status, such as camping and attending events out of town, also are foreclosed by the 15-minute response time of the second-call team, or for that matter by a one-hour response time. But attending special events such as out-of-town weddings could be arranged, even if the weddings were scheduled during on-call time, if an EMT swapped duty periods with another member of the staff. The Hospital has a flexible swap policy. Because swaps require finding another EMT willing to trade, they are hard to arrange for holidays (few EMTs are anxious to work on Thanksgiving or Christmas and give up their own family get-togethers) but easier to arrange for occasional events such as parties and weddings. The district judge concluded that the extensive list of things EMTs can do during first-out time is the legally important one—because time is not "work" if it can be used effectively for personal pursuits—and granted summary judgment to the Hospital. The district court's emphasis on the fact that the EMTs can stay at home while on call, and can do many things while there, has the support of the Department of Labor's implementing regulations.

An employee who is not required to remain on the employer's premises but is merely required to leave word at home or with company officials where he or she may be reached is not working while on call. Time spent at home on call may or may not be compensable depending on whether the restrictions placed on the employee preclude using the time for personal pursuits. Where, for example, a firefighter has returned home after the shift, with the understanding that he or she is expected to return to work in the event of an emergency in the night, such time spent at home is normally not compensable. On the other hand, where the conditions placed on the employee's activities are so restrictive that the employee cannot use the time effectively for personal pursuits, such time spent on call is compensable. 29 C.F.R. § 553.221(d). See Auer v. Robbins, 519 U.S. 452 (1997) (courts should defer to the Secretary's definitions of terms). The regulatory question is whether the employee can "use the time effectively for personal pursuits"—not for *all* personal pursuits, but for many. But then there is that weasel word "effectively." An employee who can remain at home while on call, but is called away every few hours, can't use the time "effectively" for sleeping, and probably not for many other activities. Plaintiffs, however, experience less than a 50% chance that there will be any call in a 14-to 16-hour period, so their time may be used effectively for sleeping, eating, and many other activities at home and around Tomahawk. (Over 338 on-call periods, Dinges had 184 pass without a call. Thus Dinges responded to at least one call only 46% of the time. Foster's experience was similar.)

Plaintiffs make a great deal of the 7-minute response limit, which they say is below the shortest period that any appellate court has deemed compatible with "effective" use of time for personal pursuits. Maybe so; the cases are not easy to classify. But we do not think that response time is dispositive. It sets a limit on the distance an EMT may live from the Hospital, but a person who lives nearby may have ample time to respond. A person who lived well outside Tomahawk would find a 20-minute response time as constraining as plaintiffs find a 7-minute time, while someone who lived next door to the hospital would think 7 minutes generous. Both plaintiffs live where they did before they asked for first-out status and do not say that they would have moved farther away if the time were longer; the response time has not affected residential choices. Tomahawk is rural and traffic jams are rare. A 7-minute response limit in Milwaukee would not be compatible with effective use of time for personal pursuits; things are otherwise in the countryside. Plaintiffs do not contend that the 7-minute time interferes with sleeping or the care of children. It is long enough to wake up (or finish changing a diaper) and still get to the Hospital on time. Seven minutes may be the lower limit, for it takes time to shake off the cobwebs when awakening and to jump into clothes, but we need not explore the question further.

To the extent there is uncertainty—and the open-ended regulatory standard, combined with the Supreme Court's oracular "test," ensures uncertainty—we must take account of the arrangement plaintiffs themselves chose. They sought first-out status because it created the best earnings opportunity, and they agreed to a combination of hourly pay for on-call hours plus time-and-a-half for actual emergency calls. The prospect of being paid for spending time at home (even time asleep) must have been attractive. Although the FLSA overrides contracts, in close cases it makes sense to let private arrangements endure—for the less flexible statutory approach has the potential to make everyone worse off. Suppose we were to hold that time the EMTs spend on call counts as "work." That would produce a windfall for Dinges and Foster today, but it would lead the Hospital to modify its practices tomorrow. If the EMTs are "working" 24 hours a day, then the Hospital will abolish the on-call system and have EMTs on its premises 24 hours a day, likely

PP

hiring additional EMTs so that it can limit the premium pay for overtime. This is what St. Mary's already has done at its hospital in Rhinelander, Wisconsin. The Hospital will pay more in the process, but EMTs such as Dinges and Foster will receive less, spend more time at the Hospital (and less at home), or both. Ambulatory statutory and regulatory language permits labor and management to structure their relations so that each side gains. That is what the Hospital has done in Tomahawk, and we do not think that the FLSA compels a different arrangement.

Affirmed.

NOTES

1. **Employees' Ability to Make Effective Use of Their Time.** In *Dinges*, the Seventh Circuit focused on the distinction between employees who are "waiting to be engaged" and those who are "engaged to wait." As the court explained, the core issue in drawing this distinction is whether the employee can make effective use of his or her on-call time to tend to "the ordinary activities of private life." If the requirements of their jobs prevent them from doing so, the time will be compensable.

2. **Always on Call.** Suppose that one hundred percent of an employee's time is spent on-call because the employer does not have another employee responsible for the same duties to alternate shifts or cover the on-call worker when he or she is off-duty. Would the analysis remain the same? In *Bright v. Houston Northwest Medical Center Survivors Inc.*, 934 F.2d 671 (5th Cir. 1991) (*en banc*), the court saw no distinction. Bright was a biomedical equipment repair technician required to work a standard 40-hour week at the hospital and to wear an electronic paging device (beeper) during all off-duty hours so that he could be summoned to the hospital to make emergency repairs on biomedical equipment. Bright was not compensated for his "on-call" time, although he was compensated for four hours at his regular rate if he was in fact called; the hospital accomplished this without paying him overtime by reducing his work hours the following workday or days but paying him for the regular 40-hour week. Bright was called on average two times per week during the workweek and 2–3 times on the weekend. Bright's typical call lasted sufficiently less than four hours so that an overtime premium for these hours actually worked was effectively paid. Bright contended, however, that he should be paid overtime for the hours he was on-call, but not called.

The court considered whether Bright was able to make effective use of his on-call time, and concluded that he was, along the same reasoning discussed in *Dinges*. The court dismissed the argument that Bright's status as the senior technician responsible for being on-call at all times meant that he never had any relief from his on-call status. The court observed:

> We do not deny the obvious truth that the long continued aspect of Bright's on-call status made his job highly undesirable and arguably somewhat oppressive. Clearly, it would have been vastly more pleasant from Bright's point of view had he only been on call the first week of every month, for example. But the FLSA's overtime provisions are more narrowly focused than being simply directed at requiring extra compensation for

oppressive or confining conditions of employment. A Texan working 8:30 p.m. to 3:00 a.m. six days a week (thirty-nine hours), fifty-two weeks a year, at a remote Alaska location has a most restrictive and oppressive job that as a practical matter prevents, *inter alia*, vacations, visiting relatives, and attending live operatic performances or major league sporting events, but it seems obvious that the FLSA overtime provisions provide no relief for those oppressive and confining conditions. Bright's job was oppressive and confining in many of the same ways, but it, too, did not involve more than forty hours work a week.

Id. at 678. The dissent believed that the core issue should be the lack of any relief time over a substantial period (almost one year), and described Bright as being "held on a permanent 20-minute leash." The dissent's view was that the restrictions occasioned by his on-call status prevented Bright from engaging in many ordinary personal life activities, justifying compensation:

> Bright "was not far removed from a prisoner serving a sentence under slightly relaxed house arrest terms. He never could go to downtown Houston, he never could go to Galveston and see the ocean. He never could go to a baseball or football game in the Astrodome. An out of town event, even a visit to relatives or friends in San Antonio or Austin, was totally out of the question." Bright, 888 F.2d at 1064. Further, the employer had a relatively simple and humane means of avoiding this restriction which was akin to and rather close to house arrest. The remedy is found in every single one of the cases cited by the majority opinion and relied upon by the majority opinion. The employer could have set up a system under which this onerous restrictive duty could be shared or certain periods of relief could be afforded.

Id. at 680. Does the dissent have a different definition of "the ordinary activities of private life" than the majority? Is the majority saying that Bright chose this lifestyle since he understood that these would be the requirements of the job when he assumed the position? Is this another way of saying that he waived the protections available under the FLSA? What is wrong with that reasoning? On what rationale might the court have interpreted the Act to require overtime compensation for Bright?

3. **Employees as "Prisoners."** Was Bright effectively a prisoner? Should the length of the employee's "leash" be dispositive? What about the number of times the employee is called to work or the duration of the callbacks? Is it possible to distinguish on-call situations where the employee's freedom to move about is significantly circumscribed from those where the employee works "off-the-clock"? What is the difference?

In drawing such distinctions, the Department of Labor relies upon 29 C.F.R. § 785.17, which provides that an employee's on-call time will be considered compensable if the employee must remain on the employer's premises or stay "so close thereto that he cannot use the time effectively for his own purposes." On the other hand, an employee who is "merely required" to leave word where he may be reached is not working on call.

The *Bright* court commented that cases where employees recovered overtime compensation for on-call time typically involved employees who had " 'almost no freedom at all.' " 934 F.2d at 676 (quoting *Halferty v. Pulse Drug Co.*, 864 F.2d 1185, 1190 (5th Cir. 1989)). The court cited examples of guards at a plant under strike who were required to remain at the plant 24 hours per day during the 3-month duration of the strike, and a situation where employees who worked on derrick barges for rotating 7-day shifts, 12 hours on, 12 hours off were required to stay on the barges during their 12 hours off for each 7-day shift whether the barges were offshore or docked. In both cases, the court had ruled that the off-duty, on-call time was not compensable. Can you think of any circumstances in which the *Bright* and *Dinges* courts would find on-call time compensable?

In *Gonzalez v. Tanimura & Antle, Inc.*, 14 Wage & Hour Cas. 2d (BNA) 364 (D. Ariz. 2008), the plaintiffs were agricultural workers who reported for work at a bus parking lot leased by their employer. They then rode a company bus to the fields, 10 to 40 miles from the parking lot. On cold mornings, plaintiffs were sometimes required to wait for 2–3 hours for ice on the crops to melt. Although plaintiffs were not required to wait in the parking lot and were free to leave on those mornings, most found it impractical to do so and stayed in the vicinity, drinking coffee, eating breakfast, playing cards, or playing soccer. The court found the workers' waiting time compensable. Analogizing to the on-call cases, the court observed that the workers' activities were "more akin to filling time" than to pursuing personal activities. The court emphasized that plaintiffs were unable to "watch television, eat breakfast at home with a spouse, take the children to school, do home care or car repair, or other things that would allow being at or near their home or community." *Id.* at 370.

Suppose the employee is confined to his or her own house during the on-call time. Would this make a difference? What if the employee's home is provided by the employer? In *Brigham v. Eugene Water & Electric Board*, 357 F.3d 931 (9th Cir. 2004), the Ninth Circuit held that electric utility employees who lived in employer-provided housing were owed overtime pay for a portion of the 24-hour shift they spent waiting to be called for a potential emergency. The employees worked at a power generation facility located at a remote site in a national forest. The company provided housing, furnished utilities, and transported the employees' children to school. The employees worked 4-day weeks consisting of three 10-hour maintenance shifts and one 24-hour duty shift. The duty shift entailed performing 6 hours of work and remaining available during the next 18 hours in case of emergency. During their on-call duty shifts, the employees were permitted to spend time at home but were required to remain sober and respond instantly at all times. The court found that the characterization of the duty-shift time was not an all-or-nothing proposition in the context of employees who resided on the employer's premises, and required the employer to count 4 hours per duty shift as compensable time. *Id.* at 941–42.

4. **Policies Behind the FLSA and the Role of Private Contract.** In *Dinges*, the court reasoned that the plaintiffs chose "first-out" status and should be held to their bargain. Is this rationale consistent with the purposes of the FLSA? Suppose they had chosen to work for less than minimum wage. Would the court have enforced that agreement? What about the argument that any gain attributable to ruling the on-call time compensable would ultimately be offset by the hospital's

anticipated restructuring? Dinges and Foster will earn less if the hospital chooses to hire additional EMTs, but isn't work-spreading one of the Act's primary goals? Suppose that the hospital had chosen instead to reduce Dinges and Foster's hourly rate to hold down its labor costs, would the court have allowed that? In *Parth v. Pomona Valley Hosp.*, 584 F.3d 794 (9th Cir. 2009), a group of nurses expressed a preference for 12-hour shifts instead of the 8-hour shifts they were accustomed to working. The hospital agreed to their request, but reduced the hourly rate for the 12-hour shifts to offset the increase in its labor costs attributable to overtime pay entitlement for hours worked in excess of eight per day. The court found this practice lawful, noting that it became commonplace after the enactment of the FLSA and citing the Supreme Court's decision in *Walling v. A.H. Belo Corp.*, 316 U.S. 624 (1942). *Parth*, 584 F.3d at 799. Does this seem inconsistent with the purposes of the FLSA? Questions concerning the judicial deference to be accorded to the parties' freedom to contract lurk in many cases involving entitlement to overtime pay (and, as we shall see, compensatory time in the public employment context), and we shall return to them in the final section of this chapter as we inquire whether the overtime provisions effectively further the Act's goals.

Are the purposes of the FLSA served by a narrow definition of compensable time in the on-call context? Which purposes might be served by a broader definition?

3. Rest and Meal Periods

The FLSA does not contain any requirement that employers provide rest or meal periods to workers. However, nine states require paid rest periods (California, Colorado, Illinois, Kentucky, Minnesota, Nevada, Oregon, Vermont, and Washington). Department of Labor Wage & Hour Division, *Minimum Paid Rest Period Requirements Under State Law for Adult Employees in Private Sector—* January 1, 2015, *available at* http://www.dol.gov/whd/state/rest.htm. Twenty states have some form of meal period requirement. Department of Labor Wage & Hour Division, *Minimum Length of Meal Period Required Under State Law for Adult Employees in Private Sector—*January 1, 2014, *available at* http://www.dol.gov/whd/state/meal.htm.

If the employer does provide rest or meal periods, are they compensable under the FLSA? Generally, rest periods of 20 minutes or less are included in compensable work time, but "bona fide" meal breaks of 30 minutes or longer when the employee is completely relieved of duty are not. 29 C.F.R. § 785.19(a). A lively debate has arisen among the circuit courts regarding the Department of Labor's bona fide meal period regulation. While some courts have accepted the 30-minute minimum, "completely relieved from duty" standard, *see, e.g., Kolheim v. Glynn County*, 915 F.2d 1473 (11th Cir. 1990) (holding that firefighters' mealtime is includible in hours worked because they are not completely relieved from duty, but were instead required to remain at the station and to accept emergency calls), others have insisted that the question of what is compensable work under the FLSA is for the courts. These courts have typically applied a "predominantly for the benefit of the employer" test, asking whether the meal period is used predominantly for the employer's benefit. For example, in *Henson v. Pulaski County Sheriff Department*, 6 F.3d 531 (8th Cir. 1993) the court ruled that a 30-minute meal period provided to police officers was not compensable because employees were free to go wherever they wished, including outside their patrol area, and to run personal errands, even though they were still required to monitor their radios and respond to emergency calls. Thus, the meal period was not used "predominantly for the employer's benefit." *See also Hertz v. Woodbury County Iowa*, 56 F.3d 775 (8th Cir. 2009) (holding that police officers seeking compensation for meal breaks had burden of proving that meal breaks were spent primarily for the benefit of the employer).

4. Training Time

Suppose that as a condition of employment the employer requires its employees to attend orientation sessions, occupational safety courses, or other training sessions. Do such requirements yield compensable work? In general, time spent attending employer-sponsored lectures, meetings, and training programs is compensable unless (1) it occurs outside the employee's regular working hours; (2) attendance is voluntary; (3) the course is not directly related to the employee's job; and (4) the employee performs no productive work during the training. Only when the activity meets all four criteria is the time not compensable. 29 C.F.R. § 785.27. For example, in *Chao v. Tradesmen Int'l, Inc.*, 310 F.3d 904 (9th Cir. 2002), the employer required employees to complete an occupational safety course within a reasonable time after beginning employment; employees who failed to do so were discharged. The course consisted of four 2.5-hour sessions held in the evening outside of regular working hours. The court characterized the employees' attendance as "voluntary" because the employees were informed of the training requirement at the hiring interview and chose to take the jobs anyhow. Moreover, the subject matter of the training (safety) was not directly related to their jobs, and plaintiffs performed no work during the OSHA classes. Accordingly, the training time was not compensable. *Id.* at 910. Did the court fall back on a freedom of contract rationale? Or is it simply the employer's prerogative to determine what is required as part of the job? What role does the at-will rule play in shaping this interpretation of the FLSA?

Courts have been especially likely to find training time not compensable where it is of general value to the employee beyond that particular job, and where the employee retains some choice in determining how the training will be accomplished. *See, e.g., Loodeen v. Consumers Energy Co.*, 13 Wage & Hour Cas.2d (BNA) 896, 901 (W.D. Mich. 2008) (employee time spent completing college courses not compensable, especially where he is free to select the college and the classes he takes); Wage and Hour Opinion Letter, FLSA 2006-5, March 3, 2006 (where employer required employees to learn English and provided paid work time for that purpose, time spent studying English at home with one's family not compensable). Similarly, where the employee reaps a personal benefit from the training time that is difficult to sever from the benefits reaped by the employer, courts deny compensation. For example, in *Dade County v. Alvarez*, 124 F.3d 1380 (11th Cir. 1997), the Metro-Dade Police Department required members of its Special Response Team (SRT) to adhere to physical fitness standards that necessitated an average of two hours per day of physical fitness training; SRT members were monitored to ensure that they were complying and were subject to reassignment outside the SRT if they failed to maintain adequate physical condition. The court ruled that the off-duty training time was not compensable, finding that it met all four of the criteria in § 785.27: it was off-duty; voluntary (officers were not required to spend a specific amount of time training or to perform specific exercise routines and could train at any location, any time, and for any duration); the exercise benefitted the workers in ways separate from their employment; and employees performed no other work while exercising. *Id.* at 1385–86.

On the other hand, where training activities are undertaken primarily for the benefit of the employer, the courts are likely to find them compensable. For example, in *Sehie v. City of Aurora*, 432 F.3d 749 (7th Cir. 2005), the court found that time spent attending and traveling to and from psychotherapy sessions required by the employer as a counter-measure for work-related stress was compensable. Of particular importance to the court was that the employer paid for the sessions and denied the employee her choice of therapists. *Id.* at 752. Courts have also been receptive to claims by police officers and customs officials who work with a canine teammate that time spent training their assigned dogs is compensable, because such tasks are done primarily for the benefit of the employer. *See Bull v. United States*, 68 Fed. Cl. 212 (2005), *aff'd*, 479 F.3d 1365 (Fed. Cir. 2007) (customs officers were owed additional compensation for four hours per week spent training contraband-sniffing dogs and laundering towels used in training). Time spent feeding, grooming or caring for the dogs, however, is generally not compensable. *See Id.* at 269–71. If the dogs are indispensable to the customs officers' work, why should this be the case?

5.   Travel Time

Many employees incur substantial time commuting to work from home, or driving between worksites, customer or client locations, and branch offices. Is this time compensable? The Portal-to-Portal Act of 1947 answers most of these questions. The Portal-to-Portal Act excludes from compensable time commuting time from home to work and back. 29 U.S.C. § 254(a); C.F.R. § 785.35. However, travel time incurred in connection with out-of-town work, travel while away from home on business, and travel time during the normal business day from one location to another or from office to job site is compensable. 29 C.F.R. §§ 785.36–785.41.

Because employers increasingly require employees to complete some work tasks at home or in the car on the way to their first work assignment or upon returning home after their final assignment, there is a potential for compensable work time to expand to include commuting time. Suppose, for example, that insurance appraisers are required to perform work-related tasks at the beginning and end of their workday at home, such as checking email and voicemail, calling body shops, parts suppliers, insureds, and claimants, sending materials to their employer, and downloading and reviewing assignments for the next day. The time spent doing these activities is undeniably compensable, but is the time spent driving from home to the first assignment each day and from the last assignment to home therefore compensable as well? One court has concluded that it is. *See Dooley v. Liberty Mutual Ins. Co.*, 307 F. Supp. 2d 234 (D. Mass. 2004).

Most courts, however, continue to rely heavily on the presumed non-compensability of commuting time. In *Singh v. City of New York*, 524 F.3d 361 (2d Cir. 2008), the Second Circuit rejected a claim by New York City fire alarm inspectors that their commuting time should be compensable because they were required to carry a briefcase containing 15–20 pounds of files each day as they reported to field inspection sites. The plaintiffs complained that carrying the files affected their commutes, slowing them down, causing them to miss buses or subway trains, and preventing them from attending social events after work (they were required to carry the files directly to their homes for safekeeping). The court found that the imposition of some minimal burden on the employees did not transform the commute into compensable time, noting that the plaintiffs remained free to use their commuting time for their own purposes—including reading, listening to music, or eating. *Id.* at 368. Applying the standard that compensable time must be predominantly for the employer's benefit, the court explained that in commuting contexts, the test is "whether an employer's restrictions hinder the employees' ability to use their commuting time as they otherwise would have had there been no work-related restrictions." *Id.* at 369. The court found the plaintiffs' obligation to carry inspection documents with them had only a *de minimis* effect on their commute and did not significantly impair their use of their commuting time for their own purposes.

Were the plaintiffs' lawyers too greedy in framing their claims, or was the argument simply unwinnable because of the sanctity of commuting time under the Portal-to-Portal Act? The court acknowledged in a concluding passage:

> In deciding this case, we note the practical consequences of the plaintiffs' challenge. Ruling in their favor could have a wide-ranging impact, suddenly imposing upon businesses across the country a liability to compensate employees anytime those employees must commute to work with important documents, tools, or communications devices. In the sixty years following the Portal-to-Portal Act, we are unaware of any court that has required employers to pay employees for otherwise non-compensable time simply because employees must travel with a briefcase or a small toolbox or a handheld device in order to be prepared for the workday. We are not convinced that the facts in this case warrant such groundbreaking law.

Id. at 370.

Suppose the employer assigns an unusually broad territory to which an employee is expected to travel each day from home. Are there any limits on the rule that commuting time is not compensable? In *Kavanagh v. Grand Union*, 192 F.3d 269 (2d Cir. 1999), a refrigerator repairman for Grand Union Supermarkets was assigned to an area encompassing Connecticut, New York and New Jersey. His average daily commute from his home on Long Island was seven to eight hours each day. He was required to be at various locations in his territory beginning at 8 a.m. and extending to 4:30 p.m. five days per week. He was compensated for the time spent traveling from site to site during the day, but not for the time spent traveling to his first location of the day or home from his last. The court refused his claim for overtime compensation, citing the regulations implementing the Portal-to-Portal Act. Because the extensive commute was a contemplated, normal part of the employee's job, it was not compensable. *Id.* at 272–73. The dissent argued that such a rigid interpretation allowed the employer to do an "end-run" around the FLSA, avoiding overtime simply by making unreasonable commute time a regular part of the employee's job. *Id.* at 275.

6. "Preliminary and Postliminary" Activities

Another commonly litigated question involves whether activities performed at the jobsite are excludible preliminary or postliminary activities. For example, washing-up time, time necessary to change in and out of uniforms or to put on and take off safety or protective gear (also known as "donning and doffing" time), and time spent waiting in line to obtain equipment or to clock in for work raise this question. In general, such activities are compensable if they are an integral part of the principal activities of the job. By contrast, preliminary or postliminary activities are those which are not an integral part of the principal job activities, and they are noncompensable unless made so by contract, custom or practice. Courts typically distinguish between the two types of activities by inquiring whether the employer or the employee is the primary beneficiary of the activity. While it is clear that time spent waiting for work to proceed during a workday because of a shortage of customers, breakdown of machines, or delivery delays is compensable, courts worry that drawing the line too far back from the start of the workday would begin a slide down an endless slippery slope.

IBP, Inc. v. Alvarez; Tum v. Barber Foods, Inc., 546 U.S. 21 (2005). These consolidated cases involved slaughterhouse and poultry processing employees who were required to don protective gear to perform their jobs, including smocks, hairnets, hardhats, earplugs, gloves, sleeves, aprons, leggings, and boots. Those who used knives also had to wear chain link metal aprons, vests, plexiglass armguards, and special gloves. The gear was stored in company locker rooms, where employees changed into and out of their clothes at the start and end of their shifts. Both cases presented the question whether the time workers spent walking from the changing area to the production area was compensable ("walking time"); the *Tum* case also involved the question whether the time workers spent waiting to put on and take off protective gear was compensable ("waiting time").

The Court first reviewed its own jurisprudence on how compensable work is defined under the FLSA and the history of the Portal-to-Portal Act of 1947, which established exceptions to compensable work. *Id.* at 25–30. The Court's pre-Portal-to-Portal Act cases defined work broadly, including "all time during which an employee is necessarily required to be on the employer's premises, on duty or at a prescribed workplace." *IBP, Inc. v. Alvarez; Tum v. Barber Foods, Inc.*, 328 U.S. 680, 690–91 (1946). Thus, time spent by employees walking from their time clocks near the factory entrance to their workstations was compensable. *Id.* at 691–92. One year later, concerned about the imposition of "immense" liability resulting from the Court's decision in *Anderson*, Congress enacted the Portal-to-Portal Act, which narrowed the coverage of the FLSA by excluding from compensable work time all time spent walking on the employer's premises to and from the place of performance of the principal job activity, and activities "preliminary or postliminary" to the employees' principal job activity. The Department of Labor then adopted a regulation specifying that the Portal-to-Portal Act had no effect upon the characterization of time spent "within" a continuous workday, defined as the period between commencement and completion of an employee's principal job activity on any given day. *See* 29 C.F.R. § 790.6(b) (2005).

Thereafter, the Court ruled in *Steiner v. Mitchell*, 350 U.S. 247 (1956) that workers in a battery plant were entitled to compensation for time spent incident to changing clothes prior to their shifts and showering and changing at the end of their shifts because of their potential exposure to caustic and toxic materials associated with the production of batteries. The Court construed "principal activity or activities" in the Portal-to-Portal Act as including all activities that are an integral and indispensable part of the principal job activities even though performed before and/or after the regular work shift. *Id.* at 252–53. Because the changing and showering activities in *Steiner* were an integral and indispensable part of working in a battery production facility, they were compensable. *Id.* at 256.

In *Alvarez*, the Court applied the test articulated in *Steiner* and held that the donning and doffing of specialized protective gear as well as post-donning and pre-doffing walking time was compensable because the protective gear at issue was integral and indispensable to the employees' work and the locker room was the relevant place of performance of the principal job activity. 546 U.S. at 36–37. Thus, the workday began when the workers donned the gear in the locker room and the walking time was compensable as part of the continuous workday; similarly, the workday ended when the workers doffed the gear in the locker room. The Court acknowledged that in most situations the workday will be defined by the beginning and end of the primary productive activity, reflecting the "whistle to whistle" rule used in the Department of Labor's regulation defining the limits of the workday. Nevertheless, the regulations define "workday" as the period between the commencement and completion on the same workday of an employee's principal job activity, and the donning of specialized protective gear was a principal activity. *Id.* at 37. The Court concluded:

> . . . [W]e hold that any activity that is 'integral and indispensable' to a 'principal activity' is itself a 'principal activity' under § 4(a) of the Portal-to-Portal Act. Moreover, during a continuous workday, any walking time that occurs after the beginning of the employee's first principal activity and before the end of the employee's last principal activity is excluded from the scope of that provision, and as a result is covered by the FLSA.

Id.

In *Alvarez*, this meant that the employees were entitled to compensation for 12–14 minutes of pre- and post-production work, including 3.3–4.4 minutes of walking time daily. In *Tum*, the employees argued that they should be compensated for time spent waiting to don and doff protective gear, as well. The Court applied the continuous workday rule and agreed that their pre-doffing waiting time was compensable, but held that their pre-donning time was not. *Id.* at 40–41. The Court rejected the argument that the pre-donning waiting time was itself integral and indispensable to the principal activity of donning, noting that "unlike the donning of. . . . protective gear, which is *always* essential if the worker is to do his job, the waiting may or may not be necessary in particular situations or for every employee," and is thus a preliminary activity "two steps removed from the productive activity on the assembly line" and therefore excluded from compensability by the Portal-to-Portal Act. *Id.* at 41–42. The Court noted that waiting time might be compensable if the employer required the workers to report at a particular time at the place where the principal activity is performed, and the employee was then required to wait there if for some reason beyond his control there was no work for him yet to perform, citing a Department of Labor regulation to the same effect. *Id.* at 41. In the case before the Court, however, there was no evidence of such an employer rule and thus the waiting time was not compensable.

NOTES

1.   **The Significance of *Alvarez* and *Tum* in the Industrial Context**. Because the employers in *Alvarez* and *Tum* conceded on appeal that the actual donning and doffing time was compensable, only a few minutes per employee per workday was at stake—the walking and waiting time. Why, then, was the issue so important?

Business interest groups—including the National Association of Manufacturers, the American Meat Institute, and the National Chicken Council, filed an *amicus curiae* brief warning that if the plaintiffs' interpretation of the Portal-to-Portal Act prevailed, industrial employers in the meatpacking industry would incur substantial labor costs because of the size and complexity of their facilities, which were designed with an eye toward promoting production efficiency rather than to minimize walking time for workers. Some facilities apparently involve as much as ten minutes of walking time each way to get from dressing areas to work stations. Multiplied by hundreds of workers and hundreds of days, it is easy to see how a ruling that walking and waiting time are compensable could cause labor costs to increase dramatically. Consider, for example, *Garcia v. Tyson Foods, Inc.*, 2014 U.S. App. LEXIS 15917 (10th Cir. Aug. 19, 2014), in which a plaintiff class of 7,000 workers won a $4.1 million verdict under the FLSA and state wage and hour laws because they established that the employer systematically undercompensated them by 29 minutes per worker per day for time spent donning, doffing, and walking to and from their work stations; Tyson had allocated only 4–7 minutes of compensated time per worker per day for these tasks. *See also Bouaphakeo v. Tyson Foods, Inc.*, 765 F.3d 791 (8th Cir. 2014) (upholding $5.8 million verdict on similar facts).

In addition, in some cases (including one of the two cases before the Court, *Alvarez*), overtime pay entitlements are triggered if walking time is compensable because the workers are already working 40-hour workweeks (or in some states, 8 hours per day); adding the walking time pushes them into overtime for hours worked in excess of those numbers. To further complicate matters, some state laws (including Washington state, where *Alvarez* originated), require that employees be paid for uninterrupted meal breaks. If workers must doff their protective gear in order to eat, not only the additional doffing and re-donning time for meal breaks but also the walking time must be compensated. In *Alvarez*, the 800 employee plaintiffs shared an $8.5 million judgment, with nearly half receiving checks for more than $10,000 and some receiving as much as $20,000 or more. A settlement was reached in a related case addressing compensable pay stemming from the meal break entitlement. *See IBP Workers Begin Receiving Checks Resulting from Supreme Court Ruling*, Daily Lab. Rep. (BNA) No. 75, Apr. 19, 2006.

    2. The 'Continuous Workday.' *Alvarez* and *Tum* raise important questions that resonate in many other employment contexts about when the workday begins and ends. For example, many field technicians and construction workers receive job assignments at home via electronic means, and must check e-mail, download work tickets, and communicate with the central office from their homes before leaving to drive to the worksite each day. Similarly, call center workers must start the computer, read directions and perform certain administrative tasks before making their first phone calls of the day. Bartenders may be required to report to work prior to the beginning of their shifts, straighten the restaurant and ready the bar for the shift. Are these tasks "integral and indispensable" to the "principal activity" of their jobs? If so, both the time necessary to accomplish the tasks and any drive time to the first jobsite (in the case of field technicians or others who work at variable sites) would be compensable.

    3. Compensable Donning and Doffing Time. The issue of compensable walking time post-donning and pre-doffing does not arise unless the donning and doffing activity is itself integral and indispensable to performance of the workers' jobs. The plaintiffs in *Alvarez* presented a particularly appealing factual case for compensability of donning and doffing of protective gear. The processing division knife user employees, for example, were required to don metal mesh aprons covering them from shoulder to knee or ankle, metal mesh sleeves, Kevlar gloves, a plexiglass armguard, and a scabbard and chain—an outfit that, according to the plaintiffs' brief, resembled "that worn by medieval knights." Employers worried, however, that the Court's ruling would translate into requirements that workers in other contexts be paid for time spent donning and doffing commonly required work garb mandated by state or federal safety and health laws (such as smocks, hairnets, work gloves, or helmets). In the wake of *Alvarez*, the courts have drawn a distinction between donning and doffing of "clothing" or "generic protective gear," such as protective glasses, boots, and helmets, which is not compensable, and safety gear necessary to protect against workplace dangers that transcend ordinary risks, which is compensable. Some courts explain the noncompensability of time spent donning generic protective gear as not amounting to "work" either because it does not require exertion or because it requires only *de minimis* effort. *Gorman v. The Consolidated Edison Corp.*, 488 F.3d 586, 594 (2d Cir. 2007) (characterizing the donning process associated with protective glasses, boots and helmets for nuclear power plant employees as "relatively effortless"); *De Asencio v. Tyson Foods, Inc.*, 500 F.3d 361 (3d Cir. 2007) (allowing donning and doffing claim of chicken processing employees to go forward, but remanding for determination whether time spent was *de minimis*). Are these considerations consistent with the Court's reasoning in *Alvarez*? With the policies behind the FLSA? The Court recently rejected a *de minimis* argument raised by an employer in a related donning and doffing context, observing that the FLSA "is *all about* trifles—the relatively insignificant periods of time in which employees wash up and put on various items of clothing needed for their jobs." *Sandifer v. U.S. Steel Corp.*, 134 S. Ct. 870, 880 (2014).

4. Dangerous or Lethal Work Environments. Courts seem quite reluctant to extend the Court's rulings in *Alvarez, Tum, and Steiner v. Mitchell*, 350 U.S. 247 (1956), discussed and relied upon by the Court in *Alvarez*, to less dangerous work environments than the notorious meatpacking industry profiled in Upton Sinclair's book "The Jungle." For example, in *Gorman v. The Consolidated Edison Corp.*, supra, the Second Circuit rejected a claim by nuclear power plant employees for compensation for donning, doffing, waiting and walking time prior to entering their work area. The employees sought compensation for time waiting in traffic outside the plant entrance, badge inspection, visual checks and random searches of their cars' interiors at the plant gate, parking and walking to the command post, waiting in line and passing through a radiation detector, an x-ray machine and an explosive materials detector, waiting in line to swipe an ID badge and palm a sensor, going to the locker room and donning capped safety boots, safety glasses and a helmet, and walking to the jobsite, as well as all of these activities in reverse. The security screening process was particularly time-consuming, occupying a 10- to 30-minute period for most employees. The court explained that although the employees who worked inside the nuclear containment area of the plant were entitled to compensation for donning and doffing time for their more specialized gear and dosimeters, the employees who worked outside the containment area and were required to don only generic protective gear were not. The *Gorman* court distinguished *Steiner* (involving workers in a battery plant who were entitled to compensation for time spent changing and showering) as follows:

> *Steiner* is in one sense the most apt analog, dealing as it does with donning and doffing gear that protects against workplace dangers that transcend ordinary risks. At issue in *Steiner* was exposure to corrosive and toxic substances that permeated a battery plant; at issue here is the security of a nuclear power plant. The analogy is, however, unsustainable. . . . Without the taking of the measures required, the environment of the battery plant could not sustain life—given the toxic substances in liquid, solid, powder and vapor form (and in the dust of the air) that "permeate[d] the entire [battery] plant and everything and everyone in it." [*Steiner v. Mitchell*, 350 U.S. at 249, 250 (1956)]. *Steiner* therefore supports the view that when work is done in a lethal atmosphere, the measures that allow entry and immersion into the destructive element may be integral to all work done there, just as a diver's donning of wetsuit, oxygen tank and mouthpiece may be integral to the work even though it is not the (underwater) task that the employer wishes done.

> By contrast, the activities for which plaintiffs here seek compensation, while arguably indispensable, are not integral to their principal activities. . . .

488 F.3d 586, 593.

5. The Collective Bargaining Context. The FLSA provides that employers whose workforces are represented by unions and governed by collective bargaining agreement may enforce the labor contract or an established custom or practice left intact by the contract that excludes "time spent in changing clothes or washing at the beginning or end of each workday" from compensable time. 29 U.S.C. § 203(o).

But what does "changing clothes" mean? Does it include the donning and doffing of protective gear? In *Sandifer v. U.S. Steel Corp.*, 134 S. Ct. 870 (2014), the Court answered this narrow question in the affirmative, but also shed light on which preliminary and postliminary activities are integral to the performance of workers' jobs and therefore, compensable. The unionized steelworkers in *Sandifer* sought backpay for time spent donning and doffing protective gear, including flame-retardant jackets, pants, hoods, hardhats, snoods, wristlets, work gloves, leggings, metarsal boots, safety glasses, earplugs, and respirators that the employer required them to wear due to the hazards present in steelmaking plants. Because these items were integral and indispensable to the performance of their jobs, the time spent donning and doffing would have been compensable but for the fact that the collective bargaining agreement between the employer and the union rendered it noncompensable. The agreement was enforceable to the extent that it covered "changing clothes," pursuant to the exclusion in § 203(o). Looking to the plain meaning of the word "clothes," the Court rejected the workers' effort to narrow the exclusion by distinguishing between items worn "for decency or comfort" and items used to "protect against workplace hazards," ruling that the term denotes "items that are both designed and used to cover the body and are commonly regarded as articles of dress." *Id.* at 876–77 (citing WEBSTER'S NEW INTERNATIONAL DICTIONARY OF THE ENGLISH LANGUAGE 507 (2d ed. 1950)).

Applying this definition, the Court concluded that the "petitioners' donning and doffing of the protective gear at issue qualified as 'changing clothes' within the meaning of § 203(o)," and thus was not compensable. *Id.* at 879. The only items that did not fit within the definition of clothes were the safety glasses, earplugs, and respirators. *Id.* To avoid "convert[ing] federal judges into time-study professionals" charged with separating the minutes spent clothes-changing and washing from minutes devoted to other activities the Court adopted the following standard: "whether the period at issue can, on the whole, be fairly characterized as 'time spent in changing clothes or washing.'" *Id.* at 881. Thus, where an employee devotes the "vast majority" of the time in question to putting on and taking off clothes (as opposed to equipment or other non-clothes items)—as in this case—the entire period qualifies as non-compensable. *Id.*

The *Sandifer* standard made it very difficult for unionized workers to obtain compensation for donning and doffing time. Section 203(o) applies not only in contexts where the collective bargaining agreement explicitly excludes donning and doffing time from compensability (as did the agreement in *Sandifer*), but also where the agreement is silent and there is an established custom or practice of non-compensation for such time (the idea is that the union has acquiesced in the custom or practice and it has thus become part of the agreement between the parties).

What are the larger consequences of *Sandifer*? First, recall that if donning and doffing time is compensable, under the "continuous workday" rule the travel time that follows to reach the worksite is also compensable. Thus, there was more at stake in *Sandifer* for unionized workers than simply the time spent putting items on and taking them off. What impact might *Sandifer* have on non-unionized workers? Are they better off than unionized workers? Could employers seek to negotiate individual agreements with employees excluding compensation for donning and doffing time of clothing that is an integral and indispensable part of the job? What if the clothing is not an integral and indispensable part of the job? How will the employee know the difference?

6. Security Screening as Compensable Time? Courts have not been receptive to plaintiffs' arguments that security screening time is compensable. The court in *Gorman v. The Consolidated Edison Corp., supra*, for example, characterized security screening and related activities as "modern paradigms of the preliminary and postliminary activities described in the Portal-to-Portal Act, in particular, travel time." *Gorman*, 488 F.3d at 593. Similarly, the Eleventh Circuit denied compensation for security screening time to construction workers employed on the tarmac at Miami International airport, including time spent being transported from their cars to the airport in employer-provided buses and vans, and passing through FAA-required security screening. *See Bonilla v. Baker Concrete Construction, Inc.*, 487 F.3d 1340 (11th Cir. 2007). The court reasoned that security screening was not integral and indispensable to the principal activity—construction—because it did not primarily benefit the employer, even though it was necessary for employees to perform their jobs. The integral and indispensable tests are not coextensive with necessity, observed the court; otherwise, "all commuting would be compensable because it is a practical necessity for all workers to travel from their homes to their jobs." *Id.* at 1344.

The Supreme Court reaffirmed this conclusion in *Integrity Staffing Solutions, Inc. v. Busk*, 2014 U.S. LEXIS 8293 (Dec. 10, 2014). The Court ruled unanimously that employees at Amazon warehouses were not entitled to compensation for time spent waiting for security screenings designed to prevent theft. The screenings were conducted at the end of employees' shifts, and they were required to empty their pockets and pass through metal detectors before exiting the warehouse; waiting time was sometimes as long as 25 minutes. The Court reasoned that although required and administered by the employer, the security checks were not integral and indispensable to the employees' principal job activities of retrieving products from warehouse shelves and packaging them for shipment. Instead, they were noncompensable postliminary activities. Nor did it matter that the employer could have reduced the screening time to a *de minimis* period of time by utilizing more security screening staff or staggering the ends of workers' shifts; such arguments "are properly presented to the employer at the bargaining table," said the Court, rather than in an FLSA litigation context. Slip op. at 9. The case is expected to have broad impact in the retail sector, where security searches at the end of workers' shifts are a common part of anti-theft programs. Ironically, the Obama Administration's Solicitor General filed an amicus brief supporting Integrity Staffing's position, mentioning in its statement of interest that the government—in its role as employer—"employs many employees who are covered by the FLSA . . . and requires physical-security checks in many settings." The AFL-CIO filed an amicus brief on behalf of the workers.

F. THE OVERTIME EXEMPTIONS

As discussed above in part B., the traditional white-collar exemptions cover four categories of employees: executive employees, administrative employees, professional employees, and outside salespersons. *See* 29 U.S.C. § 213(a)(1). An exemption for computer professionals was added in 1996, *see* 29 U.S.C. § 213(a)(17). We explore these five exemptions further below. Finally, the 2004 regulations established two new exemptions designed to catch employees whose duties straddled these categories or who were so highly compensated that they can be presumed to possess sufficient bargaining power to negotiate for themselves (employees must earn more than $100,000 per year to fit into this category). We discuss those briefly in the final section of this part.

Although the test for each exemption is discussed separately below, it is important to observe at the outset that more than a single exemption could be applicable to any given fact scenario, either in the alternative or in combination.

1. Traditional White-Collar Employees: Executives, Administrative Employees, Professionals, and Outside Salespersons

Employees who fall within the traditional white collar exemptions have historically been defined as possessing three types of characteristics: (1) they are compensated on a salary basis, rather than hourly; (2) they exceed a specified pay threshold; and (3) they meet certain duties tests. The FLSA does not itself define the boundaries of the exemptions; instead, the Secretary of Labor issues regulations defining the exemptions pursuant to her authority to administer and enforce the Act. When this text went to press the 2004 regulations were still the governing law, so that will be our main focus. As discussed above, in March 2014 President Obama instructed the Department of Labor to engage in rulemaking to narrow and simplify the FLSA's traditional white collar exemptions and to make more workers eligible for overtime pay. The rulemaking process is expected to take approximately one to two years. Susan J. McGolrick, *Obama Signs Memo Telling DOL to Update, Streamline White-Collar Overtime Exemption*, DAILY LAB. REP. (BNA) No. 49, Mar. 13, 2014. It will remain important to have some appreciation for the old regulations because historically courts have proceeded from premises established in case law developed under the preceding sets of regulations.

The Salary Basis Test

The simplest of the three tests that a worker must meet in order to qualify as an exempt white collar employee is compensation on a salary basis: the worker must receive a "predetermined amount" of compensation each week, regardless of hours worked. The salary generally cannot be subject to reduction because of variance in the quality or quantity of the work performed, although there are some exceptions. 29 C.F.R. § 541.2(e)(2); *see Auer v. Robbins*, 519 U.S. 452 (1997) (upholding the Secretary's interpretation of the salary basis test as requiring that any adjustments made to salaried employees' compensation be pursuant to an employer policy that clearly communicates that deductions will be made in certain circumstances). Thus, where an employer deducted monies from managers' base compensation to "reclaim" bonuses paid before their performance dropped, the jobs were no longer exempt from the overtime requirements because they failed the "salary basis" test. *See Baden-Winterwood v. Life Time Fitness, Inc.*, 566 F.3d 618, 631–32 (6th Cir. 2009).

The Pay Threshold Test

The pay threshold test effective since 2004 requires that an exempt employee's salary be at least $455 per week ($23,660 annually) exclusive of board, lodging, or other facilities. 29 C.F.R. § 541.600(a). The regulations divide employees into three categories by pay level: Salaried employees who earn less than $23,660 per year are guaranteed overtime. Those earning between $23,660 and $100,000 are still eligible for overtime if they do not satisfy the "standard duties" test described below. Those earning $100,000 or more are subject to a new "highly-compensated" duties test, under which an employee is exempt from the FLSA minimum wage and overtime provisions if the employee "customarily and regularly performs any one or more of the exempt duties or responsibilities of an executive, administrative or professional employee." 29 C.F.R. § 541.601(a).

Finally, the regulations completely exempt from the salary level test "employees engaged as teachers (*see* § 541.303); employees who hold a valid license or certificate permitting the practice of law or medicine or any of their branches and are actually engaged in the practice thereof (*see* § 541.304); or . . . employees who hold the requisite academic degree for the general practice of medicine and are engaged in an internship or resident program pursuant to the practice of the profession." 29 C.F.R. § 541.600(e).

The Duties Test

The duties test varies according to whether an employee is classified as an executive, an administrative, or a professional employee. The duties test for each exemption is discussed further in subsections (a-d), below. The regulations also explicitly exclude certain types of employees from the white-collar exemptions (meaning that they are entitled to overtime). For example, the white-collar exemptions "do not apply to manual laborers or other 'blue collar' workers who perform work involving repetitive operations with their hands, physical skill and energy," *see* 29 C.F.R. § 541.3(a), or to "police officers, detectives, deputy sheriffs, state troopers, highway patrol officers, investigators, inspectors, correctional officers, parole or probation officers, park rangers, fire fighters, paramedics, emergency medical technicians, ambulance personnel, rescue workers, hazardous materials workers and similar employees, regardless of rank or pay level," *see* 29 C.F.R. § 541.3(b)(1). Finally, the regulations include within the exempt category of professional employees "any employee with a primary duty of teaching, tutoring, instructing or lecturing in the activity of imparting knowledge and who is employed and engaged in this activity as a teacher in an educational establishment." 29 C.F.R. § 541.303(a).

As we shall see, the white-collar exemptions are not finely drawn, and employees who fall into these classifications are often relatively highly paid and frequently work in excess of 40 hours per week. Thus, an error in classifying them as exempt can produce significant liability for unpaid overtime. The following cases illustrate the application of the duties tests developed for each of the traditional white-collar exemptions.

a. Executive Employees   *(duties test)*

Under the 2004 regulations, executive employees must, in addition to meeting the salary basis and threshold tests, meet the following duties test:

(1) Have as his or her primary duty managing the enterprise in which the employee is employed, or a customarily recognized department or subdivision thereof;

(2) Customarily and regularly direct the work of two or more other employees; and

(3) Have the authority to hire and fire other employees, or make suggestions and recommendations that are given particular weight as to hiring, firing, advancement, promotion, or any other change of status of other employees.

Most litigated cases under the executive employee exemption revolve primarily around the first requirement for exemption, carried over from the pre-2004 regulations: the employee's "primary duty" must be "management of the enterprise." 29 C.F.R. § 541.100. The mere fact that an employee occupies a job with a title such as "store manager" will not automatically exempt the employee from the Act's coverage for overtime purposes. As one court put it, "simply slapp[ing] on a talismanic phrase" is not dispositive; "[w]hen it comes to deciding whether an employee is an executive within the meaning of the FLSA, the answer is in the details." *Rodriguez v. Farm Stores Grocery, Inc.*, 518 F.3d 1259, 1264 (11th Cir. 2008).

[handwritten margin notes: "most litigated exec EE issues"; "giving an EE a title is not dispositi"]

In many retail establishments, managers do the same work that lower-level hourly workers perform, but they also supervise and manage the store and its workers. Courts faced with determining whether employees who spend the majority of their time performing manual labor are nonetheless exempt executive employees have agreed that the proportion of time spent on managerial duties as opposed to routine labor is not the sole determinant of categorization. Thus, managers may perform manual labor—even for significant percentages of their working time—and still manage. In a number of cases retail store managers in major chains have argued that despite their titles, they do not qualify as executive employees and should be entitled to overtime. Compare the analyses in the following cases, which focus on the nature of the employees' primary job duties. What factors seem most persuasive to these courts in deciding how to characterize workers as executives?

Morgan v. Family Dollar Stores, 551 F.3d 1233 (11th Cir. 2008). Plaintiffs were store managers who worked 60 to 70 hours per week and sought overtime pay entitlement; Family Dollar contended that the store managers were exempt executives. The managers spent 80 to 90 percent of their time performing manual labor, including stocking shelves, running cash registers, unloading trucks, and cleaning the floors and bathrooms. The employer's job description for store managers listed under "Essential Job Functions" the same work that cashiers and clerks were expected to perform, along with supervisory tasks such as assigning work, ensuring compliance with merchandising policies, depositing monies received into the bank, and locking and unlocking the store. The store managers' discretionary powers were almost never exercised because either the operations manuals or the district managers to whom they reported controlled almost every aspect of the store's day-to-day operations. Indeed, the operations manual explained in detail how cleaning tasks were to be performed, how product should be displayed, how office drawers should be organized, and how the coffeemakers in the break room should be maintained. *Id.* at 1249–51. The district managers closely supervised the hiring and firing processes for the stores, and although store managers interviewed assistant manager candidates and had veto power over district managers' recommendations, the ultimate decisions regarding hiring and firing were typically made by the district managers and the store managers acquiesced. *Id.* at 1256–57. The court concluded that the managers were non-exempt, and affirmed the jury's verdict in favor of the plaintiffs. The court found the company's violation willful, and the jury awarded the 1,424 managers $35.6 million including back pay, liquidated damages and attorneys' fees.

Grace v. Family Dollar Stores, 637 F.3d 508 (4th Cir. 2011). The plaintiff, a store manager at Family Dollar, testified that she spent the vast majority of her time—95–99%—on nonmanagerial tasks such as freight unloading and unpacking, stocking shelves, running a cash register, and performing janitorial work. Nevertheless, the court found that she carried out managerial and nonmanagerial tasks concurrently; since no one else in the store directed others performing nonmanagerial tasks on a regular basis, she effectively never ceased exercising discretion in her job. *Id.* at 515–16. Moreover, since her compensation depended in part on increasing the store's profitability (her bonus was linked to the store's profitability), her decision to perform nonexempt work herself rather than scheduling others to do it simultaneously served her managerial interests. *Id.* at 517–18. Further, her district manager visited her store only once every two or three weeks, so that she was relatively free from supervision. Finally, her salary was higher than that of nonexempt employees—she earned $655 per week, for which she worked 50–65 hours weekly. *Id.* at 511. The court concluded that she was exempt as an executive employee, and thus was not entitled to overtime pay.

Do you agree with the Fourth Circuit's analysis or the Eleventh Circuit's analysis? Should a salaried store manager who earns roughly $10 per hour be characterized as an executive employee on the basis that the store is leanly staffed and other employees below her in the supervision chain earn only minimum wage? How much should the bonus structure of the store manager's compensation matter in assessing whether she is performing nonmanagerial or managerial tasks? On the other hand, isn't there a significant difference between a manager and nonmanagerial employee in a retail operation? Managers at Family Dollar Stores routinely supervise, discipline, terminate, and assign work to employees.

The Starbucks Cases: Mims v. Starbucks Corp., 12 Wage & Hour Cas.2d (BNA) 213 (S.D. Tex. 2007); Pendlebury v. Starbucks Coffee, 518 F. Supp. 2d 1345 (S.D. Fla. 2007). Plaintiffs were managers of Starbucks coffee stores who claimed entitlement to overtime pay, complaining that they were merely "glorified baristas" who spent 70 to 80 percent of their working time pouring coffee, waiting on customers, cleaning the restrooms, and operating the cash registers—the same tasks performed by nonmanagerial employees. Starbucks argued that the managers were exempt executive employees because they performed significant management functions that were critical to their stores' success.

In *Mims v. Starbucks,* the court ruled that the managers were indeed exempt, reasoning that managerial employees in retail contexts often perform both managerial and nonmanagerial tasks concurrently because they must lead by example and train nonsupervisory employees; thus, managers' performance of duties normally assigned to nonmanagerial employees is part of their management responsibility. 12 Wage & Hour Cas.2d at 216, 218–19. The court refused to apply a simple "clock" standard to determine what the managers' primary duty was, and emphasized instead the centrality to the employer of their management functions: they were the highest-ranking employees in their stores, they exercised discretion in interviewing, hiring, training and disciplinary decisions, supervised staffs of as many as 30 employees, made decisions about inventory, and had responsibility for increasing revenues, controlling costs, and ensuring compliance with corporate policies. Importantly, they were paid almost twice as much as employees without management duties, and were eligible for bonuses tied to their stores' financial performance and customer service as well as for training prospective store managers that were not available to baristas and shift supervisors. The court concluded: "This marked disparity in pay and benefits between Plaintiffs and the non-exempt employees [that they supervise] is a hallmark of exempt status." *Id.* at 221.

In *Pendlebury v. Starbucks,* the court certified a nationwide class action by Starbucks managers seeking overtime pay, finding that the same facts weighed against exempt executive status. The court considered the amount of time spent by store managers on non-managerial tasks such as waiting on customers, the relative importance of their managerial duties as compared with their other duties, the amount of supervision to which they were subject, their relatively low salaries which amounted to little more than those of hourly workers given their long hours and lack of overtime pay, their minimal discretion to deviate from an automated labor scheduling system used to set staffing levels, and their level of influence in personnel decisions which varied according to the management styles of their district managers. 518 F. Supp. 2d at 1361–62. The court cautioned that it was not evaluating the merits of the managers' eligibility for overtime pay, but only whether they had established sufficient similarity for class certification; nevertheless, the court framed that issue as dependent upon whether the store managers were "similarly situated for purposes of the executive exemption" because their primary duty was management, and went on to find that they were similarly situated and not likely exempt. *Id.* at 1350, 1363. The claim survived the company's subsequent motion for summary judgment and ultimately settled. Concerned by the ruling in *Morgan v. Family Dollar Store, supra,* Starbucks agreed to pay the plaintiff class of 553 current and former managers $613,000 in overtime pay and $950,000 in attorneys' fees. *Starbucks to Pay $1.55 Million to Settle Case Seeking Overtime Pay for Store Managers*, DAILY LAB. REP. (BNA) No. 163, Aug. 23, 2011.

Which of the *Starbucks'* analyses do you find more persuasive?

In order to categorize an employee as an exempt executive, the employer must also establish the two other prongs of the executive exemption: that the employee "customarily and regularly directs the work of two or more other employees," and that the employee "has the authority to hire or fire other employees or [is an individual] whose suggestions and recommendations as to the hiring, firing, advancement, promotion or any other change of status of other employees are given particular weight." 29 C.F.R. § 541.100. Cases decided under these prongs tend to be highly fact-specific and thus, not necessarily consistent. Courts resolving such cases are guided by the Department of Labor's regulation, 29 C.F.R. § 541.105, which suggests consideration of whether the employee's job duties include the making of recommendations, the frequency with which the employee makes them, and the frequency with which the employee's recommendations are relied upon. An employee may meet this test even if his or her recommendations may be overridden by a higher level manager. *See Davis v. Mountaire Farms*, 453 F.3d 554, 559 (3d Cir. 2006) (remanding for trial a case that turned on whether the crew leader of a chicken-catching operation was FLSA-exempt).

Are there steps an employer might take to better position itself on the executive exemption issue? Suppose that the employer routinely has its managers write their initials on job applications, resumes, disciplinary actions and termination letters to evidence their role in hiring, supervision and firing. Would this suffice? What difference does it make if the employer is a large nationwide retail chain with detailed hiring and discharge policies that are consistently enforced through a centralized personnel department across all of its stores?

b. Administrative Employees   *duties test*

To qualify as an exempt administrative employee under the 2004 regulations, an employee must meet the salary basis test, the salary threshold test, and satisfy the following duties test:

(1) Have the primary duty of performing office or nonmanual work directly related to the management or general business operations of the employer or the employer's customers; and

(2) Have a primary duty that includes the exercise of discretion and independent judgment with respect to matters of significance.

29 C.F.R. § 541.200.

Office or NonManual Work Directly Related to the Management or General Business Operations of the Employer or the Employer's Customers

The first prong of the administrative test—that the employee's primary duties directly relate to management or general business operations of the employer—has generated a great deal of litigation. The Secretary's interpretive regulations explain that "directly related to management policies or general business operations" means "work directly related to assisting with the running or servicing of the business, as distinguished, for example, from working on a manufacturing production line or selling a product in a retail or service establishment." 29 C.F.R. § 541.201(a). The production/administrative dichotomy has proved particularly illusory. Are there situations where service employees are the functional equivalent of production line workers in a manufacturing context? Compare the courts' analyses in the following cases.

Roe-Midgett v. CC Servs., Inc., 512 F.3d 865 (7th Cir. 2008). Plaintiffs were insurance damage appraisers who spent much of their time in the field and were charged with conducting on-site investigations of automobile claims in which determinations of liability had already been made, and settling them; their settlement authority was limited to $12,000 per claim. They drew an annual salary of between $36,952 and $55,427 per year. They sought to characterize themselves as "the postindustrial equivalent of production workers" and hence not involved in work directly related to the employer's management or business operations. The court rejected the argument, explaining that claims processing is an administrative function rather than a process of production in itself; damage appraisers administer the insurance policies for the companies that produce them:

> The plaintiffs are correct that the "directly related" test seeks to distinguish exempt administrative work from nonexempt production or sales work. 29 C.F.R. § 205(a). But their attempt to cast [damage appraisers] as service-industry "production" workers founders . . . .
>
> [T]he so-called production/administrative dichotomy—a concept that has an industrial age genesis—is only useful by analogy in the modern service-industry context. "The typical example of the . . . dichotomy is a factory setting where the 'production' employees work on the line running machines, while the administrative employees work in an office communicating with the customers and doing paperwork." *Shaw v. Prentice Hall Computer Publ'g, Inc.*, 151 F.3d 640, 644 (7th Cir.1998). The analogy is not terribly useful here. . . . [Damage appraisers] are obviously neither working on a manufacturing line nor "producing" anything in the literal sense. They are service providers, and the service they provide is the administration of insurance claims. This is the main business of CCS's Claims Division. We have no difficulty concluding that the duties of [damage appraisers] "directly relate" to CCS's "administrative operations."

512 F.3d at 872–73.

Desmond v. PNGI Charles Town Gaming LLC, 564 F.3d 688 (4th Cir. 2009). Plaintiffs officiated at horse races for a race-track operator covered by the FLSA for overtime purposes. They argued that that they served in a "production-side role" for the employer rather than in an administrative capacity. They pointed to the routine nature of the clerical work they performed, as well as their responsibilities on race days which included checking entrants' paperwork, inspecting horses to ensure the identity of the horse and the proper racing equipment, operating the jockey weight scales, observing the races, and determining the final outcome of each race using computer equipment and a photo finish system—duties that were indispensable to the race track operator but mandated by state law. Though important, the court characterized the employees' jobs as "unrelated to the general business functions of the company." The court explained:

> [A] Racing Official's work consist[s] of tasks somewhat similar to those performed "on a manufacturing production line or selling a product in a retail or service establishment." *Cf.* 29 C.F.R. § 541.201(a). Although the administrative-production dichotomy is an imperfect analytical tool in a service-oriented employment context, it is still a useful construct. Other Circuit Courts of Appeal have adopted and modified its logic to less traditional "production" situations:

> [A]pplying the administrative-production dichotomy is not as simple as drawing the line between white-collar and blue-collar workers. On the contrary, non-manufacturing employees can be considered 'production' employees in those instances where their job is to generate (i.e., 'produce') the very product or service that the employer's business offers to the public. *See, e.g., Reich v. New York*, 3 F.3d 581, 587–89 (2d Cir.1993) (police investigators conduct or 'produce' criminal investigations); *Dalheim v. KDFW-TV*, 918 F.2d 1220, 1230–31 (5th Cir. 1990) (television station's producers, directors, and assignment editors 'produced' newscast, and were thus non-exempt). . . .

> . . . Charles Town Gaming "produces" live horse races. The position of Racing Official consists of "the day-to-day carrying out of [Charles Town Gaming's] affairs" to the public, a production-side role. Because a Racing Official's duties are not directly related to the general business operations of Charles Town Gaming, the position does not satisfy the requirements for the administrative exemption under the FLSA.

Id. at 694–95. *See also Whalen v. J.P. Morgan Chase & Co.*, 587 F.3d 529, 535 (2d Cir. 2009) (finding loan underwriter not exempt as administrative employee where employee's primary duty was to evaluate whether to issue loans by referring to detailed guidelines provided by his employer and his work did not include advising customers about loan products; he functioned as a production worker "directly engaged in creating the 'goods'—loans and other financial services—produced and sold by Chase").

Does it follow from the *Roe-Midgett* court's analysis that nearly all service employees are engaged in the administration of the businesses for which they work? If not, what are the distinguishing characteristics that render particular jobs in the service sector exempt? On the other hand, is the *Desmond* court's understanding of the exemption too narrow, potentially entitling too many service-sector office workers to overtime pay?

With so many service workers involved directly or indirectly in sales, challenging cases have also arisen around the question of how to distinguish between exempt administrative employees and those who have a direct role in production as salespersons. The Second Circuit explained that employees who generally encourage an increase in sales among all customers are administrative employees exempt from overtime pay under the FLSA, while those who make specific sales to individual customers are more akin to production workers who are not exempt. Thus, a regional director of advertising sales for a complimentary magazine was not exempt as an administrative employee because she was essentially a salesperson responsible for selling specific advertising space. Since the magazine depended upon advertising revenues, the advertising space was its product, and thus the employee was on the production/sales side of the line. *See Reiseck v. Universal Communications of Miami, Inc.*, 591 F.3d 101 (2d Cir. 2010). On the other hand, the Seventh Circuit found that a sales director and product manager who assisted with promoting and marketing the company's employee benefit plans, educating employees about products and making recommendations, was exempt as an administrative employee because his work was directly related to the employer's management or general business operations. *See Blanchar v. Standard Ins. Co.*, 736 F.3d 753 (7th Cir. 2013); *see also Verkuilen v. Mediabank, LLC*, 646 F.3d 979 (7th Cir. 2011) (finding account manager for a software company exempt where her primary duties were understanding and conveying customers' needs and concerns to her employer's software developers and ensuring customer satisfaction, rather than purely sales).

A number of unlikely highly-paid plaintiffs claiming entitlement to overtime compensation have emerged from the financial services industries. Stockbrokers and financial advisers argue that they do not qualify for the administrative exemption because they were hired primarily to sell securities rather than to perform office work related to management of the employer's business operations. In addition to sales, their duties may include production of the business such as keeping abreast of the market, advising customers about financial opportunities, and managing portfolios. (Recall that employees involved in production do not qualify for the administrative exemption). Moreover, although there exists a commission sales exception to the overtime rules for employees who work in retail stores or other service establishments, are paid a wage in excess of 1.5 times the minimum wage, and who receive more than half their compensation in the form of commissions on goods and services, *see* 29 U.S.C. § 207(i), financial services businesses are excluded from the exception. Nor do the brokers and financial advisers qualify as highly compensated white-collar employees earning more than $100,000 per year; although the industry average for stockbrokers is $153,000 per year, they are paid entirely on commissions rather than a guaranteed salary (the 2004 regulations provide that at least $455 per week must be received in salary in order for an employee to fall into any of the white-collar exemptions). A number of large settlements were reached in these cases.

In 2006 the Wage and Hour Division of the Department of Labor issued an opinion letter that characterized account executives, broker-representatives, financial executives, financial consultants, financial advisors, investment professionals, and stockbrokers in the financial services industry as exempt. *See* FLSA 2006-43, Nov. 27, 2006, *available at* http://www.dol.gov/whd/opinion/FLSA/2006/2006_11_27_43_FLSA.htm. For courts inclined to defer to the DOL's interpretation, this advice proved persuasive. In 2007 a district court denied a collective action claim for overtime pay by securities brokers at PNC Financial, finding the brokers exempt administrative employees. *Hein v. PNC Fin. Servs. Group*, 511 F. Supp. 2d 563 (E.D. Pa. 2007). The court relied heavily on the Department of Labor's regulations, which provide a basis for exempting financial services employees who collect and analyze information and advise customers about financial products, but exclude from the exemption employees whose primary duty is selling financial products. 29 C.F.R. § 541.203(b). The court seemed unsympathetic to a claim by highly compensated employees whose annual income averaged over $100,000 per year, and noted the relative autonomy and freedom from supervision that was characteristic of the job as well as the fact that plaintiffs supervised subordinate employees ("licensed financial sales consultants"), who earned less than half the salaries of securities brokers. Emphasizing the FLSA's role in protecting low-waged workers from substandard wages and oppressive working hours, the court set a high bar for white-collar employees in the financial services seeking overtime pay.

In 2010, however, the DOL issued an Administrative Interpretation in which it concluded that the typical mortgage loan officer has a primary duty of making sales of loans (products) and thus performs production work, rendering loan officers non-exempt if the majority of their time is spent on making sales of loans. The Mortgage Bankers' Association (a trade association representing real estate finance companies) challenged the 2010 interpretation on the basis that the DOL had switched its position without affording the public notice and opportunity for comment. The D.C. Circuit agreed, vacating the DOL's 2010 administrative interpretation and reasoning that the DOL could not issue a definitive regulatory interpretation without affording opportunity for public comment through formal rulemaking pursuant to the Administrative Procedure Act. *Mortgage Bankers Ass'n v. Solis*, 720 F.3d 966 (D.C. Cir. 2013). The Supreme Court granted *certiorari* in consolidated cases which were pending at the time this book went to press. *Nickols v. Mortgage Bankers' Ass'n*, 134 S. Ct. 2820 (2014); *Perez v. Mortgage Bankers' Ass'n*, 134 S. Ct. 2820 (2014).

Meanwhile, lawsuits have proliferated, and some have settled quite recently. For example, Morgan Stanley agreed to pay $4.2 million to its client service associates. Merrill Lynch negotiated a $6.9 million settlement with its field financial advisers, a $12 million settlement with its client associates, who provide administrative and sales assistance to financial advisers, and a $7 million settlement with another class of financial advisers. *See* Gayle Cinquegrani, *Morgan Stanley Agrees to Pay $4.2 Million to Settle Overtime Claims of Sales Associates*, DAILY LAB. REP. (BNA) No. 161, Aug. 20, 2014; Susan J. McGolrick, *Merrill Lynch Companies, Financial Advisers Settle Overtime Allegations for $6.9 Million*, DAILY LAB. REP. (BNA) No. 97, May 20, 2014. If the Supreme Court rules that the 2010 interpretation finding mortgage loan officers non-exempt is invalid, can employers in the financial services industry breathe a sigh of relief, or should they still be concerned about such claims? Note that job descriptions in the industry vary widely, many positions involve sales, and some involve production (which as we saw above, is a somewhat slippery concept).

The Exercise of Discretion or Independent Judgment with Respect to Matters of Significance

The second prong of the duties test for the administrative exemption has also been a popular focus of litigation. Many cases have involved insurance claims adjusters, loss prevention specialists, safety and compliance officers, financial services employees, and mortgage loan officers raising the question whether their jobs involve the exercise of discretion and independent judgment when they are essentially controlled by detailed procedure manuals and/or computer software that guides the worker through an analysis and leaves little opportunity for the exercise of discretion or judgment. Although a few courts have found this argument persuasive, most have not. *See, e.g., Foster v. Nationwide Mutual Ins. Co.*, 710 F.3d 640 (6th Cir. 2013) (finding special investigators for insurance company charged with ferreting out fraudulent claims as exempt administrative employees even though their duties involve gathering factual information and applying known standards and prescribed procedures to the facts, because their primary job duty of investigating suspicious claims requires the exercise of discretion and independent judgment); *Robinson-Smith v. GEICO*, 590 F.3d 886 (D.C. Cir. 2010) (rejecting argument by insurance claims adjusters that the use of computer software to estimate claims deprived them of discretion and independent judgment); *In Re Farmers Insurance Exchange*, 481 F.3d 1119, 1130–31 (9th Cir. 2006) (analogizing software to ordinary reference tools such as manuals); *Roe-Midgett v. CC Servs. Inc.*, 512 F.3d 865, 875 (7th Cir. 2008) (finding that company manual and computer software that guided damage appraisers' estimates functioned as "tools that channel rather than eliminate the [damage appraisers'] discretion."); *Cheatham v. Allstate Ins. Co.*, 465 F.3d 578, 586–87 (5th Cir. 2006) (rejecting argument that adjusters' exercise of discretion and independent judgment was limited by computer software or obligation to consult manuals or guidelines). *But see In re American Family Mutual Ins. Co. Overtime Pay Litig.*, 2007 U.S. Dist. LEXIS 77548, at *32 (D. Colo. 2007) (finding physical damage claims analysts not exempt because computer software-generated claims estimates deprive them of discretion and independent judgment; while their job duties involved the application of skill in applying well-established "techniques, procedures or specific standards described in manuals or other sources," they did not involve the ability to make "independent choices free from immediate direction or supervision").

The debate over whether sophisticated computer software effectively deprives office workers of opportunities to exercise discretion and independent judgment is of relevance for many workers other than insurance adjusters. Most courts that have faced the question in other contexts have also concluded that such software does not render the worker nonexempt. *See, e.g., Renfro v. Indiana Mich. Power Co.*, 497 F.3d 573, 577 (6th Cir. 2007) (finding technical writers who prepare maintenance procedures for nuclear power plant workers exempt administrative employees, and describing the detailed writer's manual that the employees must follow as "ensur[ing] uniformity of the style and format of the technical writers' procedures, but not their content"—and thus, not a restriction on their discretion). *See also Hines v. State Room, Inc.*, 665 F.3d 235 (1st Cir. 2011) (finding sales managers for banquet facilities exempt administrative employees where the vast majority of their duties involved non-scripted conversations with clients in the course of event planning, even though they supervised no other employees, adhered to price schedules established by management, and had no authority to make financial decisions or to finalize contracts). Similar issues are raised in cases where employees have claimed entitlement to overtime because they are employed in a highly regulated industry that strips them of discretion and independent judgment in their job performance. Such arguments have met with mixed success.

Kennedy v. Commonwealth Edison, 410 F.3d 365 (7th Cir. 2005). Plaintiffs were nuclear power plant employees who argued that they were not exempt because they worked in an environment that was "procedure driven, routine, and strictly controlled." The Seventh Circuit rejected the argument and characterized the workers as exempt administrative employees, commenting that the fact that workers must follow regulations to perform their jobs cannot mean that they are exercising no judgment. The court explained:

> While the plaintiffs' discretion may be channeled by the regulations that apply to this industry, that does not mean ComEd employees do not exercise independent judgment. Certainly no one would contend that a tax lawyer does not exercise discretion or independent judgment just because the Internal Revenue Code contains a highly regimented set of rules.
>
> The plaintiffs' job-specific arguments fare no better. As problem solvers, the Work Planners and Lead Work Planners exercise discretion and independent judgment with respect to matters of significance. Their job is to come up with a set of instructions that will remedy reported problems around the plant. The fact that they look to past work packages for guidance and use a computer to aid their recommendations does not transform them into automatons. Judges, to name just one profession, routinely look to past decisions to determine how to resolve cases. Faced with novel or not-so-novel problems, judges and Work Planners must use their independent judgment to determine how best to respond.

Id. at 375–76. *Cf. Schaefer v. Indiana Michigan Power Co.*, 358 F.3d 394, 404 (6th Cir. 2004) (holding that a nuclear waste environmental specialist was not an exempt administrative employee because his decisions were dictated by Department of Transportation and Nuclear Regulatory Commission rules, and observing that "[t]he very purpose of such detailed regulations and procedures is to create conformity which has the practical effect of minimizing discretion."). *Id.* at 404. Which reasoning do you find more persuasive?

c. Professional Employees

Exempt professional employees fall into two categories: learned professionals and creative professionals.

Learned Professionals

(a) To qualify for the learned professional exemption, an employee's primary duty must be the performance of work requiring advanced knowledge in a field of science or learning customarily acquired by a prolonged course of specialized intellectual instruction. This primary duty test includes three elements:

(1) The employee must perform work requiring advanced knowledge;

(2) The advanced knowledge must be in a field of science or learning; and

(3) The advanced knowledge must be customarily acquired by a prolonged course of specialized intellectual instruction.

(b) The phrase "work requiring advanced knowledge" means work which is predominantly intellectual in character, and which includes work requiring the consistent exercise of discretion and judgment, as distinguished from performance of routine mental, manual, mechanical or physical work. An employee who performs work requiring advanced knowledge generally uses the advanced knowledge to analyze, interpret or make deductions from varying facts or circumstances. Advanced knowledge cannot be attained at the high school level.

(c) The phrase "field of science or learning" includes the traditional professions of law, medicine, theology, accounting, actuarial computation, engineering, architecture, teaching, various types of physical, chemical and biological sciences, pharmacy and other similar occupations that have a recognized professional status as distinguished from the mechanical arts or skilled trades where in some instances the knowledge is of a fairly advanced type, but is not in a field of science or learning.

(d) The phrase "customarily acquired by a prolonged course of specialized intellectual instruction" restricts the exemption to professions where specialized academic training is a standard prerequisite for entrance into the profession. . . . [T]the word "customarily" means that the exemption is also available to employees in such professions who have substantially the same knowledge level and perform substantially the same work as the degreed employees, but who attained the advanced knowledge through a combination of work experience and intellectual instruction. . . . The learned professional exemption . . . does not apply to occupations in which most employees have acquired their skill by experience rather than by advanced specialized intellectual instruction.

29 C.F.R. § 541.301.

The courts have diligently applied the learned professional exemption to traditional fields even where the professionals involved perform routine tasks and have limited discretion, as long as they exercise intellectual judgment within the domain of their professional expertise. *See Pippins v. KPMG LLP*, 759 F.3d 235 (2d Cir. 2014) (finding accountants employed as audit associates for a large firm exempt as learned professionals, even though they receive internal training, are constrained by formal guidelines, and perform many routine clerical and administrative tasks); *Campbell v. PricewaterhouseCoopers, LLP*, 642 F.3d 820 (9th Cir. 2011) (finding summary judgment for junior accountants employed by large accounting firm to conduct audits was inappropriate even though they lacked licenses as Certified Public Accountants and occupied the bottom two rungs on the firm's seven-tier hierarchy of white-collar job titles; employer had raised triable issues of fact as to whether they were exempt as learned professionals); *Lola v. Skadden, Arps, Slate, Meagher & Flom LLP*, 2014 U.S. Dist. LEXIS 130604 (S.D.N.Y. Sept. 16, 2014) (finding contract attorney employed to perform document review exempt as a learned professional).

There has been a fair bit of litigation over the contours of the learned professional exemption—particularly on the question of what constitutes a "prolonged course of specialized intellectual instruction." The Department of Labor traditionally emphasized the educational requirements of the profession in defining those who fall within the learned professional exemption. "Only occupations that customarily require specialized academic training are considered learned professional fields under the regulations," explained the DOL in a 2005 opinion letter. Wage and Hour Opinion Letter, FLSA2005-50, Nov. 4, 2005. Thus, social workers who are required to have a master's degree are exempt, while caseworkers who work for the same employer and are required only to have a bachelor's degree are typically not exempt, even though they provide similar services to clients. *See Id.* Similarly, paralegals and legal assistants who perform general paralegal tasks like drafting documents and performing research are generally not exempt professionals even if they possess an advanced degree such as a master's degree in business or accounting, because the degree is not a requirement for entrance to the profession or necessary for the specialized job being performed. Wage and Hour Opinion Letter, FLSA2005-54, Dec. 16, 2005. On the other hand, paralegals possessing other professional degrees that are used in the course of their legal work, such as an engineer who works on patent cases or assists with expert advice in product liability cases, would be exempt. 29 C.F.R. § 541.301(e)(7).

Under what circumstances might employees with no formal educational training beyond a bachelor's degree but who also possess considerable work experience be exempt as learned professionals? In a case involving social workers, the Ninth Circuit provided a succinct summary of the developing law in this area.

Solis v. Washington, 656 F.3d 1079 (9th Cir. 2011). Plaintiffs were social workers employed by the state of Washington to investigate allegations of child abuse and neglect, develop treatment plans, evaluate child and family progress in treatment, make child placement decisions, and make recommendations as to whether termination of parental rights is appropriate in particular cases. They sought overtime pay, which the state denied on the basis that its "rigorous educational qualifications" for social worker positions established that the plaintiffs were exempt as learned professionals. *Id.* at 1083. The state pointed to its requirement that social workers possess a bachelor's degree or higher in "social services, human services, behavioral sciences, or an allied field," plus at least 18 months' experience as a social worker. *Id.* The district court granted summary judgment to the state, finding the social workers exempt. The Ninth Circuit reversed. The court first

examined the treatment of a combination of educational qualifications and experience by other courts evaluating the availability of the exemption in various fields:

> . . . [O]ur sister circuits have concluded that positions that do not
> require a particular course of intellectual instruction directly related to the
> employee's professional duties do not come within the "learned profes-
> sional" exemption, even if they also require substantial practical experi-
> ence. In *Dybach v. State of Florida Department of Corrections*, 942 F.2d
> 1562 (11th Cir. 1991), the court held that probation officers, who were
> required to have a bachelor's degree in any field, including "nuclear
> physics" or "basketweaving," *Id.* at 1565–66, did not qualify for the "learned
> professional" exemption despite a requirement of one year of prior
> experience in law enforcement or corrections. In *Fife v. Harmon*, 171 F.3d
> 1173 (8th Cir. 1999), the Eighth Circuit considered the application of the
> exemption to aviation operation specialists, who were required to have
> either a bachelor's degree in aviation management or a directly related
> field, or four years of full-time experience in aviation administration, or
> some combination of the two. The court concluded the "learned profes-
> sional" exemption did not apply because the employees acquired their
> advanced knowledge "from a general academic education or from an
> apprenticeship" and not from a "prolonged course of specialized study," *Id.*
> at 1177. In *Vela v. City of Houston*, 276 F.3d 659 (5th Cir. 2001), the court
> held that emergency medical technicians and paramedics, who were
> required to complete 200 to 880 hours of didactic training, clinical [1085]
> experience, and field internship, did not satisfy the education prong of the
> "learned professional" exemption. *Id.* at 676.

In contrast, in situations in which applicants are required to complete a
particular course of instruction directly related to a position, even if they do
not have a specific degree, courts have concluded that the "learned
professional" exemption is applicable. In *Owsley v. San Antonio Independent School District*, 187 F.3d 521 (5th Cir. 1999), the court concluded that
state-licensed athletic trainers were exempt even though applicants could
qualify with a bachelor's degree in any field. To obtain a license, trainers
also had to complete courses in the specific areas of "(a) human anatomy;
(b) health, disease, nutrition, fitness, wellness, or drug and alcohol education; (c) kinesiology; (d) human physiology or physiology of exercise; and (e)
athletic training." The court concluded that "the brevity of the trainer's
course of specialized study [did] not preclude its inclusion under the
"learned" prong." *Id.* at 524. The court distinguished Dybach on the basis
that the trainers were required to "take a specified number of specialized
courses directly related to their professional duties." *Id.* at 525.

Other circuit courts have reached similar conclusions. In *Rutlin v. Prime
Succession, Inc.*, 220 F.3d 737 (6th Cir. 2000), the Sixth Circuit determined
that a licensed funeral director was a "learned professional" despite the
absence of a college degree requirement because licensing required a
specific course of study including completion of one year of mortuary
instruction and two years of college, with classes in chemistry and
psychology and a passing grade on national board tests in embalming,

pathology, anatomy, and cosmetology. The court concluded that a funeral director was required to "complete a specialized course of instruction directly relating to his primary duty of embalming human remains." *Id.* at 742. In *Reich v. Wyoming*, 993 F.2d 739 (10th Cir. 1993), game wardens required to have a bachelor's degree in wildlife management, wildlife biology, or a closely related field, as well as basic law enforcement training, were found to be "learned professionals." The court concluded that the curricula for such degrees contain an "emphasis on biology, zoology, botany, and other physical sciences," *Id.* at 741, which provides requisite knowledge of the tasks associated with wildlife management, *Id.* at 743.

Id. at 1085–86. The court then applied that doctrine to the case before it:

> Whether a position requires a degree in a specialized area, *see Reich*, 993 F.2d at 739, or merely a specific course of study, *see Rutlin*, 220 F.3d at 737, a "prolonged course of specialized intellectual instruction" must be sufficiently specialized and relate directly to the position. An educational requirement that may be satisfied by degrees in fields as diverse as anthropology, education, criminal justice, and gerontology does not call for a "course of specialized intellectual instruction." Moreover, in this case the net is cast even wider by the acceptance of applicants with other degrees as long as they have sufficient coursework in any of these fields.
>
> [The state of Washington] nonetheless contends that it has presented evidence that each of the acceptable degrees relates to the duties of its social workers. However, while social workers no doubt have diverse jobs that benefit from a multi-disciplinary background, the "learned professional" exemption applies to positions that require "a prolonged course of specialized intellectual instruction," not positions that draw from many varied fields. While particular coursework in each of the acceptable fields may be related to social work, [the state] admits that it does not examine an applicant's coursework once it determines that the applicant's degree is within one of those fields. For the "learned professional" exemption to apply, the knowledge required to perform the duties of a position must come from "advanced specialized intellectual instruction" rather than practical experience. 29 C.F.R. § 541.301(d). The requirement of a degree or sufficient coursework in any of several fields broadly related to a position suggests that only general academic training is necessary, with the employer relying upon apprenticeship and experience to develop the advanced skills necessary for effective performance as a social worker.
>
> The district court also gave weight to the six-week formal training program required for accepted applicants. However, such a program was determined to be insufficient in *Vela*, where the court concluded that 880 hours of specialized training in didactic courses, clinical experience, and field internship did not satisfy the education prong of the "learned professional" exemption. 276 F.3d at 659. If six weeks of additional training, only four weeks of which is in the classroom, were sufficient to qualify as a specialized course of intellectual instruction, nearly every position with a formal training program would qualify.

The district court concluded that the requirement of eighteen months of experience in social work was another factor weighing in favor of a determination of specialized instruction. However, the regulation states clearly that the exemption does not apply to "occupations in which most employees have acquired their skill by experience." 29 C.F.R. § 541.301(d). *Owsley*, upon which the district court relied, is not to the contrary, as the position at issue in that case included a requirement of specific academic courses as well as the apprenticeship requirement. 187 F.3d at 521. Indeed, *Owsley* distinguished *Dybach* on this exact point. *Id.* at 525.

Id. at 1088–89. The Ninth Circuit concluded that the employer had failed to meet its burden to establish the exemption.

Creative Professionals

(a) To qualify for the creative professional exemption, an employee's primary duty must be the performance of work requiring invention, imagination, originality or talent in a recognized field of artistic or creative endeavor as opposed to routine mental, manual, mechanical or physical work. . . .

(b) To qualify for exemption as a creative professional, the work performed must be "in a recognized field of artistic or creative endeavor." This includes such fields as music, writing, acting and the graphic arts.

(c) The requirement of "invention, imagination, originality or talent" distinguishes the creative professions from work that primarily depends on intelligence, diligence and accuracy. The duties of employees vary widely, and exemption as a creative professional depends on the extent of the invention, imagination, originality or talent exercised by the employee. Determination of exempt creative professional status, therefore, must be made on a case-by-case basis. . . .

(d) Journalists may satisfy the duties requirements for the creative professional exemption if their primary duty is work requiring invention, imagination, originality or talent, as opposed to work which depends primarily on intelligence, diligence and accuracy. Employees of newspapers, magazines, television and other media are not exempt creative professionals if they only collect, organize and record information that is routine or already public, or if they do not contribute a unique interpretation or analysis to a news product. Thus, for example, newspaper reporters who merely rewrite press releases or who write standard recounts of public information by gathering facts on routine community events are not exempt creative professionals. Reporters also do not qualify as exempt creative professionals if their work product is subject to substantial control by the employer. However, journalists may qualify as exempt creative professionals if their primary duty is performing on the air in radio, television or other electronic media; conducting investigative interviews; analyzing or interpreting public events; writing editorials, opinion columns or other commentary; or acting as a narrator or commentator.

29 C.F.R. § 541.302.

Some of the most illuminating cases arising under this exemption have involved claims made by newspaper reporters and television news writers, editors, and producers. Compare the following cases:

Dalheim v. KDFW-TV, 918 F.2d 1220 (5th Cir. 1990). The plaintiffs were general-assignment reporters, producers, directors and assignment editors employed in the news and programming departments of the Dallas-Fort Worth television Station KDFW-TV. The court ruled that they were not exempt either as executive, administrative, or professional employees. The approach reporters took to their day-to-day work was largely dictated by management ("Reporters are told the story that the station intends to cover, what they are expected to shoot, and the intended angle or focus of the story"), and "neither analytic nor interpretive nor original"; therefore, the employees were not exempt from the FLSA. _Id._ at 1228–29.

Freeman v. NBC, Inc., 80 F.3d 78 (2d Cir. 1996). Plaintiffs were television news writers, editors, producers and field producers for NBC's Nightly News. The court found them exempt from the Act's overtime provisions as creative professionals. The court commented, "The FLSA is properly considered a shield to protect unwary workers; it is not a sword by which 'writers and producers at the pinnacle of accomplishment and prestige in broadcast journalism' may obtain a benefit from their employer for which they did not bargain." _Id._ at 86.

Reich v. Gateway Press, Inc., 13 F.3d 685 (3d Cir. 1994). The plaintiffs were reporters working for small, suburban community newspapers who spent most of their time "rewriting press releases, attending municipal, school board and city council meetings, interviewing people, answering phones, and typing wedding announcements, school lunch menus, business reviews, real estate transactions, and church news." The court concluded that they were not exempt from the Act's overtime provisions because these tasks did not "require any special imagination." _Id._ at 699–700.

Sherwood v. Washington Post, 871 F. Supp. 1471 (D.D.C. 1994). The plaintiff was a reporter working for the Washington Post. The court concluded that he was exempt from the FLSA as an artistic professional because his primary duties included "originat[ing] ideas for stories, . . . decid[ing] what facts need to be gathered . . . [and] advis[ing] editors when he believed that particular topics might be newsworthy." _Id._ at 1473–74. The court noted that reporters at the Washington Post held "prestigious, competitive job[s]" and enjoyed "opportunities that most journalists only dream of having." _Id._ Finding that Sherwood exercised invention, imagination and talent in his job, the court concluded that he was exempt.

Is the deciding factor in these cases the prestige of the newspaper or television news station at which the plaintiffs work? Should it be? The Ninth Circuit shed light on this question in _Wang v. Chinese Daily News_, 623 F.3d 743 (9th Cir. 2010), _vacated and remanded on other grounds_, 132 S. Ct. 74 (2011). The court discussed the available precedents and explained the basis for its conclusion that newspaper reporters at the Chinese Daily News were not eligible for exemption as creative professionals:

> Although we have not decided a case applying the creative professional exemption to journalists, other courts have explored the circumstances

under which print journalists qualify for the exemption. In *Reich v. Gateway Press, Inc.*, 13 F.3d 685 (3d Cir. 1994), the Third Circuit concluded that none of the reporters at a chain of 19 local weeklies was exempt. The newspapers largely contained "information about the day-to-day events of their respective local communities . . . overlooked by the Pittsburgh metropolitan daily press." *Id.* at 688. The reporters primarily generated articles and features using what they knew about the local community, spent 50–60% of their time accumulating facts, and mostly filed recast press releases or information taken from public records. They wrote a feature article or editorial about once per month. *Id.* at 689. The court held that they were among the majority of reporters who were non-exempt. *Id.* at 699–700. It noted that the work was not "the type of fact gathering that demands the skill or expertise of an investigative journalist for the Philadelphia Inquirer or Washington Post, or a bureau chief for the New York Times." *Id.* at 700.

In *Reich v. Newspapers of New England, Inc.*, 44 F.3d 1060 (1st Cir. 1995), the First Circuit similarly held that reporters and other employees employed by a small community newspaper were not exempt professionals. The day-to-day duties of the reporters involved "general assignment work" covering hearings, criminal and policy activity, and legislative proceedings and business events. Employees were not "asked to editorialize about or interpret the events they covered." *Id.* at 1075. They, too, were therefore among the majority of reporters who were not exempt, even though their work occasionally demonstrated creativity, invention, imagination, or talent. *Id.*

By comparison, in *Sherwood v. Washington Post*, 871 F. Supp. 1471, 1482 (D.D.C. 1994), the district court held that a Washington Post reporter whose "job required him to originate his own story ideas, maintain a wide network of sources, write engaging, imaginative prose, and produce stories containing thoughtful analysis of complex issues" was exempt. As a high-level investigative journalist who had held multiple positions of prominence at one of the nation's top newspapers, the reporter was the sort of elite journalist whom the creative professional exemption was intended to cover.

The parties in this case submitted extensive evidence on summary judgment. Reporters stated in their depositions that they wrote between two and four articles per day, and that they very seldom did investigative reporting. The reporters proposed articles, but the editors gave considerate direction and frequently assigned the topics. One reporter explained that with having to write so much, "you didn't have enough time to—really analyze anything." Some time was spent rewriting press releases. There were no senior reporters or others with distinctive titles, and each of the reporters performed essentially the same tasks.

Editors' declarations submitted by CDN, on the other hand, stated that articles "include background, analysis and perspective on events and news," that CDN employs some of the most talented reporters in the Chinese

884   THE REGULATION OF WAGES AND HOURS   CH. 11

newspaper industry, and that the reporters have extensive control over their time, pace of work, and ideas for articles to write. They stated that reporters must cultivate sources, sift through significant amounts of information, and analyze complicated issues. Several editors stated that they approved more than 90% of the topics suggested by reporters. Reporters' salaries ranged from $2,060 to $3,700 per month.

Although the evidence submitted revealed disputes over how to characterize CDN's journalists, we agree with the district court that, even when viewing the facts in the light most favorable to CDN, the reporters do not satisfy the criteria for the creative professional exemption. CDN's Monterey Park (Los Angeles) operation, with 12 to 15 reporters and a local circulation of 30,000, is not quite as small or unsophisticated as the community newspapers described in the *Newspapers of New England* and *Gateway Press* cases. But CDN is much closer to the community newspapers described in those cases than to the New York Times or Washington Post. As the district court explored in detail, the materials submitted on summary judgment make clear that CDN's articles do not have the sophistication of the national-level papers at which one might expect to find the small minority of journalists who are exempt. Moreover, the intense pace at which CDN's reporters work precludes them from engaging in sophisticated analysis. CDN's reporters' primary duties do not involve "conducting investigative interviews; analyzing or interpreting public events; [or] writing editorial[s], opinion columns or other commentary," 29 C.F.R. § 541.302(d), even if they engage in these activities some of the time. Indeed, many CDN articles may be characterized as "standard recounts of public information [created] by gathering facts on routine community events," *Id.*, as opposed to the product of in-depth analysis. Characterizing CDN journalists as exempt would therefore be inconsistent with the Department of Labor's intent that "the majority of journalists . . . are not likely to be exempt," 69 Fed. Reg. at 22158, and with the requirement that FLSA exemptions be construed narrowly.

Id. at 752–54.

d. Outside Sales Employees

The white-collar exemptions from the overtime provisions of the FLSA also include outside sales employees. *See* 29 U.S.C. § 213(a)(1). The Department of Labor defines an outside salesperson as follows:

(a) The term "employee employed in the capacity of outside salesman" in section 13(a)(1) of the Act shall mean any employee:

    (1) Whose primary duty is:

        (i) making sales . . . or

        (ii) obtaining orders or contracts for services or for the use of facilities for which a consideration will be paid by the client or customer; and

> (2)   Who is customarily and regularly engaged away from the employer's place or places of business in performing such primary duty.

29 C.F.R. § 541.500(a). According to the regulations, any work performed "incidental to and in conjunction with the employee's own outside sales or solicitations, including incidental deliveries and collections," and "[o]ther work that furthers the employee's sales efforts" is also exempt. 29 C.F.R. § 541.500(b).

The outside sales employee exemption is based upon the incompatibility of minimum wage requirements with the individual character of the work of salespersons, including their autonomy in setting their own hours, relative freedom from supervision, and the fact that they often are paid on a commission basis. *Jewel Tea Co. v. Williams*, 118 F.2d 202, 207–08 (10th Cir. 1941). Like the other white-collar exemptions, employees in this category perform work that is difficult to standardize and could not easily be spread to other workers. Relevant factors in determining whether an employee falls into this category revolve around whether the employee is charged with soliciting new business, receives specialized sales training, was hired and denominated as a salesperson, lacks direct or constant supervision, and is paid on a commission basis. *See Nielsen v. DeVry*, 302 F. Supp. 2d 747, 756 (W.D. Mich. 2003) (finding that field representatives and recruiters for a for-profit education company were exempt from the FLSA's overtime provisions); *Meza v. Intelligent Mexican Marketing, Inc.*, 720 F.3d 577 (5th Cir. 2013) (finding route salesman for company that supplied food and beverage products to convenience stores exempt where plaintiff was hired as a salesperson, represented himself as having sales experience, was paid a base salary plus a commission that rewarded him for making sales, and was required to attend weekly sales training meetings; plaintiff's relatively low compensation—$6.66 per hour on average based upon an alleged 72-hour work week—could have been attributable to poor salesmanship).

Recent litigation has revolved around the categorization of pharmaceutical sales representatives. The plaintiffs in these cases argue that they do not actually make any direct sales, and therefore should be characterized as promoters rather than salespeople. The Supreme Court resolved a circuit split in the following case, finding the pharmaceutical sales representatives exempt.

Christopher v. SmithKline Beecham Corp. d/b/a Glaxo-SmithKline, 132 S. Ct. 2156 (2012). Michael Christopher worked as a pharmaceutical representative or "detailer" for SmithKline. In that capacity, he was responsible for calling on doctors within his assigned sales territory to provide them with details and information about the benefits and risks of the company's products. His goal was to obtain nonbinding commitments from doctors to prescribe the drugs to patients. Toward that end he spent 40 hours per week in the field and another 10–20 hours per week attending events, reviewing product information, and performing other tasks related to the job. He was subject to minimal supervision, and was not required to punch a clock. His annual gross pay was $72,000, which included a base salary and incentive pay based on his sales volume and market share of drug sales in his assigned territory. (The median gross pay for pharmaceutical detailers nationwide is over $90,000 per year. *Id.* at 2164 n.7). He did not receive overtime pay.

The district court granted summary judgment for SmithKline, finding that Christopher was exempt as an outside salesman, and the Ninth Circuit affirmed. 635 F.3d 383 (9th Cir. 2011). Meanwhile, the Second Circuit had ruled to the contrary in *In re Novartis Wage and Hour Litigation*, 611 F.3d 141 (2d Cir. 2010). The Second Circuit accorded significant deference to an amicus brief filed by the DOL in support of the plaintiffs. The DOL's previous position had been that its regulations implementing the exemption required only that an employee "in some sense" make a sale, resulting in its acquiescence in the sales practices of the drug industry for over 70 years. In its *Novartis* brief and in its brief to the Ninth Circuit in *Christopher*, however, the DOL argued that a "sale" for purposes of the exemption requires a "consummated transaction directly involving the employee for whom the exemption is sought." Secretary's *Novartis* brief, quoted at 132 S. Ct. 2166. After the Supreme Court granted *certiorari* in *Christopher*, the DOL changed course yet again, filing a brief that argued that "[a]n employee does not make a 'sale' for purposes of the 'outside salesman' exemption unless he actually transfers title to the property at issue." Brief for United States as *Amicus Curiae* 12–13, quoted at 132 S. Ct. 2166.

The Court refused to defer to the Secretary's interpretation of its regulations, reasoning that the DOL's consistent inaction despite the industry's decades-long practice of classifying pharmaceutical detailers as exempt employees effectively signaled its acquiescence in the practice. The DOL has an obligation to provide regulated entities with clear notice of the meaning of ambiguous regulations; to change its stance now would visit unfair surprise and create massive liability for the companies that employ over 90,000 pharmaceutical sales representatives, whose work has not changed in any material way for decades. *Id.* at 2167–68. Having dispensed with the DOL's interpretation, the Court explained why a broad, functional interpretation of the meaning of the word "sale" was both more consistent with the text of the statute and also in keeping with the purpose of the exemption:

> We begin with the text of the FLSA. Although the provision that establishes the overtime salesman exemption does not furnish a clear answer to the question before us, it provides at least one interpretive clue: It exempts anyone "employed . . . *in the capacity* of [an] outside salesman." 29 U.S.C. § 213(a)(1) (emphasis added). "Capacity," used in this sense, means "[o]utward condition or circumstances; relation; character; position." Webster's New International Dictionary 396 (2d ed.1934); *see also* 2 Oxford English Dictionary 89 (def.9) (1933) ("Position, condition, character, relation"). The statute's emphasis on the "capacity" of the employee counsels in favor of a functional, rather than a formal, inquiry, one that views an employee's responsibilities in the context of the particular industry in which the employee works.

> . . . .

> That petitioners bear all of the external indicia of salesmen provides further support for our conclusion. Petitioners were hired for their sales experience. They were trained to close each sales call by obtaining the maximum commitment possible from the physician. They worked away

from the office, with minimal supervision, and they were rewarded for their efforts with incentive compensation. It would be anomalous to require respondent to compensate petitioners for overtime, while at the same time exempting employees who function identically to petitioners in every respect except that they sell physician-administered drugs, such as vaccines and other injectable pharmaceuticals, that are ordered by the physician directly rather than purchased by the end user at a pharmacy with a prescription from the physician.

Our holding also comports with the apparent purpose of the FLSA's exemption for outside salesmen. The exemption is premised on the belief that exempt employees "typically earned salaries well above the minimum wage" and enjoyed other benefits that "se[t] them apart from the nonexempt workers entitled to overtime pay." Preamble 22124. It was also thought that exempt employees performed a kind of work that "was difficult to standardize to any time frame and could not be easily spread to other workers after 40 hours in a week, making compliance with the overtime provisions difficult and generally precluding the potential job expansion intended by the FLSA's time-and-a-half overtime premium." *Ibid.* Petitioners—each of whom earned an average of more than $70,000 per year and spent between 10 and 20 hours outside normal business hours each week performing work related to his assigned portfolio of drugs in his assigned sales territory—are hardly the kind of employees that the FLSA was intended to protect. And it would be challenging, to say the least, for pharmaceutical companies to compensate detailers for overtime going forward without significantly changing the nature of that position. *See, e.g.,* Brief for PhRMA as *Amicus Curiae* 14–20 (explaining that "key aspects of [detailers'] jobs as they are currently structured are fundamentally incompatible with treating [detailers] as hourly employees").

Id. at 2170–74.

The dissenting Justices argued that the primary duty of pharmaceutical representatives was not "to obtain a promise to prescribe a particular drug," but instead to "provid[e] information so that the doctor will keep the drug in mind with an eye toward using it when appropriate." *Id.* at 2177 (Justice Breyer, dissenting). Pharmacists, not pharmaceutical detailers, sell drugs. Detailers do not enter into any binding contract with the doctors—nor could they. They do not consign, ship, or sell any product at all. At most, the dissent argued, the detailer advances a concept, an idea, information, designed to obtain a " 'nonbinding commitment' [which] is, at most, a nonbinding promise to consider advising a patient to use a drug where medical indications so indicate (if the doctor encounters such a patient) and to write a prescription that will likely (but may not) lead that person to order that drug under its brand name from a pharmacy." *Id.* at 2176.

Christopher is the first white-collar exemption case that the Supreme Court has taken, and as a result it was closely watched by employers across many industries. What is the significance of the Court's determination that assessing coverage under the white-collar exemptions requires a functional inquiry viewed in the context of the particular industry rather than a formalistic reading of the regulations and the statute? Should the functional approach extend to the other white collar exemptions too? What difference would that make in the outcomes of some of the cases we have studied?

What about the Court's refusal to defer to the DOL's shifting interpretation of its regulations,might that have ramifications for other aspects of the FLSA? (The Secretary's interpretation of ambiguous regulations have historically been afforded significant deference by the courts under a doctrine announced by the Court in *Auer v. Robbins*, 519 U.S. 452 (1997)).

Finally, in a footnote to its opinion in *Christopher*, the Court also rejected the plaintiffs' reliance on the well-established canon that FLSA exemptions should be narrowly construed:

> In the past, we have stated that exemptions to the FLSA must be 'narrowly construed against the employers seeking to assert them and their application limited to those [cases] plainly and unmistakably within their terms and spirit.' *Arnold v. Ben Kanowsky, Inc.*, 361 U.S. 388, 392 (1960). Petitioners and the DOL contend that *Arnold* requires us to construe the outside salesman exemption narrowly, but *Arnold* is inapposite where, as here, we are interpreting a general definition that applies throughout the FLSA.

132 S. Ct. 2172 n.21. What difference does this canon of FLSA construction make? What effect is the Court's limitation of this canon likely to have on the burgeoning litigation over the white-collar exemptions?

2.   Computer professionals

A special exemption was added in 1996 for computer systems analysts, programmers, software engineers and similarly situated employees engaged in computer-related work who are paid on an hourly basis and are compensated at a minimum of $27.63 per hour. 29 U.S.C. § 213(a)(17). Alternatively, computer professionals may qualify for the white-collar exemption for professionals in § 213(a)(1) if they are compensated on a salary or fee basis at a rate not less than $455 per week. Under either exemption, computer professionals must also meet the duties test below. 29 C.F.R. § 541.400(a), (b). The 2004 regulations require that the employee's primary duty consist of:

> (1) The application of systems analysis techniques and procedures, including consulting with users, to determine hardware, software or system functional specifications;

> (2) The design, development, documentation, analysis, creation, testing or modification of computer systems or programs, including prototypes, based on and related to user or system design specifications;

> (3) The design, documentation, testing, creation or modification of computer programs related to machine operating systems; or

(4) A combination of the aforementioned duties, the performance of which requires the same level of skills.

29 C.F.R. §§ 541.400(b).

A fair bit of litigation has arisen around employer classification of help desk and technical support workers as exempt computer professionals. The following case, litigated under the pre-2004 standards (which were slightly narrower than the current standard, since they also required proof that the employee's primary duty involved work requiring the consistent exercise of discretion and judgment) offers a good discussion of the distinction between computer professionals who are exempt, and help desk or technical support workers who are not.

Martin v. Indiana Michigan Power Co., 381 F.3d 574 (6th Cir. 2004). Anthony Martin was an Information Technology specialist at Indiana Michigan Power (known as American Electric Power, or AEP). Martin's job was to maintain the computer workstation software on other employees' desks, responding to requests for assistance and troubleshooting, installing software and software patches, and relocating workstations. He also installed network hardware and cable and worked in the wiring closets when necessary. Martin had no computer certifications and no degree beyond a high school diploma; his only training consisted of several courses on various computer and software functions. He wore a blue short-sleeved work shirt with a name badge, blue work pants, and work boots, and his workstation was a workbench located in a common workshop area; he had no phone line of his own. AEP contended that Martin was exempt either as a computer professional or as an administrative employee. The district court ruled that Martin was exempt as a computer professional, but the Sixth Circuit reversed. The Sixth Circuit observed that not all jobs involving computers require highly specialized knowledge, and explained that the key inquiry was whether the employee's particular job duties required application of knowledge "in computer systems, analysis, programming, and software engineering," rather than simply "highly-specialized knowledge of computers and software," as the district court had been satisfied with. *Id.* at 580. The court explained:

> The district court made an understandable mistake, one that arises from the common perception that all jobs involving computers are necessarily highly complex and require exceptional expertise. . . .

> Martin does not do computer programming or software engineering; nor does he perform systems analysis, which involves making actual, analytical decisions about how Cook's computer network should function. Rather, Martin's tasks—installing and upgrading hardware and software on workstations, configuring desktops, checking cables, replacing parts, and troubleshooting Windows problems—are all performed to predetermined specifications in the system design created by others. As Martin testified, he is provided the standard "desktop" for installation on the computers he configures, but he is not involved in determining what the desktop should look like. Thornburg [Martin's supervisor] explained . . . that IT Support is "a maintenance organization that takes care of computer systems."

Id. at 580–81.

The court also concluded that Martin did not qualify for the administrative exemption because his work was not directly related to management policies or to general business operations. His job had nothing to do with servicing of the business through advising management, planning, negotiating, representing the company, purchasing, promoting sales, or business research and control mentioned in the relevant regulation, 29 C.F.R. § 541.205(b). His job was only "to assist in keeping the computers and network running to the specifications and designs of others." *Id.* at 582. The court remanded for entry of summary judgment in favor of Martin, and for calculation of damages.

———

As *Martin* suggests, employees performing computer-related work may qualify for an exemption either as computer professionals, administrative employees or as learned professionals. The computer professional exemption did not supplant these other bases for exemption. Questions continue to arise as to whether information technology support specialists who provide help desk support and troubleshoot hardware and software problems qualify for either the computer professionals' exemption or the administrative exemption. In 2006, the Department of Labor issued an opinion letter in which it explained that information technology support specialists generally do not qualify for either exemption because the job requires only a high school diploma, does not require the exercise of discretion and independent judgment necessary for the administrative exemption, and lacks the development and analysis skills required by the computer professionals' exemption. Thus, they are entitled to overtime compensation. Wage and Hour Opinion Letter, FLSA2006-42, Oct. 26, 2006. The position is apparently frequently misclassified as exempt, with resulting exposure to significant liability for employers. Ironically, both IBM and Hewlett-Packard have been sued for misclassification. IBM settled a nationwide collective action brought by its information technology workers, including systems administrators, network technicians and other technical staff for $65 million. *See IBM Agrees to Pay $65 Million to Settle Overtime Claims Involving IT Workers*, DAILY LAB. REP. (BNA) No. 226, Nov. 24, 2006. A collective action claim against Hewlett-Packard by almost 10,000 technical support specialists (who install, maintain and support computer software and hardware) received conditional certification and is pending. *See Benedict v. Hewlett-Packard Co.*, 2014 U.S. Dist. LEXIS 18594 (N.D. Cal. Feb. 13, 2014). Ultimately, employees' actual duties, not their job titles, determine whether or not they are exempt. *See* 29 C.F.R. § 541.400 ("Because job titles vary widely and change quickly in the computer industry, job titles are not determinative of the applicability of [the computer employee] exemption.").

3.   The Combination and Highly Compensated Exemptions

The Department of Labor's 2004 regulations established two other white-collar exemptions. The first is a "combination exemption," which provides that an employee who performs a combination of exempt duties as an executive, administrative, professional, computer and outside sales employee may qualify for exemption if the duties, when combined, constitute the employee's primary duty. 29

C.F.R. § 541.708. This exemption is designed to ensure that "work that is exempt under one section of this part will not defeat the exemption under any other section." *Id.* The 2004 regulations also added an exemption for "highly compensated" employees, defined as those earning at least $100,000 per year (including nondiscretionary bonuses or commissions) and who "customarily and regularly perform[] any one or more of the exempt duties of an executive, administrative or professional employee." 29 C.F.R. § 541.601(a). Some worried that these latter two new exemptions might erode the significance of the tests under the traditional white-collar exemptions, but the fears proved unfounded. *See, e.g., Intracomm, Inc. v. Bajaj*, 492 F.3d 285 (4th Cir. 2007) (employee who could not meet the salary requirement of the administrative exemption and did not qualify for the outside sales exemption based upon his duties was not exempt under the combination exemption, which permits the blending of exempt duties for purposes of defining an employee's primary duty, but does not relieve the employer of the obligation to independently establish the salary basis or compensation requirement of each exemption whose duties are combined); *Ogden v. CDI Corp.*, 2010 U.S. Dist. LEXIS 66686 (D. Ariz. June 30, 2010) (denying employer's motion for summary judgment in overtime claim based on classification of employee as a highly compensated employee; even though employee earned over $100,000 per year, employer could not establish beyond question that employee customarily and regularly performed one or more of the exempt administrative duties described in the DOL's regulations).

Chapter 12

HEALTH AND PENSION PLANS—ERISA REGULATION

Health and pension benefits are two of the most common—and most sought after—benefits that often attach to employment. One federal statute, the Employee Retirement Income Security Act (commonly known as "ERISA"), regulates both health and pension plans. 29 U.S.C. §§ 1001–1461. In this section, we will explore the provisions of ERISA that relate to health and pension plans that are of interest to employees and employers (as opposed to plan administrators or those who set up plans).

ERISA is a comprehensive federal statute that regulates pension and "welfare benefit plans." The statute defines "welfare benefit plans" to include "medical, surgical, or hospital care or benefits, or benefits in the event of sickness, accident, disability, death or unemployment, or vacation benefits, apprenticeship or other training programs, or day care centers, scholarship funds, or prepaid legal services." 29 U.S.C. § 1002(1). Health benefit plans are the most common welfare benefit plans, with other benefits, such as life insurance and disability plans, also falling within that category.

When ERISA was passed in 1974, its primary concern was pension benefits. Prior to the passage of ERISA, a number of pension funds had gone bankrupt: the Studebaker automobile company was the most notorious of the bankruptcies that deprived thousands of employees of their pension funds. *See* James A. Wooten, *"The Most Glorious Failure in Business": The Studebaker-Packard Corporation and the Origins of ERISA*, 49 BUFFALO L. REV. 683 (2001) (detailing the failure of Studebaker in 1963 where 11,000 employees lost their pensions). There were also concerns that pension funds were being mismanaged or were vulnerable to looting by their plan administrators. As a result, the statute provides for comprehensive federal regulation of pensions, and displaces almost all state regulation of pension plans. This latter part of the statute, known as the preemption clause, was designed to provide uniform regulation for employers that operated in more than one state, and was also intended to ensure a single comprehensive regulatory scheme. For a discussion of the origins of ERISA, see JOHN H. LANGBEIN & BRUCE E. WOLK, PENSION & EMPLOYEE BENEFIT LAW 68–84 (5d ed. 2010).

Although health benefit plans were widely in use by the time ERISA was passed, the legislation treated such plans as almost an afterthought. Unlike the comprehensive statutory and regulatory guidance on establishing and maintaining pension plans, there are virtually no substantive provisions within ERISA that regulate health plans, or other welfare benefit plans. The absence of substantive provisions combined with a broad preemption provision and limited remedies available under ERISA created great controversy and generated substantial litigation over health benefits. It also made it very difficult for states to regulate large plans. This has all changed under the Affordable Care Act, also known as ObamaCare or the ACA, which we will touch on below but it is worth noting at this point that the statute is just now becoming effective and it is difficult to know what issues might arise under the statute that will become the province of employment lawyers.

Many of the statutory provisions of ERISA apply to both pension and health benefit plans. All plan administrators have a fiduciary duty to act in the sole interests of plan beneficiaries, which requires both loyalty and prudence, terms that are largely borrowed from trust law where fiduciary obligations apply to those who are charged with the responsibility of administering a trust. *See* 29 U.S.C. § 1104. Section 502(a) of ERISA provides federal court jurisdiction for lawsuits brought by plan beneficiaries and limits the range of remedies available to the benefit due under the plan, as well as costs and attorney's fees. In other words, neither punitive nor consequential damages can be recovered by a plan beneficiary. The limitation on consequential damages is the result of the Supreme Court's interpretation of section 502(a), which provides for "equitable relief," a term the Supreme Court has defined so as to exclude consequential damages. *See, e.g., Mertens v. Hewitt Assocs.*, 508 U.S. 248, 255–62 (1993). Section 514 provides the broad preemption clause that supplants most state regulation. As a result of the interplay between sections 502 and 514, most employees with claims against their health or pension plans are limited to the remedies provided by section 502. One other statutory provision proves important to employees: section 510 prohibits discrimination against plan participants, an issue that arose under some health benefit plans in the past but should be largely mitigated by the comprehensive federal requirements for health benefit plans under the new legislation.

An essential aspect of the ERISA scheme, and one that is central to understanding its provisions, is that health (until recently) and pension benefits are discretionary. No employer was required to provide any such benefits, and still are not for pension plans; what ERISA does is regulate benefit plans once an employer decides to provide them.

A. HEALTH BENEFITS

As noted previously, the United States system of health insurance is principally employer-based. The American system of employer-provided insurance is unique—most industrialized nations provide insurance through a national system financed by taxes—and arose through a convergence of events. Beginning late in the 19th century, a number of employers began to provide health care to their employees, some out of beneficence but often out of self-interest as well. Healthy employees are almost always better employees, and providing health benefits was another way to tie employees to their particular employer. In 1910, Montgomery Ward and Co. instituted a health insurance plan, and what is now Blue Cross-Blue Shield originated in 1929, with Kaiser Permanente, generally considered the nation's first HMO, emerging in the 1930s. *See* Laura A. Scofea, *The Development and Growth of Employer-Provided Health Insurance*, MONTHLY LABOR REV. 3, 4–5 (MAR. 1994). However, the comprehensive system of employer-provided health insurance fell into place in the 1940s and '50s.

Wage and price controls instituted during World War II prevented employers from increasing wages. Insurance and pension contributions were not counted as wages, however, and employers began to substitute these benefits for wage increases as a way to compete for scarce labor. Around the same time, the Internal Revenue Service issued a ruling that amounts paid by employers for health insurance did not constitute income to employees, even though employers were able to deduct the amounts as business expenses. When the IRS changed its ruling ten years later, Congress responded by expressly excluding employment-based health contributions from taxable income, thus offering what amounts to a tax subsidy for providing insurance through employers. Labor unions largely followed suit by aggressively bargaining for better benefit packages, and in time, more and more employers began to add health insurance benefits to their standard package of fringe benefits. For a concise history of employer-based coverage see David A. Hyman & Mark Hall, *Two Cheers for Employment-Based Health Insurance*, 2 YALE J. HEALTH POL'Y L. & ETHICS 23 (2002).

The Affordable Care Act ("ACA"), also now commonly referred to as ObamaCare, has altered the landscape for health benefits. In a very general way, we have moved from a discretionary system of health benefits with light regulation, to a mandatory system with substantial federal regulation. The legislation requires individuals to obtain health insurance and it also requires employers with 50 or more employees to provide health insurance to their full-time employees or pay a penalty for failing to do so. Employers with fewer than fifty full-time employees are not required to provide insurance but instead are provided with financial incentives, primarily in the form of tax incentives, to do so. *See* 26 U.S.C. § 1501(b) and 4980H(a)(1).

A critical aspect of the ACA is that it preserves the employer-provided health insurance system and adds a means for individuals to obtain health insurance through a state or federal health exchange. The legislation is complex and the individual mandate took effect in 2014, while the employer mandate is phased in beginning in 2015 for employers of 100 or more employees, and 2016 for those with between 50 and 100 employees. The ACA also provides for comprehensive regulation of health plans, prohibiting, for example, what were known as exclusions for pre-existing conditions where insurers would frequently deny individuals insurance based on a health condition that existed at the time health insurance was sought. There are other coverage requirements and an employer's plan must meet both affordability (which is generally defined as having costs that are less than 9.5% of an employee's income) and value requirements in order to satisfy the employer mandate. Because the employer mandate to provide insurance applies to employers with more than 50 full-time employees, considerable attention is likely to be paid to how a full-time employee is defined.

The legislation and its implementing regulations define full-time employees with specificity. For example, regulations indicate that the common law definition of employee is to be applied, and full-time employees are defined as those who work an average of 30 or more hours in a week. Treas. Reg. § 4980H (c)(4) (2014); 79 Fed. Reg. 8552. There is no specific penalty if employers cut employee hours so that they fall below 30 hours in a week to avoid the insurance mandate, though as discussed below, such a strategy could violate ERISA. Similarly, some employers may choose to pay the penalty rather than provide health insurance but this would likely make these employers less desirable in employees' eyes since the employees would then have to purchase their own insurance to comply with the individual mandate portion of the law. The penalty for failing to comply with the employer mandate can be significant, ranging from as much as $700 per employee to $3,000 per employee when an employee seeks insurance outside of the employer-provided coverage.

One question that remains to be resolved over time is how the ACA interacts with ERISA, the law that had previously (and still does) regulated employer-provided health insurance plans. One key feature of ERISA has likely been rendered moot. Prior to the ACA, there was no federal requirement that employers provide health benefits and ERISA regulated only to the extent an employer chose to provide such benefits. Because of a concern that if the regulation proved too onerous, employers would likely opt to stop providing health insurance, ERISA imposed no real substantive regulation, such as requiring health plans to offer minimum benefits. Indeed, its most important feature was a broad preemption provision that pre-empted most state legislation intended to regulate large employer-provided plans. The broad preemption provision generated an enormous amount of complicated litigation to determine whether employers had to comply with state legislation. In recent years, that litigation had slowed and it should no longer be relevant in light of the federal mandate.

However, employers who choose to reduce the hours of their employees to avoid the insurance mandate may run afoul of Section 510 of ERISA, which makes it unlawful for an employer to take an adverse action against an employee "for the purpose of interfering with the attainment of any right to which such participant may become entitled under an employee benefit plan." 29 U.S.C. § 1140. An employee suing under section 510 would have to prove that the employer had a specific intent to deprive the employee of a benefit he would otherwise be entitled to but for the reduction in hours. Under this section, employers would appear most vulnerable if they reduced the hours of an existing employee as opposed to hiring someone to perform part-time as opposed to full-time work. The remedy for violating Section 510 is typically limited to restoring the benefit the employee seeks.

Another issue that is likely to draw early attention involves what are known as wellness programs. In an effort to reduce medical costs, the ACA includes incentives for employers to adopt programs to encourage healthy behaviors by employees. Some programs, such as those that provide discounts on gym memberships or offer incentives for employee participation in various programs, are likely to generate little controversy as long as they are made available to all employees. Other programs, however, provide rewards for employees who achieve certain health conditions, whether that is achieving a certain cholesterol or blood-pressure level or stopping smoking or some other activity. While financial incentives for participating in wellness programs were permitted before the ACA, the statute increases the level of incentives that can be offered. Employers may now offer employees a financial incentive worth up to 30% of the insurance premium for meeting the goals or the wellness plan, and up to 50% for programs designed to prevent or reduce tobacco usage. 45 C.F.R. § 146.121(f)(5).

These programs raise concerns regarding employee privacy interests and discrimination on the basis of disability. Employee privacy may be affected because in order to participate in these wellness programs, employees are often required to reveal sensitive medical information or share information about their lifestyle (e.g., diet, exercise) with their employer. The programs also raise concerns about discrimination, because employees with disabilities may have a more difficult time satisfying the program conditions. One way to address this problem would be to ensure reasonable alternatives for receiving an award are provided to any such employees but challenges under the Americans With Disabilities Act may be forthcoming.

The Supreme Court has to date issued two decisions involving the ACA. The first upheld the constitutionality of the individual mandate of the Act, though the Court invalidated the expansion of Medicaid provisions. *See Nat'l Fed'n of Indep. Business v. Sebelius*, 132 S. Ct. 2566 (2012). More recently, the Court allowed a for-profit, closely-held corporation that raised religious objections to birth control to be exempted from the ACA's requirement that insurance coverage include contraceptives. *See Burwell v. Hobby Lobby Stores, Inc.*, 134 S. Ct. 2751 (2014). It is likely that similar cases may continue to arise but that the primary concern for employers will be (1) whether they have more than 50 full-time employees and, if they do, (2) whether their plans, assuming they decide to provide insurance rather than pay the excise tax, comply with the various requirements of the ACA. This latter issue is likely to be the province of benefit lawyers and is also likely to be addressed in detail in courses on employee benefits or healthcare law so we have kept our discussion to a minimum.

Finally, we note that the healthcare law is complicated and responsibility for enforcement and implementation is divided among several agencies—the Department of Health and Human Services, the Department of Treasury which has issued some of the most important implementing regulations regarding the employer mandate, the Department of Labor which has some responsibility, including its current role with respect to ERISA regulation, and the Small Business Administration. Useful summaries of the law, as it relates to employer obligations, can be found at *Internal Revenue Service, Questions and Answers on Employer Shared Responsibility Provisions Under the Affordable Care Act, available at* http://www.irs.gov/uac/Newsroom/Questions-and-Answers-on-Employer-Shared-Responsibility-Provisions-Under-the-Affordable-Care-Act (May 13, 2014); *What Do Small Businesses Need to Know?, HealthCare.Gov*, https://www.healthcare.gov/what-do-small-businesses-need-to-know; www.dol.gov/ebsa/healthreform/.

B. PENSION BENEFITS

The system of pension benefits in the United States has three independent components: (1) social security; (2) employer-provided pension plans; and (3) private savings. This section will focus on employer-provided pension benefits, but it should be kept in mind that social security provides near universal coverage after age 65 (depending on the year of birth, for some the age will be 66 and eventually 67) and provides about 45% of average pay as a benefit.

Pension benefit plans have long been an important benefit offered by employers. For employees, pensions offer security in older age, particularly when the benefit is guaranteed throughout one's lifetime. But why do employers provide pensions? One reason is that, at least for many, pensions have, over time and largely at the behest of unions, become a common and desirable benefit, one that many employers need to offer in order to attract good employees. Yet, if it were just about attracting employees, employers might be able to offer higher wages, since pensions are effectively deferred income, and it is quite likely that many employees might readily accept higher wages in lieu of an employer-sponsored pension plan.

Pension plans, however, offer additional benefits to employers. One of the reasons pensions developed as part of an employer's compensation strategy was to aid the employer in regulating its workforce. Employees would be more willing to retire if they had a stable income available during retirement and by facilitating that security, employers were able to control their workforce turnover. In addition, because a traditional pension is commonly based on an individual's length of service and highest salary, pensions provide incentives for employees to remain with their employer.

With the decrease in career employment, traditional pension plans have waned in significance. Employer-provided pension coverage has been declining in recent years. The Department of Labor has calculated that 74% of private full-time employees have access to retirement benefits, and 58% of those employees participate in retirement plans. The coverage levels are much higher for government employees and union members where more than 90% of such employees participate in retirement plans. Among the lowest wage group, only 18% of private sector employees participated in retirement plans. *See* UNITED STATES DEPT. OF LABOR, EMPLOYEE BENEFITS IN THE UNITED STATES, March 2014, at Table 1.

Traditionally there have been two types of pension benefits. A defined benefit plan offers a fixed benefit during retirement, typically based on a formula that takes into account an employee's highest (or average) salary with the employer and length of service. At one time, these plans were the dominant form of pension, but they have now fallen out of favor, and such plans are today found almost exclusively among union members, as well as some state retirement systems.

The other form of pension is known as a defined contribution plan. In this plan, the employee, and typically the employer, make contributions into an individual account for each employee, and the employee is responsible for managing that plan. The most common form of a defined contribution plan is the 401(k), and these plans typically provide the benefits for today's workers who receive retirement benefits. In today's workforce, twice as many workers have defined contribution plans than defined benefit plans. In the late 1970s and early 1980s, those proportions were reversed.

One important difference between these two plans that helps explain the change over time is who is responsible for ensuring the benefit. In a defined benefit plan, the employer must manage the pension plan to ensure adequate resources for its retired employees. In other words, the employer assumes the risk for the plan investments. To the extent the pension plan investments do not perform as expected, employers are required to make additional contributions to ensure the plan is adequately funded. Recall that underfunded pensions were one of the strongest motivating factors behind the passage of ERISA, and there are detailed requirements for how much employers must contribute to ensure adequate funding of defined benefit plans.

In contrast, in a defined contribution plan, the employer gives the initial contribution directly to the employee, and thereafter, does not have to worry about whether the retirement account is adequate to provide a certain level of funding since only the contribution, not the benefit, is guaranteed. The employer is responsible, however, for providing an adequate array of investment opportunities (typically at least three) for employee contributions, and many employers make their own stock available as an investment option, an issue that is discussed in the material below. It is important to emphasize that in a defined contribution plan the risk of ensuring adequate retirement income falls on the employee.

From an employee's perspective, there are two significant advantages to a defined benefit plan. First, the benefit lasts throughout one's lifetime so that it is not possible for the retiree to outlive her retirement benefit. Second, defined benefit plans are insured by a federal corporation, the Pension Benefit Guaranty Corporation ("PBGC"), which is modeled on the better-known Federal Deposit Insurance Corporation. *See* 29 U.S.C. § 1302; *Pension Benefit Guaranty Corp. v. LTV Corp.*, 496 U.S. 633, 636–37 (1990) (describing PBGC's purpose and structure). The PBGC ensures plan benefits in the event of bankruptcy or severely underfunded pensions, and is only available for defined benefit plans. For employers, defined benefit plans are administratively cumbersome and can lead to substantial pension liabilities, particularly in a weak stock market, and for these reasons, and others, private employers have moved away from them. As you may be aware, over the last few years, the costs of public pensions have become a major issue, and many public pensions are facing serious shortfalls in the future, though this is always difficult to predict given the changing nature of the economy and other factors. A cogent discussion of the issues facing public pensions can be found in Jack M. Beermann, *The Public Pension Crisis*, 70 WASH. & LEE L. REV. 3 (2013).

Defined contribution plans, on the other hand, offer the potential for higher benefit returns since the employee controls the investments and can choose among varying plans and risk levels. These plans can be particularly attractive when the stock market is strong but stock markets are not always strong. However, one reason employers made the switch away from defined benefit plans is that many employees considered defined contribution plans to be more attractive because of their potentially higher returns. Defined contribution plans are also more portable because, as discussed further below, employee contributions vest immediately, and there is not the same incentive to stay with an employer throughout one's career in order to maximize one's pension. Under the traditional defined benefit plans, there were strong incentives to remain with an employer because most plans tied pension benefits to the employee's length of service. Such plans are seen as less relevant today where mobility is often stressed over longevity. From your own perspective, what kind of pension would you prefer to have? Consider further, if you were afforded the opportunity to invest your own pension funds, how would you make your investment decisions?

In recent years, a new kind of retirement plan has emerged that shares qualities of both defined benefit and defined contribution plans. Known as a cash balance plan, these pension plans establish a "hypothetical" employee account that accrues benefits for each year of service and also accrues interest on those benefits. These plans are technically defined benefit plans because they offer a guaranteed benefit and the employer is responsible for ensuring adequate funding to cover its plan obligations. However, they are more portable and they are not dependent on accumulated length in service to build an adequate retirement benefit since pension credit is awarded equally for each year of service. Cash balance plans are often see as a transitional device from a defined benefit plan to a defined contribution plan but they have also grown popular on their own, particularly for small or medium-sized businesses because they are a way to provide guaranteed income while limiting a company's potential liability since the contribution is defined.

The practices of employers have largely outgrown the original purpose of the ERISA legislation as it relates to pension benefits. ERISA was passed at a time when defined benefit plans dominated the benefits landscape, and many of the statute's substantive provisions exclusively involve defined benefits plans. Now that these plans are fading in importance, courts are left to struggle with a statute that does not neatly fit the new workplace, and most efforts to reform pension legislation have so far failed. Throughout this section, you should consider how the pension system might be improved or reformed, keeping in mind that no employer is required to provide pension benefits and one of the primary reasons pension reform has not advanced is a fear that employers might choose to stop offering pension plans rather than submit to greater governmental regulation.

1. Defined Benefit Plans

a. Vesting of Benefits

The vesting of pension benefits was one of the key legislative innovations promulgated by ERISA. Previously, no federal law had ensured any vesting of benefits, and in the case of Studebaker and other major bankruptcies, longtime employees saw their promised pensions vanish. Section 203 of ERISA mandates that benefits vest—and thus become nonforfeitable (with some minor exceptions)—after a certain period of time. There are two methods of vesting: cliff vesting where employer contributions vest after five years; alternatively, employers can establish a graded or gradual vesting, with 20% of benefits vesting after three years and 100% vesting after seven years. 29 U.S.C. § 1053. As tenure with employers has decreased over time, the vesting schedule has also adjusted. For pension plans that went into effect after 2002, cliff vesting now occurs after three years, and the gradual vesting is from 2 to 6 years. Employee contributions vest immediately, and employers may establish an earlier vesting schedule.

Once a benefit becomes "vested" it cannot be altered and must be paid to the employee at her "normal retirement" age, a term used in the ERISA statute but left to the employer to define. Most commonly, the normal retirement age is 65, but early retirement programs can advance the age, and in the near future, normal retirement ages may be increased as the workforce is currently undergoing a significant transformation to an older workforce.

2. Defined Contribution Plans, 401(k)s, and Their Investments

As noted earlier, with the exception of some cash balance plans, virtually all new retirement plan participants are enrolled in defined contribution plans. Unlike defined benefit plans, these plans do not offer any guaranteed benefit but instead require the participant to manage her investments over time to yield a satisfactory retirement income. Most defined contribution plans have two components: (1) employee contributions and (2) employer contributions, and the two components are subject to different regulatory provisions.

Employee contributions vest immediately and are not forfeitable, and plan administrators must provide a diverse array of investment opportunities from which employees choose. Employer contributions, on the other hand, typically vest after a short waiting period such as three years but employers are permitted to impose restrictions on a plan participant's ability to sell or trade those investments. The recession that plagued the United States beginning in 2008 wreaked havoc on may pension plans, and this was a particular problem for defined contribution plans since the risk of these plans is borne by the employees. The changing economic conditions, and other factors, resulted in a substantial increase in litigation, particularly concerning the responsibilities of plan fiduciaries. The next case provides some of the legal framework for such claims, and the following case and accompanying notes explores many of the current issues relating to defined contribution plans.

LaRUE v. DeWOLFF, BOBERG & ASSOCIATES, INC.
United States Supreme Court
552 U.S. 248 (2008)

JUSTICE STEVENS delivered the opinion of the Court.

In *Massachusetts Mut. Life Ins. Co. v. Russell*, 473 U.S. 134 (1985), we held that a participant in a disability plan that paid a fixed level of benefits could not bring suit under § 502(a)(2) of the Employee Retirement Income Security Act of 1974 (ERISA), 88 Stat. 891, 29 U.S.C. § 1132(a)(2), to recover consequential damages arising from delay in the processing of her claim. In this case we consider whether that statutory provision authorizes a participant in a defined contribution pension plan to sue a fiduciary whose alleged misconduct impaired the value of plan assets in the participant's individual account.[1] Relying on our decision in *Russell*, the Court of Appeals for the Fourth Circuit held that § 502(a)(2) "provides remedies only for entire plans, not for individuals. . . . Recovery under this subsection must 'inure[ ] to the benefit of the plan *as a whole*,' not to particular persons with rights under the plan." 450 F.3d 570, 572–573 (2006) (quoting *Russell*, 473 U.S., at 140).

---

[1] [n.1] As its names imply, a "defined contribution plan" or "individual account plan" promises the participant the value of an individual account at retirement, which is largely a function of the amounts contributed to that account and the investment performance of those contributions. A "defined benefit plan," by contrast, generally promises the participant a fixed level of retirement income, which is typically based on the employee's years of service and compensation.

While language in our *Russell* opinion is consistent with that conclusion, the rationale for *Russell*'s holding supports the opposite result in this case.

I

Petitioner filed this action in 2004 against his former employer, DeWolff, Boberg & Associates (DeWolff), and the ERISA-regulated 401(k) retirement savings plan administered by DeWolff (Plan). The Plan permits participants to direct the investment of their contributions in accordance with specified procedures and requirements. Petitioner alleged that in 2001 and 2002 he directed DeWolff to make certain changes to the investments in his individual account, but DeWolff never carried out these directions. Petitioner claimed that this omission "depleted" his interest in the Plan by approximately $150,000, and amounted to a breach of fiduciary duty under ERISA. The complaint sought " 'make-whole' or other equitable relief as allowed by [§ 502(a)(3)]," as well as "such other and further relief as the court deems just and proper." Civil Action No. 2:04-1747-18 (D. S. C.), p 4.

Respondents filed a motion for judgment on the pleadings, arguing that the complaint was essentially a claim for monetary relief that is not recoverable under § 502(a)(3). Petitioner countered that he "d[id] not wish for the court to award him any money, but . . . simply want[ed] the plan to properly reflect that which would be his interest in the plan, but for the breach of fiduciary duty." Reply to Defendants Motion to Dismiss, p 7. The District Court concluded, however, that since respondents did not possess any disputed funds that rightly belonged to petitioner, he was seeking damages rather than equitable relief available under § 502(a)(3). Assuming, *arguendo*, that respondents had beached a fiduciary duty, the District Court nonetheless granted their motion.

. . . The Court of Appeals [affirmed]. . . .

Section 502(a)(2) provides for suits to enforce the liability-creating provisions of § 409, concerning breaches of fiduciary duties that harm plans. The Court of Appeals cited language from our opinion in *Russell* suggesting that these provisions "protect the entire plan, rather than the rights of an individual beneficiary." 473 U.S., at 142. It then characterized the remedy sought by petitioner as "personal" because he "desires recovery to be paid into his plan account, an instrument that exists specifically for his benefit," and concluded: "We are therefore skeptical that plaintiff's individual remedial interest can serve as a legitimate proxy for the plan in its entirety, as [*§ 502(a)(2)*] requires. . . ." 450 F.3d, at 574.

II

As the case comes to us we must assume that respondents breached fiduciary obligations defined in § 409(a), and that those breaches had an adverse impact on the value of the plan assets in petitioner's individual account. Whether petitioner can prove those allegations and whether respondents may have valid defenses to the claim are matters not before us. Although the record does not reveal the relative size of petitioner's account, the legal issue under § 502(a)(2) is the same whether his account includes 1% or 99% of the total assets in the plan.

As we explained in *Russell*, and in more detail in our later opinion in *Varity Corp. v. Howe*, 516 U.S. 489, 508–512 (1996), § 502(a) of ERISA identifies six types of civil actions that may be brought by various parties. The second, which is at issue in this case, authorizes the Secretary of Labor as well as plan participants, beneficiaries, and fiduciaries, to bring actions on behalf of a plan to recover for violations of the obligations defined in § 409(a). The principal statutory duties imposed on fiduciaries by that section "relate to the proper management, administration, and investment of fund assets," with an eye toward ensuring that "the benefits authorized by the plan" are ultimately paid to participants and beneficiaries. *Russell*, 473 U.S., at 142. The misconduct alleged by the petitioner in this case falls squarely within that category.

The misconduct alleged in *Russell*, by contrast, fell outside this category. The plaintiff in *Russell* received all of the benefits to which she was contractually entitled, but sought consequential damages arising from a delay in the processing of her claim. 473 U.S., at 136–137. In holding that § 502(a)(2) does not provide a remedy for this type of injury, we stressed that the text of § 409(a) characterizes the relevant fiduciary relationship as one "with respect to a plan," and repeatedly identifies the "plan" as the victim of any fiduciary breach and the recipient of any relief. *See Id.*, at 140. The legislative history likewise revealed that "the crucible of congressional concern was misuse and mismanagement of plan assets by plan administrators." *Id.*, at 141, n 8. Finally, our review of ERISA as a whole confirmed that §§ 502(a)(2) and 409 protect "the financial integrity of the plan," *Id.*, at 142, n 9, whereas other provisions specifically address claims for benefits. We therefore concluded:

> "A fair contextual reading of the statute makes it abundantly clear that
> its draftsmen were primarily concerned with the possible misuse of plan
> assets, and with remedies that would protect the entire plan, rather than
> with the rights of an individual beneficiary." *Id.*, at 142.

Russell's emphasis on protecting the "entire plan" from fiduciary misconduct reflects the former landscape of employee benefit plans. That landscape has changed.

Defined contribution plans dominate the retirement plan scene today. In contrast, when ERISA was enacted, and when *Russell* was decided, "the [defined benefit] plan was the norm of American pension practice." J. Langbein, S. Stabile, & B. Wolk, Pension and Employee Benefit Law 58 (4th ed. 2006). Unlike the defined contribution plan in this case, the disability plan at issue in *Russell* did not have individual accounts; it paid a fixed benefit based on a percentage of the employee's salary. *See Russell v. Massachusetts Mut. Life Ins. Co.*, 722 F.2d 482, 486 (CA9 1983).

The "entire plan" language in *Russell* speaks to the impact of § 409 on plans that pay defined benefits. Misconduct by the administrators of a defined benefit plan will not affect an individual's entitlement to a defined benefit unless it creates or enhances the risk of default by the entire plan. It was that default risk that prompted Congress to require defined benefit plans (but not defined contribution plans) to satisfy complex minimum funding requirements, and to make premium payments to the Pension Benefit Guaranty Corporation for plan termination insurance.

For defined contribution plans, however, fiduciary misconduct need not threaten the solvency of the entire plan to reduce benefits below the amount that participants would otherwise receive. Whether a fiduciary breach diminishes plan assets payable to all participants and beneficiaries, or only to persons tied to particular individual accounts, it creates the kind of harms that concerned the draftsmen of § 409. Consequently, our references to the "entire plan" in *Russell*, which accurately reflect the operation of § 409 in the defined benefit context, are beside the point in the defined contribution context. . . .

We therefore hold that although § 502(a)(2) does not provide a remedy for individual injuries distinct from plan injuries, that provision does authorize recovery for fiduciary breaches that impair the value of plan assets in a participant's individual account. Accordingly, the judgment of the Court of Appeals is vacated, and the case is remanded for further proceedings consistent with this opinion.

It is so ordered.

[The concurring opinions of CHIEF JUSTICE ROBERTS, joined by JUSTICE KENNEDY, and JUSTICE THOMAS, with whom JUSTICE SCALIA joins, are omitted].

NOTES

1.   **The Significance of *LaRue*.** The Court's decision may seem rather ordinary given that it was both unanimous and short. This was also one of those decisions only the Supreme Court could render since it was necessary to distinguish a prior Supreme Court decision that appeared to be squarely on point. But the real significance of the *LaRue* decision is its connection to the rising number of breach of fiduciary duty claims that resulted when the economy weakened. While the *LaRue* decision has not caused the explosion in litigation, it has facilitated many of the claims since the Supreme Court approved of claims to recover losses in individual accounts. Those cases are discussed below.

2.   **Litigation After *LaRue*.** Most of the early cases applying the *LaRue* decision were in the context of former employees. Prior to the *LaRue* decision, it was an open question whether a former employee was still considered a "participant" for purposes of pursuing a claim for breach of fiduciary duty under ERISA. Since *LaRue*, courts have generally held that former employees can bring such claims. *See Evans v. Akers*, 534 F.3d 65, 71 (1st Cir. 2008); *In re Mutual Funds Investment Litigation*, 529 F.3d 207, 215 (4th Cir. 2008); *Nichols v. Alcatel USA, Inc.*, 532 F.3d 364, 376 (5th Cir. 2008). More recently, several courts have considered whether class action claims were permissible even though the losses were suffered by individual plan participants. In vacating two class certification orders on the basis of a lack of typicality while remanding for additional proceedings, the Seventh Circuit stated: "Nothing we have said should be understood as ruling out the possibility of class treatment for one or more better defined and more targeted classes." *Spano v. Boeing Co.*, 633 F.3d 574, 588 (7th Cir. 2011). The court went on, however, to note that, "[T]here is no denying the fact that a greater number of

issues will be suitable for class treatment in a defined benefit plan than will be in a defined contribution plan." *Id.* at 591. *See also In Re Schering Plough Corp. ERISA Litigation*, 589 F.3d 585, 605 (3d Cir. 2009) (vacating class certification and remanding for more rigorous analysis of whether class representatives satisfied typicality requirement among other issues).

FIFTH THIRD BANCORP v. DUDENHOEFFER
Supreme Court of the United States
134 S. Ct. 2459 (2014)

JUSTICE BREYER delivered the opinion of the Court.

The Employee Retirement Income Security Act of 1974 (ERISA), 29 U.S.C. § 1001 *et seq.*, requires the fiduciary of a pension plan to act prudently in managing the plan's assets. § 1104(a)(1)(B). This case focuses upon that duty of prudence as applied to the fiduciary of an "employee stock ownership plan" (ESOP), a type of pension plan that invests primarily in the stock of the company that employs the plan participants.

We consider whether, when an ESOP fiduciary's decision to buy or hold the employer's stock is challenged in court, the fiduciary is entitled to a defense-friendly standard that the lower courts have called a "presumption of prudence." The Courts of Appeals that have considered the question have held that such a presumption does apply, with the presumption generally defined as a requirement that the plaintiff make a showing that would not be required in an ordinary duty-of-prudence case, such as that the employer was on the brink of collapse.

We hold that no such presumption applies. Instead, ESOP fiduciaries are subject to the same duty of prudence that applies to ERISA fiduciaries in general, except that they need not diversify the fund's assets. § 1104(a)(2).

I

Petitioner Fifth Third Bancorp, a large financial services firm, maintains for its employees a defined-contribution retirement savings plan. Employees may choose to contribute a portion of their compensation to the Plan as retirement savings, and Fifth Third provides matching contributions of up to 4% of an employee's compensation. The Plan's assets are invested in 20 separate funds, including mutual funds and an ESOP. Plan participants can allocate their contributions among the funds however they like; Fifth Third's matching contributions, on the other hand, are always invested initially in the ESOP, though the participant can then choose to move them to another fund. The Plan requires the ESOP's funds to be "invested primarily in shares of common stock of Fifth Third." App. 350.

Respondents, who are former Fifth Third employees and ESOP participants, filed this putative class action in Federal District Court in Ohio. They claim that petitioners, Fifth Third and various Fifth Third officers, were fiduciaries of the Plan and violated the duties of loyalty and prudence imposed by ERISA. *See* §§ 1109(a), 1132(a)(2). We limit our review to the duty-of-prudence claims.

The complaint alleges that by July 2007, the fiduciaries knew or should have known that Fifth Third's stock was overvalued and excessively risky for two separate reasons. First, publicly available information such as newspaper articles provided early warning signs that subprime lending, which formed a large part of Fifth Third's business, would soon leave creditors high and dry as the housing market collapsed and subprime borrowers became unable to pay off their mortgages. Second, nonpublic information (which petitioners knew because they were Fifth Third insiders) indicated that Fifth Third officers had deceived the market by making material misstatements about the company's financial prospects. Those misstatements led the market to overvalue Fifth Third stock—the ESOP's primary investment—and so petitioners, using the participants' money, were consequently paying more for that stock than it was worth.

The complaint further alleges that a prudent fiduciary in petitioners' position would have responded to this information in one or more of the following ways: (1) by selling the ESOP's holdings of Fifth Third stock before the value of those holdings declined, (2) by refraining from purchasing any more Fifth Third stock, (3) by canceling the Plan's ESOP option, and (4) by disclosing the inside information so that the market would adjust its valuation of Fifth Third stock downward and the ESOP would no longer be overpaying for it.

Rather than follow any of these courses of action, petitioners continued to hold and buy Fifth Third stock. Then the market crashed, and Fifth Third's stock price fell by 74% between July 2007 and September 2009, when the complaint was filed. Since the ESOP's funds were invested primarily in Fifth Third stock, this fall in price eliminated a large part of the retirement savings that the participants had invested in the ESOP. (The stock has since made a partial recovery to around half of its July 2007 price.)

The District Court dismissed the complaint for failure to state a claim. 757 F. Supp. 2d 753 (SD Ohio 2010). The court began from the premise that where a lawsuit challenges ESOP fiduciaries' investment decisions, "the plan fiduciaries start with a presumption that their decision to remain invested in employer securities was reasonable." Id., at 758. The court next held that this rule is applicable at the pleading stage and then concluded that the complaint's allegations were insufficient to overcome it. 757 F. Supp. 2d, at 758–759, 760–762. The Court of Appeals for the Sixth Circuit reversed, . . . [holding] that the presumption is evidentiary only and therefore does not apply at the pleading stage, [and] the allegations in the complaint were sufficient to state a claim for breach of fiduciary duty. 692 F.3d 410, 418–19 (2012). In light of differences among the Courts of Appeals as to the nature of the presumption of prudence applicable to ESOP fiduciaries, we granted the fiduciaries' petition for certiorari. . . .

II

A

In applying a "presumption of prudence" that favors ESOP fiduciaries' purchasing or holding of employer stock, the lower courts have sought to reconcile congressional directives that are in some tension with each other. On the one hand, ERISA itself subjects pension plan fiduciaries to a duty of prudence. In a section titled "Fiduciary duties," it says:

> "(a) Prudent man standard of care
>
> (1) Subject to *sections* 1103(c) and (d), 1342, and 1344 of this title, a fiduciary shall discharge his duties with respect to a plan solely in the interest of the participants and beneficiaries and—
>
> (A) for the exclusive purpose of:
>
> (i) providing benefits to participants and their beneficiaries; and
>
> (ii) defraying reasonable expenses of administering the plan;
>
> (B) with the care, skill, prudence, and diligence under the circumstances then prevailing that a prudent man acting in a like capacity and familiar with such matters would use in the conduct of an enterprise of a like character and with like aims;
>
> (C) by diversifying the investments of the plan so as to minimize the risk of large losses, unless under the circumstances it is clearly prudent not to do so; and
>
> (D) in accordance with the documents and instruments governing the plan insofar as such documents and instruments are consistent with the provisions of this subchapter and subchapter III of this chapter." § 1104.

On the other hand, Congress recognizes that ESOPs are "designed to invest primarily in" the stock of the participants' employer, § 1107(d)(6)(A), meaning that they are *not* prudently diversified. And it has written into law its "interest in encouraging" their use. . . . . Moench v. Robertson, 62 F.3d 553, 571 (1995). The Ninth Circuit has said that to "overcome the presumption of prudent investment, plaintiffs must . . . make allegations that clearly implicate the company's viability as an ongoing concern or show a precipitous decline in the employer's stock . . . combined with evidence that the company is on the brink of collapse or is undergoing serious mismanagement." *Quan v. Computer Sciences Corp.*, 623 F.3d 870, 882 (2010). . . .

Petitioners argue that the lower courts are right to apply a presumption of prudence, that it should apply from the pleading stage onward, and that the presumption should be strongly in favor of ESOP fiduciaries' purchasing and holding of employer stock. . . . We must decide whether ERISA contains some such presumption.

III

A

In our view, the law does not create a special presumption favoring ESOP fiduciaries. Rather, the same standard of prudence applies to all ERISA fiduciaries, including ESOP fiduciaries, except that an ESOP fiduciary is under no duty to diversify the ESOP's holdings. This conclusion follows from the pertinent provisions of ERISA, which are set forth above.

Section 1104(a)(1)(B) "imposes a 'prudent person' standard by which to measure fiduciaries' investment decisions and disposition of assets." *Massachusetts Mut. Life Ins. Co. v. Russell*, 473 U.S. 134, 143, n. 10 (1985). Section 1104(a)(1)(C) requires ERISA fiduciaries to diversify plan assets. And § 1104(a)(2) establishes the extent to which those duties are loosened in the ESOP context to ensure that employers are permitted and encouraged to offer ESOPs. Section 1104(a)(2) makes no reference to a special "presumption" in favor of ESOP fiduciaries. It does not require plaintiffs to allege that the employer was on the "brink of collapse," under "extraordinary circumstances," or the like. Instead, § 1104(a)(2) simply modifies the duties imposed by § 1104(a)(1) in a precisely delineated way: It provides that an ESOP fiduciary is exempt from § 1104(a)(1)(C)'s diversification requirement and also from § 1104(a)(1)(B)'s duty of prudence, but *"only to the extent that it requires diversification."* § 1104(a)(2) (emphasis added). . . .

B

Petitioners make several arguments to the contrary. First, petitioners argue that the special purpose of an ESOP—investing participants' savings in the stock of their employer—calls for a presumption that such investments are prudent. The[y argue] . . . that the "character" and "aims" of an ESOP differ from those of an ordinary retirement investment, such as a diversified mutual fund. An ordinary plan seeks (1) to maximize retirement savings for participants while (2) avoiding excessive risk. But an ESOP also seeks (3) to promote employee ownership of employer stock. . . . Thus, a claim that an ESOP fiduciary's investment in employer stock was imprudent as a way of securing retirement savings should be viewed unfavorably because, unless the company was about to go out of business, that investment was advancing the additional goal of employee ownership of employer stock.

We cannot accept the claim that underlies this argument, namely, that the content of ERISA's duty of prudence varies depending upon the specific nonpecuniary goal set out in an ERISA plan, such as what petitioners claim is the nonpecuniary goal here. Taken in context, § 1104(a)(1)(B)'s reference to "an enterprise of a like character and with like aims" means an enterprise with what the immediately preceding provision calls the "exclusive purpose" to be pursued by all ERISA fiduciaries: "providing benefits to participants and their beneficiaries" while "defraying reasonable expenses of administering the plan." §§ 1104(a)(1)(A)(i),(ii). Read in the context of ERISA as a whole, the term "benefits" in the provision just quoted must be understood to refer to the sort of *financial* benefits (such as retirement income) that trustees who manage investments typically seek to secure for the trust's beneficiaries. *Cf.* § 1002(2)(A) (defining "employee pension benefit plan" and "pension plan" to mean plans that provide employees with "retirement income" or other "deferral of income"). The term does not cover nonpecuniary benefits like those supposed to arise from employee ownership of employer stock.

Consider the statute's requirement that fiduciaries act in accordance with the documents and instruments governing the plan *"insofar as such documents and instruments are consistent with the provisions of this subchapter."* § 1104(a)(1)(D) (emphasis added). This provision makes clear that the duty of prudence trumps the instructions of a plan document, such as an instruction to invest exclusively in employer stock even if financial goals demand the contrary. *See also* § 1110(a) (With irrelevant exceptions, "any provision in an agreement or instrument which purports to relieve a fiduciary from responsibility . . . for any . . . duty under this part shall be void as against public policy"). This rule would make little sense if, as petitioners argue, the duty of prudence is defined by the aims of the particular plan as set out in the plan documents, since in that case the duty of prudence could never conflict with a plan document. . . .

Petitioners are right to point out that Congress, in seeking to permit and promote ESOPs, was pursuing purposes other than the financial security of plan participants. See, *e.g.*, Tax Reform Act of 1976, § 803(h), 90 Stat. 1590 (Congress intended ESOPs to help "secur[e] capital funds for necessary capital growth and . . . brin[g] about stock ownership by all corporate employees"). Congress pursued those purposes by promoting ESOPs with tax incentives. *See* 26 U.S.C. §§ 402(e)(4), 404(k), 1042. And it also pursued them by exempting ESOPs from ERISA's diversification requirement, which otherwise would have precluded their creation. 29 U.S.C. § 1104(a)(2). But we are not convinced that Congress *also* sought to promote ESOPs by further relaxing the duty of prudence as applied to ESOPs with the sort of presumption proposed by petitioners. . . .

Third, petitioners argue that subjecting ESOP fiduciaries to a duty of prudence without the protection of a special presumption will lead to conflicts with the legal prohibition on insider trading. The potential for conflict arises because ESOP fiduciaries often are company insiders and because suits against insider fiduciaries frequently allege, as the complaint in this case alleges, that the fiduciaries were imprudent in failing to act on inside information they had about the value of the employer's stock.

This concern is a legitimate one. But an ESOP-specific rule that a fiduciary does not act imprudently in buying or holding company stock unless the company is on the brink of collapse (or the like) is an ill-fitting means of addressing it. While ESOP fiduciaries may be more likely to have insider information about a company that the fund is investing in than are other ERISA fiduciaries, the potential for conflict with the securities laws would be the same for a non-ESOP fiduciary who had relevant inside information about a potential investment. . . . The potential for conflict therefore does not persuade us to accept a presumption of the sort adopted by the lower courts and proposed by petitioners. We discuss alternative means of dealing with the potential for conflict in Part IV, *infra*.

Finally, petitioners argue that, without some sort of special presumption, the threat of costly duty-of-prudence lawsuits will deter companies from offering

ESOPs to their employees, contrary to the stated intent of Congress. ESOP plans instruct their fiduciaries to invest in company stock, and § 1104(a)(1)(D) requires fiduciaries to follow plan documents so long as they do not conflict with ERISA. Thus, in many cases an ESOP fiduciary who fears that continuing to invest in company stock may be imprudent finds himself between a rock and a hard place: If he keeps investing and the stock goes down he may be sued for acting imprudently in violation of § 1104(a)(1)(B), but if he stops investing and the stock goes up he may be sued for disobeying the plan documents in violation of § 1104(a)(1)(D). Petitioners argue that, given the threat of such expensive litigation, ESOPs cannot thrive unless their fiduciaries are granted a defense-friendly presumption.

Petitioners are basically seeking relief from what they believe are meritless, economically burdensome lawsuits. We agree that Congress sought to encourage the creation of ESOPs. And we have recognized that "ERISA represents a ' "careful balancing" between ensuring fair and prompt enforcement of rights under a plan and the encouragement of the creation of such plans' " *Conkright v. Frommert*, 559 U.S. 506, 517 (2010) (quoting *Aetna Health Inc. v. Davila*, 542 U.S. 200, 215 (2004)). At the same time, we do not believe that the presumption at issue here is an appropriate way to weed out meritless lawsuits or to provide the requisite "balancing." The proposed presumption makes it impossible for a plaintiff to state a duty-of-prudence claim, no matter how meritorious, unless the employer is in very bad economic circumstances. Such a rule does not readily divide the plausible sheep from the meritless goats. That important task can be better accomplished through careful, context-sensitive scrutiny of a complaint's allegations. We consequently stand by our conclusion that the law does not create a special presumption of prudence for ESOP fiduciaries.

IV

We consider more fully one important mechanism for weeding out meritless claims, the motion to dismiss for failure to state a claim. That mechanism, which gave rise to the lower court decisions at issue here, requires careful judicial consideration of whether the complaint states a claim that the defendant has acted imprudently. *See* Fed. Rule Civ. Proc. 12(b)(6); *Ashcroft v. Iqbal*, 556 U.S. 662, 677–680 (2009). Because the content of the duty of prudence turns on "the circumstances . . . prevailing" at the time the fiduciary acts, § 1104(a)(1)(B), the appropriate inquiry will necessarily be context specific.

The District Court in this case granted petitioners' motion to dismiss the complaint because it held that respondents could not overcome the presumption of prudence. The Court of Appeals, by contrast, concluded that no presumption applied. And we agree with that conclusion. The Court of Appeals, however, went on to hold that respondents had stated a plausible duty-of-prudence claim. 692 F.3d, at 419–420. The arguments made here, along with our review of the record, convince us that the judgment of the Court of Appeals should be vacated and the case remanded. On remand, the Court of Appeals should apply the pleading standard as discussed in *Twombly* and *Iqbal* in light of the following considerations.

A

Respondents allege that, as of July 2007, petitioners knew or should have known in light of publicly available information, such as newspaper articles, that continuing to hold and purchase Fifth Third stock was imprudent. The complaint alleges, among other things, that petitioners "continued to allow the Plan's investment in Fifth Third Stock even during the time that the stock price was declining in value as a result of [the] collapse of the housing market" and that "[a] prudent fiduciary facing similar circumstances would not have stood idly by as the Plan's assets were decimated." App. at 53.

In our view, where a stock is publicly traded, allegations that a fiduciary should have recognized from publicly available information alone that the market was over—or undervaluing the stock are implausible as a general rule, at least in the absence of special circumstances. Many investors take the view that " 'they have little hope of outperforming the market in the long run based solely on their analysis of publicly available information,' " and accordingly they " 'rely on the security's market price as an unbiased assessment of the security's value in light of all public information.' " *Halliburton Co. v. Erica P. John Fund, Inc.*, 189 L. Ed. 2d 339 (2014) (quoting *Amgen Inc. v. Conn. Ret. Plans & Trust Funds*, 133 S. Ct. 1184, 1192 (2013)). ERISA fiduciaries, who likewise could reasonably see "little hope of outperforming the market . . . based solely on their analysis of publicly available information," *ibid.*, may, as a general matter, likewise prudently rely on the market price.

In other words, a fiduciary usually "is not imprudent to assume that a major stock market . . . provides the best estimate of the value of the stocks traded on it that is available to him." *Summers v. State Street Bank & Trust Co.*, 453 F.3d 404, 408 (CA7 2006); cf. *Quan*, 623 F.3d, at 881 ("Fiduciaries are not expected to predict the future of the company stock's performance").

We do not here consider whether a plaintiff could nonetheless plausibly allege imprudence on the basis of publicly available information by pointing to a special circumstance affecting the reliability of the market price as " 'an unbiased assessment of the security's value in light of all public information,' " *Halliburton Co.*, *supra*, at 354, 2014 U.S. LEXIS 4305, *27 (quoting *Amgen Inc.*, 133 S. Ct. 1184, 1192), that would make reliance on the market's valuation imprudent. In this case, the Court of Appeals held that the complaint stated a claim because respondents "allege that Fifth Third engaged in lending practices that were equivalent to participation in the subprime lending market, that Defendants were aware of the risks of such investments by the start of the class period, and that such risks made Fifth Third stock an imprudent investment." 692 F.3d, at 419–420. The Court of Appeals did not point to any special circumstance rendering reliance on the market price imprudent. The court's decision to deny dismissal therefore appears to have been based on an erroneous understanding of the prudence of relying on market prices.

B

Respondents also claim that petitioners behaved imprudently by failing to act on the basis of *nonpublic* information that was available to them because they were Fifth Third insiders. In particular, the complaint alleges that petitioners had inside information indicating that the market was overvaluing Fifth Third stock and that they could have used this information to prevent losses to the fund by (1) selling the ESOP's holdings of Fifth Third stock; (2) refraining from future stock purchases (including by removing the Plan's ESOP option altogether); or (3) publicly disclosing the inside information so that the market would correct the stock price downward, with the result that the ESOP could continue to buy Fifth Third stock without paying an inflated price for it. *See* App. 17, 88–89, 113.

To state a claim for breach of the duty of prudence on the basis of inside information, a plaintiff must plausibly allege an alternative action that the defendant could have taken that would have been consistent with the securities laws and that a prudent fiduciary in the same circumstances would not have viewed as more likely to harm the fund than to help it. The following three points inform the requisite analysis.

First, in deciding whether the complaint states a claim upon which relief can be granted, courts must bear in mind that the duty of prudence, under ERISA as under the common law of trusts, does not require a fiduciary to break the law. *Cf.* Restatement (Second) of Trusts § 166, Comment a ("The trustee is not under a duty to the beneficiary to do an act which is criminal or tortious"). Federal securities laws "are violated when a corporate insider trades in the securities of his corporation on the basis of material, nonpublic information." *United States v. O'Hagan*, 521 U.S. 642, 651–652 (1997). . . . To the extent that the Sixth Circuit denied dismissal based on the theory that the duty of prudence required petitioners to sell the ESOP's holdings of Fifth Third stock, its denial of dismissal was erroneous.

Second, where a complaint faults fiduciaries for failing to decide, on the basis of the inside information, to refrain from making additional stock purchases or for failing to disclose that information to the public so that the stock would no longer be overvalued, additional considerations arise. The courts should consider the extent to which an ERISA-based obligation either to refrain on the basis of inside information from making a planned trade or to disclose inside information to the public could conflict with the complex insider trading and corporate disclosure requirements imposed by the federal securities laws or with the objectives of those laws. *Cf.* 29 U.S.C. § 1144(d) ("Nothing in this subchapter [which includes § 1104] shall be construed to alter, amend, modify, invalidate, impair, or supersede any law of the United States . . . or any rule or regulation issued under any such law"); *Varity Corp.*, 516 U.S., at 506 (reserving the question 'whether ERISA fiduciaries have any fiduciary duty to disclose truthful information on their own initiative, or in response to employee inquiries"). The U.S. Securities and Exchange Commission has not advised us of its views on these matters, and we believe those views may well be relevant.

Third, lower courts faced with such claims should also consider whether the complaint has plausibly alleged that a prudent fiduciary in the defendant's position could not have concluded that stopping purchases—which the market might take as a sign that insider fiduciaries viewed the employer's stock as a bad investment—or publicly disclosing negative information would do more harm than good to the fund by causing a drop in the stock price and a concomitant drop in the value of the stock already held by the fund.

* * * *

We leave it to the courts below to apply the foregoing to the complaint in this case in the first instance. The judgment of the Court of Appeals for the Sixth Circuit is vacated and the case is remanded for further proceedings consistent with this opinion.

It is so ordered.

NOTES

1.   **"Stock Drop Cases."** The *Fifth Third Bank* case has potentially shifted the landscape in the stock drop cases—cases in which employees sue fiduciaries when the price of employer stock declines significantly. Over the last decade, there has been a tremendous uptick in litigation involving such claims, though most have failed, largely due to the "presumption of prudence" now firmly rejected by the Supreme Court. However, in the latter part of the opinion, the Court also rejected some common claims by plaintiffs: (1) that the fiduciary should have acted on inside information, knowing that the price was likely to decline and (2) that the fiduciary should not be required to take into account publicly available information other than price information as a guide to whether the investment is prudent. As a result, it is possible that the results—most claims fail at the motion to dismiss stage—will remain the same but for different reasons. For a comprehensive discussion of the litigation that has occurred prior to *Fifth Third Bank*, see Jose Martin Jara, *What Is the Correct Standard of Prudence in Employer Stock Cases?* 45 J. MARSHALL L. REV. 541 (2012). The cases involving declining stock prices are cyclical in nature and with a strengthening economy, new cases have trailed off, although a substantial volume of cases remain in the courts. Plan fiduciaries have also, on occasion, been sued when the plan sells stock after price decreases with the plaintiffs contending that the fiduciaries should have waited until the stock rebounded rather than selling at a low point. These cases likewise generally have failed. *See, e.g., Bunch v. W.R. Grace & Co.*, 555 F.3d 1 (1st Cir. 2009) (dismissing claim that fiduciary should not have sold stock while company was in bankruptcy). In case you were wondering, the name Fifth Third Bank arose as a result of the turn of the century merger between the Third and Fifth National Banks, both of which were apparently located in Cincinnati.

2.   **ESOPs**. Although the presumption of prudence applied to individual employment account plans, the *Fifth Third Bank* case involved an ESOP or Employee Stock Ownership Plan. These plans are designed to promote employee ownership and estimates are that there are 7,000 such companies with more than 13.5 million employees, as of 2014. *See* National Center for Employee Ownership, *available at* www.esop.org. Some well known ESOPS include Publix Markets with more than 160,000 employees, Davey Tree Expert and King Arthur Flour. ESOPs are

tax-advantaged devices that are complex in their nature; there are also several different kinds of ESOPs some of which, like those noted above, provide greater employer ownership than others. However, a common feature of ESOPS, as discussed in *Fifth Third Bank*, is that they concentrate worker retirement savings in the company. The details of ESOPs are beyond the scope of this book but for a detailed article that explores the application of ERISA to ESOPs, see Lauren E. Berson & Nicholas L. Cushing, *Safeguarding Employee Stock Ownership Plans: Insurance as Assurance*, 26 HOFSTRA LAB. & EMP. L.J. 539 (2009).

3.   The Prudent Investor. A central duty imposed upon fiduciaries is that they act with prudence. Outside of the employer-stock context, the duty is typically described as that of a prudent investor. One court has summarized the duties as follows:

> Under ERISA, a fiduciary is required to act with the care, skill, prudence and diligence . . . that a prudent man acting in a like capacity and familiar with such matters would use. The test of prudence—the Prudent Man Rule—is one of conduct, and not a test of the result of performance of the investment. Whether a fiduciary's actions are prudent cannot be measured in hindsight. The test is how the fiduciary acted viewed from the perspective of the challenged decision rather than from the vantage point of hindsight.

Bunch v. W.R. Grace & Co., 555 F.3d 1, 16 (1st Cir. 2009) (citations and quotation marks omitted).

4.   Excessive Fee Litigation. The other area that has seen a significant increase over the last few years in connection with retirement plans involves claims that fiduciaries breached their duties by providing investment choices that had excessive fees. In *Hecker v. Deere Co.*, 556 F.3d 575 (7th Cir. 2009), *cert. denied*, 558 U.S. 1148 (2010), the plaintiffs alleged that the Deere company had violated "its fiduciary duty by selecting investment options with excessive fees." *Id.* at 586. They argued that Deere should have been able to negotiate lower fees given the volume of business it was providing and that it could have reduced fees by offering plans from more than a single company (Deere relied on the Fidelity company to provide a wide range of fund options). The court rejected the claims because the company had met the standard of prudence that guides investment decisions. The court also concluded that the safe harbor provision that "provides to Plan Fiduciaries a 'Safe Harbor' from liability for losses that a participant suffers in his or her 401(k) accounts to the extent that the participant exercises control over the assets in his or her 401(k) accounts" was satisfied. *Id.* at 588. Most courts have reached similar conclusions. *See, e.g., Renfro v. Unisys Corp.*, 671 F.3d 314 (3d Cir. 2011) (affirming dismissal of claims including for excessive fees); *Loomis v. Exelon Corp.*, 658 F.3d 667 (7th Cir. 2011) (affirming dismissal of claims for imprudent investment choices and excessive fees). If this is an area of interest for you, the *Exelon* case was written by JUDGE EASTERBROOK and includes an entertaining discussion of the benefits of participant-directed retirement plans. More recently, plaintiffs' class actions have made some headway on their litigation. In *Tussey v. ABB, Inc.*, 746 F.3d 327 (8th Cir. 2014), the Court upheld a district court's determination that the plan fiduciaries had paid excessive fees with respect to recordkeeping, and noted that the claims included allegations of wrongdoing. The Ninth Circuit has also recently upheld a lower court determination that plan fiduciaries violated their duties by relying entirely on an outside advisor for investment advice without exploring the possibility of obtaining lower fees through institutional as opposed to retail mutual funds. *See Tibble v. Edison Int'l*, 729 F.3d 1110 (9th Cir. 2013). At the same time, the court rejected a number of the plaintiffs' claims, including with respect to revenue sharing and challenged investments. It is noteworthy that both of these decisions followed trials rather than dismissals. Petitions for *certiorari* were pending in the *Tribble* case at the time this edition went to press.

5. Employees as Investors. The shift from defined benefit plans to defined contribution plans is all but complete. Outside of union and government workplaces, employees today are unlikely to be enrolled in a defined benefit plan and are, as a result, responsible for their own retirement savings. This shift, which was generally welcomed during strong economic times, is now the source of great concern that individuals will be left with inadequate resources to support their retirement. Two commentators summarized some of the concerns this way:

> Although workers in theory could accumulate substantial pension wealth under 401(k) plans, in practice they do not. Balances—even for long-service employees—are substantially less than those produced by even the most sophisticated simulations. The reason for these low balances appears to be that the entire burden is on employees, and they make mistakes at every step along the way. A quarter of those eligible to participate in a plan fail to do so. Less than 10 percent of those who do participate contribute the maximum. Over half fail to diversify their investments, many overinvest in company stock, and almost none rebalance their portfolios in response to age or market returns. Most important, many take cash when they change employers. And few annuitize at retirement.

Samuel Estreicher & Laurence Gold, *The Shift from Defined Benefit Plans to Defined Contribution Plans*, 11 LEWIS & CLARK L. REV. 331 (2007). One significant problem is that too few employees enroll in plans. Many employers now have what are known as automatic enrollment plans where employees are automatically enrolled in pension plans rather than having to sign up for the plan. This change alone can increase participation substantially. One study of 50 automatic enrollment plans found dramatic increases in enrollment among new employees, from 45% participation to 86%. The study also found that the increase was greatest among low-wage and younger employees, and that most new employees opted for the company's default investment option. *See* Vanguard Center for Retirement Research, MEASURING THE EFFECTIVENESS OF AUTOMATIC ENROLLMENT, Dec. 2007, at 4–5. Two researchers have highlighted a potential unintended effect of the automatic enrollment plans when their study of such plans found that employers tended to lower their own contribution rates so while more employees may join such plans they may ultimately receive lower employer contributions. *See* Mauricio Soto & Barbara Butrica, *Will Automatic Enrollments Reduce Employer Contributions TO 401(K) Plans?*, Urban Institute Report, Dec. 2009.

The other primary concern is that employees are poor investors. One reason for this is that they often do not have adequate information to make sound investment choices, and until recently employers typically provided no investment information due to a concern that providing information might lead to additional lawsuits. Some changes put in place by the Pension Protection Act of 2006 are designed to create incentives for employers to provide greater investment information. As suggested in the excerpt above, employees also make poor investment choices. For example, Susan Stabile has documented that employees significantly overinvest in employer stock when they are given the opportunity, and they do so for fairly well-documented flaws in investor behavior. *See* Susan J. Stabile, *The Behavior of Defined Contribution Plan Participants*, 77 N.Y.U. L. REV. 71, 92–93 (2002) (explaining that employees typically overinvest in company stock due to overconfidence and loyalty). Marion Crain has noted that some of the investment behavior is attributable to employers' internal branding programs that are designed to intensify employees' loyalty, which then translates into higher investments in the firm. *See* Marion Crain, *Managing Identity: Buying into the Brand at Work*, 95 IOWA L. REV. 1179 (2010). If we know that many employees will make improper investments (for example, a basic tenet of prudent investing would call for no more than 5–10% investment in any one stock), is there reason to regulate their investment behavior, or is employee autonomy a more important value? How do pensions compare to health insurance? One of the rationales for maintaining employer-based health insurance—and now rendering it mandatory—was a concern that, left on their own, employees might opt to forego health insurance altogether. Is there a similar rationale that might counsel in favor of regulating employee investments? There have been many calls for reform including requiring that employees have access to basic diversified portfolios to invest in. For a discussion of many of the issues relating to pensions see Jacob S. Hacker, *The Great Risk Shift: The Assault on American Jobs, Families, Health Care & Retirement and How You Can Fight Back* (2006); Stephen F. Befort, *The Perfect Storm of Retirement Insecurity: Fixing the Three-Legged Stool of Social Security, Pensions and Personal Savings*, 91 MINN. L. REV. 938 (2007).

If the current system proves inadequate to provide sufficient retirement income, there could be significant social costs as well. Individuals who are unable to retire may attempt to stay in the workforce, and others may be forced to come out of retirement to earn sufficient income to live on. In either case, these workers may crowd out others and may also suppress wages through increased competition, particularly in the service sector. The aging of the workforce could also lead to increased litigation over issues relating to age discrimination, as employers may be less able to induce retirement through buy-outs and more exposed to litigation regarding terminations of older workers.

6. Disability and Life Insurance Plans. In addition to health and pension plans, ERISA often comes into play with respect to Disability and Life Insurance plans. Many employers offer their employees Disability or Life Insurance plans, but the plans are only covered by ERISA to the extent the plan was offered with "an expressed intention by the employer to provide benefits on a regular and long term basis." *Wickman v. Nw. Nat'l Ins. Co.*, 908 F.2d 1077, 1083 (1st Cir. 1990). This typically requires the employer to pay some part of the benefit and to make it regularly available. When disputes arise over these ERISA-covered plans, they are primarily contract disputes with the insurance plans providing the terms of the agreements. *See Heimeshoff v. Hartford Life & Accident Ins. Co.*, 134 S. Ct. 604 (2013) (holding that ERISA plan and participant can contractually agree to a limitations period absent a controlling statutory provision). In these cases, courts typically review the benefit decisions *de novo*, unless the plan specifically provides the plan administrator with discretion to make the benefit decisions. *See Firestone Tire & Rubber Co. v. Bruch*, 489 U.S. 101, 115 (1989). The district court's determination is also reviewed *de novo*, so these cases can generate a substantial amount of litigation. For two recent examples, see *Johnson v. American United Life Ins.*, 716 F.3d 813 (4th Cir. 2013) (determining that death that resulted from drunk driving was an "accident" under the terms of an accidental death policy and thus covered under that policy); *Colby v. Union Security Ins. Co.*, 705 F.3d 58 (1st Cir. 2013) (finding that a risk of relapse due to an addiction can constitute a disability under the terms of a long-term disability policy).

Chapter 13

HEALTH AND SAFETY

Ensuring the safety of workers has long been of paramount importance, and many labor strikes or work stoppages have resulted over unsafe worker conditions. Workplace conditions have changed dramatically since the publication of Upton Sinclair's *The Jungle* in 1906, undoubtedly the most famous work highlighting just how dangerous many workplaces had become. Even so, workplace injuries, illnesses, and fatalities remain a stubborn fact of the employment sphere.

According to the Bureau of Labor Statistics, there were 4,628 fatal workplace injuries and nearly 3.8 million nonfatal injuries and illnesses in public and private industry in 2012. (These are the numbers reported by the Bureau, and many believe they underestimate the number of actual injuries, and particularly illnesses which are often difficult to trace directly to workplace exposures.) The number of fatalities has declined over the last couple of decades from a high of 6,632 in 1994, and is well below the 70,000 annual deaths that occurred in the years prior to the passage of the Occupational Safety and Health Act in 1970 ("the Act"). The most frequent causes of fatalities are transportation accidents, violent assaults, falls, and "contact with objects and equipment." Of the 3 million nonfatal injuries in private industry in 2012, about one-half resulted in lost time from work or a job transfer or restriction. The median time away from work for nonfatal injuries was nine days. For these and other statistics on workplace injury, illness and fatality statistics, see the reports posted on the United States Department of Labor website, http://www.osha.gov/oshstats/work.html.

There are two comprehensive regulatory systems designed to prevent and remedy workplace injuries. The Workers' Compensation system developed in the early twentieth century in response to rising rates of industrial accidents and their devastating economic consequences for workers disabled or killed on the job and their dependents. Workers' Compensation is a state-based scheme mandating that employers insure their workers against accidental injuries. The state statutes generally provide a modest benefit for injured workers or their surviving families without requiring them to prove employer fault. *[workers comp]*

While state Workers' Compensation laws are directed at providing income support for the victims of industrial accidents, the federal Occupational Safety and Health Act of 1970 seeks to prevent occupational injury and disease through direct regulation of working conditions. The Act created the Occupational Health and Safety Administration ("OSHA") within the Department of Labor, which is an agency designed to prevent workplace injuries with a broad mandate to "assure so far as possible every working man and woman in the nation safe and healthful working conditions. . . ." 29 U.S.C. § 651(c). In this chapter we will discuss both of *[OSHA]* these regulatory systems and explore whether they have succeeded in their missions.

A. WORKERS' COMPENSATION

1. The Origins of Workers' Compensation Laws

Around the turn of the 20th century, the United States was in the midst of what John Fabian Witt has called "an accident crisis." JOHN FABIAN WITT, THE ACCIDENTAL REPUBLIC: CRIPPLED WORKINGMEN, DESTITUTE WIDOWS, AND THE REMAKING OF AMERICAN LAW 2 (2004). As he describes,

> Workplace injuries were far and away the leading category of accidental injury and death in turn-of-the-century America, representing close to one-third of all accidental deaths and, by contemporary estimates, between one-half and two-thirds of all accidental injuries. . . . In 1890, railroad worker death rates were 314 per 100,000 workers per year. In that same year, coal miner fatality rates were comparable, ranging from 215 deaths per 100,000 workers per year in bituminous coal mines to 300 deaths per 100,000 workers per year in anthracite coal mines. Certain subsets of workers in these dangerous industries had even higher rates of accidental death. Trainmen, whose jobs required that they operate the coupling devices between cars, and brakemen, who operated the train's handbrakes, died in work-related accidents at rates of 900 and 1,141 deaths per 100,000 workers per year, respectively. . . .

> High work-accident rates led many contemporaries to think about the relationship between industrialization and accidents. Nineteenth-century observers believed both that the number of accidental injuries was increasing rapidly and that the cause of the increase was the mechanization of production. . . . Industrialization, in short, had devised myriad new and unfamiliar mechanisms for inflicting harm on the human body. . . .

> [T]he industrial accident emerged in the United States as among the most visible of social ills. For one thing, work accidents seemed to pose an especially acute problem in some of the leading occupations of the new industrial economy. Workplace accidents were the leading cause of incapacity among working-age men in railroad work, mining, logging and timber work, and bricklaying and masonry. . . . Industrial accidents also disproportionately affected wage-earning men supporting dependent wives and children. . . . Families were thus thrown by the accidental injury of a male wage-earner into the ranks of the "dispossessed," "pawning their furniture," "using up what little savings bank account they have had," and "obligated to turn in humiliation and permanent injury to the charitable societies or to relatives and friends." . . . Work accidents, it seemed, threw the ambiguous status of the industrial wage worker into bold relief, compelling victim and observer alike to ask hard questions about the relationships among capital, labor, and the public.

For all these reasons, many believed by the end of the first decade of the twentieth century that industrial accidents were one of the most important issues in American public life.

Id. at 27–28, 37–38.

a. The Common Law Approach

Prior to enactment of workers' compensation laws in the United States in the early twentieth century, the only recourse for injured workers or their survivors was a lawsuit to try to recover damages. The most immediate concern of the injured worker or his surviving family was to find some means of support to replace the lost wages. The tort system, however, was costly and slow, and the availability of damages turned on questions of fault and causation, not need. The following case illustrates some of the difficulties faced by workers in the 19th century who sought recovery from their employers for injuries sustained on the job.

FARWELL v. THE BOSTON AND WORCESTER RAIL ROAD CORP.
Supreme Judicial Court of Massachusetts
45 Mass. 49 (1842)

Shaw, C.J.

This is an action of new impression in our courts, and involves a principle of great importance. It presents a case, where two persons are in the service and employment of one company, whose business it is to construct and maintain a railroad, and to employ their trains of cars to carry persons and merchandize for hire. They are appointed and employed by the same company to perform separate duties and services, all tending to the accomplishment of one and the same purpose—that of the safe and rapid transmission of the trains; and they are paid for their respective services according to the nature of their respective duties, and the labor and skill required for their proper performance. The question is, whether, for damages sustained by one of the persons so employed, by means of the carelessness and negligence of another, the party injured has a remedy against the common employer. It is an argument against such an action, though certainly not a decisive one, that no such action has before been maintained.

It is laid down by Blackstone, that if a servant, by his negligence, does any damage to a stranger, the master shall be answerable for his neglect. But the damage must be done while he is actually employed in the master's service; otherwise, the servant shall answer for his own misbehavior. This rule is obviously founded on the great principle of social duty, that every man, in the management of his own affairs, whether by himself or by his agents or servants, shall so conduct them as not to injure another; and if he does not, and another thereby sustains damage, he shall answer for it. If done by a servant, in the course of his employment, and acting within the scope of his authority, it is considered, in contemplation of law, so far the act of the master, that the latter shall be answerable *civiliter*. But this presupposes that the parties stand to each other in the relation of strangers, between whom there is no privity; and the action, in such case, is an action sounding in tort. The form is trespass on the case, for the consequential damage. The maxim *respondeat superior* is adopted in that case, from general considerations of policy and security.

But this does not apply to the case of a servant bringing his action against his own employer to recover damages for an injury arising in the course of that employment, where all such risks and perils as the employer and the servant respectively intend to assume and bear may be regulated by the express or implied contract between them, and which, in contemplation of law, must be presumed to be thus regulated.

. . . [I]t was conceded, that the claim could not be placed on the principle indicated by the maxim respondeat superior, which binds the master to indemnify a stranger for the damage caused by the careless, negligent or unskillful act of his servant in the conduct of his affairs. The claim, therefore, is placed, and must be maintained, if maintained at all, on the ground of contract. As there is no express contract between the parties, applicable to this point, it is placed on the footing of an implied contract of indemnity, arising out of the relation of master and servant. It would be an implied promise, arising from the duty of the master to be responsible to each person employed by him, in the conduct of every branch of business, where two or more persons are employed, to pay for all damage occasioned by the negligence of every other person employed in the same service. If such a duty were established by law—like that of a common carrier, to stand to all losses of goods not caused by the act of God or of a public enemy—or that of an innkeeper, to be responsible, in like manner, for the baggage of his guests; it would be a rule of frequent and familiar occurrence, and its existence and application, with all its qualifications and restrictions, would be settled by judicial precedents. But we are of opinion that no such rule has been established, and the authorities, as far as they go, are opposed to the principle.

The general rule, resulting from considerations as well of justice as of policy, is, that he who engages in the employment of another for the performance of specified duties and services, for compensation, takes upon himself the natural and ordinary risks and perils incident to the performance of such services, and in legal presumption, the compensation is adjusted accordingly. And we are not aware of any principle which should except the perils arising from the carelessness and negligence of those who are in the same employment. These are perils which the servant is as likely to know, and against which he can as effectually guard, as the master. They are perils incident to the service, and which can be as distinctly foreseen and provided for in the rate of compensation as any others. To say that the master shall be responsible because the damage is caused by his agents, is assuming the very point which remains to be proved. They are his agents to some extent, and for some purposes; but whether he is responsible, in a particular case, for their negligence, is not decided by the single fact that they are, for some purposes, his agents. . . .

If we look from considerations of justice to those of policy, they will strongly lead to the same conclusion. In considering the rights and obligations arising out of particular relations, it is competent for courts of justice to regard considerations of policy and general convenience, and to draw from them such rules as will, in their practical application, best promote the safety and security of all parties concerned. This is, in truth, the basis on which implied promises are raised, being duties legally inferred from a consideration of what is best adapted to promote the benefit of all persons concerned, under given circumstances. To take the well known and familiar cases already cited; a common carrier, without regard to actual fault or neglect in himself or his servants, is made liable for all losses of goods confided to him for carriage, except those caused by the act of God or of a public enemy, because he can best guard them against all minor dangers, and because, in case of actual loss, it would be extremely difficult for the owner to adduce proof of embezzlement, or other actual fault or neglect on the part of the carrier, although it may have been the real cause of the loss. The risk is therefore thrown upon the carrier, and he receives, in the form of payment for the carriage, a premium for the risk which he thus assumes. . . .

We are of opinion that these considerations apply strongly to the case in question. Where several persons are employed in the conduct of one common enterprise or undertaking, and the safety of each depends much on the care and skill with which each other shall perform his appropriate duty, each is an observer of the conduct of the others, can give notice of any misconduct, incapacity or neglect of duty, and leave the service, if the common employer will not take such precautions, and employ such agents as the safety of the whole party may require. By these means, the safety of each will be much more effectually secured, than could be done by a resort to the common employer for indemnity in case of loss by the negligence of each other. Regarding it in this light, it is the ordinary case of one sustaining an injury in the course of his own employment, in which he must bear the loss himself, or seek his remedy, if he have any, against the actual wrong-doer.

In applying these principles to the present case, it appears that the plaintiff was employed by the defendants as an engineer, at the rate of wages usually paid in that employment, being a higher rate than the plaintiff had before received as a machinist. It was a voluntary undertaking on his part, with a full knowledge of the risks incident to the employment; and the loss was sustained by means of an ordinary casualty, caused by the negligence of another servant of the company. Under these circumstances, the loss must be deemed to be the result of a pure accident, like those to which all men, in all employments, and at all times, are more or less exposed; and like similar losses from accidental causes, it must rest where it first fell, unless the plaintiff has a remedy against the person actually in default; of which we give no opinion.

It was strongly pressed in the argument, that although this might be so, where two or more servants are employed in the same department of duty, where each can exert some influence over the conduct of the other, and thus to some extent provide for his own security; yet that it could not apply where two or more are employed in different departments of duty, at a distance from each other, and where one can in no degree control or influence the conduct of another. But we think this is founded upon a supposed distinction, on which it would be extremely difficult to establish a practical rule. When the object to be accomplished is one and the same, when the employers are the same, and the several persons employed derive their authority and their compensation from the same source, it would be extremely difficult to distinguish, what constitutes one department and what a distinct department of duty. It would vary with the circumstances of every case. . . .

[S]upposing the accident to have occurred, and the loss to have been caused, by the negligence of the person employed to attend to and change the switch, in his not doing so in the particular case, the court are of opinion that it is a loss for which the defendants are not liable, and that the action cannot be maintained.

Plaintiff nonsuit.

NOTES

1. **Compensating for Injury.** According to the court in *Farwell*, why isn't the railroad responsible for injuries sustained by one employee as a result of the negligence of another employee under the theory of *respondeat superior*? What agreement existed between the parties regarding who would bear the costs of any on-the-job injuries? Could the worker have contracted with the railroad for payment in the case of injury? If not, how are the worker's interests in workplace safety protected?

2. **The Market Solution.** The court in *Farwell* suggests that the employment agreement takes into account the ordinary risks of the workplace, and that "the compensation is adjusted accordingly." Under this theory, in a competitive labor market employers who operate dangerous workplaces will have to pay workers more to compensate them for the greater risk of injury. The wage premium that workers receive for working at a dangerous job compensates them for the added risk that they face. And because they are forced to pay higher wages, employers have an incentive to take measures to make their workplaces safer. However, they will only spend money to improve workplace safety up to the point where the added cost of an additional safety measure equals, but does not exceed, the savings they would gain in lower wages if they were to implement the safety measure. Thus, in a perfectly competitive labor market, employer spending on workplace safety will reach an efficient level.

Do you think the labor market actually operates in this manner? Empirical studies of the question have reached differing conclusions as to whether workers in riskier jobs in fact receive a compensating wage premium. *Compare, e.g.*, Peter Dorman & Paul Hagstrom, *Wage Compensation for Dangerous Work Revisited*, 52 INDUS. & LAB. REL. REV. 116 (1998) (finding no convincing evidence of compensating wage differentials for the risk of fatal and nonfatal work injury), *with* MICHAEL MOORE & W. KIP VISCUSI, COMPENSATION MECHANISMS FOR JOB RISKS: WAGES, WORKERS' COMPENSATION, AND PRODUCT LIABILITY (1990) (finding evidence of a wage premium for risky jobs).

Susan Rose-Ackerman suggests several reasons to doubt that the labor market will actually force employers to take into account the full cost of workplace injuries:

[T]he market will . . . only work efficiently if potential new employees can observe the riskiness of jobs. One way such information might be provided is through a learning process. The first round of employees are uninformed, but after they are injured, other members of the labor force observe their injuries and illnesses and demand that the company pay a wage premium or reduce workplace hazards.

There are many reasons why this learning process will work poorly in the real world. First, many hazards take a long time to produce injuries. Second, even if they happen quickly, participants in a large labor market will not observe many of the injured. Third, the level of hazard depends on workers as well as workplaces. Some workers are more susceptible to hazards because of their genetic characteristics or their life style—for example, whether they smoke. Therefore, it may be difficult for job applicants correctly to infer their own risk by observing the harm suffered by others. Fourth, workplace conditions change with technology—so the past may be a poor guide to the future. . . .

[T]he mere provision of information may not be sufficient for two different reasons. The first turns on the limited information-processing capacities of people, especially regarding probabilistic information. . . . A second reason why an information strategy may be inadequate concerns the production function for health and safety. Many actions employers take are "local public goods." If dust collectors are installed, they will benefit all employees on a shop floor, and if a harmless chemical is substituted for a toxic, everyone who comes in contact with the material will benefit. However, if the employees are not organized into a union, individual workers may be unwilling to modify their wage demands enough to make the health and safety investment worthwhile. If employers do not know the value workers place on safety, they may be unwilling to experiment with costly changes that may not pay off in lower wage increases or improved productivity. . . .

Susan Rose-Ackerman, *Progressive Law and Economics—And the New Administrative Law*, 98 YALE L.J. 341, 355–57 (1988). *See also* Anne Marie Lofaso, *What We Owe Our Coal Miners*, 5 HARV. L. & POL'Y REV. 87, 104–05 (2011) (describing market failures that lead to poor safety in the coal mining industry).

If Rose-Ackerman is correct that these market failures prevent efficient bargaining about workplace safety, what should the response of the law be? The appropriate response depends upon which type of market failure seems most likely. For example, lack of accurate information might argue for providing more or better information to workers. Alternatively, if more information will not produce better informed workers, direct regulation may be warranted.

What about the possibility that workplace safety is a "local public good"? Suppose the benefit of a particular safety measure cannot be isolated to a single worker, but, once adopted, will benefit all. What would be the most efficient way to aggregate the interests of all affected workers?

Identifying potential barriers to efficient bargaining over workplace safety suggests a role for unions or other vehicles for representing collective worker interests. For example, employee organizations may assist workers in obtaining and understanding information about workplace risks, particularly less visible risks such as those associated with exposure to toxic substances or repetitive stress. By aggregating workers' interests, unions potentially offer a means of dealing with the "public goods" nature of safety measures that would otherwise inhibit individual employees from expressing their risk preferences.

If robust and informed bargaining over health and safety issues takes place, preventive measures—tailored to the circumstances of the particular workplace— could in theory be adopted without the need for any government mandated safety standards.

In fact, unions have often played a critical role in raising and negotiating over issues of health and safety. Because they implicate working conditions, safety issues are a mandatory subject of bargaining in a unionized workplace, and employers are therefore obligated to provide safety information upon the union's request. Thus, unions are often the conduit for information about workplace risks to their members. In addition, unions frequently negotiate for improved safety measures, or alternatively, higher wages to compensate for the risks, through the collective bargaining process. *See, e.g.*, Lofaso, 5 HARV. L. & POL'Y REV. at 106 (documenting lower fatality rates at unionized coal mines).

Suppose that the labor market *were* perfectly efficient when it comes to rating the safety risks entailed in particular jobs. Would it then be appropriate to leave the question of workplace safety to be determined by the operation of the labor market? Or are there other objections to a purely market-based approach beyond the potential for inefficiency?

3. **Common Law Defenses.** The "fellow-servant rule," articulated by the court in *Farwell*, was one of a trilogy of common law defenses adopted by the courts in the nineteenth century that effectively barred suits by injured workers against their employers. The "assumption of risk" doctrine held that the employee, by continuing to work in the face of known dangers, voluntarily accepted those risks and could not later complain if he were injured as a result. Finally, contributory negligence was also recognized as a defense, such that even in cases in which employer negligence was clear, any showing of fault on the part of the employee would completely bar recovery.

As the process of industrialization produced increasing numbers of workplace accidents, the harshness of the common law approach became apparent, prompting some efforts at reform. A few courts judicially modified one or another of the common law defenses. More significantly, many states beginning in the mid-nineteenth century passed statutes modifying or abrogating one or more of the defenses for employers. For example, some states legislatively rejected the fellow-servant rule for railroads or for all employers. Others replaced the principle of contributory negligence with a comparative negligence approach. Arthur Larson has pointed out the limited nature of these reforms:

> All legislation prior to the Workmen's Compensation Acts accepted the basic common-law idea that the employer was liable to the employee only for the negligence or fault of himself, or, at most, of someone for whom he is generally responsible under the *respondeat superior* doctrine. These so-called "Employers' Liability Statutes" did not aspire to create any new

principle of liability applicable to the employment relation as such. The most they ever set out to accomplish was the restoration of the employee to a position no worse than that of a stranger injured by the negligence of the employer or his servants.

Arthur Larson, *The Nature and Origins of Workmen's Compensation*, 37 CORNELL L.Q. 206, 226 (1952).

Suppose that the reforms of the common law tort system had been more thorough, such that all three traditional employer defenses were abolished everywhere, and the employee could recover for workplace injuries caused by negligence just like any third party. Would such a system adequately meet the twin goals of preventing workplace accidents and compensating injured workers? Are there any problems with relying on the tort system to regulate workplace safety?

4. Workingmen's Cooperatives. In the context of limited common law remedies and high accident rates, workers in the late 19th century began to form cooperative associations to provide disability and life insurance to their members. *See* JOHN FABIAN WITT, THE ACCIDENTAL REPUBLIC: CRIPPLED WORKINGMEN, DESTITUTE WIDOWS, AND THE REMAKING OF AMERICAN LAW 71–102 (2004). The cooperative insurance movement grew quickly, such that it was the leading form of life insurance in the United States in the 1890s, and in the last two decades of the nineteenth century approximately one-third of American workingmen belonged to a cooperative insurance association. *Id.* at 71–72.

Although trade unions played an important role, their relationship to the movement was sometimes ambivalent. Providing benefit funds encouraged loyalty to the union; however, the need to insure the solvency of an insurance cooperative raised the costs of union membership, thereby conflicting with their goal of increasing membership as much as possible. *Id.* at 77. In hazardous industries, however, union participation in the cooperative movement was crucial. For example, in the first decade of the 20th century, railroad unions distributed more than 4 million dollars in death benefits and a half million dollars in disability benefits each year to their members. *Id.* at 79.

Despite its initial success, the cooperative insurance movement faced increasing difficulties in the first decades of the 20th century. The workplace became increasingly diverse with an influx of new immigrants from Europe and "the fraternal ethic" on which the associations were built "generally did not extend across racial or religious lines." *Id.* at 85. In addition, low-risk members began to leave the older cooperatives, leaving pools of high-risk workers who were unable to maintain the funds to pay meaningful benefits. By the end of the first decade of the twentieth century, momentum "had shifted decisively away from the cooperative insurance associations." *Id.* at 101.

The history of the workingmen's cooperative associations suggests that the problem of providing meaningful financial support to workers killed or injured on the job was too big and complicated for workers to address collectively without some form of government intervention. Is there any role today for a collective worker response to workplace health and safety risks?

b.   The Compensation Acts

Even with the passage of laws mitigating the harshness of the common law system, dissatisfaction with the tort system continued and eventually led to more fundamental reforms, as described in the following materials.

Arthur Larson, *The Nature and Origins*
of Workmen's Compensation
37 CORNELL L.Q. 206, 231–33 (1952)

By the end of the nineteenth century . . . the coincidence of increasing industrial injuries and decreasing remedies had produced in the United States a situation ripe for radical change, and when, in 1893, a full account of the German system written by John Graham Brooks was published, legislators all over the country seized upon it as a clue to the direction which efforts at reform might take. Another stimulus was provided by the enactment of the first British Compensation Act in 1897 which later became the model of state acts in many respects.

A period of intensive investigation ensued, carried on by various state commissions, beginning with Massachusetts in 1904, Illinois in 1907, Connecticut in 1908 and a legislatively-created commission of representatives, industrialists and other experts in New York in 1909. By 1910 the movement was in full swing, with commissions being created by Congress and the legislatures of Massachusetts, Minnesota, New Jersey, Connecticut, Ohio, Illinois, Wisconsin, Montana and Washington. In 1910 also there occurred a conference in Chicago attended by representatives of all these commissions, at which a Uniform Workmen's Compensation Law was drafted. Although the state acts which followed were anything but uniform, the discussions at this conference did much to set the fundamental pattern of legislation.

As to actual enactments, the story begins modestly with a rather narrow cooperative Accident Fund for miners passed by Maryland in 1902, which quietly expired when held unconstitutional in an unappealed lower court decision. In 1909 another miners' compensation act was passed in Montana, and suffered the same fate. In 1908 Congress passed a compensation Act covering certain federal employees.

In 1910 the first New York Act was passed, with compulsory coverage of certain "hazardous employments." It was held unconstitutional in 1911 by the Court of Appeals in Ives v. South Buffalo Railway Co., [94 N.E. 431 (1911),] on the ground that the imposition of liability without fault upon the employer was a taking of property without due process of law under the state and federal constitutions. . . . One important practical result [flowed] from these preliminary constitutional setbacks: the very fear of unconstitutionality impelled the legislatures to pass over the ideal type of coverage, which would be both comprehensive and compulsory, in favor of more awkward and fragmentary plans whose very weakness and incompleteness might ensure their constitutional validity. And so, beginning with New Jersey, "elective" or "optional" statutes became common, under which employers could choose whether or not they would be bound by the compensation plan, with the alternative of being subject to common-law actions without benefit of the three common-law defenses. Similarly, a number of states limited their coverage to "hazardous" employments because of doubt as to the extent of the police power. . . .

In New York, the *Ives* decision was answered by the adoption in 1913 of a constitutional amendment permitting a compulsory law, and such a law was passed in the same year. In 1917 this compulsory law, together with the Iowa elective-type and the Washington exclusive-state-fund-type law, was held constitutional by the United States Supreme Court, and, with fears of constitutional impediments virtually removed, the compensation system grew and expanded with a rapidity that probably has no parallel in any comparable field of law.

By 1920 all but eight states had adopted Compensation Acts, and on January 1, 1949, the last state, Mississippi, came under the system.

NEW YORK CENTRAL RAILROAD CO. v. WHITE
United States Supreme Court
243 U.S. 188 (1917)

MR. JUSTICE PITNEY delivered the opinion of the Court.

A proceeding was commenced by defendant in error before the Workmen's Compensation Commission of the State of New York, established by the Workmen's Compensation Law of that State, to recover compensation from the New York Central & Hudson River Railroad Company for the death of her husband, Jacob White, who lost his life September 2, 1914, through an accidental injury arising out of and in the course of his employment under that company. The Commission awarded compensation in accordance with the terms of the law [and the award was affirmed on appeal]. . . .

The scheme of the act is so wide a departure from common-law standards respecting the responsibility of employer to employee that doubts naturally have been raised respecting its constitutional validity. The adverse considerations urged or suggested in this case and in kindred cases submitted at the same time are: (a) that the employer's property is taken without due process of law, because he is subjected to a liability for compensation without regard to any neglect or default on his part or on the part of any other person for whom he is responsible, and in spite of the fact that the injury may be solely attributable to the fault of the employee; (b) that the employee's rights are interfered with, in that he is prevented from having compensation for injuries arising from the employer's fault commensurate with the damages actually sustained, and is limited to the measure of compensation prescribed by the act; and (c) that both employer and employee are deprived of their liberty to acquire property by being prevented from making such agreement as they choose respecting the terms of the employment.

In support of the legislation, it is said that the whole common-law doctrine of employer's liability for negligence, with its defenses of contributory negligence, fellow-servant's negligence, and assumption of risk, is based upon fictions, and is inapplicable to modern conditions of employment; that in the highly organized and hazardous industries of the present day the causes of accident are often so obscure and complex that in a material proportion of cases it is impossible by any method correctly to ascertain the facts necessary to form an accurate judgment, and in a still larger proportion the expense and delay required for such ascertainment amount in effect to a defeat of justice; that under the present system the injured workman is left to bear the greater part of industrial accident loss, which because of his limited income he is unable to sustain, so that he and those dependent upon him are overcome by poverty and frequently become a burden upon public or private charity; and that litigation is unduly costly and tedious, encouraging corrupt practices and arousing antagonisms between employers and employees.

In considering the constitutional question, it is necessary to view the matter from the standpoint of the employee as well as from that of the employer. For, while plaintiff in error is an employer, and cannot succeed without showing that its rights as such are infringed, yet . . . the exemption from further liability is an essential part of the scheme, so that the statute if invalid as against the employee is invalid as against the employer. . . .

The statute under consideration sets aside one body of rules only to establish another system in its place. If the employee is no longer able to recover as much as before in case of being injured through the employer's negligence, he is entitled to moderate compensation in all cases of injury, and has a certain and speedy remedy without the difficulty and expense of establishing negligence or proving the amount of the damages. Instead of assuming the entire consequences of all ordinary risks of the occupation, he assumes the consequences, in excess of the scheduled compensation, of risks ordinary and extraordinary. On the other hand, if the employer is left without defense respecting the question of fault, he at the same time is assured that the recovery is limited, and that it goes directly to the relief of the designated beneficiary. And just as the employee's assumption of ordinary risks at common law presumably was taken into account in fixing the rate of wages, so the fixed responsibility of the employer, and the modified assumption of risk by the employee under the new system, presumably will be reflected in the wage scale. The act evidently is intended as a just settlement of a difficult problem, affecting one of the most important of social relations, and it is to be judged in its entirety. We have said enough to demonstrate that, in such an adjustment, the particular rules of the common law affecting the subject-matter are not placed by the Fourteenth Amendment beyond the reach of the law making power of the State; and thus we are brought to the question whether the method of compensation that is established as a substitute transcends the limits of permissible state action. . . .

Briefly, the statute imposes liability upon the employer to make compensation for disability or death of the employee resulting from accidental personal injury arising out of and in the course of the employment, without regard to fault as a cause except where the injury or death is occasioned by the employee's willful intention to produce it, or where the injury results solely from his intoxication while on duty; it graduates the compensation for disability according to a prescribed scale based upon the loss of earning power, having regard to the previous wage and the character and duration of the disability; and measures the death benefits according to the dependency of the surviving wife, husband, or infant children. Perhaps we should add that it has no retrospective effect, and applies only to cases arising some months after its passage.

what the act does

Of course, we cannot ignore the question whether the new arrangement is arbitrary and unreasonable, from the standpoint of natural justice. Respecting this, it is important to be observed that the act applies only to disabling or fatal personal injuries received in the course of hazardous employment in gainful occupation. Reduced to its elements, the situation to be dealt with is this: Employer and employee, by mutual consent, engage in a common operation intended to be advantageous to both; the employee is to contribute his personal services, and for these is to receive wages, and ordinarily nothing more; the employer is to furnish plant, facilities, organization, capital, credit, is to control and manage the operation, paying the wages and other expenses, disposing of the product at such prices as he can obtain, taking all the profits, if any there be, and of necessity bearing the entire losses. In the nature of things, there is more or less of a probability that the employee may lose his life through some accidental injury arising out of the employment, leaving his widow or children deprived of their natural support; or that he may sustain an injury not mortal but resulting in his total or partial disablement, temporary or permanent, with corresponding impairment of earning capacity. The physical suffering must be borne by the employee alone; the laws of nature prevent this from being evaded or shifted to another, and the statute makes no attempt to afford an equivalent in compensation. But, besides, there is the loss of earning power; a loss of that which stands to the employee as his capital in trade. This is a loss arising out of the business, and, however it may be charged up, is an expense of the operation, as truly as the cost of repairing broken machinery or any other expense that ordinarily is paid by the employer. Who is to bear the charge? It is plain that, on grounds of natural justice, it is not unreasonable for the State, while relieving the employer from responsibility for damages measured by common-law standards and payable in cases where he or those for whose conduct he is answerable are found to be at fault, to require him to contribute a reasonable amount, and according to a reasonable and definite scale, by way of compensation for the loss of earning power incurred in the common enterprise, irrespective of the question of negligence, instead of leaving the entire loss to rest where it may chance to fall—that is, upon the injured employee or his dependents. Nor can it be deemed arbitrary and unreasonable, from the standpoint of the employee's interest, to supplant a system under which he assumed the entire risk of injury in ordinary cases, and in others had a right to recover an amount more or less speculative upon proving facts of negligence that often were difficult to prove, and substitute a system under which in all ordinary cases of accidental injury he is sure of a definite and easily ascertained compensation, not being obliged to assume the entire loss in any case but in all cases assuming any loss beyond the prescribed scale. . . .

The provision for compulsory compensation, in the act under consideration, cannot be deemed to be an arbitrary and unreasonable application of the principle, so as to amount to a deprivation of the employer's property without due process of law. The pecuniary loss resulting from the employee's death or disablement must fall somewhere. It results from something done in the course of an operation from which the employer expects to derive a profit. In excluding the question of fault as a cause of the injury, the act in effect disregards the proximate cause and looks to one more remote—the primary cause, as it may be deemed—and that is, the employment itself. For this, both parties are responsible, since they voluntarily engage in it as co-adventurers, with personal injury to the employee as a probable and foreseen result. In ignoring any possible negligence of the employee producing or contributing to the injury, the lawmaker reasonably may have been influenced by the belief that in modern industry the utmost diligence in the employer's service is in some degree inconsistent with adequate care on the part of the employee for his own safety; that the more intently he devotes himself to the work, the less he can take precautions for his own security. And it is evident that the consequences of a disabling or fatal injury are precisely the same to the parties immediately affected, and to the community, whether the proximate cause be culpable or innocent. . . .

This, of course, is not to say that any scale of compensation, however insignificant on the one hand or onerous on the other, would be supportable. In this case, no criticism is made on the ground that the compensation prescribed by the statute in question is unreasonable in amount, either in general or in the particular case. Any question of that kind may be met when it arises.

But, it is said, the statute strikes at the fundamentals of constitutional freedom of contract. . . . [W]e recognize that the legislation under review does measurably limit the freedom of employer and employee to agree respecting the terms of employment, and that it cannot be supported except on the ground that it is a reasonable exercise of the police power of the State. In our opinion it is fairly supportable upon that ground. And for this reason: The subject matter in respect of which freedom of contract is restricted is the matter of compensation for human life or limb lost or disability incurred in the course of hazardous employment, and the public has a direct interest in this as affecting the common welfare. "The whole is no greater than the sum of all the parts, and when the individual health, safety, and welfare are sacrificed or neglected, the State must suffer." *Holden v. Hardy*, 169 U.S. 366, 397. . . .

We have not overlooked the criticism that the act imposes no rule of conduct upon the employer with respect to the conditions of labor in the various industries embraced within its terms, prescribes no duty with regard to where the workmen shall work, the character of the machinery, tools, or appliances, the rules or regulations to be established, or the safety devices to be maintained. This statute does not concern itself with measures of prevention, which presumably are embraced in other laws. But the interest of the public is not confined to these. One of the grounds of its concern with the continued life and earning power of the individual is its interest in the prevention of pauperism, with its concomitants of vice and crime. And, in our opinion, laws regulating the responsibility of employers for the injury or death of employees arising out of the employment bear so close a relation to the protection of the lives and safety of those concerned that they properly may be regarded as coming within the category of police regulations. . . .

Judgment affirmed.

NOTES

1. **Constitutionality of a Compromise.** What was the basis for the railroad company's constitutional challenge to New York's Workmen's Compensation Law? How did the United States Supreme Court resolve the question of the statute's constitutionality? Explain the purposes behind the legislation and how the specific

provisions of the statute achieved those purposes.

After the Supreme Court upheld the constitutionality of New York's law, workers' compensation legislation was widely adopted by states that had not previously done so. Although the state statutes differed significantly in their coverage and details, the fundamental compromise—no fault compensation in exchange for limited liability—that the Supreme Court approved in *New York Central Railroad v. White* provided the basis for all these laws.

2. The Inevitability of Industrial Accidents. The Supreme Court's discussion in *New York Central Railroad v. White* suggests that worker injuries, and even death, are the inevitable by-products of modern industry. Did this perspective influence how the legislature chose to allocate the burden of workplace accidents? Note that New York's Workmen's Compensation Law "does not concern itself with measures of prevention." Rather, it focuses rather narrowly on the goal of providing support for injured workers. Witt argues that because of the lack of a professional civil service in either state or federal government at the time, an effective factory inspection system was "not a viable" option for addressing the problem of industrial accidents in the late nineteenth and early twentieth centuries. John Fabian Witt, The Accidental Republic: Crippled Workingmen, Destitute Widows, and the Remaking of American Law 19 (2004). It was not until many years later that government attempted comprehensive, direct regulation of workplace safety.

2. Basic Benefits and Coverage

The basic outlines of the New York Workmen's Compensation Law as described in *New York Central Railroad v. White* are typical of most workers' compensation laws today. These schemes are intended to provide prompt, but limited, relief to workers injured on the job without regard to fault. Although their overall structures are similar, the various state laws vary greatly in their details on such issues as what types of injuries are compensable and how benefit levels are determined. In addition, several federal laws establish separate compensation schemes for certain categories of workers. *See, e.g.,* Federal Employees' Compensation Act, 5 U.S.C. §§ 8101-93 (providing compensation to federal government employees); Longshore and Harbor Workers' Compensation Act, 33 U.S.C. §§ 901-50 (providing compensation to certain transportation workers such as ship, harbor and railroad employees).

A detailed exploration of the variety of rules under all these compensation laws is beyond the scope of this text. Rather, this section first outlines the typical structure of these workers' compensation schemes, and then discusses some basic questions that arise in determining whether or not a particular injury is covered by workers' compensation. In the next section, we consider the principle of exclusivity—the rule that workers' compensation should provide the exclusive remedy for workplace injuries—and how it plays out in practice.

a.   Benefits and Procedures

Typically, workers' compensation provides two basic types of benefits for injured workers. First, most state laws require that covered employers pay for the medical care necessitated by the on-the-job injury. In some states, benefits also include rehabilitation services or therapy. Vocational rehabilitation to retrain workers for a new type of job may also be covered, but is less common. Second, workers' compensation typically provides injured workers with some form of cash benefit. When a worker is temporarily rendered unable to work due to injury, he or she will typically receive a weekly cash benefit during the period of disability. The amount of the benefit is generally measured as a percentage of the worker's pre-injury wage, subject to certain statutory minimum and maximum amounts.

If it appears that a worker has become permanently disabled, he or she may also be entitled to permanent disability benefits. In cases where the resulting disability is total and permanent, rendering the individual unable to work, he or she will receive a weekly benefit amount for the duration of the disability, or for life, although some states limit either the total dollar amount or the duration of these benefits. Benefits are also available to compensate for permanent impairments, even when these do not result in total disability. Determining the appropriate amount of benefits in cases of partial disability, however, can be difficult. Some states have resorted to schedules of benefits, so that, for example, a worker in New York is entitled to 244 weeks of compensation for the loss of a hand, 160 weeks for the loss of an eye, 75 weeks for the loss of a thumb, and so on. N.Y. WORKERS' COMP. LAW § 15(3). Another method for calculating benefits requires a determination of a worker's level of permanent impairment as compared to one who is totally disabled. Thus, if a worker's permanent disability is rated as 75% of a totally disabling loss, her benefits would be set at 75% of the benefits given in cases of total disability.

Finally, workers' compensation also provides benefits for the survivors of a worker killed on the job. Once again, benefits are based on a percentage of the worker's prior wage, subject to statutory minimum and maximum amounts. The level of benefits may also vary depending upon the number of dependents. In addition, workers' compensation pays funeral and burial expenses of the deceased worker, up to a certain fixed maximum amount.

One crucial aspect of the workers' compensation benefit system is that it does not, and is not intended to, provide complete compensation for the loss incurred. In most states, the level of weekly benefit is two-thirds of the worker's pre-injury wage. With statutory maximums, the actual amount received by the average worker may be even less. In addition, there is no attempt to compensate workers for pain and suffering or any consequential damages; rather, the loss is measured by reference to a worker's prior earnings. Although a few states provide penalties for particularly egregious behavior, these penalties are typically quite modest, see, e.g., CAL. LAB. CODE § 4553 (penalty of 1 and 1/2 times benefit amount in cases of willful violation), and thus, the concepts of punishment and deterrence that lie behind punitive damages are absent from the system.

Employers are required to provide the benefits spelled out under state workers' compensation laws and may do so in one of three ways. They may purchase private insurance, participate in a state administered workers' compensation fund or self-insure. Depending upon the state, employers may be able to choose how they will finance their compensation obligations, or the law may require one particular form. Each of these forms of insurance is experience rated in the sense that an increase in claims will result in increasing premium costs, although the degree of experience rating, and therefore the incentives to take preventive measures, vary significantly.

In addition to establishing basic benefit levels, state workers' compensation laws also create some sort of administrative structure for overseeing the entire system, although, again, the details differ significantly from state to state. Typically, disputes about compensability or the level of benefits are first heard by an administrative law judge, who holds a hearing in which the parties can present their evidence. Either party can appeal the ALJ's decision to a state workers' compensation appeals board. The board's decision can then be appealed to the state's general courts of appeal. Thus, many workers' compensation issues are resolved in state court, although the disputes typically start in the administrative system.

In many cases, a worker's claim for benefits is uncontested, and payment occurs as a matter of course. For example, the train engineer injured when a brake fails and the factory worker hurt by a malfunctioning machine are clearly entitled to compensation. Certain other types of injuries, however, have proven more problematic for the compensation system. In particular, coverage of occupational diseases, repetitive stress injuries and mental injuries have proven controversial.

In the case of occupational diseases or repetitive injuries, several factors complicate the coverage determination. State statutes typically speak in terms of "accidental injuries" or "injury by accident." Because many occupational diseases result from exposure—often over a long period of time—to a harmful substance rather than a specific incident, they do not obviously fall within the definition of an "injury arising by accident." Similarly, repetitive stress injuries like carpal tunnel or bursitis result not from a single identifiable event, but the accumulated effects of low-level trauma over months or years. All states now include coverage of "disease" in addition to "injury," either through specific statutory language or judicial interpretation. However, those suffering from work-related diseases still face considerable hurdles. Occupational diseases like asbestosis often have long latency periods, such that symptoms may not appear until well after the exposure or even the employment has ended. Lack of information about the causes of disease and strictly applied statutes of limitations may prevent workers from asserting claims for benefits. For both diseases and repetitive injuries, proving causation can be difficult, given that many diseases and conditions are of unknown origin or may have multiple contributing causes. A number of statutes specifically limit compensation to diseases "characteristic of" or "peculiar to" a particular type of job and exclude "ordinary diseases of life," further restricting the availability of benefits for diseases whose work connection cannot be conclusively proven.

Mental stress claims have also proven controversial. Although compensation is generally available when mental illness or disability accompanies or results from a physical injury sustained at work, mental injuries having a non-physical origin, such as pure stress claims, are much less likely to be covered. Courts and legislatures have expressed concerns about the difficulty of proving causation in purely mental

[handwritten margin note: how states deal w/ mental stress]

cases and raised fears of malingering by claimants. Some states have responded by drawing a distinction between mental injuries caused by a particular, identifiably stressful event at work, such as witnessing the death of a co-worker, and those caused by the cumulative effects of on-going mental stress and tension. These states limit compensation to the former type of injury. State legislatures have also enacted a variety of limitations on stress claims, such as imposing a higher standard of proving causation in pure mental stress cases, or limiting benefits for this category of claims. A few states exclude stress claims entirely from coverage.

In recent years, the number of compensation cases involving illnesses and injuries falling within these problem areas has grown. As scientific understanding of the cause of illness and disease has expanded, so too has the potential scope of employers' compensation liability. Similarly, the pressures of global competition and the drive for ever-increasing levels of productivity have contributed to growing numbers of stress-related compensation claims. A full exploration of the impact of these developments on the compensation system lies beyond the scope of this text; however, the difficulties raised by these types of cases should be kept in mind as we consider basic coverage issues in the next sections.

b.   Who Is an Employee?

In order to be eligible to receive workers' compensation benefits, a worker must show that an employer-employee relationship exists. As we have seen in other contexts (e.g., Chapter 2 and Chapter 11), disputes sometimes arise over whether a particular worker is an employee or independent contractor. These disputes are especially common in certain industries, where the work to be performed either does not require close supervision or such supervision is impractical, such as in the taxi and delivery industries. Most workers' compensation statutes do not contain definitions that are helpful in distinguishing covered employees from independent contractors, and as a result, courts have relied on other tests, such as a "right to control" test and a "relative nature of the work" test.

The "right to control" test is derived from the common law of agency and aims to answer the "pivotal question" "whether the employer had the right to control the means and manner of the service, as distinguished from controlling the ultimate results of the service." *Chouteau v. Netco Construction*, 132 S.W.3d 328, 332 (Mo. Ct. App. 2004). Because the right to control test turns on multiple factors, outcomes are often difficult to predict. As we saw in Chapter 2, the result may be that workers in the same industry, or even workers doing the same job for the same company, may have different statuses. In addition to its uncertainty, the "right to control" test has been criticized as incompatible with the basic theory of workers' compensation. As Larson argues,

> The "servant" concept at common law performed one main function: to delimit the scope of a master's vicarious tort liability. This tort liability arose out of detailed activities carried on by the servant, resulting in some kind of harm to a third person. The extent to which the employer had a right to control these detailed activities was thus highly relevant to the question whether the employer ought to be legally liable for them. . . . By contrast, compensation law is concerned not with injuries *by* the employee

in his or her detailed activities, but with injuries *to* him or her as a result not only of his or her own activities (controlled by the employer as to details) but those of co-employees, independent contractors and other third persons (some controlled by the employer, and others not). To this issue, the right of control of details of his work has no such direct relation as it has to the issue of vicarious tort liability.

Lex K. Larson, Larson's Workers' Compensation, Desk Edition § 60.04 (2014).

Unlike the common law right to control test, the "relative nature of the work" test is one that has developed specifically in the context of determining coverage under workers' compensation statutes. The test generally consists of two elements. The first looks at the character of the alleged employee's work. The second examines the relationship between the individual's work and the purported employer's business. These elements in turn rest on several independent factors. The court in *Odsather v. Richardson*, 96 P.3d 521 (Alaska 2004), explained the structure of the test as follows:

> The inquiry into the character of the claimant's business can further be broken into three factors: (1) the degree of skill involved, (2) whether the claimant holds himself out to the public as a separate business, and (3) whether the claimant bears the accident burden. The inquiry into the relationship between the claimant's work and the work of the purported employer can also be broken into three factors: (1) extent to which claimant's work is a regular part of the employer's regular work, (2) whether claimant's work is continuous or intermittent, and (3) whether the duration of the work is such that it amounts to hiring of continuing services rather than a contract for a specific job.

Id. at 523. Although this test overlaps with the "right to control" test, it focuses on a different ultimate question. As one court explained,

> [B]ecause the theory of workmen's compensation legislation is that the cost of industrial accidents should be borne by the consumer as a part of the cost of the product, this court has held that a worker whose services form a regular part of the cost of the product, and whose work does not constitute a separate business which allows a distinct channel through which the cost of an accident may flow, is presumptively within the area of intended protection of the compensation act.

Ware v. Industrial Commission, 743 N.E.2d 579, 584–85 (Ill. App. Ct. 2000) (citation omitted).

Whether a worker is an employee or independent contractor matters because it will determine not only whether that worker is entitled to compensation benefits, but also, as will see in section 3, whether the worker will be barred by the exclusivity rule from bringing a tort action for a workplace injury.

In addition to independent contractors, other non-employees are also excluded from coverage under the workers' compensation laws. For some, the question turns on whether they worked under a contract "of hire" or were volunteers not eligible for benefits. For example, in *Hoste v. Shanty Creek Management, Inc.*, 592 N.W.2d

360 (Mich. 1999), a ski patroller who suffered a totally disabling accident while on a ski run at a resort, was denied compensation benefits on the grounds that he was not an employee of the resort. Hoste was a member of the National Ski Patrol System (NSPS) and worked at the resort on weekends. He did not receive any wages; however, in exchange for his patrolling services, he received free lift tickets, skiing privileges for family members, free hot beverages and reduced prices on certain meals and merchandise. Interpreting the definition of "employee" in the statute, the Supreme Court of Michigan held that in order to be covered,

> [an] individual must be employed pursuant to a contract "of hire," where the benefit received by the individual is payment intended as wages. In other words, workers' compensation provides benefits to those who have lost a source of income; it does not provide benefits to those who can no longer take advantage of a gratuity or privilege that serves merely as an accommodation.

Id. at 366. Finding that the benefits provided by the resort were an "accommodation" to the claimant rather than a payment intended as wages, the court concluded he was a "gratuitous worker" not entitled to workers' compensation benefits.

The dissent argued that the resort relied on the "volunteer" ski patrol in the sense that it could not operate without its presence. During the week, the company hired ski patrollers who performed the exact same function as the weekend "volunteers," and were clearly acknowledged to be employees. Regarding the benefits received by the claimant as "meaningful compensation," the dissent argued that the initial determination that Hoste was a covered employee should have been upheld.

If accidents are an inevitable part of the business of running a ski resort, who should bear the risk that ski patrol members like Hoste may get injured?

c. "Arising out of and in the Course of Employment"

Although the workers' compensation system was intended to avoid the complexity and uncertainty of determining "fault," litigation persists, often focused on the issue of whether a particular injury is covered under the compensation statute. Every jurisdiction requires some measure of connection to work in order for an injury to be covered, and most have adopted the same test for establishing coverage: whether an injury is one "arising out of and in the course of employment." In many cases, coverage is clear—for example, when an employee is injured while using the employer's tools to perform her assigned job responsibilities during working hours. Other situations present more marginal cases, such as cases in which the injury occurred during breaks or after hours, or resulted from forces like lightning that are external to the employment. In addressing these types of claims, administrative agencies and the courts have developed an extensive body of law interpreting when an injury "arises out of and in the course of employment."

Clear cases & obscure examples

PROWS v. INDUSTRIAL COMMISSION OF UTAH
Supreme Court of Utah
610 P.2d 1362 (1980)

WILKINS, JUSTICE:

This is an appeal from an Order of the Industrial Commission (hereafter "Commission") denying the application for Workmen's Compensation benefits by Michael Prows (hereafter "Petitioner").

The facts of this case are essentially undisputed. Petitioner was employed as a truck driver by Respondent Bergin Brunswig Company (hereafter "Bergin"). His duties included loading medical supplies onto his delivery truck and making deliveries to doctors, hospitals, and clinics.

The boxes containing the medical supplies measured approximately eleven and one-half by twenty-four inches, and each box was secured by elastic bands (also described as "rubber bands"). Each rubber band was approximately twelve inches long by three-eighths inch wide.

Testimony before the administrative law judge established that the rubber bands were used by some of Bergin's employees for "rubber bands fights." Petitioner and one of his co-employees testified that the "fights" were an almost daily occurrence. One of Bergin's supervisors testified that he observed such "fights" perhaps two or three times a month, and that when he observed one he discouraged its continuation.

On March 3, 1978, Petitioner was engaged in his usual assigned duties and was loading supplies on his delivery truck. As he was unloading boxes of supplies from a hand truck and onto his delivery truck, he was hit by one or two rubber bands which were flipped at him by two co-employees standing nearby. Petitioner thereupon flipped a rubber band back at his "attacker." One of the co-employees then ripped an approximately eighteen inch long piece of wood off a nearby pallet and came toward Petitioner brandishing the wood like a sword. Petitioner took the wood from his co-employee, placed a rubber band between the handles of his hand truck and attempted to shoot the wood into the air in a slingshot fashion. The piece of wood, instead of sailing into the air, struck Petitioner in the right eye, severely injuring him.

In denying compensation the administrative law judge found, inter alia, that there had been numerous incidents of "horseplay" indulged in by Bergin's employees, including flipping rubber bands, and that this type of activity had been discouraged and was not condoned by Bergin; that the horseplay represented a "complete abandonment of the employee's duties"; and that the petitioner had "failed to prove that his accident arose out of or was in the scope of his employment."[1] In denying Petitioner's Motion for Review, the Commission adopted

---

[1] [n. 1] The concept of "Scope of Employment" is one foreign to the law of workmen's compensation belonging rather in the law of master and servant. Therefore, petitioner can in no way be considered to have the burden of proving that the accident "was in the scope of his employment."

the administrative law judge's Findings of Fact, Conclusions of Law, and Order.

Section 35-1-45 of Utah's Workmen's Compensation Act provides in pertinent part:

> Every employee . . . who is injured . . . by accident arising out of or in the course of his employment, wheresoever such injury occurred, provided the same was not purposely self-inflicted, shall be entitled to receive and shall be paid, such compensation for loss sustained on account of such injury . . . as is herein provided.[2]

In discussing construction of the act and the underlying purposes of the act this Court in *Chandler v. Industrial Commission,* 184 P. 1020, 1021–1022 (1919) stated:

> We are also reminded that our statute requires that the statutes of this state are to be "liberally construed with a view to effect the objects of the statutes and to promote justice."
>
> In this connection it must be remembered that the compensation provided for in the act is in no sense to be considered as damages for the injured employee or to his dependents in case death supervenes. The right to compensation arises out of the relation existing between employer and employee, and that the injury arises out of (or) in the course of the employment. Under such an act the costs and expenses of conducting the business or enterprise, including compensation for injuries to employees or other casualties, must be taxed to the business. The theory of the Compensation Act is that the whole cost and expense of conducting the business as aforesaid is added to the cost of the articles that are produced and sold, and hence, in the long run, such costs and expenses are borne by the public; that is, by the consumers of the articles produced. The purpose of such an act, therefore, is to protect the employee and those dependent upon him, and in case of his serious injury or death to provide adequate means for the support of those dependent upon him. In view, therefore, that in case of total disability or death of the employee his dependents might become the objects of public charity, such a calamity is avoided by requiring the business or enterprise to provide for such dependents, with the right of the employer to add the amount that is paid out to the cost of producing and selling the product of such business or enterprise. The beneficent purposes of such acts are therefore apparent to all, and for that reason, if for no other, should receive a very liberal construction in favor of the injured employee. We are all united upon the proposition that in view of the purposes of such acts, in case there is any doubt respecting the right to compensation, such doubt should be resolved in favor of the employee or of his dependents as the case may be.

This Court, along with the courts of other jurisdictions, has recognized that

---

[2] [n. 3] It must be kept clearly in mind that the statute requires that the injury arise in the course of employment, not that the injured worker be in the course of his employment. A definition of the term "course of employment" is found in 1 Larson, *The Law of Workmen's Compensation* (1979), § 14: "when it takes place within the period of the employment at a place where the employee reasonably may be, and while he is fulfilling his duties or engaged in doing something incidental thereto."

concepts of negligence, contributory negligence, fault, and similar tort concepts have no place within the remedial framework of the compensation act. In *Twin Peaks Canning Co. v. Industrial Commission,* [196 P. 853, 859 (1921)] this Court stated:

> Our statute only exclude(d) those injuries which are "purposely self-inflicted." As we read the statute, therefore, it is not enough that the employee merely disregards some rule, regulation, or order of the master, since such conduct may constitute nothing more than ordinary negligence on the part of the employee, and mere negligence does not destroy the right to compensation.

. . . .

With these basic principles in mind, we turn now to an analysis of whether and under what circumstances injuries sustained as a result of "horseplay" on the part of an employee may not be compensated under the act. . . .

Larson proposes a four-part test to analyze any particular act of horseplay to determine whether the horseplay constitutes such a substantial deviation as to justify denying compensation to a participant therein. Whether initiation of or participation in horseplay is a deviation from course of employment depends on (1) the extent and seriousness of the deviation, (2) the completeness of the deviation (i.e., whether it was commingled with the performance of duty or involved an abandonment of duty), (3) the extent to which the practice of horseplay had become an accepted part of the employment, and (4) the extent to which the nature of the employment may be expected to include some such horseplay. [ARTHUR LARSON, THE LAW OF WORKMEN'S COMPENSATION (1979).]

This Court has heretofore had only one occasion to examine the issue of horseplay in the workmen's compensation setting. In *Twin Peaks Canning Company v. Industrial Commission, supra,* an award of compensation to the dependents of a worker who was killed as a result of horseplay in which "the deceased was the instigator and the principal, if not the sole actor" [196 P. at 858.] was affirmed by this Court. The analysis in *Twin Peaks* turned on whether the deceased employee could be said to have been killed while "in the course of" his employment in light of his activities in using an elevator located on the premises of his employer, the use of which elevator by the deceased was allegedly forbidden by the employer. . . . In our view, the analysis in *Twin Peaks* though lacking the formal structure of the test proposed by Larson, *supra,* is founded on the same general principles. We therefore adopt Larson's four-part test to determine whether a particular act of horseplay constitutes such a deviation that it can be said that the resulting injury did not arise in the course of the employment and hence is not compensable.

(1) Extent and seriousness of the deviation.

In *Twin Peaks, supra,* the Court observed:

A careful reading of the decided cases will, however, disclose that the mere fact that the injured employee, at the time of the accident, was not in the discharge of his usual duties or was not directly engaged in anything connected with those duties, does not necessarily prevent him from recovering compensation in case of accidental injury. In that connection it must be remembered that, while a human being may do no more than what a machine might do, yet he can not be classed as a machine merely. [*Id.* at 858.]

Recognizing that "a little nonsense now and then is relished by the best of (workers)," it is clear that the better reasoned decisions make allowances for the fact that workers cannot be expected to attend strictly to their assigned duties every minute they are on the job. That is not to say that substantial excursions from job assignments need be tolerated or if injury occurs during such excursions, compensation need be paid. In the case at bar, Petitioner was engaged in the performance of his assigned duties when he was playfully "attacked" by co-workers flipping rubber bands. Petitioner then momentarily set aside his duties and took up the challenge. In an exchange lasting a matter of minutes, Petitioner was injured. As Larson points out:

> The substantial character of a horseplay deviation should not be judged by the seriousness of its consequences in the light of hindsight, but by the extent of the work-departure in itself. This is not always easy to do, especially when a trifling incident escalates or explodes into a major tragedy. [1A Larson at 5-152.]

We think the converse of this principle is likewise true; the fact that a major tragedy has occurred should not dictate an award of compensation when that tragedy resulted from a deviation so extensive and serious that the employment can be said to have been abandoned. However, it is our opinion that the deviation involved in the case at bar was short in duration and when disassociated from the serious consequences which resulted, relatively trivial.

(2) Completeness of the deviation.

Petitioner was, at the time he was "attacked" by his co-employees, engaged in the discharge of his duties. Had he not been injured, he would presumably have completed loading the truck and carried on with his deliveries. The horseplay he engaged in was clearly "commingled with the performance of duty" and hence did not constitute an "abandonment of duty." Larson points out:

> . . . the particular act of horseplay is entitled to be judged according to the same standards of exten[t] and duration of deviation that are accepted in other fi[e]lds, such as resting, seeking personal comfort, or indulging in incidental personal errands. If an employee momentarily walks over to a co-employee to engage in a friendly word or two, this would nowadays be called an insubstantial deviation. If he accompanies this friendly word with a playful jab in the ribs, surely it cannot be said that an entirely new set of principles has come into play. The incident remains a simple human diversion subject to the same tests of extent of departure from the employment as if the playful gesture had been omitted.

At the other extreme, there are cases in which the prankster undertakes a practical joke which necessitates the complete abandonment of the employment and the concentration of all his energies for a substantial part of his working time on the horseplay enterprise. When this abandonment is sufficiently complete and extensive, it can only be treated the same as abandonment of the employment for any other personal purpose, such as an extended personal errand or an intentional four-hour nap. [Id. at 5-142 to 5-143]

(3) Extent to which horseplay has become a part of the employment.

The evidence adduced at the hearing before the administrative law judge was conflicting on the frequency of "rubber band fights," but clearly such "fights" had become a part of the employment, whether the "fights" occurred "daily" or "two or three times a month."

As Larson points out:

The controlling issue is whether the custom had *in fact* become a part of the employment; the employer's knowledge of it can make it neither more nor less a part of the employment—at most it is evidence of incorporation of the practice into the employment. [Id. at 5-133.] (italics in original)

We do not consider the fact that apparently no employee of Bergin had ever attempted before to flip a piece of wood with a rubber band as indicating that such a practice could not be considered a part of the employment. The elements of the practice, which must be conceded to have been part of the employment, were not significantly enlarged or so modified so as to no longer constitute a part of the employment.

(4) Extent to which nature of employment may be expected to include some such horseplay.

This element of Larson's approach focuses on the foreseeability of horseplay in any given employment environment and on the particular act of horseplay involved. Considerations which may enter into the analysis of this point include whether the work involves lulls in employment activity or is essentially continuous, and the existence of instrumentalities which are part of the work environment and which are readily usable in horseplay situations. This list is not intended to be exhaustive but rather illustrative of the possibilities. In the present case all of the elements which joined to result in Petitioner's injury—the hand truck, the rubber bands, and the piece of wood—were part and parcel of the work environment. It therefore is not difficult to foresee that horseplay of the type engaged in by Petitioner was to be expected. . . .

[U]nder the facts of this case we believe as a matter of law that there was not a substantial deviation such that it can be said that the resulting injury did not arise in the course of the employment and hence is not compensible. The record herein reveals no substantial evidence supporting the finding of the Commission that by engaging in horseplay, Petitioner "completely abandoned" his duties and hence was not injured in the course of his employment. Therefore the Order of the Commission is reversed. . . .

HALL, JUSTICE (dissenting):

. . . [T]he facts in *Twin Peaks* are readily distinguishable in several particulars. For example, in *Twin Peaks*, the fatal injury occurred during a lull in the work, at a time when there was no work to perform; in the instant case, petitioner was actively engaged in his work when he abandoned it for the purpose of "horseplay." . . .

In the instant case, the petition admitted that at the time of the accident he was not performing an assigned duty. He also admitted that his injury resulted from his own act and that he was the "aggressor" in flipping the piece of wood, i.e., that his flipping of the wood was not a reaction of having been hit with an elastic band but was rather an independent, playful gesture. Testimony indicated that the employees had been warned about flipping elastic bands at each other and that apparently no employee of the company had ever before attempted to flip a projectile with an elastic band while on the job. Based on the evidence presented, the administrative law judge found as follows:

> The horseplay was not related in any way to the performance of the applicant's job duties but rather represents a complete abandonment of the employee's duties. At the time of the accident neither the applicant nor any of the other employees involved in the horseplay were carrying out their assigned tasks.
>
> The applicant has failed to prove that his accident arose out of or was in the scope of his employment.

. . . .

I would affirm.

NOTES

1. **Scope vs. Course of Employment.** In a footnote, the court in *Prows* suggests that the administrative law judge erred in asking whether the accident was "in the scope of his employment." What is the difference between the "scope of employment" test developed in the law of master and servant and the "course of employment" test? Why was it inappropriate for the ALJ to use the "scope of employment" rather than the "course of employment" test?

2. **Compensating Horseplay.** The claimant in *Prows* was injured as a result of an accident that occurred while he was fooling around *instead* of doing his job. Why should his injury be compensated at all? What test does the court use to determine whether or not Prows should be compensated? Why are the factors it identifies relevant to the question of *whether* Prows should be compensated?

3. **Two Tests?** The Utah workers' compensation statute speaks in terms of the employee injured "by accident arising out of or in the course of his employment." In *Prows*, the court appears to treat this language as describing a single test. Other courts, however, have separated the two parts of the phrase, making each an independent and necessary test for compensation. The following case illustrates the distinction.

HOUSER v. BI-LO, INC.
Supreme Court of Tennessee
36 S.W.3d 68 (2001)

ANDERSON, C.J.

In this workers' compensation case, the widow of the employee, Phil Houser, has appealed from a circuit court judgment denying the employee's claim for benefits filed against the employer, Bi-Lo, Inc. . . .

The employee, Phil Houser, was the manager of a grocery store owned by the employer, Bi-Lo, Inc. As manager of the store, he was responsible for ordering stock. On December 17, 1996, he arrived at work to discover that another employee had also ordered stock for the store, resulting in the receipt of an excessively large order. Not long after he discovered the extra stock, he suffered a stroke while reaching down to pick up a box. After a period of hospitalization and recovery, the employee resumed working in the store under light duty restrictions. He suffered a second, fatal stroke on October 16, 1998, several months after he no longer worked for the employer.

At trial, a former Bi-Lo employee, Burt Cannon, testified that he was working as a stock person on the night the extra stock arrived at the store. Cannon said that when the manager discovered the extra stock, he went "ballistic" and became "red, real red-faced." Cannon also stated that the extra stock caused much confusion and caused the stock room to appear "messy." According to Cannon, it was not normal for an unauthorized employee to order stock.

Andrew White, another worker on duty that night, testified that the manager was "upset" and "real mad" about receiving the extra stock. He stated that other employees in the store were upset as well. White, who was the manager of the store at the time of trial, testified that it was not unusual to have extra stock come in around the holidays and special events. Moreover, he stated that it was part of the manager's job to handle extra stock. White testified that when he became manager of the store, he thought about quitting because the duty of ordering stock was too much for him to handle.

Three physicians testified by deposition. The first of these was Dr. Gregory Wheatley, the employee's treating neurologist. Dr. Wheatley testified that the employee had several risk factors for a stroke, including a history of cerebral vascular disease; heart disease; high blood pressure; and smoking. It was his opinion that the episode of anger and stress on December 17, 1996, contributed to the employee's stroke. Dr. Wheatley also believed that "the injury from the initial stroke predisposed the employee to having bleeding in that area [of the brain] which then . . . was the event that caused his death."

Another neurologist, Dr. Jack Scariano, testified that the employee's first stroke was caused by multiple pre-existing factors such as high blood pressure; alcohol use; smoking; and a history of cardiac disease. Dr. Scariano said that nothing in the employee's medical records indicated that the first stroke was causally related to his employment, and that anger was not a risk factor for having a stroke. He also testified that the second stroke was not causally related to the employee's work. Dr. Scariano stated that the first and second strokes were different types of strokes occurring at different areas in the brain and had no causal connection to each other.

Dr. Cleland Blake, a forensic pathologist, performed an autopsy on the employee and testified that the cause of the employee's death was a massive cerebral hemorrhage, i.e. a stroke. When asked whether he had an opinion as to whether the second stroke was causally related to the first stroke, Dr. Blake testified that the two were causally related in that the first one softened and weakened the brain.

After considering the evidence, the trial court denied the plaintiff's claim for benefits. The trial court reasoned that receiving a large shipment of stock did not constitute an unusual or abnormal circumstance for the manager of a grocery store. The plaintiff appealed. . . .

In order to be eligible for workers' compensation benefits, an employee must suffer an "injury by accident arising out of and in the course of employment which causes either disablement or death. . . ." Tenn. Code Ann. § 50-6-102(12) (1999). The statutory requirements that the injury "arise out of" and occur "in the course of" the employment are not synonymous. An injury occurs "in the course of" employment if it takes place while the employee was performing a duty he or she was employed to perform. Put another way, "the injury must have substantially originated from the 'time and space' of work, resulting in an injury directly linked to the work environment or work-related activities." *Harman v. Moore's Quality Snack Foods*, 815 S.W.2d 519, 527 (Tenn. Ct. App. 1991). Accordingly, the course of employment requirement focuses on the "time, place and circumstances" of the injury.

In contrast, "arising out of" employment refers to "cause or origin." An injury arises out of employment "when there is apparent to the rational mind, upon a consideration of all the circumstances, a causal connection between the conditions under which the work is required to be performed and the resulting injury." *Fink v. Caudle*, 856 S.W.2d [952,] 958. The mere presence of the employee at the place of injury because of the employment is not sufficient, as the injury must result from a danger or hazard peculiar to the work or be caused by a risk inherent in the nature of the work. As one court has put it, the "danger must be peculiar to the work. . . . An injury purely coincidental, or contemporaneous, or collateral, with the employment . . . will not cause the injury . . . to be considered as arising out of the employment." *Jackson v. Clark & Fay, Inc.*, 270 S.W.2d [389,] 390.

The present case focuses on whether the employee's injury arose out of his employment, as there is no question that it occurred in the course of the employment. Relying on *Reeser v. Yellow Freight Sys.*, Inc., 938 S.W.2d 690 (Tenn. 1997), the plaintiff argues that her husband's stroke on December 17, 1996, arose out of his employment because receiving the shipment of overstock, which caused the employee to become angry, was an abnormal or unusual event. The employer responds that dealing with overstock such as occurred on December 17, 1996, was part of the employee's job and should be considered normal stress and therefore not compensable. The employer thus urges this Court to affirm the trial court's denial of benefits.

We agree with the parties that this case is controlled largely by our decision in *Reeser*, which is the seminal case in this jurisdiction regarding the compensability of strokes. In *Reeser*, the employee suffered a stroke while driving a large truck through one of the worst ice storms to ever hit the area. 938 S.W.2d at 691. The employee had to navigate his truck through "horrendous" weather and road conditions and around vehicles and trees, at times in the dark. *Id.* at 692–93. We affirmed the trial court's finding that the employee's stroke arose out of his employment. *Id.* at 693. In doing so, we relied upon the settled rule that "injuries are generally compensable as accidental injuries when they are precipitated by physical exertion or strain *or* a specific incident or series of incidents involving mental or emotional stress of an unusual or abnormal nature." *Id.* at 692.

With regard to injuries caused by a mental or emotional stimulus, we stated in *Reeser* that "excessive and unexpected mental anxiety, stress, tension or worry attributable to the employment can cause injuries sufficient to justify an award of benefits." *Id.* However, the ordinary stress of one's occupation does not meet this standard because "emotional stress, to some degree, accompanies the performance of any contract of employment." *Allied Chem. Corp. v. Wells*, 578 S.W.2d 369, 373 (Tenn. 1979). In other words, "normal ups and downs are part of any employment relationship and, as we have said on many previous occasions, do not justify finding an 'accidental injury' for purposes of worker[s'] compensation law." *Bacon v. Sevier County*, 808 S.W.2d [46,] 53 (citations omitted). Thus, the rule is settled in this jurisdiction that physical or mental injuries caused by worry, anxiety, or emotional stress of a general nature or ordinary stress associated with the worker's occupation are not compensable. The injury must have resulted from an incident involving mental stress of an unusual or abnormal nature, rather than the day-to-day mental stresses and tensions to which workers in that field are occasionally subjected.

With these principles in mind, we review the record in the present case to determine whether the employee's stroke on December 17, 1996, arose out of his employment. We note first that there was no physical exertion or strain involved in precipitating the stroke. Instead, according to some of the medical proof, the mental stress or tension of having to deal with the unexpected shipment of overstock caused the stroke. However, the record is uncontradicted that handling overstock was part of the employee's job as the manager of the store. Moreover, evidence was presented that it was normal for extra stock to arrive at the store during holidays. The stock involved here arrived at the store shortly before Christmas. Accordingly, it cannot be said that the evidence preponderates against the trial court's finding that the employee's stroke did not arise out of his employment. The reason, simply put, is that the stroke was not caused by a mental or emotional stimulus of an unusual or abnormal nature, beyond what is typically encountered by the manager of a grocery store.

We thus reiterate the rule again in this case that physical or mental injuries caused by a mental or emotional stimulus; excessive and unexpected mental anxiety; or stress, tension, or worry attributable to the employment can justify an award of benefits, but the ordinary mental stresses and tensions of one's occupation do not because "emotional stress, to some degree, accompanies the performance of any contract of employment." *Allied Chem. Corp. v. Wells*, 578 S.W.2d at 373. If the rule were otherwise, workers' compensation coverage would become as broad as general health and accident insurance, which it is not. . . .

We conclude that neither stroke, and hence the employee's death, arose out of his employment. Accordingly, the trial court correctly denied benefits.

NOTES

1. **"Arising out of."** How does the "arising out of" test differ from the "in the course of employment" test? Which test caused problems for the claimant in this case and why?

In interpreting the "arising out of" phrase, courts have developed several different tests for determining whether a particular risk resulted from the employment or not. The three tests most commonly utilized currently are: "increased-risk," "actual risk" and "positional-risk." LEX K. LARSON, LARSON'S WORKERS' COMPENSATION, DESK EDITION § 3.01 (2014). The increased-risk doctrine focuses on whether the employment increased the *quantity* of a risk, even if that risk is *qualitatively* not peculiar to the employment. *Id.* at § 3.03. The "actual risk" doctrine simply asks whether the employment subjected the claimant to the actual risk that caused the injury. Adoption of this test has the effect of "permit[ting] recoveries in most street-risk cases and in a much greater proportion of act-of-God cases." *Id.* at § 3.04. The "positional-risk" test requires only that the injury "would not have occurred *but for* the fact that the conditions and obligations of the employment placed claimant in the position where he was injured." *Id.* at § 3.05. According to Larson, this test supports compensation "in cases of roving lunatics, and other situations in which the only connection of the employment with the injury is that its obligations placed the employee in the particular place at the particular time when he or she was injured by some neutral force." *Id.*

Despite their differences, what these tests try to capture is whether the injury that occurred is sufficiently connected to the work that it should be compensable. This notion of work connection is considerably broader than the traditional tort notion of "proximate cause," which links a negligent or reckless act with its foreseeable consequences.

The broader concerns of compensation law are perhaps best illustrated by another case. In *Carroll v. Workers' Compensation Appeal Board*, 750 A.2d 938 (Pa. Commw. Ct. 2000), the claimant, the Director of the Administrative Computer Center at the University of Pennsylvania, was attending a meeting when he "felt a sneeze coming on." *Id.* at 939. He tried to suppress the sneeze and failed, but as a result of the attempt he suffered a detached retina and lost his vision in his left eye. *Id.* at 940. The court held that the injury occurred while the claimant was acting in furtherance of his employer's affairs—he tried to suppress the sneeze in order to avoid spreading germs—and was therefore compensable. Clearly, the result in a case like *Carroll* cannot be explained by any concept of "proximate cause" or "fault," but rather turns on the injury's connection to the claimant's work.

2. **How Much Stress?** In cases involving strokes, heart attacks, and similar types of physical illness, the challenge for the compensation system is to determine when conditions ordinarily found in the population at large are sufficiently

connected to the particular employment that compensation benefits are warranted. Where physical consequences immediately follow a sudden, traumatic event—for example, when an employee has a heart attack upon being held up at gunpoint at work—the connection seems obvious, and most states will award compensation. More difficult are allegations that physical illness or injury has resulted from less dramatic events, or even gradual or sustained periods of stress. In these situations, compensation often turns on whether there is some evidence that the conditions of work played a contributing role in precipitating the worker's illness. Courts have found compensable the heart attack of an employee brought on by a rigorous cross-examination when he was testifying on behalf of his employer at trial, *Church v. Westchester County*, 253 A.D. 859 (N.Y. App. Div. 1938), and the fatal stroke of a sportswriter whose job repeatedly required that he meet very tight deadlines for producing articles, *Mulcahey v. New England Newspapers, Inc.*, 488 A.2d 681 (R.I. 1985). Would the claims of these employees be compensable under the test set out in *Houser*? Should they be compensable?

3. **"Arising out of" but Not "In the Course of" Employment.** Because an injury must "arise out of" and "in the course of" employment to be covered, satisfying only one test is not sufficient to prove compensability. For example, a flight attendant who was originally scheduled to work on September 11, 2001, on the flight that was hijacked and then crashed in Pennsylvania could not recover workers' compensation for post-traumatic stress syndrome because she failed to meet both tests. *Stroka v. United Airlines*, 835 A.2d 1247 (N.J. Super. Ct. App. Div. 2003). Several days before the flight, she had requested the day off in order to care for her child. While she was off duty that day, she learned of the crash and subsequently suffered post-traumatic stress syndrome as a result of learning of the manner of death of her co-workers and her feelings of guilt that one of them had replaced her on the flight. The court found that although her condition did "arise out of" her employment, it did not occur "in the course of" employment, as she was not working nor in a place she was reasonably expected to be in relation to her employment at the time she learned of the crash, and therefore, it denied compensation.

3.   Exclusivity of Remedies

a.   The Fundamental Bargain

ECKIS v. SEA WORLD CORP.
California Court of Appeal
134 Cal. Rptr. 183 (1976)

AULT, J.

Defendants Sea World and Kent Burgess have appealed from a judgment entered on a jury verdict awarding Anne E. Eckis $75,000 in compensatory damages. Plaintiff had sought both compensatory and punitive damages for personal injuries she sustained while riding "Shamu the Whale," framing her complaint on three theories: fraud, negligence, and liability for an animal with vicious or dangerous propensities. . . .

The major issue raised on appeal is the contention there was no substantial evidence to support the jury's finding that plaintiff's injuries did *not* occur in the course of her employment by Sea World. The facts which govern this issue are not in dispute.

When injured on April 19, 1971, plaintiff Anne E. Eckis, then 22 years old, was a full-time employee of Sea World. First hired by Sea World in 1967, she had worked variously as ticket sales girl, receptionist, in the accounting department, and in 1970 became the secretary for Kent Burgess, the director of Sea World's animal training department. From then on her job title was secretary, and that is what she considered herself to be, although from time to time she did other tasks at Burgess' request, such as taking the water temperature, doing research, and running errands. She worked five days a week, for which she was paid a salary of $450 per month. When first hired plaintiff, like all other Sea World employees, had signed an authorization for reproduction of her physical likeness. Plaintiff was also an excellent swimmer, with some scuba diving experience, and had occasionally worked as a model, sometimes for pay.

In April 1971 Gail MacLaughlin, Sea World's public relations director, and Kent Burgess asked plaintiff if she would like to ride Shamu, the killer whale, in a bikini for some publicity pictures for Sea World. Although the ride was not made a condition of her keeping her job, plaintiff eagerly agreed, thinking it would be exciting. Although warned in general terms that the ride involved dangers and aware that she might fall off, plaintiff was confident of her swimming ability and anxious to do it. She had never heard of whales pushing riders around.

Burgess had been responsible for training Shamu ever since Sea World first acquired the animal. He knew Shamu was conditioned to being ridden only by persons wearing wetsuits, and that Shamu had in the past attacked persons who attempted to ride her in an ordinary bathing suit: first a Catalina swimsuit model and then Jim Richards, one of the trainers at Sea World. In addition, Burgess had read training records which showed Shamu had been behaving erratically since early March 1971. This information he did not disclose to plaintiff.

Plaintiff was trained for the ride by Sea World trainers in the tank at Sea World during normal office working hours. First she practiced riding Kilroy, a smaller, more docile whale, while wearing a bathing suit. During her one practice session on Shamu, she wore a wetsuit, fell off, but swam to the edge of the tank without incident.

On April 19 plaintiff became apprehensive for the first time when one of Sea World's trainers said he was not going to watch her ride Shamu because it was "really dangerous." Plaintiff then went to Burgess and told him of her concern. He told her not to worry, said there was nothing to be concerned about, and that the ride was "as safe as it could be." He still did not tell her about the problems they had been having with Shamu or about the earlier incidents involving Richards and the swimsuit model. Thus reassured, plaintiff, wearing a bikini Sea World had paid for, then took three rides on Shamu. During the second ride one of the trainers noticed

Shamu's tail was fluttering, a sign the animal was upset. During the third ride plaintiff fell off when Shamu refused to obey a signal. Shamu then bit her on her legs and hips and held her in the tank until she could be rescued.

Plaintiff suffered 18 to 20 wounds which required from 100 to 200 stitches and left permanent scars. She was hospitalized five days and out of work several weeks. She also suffered some psychological disturbance. Sea World paid all her medical expenses and continued to pay her salary as usual during this period. On advice of her counsel, she filed this civil action and a workers' compensation claim.

injury

When an employee's injuries are compensable under the Workers' Compensation Act, the right of the employee to recover the benefits provided by the Act is his exclusive remedy against the employer.

Under [Labor Code] section 3600, with exceptions not applicable here, liability of the employer to pay compensation under the Act, "in lieu of any other liability whatsoever," attaches:

> "(b) Where, at the time of the injury, the employee is performing service growing out of and incidental to his employment and is acting within the course of his employment," and

> "(c) Where the injury is proximately caused by the employment, either with or without negligence."

The provisions of the Act must be ". . . liberally construed by the courts with the purpose of extending their benefits for the protection of persons injured in the course of their employment." (§ 3202.) . . .

Where a reasonable doubt exists as to whether an act of an employee is contemplated by the employment, or as to whether an injury occurred in the course of the employment, section 3202 requires courts to resolve the doubt against the right of the employee to sue for civil damages and in favor of the applicability of the Compensation Act. The importance of adhering to the rule requiring a liberal construction of the Act in favor of its applicability in civil litigation was emphasized by the court in *Scott* [*v. Pacific Coast Borax Co.*, 140 Cal. App. 2d 173].

> "Though it may be more opportunistic for a particular plaintiff to seek to circumscribe the purview of compensation coverage because of his immediate interest and advantage, the courts must be vigilant to preserve the spirit of the act and to prevent a distortion of its purposes. That the question before us in this case arises out of litigation prosecuted in the superior court is all the more reason for care lest rules of doubtful validity, out of harmony with the objectives of the act, be formulated."

(Scott v. Pacific Coast Borax Co., supra, 140 Cal. App. 2d 173, 178.) . . . .

Governed by these legal principles, we examine the evidence to determine whether it supports the finding plaintiff was not acting within the course and scope of her employment at Sea World when she sustained her injuries.

The undisputed evidence shows: at the time she was injured plaintiff was an employee of Sea World; she was injured on the employer's premises during what were her regular working hours; she was injured while engaging in an activity which her employer had requested her to perform and for which it had provided her with the training and the means to perform; in riding Shamu the Whale for publicity pictures, plaintiff was not engaged in an activity which was personal to her, but rather one which was related to, furthered, and benefited the business of her employer.

Despite this formidable array of factors which indicate her injuries did arise out of and occurred in the course and scope of her employment, plaintiff maintains substantial evidence supports the special finding to the contrary. She premises her position on the claim she was hired to be a secretary, not to ride a whale. Since her injuries were unrelated to the secretarial duties she was originally hired to perform, she argues her employment "had nothing whatsoever to do with her injury" and that her case does not come within the purview of the Compensation Act. Because of the highly unusual circumstances under which she was injured, she maintains the rules and formulas traditionally used to determine whether injuries have arisen out of or occurred in the course of employment are neither applicable nor helpful.

These arguments are without merit. The right to compensation is not limited to those cases where the injury occurs while the employee is performing the classical duties for which he was originally hired. Far less than a direct request by the employer operates to bring an injury-causing activity within the provisions of the Compensation Act. For example, in *Lizama v. Workmen's Comp. Appeals Bd.*, 40 Cal. App. 3d 363, the employee was injured on the employer's premises after he had clocked out from work while using a table saw to construct a bench to sit on at lunch time. Although his assigned duties did not include use of the saw and he had never used it before, the injury was held compensable because the employer had expressly or impliedly permitted such use of equipment. . . .

Where, as here, an employee is injured on the employer's premises during regular working hours, when the injury occurs while the employee is engaged in an activity which the employer has requested her to undertake, and when the injury-causing activity is of service to the employer and benefits the employer's business, the conditions imposing liability for compensation under Labor Code section 3600 are met as a matter of law, and it is immaterial that the activity causing the injury was not related to the employee's normal duties or that the circumstances surrounding the injury were unusual or unique.

It would be wholly incongruous and completely at variance with the long declared purposes and policies of the workers' compensation law to say that an employee who sustained injuries under the circumstances of this case is not entitled to the benefits of the Workers' Compensation Act. Since her injuries fall within the scope of the Act, a proceeding under it constitutes plaintiff's exclusive remedy.

The concluding remarks of the court in *Scott v. Pacific Coast Borax Co.*, *supra*, 140 Cal. App. 2d 173, 184, are appropriate here.

> "We are cognizant of the fact that plaintiff, believing himself without fault, regards it to his decided advantage to maintain an action for damages against his employer rather than to receive an award of workmen's compensation. But in deciding whether an injury is compensable, we must disregard completely the question of fault and be mindful that the rules we

lay down in this particular case must be salutary and consonant with the spirit and purpose of the compensation act, since they will govern other cases where the act will provide the worker disabled by industrial injury with his sole remedy. Inasmuch as this state is committed to the view that the Workmen's Compensation Act must be liberally construed in favor of coverage for the employee and jurisdiction in the commission and since the facts adduced show there existed a concurrence of the conditions of section 3600 of the Labor Code, the trial court correctly ruled that the commission was the exclusive tribunal for the prosecution of plaintiff's rights."

(*Scott v. Pacific Coast Borax Co.*, *supra*, 140 Cal. App. 2d 173, 184.) . . .

The judgment is reversed; the trial court is directed to enter a judgment in favor of Sea World.

NOTES

so it was in course scope of employ

1. **Limited Remedies.** After Eckis was injured, Sea World paid for all of her medical expenses and continued to pay her full salary until she returned to work. Why then did she bring a civil action? What losses did she suffer that would *not* be covered by workers' compensation?

Given the facts described in the opinion, did Eckis establish Burgess's fault in causing her injuries? Why did the court reverse the jury verdict in her favor? In cases of egregious employer misconduct, is it fair to limit the remedies available to a worker injured as a result?

2. **An Absence of Remedy.** Under the "compensation bargain," all work-related injuries are compensated exclusively through the workers' compensation system. But what if a worker has sustained an injury at the workplace and under the requirements of the state statute, no compensation is available for that particular injury? Such a situation can arise because a statute excludes certain types of injuries, for example mental stress, or because the injury was not disabling, and therefore did not affect the worker's ability to earn wages, even though it may have injured him in other ways. Should exclusivity bar a tort suit to recover for injuries if the worker will otherwise receive nothing under the compensation system?

Courts have taken different approaches to this question. In *Kleinhesselink v. Chevron,* 920 P.2d 108 (Mont. 1996), the court held that because the workers' compensation statute does not provide benefits for mental or physical conditions caused by mental stress, the employee's tort suit alleging that the employer's negligence caused such harm should not be barred. According to the court, "the quid pro quo between employers and employees is central to the Act; thus, it is axiomatic that there must be some possibility of recovery by the employee for the compromise to hold." *Id.* at 111. In contrast, the California Supreme Court in *Livitsanos v. Superior Court*, 828 P.2d 1195 (Cal. 1992), held that where an employee suffers mental distress, but is not disabled, as a result of an employer's conduct, the injury will not result in "any occupational impairment compensable under the workers' compensation law," *and* the worker will still be barred from bringing a tort suit. It concluded that "the possibility of a lack of a remedy in a few cases does not abrogate workers' compensation exclusivity." *Id.* at 1203. *See also*

Bias v. E. Associated Coal Corp., 640 S.E.2d 540 (W. Va. 2006).

In Oregon, the legislature took on the issue directly, adding the following language to the state's workers' compensation statute: "The exclusive remedy provisions . . . apply to all injuries and to diseases, symptom complexes or similar conditions of subject workers arising out of and in the course of employment whether or not they are determined to be compensable under this chapter." OR. REV. STAT. § 656.018(7) . The Oregon Supreme Court, however, held that the provision is unconstitutional as applied in certain circumstances. In *Smothers v. Gresham Transfer, Inc.*, 23 P.3d 333 (Or. 2001), the plaintiff alleged that workplace exposure to sulfuric acid and other chemical mists had caused damage to his respiratory system. His claim for workers' compensation benefits was denied because he could not prove that his work exposure was the major contributing cause of his illness, as required under Oregon's compensation law. When he sued for damages alleging negligence, the employer argued that his claim was barred by the exclusivity provision. The Oregon Supreme Court held the exclusivity provision unconstitutional to the extent that it leaves "a worker with no process through which to seek redress for an injury for which a cause of action existed at common law." *Id.* at 362.

b. Exception for Intentional Acts

Because of the rather limited remedies available under workers' compensation, injured employees, like Eckis, sometimes try to escape the exclusivity bar in cases of clear employer fault. One way to avoid exclusivity is to show that their injury was not covered by workers' compensation at all—for example, by arguing, as Eckis tried unsuccessfully to do, that it did not arise out of or in the course of employment.

Another way workers can sometimes avoid exclusivity is by alleging that their injuries resulted from an intentional tort by the employer. Most states recognize an exception to exclusivity for intentional torts. In some states, the exception for intentional torts is spelled out in the statute. In others, the exception is created judicially. Typically, the courts recognizing such an exception focus on statutory language specifying that worker injuries and death resulting from "accident" are covered by workers' compensation. Because intentional torts are not accidental, these courts reason that the exclusivity bar does not apply. Often, policy concerns underscore this interpretation of the state statute. As the court in *Zimmerman v. Valdak Corp.*, 570 N.W.2d 204 (N.D. 1997), explained:

> An underlying objective of workers' compensation is to promote a safe work environment. Affording employers immunity for intentional acts does not promote that objective. If intentional torts were covered by workers' compensation, it would allow "an intentional tortfeasor to shift his liability to a fund paid for with premiums collected from innocent employers." Employers would not be held individually responsible for their intentional actions. In effect, it would allow an employer to buy the right to hit an employee.

Id. at 207 (citation omitted).

Even though a majority of states recognizes an exception to exclusivity for intentional torts, courts are often quite reluctant to find that the exception applies.

Even cases involving egregious employer conduct, such as knowingly ordering employees to perform extremely dangerous work, willfully violating safety statutes, or deliberately removing safety devices, have been held to fall within the exclusive remedy rule. In a handful of states, the intentional exception to the exclusivity rule has been broadened, but only slightly, as the next case illustrates.

WHITAKER v. TOWN OF SCOTLAND NECK
Supreme Court of North Carolina
597 S.E.2d 665 (2003)

WAINWRIGHT, JUSTICE.

. . . The Town of Scotland Neck (Town) is a North Carolina municipality that provides general governmental services including, among other things, garbage collection. Decedent Carlton Whitaker was employed by the Town as a general maintenance worker assigned to assist in the operation of a garbage truck.

On 30 July 1997, decedent and two other maintenance workers were emptying a dumpster at a private school. The garbage truck backed up to the dumpster, with decedent positioned at the rear of the truck. Decedent's job was to attach the dumpster to the truck's lifting equipment so that the dumpster could be emptied. In order to secure the dumpster for lifting, decedent and his co-worker attached a trunnion bar on the front of the dumpster to latching mechanisms located at the rear of the truck. Decedent hooked the truck's cable winch to the rear of the dumpster. Coupled to the truck in this fashion, the winch hoisted the dumpster into the air, pivoting the dumpster on its trunnion bar, and allowing its contents to fall into the truck's rear compactor.

As the dumpster was being hoisted, the latching mechanism on decedent's side of the garbage truck gave way, releasing the trunnion bar and allowing the raised container to swing free of its restraints. The dumpster swung around to decedent's side of the truck, striking decedent and pinning him against the truck. Decedent's co-workers rushed to his aid, manually pushing the dumpster aside and lowering decedent to the ground. Following the accident, decedent was conscious and could talk.

Rescue personnel responded and transported decedent to the hospital. Twenty-eight days after the accident, decedent died as a consequence of a crush injury to his chest.

On the day of the accident, Scotland Neck Safety Director C.T. Hasty began his investigation. He found that the dumpster latching mechanism on the truck could not, in fact, be latched by hand and that the dumpster was bent. He interviewed a number of decedent's co-workers, several of whom reported that both the dumpster and the truck's latching mechanism had been broken for at least two months and that such defects had been reported to their supervisor. The supervisor, however, denied any prior knowledge of defects in the truck or dumpster. Based upon his investigation, Hasty concluded that the broken latch and the bent dumpster were the direct cause of the accident.

In August 1997, the North Carolina Department of Labor's Division of Occupational Safety and Health (OSHANC) also investigated the accident and similarly concluded that "defective equipment was the proximate cause of the accident" and that "the accident . . . was a result of employment conditions that were not in compliance with the safety standards of OSHA." More specifically, the OSHANC investigator found five "serious" violations of state labor law. These violations included: failure to train employees in the safe operation of garbage truck equipment, failure to properly supervise employees in the operation of garbage truck equipment, failure to implement a program for inspection of garbage truck equipment, operation of defective garbage truck equipment, and unsafe operation of garbage truck equipment. As a result of these OSHANC violations, the Town was assessed penalties totaling $10,500.

On 20 August 1999, plaintiffs Donald Whitaker and Thomas Whitaker, Jr., as co-administrators of the estate of decedent, filed a civil action against the Town; Scotland Neck Safety Director C.T. Hasty, in his individual and official capacity; and Scotland Neck Public Works Superintendent Douglas Braddy, in his individual and official capacity. Plaintiffs alleged "willful, wanton, reckless, careless and gross negligence" and demanded compensatory and punitive damages.

Defendants denied all negligence. As an additional defense, defendants responded that plaintiffs' civil action was barred by the North Carolina Workers' Compensation Act, which limits remedies for work-related injuries to those expressly provided by the Act.

The trial court agreed that plaintiffs' claim was barred by the Workers' Compensation Act and granted defendants' motion for summary judgment on 15 August 2001. Plaintiffs thereafter appealed to the Court of Appeals, which reversed the trial court, concluding that plaintiffs had raised a genuine issue of material fact under *Woodson* [*v. Rowland*, 407 S.E.2d 222 (1991),] as to whether defendants' actions were substantially certain to cause decedent's death. . . .

As this Court has often discussed, the North Carolina Workers' Compensation Act was created to ensure that injured employees receive sure and certain recovery for their work-related injuries without having to prove negligence on the part of the employer or defend against charges of contributory negligence. In exchange for these "limited but assured benefits," the employee is generally barred from suing the employer for potentially larger damages in civil negligence actions and is instead limited exclusively to those remedies set forth in the Act.

This Court, however, recognizes an important exception to the general exclusivity provisions of the Workers' Compensation Act where an employee is injured or killed as a result of the intentional misconduct of the employer. In *Woodson*, this Court slightly expanded this exception to include cases in which a defendant employer engaged in conduct that, while not categorized as an intentional tort, was nonetheless substantially certain to cause serious injury or death to the employee. 407 S.E.2d at 226-30. In such cases, the injured employee may proceed outside the exclusivity provisions of the Act and maintain a common law tort action against the employer.

In *Woodson v. Rowland*, the defendant-employer was a construction company that specialized in trench excavation. *Id.* at 225. An employee of the defendant-employer was killed when a fourteen-foot-deep trench in which he was working collapsed. The factual circumstances surrounding the employee's death in *Woodson* were particularly offensive to this Court. In flagrant disregard of safety regulations and industry-wide standards, the defendant-employer's president had knowingly directed his employees to work in a deep trench with sheer, unstable walls that lacked proper shoring. *Id.* at 231. The hazard of a cave-in was so obvious that the foreman of another construction crew working on the project had emphatically refused to send his men into the trench until it was properly shored. *Id.* at 225. Moreover, the defendant-employer had been cited at least four times in the preceding six and a half years for multiple violations of trenching-safety regulations. *Id.* at 231. Thus, there was sufficient evidence from which "a reasonable juror could determine that upon placing a man in this trench serious injury or death as a result of a cave-in was a substantial certainty rather than an unforeseeable event, mere possibility, or even substantial probability." *Id.*

Based on these specific facts, this Court in *Woodson* defined a narrow exception to the general exclusivity provisions of the North Carolina Workers' Compensation Act. We specifically held that when an employer intentionally engages in misconduct knowing it is substantially certain to cause serious injury or death to employees and an employee is injured or killed by that misconduct, that employee, or the personal representative of the estate in case of death, may pursue a civil action against the employer. Such misconduct is tantamount to an intentional tort, and civil actions based thereon are not barred by the exclusivity provisions of the Act.

The *Woodson* exception represents a narrow holding in a fact-specific case, and its guidelines stand by themselves. This exception applies only in the most egregious cases of employer misconduct. Such circumstances exist where there is uncontroverted evidence of the employer's intentional misconduct and where such misconduct is substantially certain to lead to the employee's serious injury or death.

In the present case, there is insufficient evidence to reasonably support plaintiffs' contention that defendants intentionally engaged in misconduct knowing that it was substantially certain to cause serious injury or death to decedent. Indeed, the facts of the present case are readily distinguishable from those that gave rise to our holding in *Woodson*.

In *Woodson*, the defendant-employer's president was on the job site and observed first-hand the obvious hazards of the deep trench in which he directed the decedent-employee to work. *Id.* at 225. Knowing that safety regulations and common trade practice mandated the use of precautionary shoring, the defendant-employer's president nonetheless disregarded all safety measures and intentionally placed his employee into a hazardous situation in which experts concluded that only one outcome was substantially certain to follow: an injurious, if not fatal, cave-in of the trench. *Id.* at 231–32.

In the present case, there is no similar evidence that defendants were manifestly indifferent to the health and safety of their employees. The Town has a long history of garbage collection, yet there is no evidence of record that the Town had been previously cited for multiple, significant violations of safety regulations, as in *Woodson*. On the day of the accident, none of the Town's supervisors were on-site to monitor or oversee the workers' activities. Decedent was not expressly instructed to proceed into an obviously hazardous situation as in *Woodson*. There is no evidence that defendants knew that the latching mechanism on the truck was substantially certain to fail or that if such failure did occur, serious injury or death would be substantially certain to follow. As discussed in *Woodson*, simply having knowledge of some possibility, or even probability, of injury or death is not the same as knowledge of a substantial certainty of injury or death.

In *Woodson*, evidence was presented from which a jury could reasonably conclude that the defendant-employer's president recognized the immediate hazards of his operation and consciously elected to forgo critical safety precautions. *Id.* at 231. Here, there is no such evidence. Moreover, in Woodson, the employee worked in a deep, narrow trench in which it was impossible for him to escape or avoid injury once the soil around him began to cave in. Here, however, decedent was not so helpless. In sum, the forecast of evidence in the present case fails to establish that defendants intentionally engaged in misconduct knowing that it was substantially certain to cause serious injury or death to decedent. The facts of this case involve defective equipment and human error that amount to an accident rather than intentional misconduct.

We therefore conclude that plaintiffs failed to raise a genuine issue of material fact as to defendants' civil liability under the *Woodson* exception to the general exclusivity provisions of the North Carolina Workers' Compensation Act. Accordingly, we reverse the ruling of the Court of Appeals and instruct that court to reinstate the original order of the Superior Court, Halifax County, granting summary judgment in favor of defendants.

Reversed.

NOTES

1. **Discerning Intent.** According to the Supreme Court of North Carolina, what showing of intent on the part of the employer is necessary in order for a plaintiff to avoid the exclusivity bar and proceed in a tort action? How does the court in *Whitaker* distinguish its earlier ruling in *Woodson*?

2. **Substantial Certainty.** Although a handful of states do not recognize any exception to workers' compensation exclusivity for intentional acts, most states do permit common law actions based on intentional torts in certain circumstances. However, these jurisdictions differ significantly regarding what showing of intent is sufficient to remove a case from the exclusivity bar. Many require that the employer actually intended to cause injury. In these jurisdictions, even gross negligence or willful and wanton conduct will not result in tort liability without a showing that the employer intended to cause harm, a nearly impossible hurdle in most cases. This traditional position is explained in Larson's treatise on workers' compensation law:

> Even if the alleged conduct goes beyond aggravated negligence, and includes such elements as knowingly permitting a hazardous work condition to exist, knowingly ordering employees to perform an extremely dangerous job, wilfully failing to furnish a safe place to work . . . wilfully violating a safety statute, failing to protect employees from crime, negli-

gent hiring, refusing to respond to an employee's medical needs and restrictions, allowing excessive levels of employee horseplay or withholding information about worksite hazards, the conduct still falls short of the kind of actual intention to injure that robs the injury of accidental character. . . .

If these decisions seem rather strict, one must remind oneself that what is being tested here is not the degree of gravity or depravity of the employer's conduct, but rather the narrow issue of the intentional versus the accidental quality of the precise event producing injury. The intentional removal of a safety device or toleration of a dangerous condition may or may not set the stage for an accidental injury later. But in any normal use of the words, it cannot be said, if such an injury does happen, that this was deliberate infliction of harm comparable to an intentional left jab to the chin.

LEX K. LARSON, LARSON'S WORKERS' COMPENSATION, DESK EDITION § 103.03 (2014).

Although it represents the traditional approach, strict application of the intent standard has been criticized as unduly harsh. As the court in *Delgado v. Phelps Dodge Chino, Inc.*, 34 P.3d 1148 (N.M. 2001), wrote:

[The actual intent test] provides employers with virtually absolute immunity, and "an employer who knows his acts will cause certain harm or death to an employee may escape personal responsibility for an act by merely claiming that he/she hoped the employee would make it." Even more disturbingly, the actual intent test encourages an employer, motivated by economic gain, to knowingly subject a worker to injury in the name of profit-making. As long as the employer is motivated by greed, rather than intent to injure the worker, the employer may abuse workers in an unlimited variety of manners while still enjoying immunity from tort liability.

Id. at 1154. Despite its harshness, courts have been reluctant to move away from a strict requirement of actual intent to harm, fearing that too expansive a reading of the intentional exception to exclusivity could end up undermining the principle of workers' compensation exclusivity altogether.

In *Millison v. E.I. du Pont de Nemours & Co.*, 501 A.2d 505 (N.J. 1985), one of the leading cases adopting the "substantially certain" standard, the court struggled with the question of how an "intentional wrong" should be defined for purposes of avoiding workers' compensation exclusivity. The court in that case wrote:

Although we are certain that the legislature could not have intended that the system of workers' compensation would insulate actors from liability outside the boundaries of the Act for all willful and flagrant misconduct short of deliberate assault and battery, we are equally sure that the statutory scheme contemplates that as many work-related disability claims as possible be processed exclusively within the Act. Moreover, if "intentional wrong" is interpreted too broadly, this single exception would swallow up the entire "exclusivity" provision of the Act, since virtually all employee accidents, injuries, and sicknesses are a result of the employer or a co-employee intentionally acting to do whatever it is that may or may not lead to eventual injury or disease. Thus in setting an appropriate standard by which to measure an "intentional wrong," we are careful to keep an eye fixed on the obvious: the system of workers' compensation confronts head-on the unpleasant, even harsh, reality—but a reality nevertheless—that industry knowingly exposes workers to the risks of injury and disease.

The essential question therefore becomes what level of risk-exposure is so egregious as to constitute an "intentional wrong." We are confident that the *quid pro quo* of workers' compensation—employer makes swift and certain payment without regard to his own fault in exchange for immunity from liability at law—can best be preserved by applying the "intent" analysis of Dean Prosser to determine what is an "intentional wrong" within the meaning of the Act. According to Prosser, the mere knowledge and appreciation of a risk—something short of substantial certainty—is not intent. The defendant who acts in the belief or consciousness that the act is causing an appreciable risk of harm to another may be negligent, and if the risk is great the conduct may be characterized as reckless or wanton, but it is not an intentional wrong. [W. Prosser and W. Keeton, supra, § 8 at 36.] *See also Restatement 2d of Torts*, § 8A (meaning of intent is that actor desires to cause consequences of his act or is substantially certain that such consequences will result from his actions).

In adopting a "substantial certainty" standard, we acknowledge that every undertaking, particularly certain business judgments, involve some risk, but that willful employer misconduct was not meant to go undeterred. The distinctions between negligence, recklessness, and intent are obviously matters of degree, albeit subtle ones, as the thoughtful dissent so power- fully points out. . . . [T]he dividing line between negligent or reckless conduct on the one hand and intentional wrong on the other must be drawn with caution, so that the statutory framework of the Act is not circumvented simply because a known risk later blossoms into reality. We must demand a virtual certainty.

Id. at 513–14. For those courts adopting a "substantial certainty" standard, the difficult question then becomes how to distinguish recklessness from intentional conduct, or a serious risk from a substantial certainty.

The Supreme Court of Utah declined to adopt the "substantial certainty" test, arguing that it "conflates probability with intent." *Helf v. Chevron*, 203 P.3d 962, 973 (Utah 2009). It reasoned that the mere fact that a high probability of injury exists such that "the employer knew that harm was substantially likely to occur sometime to some employee" should not be enough to establish intent, because "almost every form of employment bears some risk of injury." *Id.* On the other hand, the court found that the intent required is broader than motive or desire, and therefore, an injured employee might be able to bring a tort claim even when the employer did not wish to harm the employee, but was only motivated to cut costs or increase profits. The court then framed a different test, one that focuses on "whether the actor knew or expected that injury would occur to a particular employee performing a specific task in determining whether an injury was intentional." *Id.* at 974. Is the approach of the court in *Helf* likely to produce different results than the test articulated in *Whitaker* and *Millison*? Which test best comports with the purposes behind the rule that workers' compensation should provide the exclusive remedy for workplace injuries?

3. Fraudulent Concealment. The *Millison* case, quoted above, is one of a number of cases brought by workers facing devastating disease due to occupational exposure to asbestos. In *Millison*, the workers brought a tort suit alleging two distinct wrongs: first, that their employer had deliberately exposed them to a hazardous work environment with full knowledge of the health risks posed by asbestos; and second, that the employer had fraudulently concealed from them the results of medical exams showing that they were suffering from asbestos-related diseases. Addressing these two different claims, the New Jersey Supreme Court wrote:

> [C]ount one of plaintiffs' complaints seeking damages beyond those available through workers' compensation for their initial work-related occupational diseases must fall. Although defendants' conduct in knowingly exposing plaintiffs to asbestos clearly amounts to deliberately taking risks with employees' health, as we have observed heretofore the mere knowledge and appreciation of a risk—even the strong probability of a risk—will come up short of the "substantial certainty" needed to find an intentional wrong resulting in avoidance of the exclusive-remedy bar of the compensation statute. In the face of the legislature's awareness of occupational diseases as a fact of industrial employment, we are constrained to conclude that plaintiffs-employees' initial resulting occupational diseases must be considered the type of hazard of employment that the legislature anticipated would be compensable under the terms of the Compensation Act and not actionable in an additional civil suit. . . .

> Plaintiffs have, however, pleaded a valid cause of action for aggravation of their initial occupational diseases under the second count of their complaints. Count two alleges that in order to prevent employees from leaving the workforce, defendants fraudulently concealed from plaintiffs the fact that they were suffering from asbestos-related diseases, thereby delaying their treatment and aggravating their existing illnesses. As noted earlier, du Pont's medical staff provides company employees with physical examinations as part of its package of medical services. Plaintiffs contend that although plaintiffs' physical examinations revealed changes in chest x-rays indicating asbestos-related injuries, du Pont's doctors did not inform plaintiffs of their sicknesses, but instead told them that their health was fine and sent them back to work under the same hazardous conditions that had caused the initial injuries.

> These allegations go well beyond failing to warn of potentially-dangerous conditions or intentionally exposing workers to the risks of disease. There is a difference between, on the one hand, tolerating in the workplace conditions that will result in a certain number of injuries or illnesses, and, on the other, actively misleading the employees who have already fallen victim to those risks of the workplace. An employer's fraudulent concealment of diseases already developed is not one of the risks

an employee should have to assume. Such intentionally-deceitful action goes beyond the bargain struck by the Compensation Act. But for defendants' corporate strategy of concealing diseases discovered in company physical examinations, plaintiffs would have minimized the dangers to their health. Instead, plaintiffs were deceived—or so they charge—by corporate doctors who held themselves out as acting in plaintiffs' best interests. The legislature, in passing the Compensation Act, could not have intended to insulate such conduct from tort liability. We therefore conclude that plaintiffs' allegations that defendants fraudulently concealed knowledge of already-contracted diseases are sufficient to state a cause of action for aggravation of plaintiffs' illnesses, as distinct from any claim for the existence of the initial disease, which is cognizable only under the Compensation Act.

501 A.2d at 514–16. A similar approach was taken by the California Supreme Court in *Johns-Manville Products Corp. v. Superior Court*, 612 P.2d 948 (Cal. 1980) (holding that employee's claim that his employer had fraudulently concealed that he suffered from asbestos-related disease, resulting in aggravation of the disease, was not barred), and was later codified by the California legislature, *see* CAL. LAB. CODE § 3602(b)(2) (permitting an action at law where "the employee's injury is aggravated by the employer's fraudulent concealment of the existence of the injury and its connection with the employment").

Are the employer's actions giving rise to the fraudulent concealment claim distinguishable from its initial conduct in knowingly exposing its employees to the hazards of working with asbestos? Do you agree that the plaintiff's claim for fraudulent concealment falls outside the "compensation bargain" and should be permitted to proceed in tort?

c.   Non-Physical Torts

As we saw in Chapters 4 and 7, *supra*, employees may bring a number of common law or statutory claims, such as wrongful discharge, defamation, or intentional infliction of emotional distress, against their employers. In some cases, plaintiffs bringing these claims include allegations that the employer's wrongful act has caused them personal injury in the form of mental distress or even resulting physical injury. As we have seen, however, physical injuries "arising out of and in the course of employment" are also covered by workers' compensation. In addition, many states have extended workers' compensation benefits to encompass claims of disabling mental injury that results from emotional trauma or stress encountered on the job. Where the claimed physical or mental injuries are compensable under workers' compensation, should the exclusivity rule bar these common law or statutory claims? The following materials address this question.

COLE v. FAIR OAKS FIRE PROTECTION DISTRICT
Supreme Court of California
729 P.2d 743 (1987)

The main issue presented is whether an employee may maintain a civil action in the courts for intentional infliction of emotional distress against his employer and fellow employee when the conduct complained of has caused total, permanent, mental and physical disability compensable under workers' compensation law. We conclude that when the employee's claim is based on conduct normally occurring in the workplace, it is within the exclusive jurisdiction of the Workers' Compensation Appeals Board. . . .

Leonard Cole enlisted as a volunteer firefighter in 1964 with the district, and in the next year he was appointed a full-time firefighter. In 1970 he was appointed engineer, and in 1977 he was promoted to captain. In March 1981 he was elected union representative and continued to serve in that capacity until April 1982.

In October 1981, he was diagnosed as having high blood pressure. His physician recommended rest and recreation. In February 1982 he was examined and again found to have elevated blood pressure. He was placed on medication. The elevated blood pressure was due to unreasonable stress and pressure by the assistant chief. As union representative Cole negotiated questions of contractual interpretation with management, and the assistant chief, although formerly the union representative, deliberately harassed him in the negotiations.

On one occasion the assistant chief demanded that Cole report to a meeting for performance evaluation and possible disciplinary action and refused to excuse him to attend a funeral.

Although Cole had repeatedly received superior performance ratings, the assistant chief devised a novel personnel evaluation procedure for Cole for the purpose of punishing him for his union activities. Cole was informed by various members of the fire department that the assistant chief and members of the management intended to take punitive action against him because of his union activities.

On May 11, Cole was placed on sick leave because of his hypertension. A doctor employed by the assistant chief reported that the level of hypertension disabled Cole from performing heavy duty and that he should be restricted to light duty until his blood pressure was better controlled.

Thereafter, the assistant chief notified him by mail that he was to present himself at a disciplinary hearing on June 3, 1982. The letter falsely asserted dishonesty as one of the grounds for the hearing. It stated that Cole had stated falsely that he was on workers' compensation and that he had been told by a county safety official not to report to work. The assistant chief conducted the hearing before a panel of battalion chiefs. The hearing was a "kangaroo" proceeding.

Thereafter, on June 28, 1982, Cole was demoted to engineer, and was publicly stripped of his captain's badge. The assistant chief assigned him to perform "humiliating and menial duties," and he was ordered to return to duty from sick leave and assigned to work as a dispatcher, an entry level position.

On October 18, 1982, the Board of Directors of the Fair Oaks Fire Protection District reversed Cole's demotion and reinstated him as a captain at a reduced salary and placed him on probationary status. The assistant chief continued his harassment and sometime between July and September 1982, the assistant chief filed an application with the state to force Cole to retire involuntarily.

Cole's blood pressure was elevated by the continuous harassment, and on November 8, 1982, he suffered a severe and totally disabling cerebral vascular accident. He cannot move, care for himself, or communicate other than by blinking. . . .

In *Johns-Manville Products Corp. v. Superior Court* (1980) 612 P.2d 948, we held that an employee could state a cause of action against the employer where the employer fraudulently concealed from him, from his doctors and from the state that he was suffering from a work-related disease thereby preventing treatment and inducing him to continue working under hazardous conditions. . . .

[The court in *Johns-Manville* wrote:]

> [Workers' compensation] is the sole remedy for additional compensation against an employer whose employee is injured in the first instance as the result of a deliberate failure to assure that the physical environment of the work place is safe.

> Thus, if the complaint alleged only that plaintiff contracted the disease because defendant knew and concealed from him that his health was endangered by asbestos in the work environment, failed to supply adequate protective devices to avoid disease, and violated governmental regulations relating to dust levels at the plant, plaintiff's only remedy would be to prosecute his claim under the workers' compensation law.

> But where the employer is charged with intentional misconduct which goes beyond his failure to assure that the tools or substances used by the employee or the physical environment of a workplace are safe, some cases have held that the employer may be subject to common law liability.

The court [in *Johns-Manville*] pointed out that cases had permitted action for damages by the employee for an assault by the employer, for fraudulent misrepresentations made as part of a conspiracy with a third party which concealed that the industrial injury was caused by the third party against whom the employee had recourse, and for assault, battery and intentional infliction of emotional distress based on an insurer's deceitful investigation. Those cases relied upon the factors that the employer's and insurer's misconduct had a questionable relationship to the employment and was not considered a risk of the employment. The court concluded that the cases reflect "a trend toward allowing an action at law for injuries suffered in the employment if the employer acts deliberately *for the purpose of injuring the employee* or if the harm resulting from the intentional misconduct consists of aggravation of an initial work-related injury." 27 Cal. 3d at 476. . . .

Plaintiffs urge that the reasoning of *Johns-Manville* permits maintenance of an action for intentional infliction of emotional distress whether or not physical injury resulted where the tortious conduct has aggravated a compensable injury. Plaintiffs' contention appears too broad. . . . [T]he intent element for such a [claim of intentional infliction of emotional distress] may consist of an intention to cause emotional distress or reckless disregard of the probability of causing emotional distress. To permit liability where the employer did not specifically intend to cause distress but his misconduct reflected a reckless disregard of the probability of injury would to be contrary to [our precedent]. As [we] pointed out: "It is not uncommon for an employer to 'put his mind' to the existence of a danger to an employee and nevertheless fail to take corrective action. . . . The focus of the inquiry in a case involving work-related injury would often be not whether the injury arose out of and in the course of employment, but the state of knowledge of the employer and the employee regarding the dangerous condition which caused the injury. Such a result would undermine the underlying premise upon which the workers' compensation system is based." (612 P.2d 948.) Since awareness of the danger by the employer is not a basis for liability for damages, it follows that reckless disregard of the probability of injury should not warrant exemption from the exclusive remedy provisions of the Labor Code. . . .

Nevertheless, the question remains whether the exclusive remedy provisions exclude liability in a limited class of cases of intentional infliction of emotional distress causing disability, namely, where the employer acts with the purpose of causing emotional distress. Permitting such an action would throw open the doors to numerous claims already compensable under the compensation law. An employer's supervisory conduct is inherently "intentional." In order to properly manage its business, every employer must on occasion review, criticize, demote, transfer and discipline employees. Employers are necessarily aware that their employees will feel distressed by adverse personnel decisions, while employees may consider any such adverse action to be improper and outrageous. Indeed, it would be unusual for an employee *not* to suffer emotional distress as a result of an unfavorable decision by his employer.

We have concluded that, when the misconduct attributed to the employer is actions which are a normal part of the employment relationship, such as demotions, promotions, criticism of work practices, and frictions in negotiations as to grievances, an employee suffering emotional distress causing disability may not avoid the exclusive remedy provisions of the Labor Code by characterizing the employer's decisions as manifestly unfair, outrageous, harassment, or intended to cause emotional disturbance resulting in disability. The basis of compensation and the exclusive remedy provisions is an injury sustained and arising out of the course of employment, and when the essence of the wrong is personal physical injury or death, the action is barred by the exclusiveness clause no matter what its name or technical form if the usual conditions of coverage are satisfied.

If characterization of conduct normally occurring in the workplace as unfair or outrageous were sufficient to avoid the exclusive remedy provisions of the Labor Code, the exception would permit the employee to allege a cause of action in every case where he suffered mental disability merely by alleging an ulterior purpose of causing injury. Such an exception would be contrary to the compensation bargain and unfair to the employer. . . .

The cases that have permitted recovery in tort for intentional misconduct causing disability have involved conduct of an employer having a "questionable" relationship to the employment, an injury which did not occur while the employee was performing service incidental to the employment and which would not be viewed as a risk of the employment, or conduct where the employer or insurer stepped out of their proper roles. Such circumstances are not alleged in the complaint before us.

To the contrary, the allegations in the instant case as to the *conduct* of the employer and the assistant chief reflect matters which can be expected to occur with substantial frequency in the working environment. Some harassment by superiors when there is a clash of personality or values is not uncommon. Disciplinary hearings and demotions and friction in negotiations as to grievances are also an inherent part of the employment setting as are decisions to seek disability retirement and demands to appear at meetings which interfere with personal arrangements. . . .

NOTES

1. **A Normal Risk of Employment?** In *Johns-Manville Products Corp. v. Superior Court*, 612 P.2d 948 (Cal. 1980), the California Supreme Court had held that a tort action for employment-related injuries could proceed if the employer had acted deliberately for the purpose of injuring the employee. In *Cole*, however, the court found that this exception did not apply to the tort of intentional infliction of emotional distress? Why not?

Chief Justice Bird dissented in *Cole*, asserting that the defendants "conspired to humiliate, harass and intimidate" Cole, and that "[s]uch a sustained and deliberate psychological assault designed to injure an employee is not a normal risk or condition of employment and is not 'conduct normally occurring in the workplace.' " *Id.* at 753. She further argued that because workers' compensation provides no compensation for pain and suffering and does not allow for punitive damages, "it does not sufficiently deter employers from engaging in such egregious conduct." *Id.* In cases in which the employee could establish that the employer acted, not merely recklessly, but "deliberately for the purpose of injuring the employee," Justice Bird would have permitted the employee to file a tort suit.

Recall the elements of the tort of intentional infliction of emotional distress. Should employer actions that are sufficiently egregious to satisfy the elements of the tort be considered part of the compensation bargain? What reasons are there not to permit such tort claims to proceed?

State courts are divided on the issue whether claims for intentional infliction of emotional distress are barred by workers' compensation exclusivity. Some courts look at the nature of the injury alleged, and, to the extent that mental distress is compensable under workers' compensation, find these claims barred. *See, e.g., Green v. Wyman-Gordon Co.*, 664 N.E.2d 808 (Mass. 1996) (barring claim of intentional infliction of emotional distress where plaintiff's alleged injury was compensable by workers' compensation). Others permit such claims on the grounds that they fall within the exception for intentionally caused injuries. *See, e.g., Coates v. Wal-Mart Stores, Inc.*, 976 P.2d 999 (N.M. 1999) (finding sufficient evidence to show that employer acted intentionally, such that common-law tort action fell outside the workers' compensation exclusivity provision).

2. Intentional Acts of Co-Workers. One reason employees have difficulty bringing claims for intentional infliction of emotional distress under the exception for intentional acts is that such claims are often based on the actions of a co-worker rather than the employer, and courts are generally reluctant to permit common-law claims against an employer based on co-employee conduct. As the court in *Meerbrey v. Marshall Field & Co.*, 564 N.E.2d 1222 (Ill. 1990), explained:

> The legal justification for allowing a common law cause of action against an employer who personally commits an intentional tort does not apply where a plaintiff-employee seeks to impose liability upon his or her employer solely under the principle of *respondeat superior*. As Professor Larson explained: "The legal reason for permitting the common-law suit for direct assault by the employer . . . is that the same person cannot commit an intentional assault and then allege it was accidental. This does not apply when the assailant and the defendant are two entirely different people. Unless the employer has commanded or expressly authorized the assault, it cannot be said to be intentional from his standpoint any more than from the standpoint of any third person. Realistically, it to him is just one more industrial mishap in the factory, of the sort he has the right to consider exclusively covered by the compensation system." (SA A. Larson, Law of Workmen's Compensation § 68.21 (1988).)

Id. at 1227. Thus, while a number of states permit tort actions against an employer for intentionally inflicted injury, they often require that the intentional act be one commanded or directly authorized by the employer.

3. Other Non-Physical Torts. In contrast to claims of intentional infliction of emotional distress, other common law torts such as defamation, invasion of privacy and malicious prosecution are generally *not* barred by workers' compensation exclusivity because the essence of these torts is not physical or mental injury. *See, e.g., Mounteer v. Utah Power & Light Co.*, 823 P.2d 1055 (Utah 1991) (holding that employee's claim against employer for slander is not barred by workers' compensation exclusivity); *Howland v. Balma*, 143 Cal. App. 3d 899 (1983) (same); *Branham*, 744 N.E.2d 514 (Ind. Ct. App. 2001) (holding defamation and invasion of privacy claims not barred by workers' compensation exclusivity); *Cole v. Chandler*, 752 A.2d 1189 (Me. 2000) (holding that mental and physical injuries resulting from defamation, invasion of privacy and interference with advantageous economic relations are barred by exclusivity, while economic and reputational injuries resulting from these torts are not).

The court in *Foley v. Polaroid Corp.*, 413 N.E.2d 711 (Mass. 1980), found that "the gist of an action for defamation is injury to reputation irrespective of any physical or mental harm," and therefore, held that a common law claim for defamation was not barred. *Id.* at 715. Similarly, it concluded that "the essence of the tort [of malicious prosecution] is not physical or mental injury, but interference with the right to be free from unjustifiable litigation. Any physical or mental harm is incidental, and is not an indispensable ingredient of the tort." *Id.* at 716. The court then explained:

At this point the distinction between the employee's claims for malicious prosecution and defamation on the one hand, and intentional infliction of mental distress on the other hand, becomes clear: mental harm is the essence of the tort of intentional infliction of mental distress; it is an indispensable element of the tort. It matters not that all three claims are based upon the same alleged conduct of the defendant for "the key to whether the Workmen's Compensation Act precludes a common law right of action lies in the nature of the injury for which plaintiff makes claim, not the nature of the defendant's act which the plaintiff alleges to have been responsible for that injury."

Id. at 715 (citation omitted).

4. **Limits of the Compensation Bargain.** Although the exclusive remedy bar to personal injury suits against an employer can be quite extensive, it does have limits. As the California Supreme Court explained in *Shoemaker v. Myers*, 801 P.2d 1054 (Cal. 1990):

> [T]he exclusive remedy provisions are not applicable under certain circumstances, sometimes variously identified as "conduct where the employer or insurer stepped out of their proper roles", or "conduct of an employer having a 'questionable' relationship to the employment", but which may be essentially defined as not stemming from a risk reasonably encompassed within the compensation bargain. (*Cole, supra*, 43 Cal. 3d at pp. 159, 161). . . .

Id. at 1063. The plaintiff in *Shoemaker* sued his former employer pursuant to a state statute prohibiting retaliation against government employees who report actual or suspected violations of the law on the job. Because he alleged that his termination caused him to suffer physical illness and disability, the trial court found his statutory whistleblower claim barred by the workers' compensation exclusivity provisions. On appeal, the California Supreme Court considered the purposes served by the two statutes at issue:

> [T]he purpose of the workers' compensation law is to provide a comprehensive scheme of compensation for all employees for industrial personal injury or death. The purpose of an action under the whistleblower protection statute, however, is to provide redress to a certain limited class of employees (state employees), for damages suffered as a consequence of the specific use of official power to deter a particular protected activity— the proper reporting of on-the-job or job-related unlawful government actions. . . . [T]he evils addressed by the whistle-blower statute are different from those addressed by the workers' compensation law, and the Legislature cannot have " 'intend[ed] that the objectives [to] be defeated by the bar of the exclusive remedy provision.' " (Id. at p. 807.) Thus, the Legislature's enactment of specific statutory protection for whistleblowing activity, including a civil action *for damages* incurred from official retaliatory acts, defines the protected activity as a specific statutory exception to the provisions of the workers' compensation law; such conduct lies well outside the compensation bargain.

Id. at 1066–67.

What about claims by employees that they suffered mental injuries and perhaps even physical illness because they were terminated in violation of public policy? Or that they suffered injuries as a result of unlawful discrimination? Should these types of claims be barred by workers' compensation exclusivity or do they fall outside "the compensation bargain"?

Consider the reasoning of the California Supreme Court in *Gantt v. Sentry Insurance*, 824 P.2d 680 (Cal. 1992):

> When an employer's decision to discharge an employee results from an animus that violates the fundamental policy of this state . . . such misconduct cannot under any reasonable viewpoint be considered a "normal part of the employment relationship" (*Cole v. Fair Oaks Fire Protection Dist.*, 729 P.2d 743) or a "risk reasonably encompassed within the compensation bargain." (*Shoemaker v. Myers*, 801 P.2d 1054.) The obligation to refrain from such conduct is a "duty imposed by law upon all employers to implement the fundamental public policies" of the state; it cannot be bargained away; it is not preempted by other statutory remedies; and its breach is most assuredly not a "normal" risk of the employment relationship subject to the exclusive remedy provisions of the Labor Code.

> . . . As we explained in *Foley v. Interactive Data Corp.*, supra: "What is vindicated through the [public policy tort] cause of action is not the terms or promises arising out of the particular employment relationship involved, but rather the public interest in not permitting employers to impose as a condition of employment a requirement that an employee act in a manner contrary to fundamental public policy." (765 P.2d 373.) Just as the individual employment agreement may not include terms which violate fundamental public policy, so the more general "compensation bargain" cannot encompass conduct, such as sexual or racial discrimination, "obnoxious to the interests of the state and contrary to public policy and sound morality."

Id. at 691–92.

Other courts have similarly concluded that employee claims based on discrimination or harassment are not barred by workers' compensation exclusivity. *See, e.g., Perry v. Stitzer Buick GMC, Inc.*, 637 N.E.2d 1282 (Ind. 1994); *Karch v. Baybank FSB*, 794 A.2d 763 (N.H. 2002).

B. OSHA

Regulating worker safety is no easy task. OSHA was created as part of the comprehensive 1970 legislation designed to regulate workplace conditions, and OSHA is charged with promulgating regulations, inspecting workplaces and prosecuting violations of its regulations and standards. Today OSHA is perhaps best known for being one of the most criticized of all federal agencies, certainly the most criticized agency that regulates the workplace. Given its mandate, the criticism is not all that surprising.

OSHA, along with its state partners, governs virtually all private workplaces—regulating the work conditions of more than 130 million workers in more than eight million workplaces. To accomplish its work, OSHA and the state OSHAs have just over 2,200 inspectors, which represents a significant increase in the last few years. Because of its broad scope, OSHA's regulatory process is frequently challenged by both employers and unions. Employers will often challenge OSHA regulations as being too cumbersome, while unions often seek more stringent recommendations and workplace oversight. As a result, the regulatory process can quickly grind to a halt. Largely because of the difficulty it has in promulgating regulations, OSHA commonly relies on what is known as the general duty clause (see below) rather than specific regulations for its enforcement actions. In this section, we will discuss the general structure of the statute as well as two of the issues that frequently arise relating to enforcement actions and worker rights regarding a dangerous workplace.

In addition to the federal OSHA agency, the Act authorizes states to create their own OSHA agencies so long as the agencies and their standards are at least as effective as the federal act. Currently, twenty-two states and two territories have established their own state OSHAs, and two other states have authority over their public sectors. Unless the state has an approved plan, OSHA generally preempts state health and safety regulations. *See Gade v. National Solid Wastes Mgt. Ass'n*, 505 U.S. 88 (1992).

1.   The Structure of the Statute

a.   Promulgating Standards

When the Act was originally passed, OSHA was charged with responsibility for promulgating permanent health and safety standards after going through formal notice and comment procedures pursuant to the Administrative Procedure Act ("APA"). The APA requires a formal notice and a comment period, with subsequent review typically performed by the Office of Management and Budget. Any party adversely affected by the standard may then file a challenge to its validity, either for a procedural irregularity or to the substance of the standard as insufficiently documented or inconsistent with the statute's mandate.

This process can be cumbersome under the best of circumstances, but as noted earlier, it has become a focal point of litigation by employers and unions. Most standards promulgated by OSHA have been subject to litigation, much of it lengthy, and it now takes on average about six years for OSHA to promulgate a new standard. As a result, OSHA has promulgated far fewer permanent standards than was originally contemplated, and it often relies on other means to enforce its statutory mandate.

i.   Ergonomics Standards

As an illustration of the difficulty the agency has in promulgating regulations, consider the case of its ergonomics standard. A large number of workers—how large is a matter of dispute—have suffered from a variety of musculoskeletal disorders or injuries from their jobs, including carpal tunnel syndrome and other forms of repetitive stress syndrome. Many occupations are plagued by repetitive motion injuries, including those who work on assembly lines, operators, secretaries, cashiers, machine operators, nurses, hairdressers, and many others. The injuries do not have a common source or even common symptoms, but instead ergonomics involves ways to structure the workplace to reduce such injuries by, among other approaches, adjusting workstations, changing heights on assembly lines, and allowing frequent rest periods. In 1990, after determining that musculoskeletal injuries were the fastest growing category of workplace injury accounting for about one-third of all such injuries, OSHA began work on establishing a comprehensive ergonomics standard.

From the outset, OSHA's efforts were controversial and the business community expressed great concern over the potential cost of any standard. Under the Clinton Administration, OSHA originally committed to issuing a proposed standard by September 30, 1994, but it failed to meet that deadline. Thereafter, the Republican-controlled Congress sought to prevent OSHA from issuing an ergonomics standard, and on several occasions attempted to withhold OSHA's budget if the agency issued a standard. It was not until February 1999, nine years after the process began, that OSHA released its draft proposed ergonomics standard and public hearings were concluded the following year (during which more than 1,000 witnesses testified). In November 2000, towards the end of the Clinton Administration, OSHA issued a final ergonomics standard that included an 11-page rule and nearly 600 pages of interpretation and explanations. OSHA estimated that it would cost businesses approximately $4.5 billion in the first year to comply with its regulation, but at a savings of almost $9 billion a year in workers' compensation costs and lost work days. Business groups countered that the regulation would cost more than $6 billion in the first year, with costs eventually rising to total more than $100 billion with far lower projected savings. The rule took effect on January 16, 2001.

Less than two months after it was issued, President Bush rescinded the standard, and the Department of Labor began new proceedings to establish ergonomics guidelines for certain industries. During the Bush Administration, the Department subsequently promulgated guidelines for four industries: poultry processing, retail grocery stores, nursing homes and shipyard employment. Meanwhile, several states (including California and Washington) under the authority of their state OSHAs issued ergonomics standards of their own. The Department of Labor has claimed that musculoskeletal disorder injuries have decreased considerably (with carpel tunnel syndrome decreasing by a third during the 1990s) but such disorders still account for 34% of all injuries and illnesses that lead to time off from work. *See Bureau of Labor Statistics, Nonfatal Occupational Injuries and Illnesses Requiring Days Away from Work*, 2012 (Nov. 26, 2013), *available at* http://www.bls.gov/news.release/pdf/osh2.pdf This short summary should offer you some insight into the difficulty OSHA frequently encounters issuing permanent standards both because of its scope and the varied interests with which it must work. It also raises some important questions: what justification could there be for 600 pages on the regulation? If the regulation would save so much money, why would employers be hesitant to adopt the standards?

A great deal of law has developed over the process for promulgating workplace standards, and that law is frequently an important part of administrative law courses. Most of the issues relate to procedural aspects of the statute, or the proper standard OSHA must use to effectuate regulations, issues that are only tangentially related to employment law. (They are obviously relevant to the extent the standards are or are not implemented in the workplace, but the concerns are more administrative in nature than substantive.) We have thus elected not to cover those issues in this book. Students who are interested in the specific cases should see *Industrial Union Dep't v. American Petroleum Inst.*, 448 U.S. 607 (1980) (The Benzene Case); *American Textile Manufacturers Institute v. Donovan*, 452 U.S. 490 (1981) (The Cotton Dust case), and *AFL-CIO v. OSHA*, 965 F.2d 962 (11th Cir. 1992) (generic rulemaking).

ii.   Other Enforcement Means

As a result of its difficulty in promulgating permanent standards, OSHA typically relies on two other regulatory provisions to enforce safety standards. When the Act was originally passed, OSHA was authorized to issue "temporary" standards, and in 1971 it issued more than 4,000 temporary standards, most of which were based on industry standards that were in place at the time. Some of those standards were subsequently deleted, but many remain in place today as interim, but enforceable standards.

The other primary means of enforcement is section 5(a), what is known as the "general duty clause." Section 5(a)(1) creates a general duty for an employer to

> furnish to each of his employees employment and a place of employment that are free from recognized hazards that are causing or are likely to cause death or serious physical harm to his employees.

29 U.S.C. § 654(a)(1). Many enforcement actions are brought pursuant to the general duty clause, and rules have emerged to guide enforcement under that section, an issue we will turn to shortly.

b.   Inspection and Enforcement Scheme

OSHA's standards, and the general duty clause, are enforced through inspections. There are four types of investigations: (1) investigations targeting workplaces where hazards posing imminent danger are present; (2) investigations that follow documented injuries or deaths; (3) inspections prompted by employee (or union) complaints; (4) programmed complaints. In Fiscal Year 2012, OSHA completed just over 40,000 inspections, 17,000 of which were in connection with workplace accidents or complaints. State OSHAs conducted just over 50,000 investigations.

The Supreme Court has held that the Department of Labor must obtain an administrative warrant to conduct a search to which the employer does not consent. *See Marshall v. Barlow's*, Inc., 436 U.S. 307 (1978). The warrant can be issued ex parte by a magistrate, and warrants are routinely granted where there is "specific evidence of an existing violation" or where the inspection is conducted pursuant to a valid regulation (such as for a programmed inspection). *Id.* at 320. *See also Reich v. Montana* Sulphur & *Chemical* Co., 32 F.3d 440 (9th Cir. 1994) (discussing standards for OSHA subpoenas and warrants); *Reich v. Kelly-Springfield Tire Co.*,

13 F.3d 1160 (7th Cir. 1994) (upholding warrant based on employee complaint to investigate violation of general duty clause on ergonomics issue).

OSHA provides no advanced notice of its investigations and requires employers to be in compliance with the Act at the time of the inspections; in other words, no warnings are provided but instead OSHA issues citations for any workplace violations uncovered during the inspection. In 2012, OSHA cited employers for more than 78,000 workplace violations with more than 73% issued for serious violations (but only 423 for willful violations). OSHA's penalties depend on the nature of the violation: if the violation is not labeled as serious, the fine ranges from $0 to $1,000 for each violation, while serious violations are assessed a penalty ranging from $1,500 to $7,000, and willful violations may be penalized a minimum of $5,000 to a maximum of $70,000. Criminal penalties are also possible for knowing violations that result in the death of an employee, though the criminal penalty is only a misdemeanor with a maximum six-month jail term. States may also prosecute workplace deaths under their general criminal laws, and some states do so. In addition to these penalties, employers are typically required to abate the hazardous conditions, and the costs of the abatement frequently exceed the monetary penalties.

An employer may contest a citation before an independent commission, the Occupational Safety and Health Review Commission ("OSHRC"), which then assigns an administrative law judge to schedule a hearing. After the ALJ issues a ruling, any party may seek further review before the OSHRC. Limited judicial review of the OSHRC decision is then available in the United States Courts of Appeals.

The Department of Labor, and state OSHAs, are fully responsible for enforcing the Act. The Act provides for no private causes of action, and the main outlet available for workers and their representatives to complain about workplace hazards is to file a complaint with OSHA. Why do you think this might be? Why not allow private entities to bring enforcement actions?

2. The General Duty Clause

SEAWORLD v. PEREZ
United States Court of Appeals for the District of Columbia
748 F.3d 1202 (2014)

ROGERS, CIRCUIT JUDGE.

SeaWorld of Florida, LLC, operates a theme park in Orlando, Florida, that is designed to entertain and educate paying customers by displaying and studying marine animals. Following the death of one of SeaWorld's trainers while working in close contact with a killer whale during a performance, the Occupational Safety and Health Review Commission found that SeaWorld had violated the general duty clause, § 5(a)(1) of the Occupational Safety and Health Act of 1970, 29 U.S.C. § 654(a)(1), by exposing the trainers to recognized hazards when working in close contact with killer whales during performances, and that the abatement procedures recommended by the Secretary of Labor were feasible. SeaWorld challenges the order with respect to one citation. Concluding its challenges are unpersuasive, we deny the petition for review.

I.

On February 24, 2010, SeaWorld trainer Dawn Brancheau was interacting with Tilikum, a killer whale, during a performance before a live audience in a pool at Shamu Stadium in Orlando. Ms. Brancheau was reclined on her back on a platform a few inches below the water surface. Tilikum was supposed to mimic her behavior by rolling over. Instead, the killer whale grabbed her and pulled her off the platform into the pool, refusing to release her. She suffered traumatic injuries and drowned as a result of Tilikum's actions.

The Secretary of Labor issued three citations to SeaWorld after an investigation by an Occupational Safety and Health Administration ("OSHA") compliance officer. Only the second citation is at issue. It alleged two instances of a "willful" violation of the general duty clause for exposing animal trainers to the recognized hazards of drowning or injury when working with killer whales during performances. The first instance related to animal trainers working with Tilikum being exposed to "struck-by and drowning hazards" by being "allowed unprotected contact with Tilikum" while conducting " 'drywork' performances on pool ledges, slideouts and platforms." Citation 2, Instance (a). In SeaWorld's terms, when trainers are out of the pool or on submerged ledges called "slideouts" in water no deeper than their knees, their interactions with killer whales are called "drywork." Any interaction in deeper water is "waterwork." According to the Secretary, "[a]mong other methods, one feasible and acceptable means of abatement would be to not allow animal trainers to have any contact with Tilikum unless they are protected by a physical barrier." *Id.* The second instance concerned animal trainers working with killer whales other than Tilikum who were exposed to struck-by and drowning hazards when they were "allowed to engage in 'waterwork' and 'drywork' performances with the killer whales without adequate protection." Citation 2, Instance (b). The Secretary listed as possible abatement methods "prohibit[ing] animal trainers from working with killer whales, including 'waterwork' or 'dry work,' unless the trainers are protected through the use of physical barriers or through the use of decking systems, oxygen supply systems or other engineering or administrative controls that provide the same or greater level of protection for the trainers." Id. The Secretary proposed a penalty of $70,000.

Following an evidentiary hearing, the Administrative Law Judge ("ALJ") . . . found that the first and third elements of a violation of the general duty clause—existence of a workplace condition presenting a hazard that likely caused death or serious physical harm—were established by the events on February 24, 2010: Ms. Brancheau's death demonstrated that close contact with killer whales was a hazard likely to cause death or serious injury. Based on evidence regarding three previous deaths involving killer whales (beginning in 1991 with Tilikum), SeaWorld's written training manuals and safety lectures as implemented specifically to Tilikum, and SeaWorld's incident reports, the ALJ found that the Secretary had established by "abundant" record evidence that "SeaWorld recognized the hazard created when its trainers worked in close contact with Tilikum during drywork performances," satisfying the second element of a violation. 2012 OSAHRC LEXIS 40 at 51. . . .

The ALJ also found that the Secretary had established the fourth element of a violation: feasible abatement of the hazard for trainers working with Tilikum and other killer whales. . . . Additionally, the ALJ noted that SeaWorld had already implemented the means of abatement recommended by the Secretary for trainers working with Tilikum—namely, maintaining a minimum distance from the killer whale, or imposing a physical barrier between the killer whale and trainers—and concluded the same or similar abatement involving other killer whales was no less feasible.

. . . Observing that OSHA has "no specific standard" regulating employees working in close contact with killer whales, and that the Secretary had presented no evidence SeaWorld had a "heightened awareness of the illegality of its conduct" or manifested "plain indifference to employee safety," the ALJ found that violations were "serious," not "willful," and imposed a fine of $7,000 for the general duty clause violation in Citation 2, emphasizing that his order was limited to show performances. 2012 OSAHRC LEXIS 40 at 92. SeaWorld unsuccessfully sought discretionary review by the Commission, whereupon the ALJ's decision and order became final. *See* 29 C.F.R. § 2200.90(d). SeaWorld petitions for review of the general duty violation.

II.

The general duty clause, § 5(a)(1) of the Occupational Safety and Health Act, provides: "Each employer [ ] shall furnish to each of his employees employment and a place of employment which are free from recognized hazards that are causing or are likely to cause death or serious physical harm to his employees." 29 U.S.C. § 654(a)(1). As explained by the House Committee on Education and Labor, "[b]earing in mind the fact that there is no automatic penalty for violation of the general duty, this clause enables the Federal Government to provide for the protection of employees who are working under such *unique* circumstances that no standard has yet been enacted to cover this situation." H.R. Rep. No. 91-1291, at 21–22 (1970) (emphasis in original). In a seminal case this court, in turn, observed that "[t]hough novel in approach and sweeping in coverage, the legislation is no more drastic than the problem it aims to meet." *Nat'l Realty & Constr. Co. v. OSHRC*, 489 F.2d 1257, 1260–61 (D.C. Cir. 1973). Notwithstanding the "unqualified and absolute" textual imperative that the workplace be "free" of the recognized hazard, *id.* at 1265, the court further observed that "Congress quite clearly did not intend the general duty clause to impose strict liability: The duty was to be an achievable one," *id.* at 1265–66. So understood, the court held that "[a]ll preventable forms and instances of hazardous conduct must . . . be entirely excluded from the workplace." Id. at 1266–67.

"To establish a violation of the General Duty Clause, the Secretary must establish that: (1) an activity or condition in the employer's workplace presented a hazard to an employee, (2) either the employer or the industry recognized the condition or activity as a hazard, (3) the hazard was likely to or actually caused death or serious physical harm, and (4) a feasible means to eliminate or materially reduce the hazard existed." *Fabi Constr. Co. v. Sec'y of Labor*, 508 F.3d 1077, 1081 (D.C. Cir. 2007). Tempering the range of potential remedies that might be imposed upon finding a violation of the clause, the court explained: "In other words, the Secretary must prove that a reasonably prudent employer familiar with the circumstances of the industry would have protected against the hazard in the manner specified by the Secretary's citation." *Id.*

SeaWorld contests only the second and fourth elements regarding recognized hazard and feasibility. In challenging the general duty citation, SeaWorld does not perforce contend that the Secretary of Labor or the Occupational Safety and Health Review Commission lack legal authority to require employers to provide a reasonably safe working environment for employees. Rather, SeaWorld takes issue with the interpretation by these officials of what constitutes a recognized hazard that would subject an employer to citation under the Occupational Safety and Health Act. First, SeaWorld contends that the finding that it exposed its employees to a "recognized hazard" is unsupported by substantial evidence. Second, it contends that "when some risk is inherent in a business activity, that risk cannot constitute a 'recognized hazard.'" Pet'r Br. at 33. Third, it contends . . . that the Secretary failed to prove feasible abatement methods (or that SeaWorld had already implemented these measures), and that the ALJ failed to consider evidence these abatement measures present additional hazards and erred because eliminating close contact changes the nature of a trainer's job. Finally, SeaWorld contends the general duty clause is unconstitutionally vague as applied because SeaWorld lacked fair notice of the Secretary's abatement measures.

The court must uphold the Commission's decision unless it is "arbitrary, capricious, an abuse of discretion, or otherwise not in accordance with law." *Fabi Constr. Co.*, 508 F.3d at 1080. The factual findings of the Commission, "if supported by substantial evidence on the record considered as a whole, shall be conclusive." 29 U.S.C. § 660(a). Likewise, the court "must accept the ALJ's credibility determinations . . . unless they are patently unsupportable." Id. (ellipsis in original). The court will "defer to the Secretary's interpretation of the Act and regulations, upholding such interpretations so long as they are consistent with the statutory language and otherwise reasonable." *Anthony Crane Rental, Inc. v. Reich*, 70 F.3d 1298, 1302, (D.C. Cir. 1995).

A.

Whether a work condition poses a recognized hazard is a question of fact. *See Baroid Div. of NL Indus., Inc. v. OSHRC*, 660 F.2d 439, 446 (10th Cir. 1981). Substantial evidence supports the finding that "drywork" and "waterwork" with killer whales were recognized hazards. Tilikum is a 32-year-old male killer whale with known aggressive tendencies who in 1991 killed a whale trainer at a marine park in Vancouver, British Columbia. SeaWorld had established special protocols for Tilikum, which prohibited "waterwork" and, among other things, required non-killer whale personnel and guests to stay five feet behind pool walls or three feet from Tilikum's head, indicating that SeaWorld recognized the possibility of harm to people standing outside of the pool on land. Although "drywork" with Tilikum continued, SeaWorld limited it to a team of experienced trainers who used extra caution. The caution with which SeaWorld treated Tilikum even when trainers were poolside or on "slideouts" in the pool indicates that it recognized the hazard the killer whale posed, not that it considered its protocols rendered Tilikum safe.

As to other killer whales, SeaWorld suggests that close contact with these whales was not a recognized hazard because all whales behave differently and its incident reports help SeaWorld improve training. But SeaWorld's incident reports demonstrate that it recognized the danger its killer whales posed to trainers notwithstanding its protocols. At the time of Ms. Brancheau's death, seven killer whales were at the Orlando park. Even though SeaWorld had not recorded incident reports on all of its killer whales, a substantial portion of SeaWorld's killer whale population had at least one reported incident. . . . Killer whales bit trainers' body parts on several occasions (although not generally puncturing skin) and in 2006 a killer whale pulled a trainer underwater by the foot and submerged him repeatedly for approximately 10 minutes. . . . On numerous occasions, trainers fell or were pulled into the water, as later happened with Tilikum and Ms. Brancheau, or killer whales lunged out of the water toward trainers. These incidents constitute substantial evidence to support the ALJ's finding that "drywork" was also a recognized hazard.

SeaWorld's position is that working with killer whales was not a recognized hazard because its training and safety program adequately controlled the risk. To train its killer whales, SeaWorld uses "operant conditioning" to reinforce desired behaviors with food or other rewards. It also trains its employees who work with killer whales to recognize particular behaviors that it calls "precursors," which indicate that the killer whales may act aggressively, and keeps detailed incident reports of when its killer whales had behaved aggressively or otherwise undesirably toward trainers, including pulling trainers into the pool. The Secretary presented evidence that the killer whales posed a hazard in spite of SeaWorld's safety measures. On multiple occasions, including the death of Ms. Brancheau, SeaWorld's incident reports indicated that the killer whales showed no immediate precursors of aggressive behavior or ignored SeaWorld's emergency procedures designed to make them cease aggressive behavior. Statements by SeaWorld managers do not indicate that SeaWorld's safety protocols and training made the killer whales safe; rather, they demonstrate SeaWorld's recognition that the killer whales interacting with trainers are dangerous and unpredictable and that even senior trainers can make mistakes during performances, and the managers repeatedly urged caution in working with the killer whales. The evidence thus supports the ALJ's finding that a recognized hazard existed, even beyond the impact of SeaWorld's safety protocols.

. . . Here, there was substantial record evidence that SeaWorld recognized its precautions were inadequate to prevent serious bodily harm or even death to its trainers and that the residual hazard was preventable.

The remedy imposed for SeaWorld's violations does not change the essential nature of its business. There will still be human interactions and performances with killer whales; the remedy will simply require that they continue with increased safety measures. SeaWorld itself has limited human interactions. After Ms. Brancheau's death in 2010, SeaWorld ceased "waterwork" with all of its killer whales. It also imposed distance between trainers and Tilikum during drywork and, to a lesser degree, between other killer whales and trainers during drywork. These self-imposed limitations are relevant to the assessment of which aspects of SeaWorld's business are essential and indicate that the Secretary's remedy will not eliminate any essential element. SeaWorld does not assert (and at oral argument disavowed) that a public perception of danger to its trainers is essential to its business. Nor has SeaWorld ever argued that limiting interactions in the way that the remedy requires would have a detrimental economic impact on its profits. And SeaWorld is, after all, a for-profit entity owned, at times relevant to the Commission proceedings, by the Blackstone Group, an investment firm.

Pelron Corp., 12 BNA OSHC 1833 (1986), on which SeaWorld relies, is inapposite. That case involved an enforcement action against a company that manufactured products by mixing, *inter alia*, ethylene oxide. *See* 1986 OSAHRC LEXIS 114. The ALJ had defined the alleged hazard as the "possibility" of accumulations of unreacted ethylene oxide, which the Commission found could never be prevented. *See* 1986 OSAHRC LEXIS 114. Thus, impliedly, the only remedy would have been to close the plant. Here, the Secretary and the Commission could reasonably conclude that the danger to SeaWorld's trainers during performances from killer whales can be prevented by use of physical barriers and distance, and closing SeaWorld is not at issue. The hazard killer whales pose during performances is not "so idiosyncratic and implausible" that it cannot be considered preventable. *Nat'l Realty & Constr. Co.*, 489 F.2d at 1266. . . .

SeaWorld's suggestion that because trainers "formally accepted and controlled their own exposure to . . . risks," the hazard of close contact with killer whales cannot be recognized, contravenes Congress's decision to place the duty to ensure a safe and healthy workplace on the employer, not the employee. This court has long held "this duty is not qualified by such common law doctrines as assumption of risk, contributory negligence, or comparative negligence." *Nat'l Realty & Constr. Co.*, 489 F.2d at 1266 n.36. . . .

The Secretary and the Commission could also reasonably determine that the remedy does not go to the essence of SeaWorld's productions. SeaWorld has had no "waterwork" performances since Ms. Brancheau's death in 2010, and it temporarily suspended "waterwork" after other incidents, such as the killing of a trainer by a killer whale in 2009 at a non-SeaWorld park in Spain. With distance and physical barriers between Tilikum and trainers during drywork, Tilikum can still perform almost the same behaviors performed when no barriers were present. The nature of SeaWorld's workplace and the unusual nature of the hazard to its employees performing in close physical contact with killer whales do not remove SeaWorld from its obligation under the General Duty Clause to protect its employees from recognized hazards. . . .

. . . Although this case is only about a single "entertainment show," our [dissenting] colleague repeatedly characterizes this case as being about the "*sports and* entertainment *industries*." Dissent at 2 (emphasis added). No one has described SeaWorld's killer whale performances as a "sport," and a *legal* argument that the "sports industry" should not be regulated by OSHA can be raised when and if OSHA attempts to do so. Until then, this court will not find that OSHA acted arbitrarily based on a few responses to hypotheticals in briefing or oral argument. . . .

[Section B is omitted]

C.

Substantial evidence supports the ALJ's findings that it was feasible for SeaWorld to abate the hazard to its employees by using barriers or minimum distance between trainers and killer whales, most notably because SeaWorld has implemented many of these measures on its own. When an employer has existing safety procedures, the burden is on the Secretary to show that those procedures are inadequate. *See Cerro Metal Prods. Div., Marmon Grp., Inc.*, 12 BNA OSHC 1821. The record evidence showed that SeaWorld's training and protocols did not prevent continued incidents, including the submerging and biting of one trainer in 2006, the killing of a trainer by a SeaWorld-trained and -owned killer whale in 2009 at an amusement park in Spain, and Ms. Brancheau's death in 2010. SeaWorld employees repeatedly acknowledged the unpredictability of its killer whales. This record evidence supports the ALJ's finding that existing protocols were inadequate to eliminate or materially reduce the hazard to SeaWorld's trainer employees performing with killer whales.

Abatement is "feasible" when it is "economically and technologically capable of being done." *Baroid*, 660 F.2d at 447. After Ms. Brancheau's death, SeaWorld required that all trainers work with Tilikum from a minimum distance or behind a barrier, and "waterwork" ceased with all of its killer whales. As in *ConAgra, Inc., McMillan Co. Div.*, 11 BNA OSHC 1141, . . . (No. 79-1146, 1983), implementing the ordered abatement is feasible because it would involve extending these practices to all killer whales and into the future. *See id.* at 1145, 5. As the ALJ noted, SeaWorld had not argued the Secretary's proposed abatement was not economically or technologically feasible and had already implemented abatement for at least one of its killer whales and needed only to apply the same or similar protective contact measures it used with Tilikum to other killer whales. . . .

D.

. . . SeaWorld contends the general duty clause is unconstitutionally vague as applied because it lacked fair notice that the abatement measures would be required. But the administrative record establishes that SeaWorld did not lack fair notice because the hazard arising from trainers' close contact with killer whales in performance is preventable. Given evidence of continued incidents of aggressive behavior by killer whales toward trainers notwithstanding SeaWorld's training, operant conditioning practices, and emergency measures, SeaWorld could have anticipated that abatement measures it had applied after other incidents would be required. SeaWorld suggests that it was entitled to rely on the fact that the State of California's Division of Occupational Safety and Health ("Cal/OSHA") did not issue a citation for killer whale hazards after a killer whale bit and dragged a trainer underwater during a performance, puncturing the trainer's skin on both feet and breaking the metatarsal in his left foot. Cal/OSHA, however, inspected a different SeaWorld facility (in San Diego) and it, not the federal OSHA, resolved the citation question. In any event, the State inspection report included a warning on point. Although noting that SeaWorld had been following industry standards and was a recognized leader in training killer whales for performance, and that its employees were well-trained and followed emergency procedures, Cal/OSHA concluded that SeaWorld of San Diego's procedures "were not entirely effective at stopping the unwanted behaviors of the killer whale during this attack" and that "[s]hort of eliminating all of the water interactions with the killer whales, there is no guarantee that employees can be kept safe from an attack by the killer whale once they get in the water with the animal." Cal/OSHA

Accordingly, we deny the petition for review.

KAVANAUGH, CIRCUIT JUDGE, dissenting.

Many sports events and entertainment shows can be extremely dangerous for the participants. Football. Ice hockey. Downhill skiing. Air shows. The circus. Horse racing. Tiger taming. Standing in the batter's box against a 95 mile per hour fastball. Bull riding at the rodeo. Skydiving into the stadium before a football game. Daredevil motorcycle jumps. Stock car racing. Cheerleading vaults. Boxing. The balance beam. The ironman triathlon. Animal trainer shows. Movie stunts. The list goes on.

But the participants in those activities want to take part, sometimes even to make a career of it, despite and occasionally because of the known risk of serious injury. To be fearless, courageous, tough—to perform a sport or activity at the highest levels of human capacity, even in the face of known physical risk—is among the greatest forms of personal achievement for many who take part in these activities. American spectators enjoy watching these amazing feats of competition and daring, and they pay a lot to do so. Americans like to witness the thrill of victory, to cheer the linebacker who hammers the running back at the goal line, to yell with admiration as Derek Jeter flies into the stands down the left-field line to make a catch, to applaud the gymnast who nails the back flip off the balance beam, to hold their collective breath as Jack Hanna plays with pythons, to root on the marathoner who is near collapse at the finish line, to scream "Foreman" when the announcer says "Down goes Frazier." And American spectators also commiserate during the "agony of defeat," as immortalized in the Wide World of Sports video of a ski jumper flying horribly off course.

The broad question implicated by this case is this: When should we as a society paternalistically decide that the participants in these sports and entertainment activities must be protected from themselves—that the risk of significant physical injury is simply too great even for eager and willing participants? And most importantly for this case, *who decides* that the risk to participants is too high?

In the first instance, the sports and entertainment industries regulate themselves, often through collaboration between management and participants, to ensure that the risks are at least known to all. Often, the sports and entertainment industries take affirmative steps to make the sports or activities safer for participants. Major League Baseball has required batters to wear increasingly protective helmets; just this offseason, it issued a new rule about home-plate collisions. The NFL has prohibited certain hits to the head. NASCAR has mandated roll cages, fire retardant uniforms, and window netting. And so on.

Sometimes Congress, state legislatures, or state regulators jump into the fray by prohibiting or otherwise regulating certain sports or entertainment activities. State tort law also looms as a significant constraint in most jurisdictions. . . .

On the other hand, the bureaucracy at the U.S. Department of Labor has not traditionally been thought of as the proper body to decide whether to ban fighting in hockey, to prohibit the punt return in football, to regulate the distance between the mound and home plate in baseball, to separate the lions from the tamers at the circus, or the like. . . .

In this case, however, the Department departed from tradition and stormed headlong into a new regulatory arena. The Department issued a citation to SeaWorld that effectively bans SeaWorld from continuing a longstanding and popular (albeit by definition somewhat dangerous) show in which SeaWorld trainers play with and interact with whales. . . .

Whether SeaWorld's show is unreasonably dangerous to participants and should be banned or changed is not the question before us. The question before us is whether the Department of Labor has authority under current law to make that decision—in addition to the authority already possessed by Congress, state legislatures, state regulators, and courts applying state tort law.

The courts and the Department of Labor have recognized that the broad terms of the General Duty Clause must be applied reasonably lest the Clause morph into a blunt instrument by which absolute workers'-compensation-like liability is imposed on employers for all workplace injuries. The courts and the Department have stated that it must have been "feasible" for the employer to eliminate or materially reduce the recognized hazard at issue. *See, e.g., Fabi Construction Co., Inc. v. Secretary of Labor*, 508 F.3d 1077, 1081 (D.C. Cir. 2007). And importantly, the Department has acknowledged that hazards posed by the normal activities intrinsic to an industry cannot be "feasibly" eliminated and so may not form the basis of a General Duty Clause citation.

. . . In the sports and entertainment fields, the activity itself frequently carries some risk that cannot be eliminated without fundamentally altering the nature of the activity as defined within the industry. Tackling is part of football, speeding is part of stock car racing, playing with dangerous animals is part of zoo and animal shows, and punching is part of boxing, as those industries define themselves.

Management and participants in the relevant sports or entertainment industry must initially decide what their competition or show consists of and how to market it to spectators—subject to appropriate regulation by Congress, state legislatures, state regulators, or state tort law. Here, SeaWorld has decided that close contact between SeaWorld trainers and whales is an important aspect of its shows.

. . . To allay concerns about the breadth of its assertion of regulatory authority in this case, the Department—consistent with its traditional practice—has repeatedly disclaimed authority under the General Duty Clause to ban, for example, tackling in the NFL or excessive speed in NASCAR races. *See* Br. for Secretary of Labor 52; Oral Arg. at 19:15–19:29, 33:05–33:25. . . . Yet the line the Department has drawn . . . is entirely arbitrary and unreasonable. The Department cannot reasonably distinguish close contact with whales at SeaWorld from tackling in the

NFL or speeding in NASCAR. The Department's sole justification for the distinction is that SeaWorld *could* modify (and indeed, since the Department's decision, has had to modify) its shows to eliminate close contact with whales without going out of business. But so too, the NFL *could* ban tackling or punt returns or blocks below the waist. . . . The Department assures us, however, that it would never dictate such outcomes in those sports because "physical contact between players is intrinsic to professional football, as is high speed driving to professional auto racing." Br. for Secretary of Labor 52. But that ipse dixit just brings us back to square one: Why isn't close contact between trainers and whales as intrinsic to SeaWorld's aquatic entertainment enterprise as tackling is to football or speeding is to auto racing? The Department offers no answer at all. . . . I respectfully dissent.

NOTES

1. **The Purpose of the General Duty Clause.** OSHA has often been criticized for relying on the general duty clause to enforce workplace safety in lieu of promulgating specific standards, but might this be a circumstance where relying on the general duty clause makes sense? Why or why not? And how might one distinguish the various sporting analogies raised by Judge Cavanaugh in dissent? Note that a violation of the general duty clause requires establishing that the employer was aware of the hazard, and in this case, as in many cases, the company's past experience provided sufficient knowledge. However, neither courts nor the Commission requires specific knowledge of the hazard. Instead, they rely on an objective standard to determine whether "the employer knew, or through the exercise of reasonable diligence, could have known of the violative condition." *D.A. Collins Constr. Co. v. Secretary of Labor*, 117 F.3d 691, 694 (2d Cir. 1997); *Fabi Constr. Co. v. Sec'y of Labor*, 508 F.3d 1077, 1081 (D.C. Cir. 2007) ("[T]he Secretary must prove that a reasonably prudent employer with the circumstances of the industry would have protected against the hazard.").

2. **General Duty Clause and Specific Standards.** As a general matter, it is inappropriate to cite an employer for a violation of the general duty clause when the employer is in compliance with a specific standard designed to address the hazard that is at issue. But in some limited circumstances, the general duty clause can be used where the specific standard is known to be inadequate. In *International Union, UAW v. General Dynamics Land Systems Div.*, 815 F.2d 1570, 1577 (D.C. Cir. 1987), the court explained: Importantly, the court stated that without specific knowledge of the inadequacy of the specific standard, compliance with that standard will satisfy the employer's duty under the general duty clause. *Id.*

> [I]f (as is alleged in this case) an employer knows a particular safety standard is inadequate to protect his workers against the specific hazard it is intended to address, or that the conditions in his place of employment are such that the safety standard will not adequately deal with the hazards to which his employees are exposed, he has a duty under section 5(a)(1) to take whatever measures may be required by the Act, over and above those mandated by the safety standard, to safeguard his workers.

Importantly, the court stated that without specific knowledge of the inadequacy of the specific standard, compliance with that standard will satisfy the employer's duty under the general duty clause. *Id.*

3. Abatement of the Hazard. One requirement of a general duty clause violation is that the hazard could have reasonably been abated. Here the feasibility of abatement depends in large part on the remedial measures instituted by the employer. What would you expect Sea World to do? Would it need to do more than it had already done? Do you think Judge Cavanaugh is correct that the citations might mean the end of the killer whale shows? The incident received widespread media coverage. For some of the news reports, see Vivian Kuo, *SeaWorld Appeal of OSHA Citations Denied*, CNN, Apr. 13, 2014, *available at* http://www.cnn.com/2014/04/11/us/seaworld-ruling/index.html; Damian Cave, *Intentions of Whale in Killing are Debate*, N.Y. TIMES, Feb. 25, 2010, at A10. Some have advocated increasing OSHA's role in investigating and limiting sports injuries, such as concussions in football. *See* Rodney K. Smith, *Solving the Concussion Problem and Saving Professional Football*, 35 T. JEFFERSON L. REV. 127, 168–72 (2013).

4. Unforeseeable Employee Misconduct. Employers frequently contend that employee misconduct caused the particular injury, and courts have developed a defense in cases of employee misconduct. To establish the defense of "unforeseeable employee misconduct," an employer must prove that (1) it established work rules to prevent the violation; (2) these rules were adequately communicated to the employees; (3) it took steps to discover violations; and (4) it effectively enforced the rules when infractions were discovered. *See W.G. Yates & Sons. Constr. Co. v. OSHRC*, 459 F.3d 604, 609 n.7 (6th Cir. 2006). Most courts treat this as an affirmative defense, although two courts require the Secretary of Labor to establish that the employee's act was not idiosyncratic and unforeseeable. *See L.R. Willson & Sons, Inc. v. OSHRC*, 134 F.3d 1235, 1241 n.30 (4th Cir. 1998); *Pennsylvania Power & Light Co. v. OSHRC*, 737 F.2d 350, 358 (3d Cir. 1984). One court recently considered whether the legal analysis should be different when the misconduct arises from a supervisor, specifically whether the supervisor's misconduct (in this case an improper excavation) should be imputed to the employer as a way of satisfying the knowledge requirement. The court joined several other Circuit Courts in holding that the supervisor's actions should not be imputed to the employer, noting instead that without actual or constructive knowledge on the employer's part "a supervisor's misconduct may be viewed as an isolated incident of unforeseeable or idiosyncratic behavior." *Comtran Group v. United States Dept. of Labor*, 722 F.3d 1304 (11th Cir. 2013). Consistent with the broad purpose of the statute, the defense turns on whether there was a recognized hazard that the employer failed adequately to address rather than whether the particular injury was caused by the employee misconduct. For example, in *Safeway, Inc. v. OSHRC*, 382 F.3d 1189 (10th Cir. 2004), the employer held an employee barbeque and used a propane gas tank that was too large for the gas grill. When one employee sought to reposition the tank, fuel escaped and a ball of fire erupted that severely burned the two employees working the grill. The employer argued that the injuries resulted from "unforeseeable employee misconduct" because the employee who set up the grill was under the influence of narcotics. The court summarily rejected the argument noting that "the cause of the accident in this case does not bear on whether the citation should be affirmed." The court explained, "The relevant inquiry is not the proximate cause of this particular accident, but the risk of accident or injury as a result of the alleged violations and the seriousness of the potential injuries." *Id.* at n.5 (citation omitted).

5. **Obvious Hazard.** Related to the unforeseeable employee misconduct defense is the question of whether an employer has a duty to protect against obvious injuries. In one case, the employee was digging a trench beside a six-lane highway when the crew struck a cable. To check on the status of the cable, the employee, Floyd Wolfe, walked across three lanes of traffic to inspect a junction box. Unable to trace the cable, he then sought to cross the other three lanes of traffic when he was struck by a car and killed. OSHA cited the employer under a regulatory provision that was analogous to the general duty clause, and the employer argued that it should not have been required to instruct the employee not to cross the highway where cars were moving at upwards of 70 miles per hour. The court rejected the defense explaining:

> There is no dispute that being struck by traffic . . . is an obvious hazard. What's at issue is whether the hazard of crossing an active roadway was so obvious that no instruction about doing so safely was required. . . . As both sides note, the decedent, Wolfe, was an experienced highway worker with a history of sound judgment. The fact that he attempted to cross a road, as he and other employees had done in the past, in the face of credible testimony by two witnesses that doing so at the time was not safe, suggests that the dangers inherent in crossing an active roadway were not so obvious that employees would not have benefitted from systematic instruction.

W. G. Fairfield Co. v. OSHRC, 285 F.3d 499, 508 (6th Cir. 2002). What should the employer have done? The court notes a few options: it could have had a car available to the employees for crossing the road, or it could have provided instruction on how to determine when it was safe to cross the highway on foot. In Massachusetts, public works contractors are required to hire police officers on many projects for safety purposes. The company was fined $3,500 for its violation, a fine the company contested through two levels of appeal.

6. **Enforcement.** Both the *Sea World* and the *W.G. Fairfield Co.* case provide some insight into OSHA's enforcement process. In both cases, the inspections arose after serious accidents. Could the agency have proceeded in any other way? Would a routine inspection have turned up any danger at Sea World? Was it necessary to wait for an accident to occur? How about on the roadside construction? How could OSHA have even known about the gas grill in the *Safeway* case? What else could be done? One possibility would be for the employer to have a safety inspector on staff as many employers do, but what is to ensure that the inspector would be primarily concerned with safety rather than taking into account cost or other concerns? In a workplace where a union is present, the union might have a safety inspector and the collective bargaining agreement might also set forth certain safety requirements, such as requiring police officers for construction sites. What other options might there be?

When a union is present, the union can demand information regarding safety issues through the collective bargaining process. Job safety has been defined as a

B. OSHA 985

working condition, and thus is a mandatory subject for bargaining. As a mandatory subject, employers must provide information on job safety. Without a union, would employees likely have the bargaining power to demand safety measures, or to demand information on workplace hazards? How would they obtain information necessary to know of workplace hazards, particularly concerning risks posed by chemical exposure, and other issues that may not be immediately apparent to the workers? For a discussion of coal miners with a particular focus on the differences between union and non-union mines, see Anne Marie Lofaso, *What We Owe Our Coal Miners*, 5 HARV. L. & POL'Y REV. 87 (2011).

3. Employee Rights

WHIRLPOOL CORP. v. MARSHALL, SECRETARY OF LABOR
United States Supreme Court
445 U.S. 1 (1980)

MR. JUSTICE STEWART delivered the opinion of the Court.

The Occupational Safety and Health Act of 1970 (Act) prohibits an employer from discharging or discriminating against any employee who exercises "any right afforded by" the Act. The Secretary of Labor (Secretary) has promulgated a regulation providing that, among the rights that the Act so protects, is the right of an employee to choose not to perform his assigned task because of a reasonable apprehension of death or serious injury coupled with a reasonable belief that no less drastic alternative is available. The question presented in the case before us is whether this regulation is consistent with the Act.

I

The petitioner company maintains a manufacturing plant in Marion, Ohio, for the production of household appliances. Overhead conveyors transport appliance components throughout the plant. To protect employees from objects that occasionally fall from these conveyors, the petitioner has installed a horizontal wire-mesh guard screen approximately 20 feet above the plant floor. This mesh screen is welded to angle-iron frames suspended from the building's structural steel skeleton.

Maintenance employees of the petitioner spend several hours each week removing objects from the screen, replacing paper spread on the screen to catch grease drippings from the material on the conveyors, and performing occasional maintenance work on the conveyors themselves. To perform these duties, maintenance employees usually are able to stand on the iron frames, but sometimes find it necessary to step onto the steel mesh screen itself.

In 1973, the company began to install heavier wire in the screen because its safety had been drawn into question. Several employees had fallen partly through the old screen, and on one occasion an employee had fallen completely through to the plant floor below but had survived. A number of maintenance employees had reacted to these incidents by bringing the unsafe screen conditions to the attention of their foremen. The petitioner company's contemporaneous safety instructions admonished employees to step only on the angle-iron frames.

On June 28, 1974, a maintenance employee fell to his death through the guard screen in an area where the newer, stronger mesh had not yet been installed. Following this incident, the petitioner effectuated some repairs and issued an order strictly forbidding maintenance employees from stepping on either the screens or the angle-iron supporting structure. An alternative but somewhat more cumbersome and less satisfactory method was developed for removing objects from the screen. This procedure required employees to stand on power-raised mobile platforms and use hooks to recover the material.

On July 7, 1974, two of the petitioner's maintenance employees, Virgil Deemer and Thomas Cornwell, met with the plant maintenance superintendent to voice their concern about the safety of the screen. The superintendent disagreed with their view, but permitted the two men to inspect the screen with their foreman and to point out dangerous areas needing repair. Unsatisfied with the petitioner's response to the results of this inspection, Deemer and Cornwell met on July 9 with the plant safety director. At that meeting, they requested the name, address, and telephone number of a representative of the local office of the Occupational Safety and Health Administration (OSHA). Although the safety director told the men that they "had better stop and think about what [they] were doing," he furnished the men with the information they requested. Later that same day, Deemer contacted an official of the regional OSHA office and discussed the guard screen.

The next day, Deemer and Cornwell reported for the night shift at 10:45 p.m. Their foreman, after himself walking on some of the angle-iron frames, directed the two men to perform their usual maintenance duties on a section of the old screen. Claiming that the screen was unsafe, they refused to carry out this directive. The foreman then sent them to the personnel office, where they were ordered to punch out without working or being paid for the remaining six hours of the shift. The two men subsequently received written reprimands, which were placed in their employment files.

A little over a month later, the Secretary filed suit in the United States District Court for the Northern District of Ohio, alleging that the petitioner's actions against Deemer and Cornwell constituted discrimination in violation of § 11(c)(1) of the Act. As relief, the complaint prayed, *inter alia*, that the petitioner be ordered to expunge from its personnel files all references to the reprimands issued to the two employees, and for a permanent injunction requiring the petitioner to compensate the two employees for the six hours of pay they had lost by reason of their disciplinary suspensions.

Following a bench trial, the District Court found that the regulation in question justified Deemer's and Cornwell's refusals to obey their foreman's order on July 10, 1974. The court found that the two employees had "refused to perform the cleaning operation because of a genuine fear of death or serious bodily harm," that the danger presented had been "real and not something which [had] existed only in the minds of the employees," that the employees had acted in good faith, and that no reasonable alternative had realistically been open to them other than to refuse to work. The District Court nevertheless denied relief, holding that the Secretary's regulation was inconsistent with the Act and therefore invalid. *Usery v. Whirlpool Corp.*, 416 F. Supp. 30, 32–34.

The Court of Appeals for the Sixth Circuit reversed the District Court's judgment . . . disagree[ing] with the District Court's conclusion that the regulation [was] invalid. 593 F.2d 715, 721–736. . . . We granted certiorari because the decision of the Court of Appeals in this case conflicts with those of two other Courts of Appeals on the important question in issue. That question, as stated at the outset of this opinion, is whether the Secretary's regulation authorizing employee "self-help" in some circumstances, 29 CFR § 1977.12(b)(2) (1979), is permissible under the Act.

II

The Act itself creates an express mechanism for protecting workers from employment conditions believed to pose an emergent threat of death or serious injury. Upon receipt of an employee inspection request stating reasonable grounds to believe that an imminent danger is present in a workplace, OSHA must conduct an inspection. 29 U.S.C. § 657(f)(1). In the event this inspection reveals workplace conditions or practices that "could reasonably be expected to cause death or serious physical harm immediately or before the imminence of such danger can be eliminated through the enforcement procedures otherwise provided by" the Act, 29 U.S.C. § 662(a), the OSHA inspector must inform the affected employees and the employer of the danger and notify them that he is recommending to the Secretary that injunctive relief be sought. § 662(c). At this juncture, the Secretary can petition a federal court to restrain the conditions or practices giving rise to the imminent danger. By means of a temporary restraining order or preliminary injunction, the court may then require the employer to avoid, correct, or remove the danger or to prohibit employees from working in the area. § 662(a).

To ensure that this process functions effectively, the Act expressly accords to every employee several rights, the exercise of which may not subject him to discharge or discrimination. An employee is given the right to inform OSHA of an imminently dangerous workplace condition or practice and request that OSHA inspect that condition or practice. 29 U.S.C. § 657(f)(1). He is given a limited right to assist the OSHA inspector in inspecting the workplace, §§ 657(a)(2), (e), and (f)(2), and the right to aid a court in determining whether or not a risk of imminent danger in fact exists. See § 660(c)(1). Finally, an affected employee is given the right to bring an action to compel the Secretary to seek injunctive relief if he believes the Secretary has wrongfully declined to do so. § 662(d).

In the light of this detailed statutory scheme, the Secretary is obviously correct when he acknowledges in his regulation that, "as a general matter, there is no right afforded by the Act which would entitle employees to walk off the job because of potential unsafe conditions at the workplace." By providing for prompt notice to the employer of an inspector's intention to seek an injunction against an imminently dangerous condition, the legislation obviously contemplates that the employer will normally respond by voluntarily and speedily eliminating the danger. And in the few instances where this does not occur, the legislative provisions authorizing prompt judicial action are designed to give employees full protection in most situations from the risk of injury or death resulting from an imminently dangerous condition at the worksite.

As this case illustrates, however, circumstances may sometimes exist in which the employee justifiably believes that the express statutory arrangement does not sufficiently protect him from death or serious injury. Such circumstances will probably not often occur, but such a situation may arise when (1) the employee is ordered by his employer to work under conditions that the employee reasonably believes pose an imminent risk of death or serious bodily injury, and (2) the employee has reason to believe that there is not sufficient time or opportunity either to seek effective redress from his employer or to apprise OSHA of the danger.

Nothing in the Act suggests that those few employees who have to face this dilemma must rely exclusively on the remedies expressly set forth in the Act at the risk of their own safety. But nothing in the Act explicitly provides otherwise. Against this background of legislative silence, the Secretary has exercised his rulemaking power under 29 U.S.C. § 657(g)(2) and has determined that, when an employee in good faith finds himself in such a predicament, he may refuse to expose himself to the dangerous condition, without being subjected to "subsequent discrimination" by the employer.

The question before us is whether this interpretative regulation constitutes a permissible gloss on the Act by the Secretary, in light of the Act's language, structure, and legislative history. Our inquiry is informed by an awareness that the regulation is entitled to deference unless it can be said not to be a reasoned and supportable interpretation of the Act. *Skidmore v. Swift & Co.*, 323 U.S. 134, 139–140.

A

The regulation clearly conforms to the fundamental objective of the Act—to prevent occupational deaths and serious injuries. The Act, in its preamble, declares that its purpose and policy is "to assure so far as possible every working man and woman in the Nation safe and healthful working conditions and to *preserve* our human resources. . . ." 29 U.S.C. § 651(b). (Emphasis added.)

To accomplish this basic purpose, the legislation's remedial orientation is prophylactic in nature. *See Atlas Roofing Co. v. Occupational Safety and Health Review Comm'n*, 430 U.S. 442, 444–445. The Act does not wait for an employee to die or become injured. It authorizes the promulgation of health and safety standards and the issuance of citations in the hope that these will act to prevent deaths or injuries from ever occurring. It would seem anomalous to construe an Act so directed and constructed as prohibiting an employee, with no other reasonable alternative, the freedom to withdraw from a workplace environment that he reasonably believes is highly dangerous.

Moreover, the Secretary's regulation can be viewed as an appropriate aid to the full effectuation of the Act's "general duty" clause. That clause provides that "[each] employer . . . shall furnish to each of his employees employment and a place of employment which are free from recognized hazards that are causing or are likely to cause death or serious physical harm to his employees." 29 U.S.C. § 654(a)(1). As the legislative history of this provision reflects, it was intended itself to deter the occurrence of occupational deaths and serious injuries by placing on employers a mandatory obligation independent of the specific health and safety standards to be promulgated by the Secretary. Since OSHA inspectors cannot be present around the clock in every workplace, the Secretary's regulation ensures that employees will in all circumstances enjoy the rights afforded them by the "general duty" clause.

The regulation thus on its face appears to further the overriding purpose of the Act, and rationally to complement its remedial scheme. In the absence of some contrary indication in the legislative history, the Secretary's regulation must, therefore, be upheld, particularly when it is remembered that safety legislation is to be liberally construed to effectuate the congressional purpose. *United States v. Bacto-Unidisk*, 394 U.S. 784, 798.

B

In urging reversal of the judgment before us, the petitioner relies primarily on two aspects of the Act's legislative history.

1

Representative Daniels of New Jersey sponsored one of several House bills that led ultimately to the passage of the Act. As reported to the House by the Committee on Education and Labor, the Daniels bill contained a section that was soon dubbed the "strike with pay" provision. This section provided that employees could request an examination by the Department of Health, Education, and Welfare (HEW) of the toxicity of any materials in their workplace. If that examination revealed a workplace substance that had "potentially toxic or harmful effects in such concentration as used or found," the employer was given 60 days to correct the potentially dangerous condition. Following the expiration of that period, the employer could not require that an employee be exposed to toxic concentrations of the substance unless the employee was informed of the hazards and symptoms associated with the substance, the employee was instructed in the proper precautions for dealing with the substance, and the employee was furnished with personal protective equipment. If these conditions were not met, an employee could "absent himself from such risk of harm for the period necessary to avoid such danger without loss of regular compensation for such period."

This provision encountered stiff opposition in the House. . . . In response, Representative Daniels offered a floor amendment that, among other things, deleted his bill's "strike with pay" provision. He suggested that employees instead be afforded the right to request an immediate OSHA inspection of the premises, a right which the Steiger bill did not provide. The House ultimately adopted the Steiger bill. . . . The bill that was reported to and, with a few amendments, passed by the Senate never contained a "strike with pay" provision. . . .

. . . The petitioner argues that Congress' overriding concern in rejecting the "strike with pay" provision was to avoid giving employees a unilateral authority to walk off the job which they might abuse in order to intimidate or harass their employer. Congress deliberately chose instead, the petitioner maintains, to grant employees the power to request immediate administrative inspections of the workplace which could in appropriate cases lead to coercive judicial remedies. As the petitioner views the regulation, therefore, it gives to workers precisely what Congress determined to withhold from them.

We read the legislative history differently. Congress rejected a provision that did not concern itself at all with conditions posing real and immediate threats of death or severe injury. The remedy which the rejected provision furnished employees could have been invoked only after 60 days had passed following HEW's inspection and notification that improperly high levels of toxic substances were present in the workplace. Had that inspection revealed employment conditions posing a threat of imminent and grave harm, the Secretary of Labor would presumably have requested, long before expiration of the 60-day period, a court injunction pursuant to other provisions of the Daniels bill. Consequently, in rejecting the Daniels bill's "strike with pay" provision, Congress was not rejecting a legislative provision dealing with the highly perilous and fast-moving situations covered by the regulation now before us.

It is also important to emphasize that what primarily troubled Congress about the Daniels bill's "strike with pay" provision was its requirement that employees be paid their regular salary after having properly invoked their right to refuse to work under the section. It is instructive that virtually every time the issue of an employee's right to absent himself from hazardous work was discussed in the legislative debates, it was in the context of the employee's right to continue to receive his usual compensation.

When it rejected the "strike with pay" concept, therefore, Congress very clearly meant to reject a law unconditionally imposing upon employers an obligation to continue to pay their employees their regular paychecks when they absented themselves from work for reasons of safety. But the regulation at issue here does not require employers to pay workers who refuse to perform their assigned tasks in the face of imminent danger. It simply provides that in such cases the employer may not "discriminate" against the employees involved. An employer "discriminates" against an employee only when he treats that employee less favorably than he treats others similarly situated.

2

The second aspect of the Act's legislative history upon which the petitioner relies is the rejection by Congress of provisions contained in both the Daniels and the Williams bills that would have given Labor Department officials, in imminent-danger situations, the power temporarily to shut down all or part of an employer's plant. These provisions aroused considerable opposition in both Houses of Congress. . . . The Steiger bill that ultimately passed the House gave the Labor Department no such authority. The Williams bill, as approved by the Senate, did contain an administrative shutdown provision, but the Conference Committee rejected this aspect of the Senate bill.

The petitioner infers from these events a congressional will hostile to the regulation in question here. The regulation, the petitioner argues, provides employees with the very authority to shut down an employer's plant that was expressly denied a more expert and objective United States Department of Labor.

As we read the pertinent legislative history, however, the petitioner misconceives the thrust of Congress' concern. Those in Congress who prevented passage of the administrative shutdown provisions in the Daniels and Williams bills were opposed to the unilateral authority those provisions gave to federal officials, without any judicial safeguards, drastically to impair the operation of an employer's business. Congressional opponents also feared that the provisions might jeopardize the Government's otherwise neutral role in labor-management relations.

Neither of these congressional concerns is implicated by the regulation before us. The regulation accords no authority to Government officials. It simply permits private employees of a private employer to avoid workplace conditions that they believe pose grave dangers to their own safety. The employees have no power under the regulation to order their employer to correct the hazardous condition or to clear the dangerous workplace of others. Moreover, any employee who acts in reliance on the regulation runs the risk of discharge or reprimand in the event a court subsequently finds that he acted unreasonably or in bad faith. The regulation, therefore, does not remotely resemble the legislation that Congress rejected.

C

For these reasons we conclude that 29 CFR § 1977.12(b)(2) (1979) was promulgated by the Secretary in the valid exercise of his authority under the Act. Accordingly, the judgment of the Court of Appeals is affirmed.

NOTES

1. **Governing Standard.** What standard does the Court determine for when an employee has the right to refuse to work because of unsafe working conditions? Do you believe the Agency has established sufficient protections against employee abuse?

2. **Antidiscrimination Provision.** The Supreme Court distinguishes the "strike with pay" provision from the antidiscrimination regulation at issue in Whirlpool. What is the distinction the Court makes?

3. **Alternative Approaches.** As we have seen previously, *see* Chapter 8, section E, a walkout by nonunion workers to protest an unsafe workplace can be considered concerted activity under § 7 of the NLRA. *See NLRB v. Washington Aluminum Co.*, 370 U.S. 9 (1962). In the context of unionized workers, one court has interpreted § 502 of the LMRA as protecting union workers from being replaced when employees in good faith refuse to work in abnormally dangerous conditions, and there is objective evidence to support their belief. Section 502 protects such workers despite the existence of a no-strike clause in their collective bargaining agreement. *See TNS, Inc. v. NLRB*, 296 F.3d 384, 393–94 (6th Cir. 2002), *cert. denied*, 537 U.S. 1106 (2003). Courts have also concluded that employees need not follow the OSHA complaint procedures in order to be protected under § 502, which can afford

superior protection to employees in exigent circumstances. *See NLRB v. Tamara Foods, Inc.*, 692 F.2d 1171, 1182 (8th Cir. 1982), *cert. denied*, 461 U.S. 928 (1983).

4. **Section 11(c) of the Act.** The regulation at issue in *Whirlpool* was passed under the authority of § 11(c)(1), which reads:

(c) (1) No person shall discharge or in any manner discriminate against any employee because such employee has filed any complaint or instituted or caused to be instituted any proceeding under or related to this Act or has testified or is about to testify in any such proceeding or because of the exercise by such employee on behalf of himself or others of any right afforded by this Act.

Employees who feel they have been subjected to conduct in violation of § 11(c) can file a complaint with OSHA to obtain appropriate equitable relief. For a thorough discussion of this section and how it can be used to protect whistleblowers, see Monique C. Lillard, *Exploring the Paths to Recovery for OSHA Whistleblowers: Section 11(c) of the OSHAct and the Public Policy Tort*, 6 EMPL. Rts. & EMPLOY. POL'Y J. 329 (2002).

C. REFLECTIONS ON WORKER SAFETY

The materials on workers' compensation and OSHA provide important insights into the way in which, as a society, we have chosen to regulate an important facet of employees' work lives. It is often said that just one fatality is too many, but that seems true only as an abstract proposition for it seems unlikely that we would be willing to expend the necessary resources to eliminate all workplace fatalities. And, as noted earlier, workplace fatalities have decreased significantly—even in absolute numbers—since OSHA was founded, even though the workforce has grown substantially. Workplace injuries and illnesses have also declined, although days lost from work have not significantly decreased.

Despite the decline in workplace injuries and fatalities since the early twentieth century, there remains widespread dissatisfaction with the way in which worker safety is regulated. By establishing a no-fault insurance system, Workers' Compensation was intended to provide a quick, low-cost mechanism for providing basic support to injured workers and their families. Over the last several decades, the costs of the workers' compensation system have ballooned, now exceeding $77 billion annually. *See* National Academy of Social Insurance Workers' Compensation Benefits, Coverage, and Costs, 2011, at 1 (2013). A substantial proportion of these funds is going to health care providers hired to assess the extent of disability and to lawyers, rather than providing treatment to injured workers. Despite the high costs of the system, many argue that the levels of compensation are inadequate to meet the needs of disabled workers and that employers have failed to respond to rising costs by taking more affirmative steps to prevent injuries.

Similarly, OSHA has been widely criticized from all sides. Employers argue that its regulations are unduly burdensome, entailing costly mandates that do little to improve workplace safety. Employee advocates assert that the agency is ineffective in protecting workers' health and safety because of the limitations on the agency's authority and funding, leaving the agency underequipped to provide adequate safety regulation.

In a Pulitzer prize-winning series, the New York Times highlighted the difficulty OSHA has in regulating the most dangerous workplaces and in preventing workplace fatalities. Reviewing agency records, the newspaper identified 2,197 deaths over two decades and found,

> "For those 2,197 deaths, employers faced $106 million in civil OSHA fines and jail sentences totaling less than 30 years. . . . Twenty of those years were from one case, a chicken-plant fire in North Carolina that killed 25 workers in 1991. By contrast, one company, WorldCom, recently paid $750 million in civil fines for misleading investors. The Environmental Protection Agency, in 2001 alone, obtained prison sentences totaling 256 years."

David Barstow, *U.S. Rarely Seeks Charges for Deaths in Workplace*, N.Y. TIMES, Dec. 22, 2003, at A1. As noted previously, the criminal penalty for causing a worker's death remains a misdemeanor, which has hampered prosecution efforts. A former OSHA administrator explained, "After you do all the work, get the file perfect . . . you take it to a U.S. Attorney, and they say, 'It's a misdemeanor?' " *Id.* The article noted, "There have been repeated efforts to make it a felony to cause a worker's death. But strong opposition from Republicans and many Democrats doomed every effort." *Id.* The New York Times pointed out that the maximum sentence for killing a worker was "half the maximum for harassing a wild burro on federal lands." *Id.* There are more than 7,500 federal inspectors to ensure the safety of our meat and poultry supply, while slightly more than 2,200 OSHA inspectors regulate the safety of workers.

Why do you think it is so difficult to change the penalties for serious injuries or worker deaths? Is this an area where employer clout in the political process explains why it is so difficult to obtain legislative reform, or additional financial support for OSHA? Relatedly, who speaks for employees on safety issues when most workplaces are without a union presence?

One possible explanation for the failure of legislative reform has to do with existing incentives, an issue we have discussed in various forms throughout the book. First, many believe the workers' compensation system provides a stronger basis for encouraging workplace safety than governmental regulatory enforcement, in that the costs associated with workers' compensation far exceeds the penalties OSHA exacts (approximately $100 million annually with some variations). Large employers can reduce their workers' compensation insurance premiums significantly by reducing their injury rates (for smaller employers, the premiums are not as directly tied to specific injury rates).

Second, there are substantial market incentives pressing employers to ensure safe workplaces. When employees are injured, they not only obtain compensation, but they frequently lose time away from work, which ought to result in lower productivity. The labor market may also punish employers who acquire a poor reputation for worker safety. Under what conditions will this likely occur? How will employees obtain this information? Employees, themselves, also have strong incentives to ensure a safe workplace, and under *Whirlpool v. Marshall*, they have the ability to walk off the job under certain circumstances where the workplace is demonstrably dangerous.

Certainly not all employees will be able or willing to exercise this right, and indeed, one of the most troubling aspects of the existing system of worker safety is that low-wage, low-skill workers are the most vulnerable to dangerous workplace conditions. Latino workers, for example, have a significantly higher injury rate than non-Latinos, and foreign-born Latinos have a fatality rate much higher than any other group. *See* Christen G. Byler, *Hispanic/Latino Fatal Occupational Injury Rates*, MONTHLY LAB. REV., Feb. 2013. This may be attributable in part to language barriers, but it may also be due to a greater fear of retribution by immigrant workers for reporting dangerous work conditions. Indeed, a government report suggested that serious disincentives exist for employees to report injuries, including that they might be fired and these disincentives are more prevalent among low-wage workers. *See* Government Accountability Office, *Workplace Safety and Health: Enhancing OSHA's Records Audit Process Could Improve the Accuracy of Worker Injury & Illness Data*, at 17–19 (Oct. 2009).

Sometimes, it is simply a lack of alternatives that compels workers into dangerous jobs. This sentiment was captured in a news report regarding an explosion at a medical-supply plant in Goldsboro, North Carolina that killed three workers and injured 37, many of whom were severely burned in the explosion. Despite the catastrophic experience, the impulse by the state and the community was to get the jobs back. The state labor commissioner stated, "We need to convince this company very quickly to rebuild this plant," and one of the employees observed, "There's really no jobs here. And that was one of the best companies here that was paying any money. Now we don't know what we're going to do. Lord knows, I hope they rebuild it." David M. Halbfinger, *Explosion Extinguishes One of a North Carolina Town's Few Bright Spots*, N.Y. TIMES, Jan. 21, 2003, at A19.

What alternatives exist to the current system? Would it be desirable to increase the level of fines available for safety violations, and if so, to what level? One problem that currently exists is that OSHA investigators frequently reduce the fines, and the seriousness of the charges, as a way of avoiding contested proceedings. Would raising the fines help in that context? Would increasing the number of inspectors, or OSHA's budget, make a significant difference? One scholar has recently suggested that the agency's strategic plan for investigations could be enriched by improving the focus on information technology to harvest the agency's vast data and she observes that OSHA is particularly important today given the declining role of unions. *See* Alison D. Morantz, *Putting Data to Work for Workers: The Role of Information Technology in U.S. Worker Protection Agencies*, 67 IND. & LAB. REL. REV. 675 (2014). Another possibility would be to return to a fault-based system for worker's compensation, returning worker injuries to the tort system. Does that seem like a preferable alternative? Would it offer a stronger deterrent for employers? Finally, the workplace might borrow from the existing system that regulates food safety. In many food plants around the country, federal employees are present to inspect and grade the products, and the inspectors are paid by fees collected from the regulated industries. Might this model be more appropriate than the existing inspection system?

Part Five

SYSTEMS OF JUSTICE: PUBLIC VERSUS PRIVATE, COLLECTIVE VERSUS INDIVIDUAL

So far, we have discussed the law as if it included only the common law developments in the courts and legislative enactments. In fact, however, the employment relation is governed by a great deal of contractual "law"—arrangements between the parties that apply only to those parties. Because these arrangements are private and sheltered from the public view unless disputed, it is easy to discount or ignore this system of workplace regulation. In fact, however, it is central to the day-to-day lives of workers and managers at the firm level.

One example of such private regulation of the employment relation that we have studied thus far is collective bargaining. If successful, collective bargaining yields a labor contract that both settles the most fundamental aspects of the wage-labor bargain and creates a privatized system of dispute resolution, the grievance and arbitration machinery. Disputes as to contract interpretation (for example, over what conduct amounts to just cause for discharge) are funneled into labor arbitration before a neutral arbitrator chosen jointly by the parties and bound by a set of procedural rules negotiated by the parties; the arbitrator's fee is typically split equally between the parties. The union represents the workers' interest and the employer designates personnel to represent its interests. Attorneys are frequently involved on both sides. Dispute resolutions achieved through this process receive a high degree of judicial deference, so that the system remains truly private. Thus, unionized employees obtain protection for the core interests we have discussed throughout this book—job security, voice, dignity, autonomy, and free-dom from discrimination—through arbitration under their labor contracts.

But what about the 93% of private sector workers who are not unionized? Is there a private system of justice applicable to them, as well? Indeed there is, although one must look closely at the patchwork of employer and employee responses to common law developments and legislative enactments to appreciate it. This Part surveys the evolving private system of justice applicable to the workforce as a whole. Just as a private dispute resolution system was needed in the labor arena to interpret and implement the rights guaranteed in collective bargaining agreements, a similar system has evolved in the nonunion sector to respond to the rights created by common law and statute. Chapter 14 examines the most well-established device for privatizing workplace disputes in the nonunion sector: predispute arbitration agreements that channel litigation over workplace rights into arbitration. Initially intended by employers as a tool to reduce the costs and risks inherent in litigation, predispute arbitration agreements have been transformed into a private system of justice complete with their own common law of enforceability. Nevertheless, questions remain about whether the public interest is jeopardized by the privatization of these disputes, and whether the process is adequately policed in order to produce substantively fair outcomes. Chapter 15 takes up these policy questions at a macro level, describing the pressure toward employer self-regulation that is exerted by various doctrines we have studied throughout the course. How does this evolving private system of justice compare with the public law system of individual rights enforcement through litigation? How does it compare with the private dispute resolution system available in the collective bargaining context?

Chapter 14

ARBITRATION OF WORKPLACE DISPUTES

Litigation is no longer the sole or even the primary dispute resolution system in the United States. Arbitration pursuant to predispute arbitration agreements, typically imposed on employees as a condition of employment, has supplanted litigation in many workplaces. This chapter explores this workplace dispute resolution device. Part A offers an overview of arbitration in the labor and employment context. Part B traces the origins of arbitration in the workplace to the collective bargaining context, addressing the problems that arise when unionized workers' rights to arbitrate disputes under their labor contracts overlap with statutory rights to proceed in public fora. Part C takes up the question of the enforceability of individual employee contracts to waive statutory forum rights in exchange for private arbitration processes unilaterally established and administered by the employer. Part D explores the jurisprudence that has evolved as courts struggled to police individual arbitration agreements. Part E surveys the policy debate that has grown up around this particular form of private justice.

A. ARBITRATION AS A WORKPLACE DISPUTE RESOLUTION MECHANISM: ORIGINS AND EVOLUTION

We begin with an overview of arbitration's history and role in the workplace setting.

RICHARD A. BALES, COMPULSORY ARBITRATION: THE GRAND EXPERIMENT IN EMPLOYMENT
3–10 (1997)

Arbitration is a "simple proceeding voluntarily chosen by parties who want a dispute determined by an impartial judge of their own mutual selection, whose decision, based on the merits of the case, they agree in advance to accept as final and binding." A compulsory employment arbitration agreement is an agreement between employer and employee to resolve future employment disputes by arbitration. Compulsory arbitration provisions can be created as stand-alone agreements, or inserted as part of broader written employment agreements. They can be broad enough to encompass virtually every employment dispute imaginable, or drawn narrowly to encompass only a limited range of disputes (such as those involving discharge from employment). They can incorporate original rules to govern arbitral procedure, or adopt the rules promulgated by a neutral agency such as the American Arbitration Association (AAA) or the Center for Public Resources (CPR).

An arbitration agreement, by itself, does not affect the substantive legal rules that govern the employment relationship. If an employee is employed at-will, that is, she can quit or be fired at any time without notice for any reason (other than one proscribed by law, such as her race), an arbitration agreement does not affect her at-will status. Similarly, an employee does not sign away her right to be free from invidious workplace discrimination or to recover certain damages specified by statute to compensate her for discrimination she has suffered, merely by signing an arbitration agreement. An arbitration agreement, by itself, merely changes the forum where the parties' substantive rights are adjudicated from the courthouse to arbitration, and does not affect those underlying rights. . . .

The primary distinctive feature of a compulsory arbitration agreement is that both parties, the employer and the employee, agree to submit to binding arbitration any employment dispute that arises in the future. Because this is the final adjudication of a dispute, it operates to the exclusion of other forms of adjudication, such as litigation. As such, compulsory arbitration is a mutually exclusive alternative to litigation, because one signatory to such an agreement can compel the other to submit a claim to arbitration in lieu of litigation, and because an arbitration award is as final and binding as a case that has been litigated to final judgment with virtually all appeals exhausted. . . .

By far the most significant use of arbitration in the twentieth-century United States has been in the workplace. There have been three major transformations in the way workplace disputes have been resolved. The first was the unionization of the American workforce in the 1940s and 1950s, and the concomitant use of arbitration to settle disputes between employers and unions. The second was congressional passage of individual employment rights statutes, such as those prohibiting discrimination, which shifted the resolution of employment disputes from arbitration by the union and the employer, to resolution by litigation brought by an employee against the employer. The third . . . is the return to arbitration for resolving disputes concerning these individual rights.

Although labor arbitration began during the latter part of the nineteenth century, its most rapid advance occurred during World War II through the National War Labor Board. The NWLB decided approximately 20,000 labor dispute cases, most of which were disputes over the terms of collective bargaining agreements. As a precondition to issuing a decision in a labor dispute, the NWLB required the parties to insert into their collective bargaining agreement a clause providing for arbitration of all future disputes. This laid the foundation for the current labor practice of terminating the contract grievance procedure with the final step of arbitration.

The preeminent role of arbitration in resolving labor disputes was confirmed by the United States Supreme Court's 1960 *Steelworkers* Trilogy.[1] In these cases, the

---

[1] [n. 42] *United Steelworkers of Am. v. American Mfg. Co.*, 363 U.S. 564 (1960) (holding that arbitrators, not courts, should decide the arbitrability of grievances); *United Steelworkers of Am. v. Warrior & Gulf Navigation Co.*, 363 U.S. 574 (1960) (holding that courts should refuse to order a grievance to arbitration only if the collective bargaining agreement's arbitration clause cannot be interpreted to cover the dispute); *United Steelworkers of Am. v. Enterprise Wheel & Car Co.*, 363 U.S. 593 (1960) (holding that courts should not review the merits of an arbitrator's award so long as the award

Court created a virtually irrebuttable presumption that disputes between employers and unions were arbitrable, and sharply restricted the role of courts in resolving such disputes. The Court also articulated its vision of the American workplace as entirely autonomous—a place where unions and employers would collectively bargain and agree to rules governing the workplace, where all workplace disputes would be settled by arbitration, and where there was very little room (or need) for judicial intervention. . . .

The trend to legislate in the employment sector began in the first decades of this century, when states began passing workers' compensation statutes. . . . [Congressional enactment of the FLSA, Equal Pay Act, Title VII, the ADEA, OSHA, ERISA, and the FMLA followed.]

These new minimum terms of employment are called "individual rights" because the individual employee, rather than a union, is responsible for their enforcement. Unlike the grievance mechanism of a collective bargaining agreement, in which conflicts are resolved jointly by employer and union, individual rights rely for enforcement on lawsuits brought by employees against employers. The number of such lawsuits has exploded recently, as press coverage of highly publicized cases has made employees aware of their rights and of the possibility of receiving large damage awards.

Not everyone, however, welcomes the prospect of enforcing these new individual employment rights through litigation. Judges see the employment litigation explosion as adding a backlog that forces litigants to wait years before getting to trial. . . . This may explain, at least in part, the recent judicial embrace of compulsory employment arbitration.

Many employers are equally happy with compulsory arbitration. They dislike the jury system because they believe that juries are unpredictable, that jurors often decide cases on the basis of sympathy rather than legal merit, and that jurors are "the 'peers' of employees, not employers." Moreover, because arbitration is faster and less formal than litigation, it is a substantially less expensive means of resolving employment disputes. . . .

Employees and their advocates often are less enthusiastic. This hesitation no doubt stems from the (often justified) fear that employers will draft arbitration agreements that deprive employees of their basic employment rights, and then offer these one-sided agreements to current and prospective employees on a sign-it-or-be-fired basis. . . .

A fairly designed compulsory arbitration system has a great deal to offer to employees. Many employees, especially lower-income workers, are shut out of the current litigation process because their low salaries make their receiving large damage awards unlikely, and this in turn makes it difficult to attract attorneys who will handle these cases on a contingency basis. The speed and low cost of an arbitration award may make even a low-damage case attractive to plaintiff attorneys. Moreover, even if the employee still cannot find an attorney, the relative informality of arbitration makes it far easier to arbitrate a claim without the aid of

---

"draws its essence" from the collective bargaining agreement).

an attorney rather than satisfy the procedural roadblocks imposed by federal antidiscriminatory statutes as a prerequisite to litigation. Further, the adversarial litigation process forces employees to jeopardize or sever current employment relationships; to pay for attorneys' retainers, expert witness fees, and protracted discoveries; and to put their professional lives on hold for years. Arbitration offers a way to resolve disputes quickly, often before the parties are so entrenched that reconciliation becomes impossible. For these reasons, employers and employees increasingly are entering into, and courts increasingly are enforcing, compulsory arbitration agreements.

This use of compulsory arbitration to resolve disputes concerning individual employment rights represents the third transformation in the way employment disputes are resolved. This transformation, however, is far from complete. . . .

NOTES

1. **An Autonomous System of Dispute Resolution for Unionized Workers.** What is the justification for judicial deference to the private system of dispute resolution in the collective bargaining context? The Supreme Court explained:

> . . .The present federal policy is to promote industrial stabilization through the collective bargaining agreement. A major factor in achieving industrial peace is the inclusion of a provision for arbitration of grievances in the collective bargaining agreement.

> [In] the run of arbitration cases . . . the choice is between the adjudication of cases or controversies in courts with established procedures or even special statutory safeguards on the one hand and the settlement of them in the more informal arbitration tribunal on the other. In the commercial case, arbitration is the substitute for litigation. Here arbitration is the substitute for industrial strife. Since arbitration of labor disputes has quite different functions from arbitration under an ordinary commercial agreement, the hostility evinced by courts toward arbitration of commercial agreements has no place here. For arbitration of labor disputes under collective bargaining agreements is part and parcel of the collective bargaining process itself.

United Steelworkers v. Warrior & Gulf Navigation Co., 363 U.S. 574, 578 (1960). The source of an arbitrator's authority to render an award is the collective bargaining agreement. Thus, as long as the arbitrator's decision is predicated on the contract—or as the Court put it, as long as the award "draws its essence from the collective bargaining agreement," courts must refuse to review the merits of arbitral rulings in labor cases. *United Steelworkers v. Enterprise Wheel & Car Corp.*, 363 U.S. 593, 597 (1960). This is true even where the arbitrator's decision "rests on factual errors or misinterprets the parties' agreement," *Paperworkers v. Misco, Inc.*, 484 U.S. 29, 36 (1987), or where the reviewing court "is convinced [that the arbitrator] committed serious error." *Eastern Associated Coal Corp. v. Mine Workers*, 531 U.S. 57, 62 (2000). The rationale for this judicial deference is that arbitration is a continuation of the collective bargaining process, and the arbitrator is functioning as the parties' surrogate. Consequently, "[i]n the absence of fraud or an overreaching of authority on the part of the arbitrator, [the arbitrator] is speaking for the parties, and his award is their contract." Theodore J. St. Antoine, *Judicial Review of Labor Arbitration Awards: A Second Look at Enterprise Wheel and Its Progeny*, 75 Mich. L. Rev. 1137, 1140 (1977).

2. Finality of Arbitration Awards Outside the Collective Bargaining Context. Predispute employment arbitration agreements outside the collective bargaining context are also entitled to a strong presumption of finality to which the courts must defer. Section 10(a) of the Federal Arbitration Act, which governs individual employment arbitration agreements, describes the narrow grounds upon which arbitration awards may be vacated:

(1) Where the award was procured by corruption, fraud, or undue means.

(2) Where there was evident partiality or corruption in the arbitrators. . . .

(3) Where the arbitrators were guilty of misconduct in refusing to postpone the hearing, upon sufficient cause shown, or in refusing to hear evidence pertinent and material to the controversy; or of any other misbehavior by which the rights of any party have been prejudiced.

(4) Where the arbitrators exceeded their powers, or so imperfectly executed them that a mutual, final, and definite award upon the subject matter submitted was not made.

These grounds for vacating or modifying an arbitration ruling are the exclusive grounds for judicial review; the parties may not expand the grounds by private agreement. *Hall St. Assocs., L.L.C. v. Mattel, Inc.*, 552 U.S. 576 (2008). Nor can they contract the grounds for review; the FAA's grounds for review were designed by Congress to ensure a minimum level of due process for parties to arbitration. *In re Wal-Mart Wage & Hour Empl. Practices Litig.*, 737 F.3d 1262, 1268–69 (9th Cir. 2013).

Subsection (4) above might seem to offer a flexible avenue for obtaining review, but the Court has made it clear that its scope is very narrow. In *Oxford Health Plans LLC v. Sutter*, 133 S. Ct. 2064 (2013), the Court summarized its decisions from the collective bargaining context and applied them to arbitration decisions governed by the FAA:

> [Section] 10(a)(4) of the [FAA] . . . authorizes a federal court to set aside an arbitral award "where the arbitrator[] exceeded [his] powers." A party seeking relief under that provision bears a heavy burden. "It is not enough to show that the [arbitrator] committed an error—or even a serious error." Because the parties "bargained for the arbitrator's construction of their agreement," an arbitral decision "even arguably construing or applying the contract" must stand, regardless of a court's view of its (de)merits. Only if "the arbitrator act[s] outside the scope of his contractually delegated authority"—issuing an award that "simply reflect[s] his own notions of [economic] justice" rather than "draw[ing] its essence from the contract"— may a court overturn his determination. So the sole question for us is whether the arbitrator (even arguably) interpreted the parties' contract, not whether he got its meaning right or wrong.

Id. at 2069–72.

What is the rationale for the narrow standard of review applicable to individual employment agreements under the FAA? Is it reasonable to apply a doctrine developed in a context where a union negotiates for an arbitration and grievance process, plays a central role in selecting the arbitrator, and frames the case before the arbitrator to a situation where an individual employee is covered by a predispute arbitration agreement? On a broader note, if courts refuse to review employment arbitration awards construing statutory rights for errors of law, is the public law essentially transformed into a system of private justice? Is there anything wrong with this from the standpoint of labor and employment policy?

3. **Comparing Labor Arbitration with Employment Arbitration: Apples and Orangutangs.** As we shall see, the Court increasingly applies doctrines developed in the labor arbitration context to the employment arbitration context. It may be helpful here to recall some of the differences between the two. It would be fair to characterize labor and employment arbitration as not just apples and oranges, but apples and orangutangs! Labor arbitration grievants are represented by the union (which usually employs a lawyer for this purpose). The union typically "owns" the grievance, since the union rather than the employee was signatory to the labor contract (employees are beneficiaries of the agreement rather than signatories). That is, the union decides which grievances to take forward to arbitration, and represents the individual grievant with an eye toward the impact of a particular construction of the labor contract on all the employees that it represents. Both sides usually have significant experience with particular arbitrators, and will bring that to bear during the arbitral selection process (the "repeat player" effect). Procedural rules governing labor arbitration are established through collective bargaining, including time limits for grievance filing, the process for choosing the arbitrator, and limitations on available remedies. In discipline or discharge cases arising under a labor contract's just cause provision, the employer bears the burden of proof. Labor arbitrations center on issues of contractual interpretation that affect individuals or groups of employees, and (as we saw in Chapter 3) are governed not only by the labor contract but by implied rights imposed by arbitrators as a matter of practice, including the meaning of just cause, a requirement of progressive discipline, and requirements of notice and due process.

Claimants in individual employment arbitration proceedings are often not represented by a lawyer, particularly if the claimant is a low wage employee so that there is relatively little financial recovery at stake. Pro se claimants or even the lawyers representing individual claimants may not know the arbitrators, while large employers are more likely to be familiar with them; this has consequences for the arbitral selection process, and the "repeat player" effect is typically present on only one side of the equation. Procedural rules applicable to employment arbitration are established by the employer, including time limitations, arbitral selection processes, and limits on remedies. The claimant always bears the burden of proof in employment arbitration. Employment arbitrations typically focus on statutory rights, contractual rights (under the employee handbook or an individual contract, if one is present) or, less commonly, rights derived from the common law (e.g., wrongful discharge claims).

Outcomes in labor arbitration cases fall into three categories. Employers obtain outright wins in about half of all grievances; the other half of the decisions are divided between grievant outright wins and so-called "split" cases, in which grievants prevail but do not obtain the full relief sought (e.g., they win reinstatement, but without back pay). *See* Laura J. Cooper, *Discipline and Discharge of Public Sector Employees: An Empirical Study of Arbitration Awards*, 27 ABA J. Lab. & Emp. L. 195 (2012); Laura J. Cooper, Mario F. Bognanno, & Stephen Befort, *How and Why Labor Arbitrators Decide Discipline and Discharge Cases: An Empirical Examination*, Arbitration 2007: Workplace Justice for a Changing Environment, Proceedings of the Sixtieth Annual Meeting, National Academy of Arbitrators, Bureau of National Affairs 420 (2008).

Win rates in employment arbitrations are difficult to summarize because studies sometimes lump together highly compensated executives and low wage employees, whose circumstances are disparate. Recent studies indicate that in cases based on employer-promulgated arbitration clauses, employee-claimants win 24.7% of the time (this includes a broad range of cases where the amount of damages awarded may be considerably less than the amount claimed). In cases arising under individually-negotiated agreements (typically involving relatively highly compensated executives), employee-claimants won 64.6% of the time. Alexander J.S. Colvin, *Saturns and Rickshaws Revisited: What Kind of Arbitration System Has Developed?*, 29 Oh. St. J. on Disp. Res. 59, 74 (2014). Because of the differences between labor arbitration and employment arbitration, these comparisons in win rates are of limited utility; the more relevant comparison is between outcomes in employment litigation and outcomes in employment arbitration. We will explore that question further in Part E.

B. LABOR ARBITRATION AND THE PROBLEM OF OVERLAPPING REMEDIES

Perhaps the most commonly arbitrated dispute in the collective bargaining context is whether an individual employee has been discharged for "just cause" within the meaning of the job security provision in the typical labor contract. Suppose, however, that the employee's termination also offends a statutory right contained in one of the individual rights statutes that we have studied, such as Title VII. The question early arose whether a unionized employee covered by a collective bargaining agreement could proceed in court on a Title VII claim and through labor arbitration on a claim that the discharge or discipline violated his or her contractual right to be discharged only for just cause; and if so, what effect the resolution in one forum—typically the labor arbitration forum due to its relative speed—should have on a case pending in the other forum. A related question was the relevance of provisions in the labor contract reiterating rights established in individual rights statutes, such as antidiscrimination clauses tracking the language of Title VII.

***Alexander v. Gardner-Denver Co.*, 415 U.S. 36 (1974).** Harrell Alexander was an African American maintenance worker who was promoted to a position as a drill operator trainee in 1968. A little over a year later, he was discharged for producing too many defective or unusable parts that had to be scrapped. Alexander filed a grievance alleging that his termination was in breach of the collective bargaining agreement, stating simply "I feel that I have been unjustly discharged and ask that I be reinstated with full seniority and pay." Three provisions in the contract had potential applicability to his case: Article 4, in which the company retained "the right to hire, suspend or discharge [employees] for proper cause;" Article 5, which proclaimed that "there shall be no discrimination against any employee on account of race, color, religion, sex, national origin, or ancestry;" and Article 23, which stated that "no employee will be discharged, suspended or given a written warning notice except for just cause." The union processed his grievance, arguing that the company's usual practice was to transfer unsatisfactory trainees back to their former positions rather than discharging them. In the final pre-arbitration step of the grievance process, Alexander for the first time raised the claim that his discharge resulted from racial discrimination. He also filed a charge of racial discrimination with the Colorado Civil Rights Commission, which in turn referred the complaint to the EEOC.

At the arbitration hearing Alexander testified that his discharge was the result of racial discrimination and informed the arbitrator that he had filed a charge with the Colorado Commission because he "could not rely on the union." The arbitrator ruled that petitioner had been "discharged for just cause," finding that the union's evidence of the company's normal transfer policy was insufficient; he made no reference to petitioner's claim of racial discrimination. Meanwhile, Alexander's race discrimination claim proceeded to federal district court. The district court granted the company's motion for summary judgment, reasoning that Alexander's race discrimination claim had been resolved in arbitration and was binding upon him. The Tenth Circuit affirmed.

The Supreme Court reversed, reasoning that Title VII evinced a legislative intent to authorize parallel and overlapping remedies for discrimination in employment. The Court explained that two independent sources of rights existed, even if they arose out of the same factual setting. Grievance arbitration under a collective bargaining agreement seeks to vindicate contractual rights, while lawsuits under federal antidiscrimination statutes assert independent statutory rights. The Court explained:

> We are . . . unable to accept the proposition that petitioner waived his cause of action under Title VII [by proceeding in arbitration]. To begin, we think it clear that there can be no prospective waiver of an employee's rights under Title VII. It is true, of course, that a union may waive certain statutory rights related to collective activity, such as the right to strike. . . . These rights are conferred on employees collectively to foster the processes of bargaining and properly may be exercised or relinquished by the union as collective-bargaining agent to obtain economic benefits for union members. Title VII, on the other hand, stands on plainly different ground; it concerns not majoritarian processes, but an individual's right to equal employment opportunities. Title VII's strictures are absolute and represent a congressional command that each employee be free from discriminatory practices. Of necessity, the rights conferred can form no part of the collective-bargaining process since waiver of these rights would defeat the paramount congressional purpose behind Title VII.

Id. at 51–52. In addition, the Court explained, the role of the arbitrator in grievance resolution under a collective bargaining agreement is completely different from that of a court enforcing statutory rights. The arbitrator—often himself not a lawyer—derives his authority solely from the labor contract, and sits as the proctor of the parties' bargain, seeking to effectuate their intent. He has no authority to invoke public laws that might conflict with the contract's provisions; indeed, if he grounds his award on what he believes is required by statute, his award can be set aside on the grounds that he has exceeded the scope of his authority. *Id.* at 53–54.

The Court also rejected the employer's argument that federal courts should defer to arbitral decisions on discrimination claims where the collective bargaining agreement contains an antidiscrimination clause tracking the language of the statutory right. The Court explained:

> Arbitral procedures, while well suited to the resolution of contractual disputes, make arbitration a comparatively inappropriate forum for the final resolution of rights created by Title VII. This conclusion rests first on the special role of the arbitrator, whose task is to effectuate the intent of the parties rather than the requirements of enacted legislation. . . .

> Moreover, the fact-finding process in arbitration usually is not equivalent to judicial fact-finding. The record of the arbitration proceedings is not as complete; the usual rules of evidence do not apply; and rights and procedures common to civil trials, such as discovery, compulsory process, cross-examination, and testimony under oath, are often severely limited or unavailable. And as this Court has recognized, "arbitrators have no obligation to the court to give their reasons for an award." United Steelworkers of America v. Enterprise Wheel & Car Corp., 363 U.S., at 598. Indeed, it is the informality of arbitral procedure that enables it to function as an efficient, inexpensive, and expeditious means for dispute resolution. This same characteristic, however, makes arbitration a less appropriate forum for final resolution of Title VII issues than the federal courts.

Id. at 56–58. The Court explained in a footnote that an additional argument against deferral stems from the union's exclusive control over the manner and extent to which any individual grievance is processed. Because the union's role is to represent the interests of all the employees in the bargaining unit, individual interests are subordinated to collective interests and the union may make decisions that are adverse to the individual's interests. The Court took judicial notice of the fact that conflicts of interest among workers are particularly likely where a claim of race discrimination is made, alluding to the legacy of racial discrimination by some unions. The Court observed that it could be difficult for an individual employee to establish a breach of the union's duty of fair representation, and noted that Congress thought it necessary to afford Title VII protections against unions as well as against employers. *Id.* at 58 n.19.

The Court concluded:

> We think, therefore, that the federal policy favoring arbitration of labor disputes and the federal policy against discriminatory employment practices can best be accommodated by permitting an employee to pursue fully

both his remedy under the grievance-arbitration clause of a collective-bargaining agreement and his cause of action under Title VII. The federal court should consider the employee's claim *de novo*. The arbitral decision may be admitted as evidence and accorded such weight as the court deems appropriate.

Id. at 59–60.

NOTE

The Union Role in Combatting Workplace Discrimination. At its core, discrimination occurs because of an individual's membership in a group defined by race, sex, national origin or religion. Yet its impact may be felt most keenly by an individual worker. Is discrimination an individual injury or a collective injury? If collective, would it not be best redressed through collective action and collective bargaining? Where employees are unionized, what are the problems with committing discrimination claims to the grievance processes available under the collective bargaining agreement?

The Court's analysis in *Gardner-Denver* was predicated in part upon its desire to protect minority employees from the strictures of the labor law principle of exclusivity where the union might itself be discriminating, or choosing to protect certain employee interests over others. As the exclusive representative of the employees in workplace disputes, the union rather than the individual employee controls the grievance and arbitration process. By classifying Title VII claims as individual claims, the Court was able to distinguish them from the collective (majoritarian) claims that are suitable for resolution by the union under the grievance and arbitration process specified in most collective bargaining agreements. The risk of characterizing them in this way, of course, is that it reinforces the historical tendency of unions to see battling discrimination as peripheral to their mission. *See* Marion Crain & Ken Matheny, *Labor's Identity Crisis*, 89 CALIF. L. REV. 1767, 1800–02 (2001).

Although *Alexander v. Gardner-Denver* has never been overruled, its reasoning has been severely undermined by subsequent developments. Those developments occurred first in the nonunion context, and eventually circled back to the union context. We consider those developments in the next section.

C. ARBITRATION IN THE NONUNION WORKPLACE

GILMER v. INTERSTATE/JOHNSON LANE CORP.
United States Supreme Court
500 U.S. 20 (1991)

JUSTICE WHITE delivered the opinion of the Court.

The question presented in this case is whether a claim under the Age Discrimination in Employment Act of 1967 (ADEA), can be subjected to compulsory arbitration pursuant to an arbitration agreement in a securities registration application. The Court of Appeals held that it could, and we affirm.

I

Respondent Interstate/Johnson Lane Corporation (Interstate) hired petitioner Robert Gilmer as a Manager of Financial Services in May 1981. As required by his employment, Gilmer registered as a securities representative with several stock exchanges, including the New York Stock Exchange (NYSE). His registration application, entitled "Uniform Application for Securities Industry Registration or Transfer," provided, among other things, that Gilmer "agreed to arbitrate any dispute, claim or controversy" arising between him and Interstate "that is required to be arbitrated under the rules, constitutions or by-laws of the organizations with which I register." Of relevance to this case, NYSE Rule 347 provides for arbitration of "any controversy between a registered representative and any member or member organization arising out of the employment or termination of employment of such registered representative."

Interstate terminated Gilmer's employment in 1987, at which time Gilmer was 62 years of age. After first filing an age discrimination charge with the Equal Employment Opportunity Commission (EEOC), Gilmer subsequently brought suit in the United States District Court for the Western District of North Carolina, alleging that Interstate had discharged him because of his age, in violation of the ADEA. In response to Gilmer's complaint, Interstate filed in the District Court a motion to compel arbitration of the ADEA claim. In its motion, Interstate relied upon the arbitration agreement in Gilmer's registration application, as well as the Federal Arbitration Act (FAA), 9 U.S.C. § 1 et seq. The District Court denied Interstate's motion, based on this Court's decision in *Alexander v. Gardner-Denver Co.*, 415 U.S. 36 (1974), and because it concluded that "Congress intended to protect ADEA claimants from the waiver of a judicial forum." The United States Court of Appeals for the Fourth Circuit reversed, finding "nothing in the text, legislative history, or underlying purposes of the ADEA indicating a congressional intent to preclude enforcement of arbitration agreements." We granted certiorari to resolve a conflict among the Courts of Appeals regarding the arbitrability of ADEA claims.

II

The FAA was originally enacted in 1925, 43 Stat. 883, and then reenacted and codified in 1947 as Title 9 of the United States Code. Its purpose was to reverse the longstanding judicial hostility to arbitration agreements that had existed at English common law and had been adopted by American courts, and to place arbitration agreements upon the same footing as other contracts. Its primary substantive provision states that "[a] written provision in any maritime transaction or a contract evidencing a transaction involving commerce to settle by arbitration a controversy thereafter arising out of such contract or transaction . . . shall be valid, irrevocable, and enforceable, save upon such grounds as exist at law or in equity for the revocation of any contract." 9 U.S.C. § 2. The FAA also provides for stays of proceedings in federal district courts when an issue in the proceeding is referable to arbitration, § 3, and for orders compelling arbitration when one party has failed, neglected, or refused to comply with an arbitration agreement, § 4. These provisions manifest a "liberal federal policy favoring arbitration agreements." *Moses H. Cone Memorial Hospital v. Mercury Construction Corp.*, 460 U.S. 1, 24, (1983).[2]

It is by now clear that statutory claims may be the subject of an arbitration agreement, enforceable pursuant to the FAA. Indeed, in recent years we have held enforceable arbitration agreements relating to claims arising under the Sherman Act, 15 U.S.C. §§ 1–7; § 10(b) of the Securities Exchange Act of 1934, 15 U.S.C. § 78j(b); the civil provisions of the Racketeer Influenced and Corrupt Organizations Act (RICO), 18 U.S.C. § 1961 et seq.; and § 12(2) of the Securities Act of 1933, 15 U.S.C. § 771(2). *See Mitsubishi Motors Corp. v. Soler Chrysler-Plymouth, Inc.*, 473 U.S. 614 (1985); *Shearson/American Express Inc. v. McMahon*, 482 U.S. 220 (1987); *Rodriguez de Quijas v. Shearson/American Express, Inc.*, 490 U.S. 477 (1989). In these cases we recognized that "by agreeing to arbitrate a statutory claim, a party does not forgo the substantive rights afforded by the statute; it only submits to their resolution in an arbitral, rather than a judicial, forum." *Mitsubishi*, 473 U.S. at 628.

Although all statutory claims may not be appropriate for arbitration, "having made the bargain to arbitrate, the party should be held to it unless Congress itself has evinced an intention to preclude a waiver of judicial remedies for the statutory rights at issue." *Ibid.* In this regard, we note that the burden is on Gilmer to show that Congress intended to preclude a waiver of a judicial forum for ADEA claims. See McMahon, 482 U.S. at 227. If such an intention exists, it will be discoverable in the text of the ADEA, its legislative history, or an "inherent conflict" between arbitration and the ADEA's underlying purposes. See *ibid.* Throughout such an inquiry, it should be kept in mind that "questions of arbitrability must be addressed with a healthy regard for the federal policy favoring arbitration." *Moses H. Cone, supra*, at 24.

III

Gilmer concedes that nothing in the text of the ADEA or its legislative history explicitly precludes arbitration. He argues, however, that compulsory arbitration of ADEA claims pursuant to arbitration agreements would be inconsistent with the statutory framework and purposes of the ADEA. Like the Court of Appeals, we disagree.

---

[2] [n. 2] Section 1 of the FAA provides that "nothing herein contained shall apply to contracts of employment of seamen, railroad employees, or any other class of workers engaged in foreign or interstate commerce." 9 U.S.C. § 1. Several *amici curiae* in support of Gilmer argue that that section excludes from the coverage of the FAA *all* "contracts of employment." Gilmer, however, did not raise the issue in the courts below; it was not addressed there; and it was not among the questions presented in the petition for certiorari. In any event, it would be inappropriate to address the scope of the § 1 exclusion because the arbitration clause being enforced here is not contained in a contract of employment. . . . [T]he arbitration clause at issue is in Gilmer's securities registration application, which is a contract with the securities exchanges, not with Interstate. . . . [W]e therefore hold that § 1's exclusionary clause does not apply to Gilmer's arbitration agreement. Consequently, we leave for another day the issue raised by *amici curiae*.

A

Congress enacted the ADEA in 1967 "to promote employment of older persons based on their ability rather than age; to prohibit arbitrary age discrimination in employment; [and] to help employers and workers find ways of meeting problems arising from the impact of age on employment." 29 U.S.C. § 621(b). To achieve those goals, the ADEA, among other things, makes it unlawful for an employer "to fail or refuse to hire or to discharge any individual or otherwise discriminate against any individual with respect to his compensation, terms, conditions, or privileges of employment, because of such individual's age." § 623(a)(1). This proscription is enforced both by private suits and by the EEOC. In order for an aggrieved individual to bring suit under the ADEA, he or she must first file a charge with the EEOC and then wait at least 60 days. § 626(d). An individual's right to sue is extinguished, however, if the EEOC institutes an action against the employer. § 626(c)(1). Before the EEOC can bring such an action, though, it must "attempt to eliminate the discriminatory practice or practices alleged, and to effect voluntary compliance with the requirements of this chapter through informal methods of conciliation, conference, and persuasion." § 626(b); *see also* 29 CFR § 1626.15 (1990).

As Gilmer contends, the ADEA is designed not only to address individual grievances, but also to further important social policies. We do not perceive any inherent inconsistency between those policies, however, and enforcing agreements to arbitrate age discrimination claims. It is true that arbitration focuses on specific disputes between the parties involved. The same can be said, however, of judicial resolution of claims. Both of these dispute resolution mechanisms nevertheless also can further broader social purposes. The Sherman Act, the Securities Exchange Act of 1934, RICO, and the Securities Act of 1933 all are designed to advance important public policies, but, as noted above, claims under those statutes are appropriate for arbitration. "So long as the prospective litigant effectively may vindicate [his or her] statutory cause of action in the arbitral forum, the statute will continue to serve both its remedial and deterrent function." *Mitsubishi, supra,* at 637.

We also are unpersuaded by the argument that arbitration will undermine the role of the EEOC in enforcing the ADEA. An individual ADEA claimant subject to an arbitration agreement will still be free to file a charge with the EEOC, even though the claimant is not able to institute a private judicial action. Indeed, Gilmer filed a charge with the EEOC in this case. In any event, the EEOC's role in combating age discrimination is not dependent on the filing of a charge; the agency may receive information concerning alleged violations of the ADEA "from any source," and it has independent authority to investigate age discrimination. *See* 29 CFR §§ 1626.4, 1626.13 (1990). Moreover, nothing in the ADEA indicates that Congress intended that the EEOC be involved in all employment disputes. Such disputes can be settled, for example, without any EEOC involvement. Finally, the mere involvement of an administrative agency in the enforcement of a statute is not sufficient to preclude arbitration. For example, the Securities Exchange Commission is heavily involved in the enforcement of the Securities Exchange Act of 1934 and the Securities Act of 1933, but we have held that claims under both of those statutes may be subject to compulsory arbitration. *See Shearson/American Express Inc. v. McMahon,* 482 U.S. 220 (1987); *Rodriguez de Quijas v. Shearson/American Express, Inc.,* 490 U.S. 477 (1989).

Gilmer also argues that compulsory arbitration is improper because it deprives claimants of the judicial forum provided for by the ADEA. Congress, however, did not explicitly preclude arbitration or other nonjudicial resolution of claims, even in its recent amendments to the ADEA. "If Congress intended the substantive protection afforded [by the ADEA] to include protection against waiver of the right to a judicial forum, that intention will be deducible from text or legislative history." *Mitsubishi*, 473 U.S. at 628. Moreover, Gilmer's argument ignores the ADEA's flexible approach to resolution of claims. The EEOC, for example, is directed to pursue "informal methods of conciliation, conference, and persuasion," 29 U.S.C. § 626(b), which suggests that out-of-court dispute resolution, such as arbitration, is consistent with the statutory scheme established by Congress. In addition, arbitration is consistent with Congress' grant of concurrent jurisdiction over ADEA claims to state and federal courts, *see* 29 U.S.C. § 626(c)(1) (allowing suits to be brought "in any court of competent jurisdiction"), because arbitration agreements, "like the provision for concurrent jurisdiction, serve to advance the objective of allowing [claimants] a broader right to select the forum for resolving disputes, whether it be judicial or otherwise." *Rodriguez de Quijas, supra*, at 483.

B

In arguing that arbitration is inconsistent with the ADEA, Gilmer also raises a host of challenges to the adequacy of arbitration procedures. Initially, we note that in our recent arbitration cases we have already rejected most of these arguments as insufficient to preclude arbitration of statutory claims. Such generalized attacks on arbitration "rest on suspicion of arbitration as a method of weakening the protections afforded in the substantive law to would-be complainants," and as such, they are "far out of step with our current strong endorsement of the federal statutes favoring this method of resolving disputes." *Rodriguez de Quijas, supra*, at 481. Consequently, we address these arguments only briefly.

Gilmer first speculates that arbitration panels will be biased. However, "we decline to indulge the presumption that the parties and arbitral body conducting a proceeding will be unable or unwilling to retain competent, conscientious and impartial arbitrators." *Mitsubishi, supra*, at 634. In any event, we note that the NYSE arbitration rules, which are applicable to the dispute in this case, provide protections against biased panels. The rules require, for example, that the parties be informed of the employment histories of the arbitrators, and that they be allowed to make further inquiries into the arbitrators' backgrounds. In addition, each party is allowed one peremptory challenge and unlimited challenges for cause. Moreover, the arbitrators are required to disclose "any circumstances which might preclude [them] from rendering an objective and impartial determination." The FAA also protects against bias, by providing that courts may overturn arbitration decisions "where there was evident partiality or corruption in the arbitrators." 9 U.S.C. § 10(b). There has been no showing in this case that those provisions are inadequate to guard against potential bias.

Gilmer also complains that the discovery allowed in arbitration is more limited than in the federal courts, which he contends will make it difficult to prove discrimination. It is unlikely, however, that age discrimination claims require more extensive discovery than other claims that we have found to be arbitrable, such as RICO and antitrust claims. Moreover, there has been no showing in this case that the NYSE discovery provisions, which allow for document production, information requests, depositions, and subpoena . . . will prove insufficient to allow ADEA claimants such as Gilmer a fair opportunity to present their claims. Although those procedures might not be as extensive as in the federal courts, by agreeing to arbitrate, a party "trades the procedures and opportunity for review of the courtroom for the simplicity, informality, and expedition of arbitration." *Mitsubishi*, *supra*, at 628. Indeed, an important counterweight to the reduced discovery in NYSE arbitration is that arbitrators are not bound by the rules of evidence. A further alleged deficiency of arbitration is that arbitrators often will not issue written opinions, resulting, Gilmer contends, in a lack of public knowledge of employers' discriminatory policies, an inability to obtain effective appellate review, and a stifling of the development of the law. The NYSE rules, however, do require that all arbitration awards be in writing, and that the awards contain the names of the parties, a summary of the issues in controversy, and a description of the award issued. In addition, the award decisions are made available to the public. Furthermore, judicial decisions addressing ADEA claims will continue to be issued because it is unlikely that all or even most ADEA claimants will be subject to arbitration agreements. Finally, Gilmer's concerns apply equally to settlements of ADEA claims, which, as noted above, are clearly allowed.

It is also argued that arbitration procedures cannot adequately further the purposes of the ADEA because they do not provide for broad equitable relief and class actions. As the court below noted, however, arbitrators do have the power to fashion equitable relief. Indeed, the NYSE rules applicable here do not restrict the types of relief an arbitrator may award, but merely refer to "damages and/or other relief." The NYSE rules also provide for collective proceedings. But "even if the arbitration could not go forward as a class action or class relief could not be granted by the arbitrator, the fact that the [ADEA] provides for the possibility of bringing a collective action does not mean that individual attempts at conciliation were intended to be barred." *Nicholson v. CPC Int'l Inc.*, 877 F.2d 221, 241 (CA3 1989) (Becker, J., dissenting). Finally, it should be remembered that arbitration agreements will not preclude the EEOC from bringing actions seeking class-wide and equitable relief.

C

An additional reason advanced by Gilmer for refusing to enforce arbitration agreements relating to ADEA claims is his contention that there often will be unequal bargaining power between employers and employees. Mere inequality in bargaining power, however, is not a sufficient reason to hold that arbitration agreements are never enforceable in the employment context. Relationships between securities dealers and investors, for example, may involve unequal bargaining power, but we nevertheless held in *Rodriguez de Quijas* and *McMahon* that agreements to arbitrate in that context are enforceable. As discussed above, the FAA's purpose was to place arbitration agreements on the same footing as other contracts. Thus, arbitration agreements are enforceable "save upon such grounds as exist at law or in equity for the revocation of any contract." 9 U.S.C. § 2. "Of course, courts should remain attuned to well-supported claims that the agreement to arbitrate resulted from the sort of fraud or overwhelming economic power that would provide grounds 'for the revocation of any contract.' " *Mitsubishi*, 473 U.S. at 627. There is no indication in this case, however, that Gilmer, an experienced businessman, was coerced or defrauded into agreeing to the arbitration clause in his registration application. As with the claimed procedural inadequacies discussed above, this claim of unequal bargaining power is best left for resolution in specific cases.

In addition to the arguments discussed above, Gilmer vigorously asserts that our decision in *Alexander v. Gardner-Denver Co.*, 415 U.S. 36 (1974), and its progeny— *Barrentine v. Arkansas-Best Freight System, Inc.*, 450 U.S. 728 (1981) [ruling that FLSA rights are nonwaivable by unions in the collective bargaining context], and *McDonald v. West Branch*, 466 U.S. 284 (1984) [ruling that section 1983 rights are nonwaivable in the collective bargaining context]—preclude arbitration of employment discrimination claims. Gilmer's reliance on these cases, however, is misplaced.

. . . .

There are several important distinctions between the *Gardner-Denver* line of cases and the case before us. First, those cases did not involve the issue of the enforceability of an agreement to arbitrate statutory claims. Rather, they involved the quite different issue whether arbitration of contract-based claims precluded subsequent judicial resolution of statutory claims. Since the employees there had not agreed to arbitrate their statutory claims, and the labor arbitrators were not authorized to resolve such claims, the arbitration in those cases understandably was held not to preclude subsequent statutory actions. Second, because the arbitration in those cases occurred in the context of a collective-bargaining agreement, the claimants there were represented by their unions in the arbitration proceedings. An important concern therefore was the tension between collective representation and individual statutory rights, a concern not applicable to the present case. Finally, those cases were not decided under the FAA, which, as discussed above, reflects a "liberal federal policy favoring arbitration agreements." *Mitsubishi*, 473 U.S. at 625. Therefore, those cases provide no basis for refusing to enforce Gilmer's agreement to arbitrate his ADEA claim.

V

We conclude that Gilmer has not met his burden of showing that Congress, in enacting the ADEA, intended to preclude arbitration of claims under that Act. Accordingly, the judgment of the Court of Appeals is *Affirmed*.

[Justices Stevens and Marshall dissented. Their dissent expressed the view that arbitration clauses in employment agreements are exempt from coverage under the FAA and that compulsory arbitration of age discrimination claims conflicted with the Congressional purpose behind the ADEA, "eviscerating the important role played by an independent judiciary in eradicating employment discrimination" and "ma[king] the foxes guardians of the chickens." The dissent thought it particularly significant that the ADEA authorizes courts to order broad, class-wide relief to achieve its goals, and most arbitration proceedings do not provide for such relief.]

NOTES

1.   Broad Applicability of the FAA's Pro-Arbitration Policy. Ten years after its decision in *Gilmer*, the Court resolved the question left open in footnote 2. In *Circuit City Stores, Inc. v. Adams*, 532 U.S. 105 (2001), the Court ruled 5-4 that the FAA's exclusion from the Act's coverage of "contracts of employment of seamen, railroad employees, or any other class of workers engaged in foreign or interstate commerce" was limited to exempting contracts of employment of transportation workers. The Court's narrow reading of the exemption was based upon a strict textual analysis of the statute. The Court justified its interpretation with a strong defense of arbitration in the employment context, noting that many employers had adopted alternative dispute resolution procedures in the wake of *Gilmer* and expressed its reluctance to cast doubt upon the enforceability of those agreements. *See id.* at 123. The Court remanded the case to the Ninth Circuit to apply the FAA to the plaintiff's sexual harassment claim under the California Fair Employment and Housing Act. The dissenting Justices argued that both legislative history and historical context supported the opposite reading of the FAA's exclusion, such that all contracts of employment would be exempted.

On remand, the Ninth Circuit concluded that the Circuit City arbitration agreement was nonetheless unenforceable because it was a contract of adhesion between parties of unequal bargaining power that conferred asymmetrical rights on employees and the employer and limited damages, and thus was both procedurally and substantively unconscionable under California state law. *Circuit City Stores, Inc. v. Adams*, 279 F.3d 889 (9th Cir.), *cert. denied*, 535 U.S. 1112 (2002). We will study this basis for refusing to enforce an arbitration agreement further in section D.

2.   Extension of *Gilmer* to Rights Guaranteed by Other Statutes. Should the *Gilmer* reasoning apply to antidiscrimination rights arising under other statutes? The circuit courts' answer to this question is now unequivocally "yes" as to both Title VII and the ADA. *See, e.g., EEOC v. Luce, Forward, Hamilton & Scripps*, 345 F.3d 742 (9th Cir. 2003) (*en banc*) (Title VII); *Miller v. Public Storage Management, Inc.*, 121 F.3d 215 (5th Cir. 1997) (ADA). The *Gilmer* reasoning has also been extended to predispute arbitration agreements involving waivers of statutory forum rights created by employment legislation guaranteeing minimum terms, such as the FLSA and ERISA. *See, e.g., Adkins v. Labor Ready Mid-Atlantic, Inc.*, 303 F.3d 496 (4th Cir. 2002) (enforcing predispute arbitration agreement to block a proposed class action brought by manual day laborers alleging violations of the FLSA and the West Virginia minimum wage and wage collection statutes, and reasoning that the FLSA's remedial purposes and enforcement scheme are similar to the ADEA's); *Bird v. Shearson Lehman/American Express, Inc.*, 926 F.2d 116 (2d Cir. 1991) (enforcing predispute arbitration agreement covering breach of fiduciary duty claims arising under ERISA).

3.   A Statutory Bar on Arbitration Agreements. The *Gilmer* court suggested that an employee who signs a predispute arbitration agreement "should be held to it unless Congress itself has evinced an intention to preclude a waiver of judicial remedies." In the Dodd-Frank Wall Street Reform and Consumer Protection Act of 2010, Congress did exactly that with regard to certain whistleblower protection claims. As discussed in Chapter 8, *supra*, Dodd-Frank amended the whistleblower protections established by the Sarbanes-Oxley Corporate Reform Act of 2002 in several ways, including the addition of a prohibition on mandatory arbitration agreements. Dodd-Frank also creates new whistleblower protections for employees who report violations of the Commodity Exchange Act, federal consumer financial protection law or federal securities laws to certain government agencies and it forbids mandatory predispute arbitration agreements of these claims as well.

Interesting issues have arisen regarding whether the Dodd-Frank amendment prohibiting predispute arbitration agreements should apply retroactively to contracts signed before its enactment. The lower courts are split on the question. *Compare Taylor v. Fannie Mae*, 839 F. Supp. 2d 259 (D.D.C. 2012) (refusing to apply Dodd-Frank retroactively to bar arbitration because doing so would alter parties' substantive rights in force at the time of contract formation) and *Kahzin v. TD Ameritrade Holding Corp.*, 2014 U.S. Dist. LEXIS 31142 (D.N.J. Mar. 11, 2014) (holding that to apply Dodd-Frank retroactively would frustrate parties' expectations regarding substantive rights), *with Pezza v. Investors Capital Corp.*, 767 F. Supp. 2d 225 (D. Mass. 2011) (applying Dodd-Frank retroactively to bar mandatory arbitration of Sarbanes-Oxley claim, reasoning that Congress did not expressly limit Dodd-Frank's temporal reach and the issue was merely a procedural question of jurisdiction that did not affect the parties' substantive rights). Should an agreement to arbitrate questions arising out of the employment relation be viewed as a substantive right that should not be altered retroactively, or as a procedural question in which only the forum for the claim is at stake?

4. The Union Role. As unions undertook to represent an ever-more diverse membership, they negotiated anti-discrimination clauses in collective bargaining agreements that tracked the language of federal or state statutory schemes. Unions assumed that under *Alexander v. Gardner-Denver* such efforts to expand employee rights in the labor contract and in grievance arbitration thereunder would not undermine employees' individual rights to proceed in court on statutory claims. It soon became apparent, however, that this was a risky strategy: by including clauses specifically protecting the statutory rights of employees, the union risked waiving employees' rights to proceed in court. In *14 Penn Plaza LLC v. Pyett*, 556 U.S. 247 (2009), the Court applied *Gilmer* to the collective bargaining context and found that a clear, "explicitly stated" clause in the labor contract agreeing to arbitrate statutory employment claims was effective to waive the individual worker's right to proceed in court because the agreement to arbitrate did not entail waiver of the underlying substantive right. *Id.* at 259–60. The Court did not establish guidelines for determining whether a particular waiver meets the "clear and unmistakable" waiver standard. The Court's subsequent decisions in the arbitration context suggest, however, that it would be likely to interpret such waivers broadly. *See* Martin H. Malin, *The Employment Decisions of the Supreme Court's 2012–13 Term*, 29 ABA J. Lab. & Emp. L. 203, 211 (2014).

How should unions desiring to represent an increasingly diverse workforce respond? Should they continue to negotiate for such clauses in order to advance antidiscrimination protections through collective bargaining and grievance arbitration? Might employers be eager to agree to these clauses? Would such an interpretation empower unions at the expense of individual employees? *See*

Deborah A. Widiss, *Divergent Interests: Union Representation of Individual Employment Discrimination Claims*, 87 IND. L.J. 421 (2012). On the other hand, might employers respond by imposing on individual unionized workers predispute arbitration agreements covering statutory claims not addressed by the labor contract, so that arbitration becomes the sole channel for dispute resolution anyhow? Aren't workers as a class better served by an arbitration mechanism negotiated by a union and likely to include stronger procedural protections? *See* Marion Crain & Ken Matheny, *Labor's Identity Crisis*, 89 CALIF. L. REV. 1767 (2001).

Alternatively, could unions market themselves to employees by offering their services to employees seeking representation in individual employment arbitration? Could these efforts expand beyond the unionized sector? *See* Ann C. Hodges, *Trilogy Redux: Using Arbitration to Rebuild the Labor Movement*, 98 MINN. L. REV. 1682 (2014).

D. THE USES AND LIMITS OF PREDISPUTE EMPLOYMENT ARBITRATION AGREEMENTS

Following the Supreme Court's endorsement of mandatory predispute arbitration in *Gilmer*, many employers conditioned employment on an agreement to arbitrate rather than litigate claims arising out of employment. Estimates are that only 2.1% of employers used predispute arbitration agreements in 1992, compared with 22.7% by 2003 and 25% by 2014. Alexander J.S. Colvin & Kelly Pike, *Saturns and Rickshaws Revisited: What Kind of Arbitration System Has Developed?*, 29 OH. STATE J. ON DISP. RES. 59 (2014); Alexander J.S. Colvin, *Empirical Research on Employment Arbitration: Clarity Amidst the Sound and Fury?*, 11 EMP. RTS. & EMPLOY. POL'Y J. 405, 408–11 (2007). Employers were drawn to arbitration because it was perceived as saving time and money, limited the extent of discovery, preserved confidentiality and avoided adverse legal precedents. Thomas J. Stipanowich & J. Ryan Lamare, *Living with ADR: Evolving Perceptions and Use of Mediation, Arbitration, and Conflict Management in Fortune 1,000 Corporations*, 19 HARV. NEGOT. L. REV. 1, 10 (2013). In addition, some employers utilized lopsided agreements, which implemented procedures that disadvantaged plaintiff-employees relative to those available in court litigation.

Most of the increase in adoption of employment arbitration policies occurred in the first decade following *Gilmer*. Beginning in the 2000s, the adoption rate declined. There were several reasons for the fall-off. First, employers lost interest in arbitration as courts reined in some of the more outrageous practices that employers had adopted after *Gilmer*, including shifting the costs of arbitration to the employee, severely limiting the time frame during which claims might be filed, blocking employees from suing employers in court but preserving employer rights to sue employees, and appointing arbitrators biased in favor of the company. We explore this doctrine further below. Second, arbitration mechanisms, especially even-handed systems, proved to be no panacea for employers: employees who had been educated about the policies by their employers took advantage of low costs and the opportunity to proceed without legal representation to bring more claims, trial elements were imported into arbitration, increasing costs and time, and win rates were higher in arbitration for some groups of employees (particularly higher-paid employees represented by counsel) than they were in litigation. We consider empirical data on arbitration relative to litigation use and outcomes further in part E, *below*. Third, large employers became increasingly sophisticated at managing workplace conflict and adopted strategies aimed at resolving conflict at earlier points, such as peer-review and in-house grievance systems, mediation, and third-party evaluation and fact-finding by neutrals as ways to encourage settlement. *See* Stipanowich & Lamare, *supra*, at 3. We explore these strategies further in Chapter 15.

Nevertheless, predispute arbitration policies have become firmly entrenched as systems of workplace dispute resolution. In the years after *Gilmer*, a jurisprudence evolved on the enforceability of predispute arbitration agreements. This Part explores the three bases that emerged for challenging the validity of those agreements. First, some federal courts ruled that in order to be enforceable as effective mechanisms for the vindication of the individual employee's rights under federal labor and employment statutes, predispute arbitration agreements must as a matter of fairness satisfy certain minimum standards. Second, courts utilized state law contract principles of unconscionability, lack of consideration or lack of assent (including notice and acceptance) to set aside agreements. Third, and closely related to the first line of cases, provisions barring class claims were challenged where they operated to undermine attainment of the public policy goals and enforcement mechanisms of particular statutory schemes.

1. Effective Vindication of Statutory Rights

The *Gilmer* court qualified its ruling, indicating that it was applicable to valid arbitration agreements that enable plaintiffs "effectively [to] vindicate" their substantive federal statutory rights. *Gilmer*, 500 U.S. at 28 (citing *Mitsubishi Motors Corp. v. Soler Chrysler-Plymouth, Inc.*, 473 U.S. 614, 637 (1985)). In the wake of *Gilmer*, arbitrator-appointing organizations developed rules designed to ensure fairness in arbitration, both procedurally and substantively. Three organizations—the American Arbitration Association (AAA), the Judicial Arbitration & Mediation Services (JAMS) and the Center for Public Resources (CPR)—were at the forefront of evolving such guidelines. Self-policing by the third party neutral community was not entirely adequate to the task, however. *See* Margaret M. Harding, *The Limits of the Due Process Protocols*, 19 OH. ST. J. ON DISP. RESOL. 369, 421–37 (2004) (warning against reliance on self-regulation because of lack of universal commitment to turn away business from those who fail to comply, and lack of monitoring and sanctions against those who renege on promises to comply). The federal judiciary soon stepped in.

***Cole v. Burns International Security Servs.*, 105 F.3d 1465 (D.C. Cir. 1997).** Cole was a security guard at Union Station in Washington, D.C., who filed a complaint in federal court alleging race discrimination and retaliatory discharge claims under Title VII. His employer moved to compel arbitration and dismiss Cole's complaint pursuant to a predispute resolution agreement channeling all employment-related disputes to arbitration proceedings conducted in accord with the rules of the AAA, which did not prescribe any particular allocation of responsibility for payment of the arbitrator's fees (estimated to be $500 to $1,000 or more per day). The district court granted the employer's motion and dismissed Cole's complaint.

Writing for the D.C. Circuit, Judge Harry Edwards applied *Gilmer* and upheld the arbitration agreement but limited enforceable predispute arbitration agreements to those that "do not undermine the relevant statutory scheme." *Id.* at 1468. The court relied heavily upon the *Gilmer* Court's statement that prospective litigants' substantive statutory rights would be preserved and the statute would continue to serve its remedial and deterrent function only " '[s]o long as the prospective litigant effectively may vindicate [his or her] statutory cause of action in the arbitral forum . . . .' " *Id.* at 1478 (quoting *Gilmer, supra*, at 28). Because employers routinely paid all arbitral fees under the agreement in the securities industry at issue in *Gilmer*, the question whether an enforceable agreement could require an employee to pay all or part of the arbitration fee was a novel one. The court construed the ambiguity in the arbitration agreement regarding the party responsible for payment of arbitration fees against the employer as drafter, and interpreted it to require the employer to pay all arbitrator fees associated with resolution of the dispute. The court explained:

> In our view, an employee can never be required, as a condition of employment, to pay an arbitrator's compensation in order to secure the resolution of statutory claims under Title VII (any more than an employee can be made to pay a judge's salary). If there is any risk that an arbitration agreement can be construed to require this result, this would surely deter the bringing of arbitration and constitute a *de facto* forfeiture of the employee's statutory rights. The only way that an arbitration agreement of the sort at issue here can be lawful is if the employer assumes responsibility for the payment of the arbitrator's compensation.

Id.

The court went on to articulate a set of standards for assessing the enforceability of a predispute arbitration agreement. The court ruled that a predispute arbitration agreement is enforceable only if it:

> (1) provides for neutral arbitrators, (2) provides for more than minimal discovery, (3) requires a written award, (4) provides for all of the types of relief that would otherwise be available in court, and (5) does not require employees to pay either unreasonable costs *or* any arbitrators' fees or expenses as a condition of access to the arbitration forum.

Id. at 1482. Distinguishing arbitration clauses in collective bargaining agreements, which are not generally reviewed by courts under any sort of due process standards, the court justified the expanded oversight role for federal courts evaluating predispute waivers of statutory forum rights in this way:

> The fundamental distinction between contractual rights [such as those at issue in arbitration under collective bargaining agreements], which are created, defined, and subject to modification by the same private parties participating in arbitration, and statutory rights, which are created,

defined, and subject to modification only by Congress and the courts, suggests the need for a public, rather than private, mechanism of enforcement for statutory rights.

Id. at 1476.

NOTE

Federal Judicial Oversight of Individual Employment Arbitration. Prior to his appointment to the bench, Judge Edwards was a highly respected labor law professor and labor arbitrator. For these reasons—as well as the logic and comprehensiveness of the *Cole* court's analysis—the decision proved very influential. *See* Martin H. Malin, *Due Process in Employment Arbitration: The State of the Law and the Need for Self-Regulation*, 11 EMP. RTS. & EMPLOY. POL'Y J. 363, 366 (2007).

In the years following *Cole*, some federal courts refused to enforce agreements that overreached in ways that undermined the remedial or deterrent purposes of federal employment statutes, particularly by imposing the costs of arbitration on the employee. *See, e.g., Morrison v. Circuit City Stores, Inc.*, 317 F.3d 646 (6th Cir. 2003) (*en banc*) (finding agreement unenforceable where it contained a cost-splitting provision that would operate to deter similarly situated employees from vindicating statutory rights and limited remedies to injunctive relief, reinstatement, one year of back pay, two years of front pay, compensatory damages, and punitive damages capped at $5,000 or the sum of the back pay and front pay awards, whichever was greater); *Shankle v. B-G Maintenance Mgmt. of Colorado, Inc.*, 163 F.3d 1230 (10th Cir. 1999) (ruling that agreement requiring claimant to pay one-half of arbitration costs "failed to provide an accessible forum in which [claimant] could resolve his statutory rights").

However, predispute arbitration agreements are now enforced in the vast majority of cases, even if they contain cost-splitting provisions. The shift in outcomes was largely attributable to the Supreme Court's ruling in *Green Tree Financial Corp. v. Randolph*, 531 U.S. 79 (2000), a commercial arbitration case involving a consumer financing agreement channeling all disputes to arbitration. The Court enforced the arbitration agreement even though it did not specify which party would be liable for costs of the proceeding and thus posed a risk that plaintiff might incur substantial costs to vindicate her statutory rights under the Truth in Lending Act and the Equal Credit Opportunity Act. Reiterating the strong federal policy favoring arbitration, the Court held that just as a party seeking to resist arbitration must carry the burden to show that the particular statutory claim at issue is not appropriate for arbitral resolution, so the same party carries the burden of establishing that excessive costs impede access to the arbitral forum in that particular factual context. *Id.* at 81. Courts addressing the issue of cost-splitting post-*Randolph* seized on this, employing a case-by-case analysis that assesses the impact of fees on individual plaintiffs. *See, e.g., E.E.O.C. v. Woodmen of the World Life Insurance Society*, 479 F.3d 561 (8th Cir. 2007) (enforcing arbitration clause that provided for fee-splitting despite plaintiffs' bankruptcy where fee-splitting provision was severable from arbitration agreement and defendant employer had agreed to pay arbitration costs in full); *James v.*

McDonald's Corp., 417 F.3d 672 (7th Cir. 2005) (compelling arbitration despite proof that arbitration fees and costs would range from $38,000 to $80,500 and affidavit from plaintiff that she lacked financial resources to pay them, because plaintiff did not apply to AAA for a fee waiver). The combination of the heavy burden of persuasion and the focus on the individual plaintiff's financial circumstances imposed by *Randolph* and its progeny has made it far more difficult for would-be plaintiffs to challenge arbitration agreements on the basis of costs.

2. State Contract Law Principles

As a federal statute, the FAA preempts inconsistent state law. It does not, however, preempt generally applicable state contract law. Recall that section 2 of the FAA requires enforcement of arbitration agreements "save upon such grounds as exist at law or in equity for the revocation of any contract." 9 U.S.C. § 2. Accordingly, state contract law defenses such as fraud, duress, unconscionability, or lack of consideration may be applied to invalidate arbitration agreements, as long as they are of general applicability and are not applied only to arbitration agreements.

The most common ground for voiding an arbitration agreement is unconscionability. The following cases are illustrative.

***Hooters of America, Inc. v. Phillips*, 173 F.3d 933 (4th Cir. 1999).** Annette Phillips alleged that she was sexually harassed by a Hooters official while working as a bartender at a Hooters restaurant in Myrtle Beach, quit her job, and hired an attorney who threatened to sue Hooters. Hooters filed a preemptive suit to compel arbitration under the FAA pursuant to a dispute resolution process (DRP) that included a predispute arbitration agreement. The court found the DRP "utterly lacking in the rudiments of even-handedness," ordered rescission of the contract, and affirmed the district court's refusal to compel arbitration. *Id.* at 935.

The court described Hooters' DRP as follows:

> The Hooters rules . . . are so one-sided that their only possible purpose is to undermine the neutrality of the proceeding. The rules require the employee to provide the company notice of her claim at the outset, including "the nature of the Claim" and "the specific act(s) or omission(s) which are the basis of the Claim." Hooters, on the other hand, is not required to file any responsive pleadings or to notice its defenses. Additionally, at the time of filing this notice, the employee must provide the company with a list of all fact witnesses with a brief summary of the facts known to each. The company, however, is not required to reciprocate.
>
> The Hooters rules also provide a mechanism for selecting a panel of three arbitrators that is crafted to ensure a biased decisionmaker. The employee and Hooters each select an arbitrator, and the two arbitrators in turn select a third. Good enough, except that the employee's arbitrator and the third arbitrator must be selected from a list of arbitrators created exclusively by Hooters. This gives Hooters control over the entire panel and places no limits whatsoever on whom Hooters can put on the list. Under the

rules, Hooters is free to devise lists of partial arbitrators who have existing relationships, financial or familial, with Hooters and its management. In fact, the rules do not even prohibit Hooters from placing its managers themselves on the list. Further, nothing in the rules restricts Hooters from punishing arbitrators who rule against the company by removing them from the list. Given the unrestricted control that one party (Hooters) has over the panel, the selection of an impartial decisionmaker would be a surprising result.

Nor is fairness to be found once the proceedings are begun. Although Hooters may expand the scope of arbitration to any matter, "whether related or not to the Employee's Claim," the employee cannot raise "any matter not included in the Notice of Claim." Similarly, Hooters is permitted to move for summary dismissal of employee claims before a hearing is held whereas the employee is not permitted to seek summary judgment. Hooters, but not the employee, may record the arbitration hearing "by audio or video taping or by verbatim transcription." The rules also grant Hooters the right to bring suit in court to vacate or modify an arbitral award when it can show, by a preponderance of the evidence, that the panel exceeded its authority. No such right is granted to the employee.

In addition, the rules provide that upon 30 days notice Hooters, but not the employee, may cancel the agreement to arbitrate. Moreover, Hooters reserves the right to modify the rules, "in whole or in part," whenever it wishes and "without notice" to the employee. Nothing in the rules even prohibits Hooters from changing the rules in the middle of an arbitration proceeding.

If by odd chance the unfairness of these rules were not apparent on their face, leading arbitration experts have decried their one-sidedness. George Friedman, senior vice president of the American Arbitration Association (AAA), testified that the system established by the Hooters rules so deviated from minimum due process standards that the Association would refuse to arbitrate under those rules. George Nicolau, former president of both the National Academy of Arbitrators and the International Society of Professionals in Dispute Resolution, attested that the Hooters rules "are inconsistent with the concept of fair and impartial arbitration." . . . Additionally, Dennis Nolan, professor of labor law at the University of South Carolina, declared that the Hooters rules "do not satisfy the minimum requirements of a fair arbitration system." He found that the "most serious flaw" was that the "mechanism [for selecting arbitrators] violates the most fundamental aspect of justice, namely an impartial decision maker." Finally, Lewis Maltby, member of the Board of Directors of the AAA, testified that "This is without a doubt the most unfair arbitration program I have ever encountered."

Id. at 938–39.

The court reasoned that Hooters had undertaken to establish a dispute resolution system in which disputes would be fairly resolved by an impartial third party, and "[b]y creating a sham system unworthy even of the name of arbitration,"

Hooters breached the contract. *Id.* Moreover, the Hooters rules also violated Hooters' contractual good faith obligation because they amounted to "evasion of the spirit of the bargain" and demonstrated an "abuse of a power to specify terms." *Id.* at 940 (quoting Restatement (Second) of Contracts § 205 (1981)). A set of procedures "so wholly one-sided as to present a stacked deck" frustrated Phillips' reasonable expectations of fair, prompt and economical resolution of her claims. *Id.*

———————

Alexander v. Anthony Int'l, L.P., 341 F.3d 256 (3d Cir. 2003). In a case involving discrimination claims under Virgin Islands law, the Third Circuit applied state contract law and found a predispute arbitration agreement unconscionable. The court described the two-tiered framework for unconscionability analysis as follows:

> Courts have generally recognized that the doctrine of unconscionability involves both "procedural" and "substantive" elements. Procedural unconscionability pertains to the process by which an agreement is reached and the form of an agreement, including the use therein of fine print and convoluted or unclear language. This element is generally satisfied if the agreement constitutes a contract of adhesion. A contract of adhesion is one which is prepared by the party with excessive bargaining power who presents it to the other party for signature on a take-it-or-leave-it basis. A contract, however, is not unconscionable merely because the parties to it are unequal in bargaining position. An adhesion contract is not necessarily unenforceable.
>
> The party challenging the contract therefore must also establish "substantive unconscionability." This element refers to terms that unreasonably favor one party to which the disfavored party does not truly assent. According to the commentary accompanying section 208 [of the Restatement (Second) of Contracts]:
>
>> [G]ross inequality of bargaining power, together with terms unreasonably favorable to the stronger party, may confirm indications that the transaction involved elements of deception or compulsion, or may show that the weaker party had no meaningful choice, no real alternative, or did not in fact assent or appear to assent to the unfair terms.
>
> RESTATEMENT (SECOND) OF CONTRACTS, *supra*, section 208 cmt. d. In the end, unconscionability requires a two-fold determination: that the contractual terms are unreasonably favorable to the drafter and that there is no meaningful choice on the part of the other party regarding acceptance of the provisions.

Id. at 265–66. The court concluded that the agreement was presented on a take-it-or-leave-it basis to low level employees with limited education, allowed only 30 days to file employment-related claims, restricted available remedies to reinstatement, did not allow the prevailing claimant to recover attorneys' fees, and required the loser to pay all arbitration costs; thus, it was procedurally and substantively unconscionable.

NOTES

1. **Standards of Unconscionability.** Neither *Hooters* nor *Alexander* identifies a clear standard for determining whether an agreement is unconscionable. How do these decisions compare with the framework established by the *Cole* court? Some state courts adopted the *Cole* standards, pulling them into unconscionability analysis. *See, e.g., Armendariz v. Foundation Health Psychcare Services, Inc.*, 6 P.3d 669, 682 (Cal. 2000) (citing *Cole* and establishing the procedural protections that it considered essential to the integrity of the arbitration process: a neutral arbitrator; provision of adequate discovery; a written award subject to judicial review; permitting recovery of all relief otherwise available in court, including punitive damages and attorneys' fees; and no requirement that the employee bear expenses that he would not be required to incur if he were free to bring the action in court—thus, the employer is impliedly obligated to pay all costs unique to the arbitral forum).

Note that the *Armendariz* court included "adequate discovery" on the list of essential procedural protections. Dramatic differences exist between discovery available in court litigation as opposed to arbitration. Under the Federal Rules of Civil Procedure, litigants have the right to engage in broad discovery, including compelling participation by non-parties, backed by the court's power to impose contempt sanctions for failure to comply. By contrast, discovery proceedings in arbitration are limited to what the parties have agreed to in advance. Moreover, the arbitral power to compel non-party participation stems from the FAA and is relatively limited. *See* Jason F. Darnall & Richard Bales, *Arbitral Discovery of Nonparties*, 2001 J. OF DISP. RESOL. 321. Some arbitration agreements further restrict or even eliminate discovery. How important is "adequate discovery" to a fair arbitration process? Isn't avoiding costly and time-consuming discovery one of the potential benefits of arbitration? Does protecting discovery convert arbitration into a form of mini-litigation?

2. **Traditional Defenses to Contract Formation.** Claimants may also challenge arbitration agreements on other traditional contract grounds, including lack of consideration and lack of notice and acceptance. Courts generally consider the promise to arbitrate itself adequate consideration. *See, e.g., Soto-Fonalledas v. Ritz-Carlton San Juan Hotel Spa & Casino*, 640 F.3d 471 (1st Cir. 2011) (bilateral promises to arbitrate constitute adequate consideration). Suppose, however, that the arbitration agreement is contained in an employee handbook and the employer reserves the right to alter, modify, amend or revoke at any time and without notice—including retroactively, such that the revised provision can be made applicable to a dispute already pending. Is the promise then illusory? Some courts have held that such qualified promises to arbitrate are unenforceable for lack of consideration. *See, e.g., Carey v. 24 Hour Fitness, USA, Inc.*, 669 F.3d 202 (5th Cir. 2012) (applying Texas law).

In order to find a meeting of the minds, courts typically require notice and informed consent, looking to the circumstances surrounding notice to determine its adequacy. What notice is sufficient? Though notice by email is generally acceptable, context matters. *See, e.g., Skirchak v. Dynamics Research Corp.*, 508 F.3d 49, 60 (1st Cir. 2007) (striking down arbitration agreement where employer provided notice via email two days before Thanksgiving and distributed agreement in appendices to a 15-page description of a new dispute resolution program, and noting that although "there was nothing objectionable about the use of email itself," "[t]he timing, the language, and the format of the presentation of the [DRP] obscured, whether intentionally or not, the waiver of class rights"); *Campbell v. General Dynamics Gov't Sys. Corp.*, 407 F.3d 546, 556–559 (1st Cir. 2005) (finding mass email containing web links to information about the company's new dispute resolution policy insufficient notice where the company had no history of communicating significant personnel matters to employees via email, the email did not explicitly state that the new dispute resolution policy contained a mandatory arbitration clause, and the email required no affirmative response from employees).

Another question that arises with increasing frequency is whether notice in English will suffice when the workforce is composed of employees who are not fluent in English. Must the employer translate the arbitration provision in order for it to be binding? Most courts say no, placing the burden on the employee to undertake translation before signing. *See, e.g., Morales v. Sun Constructors, Inc.*, 541 F.3d 218 (3d Cir. 2008) (holding arbitration clause binding upon Spanish speaking welder who could not read English and understood little spoken English, where manager who conducted orientation session asked a coworker to translate for the plaintiff and the coworker failed to convey the arbitration clause). *But see Samaniego v. Empire Today, LLC*, 205 Cal. App. 4th 1138 (2012) (finding that arbitration provision contained in an 11-page, single-spaced document presented only in English to non-English reading workers was unenforceable under California law; the workers were not provided with a copy of the arbitration rules and were told that no Spanish translation was available).

As for consent, courts typically find that where the employee receives adequate notice, failure to opt out and continuing to work constitutes acceptance. *See Tillman v. Macy's, Inc.*, 735 F.3d 453 (6th Cir. 2013).

3.   Severability and Drafting Issues. As we saw in the context of covenants not to compete in Chapter 6, *supra*, one question that arises in employment contract cases is whether portions of the contract that over-reach can be severed from the remainder of the contract or "blue-penciled," so that the remaining portions are still enforceable. Should courts sever or rewrite parts of an arbitration agreement that the court deems unconscionable? In *Nino v. The Jewelry Exchange, Inc.*, 609 F.3d 191 (3d Cir. 2010), the arbitration agreement included a five-day deadline for employees to file grievances or lose the right to arbitration, required employees to bear their own costs including attorneys' fees, and contained an arbitrator selection procedure so one-sided that it was both procedurally and substantively unconscionable under Virgin Islands law. The court refused to sever the unconscionable portions, finding the entire agreement unenforceable. The court explained that severance is inappropriate in two circumstances: (1) where the unconscionable aspects constitute an essential part of the agreed exchange of promises; or (2) where the unconscionability of the clause evidences "a deliberate attempt to impose an arbitration scheme designed to discourage an employee's resort to arbitration or to produce results biased in the employer's favor." (citation omitted). Citing *Hooters*, the court concluded that the arbitration provisions before it were "baldly one-sided, with only one discernible purpose—to create advantages for the employer that are not afforded to the employee." 609 F.3d 191, at 208.

What ethical issues might arise in drafting arbitration clauses? Should the company lawyer draft the most employer-advantageous agreement possible in an effort to chill claims, or does the attorney's duty as an officer of the court to maintain the integrity of the public justice system impose limits on the duty to zealously advocate on behalf of the client? *See* Martin H. Malin, *Ethical Concerns in Drafting Employment Arbitration Agreements After* Circuit City *and* Green Tree, 41 BRANDEIS L.J. 779 (2003). If the court is willing to sever or "blue-pencil" the agreement to eliminate any clauses that over-reach, or if the employer can preserve the validity of the agreement by waiving enforcement of portions that over-reach, what is the incentive for the employer or its counsel to police itself at the drafting stage? *See* Cynthia L. Estlund, *Between Rights and Contract: Arbitration Agreements and Non-Compete Covenants as a Hybrid Form of Employment Law*, 155 U. PA. L. REV. 379, 435 (2006).

4. Predispute Arbitration Agreements at Law Firms. A number of the predispute arbitration clause cases have arisen in the law firm context. The reason was succinctly stated by a partner at Paul, Hastings, Janofsky, & Walker, who commented: "We recommend [alternative dispute resolution] to our clients, and we practice what we preach." *Judge Orders Fired Law Firm Receptionist to Arbitrate FMLA, Disability Bias Claims*, DAILY LAB. REP. (BNA) No. 100, May 23, 2002, at A-1, reporting on *Stewart v. Paul, Hastings, Janofsky & Walker, LLP*, 201 F. Supp. 2d 291 (S.D.N.Y. 2002) (ruling that former law firm receptionist must arbitrate her FMLA and disability discrimination claims pursuant to predispute arbitration agreement drafted by law firm). Should it matter to the analysis of procedural unconscionability that the agreements are drafted by highly sophisticated lawyers? *See Davis v. O'Melveny & Myers*, 485 F.3d 1066 (9th Cir. 2007) (finding law firm's dispute resolution procedurally and substantively unconscionable as applied to paralegal, and observing that it was "written by a sophisticated employer—a national and international law firm, no less . . . .").

3. Provisions Barring Class Claims

When predispute arbitration agreements bar class claims, they may undermine the enforcement of statutory rights in ways that sweep beyond the individual employee's rights. This is particularly likely where recoveries under the statute can be minimal and the statute provides for class litigation as a practical mechanism for enforcing statutory rights (e.g., the FLSA), or where the statute explicitly protects group rights (e.g., the NLRA). Do arbitration agreements that bar class claims interfere with the vindication of statutory rights? Are they unconscionable?

a. Statutes That Provide for Group Litigation as an Enforcement Mechanism

SUTHERLAND v. ERNST & YOUNG LLP
United States Court of Appeals for the Second Circuit
726 F.3d 290 (2013)

Per Curiam:

The question presented in this appeal is whether an employee can invalidate a class-action waiver provision in an arbitration agreement when that waiver removes the financial incentive for her to pursue a claim under the Fair Labor Standards Act of 1938 ("FLSA"), 29 U.S.C. § 201, *et seq.* In light of the supervening decision of the Supreme Court in *American Express Co. v. Italian Colors Restaurant*, 133 S. Ct. 2304 (2013), we answer that question in the negative, and reverse the contrary decision of the United States District Court for the Southern District of New York (Kimba M. Wood, Judge).

Defendant-appellant Ernst & Young ("E&Y") appeals from an order of the District Court denying its Rule 12(b)(1) motion to dismiss or stay the proceedings, and to compel arbitration pursuant to the Federal Arbitration Act, 9 U.S.C. § 1, *et seq.* E&Y seeks to dismiss or stay this putative class action brought by its former employee, Stephanie Sutherland, on behalf of herself and others similarly situated to recover "overtime" wages pursuant to the FLSA, and the New York Department of Labor's Minimum Wage Order, N.Y. Comp. Codes R. & Regs. tit. 12, § 142-2.2, promulgated pursuant to the New York Labor Law ("NYLL") § 650, *et seq.*

The District Court denied E&Y's motion to compel arbitration because it found that the underlying class-action waiver provision in the arbitration agreement between E&Y and Sutherland was unenforceable pursuant to our decision in *In re American Express Merchants' Litigation*, 554 F.3d 300 (2d Cir. 2009) ("*Amex I*"). In that case, we invalidated a class-action waiver provision in an arbitration agreement because (1) the plaintiffs had shown that "they would incur prohibitive costs if compelled to arbitrate under the class action waiver," and (2) enforcing the arbitration agreement would "deprive them of substantive rights under the federal antitrust statutes." *Id.* at 315–16. But *Amex I* and the subsequent decisions that followed in our Circuit are no longer good law[3] in light of the Supreme Court's

---

[3] [n. 2] After we decided *Amex I*, the Supreme Court vacated our decision and remanded the case to us in light of its subsequent decision in *Stolt-Nielsen S.A. v. AnimalFeeds Int'l Corp.*, 559 U.S. 662, 130 S. Ct. 1758, 1775 (2010) (holding that "a party may not be compelled under the FAA to submit to class arbitration unless there is a contractual basis for concluding that the party agreed to do so."). See *Am. Express Co. v. Italian Colors Rest.*, 559 U.S. 1103 (2010) (Mem.). On remand, we adhered to our original conclusions in *Amex I* but placed a hold on the mandate to allow American Express to file a petition for a writ of certiorari. *In re Am. Express Merchants' Litig.*, 634 F.3d 187 (2d Cir. 2011) ("*Amex II*"). While the mandate was on hold, the Supreme Court decided *AT&T Mobility LLC v. Concepcion*, 131 S. Ct. 1740 (2011), in which the Supreme Court held that the Federal Arbitration Act preempted a California judicial rule barring as unconscionable the enforcement of class-action waivers in consumer contracts.

Upon a panel rehearing of *Amex II*, we held that *Concepcion* did not alter our analysis and again adhered to our *Amex I* decision. *In re Am. Express Merchants' Litig.*, 667 F.3d 204 (2d Cir. 2012) ("*Amex*

recent decision in *American Express Co. v. Italian Colors Restaurant*, 133 S. Ct. 2304 (2013), which held that plaintiffs could not invalidate a waiver of class arbitration under the so-called "effective vindication doctrine" by showing that "they ha[d] no economic incentive to pursue their antitrust claims individually in arbitration." *Id.* at 2310; *see Id.* at 2311 ("But the fact that it is not worth the expense involved in proving a statutory remedy does not constitute the elimination of the right to pursue that remedy.").

Because *Italian Colors* abrogated the District Court's basis for invaliding the class-action waiver provision in this case, we conclude that the District Court erred in denying E&Y's motion to compel arbitration. Accordingly, we reverse the District Court's March 3, 2011 order and remand the cause for further proceedings consistent with this opinion.

Background

Sutherland was employed by E&Y from September 2008 through December 2009. During her tenure at E&Y, she worked as a "Staff 1" and later as a "Staff 2" audit employee. Most of her responsibilities involved "pre-professional training" and "low level clerical work." Sutherland was compensated by E&Y on a "salary only" basis, which meant that she was paid a fixed salary of $55,000 per year, regardless of how many hours she worked. As relevant here, because Sutherland was a "salary only" employee, she did not receive any additional compensation for working "overtime"—i.e., more than 40 hours per week. Sutherland alleges that she "regularly worked in excess of 40 hours in a work week, often 45 to 50 hours in one week."

When Sutherland accepted her offer of employment with E&Y, she signed a so-called offer letter. That offer letter stated, inter alia, that "if an employment related dispute arises between you and the firm, it will be subject to mandatory mediation/arbitration under the terms of the firm's alternative dispute resolution program, known as the Common Ground Program, a copy of which is attached." Sutherland also signed a confidentiality agreement, which listed the terms of the "Alternative Dispute Resolution" policy and stated:

> I further agree that any dispute, controversy or claim (as defined in the E&Y Common Ground Dispute Resolution Program (AA7521)) arising between myself and the Firm will be submitted first to mediation and, if mediation is unsuccessful, then to binding arbitration in accordance with the terms and conditions set forth in AA7521, which describes the Firm's Common Ground Dispute Resolution Program. I acknowledge that I have read and understand the E&Y Common Ground Dispute Resolution Program (AA7521) and that I shall abide by it.

III"). We declined to review *Amex III* en banc on May 29, 2012. *See In re Am. Express Merchants' Litig.*, 681 F.3d 139 (2d Cir. 2012) (order denying en banc review). On November 9, 2012, the Supreme Court granted *certiorari* to review *Amex III*, *see Am. Express Co. v. Italian Colors Rest.*, 133 S. Ct. 594 (2012) (Mem.), and on June 20, 2013, the Court reversed our decision in *Amex III*, *see Am. Express Co. v. Italian Colors Rest.*, 133 S. Ct. 2304 (2013). That final decision of the Supreme Court dictates the outcome here.

As noted, a copy of the E&Y Common Ground Dispute Resolution Program ("Arbitration Agreement") was attached to the offer letter and the confidentiality agreement. As relevant here, the Arbitration Agreement specifically states that "[c]laims based on federal statutes such as . . . the Fair Labor Standards Act," "[c]laims based on state statutes and local ordinances, including state and local anti-discrimination laws," and "[c]laims concerning wages, salary, and incentive compensation programs" are subject to the terms of the Arbitration Agreement. The terms of the Arbitration Agreement also include the following two relevant provisions: (1) "Neither the Firm nor an Employee will be able to sue in court in connection with a Covered Dispute," (emphasis omitted); and (2) "Covered Disputes pertaining to different [e]mployees will be heard in separate proceedings."

Despite the terms of the Arbitration Agreement, which the parties agree bars both civil lawsuits and "any class or collective proceedings in the arbitration," Sutherland filed this putative class action against E&Y to recover, *inter alia*, 151.5 hours of unpaid overtime wages, amounting to $1,867.02. In particular, Sutherland claimed that E&Y had wrongfully classified her as "exempt" from the overtime requirements of the FLSA and the NYLL.

After Sutherland filed her putative class action, E&Y filed a motion to dismiss, or stay the proceedings, and to compel arbitration of Sutherland's claims on an individual basis in accordance with the terms of the Arbitration Agreement. Sutherland responded by arguing that the entire provision requiring individual arbitration was unenforceable because the requirement that she arbitrate her claims individually, rather than collectively, prevented her from "effectively vindicating" her rights under the FLSA and the NYLL. In particular, she argued that the costs and fees associated with prosecuting her claims an individual basis would dwarf her potential recovery of less than $2,000. In support of this argument, Sutherland filed an uncontested estimate that her attorney's fees during arbitration would be $160,000 and that her costs would exceed $6,000. She also claimed that expert testimony would be necessary and would cost at least $25,000. In sum, she argued that to "effectively vindicate" her claims in an individual arbitration, she would be required to expend approximately $200,000 to recover less than $2,000.

The District Court was persuaded by Sutherland's arguments and, on March 3, 2011, denied E&Y's motion to dismiss, or stay the proceedings, and to compel arbitration on an individual basis. In doing so, the District Court relied in large part on our analysis in *Amex I*, 554 F.3d 300, which invalidated a provision barring class actions in the antitrust context where plaintiffs demonstrated that they would be unable to vindicate their statutory rights if that provision was enforced. *See Sutherland v. Ernst & Young LLP*, 768 F. Supp. 2d 547, 549 (S.D.N.Y. 2011). Specifically, the District Court stated that "[e]nforcement of the class waiver provision in this case would effectively ban all proceedings by Sutherland against E&Y," *Id.* at 554, because of the nature of her "low-value, high-cost claim," *Id.* at 552.

On March 31, 2011, E&Y moved for reconsideration of the District Court's March 3, 2011 order in light of the Supreme Court's subsequent decision in *AT&T Mobility LLC v. Concepcion*, 131 S. Ct. 1740 (2011). The District Court denied that motion on January 17, 2012, concluding, inter alia, that "Sutherland, unlike the [plaintiffs in

Concepcion], is not able to vindicate her rights absent a collective action." *Sutherland v. Ernst & Young LLP*, 847 F. Supp. 2d 528, 535 (S.D.N.Y. 2012).

This appeal now presents the following question: May an employee invalidate a class-action waiver provision in an arbitration agreement when that waiver removes the financial incentive for her to pursue her FLSA claim?

DISCUSSION

A. Standard of Review

We have jurisdiction over this appeal because the Federal Arbitration Act ("FAA") authorizes interlocutory appeals from denials of motions to compel arbitration. *See* 9 U.S.C. § 16(a)(1)(A)-(B). "We review de novo a district court's refusal to compel arbitration." *Parisi v. Goldman, Sachs & Co.*, 710 F.3d 483, 486 (2d Cir. 2013).

B. The Class Action Waiver Must Be Enforced

The FAA, which was "enacted in 1925 in response to judicial hostility to arbitration agreements," *Concepcion*, 131 S. Ct. at 1745, provides that:

> A written provision in any maritime transaction or a contract evidencing a transaction involving commerce to settle by arbitration a controversy thereafter arising out of such contract or transaction . . . shall be valid, irrevocable, and enforceable, save upon such grounds as exist at law or in equity for the revocation of any contract.

9 U.S.C. § 2. In analyzing this provision of the FAA, the Supreme Court has remarked on several occasions that it establishes " 'a liberal federal policy favoring arbitration agreements,' " *CompuCredit Corp. v. Greenwood*, 132 S. Ct. 665, 669 (2012) (quoting *Moses H. Cone Mem'l Hosp. v. Mercury Constr. Corp.*, 460 U.S. 1, 24 (1983)), and that arbitration agreements should be enforced according to their terms "unless the FAA's mandate has been 'overridden by a contrary congressional command,' " *Id.* (quoting *Shearson/American Express Inc. v. McMahon*, 482 U.S. 220, 226 (1987)). In *American Express Co. v. Italian Colors Restaurant*, 133 S. Ct. 2304 (2013), the Court recently reminded lower courts to "rigorously enforce arbitration agreements according to their terms, including terms that specify with whom [the parties] choose to arbitrate their disputes, and the rules under which that arbitration will be conducted." *Id.* at 2309 (internal quotation marks and citations omitted; emphasis and brackets in original).

Consistent with the Supreme Court's recent analysis in *Italian Colors*, we first consider whether the FLSA contains a "contrary congressional command" barring waivers of class arbitration. Because no "contrary congressional command" exists, we then proceed to analyze Sutherland's argument that she cannot "effectively vindicate" her rights in an individual arbitration, inasmuch as such a proceeding would be "prohibitively expensive."

i. The FLSA Does Not Contain a "Contrary Congressional Command"

As in the antitrust context, "[n]o contrary congressional command requires us to reject the waiver of class arbitration" in the FLSA context. *Id.* Although we have not directly or specifically addressed whether an employee's ability to proceed collectively under the FLSA can be waived in an arbitration agreement, every Court of Appeals to have considered this issue has concluded that the FLSA does not preclude the waiver of collective action claims. *See Owen v. Bristol Care, Inc.*, 702 F.3d 1050, 1055 (8th Cir. 2013); *Carter v. Countrywide Credit Indus., Inc.*, 362 F.3d 294, 298 (5th Cir. 2004); *Adkins v. Labor Ready, Inc.*, 303 F.3d 496, 503 (4th Cir. 2002). We agree with this consensus among our sister Circuits for multiple reasons.

First, the text of the FLSA does not " 'envinc[e] an intention to preclude a waiver' of class-action procedure." *Italian Colors*, 133 S. Ct. at 2309 (quoting *Mitsubishi Motors Corp. v. Soler Chrysler-Plymouth, Inc.*, 473 U.S. 614, 628 (1985) (alteration in original)). Sutherland argues to the contrary, asserting that Section 16(b) of the FLSA creates a "right" to bring a collective action because the statute provides that "[a]n action to recover the liability . . . may be maintained against any employer . . . in any Federal or State Court of competent jurisdiction by any one or more employees for and in behalf of himself or themselves or other employees similarly situated," 29 U.S.C. § 216(b) (emphasis supplied). But Sutherland's argument neglects the fact that § 216(b) also requires an employee with a FLSA claim to affirmatively opt-in to any collective action. 29 U.S.C. § 216(b) ("No employee shall be a party plaintiff to any such action unless he gives his consent in writing to become such a party and such consent is filed in the court [297] in which such action is brought."). As the Eighth Circuit noted in *Owen*, "[e]ven assuming Congress intended to create some 'right' to class actions, if an employee must affirmatively opt in to any such class action, surely the employee has the power to waive participation in a class action as well."[4] 702 F.3d at 1052–53.

Second, Supreme Court precedents inexorably lead to the conclusion that the waiver of collective action claims is permissible in the FLSA context. In *Concepcion*, the Court held that the FAA preempted a California judicial rule regarding the unconscionability of class arbitration waivers in consumer contracts because "[r]equiring the availability of classwide arbitration [would] interfere[ ] with fundamental attributes of arbitration and thus create[ ] a scheme inconsistent with the FAA." 131 S. Ct. at 1748. Moreover, in *Gilmer v. Interstate/Johnson Lane Corp.*, 500 U.S. 20 (1991), the Court upheld the waiver of a collective action provision in the Age Discrimination in Employment Act ("ADEA"), 29 U.S.C. § 621 *et seq. Gilmer*, 500 U.S. at 32. In doing so, the Court noted that "even if the arbitration could not go forward as a class action or class relief could not be granted by the arbitrator, the fact that the [ADEA] provides for the possibility of bringing a collective action

---

[4] [n. 6] Our conclusion that nothing in the text of the FLSA prevents an employee from waiving his or her ability to proceed collectively under the FLSA is reinforced by our earlier decision referring to the FLSA collective action "right" as a "procedural mechanism[ ]." *Shahriar v. Smith & Wollensky Rest. Grp., Inc.*, 659 F.3d 234, 244 (2d Cir. 2011). We have previously explained that the procedural "right" to proceed collectively presupposes, and does not create, a non-waivable, substantive right to bring such a claim." *See Parisi*, 710 F.3d at 488. Indeed, as the Supreme Court noted in *Italian Colors*, "[o]ne might respond, perhaps, that federal law secures a nonwaivable opportunity to vindicate federal policies by satisfying the procedural strictures of Rule 23 or invoking some other informal class mechanism in arbitration. But we have already rejected that proposition . . . ." 133 S. Ct. at 2310 (citing *Concepcion*, 131 S. Ct. at 1748).

does not mean that individual attempts at conciliation were intended to be barred." *Id.* (internal quotation marks omitted; alteration in original)).[5]

For these reasons, the FLSA does not include a "contrary congressional command" that prevents the underlying arbitration agreement from being enforced by its terms.

ii. Sutherland Is Not Prevented from Effectively Vindicating Her Rights by Pursuing Arbitration on an Individual Basis

"Our finding of no 'contrary congressional command' does not end the case" because Sutherland invokes the "judge-made" exception to the FAA which "allow[s] courts to invalidate agreements that prevent the 'effective vindication' of a federal statutory right."[6] *Italian Colors*, 133 S. Ct. at 2310. In particular, Sutherland argues that pursuing individual arbitration would be "prohibitively expensive" because the recovery she seeks is dwarfed by the costs of individual arbitration.

Despite the obstacles facing the vindication of Sutherland's claims, the Supreme Court's recent decision in *Italian Colors*, which reversed our decision in *In re American Express Merchants' Litigation*, 667 F.3d 204 (2d Cir. 2012) ("*Amex III*"), compels the conclusion that Sutherland's class-action waiver is not rendered invalid by virtue of the fact that her claim is not economically worth pursuing individually.

Although the "effective vindication doctrine" could be used to invalidate "a provision in an arbitration agreement forbidding the assertion of certain statutory rights . . . . [and] would perhaps cover filing and administrative fees attached to arbitration that are so high as to make access to the forum impractical," *Italian Colors*, 133 S. Ct. at 2310–11 (relying on *Green Tree Fin. Corp.-Ala. v. Randolph*, 531 U.S. 79, 90 (2000)), plaintiffs cannot use the doctrine to invalidate class-action waiver provisions by showing that "they ha[d] no economic incentive to pursue their [FLSA] claims individually in arbitration," *Id.* at 2310. In other words, "the fact that it is not worth the expense involved in proving a statutory remedy does not constitute the elimination of the right to pursue that remedy."[7] *Id.* at 2311.

---

[5] [n. 7] Although Sutherland asks us to limit the scope of *Gilmer*, we see no valid basis upon which to do so, especially considering that the Supreme Court referred to *Gilmer* with approval in *Italian Colors*, noting that "[i]n *Gilmer*, we had no qualms in enforcing a class waiver in an arbitration agreement even though the federal statute at issue, the [ADEA], expressly permitted collective actions. We said that statutory permission did 'not mean that individual attempts at conciliation were intended to be barred.'" *Italian Colors*, 133 S. Ct. at 2311 (quoting *Gilmer*, 500 U.S. at 32) (citations omitted).

[6] [n. 9] In describing the "effective vindication doctrine," the Court remarked that the doctrine "originated as dictum in *Mitsubishi Motors*, where we expressed a willingness to invalidate, on 'public policy' grounds, arbitration agreements that 'operat[e] . . . as a prospective waiver of a party's right to pursue statutory remedies." *Italian Colors*, 133 S. Ct. at 2310 (quoting *Mitsubishi Motors*, 473 U.S. at 637 n.19) (alterations and emphasis in original). The Court went on to note that although "[s]ubsequent cases have similarly asserted the existence of an 'effective vindication' exception, . . . [all of those cases] have similarly declined to apply it to invalidate the arbitration agreement at issue." *Id.*

[7] [n. 10] The Supreme Court explained that:

> [t]he class action waiver merely limits arbitration to the two contracting parties. It no more eliminates those parties' right to pursue their statutory remedy than did federal law before its adopting of the class action for legal relief in 1938. . . . Or, to put it differently, the individual suit that was considered adequate to assure "effective vindication" of a federal right before

Accordingly, in light of the Supreme Court's holding that the "effective vindica- tion doctrine" cannot be used to invalidate class-action waiver provisions in circumstances where the recovery sought is exceeded by the costs of individual arbitration, we are bound to conclude that Sutherland's arguments are insufficient to invalidate the class-action waiver provision at issue here.[8]

CONCLUSION

To summarize, we hold that:

(1) The Fair Labor Standards Act of 1938 does not include a "contrary congressional command" that prevents a class-action waiver provision in an arbitration agreement from being enforced by its terms; and

(2) In light of the Supreme Court's recent decision in *American Express Co. v. Italian Colors Restaurant*, 133 S. Ct. 2304 (2013), Sutherland's argument that proceeding individually in arbitration would be "prohibitively expensive" is not a sufficient basis to invalidate the class-action waiver provision at issue here under the "effective vindication doctrine."

For these reasons, we REVERSE the March 3, 2011 order of the District Court, which denied defendant-appellant Ernst & Young's motion to dismiss or stay the proceedings, and to compel arbitration pursuant to the Federal Arbitration Act, 9 U.S.C. § 1, *et seq.*, and we REMAND the cause to the District Court for further proceedings consistent with this opinion.

NOTES

1. Class Waivers. The *Sutherland* court lays out the analysis applicable to waivers of class claims deriving from three Supreme Court decisions in the commercial law area: *Stolt-Nielsen S. A. v. AnimalFeeds Int'l Corp.*, 559 U.S. 662, 684 (2010) (finding that parties to arbitration agreements cannot be compelled to submit to class arbitration unless there is a contractual basis for finding that they agreed to be bound, because class action claims alter the fundamental nature of the arbitration bargain, which traditionally meant one plaintiff and one defendant); *AT&T Mobility v. Concepcion*, 131 S. Ct. 1740, 1752 (2011) (reaffirming that the shift from bilateral arbitration to class action arbitration is fundamental, and thus a ban on class arbitration in an arbitration agreement is enforceable; the Court noted that class arbitration would subject defendants to the "high stakes of class litigation," and doubted that defendants would have "bet the company" with no effective review mechanism, given the limited review afforded to arbitral decisions);

---

adoption of class-action procedures did not suddenly become "ineffective vindication" upon their adoption.

Italian Colors, 133 S. Ct. at 2311.

[8] [n. 11] We need not consider E&Y's various arguments about the cost-sharing provisions that may be available to individuals like Sutherland inasmuch as the Supreme Court rejected the use of the "effective vindication doctrine" in situations where the cost of proving a statutory remedy exceeds the remedy itself. *See Italian Colors*, 133 S. Ct. at 2311 n.4 (rejecting the conclusion that class-action waiver was unenforceable because other forms of cost sharing were not economically feasible).

and *American Express Co. v. Italian Colors Restaurant*, 133 S. Ct. 2304, 2311 (2013) (upholding a waiver of class action rights and characterizing the effective vindication of statutory rights analysis as inapplicable to an agreement that would render prohibitive the costs of proving the statutory claim individually because the law guarantees only the right to pursue the remedy; "the fact that it is not worth the expense involved in *proving* a statutory remedy does not constitute the elimination of the right to *pursue* that remedy.").

Other courts have agreed with *Sutherland* that class claims are waivable in the employment context because the "right" at stake is a procedural rather than substantive right. *See, e.g., Walthour v. Chipio Windshield Repair, LLC*, 745 F.3d 1326 (11th Cir. 2014) (applying *Italian Colors* to compel individual arbitration under the FLSA and enforce a class and collective action waiver because nothing in the FLSA's text or legislative history establishes a contrary congressional intent; the FLSA creates a procedural right to bring collective actions rather than a substantive, non-waivable right).

Sutherland and *Walthour* involved waivers of class claims presented as part of a predispute arbitration policy. But suppose the waiver of class claims is not part of an arbitration agreement? In *Killion v. KeHE Distribs.*, 761 F.3d 574 (6th Cir. 2014) the employer terminated a group of sales representatives as part of a corporate restructuring, and then sent them separation agreements offering a retention bonus if they would work for another month and agree to "release all claims" against the employer "arising out of [their] employment," as well as promising "not to consent to become[] a member of any class or collective action in a case in which claims are asserted against the Company that are related in any way to [their] employment or the termination of [their] employment with the Company." *Id. at* 579. Some of the sales representatives brought a collective action under the FLSA for failure to pay overtime, and the district court excluded from its conditional certification of the claim those employees who had signed the separation agreements containing the class waiver. The Sixth Circuit disagreed, finding the waivers invalid. The court reasoned that FLSA rights to a judicial forum cannot be waived unless the alternative forum allows for the effective vindication of the employee's claim. Arbitration is such a forum, but where the waiver is presented without an arbitration provision, the FAA's countervailing federal policy does not apply, and the analysis in *Sutherland* and *Walthour* is inapposite. *Id.* at 591–594. Is this a fair reading of *Sutherland*?

2. Continued Viability of the Effective Vindication of Statutory Rights Analysis. What, if anything, remains of the "effective vindication of statutory rights" line of analysis developed in *Cole, supra*, requiring fairness in employment arbitration? *See* Imre Stephen Szalai, *More Than Class Action Killers: The Impact of Concepcion and American Express [Italian Colors] on Employment Arbitration*, 35 BERKELEY J. EMP. & LAB. L. 31 (2014) (arguing that the legal framework that had developed previously under the effective vindication line of argument has been destabilized). In *Italian Colors*, the Court acknowledged the origins of the effective vindication line of analysis in *Mitsubishi Motors Corp. v. Soler Chrysler-Plymouth, Inc.*, 473 U.S. 614, 628 (1985), but characterized it as dicta. *Italian Colors*, 133 S. Ct. 2304, 2310 (2013). Should challenges to arbitration agreements on the basis that they frustrate the effective vindication of statutory rights continue to be viable in cases that don't involve waivers of class claims?

    3. Employer Responses. How should counsel for management advise clients to respond to these cases? It seems settled that class and collective action waivers will be upheld, assuming adequate notice is given. *See Davis v. Nordstrom, Inc.*, 755 F.3d 1089 (9th Cir. 2014) (employer that revised its policy after *Concepcion* to add a waiver of most class and collective action claims provided sufficient notice where it gave written notification and 30-day notice; employer was not required to inform workers that continued employment constituted acceptance). Thus, employers seeking to avoid costly class and collective action litigation are likely to insert an explicit waiver of class and collective actions in arbitration agreements. *See Using* Comcast *and Arbitration Agreements to Avoid Class Actions: The New Wave of Supreme Court Cases*, DAILY LAB. REP. (BNA) No. 165, Aug. 26, 2013. Although this may seem prudent, could a class action waiver in an arbitration agreement backfire? Consider a scenario in which the same law firm files separate but identical wage and hour claims on behalf of 40 different employees (as could easily happen if the employer has misclassified an entire occupational group as exempt from the FLSA's overtime pay requirements, for example). If the arbitration provision bars class arbitration, the employer will be required to bear the costs of 40 arbitration proceedings with different arbitrators assigned to each proceeding, including the lost time entailed in 40 separate depositions of the same managers and 40 hearings in which the company is represented by its lawyers or human resources personnel. In addition, the company may be required to deposit the estimated fee for each arbitrator up front, as for example the AAA rules require, necessitating significant out-of-pocket costs (one arbitrator estimated that the total deposit for 40 arbitrations might be as high as $500,000 to $1,000,000). *See* Martin H. Malin, *The Employment Decisions of the Supreme Court's 2012–13 Term*, 29 ABA J. LAB. & EMP. L. 203, 213–14 (2014). As a case in point, the ABA Journal reported that AT&T Mobility's win in the *Concepcion* case was ultimately a "Pyrrhic victory." The company subsequently faced over 700 individual notices of dispute and arbitration demands from consumers complaining that its merger with T-Mobile violated the antitrust laws. The same law firm represented all the consumers. Martha Neil, *Law Firm Makes Lemonade After Supremes Nix AT&T Class Action, Now Pursues Individual Arbitrations*, ABA JOURNAL, July 2011.

    Another question that courts must face after *Concepcion* and *Italian Colors* is how these decisions will impact state law-based unconscionability doctrine under the FAA's saving clause. The following decision and notes explore that question.

    ***Chavarria v. Ralphs Grocery Co.*, 733 F.3d 916 (9th Cir. 2013).** The plaintiff, a deli clerk at Ralph's Grocery, filed an action on behalf of herself and all similarly situated employees alleging that Ralph's had failed to pay her and other employees for rest and meal breaks in violation of the California Labor Code and the California Business and Professions Code. Ralph's moved to compel arbitration of her individual claim under its predispute arbitration agreement, which was incorporated into the employment application and presented on a take-it-or-leave-it basis to all applicants. The agreement precluded the use of institutional arbitration administrators affiliated with a list of organizations (such as the AAA), all of which adhered to rules designed to produce a neutral arbitration. It also gave an advantage in arbitrator selection to the party who did not initiate arbitration, effectively guaranteeing that Ralph's would determine the arbitrator in the vast majority of cases. Further, the agreement prohibited the arbitrator from awarding attorneys' fees to the employee unless a Supreme Court decision expressly required the award, required the arbitrator to determine at the outset of arbitration how the fee (ranging from $7,000 to $14,000 per day) would be apportioned between the parties without regard to the claim's merits, and allowed the employer to amend the agreement unilaterally without notice to the employee, with continued employment serving as assent to the new terms.

The Ninth Circuit found the agreement both procedurally and substantively unconscionable. It found procedural unconscionability because submission of an application for employment bound applicants to the policy's terms, and Ralph's did not provide the terms of the policy until three weeks after the applicant had consented to be bound. *Id.* at 923–24. It also found substantive unconscionability because the arbitrator selection procedure would nearly always produce an arbitrator chosen by Ralph's, the exclusion of arbitrators provided by AAA or JAMS avoided their neutral arbitrator selection processes and due process protocols, and the fee apportionment provision was designed to price employees out of the arbitration dispute resolution process. *Id.* at 924–27.

The court then discussed the employer's argument that the FAA preempted California state law-based unconscionability doctrine:

> Federal law preempts state laws that stand as an obstacle to the accomplishment of Congress's objectives. *Concepcion*, 131 S. Ct. at 1753. Accordingly, the FAA preempts state laws that in theory apply to contracts generally but in practice impact arbitration agreements disproportionately. *Id.* at 1747.

> California's unconscionability doctrine applies to all contracts generally and therefore constitutes "such grounds at law or in equity for the revocation of [a] contract." 9 U.S.C. § 2. But specific application of rules within that doctrine may be problematic. *See Concepcion*, 131 S. Ct. at 1753 (holding that California's rule making class waivers unconscionable was preempted by the FAA).

> In this case, California's procedural unconscionability rules do not disproportionately affect arbitration agreements, for they focus on the parties and the circumstances of the agreement and apply equally to the formation of all contracts. The application of California's general substantive unconscionability rules to Ralphs' arbitration policy, however, warrants more discussion.

> The Supreme Court's recent decision in *American Express Corp. v. Italian Colors Restaurant*, 133 S. Ct. 2304 (2013), does not preclude us from considering the cost that Ralphs' arbitration agreement imposes on employees in order for them to bring a claim. In that case, plaintiffs argued that the class waiver term of the arbitration agreement at issue effectively

foreclosed vindication of the plaintiffs' federal rights: specifically, their rights under the Sherman Antitrust Act. *Id.* at 2310. Plaintiffs could not pursue their antitrust claims, they argued, because the experts required to prove an antitrust claim would cost hundreds of thousands of dollars, while the individual recovery would not exceed $40,000. *Id.* The class waiver provision did not foreclose effective vindication of that right, the Court reasoned, because "the fact that it is not worth the expense involved in *proving* a statutory remedy does not constitute an elimination of the *right to pursue* that remedy." *Id.* at 2311. The Court explicitly noted that the result might be different if an arbitration provision required a plaintiff to pay "filing and administrative fees attached to arbitration that are so high as to make access to the forum impracticable." *Id.* at 2310–11.

Ralphs' arbitration policy presents exactly that situation. In this case, administrative and filing costs, even disregarding the cost to prove the merits, effectively foreclose pursuit of the claim. Ralphs has constructed an arbitration system that imposes non-recoverable costs on employees just to get in the door.

The Supreme Court's holding that the FAA preempts state laws having a "disproportionate impact" on arbitration cannot be read to immunize all arbitration agreements from invalidation no matter how unconscionable they may be, so long as they invoke the shield of arbitration. Our court has recently explained the nuance: "*Concepcion* outlaws discrimination in state policy that is *unfavorable* to arbitration." *Mortensen v. Bresnan Communs., LLC*, 722 F.3d 1151, 1160 (9th Cir. 2013) (emphasis added). We think this is a sensible reading of *Concepcion*.

This case illustrates the distinction. In addition to the problematic cost provision, Ralphs' arbitration policy contains a provision that unilaterally assigns one party (almost always Ralphs, in our view, as explained above) the power to select the arbitrator whenever an employee brings a claim. Of course, any state law that invalidated this provision would have a disproportionate impact on arbitration because the term is arbitration specific. But viewed another way, invalidation of this term is agnostic towards arbitration. It does not disfavor arbitration; it provides that the arbitration process must be fair.

If state law could not require some level of fairness in an arbitration agreement, there would be nothing to stop an employer from imposing an arbitration clause that, for example, made its own president the arbitrator of all claims brought by its employees. Federal law favoring arbitration is not a license to tilt the arbitration process in favor of the party with more bargaining power. California law regarding unconscionable contracts, as applied in this case, is not unfavorable towards arbitration, but instead reflects a generally applicable policy against abuses of bargaining power. The FAA does not preempt its invalidation of Ralphs' arbitration policy.

733 F.3d at 927–28.

NOTES

1. **Impact of *Concepcion* and *Italian Colors* on State Law Unconscionability Analysis.** How does the Ninth Circuit distinguish the Supreme Court precedents in *Chavarria*? Is the court's analysis persuasive? If not, are there any judicial limits on employer power to tilt the arbitration process in its favor?

Other courts have limited *Concepcion*'s preemptive effect to the class waiver context, leaving the remainder of unconscionability doctrine intact. *See, e.g., Hill v. Garda CL Nw., Inc.*, 308 P.3d 635 (Wash. 2013) (*en banc*) (finding employment arbitration agreement unconscionable where it imposed a two-week limitations period, limited back pay in wage claims to two or four months, and imposed a cost-prohibitive fee-sharing arrangement).

Outside the employment context, some courts have read *Concepcion*'s broad preemption analysis as severely circumscribing unconscionability analysis. *See, e.g., Lucas v. Hertz Corp.*, 875 F. Supp. 2d 991 (N.D. Cal. 2012) (enforcing consumer arbitration agreement that barred discovery and finding unconscionability analysis preempted where agreement would have been unconscionable under pre-*Concepcion* California law). The Sixth Circuit concluded that the Court's precedents completely obviate judicial oversight under the unconscionability doctrine, and suggested that the solution to the dilemma of lopsided arbitration clauses should come from the market. *See Reed Elsevier, Inc. v. Crockett*, 734 F.3d 594, 600 (6th Cir. 2013) (ruling that *Italian Colors* required enforcement of an adhesive arbitration agreement to bar class claims of a lawyer who had a billing dispute with LexisNexis, and noting that Westlaw's agreement with its customers does not include an arbitration clause). What would a market solution look like in the employment context?

2. **Comparing Effective Vindication and Unconscionability Doctrine.** What difference does it make whether a challenge to an arbitration agreement is framed as interfering with the effective vindication of statutory rights, or as imposing an unconscionable contract? Recall that standards for evaluating the fairness of arbitration agreements under the vindication of statutory rights doctrine were developed by the federal courts and allowed for judicial oversight of arbitration agreements at the federal level, ensuring some degree of uniformity across states. *See Cole, supra.* By contrast, unconscionability doctrine is a creature of state law, and varies from state to state. If *Concepcion* and *Italian Colors* block effective vindication challenges but do not block challenges based upon state law outside the waiver context, the enforceability of arbitration agreements will vary according the plaintiff-friendliness of the state law regime.

b. NLRA Rights

As we saw in Chapter 8, employee rights to engage in concerted activity protected under § 7 of the NLRA arguably include the right to solicit and maintain class action litigation to enforce statutory or contractual employment rights. It is well-established that employers cannot require employees to waive their rights to engage in concerted activity. Do provisions in arbitration clauses blocking class claims thus violate the NLRA by requiring waiver of § 7 rights or otherwise interfering with concerted activity?

D.R. Horton, Inc., 357 N.L.R.B. No. 184 (2012), *reversed in part*, 737 F.3d 344 (5th Cir. 2013). D.R. Horton required new and current employees to sign a predispute arbitration agreement that restricted the arbitrator to hearing individual claims, explicitly depriving the arbitrator of the authority "to fashion a proceeding as a class or collective action or to award relief to a group or class of employees in one arbitration proceeding." In exchange for the right to arbitrate claims, employees waived the right to file a lawsuit or other civil proceedings relating to employment, including the right to trial by a judge or jury. 357 N.L.R.B. No. 184, at 2. An employee who had signed the arbitration agreement asserted that he had been misclassified as exempt from the overtime pay requirements of the Fair Labor Standards Act, and sought to initiate arbitration on behalf of a nationwide class of similarly classified employees. When the employer refused, citing the contractual language barring arbitration of collective claims, the employee filed an unfair labor charge with the NLRB, alleging that the arbitration agreement interfered with employees' rights to engage in concerted activities for the purpose of collective bargaining or other mutual aid or protection.

The NLRB found that the class action waiver violated § 8(a)(1) of the NLRA because the contractual language would lead employees reasonably to believe that they were prohibited from exercising their associational rights under § 7 of the NLRA:

> The Board has long held, with uniform judicial approval, that the NLRA protects employees' ability to join together to pursue workplace grievances, including through litigation. Not long after the Act's passage, the Board held that the filing of a Fair Labor Standards Act suit by three employees was protected concerted activity, . . . as was an employee's circulation of a petition among coworkers, designating him as their agent to seek back wages under the FLSA. . . . In the decades that followed, the Board has consistently held that concerted legal action addressing wages, hours, or working conditions is protected by Section 7.

> Collective pursuit of a workplace grievance in arbitration is equally protected by the NLRA. When the grievance is pursued under a collectively-bargained grievance-arbitration procedure, the Supreme Court has observed, "No one doubts that the processing of a grievance in such a manner is concerted activity within the meaning of § 7." *NLRB v. City Disposal Systems, Inc.*, 465 U.S. 822, 836 (1984). And the same is true when the grievance is pursued under a unilaterally created grievance/arbitration procedure so long as its pursuit is concerted. . . . Thus, employees who join together to bring employment-related claims on a classwide or collective basis in court or before an arbitrator are exercising rights protected by Section 7 of the NLRA.

> . . . .

> That this restriction on the exercise of Section 7 rights is imposed in the form of an agreement between the employee and the employer makes no

difference. From its earliest days, the Board, again with uniform judicial approval, has found unlawful employer-imposed, individual agreements that purport to restrict Section 7 rights—including, notably, agreements that employees will pursue claims against their employer only individually.

. . . .

357 N.L.R.B. No. 184, at 2–6.

The Board offered the following analysis of the potential conflict between the FAA and its interpretation of the NLRA:

> Holding that the [arbitration agreement at issue here] violates the NLRA does not conflict with the FAA or undermine the pro-arbitration policy underlying the FAA under the circumstances of this case for several reasons. First, the purpose of the FAA was to prevent courts from treating arbitration agreements less favorably than other private contracts. The Supreme Court . . . has made clear that "[w]herever private contracts conflict with [the] functions" of the National Labor Relations Act, "they obviously must yield or the Act would be reduced to a futility." *J.I. Case Co.*, [*v. NLRB*, 321 U.S. 332 (1944)] *supra*, at 337. To find that an arbitration agreement must yield to the NLRA is to treat it no worse than any other private contract that conflicts with Federal labor law. . . .

> Second, the Supreme Court's jurisprudence under the FAA, permitting enforcement of agreements to arbitrate federal statutory claims, including employment claims, makes clear that the agreement may not require a party to "forgo the substantive rights afforded by the statute." *Gilmer, supra*, at 26. The question presented in this case is *not* whether employees can effectively vindicate their rights under the Fair Labor Standards Act in an arbitral forum. *See Gilmer, supra*. Rather, the issue here is whether [the arbitration agreement's] categorical prohibition of joint, class, or collective federal or state employment law claims in any forum directly violates the substantive rights vested in employees by Section 7 of the NLRA.

> *Gilmer* addresses neither Section 7 nor the validity of a class action waiver. The claim in *Gilmer* was an individual one, not a class or collective claim, and the arbitration agreement contained no language specifically waiving class or collective claims. Here, although the underlying claim the Charging Party sought to arbitrate was based on the FLSA . . . the right allegedly violated by [the arbitration agreement] is not the right to be paid the minimum wage or overtime under the FLSA, but the right to engage in collective action under the NLRA. Thus, the question presented is not whether employees can effectively vindicate their rights under the FLSA in arbitration despite a prohibition against class or collective proceedings, but whether employees can be required, as a condition of employment, to enter into an agreement waiving their rights under the NLRA.

> Any contention that the Section 7 right to bring a class or collective action is merely "procedural" must fail. The right to engage in collective action—including collective *legal* action—is the core substantive right

protected by the NLRA and is the foundation on which the Act and Federal labor policy rest. . . .

Id. at 2–12.

The Fifth Circuit refused to enforce this part of the Board's order, finding that the NLRB had failed to give sufficient weight to the FAA. Applying *AT&T Mobility v. Concepcion*, 131 S. Ct. 1740 (2011), the court found that neither the FAA's saving clause nor the NLRA's policy favoring group action justified invalidation of the waiver of class procedures in the arbitration agreement. Although the court acknowledged that NLRA section 7 protects collective suit filings whether in litigation or in arbitration as an exercise of concerted activity, the right to bring class claims is not a substantive right. 737 F.3d at 357. Nor does the NLRA itself contain a textual or legislative command sufficient to override the FAA; indeed, the NLRA permits and encourages arbitration through collective agreements. Thus, the NLRA does not trump the FAA. *Id.* at 361–62. The court did rule, however, that because Horton's agreement might reasonably be understood as barring employees from engaging more generally in activity protected under section 7 of the NLRA, the Board was entitled to enforce its order requiring that D.R. Horton revise the agreement to clarify that it would not preclude employees from engaging in protected activity, including the right to file unfair labor practice charges with the NLRB. *Id.* at 364–65.

NOTES

1. **Federal Court Unanimity; NLRB Nonacquiescence.** At least three other circuit courts have reached the same conclusion as the Fifth Circuit. *See Richards v. Ernst & Young, LLP*, 744 F.3d 1072 (9th Cir. 2013); *Sutherland v. Ernst & Young LLP*, 726 F.3d 290 (2d Cir. 2013); *Owen v. Bristol Care, Inc.*, 702 F.3d 1050 (8th Cir. 2013). Why do you think they are unanimous in this regard? Nevertheless, the NLRB has pursued a policy of "nonacquiescence." As an expert agency charged with administering a statute, the NLRB is entitled to persist in its own interpretation in the face of contrary judicial precedent. *See* Ross Davies, *Remedial Nonacquiescence*, 89 Iowa L. Rev. 65 (2003) (describing and critiquing the phenomenon). Accordingly, the Board has continued to press its view in cases asserting unfair labor practices under the NLRA—even in cases arising in the same judicial territory where the courts have ruled against it (indeed, the Board will not know in advance which circuit may be presented with a petition to enforce or review the Board's order). Deborah Maranville, *Nonacquiescence: Outlaw Agencies, Imperial Courts, and the Perils of Pluralism*, 39 Vand. L. Rev. 471, 471 (1986). Administrative law judges for the NLRB are bound to enforce the Board's *D.R. Horton* ruling unless and until it is reversed by the Board or by the Supreme Court. Rebecca Hanner White, *Time for a New Approach: Why the Judiciary Should Disregard the "Law of the Circuit" When Confronting Nonacquiescence by the National Labor Relations Board*, 69 N.C.L. Rev. 639 (1991).

2. **Vindication of Statutory Rights Theory and the NLRA.** In *D.R. Horton*, the Board relied to some degree on the "vindication of statutory rights" argument derived from *Gilmer* and *Mitsubishi*, and discussed in *Cole* and *Sutherland*, *supra*—i.e., that arbitration is an adequate substitute for a judicial forum only

where the employee can effectively vindicate her statutory rights through the arbitral process. The substantive rights at issue in *D.R. Horton* were NLRA rights, not FLSA rights, although the employees sought to bring FLSA claims. Both the NLRA and the FLSA are federal statutes, so what difference should this make? Is there something distinctive about NLRA rights? Would the Court see any distinction between them in the context of an agreement to arbitrate? *See* Katherine V.W. Stone, *Procedure, Substance, and Power: Collective Litigation and Arbitration Under the Labor Law*, 61 UCLA L. Rev. Disc. 164, 179–80 (2013) (suggesting that *Italian Colors* heralds the destruction of the protection for collective action that lies at the heart of the labor laws). Can the NLRB's decision in *D.R. Horton* be distinguished because it conflated the power of employees to collectively assert their legal rights, which the NLRA protects, with the ability of workers to have their claims collectively adjudicated, which it does not?

3. **Coercive Grants of Benefits Under the NLRA.** As employers have responded to *Italian Colors* and *Concepcion* by adding waivers of class claims to their employment policies, some plaintiffs have brought unfair labor practice claims under the NLRA, asserting that the modified policies violate § 8(a)(1) by interfering with, restraining or coercing them in the exercise of their § 7 rights to engage in concerted activity. The Ninth Circuit faced such a claim in *Johnmohammadi v. Bloomingdale's, Inc.*, 755 F.3d 1072 (9th Cir. 2014). The court acknowledged that bringing a class action on behalf of other employees might be a form of concerted activity protected under the NLRA, but concluded that the employee could not show that the employer had interfered with, restrained or coerced her in any way, since she had "freely consented" to an arbitration policy containing a class waiver which allowed employees to opt-out by returning a form within 30 days of presentation of the agreement, and she had not opted out. Nor could she establish that coercion was implicit in offering the arbitration policy as a benefit in exchange for the waiver of section 7-protected rights. The court explained:

> To prevail on this argument, Johnmohammadi would need to show that offering the arbitration agreement constitutes "conduct immediately favorable to employees," which Bloomingdale's undertook with the express purpose of impinging upon its employees' "freedom of choice" in deciding whether to waive or retain their right to participate in class litigation. *NLRB v. Exch. Parts Co.*, 375 U.S. 405, 409 (1964). We don't doubt that offering the arbitration agreement could be viewed as conduct favorable to employees, since the benefits of having an arbitral forum available to resolve workplace disputes can be substantial. For certain types of disputes the speed, informality, and lower costs of arbitration provide real advantages over litigating in court. *See Concepcion*, 131 S. Ct. at 1749, 1751. But arbitration comes with disadvantages of its own, which, depending on the nature of the dispute, may make it a less attractive forum for employees. At the outset of the employment relationship, before an employee knows what types of workplace-related disputes she may later encounter, the benefits (and costs) of prospectively agreeing to arbitrate all such disputes are decidedly uncertain, even putting aside the class-action waiver. We don't think the offer of those benefits is of such a character that it would tend to interfere with an employee's freedom of choice about whether to forgo

future participation in class actions. And Johnmohammadi has offered no evidence that Bloomingdale's offered those benefits with the express purpose of curtailing its employees' freedom of choice. Indeed, it would be difficult for Johnmohammadi to make such a showing here, given that the presumed benefits of agreeing to arbitrate all employment-related disputes would largely be lost if the agreement permitted class-wide arbitration.

Id. at 1076. The plaintiff's argument rested upon precedent under the NLRA that establishes that an employer violates NLRA section 8(a)(1) when it offers a promise of benefit—for example, a wage increase or an improvement in working conditions or benefits—in an effort to dissuade employees from asserting their section 7 rights to organize. *NLRB v. Exchange Parts Co.*, 375 U.S. 405, 409 (1964). Are you persuaded by the Ninth Circuit's analysis of the questionable benefits of arbitration? Is the court's reasoning on this point consistent with its earlier conclusion that the plaintiff freely consented to the policy?

4.   The Impact of Arbitration Agreements on the Public Interest

Some labor and employment statutes provide for an administrative agency that—along with individuals—enforces the statute. If an individual employee or group of employees is bound by a predispute arbitration agreement, may the agency still proceed with its own enforcement action? Does it matter what sort of relief it seeks? The Supreme Court took up this question in the following case involving the EEOC.

Equal Employment Opportunity Commission v. Waffle House, Inc., 534 U.S. 279 (2002). Eric Baker, a grill operator at Waffle House, suffered a seizure at work and was discharged shortly thereafter. Baker filed a charge of discrimination with the EEOC alleging that his discharge violated the ADA. The EEOC filed an enforcement action in federal district court alleging ADA violations and seeking make-whole relief (including backpay, reinstatement, and compensatory damages) as well as punitive damages. The employer invoked a predispute arbitration agreement and sought to compel arbitration under the FAA in lieu of the EEOC action in court. The Court of Appeals for the Fourth Circuit found that although the arbitration agreement did not foreclose the enforcement action because the EEOC was not a party to the contract, it precluded the EEOC from seeking victim-specific relief in order to give effect to the arbitration agreement and the policies articulated in the FAA, limiting the EEOC's remedies to injunctive relief. The Supreme Court considered the policies behind the enforcement scheme provided in Title VII (which are applicable to ADA enforcement actions by the EEOC) and reviewed the policies behind the FAA. Noting that the EEOC files fewer than 2% of all antidiscrimination claims in federal court, the Court reasoned that permitting the EEOC to pursue victim-specific relief in court would have a negligible effect on the federal policy favoring arbitration. *Id.* at 290 n.7. Moreover, once the plaintiff files a charge with the EEOC, it is in command of the investigation, conciliation, and suit-filing process: If the EEOC chooses to file suit, the employee has no independent cause of action. *Id.* at 291. The Court explained:

The statute clearly makes the EEOC the master of its own case and confers on the agency the authority to evaluate the strength of the public interest at stake. Absent textual support for a contrary view, it is the public agency's province—not that of the court—to determine whether public resources should be committed to the recovery of victim—specific relief. And if the agency makes that determination, the statutory text unambiguously authorizes it to proceed in a judicial forum. . . .

Even if the policy goals underlying the FAA did necessitate some limit on the EEOC's statutory authority, the line drawn by the Court of Appeals between injunctive and victim-specific relief creates an uncomfortable fit with its avowed purpose of preserving the EEOC's public function while favoring arbitration. For that purpose, the category of victim-specific relief is both overinclusive and underinclusive. For example, it is overinclusive because while punitive damages benefit the individual employee, they also serve an obvious public function in deterring future violations. Punitive damages may often have a greater impact on the behavior of other employers than the threat of an injunction, yet the EEOC is precluded from seeking this form of relief under the Court of Appeals' compromise scheme. And, it is underinclusive because injunctive relief, although seemingly not "victim-specific," can be seen as more closely tied to the employees' injury than to any public interest. . . .

[W]e are persuaded that, pursuant to Title VII and the ADA, whenever the EEOC chooses from among the many charges filed each year to bring an enforcement action in a particular case, the agency may be seeking to vindicate a public interest, not simply provide make-whole relief for the employee, even when it pursues entirely victim-specific relief. To hold otherwise would undermine the detailed enforcement scheme created by Congress simply to give greater effect to an agreement between private parties that does not even contemplate the EEOC's statutory function.

Id. at 291–92, 294–96. Justices Thomas, Rehnquist and Scalia dissented. The dissent complained that permitting the EEOC to pursue victim-specific remedies for Baker amounted to an end run around the arbitration agreement by allowing employees two bites at the apple—one in arbitration and one in litigation conducted by the EEOC. Such a result would discourage the use of arbitration agreements, and had no basis in Title VII, which only confers upon the EEOC the right to bring suit, not the right to obtain any particular remedy. *Id.* at 300–01, 309–10.

NOTES

1.   **The Continuing Significance of *Waffle House*.** Is the Court's reasoning in *Waffle House* undercut by its decision in *AT&T Mobility v. Concepcion*, 131 S. Ct. 1740 (2011), where the Court found class action waivers in predispute arbitration agreements enforceable because they facilitate the streamlined proceedings characteristic of the arbitration scheme protected by the FAA?

2.   **State Enforcement Schemes.** The Court in *Waffle House* also emphasized the fact that the EEOC was not a party to the private employment agreement in

which the individual employee waived statutory rights to proceed in court, and so should not be bound by it. 534 U.S. at 288–89. Nor was the EEOC a proxy for the individual employee; the EEOC was the "master of its own case" and could prosecute the action without the employee's consent. *Id.* at 291. What about the mirror image of *Waffle House*, where instead of the government seeking victim-specific relief on behalf of an employee who is bound by an arbitration agreement, an employee bound by an arbitration agreement seeks redress beyond victim-specific relief, most of which is paid into the state's treasury? California authorizes private citizens to act in a representative capacity as private attorneys general, taking on the state's enforcement role. Plaintiffs may seek civil penalties for violation of the state's labor and employment laws as a proxy for the state, with 75% of the penalty assessed going to the state, and the remaining 25% to the plaintiff(s). Private Attorneys General Act, CAL. LABOR CODE § 2698 *et seq.* (2004) (PAGA). The California Supreme Court ruled in *Iskanian v. CLS Transp. of Los Angeles, LLC*, 327 P.3d 129 (Cal. 2014) that arbitration agreements that purport to condition employment on giving up the right to bring representative PAGA claims in any forum contravene public policy and are unenforceable. The court reasoned that such claims do not involve a dispute between private parties; instead, the dispute is between the employer and the state, with the employee serving as proxy for the state and advancing its enforcement capabilities. Thus, *Concepcion* is inapposite and the FAA does not preempt a state's refusal to permit waiver of PAGA representative actions in an employment contract. The court explained:

> Nothing in the text or legislative history of the FAA nor in the Supreme Court's construction of the statute suggests that the FAA was intended to limit the ability of states to enhance their public enforcement capabilities by enlisting willing employees in *qui tam* actions. Representative actions under the PAGA, unlike class action suits for damages, do not displace the bilateral arbitration of private disputes between employers and employees over their respective rights and obligations toward each other. Instead, they directly enforce the state's interest in penalizing and deterring employers who violate California's labor laws.

Id. at 63.

Are you persuaded? Or does the *Concepcion* analysis suggest that refusing to enforce waivers of PAGA rights in predispute arbitration clauses would be fundamentally inconsistent with the FAA's pro-arbitration policy?

E. RECONSIDERING EMPLOYER-PROMULGATED ARBITRATION SYSTEMS

Predispute employment arbitration is now a more widespread dispute resolution system than collective bargaining and labor arbitration: less than 12% of employees are covered by a collective bargaining agreement containing a labor arbitration clause, while approximately 25% of nonunion employers have adopted employment arbitration for nonunion employees. Alexander J.S. Colvin & Kelly Pike, *Saturns and Rickshaws Revisited: What Kind of Arbitration System Has Developed?*, 29 OH. STATE J. ON DISP. RES. 59, 82 (2014). What are the consequences of the channeling of workplace issues governed by statute to a private dispute resolution system promulgated by employers and applicable to workers not represented by unions?

Katherine Van Wezel Stone, *Mandatory Arbitration of Individual Employment Rights: The Yellow Dog Contract of the 1990s*
73 Denv. U. L. Rev. 1017, 1036–37, 1039–43, 1046–50 (1996)

While mandatory arbitration of statutory rights is troublesome in any context, in the nonunion setting it is particularly problematic. Many pre-hire arbitral agreements are blatant contracts of adhesion. . . . At the moment of hire, employees lack bargaining power and are needful of employment, so they frequently agree to such terms without giving them much thought. . . . [T]hese *Gilmer* pre-hire arbitration agreements discourage workers from asserting statutory rights. They operate like the early nineteenth century "yellow dog contracts"—contracts in which employees had to promise not to join a union in order to get a job. Today's "yellow dog contracts" require employees to waive their statutory rights in order to obtain employment.

Like the yellow dog contracts of the past, the new mandatory arbitration provisions are often imposed on workers without even the illusion of bargaining or consent. They are designed by employers unilaterally, and given to employees at the time of hire or inserted in employee handbooks, without mention of their existence and without discussion as to their terms. . . .

The increased judicial deference to arbitration to resolve the statutory claims of nonunion workers and to preclude the statutory claims of unionized workers makes it exceedingly difficult for legislatures to enact meaningful statutes that give employees protection. Imagine, for example, that courts were to hold that workers' complaints under the Occupational Safety and Health Act of 1970 (OSHA) are subject to mandatory arbitration provisions. Such a result, which is possible under an expansive interpretation of *Gilmer*, would vitiate Congress's intent in enacting OSHA in the first place. Congress enacted OSHA in order to provide uniform standards for employee health and safety. To subject its provisions to mandatory arbitration would subject unionized as well as nonunion workers to the variable, unpredictable, and invisible outcomes of private arbitration. Further, such a requirement would make it difficult, if not impossible, for Congress to monitor the effectiveness of its legislative efforts, or to revise legislation to better address pressing social problems. In a similar fashion, compelled arbitration of statutory claims threatens to nullify all employee protection legislation. It also makes it impossible for Congress to enact effective legislation for worker protection because whatever is stipulated by statute can be compromised away by employer-designated arbitrators. In addition, by removing labor cases to private arbitral tribunals, courts are taking employment concerns out of the public arena, away from public scrutiny and political accountability. Because the arbitral tribunal is invisible, no one knows to what extent arbitration enforces these publicly conferred employment rights, if at all.

A related problem with mandatory arbitration of statutory rights is that statutory disputes are being decided in private tribunals which generate no publicly available norms to guide actors or decisionmakers in the future. . . . This will mean that arbitrators who want to interpret the statutes correctly will have no authoritative statutory interpretations to look to for guidance. It also means that the law cannot play an educational role of shaping parties' norms and sense of right and wrong, and therefore it cannot shape behavior in its shadow.

Furthermore, statutory employment rights are enacted when a legislature believes that workers cannot adequately protect themselves simply by bargaining with their employers. That is, they reflect a legislature's view of market failure in the contracting process. Legislatures act to ensure healthy and safe workplaces, protect privacy on the job, or to provide other protections when they believe that there is a public policy concern so compelling that it warrants intervening in the wage bargain. To then relegate enforcement or interpretation of these employment rights to a privatized tribunal—a tribunal whose composition and internal rules reflect and instantiate the very power imbalances that gave rise to the need for legislation in the first place—permits, indeed invites, de facto nullification. . . .

There is a significant and growing sentiment in the legal community that arbitration is an inadequate enforcement mechanism for employees' statutory rights. Some focus on the procedural deficiencies in the arbitral process, stressing that arbitration is a privately created, do-it-yourself tribunal, which rarely provides rights to discovery, compulsory process, cross examination, or other due process protections common to civil trials. Thus, some claim, arbitration relegates workers to second-class justice.

Other critics focus on the privatization of disputes in arbitration. These critics argue that arbitral decisions are invisible documents—they do not receive media attention or public scrutiny and therefore engender no public debate. Arbitrators are not public officials, not accountable to a larger public, nor required to apply public law. And there is no legislative arena in which unpopular decisional trends can be challenged. Arbitration is a privatized forum, designed by the parties, and out of the public eye. . . .

The nature of the tribunal where suits are tried is an important part of the parcel of rights behind a cause of action. The change from a court of law to an arbitration panel may make a radical difference in ultimate result. Arbitration carries no right to trial by jury. . . . Arbitrators do not have the benefit of judicial instruction on the law; they need not give their reasons for their results; the record of their proceedings is not as complete as it is in a court trial; and judicial review of an award is more limited than judicial review of a trial. . . .

The state of labor and employment law today stands as a distorted reflection of that which existed one hundred years ago. In the past, workers had few workplace rights other than those they could secure and enforce through collective muscle and labor market power. Today, workers have many de jure rights, but often these rights cannot be enforced due to mandatory pre-dispute arbitration systems. . . . The result is a bitter irony for the worker—she has more rights and less protection than ever.

Samuel Estreicher, *Saturns for Rickshaws: The Stakes in the Debate over Predispute Employment Arbitration Agreements*
16 Oh. St. J. on Disp. Resol. 559, 563–64 (2001)

In a world without employment arbitration as an available option, we would essentially have a "cadillac" system for the few and a "rickshaw" system for the many. The unspoken (yet undeniable) truth is that most claims filed by employees do not attract the attention of private lawyers because the stakes are too small and outcomes too uncertain to warrant the investment of lawyer time and resources. These claims have only one place to go: filings with administrative agencies where they essentially languish, for the agencies themselves lack the staffing (and often even the inclination) to serve as lawyers for average claimants. The people who benefit under a litigation-based system are those whose salaries are high enough to warrant the costs and risks of a law suit undertaken by competent counsel; these are the folks who are likely to derive benefit from the considerable upside potential of unpredictable jury awards. Very few claimants, however, are able to obtain a position in the "litigation lottery."

Most plaintiff lawyers understandably value this system because it enables them to be highly selective about the cases they take on. Moreover, the sheer costs of defending a litigation and the risks of a jury trial create considerable settlement value irrespective of the substantive merits of the underlying claim. Thus, most cases where claimants obtain competent counsel will settle, and at sufficiently high values to give plaintiff lawyers ample economic rewards without actually having to try many law suits. Thus, the system works well for high-end claimants and most plaintiff lawyers, and not very well for average claimants.

A properly designed arbitration system, I submit, can do a better job of delivering accessible justice for average claimants than a litigation-based approach. It stands a better chance of providing Saturns for average claimants, in place of the rickshaws now available to the many so that a few can drive Cadillacs. Average claimants will benefit under an arbitration system because the lower costs of the forum also mean lower costs for their representatives (which could include unions). Moreover, unlike litigation where resolution often comes too late and the process itself is so divisive that reinstatement is rarely practicable, arbitration holds out the promise of a prompt resolution more suitable for claims by incumbent employees or even former employees truly desiring reinstatement.

Alexander J.S. Colvin & Kelly Pike, *Saturns and Rickshaws Revisited: What Kind of Arbitration System Has Developed?*
29 Oh. State J. on Disp. Res. 59, 59–62, 80–84 (2014)

In an influential 2001 article, Prof. Samuel Estreicher analogized employment arbitration to a "Saturn" system of justice, referring to the then prominent economy car line produced by General Motors. He contrasted this to the inequality in the employment litigation system, where a few who were successfully able to access it would receive a Cadillac system of justice with high levels of due process, whereas the larger group of employees who were unable to obtain access to the courts would be left with a Rickshaw system providing no effective access to justice for their claims.

Estreicher's argument resonates powerfully because it provides a positive public policy vision justifying the use of employment arbitration and guiding its development. It moves beyond the at times formalistic and simplified assumptions of many of the court decisions that led to the expanded deferral of the courts to arbitration. Rather than simply arguing that interpretation of the Federal Arbitration Act requires enforcement of arbitration agreements, Estreicher is arguing that as a matter of public policy we should be supporting the expansion of mandatory employer promulgated arbitration procedures because they will enhance the access by employees to justice in the workplace. If correct, this provides perhaps the strongest rationale for mandatory arbitration and should lead to both legislative and judicial actions directed at removing impediments to its adoption.

Estreicher was able to marshal some empirical evidence about employment arbitration in support of his argument. However, he was writing at a time when empirical research on employment arbitration was in its infancy with only a small number of researchers having examined relatively small samples of arbitration cases. During the 1990s when this early research was conducted, relatively fewer employers had yet adopted mandatory arbitration procedures and few cases had been heard in arbitration based on these employer promulgated procedures. Indeed, the larger number of employer arbitration cases during this period were based on individually negotiated agreements, typically involving higher level employees such as senior executives who are able to negotiate detailed individual contracts, often with the assistance of their own legal counsel.

Since that time, employer promulgated procedures have spread more widely and we have seen larger numbers of cases in arbitration based on these procedures. . . .

. . . With the availability of [larger scale datasets that feature cases based on employer promulgated procedures] . . . , we are able to revisit Estreicher's argument . . . .

[The authors describe data drawn from 449 employment arbitration cases administered by the AAA nationally and terminating in 2008, and detail the following findings for arbitrations held pursuant to employer-promulgated procedures: 83% of claimants earned less than $100,000 per year; the median claim was $167,880; the majority of cases involved statutory claims (54.1%); claimants were not represented by attorneys in 31.4% of claims (compared with just under 25% of plaintiffs in employment litigation); employers were much more likely than claimants to be represented by attorneys that specialized in employment law and by firms that handle employment arbitration cases frequently, yielding a "repeat player" effect; employment arbitration cases take approximately one year from claim to hearing (compared with two years for litigation cases to reach trial); the average arbitration takes 2.3 hearing days and the median arbitrator fee is $8,890; employees win 24.7% of the time, using a broad definition of "win" as including any degree of employer liability, even if the remedy awarded was significantly less than that sought; the median damage award in cases where employees prevailed was $39,609, and the average damage award across all cases involving employee claimants, won and lost, was $19,967; and attorney fees were awarded in 24% of the cases where there was an award of damages, with a typical fee of $51,710. Win rates were lowest in cases involving employment discrimination, but recoveries in successful cases were highest. *Id.* at 59–79].

Some aspects of the current employment arbitration system do accord with Estreicher's vision. The time it takes to get a hearing, while arguably still too long at around a year, is shorter than typical in the litigation system. The employees bringing claims under employer promulgated procedures are mostly of lower to middle income levels, earning less than $100,000 a year. Employees do win some cases, just under a quarter of all hearings, and recover some substantial damages, albeit the employee win rates and damage amounts are lower than those found in litigation cases that manage to get to the trial stage. Under the AAA's rules, employers are paying the arbitration fees, which at almost $10,000 per case could otherwise be a substantial barrier to access.

In other respects, however, the picture is less encouraging for Estreicher's vision of a simple, effective, and accessible system. The typical case in employer promulgated arbitration is a statutory claim based case with a fairly substantial damage claim of well over $100,000, which is the type of case we also typically see in litigation. There are relatively few of the smaller claims that are often seen as excluded from accessibility in the litigation system. Although a third of employees are going to arbitration pro se, not much higher than the one- quarter pro se rate seen in employment litigation, the majority of two-thirds of employees are proceeding in employment arbitration with representation from attorneys. Furthermore, the self-represented employees have lower success rates and receive much smaller damages. What we are seeing is in some ways a replication of the structure of the litigation system, where employees mostly need attorney representation to successfully proceed with claims.

It is also striking [how] the structural features of the litigation system . . . are replicated in arbitration. Settlement is the predominant mechanism for resolving cases in litigation, with a smaller number of cases being resolved on preliminary motions and relatively few proceeding to a hearing. Settlement is similarly the resolution mechanism for most cases in arbitration. The perennial problem of how to compare litigation and arbitration outcomes, given that different types of cases may proceed to a hearing, is exacerbated because most cases in both systems are resolved through private settlements where we have limited information on the outcomes. It may be that only the stronger cases in litigation end up going to trial, but it could also be that settlement exerts a similar filtering effect on the cases that proceed to a hearing in arbitration. One important structural difference that is often pointed to in litigation is the availability of summary judgment motions, which result in many cases being dismissed before trial, often to the defendant employer's advantage. Traditionally, summary judgment motions were seen as incompatible with the arbitral forum, where the opportunity to obtain a hearing on the merits of the case was seen as an important strength of the process. However, we find that summary judgment motions have become a feature of the employment arbitration process as well, with such motions being brought in a quarter of the cases we examined and most of these motions being successful. It appears that the idea of employment arbitration ensuring a claimant a hearing on the merits of the case is eroding.

A key aspect of accessibility is whether the costs of proceeding with a case through the system are low enough to be justifiable given the likely outcomes of the case. The criticism of litigation as a Cadillac system is grounded in the idea that this will only be true in the court system for a strong case with a relatively large damage claim. [But] . . . our results tell us [that under employer-promulgated procedures] . . . the average award across all cases . . . is just under $20,000. . . . Although we do not have direct evidence on [the costs of representation] . . . our results provide some suggestive parameters to work with. . . . [We find that] in most cases the cost of obtaining representation to proceed with a case in employment arbitration under employer promulgated procedures will outweigh the potential damages that can be expected to be recovered in these cases. . . .

. . . .

CONCLUSION

Overall, the system of employment arbitration under employer promulgated procedures appears to us to be strikingly similar to the litigation system in providing relatively little accessibility to employees who do not have strong cases and large provable damages. . . . Instead of a new Saturn system of justice, it appears that employment arbitration [has] become another Cadillac system for a few plaintiffs and another Rickshaw system for most employees who still do not have access to justice in employment disputes.

NOTES

1. **Privatizing Justice.** Stone argues that the privatization of public law through mandatory predispute arbitration agreements is especially troubling where the parties have unequal bargaining power. What, exactly, is she concerned about?

In a subsequent article, Stone elaborated on her argument, asserting that judicial deference to mandatory predispute arbitration is most troubling in situations where there is no shared normative community to facilitate self-regulation. This is so in the nonunion employment context, she explains, because employees do not participate in constructing the rules, norms and customs of the community; "[r]ather, the arbitration agreement [is] the ticket of entrance into the community." Katherine Van Wezel Stone, *Rustic Justice: Community and Coercion Under the Federal Arbitration Act*, 77 N.C.L. REV. 931, 1029–30 (1999). Does Estreicher provide a satisfactory answer to her concerns?

2. **Arbitration Outcomes and Workplace Justice.** Estreicher's argument is appealing because it offers a positive policy justification for arbitration as superior to litigation in affording employees access to a system of workplace justice. As Colvin notes, however, Estreicher's analysis was based upon early empirical research skewed toward arbitration results under individually-negotiated processes in which relatively highly-compensated employees were represented by counsel. The study results that Colvin reports are based upon a more representative database of AAA arbitrations terminating in 2008, of which roughly 72% were employer-promulgated procedure cases. While the earlier results on which Estre-

icher relied found an employee win rate of 63% in arbitration compared with a win rate of 14.9% in court, *see, e.g.*, Lewis Maltby, *Private Justice: Employment Arbitration and Civil Rights*, 30 COLUM. HUM. RTS. L. REV. 29, 46 (1998), Colvin's study found a 24.7% win rate in arbitration, compared with a 23.1% win rate in litigation (win rates in litigation were higher in states with employee-friendly legislation, such as California, where the win rates in litigation were 35.1%). Self-represented employees did particularly poorly in arbitration, enjoying only a 17% win rate and an $11,071 average recovery. Colvin & Pike, *Saturns and Rickshaws Revisited, supra*, at 74–76, 79–80. Although Colvin endeavored to control for merit of the claim, one possible explanation for these disparate results is that attorneys perform a screening function in litigation contexts, taking only cases that they evaluate as winnable and which have potential for relatively significant damage recoveries.

Note, however, that Colvin's own data establish that win rates in arbitration are slightly higher than win rates in litigation, even though employees are less likely to be represented by an attorney in arbitration than they are in litigation. Doesn't that undercut Colvin's conclusions? Does Estreicher's argument still have persuasive force?

3. A Self-Serving Judiciary? Do courts have a vested interest in routing employment claims away from the court system and into arbitration? David Schwartz thinks so. He argues that any employment dispute resolution system should be developed with input from all parties, through the political process:

> The problem with FAA arbitration is that an entire dispute resolution system, one that effectively works a major judicial reform, has been undertaken in a way that bypasses normal political processes. Courts have authorized defendants to create the system and write the rules subject to limited judicial oversight. Defendants can look after their interests in writing the contracts; courts have looked after their interests in docket control by the doctrine of vigorous enforcement of arbitration clauses. But the other side of the litigation—employees and consumers—has not had much of a seat at that table. Their interests have been accounted for only indirectly, filtered through the more "enlightened" arbitration vendors.
>
> . . . .
>
> [The courts] are not neutral arbiters of this controversy, but have a stake in promoting arbitration. Simply put, the FAA regime makes judges' lives easier by reducing their case loads, and more lucrative by giving them post-judicial career opportunities as arbitrators. They should not be entrusted with this important policy choice.

David S. Schwartz, *Mandatory Arbitration and Fairness*, 84 NOTRE DAME L. REV. 1247, 1339–1340 (2009). Do you agree? Is private judging in this context inconsistent with democracy? *See* Matthew W. Finkin, *Workplace Justice: Does Private Judging Matter?, available at* http://papers.ssrn.com/sol3/papers.cfm?abstract_id=2425717 (2014).

4. The Cost/Benefit Calculation for Employers. As Colvin notes, employment arbitration has become increasingly similar in structure and outcomes to litigation.

Does this help to explain why more employers have not adopted predispute arbitration policies?

Some companies, concerned about the number of claims filed and the rising cost of defending themselves against these claims in arbitration have substituted predispute "jury waivers" for arbitration clauses. In so doing, they hope to protect themselves from large damage awards; median awards after jury trials are 32% higher than those after bench trials. *See* Jane Spencer, *Waiving Your Right to a Jury Trial*, WALL ST. J., Aug. 17, 2004. Jury trial waivers are generally enforceable, but the waiver must be voluntary, knowing and intentional. *See* Jean Sternlight, *Mandatory Binding Arbitration and the Demise of the Seventh Amendment Right to a Jury Trial*, 16 OH. ST. J. ON DISP. RESOL. 669, 678–89 (2001). Alternatively, employers may include clauses that limit the filing of claims to courts in a particular venue that is perceived as business-friendly, and which may not be particularly convenient for most employees.

Many employers also use mediation as a precursor or complement to arbitration, rather than as an alternative. Even "unsuccessful" mediation processes can narrow the issues for arbitration, saving money and time. *See* Leslie A. Gordon, *Clause for Alarm: As Arbitration Costs Rise, In-House Counsel Turn to Mediation or a Combined Approach*, ABA J., Nov. 2006, at 19, 20. Others use a range of more informal conflict management systems that allow for intervention much earlier in the dispute resolution process, including open door policies, ombudspersons, peer review, and other conflict facilitation mechanisms. Thomas J. Stipanowich & J. Ryan Lamare, *Living with ADR: Evolving Perceptions and Use of Mediation, Arbitration, and Conflict Management in Fortune 1,000 Corporations*, 19 HARV. NEGOT. L. REV. 1, 41–44 (2013).

5. Legislative Reform? The Arbitration Fairness Act, introduced in Congress most recently in 2013, would amend the FAA to provide that "No predispute arbitration agreement shall be valid or enforceable if it requires arbitration of an employment dispute, consumer dispute, antitrust dispute, or civil rights dispute." Arbitration under collective bargaining agreements is exempted. *See* H.R. 1844, 113th Cong. (2013), S. 878, 113th Cong. (2013). The Act has not progressed in previous legislative sessions, and seems unlikely to gain traction in the future.

Zev Eigen, Nicholas Menillo and David Sherwin have proposed a Mandatory Arbitration Act that would retain the best aspects of arbitration (flexibility, speed, and reduced costs) while making it more difficult for exploitative employers to hide from the disciplining effect of public law; they would also impose a for-cause requirement for termination or severance pay in lieu of proof of cause. *See* Zev Eigen, Nicholas Menillo & David Sherwyn, *Shifting the Paradigm of the Debate: A Proposal to Eliminate At-Will Employment and Implement a "Mandatory Arbitration Act"*, 87 IND. L.J. 271 (2014). Jean Sternlight has proposed a system that she calls "governmental mandatory arbitration." Under this system, arbitration would be mandatory for employers, but not for workers; workers would choose whether to pursue claims through arbitration or litigation post-dispute. If they chose arbitration, companies would have to agree, and the results would then be binding on both parties. The parameters of the arbitration system would be spelled out by Congress in legislation. *See* Jean R. Sternlight, *In Defense of Mandatory*

Binding Arbitration (If Imposed on the Company), 8 NEV. L.J. 82, 85–87 (2007). Michael Green has proposed an amendment to Title VII to create a new defense to punitive damage claims for employers who offer to arbitrate disputes after they arise. *See* Michael Z. Green, *Debunking the Myth of Employer Advantage from Using Mandatory Arbitration for Discrimination Claims*, 31 RUTGERS L.J. 399, 468–70 (2000). Do these suggestions have any appeal?

Chapter 15

SELF-REGULATION

We began this course with a survey of the evolution of the law governing the employment relation, moving from freedom of contract to protection of the right to organize and collectively bargain, to regulatory regimes designed to ensure minimum standards in employment, to protection of individual rights against discrimination. It seems fitting to conclude with some thoughts about the direction in which current law now seems to be moving: toward a system of "monitored self-regulation," as Cynthia Estlund has dubbed it. *See* Cynthia Estlund, *Rebuilding the Law of the Workplace in an Era of Self-Regulation*, 105 COLUM. L. REV. 319, 324 (2005). The materials on arbitration as a workplace dispute mechanism in Chapter 14 provide a powerful illustration of this shift and its consequences.

As you read the materials that follow, consider the sociolegal forces that have combined to press the law in this direction (demographic, economic, political, and doctrinal). Are these forces shifting even as we ask this question? What directions do these shifts portend for the law of the workplace?

A. EMPLOYER SELF-REGULATION

Cynthia Estlund, *Rebuilding the Law of the Workplace in an Era of Self-Regulation*
105 COLUM. L. REV. 319, 320–26 (2005)

In workplaces around America, reform is in the air. Not, to be sure, "labor law reform" . . . the prospect of federal labor law reform of the sort long sought by organized labor and its allies is negligible. But another kind of workplace reform is gaining ground in some surprising places. For example, Wal-Mart, Inc., the world's largest private employer and reigning nemesis of organized labor and other employee advocates, recently announced the creation of a "Corporate Compliance team." Frustrated by labor and community opposition to its expansion plans and battered by legal challenges under wage and hour laws, immigration laws, labor laws, and discrimination laws—including the certification of an unprecedented multi-million member class action—the firm has vowed to use its legendary organizational capabilities, along with new technology and compensation policies, to become "a corporate leader in employment practices." According to the company, new software will ensure that workers are taking required breaks and not working "off the clock"; a new job classification and pay structure will ensure pay equity; and managers' compensation will reflect in part their achievement of "diversity goals."

What are we to make of Wal-Mart's vowing to reorganize itself into a model corporate citizen in its labor practices? Is this a superficial public relations gesture?

A genuine and public-spirited embrace of corporate responsibility? Or perhaps simply a rational set of precautions against future accidents and attendant liability? Are these measures diversionary tactics to be exposed and discounted, or do they show the law working just as it should by inducing compliance? Or do they represent something new and important in the evolution of the law of the workplace?

What is new lies not so much in Wal-Mart's organizational response to the external legal environment—the corporate compliance bandwagon has been on the road for some time—but in the interaction between the external law of the workplace and internal compliance programs like Wal-Mart's. Such programs are no longer merely compliance (or litigation avoidance) schemes instituted under the "shadow of the law." Rather, they seek to meet explicit demands of external law and to earn distinct legal benefits. The coordination of internal or self-regulatory compliance structures with the external law of the workplace has the potential to create new mechanisms for the enforcement of employee rights and labor standards—mechanisms that engage employees and revive the prospects for employee voice in the wake of declining unionization. But it also has the potential to divert crucial public resources from the task of securing compliance with public norms, and to enfeeble the few fearsome legal weapons that worker advocates have in their efforts to enforce basic employee rights and labor standards. It all depends.

To understand on what it depends, and to shape the divergent possibilities that are presented by the movement toward self-regulation in the workplace, it will be helpful to look back from whence it came. Self-regulation resonates with rather old ideas in workplace governance. The New Deal model of industrial relations, with its reliance on self-organization of workers and voluntary collective bargaining over most terms and conditions of employment, is itself a system of self-governance. As the New Deal model of industrial self-governance in the United States has grown old and ossified, however, the problems to which collective bargaining was to be the answer have not disappeared. Nor has the law ceased to grapple with them. On the contrary, the role of external law—of courts, of legislation, and of regulatory bodies—has burgeoned as the New Deal system of internalized lawmaking and dispute resolution has shrunk.

Since the 1960s, the New Deal collective bargaining system has been supplemented, and largely supplanted, by other models of workplace governance: a regulatory model of minimum standards enforceable mainly by administrative agencies and a rights model of judicially enforceable individual rights. The former is exemplified by the wage and hour laws and the Occupational Safety and Health Administration (OSHA); the latter, by the civil rights laws and the employee rights underlying the law of wrongful discharge. These two bodies of law, which make up much of what we call "employment law," each mobilized institutions and resources that were not central to the collective bargaining model constituted by "labor law." The regulatory model harnessed the coercive power and comprehensive reach of the government, while the rights model made courts central to the articulation and enforcement of employee rights, and tapped into the self-interest and indignation of aggrieved individuals and the professional and entrepreneurial energies of their attorneys.

Much as they resisted the constraints of collective bargaining, employers have fought back against the burdens of regulatory compliance and litigation; they have proclaimed the virtues of deregulation and the need to curb the "litigation crisis." But challenges to the efficacy of regulation and litigation of workplace rights and standards have come not only from employers, but from scholars and employee advocates as well. Observers from a range of perspectives have argued that the postwar regime of command-and-control regulation is losing its grip in the face of rapidly changing markets, technology, and firm structures; and that civil litigation is a costly, slow, and often inaccessible mechanism for securing workplace rights.

These critiques have begun to converge on the concept of self-regulation, and to make their mark on the external law of the workplace. Agencies responsible for enforcing labor standards have experimented with cooperative programs designed to bring about self-regulation and voluntary compliance. Courts responsible for enforcing employee rights have begun to formalize the role of internal compliance procedures, and to defer to private dispute resolution schemes (including arbitration), according employers a partial shield against litigation and liability based on those schemes. These developments bring the locus of enforcement of both rights and regulations inside the firm or under the firm's control. The internal compliance regimes of Wal-Mart and many other employers must be seen in that light: as efforts not simply to comply with the law but to secure the legal advantages of self-regulation and to erect a partial shield against regulatory and judicial intervention.

The move away from command and control, and toward more and less regulated versions of self-regulation, has swept across a wide range of regulatory arenas in recent decades. Detractors see in these moves toward self-regulation a disguised form of deregulation. Proponents see the evolution of more efficient and effective systems for enforcing legal norms. Much turns on how self-regulation works—what standards of efficacy and what institutional safeguards regulators require of self-regulating firms. In the workplace setting in particular, much turns on whether employees themselves play an effective part in firms' self-regulation of their labor practices. Regulatory theory and experience teach that effective self-regulation in the workplace should be "tripartite" in structure: It requires the participation of the government, the regulated firm, and the workers for whose benefit the relevant legal norms exist. Self-regulatory processes in which workers participate can introduce flexibility and responsiveness into the regulatory regime, and can reduce the costs and contentiousness associated with litigation, while promoting the internalization of public law norms into the workplace itself.

The problem, of course, is that the move toward self-regulation has coincided with a drastic decline in unionization, the only legally sanctioned vehicle in the United States for employee representation within the firm. Even apart from the trend toward self-regulation, both employee rights and workplace regulations are often underenforced in the absence of union representation, especially where employers are committed to competing through the minimization of labor costs. The movement toward self-regulation, and the attendant retreat of public agencies and of courts from the front lines of enforcement, exacerbates this vulnerability. Yet the prospects for reviving and dramatically extending the New Deal collective bargaining model seem bleak.

The story so far—like many labor law stories these days—threatens to become a lamentation: The same relentless forces of capital and competition that have eroded unionization have led employers to push for the internalization and domestication of both rights and regulatory enforcement. That process of internalization exacerbates the vulnerability of employees who lack a collective voice within firms, and threatens to collapse into deregulation. That is the fatalistic version of the story.

I aim instead to retell the story as one of possibility. The movement of employment law and its enforcement inside firms creates not only the need, but also the opportunity to revive employees' voice inside firms. That is because the law can and does impose conditions on firms' ability to secure the legal advantages of self-regulation—conditions that aim to ensure the efficacy of self-regulation. . . . [O]ne of those conditions could and should be the effective participation of the employees whose rights and working conditions are at stake. The challenge is to reconfigure [this system] for the overwhelmingly nonunion environment that exists, and is likely to persist, in the United States. . . .

At the center of the constellation [of actors and mechanisms involved in self-regulation] are independent monitors who oversee the self-regulatory system and safeguard its integrity. Monitors who are independent of employers and accountable to workers and the public can both leverage limited public enforcement resources and serve some of the watchdog functions that employees in the nonunion setting cannot do alone. Outside monitors can also help to give voice to employees themselves, who are in the best position to monitor employer compliance with the labor and employment laws. The periodic presence of independent monitors inside the workplace represents a small but tangible breach of employer sovereignty over the workplace, and may help dispel the fear that inhibits both employees' participation in law enforcement and their impulses toward self-organization. Independent monitoring of workplaces can give voice to workers by serving both as a conduit for what they know, and as protection against employer reprisals. Alongside independent monitors and individual employee whistleblowers, employees and their private attorneys also play important roles, both in bolstering the efforts of public agencies and in ensuring against their capture. The existence of private rights of action is thus a key component of monitored self-regulation. Indeed, through private rights of action it may be possible to induce firms to enter into monitored self-regulation even without direct state enforcement.

My aim here is to chart a strategy for reforming the law of the workplace that straddles the conventional divide between labor law and employment law—one that finds footholds within employment law for the pursuit of the core normative commitment of New Deal labor law to workplace democracy. It is grounded in the observation that workers' freedom of association and self-determination are not only of intrinsic value in a democratic society—that proposition has been much mooted and will not be further elaborated upon here—but of instrumental value in realizing the rights and the regulatory norms governing the workplace. That is especially true in an era of self-regulation, in which the locus of enforcement is moving inside the workplace and away from direct public oversight. Giving employees an institutionalized role in self-regulatory processes will help both to make rights more real and regulatory standards more effective, and also to rebuild mechanisms for effective worker participation in self-governance. In other words, the models of workplace governance that have emerged in the wake of the decline of the collective bargaining model can be both improved by and turned to the cause of promoting democratic self-governance within the workplace.

Susan Sturm, *Second Generation Employment Discrimination: A Structural Approach*
101 COLUM. L. REV. 458, 475–76, 479, 492–99, 521–22, 527–28, 530, 533 (2001)

The architecture of a multi-sector regulatory system for addressing second generation workplace problems is emerging through the interplay among the judiciary, workplaces, and nongovernmental actors playing an intermediary role. . . . Responsive employers have instituted internal systems for preventing and remedying problems stemming from complex workplace relationships. These systems develop the information and capacity necessary to understand the nature of the problem, respond at the appropriate organizational level to remedy it, and learn from previous problem-solving efforts. These pathbreaking organizations demonstrate that internal dispute resolution and problem-solving systems can be robust, if they are designed to provide for accountability and effectiveness. . . .

Deloitte & Touche, America's third largest accounting, tax, and management consulting firm, implemented a major Women's Initiative that dramatically increased women's advancement in the company and reduced the turnover rate of women in particular and employees in general. The firm accomplished this by forming ongoing, participatory task forces with responsibility for determining the nature and cause of a gender gap in promotion and turnover, making recommendations to change the conditions underlying these patterns, developing systems to address those problems and to make future patterns transparent, and monitoring the results. The task force recommendations were implemented through ongoing data gathering and analysis, operational change through line management, and accountability in relation to benchmarks.

The Women's Initiative resulted not from the threat of litigation, but rather from the CEO's perception that a gender gap in the promotion and turnover rate signaled a problem with the firm's capacity to compete effectively for talent. In 1991, Mike Cook, Chairman and CEO of Deloitte & Touche, discovered that, although Deloitte had been hiring women at an aggressive rate—50% or more—for more than ten years, the rate of promotion hovered at around 10%. The data also revealed "a significant and growing gap in turnover" between the percentage of women and men. . . .

In response to this problem, Deloitte's Board established the Task Force on Retention and Advancement of Women. Cook charged the Task Force with the mission of explaining the high turnover rate for women, and figuring out how to reverse the trend. He was careful to include a cross-section of the organization that was diverse based on age, sex, geography, department, and family status. The CEO chaired the Task Force and attended all of its meetings.

The Task Force began by analyzing the personnel records for the previous three years to identify overall patterns in hiring, promotion, and retention. This analysis revealed that, "although men and women left the firm in roughly equal numbers at the entry level, at higher and higher levels, women were leaving at an ever-increasing rate." The Task Force then hired a nonprofit research organization, called Catalyst, to help the members to understand better the problem and how to respond. . . . The Task Force incorporated Catalyst's findings into its report, which identified three obstacles to the advancement and retention of women:

(1) "A male-dominated culture, particularly in senior leadership and partner positions, which perpetuated stereotypes and assumptions about women";

(2) "Built in systems for advancement—mentoring, coaching, counseling, networking—that worked for the men didn't work for the women";

(3) "A company-wide need for a more balanced work-life approach."

The Task Force presented these findings, along with preliminary recommendations for addressing the problems, to the Management Committee in January, 1993. . . . In April of 1993, the firm's CEO held a press conference to announce the Initiative for the Retention and Advancement of Women. He also announced the formation of an external advisory group, the "Council on the Advancement of Women," which would meet quarterly to monitor the firm's performance with respect to the Women's Initiative and to continue to push for change. The Council's members included highly visible business and public figures; Lynn Martin, the former Secretary of Labor and head of the Glass Ceiling Commission, was appointed chair. The firm also created an internal Task Force on the Retention and Advancement of Women, headed by a respected partner who served on the initial task force that studied the problem and developed recommendations. Deloitte created a full time position of chief of staff for national human resources (HR), which served as a liaison between the women's initiative and HR. The Task Force undertook the process of translating Catalysts' findings into an agenda for change.

Three basic principles guided the implementation process. First, line management, rather than Human Resources, would drive the operational changes. Second, accountability and commitment had to be expressed both internally and externally to assure follow-through. Finally, an accountability structure was developed to make the Women's Initiative matter to each partner's success. Responsibility for implementing the changes was decentralized to each individual office. . . .

One of the key issues addressed by the Task Force was the assignment process. . . . At th[e] time, the assignment process was not clearly defined, and the assignment directors acted largely on their own. The Task Force audited the assignment process—how assignments were made, who was considered, what criteria were used, what results emerged, and whether gender bias existed. "The Task Force found that on the accounting side, women's assignments tended to be clustered in not-for-profit companies, health care, and retail. . . . Women were rarely assigned to such high-potential areas as mergers and acquisitions."

One of the changes instituted by the Task Force was to make the process and its results visible by instituting annual assignment reviews. These reviews required office managing partners to list the nature and quantity of the assignments, who got the best ones, and how that broke down by gender. Until then, many offices had no idea that disparities existed.

The Task Force also adopted changes to make flexible work arrangements viable without threatening an individual's advancement. This was done by calibrating the timing of promotion decisions based on experience and performance, and following through in partnership decisions . . . [and] reduc[ing] the amount of time that Deloitte consultants would be on the road. The Task Force reviewed every policy to identify and minimize gender bias. The Initiative also introduced succession and formal career planning for women. The process encouraged the formation of women's management groups, "in which women would assemble to identify issues in their own offices, as well as to provide another opportunity for networking." . . .

The Women's Initiative produced swift and observable results, both in women's participation and in the firm's overall retention rate. The combination of increased communication and programmatic change contributed to what many called a culture change. Flexible work has become acceptable at Deloitte for women and men. "By 1995, 23% of senior managers were women, the percentage of women admitted to partner rose from 8% in 1991 to 21%; the turnover rate for female senior managers dropped from 26% to 15%." In 1993, the U.S. firm had 88 women partners; in 1999, the total was 246. The turnover rate fell for both men and women between 1995 and 1998. Cook credits his firm's thirty percent growth rate in 1999, the best among the "Big Five [accounting firms]," to lower turnover. Deloitte's success has attracted attention and awards, and has itself become an effective recruitment tool.

The Deloitte & Touche story illustrates one method of building accountability and ongoing adaptation into an internal problem-solving system—a method that fit its project-oriented work ethic. The company institutionalized a change process by creating a combination of inside and outside deliberative groups comprised of diverse stakeholders and then investing those groups with the legitimacy, capacity, and resources to solve problems effectively. The internal problem-solving group included key partners with local knowledge of the dynamics and culture of the firm and the skills needed to uncover root causes of the gender gap. The composition of the group itself linked the concerns of equity and effectiveness, by bringing together people concerned with women's participation and those concerned with more general personnel issues. This permitted the group to address both gender dynamics and broader concerns made visible by their particularly strong impact on women. . . .

Significantly, the group involved outsiders with expertise and legitimacy, such as Catalyst and the Center for Gender in Organizations, which provided the information and processes needed to develop workable (and revisable) solutions. These outsiders were effective boundary negotiators who could place the firm's experience in a broader context and help to identify recurring patterns. The company's external advisory group, with its highly visible, credible, and public participants, provided a continual source of reflection, and protected the process from internal capture.

The process also created a constituency for change, both inside and outside the organization. Women developed an internal (and external) presence and a vehicle for expressing their concerns as a group. This enabled women who were reluctant to raise concerns individually to participate without creating an adversarial relationship with the firm or risking their personal position. The problem-solving process created an immediate and direct focus for women's (and men's) concerns, which provided incentives for collective action. This in turn helped constitute this group as an internal source of accountability. . . .

. . . [L]aw interacted with internal change initiatives in both complementary and contradictory ways. It served as a catalyst, and provided legitimacy, clout, and regular consideration for human resource concerns that are typically neglected or undervalued. At the same time, however, "legal" sometimes came to symbolize the risk involved in taking proactive steps to address problems with legal implications. Law helped make the vocabulary of norms a part of the day-to-day language of the workplace, and to inject normative considerations into decisions about how to structure the day-to-day operations of the business. But it also threatened to relegate these same concerns to the category of liability avoidance and thus marginalize both their ethical and economic dimensions. Law encouraged the development of internal systems of accountability, even as it sometimes stifled creativity and risk-taking out of concern that revealing problems or mistakes would fuel legal "punishment." In [the Deloitte & Touche example], individual and organizational intermediaries played a crucial role in mediating this tension between the coercive and aspirational character of law. . . .

Creative lawyers on both sides of the employment discrimination divide also play an important role as catalysts, poolers of information, and sources of accountability. . . . The evolution of the role of plaintiffs' counsel who function as repeat players in structural reform regimes is particularly striking. The involvement of plaintiffs' counsel in the negotiation of [consent decrees in litigated cases] illustrates this development. The . . . Saperstein, Goldstein, Demchak, & Baller [firm] is one of the nation's most successful firms handling plaintiffs' discrimination cases. . . . Barry Goldstein . . . spent years at the NAACP Legal Defense and Educational Fund litigating employment discrimination cases before he joined the firm. . . .

Goldstein employs a problem-oriented approach to case investigation and selection. The firm has developed substantial capacity to identify employment patterns within a sector of the economy, and to generate hypotheses about why women or people of color fare less well in that sector. It has also developed a network of experts in various fields and disciplines, enabling the lawyers to facilitate interdisciplinary teams for both problem identification and remedial development. They conduct a substantial investigation to develop and test their causal hypotheses prior to determining whether to pursue litigation or settlement. This approach has enabled them to get to know patterns in particular industries, and to use their knowledge and position as repeat players to translate and apply changes from one company to another.

. . . Once settlement negotiations [in litigated cases begin] in earnest, Goldstein . . . [effectively deploys his] tremendous credibility as a result of his track record, his knowledge derived from years of experience addressing companies' human resource practices, and his appreciation of the importance of designing a system that would be consistent with [the firm's] culture, mission, and economic goals. . . . [H]is role [is] to help structure a process for developing a system that would work, that would be sufficiently transparent so that the information would provide a continual check on the process, and that would institutionalize regular occasions for evaluating the system's effectiveness. . . .

Employee groups operating both within and across workplace boundaries provide another important source of accountability, information sharing, and pressure to adopt equitable employment practices. This role has not been widely embraced by many traditional unions, many of which themselves have had a history of excluding women, immigrants, and people of color. However, new forms of worker organization, both union and nonunion, have emerged as potential catalysts for improving access, knowledge, opportunity, and decisionmaking within workplaces.

. . . Some companies have encouraged formation of employee identity groups, and they have included them as key participants in developing and monitoring innovations designed to address bias. For example, at Deloitte & Touche, networks of female managers have developed both within the company and among professional women within the local business community. These groups help identify issues of shared concern, evaluate the effectiveness of internal initiatives, and design effective strategies for new types of problems. Management's adoption of problem-solving processes to address diversity and inclusion itself encouraged the formation of these groups, which then provide an important source of accountability for those same processes as long as the groups maintain financial and substantive independence.

NOTES

1. **Examples of Employer Self-Regulation.** Estlund discusses several examples of employer self-regulation instituted as a "shield against litigation and liability," including progressive discipline systems to ward off wrongful discharge claims; adoption of affirmative action programs designed to enhance workforce diversity and ensure compliance with Title VII; the implementation of internal reporting systems to address sexual harassment in the workplace (which serves as a defense to liability under *Faragher v. City of Boca Raton*, 524 U.S. 775 (1998) and *Burlington Industries v. Ellerth*, 524 U.S. 742 (1998)); the development of private dispute resolution systems including—though not limited to—arbitration; and cooperative relations with governmental agencies like OSHA that are interested in enhancing their enforcement efforts through incentivizing voluntary compliance with the law. Can you think of other examples that we have studied? Does the efficacy of such self-regulatory reforms turn upon whether they are instituted in response to a lawsuit or independent of one? What is the role of judicial oversight in maintaining their efficacy?

2. **Law's Deterrent Function.** Is the move toward using law as a carrot and/or a stick to incentivize compliance and punish noncompliance in the employment realm any different than the way that law functions in other areas of law? Should it be regarded differently here? Why or why not?

Within the employment realm, does law's deterrent and incentive function differently with regard to corporate efforts to eradicate discrimination like those that Sturm describes than it does with respect to enforcement of wage and hour laws? Other than concerns with legal liability, do employers have affirmative interests in eradicating discrimination and promoting diversity in the workforce? What are they? Do they have affirmative interests (aside from avoiding legal liability) in ensuring payment of minimum wages and overtime pay? What would those interests be? Are the interests in each case consistent or inconsistent with a goal of profitability?

3. Conditions for Success. In the excerpt from Sturm's article, can you identify the conditions necessary for successful implementation of the workplace reform initiatives that she discusses? What are her criteria for measuring change? Sturm cautions against the possibility of changes that lack meaning or are primarily for symbolic purposes:

> Recent scholarship has drawn attention to the risk that employers will adopt legalistic, sham, or symbolic internal processes that leave underlying patterns of bias unchanged. This literature brings to the surface serious questions about the legitimacy, accountability, and effectiveness of workplace dispute resolution and problem-solving systems. What will prevent the adoption of sham or purely symbolic processes that leave the status quo intact? What keeps these processes from simply replicating the power dynamics that produced the complaints about harassment in the first place? Will these processes become captive to managerial concerns that may be inconsistent with legal aspirations? Much of the scholarship on workplace dispute resolution has evaluated internal dispute resolution processes in the aggregate, without attempting to distinguish the impact of different types of internal processes. Yet, internal dispute resolution processes vary widely in their features and effectiveness. In part because of the reluctance of many companies to open up their internal processes to scrutiny, most scholars have not analyzed particular dispute resolution or problem-solving processes in depth to begin to differentiate between robust and sham processes.

Sturm, *supra*, at 490–91. How does one ensure the process is accountable?

4. The Role of Independent Monitors. Estlund suggests that Wal-Mart's organizational response to pending class litigation contains the seeds of a self-regulatory compliance structure with "potential to create new mechanisms for the enforcement of employee rights and labor standards—mechanisms that engage employees and revive the prospects for employee voice in the wake of declining unionization." *Id.* at 321. These possibilities will be realized, she argues, only if the new self-regulatory system features independent monitors who can be trusted to oversee the system, safeguard its integrity, and serve as watchdogs for the vast majority of workers who no longer have unions to perform this role. Individual employee whistleblowers and the plaintiffs' bar are thus critical players in ensuring that the external law continues to structure employer efforts at self-regulation.

Suppose that Estlund's recommendations were taken to heart. Who might perform the monitoring role? What about unions, would they be interested in serving as monitors in appropriate cases? Would employers be receptive to their appointment? What about worker centers and advocacy groups that promote the particular interests of low-wage workers, women or minorities? *See* Janice Fine & Jennifer Gordon, *Strengthening Labor Standards Enforcement Through Partnership and Workers' Organization*, 38 POLITICS & SOC'Y 552, 559, 561 (2010) (suggesting deputizing nonprofit advocacy groups and unions to inspect workplaces to detect violations). What about academics or consultants with expertise in the area, would they likely be effective? In a settlement of a class action sex discrimination claim by female financial advisors against Smith Barney, the parties proposed and the court approved appointment of an industrial psychologist charged with devising new procedures to guard against gender bias in compensation, distribution of accounts, partnerships, and other business opportunities. *See Federal Judge OKs $33 Million Settlement in Suit Alleging Sex Bias by Smith Barney*, DAILY LAB. REP. (BNA) No. 157, Aug. 14, 2008 (describing settlement in *Amochaev v. CitiGroup Global Markets, Inc.*, No. 05-cv-01298-PJH (N.D. Cal. Aug. 13, 2008)).

Sturm mentions plaintiffs' counsel as possible sources of accountability, particularly where they function as repeat players litigating against an industry or a particular practice (consider, for example, the role of plaintiffs' lawyers in intern litigation; one firm has been particularly active in these suits, and has developed significant experience with the practice of internships). How effective do you think the firm might be in constructing a system that would institutionalize the benefits gained through litigation? Michael Selmi is skeptical; he contends that class action litigation in the discrimination context is unduly focused on providing monetary compensation for past discrimination rather than seeking forward-looking institutional reform, that there is precious little judicial oversight of settlements, that incentive structures for attorneys do not encourage monitoring post-settlement, and that monitoring by task forces has been largely a form of whitewashing to enhance the public image of the corporation, with no real incentive for substantive reform. Michael Selmi, *The Price of Discrimination: The Nature of Class Action Employment Discrimination Litigation and its Effects*, 81 TEX. L. REV. 1249 (2003).

5.   **Back to the Future?** Estlund references the arguments made by detractors regarding private law systems that function as substitutes for public law. Several of these commentators have argued that the shift toward employer self-regulation and increased reliance upon private dispute resolution systems amounts to a "resurrect[ion of] 'freedom of contract' principles" reminiscent of the *Lochner* era. *See, e.g.*, Kathryn A. Sabbeth & David C. Vladeck, *Contracting (out) Rights*, 36 FORDHAM URB. L.J. 803, 805–08 (2009); Richard A. Bales, *The Laissez-Faire Arbitration Market and the Need for a Uniform Federal Standard Governing Employment and Consumer Arbitration*, 52 KAN. L. REV. 583, 584 (2004). Can you think of doctrines or cases we have studied that seem heavily influenced by Lochnerian values? Why is the freedom of contract imagery so powerful in American law?

What would be wrong with a return to a freedom of contract regime?

B.   WORKER REPRESENTATION AND SELF-GOVERNANCE

In the previous section, Cynthia Estlund argued that the shift toward self-regulation has hopeful possibilities for reviving worker voice mechanisms inside companies that could function as union substitutes: watchdogs for workers' rights, and conduits for workers' voice. Estlund, *supra*, at 324–25. Sturm suggested a variety of forms that worker representation might assume, including identity groups, nonprofit organizations working with employees, and of course, unions.

Why is worker participation and voice in the regulation of the workplace so important? What pragmatic effects does it have? What values does it further? *See* CYNTHIA ESTLUND, REGOVERNING THE WORKPLACE: FROM SELF-REGULATION TO CO-REGULATION (2010).

This section surveys a few of the nontraditional forms that employee participation in workplace governance has assumed: identity caucuses, workers' centers, employee involvement mechanisms, and works councils modeled on the EU system. Which forms do you think would be most effective in furthering the goals served by worker participation, and why?

1.   Identity Caucuses and Worker Centers

Unlike traditional unions, which rely upon solidarity predicated on common class and occupational characteristics, identity caucuses are based on common interests arising out of social identities that transcend the workplace. Initially worksite-based organizations, such caucuses have evolved into nationwide constituency groups, some of which are affiliated with the AFL-CIO (examples include the Coalition of Black Trade Unionists, the Labor Council on Latin American Advancement, the Coalition of Labor Union Women, the Asian Pacific American Labor Alliance, and Pride At Work). These groups press existing labor unions to respond to the interests of their constituencies. *See* Ruben J. Garcia, *New Voices at Work: Race and Gender Identity Caucuses in the U.S. Labor Movement*, 54 HASTINGS L.J. 79 (2002).

Some caucuses have been successful in directly challenging workplace discrimination and changing employer practices, often by invoking statutory rights and utilizing litigation as the leverage to advance their constituents' interests. *See* Michael J. Yelnosky, *Title VII, Mediation, and Collective Action*, 1999 U. ILL. L. REV. 583, 615–17. Because caucuses are not constrained by majoritarian interests in the same way that unions are, such activities do not create the same conflicts of interest that they might in the union context. Nevertheless, caucus activities may risk heightening inter-group conflict among workers and could interfere with the formation of bonds of class solidarity among workers. On the other hand, caucuses might serve as "waystations" for employees not yet ready to unionize, offering them the opportunity to develop a "taste for collective action." *See id.* at 619.

Alternatively, community-based membership organizations known as worker centers have sprung up to organize workers at a grassroots level. Worker centers are nonprofit organizations committed to building democratic organizations that are accountable to the interests, needs, and goals of the workers being organized. They emphasize that the workers themselves must assume leadership roles in organizing and transform themselves from victims to advocates. Workers typically serve on the organizations' boards of directors, participate in making strategy decisions in organizing campaigns, plan demonstrations, raise funds and speak to the press. *See* Jennifer Gordon, *We Make the Road by Walking: Immigrant Workers, the Workplace Project, and the Struggle for Social Change*, 30 HARV. C.R.-C.L. L. REV. 407 (1995). Worker centers are particularly effective in immigrant communities, where workers tend to live in close proximity to one another and work in similar service jobs that systematically exploit the workers' undocumented status and lack of familiarity with U.S. laws and the English language. These organizations provide the foundation for labor union organizing, but do not themselves seek to supplant labor unionism; indeed, they often collaborate with unions. *See generally* JANICE FINE, WORKER CENTERS: ORGANIZING COMMUNITIES AT THE EDGE OF THE DREAM (2006); JENNIFER GORDON, SUBURBAN SWEATSHOPS: THE FIGHT FOR IMMIGRANT RIGHTS (2005).

Worker centers have been increasingly active in assisting workers with filing claims in court, and have achieved some measure of success particularly in wage and hour claims. *See* Steven Greenhouse, *A Union in Spirit: Worker Centers Bring Together Immigrants Where Traditional Labor Hasn't. The Result? Back Pay, Rest Breaks and Self-Respect*, N.Y. TIMES, Aug. 11, 2013. By 2013, there were at least 139 worker centers in 32 states. Gayle Cinquegiani, *House Republicans Ask Perez to Clarify LMRDA Filing Terms for Worker Centers*, DAILY LAB. REP. (BNA) No. 148, Aug. 1, 2013.

A vexing challenge for all of these groups is how to leverage worker power to accomplish change. Workers' social power may be negligible where workers are fungible, employers are mobile or enjoy the economic resources to outlast a strike, or where legal strategies are available to outmaneuver worker activism—for example, where workers are undocumented. Thus, although identity caucuses and worker centers may offer extraordinary potential to articulate workers' collective voice, their prospects as economic empowerment devices are less certain. Can the goal of furthering workers' voice be separated from the substantive goal of economic empowerment? Should the priority be simply maximizing voice, or maximizing voice with an eye toward leveraging power?

The dilemma is particularly well-illustrated in situations where government agencies and legal advocacy groups for immigrant and ethnic workers have effectively become workers' representatives in the absence of a union presence. As union density has declined, low-wage service workers have increasingly been represented by some combination of unions, government or public officials, legal advocacy groups, and immigrant or ethnic groups. These groups then "negotiate" agreements with employers who consistently violate employment laws, using waivers of prosecution of previous violations as leverage to obtain the agreement. The advocacy efforts that produced the New York City Greengrocer Code of Conduct are illustrative. The New York State Attorney General's office agreed to refrain from investigating past violations of state employment laws if the small grocers that populate New York City agreed to the "Greengrocer Code of Conduct." The Code established minimum terms and conditions for employment, including provisions regarding pay and sick and vacation leave. Some of the terms simply replicated the existing law regarding minimum wage and overtime, but other terms went beyond existing law, including establishing sick leave and vacation benefits for workers employed for more than a year. Grocers who signed the Code were immune from prosecution for past state law violations but not from any future violations. The signatories also agreed to unannounced monitoring by an independent company. Part of the motive for the Code was a sense that many of the grocers, who were predominantly Korean immigrants, were unfamiliar with the laws. *See* Alan Hyde, *Who Speaks for the Working Poor?: A Preliminary Look at the Emerging Tetralogy of Representation of Low-Wage Service Workers*, 13

CORNELL J. L. & PUB. POL'Y 599, 603–606 (2004). For a thorough discussion of the Code's provisions, see Matthew T. Bodie, *The Potential for State Labor Law: The New York Greengrocer Code of Conduct*, 21 HOFSTRA LAB. & EMP. L.J. 183 (2003).

Alan Hyde is critical of the process that produced the Greengrocer Code because the collaborations between advocacy groups and governmental officials who took the laboring oars on the Code are fragile and fail to institutionalize a vehicle for worker voice that would leverage workers' collective power in the future. He writes:

> . . . [R]esolution [of the workers' claims] has largely been driven by the alliance between legal or ethnic advocacy groups and governmental entities like the State Attorney General or City Council. The advocacy groups are self-designated. Nobody elected them and they are not responsible to anyone. They have no legal basis to compel their own recognition. Consequently, their legitimacy depends on their ability to extract benefits from government, and they must accept relatively small amounts. The governmental entities, in turn, seem largely motivated by some public officials' desire for a favorable image as friends of poor workers. They have no institutional capacity or interest in creating or sustaining systems of representation that will survive the particular advocacy campaign in which they are involved. . . .

Hyde, *supra*, at 613. Hyde faults the New York City labor unions that might have organized the workers for passivity and ineffective strategies, and observes that the signing of the Code seems to have halted any nascent union organizing drives. *Id.* at 605. He worries that unless new worker organizations can institutionalize themselves as unions can, and thus provide continuing representation, workers' rights will be subject to the political whims of the Attorney General. *See* Alan Hyde, *New Institutions for Worker Representation in the United States: Theoretical Issues*, 50 N.Y.L. SCH. L. REV. 385, 401–02 (2005–06).

On the other hand, Cynthia Estlund characterizes the Greengrocer Code as "a step toward employee empowerment" because the Code provides for independent monitors who are accountable to the employee advocacy organizations and to the Attorney General. Monitors, she explains, "multiply regulatory eyes within the workplace" and meetings between monitors and workers afford workers "not a collective voice, [but] at least a chance of exercising their individual voices," ultimately "formalizing and protecting employee whistleblowing." Cynthia Estlund, *Rebuilding the Law of the Workplace in an Era of Self-Regulation*, 105 COLUM. L. REV. 319, 373 (2005).

Are collaborations between advocacy groups and government officials like the one that produced the Greengrocer Code dangerous illusions, or steps along the road to employee representation? Are they better than nothing, or worse than nothing? If they are worse than nothing, what are the alternatives? More vigorous unionism? More advantageous deals for workers forged by other advocacy organizations with more leverage? What about a system in which employers might receive a designation or label that would signal to consumers their progressive social values, including providing well-paying jobs and benefits? *See* Michael Selmi, *Hostess and the Search for Workplace Dignity*, 52 WASHBURN L.J. 517 (2013) (arguing for the development of a "Humanely Produced" label requiring certification related to progressive workplace policies).

Some commentators worry that where worker centers or advocacy groups become too effective, they will be categorized as "labor organizations" and subjected to restrictions on picketing and boycott activities under the NLRA. *See* David Rosenfeld, *Worker Centers: Emerging Labor Organizations—Until They Confront the National Labor Relations Act*, 27 BERKELEY J. EMP. & LAB. L. 469 (2006). We explore issues relating to the NLRA as an impediment to alternative vehicles for collective voice further below.

2.   Employer-Initiated Vehicles for Collective Voice

A number of employers—both unionized and nonunionized—have instituted employee involvement ("EI") programs. Most EI programs are initiated in an effort to increase productivity and/or quality in response to global competition. EI programs generally fall into one of four categories: (1) production and quality-centered initiatives, usually called "quality circles," in which supervisors solicit and review employee suggestions for improving quality and efficiency; (2) "total quality management" teams, another form of production and quality-centered initiative which features blurred status distinctions between managers and employees; (3) job enrichment and redesign programs, which take the form of innovations in work organization that are more holistic, allowing workers to obtain skill training or to be involved in the production of the entire product rather than one isolated aspect of it; and (4) workplace committees and partnerships, structured as cooperative ventures in which managers and employees meet to discuss shared concerns, ranging from health and safety issues to issues of worker satisfaction. The common denominator of all EI programs is the conceptualization of the workplace as collaborative and of management-employee relationships as cooperative rather than adversarial. In this sense, they are fundamentally at odds with the NLRA, which presupposes an adversarial, arm's-length relationship between the employer and its employees. *See* Johanna Oreskovic, *Capturing Volition Itself: Employee Involvement and the TEAM Act*, 19 BERKELEY J. EMP. & LAB. L. 229, 248–52 (1998).

The NLRA is hostile to such programs where they trench upon traditional collective bargaining functions performed by labor unions. The rationale for the Act's hostility to them is that they offer a promise of workplace democracy and worker participation and power that is largely illusory, engendering "false consciousness." If employer and worker interests are at odds, then emphasizing "cooperation" risks cloaking the reality of the adverse interests in attractive, but ultimately false, garb. "Employee involvement" is not necessarily the equivalent of workplace democracy. On the other hand, proponents of EI programs ask, why should we question workers' choice of vehicles for voice? If workers choose not to unionize, why should they be denied this alternative avenue for voice, especially where the alternative is no voice at all?

EI programs have been shown to improve workers' affective response to work. Benefits for employers include higher productivity (as much as 2 to 5% improvement), enhanced morale and commitment to the firm, and lower turnover. EI programs also reduce the desire to unionize. *See* RICHARD B. FREEMAN & JOEL

ROGERS, WHAT WORKERS WANT 105, 108, 113–14 (1999). Although most EI programs focus initially on production or quality issues, they frequently expand to encompass topics traditionally dealt with in collective bargaining: wages, hours, and conditions of employment. Some commentators are convinced that modern employers deliberately utilize EI programs as a sophisticated anti-union tool, hoping to supplant collective bargaining with a system that offers management the opportunity to exercise more control over front-line workers and to increase demands regarding job performance. *See, e.g.*, Michael C. Harper, *The Continuing Relevance of § 8(a)(2) to the Contemporary Workplace*, 96 MICH. L. REV. 2322, 2338 (1998). A study by the Economic Policy Institute in 2009, however, indicated that employers' use of EI programs as a union-avoidance device have been gradually decreasing. Kate Bronfenbrenner, *No Holds Barred: The Intensification of Employer Opposition to Organizing*, 235 ECON. POL'Y INST. BRIEFING PAPER 14, 24 (2009).

Employers are not the only advocates of EI programs, however. According to the empirical survey data collected by Richard Freeman and Joel Rogers, the majority of workers want more opportunity to participate in workplace decision making, and most prefer a system of workplace representation that management supports—a cooperatively run management relationship rather than the traditional adversarial system implicit in unionization and collective bargaining under the NLRA. *See* FREEMAN & ROGERS, SUPRA, at 41–43, 152.

Why, then, doesn't every employer initiate an employee involvement program? One barrier to such programs is the labor law. Employee involvement programs potentially violate the so-called "company union prohibition" contained in § 8(a)(2) of the NLRA. During the 1920s and early 1930s, many employers established employee representation programs, or "company unions." Company unions emulated the structure of independent unions but were controlled and financed by management. Management authored the union's constitutions and bylaws and was integrally involved in the internal affairs of the union. Management controlled the eligibility of members to run for representative status and the tenure of such employee representatives. Management funded the company union, and without dues company unions had no treasuries and therefore no strike funds. Moreover, because company unions were organized on a plant-wide rather than an industry-wide basis, workers lacked economic data about wages and prices in the industry and could not make common cause with other workers to leverage the power of their labor.

Company unionism became a central issue during the debates on the Wagner Act. Senator Wagner believed that company unions were inherently incompatible with collective bargaining because they undermined arm's-length bargaining, placing management on both sides of the bargaining table. Worse, Wagner argued, company unionism bred a false consciousness in workers who were duped into believing that they had a voice in workplace decision making when in fact management controlled every outcome. When Congress enacted the Wagner Act, it included a provision (now codified as § 8(a)(2)), which makes it an unfair labor practice for an employer "to dominate or interfere with the formation or administration of any labor organization or contribute financial or other support to it." A *labor organization* is defined in § 2(5) as "any organization . . . or employee representation committee or plan, in which employees participate and which exists for the purpose, in whole or in part, of dealing with employers concerning grievances, labor disputes, wages, rates of pay, hours of employment, or conditions of work." *See NLRB v. Cabot Carbon Co.*, 360 U.S. 203 (1959) (employee committees established by the employer to discuss "ideas and problems of mutual interest" and which made suggestions, proposals and requests concerning seniority, overtime, scheduling, wages, sick leave, and improvements in working conditions or facilities were "labor organizations"). Thus, in order for a violation of § 8(a)(2) to occur, the Board must first conclude that the employee organization or committee is a "labor organization" within the meaning of § 2(5) and then find that it has been either dominated or assisted by the employer in violation of § 8(a)(2). Such organizations are ordered disestablished (if employer-dominated) or required to cease and desist in their dealings with the employer (if employer-supported).

Modern EI programs have presented the Board with increasingly difficult issues in determining whether programs are permissible, and not all of the programs have been found violative of § 8(a)(2). The Labor Board views the critical factors as the degree of control exercised by the employer over the composition of the committee, the subjects it discusses, the selection of its membership, and its financial support. Where these aspects are controlled by the employer, a violation will typically be found regardless of the employer's motive in establishing the committee. The Seventh Circuit explained the rationale for the Act's prohibition of such employer-controlled organizations in this way:

> [T]he principal distinction between an independent labor organization and an employer-dominated organization lies in the unfettered power of the independent organization to determine its own actions. [Worker] committees . . . wholly created by the employer, whose continued existence depend[s] on the employer, and whose functions [are] essentially determined by the employer, lack[ ] the independence of action and free choice guaranteed by § 7.

Electromation, Inc. v. NLRB, 35 F.3d 1148, 1170–71 (7th Cir. 1994) (finding that employee action committees formed in response to worker complaints were labor organizations dominated by the employer in violation of § 8(a)(2) where the employer defined the committees' goals, determined how many employees would serve on each committee, and appointed management participants who retained final authority with respect to any committee recommendations). *See also Polaroid Corp.*, 329 N.L.R.B. 424 (1999) (finding employee-owners' influence council that dealt bilaterally with the employer over medical insurance benefits, vacation and family/medical leave benefits, policies regarding termination, transfer policies, and employee stock option plan dispositions to be a "labor organization" dominated by the employer in violation of § 8(a)(2)).

Similarly, employee-management safety committees formed by employers to discuss safety issues and to submit recommendations to management have been found to be unlawfully employer-dominated labor organizations where the employer controlled their composition and continuing existence. *See E.I. Du Pont de Nemours & Co.*, 311 N.L.R.B. 893 (1993) (noting that the employer determined the number of employee participants, decided which employees would be selected to serve on the committee, and reserved the right to abolish any of the committees). State law in some jurisdictions requires employers to establish employee safety committees for the purposes of addressing safety problems in the workplace and finding ways to enforce safety policies. In addition, the Occupational Safety and Health Act places legal responsibility on employers to maintain workplace safety, and acknowledges the need for employees to play a role. If an employer establishes workplace safety committees to conform to these requirements and to advance health and safety issues in the workplace, does it risk violating § 8(a)(2)? *See EFCO Corp.*, 327 N.L.R.B. 372 (1998), *enforced*, 215 F.3d 1318 (4th Cir. 2000) (holding employer-established safety committees were labor organizations unlawfully dominated by the employer).

On the other hand, less ambitious EI programs that do not create any committee or organization giving rise to an appearance of employee representation and consist instead of one-way solicitation of employee input by the employer generally do not violate the Act. Employee suggestion boxes, conferences conducted by management with employees which amount merely to "brainstorming" sessions in which the employer receives employee input, or isolated instances of committee proposals and the lack of a pattern or practice of bilateral dealing do not constitute "dealing with" the employer, so § 8(a)(2) will not be violated. *See E.I. Du Pont de Nemours & Co.*, 311 N.L.R.B. 893 (1993) (holding that safety conferences conducted by management officials with employees in attendance did not violate § 8(a)(2)); *NLRB v. Peninsula Gen. Hosp.*, 36 F.3d 1262 (4th Cir. 1994) (ruling that nurses' committee formed to discuss practice issues lacked pattern or practice of dealing with employer over committee proposals and therefore did not violate the Act). Alternatively, complete delegation of managerial functions to an employee group also avoids liability under § 8(a)(2) because the organization does not exist to "deal with" the employer. *See In Re Crown Cork & Seal Co., Inc.*, 334 N.L.R.B. 699 (2001) (holding that employee safety production teams with authority to investigate and correct safety-related problems were essentially performing "managerial functions" rather than "dealing" with the employer in violation of the Act).

What about internal complaint procedures established by employers seeking to channel potential litigation to alternative dispute resolution systems—do these violate § 8(a)(2)? In *Syracuse University*, 350 N.L.R.B. 755 (2007), the Board considered a staff complaint procedure developed by the university to resolve labor issues between non-union employees and their supervisors. The complaint process involved a three-step grievance procedure for disciplinary actions that included mediation, a formal hearing, and an appeal stage. Because the complaint procedure did not entail the "bilateral process involving employees and management in order to reach bilateral solutions on the basis of employee-initiated proposals" contemplated by *Electromation*, the process did not violate the NLRA.

The application of § 8(a)(2) to invalidate many EI programs has produced pressure for legislative change. The Dunlop Commission, a blue ribbon panel appointed in 1993 by President Clinton and charged with making recommendations addressing the state of labor-management relations, concluded that it was in the national interest to promote the expansion of EI programs and offered a qualified endorsement of them. *See* REPORT AND RECOMMENDATIONS OF THE COMMISSION ON THE FUTURE OF WORKER-MANAGEMENT RELATIONS (1995) (recommending legislative clarification of § 8(a)(2)). The most notable of the ensuing legislative amendment efforts is the Teamwork for Employees and Management Act, known as the TEAM Act, first introduced before the House of Representatives in 1993. In its most recent incarnation, the TEAM Act would retain the core language of § 8(a)(2) but would amend it to authorize the establishment of EI programs designed "to address matters of mutual interest, including, but not limited to, issues of quality, productivity, efficiency, and safety and health" in nonunion workplaces. In September 1995, the House of Representatives passed a version of the TEAM Act by a slim margin, and in July of 1996 the Senate passed the bill by a vote of 53-46 following a heated debate along largely partisan lines. *See Dole Pushes Little Understood Labor Bill into the Limelight and Unions Loath It*, WALL ST. J., May 10, 1996. President Clinton vetoed the Act later that month, claiming that it would "undermine the system of collective bargaining that has served this country so well for many decades." *Clinton Kills Bill Favoring Labor-Management Teams*, WALL ST. J., July 31, 1996. The TEAM Act remains on the legislative agenda of many lawmakers, but it has been unable to gain traction.

NOTES

1. **Union Absence.** Is there something inherently flawed about an EI program that is created in the absence of a union? Is the problem simply that we don't trust employers to be fair? Even if the employer's goal is to supplant collective bargaining, shouldn't the most important question be whether the program benefits employees? Why doesn't the Board review the programs to determine whether they have, in fact, resulted in the implementation of valuable workplace benefits or reforms? Is § 8(a)(2) simply a union protection device?

2. **EI in the Modern Workplace.** Should a legal doctrine developed for application to the workplace as it existed in the 1930s be applied to today's workplace? Is the analysis developed by the Board in *Electromation* and *E.I. Du Pont* adequate to the challenge of distinguishing between employee organizations that undermine worker agency by creating an aura of false consciousness among workers and those that do not? If an employer seeks to comply with the Act as interpreted by the Board, how should it cabin discussions of production and quality issues (permissible) and prevent them from growing into discussions about employment practices, wages, hours and working conditions (impermissible)?

3. **EI as an Alternative to No Representation.** Does the application of § 8(a)(2) to ban employer-initiated EI programs ultimately hurt employees by leaving them with a choice between independent union representation and no representation at all? What sort of choice is this in a private sector market characterized by less than 8% union density? Should it matter whether the employees support the EI program? Some have suggested that it is paternalistic to ignore the employees' subjective perceptions of employer-initiated EI programs. Why shouldn't we trust the employees' judgments about their own needs and interests? Who will complain about an employee group that potentially violates § 8(a)(2)? Should public policy seek to effectuate employee preferences or union preferences in this area? *See generally* Johanna Oreskovic, *Capturing Volition Itself: Employee Involvement and the TEAM Act*, 19 BERKELEY J. EMP. & LAB. L.

229 (1998) (defending § 8(a)(2) prohibition on EI programs and arguing that EI programs are a modern manifestation of employer-controlled welfare capitalism, fundamentally inconsistent with the NLRA's vision of industrial democracy); Samuel Estreicher, *Employee Involvement and the "Company Union" Prohibition: The Case for Partial Repeal of § 8(a)(2) of the NLRA*, 69 N.Y.U. L. REV. 125 (1994) (proposing partial repeal of § 8(a)(2) as part of an integrated package of labor law reforms bolstering protections for workers who desire independent unions).

Might worker organizations initiated and supported by the employer provide a breeding ground for incipient union organizing efforts rather than a barrier to collective action? Some commentators think so, although others express doubts. *Compare* Alan Hyde, *Employee Caucus: A Key Institution in the Emerging System of Employment Law*, 69 CHI-KENT L. REV. 149 (1993) (suggesting potential role for identity-based employee caucuses), *with* Carol Brooke, Note, *Nonmajority Unions, Employee Participation Programs, and Worker Organizing: Irreconcilable Differences?*, 76 CHI-KENT L. REV. 1237 (2000) (contrasting empowering effects of nonmajority unions with disempowering effects of employee participation programs).

   4. EI in the Unionized Workplace. One might assume that EI programs are more likely to be found in nonunion workplaces, but the opposite is true: 55% of unionized workers in the firms surveyed by Freeman and Rogers had an EI program at their workplace, and 33% of workers participated in it, as compared with 49% of nonunion workers with an EI program and only 28% participating. It appears that employee involvement programs complement unionism. *See* RICHARD B. FREEMAN & JOEL ROGERS, WHAT WORKERS WANT 115 (1999).

3. Works Councils

Works councils are elected by employees to represent the interests of all employees in a particular branch or office, exercising information, consultation, and co-determination rights with management. They function to furnish the employer with meaningful employee input and to boost employee morale by offering the opportunity to impact the company's operations. Works councils are common in the European Union where they are required of employers of a certain size upon petition by a group of employees or a union.

In the EU works councils exist side-by-side with labor unions. Although they operate independently, there are strong ties between the two groups. Traditionally labor unions organize entire sectors or industries and negotiate collective bargaining agreements with employer associations that cover the industry as a whole; among other things, these agreements typically set wage levels. Works councils are elected at the local level and represent all the workers in that shop. Their role is to apply and adjust the labor agreement reached at the national level by employer and union to local shop conditions. Works councils are typically involved in a variety of workplace governance issues, including staffing and promotion below the senior management level, discipline and discharge, the allocation of work hours to groups of employees, work organization, and issues surrounding the introduction of new technology. The division of labor between labor unions and works councils allows works councils to engage in a collaborative relationship with local management, while more militant and adversarial postures are left to unions in collective bargaining negotiations at the national and industry level.

To date, works councils do not exist in the United States. Because they involve employee participation in a group setting, convey proposals and ideas to management, and engage in back-and-forth dialogue over time with management on mandatory subjects of bargaining (wages, hours, and working conditions), they qualify as labor organizations governed by the NLRA. To the extent that the employer dominates, supports or assists the group, violation of section 8(a)(2) is therefore likely.

Germany's works councils are particularly robust and the relationship between unions and works councils has historically been close. Martin Behrens, *Still Married After All These Years? Union Organizing and the Role of Works Councils in German Industrial Relations*, 62 INDUS. & LAB. REL. REV. 275, 277–79 (2009). When the German company Volkswagen opened a new plant in Chattanooga, Tennessee, it sought to establish the forms of workplace governance with which it had positive experience. Accustomed to dealing with unions, VW expressed support for unionization during the representation election held in early 2014. Resistance from local and state-level elected officials who conditioned the receipt of tax benefits on the plant remaining non-union combined with southern workers' unfamiliarity with and hostility toward unions, however, and the union lost the election by a narrow margin. Steven Greenhouse, *Defeat of Auto Union in Tennessee Casts Its Strategy into Doubt*, N.Y. TIMES, Feb. 15, 2014. Despite the union election loss, the company indicated its continuing interest in establishing a German-style works council in the plant. Its CEO touted the company's relationship with works councils in Germany as vital to the productivity that helped make Volkswagen the second largest car manufacturer in the world. Steven Greenhouse, *Labor Regroups in South After VW Vote*, N.Y. TIMES, Feb. 16, 2014. The UAW responded to Volkswagen's embrace of works councils by chartering a "members-only" local union in order to create a base for future full unionization, which it hopes will in turn facilitate the works council. Steven Greenhouse, *Despite Earlier Loss, U.A.W. Creates Union at VW Plant*, N.Y. TIMES, July 11, 2014. A members-only union is one where the union represents only its own members, and does not bargain for others.

Union advocates, management and labor experts are watching the VW experiment with works councils closely. Many questions remain. Would a works council violate NLRA section 8(a)(2)? Is this more likely without a union in the plant? Can a members-only union adequately substitute for a majority union with exclusive bargaining rights in this context? Will American workers in the south join a members-only union? Will they embrace a majority union, given time and familiarization with the functions of unions? How transferrable are works councils to the American system, particularly in the absence of a strong labor union with collective bargaining rights?

Because American workers desire voice in a collaborative system, a number of scholars have been inspired to propose legislative reforms based upon the works council system. *See, e.g.,* Stephen F. Befort, *A New Voice for the Workplace: A*

Proposal for an American Works Councils Act, 69 Mo. L. REV. 607, 642 (2004) (discussing limitations that 8(a)(2) poses for employee participatory programs and exploring possibilities for NLRA reform and creation of works councils to empower workers' voice in the workplace); Charles Craver, *Mandatory Worker Participation is Required in a Declining Union Environment to Provide Employees with Meaningful Industrial Democracy*, 66 GEO. WASH. L. REV. 135 (1997–98) (arguing that such forms of representation could replace traditionally adversarial labor-management relationships and foster better appreciation among employees for the competitive pressures facing their employers, as well as enhancing the enforcement of safety and health legislation and wage and hour law). Though politically unlikely at present, these reform proposals offer new strategies for self-regulation and systems of workplace governance that might combine the best of the old and new worlds.

TABLE OF CASES

[References are to pages]

[References are to pages]

[References are to pages]

[References are to pages]

[References are to pages]

[References are to pages]

[References are to pages]

N

[References are to pages]

[References are to pages]

Q

R

[References are to pages]

[References are to pages]

[References are to pages]

[References are to pages]

Y

Z

INDEX

[References are to sections.]

A

ADA (See AMERICANS WITH DISABILITIES ACT (ADA))

AGE DISCRIMINATION
Generally . . . 9[F][1]

AMERICANS WITH DISABILITIES ACT (ADA)
Generally . . . 9[E]
Defining disability . . . 9[E][1]
Duty to accommodate . . . 9[E][2]

ARBITRATION
Employer-promulgated arbitration systems reconsideration . . . 14[E]
Labor arbitration and problem of overlapping remedies . . . 14[B]
Nonunion workplace, in . . . 14[C]
Predispute employment arbitration agreements
  Generally . . . 14[D]
  Effective vindication of statutory rights . . . 14[D][1]
  State contract law principles . . . 14[D][2]
  Statutory rights, effective vindication of . . . 14[D][1]
Provisions barring class claims
  Generally . . . 14[D][3]
  Group litigation as enforcement mechanism, statutes for . . . 14[D][3][a]
  National Labor Relations Act (NLRA) rights . . . 14[D][3][b]
Public interest, arbitration agreements impact on . . . 14[D][4]
Resolution mechanism, arbitration as workplace dispute . . . 14[A]

ATTORNEYS
Public policy protections for individual job security . . . 4[E]

AT-WILL EMPLOYMENT
Contract-based limits on
  Fair dealing, implied covenant of . . . 3[D][2]
  Good faith and fair dealing, implied covenant of . . . 3[D][2]
  Implied covenant of good faith and fair dealing . . . 3[D][2]
  Promissory estoppel . . . 3[D][1]
Presumption of
  Generally . . . 3[A][1]
  Alternative models
    Generally . . . 3[A][2]
    Public employment . . . 3[A][2][b]
    Union sector . . . 3[A][2][a]
  Contemporary era . . . 3[A][3]
Revisiting presumption of . . . 4[F]

C

CAT'S PAW THEORY
Generally . . . 9[B][3]

CHILD LABOR PROVISIONS
Fair Labor Standards Act (FLSA) . . . 11[B][3]

COLLECTIVE BARGAINING
Practice of . . . 1[C][3]

COLLECTIVE JOB SECURITY
Common law contract, property, and tort claims . . . 5[A]
National Labor Relations Act (NLRA), under (See NATIONAL LABOR RELATIONS ACT (NLRA), subhead: Collective job security under)
Property . . . 5[A]
Tort claims . . . 5[A]
Unemployment insurance system . . . 5[D]
Worker Adjustment and Retraining Notification Act (WARN) (See WORKER ADJUSTMENT AND RETRAINING NOTIFICATION ACT (WARN))

COMMON LAW
Collective job security, contract in . . . 5[A]
Employee voice . . . 8[C]
Private employees, protections for (See PRIVACY, subhead: Private employees, common law protections for)
Statutory and common law remedies, relationship between . . . 4[D]
Workers' compensation . . . 13[A][1][a]

CONTRACTS
At-will employment, contract-based limits on (See AT-WILL EMPLOYMENT, subhead: Contract-based limits on)
Freedom to contract, rise and fall of . . . 1[B]
Independent contractors . . . 11[D][4][a]
Presumption by agreement, overcoming (See INDIVIDUAL JOB SECURITY, subhead: Agreement, overcoming presumption by)

D

DIGNITARY INTERESTS
Drug testing . . . 7[D]; 7[D][2]
Emotional harm, avoiding . . . 7[A]
Genetic testing . . . 7[D]; 7[D][1]
Monitoring and data analytics . . . 7[D]; 7[D][3]
Off-duty conduct and associations . . . 7[C]
Privacy (See PRIVACY)
Reputation . . . 7[E]

DISCHARGE
Individual job security, public policy protections for . . . 4[C]

DISCRIMINATION
Generally . . . 9[A]

[References are to sections.]

[References are to sections.]

[References are to sections.]

[References are to sections.]

T

U

W

[References are to sections.]